WORLD RESOURCES

1992-93

WORLD RESOURCES

1992-93

**A Report by
The World Resources Institute**

in collaboration with

**The United Nations
Environment Programme**

and

**The United Nations
Development Programme**

New York   Oxford
Oxford University Press
1992

The cover shows sunset, lit by Earth's atmosphere, in a photograph taken by cosmonauts V. Kovalyonok and A. Ivanchenkov on board an orbital space complex Salyut 6-Soyuz 29-Soyuz 31. Photo courtesy of Kevin Kelly.

The World Resources Institute, The United Nations Environment Programme, and the United Nations Development Programme gratefully acknowledge permission to reprint from the following sources:

Part I: Box 2.1, Figure 1, Joint Center for Political and Economic Studies.

Part II: Box 5.2, Figure 1, *Politische Ökologie* magazine.

Part III: Figures 8.1 and 8.2, and Box 8.3, Figure 1, International Soil Reference and Information Centre; Figure 9.3, *Oceanus*, Woods Hole Oceanographic Institution (source should read p. 27, not p. 29); Figure 11.1, Peter J. Lamb, Cooperative Institute for Mesoscale Meterological Studies; Figure 12.1, Benjamin L. Peierls, Institute of Ecosystem Studies, The New York Botanical Gardens; Figure 12.5, Coastal Resources Management Project; Figure 12.6, U.S. Environmental Protection Agency, Chesapeake Bay Program; Figure 12.7, United Nations Environment Programme.

Printed in the United States of America on recycled paper.

Oxford University Press

Oxford   New York   Toronto
Delhi   Bombay   Calcutta   Madras   Karachi
Kuala Lumpur   Singapore   Hong Kong   Tokyo
Nairobi   Dar es Salaam   Cape Town
Melbourne   Auckland

and associated companies in
Berlin   Ibadan

ISBN 0-19-506230-2

ISBN 0-19-506231-0 (PBK)

Library of Congress Cataloging Number: 86-659504
ISSN 0887-0403

World Resources is a biennial publication of the World Resources Institute, 1709 New York Ave., NW, Washington, DC, 20006.

Printing (last digit): 9 8 7 6 5 4 3 2 1

Contents

PART I   Sustainable Development

PART II   Regional Focus

Preface

The *World Resources* series is intended to meet the critical need for accessible, accurate information on some of the most pressing issues of our time. Wise management of natural resources and protection of the global environment are essential to achieve sustainable economic development and hence to alleviate poverty, improve the human condition, and preserve the biological systems on which all life depends.

Publication of *World Resources 1992-93*, the fifth in the series, reflects an ongoing collaborative effort of the United Nations Environment Programme (UNEP), the United Nations Development Programme (UNDP), and the World Resources Institute (WRI) to produce and disseminate the most objective and up-to-date report of conditions and trends in the world's natural resources and in the global environment.

This volume has a special focus on sustainable development, in support of the upcoming 1992 United Nations Conference on Environment and Development (UNCED). Part I consists of four special chapters on sustainable development: an overview chapter and three case studies of what sustainable development might mean in industrial countries, low-income countries, and rapidly industrializing countries. Additional material pertinent to this topic is found throughout the volume. Part II continues the tradition of examining in each volume a particular region in more detail—in this case, an overview of the severe environmental and resource problems faced by Central Europe as that region makes a difficult transition to more democratic governments and more market-oriented economies. Part III reports on basic conditions and trends, key issues, major problems and efforts to resolve them, and recent developments in each of the major resource categories, from population and human development to energy to atmosphere and climate. Where data exist, the chapters give a 20-year perspective on trends in the physical environment—spanning the time between the first United Nations Conference on the Environment and UNCED. Supporting data, as well as the core data tables from the World Resources Data Base, are found in Part IV.

Additional information and data can be found in the *Environmental Data Report*, published every other year by UNEP in cooperation with WRI and the U.K. Department of the Environment. The *Environmental Data Report* and *World Resources* are published in alternating years. The forthcoming volume of the *Human Development Report 1992*, published by UNDP, will also have a special chapter on the environment that bears directly on the issues discussed in this volume of *World Resources*. Also forthcoming are UNEP's *State of the Environment Report* and the World Bank's *World Development Report 1992*, which this year will focus on the environment.

In an effort to make an expanded set of data accessible to policymakers, scholars, and nongovernmental organizations, WRI is also publishing the World Resources Data Base—expanded to include 20-year data sets where possible—on diskette.

The audience for the *World Resources* series is steadily expanding, with English, Spanish, Arabic, German, Japanese, and Chinese editions now in print. With this volume, French and Dutch translations will also be added. A *Teacher's Guide to World Resources* is also helping to make the series accessible and useful to teachers and students.

WRI, UNEP, and UNDP share the conviction that the *World Resources* series can best contribute to management of the world's natural resources and to a broadened awareness of environmental concerns by providing an independent perspective on these critical global issues. Accordingly, while both UNEP and UNDP have provided essential information and invaluable critical advice, *final responsibility for substance and editorial content of the series remains with WRI*.

We commend the *World Resources* staff for their efforts in assembling and analyzing this unique collection of information on natural resources and the global environment and in producing the volume in a timely fashion. The Editorial Advisory Board, chaired by Dr. M.S. Swaminathan, provided active advice and support at all stages of the project. Its call to action on the issues discussed in this volume—in a signed statement on the following page—deserves broad consideration.

We wish to thank the John D. and Catherine T. MacArthur Foundation and the Ford Foundation for their support in this endeavor. Their financial commitment to the continuation of the *World Resources* series and its distribution throughout the developing world help to make it all possible. Thanks are also due to the World Bank for assistance in distribution of the report, to the Inter-American Development Bank and the African Development Bank for support of the Spanish and French editions, respectively, to the Swedish International Development Authority and the U.S. Environmental Protection Agency for support to expand and strengthen the World Resources Data Base, and to the Geraldine R. Dodge Foundation and the National Geographic Society for support of the *Teacher's Guide*.

James Gustave Speth
President
World Resources Institute

Mostafa K. Tolba	William H. Draper III
Executive Director	Administrator
United Nations	United Nations
Environment Programme	Development Programme

Statement by Members of the Editorial Advisory Board

"Let the facts speak for themselves." That has been the principle guiding the *World Resources* series from its first volume through this latest edition.

It is time, we believe, for one limited exception. As members of *World Resources* Editorial Advisory Board, we have supervised an outpouring of data and information that underscores the alarming degree to which current patterns of human activity are impoverishing and destabilizing the natural environment and undermining the prospects of future generations.

Fortunately, the opportunity is now at hand for the governments of the world's nations and others to come together in recognition of these disturbing trends and to act to reverse them. The United Nations Conference on Environment and Development (UNCED) in Rio de Janeiro, Brazil, in June 1992 presents the opportunity for a generation to focus world attention on the planet's needs and on those of current and future generations and to chart a new direction for future development.

To support these efforts, this issue of *World Resources* accords central attention to issues relevant to UNCED. The opportunity for action provided by UNCED also prompts this special statement. For while the agenda requiring international attention is now widely, if not universally acknowledged, we are deeply concerned that a sense of urgency is lacking and that the costs of delay are not adequately appreciated by governments.
■ Indications abound that the global soil resource base is rapidly being degraded. Over the past 50 years, the productivity of more than 1.2 billion hectares of land—an area larger than China and India together—has been significantly lowered. If such human-caused losses continue, it will make even harder the task of providing food for a world population projected to nearly double by the middle of the next century.
■ Atmospheric accumulations of climate-threatening greenhouse gases continue to rise. Of particular concern is carbon dioxide from the combustion of fossil fuels, which now supply 95 percent of the world's commercial energy. To stabilize atmospheric concentrations of carbon dioxide, the Intergovernmental Panel on Climate Change concluded that emissions must be cut by 60 percent from present levels. Yet, the world economy is expected to grow at least fivefold by 2050. If that growth is based on expanded use of fossil energy, the likelihood of global climate change will increase significantly.
■ The biological heritage of the planet is increasingly at risk. Habitat losses stemming from clearing of forests or draining of wetlands or from the degradation of ecosystems through destructive fishing, farming, and grazing practices are leading to reductions in natural populations and the extinction of species at extraordinary rates. Industrial and urban pollution are putting additional stresses on the world's biological diversity. Without urgent measures to conserve these irreplaceable resources, our descendants will inherit a biologically impoverished world.

Just as these and other problems are now better understood, so we are beginning to sense the broad outlines of what must be done to find solutions. We must seek a series of transitions or transformations to more sustainable paths of development, including:
■ A technological transition away from today's resource-intensive, pollution-prone technologies to a new generation that places less stress on the environment;
■ An economic transition to a world economy based on reliance on nature's "income" and not on depletion of its "capital;"
■ A transition to greater social equity aimed at alleviating poverty;
■ A demographic transition to a stable human population no more than twice the level of today;
■ A transition in consciousness to a more profound and widespread understanding of global sustainability;
■ An institutional transition to new arrangements—among governments and peoples—that can achieve environmental security.

Each nation, developed and developing, must begin to plot a course toward sustainability on their own, without waiting for others. But much more will be achieved if all countries move in partnership together. The transitions referred to above are needed by both developed and developing countries.

We appeal to governments, to industry and institutions, and to individuals everywhere to respond to this urgent agenda in ways commensurate with the scale of the problems.

Abdlatif Y. Al-Hamad
Serge Antoine
William H. Draper III
Nikita Glazovsky
Yolanda Kakabadse
T.N. Khoshoo
Thomas A. Lambo
István Láng

Uri Marinov
Robert McNamara
Liberty Mhlanga
Akio Morishima
José Sarukhán
James Gustave Speth
M.S. Swaminathan
Mostafa K. Tolba
Brian Walker

Acknowledgments

World Resources 1992-93 is the product of a unique international collaboration involving many institutions and individuals. Without their advice, support, and hard work, this volume could not have been produced.

We are especially grateful for the advice and assistance of our many colleagues at the World Resources Institute (WRI), the United Nations Environment Programme (UNEP), and the United Nations Development Programme (UNDP). Their advice on the selection of material to be covered and their diligent review of manuscript drafts and data tables, often under time pressure, have been invaluable.

Institutions
We wish to recognize and thank the many other institutions that have contributed data, reviews, and encouragement to this project. They include:

The Food and Agriculture Organization of the United Nations (FAO)
The Global Environment Monitoring System of UNEP (GEMS)
The World Bank
The Monitoring and Assessment Research Centre (MARC)
The United Nations Statistical Office
The United Nations Population Office
The Organisation for Economic Co-operation and Development (OECD)
The Carbon Dioxide Information Analysis Center (CDIAC)
The World Conservation Union, formally the International Union for Conservation of Nature and Natural Resources (IUCN)
The World Conservation Monitoring Centre (WCMC)

Individuals
Many individuals contributed to the development of this volume by providing expert advice, data, or careful review of manuscripts. While final responsibility for the chapters rests with the *World Resources* staff, the contributions and help of these colleagues are reflected throughout the book. Special thanks go to UNEP colleagues Joan Martin-Brown, special advisor to the UNEP executive director, who coordinated help from Washington, and to Danielle Mitchell, who coordinated access to pertinent UNEP experts in Nairobi. Special thanks also go to Dan Tunstall of WRI, who advised on and reviewed data chapters. We also thank our authors, who performed diligently and then endured patiently our numerous queries and often substantial editorial changes. The primary authors are listed at the end of each chapter. Reviewers, consultants, and major sources include:

Dimensions of Sustainable Development
Mona Bjorklund, UNEP; Philip Burgess, MARC; Roger Dower, WRI; Tom Fox, WRI; Taka Hiraishi, UNEP; Jeff Leonard, Global Environment Fund (Washington); Kenton Miller, WRI; Ralph Schmidt, UNDP; G. Schneider, UNEP; Manfred Schneider, UNEP; Martin Smith, UNEP; Peter Thacher, WRI; Ann Willcocks, MARC.

Industrial Countries Mona Bjorklund, UNEP; Philip Burgess, MARC; Roger Dower, WRI; Taka Hiraishi, UNEP; Jessica Tuchman Mathews, WRI; Walter Reid, WRI; Ralph Schmidt, UNDP; Manfred Schneider, UNEP; Martin Smith, UNEP; Peter Thacher, WRI; Tony Zamparutti, WRI.

Poor Countries Herbert Acquay; Robert Blake, WRI; Jacqueline Carless, MARC; Willie Cruz, WRI; Arthur Dommen, U.S. Department of Agriculture; Dorothy Etoori, Environmental Ministry (Uganda); Tom Fox, WRI; Michael Gucovsky, UNDP; Taka Hiraishi, UNEP; Jeff Leonard, Global Environment Fund (Washington); John Lewis, Center for International Studies (Princeton); Carlos Lopez-Ocana, Inter-American Development Bank; Joan Martin-Brown, UNEP; Bill Nagle; Manfred Schneider, UNEP; John Sewell, Overseas Development Council; Jonas Svensson, UNEP; B.M. Taal, UNEP; Peter Thacher, WRI; Dan Tunstall, WRI; Ann Willcocks, MARC.

Rapidly Industrializing Countries Chip Barber, WRI; Walden Bello, Institute for Food (San Francisco); Zbigniew Bochniarz, Hubert Humphrey Institute of Public Affairs; Robin Broad; Jacqueline Carless, MARC; John Cavanaugh, Institute for Policy Studies (Washington); Uttam Dabholkar, UNEP; Aloisi de Laarderel, UNEP; Richard Feinberg, Overseas Development Council; Tom Fox, WRI; Steven Glovinsky, UNDP; Taka Hiraishi, UNEP; Jorge Illueca, UNEP; John Lewis, Center for International Studies (Princeton); Robert Repetto, WRI; José Sarúkhan, Universidad Nacional Autonoma de Mexico; Manfred Schneider, UNEP; John Sewell, Overseas Development Council; Martin Smith, UNEP; B.M. Taal, UNEP; Tony Zamparutti, WRI; Aaron Zazueta, WRI.

Regional Focus: Central Europe Richard Ackermann, the World Bank; Walter Arensberg, WRI; Matthew Auer, U.S. Agency for International Development; Zbigniew Bochniarz, Hubert Humphrey Institute of Public Affairs; William Chandler, Battelle Pacific Northwest Laboratories; G. Shabbir Cheema, UNDP; Amy Evans, U.S. Environmental Protection Agency; Duncan Fisher, Ecological Studies Institute (London); Hilary French, Worldwatch Institute; P. Garan, UNEP; N. Gebremedhin, UNEP; Nikita Glazovsky, Institute of Geography (Moscow); Peter Hardi, Regional Environmental Center (Budapest); Z. Karpowicz, IUCN; Stan Kolar, Kolar Associates; István Láng, Hungarian Academy of Science; Barry Levy, Management Sciences for Health (Boston); Richard Liroff, World Wildlife Fund; Joan Martin-Brown, UNEP; Jeff Michel; Bedrich Moldan; Miklos Persanyi, Cornell University; Peter Peterson, MARC; Jeremy Russell, Royal Institute of International Affairs (London); Dan Tunstall, WRI; Michael Walsh; Steven Wassersug, Regional Environmental Center (Budapest); Piotr Wilczysnki, Oscar Lange Academy of Economics (Poland).

Population and Human Development
Mary Barberis, Population Crisis Committee (Washington); Robert Black, The Johns Hopkins School of Hygiene and Public Health; Arleen Cannata; Jacqueline Carless, MARC; Joseph Chamie, United Nations Population Division; Patrick Cornu, International Labor Office (Geneva); Uttam Dabholkar, UNEP; Steven Esrey, Water and Sanitation for Health Project (Washington); Tom Fox, WRI; N. Gebremedhin, UNEP; Steven Glovinsky, UNDP; O. Gritsai, Institute of Geography (Moscow); Michael Gucovsky, UNDP; H.R. Haspara, World Health Organization; Carl Haub, Population Reference Bureau (Washington); Larry Heligman, United Nations Population Division; Kenneth Hill, The Johns Hopkins School of Hygiene and Public Health; Pamela Johnson; Alan Lopez, World Health Organization; Joan Martin-Brown, UNEP; Monika Mentzingen, UNEP; Thomas Merrick, Population Reference Bureau (Washington); T. Nefedova, Institute of Geography (Moscow); Renate Plaut, Pan American Health Organization; Beth Ann Plowman, International Science and Technology Institute; Robert Repetto, WRI; Steven Sinding, the World Bank; Alfred Sommer, The Johns Hopkins School of Hygiene and Public Health; Katherine Springer, UNDP; Peter Thacher, WRI; Philip van Hacke, United Nations International Children's Emergency Fund; Veerle Vanderweerd, UNEP; My T. Vu, the World Bank; Greg Watters, World Health Organization; Kevin Wayne; Mary Beth Weinberger, United Nations Population Division; Robert Weisell, FAO; Nancy Yinger, Population Reference Bureau (Washington).

Food and Agriculture A. Ayoub, UNEP; David Baldock, Institute for European Environmental Policy (London); Ed Barbier, International Institute for Environment and Development (London); Bill Barclay, Greenpeace International; Robert Blake, WRI; Robert Brinkman, FAO; Jacqueline Carless, MARC; Chris Chung, OECD; R. James Cook, U.S. Department of Agriculture; Walter Couto, FAO; Michael Dover; Alex Dubgaard, Royal Veterinary and Agricultural University (Denmark); Ron Duncan, the World Bank; David Ervin, U.S. Department of Agriculture; Paul Faeth, WRI; Tom Fox, WRI; Brian Gardner, European Policy Analysis (Belgium); Michael Gucovsky, UNDP; Kim Hjort, U.S. Department of Agriculture; Nurul Islam, International Food Policy Research Institute

(Washington); Kim Kroll, Rodale Research Center; Rattan Lal, Ohio State University; Nicolas Lampkin, University College of Wales; Bjorn Lundgren, International Council for Research in Agroforestry (Nairobi); Joan Martin-Brown, UNEP; T. Maukonen, UNEP; John Mellor; Monika Mentzingen, UNEP; Francesco Pariboni, FAO; Leonardo Paulino, International Food Policy Research Institute (Washington); Peter Peterson, MARC; Katherine Reichelderfer, Resources for the Future; Barbara Rose, International Food Policy Research Institute (Washington); Mark Rosegrant, International Food Policy Research Institute (Washington); Pedro Sanchez, International Council for Research in Agroforestry (Nairobi); D.W. Sanders, FAO; J. Skoupy, UNEP; Ann Thrupp, WRI; James Tobey, U.S. Department of Agriculture; Dan Tunstall, WRI; Heino von Meyer, Institut Für Ländliche Strukturforschung (Germany); Friedrich von Mallinckrodt, UNDP; B. Waiyaki, UNEP; Mark Wenner, U.S. Department of Agriculture; Michael Young, Commonwealth Science and Industrial Research Organization (Australia); Garth Youngberg, Institute for Alternative Agriculture (Washington); Tony Zamparutti, WRI.

Forests and Rangelands Barrie Adams, Alberta Forestry Land and Wildlife; Manuel Paveri Anziani, FAO; Richard Arnold, U.S. Department of Agriculture; A. Ayoub, UNEP; Marc Dourojeanni, Inter-American Development Bank; Harold Dregne, Texas Tech University; Philip Fearnside, National Institute for Research in Amazonas (Brazil); Luiz Meira Filho, Instituto Nacional De Pesquisais Espaciais (Brazil); Tom Fox, WRI; José Goldemberg, Universade de Saõ Paulo; Luis Gomez-Echeverri, UNDP; David Gow, WRI; Alan Grainger, University of Salford; Christine Haugen, WRI; Harold Heady, University of California, Berkeley; Jörg Henninger, Gesellschaft für Technische Zusammenarbeit (Paraguay); Klaus Janz, FAO; David Kummer, Clark University; James LaFleur, ECOTEC (Brazil); J.P. Lanly, FAO; Carlos Lopez-Ocana, Inter-American Development Bank; Joan Martin-Brown, UNEP; Egnankou Wadja Mathieu, Institut de la Carte International de la Vegetation (France); Dan Yit May, Forestry Department Headquarters (Malaysia); C. Hollis Murray, FAO; M. Norton-Griffiths, UNEP; L.R. Oldeman, International Soil Reference and Information Centre (the Netherlands); Richard Pardo, International Conservation Fund; T.J. Peck, FAO; Peter Peterson, MARC; Gareth Porter, U.S. Environmental and Energy Study Institute; M. Reimers, UNEP; James Romo, University of Saskatchewan; Alberto Setzer, Instituto Nacional De Pesquisas Espaciais (Brazil); K.D. Singh, FAO; David Smith, Yale University; Jonas Svensson, UNEP; Juan Torres-Rojo, Secretaria de Agricultura y Recursos Hidraulicos (Mexico); Dan Tunstall, WRI; Philip Wardle, FAO; Manuel Winograd, WRI; Robert Winterbottom, U.S. Agency for International Development (Rwanda).

Wildlife and Habitat W. James Batten; Mona Bjorklund, UNEP; Ian Bowles, Conservation International; Philip Burgess, MARC; Tom Fox, WRI; Brian Groombridge, WCMC; Michael Gucovsky, UNDP; Jeremy Harrison, WCMC; Barbara Hoskinson, World Wildlife Fund; Daniel Janzen, University of Pennsylvania; Richard Luxmoore, WCMC; Kathy MacKinnon, Joan Martin-Brown, UNEP; John McComb, WCMC; Jeff McNeely, IUCN; Kenton Miller, WRI; Robin Pellew, WCMC; Peter Peterson, MARC; Walter Reid, WRI; Christina Robinson, The Nature Conservancy; Ralph Schmidt, UNDP; Jonas Svensson, UNEP; Jim Thorsell, IUCN; Dan Tunstall, WRI; Kerry Walter, WCMC; Ann Willcocks, MARC; Ted Wolf, Conservation International; Peter Wyse-Jackson, Botanic Gardens Conservation International (United Kingdom).

Energy and Materials Christian Avérous, OECD; Fritz Balkau, UNEP; Gustavo Best, FAO; Peter Blair, U.S. Office of Technology Assessment; John Blossom, U.S. Bureau of Mines; James Carlin, Jr., U.S. Bureau of Mines; John Christensen, UNEP; William Clive, United Nations Statistical Office; Elizabeth Creel, U.S. Environmental Protection Agency; Aloisi de Laarderel, UNEP; Dan Edelstein, U.S. Bureau of Mines; Tom Fox, WRI; Sam Fraser, U.S. Bureau of Mines; José Goldemberg, Universade de Saõ Paulo; Luis Gomez-Echeverri, UNDP; Henry Hilliard, U.S. Bureau of Mines; David Jhirad, U.S. Agency for International Development; James Jolly, U.S. Bureau of Mines; Janice Jolly, U.S. Bureau of Mines; Thomas Jones, U.S. Bureau of Mines; William Kirk, U.S. Bureau of Mines; Debbie Kramer, U.S. Bureau of Mines; Peter Kuck, U.S. Bureau of Mines; Camilo Lim, UNEP; Harry Makar, U.S. Bureau of Mines; Joan Martin-Brown, UNEP; Alan Miller, Center for Global Change (Maryland); Joyce Ober, U.S. Bureau of Mines; John Papp, U.S. Bureau of Mines; Dianna Richards, U.S. National Academy of Engineering; Errol Sehnke, U.S. Bureau of Mines; Kim Shedd, U.S. Bureau of Mines; Gerald Smith, U.S. Bureau of Mines; Dan Tunstall, WRI; Ann Willcocks, MARC; William Woodbury, U.S. Bureau of Mines; William Zajac, U.S. Bureau of Mines.

Freshwater Martine Allard, National Water Research Institute (Canada); Alexander Belyaev, Institute of Geography (Moscow); Philip Burgess, MARC; Debbie Chapman; R.J. Daley, Canada Centre for Inland Waters; Luis Gomez-Echeverri, UNDP; Erik Helland-Hansen, UNDP; Richard Helmer, World Health Organization; Maynard Hufschmidt, Environmental Policy Institute (Honolulu); John Jackson, MARC; Allen Kneese, Resources for the Future; Joan Martin-Brown, UNEP; David Moody, U.S. Geological Survey; Bruce Newton, U.S. Environmental Protection Agency; Martin Smith, UNEP; Joyce Starr, Global Water Summit Initiative (Washington); Veerle Vanderweerd, UNEP; J.A. Veltrop, Harza Engineering Company.

Oceans and Coasts Philip Burgess, MARC; Donna Busch, National Marine Fisheries Service (United States); Adele Crispoldi, FAO; Clif Curtis, Oceanic Society; Arthur Dahl, UNEP; James Dobbin, James Dobbin Associates; Nancy Foster, National Marine Fisheries Service (United States); Tom Fox, WRI; Luis Gomez-Echeverri, UNDP; Dan Grosse, National Marine Fisheries Service (United States); Erik Helland-Hansen, UNDP; John Jackson, MARC; Graeme Kelleher, Great Barrier Reef Marine Park Authority; R.A. Kenchington, Coastal Zone Inquiry Resource Assessment Commission (Australia); Lee Kimball, WRI; Virginia Lee, University of Rhode Island Coastal Resources Center; Danielle Lucid, National Oceanic and Atmospheric Administration (United States); Joan Martin-Brown, UNEP; A.D. McIntyre, University of Aberdeen; Stephen Olsen, University of Rhode Island Coastal Resources Center; Peter Peterson, MARC; Walter Reid, WRI; Kenneth Sherman, National Marine Fisheries Service (United States); Martin Smith, UNEP; Michael Weber, National Marine Fisheries Service (United States); Miranda Wecker, Council on Ocean Law; Harold Weeks, Oregon Department of Fish and Wildlife; Ann Willcocks, MARC; John Wise; Donna Wise, WRI.

Atmosphere and Climate V. Adebayo, UNEP; A. Alusa, UNEP; Tom Boden, Carbon Dioxide Information Center, Oak Ridge National Laboratory; James Crowfoot, University of Michigan; Roger Dower, WRI; Tom Fox, WRI; James Galloway, University of Virginia; Luis Gomez-Echeverri, UNDP; Robert Hangebrauck, U.S. Environmental Protection Agency; Erik Helland-Hansen, UNDP; Charles Keeling, Scripps Institute of Oceanography; R.A. Kenchington, Coastal Zone Inquiry Resource Assessment Commission (Australia); M.A.K. Khalil, Center for Atmospheric Studies (Oregon); David Korten, People-Centered Development Forum (Philippines); Jin Kui, World Meteorological Organization (Switzerland); Alan Lloyd, California South Coast Air Quality; P.S. Low, UNEP; Jim MacKenzie, WRI; Gregg Marland, Carbon Dioxide Information Center, Oak Ridge National Laboratory; Joan Martin-Brown, UNEP; R.K. Pachauri, TATA Energy Research Institute (India); Larry Parker, U.S. Congressional Research Service, Lucio Reca, Inter-American Development Bank; John Reuther, Pittsburgh Energy Technology Center; David Richards, Experiment in International Living (Vermont); Kirk Smith, Environmental & Policy Institute (Hawaii); James Speth, WRI; Dan Tunstall, WRI; Veerle Vanderweerd, UNEP; Tony Webster, MARC; Ann Willcocks, MARC; Donna Wise, WRI.

Policies and Institutions Janet N. Abramovitz, WRI; Y. Ahmed, UNEP; Sheldon Annis, Boston University; Gilbert Arum, Kenya Energy and Environmental Organizations; David Beckmann, Bread for the World; Diane Bendahmane, Inter-American Foundation; Clare Billington, WCMC; Michael Bratton, Michigan State University; L. David Brown, Institute for Development Research (Boston); Tom Carroll, George Washington University; Susan Casey-Lefkowitz, IUCN; Michael Cernea, the World Bank; Manab Chakraborty, OXFAM; John Clark, OXFAM; James Crowfoot, University of Michigan; Uttam Dabholkar, UNEP; Christine Debrah, Environmental Protection Council (Ghana); Mohamed El-Ashry, the World Bank; Laurie Esposito, UNDP; Juan Flavier, International Institute for Rural Reconstruction (Philippines); Tom Fox, WRI; Ellis Franklin, CARE; Alfonso Gonzalez Martinez, Grupo De Estudios Ambientales (Mexico City); Robert Goodland, the World Bank; Enrique Iglesias, Inter-American Development Bank; Jane Jacqz, UNDP; Calestous Juma, African Center for Technology Studies; Yolanda Kakabadse, UNCED Secretariat; T.N. Khoshoo, TATA Energy Research Institute (India); David Korten, People-Centered Development Forum (Philippines); Wangari Maathai, National Council of Women in Kenya; Mik Magnusson, UNEP; Maria Marotta, UNEP; Joan Martin-Brown, UNEP; Kathleen McCarthy, City University of New York; Monika Mentzingen, UNEP; Carlos Pimentel; Lucio Reca, Inter-American Development Bank; Walter Reid, WRI; Charles Reilly, Inter-American Foundation; David Richards, Experiment in International Living (Vermont); Deodoro Roca, FAO; Robin Sharp, International Institute for Environment and Development (London); Jennifer Smith, Philippine Development Forum; M.S. Swaminathan; Kirk Talbott, WRI; Sally Timpsom, UNDP; Dan Tunstall, WRI;

Norman Uphoff, Cornell University; Steve Vetter, Inter-American Foundation; Ann Willcocks, MARC; Sally Yudelman, International Center for Research (Washington); Aaron Zazueta, WRI.

Basic Economic Indicators Jacqueline Carless, MARC; Betty Dow, the World Bank; Reza Farivari, the World Bank; Tom Fox, WRI; Monika Mentzingen, UNEP; John O'Connor, the World Bank; Dan Tunstall, WRI.

Land Cover and Settlements Jeffrey Allen, Jane's World Railways; A. Andreas, International Road Federation (Geneva); Philip Burgess, MARC; G. Dente, United Nations Economic Commission for Europe; Flemming Leicht, International Civil Aviation Organization (Montreal); Francesco Pariboni, FAO; S. Zarqa, FAO.

Production Staff

A talented team of copyeditors, fact-checkers, proofreaders and production editors, and desktop publishing experts accomplished the enormous task of making this volume ready for the printer in record time. We thank them for their dedication, hard work, long hours, and high professional standards. In addition to the *World Resources* staff, they include:

Additional Fact Checking and Research William Foerderer, W. James Batten
Copyeditors Martha Gottron, Sheila Mulvihill, Paul Phelps, Julie Philips, Roseanne Price
Proofreaders Evelyn Harris, Alden Lewis, Ann L. Martin
Manuscript Processing Kathryn Solee
Graphics Assistant James R. Mangani
Index Julie Philips
Desktop Production Robert Llewellyn, Vincent Llewellyn, Technology & Design, Inc., Washington, D.C.
Mechanical Production The Forte Group, Inc., Alexandria, Virginia

We are especially grateful to WRI Librarian Sue Terry for assisting us with research and materials.

It has been a privilege to work with so many outstanding individuals throughout the world in producing *World Resources 1992-93*.

Allen L. Hammond
Editor-in-Chief

1. Dimensions of Sustainable Development

The world faces a wide variety of critical environmental threats: degradation of soil, water, and marine resources essential to increased food production; widespread, health-threatening pollution; stratospheric ozone depletion; global climate change; and loss of biodiversity. At the same time, it faces enormous human problems in the form of widespread, persistent poverty and human misery—despite growing affluence for many—and a pattern of economic growth that is worsening rather than remedying such disparities.

Such problems are troubling enough. But if human societies in decades to come are to inhabit a world that is environmentally secure, economically prosperous, and characterized by growing peace, freedom, and human welfare, then current generations must also come to grips with underlying trends that threaten to make these problems far worse. One of the most basic trends is that world population has doubled since 1950 and is expected to roughly double again by the middle of the next century. Similarly, as people everywhere have struggled to improve their standards of living, world economic activity has grown at about 3 percent per year since 1950; if this rate continues in the de-

cades ahead, then the world economy will be 5 times larger in the year 2050 than it is today.

Such growth in population and economic activity has the potential to increase dramatically the pressure on natural resources and natural systems—from farmland to fisheries to the global atmosphere—which are already suffering serious levels of degradation. Consider just two examples:

■ Well over 1 billion people in the world are malnourished. To provide an adequate level of nutrition as the population doubles will require more than doubling current food production. Under the best conditions, that would require making very productive use of the world's stock of arable land. Yet according to new estimates by the world's leading soil scientists, more than 1.2 billion hectares of vegetated land—an area as large as India and China put together—have been significantly degraded since World War II. (See Chapter 8, "Forests and Rangelands.") If such degradation continues or accelerates, expansion of food production on the scale required will be extremely difficult, if not impossible, and greatly worsened human misery will be increasingly likely. In the last decade, in fact, per capita food production has declined in 69 developing countries. (See Chapter 18, "Food and Agriculture," Table 18.1.)

■ Fossil fuels provide about 95 percent of the commercial energy used in the world economy, and their use is growing worldwide at the rate of about 20 percent per decade. (See Chapter 10, "Energy," Table 10.1.) Combustion of those fuels constitutes the largest source of emissions of climate-altering greenhouse gases to the atmosphere. Scientists convened by the Intergovernmental Panel of Climate Change under the auspices of the United Nations Environmental Programme and the World Meteorological Organization concluded that a 60 percent reduction in carbon dioxide emissions would be necessary to stabilize carbon dioxide concentrations in the atmosphere at current levels. Protecting the Earth's climate therefore may require significant reductions in global fossil fuel use, even as the world economy expands; alternately, continued expansion of fossil fuel use at current rates will double atmospheric levels well before the middle of the next century and thus increase the risk of significant climate change [1].

As these examples illustrate, the world is not now headed toward a sustainable future, but rather toward a variety of potential human and environmental disasters. Over the past 20 years, since the Stockholm Conference on the Human Environment, the world has started to recognize that environmental problems are inseparable from those of human welfare and from the process of economic development in general and that many present forms of development erode the environmental resources on which human livelihoods and welfare ultimately depend. With this recognition, the United Nations established the World Commission on Environment and Development to examine these issues and make recommendations.

In *Our Common Future*, the Commission concluded that "a new developmental path was required, one that sustained human progress not just in a few places for a few years, but for the entire planet into the distant future." Sustainable development, as the Commission defined it, is development that "meets the needs of the present without compromising the ability of future generations to meet their own needs" [2].

In its broadest outlines, the concept of sustainable development has been widely accepted and endorsed. However, translating this concept into practical goals, programs, and policies around which nations could coalesce has proved to be harder to accomplish—in part because nations face widely varying circumstances.

A critically important effort to find common ground and to begin the process of change that sustainable development will require is the United Nations Conference on Environment and Development (UNCED). To take place in Rio de Janeiro, Brazil, in June 1992, this conference—and the extensive process of planning and consultation leading up to it—is perhaps the world's best near-term chance to forge a new consensus that can facilitate sustainable development. In support of UNCED, the first four chapters of this edition

of *World Resources* constitute a special report on sustainable development.

THE CONCEPT OF SUSTAINABLE DEVELOPMENT

In an attempt to make the concept of sustainable development more specific, some authors have given a narrow definition focused on the physical aspects of sustainable development. They stress using renewable natural resources in a manner that does not eliminate or degrade them or otherwise diminish their "renewable" usefulness for future generations [3] while maintaining effectively constant or nondeclining stocks of natural resources such as soil, groundwater, and biomass [4] [5]. Some economic definitions of sustainable development have also focused on optimal resource management, by concentrating on "maximizing the net benefits of economic development, subject to maintaining the services and quality of natural resources" [6].

Other economic definitions have focused on the broader notion that "the use of resources today should not reduce real incomes in the future" [7]. Underlying this notion "is the concept that current decisions should not impair the prospects for maintaining or improving future living standards . . . .This implies that our economic systems should be managed so that we live off the dividend of our resources, maintaining and improving the asset base" [8].

Economic development does not necessarily mean economic growth; the type of economic activity can change without increasing the quantity of goods and services. But many authors argue that not only is economic growth compatible with sustainable development—as long as it is the right kind of economic growth—it is in fact greatly needed to relieve poverty and generate the resources for development [9] and hence to prevent further environmental degradation [10]. The issue is the quality of the growth and how its benefits are distributed, not mere expansion. Some, however, argue that "sustainable growth" is a contradiction in terms, and that redistribution of wealth not growth is the way to combat poverty [11].

But economic growth, even growth that meets environmental criteria and does not increase consumption of natural resources or production of waste, may not be enough to prevent long-term environmental collapse. Constraints on human behavior also apply: on a finite Earth, population cannot grow indefinitely.

Sustainable development is also often defined as development that improves health care, education, and social well-being. Such human development is now recognized as critical to economic development [12] and to early stabilization of population [13]. As the *Human Development Report 1991* of the United Nations Development Programme put it, "men, women, and children must be the centre of attention—with development woven around people, not people around development" [14]. Increasingly, definitions of sustainable development stress that development must be participatory and must involve local peoples in decisions

Resource Sustainability: Land Degradation

Over the past 45 years, the soils of a significant portion of the world's productive lands have been degraded by human activities. Water and wind erosion, land compaction, loss of nutrients, and chemical contamination are limiting productive capacity and making it more difficult and expensive for farmers to increase production of food and fiber.

According to a new assessment, 1.2 billion hectares—an area larger than India and China together representing 11 percent of the Earth's vegetated surface—have been moderately or severely degraded since 1945. (See Figure 1.) In some instances, degradation means that farmers must increase fertilizer use just to produce the same amount of crops; some 300 million hectares, however, are so damaged that they have lost nearly all of their original biological function. Rehabilitation of even moderately degraded land would require more investment and care than farmers can afford.

There is no simple threshold that determines whether we have sufficient land left in the world to produce food for future generations. Agricultural production, both crop and livestock, are at all time highs. (See Figure 2.) But the world's population is expected to double by about the middle of the next century and there is little good land left for agricultural expansion. Thus continued degradation could make providing an adequate food supply for growing populations extremely difficult.

Figure 1 Moderate, Severe, and Extreme Land Degradation as a Percent of Vegetated Land, 1945-90

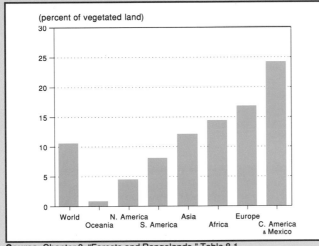

(percent of vegetated land)

Source: Chapter 8, "Forests and Rangelands," Table 8.1.
Note: Figures for European and Asian parts of the Soviet Union are included with Europe and Asia.

Figure 2 World Agricultural Production, 1961-90

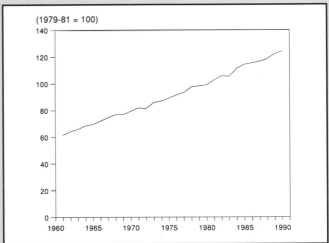

(1979-81 = 100)

Source: Food and Agriculture Organization of the United Nations (FAO), *Agrostat PC* (FAO, Rome, July 1991).

that affect their lives. (See Chapter 14, "Policies and Institutions.")

Some authors have expanded the definition of sustainable development still further to include a rapid transformation of the technological base of industrial civilization (15). They point out that new technology is needed that is cleaner, more efficient, and more sparing of natural resources in order to reduce pollution, help stabilize climate, and accommodate growth in populations and economic activity (16).

An important component of virtually all definitions of sustainable development has to do with equity. Two types are embodied in the World Commission's definition—equity for human generations yet to come, whose interests are not represented by standard economic analyses or by market forces that discount the future, and equity for people living now who do not have equal access to natural resources or to social and economic "goods." There is, in fact, some conflict between these two types of equity. Some authors point out that environmental issues in developing countries cannot be resolved without alleviating poverty and call for redis-

tribution of wealth or incomes both within countries and between rich and poor nations. Others stress intergenerational equity—the "sharing of well-being between present people and future people"—and focus on the need for reducing current consumption to provide for investments that build up resources such as knowledge or technology for the future. This conflict—between increased consumption now for poor people and increased investment for future generations—can also be stated in environmental terms. It is a conflict between increased burning of fossil fuels (or conversion of forests to agricultural uses as poor countries develop) and efforts on behalf of future generations to curb those actions to slow greenhouse warming and the loss of biological resources. Even if "an obligation to conduct ourselves so that we leave to the future the option or the capacity to be as well off as we are" is understood, the values, preferences, and technologies of future generations can only be guessed (17).

Increasingly, definitions of sustainable development attempt to cut across or encompass several aspects or dimensions. The new strategy outlined by the World

Conservation Union, *Caring for the Earth*, defines sustainable development as "improving the quality of human life while living within the carrying capacity of supporting ecosystems" (18). This report focuses on sustainable development as a process requiring simultaneous global progress in a variety of dimensions: economic, human, environmental, and technological.

In practice, however, sustainable development means different things for an African village than for a South American megacity or an industrialized European nation. In this and succeeding chapters, the attempt is to present some sense of the differing meanings and opportunities for sustainable development in different communities and nations worldwide, from the poorest to the most highly developed.

ENVISIONING SUSTAINABLE DEVELOPMENT

All countries are different, and in particular there are profound differences in the conditions of life and in outlook between the rich, industrialized countries and the poor, primarily rural, countries of the world. On closer examination, even a division into rich and poor is simplistic: there are a multiplicity of conditions and outlooks among and within countries, although it is often convenient to use such groupings for purposes of discussion. But in all contexts, there is a need for simultaneous progress along each of several different dimensions of sustainable development. This report identifies four critical, interacting dimensions: economic, human, environmental, and technological. These dimensions provide a way to discuss in more specific detail what sustainable development would look like in countries at various stages of development and, perhaps, a way to gauge progress toward that goal.

Economic Dimensions

On a per capita basis, inhabitants of industrial countries use many times more of the world's natural resources than do inhabitants of developing countries. Consumption of energy from fossil fuels, for example, is 33 times higher in the United States than in India and 10 times higher in countries of the Organisation for Economic Co-operation and Development (OECD), on average, than in developing countries (19). (See Chapter 21, "Energy and Materials," Table 21.2.) For rich countries, then, sustainable development means steady reductions in wasteful levels of consumption of energy and other natural resources through improvements in efficiency and through changes in life-style. In this process, care needs to be taken to ensure that environmental stresses are not simply exported to developing countries. Sustainable development also means changing consumption patterns that needlessly threaten the biodiversity of other countries.

Industrial countries have a special responsibility for leadership in sustainable development, because their cumulative past consumption of natural resources such as fossil fuels—and hence their contribution to global pollution problems—is disproportionately large. In addition, rich countries have the financial, technical, and human resources to take the lead in developing cleaner, less resource-intensive technologies, in transforming their economies to protect and work with natural systems, and in providing more equitable access to economic opportunities and social services within their societies. Leadership also means providing—as an investment in the future of the planet—technical and financial resources to support sustainable development in other countries. In addition, reducing the import barriers or protectionist pricing policies in rich countries that limit the access of poor economies to markets for their products would accelerate economic development worldwide.

One aspect of the international links among rich and poor countries needs careful consideration. To the extent that consumption of natural resources in industrial countries declines, it could slow the growth of exports of such products from developing countries and depress commodity prices still further, depriving developing countries of badly needed revenues. Expanded regional cooperation and trade among developing countries, heavy investments in human capital, and widespread adoption of improved technology would help to offset such losses.

In poor countries, sustainable development would mean the commitment of resources toward continued improvement in living standards. As an ethical matter, rapid improvement is especially critical for the more than 20 percent of the world's population now destitute. Alleviating absolute poverty also has important practical consequences for sustainable development, since there are close links between poverty, environmental degradation, and rapid population growth. People whose basic needs are unmet and whose survival may be in doubt perceive no stake in the future of the planet and have no reason to consider the sustainability of their actions. They also tend to have more children in an effort to increase the family labor force and provide security for their old age.

One means of alleviating poverty and improving living standards that applies to both rich and poor countries is also an end in itself: making access to resources among all people within a society more equal. The need goes beyond access to economic resources such as credit: unequal access to education and social services, to land and other natural resources, and to freedom of choice and other political rights is a major barrier to development. Correspondingly, more equal access helps to stimulate development and the economic growth needed to improve living standards.

Thus, sustainable development means reducing the growing disparity of incomes and access to health care in industrialized countries such as the United States (see Chapter 2, "Industrial Countries") making unproductive, large landholdings available to the landless poor in regions such as South America; extending credit and legitimacy to the informal economic sectors of many countries; and improving education and health care opportunities for women everywhere. It is worth noting that improved access to land, education, and other social services played a critical role in stimu-

Resource Stabilization: Climate Change

The Earth's carbon cycle is being stressed by increasing emissions of carbon dioxide from burning fossil fuels and rapid changes in land use. Emissions from fossil fuel use alone have increased 3.6 times since 1950. (See Figure 1.) Atmospheric concentrations of carbon dioxide in the atmosphere are increasing at 0.5 percent per year. (See Figure 2.)

The Intergovernmental Panel on Climate Change concluded that such emissions, if continued, will enhance the greenhouse effect, resulting on average in an additional warming of the Earth's surface. The Panel estimated that an immediate, 60 percent reduction in emissions would be required to stabilize atmospheric concentrations of carbon dioxide at present levels. (See Figure 1.)

Figure 1 Worldwide Annual Emission of CO_2 from Industrial Sources, 1860–1989

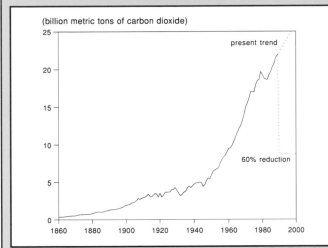

Source: Carbon Dioxide Information Analysis Center (CDIAC) (Oak Ridge National Laboratory, Oak Ridge, Tennessee, unpublished data, July 1991). See also Chapter 24, "Atmosphere and Climate," Table 24.4.

Figure 2 Atmospheric CO_2 Concentrations, 1860–1990

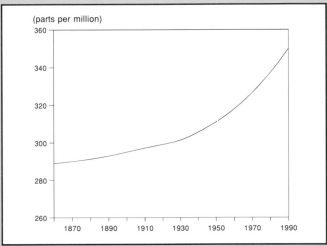

Source: Intergovernmental Panel on Climate Change (IPCC), *Climate Change: The IPCC Scientific Assessment*, J.T. Houghton, G.J. Jenkins, and J.J. Ephraums, eds. (Cambridge University Press, Cambridge, U.K., 1990), p. xvi.

lating rapid development and growth in economies such as the Republic of Korea and Taiwan. (See Chapter 4, "Rapidly Industrializing Countries.")

In all countries, sustainable development means transferring money from military and state security expenditures to development needs. Reallocating even a small portion of the resources now devoted to the military could markedly accelerate development (20).

Human Dimensions

Sustainable development means significant progress toward stable populations. This is important not only because continued growth of the human population for long at anything like current global rates is clearly impossible, but also because rapid growth puts severe strains on natural resources and on the ability of governments to provide services. Within a given country or region, rapid population growth undercuts development and dilutes the natural resource base available to support each inhabitant (21).

The final size attained by Earth's human population is also important, because the limits of Earth's carrying capacity for human life are not known with any accuracy. Current projections suggest that, given present trends in fertility, world population will stabilize at about 11.6 billion, which would more than double the current population. (See Chapter 6, "Population and Human Development.") Even at present levels, population pressure is a growing factor in deforestation, land degradation, and the overexploitation of wildlife and other natural resources; as expanding populations are driven to marginal lands or must overuse resources.

Distribution of population is important too: present trends toward increasing urbanization, especially the development of megacities, have massive environmental implications. With currently employed technologies, cities concentrate wastes and pollutants and thus often generate conditions hazardous to people and damaging to surrounding natural systems. Thus, sustainable development would mean vigorous rural development to help slow migration to cities and adoption of policy measures and technologies to minimize the environmental consequences of urbanization.

Sustainable development also entails making full use of human resources by improving education and health services and by combating hunger. It is especially important that basic services reach those living in extreme poverty; thus, sustainable development would mean redirecting or reallocating resources to ensure that basic human needs, such as literacy, primary health care, and clean water, are met first (22). Beyond basic needs, sustainable development means improving social well-being, protecting cultural diversity, and investing in human capital—training the educators, health-care workers, technicians and scientists, and other specialists needed for continuing development.

Human development also interacts strongly with other dimensions of sustainable development. A population healthy and well-fed enough to work and a better educated work force, for example, assist economic development (23). Education can help farmers and other rural inhabitants to better protect forests, soil resources, and biodiversity.

The role of women is particularly critical. In many developing countries, women and children grow the subsistence crops, graze animals, gather wood and water, use most of the household's energy in cooking, and care for the household's immediate environment. In other words, women are the primary resource and environmental managers in the household—as well as the primary care-givers for children—yet their health and education are often neglected in comparison to those of men. More-educated women have greater access to contraception and, on average, lower fertility rates, as well as healthier babies. (See Chapter 6, "Population and Human Development.") Investing in the health and education of women can have multiple benefits for sustainability.

Sustainable development also requires the participation of those affected by decisions in their planning and execution, for the practical reason that development efforts that do not involve local groups often fail.

Environmental Dimensions

Soil erosion and loss of soil productivity reduce yields and remove large areas of agricultural land from production every year. Overuse of fertilizers and pesticides pollutes surface and groundwater. Human and livestock pressures damage or destroy vegetation and forests. Many freshwater and marine fisheries are already being harvested at levels that are now, or are close to becoming, unsustainable.

Sustainable development necessitates protecting the natural resources needed for food production and cooking fuels—from soils to woodlots to fisheries—while expanding production to meet the needs of growing populations. These are potentially conflicting goals, and yet failure to conserve the natural resources on which agriculture depends would ensure future shortages of food. Sustainable development means more efficient use of arable lands and water supplies, as well as development and adoption of improved agricultural practices and technologies to increase yields. It requires avoiding overuse of chemical fertilizers and pesticides, so that they do not degrade rivers and lakes, threaten wildlife, and contaminate human food and water supplies. It means careful use of irrigation, to avoid salinization or waterlogging of cropland. It means avoiding the expansion of agriculture onto steep hillsides or marginal soils that would rapidly erode. (See Chapter 7, "Food and Agriculture.")

In some regions, water is in as short supply as land, with withdrawals from rivers threatening to exhaust the available supply and groundwater being pumped at unsustainable rates. Industrial, agricultural, and human wastes are polluting surface and groundwater and threatening lakes and estuaries in virtually every country. Sustainable development means conserving water by ending wasteful uses and improving the efficiency of water systems. It also means improving water quality and limiting surface water withdrawals to a rate that would not disrupt ecosystems dependent on those waters, and limiting groundwater withdrawals to the rate of regeneration. (See Chapter 11, "Freshwater.")

The area of wildlands—lands not appropriated to human use—continues to decline, reducing the habitat available for species other than the few that humans manage intensively or that can survive in the domesticated environment. Tropical forests, coral reef ecosystems, coastal mangrove forests and other wetlands, and many other unique habitats are being rapidly destroyed, and species extinction is accelerating. Sustainable development means that the richness of Earth's biodiversity would be conserved for future generations by greatly slowing—and, if possible, halting—extinctions and habitat and ecosystem destruction. (See Chapter 9, "Wildlife and Habitat.")

Sustainable development also means not risking significant alterations of the global environment that might—by increasing sea level or changing rainfall and vegetation patterns or increasing ultraviolet radiation—alter the opportunities for future generations. That means preventing the destabilization of climate or other global biogeophysical systems or the destruction of the Earth's protective ozone layer by human actions (see the following section).

Technological Dimensions

Industrial facilities have often polluted surrounding air, water, and land. In developed countries, control of effluent streams and pollution cleanup are accomplished at great expense; in many developing countries, effluents are largely uncontrolled. Yet, pollution is not an inevitable consequence of industrial activity. Such effluents reflect inefficient technologies or wasteful processes as well as carelessness and lack of economic penalties. Sustainable development means shifting to technologies that are cleaner and more efficient—as close to "zero emissions" or "closed" processes as possible—and that minimize consumption of energy and other natural resources. The goal should be processes or technological systems that create few wastes or pollutants in the first place, that recycle wastes internally, and that work with or support natural systems. In some instances, traditional technologies meet these criteria well and should be preserved.

Prototypes and possibilities for many such ecologically modern technologies exist and are beginning to be exploited. The transition to such technologies would be supported by expansion of the highly developed economies—because these sectors are often less resource intensive (24). The private sector has a critical role in sustainable development because it is the primary agent in developing and deploying improved technologies. Despite many abuses, private firms often

Resource Sustainability: Marine Fish Catch

For the first time in history, stocks of most marine fish species are now being fully exploited. Annual marine fish catch in 1990 was 84.2 million metric tons, representing a 35 percent increase since 1980 and more than a fourfold increase since 1950. As signs of severe pressure on this resource accumulate, there is growing concern that these tremendous gains cannot be sustained. In 8 of the world's 17 ocean fisheries, the amount of fish caught exceeded the lower range of the estimated sustainable catch. (See Figure 1.) In 1980, only 5 areas were fished so heavily.

Increasing pollution in coastal waters and destruction of coastal estuaries, which provide reproduction grounds for 90 percent of the world's marine catch, are also degrading the fisheries. Under these circumstances, expanding the catch will prove difficult; it may take years of rehabilitation just to maintain current production levels. (See Chapter 12, "Oceans and Coasts.")

Figure 1 Marine Fish Catch as a Percent of Estimated Average Sustainable Catch, 1987–89

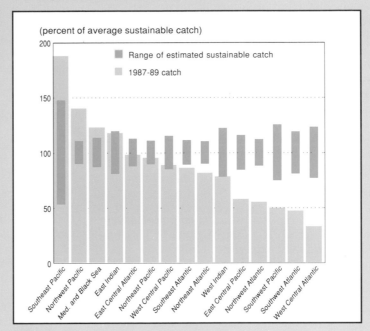

(percent of average sustainable catch)

■ Range of estimated sustainable catch
□ 1987-89 catch

Source: Chapter 23, "Oceans and Coasts," Table 23.3.
Note: Maximum sustainable yields are not defined for Arctic and Antarctic regions.

have a better environmental record than do government-run industries in market economies; nonmarket economies have often produced even worse environmental abuse. (See Chapter 5, "Regional Focus: Central Europe.") Many major industries—particularly multinational firms—are cutting effluents and emissions, reducing unnecessary packaging, or recycling materials after consumer use. Sustainable development means encouraging such trends and finding additional incentives for responsible corporate behavior on a global basis.

In developing countries, the technologies now in use are frequently less efficient and much more highly polluting than those available in industrial countries (25). Sustainable development means rapid introduction of improved technologies, as well as improved government regulation and enforcement. Technology cooperation—joint development or adaptation of cleaner and more efficient technologies to fit local needs—to close the gap between industrialized and developing countries would raise economic productivity as well as prevent further deterioration in environmental quality. (See Chapter 10, "Energy," Focus On Technology Cooperation in Energy Efficiency.) Such efforts, to be successful, also require significant investments in education and human development, particularly in poorer countries. Technology cooperation illustrates the interaction of the economic, human, environmental, and technological dimensions in achieving sustainable development.

Of particular concern are fossil fuels, the use of which is a prime example of an unclosed industrial process. These fuels are mined and burned, and the waste is discarded into the environment. As a result, they are a major source of urban air pollution, of the acid rain affecting large regions, and of the trace greenhouse gases that threaten to alter the climate. Current levels of emissions of greenhouse gases from human activities exceed the Earth's ability to absorb them; short-term effects are uncertain, but most scientists agree that such emissions cannot be continued indefinitely at current or increasing levels without causing a global warming of the climate. The resulting changes in temperatures, rainfall patterns, and eventually sea levels—particularly if rapid—would have devastating effects on ecosystems and on the well-being and livelihoods of people, especially those directly dependent on natural systems. (See Chapter 13, "Atmosphere and Climate.")

Sustainable development means limiting the global rate of increase of greenhouse gases and, eventually, stabilizing the atmospheric concentrations of these gases. The most important greenhouse gas arising from human activity is carbon dioxide, which accounts for about half of the atmospheric warming potential of current greenhouse gas emissions; combustion of fossil fuels accounts for about three fourths of such carbon dioxide emissions. Thus, sustainable development has profound implications for world energy supplies: it means that, over time, use of fossil fuels must be greatly curtailed and other sources of energy found to support industrial societies. The industrial countries will need to take the initial steps to limit carbon dioxide emissions and to develop new technologies for using fossil energy more efficiently and for providing safe and affordable supplies of nonfossil energy. Until such technologies are in place, however, sustainable development means using fossil fuels as efficiently as possible in all countries.

Sustainable development also means preventing degradation of the Earth's protective ozone layer. Actions taken to deal with this problem provide an encouraging precedent: the Geneva Convention and the subsequent Montreal Protocol, which require a phase out of ozone-threatening chemicals, show that international cooperation to deal with global environmental threats is possible.

POLICY IMPLICATIONS

The dimensions of progress toward sustainable development outlined in the preceding section are demanding and will not be achieved without international cooperation, political will, and improved policies. But policy levers do exist that could move the world in the direction of sustainable development. Although the particulars of any policy must be adapted for specific countries and situations, the policy directions outlined in this section provide a starting point.

Economic Policies

Proper Resource Pricing

Resources that are undervalued are often wasted. Price signals are thus a powerful policy tool to support more sustainable development.

Many industrial countries have natural resource subsidies, established in another era, that encourage production or support often wasteful levels of consumption. Proper resource pricing may mean elimination of subsidies for irrigation water, grazing rights, use of fertilizer, timber cutting, and production of fossil fuels. The fact that some resources, such as clean air and water, are unpriced has encouraged pollution. Although regulations can restrict such behavior, pricing policies such as direct pollution taxes (based on the principle of "the polluter pays") and tradable emission permits may be more efficient and more effective. Energy taxes based on the carbon content of the fuel, such as those proposed by the European Community to stabilize carbon dioxide emissions, are an example of the type of pricing policies that could support more sustainable economic development.

Proper resource pricing is equally important in developing countries. For example, forest resources have been undervalued, which has led to chaotic exploitation of timber, with little development benefit and serious ecological damage. Realistic resource pricing and recognition of the value of nontimber commodities and ecological services, along with enforcement of conservation policies, would promote more sustainable

development. Similar considerations apply to other natural resources.

Access to Resources

Many of the rural poor do not own the land they farm or have only insecure rights at best. Yet secure rights to land, trees, and other resources encourage people to invest in and conserve such resources. In addition, the distribution of land and other natural resources is often extremely skewed: much good land is underutilized while the rural poor crowd onto hillsides with fragile soils or pour into forests. Where large tracts of productive land lie idle, breaking these lands into smaller holdings to be farmed more actively would often be even more productive and could provide some of the rural poor with better livelihoods. Land reform and similar policies are controversial and politically difficult, yet have proved to be an important stimulus to development where they have occurred. (See Chapter 4, "Rapidly Industrializing Countries.")

Policies that reduce the value of large underutilized holdings as inflation hedges and tax shelters facilitate land reform. Such policies include increases in land taxes, elimination of credit subsidies, especially to livestock operations, and lasting control over inflation.

Because sustainable development can be considered a form of investment in the future, many policies that favor investment—including investment in new knowledge or improved technologies—or environmental protection at the expense of current consumption can assist sustainable development.

People-Oriented Policies

Setting Priorities

Many development programs have neglected the poorest segments of societies. Priorities need to be reordered to commit public funds first to provide a basic level of services for all. Policies that favor urban over rural development or that discriminate against agricultural development also need to be reconsidered. Those who are better off should be required to pay for services beyond the basic level in education, health, urban services, transportation, and other development sectors. Giving priority to alleviating poverty is appropriate on both moral and practical grounds. Rural development is critical to initiating economic development, to stabilizing population growth, and to preventing further degradation of soils, forests, and other natural resources.

Investing in Human Development

Providing more and better education, health care, and related social services is an essential strategy for achieving sustainable development. There is evidence in the performance of rapidly growing economies that investment in human development is also one of the most effective ways to accelerate economic growth (26).

A recent report concluded that developing countries could usefully redirect much current spending—in excess of 2 percent of gross domestic product—toward

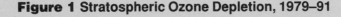

Resource Stabilization: Stratospheric Ozone

Stratospheric ozone, which absorbs much of the sun's damaging ultraviolet rays, is being depleted by the production and use of chlorofluorocarbons and other related compounds. Increases in ultraviolet radiation cause skin cancers and cataracts, and may disrupt the marine food chain and damage crops.

Recent measurements indicate that peak ozone destruction (during polar spring) has reached 60 percent over Antarctica. (See Figure 1.) For the first time, significant ozone losses have also been found at mid-latitudes (45° corresponds to Christchurch, New Zealand in the south and Minneapolis, Minnesota in the north). There are preliminary indications of an Arctic ozone hole over the North Pole. Only equatorial regions so far show no significant ozone losses.

Because chlorine and bromine chemicals already released to the atmosphere will reach the stratosphere in coming years, ozone losses are expected to increase at least through the end of the century. Even if use of such chemicals is rapidly eliminated, full recovery of the ozone layer is not expected until about the year 2100. (See Chapter 13, "Atmosphere and Climate.")

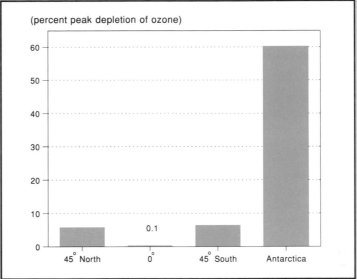

Figure 1 Stratospheric Ozone Depletion, 1979–91

(percent peak depletion of ozone)

Source: World Meteorological Organization (WMO) and United Nations Environment Programme (UNEP), "Scientific Assessment of Stratospheric Ozone, 1991," executive summary (WMO, October 22, 1991), pp. 2 and 4.

---

human development. Because so much spending is misdirected or inefficiently used, efforts to reduce military or state security expenditures, halt capital flight, combat corruption, and reform or privatize unsuccessful public enterprises could make available large amounts of money to support human development (27).

Industrial countries, too, have many unmet human needs among their populations. Reducing military expenditures could provide the resources to meet those needs. Concentrating foreign assistance on human and economic development rather than on armaments would better help the populations of recipient countries—and probably the cause of peace.

A wide range of policies can support human development. Low-cost, community-based health, nutrition, and family planning programs have achieved remarkable reductions in birth and death rates in unpromising settings. Urban self-help and community improvement programs that are largely self-financing have dramatically improved urban environments. (See *World Resources 1990–91*, Chapter 5, "Human Settlements.") Small credit programs have reduced poverty. Providing seedlings, credit, and land to landless peasants has raised incomes and promoted reforestation.

Grasping these opportunities on the scale needed will require significant policy and institutional changes. Among the most important of these changes is the need to decentralize responsibility for planning and executing development programs, since centralized agencies often lack the information or resources to deal with many dispersed small activities. Policies that empower community organizations—to ensure that the

disadvantaged benefit and that local capabilities are involved—also favor sustainable development. (See Chapter 14, "Policies and Institutions.")

Stabilizing Populations

The essential elements of policy to slow population growth are known. Stated broadly, a shift in priorities to alleviate poverty, a focus on human development—especially for women and children—and the proliferation of basic health and family planning services are needed. The first two of these are discussed above; the third is discussed here.

There are now adequate models of low-cost, community-based health and family planning programs on which to build. Successful programs tend to integrate health and family planning services; they use community organizations, leaders, and workers extensively; invest heavily in training of paraprofessionals, local facilities, outreach, and education; and emphasize cost-effective interventions such as immunization, pre- and postnatal care, and nutrition and family planning education. Expanding such programs rapidly through increases in trained personnel, facilities, and funding and providing contraceptives to all women who want them, would help stabilize populations.

Environmental Policies

Stabilizing Climate

The policy change most fundamental to climate stabilization is an international commitment to reduce use of fossil fuels for energy, at least in industrial countries. One means of accomplishing this is higher prices for fossil fuels (28). Such a policy might take the form of escalating energy taxes based on the carbon content of fuels. Gradually rising prices would promote both energy efficiency and more rapid development of renewable energy resources. Such policies are often opposed on the grounds that they would retard economic growth. If the revenues from such taxes were offset by reduced taxes of other kinds, however, they could have a profoundly positive environmental effect without slowing economic growth.

A recent study by the U.S. National Academy of Sciences concluded that 10–40 percent of current U.S. greenhouse gas emissions might be abated at modest cost; half those emissions might be eliminated with net economic savings, through cost-effective improvements in energy efficiency (29). Significant energy efficiency gains are possible in many countries, with consequent reductions in both local pollution and greenhouse gas emissions.

It is critical that international agreements be reached on steps to stabilize concentrations of greenhouse gases. Without such agreement, decisive national actions cannot be expected. It is also important for countries to pursue policies that would yield national benefits even in the absence of climate change, but which also reduce greenhouse gas emissions. Examples include energy efficiency improvements, arresting deforestation, and expanded technology cooperation to provide access to resource-efficient, low-polluting technologies for developing countries.

Sustaining Agriculture

Soil deterioration can be stopped only if farmers and agribusinesses adopt soil-conserving farming systems and invest in soil conservation. Most current incentives promote the opposite. Subsidies for agricultural chemicals, for example, encourage many farmers (but not those who are too poor to buy fertilizers and pesticides) to stick with soil-depleting monocultures, and make the cost of maintaining yields in the face of declining soil productivity artificially cheap. These subsidies are widespread in developing countries and discourage sustainable farming practices.

In Europe, the United States, and Japan, farm subsidies in the form of commodity support programs also encourage very high use of fertilizers and pesticides on cultivated land; the resulting runoff into streams and rivers makes agriculture the largest source of nonpoint pollution. Import barriers also keep many foreign products off store shelves. Elimination of domestic subsidies and removal of trade barriers in farm products would encourage farmers to adopt more sustainable and less environmentally damaging farming systems in developed and developing countries. (See Chapter 7, "Food and Agriculture.")

In addition, agriculture is the only major sector largely exempt from the "polluter pays" principle. Although the substantial damages that result from agricultural runoff cannot be reflected directly in pollution charges, they could be addressed through taxes on agricultural chemicals, water charges, and other inputs.

In very poor countries, however, where poverty and subsistence agriculture are widespread and food production is inadequate, rather different policies—those that support rural development and expanded food production—are needed. (See Setting Priorities, above.)

Conserving Biodiversity

Using biological resources without diminishing biodiversity will require improved efforts to prevent degradation of key natural habitats and to preserve the health of ecosystems. Attention must be focused not only on protected areas, threatened species, and seed banks, but also on striking a balance between people's needs and nature's in many human activities. Adoption of a "convention on biodiversity" would provide a critically needed international framework for such efforts. National policies in such areas as forestry, fisheries, and wildlife management need to be reconsidered to be sure that they provide economic incentives and legal frameworks that support biodiversity conservation. In addition, virtually all countries need to improve their institutional and human capacity to manage and conserve biodiversity; the need is particularly acute in developing countries. Local community involvement is essential to ensure that those directly affected will both support biodiversity conservation and receive a greater share of the benefits from biological resources.

Biotechnology is radically altering the value of genetic resources. Treating such resources as "the common heritage of humankind" has provided little conservation incentive and has led to inequities in the distribution of benefits from biodiversity. Countries may need to declare sovereignty over genetic resources and adopt clear regulations concerning their collection. Private companies need to recognize such rights and negotiate royalties or other forms of participation for products derived from a country's genetic resources; a recent agreement between a major drug company and Costa Rica deserves to be widely copied. (See Chapter 9, "Wildlife and Habitat.")

Creating Sustainable Systems

Incentives to Reduce Pollution and Wastes

As long as households and enterprises can dispose of wastes into the environment freely or with little restriction, demand for cleaner technologies will lag. As long as energy, water, timber, and other natural resources are underpriced, demand for energy- and resource-efficient technologies will be depressed. In industrial countries, environmental regulations and price signals need to be strengthened. In developing and formerly socialist countries, governments need to be persuaded and helped to put in place effective systems of environmental management, relying on market incentives to a much greater extent.

In addition to economic incentives, the pressure of public opinion can be an extremely strong force supporting the adoption of cleaner, more efficient technologies. Citizens' groups and nongovernmental organizations can play a key role here. (See Chapter 14, "Policies and Institutions.") In the United States, laws requiring disclosure of toxic releases have been a more potent force for emission reduction than any other toxic-substance regulatory requirement. In contrast, the absence of information available to the public in Eastern and Central Europe was a factor in allowing pollution to grow to dangerous levels with little public opposition. (See Chapter 5, "Regional Focus: Central Europe.")

Market processes can be brought to bear on natural resource valuation through mechanisms such as privatization, deregulation, creation of markets (e.g., for water rights), and use of auctions for rights to use resources in the public domain. In addition, environmental costs need to be reflected in market prices by applying the "polluter pays" principle, using environmental charges and taxes. Monitoring and information technologies have progressed to the extent that charges based on actual emissions, congestion, and other forms of environmentally damaging behavior can be administered successfully, at least in industrial countries. Raising revenues by taxing social "ills," such as pollution, instead of social "virtues," such as work and savings, can raise economic productivity and promote sustainability.

Technology Development and Cooperation

Many unexploited opportunities for adopting cleaner, more efficient technology or practices already exist in industrial and developing countries alike. More are rapidly being created. A key question is: which policies will promote their use, both in the country of origin and in other countries.

Creating demand for such technologies, as described above, is one important approach. Strengthening environmental management capacity and enforcement practices in developing countries through technical assistance will also increase demand for improved technology. Reducing disincentives for licensing and other commercial transfers is another approach. For example, greater global acceptance of and adherence to patent treaties that protect innovations (which some developing countries have not yet signed) will speed diffusion of technology. So will reducing barriers to private investment.

Many technologies, however, need to be adapted or developed to meet local conditions and preferences. Improved technology cooperation among countries will improve access to new ideas—on everything from monitoring and testing systems, to energy efficiency, to regulatory design—and accelerate their use. Information sharing, joint ventures, and new international institutions such as technology "extension services" or development institutes are needed. Few programs now exist to facilitate such technology cooperation. (See Chapter 10, "Energy," Focus On Technology Cooperation in Energy Efficiency.)

GLOBAL ISSUES

Effects of War on Development and the Environment

The 1991 Persian Gulf War was a dramatic reminder that environmental destruction can be swift and deliberate rather than gradual and inadvertent. Equally, the war and its aftermath underscored the extent to which military conflict—and preparations for it—are a continuing threat to sustainable development.

The war brought widespread damage to the region's air, water, land, vegetation, animal life, and people. The environmental damage included:

■ Smoke, soot, and a mist of unburned oil droplets from burning oil wells that created potentially hazardous air pollution and covered vegetation and virtually everything else with oil;

■ Huge lakes of spilled oil and a land surface pulverized by bombs and plowed up by military vehicles, leaving badly disturbed and easily eroded soils;

■ The largest oil spill in history, into the very slowly replenished waters of the Persian Gulf, damaging beaches and birds and raising the possibility of accumulation of toxic materials in the food chain of a fishery on which many people depend for food;

■ Similar damage to crops and other vegetation and to animals from contaminated forage and water; and

■ Release into the environment of radioactive materials and toxic chemicals when an Iraqi nuclear reactor, chemical warfare factories, and refineries were bombed.

War is the antithesis of development; both Iraq and Kuwait must rebuild a substantial portion of their industrial plant and infrastructure. Even less dramatic wars, however, make development efforts next to impossible and, especially in poor countries, cause widespread destitution, famine, and social disruption. By one accounting, there have been 127 wars and violent internal conflicts since 1945, all but two of them in the developing world, although often with industrial countries' direct involvement (30). Such conflicts have a direct effect on economic performance and development. One study found that most precipitous declines in economic growth could be traced to serious political disturbances and civil or international violence (31). A partial list of victims in just the last decade is long: Sudan, Ethiopia, Chad, Somalia, Nigeria, Uganda, Mozambique, Angola, Afghanistan, Iran, Iraq, Lebanon, Haiti, Peru, El Salvador, Nicaragua, Cambodia, and Myanmar. That these are among the world's poorest countries and also rank relatively low in human development is no accident (32).

Warfare and the preparations for it have indirect effects on environment and development as well. The preparations for war consume a large proportion of national budgets, spending that could be better directed to development efforts. Over the past three decades, spending on military and state security in developing countries has risen three times faster than in industrial countries, growing at a rate of 7.5 percent per year. In 1987, annual military spending in developing countries amounted to $173 billion; in some poor countries, arms expenditures are now two to three times the spending on education and health (33). In the wake of war, poor people desperate for food and livelihood often further degrade their environment. Sustainable development means reversing such spending priorities and reducing military conflicts.

The Debt Burden

Much of what needs to be done to move toward sustainable development is within the power of individual nations, including setting new policies and reallocating their resources. For many nations, however, one major barrier to development is the size of their external debts. Debt payments often constitute a large share of the national budget, squeezing out needed investments in environmental protection or economic and human development. In some countries, debt service obligations are so large that they exceed new loans and private external investment, meaning that financial resources are flowing out of, rather than into, the country. The need to make debt payments can also lead government officials to focus on short-term problems to the exclusion of the longer-term issues on which sustainability ultimately depends. Rescheduling or canceling debt can help progress toward sustainable development.

CONCLUSION

Reaching the goal of sustainable development requires simultaneous progress along at least four dimensions —economic, human, environmental, and technological. There are close linkages among these different dimensions, and actions in one area can reinforce goals in another. For example, heavy investment in human capital, especially among the poor, supports efforts to reduce poverty, to rapidly stabilize population, to narrow economic inequalities, to prevent further degradation of land and biological resources, and to allow rapid development and use of more efficient technologies in all countries.

Technological innovation is itself an important cross-cutting theme. Sustainability will require continuing technological change in industrial countries to reduce emissions and resource use per unit of output. It will also require rapid technological change in developing countries, especially those that are industrializing, to avoid repeating the developmental mistakes and multiplying the environmental damage of industrial countries. Technological improvement is also critical to reconciling development objectives and environmental constraints.

Sustainable development will require a fundamental change in existing policies and practices. Such change will not come easily, and will not come at all without strong leadership and the continued efforts of people in many countries.

This chapter is based on a background paper by Robert Repetto; it includes additional contributions from other senior staff members of the World Resources Institute.

References and Notes

1. Intergovernmental Panel on Climate Change (IPCC), *Climate Change: The IPCC Scientific Assessment*, T. Houghton, G.J. Jenkins, and J.J. Ephraums, eds. (Cambridge University Press, Cambridge, U.K., 1990), pp. xi and xvii.
2. World Commission on Environment and Development, *Our Common Future* (Oxford University Press, New York, 1987), pp. 4 and 8.
3. Robert Goodland and George Ledec, "Neoclassical Economics and Principles of Sustainable Development," *Ecological Modelling*, Vol. 38 (1987), p. 36.
4. David W. Pearce, Edward B. Barbier, and Anil Markandya, *Sustainable Development and Cost Benefit Analysis* (London Environmental Economics Centre, London, 1988), p. 6.
5. Charles Howe, *Natural Resource Economics* (Wiley, New York, 1979), p. 337.
6. Edward B. Barbier, *Economics, Natural Resources, Scarcity and Development: Conventional and Alternative Views* (Earthscan Publications Ltd., London, 1989), p. 185.
7. Anil Markandya and David W. Pearce, "Natural Environments and the Social Rate of Discount," *Project Appraisal*, Vol. 3, No. 1 (1988), p. 11.
8. Robert Repetto, *World Enough and Time* (Yale University Press, New Haven, Connecticut, 1986), pp. 15-16.
9. Jim MacNeill, "Strategies for Sustainable Economic Development," Scientific American, Vol. 261, No. 3 (September 1989), pp. 155-156.

10. *Op. cit.* 2, p. 89.
11. Herman E. Daly, "Towards Some Operational Principles of Sustainable Development," *Ecological Economics*, Vol. 2 (1990), pp. 1 and 5.
12. United Nations Development Programme, *Human Development Report 1991* (Oxford University Press, New York, 1991), pp. 1-2.
13. *Op. cit.* 2, pp. 55-56.
14. *Op. cit.* 12, p. 1.
15. James Gustave Speth, "The Environment: The Greening of Technology," *Development*, Vol. 2, No. 3 (1989), pp. 30-32.
16. George Heaton, Robert Repetto, and Rodney Sobin, *Transforming Technology: An Agenda for Environmentally Sustainable Growth in the 21st Century* (World Resources Institute, Washington, D.C., 1991), p. ix.
17. Robert M. Solow, "Sustainability," J. Seward Johnston Lecture (Woods Hole Oceanographic Institution, Woods Hole, Massachusetts, 1991), pp. 1-13.
18. IUCN-the World Conservation Union, United Nations Environment Programme (UNEP), and World Wide Fund for Nature (WWF), *Caring for the Earth* (IUCN, UNEP, and WWF, Gland, Switzerland, 1991), p. 10.
19. The OECD member countries are Australia, Austria, Belgium, Canada, Denmark, Finland, France, Germany, Greece, Iceland, Ireland, Italy, Japan, Luxembourg, the Netherlands, New Zealand, Norway, Portugal, Spain, Sweden, Switzerland, Turkey, the United Kingdom, and the United States. The developing countries include all coun-

tries except for OECD members, the Soviet Union, and Central European countries.
20. *Op. cit.* 12, p. 10.
21. Robert Repetto, "Population, Resources, Environment: An Uncertain Future," reprinted from *Population Bulletin*, Vol. 42, No. 2 (1989), pp. 14-34.
22. *Op. cit.* 12, pp. 49-53.
23. *Op. cit.* 12.
24. *Op. cit.* 16, pp. 7-9.
25. U.S. Congress, Office of Technology Assessment (OTA), *Energy in Developing Countries* (OTA, Washington, D.C., January 1991), pp. 64-66.
26. *Op. cit.* 12.
27. *Op. cit.* 12, p. 5.
28. James J. MacKenzie, *Toward a Sustainable Energy Future: The Critical Role of Rational Energy Pricing* (World Resources Institute, Washington, D.C., May 1991), p. 7.
29. National Academy of Sciences, *Policy Implications of Greenhouse Warming* (National Academy Press, Washington, D.C., 1991), pp. 59 and 63.
30. Ruth L. Sivard, *World Military and Social Expenditures 1989* (War Priorities, Washington, D.C., 1989), p. 22.
31. Robert Repetto, "Coping with the Eighties: Lessons from the Seventies," report prepared for the United Nations Department of International Economic and Social Affairs, New York, 1981, p. 6.
32. *Op. cit.* 12, Table 1, pp. 119-121.
33. *Op. cit.* 12, p. 82.

Introduction
to Case Studies

The preceding chapter argues that economic development, to be sustainable, cannot neglect environmental constraints nor be based on the destruction of natural resources; that it cannot succeed without the parallel development of human resources; and that, to be sustainable on a global level, it will require transformation of the existing industrial base and the development and diffusion of more Earth-friendly technologies.

Yet sustainable development remains a difficult, confusing, and even controversial idea. One of the problems is that, quite literally, there are no extant examples of sustainable development on a national level. Neither the industrial countries of the Organisation for Economic Co-operation and Development (OECD) nor the planned economies of Central Europe nor the newly industrialized economies of Southeast Asia offer adequate models: all achieved rapid industrial and economic growth at the expense of widespread environmental degradation and a continuing record of disasters, from the poisoning of Minamata Bay in Japan in the 1960s to Chernobyl in the Soviet Union and the *Exxon Valdez* oil spill in the United States in the 1980s. In the absence of explicit, widely recognized models, the concept of sustainable development and the policies needed to put it into practice are still evolving and open to debate.

A second problem is that sustainable development means different things to different people. To a village-level official in sub-Saharan Africa, it may mean, first and foremost, dealing with poverty and human misery through health and education services to get development started; to an environmental minister in Europe, it may mean protecting the physical environment by limiting emissions of both greenhouse gases and other effluents that cause acid rain; to an economic planner in Latin America or Southeast Asia, it may mean seeking to invest the income from logging operations in reforestation programs, so that the forest resource can be renewed. The resulting diversity of perceptions does not make coherent discussion easy, and the diversity of actual situations makes generalizations dangerous.

LEVELS OF ECONOMIC DEVELOPMENT

The following three chapters present three case studies that amplify the dimensions of sustainable development proposed in Chapter 1 and apply them to countries exemplifying three different levels of development. These case studies are designed to illustrate the very different challenges that confront countries at different levels of development, to offer examples of successful steps some countries, regions, or villages have taken toward more environmentally sustainable forms of development, and to suggest opportunities for additional policies and actions specific to each level of development.

The case studies focus on three groups of countries:

Industrial countries, as exemplified by OECD countries as a group and, in particular, by the United States;

Poor countries, as exemplified by countries in Africa, Asia, and the Americas that have been identified by international development agencies as ranking low on indicators of income or human development. For purposes of statistical comparisons, this grouping includes some 40 low-income countries as identified by the World Bank; China and India are included in this group but are shown separately because of their size and extensive industrial sectors.

Rapidly industrializing countries (RICs), as exemplified by three Southeast Asian countries (Thailand, Indonesia, and Malaysia) and three Latin American countries (Mexico, Brazil, and Chile). A number of other countries are also industrializing rapidly or have strong industrial sectors, and much of this chapter may also apply to those countries.

These groupings were chosen to provide examples from the extremes of economic development—both very rich countries and countries that are very poor or have large concentrations of very poor people—as well as examples from countries that are in between these extremes. Some countries—such as China and India—have both large rural populations facing one set of development problems and vigorous industrial sectors facing another set of development problems. The case studies are in no sense comprehensive. Rather, they are intended to further discussion by giving a more concrete sense of what sustainable development might mean and by illustrating in specific contexts both the problems and some starting points for solutions.

COMPARING KEY TRENDS

The case study groupings can be delineated more clearly by comparing trends among them. Although statistical comparisons may mask complex realities, they also reveal striking trends in how regions have progressed over the past 20 years and in how they compare with each other. Clearly, there has been progress in many areas, but there has been no narrowing of the gap between rich and poor countries— economically the gap is widening. It is also clear that the RICs

Figure 1 Trends in Gross National Product Per Capita, 1969–89

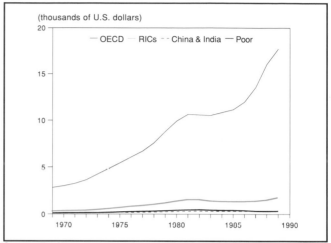

Source: The World Bank, unpublished data (The World Bank, Washington, D.C., 1991).

Figure 2 Trends in Primary School Enrollment, 1970–88

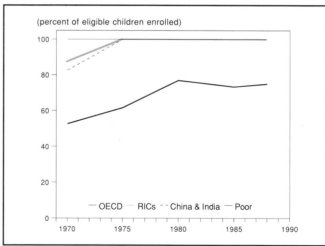

Source: The World Bank, unpublished data (The World Bank, Washington, D.C., 1991).

and China and India show progress in human development that surpasses their economic progress.

Finding broad, widely monitored indicators of the four dimensions of sustainable development is difficult. Worldwide country-level data on economic and human development trends is more available than data on environmental or technological trends. GNP per capita is a broad measure of a country's economic development although it says nothing of the distribution of wealth within the country. Primary school enrollment and child mortality are generally accepted indicators of a population's relative education and health, two criteria for human development. Globally, a comparison of commercial energy use per capita indi-

Figure 3 Trends in Under-Five Mortality, 1970–90 {a}

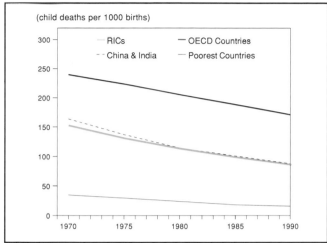

Source: The World Bank, unpublished data (The World Bank, Washington, D.C., 1991).
Note: a. 1990 data are projected.

Figure 4 Trends in Fertility, 1969–89

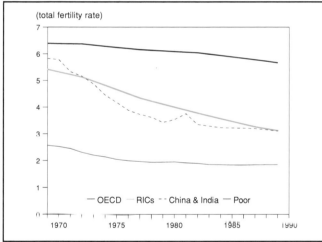

Source: The World Bank, unpublished data (The World Bank, Washington, D.C., 1991).
Note: The total fertility rate is an estimate of the number of children that an average woman would have if current age-specific fertility rates remained constant during her reproductive years.

cates both the relative level of industrialization of countries or regions and their consumption of resources.

Economic Growth

For the past 20 years, gross national product (GNP) per capita has grown significantly in the OECD countries and also (especially in percentage terms) in the RICs, and in low-income countries. (See Figure 1.) Nonetheless, the disparity in incomes between rich and poor is increasing. In a world where information and television images are widely communicated, such

Figure 5 Trends in Energy Consumption Per Capita, 1970–89

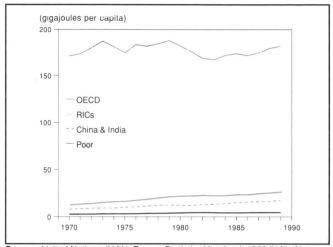

Source: United Nations (U.N.) *Energy Statistics Yearbook 1989* (U.N., New York, 1989) and previous volumes.

a divergent trend is a source of contention and concern.

Human Development

The trend to universal primary school enrollment over the past 20 years has continued, with the RICs and China and India joining the OECD countries. (See Figure 2.) Low-income countries have made significant gains, but progress has plateaued in recent years. Under-five child mortality rates show a somewhat different picture. All countries have reduced child mortality over the past 20 years, in some cases dramatically. (See Figure 3.) The OECD countries are now at very low levels. The RICs, although still showing high child mortality rates, have made remarkable progress, as has China. Low-income countries have made some progress, as has India, but these countries still have very high child mortality rates.

Population Growth

A key demographic variable is fertility rate, which is the number of children an average woman would bear during her reproductive years. For most of the past 20 years, fertility rates in OECD countries have been stable at nearly a replacement rate (about two births per woman). (See Figure 4.) Fertility rates in the RICs have declined significantly, as have those in India and (especially) China. Fertility rates in low-income countries are still very high and have declined only slightly over the period.

Energy Use

Figure 5 reflects the enormous disparities in per capita energy consumption between the industrial OECD countries and all other countries. Energy use is growing in the RICs and in India and China, but at a much lower level. Low-income countries still use very little commercial energy.

2. Industrial Countries:

Promoting Sustainable Growth in a Global Economy

Taken together, the 24 countries of the Organisation for Economic Co-operation and Development (OECD) represent an immense concentration of economic activity (1). In 1989, these industrialized countries had a combined gross national product (GNP) of $15 trillion and an average per capita income of $17,500 (2).

The OECD countries also place a huge demand on the natural resources of the planet and contribute a very large share of the global pollution burden. In 1989, the seven largest OECD economies consumed 43 percent of the world's production of fossil fuels, most of the world's production of metals, and a large share of other industrial materials and forest products. (See Table 2.1A.) On a per capita basis, the share of consumption of the largest OECD economies is often several times that of the world average. (See Table 2.1B.) In 1989, the OECD countries released approximately 40 percent of global sulfur oxides emissions and 54 percent of nitrogen oxides emissions—the primary sources of acid precipitation (3). They generated 68 percent of the world's industrial waste as measured by weight (4) and accounted for 38 percent of the global potential warming impact on the atmosphere from emissions of greenhouse gases (5). Yet the combined population of the OECD countries, 849 million, represents only 16 percent of the world's population (6).

A critical question is whether such patterns of production, consumption of natural resources, and pollution can be sustained in the future, as economic activity increases. The OECD countries and their industrial economies are directly responsible for many kinds of environmental stress—local, regional, and global. In addition, because they not only are heavy consumers of natural resources from developing countries but also tend to shift their pollution-intensive industries to those countries, the OECD countries also contribute indirectly to environmental stresses in developing regions.

DIMENSIONS OF SUSTAINABLE DEVELOPMENT

As described in Chapter 1, sustainable development is economic development that does not degrade the quality of the environment or the world's natural resource base and that "sustain[s] human progress not just in a few places for a few years" (7). The evidence is that OECD countries—and the United States in particular—do not yet meet these criteria.

Table 2.1 Apparent Consumption of Selected Materials in the Largest OECD Economies {a}

A. As Percentage of World Consumption

	Year of Data	World Con-sumption	Total	Canada	Germany	France	Italy	Japan	United Kingdom	United States	Source
Energy (exajoules)											
Total fossil fuels	1989	283.7	43.4	2.5	4.5	1.9	2.2	4.8	2.9	24.8	1
Solids	1989	97.0	35.5	1.2	6.0	0.8	0.6	3.4	2.8	20.6	1
Liquids	1989	116.6	50.2	2.9	3.9	2.9	3.4	7.1	2.8	27.1	1
Gas	1989	70.1	43.3	3.7	3.2	1.6	2.2	2.7	3.0	26.8	1
Metals (million metric tons)											
Crude steel	1989	794.5	39.9	1.8	5.6	2.2	3.5	11.7	2.2	12.9	2
Aluminum, refined	1990	17.9	58.0	2.3	7.7	4.0	3.6	13.5	2.5	24.2	3
Copper, refined	1990	10.8	57.6	1.7	9.5	4.4	4.4	14.6	2.9	19.9	3
Lead, refined	1990	5.5	55.2	1.6	8.1	4.6	4.7	7.5	5.4	23.2	3
Nickel, refined	1990	0.8	58.6	1.4	11.1	5.3	3.2	18.9	3.9	14.8	3
Tin, refined	1990	0.2	52.7	1.3	9.4	3.6	2.7	15.2	4.5	16.0	3
Zinc, slab	1990	7.0	45.9	1.8	7.6	4.1	3.9	11.7	2.7	14.2	3
Industrial Materials (million metric tons)											
Cement	1983-85	938 {b}	27.8	0.6	4.2 {c}	2.2	4.1	7.0	1.5	8.2	4,5
Fertilizer	1989/90	143	26.3	1.5	3.2	4.3	1.3	1.4	1.6	13.1	6
Forest Products											
Roundwood (million cubic meters)	1989	3,470	25.2	5.1	1.3	1.1	0.4	2.4	0.2	14.7	7
Paper and paperboard (million metric tons)	1989	230	64.6	2.7	6.2	3.6	2.9	11.9	4.2	33.1	7

B. Average Annual Consumption Per Capita

	Year of Data	World	Total	Canada	Germany	France	Italy	Japan	United Kingdom	United States	Source
Energy (gigajoules)											
Total fossil fuels	1989	54.71	190.32	270.95	160.98	94.98	106.56	109.80	142.11	282.93	1
Solids	1989	18.71	53.13	44.65	74.41	14.48	10.01	26.96	47.94	80.15	1
Liquids	1989	22.48	90.27	127.06	57.75	60.24	69.35	67.51	56.97	127.21	1
Gas	1989	13.53	46.92	99.25	28.82	20.26	27.19	15.33	37.20	75.57	1
Metals (kilograms)											
Crude steel	1989	153.20	489.09	529.72	563.08	312.77	486.71	757.64	304.00	411.44	2
Aluminum, refined	1990	3.39	15.94	15.66	17.83	12.77	11.32	19.55	7.89	17.24	3
Copper, refined	1990	2.04	9.54	6.95	13.29	8.46	8.24	12.76	5.52	8.54	3
Lead, refined	1990	1.05	4.71	3.44	5.79	4.51	4.48	3.38	5.25	5.13	3
Nickel, refined	1990	0.16	0.76	0.46	1.21	0.79	0.47	1.29	0.57	0.50	3
Tin, refined	1990	0.04	0.19	0.11	0.28	0.15	0.11	0.28	0.18	0.15	3
Zinc, slab	1990	1.32	4.93	4.75	6.85	5.03	4.69	6.59	3.29	3.95	3
Industrial Materials (kilograms)											
Cement	1983-85	197.72 {b}	416.06	239.86	502.67 {c}	376.17	670.11	550.66	242.85	327.23	4,5
Fertilizer	1989/90	27.63	58.18	82.67	58.39	108.67	31.52	15.74	41.22	75.21	6
Forest Products											
Roundwood (cubic meters)	1989	0.67	1.35	6.71	0.56	0.70	0.27	0.68	0.12	2.04	7
Paper and paperboard (kilograms)	1989	44.39	229.61	236.09	181.62	148.17	116.05	221.84	168.15	306.71	7

Sources:
1. United Nations Statistical Office, *U.N. Energy Tape* (United Nations, New York, May 1991).
2. International Iron and Steel Institute (IISI), *Steel Statistical Yearbook 1990* (IISI, Brussels, 1990), pp. 35-37.
3. World Bureau of Metal Statistics (WBMS), *World Metal Statistics* (WBMS, Ware, U.K., 1991).
4. United Nations Industrial Development Organization (UNIDO), *Handbook of Industrial Statistics 1988* (UNIDO, Vienna, 1988), Table 13, pp. 455-458.
5. U.S. Bureau of Mines (U.S. BOM), *Minerals Yearbook*, Vol. 1, *Metals and Minerals* (U.S. Government Printing Office, Washington, D.C., 1988), pp. 221-222.
6. Food and Agriculture Organization of the United Nations (FAO), *Fertilizer Yearbook 1990* (FAO, Rome, 1991), Table 1, p. 1, and Table 29, pp. 113-114.
7. Food and Agriculture Organization of the United Nations (FAO), *Forest Products Yearbook 1989* (FAO, Rome, 1991), pp. 2-9 and 234-243.

Notes:
a. Apparent Consumption = production plus imports minus exports.
b. World consumption assumed to be equal to world production.
c. Consumption in Federal Republic of Germany plus production in German Democratic Republic.
Totals may not add because of independent rounding.

Despite some improvements, air and water pollution and disposal of large quantities of waste remain serious problems in virtually all OECD countries. Industrial residues—acidic materials, heavy metals, and toxic chemicals—degrade soils, damage plants, and endanger food supplies. On a per capita basis, the OECD countries are overwhelmingly the world's major polluters, both within their own borders and in their contribution to global environmental degradation.

Economic disparities have increased over the past decade within most OECD countries. (See Box 2.1.) Disparities between rich and poor countries are grow-

Box 2.1 Poverty Amidst Wealth

Problems of poverty and human development worsened in industrialized countries in the past decade, despite steady economic growth between 1983 and 1990. In the past, economic growth had reduced poverty. But in the 1980s, rapid technological change and the increasing globalization of trade and production introduced structural changes in national economies that reduced job security, especially for low-skill workers.

According to a recent study of the United States, Canada, and several European Countries, poverty as measured relative to median income levels increased in the 1980s. As Figure 1 indicates, the percentage of low-income, working-age households (those with incomes less than 50 percent of the national median income and with heads of households who are 20 to 55 years old) increased during this period in all but two of the countries studied. The United States experienced steadier growth and lower unemployment than most European countries in the 1980s, yet the percentage of low-income households was nearly double that of the continental European countries by mid-decade (1).

In some cases, absolute poverty increased. For example, the mean income of the bottom 20 percent of U.S. families declined from $10,176 in 1970 to $9,833 in 1990. In this same period, the mean income of the top 5 percent rose from $116,555 to $148,124 (2).

In all countries, young people, single-parent households, and members of ethnic minorities were especially vulnerable to poverty (3). For example, the rate of poverty was at least three times higher for single-parent compared with couple-headed households in West Germany and Canada in the mid-1980s (4).

Governments have chosen a variety of human development strategies to combat poverty. To attack the problem of youth unemployment, France and Germany considerably improved the performance of their public school systems in the 1980s. In addition, the German government has joined with private business to create an apprenticeship program that integrates young people into the work force. Italy and France developed similar programs in the 1980s. In contrast, the performance of U.S. public schools declined over the past decade and the U.S. government devoted few resources to helping students make the school-to-work transition (5).

Figure 1 Changes in Poverty Among Working-Age Heads of Households in Selected Countries During the 1980s

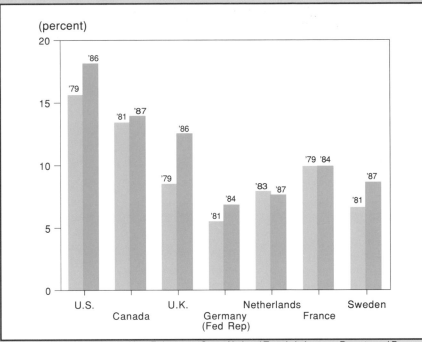

Source: Timothy Smeeding and Lee Rainwater, "Cross-National Trends in Income, Poverty and Dependency," paper prepared for the Joint Center for Political and Economic Studies, Washington, D.C., September 1991, cited in Katherine McFate, *Poverty, Inequality and the Crisis of Social Policy: Summary of Findings* (Joint Center for Political and Economic Studies, Washington, D.C., 1991), p. 27.

Note: Included are all heads of households 20 to 55 years old and with incomes less than 50 percent of the adjusted national median income after taxes and public assistance transfers.

All the continental European systems invest in child health and welfare by providing income security to families with children, universal access to health care, and high-quality public day care for children of working mothers. Many provide parental leave so mothers can return to work more easily after childbearing (6).

The effectiveness of income support programs varies considerably among countries. The United Kingdom, West Germany, the Netherlands, France, and Sweden used their powers to tax and transfer income to lift anywhere from one third to two thirds of poor households out of poverty. Canada moved only one fifth of poor households out of poverty; the United States did not lift any out of poverty (7).

Although poverty is not as pressing a problem in the OECD countries as in the developing countries, declining living standards in the OECD countries have exacerbated social tensions and focused attention on domestic rather than international concerns.

References and Notes

1. Katherine McFate, *Poverty, Inequality and the Crisis of Social Policy: Summary of Findings* (Joint Center for Political and Economic Studies, Washington, D.C., 1991), p. 1.
2. U.S. Census Bureau, *Current Population Reports*, Series P-650, No. 174 (U.S. Government Printing Office, Washington, D.C., 1991), Table B-5, p. 2202.
3. *Op. cit.* 2, p. 6.
4. *Op. cit.* 2, Figure 8, p. 32.
5. *Op. cit.* 2, pp. 10-11 and 23.
6. *Op. cit.* 2, p. 23.
7. *Op. cit.* 2, Figure 3, p. 29.

ing ever greater. (See "Introduction to Case Studies," Figure 1.) Because rich countries tend to dominate trade relationships, they bear some responsibility for this widening gap. Virtually all OECD countries, for example, have erected trade barriers against agricultural products that deny developing countries access to OECD markets. Yet with few exceptions, OECD countries do not provide financial assistance to developing countries even at the modest levels recommended by the United Nations—0.7 percent of GNP (8).

Chapter 1 also argues that the technological base of industrial societies must be transformed—replaced

Figure 2.1 Global Fossil Fuel Consumption, 1950–89

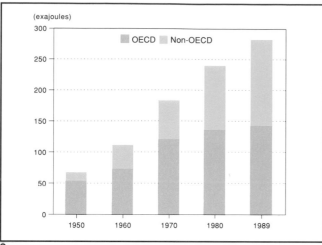

Sources:
1. United Nations (U.N.), *Energy Statistics Yearbook 1982* (U.N., New York, 1984).
2. United Nations (U.N.), *Energy Statistics Yearbook 1989* (U.N., New York, 1991).

with cleaner, more resource-sparing technologies—if sustainable development is to occur. Development of improved industrial technologies by OECD countries and their rapid diffusion and deployment in other countries through public and private mechanisms could play a critical role in sustainable development.

The opportunities are wide-ranging. When coupled with appropriate social and institutional changes, agricultural innovations could help feed growing populations, as they have in the past, and could reduce chemical inputs to the environment. New forms of pest control, including neutralization of the tsetse fly, for example, might open large areas of Africa to food production. New energy technologies could greatly reduce pollution from fossil fuels or provide renewable sources of energy well adapted to the needs of developing countries. New vaccines and new information technologies could improve health and expand educational opportunities. Harnessed to the needs of sustainable development, technological innovation represents a hopeful investment in the future, a gift of knowledge to ensure that future generations also have opportunities to meet their needs—albeit perhaps in different ways than at present. At the same time, new policies that encourage the adoption of new technologies are badly needed.

Sustainable development in industrial countries is not a question of growth or no growth. Limits to economic growth, while they probably exist, are likely to be very elastic and determined by the state of technology and the forms of social organization. It is the kind, not the amount, of economic growth that is critical to sustainable development.

This chapter considers new policies and technologies that—within the context of OECD countries—could reduce environmental degradation and promote more sustainable economic development. The discus-

sion focuses on the United States because it is the largest economic unit within the OECD and, by some measures, the least efficient and most wasteful in its use of natural resources. Examples and comparisons are drawn from other OECD countries as appropriate, and the global consequences of actions by OECD countries are considered.

ENERGY RESOURCES

Energy Transitions

Until the middle of the 19th Century, humankind depended largely on renewable energy resources—human and animal power, supplemented by wood, wind, and water power. In 1850, wood supplied more than 90 percent of energy in the United States. By the end of the century, the number of horses and mules on U.S. farms had grown to more than 20 million (9).

But the energy demands of the newly industrializing countries of the 19th Century could not be met by renewable resources with the technologies then available. The steam engines of the past century converted at best a few percent of the energy in wood into useful work. The need to concentrate large amounts of energy in industrial furnaces and electric utility boilers set the stage for a transition from renewable energy resources to fossil fuels—first to coal, then to oil and natural gas (10). By 1989, fossil fuels accounted for about 95 percent of the world's commercial energy supply. (See Chapter 21, "Energy and Materials," Table 21.1.)

As the world nears the end of the 20th Century, it finds itself facing the beginnings of a third major transition, away from fossil fuels. The candidate replacement energy technologies include those powered ultimately by the sun or by nuclear fission. Although scarcity would eventually force such a transition, the growing environmental consequences of burning fossil fuels may bring it sooner. In the United States, local air pollution has been held at bay by new control technologies and ever-tighter regulations, but most major urban areas still fail to meet national standards for ozone levels (11). Worldwide, growing urban centers concentrate energy use and the resultant pollution to such an extent—particularly where unfavorable geography or weather patterns are a factor—that they are increasingly hazardous places to live. Regional effects such as acid precipitation are damaging trees, soils, and lakes. Globally, use of fossil fuels is the largest source of greenhouse gas emissions and thus a major contributor to the threat of climate change. (See Chapter 13, "Atmosphere and Climate.")

Since 1950, use of fossil fuels has more than quadrupled, with a substantial part of the increase occurring in OECD countries. (See Figure 2.1.) Even if consumption continues to grow as industrial development occurs in more countries, it may be possible to mitigate local and regional effects to some extent through vigorous use of control technologies and regulations. But continued significant increases of fossil-fuel-related carbon dioxide emissions would enormously increase

Figure 2.2 Manufacturing Energy Intensities for Selected Countries, 1971–88

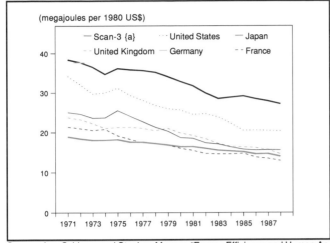

Source: Lee Schipper and Stephen Meyers, "Energy Efficiency and Human Activity: Past Trends, Future Prospects," draft, Lawrence Berkeley Laboratory (University of California, Berkeley, October 1991).
Note: a. Scan-3 = Denmark, Norway, and Sweden.

Figure 2.3 Petrol Prices and Light-Duty Vehicle Fleet Efficiencies, 1987

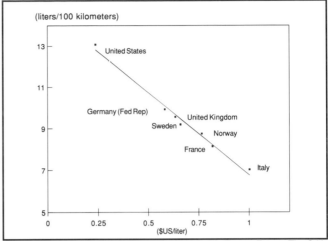

Source: James J. MacKenzie, "Toward a Sustainable Energy Future: The Critical Role of Rational Energy Pricing," in *WRI Issues and Ideas* (World Resources Institute, Washington, D.C., May 1991), p. 6.

the likelihood of devastating climate change. In contrast, the Intergovernmental Panel on Climate Change estimated that a 60–80 percent reduction in carbon dioxide emissions from present levels would be required to stabilize atmospheric concentrations of carbon dioxide (12). Hence a transition from fossil fuels appears to be urgently needed, a transition that must be led by OECD countries if it is to occur.

Such a transition can take place only over many years. For the next 10–20 years, the most effective strategy for reducing carbon dioxide emissions is to improve the efficiency of energy production and use, a strategy that would help reduce other pollution problems as well.

Energy Efficiency

Improving energy efficiency does not mean doing without energy or economic growth. From 1973 to 1988, the United States built 20 million new homes, put 50 million more vehicles on its roads, and increased its GNP by 46 percent. Yet energy consumption increased only 7 percent. The economic benefits of higher energy efficiency were enormous: cumulative energy savings worth more than $1 trillion, in addition to the pollution avoided. According to the U.S. Department of Energy, these improvements were stimulated in large measure by higher energy prices (13).

A useful measuring stick for energy efficiency is the concept of energy intensity, defined as energy consumption per unit of gross domestic product, for specific economic sectors (14). By this measure, for example, the energy intensity of manufacturing, excluding structural changes (i.e., by holding constant the 1973 production mix), declined by 33 percent in the United States, 37 percent in Japan, and an average of 29 percent in six European countries between 1973 and 1987 (15). For the same group of countries, improvements

also occurred in the efficiency of energy use in the home, as a result of more insulation and more efficient furnaces and appliances, and in most other sectors (16). Only in transportation did energy intensity increase, as a result of more cars, more kilometers driven per car, and a higher percentage of travel in cars and airplanes instead of buses and trains (17).

The United States is still one of the least energy-efficient countries in the OECD. Cars, appliances, and commercial buildings in the United States use 20–33 percent more energy per unit of activity, and U.S. industries 10–25 percent more, than in most other industrial countries. (See Figure 2.2.) The U.S. auto fleet, for example, averaged 11 liters per 100 kilometers (21 miles per U.S. gallon (mpg)) (18), compared with 9 liters per 100 kilometers (26 mpg) in Europe in 1990 (19).

A primary reason for the more wasteful use of petrol in the United States is that the average price is extraordinarily low by industrial world standards. In 1990, petrol prices hovered around $0.30 per liter in the United States. In other OECD countries they ranged from above $0.50 per liter in Germany to about $1 per liter in Italy (20). The fleet efficiencies of cars and light vehicles show a similar distribution, ranging from the United States (least efficient) to Italy (most efficient). (See Figure 2.3.) Clearly, higher fuel prices and more efficient energy use go hand in hand.

In addition, U.S. residents travel well over twice as far by car each year as Europeans and almost four times as far as Japanese. Such high automobile use is sometimes attributed to the greater geographical size of the United States. As Figure 2.4 shows, however, about 85 percent of all auto trips taken by U.S. residents are within short distances of home. Indeed, fully 97 percent of the kilometers traveled each year by U.S. residents in their cars are for trips of 18 kilometers or less (21). Lack of adequate public transportation systems, lower energy prices, and the urban sprawl of the

Figure 2.4 U.S. Motor Vehicle Trips by Purpose and Length, 1983–84

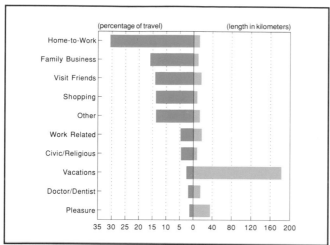

Source: James J. MacKenzie, "Toward a Sustainable Energy Future: The Critical Role of Rational Energy Pricing," in *WRI Issues and Ideas* (World Resources Institute, Washington, D.C., May 1991), p. 8.

past 40 years are larger factors in fuel use than the overall size of the country (22).

There is no lack of technological opportunity for more efficient energy use in the United States and other OECD countries. Several major automobile manufacturers have built prototypes that can achieve about 3.8 liters per 100 kilometers (63 mpg) in city driving and about 2.9 liters per 100 kilometers (81 mpg) on the highway (23). With appropriate policies, automobile fleet efficiency could double, at least in the United States, and public transportation systems could greatly expand. The U.S. Environmental Protection Agency estimates that a shift to new high-energy fluorescent lighting in commercial buildings could alone cut U.S. electricity demand 10 percent, save nearly $19 billion per year, and cut carbon dioxide emissions by 4 percent per year (24). Appliances and electric motors that are significantly more efficient than those now in general use are available. A study by the Electric Power Research Institute for the utility industry concluded that a shift to the most efficient electrical equipment now commercially available could save utility customers between 24 and 44 percent of U.S. electricity consumption by the year 2000 (25). A new generation of more efficient technologies for generating electricity, including gas turbine combined-cycle systems and fuel cells, are also poised to enter commercial use (26). What is lacking are the energy policies and pricing signals that can realize these efficiencies—and with them, at least temporary reductions in pollution levels and carbon dioxide emissions.

Renewable Energy Resources

Cleaner, more efficient energy technologies can significantly reduce pollution and greenhouse warming contributions from fossil fuels, particularly over the next 20 years. Once these efficiencies are achieved, however, expanded energy use will again increase the

greenhouse burden. In the long run, renewable energy resources offer an alternative to fossil fuels. Nuclear power offers another—albeit still controversial—option.

The world is gradually shifting away from direct use of fuels to indirect consumption in the form of electricity (27). In 1989, over 41 percent of commercial global energy consumption was dedicated to electric power production (28)—an increase from 28 percent in 1970 and 16 percent in 1950 (29). The U.S. trend is similar—electric generation consumed 45 percent of primary energy in 1989 (30), up from 14 percent in 1950 (31). That almost two thirds of the world's electricity (73 percent in the United States) is provided by power plants burning fossil fuels underscores the importance of controlling carbon dioxide emissions from the electric power sector (32).

The trend toward electrification of the global economy is perhaps fortunate, since some of the most promising future energy technologies are producers of electricity. The most attractive of these are the renewable energy technologies of wind turbines, photovoltaic cells, hydropower plants, and high-temperature solar thermal collectors. Powered ultimately by the sun, none of these energy sources emits carbon dioxide or air pollutants, and their use would thus not contribute to air pollution or global warming, although large dams built to tap hydropower resources often cause other environmental problems.

Most of the renewable technologies, by nature of the diffuse resources on which they depend, require large collection areas. Such a requirement may not in practice be a major impediment. An analysis by the World Resources Institute (WRI) showed that for the United States—the world's largest energy consumer—only about 0.4 percent of the land area of the continental United States would be needed to meet all U.S. energy needs using photovoltaic cells (33). Such a step would be uneconomical at present, but efficiencies are rising and prices have fallen drastically. In contrast, 21 percent of U.S. lands are devoted to cropland and 26 percent to pastures. (See Chapter 17, "Land Cover and Settlements," Table 17.1.) Many of the solar cells, moreover, could be placed on the walls and roofs of existing structures.

Some renewable technologies such as wind power, however, are already becoming economically competitive. The installation of commercial wind turbines is growing rapidly in the United States. The wind resource in 12 midcontinent states alone could produce more than three times the 1987 U.S. electrical energy consumption (34). The cost of electricity from wind machines has been dropping because of improved designs and increased reliability. According to the California Energy Commission, wind turbines located at good sites can now generate power at costs equal to or lower than the cost of power from either nuclear or coal-fired plants, if similar utility financing is made available (35).

California supplies 1 percent of its electricity needs from wind power and plans to increase that share to 10 percent over the next decade. Denmark supplies 1.5 percent of its electricity needs from wind power and also plans to increase that share to 10 percent over the next decade. In 1990, more than 12 countries had wind energy programs (36).

The transportation sector poses a major challenge for renewable energy technology. Carbon dioxide emissions from motor vehicles worldwide have been growing by 3 percent per year from about 510 million metric tons of carbon in 1971 to more than 830 million metric tons of carbon in 1987 (37). Cars and trucks are also the major sources of the constituents that give rise to urban smog. Curbing these emissions will be extremely difficult as long as most motor vehicles are powered by petrol: growth in the number of vehicles and miles traveled now overwhelms improvements in fuel economy (38). Additional public transit systems— particularly those powered by electricity— offer one means of improvement.

Electric vehicles are an attractive option for the future. In the next decade or two, if battery technology improves, they could fill an important niche as commuting and urban fleet vehicles. When charged at night by clean, efficient power plants, such vehicles would offer significant air pollution benefits; they would also reduce carbon dioxide emissions, unless charged by electricity from a coal-fired power plant. Electric vehicles would mesh easily with the primarily electric, nonfossil energy sources that will be needed in the next century (39).

Hydrogen vehicles are a promising longer term option. In addition to powering motor vehicles, hydrogen can be used as an airplane fuel and to supply energy to buildings. Burning hydrogen in internal combustion engines is virtually pollution free: no carbon monoxide or carbon dioxide and only trace amounts of hydrocarbons (from the crankcase oil) and nitrogen oxides are produced. Hydrogen is, in principle, a nearly ideal way to store the energy from intermittent renewable technologies (such as wind turbines and photovoltaic cells) or from nuclear power plants. Research will be needed, however, to lower costs and improve means of storage before hydrogen can become a viable option (40).

Economic and Regulatory Policies

A serious shortcoming of world energy markets, and of U.S. transportation markets in particular, is the failure to fully incorporate the environmental and social costs of energy use in energy prices. Fuel and electricity prices reflect pollution control costs but do not reflect the billions of dollars worth of damage caused by energy-related pollution (from drilling, mining, refining, oil spills, and combustion of energy), the risk of global warming, and the threat to national security of dependence on oil imports.

Many policy proposals that seek to mitigate the environmental damage of fossil fuel combustion have focused on regulatory measures. Examples include requirements for higher fleet vehicle efficiencies, minimum performance standards for major appliances, and tighter codes for new buildings. These measures are important for increasing efficiency and reducing

operating costs. But energy efficiency improvements alone will not reduce fossil fuel consumption sufficiently to significantly clean up urban pollution or to stabilize the climate, if only because of the human tendency to use more of commodities, including energy, that are less expensive. More efficient technologies also lower the effective price of energy use. Improvements in energy efficiency will buy time for more fundamental changes. But energy pricing reforms will be essential to reduce fossil fuel consumption and to increase use of renewable energy technologies.

One frequently discussed option for energy price reform is sharply higher direct taxes on petrol. Another option is a national tax on the carbon content of all fossil fuels. A carbon tax would fall most heavily on those fuels, such as coal, that contribute the most carbon dioxide to the atmosphere and that are a major source of other pollutants such as sulfur dioxide, and least heavily on carbon-poor (and generally cleaner) fuels such as natural gas.

Energy taxes are frequently opposed on the grounds that they would slow economic growth and be regressive. But energy price reform need not have that effect. Energy taxes could be economically neutral if the proceeds were used to reduce other taxes such as income or social security taxes, and might, by encouraging a more efficient economy, even be advantageous. Shifting the tax burden from "virtues"—such as labor, savings, and investment—to "ills"—such as the use of polluting fuels—makes use of market incentives to steer economic growth into more sustainable patterns.

Still another policy approach is to reduce demand. Utilities in some parts of the United States, with the encouragement of state utility commissions, are already offering their customers financial incentives to install high-efficiency appliances, lights, and cooling systems. These efforts, known as demand-side management, avoid the need to build additional generating capacity and reduce both energy costs and pollution.

AGRICULTURAL AND FOREST RESOURCES

Although conversion of forests, wetlands, and deserts to agricultural land is not now a significant activity in most OECD countries, that has not been the case in the past. As recently as 1950–1970, for example, the United States cleared 1.3 million hectares of southwestern piñon-juniper woodlands to expand pastureland (41). Earlier in the century, an ambitious, government-subsidized system of dams and canals was constructed to irrigate some 6 million hectares of western drylands and desert (42). Late in the 19th Century, more than 21 million hectares of midwestern wetlands were drained to expand cropland (43). Still earlier, in medieval times and before, large areas of the once vast European forests were cleared. The Mediterranean region, in particular, suffered almost complete degradation of natural plant and animal communities (44). These changes are similar to land conversions now under way in many developing countries.

Effects of Present Policies

Forests

A recent assessment found that careful management has restored the usefulness of many U.S. forests over the past 100 years (45). Nonetheless, the United States is the largest producer of forest products in the world and the second largest exporter of raw timber. (See Chapter 19, "Forests and Range lands," Table 19.2.) From the point of view of sustainable development, however, these high rates of cutting have complex consequences, which are exemplified by a controversy over logging of old-growth forests in the U.S. Pacific Northwest. These forests contain many of the largest tree species in the world and are also the habitat for an endangered species, the spotted owl.

Old-growth forests are stable ecosystems with trees of all ages. When such a forest is cut, it takes at least 200 years for the large trees to regrow—far longer than current logging cycles. Even so, harvesting on a 200-year cycle would not be sustainable, because the forest also requires large fallen logs on the forest floor. The trees depend on fungi that live in their roots for their nutrients. The fungi, in turn, depend on small rodents that live on the forest floor to distribute their spores and help them reproduce and spread. The rodents need fallen logs for protection and as a source of moisture during long, dry summers. Thus, harvesting cycles much longer than 200 years would be required to preserve these old-growth forests as natural and stable ecosystems (46).

Agriculture

Agricultural production, like any other economic activity, responds to market signals. When those signals are distorted by subsidies, fixed prices, or protection from competition, as is the case in virtually all OECD countries, the result is overproduction and high social and environmental costs. In the United States, direct fiscal costs to taxpayers are approximately $12 billion per year. Indirect costs of $5–$10 billion per year to U.S. consumers are added in the form of higher prices (47) (48). Still other indirect costs include soil depletion and erosion, contamination of underground and surface waters arising from the overuse of agricultural chemicals, and loss of wildlife habitat.

Similar fiscal and environmental costs are borne by the citizens of Japan and Western Europe, where governments subsidize agriculture even more substantially than in the United States. Agricultural subsidies (direct and indirect) in the world's industrial economies have been estimated at $150 billion annually (49).

The impact of such policies extends beyond national borders. By limiting imports of many agricultural commodities grown in developing countries and producing surpluses that, when exported, drive down prices, the agricultural policies of most OECD countries deprive food-exporting developing countries of markets. Such policies undercut efforts to improve the livelihoods of developing world farmers, who make up the vast majority of the world's poor.

Unsustainable Practices

Many farm practices, by reducing soil fertility or causing excessive soil loss, significantly lower the true income to the farmer. Examples include excessive use of herbicides and pesticides that kill off soil microbes, repeated planting of crops that deplete soil nutrients, and high-tillage systems that add to erosion. Such practices degrade the farm's resource base, wasting its soil "capital" and thus reducing its future income-producing potential. The costs of soil loss in lower farm productivity are often temporarily masked by rapid technological change and increasing use of inputs. Eventually, however, farmers who degrade their soil will impoverish themselves. From an environmental perspective, such resource-degrading practices are both unsustainable and unwise in a world facing at least a two-fold increase in the number of mouths to feed.

Soil-eroding and chemically intensive practices can have a more immediate environmental impact off the farm. In the United States, more than half of the suspended sediment and nutrient pollution of freshwater comes from agriculture (50). Annual damage to hydrological resources in the United States from farmland is estimated at $3.5 billion per year (51). Additional, unquantified damages include poisoning of wildlife, contamination of groundwater, and health effects from pesticide residues in food.

Existing farm policies in the United States discourage farmers from shifting to resource-conserving practices. Some farmers have nonetheless experimented with alternatives to conventional, chemically intensive practices. A detailed comparative analysis of conventional and resource-conserving practices under two different sets of conditions showed that alternative production systems can compete economically. In Pennsylvania, where shallow soils and hillside fields give rise to relatively high on-farm and off-farm environmental costs, organic farming rotations are clearly superior to conventional practices—agronomically, environmentally, and economically. In Nebraska, where thick topsoil and flat fields limit on-farm and off-farm environmental damage, resource-conserving practices were still found to be environmentally superior and economically competitive (52).

Needed Policy Reform

A shift to farm policies that encourage rather than discourage resource-conserving practices would reduce the resource costs of farming, raise agricultural productivity, and lower the burden of farm subsidies. Likewise, a move to freer trade in agricultural commodities would not only lower subsidy costs but also provide food-exporting developing countries with greater access to markets for their products. Farmers should not be exempt from the "polluter pays" principle. If tax or other incentives that force producers to absorb the costs of the off-farm damage they cause were put in place, agriculture would come to rely more on resource-conserving methods of fertilization and pest management. Sustainable agricultural practices, their promise, and the policies needed for their widespread realization are discussed in more detail in Chapter 7, "Food and Agriculture."

WASTE, POLLUTION, AND SUSTAINABLE TECHNOLOGIES

Cleanup Strategies

Over the past several decades, most OECD countries have adopted environmental strategies designed to control a growing number of specific pollutants. The concerns behind these actions have expanded to encompass not only direct, local contamination of air, water, and land but also indirect and regional effects such as the damage to forests from acid precipitation, the overfertilization of estuaries and regional seas, and the growing shortage of toxic and solid waste disposal sites. Environmental strategies, expressed in legislation and regulations, have had tangible effects, reducing emissions of some targeted pollutants into the environment. The quality of the air and the water in many communities has improved. But overall, these pollution control efforts have resulted in little more than a holding action. New pollutants and new threats to the environment have emerged, from local concerns over toxic emissions to global problems such as stratospheric ozone depletion and climate change.

The environmental strategies adopted by OECD countries to date have been for the most part "end-of-the-pipe" controls designed to contain or neutralize pollutants and hazardous waste already created. These strategies have been expensive: in the United States, for example, estimates are that public and private expenditures for pollution control now amount to just over 2 percent of the GNP, or over $115 billion annually, and are likely to rise significantly (53). Comparatively less attention has been given to altering the industrial, agricultural, and consumer technologies and practices that give rise to waste and pollutants in the first place.

Widely replicated, present technology and practices would choke the world in waste and pollutants: OECD countries now release to the atmosphere 76.5 million metric tons of the substances that cause acid rain (54), produce 1,430 million metric tons of industrial waste every year (55) and generate 2.3 billion metric tons of carbon dioxide or its equivalent in other greenhouse gases. A significant increase in these wastes and emissions as non-OECD economies expand would severely exacerbate waste disposal and health problems in urban areas, increase pollution damage to crops and forests, and increase the potential for global warming. Clearly, continued increases in wastes and emissions cannot be sustained indefinitely.

Fundamental changes in technology—and in the structure of economic activity—are the only realistic strategies. Fortunately, technology is not static, but rather changes continually. A recent analysis by WRI found a "uniquely rich" climate for more sustainable energy, agricultural, and manufacturing approaches from both existing and emerging technologies (56). The policies that influence technology development and

use in the United States, Japan, and the European Community have global implications because technological innovation is concentrated in the OECD countries and their technologies are often eventually deployed worldwide.

More Efficient Manufacturing

From an environmental point of view, preventing waste or the creation of pollutants in the first place is best. When some waste is inevitable, it should be minimized. Next, waste or by-products should be reused or recycled, at the factory level or at the consumer level. Only after all such measures have been exploited should waste treatment and disposal—the traditional end-of-the-pipe approach—be considered.

Many industrial companies have found that pollution prevention costs less if it is designed into the product or system from the start. Companies such as Minnesota Mining & Manufacturing Company (3M), with its "Pollution Prevention Pays" program, report that they have been able to reduce costs and pollution simultaneously by introducing improved technology or by using resources more efficiently. The potential for waste prevention or reduction is enormous. The U.S. Office of Technology Assessment estimated that many U.S. industries could eliminate 50 percent of their hazardous waste with available technology (57).

A few companies, particularly major chemical companies, have already set sweeping environmental strategies and targets for reduction of waste and toxic emissions, often far in excess of regulatory requirements. Monsanto Company, for example, has pledged to reduce toxic air emissions by 90 percent by 1992 and to work toward zero emissions (58). Moreover, major international companies are increasingly attempting to apply environmental strategies in every country in which they operate, irrespective of the differences in or lack of regulations and enforcement among them (59).

One incentive for companies to adopt such strategies, even when the costs exceed the immediate savings, is the growing requirement for full disclosure, particularly in the United States (60). No company likes to publish the fact that it releases millions of pounds of toxic waste to the environment, nor do such disclosures help to recruit new employees, sell products, or get permits for new plants.

A second incentive is the fear of costly legal liability for spills and waste dumps and even criminal penalties that, at least in the United States, can send managers to jail. Even without lawsuits, waste disposal costs are rising rapidly in most OECD countries, in part because no one wants a landfill or an incinerator in their neighborhood (61).

An additional motivation for many companies is the perception that it pays to prepare now for the transition to sustainability, because laws embodying tougher environmental regulations or taxes based on the "polluter pays" concept are inevitable. The director of the Swedish engineering company Fläkt AB made an apt comparison at a 1990 conference on sustainable development that bears on the question of inevitabil-

Table 2.2 Climate Change Action Program for the 21st Century

Year	Program	Actions
By 2000	World Energy Conservation	Intensified research on climate change. Accelerated energy conservation. Chlorofluorocarbons (CFCs) phased out.
By 2010	Accelerated Introduction of Clean Energy	Reduction in use of fossil fuels. Increased use of nuclear power. Increased use of new or renewable energy sources.
By 2020	Development of Environment-Friendly Technology	Spread of third-generation CFC substitutes.
By 2030	Expanding Carbon Dioxide Sinks	Net gains from reforestation. Desertification reversed through biotechnology. Enhanced oceanic sinks.
By 2040	Advanced Nonfossil Fuel Energy Technologies	Introduction of such new energy technologies as fusion, orbiting solar power plants, magma electricity generation, and energy applications of super-conductivity technology.

Source: Japanese Ministry of International Trade and Industry, "'The New Earth 21'—Action Program for the Twenty-First Century," paper presented at the U.S.-Japan Conference on Global Warming, Atlanta, June 3, 1991.

ity: "We treat nature like we treated workers a hundred years ago. We included then no cost for the health and social security of workers in our calculations, and today we include no cost for the health and security of nature" (62).

At the level of the individual company, reducing pollution at its source is simply one aspect of creating a more efficient manufacturing process, which has broader competitive advantages for a company. Competitive pressures, largely from very efficient Japanese companies, are now leading to rapid changes in manufacturing systems. A recent study by the Massachusetts Institute of Technology, focused on the auto industry, found that the "lean manufacturing" system introduced by Toyota and now spreading into many companies is creating a virtual revolution in how things are made—reducing labor, waste, manufacturing defects, and the time required to bring new products to market (63). These new technologies—and the management techniques and corporate attitudes they require—can also be harnessed to serve the goal of sustainability. Encouraging worker-led continuous incremental improvements in manufacturing processes toward a goal of "zero emissions," for example, would work as well as it has for a goal of "zero defects."

At the level of national governments, there is a need to develop comprehensive energy and environmental policies that provide industry with clear signals to guide their investment. One example of such a strategy is that proposed by Japan's Ministry of International Trade and Industry for dealing with greenhouse gases (64). The plan gives a 50-year timetable for the development and deployment of specific technologies, decade by decade. (See Table 2.2.)

Emerging Technologies

In 1991, the U.S. Government issued a list of technologies judged to be critical for economic competitiveness (65). Separately, so did an industry council (66), whose list was very similar. Significantly, both lists include many technologies of interest to environmentalists, and point out that efficiency, economic productivity, and improvements in product quality can go hand-in-hand with superior environmental performance. Consider three examples from a recent WRI study (67):

Biotechnology, still in its commercial infancy, could fuel a new and environmentally sounder "green revolution," freeing farming from heavy dependence on agrichemicals. Although widely recognized for their pharmaceutical potential, biological tools are also likely to profoundly affect a wide variety of industrial activities. Enzymes used as industrial catalysts, microbial recovery of metals (biohydrometallurgy), waste degradation, and biomass fuels and feedstocks are but a few examples. These applications could lower the energy- and pollution-intensity of production, while decreasing dependence on fossil fuels. Like other new technologies, biotechnology may not represent an unequivocal environmental gain. Fears that poorly designed or poorly understood genetically engineered organisms might become pests—a self-replicating environmental hazard—once released into the environment are reinforced by limits to our understanding of ecology.

Materials technology, equally dynamic, shows even more immediate application. Products based on specially engineered materials probably now constitute more than one third of United States GNP—over $1 trillion yearly. Because composite materials typically perform better than conventional materials per unit of weight, they require less raw material and produce less waste. Perhaps most important, materials design has become so highly sophisticated that engineers can now incorporate environmental criteria rather than deal with them as an afterthought. Here too, though, potential environmental drawbacks need consideration. Composites and other specially engineered materials are usually very difficult to recycle and may use more toxic substances.

The term "information technology"—encompassing developments as diverse as real-time monitoring of effluent streams, computer-controlled manufacturing, software development, and chemical and biological sensors—undoubtedly covers the broadest range of potentially important new technologies. All these technologies could have an enormous impact on pollution prevention and control. The application of computers to manufacturing systems not only greatly increases their efficiency and flexibility but also makes possible real-time monitoring of reaction conditions and effluent streams. When coupled with sensors that recognize changes in such conditions, automated processes can both prevent pollution and use input materials and energy more efficiently.

As these examples and others make clear, technology is not the limiting factor. What are needed are policies to enable and speed technological development and to ensure its emergence in the marketplace in sustainable, environmentally friendly forms. Also needed are more research and development on environmentally sound technologies, renewed management attention to the actual environmental behavior of firms, and an emphasis on making environmental concerns central to the education of future managers and engineers.

A GLOBAL CONTEXT

Although there is dispute about the extent and timing of climate change caused by emissions of greenhouse gases such as carbon dioxide, there is little doubt that continued emissions will eventually have significant consequences. Eventually, then, serious cuts in consumption of fossil fuels are likely to be necessary. The OECD countries have historically contributed disproportionately to global pollution and continue to do so. Therefore, to stabilize atmospheric concentrations of carbon dioxide, OECD countries may have to reduce emissions not only to cover their share of the necessary reduction in current emissions but also to allow for growth in developing countries that, on a per capita basis, emit far less.

Similar arguments apply to virtually all industrial activities that consume natural resources or produce pollution. There are indications that consumption of nonrenewable natural resources is beginning to plateau in the more advanced economies (see Figure 2.1), but continuation of this trend is far from certain. The OECD countries can reduce consumption of these resources by increasing recycling and reuse of such materials as metals and by encouraging transitions to less material-intensive technologies to reduce their consumption.

Because OECD consumption levels are so high, the impact of consumption choices can have a profound and sometimes destructive impact on natural resources in developing countries, inflating demand beyond what can be supplied on a sustainable basis. For example, in the United States, a fashion for parrots and other tropical birds as pets has put pressure on the birds' wild populations in several countries. And continuing demand for tropical hardwoods in industrial countries, especially Japan, has led to extensive and often destructive cutting of forests in Southeast Asia.

Non-OECD countries urgently need to expand their economic activity. Because most of these countries are or hope to be in the process of building an industrial base and a modern infrastructure, their consumption of energy and natural resources will have to increase

(68). If such expansion extends OECD-style consumption and pollution patterns across a much wider population base and increases these impacts in proportion to the fourfold or fivefold expansion in economic activity expected by the middle of the next century, the environmental impact could be devastating. A $50 trillion economy based on the technologies now in place would consume staggering amounts of natural resources and generate waste and pollution in unprecedented quantities (69).

A transition to more efficient, more sustainable technologies must occur first in the OECD countries, which have the scientific and technological base for innovation and the wealth to make the necessary investments. But more efficient technologies must also be spread rapidly to developing countries. OECD countries have an obligation to increase financial support and technical assistance in support of such technology transfers.

In addition, OECD countries need to take action to curb exports to developing countries of hazardous materials and unsafe technologies that are no longer allowed to be sold within the OECD. Individual multinational companies should be encouraged to apply the same emission and safety standards to plants operating in developing countries as in OECD countries, even in the absence of regulatory enforcement.

CONCLUSION

The United States could markedly improve its efficiency in using energy and other natural resources and, at the same time, reduce local and regional pollution, avoid waste, and lower its contribution to the threat of global warming. With appropriate, market-based policies, including price reforms and enlightened regulatory measures, these steps need not carry heavy economic penalties and could indeed improve the country's economic competitiveness. To a large degree, similar steps could be taken, with equal benefit, in other OECD countries.

Many promising new technologies exist that are both more efficient and more sustainable. These technologies characteristically enhance both economic growth and environmental improvement. The United States and other OECD countries will need to move toward such technologies, and toward policies that encourage their development and use, to improve not only their own destinies but also those of other countries.

This chapter is based on initial drafts prepared by Allen Hammond and James MacKenzie of the World Resources Institute, but includes contributions by many senior WRI staff members.

References and Notes

1. The OECD member countries are Australia, Austria, Belgium, Canada, Denmark, Finland, France, Germany, Greece, Iceland, Ireland, Italy, Japan, Luxembourg, the Netherlands, New Zealand, Norway, Portugal, Spain, Sweden, Switzerland, Turkey, the United Kingdom, and the United States.

2. Chapter 15, "Basic Economic Indicators," Table 15.1, and Chapter 16, "Population and Human Development," Table 16.1.

3. Organisation for Economic Co-operation and Development (OECD), *The State of the Environment* (OECD, Paris, 1991), p. 34.

4. *Ibid.*, p. 146.

5. Calculation of greenhouse gases global warming potential is based on the Intergovernmental Panel on Climate Change (IPCC) parameters for integrated heating values over a 100-year period. See Chapter 13, "At-

mosphere and Climate," Table 13.4, for further discussion.

6. Chapter 16, "Population and Human Development," Table 16.1.

7. The World Commission on Environment and Development, *Our Common Future* (Oxford University Press, New York, 1987), p. 4.

8. United Nations Development Programme, *Human Development Report 1991* (Oxford University Press, New York, 1991), p. 53.

9. Chauncey Starr, "Energy and Power," in *Energy and Power: A Scientific American Book* (W.H. Freeman and Company, San Francisco, 1971), pp. 5-7.

10. *Ibid.*, p. 7.

11. U.S. Environmental Protection Agency (U.S. EPA), *National Air Quality and Emissions Trends Report, 1989* (U.S. EPA, Washington, D.C., 1991), pp. 3-26.

12. Intergovernmental Panel on Climate Change, *Climate Change: The IPCC Scientific Assessment,* J.T. Houghton, G.J. Jenkins, and J.J. Ephraums, eds. (Cambridge University Press, Cambridge, U.K., 1990), p. 5.

13. U.S. Department of Energy (U.S. DOE), *Energy Conservation Trends: Understanding the Factors that Affect Conservation Gains in the U.S. Economy* (U.S. DOE, Washington, D.C., 1989), pp. 2, 3, and 5.

14. Lee Schipper, "Improved Energy Efficiency in the Industrialized Countries: Past Achievements, CO2 Emission Prospects," *Energy Policy*, Vol. 19, No. 3 (1991), p. 127.

15. *Ibid.*, p. 129.

16. *Ibid.*, pp. 130-132.

17. *Ibid.*, p. 127.

18. Energy Information Agency of the U.S. Department of Energy (DOE), *Monthly Energy Review: October 1991* (DOE, Washington, D.C., 1991), p. 15.

19. *Op. cit. 14*, p. 129.

20. International Energy Agency of the Organisation for Economic Co-operation and Development (OECD), *Energy Prices and Taxes: Fourth Quarter 1990* (OECD, Paris, 1991), p. 297.

21. Motor Vehicle Manufacturing Association of the United States, Inc. (MVMA), *MVMA Motor Vehicle Facts and Figures '90* (MVMA, Detroit, 1990), p. 49.

22. James J. MacKenzie, "Toward a Sustainable Energy Future: The Critical Role of Rational Energy Pricing," in *WRI Issues and Ideas* (World Resources Institute, Washington, D.C., May 1991), p. 8.

23. Deborah L. Bleviss, *The New Oil Crisis and Fuel Economy Technologies: Preparing the Light Transportation Industry for the 1990s* (Quorum Books, Westport, Connecticut, 1988), p. 102.

24. U.S. Environmental Protection Agency (U.S. EPA), "Green Lights: A Bright Investment in the Environment" (U.S. EPA, Washington, D.C., 1991), p. 1.

25. Electric Power Research Institute (EPRI), *Efficient Electricity Use: Estimates of Maximum Energy Savings* (EPRI, Palo Alto, California, 1990), pp. 1-3.

26. World Resources Institute in collaboration with the United Nations Environment Programme and the United Nations Development Programme, *World Resources 1990-91*

(Oxford University Press, New York, 1990) pp. 206-207.

27. Energy consumption figures in this paragraph are calculated on the basis of conventional fuel equivalents, such that primary electricity is valued on a fossil-fuel-avoided basis rather than an energy-output basis. See Chapter 21, "Energy and Materials" and accompanying note to Table 21.2 for further explanation.

28. United Nations (U.N.), *1989 Energy Statistics Yearbook* (U.N., New York, 1991), Table 4, p. 90, and Table 34, p. 386.

29. United Nations (U.N.), *1982 Energy Statistics Yearbook* (U.N., New York, 1984), Table 4, p. 144 and Table 39, p. 684.

30. *Op. cit. 28*, Table 4, p. 96, and Table 34, p. 398.

31. *Op. cit. 29*, Table 4, p. 155, and Table 39, p. 695.

32. *Op. cit. 28*, Table 34, pp. 386 and 398.

33. James J. MacKenzie, Senior Associate, World Resources Institute, Washington, D.C., 1991 (personal communication).

34. D.L. Elliot, L.L. Wendell, and G.L. Gower, "U.S. Areal Wind Resource Estimates Considering Environmental and Land-use Exclusions," paper presented at the American Wind Energy Association Windpower '90 Conference, Washington, D.C., September 1990.

35. Sam Rashkin *et al., Energy Technology Status Report, Final Report* (California Energy Commission, Sacramento, California, 1991), Table 4, p. 73.

36. Alexi Clark, "Wind Energy: Progress and Potential," *Energy Policy*, Vol. 19, No. 3 (1991), pp. 742-743.

37. James J. MacKenzie and Michael P. Walsh, *Driving Forces: Motor Vehicle Trends and Their Implications for Global Warming, Energy Strategies, and Transportation Planning* (World Resources Institute, Washington, D.C., December 1990), p. 17.

38. *Ibid.*, pp. 33-34.

39. *Ibid.*, pp. 41-42.

40. Joan M. Ogden and Robert H. Williams, *Solar Hydrogen: Moving Beyond Fossil Fuels* (World Resources Institute, Washington, D.C., 1989), pp. 1-3.

41. John F. Richards, "Global Patterns of Land Conversion," *Environment*, Vol. 26 No. 9 (1984), p. 11.

42. *Ibid.*, p. 13.

43. *Ibid.*, p. 12.

44. Robert L. Peters and Thomas E. Lovejoy, "Terrestrial Fauna," in *The Earth As Transformed by Human Action: Global and Regional Changes in the Biosphere over the Past 300 Years*, B.L. Turner, William C. Clark, Robert W. Kates *et al.*, eds. (Cambridge University Press with Clark University, New York, 1990), pp. 362-363.

45. Resources for the Future, *America's Renewable Resources,* Kenneth D. Frederick and Roger A. Sedjo, eds. (Resources for the Future, Washington, D.C., 1991), pp. 7-9.

46. Gordon H. Orians, "Ecological Concepts of Sustainability," *Environment*, Vol. 32, No. 9 (1990), pp. 11-39.

47. Paul Faeth, Robert Repetto, Kim Kroll *et al., Paying the Farm Bill: U.S. Agricultural Policy and the Transition to Sustainable Agriculture*

(World Resources Institute, Washington, D.C., 1991), p. 1.

48. A. Barry Carr, William H. Meyers, Tim T. Phipps *et al., Decoupling Farm Programs* (Resources for the Future, Washington, D.C., 1988), Table 1, p. 3.

49. *Ibid.*, pp. 2-3.

50. National Research Council, *Alternative Agriculture* (National Academy Press, Washington, D.C., 1989), pp. 98-99.

51. Richard A. Smith, Richard B. Alexander, and M. Gordon Wolman, "Water- Quality Trends in the Nation's Rivers," *Science*, Vol. 235, No. 4796 (1987), pp. 1611-1612.

52. *Op. cit. 47*, p. 11.

53. U.S. Environmental Protection Agency (U.S. EPA), *Environmental Investments: The Cost of a Clean Environment* (U.S. EPA, Washington, D.C., 1990), p. 2.

54. *Op. cit. 3*, p. 33.

55. *Op. cit. 3*, p. 146.

56. George Heaton, Robert Repetto, and Rodney Sobin, *Transforming Technology: An Agenda for Environmentally Sustainable Growth in the 21st Century* (World Resources Institute, Washington, D.C., 1991), pp. 5-7.

57. U.S. Congress, Office of Technology Assessment (OTA), *Serious Reduction of Hazardous Waste: For Pollution Prevention and Industrial Efficiency* (U.S. Government Printing Office, Washington, D.C., 1986), p. 106.

58. Frances Cairncross, "Cleaning Up: A Survey of Industry and the Environment," *The Economist* (September 6, 1990), p. 6.

59. International Chamber of Commerce (ICC), *The Business Charter for Sustainable Development* (ICC, Paris, 1990) n.p.

60. U.S. Senate, Committee on Environment and Public Works, "Title III— Emergency Planning and Community Right to Know," in *Superfund Amendments and Reauthorization Act of 1986 (P.L. 99-499)* (U.S. Government Printing Office, Washington, D.C., 1987), pp. 169-201.

61. *Op. cit. 58*, p. 10.

62. *Op. cit. 58*, p. 4.

63. James B. Womack, Daniel T. Jones, and Daniel Roos, *The Machine That Changed the World* (Rawson Associates, MacMillan Publishing Company, New York, 1990), pp. 71-222,

64. Japanese Ministry of International Trade and Industry, "'The New Earth 21'—Action Program for the Twenty-first Century," paper presented at the U.S.-Japan Conference on Global Warming, Atlanta, June 3, 1991, pp. 1-4.

65. National Critical Technologies Panel, *Report of the Critical Technologies Panel* (U.S. Government Printing Office, Washington, D.C., March 1991), pp. 1-118.

66. Council on Competitiveness, *Gaining New Ground: Technology Priorities for America's Future* (Council on Competitiveness, Washington, D.C., 1991), pp. 23-29.

67. *Op. cit. 56*, pp. 14-15.

68. Amulya K.N. Reddy and José Goldemberg, "Energy for the Developing World," *Scientific American*, Vol. 263, No. 3 (1990), pp. 62-65.

69. *Op. cit. 7*, pp. 4-5.

3. Poor Countries:

Breaking the Cycle of Poverty, Environmental Degradation, and Human Deprivation

The World Bank identifies low-income countries as those having an average annual per capita gross national product (GNP) of less than $580 in 1989 (1). Among the 41 countries meeting this criterion, a dozen have an average per capita GNP of less than $250 (2). These 41 low-income countries are the primary focus of this chapter.

Per capita GNP is one measure of development but by no means the only appropriate one. According to the United Nations Development Programme (UNDP), the quality of life as measured by longevity and literacy is also of critical importance in the development process. In 1990, the UNDP proposed a new measure—the Human Development Index (HDI)— that considers these factors in addition to per capita GNP. The UNDP finds some 63 low-human-development countries, including most of the low-income countries and 25 other countries whose per capita GNP puts them above the low-income line (3) (4). These 25 additional countries are also included in the focus of this chapter because although they may not be poor in terms of per capita GNP, they are poor in the quality of life they provide their citizens. Thus, these countries face many of the same problems as low-income countries. (For convenience, low-income countries serve as the basis for the statistics reported here, unless otherwise identified. Because China and India differ from other low-income countries in a number of respects—including their size, degree of development of human resources, and possession of significant industrial sectors—data are sometimes presented separately for China and India.)

The low-income countries are congregated in sub-Saharan Africa and South Asia, but include Haiti in the Americas and several countries in East and Southeast Asia (5). Low-human-development countries include additional countries in North and sub-Saharan Africa, South and Central America, and the Middle East.

For the poor countries, the challenge of sustainable development is different from that facing more modern economies, but no less urgent. They face the need to provide for basic human necessities, stabilize populations, and stimulate the economic development that can alleviate poverty, all while conserving natural resources essential to economic growth.

Poor countries are often those with the lowest levels of education, the poorest health, the least access to safe water and sanitation, and the most impoverished natural resource base. Almost half (44 percent) of the aggregate population of the low-income countries is illiterate (51 percent if China and India are excluded), and in some of these countries three quarters or more of the people are unable to read and write. The low-income countries combined have an average life expectancy of 62 years (55 if China and India are excluded); high-income countries have average life expectancies of 76 or more years. The infant mortality rate is 70 deaths per 1,000 live births (94 if China and India are excluded), compared with 8 deaths per 1,000 live births for the industrial countries (6).

The low-income countries contain most of the world's poor people, but not all. Throughout the world, according to the World Bank, more than 1.1 billion people live in poverty, and, of those, 630 million are "extremely poor," having an average annual per capita income of less than $275 (7). Other estimates put the number of poor at nearly 2 billion of the world's 5.3 billion people (8). There are also about 1 billion adults unable to read and write, over 1.5 billion people without safe drinking water (9), about 100 million people who are completely homeless, 1 billion people suffering from hunger (10), 150 million children under age five (one in three) who are malnourished, and 12.9 million children each year who die before their fifth birthday. (See Chapter 6, "Population and Human Development.") Not just the poor countries that are the focus of this chapter but also poor populations in every country would benefit from strategies aimed directly at attacking poverty and deprivation while protecting the natural resource base on which those populations often depend.

The poor countries encompass an enormous range of conditions and a vast share of humanity. Cultural, religious, and ethnic preferences and conflicts play a major role in many societies: often the poor are set apart by such differences. Thus, development strategies must take such factors into account. Governments are sometimes part of the problem, not part of the solution to development needs, so that "empowerment" of poor people—and their direct and active involvement in planning and managing projects that affect them—is essential if development is to succeed. (See Chapter 14, "Policies and Institutions.") Because every country is different, the policies discussed in this chapter cannot do justice to the diversity of conditions and needs among poor countries. The intent is rather to illustrate what sustainable development might mean in poor countries and to suggest, through specific examples, the range of opportunities for action.

POVERTY AND ENVIRONMENTAL DEGRADATION

The evidence of human poverty and deprivation in the world is unmistakable, as is the evidence of the worsening environmental conditions caused by and contributing to poverty. In poor countries, sustainable development means first and foremost addressing these intertwined problems. That in turn means progress along each of the dimensions outlined in Chapter 1: economic development to provide jobs and alleviate poverty; investments in human development to stabilize populations and enable people to improve their well-being and their livelihoods; protection for natural resources, in large part by providing poor and landless peoples with alternatives to the overexploitation of marginal lands; and support for improved practices and technologies that are appropriate and efficient in local contexts.

Many of the poor countries are experiencing rapid population growth. Sub-Saharan Africa as a whole had an average annual population growth rate of 3 percent between 1985 and 1990, with some countries—Côte d'Ivoire, Botswana, Kenya, Tanzania, Uganda, and Zambia—having rates considerably higher. (See Chapter 16, "Population and Human Development," Table 16.1.)

In many poor countries, rapid population growth, agricultural modernization, and inequalities in land tenure are creating increasingly large populations with little or no access to productive land. Without jobs and without productive land, poor people are forced onto marginal lands in search of subsistence food production and fuelwood, or they move to the cities. Those who stay on the land are forced to graze livestock herds where vegetation is sparse or soils and shrubs are easily damaged and to create agricultural plots on arid or semiarid lands, on hillsides, in tropical forests, or in other ecologically sensitive areas. It has been estimated that 60 percent of the developing world's poorest people live in areas that are ecologically vulnerable (11). As more and more people exploit open-access resources in an often desperate struggle to provide for themselves and their families, they further degrade their environment (12).

The toll on natural resources takes many forms, including soil erosion, loss of soil fertility, desertification, deforestation, depleted game and fish stocks from overhunting and overfishing, loss of natural habitats and of species, depletion of groundwater resources, and pollution of rivers and other water bodies. The result is to reduce the carrying capacity and productivity of the land and its biological resources. This degradation further exacerbates poverty and threatens not only the economic prospects of future generations, but also the livelihoods, health, and well-being of current populations.

It is in the rural areas that poverty and environmental degradation come together most acutely. Most of the low-income countries are still primarily rural; in sub-Saharan Africa, 69 percent of the population lives in rural areas; and in South Asia, 74 percent. (See Figure 3.1.) By far, the greatest proportion—in some places as many as 80–90 percent—of the poor live in rural areas, depending on agriculture and related activities for their daily subsistence. Even in highly urbanized Latin America, 60 percent of the poorest people reside in rural areas (13). Because urban populations are growing rapidly, however—at an annual rate of 6

Figure 3.1 Rural Populations as a Percentage of Total, 1989

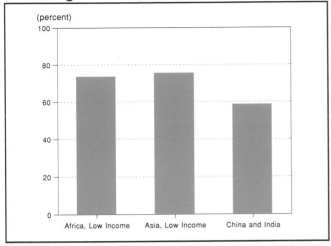

Source: United Nations (U.N.), U.N. Population Division, *World Population Prospects 1990* (U.N., New York, 1991).

percent in sub-Saharan Africa and 4 percent in South Asia—urban poverty and urban environmental problems will be increasingly important in the future (14).

A contributing factor to poverty and environmental degradation is that rural areas lag behind urban areas in human development terms, with rural infant mortality in some countries 30–50 percent higher, and rural malnutrition in one study an average of 50 percent higher (15). In every society, the poor live shorter, less healthy lives than those who are better off financially. For example, in Colombia, infants from poor families are twice as likely to die as infants from the country's wealthiest families. In rural Punjab in India, child mortality among the landless is 36 percent higher than among the landowning classes (16).

These disparities are aggravated by disparities in the delivery of social services. In low-human-development countries, 72 percent of the population live in rural areas, but the rural population is only half as likely to have access to health, safe water, and sanitation services (17). Education is also less available in rural areas; in some African and Asian countries, rural literacy rates are less than half those in urban areas (18).

Women are particularly hard hit by the accelerating spiral of poverty and environmental degradation. When they have to devote more and more time to obtaining fuel and water, they have less time to devote to food production, to increase the household income, to pursue their own education, and to improve family welfare. These growing burdens can cause still further adverse social and economic consequences for themselves and their families (19).

INVESTING IN HUMAN DEVELOPMENT

Improvements in human health and educational opportunities are important for their own sake, but they also play a critical role in achieving economic development and protecting the environment. Yet in countries with some of the most urgent needs for investment in

education and health, expenditures in these priority areas have been declining. Half the African countries had lower real social expenditures per capita in 1985–87 than in 1979–81 (20).

Education

In both education and health, the most urgent priority is to provide basic services for the poor majority. In many poor countries, the economic returns from primary education for both the individual and the society are almost twice as high as those from higher education. Moreover, spending on primary education is one means of specifically providing resources to the poor. Many poor countries, however, spend more on higher education than on primary; over 100 million children receive no primary education at all (21).

Yet changes are taking place. The share of primary schooling in education budgets increased during the 1980s in 15 of 22 African countries examined, and countries in Africa and elsewhere are finding creative ways of both reducing costs and expanding services. Using teachers with less formal training (for example, as assistant teachers, as in Senegal and Colombia), increasing the size of classes, operating double (or even triple) shifts to save on the capital costs of buildings, equipment, and libraries, and recovering at least some of the costs of higher education through user charges all offer the potential for significant savings (22). Such savings allow more children to be reached without major increases in education budgets.

Community resources and parental involvement also can make a significant difference. The Bangladesh Rural Advancement Committee (BRAC) is a nongovernmental organization providing a three-year basic curriculum at a cost of $15 per pupil per year. By involving village leaders and parents, and using simple classrooms and teachers who are not fully trained, BRAC prepares children who might not otherwise have access to schooling (especially girls from poor families) for entry into the official school system in the fourth year. Growing evidence suggests that schools managed, and to some extent financed, by local communities are more efficient than those run as part of a centralized system (23).

Health

In health, as in education, decentralization is the key to both more efficient and more effective services. Primary health care—consisting of a broad network of community health clinics and community-based health workers providing basic preventive care and health education as well as treatment for the most common illnesses—offers an effective, quick, and relatively inexpensive way of improving the health of the majority of the population in poor countries. The UNDP estimates that it costs between $100 and $600 to save each additional life through preventive health care, compared with $500–$5,000 for curative care (24).

Many poor countries spend as much as 80–90 percent of their health budgets on hospitals and, at the same time, have some of the highest infant mortality rates in the world. Restructuring these health expenditures offers significant opportunities for improving a population's health. Bangladesh, for example, redirected its health care spending from a largely urban and curative focus toward grassroots health services to the poor throughout the country. Between 1978 and 1988, the share for rural health clinics in the budget rose from 10 percent to 60 percent; in the same time period (1981 through 1988–89), the proportion of 1-year-olds immunized against the major causes of death in childhood increased from 1 percent to 60 percent (25).

Switching to lower-cost drugs (e.g., generic rather than name-brands), buying them more efficiently (e.g., by purchasing through competitive bidding), choosing more appropriate therapies (e.g., oral rehydration therapy rather than intravenous feeding for diarrhea) (see Chapter 6, "Population and Human Development"), employing traditional healers and other personnel with fewer formal qualifications, and involving communities in building or paying for health clinics all offer the potential for significant savings in health expenditures and thus could enable more people to be reached (26).

Stabilizing Populations

Improved health and education will have positive effects on population, but only if the opportunities are available for women to choose the family size they want. There is considerable evidence that strong, well-managed family planning programs are highly effective; they reduce family size, improve the health of mothers and children, and result in more balanced rates of population growth. The voluntary use of contraception in poor countries has risen from 10 percent of couples in the 1960s to 51 percent today (27 percent excluding China and India) (27). (See Chapter 16, "Population and Human Development," Table 16.6.) The average number of births per woman dropped from six in 1960 to four in 1990. If all the women who say that they want no more children had full access to family planning services, the number of births could be sharply reduced: by an estimated 27 percent in Africa, 33 percent in Asia, and 35 percent in Latin America (28).

The availability of a wide range of convenient and low-cost contraceptive options, noncoercive incentives to lower fertility, cultural sensitivity and adaptation to community needs, and effective dissemination of information about the advantages of family limitation and birth spacing and about the contraceptives themselves all contribute to success in slowing population growth (29). Ultimately, however, use of contraception depends on a wide range of social and economic factors, including the availability of security in old age, the role of children in providing the family's livelihood, and the role of religious institutions in the society. Family planning programs work best when offered in combination with other social and economic development efforts.

Nongovernmental organizations (NGOs) and the media have particularly important roles to play. NGOs can often cost-effectively reach local populations; and they often pioneer new approaches. Radio, television, films, and, increasingly, video cassette recorders offer the means of reaching even illiterate populations. Making family planning information available through such media can significantly influence behavior (30).

ENCOURAGING ECONOMIC DEVELOPMENT

The poor countries were severely affected by economic stagnation in the 1980s. Their economies suffered from the growing debt burden, the decline in primary product prices, and the hardships of economic restructuring imposed by international development agencies. In sub-Saharan Africa, where per capita GNP growth was low even in the "good years" between 1965 and 1980 (2.8 percent compared with 3.7 percent for developing countries as a whole), per capita GNP *declined* an average of 2.6 percent per year between 1980 and 1988. By 1988, per capita GNP in sub-Saharan Africa was 19 percent lower than in 1980. Many poor countries' debt in 1988 was larger than their income, in some cases three times as large (31).

These difficulties have intensified a long-running debate about the role of economic growth in development and how best to achieve it. Achieving effective development collaboration among the many actors involved in poor countries' development—the governments, bilateral and multilateral donor agencies, local and foreign NGOs, communities, and, where it exists, the private sector—has proved to be an elusive, if not impossible, task. Yet the divergence in views may not be as wide as the intensity of the debate has at times suggested (32).

Stabilization and Structural Adjustment

The policies of stabilization and structural adjustment pursued by the International Monetary Fund and the World Bank have been a focus of much current discontent with development policy. Intended to maintain foreign exchange balances and promote economic modernization and growth, adjustment programs generally include measures to manage demand, improve the incentive system, increase market efficiency, and promote investment. Specific policy measures include exchange-rate devaluation, wage reductions, trade liberalization, financial liberalization, public sector reform, tax reform, privatization of public enterprises, land reform, and the removal of price distortions of inputs and outputs in agriculture, forestry, and energy (33).

Whatever their successes in achieving macroeconomic goals, structural adjustment policies have been criticized by other international agencies, developing-country governments, and an increasingly vocal and active community of grassroots organizations for their harmful effects on both poor people and the environment (34) (35). The Economic Commission for Africa (ECA), for example, charged that "structural adjustment programs are rending the fabric of African society," with greatest impact on "the vulnerable groups –children, women, and the aged." The ECA cited the social consequences of adjustment policies as declining per capita GNP and wages, rising unemployment

Box 3.1 Community Institutions in Resource Management: Agroforestry in Ghana

In the village of Goviefe-Agodome, in Ghana's Volta region, a government-initiated local self-development cooperative has successfully turned land that was considered marginal into productive farmland through various agroforestry practices. In a country that is still recovering from the political instability and economic upheaval of the 1970s and early 1980s and that is heavily dependent on its rural population for food and foreign exchange, grassroots participation in solving local problems and carrying out self-help community improvement activities is crucial. In 1984, the government's National Mobilization Programme was established to encourage the formation of village mobilization squads (locally called "mobisquads") for purposes of community development and national economic recovery.

Goviefe-Agodome's mobisquad was initiated in 1983–84 by six villagers returning from Nigeria, when that country expelled nearly 1 million Ghanaians. At the time, the community's village leaders were not actively engaged in community development work. When presented with the opportunity provided by the newly formed mobisquad, however, village leaders and other organizations willingly joined in the effort, making the mobisquad one of the

most widely representative organizations in operation.

In 1986, the 41-member Goviefe-Agodome mobisquad's first operational year, it established a 4.8-hectare communal farm of cassava, maize, and cocoyam and intercropped with teak and leucaena trees. The sale of the crops earned the mobisquad 750,000 cedis (US$2,500). The mobisquad divided most of the profits equally among its members, but used 30,000 cedis for two community projects, an improved latrine and a clinic.

In the next three years, the mobisquad grew both in membership (to 71 members) and in the range of activities undertaken. In its first four years of operation, it developed a 37.6-hectare agroforestry farm, planted 19.2 hectares of cotton, nursed approximately 14,000 tree seedlings, and transplanted about 17,000 seedlings. From these and related activities, the mobisquad netted more than 3.28 million cedis (US$10,000).

Four elements contributed to the success of Goviefe-Agodome's community development efforts:
■ The mobisquad, with support of the local leaders and other institutions, has enabled the villagers to design, implement, and manage their own development efforts;

■ Their efforts yield immediate and significant financial benefits to the cooperative members and their households; only a small percentage of the mobisquad's profits are for community-wide efforts;
■ The resource management activities are locally sustainable and involve practices and techniques familiar to the members; and
■ The community has benefited from its proximity to an important road, linking it to major urban areas and facilitating external assistance in its development activities.

The Goviefe-Agodome experience shows that the collective decision and action power of the community regarding resource use and abuse is key to attaining sustainable development. Communities with viable village institutions and committed local leadership can mobilize local labor and resources and, with modest external assistance, can make important contributions to local development [1].

References and Notes

1. Clement Dorm-Adzobu, Okyeame Ampadu-Agyei, and Peter G. Veit, *Community Institutions in Resource Management: Agroforestry by Mobisquads in Ghana*, From the Ground Up Case Study Series, No. 3 (World Resources Institute, Washington, D.C., 1991), pp. 1-20.

---

and underemployment, deterioration in the level of social services, falling educational and training standards, rising malnutrition and health problems, and rising poverty levels and income inequalities (36).

While the debate continues, there is growing consensus that structural adjustment policies are indeed necessary but should be designed not only to minimize their adverse impact on the poor but also to reduce future poverty (37) (38) and contribute to sustainable natural resource management (39). In Africa, the Social Dimensions of Adjustment Project is a joint effort by the UNDP Regional Bureau for Africa, the African Development Bank, and the World Bank to integrate poverty reduction programs into the design of adjustment and development plans (40). The policy leverage of adjustment programs could also be used in support of land reform, health, education, agricultural priorities, environmental regeneration, family planning, constructive public works projects, and the creation of rural economic centers (41).

Importance of Local Participation

Another area of emerging consensus is that to be sustainable, development must be participatory and community-based. Throughout the poor countries, successful development initiatives share a number of characteristics. They address needs identified by local people, involve people in the design as well as the implementation of projects, use techniques and princi-

ples suited to local conditions, and respond flexibly to changing circumstances, either correcting previous mistakes or incorporating new information (42) (43).

Whether initiated by local communities themselves or by outside donors, the most successful and sustainable development efforts have been those in which the intended beneficiaries had the opportunity to participate both in defining the problem and in choosing solutions. (See Box 3.1.)

Some of the most successful projects are those initiated and run by local communities and indigenous NGOs. (See Chapter 14, "Policies and Institutions.") The provision of credit is just one area in which informal organizations—in which the participants themselves put up the money—have been more successful than modern commercial institutions in encouraging self-employment and microenterprise development. The Grameen (meaning "rural" in Bengali) Bank of Bangladesh is perhaps the most well-known of the small-loan, self-help credit institutions. Founded in 1976 and formally established by government order in 1983 (44), the bank now provides up to $10 million per month in loans averaging about $70; it has a 98 percent repayment record. Over 90 percent of its loans are to women (45) (46). According to the International Fund for Agricultural Development (IFAD)—which has similar activities throughout the developing world—to be successful, credit programs must target women as well as men, foster the active and ongoing participation of the poor not just as recipients of loans but as integral partners in development, and draw on the experiences of grassroots NGOs (47).

Assisted Self-Reliance

As a result of such experiences, old distinctions between "top-down" and "bottom-up" development are increasingly viewed as no longer relevant. The emerging consensus is that the role of governments is not so much to "do" development but to create the conditions that allow self-reliant development to take place—what Norman Uphoff calls "assisted self-reliance" (48).

Only governments have the resources, authority, and organizational capacity to build roads, bridges, and secondary schools and to enact broad social and financial policies. An important strategy, therefore, might be for governments of poor countries to implement policies to foster broad-based participatory and sustainable economic growth; that is, to establish large-scale policies that encourage and support small-scale development (49). In addition to investing in human development, as discussed above, this strategy might involve, among other things, maintaining infrastructure, improving trade, reforming land tenure, fostering public accountability, improving the position of women, and focusing aid on the poorest segments of society.

Because roads, railroads, ports, utilities, and other facilities in many poor countries have been poorly maintained in recent years, for example, rehabilitation of infrastructure is a more pressing need than investment in new facilities, and use of domestic contractors can simultaneously increase employment.

Similarly, most poor countries, especially in Africa, have markets that are too small to achieve economies of scale without trade, and industries that are too new and inexperienced to compete without protection from established overseas industries. Increased regional trade, which is already taking place informally in many cases (50), provides an excellent opportunity to expand markets. Moving in this direction would require removing obstacles to the movement of capital, labor, and goods and establishing simpler administrative procedures (51).

Employment Opportunities

In many poor countries—especially in Asia, where shortages of land mean that farming and other agricultural activities are not able to absorb growing populations—generating employment is an urgent priority. Faster rural employment growth can simultaneously increase people's earnings, reduce rural-to-urban migration, reduce resource and environmental pressures, and improve the position of women. Establishing pricing policies in poor countries that encourage agricultural production would also encourage employment growth. At present, however, agricultural prices in most developing countries discourage agricultural production (52). Decentralizing government programs to regional and local authorities and creating the climate (through economic incentives and political stability) to

draw increased official and private capital flows would also increase employment (53).

Developed countries also have a role to play. Removal of industrial countries' trade barriers to labor-intensive manufactures such as textiles, apparel, and footwear would do more to expand employment in low-income countries than any other measure. It would simultaneously have significant benefits for consumers in advanced countries (54).

Land Tenure Reform

In many poor countries, land ownership is extremely concentrated, with 20 percent of the rural population landless, about one half of the farmers (with average landholdings of less than 2 hectares) together occupying 3–4 percent of the total agricultural area, and as few as 10 percent of the farmers (each holding thousands of hectares) together occupying one half to three quarters of the total agricultural area. Large holdings are often used inefficiently and in some instances sit idle. In areas where these conditions prevail, land redistribution and tenurial reform would both reduce pressure on resources and dramatically reduce poverty (55).

Removing Subsidies

Charging users for the services they receive—whether in education, health, transportation, water, or sanitation—can encourage more careful use of the services. User charges, provided they are imposed equitably (e.g., those with higher incomes pay more, or charges are imposed for higher levels of service but not for lower), may be an effective way of both limiting costs and increasing the number of people with access to the services (56).

Food subsidies are an example of a potentially inefficient policy. Food subsidies that are available to even the relatively wealthy may continue to receive political support, but they are a highly inefficient way of helping the poor. Approaches that target the most needy as part of an integrated nutrition strategy including nutrition education and primary health care are much more effective (57).

Women's Economic Opportunities

The enormous disparities that exist between opportunities for men and women and the disproportionate burden that rural poverty and environmental degradation poses for women mean that expanded opportunities for women can result in significant returns for them, their families, and their communities. The disparities between men and women in the poor countries begin in childhood, when girls have less access than boys to education, and sometimes even less food and health care. In Nepal, to cite an extreme case, only 57 percent of girls are enrolled in primary school while the number for boys is over 90 percent; in Chad, enrollment is 29 percent for girls and 73 percent for boys (58). (See Figure 3.2.) In Bangladesh, malnutrition is three times more common among young girls than boys. Maternal mortality rates—as high as 1,000 per 100,000

Figure 3.2 Percentage of Male and Female Children Enrolled in Primary School, 1988

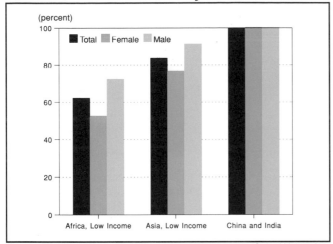

Source: The World Bank, *World Development Report 1991* (Oxford University Press, New York, 1991), Table 29, pp. 260—261.

live births in low-human-development countries compared with 10 or fewer in most developed countries—are dramatic evidence of the neglect of women's health. The literacy rate of women in the developing world as a whole is three quarters that of men (59).

In poor countries, development efforts in the informal sector have been particularly effective in increasing women's earnings. The elimination of laws and customs preventing women's participation in training and other development programs and their access to credit, education, and housing and property ownership could do much to increase women's opportunities (60). Increases in women's status, education, and earnings, along with the availability of maternal and child health care, also are significant factors in improving child nutrition and health, as well as reducing family size (61).

PROTECTING THE ENVIRONMENT

In poor countries, because of the close relationship between poverty, population growth, and environmental degradation, the most important actions to conserve natural resources are those that are aimed at stabilizing populations and alleviating poverty. However, specific efforts to maintain as much as possible of each country's natural and modified ecosystems, to halt deforestation, and to conserve biological diversity are also badly needed. Creating and maintaining protected areas and protecting threatened species are important components of the necessary strategy (62). Using both wild and managed biological resources in ways that allow stocks to renew themselves is also important.

The spiral of poverty, population growth, and environmental degradation that characterizes many poor countries is frequently aggravated by policies that actively encourage waste and resource degradation, particularly in agriculture, forestry, and energy (63). For example, holding agricultural prices artificially low to

benefit the urban minority discourages investment in soil and tree conservation. Subsidizing pesticides, fertilizers, and other agricultural inputs encourages their use and leads to residues and runoff that can be environmentally detrimental. And providing tax incentives that encourage forest clearing for timber and ranching creates short-term profits for a few while seriously degrading the environment.

Many developing countries subsidize the cost of fuel. Protecting the environment in poor countries would require economic incentives, including prices and tax policies, that favor resource conservation rather than resource degradation. However, the direction and impact of policy change are not always clearcut and must be carefully suited to local conditions (64).

An especially important ingredient in successful natural resource management is community participation in the design as well as the execution of development initiatives. Governments and international agencies serious about protecting the environment can take a number of measures to foster decentralized, small-scale natural resource management. Planning would begin with input from local individuals and institutions identifying needs, problems, and priorities rather than with decisions made by outsiders.

Governments and international organizations can train local officials in the tools and methodologies of planning, finance, and materials acquisition; they can provide small development funds to catalyze local initiatives; they can conduct research to improve locally known and accepted techniques rather than promoting new and foreign practices; and they can train village-based and local specialists in terracing, reforestation, water development, and land management, instead of supplying outside experts. In addition, they can promote linkages between local communities and central authorities by integrating community plans into regional contexts; such linkages can then contribute to creating regional markets for both agricultural and other products.

Building the institutional capacity of societies to monitor and correct environmental abuses is an important long-term strategy. Well-trained government regulators are essential. A reliable legal framework, in which the judiciary has the capacity to enforce laws, can allow the people themselves to play an enforcement role (65). A free and independent press, capable of asking hard questions and monitoring progress, can provide people with the information they need to oppose environmental degradation. It is encouraging that in some of the world's poorest countries in West Africa, where what little press there was has always been subject to total state control, there are now dozens of "hard-hitting, well-produced" independent newspapers (66).

BUILDING ON LOCAL TECHNOLOGIES

The process of sustainable development would be advanced by the development and use of labor-intensive, energy-efficient, low-cost technologies that improve productivity or conserve natural resources in poor

Box 3.2 Combining Traditional Agricultural Techniques and Modern Expertise

A growing body of experience suggests that traditional knowledge offers an important contribution to sustainable development in poor countries. Because they are locale-specific and ecologically rational, traditional farming, water use, and agroforestry practices often provide an important starting point. Some of the most successful breakthroughs occur where researchers work with small farmers, learning from their experience, and helping them improve the traditional practices described below.

Intercropping is the growing of two or more crops that have complementary needs for light, soil, or water in the same field; it reduces the risk of single crop failures and provides a regular supply of food over the year. When sorghum and groundnuts are grown together, the combined yield is 25 percent higher than when they are grown separately in the same area; millet and cowpea together have a yield more than 50 percent higher than when they are grown as monocrops; and cassava can be added to maize without any reduction in the maize yield. These techniques, long known particularly to West Africans, who intercrop as much as 80 percent of their farmland, are now beginning to be appreciated by researchers and scientists as well (1) (2).

Agroforestry involves combining tree growing with agriculture and is widely considered to offer significant potential, especially for those who cannot afford pesticides, fertilizers, and irrigation (3). Forest farmers have developed sophisticated systems of tree and crop farming that mimic the surrounding multistoried vegetation (4).

One widely heralded agroforestry technique is the *alley cropping* (i.e., alternating rows of crops and trees) of a tree species known as *Leucaena leucocephala*. Although it is cited as having excellent results in Nepal (5) and in Tanzania, the results elsewhere have been mixed (6) (7). More successful in Asia than in Africa, the best alley cropping efforts offer farmers substantial immediate benefits in the form of food, fodder, fuelwood, poles, or cash (8).

Small-scale irrigation. In Burkina Faso, lines of stone were arranged along the contour to hold back rainwater, making it pool uphill and giving it time to sink into the soil. These stone lines have resulted in yield increases averaging more than 50 percent and have been estimated to have the potential to turn most of Burkina Faso's barren expanses back into usable cropland (9). Similar examples can be found in other parts of the world. By developing a minor irrigation tank, the people of the village of Sukhomajri in India succeeded in reducing soil erosion, tripling average annual crop yields, and greatly increasing grass and fodder availability and thus milk production (10). In Chambrum, Haiti, the people built a dam and dug a network of ditches that enabled them to divert water from a canal carrying irrigation runoff from the nearby sugar plantation. In a previously completely arid area, there is now "row after row of sweet potato plants, corn, sugar cane, and sorghum" (11).

Organic recycling—the use of crop residues and manure—is another low-cost technique that can significantly increase productivity. In the Guinope area of Honduras, the introduction of organic fertilizers (chicken manure and green manure derived from the intercropping of leguminous plants) and some chemical fertilizers and traditional soil conservation techniques produced increased yields as well as increases in employment opportunities, reduced water pollution, and protection of forest cover (12).

Minimum tillage, a traditional method involving limited land disturbance, was once dismissed as unscientific but is now recognized by agricultural researchers to be an environmentally sound and productive approach for most of the humid tropics, where deep plowing can speed erosion and soil degradation (13). (See Chapter 7, "Food and Agriculture.")

References and Notes

1. Paul Harrison, *The Greening of Africa: Breaking Through in the Battle for Land and Food* (Paladin, London, 1987), pp. 108-109.
2. Bill Rau, *From Feast to Famine: Official Cures and Grassroots Remedies to Africa's Food Crisis* (Zed Books, London and Atlantic Highlands, New Jersey, 1991), pp. 146-147.
3. Geoffrey Barnard, "Agroforestry: Behind the Buzzwords," *Panoscope*, No. 19 (July 1990), p. 9.
4. *Op. cit.* 1, p. 75.
5. Kenneth Tull, Michael Sands, and Miguel Altieri, *Experiences in Success: Case Studies in Growing Enough Food Through Regenerative Agriculture* (Rodale International, Emmaus, Pennsylvania, 1987), pp. 5-13.
6. Paul Kerkhof, *Agroforestry in Africa: A Survey of Project Experience* (Panos, Washington, D.C., and London, 1990), p. 8.
7. "Beware of Miracle Trees," *Panoscope*, No. 19 (July 1990), p. 20.
8. John B. Raintree, "Agroforestry: Looking for the Wood in the Trees," *Panoscope*, No. 19 (July 1990), p. 21.
9. *Op. cit.* 1, pp. 165-170.
10. Anil Agarwal and Sunita Narain, *Towards Green Villages: A Strategy for Environmentally-Sound and Participatory Rural Development* (Centre for Science and Environment, New Delhi, 1989), pp. 17-18.
11. Patrick Breslin, *Development and Dignity* (Inter-American Foundation, Rosslyn, Virginia, 1987), pp. 48-49.
12. Walter V. Reid, James N. Barnes, and Brent Blackwelder, *Bankrolling Successes: A Portfolio of Sustainable Development Projects* (Environmental Policy Study Institute and National Wildlife Federation, Washington, D.C., 1988), pp. 21 and 26-27.
13. *Op. cit.* 1, pp. 135-137.

countries. However, one of the central lessons gained from many small-scale development projects is that technologies already known and accepted by the people have a much higher rate of success than new and unfamiliar technologies. Thus, development of technologies for the poor countries needs to give a high priority to increasing the effectiveness and efficiency of locally known techniques (67).

Nonetheless, further research on improved technologies—especially those applicable to agriculture or to rural life—is important. Because farming itself is the source of much environmental degradation, improvements in agriculture—and in the resource base on which agriculture depends—are badly needed. In Africa, in particular, raising agricultural production among small farmers has the potential to combat poverty and promote economic growth (68). Building on

the knowledge of rural peoples has already led to successes with intercropping, agroforestry, small-scale irrigation systems, organic recycling, and improved tillage methods. (See Box 3.2.) To fully use the knowledge that local farmers have of their land and of ways to manage it, however, development agencies need to shift from a technical or bureaucratic approach to a participatory one (69).

Energy technologies are also of critical importance to poor countries. Poor rural populations throughout the developing world depend heavily on traditional biomass fuels—fuelwood, charcoal, dung, and crop residues—for energy. (See Chapter 10, "Energy.") Such fuels provide approximately 60 percent of fuel needs in poor countries excluding China and India (22 percent including China and India) (70). In sub-Saharan Africa, such fuels account for two thirds of the energy

Figure 3.3 Energy Sources in Poor Countries, 1989

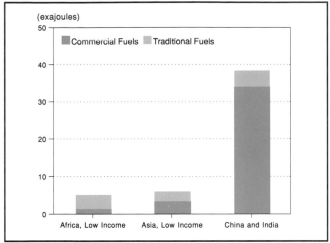

Source: United Nations (U.N.), *U.N. Energy Yearbook 1989* (U.N., New York, 1991).

consumption, with some four fifths of the population relying wholly or partly on them (71). (See Figure 3.3.) In very poor countries, the proportion of traditional fuels is even higher, exceeding 90 percent of primary energy supplies in countries such as Ethiopia, Nepal, and Bangladesh. (See Chapter 21, "Energy and Materials," Table 21.2.) More than 50 million Africans already face acute fuelwood scarcities (72). This situation is getting worse as increased prices for other fuels, especially petroleum and electricity, result in greater reliance on biomass in urban areas as well (73). Fuelwood shortages require rural women to spend increasing amounts of time collecting wood, causing a host of negative social and economic consequences, such as decreases in child nutrition (74). Moreover, as farmers begin to burn dung and agricultural residues instead of using them as fertilizers, the cycle of poverty and environmental destruction is further aggravated (75). Development of more efficient domestic stoves or cooking methods would help to minimize fuelwood needs.

Most of the commercial fuel used by poor countries is in the form of oil (76). In some countries—including Ethiopia, India and Viet Nam—energy imports and the interest on the money borrowed to buy energy represent nearly 25 percent or more of export earnings (77).

Thus there are severe environmental and foreign exchange constraints on increasing the availability of energy in poor countries. Yet energy is essential to addressing other priority issues confronting these countries, including the provision of adequate supplies of safe water, the building of physical infrastructure, the generation of nonfarm sources of employment, and increased agricultural production.

In many poor countries, the best prospects in the near term for increasing energy supplies may be from increased biomass production. However, this same biomass is also needed for food, fodder, building materials, and industrial raw materials (78). Increased biomass production can buy time for the development of

other renewable technologies, including biogas and biomethanization, that appear to offer some potential for both meeting rural energy needs and providing organic fertilizer for agriculture (79).

MOBILIZING RESOURCES

The biggest barrier to sustainable development may be the lack of political commitment. Investing in human development, creating the climate and incentives for economic growth, and implementing measures to protect the environment will cost a lot of money. But the money can be found, if difficult choices are made. Reallocation of existing government expenditures in poor countries combined with some increases and some redirection of foreign assistance could provide much of the necessary financing (80). What is needed, however, is the political commitment—by both national governments and development agencies—to reverse the cycle of poverty, environmental degradation, and human deprivation that characterizes poor countries.

Opportunities for more participatory and equitable development appear to be increasing. There is increasing recognition that development as practiced to date has failed to reach the world's poor people and an emerging consensus about the linkage between poverty and environmental degradation. Combined with an upsurge in the number of democratically elected governments, such trends could make possible changes in policies previously impossible. Nonetheless, many governments will face profound opposition from those whose interests are challenged. Encouraging democratic freedom, invoking common interests, compensating powerful groups, empowering weaker groups, channeling credit to the poor, and allowing a free press are all methods of overcoming such opposition (81). In addition, by computing the costs of economic activity in ways that show their true costs, including their environmental effects, governments can encourage the search for and use of more sustainable options (82) (83).

The resources for supporting sustainable development in poor countries can come from the poor countries themselves, in large measure. But carefully directed resources from industrial countries—and reexamined policies within those countries—are also needed.

National Policies

Nearly $50 billion—2 percent of the combined GNP of developing countries— could be made available for development purposes by reducing military spending, halting capital flight, eliminating corruption, reforming public enterprises, and reducing internal policing. Military expenditures absorb 5.5 percent of the GNP of the developing world (84); in some of the poor countries, including Sudan, Uganda, Pakistan, and India, military spending exceeds spending on education and health combined. (See Chapter 15, "Basic Economic Indicators," Table 15.3.) Simply by freezing their military expenditures at current levels, developing countries could release $10–$15 billion per year—as much as $150 billion by the year 2000 (85).

Significant additional resources could also be obtained if basic services— e.g., in health, education, credit, transportation, communications, water, and sanitation—were provided to all before more advanced services were provided for the smaller middle- and upper-middle-income groups (86).

As noted above, in health, this redirection means restructuring in favor of primary care; in education, it means diverting some resources from secondary and tertiary education toward primary schools. Similar gains are possible with respect to water and sanitation services. Of the $10 billion now spent annually on these services in developing countries, 80 percent goes to schemes costing $550 or more per person; less than 20 percent goes to low-cost strategies costing less than $30 per person served (87).

Policies for Development Assistance

As with national budgets, simply restructuring foreign assistance priorities in favor of social sector expenditures—and within the social sector, in favor of the provision of basic services—could significantly increase the prospects for sustainable development. In some poor countries, aid provides such a high proportion of the development budget (in Chad, for example, aid provides 53 percent of total expenditures on health and education), that foreign assistance priorities are a major determinant of national priorities (88). According to one estimate, if only the *increases* in aid over the next few years were allocated to primary health care, primary education, and low-cost water and sanitation schemes, the annual amount of aid available for these purposes would double (89).

Development agencies and other donors could decide to provide aid only to countries that have pledged to make social and environmental concerns priority areas. A less intrusive way of achieving the same objective is for donors simply to direct more of their aid toward countries that are already making people-oriented, ecologically sound development a priority. UNICEF, UNDP, and others have argued that the problem with adjustment assistance is not the fact that conditions have been attached to the provision of aid but the fact that those conditions have worked against the poor. "Human adjustment assistance" would provide development aid to countries pursuing policies such as investing in social infrastructure, promoting growth in employment, and providing credit to the poor (90).

Debt relief offers another major opportunity for promoting sustainable development. Although the absolute amount of money owed by poor countries is small in relation to that owed by the major debtors, in relation to the poor countries' exports and incomes, it is staggering. The countries with low human development, for example, have an average debt service ratio— that is, the total debt service as a percentage of exports of goods and services—of 28.4 percent, with many countries considerably higher (for example, Ethiopia at 37.4 percent and Indonesia at 34.1 percent) (91).

"Debt for nature" swaps, in which commercial and official creditors cancel the debt on the condition that those resources be invested in programs to promote environmental sustainability, could be supplemented by similar programs to invest in social expenditures. Two such measures—UNICEF's Debt for Child Development program and the Inter-American Development Bank's Social Investment Fund—are already in place (92).

Industrial country donors need to take steps to modify domestic policies that work against their development assistance. Industrial countries, for example, subsidize their own domestic agricultural activities on a scale of $300 billion per year (93), creating enormous agricultural surpluses. These surpluses not only deny developing countries markets for their products but also are periodically supplied to poor countries in the form of food aid, which can depress the local markets and perhaps postpone agricultural reform. At the same time, tariff barriers in industrial countries keep out many agricultural products from developing countries. The removal of such subsidies and trade barriers would increase export markets for poor countries.

CONCLUSION

In the poor countries, where poverty, environmental degradation, and human deprivation are closely linked and are aggravated by high population growth, measures to address these problems can be mutually reinforcing. Improvements in people's health and skills contribute to economic progress and—when available to women—to reduced births. Slower population growth increases the opportunities available to the current population, which in turn increases the people's capacity for responding to opportunities and incentives that protect the environment and promote economic development. A secure resource base and increases in nonagricultural employment opportunities—again, especially for women—in turn contribute to economic growth and to improved human prospects. Because of these synergistic relationships, simultaneously pursuing action on all fronts—investing in the development of people, promoting economic growth, and arresting massive environmental destruction—offers the possibility of turning a vicious cycle into a virtuous cycle.

But the challenge is formidable and will require political commitment and a host of policies to foster equity, participation, and resource conservation. The alternative, however, may well be increased ecological disaster and poverty—and the social cleavages they create—in poor countries.

People are their own best advocates when they have the opportunity. They know what they want and understand better than outsiders the local ecological, social, political, and cultural context. Initiatives that respect local knowledge, support rather than supplant local leadership, and work within existing institutions, supplementing but not replacing local wisdom with technical expertise, have the best chances of success.

Sustainable development on a global scale is inseparable from the problems of the poor countries. A better
life for their populations is a step toward sustainable
improvement in the quality of life for the world as a
whole, both rich and poor (94).

*This chapter was written by Rosemarie Philips, a writer and editor
in Alexandria, Virginia, who specializes in development issues, with
input from several senior WRI staff members and assistance from
WRI Research Assistant Tim Johnston.*

References and Notes

1. These countries are Afghanistan,
Bangladesh, Benin, Bhutan, Burkina Faso,
Burundi, Cambodia, the Central African Re-
public, Chad, China, Ethiopia, Ghana,
Guinea, Haiti, India, Indonesia, Kenya, the
Lao People's Democratic Republic, Lesotho,
Liberia, Madagascar, Malawi, Mali, Maurita-
nia, Mozambique, Myanmar, Nepal, Niger,
Nigeria, Pakistan, Rwanda, Sierra Leone, So-
malia, Sri Lanka, Sudan, Tanzania, Togo,
Uganda, Viet Nam, Zaire, and Zambia.

2. The World Bank, *World Development Report
1991* (Oxford University Press, New York,
1991), pp. 199 and 204.

3. United Nations Development Programme,
Human Development Report 1991 (Oxford
University Press, New York, 1991), p. 153.

4. Countries that appear on the low-human-
development list that are not listed as having low incomes are as follows: Algeria,
Angola, Bolivia, Cameroon, Cape Verde,
the Comoros, the Congo, Côte d'Ivoire,
Djibouti, Egypt, Equatorial Guinea, the
Gambia, Guatemala, Guinea-Bissau, Honduras, Morocco, Namibia, Papua New Guinea,
the Republic of Yemen, São Tomé and
Principe, Senegal, Swaziland, Vanuatu, and
Zimbabwe.

5. Indonesia, a poor country that is also rapidly industrializing, is discussed in more detail in Chapter 4, "Rapidly Industrializing
Countries."

6. *Op. cit.* 2, pp. 204-205 and 258-259.

7. The World Bank, *World Development Report
1990* (Oxford University Press, New York,
1990), p. 28.

8. H. Jeffrey Leonard, *Environment and the
Poor: Development Strategies for a Common
Agenda* (Transaction Books, New Bruns-
wick, New Jersey, 1989), pp. 9-10.

9. *Op. cit.* 3, pp. 2 and 24.

10. Robert W. Kates, "Hunger, Poverty and the
Human Environment," paper presented at
the Michigan State University Center for
Advanced Study of International Development, East Lansing, Michigan, May 6, 1990.

11. *Op. cit.* 8, pp. 5-7 and 19.

12. Wilfrido Cruz and Christopher Gibbs,
"Resource Policy Reform in the Context of
Population Pressure: The Philippines and
Nepal," *American Journal of Agricultural Eco-
nomics*, Vol. 72, No. 5 (1990), pp. 1264-1268.

13. John W. Mellor, "The Intertwining of Environmental Problems and Poverty," *Environment*, Vol. 30, No. 9 (November 1988), p. 8.

14. *Op. cit.* 2, p. 265.

15. United Nations Development Programme,
Human Development Report 1990 (Oxford
University Press, New York, 1990), p. 30.

16. *Op. cit.* 3, pp. 26, 33.

17. *Op. cit.* 3, p. 137.

18. *Op. cit.* 3, p. 27.

19. Shubh K. Khumar and David Hotchkiss,
"Consequences of Deforestation for
Women's Time Allocation, Agricultural Pro-
duction, and Nutrition in Hill Areas of
Nepal," in *IFPRI Research Report* (Interna-

tional Food Policy Research Institute, Washington, D.C., 1988), p. 9.

20. *Op. cit.* 3, pp. 45-46.

21. *Op. cit.* 3, p. 51.

22. *Op. cit.* 3, pp. 51 and 62.

23. *Op. cit.* 3, pp. 62-63.

24. *Op. cit.* 3, pp. 50-51.

25. *Op. cit.* 3, pp. 51 and 141.

26. *Op. cit.* 3, p. 63.

27. United Nations Fund for Population Activities (UNFPA), *The State of World Population
1991* (UNFPA, New York, 1991), p. 1.

28. World Conservation Union (IUCN), United
Nations Environment Programme (UNEP),
and World Wide Fund for Nature (WWF),
Caring for the Earth (IUCN, UNEP, and
WWF, Gland, Switzerland, 1991), p. 51.

29. *Op. cit.* 27, pp. 19-29.

30. *Op. cit.* 27, pp. 22-23.

31. Stuart K. Tucker, "The Legacy of Debt: A
Lost Decade of Development," Policy Focus
No. 3 (Overseas Development Council,
Washington, D.C., 1989), pp. 1-4.

32. The World Bank, *Sub-Saharan Africa: From
Crisis to Sustainable Growth* (The World
Bank, Washington, D.C., 1989), p. 185.

33. Stein Hansen, "Structural Adjustment Programs and Sustainable Development" (The
World Bank for the Committee of International Development Institutions on the Environment, Washington, D.C., 1988), pp. 1-2.

34. United Nations Economic Commission for
Africa (ECA), "African Alternative Framework to Structural Adjustment Programmes
for Socio-Economic Recovery and Transformation" (ECA, Addis Ababa, 1989), p. i.

35. For the grassroots and nongovernmental organization critique, see, for example, Robin
Broad, John Cavanagh, and Walden Bello,
"Development: The Market is Not Enough,"
Foreign Policy, No. 81 (Winter 1990 91), pp.
144-162; Fantu Cheru, *The Silent Revolution
in Africa: Debt, Development and Democracy*
(Zed Books, London and Atlantic Highlands, New Jersey, 1989); David C. Korten,
Getting to the Twenty-First Century (Kumarian Press, West Hartford, Connecticut 1990);
and Bill Rau, *From Feast to Famine: Official
Cures and Grassroots Remedies to Food Crises*
(Zed Books, London and Atlantic Highlands, New Jersey, 1991).

36. *Op. cit.* 34, p. 24.

37. Helena Ribe, Soniya Carvalho, Robert
Liebenthal *et al.*, *How Adjustment Programs
Can Help the Poor: The World Bank's Experience* (The World Bank, Washington, D.C.,
1990), p. 1.

38. African Development Bank, United Nations
Development Programme, and The World
Bank, *The Social Dimensions of Adjustment: A
Policy Agenda* (The World Bank, Washing-
ton, D.C., 1990), p. 8.

39. *Op. cit.* 33, p. 22.

40. *Op. cit.* 38, p. iii.

41. John P. Lewis, "Strengthening the Poor:
Some Lessons for the International Community," in *Strengthening the Poor: What Have

We Learned?* John P. Lewis, ed. (Transaction
Books, New Brunswick, New Jersey, 1988),
pp. 23-24.

42. Barbara Thomas-Slayter, Charity Kabutha,
and Richard Ford, *Traditional Village Institutions in Environmental Management: Erosion
Control in Katheka, Kenya*, From the Ground
Up Case Study Series, No. 1 (World Resources Institute, Washington, D.C., 1991).

43. See also Walter V. Reid, James N. Barnes,
and Brent Blackwelder, *Bankrolling Suc-
cesses: A Portfolio of Sustainable Development
Projects* (Environmental Policy Institute and
National Wildlife Federation, Washington,
D.C., 1988), pp. 29-35; Kenneth Tull and Michael Sands, *Experiences in Success* (Rodale
International, Emmaus, Pennsylvania,
1987); Roland Bunch, *Two Ears of Corn: A
Guide to People-Centered Agricultural Improvement* (World Neighbors, Oklahoma City,
Oklahoma 1982); and Michael Hansen, *Escape from the Pesticide Treadmill: Alternative to
Pesticides in Developing Countries* (Institute
for Consumer Policy Research, Mount Ver-
non, New York, 1988), pp. 1-7.

44. Mahabub Hossain, *Credit for Alleviation of
Rural Poverty: The Grameen Bank in
Bangladesh* (International Food Policy Research Institute, Washington, D.C., 1988),
p. 12.

45. Muhammed Yunus, "Grameen Bank: Organization and Operation," paper presented
at World Conference on Support for Micro-
enterprises, Committee of Donor Agencies
for Small Enterprise Development, Washington, D.C., June 1988, p. 2.

46. Muhammed Yunus, ed., *Grameen Dialogue*,
No. 8 (Grameen Trust, Dhaka, Bangladesh,
September 1991), p. 16.

47. Idriss Jazairy, "Preface," in *Banking the Unbankable: Bringing Credit to the Poor*, Ibrahima Bakhoum, Harry Bhaskara, Chola
Chimbano, *et al.*, eds. (Panos, Washington,
D.C., and London, 1989), pp. ii-iii.

48. Norman Uphoff, "Assisted Self-Reliance:
Working with, Rather Than for, the Poor,"
in *Strengthening the Poor: What Have We
Learned?* John P. Lewis, ed. (Transaction
Books, New Brunswick, New Jersey, 1988),
p. 47.

49. Sheldon Annis, "Can Small-Scale Development Be Large-Scale Policy?" in *Direct to the
Poor: Grassroots Development in Latin America*, Sheldon Annis and Peter Hakim, eds.
(Lynne Rienner Publishers, Boulder, Colorado, and London, 1988), p. 210.

50. Fantu Cheru, *The Silent Revolution in Africa:
Debt, Development and Democracy* (Zed
Books, London and Atlantic Highlands,
New Jersey, 1989), pp. 19-20.

51. *Op. cit.* 32, pp. 11-12.

52. Paul Faeth and Robert Repetto, "Agricultural Policy and the Development of Sustainable Agriculture," prepared for the
Business Council for Sustainable Development Discussion Workshop, Washington,
D.C., September 18, 1991, p. 11.

53. Robert Repetto, "Population, Resource Pressures, and Poverty," in *The Global Possible: Resources, Development and the New Century*, Robert Repetto, ed. (Yale University Press, New Haven, 1985), pp. 158-160.

54. *Ibid.*, pp. 161-162.

55. *Ibid.*, p. 164.

56. *Op. cit.* 3, pp. 65-66.

57. *Op. cit.* 3, pp. 64-65.

58. The World Bank, *World Development Report 1991* (The World Bank, Washington, D.C., 1991), p. 260.

59. *Op. cit.* 15, p. 31.

60. Ibrahima Bakhoum, Harry Bhaskara, Chola Chimbano *et al., Banking the Unbankable: Bringing Credit to the Poor* (Panos, Washington, D.C., and London, 1989), p. ix.

61. Mayra Buveni and Margaret A. Lycettc, "Women, Poverty, and Development in the Third World," in *Strengthening the Poor: What Have We Learned?* John P. Lewis, ed. (Transaction Books, New Brunswick, New Jersey, 1989), pp. 153-158.

62. World Conservation Union (IUCN), United Nations Environment Programme (UNEP), and World Resources Institute (WRI), *Global Biodiversity Strategy: Guidelines for Action to Save, Study, and Use Earth's Biotic Wealth Sustainably and Equitably* (IUCN, UNEP, and WRI, Washington, D.C., forthcoming).

63. N. Vijay Jagannathan, "Poverty, Public Policies and the Environment," Environment Working Paper No. 24, The World Bank, Washington, D.C., December 1989, p. 4.

64. *Op. cit.* 33, pp. iv-v.

65. *Op. cit.* 32, p. 192.

66. Jon Tinker, "Swallows Herald New Spring for West African Press," *Panoscope*, No. 24 (May 1991), pp. 26-27.

67. *Op. cit.* 42, p. 27.

68. *Op. cit.* 32, p. 8.

69. John Thompson, *Combining Local Knowledge and Expert Assistance in Natural Resource Management: Small-Scale Irrigation in Kenya*, From the Ground Up Case Study Series, No. 2 (World Resources Institute, Washington, D.C., 1991), p. 25.

70. United Nations (U.N.) Statistical Office, *1989 Energy Statistics Yearbook* (U.N., New York, 1991), pp. 90-111.

71. *Op. cit.* 32, p. 129.

72. *Op. cit.* 32, p. 129.

73. Dorothy Etoori, Environmental Officer, Ministry of Energy, Minerals, and Environment, Kampala, Uganda, July 1991 (personal communication).

74. *Op. cit.* 19, pp. 46-60.

75. Edward B. Barbier, "Sustaining Agriculture on Marginal Land: A Policy Framework," *Environment*, Vol. 31, No. 9 (1989), p. 16.

76. U.S. Congress, Office of Technology Assessment (OTA), *Energy in Developing Countries* (U.S. Government Printing Office, Washington, D.C., 1991), pp. 8 and 13.

77. *Op. cit.* 2, p. 212.

78. Anil Agarwal and Sunita Narain, *Towards Green Villages: A Strategy for Environmentally-Sound and Participatory Rural Development* (Centre for Science and Environment, New Delhi, 1989), p. 1.

79. Rene Rabezandrina, "Biogas: Evolution of Actions and Prospects for the Rural Environment in Africa," *Ambio*, Vol. 19, No. 8 (1990), pp. 424-426.

80. *Op. cit.* 3, p. 78.

81. *Op. cit.* 3, p. 9.

82. Robert Repetto, William Magrath, Michael Wells *et al., Wasting Assets: Natural Resources in the National Income Accounts* (World Resources Institute, Washington, D.C., 1989), p. 3.

83. *Op. cit.* 73.

84. *Op. cit.* 3, p. 5.

85. *Op. cit.* 3, pp. 81-83.

86. *Op. cit.* 53, pp. 162-164.

87. United Nations Children's Fund, *The State of the World's Children 1991* (Oxford University Press, New York, 1991), p. 16.

88. *Op. cit.* 3, pp. 56-57.

89. *Op. cit.* 87, p. 17.

90. *Op. cit.* 3, p. 76.

91. *Op. cit.* 3, p. 155.

92. *Op. cit.* 3, p. 80.

93. Jim MacNeill, "Strategies for Sustainable Economic Development," *Scientific American*, Vol. 261, No. 3 (September 1989), p. 159.

94. *Op. cit.* 73.

4. Rapidly Industrializing Countries:

Forging New Models

Rapidly industrializing countries (RICs) face a dual challenge. If their development is to be sustainable, they need to manage the process of industrialization better than other industrial countries have. At the same time, they need to combat poverty and protect the natural resources that are still the primary base of their economies and a significant source of employment. These are immense challenges.

Rapidly industrializing countries are thus poised at a unique juncture. They have an unparalleled opportunity to find different paths to development and in so doing to provide models that other countries could follow. With the right policies, they can achieve rapid economic development and yet avoid creating environmental problems on the scale of those created by the United States, European countries, Japan, and others. Doing it right the first time—by installing clean, efficient technologies as well as developing the institutional capacity to enforce environmental regulations —could lead to "leapfrogging" the development process and building industrial economies that are both competitive and more sustainable than those of coun-

tries with an older industrial base. Thus, some of the policies discussed in Chapter 2 are relevant to RICs.

At the same time, RICs would benefit from sharing the fruits of economic growth with all segments of their societies and from protecting their forests, soils, fisheries, and other productive natural resources. With the right policies, such countries can combat poverty, promote rural development, and build the skilled work force needed to support industrialization—while maintaining the jobs and revenues that natural resources provide and ensuring that future generations will also have access to them. Thus, some of the policies discussed in Chapter 3 are also relevant to RICs.

Although no officially sanctioned category of rapidly industrializing countries exists, this chapter uses as examples Brazil, Chile, and Mexico in Latin America and Indonesia, Malaysia, and Thailand in Asia. (The discussion applies, however, to many other countries that face similar challenges, including the rapidly industrializing regions within China and India.)

As described in Chapter 1, sustainable development means simultaneous progress toward broad-based economic development, increased human development and stable populations, a secure ecological base, and technology that is efficient and sparing of natural resources. Although by no means a homogeneous group, the RICs generally have made rapid economic progress. These six countries had gross national product (GNP) growth rates well above the world average in the 1970s. Some slipped during the economic stagnation of the 1980s, but all have productive natural resources and growing industrial sectors, including energy production, manufacturing, and transportation. Progress toward reducing absolute poverty and narrowing income inequality has been impressive but less even, with income inequality remaining a serious problem in some countries. The RICs have also made progress on human dimensions—improving health care and education and moving toward stable populations—but much remains to be done.

The RICs have been least successful along the ecological and technological dimensions of sustainable development. The RICs have abundant natural resources, but those riches—their forest and soil reserves, for example—are being rapidly depleted. These countries also face new environmental challenges from urbanization and industrial growth. They need to improve their energy efficiency, develop nonfossil energy resources where possible, reduce air and water pollution, and encourage new technologies that minimize or prevent pollution. The importance of these aspects of sustainable development—and the costs of ignoring them—are graphically illustrated by the environmental disasters that Central Europe now confronts. (See Chapter 5, "Regional Focus: Central Europe.") In less dramatic form, the same lessons emerge from the experience of the most recent group of countries to make the leap to industrial economies.

THE NIC EXPERIENCE

Over the past few decades, the world has seen the stunning transformation of Hong Kong, Singapore, the Republic of Korea (South Korea), and Taiwan from impoverished developing countries into bustling, expanding economies. Since 1965, these four economies, known collectively as the newly industrializing countries (NICs) or the four "dragons" or "tigers" of Asia, have quadrupled their share of world production and trade (1) and quintupled their per capita incomes (2). Between 1965 and 1986, the per capita GNP in each one grew at least 6 percent per year; Japan and the United States, by comparison, registered annual increases of 4.3 and 1.6 percent, respectively, during these years (3). (For the sake of simplicity, the NICs are considered here to be nations, although by some measures they are not all full-fledged nations. Only Singapore and South Korea, for example, are members of the United Nations. Hong Kong is a colony of the United Kingdom until 1997, when it will become part of China. China also claims Taiwan. Moreover, Hong Kong and Singapore are essentially city-states and do not confront many of the sharp rural-urban divisions characteristic of most developing countries.)

The NIC record is seriously flawed, however. The growth that these countries achieved came at the expense of severe environmental degradation, just as it had in the United States and Japan. Industrial air and water pollution in Taiwan, for example, has been so severe that it has damaged crop yields and poses risks to human health. In 1989, a group of environmentalists and academics released a major report on balancing Taiwan's economic growth and environmental protection. "Taiwan is now in a time of transition with respect to environmental management. In the 1950s, 1960s, and early 1970s economic growth was given priority over environmental issues almost without question . . .. If we continue to allow the harmful by-products of advanced industrial production systems to penetrate every cell of the body of the island of Taiwan, complete recovery will be impossible, and partial recovery will entail very great cost" (4).

Virtually all rivers on the island are polluted in their lower reaches, with most of them heavily polluted (5). Less than 1 percent of human waste receives primary sewage treatment. Probably as a result, the island has the highest incidence of hepatitis B in the world (6).

Taiwan is one of the top users of pesticides and fertilizers per hectare in the world, and this load contributes to the contamination of surface water and groundwater (7). Emissions of nitrogen oxides from motor vehicles in Taiwan tripled between 1977 and 1985 and may double again by the end of this decade (8). Pollution is bad enough to make the air hazardous to breathe on 62 days a year (9); asthma cases among children have quadrupled in the last decade (10). Thus, even though access to health care has improved, health itself can be undermined by environmental degradation.

In South Korea, the situation is not much better. In August 1989, government investigators discovered that a significant portion of the tap water in the country is unfit to drink—contaminated with heavy metals and other pollutants, a problem that will require $5.3 billion to fix (11). Only one quarter of the country's sewage is treated (12). With some industrial complexes discharging effluents directly into the ocean, fishing grounds have also suffered: by the early 1980s, Masan Bay was off limits for fishing and shellfishing, and Inchon Harbor had been closed to commercial fishing (13).

Groundwater is being polluted with pesticide and fertilizer runoff, because South Korea, like Taiwan, is one of the heaviest users of these agricultural inputs per hectare in the world (14).

Air pollution from the industrial and commercial sectors and from motor vehicles has earned Seoul fourth place on the World Health Organization's list of major cities with the worst sulfur dioxide ratings. Crop yields on farms near factories have also been reduced by air pollution, and several industries in one area were ordered to compensate nearby farmers for their losses (15).

In addition, like the rest of the industrial world, the NICs for a long time paid scant attention to the need for more efficient use of energy and other natural resources. In Singapore and South Korea, commercial energy consumption per dollar of GNP is among the highest in the world. In 1989, for example, South Korea consumed 18 megajoules of commercial energy per dollar of GNP, higher than the U.S. level of 15 megajoules per dollar and nowhere near as efficient as Japan's 5 megajoules. (See Chapter 21, "Energy and Materials," Table 21.2.) And Hong Kong's air quality has deteriorated with industrial growth and increasing energy use. A 1988 World Health Organization study of 33 major cities showed Hong Kong to be one of only six cities in which sulfur dioxide levels were increasing (16).

The NICs are therefore not a model of sustainable development, even though they are often cited as a model of economic development. Yet they have done well in stabilizing their populations, in spreading education and access to health care, in improving income distribution, and (in South Korea and Taiwan) in land reform—that is, in the human and economic dimensions of sustainable development that are beyond the narrow measure of economic growth. It is in these areas that their experience does indeed hold important lessons for other developing countries concerned with stimulating economic growth and achieving a more sustainable development path.

Attention in the NICs was directed early to education and health care. In South Korea, for example, the literacy rate rose from 30 percent in 1953 to 80 percent in 1963. By 1965, the nation was spending more on human resource development than the average for countries with GNPs three times as large (17), creating a relatively well educated and healthy work force that served as the foundation for industrialization. Reflecting in part this high level of investment in human resources, South Korea's population growth rate declined from 3.04 percent in 1955–60 (18) to 0.95 percent in 1985–90. (See Chapter 16, "Population and Human Development," Table 16.1.)

The successes of the two NICs that are not city-states were preceded by extensive land reform in the late 1940s and 1950s. In Taiwan during the late 1940s, the government imposed ceilings on landholdings and purchased excess land at below-market prices, eliminating Taiwan's landed elite (19). Between 1949 and 1953, one quarter of the privately held farmland changed hands; the share of families owning some or all of the land they worked rose to 88 percent (20). In South Korea, the land reform that had been promised in the late 1940s was finally carried out under prodding from the U.S. Government after the outbreak of the Korean War in the summer of 1950. Although more than 40 percent of the land scheduled for redistribution stayed in former owners' hands, the percentage of farm families that were tenants dropped from 86 percent in 1945 to 26 percent 1960 (21). These reforms laid the basis for better income distribution in both countries, roughly equalizing rural and urban incomes

(22). Equitable income distribution helped strengthen domestic markets. In Taiwan, this created a decentralized pattern of industrialization (23). Countless small-to medium-size industries sprang up to serve the needs of the rural population, including provision of agricultural inputs and processing. By 1961, only 16 percent of industrial jobs were located in Taipei, the capital.

The NICs, by laying an adequate foundation with investments in human development and with improved sharing of the benefits of economic growth, did increase the welfare of current generations. Environmental problems, however, could hinder their ability to meet the needs of future generations.

If the RICs are to match the economic successes of the Asian dragons, they need to invest heavily in human development and in broad-based economic development. If they are to avoid the problems of the NICs (and of other industrial countries before them), they also need to protect their ecological base and invest in more efficient technology.

HUMAN DEVELOPMENT

The six RICs examined here have unquestionably made progress in improving the health and education of their populations over the past 20 years, although there are significant country-by-country variations. (See Boxes 4.1 to 4.6.) Between 77 and 93 percent of the adult population of the RICs is literate, for example, compared to an average of 65 percent for all developing countries. (See Figure 4.1.) The child mortality rate (an indicator of the general health of a population) is also better in the RICs than the developing country average.

Concerted government policies to support education can make a difference. In Indonesia, such efforts over the last decade have meant that virtually all children of primary school age now attend school—one of the most successful cases of large-scale school system expansion on record, according to the World Bank (24). However, only about 48 percent of those eligible for

Figure 4.1 Adult Literacy Rates, 1970 and 1990

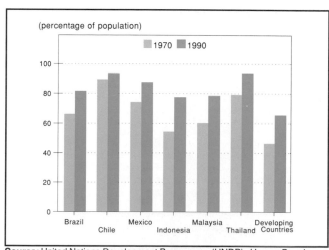

Source: United Nations Development Programme (UNDP), *Human Development Report 1991* (Oxford University Press, New York, 1991), Table 4, pp. 126–127.

Box 4.1 Malaysia

Over the past few decades Malaysia has made outstanding progress in economic growth and in raising standards of health and education while reducing poverty. Economic growth has averaged 6–7 percent annually over the past two decades. (See Chapter 15, "Basic Economic Indicators," Table 15.1.) Per capita production has far outstripped the developing country average. (See Figure 1.)

The Malaysian Government, a constitutional monarchy, has encouraged private industry to provide economic growth while devoting a relatively high share of public resources to human services such as health, education, and reduction of poverty. Of the three Asian rapidly industrializing countries (RICs), Malaysia has the smallest percentage of population below the poverty line (26 percent) (1) and the highest gross national product (GNP) per capita ($2,130) and spends the largest percentage of its GNP on human services (2). (See Chapter 15, "Basic Economic Indicators," Table 15.1.) These expenditures are having an effect: life expectancy, for example, has increased from 63 to nearly 71 years since the early 1970s. (See Chapter 16, "Population and Human Development," Table 16.2.) Virtually all Malaysian children attend primary school and more than half also attend secondary school. These are remarkable achievements for a country formed in the early 1960s amidst a civil war and severe racial tensions (3).

Once dependent on commodities such as palm oil, rubber, timber, and oil, for export earnings Malaysia's economy now increasingly relies on manufacturing. The electronics industry has led the way; Malaysia is now the world's biggest exporter of semiconductor devices (4).

The government officially encourages population growth (5), yet growth rates have been relatively modest and birth rates have been falling. Some 92 percent of the urban population and 68 percent of those in rural areas have access to clean water supplies. (See Chapter 16, "Population and Human Development," Tables 16.1 and 16.4.)

Malaysia is well endowed with natural resources, from tropical forests to offshore oil fields. More than half of Malaysia's merchandise exports are still primary products such as timber and oil. Both the government and citizens' groups are beginning to define sustainable development plans. The government's forest management system on the Malay Peninsula, for instance, is considered one of the few examples of sustainable forestry in the world (6). Nevertheless, in outlying regions such as Sabah and Sarawak, where local officials control large concessions, forests are being rapidly cut. In addition to damaging

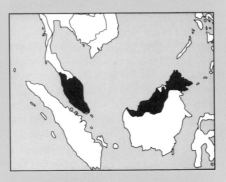

natural resources, deforestation threatens the livelihood of native peoples (7).

References and Notes

1. Calculations based on United Nations Development Programme, *Human Development Report 1991* (Oxford University Press, New York, 1991), Table 3, p. 124; and

Chapter 16, "Population and Human Development, Table 16.1.

2. United Nations Development Programme, *Human Development Report 1991* (Oxford University Press, New York, 1991), Table 3.1, p. 41.

3. The Economist Intelligence Unit (EIU), *Malaysia Country Profile 1990-91* (EIU, London, 1990), p. 4.

4. Carl Goldstein, "Chips of Change," *Far Eastern Economic Review* (September 7, 1989), p. 98.

5. *Op. cit.* 3, p. 8.

6. Duncan Poore, "Overview," in *Natural Forest Management for Sustainable Timber Production* (International Institute for Environment and Development, London, 1988), pp. 17-18.

7. "The Dwindling Forest beyond Long San," *The Economist* (August 18, 1990), pp. 23-24.

Figure 1 Gross National Product Per Capita

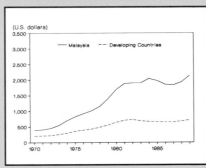

(U.S. dollars)

Source: The World Bank, unpublished data (The World Bank, Washington, D.C., 1991).

Figure 2 Total Fertility Rate

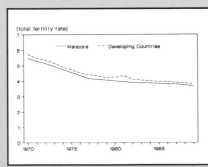

(total fertility rate)

Source: The World Bank, unpublished data (The World Bank, Washington, D.C., 1991).

Note: The total rate is an estimate of the number of children that an average woman would have if current age specific fertility rates remained constant during her reproductive years.

Figure 3 Mortality of Children Under Age 5

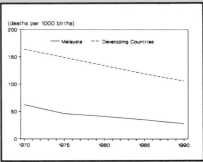

(deaths per 1000 births)

Source: United Nations (U.N.), *Mortality of Children Under 5: World Estimates and Projections* (U.N., New York, 1988), pp. 30-31.

Figure 4 Energy Consumption Per Capita

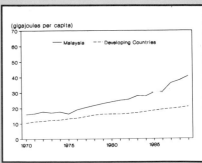

(gigajoules per capita)

Source: United Nations Statistical Office, *U.N. Energy Tape* (United Nations, New York, May 1991).

secondary school were enrolled in 1988 (25) (26). A shortage of skilled laborers and qualified managers constrains the expansion of domestic businesses (27), and so further public and private investment in education could yield substantial benefits.

In Malaysia, virtually all children of primary school age are also registered for classes, but Malaysian children are more likely to continue their schooling, with 57 percent enrolled in secondary schools (28). The country's relatively high level of education, health care, and basic services is the result of government decisions in the 1970s to invest in these areas and to alleviate rural poverty (29). (See Box 4.1, Malaysia.)

Chile, too, has made considerable progress in human development. Life expectancy at birth is nearly equal to that in the United States, the infant mortality rate is one of the lowest in the developing world, and the overall literacy rate of 93 percent is impressive (30).

Improvements in human development, to be effective, need to be coupled with progress in other dimensions of sustainable development. Mexico, for example, has a high literacy rate and has made great progress over the last 25 years in increasing the proportion of Mexicans who receive secondary and higher education. Yet the pressures of poverty, compounded in the 1980s by economic stagnation, have meant that many who start school cannot afford to stay: a United Nations study noted that more than 5 million children dropped out of primary school between 1982 and 1988 (31).

Moreover, rapidly growing populations mean that economies must continue to increase the resources they invest in education, health, and housing needs. Even though all the RICs except Indonesia have dramatically lowered their population growth rates over the past four decades, the rates still translate into annual additions of 3 million in Brazil and 1.8 million in Mexico. (See Chapter 16, "Population and Human Development," Table 16.1.)

Here again, government policies can make a profound difference. In Thailand, where the government launched a vigorous family planning program in 1971 (32), the percent of married couples using contraceptives rose from 14 in 1970 to 68 in the late 1980s and the average fertility rate fell from 5.4 in 1970 to 2.5 in 1990 (33) (34). In Indonesia, the share of married couples using contraceptives rose from 18 percent in the late 1970s to 48 percent a decade later, helped by a family planning program strongly supported by the government (35). (See Chapter 16, "Population and Human Development," Tables 16.2 and 16.6.)

Birth rates have been falling in Malaysia since the late 1950s, although not through any campaign of the government, which is one of the few to actively promote population growth. The government provides tax incentives for larger families (36). Nevertheless, as incomes improved and as education and health care became more widely available, the average fertility rate dropped from 5.4 in 1970 to 13.3 in 1990 (37). (See Box 4.1, Figure 2.)

Many of the RICs are finding new ways to promote family planning. Mass media—radio, television, and newspapers—can all present family planning information effectively. At the Pro-Pater male health clinics in three Brazilian cities, a mass media vasectomy campaign resulted in an 80 percent increase in the average number of vasectomies performed monthly, a 97 percent increase in the number of new clients visiting the clinics, and a 174 percent increase in the number of telephone inquiries about vasectomy (38).

BROADENING ECONOMIC DEVELOPMENT

Alleviating poverty and extreme income disparities are central to sustainable development. The RICs still have much to do in this regard, although some of these countries are making significant progress. Others, especially in Latin America, lost ground during the economic stagnation of the 1980s.

In Mexico, for example, income disparities widened during the 1980s. According to the government's own definition, about half the country suffers from poverty (39). Among the RICs, the need to tackle income disparities may be greatest in Brazil. (See Box 4.2, Brazil.) An estimated 58 percent of all Brazilians (or almost 90 million out of a total population of 150 million) are either poor or indigent, according to government standards (40). Rapid creation of new jobs is the key to reducing income inequalities.

Ownership of land in Brazil is also among the most concentrated in the world, a situation that has led to growing violence between large landowners and rural workers' unions (41). Nearly 11 million Brazilians who work the land have either holdings too small to support their families or no land at all. Two percent of all farms are holdings of more than 1,000 hectares, accounting for 57 percent of the agricultural land, whereas 30 percent of the farms are smaller than 1 hectare and together occupy just 1 percent of the farmland. Much of the farmland in large landholdings is held as a real estate investment rather than used productively (42). Recent attempts to expropriate and redistribute land have been generally ineffective (43). The NIC experience suggests that land reform would accelerate economic growth, as well as help combat poverty.

In Thailand, some 40 percent of agricultural land is untitled. One World Bank study found that only a "full, secure, exclusive, and indefinite title to land" would lead to increased investment and productivity. To provide such titles, a program has been in place for several years that gives squatters on reserved forest land "rights to farm" for 5–25 years (44). A recent review of Thailand's needs and prospects found that it has the widest disparity between agricultural and nonagricultural income of 12 Asian economies, in a country whose population remains 80 percent rural (45).

In Indonesia, according to the World Bank, the incidence of poverty was substantially reduced over the last decade, dropping from 22 percent in 1984 to 17 percent in 1987. Credit for this reduction is given to government policies that protected the agricultural sector during structural adjustment, to trade reform and industrial deregulation, which spurred private sector

Box 4.2 Brazil

Brazil's "economic miracle" occurred most dramatically in the late 1960s and early 1970s and then continued at a somewhat slower pace through the 1970s when average annual growth in real gross national product (GNP) was an impressive 8.4 percent. By 1978, Brazil was producing steel, petrochemicals, pulp and paper, fertilizers, and nonferrous metals plus other basic raw materials. However, in the 1980s (1979–89), growth turned sluggish, averaging just 2.7 percent annually. (See Chapter 15, "Basic Economic Indicators," Table 15.1.)

In the 1980s, a series of external shocks—a massive rise in oil prices, increased world interest rates, and a recession among major trading partners—undermined the growth of the previous two decades. Brazil's external debt problems grew worse, causing the government to seek help from the International Monetary Fund and international commercial banks. Chronic problems with inflation worsened in the 1980s (1). The election in March 1990 of Fernando Collor de Mello to Brazil's presidency marked a return to peaceful direct elections and a resurgence of interest in a private market economy. Nevertheless, economic problems worsened. In 1990, the economy shrank by 4.3 percent, while inflation approached 3,000 percent (2).

Brazil's two-decade record of economic growth, though impressive, was not shared by most of the country's population. The government has shown little willingness to undertake land reform or redirect resources to combat the country's extensive poverty (3). Income disparities have long been among the worst in the world, and the problem has worsened since 1980. By 1988, GNP per capita was estimated to be $2,160 annually, yet for the lowest 40 percent of households it was only $350 (4). Government spending reinforced this pattern: over one quarter of national income has been channeled through the government budget, yet less than 2 percent of GNP goes into human priority concerns (5). The pattern of land ownership is similarly skewed.

Brazil's growth has inflicted severe costs on its environment, especially in the Amazon Basin, the world's largest remaining tropical forest and a critical source of global biological diversity. Since the 1960s, a series of ambitious plans to develop and colonize the Amazon Basin have taken a heavy toll on the forest environment and met with mixed success economically.

In 1988, Brazil announced a new policy designed to protect the environment of tribal peoples and other forest dwellers, suspend subsidies for cattle ranching and other enterprises, create new national parks and national forests, and implement agroeco-logical zoning (6). President Collor has strengthened environmental protections, creating a new environmental secretariat, suspending subsidies that encourage deforestation and banning the export logs. Although critics

say many features of the 1960s development policies are continuing, a combination of new policies and economic recession has slowed deforestation (7). The Brazilian Government estimated deforestation in the Amazon at about 1.4 million hectares in 1990, down from 1.8 million in 1988–89 and well below a mean annual deforestation rate of 2.2 million hectares for 1979–90. (See Chapter 19, "Forests and Rangelands," Table 19.1.)

Brazilian policymakers seem increasingly interested in developing a model that synthesizes development and protection in the Amazon Basin. A May 1991 draft of a proposed government pilot program to protect Brazil's tropical forests listed biodiversity and carbon sequestra-

tion (which helps control global warming) as reasons to justify aid to Brazil from the international community (8). Such a "global bargain" is likely to gain increased international attention, especially when Brazil hosts the United Nations Conference on Environment and Development in 1992.

References and Notes

1. The Economist Intelligence Unit (EIU), *Brazil Country Profile 1990- 91* (EIU, London, 1990), pp. 10 and 13.
2. The World Bank, *Trends in Developing Economies 1991* (The World Bank, Washington, D.C., 1991), p. 57.
3. Ben Ross Schneider, "Brazil under Collor: Anatomy of a Crisis," *World Policy Journal*, Vol. viii, No. 2 (Spring 1991), p. 327.
4. *Op. cit.* 2, Table 17, p. 152.
5. United Nations Development Programme, *Human Development Report 1991* (Oxford University Press, New York, 1991), p. 6.
6. Kenton Miller and Laura Tangley, *Trees of Life: Saving Tropical Forests and Their Biological Wealth* (Beacon Press, Boston, 1991), pp. 55-57.
7. David Cleary, *The Brazilian Rainforest: Politics, Financing, Mining, and the Environment* (The Economist Intelligence Unit, London, 1991), pp. 28-30.
8. Kenton Miller, Director, Program in Forestry and Biodiversity, World Resources Institute, Washington, D.C., 1991 (personal communication).

Figure 1 Gross National Product Per Capita

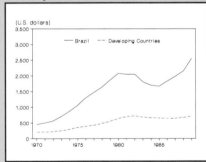

Source: The World Bank, unpublished data (The World Bank, Washington, D.C., 1991).

Figure 2 Total Fertility Rate

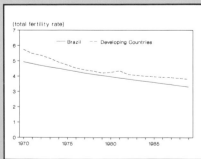

Source: The World Bank, unpublished data (The World Bank, Washington, D.C., 1991).

Figure 3 Mortality of Children Under Age 5

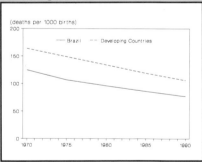

Source: United Nations (U.N.), *Mortality of Children Under 5: World Estimates and Projections* (U.N., New York, 1988), pp. 30-31.

Figure 4 Energy Consumption Per Capita

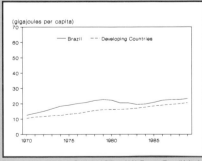

Source: United Nations Statistical Office, *U.N. Energy Tape* (United Nations, New York, May 1991).

efficiency, and to the maintenance of preexisting levels of expenditure on poverty-related programs when other public expenditures were being cut (46). Poverty alleviation remains a government priority (47). Similar progress in poverty alleviation has been recorded in Malaysia: by 1987, just under 20 percent of the population in rural areas, and 4.5 percent in the cities, were living below the poverty line (48).

A trend to open RIC economies in Latin America to outside investment and trade and to sell government-owned companies to private interests may help to stimulate economic development in the 1990s.

CONSERVING NATURAL RESOURCES

Although the RICs have expanded their industrial sectors rapidly in the last two decades, they are still highly dependent on the products of their natural resource base. Some 46–90 percent of their merchandise exports continue to be primary products, including fuels, minerals, and metals. (See Figure 4.2.) Malaysia, for example, carns more than $2 billion per year from timber exports (49). In addition, a disproportionate share of employment is in areas, such as agriculture, that depend critically on the health of resources such as soil and water. In Malaysia, 31 percent of the labor force is still involved with agriculture; in Indonesia, the figure is 54 percent (50).

Protection of resources therefore remains paramount in the RICs' efforts to achieve sustainable development. And given the wealth of biological diversity contained in many of the RICs, conservation of these genetic resources is important for future generations.

Agriculture

Failure to protect resources entails high costs. In Indonesia, for example, soil erosion stemming from deforestation is a critical problem in 36 of 125 river basins. On the island of Java, at least one third of cultivated mountainous areas are eroding seriously, with some 1 million hectares rendered useless for farming at a cost of $350 million to $410 million per year in lost agricultural productivity and damage to reservoirs, harbors, and irrigation sites (51).

As discussed in Chapter 1, scarce resources should be treated as if they were scarce, not as if they were free. Numerous studies have pointed out the problems created by below-cost pricing of irrigation water for example (52). The water is overused and wasted as a result. A study by the Thailand Development Research Institute concluded that "full-cost pricing of water . . . is an indispensable component of the policy package for resolving resource conflicts, averting growth-constraining shortages, and improving efficiency and income distribution" (53).

Subsidies are also used to promote practices that degrade the environment, such as the use of pesticides. In Indonesia, high pesticide use led to the spread of the rice-crop-destroying brown planthopper by killing its natural predators. In 1986, the Indonesian government reduced pesticide subsidies and began to pro-

Figure 4.2 Percent Share of Merchandise Exports that are Primary Products

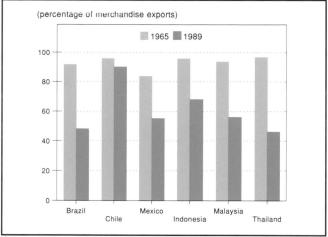

Source: The World Bank, *World Development Report 1991* (Oxford University Press, New York, 1991), Table 16, p. 234–235.

mote integrated pest management (IPM) to deal with pests by using environmentally safe biological methods. In early 1989, the government withdrew pesticide subsidies entirely. Since 1986, farmers trained in IPM have reduced pesticide applications from 4.5 to 0.5 per season while rice yields increased. In addition, decreased pesticide imports have saved the country more than $100 million per year (54) (55). (See Box 4.3, Indonesia.)

Forests

Tropical deforestation rates are still extremely high. In Indonesia, the deforestation rate has quadrupled since 1970 (56); 1 million hectares of rainforest are now destroyed annually. Forest loss slowed in Brazil in 1988 and 1989 to about 1.4 million hectares annually in the Amazon region. In Thailand, where forests covered 55 percent of the land surface as recently as 1961, they now cover only 28 percent (57). (See Box 4.4, Thailand.) In Mexico, the annual loss is estimated at 1 million hectares. In Chile, 75 percent of the forests designated for sustained yield production and 57 percent designated for protection have already been cleared (58). (See Chapter 19, "Forests and Rangelands," Table 19.2.)

Deforestation stems from a variety of causes, and so a range of policies will be required to preserve the forest resources. In Thailand, the government banned logging in January 1989. The effort has met with only mixed success; a government report found that nearly 40,000 hectares of forest had been wiped out and encroached on by the following year. Local environmental groups have declared the ban a failure (59). A recent study of the country's natural resources concluded that "any attempts to halt deforestation and to accelerate reforestation must deal with poverty first, or at least concurrently. Otherwise, the plan is bound to fail" (60).

Indonesia has followed a more phased approach. Seeking to slow forest loss and to stimulate domestic industries such as furniture production that add value

Box 4.3 Indonesia

Spread across an archipelago of more than 13,000 islands, Indonesia is the world's fifth most populous nation. Although the country is developing an industrial sector, most of its growth is still based on natural resources (primarily oil, natural gas, timber, fish, and agricultural products) (1).

Like those of Malaysia and Thailand, Indonesia's economy has grown steadily over the past two decades, averaging a 7.1 percent annual increase in real gross national product in the 1970s and a 6.5 percent increase in the 1980s. (See Chapter 15, "Basic Economic Indicators," Table 15.1.) Growth of per capita production, as shown in Figure 1, was similar to the average for all developing countries through the early 1980s. A fall in world oil prices contributed to a nearly 20 percent decline in per capita GNP between 1982 and 1989. Indonesia's economy slowed slightly in 1991, but it is considered an attractive country for foreign investment because of its stable government, low labor and land costs, and a population that provides Asia's third largest market (after China and India) (2).

Two decades ago, Indonesia was one of the poorest countries in the world. With the help of relatively broad-based economic development policies, the proportion of people living below the poverty line has fallen considerably (although many people still have incomes only slightly above the poverty line, and the incidence of poverty remains much higher in the eastern parts of the archipelago) and the number of children enrolled in primary schools has increased (3). However, Indonesia still lags behind its neighbors by many measures: life expectancy at birth has increased dramatically since the early 1970s but still is below the average for Asia. Mortality of children under five, now estimated at 99 per 1,000, is slightly above the regional average of 94. (See Chapter 16, "Population and Human Development," Tables 16.2 and 16.3.)

By 1988, it was estimated that 60 percent of urban residents and 40 percent of rural residents had access to safe drinking water. (See Table 16.4.) The government has launch-ed a major initiative to make safe water more accessible to the poor by, for instance, increasing the number of standpipes and deregulating the sale of water in Jakarta (4). As part of a campaign for preventive health care, 320,000 water supply projects were completed between 1983–84 and 1988–89 (5).

The country has made some effort to improve environmental management: it has a state environment minister, laws requiring environmental impact assessment of all ma-jor development projects, and a program to introduce integrated pest management (6). Nevertheless serious problems remain. Deforestation, which is occurring at a rate of about 1 million hectares annually, has claimed large areas of forest and caused serious soil erosion problems.

(See Chapter 19, "Forests and Range—lands," Table 19.1.) Settlers, many of whom are moved to the outer islands through ansmigration project partially funded by the World Bank, enter forests through logging roads and contribute to forest loss through slash-and-burn agricultural practices. To slow deforestation and to strengthen the domestic wood processing industry, Indonesia banned the export of raw logs in 1985 (7). It also banned the practice of clear-cutting forests and started a large-scale tree-planting program. But critics say that logging operations are expected to expand greatly in the 1990s, that about 400,000 hectares of forest are lost each year because of wasteful logging

practices, fire, and illegal cutting, that almost all loggers ignore logging regulations (8), and that the tree-planting program has in some cases replaced complex forest ecosystems with fast-growing species in monoculture plantations (9).

References and Notes

1. The Economist Intelligence Unit (EIU), *Indonesia Country Profile 1990-91* (EIU, London, 1990), p. 16.
2. Adam Schwarz, "Growth Strains Superstructure," *Far Eastern Economic Review* (April 18, 1991), p. 36.
3. United Nations Development Programme, *Human Development Report 1991* (Oxford University Press, New York, 1991), p. 60.
4. The World Bank, *Indonesia: Poverty Assessment and Strategy Report* (The World Bank, Washington, D.C., 1990), p. xv.
5. *Op. cit.* 1, p. 11.
6. The World Bank, "Indonesia: Forest, Land and Water: Issues in Sustainable Development" (draft), The World Bank, Washington, D.C., June 5, 1989, p. viii.
7. *Op. cit.* 1, p. 33.
8. Peter Halesworth, "Plundering Indonesia's Rainforests," *Multinational Monitor* (October 1990), p. 9.
9. Charles V. Barber, Associate, World Resources Institute, Washington, D.C., 1991 (personal communication).

Figure 1 Gross National Product Per Capita

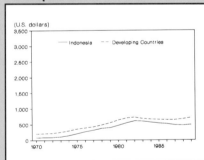

Source: The World Bank, unpublished data (The World Bank, Washington, D.C., 1991).

Figure 2 Total Fertility Rate

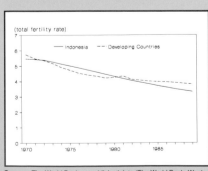

Source: The World Bank, unpublished data (The World Bank, Washington, D.C., 1991).

Figure 3 Mortality of Children Under Age 5

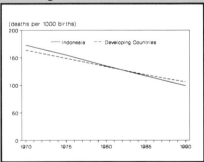

Source: United Nations (U.N.), *Mortality of Children Under 5: World Estimates and Projections* (U.N., New York, 1988), pp. 30-31.

Figure 4 Energy Consumption Per Capita

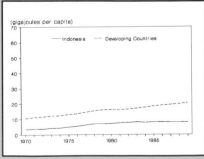

Source: United Nations Statistical Office, U.N. Energy Tape (United Nations, New York, May 1991).

Box 4.4 Thailand

Thailand built its economic wealth on its abundant natural resources (including teak, fish, rice, and tin) but now gets an increasing share of its gross national product (GNP) from manufacturing and services [1].

In several cases, Thailand nearly destroyed the resource base that fueled its growth. Logging reduced Thailand's forest cover from 55 percent of the country in 1961 to about 28 percent by 1988. Deforestation left large areas of bare soil, contributing to mud slides, floods, and loss of life. As a result of the disastrous floods, Thailand banned logging as of January 1989. But reforestation efforts still fall short of the goal of 40 percent forest cover. The Thai fishing fleet, which brings in the world's third largest catch, has decimated fish populations in the Gulf of Thailand and can maintain its catch only by building larger vessels that go further offshore. The rapid expansion of brackish water prawn culture on the southeast coast has led to the widespread destruction of mangrove forests [2] [3].

The natural beauty of Thailand's coastline helps make tourism Thailand's leading source of foreign exchange [4]. Although tourism may provide an incentive to protect scenic areas, it also causes pollution in resort towns such as Pattaya [5].

Thailand is more ethnically homogeneous than the other Asian rapidly industrializing countries (RICs), Malaysia and Indonesia. All but 5 percent of the population is made up of Thai-speaking Buddhists. Since the 1930s, the country has mostly been ruled by a succession of military governments; in 1988, Thailand elected its first prime minister in 12 years, suggesting that democracy may be maturing [6].

Thailand has invested heavily in human development. Literacy now stands at 90 percent for women and 96 percent for men, comparable to that of South Korea. As Figure 3 indicates, deaths of children under five have dropped from 91 per 1,000 in 1970 to 39 per 1,000 in 1990, far below the Asian average of 94. Assisted by a vigorous family planning program and rising living standards, Thailand has undergone a demographic transition to lower birth rates [7]. (See Chapter 16, "Population and Human Development," Table 16.3.)

Thailand has branched into labor-intensive industries such as integrated circuit and electronics assembly, footwear manufacturing, toy making, and textiles. Such industries have attracted considerable investment from Japan and Taiwan. Agriculture, still an important economic sector, employs the largest number of people, 18 million, or perhaps 70 percent of the work force [8] [9]. Northern rural areas are considerably poorer and have fewer services

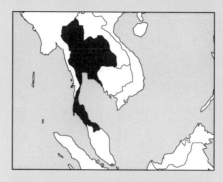

than metropolitan Bangkok (with 8.5 million people). On the other hand, Bangkok is choked by traffic and pollution, has no mass transit, and is home to at least 1 million squatters and slum dwellers [10].

Energy use, and especially electricity use, is growing rapidly. More efficient energy practices could ease the pressures for additional energy supplies (See Chapter 10, "Energy".) Thailand has considerable reserves of natural gas, a clean-burning fuel that could be tapped for both domestic use and exported in liquefied form [11].

References and Notes

1. The Economist Intelligence Unit (EIU), *Thailand, Burma Country Profile 1990-91* (EIU, London, 1990), p. 8.
2. *Ibid.*, pp. 15-16.
3. Theodore Panayotou and Chartchai Parasuk, *Land and Forest: Projecting Demand and Managing Encroachment* (Thailand Development Research Institute, Ambassador City, Jomtien, Chon Buri, Thailand, 1990), Appendix B, p. 74.
4. *Op. cit.* 1, p. 22.
5. *Op. cit.* 1, p. 22.
6. *Op. cit.* 1, pp. 4-5, and 7.
7. *Op. cit.* 1, p. 6.
8. The World Bank, *Trends in Developing Economies 1991* (The World Bank, Washington, D.C., 1991), p. 521.
9. *Op. cit.* 1, pp. 13 and 20.
10. *Op. cit.* 1, pp. 6-8.
11. *Op. cit.* 1, p. 18.

Figure 1 Gross National Product Per Capita

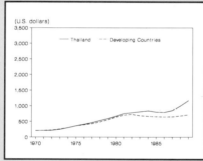

Source: The World Bank, unpublished data (The World Bank, Washington, D.C., 1991).

Figure 3 Mortality of Children Under Age 5

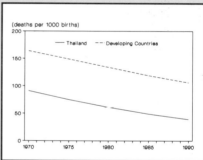

Source: United Nations (U.N.), *Mortality of Children Under 5: World Estimates and Projections* (U.N., New York, 1988), pp. 30-31.

Figure 2 Total Fertility Rate

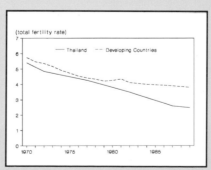

Source: The World Bank, unpublished data (The World Bank, Washington, D.C., 1991).

Figure 4 Energy Consumption Per Capita

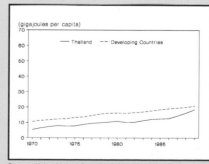

Source: United Nations Statistical Office, *U.N. Energy Tape* (United Nations, New York, May 1991).

Box 4.5 Chile

Chile, unlike most countries in Latin America, has followed a consistent export-based free market economic strategy. First implemented under the military rule of General Augusto Pinochet (1973–90) and continued since March 1990 under the democratic government of President Patricio Aylwin, this strategy helped make the public and private sectors more efficient and producers more internationally competitive. Economic growth was strong in the late 1970s. In the early 1980s, a drastic fall in copper prices (a critical export for Chile), a sharp decrease in foreign lending, and the overvaluation of the peso all conspired to send the economy reeling (1). Gross national product per capita fell sharply in the mid-1980s but has recovered strongly in the late 1980s. (See Figure 1.)

Over the past two decades, the country has exploited its natural resources (including copper, timber, and fisheries) but has also built an industrial base (2).

About 80 percent of Chile's 13 million people live in urban areas, including about 5 million in the metropolitan region of Santiago (3). Population growth was estimated at about 1.7 percent annually in 1985–90 and is expected to slow to 1.4 percent in 1995–2000. Standards of health and education are high; deaths of children under 5, shown in Figure 3, have declined dramatically, from 79 per 1,000 in 1970 to 23 in 1990. Rapid urbanization has caused housing shortages, however, and many Chileans still live in slums around Santiago (4).

Industrial pollution (from mining, smelting, fossil fuel emissions, and paper processing) and urban air and water pollution have been largely unregulated in Chile. Thick smog frequently settles over Santiago due to prevailing winds and the city's location surrounded by mountains on three sides. Produced by the combination of automobile and bus exhausts, industrial emissions, and dust particles from the severely eroded surrounding hillsides, air pollution often reaches dangerous levels during winter months. Although 90 percent of Santiago is served by sewage lines, none of the sewage is treated. Sewage is discharged into a river from which irrigation water is taken—a situation that has caused outbreaks of typhoid fever (5).

The government has estimated that nearly three fourths of the harmful elements in Santiago's smog come from the city's fleet of roughly 14,500 privately owned and operated diesel-engine buses. To address the problem, the new Aylwin government decided to remove 2,600 buses from the streets by buying them. The government also has instituted a license plate system that on any given day bars one fifth of the city's private cars from coming downtown (6).

Unlike the Pinochet regime, which gave environmental matters a relatively low priority, the Aylwin government has created an interministerial commission to define and coordinate environmental policy and a special commission to coordinate efforts to improve environmental conditions in Santiago. It has taken initiatives to train technicians in pollution control, explored methods of accounting for the role of natural resources and pollution in its economic planning, and supported public environmental awareness activities (7).

Although a University of Chile study found ample room for energy conservation in housing and transportation, not much has been done to encourage such conservation. Chile is developing large hydropower resources, which will help limit its dependence on imported oil and avoid additional air pollution, but thus far none of Chile's electric utilities has adopted any major conservation activities (8).

References and Notes

1. The Economist Intelligence Unit (EIU), *Chile Country Profile 1990- 91* (EIU, London, 1990), pp. 10-12.

2. *Ibid.*

3. *Ibid.*, p. 8.

4. *Ibid.*, p. 8.

5. Walter Arensberg, Mary Louise Higgins, Rafael Asenjo *et al.*, "Environment and Natural Resources Strategy in Chile" (draft), prepared for the U.S. Agency for International Development/Chile, World Resources Institute, Washington, D.C., November 8, 1989, pp. 33-34.

6. Eugene Robinson, "Chile Weighs Free Market's Costs," *Washington Post* (November 13, 1991), p. A24.

7. Walter Arensberg, Deputy Director, Center for International Development and Environment, World Resources Institute, Washington, D.C., 1991 (personal communication).

8. Michael Philips, *Energy Conservation Activities in Latin America and the Caribbean* (International Institute for Energy Conservation, Washington D.C., 1990), pp. 15-16.

Figure 1 Gross National Product Per Capita

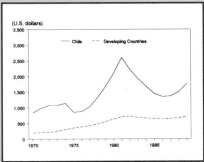

Source: The World Bank, unpublished data (The World Bank, Washington, D.C., 1991).

Figure 2 Total Fertility Rate

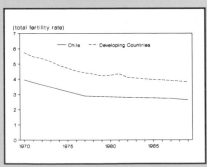

Source: The World Bank, unpublished data (The World Bank, Washington, D.C., 1991).

Figure 3 Mortality of Children Under Age 5

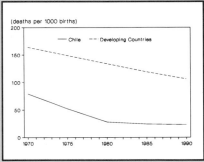

Source: United Nations (U.N.), *Mortality of Children Under 5: World Estimates and Projections* (U.N., New York, 1988), pp. 30-31.

Figure 4 Energy Consumption Per Capita

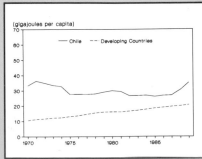

Source: United Nations Statistical Office, *U.N. Energy Tape* (United Nations, New York, May 1991).

to exported wood products, the government imposed a tax on log exports in 1979, then banned the export of raw logs in 1985 (61), and, finally, levied a high tax on sawn timber (except in Irian Jaya) that effectively banned export of such products. Nevertheless, the deforestation rate has increased in recent years. (62).

The Malaysian government has sought to limit deforestation since introducing the National Forestry Policy in 1978. Under government regulations for the Malay Peninsula, where about 30 percent of the country's timber is harvested, sections of forest are harvested on a cycle of 30 years or more, some areas are protected and only mature trees are felled. According to Mikaail Kavanagh of the World Wide Fund for Nature, in the Malay Peninsula, use of the forests is closer to being sustainable than it is in most other tropical rainforests (63). In the outlying Malaysian states of Sabah and Sarawak, however, where control is in the hands of local officials, deforestation is rampant: Sarawak is now the source of one half of the world's hardwood logs (64). If the pace of logging there is not slowed, according to a 1990 report by the International Tropical Timber Organization, all the primary forests open for logging in the region will be gone in 11 years (65).

In June 1991, Brazil's President Fernando Collor de Mello permanently suspended tax subsidies that encouraged clearing the Amazon rainforest for cattle ranching or farming. Brazil has also agreed to allow $100 million of its debt every year to be exchanged for financing of environmental projects such as training park guards or surveying park boundaries (66).

Governments can also subsidize reforestation, as Chile does. Since 1974, the government has paid a direct cash subsidy for reforestation that covers 75 percent of the planting costs. The result has been the establishment of more than 70,000 hectares of pine plantations per year (67).

Air Quality

Air quality is another part of the resource base that is being degraded in many countries, especially in urban areas. The severe pollution that envelops Mexico City nearly year-round can be traced to 36,000 factories and 3 million motor vehicles that spew some 5.5 million metric tons of contaminants into the air each year (68). A 1988 study showed that over half the newborns in Mexico City had lead levels in their blood high enough to impair neurological and motor-physical development (69). To attack this problem, a pollution control system limits the number of days individuals can drive, but the initial benefits have disappeared in dirty air as the fleet size continues to grow (70).

Kuala Lumpur is starting to experience similar pollution hazes, partly as the result of industrialization and growing motor vehicle fleets. Car sales in Malaysia were expected to reach 80,000 in 1990, up from 35,000 just three years earlier. So far, the government has established pollution emission standards only for diesel trucks (71). Santiago, too, is experiencing dangerous levels of air pollution in the winter as a result of cars,

Table 4.1 Change in Per Capita Commercial Energy Consumption 1950–89

(percent change per year)

Country	1950—60	1960—70	1970—80	1980—89
Brazil	5.4	3.6	5.8	0.7
Chile	1.6	5.1	-1.2	2.0
Mexico	4.1	3.8	4.8	0.4
Indonesia	9.3	-0.5	6.8	2.6
Malaysia	X	X	6.2	3.6
Thailand	11.3	11.9	7.2	6.5
World Total	**3.2**	**3.0**	**0.9**	**0.4**

Sources: United Nations (U.N.), *Energy Statistics Yearbook 1982* (U.N., New York, 1984)., Table 2, pp.50-97, United Nations (U.N.) *Energy Statistics Yearbook 1989* (U.N., New York, 1991), Table 2, pp. 32-61
Note: Commercial energy consumption calculated on oil equivalent basis.
X= not available.

factories, and dust that rises from surrounding eroded hillsides (72). (See Box 4.5, Chile.)

ENERGY CONSUMPTION

Energy consumption in the six RICs has skyrocketed, as is usually the case during the industrialization phase of a country's economic development. Table 4.1 shows that per capita commercial energy consumption has increased at a much higher rate than the world average over the past 40 years. All six RICs are still below the world average per capita consumption of 57 gigajoules in 1989. (See Chapter 21, "Energy and Materials," Table 21.2.)

As a country modernizes, consumption of electricity tends to rise. Recent growth in consumption and projections of future growth in demand have reached daunting proportions in the RICs. In Indonesia, for example, electricity use grew 16 percent annually from 1980 to 1987, more than twice the average rate in Asia (73). Yet, the *Far Eastern Economic Review* reports that "a power shortage is now a major concern for the government and would-be investors" (74). In Brazil, the equivalent annual rates were 12 percent from 1970 to 1980 and 6.5 percent from 1980 to 1988 (75). Malaysia recently raised its forecast of electricity consumption increases through 1995 from 8 percent per year to 12–13 percent (76). In Thailand, electricity demand nearly tripled in the 1980s, growing almost twice as fast as government planners had forecast (77).

Policies that increase the efficiency with which electricity is used help to moderate this growth demand. One such policy is to reduce or eliminate government subsidies. In oil-exporting countries, for example, energy prices are often kept below the world market level. In a step away from this practice, Indonesia has now reduced subsidies for domestic fuel prices (78) to encourage efficiency.

USING MORE EFFICIENT TECHNOLOGY

In a rapidly industrializing economy, there is a natural tendency to focus first on expanding output and only later on such seemingly secondary concerns as efficiency or pollution control. Yet attention to such matters is critical to "technological leapfrogging" and to

Box 4.6 Mexico

Mexico enjoyed steady economic growth in the four decades through 1980. In the 1969–79 period, for example, real gross national product (GNP) increased by an average 9.2 percent annually, helped to a large extent by the discovery and development of oil in the late 1970s in the Gulf of Campeche and the states of Tabasco and Chiapas (1). (See Chapter 15, "Basic Economic Indicators," Table 15.1.) However, the fruits of economic growth were not evenly distributed among the population and the environmental costs (including urban pollution and deforestation) were substantial.

In the early 1980s, economic problems became apparent. Massive borrowing drove Mexico's external debt to unmanageable levels. This, combined with other factors such as economic slowdown in industrial countries, high international interest rates, and high fiscal deficits at home, led to a crisis in 1982. The government declared that it was unable to service the country's external debt and subsequently imposed strict exchange and trade controls. Inflation accelerated rapidly, approaching almost 100 percent in 1982 (2).

The retrenchment efforts instituted in the mid-1980s had mixed success. During the 1982–85 period, real wages were reduced by 30 percent, forcing wage earners to work longer hours or find additional sources of income, and social expenditures fell on average by 19 percent. Middle-class families, which were most reliant on wage income, may have proportionately lost the most, but the incidence of poverty rose as well. There was a rise in infant illness associated with nutritional deficiencies, and more students dropped out of school (3). From 1979 to 1989, real GNP growth increased a dismal 2 percent annually. (See Table 15.1.) However, there were substantial improvements in broad health indicators such as child mortality rates. (See Figure 3.)

Since the new administration of President Carlos Salinas de Gortari took office in mid-1988, the government has made progress in controlling inflation and restructuring its external debt (4). The economy is beginning to respond to the most recent program, which includes some social and environmental components. For example, some polluting industries have been closed or fined. From 1988 to January 1991, 77 new national regulations were issued on environmental matters. Some $2.5 billion will be invested to control air pollution in Mexico City, with 42 percent of the money provided by foreign governments and multilateral banks (5).

Environmental groups are pressuring Mexico to toughen enforcement of environmental standards. Already a mushrooming of unregulated assembly plants along the U.S.-Mexican border has produced serious pollution and substandard

living conditions (6). In response, the Mexican environmental agency (SEDUE) has worked with the U.S. Environmental Protection Agency (U.S. EPA) to develop a Comprehensive Mexico-United States Environmental Border Program. Under the program, the Mexican Government plans to spend $460 million in 1992–94 in the border region on water treatment plants and enforcement actions such as tracking movements of hazardous wastes (7).

Mexico is working towards a free trade agreement with the United States and Canada. This agreement could stimulate Mexican growth by attracting investment and opening rich new markets. Environmental groups are concerned that the agreement could encourage U.S. companies to move to Mexico to take advantage of lax environmental regulations, but Mexican officials

contend that new firms will face strict environmental codes (8). Others are concerned with equity issues, such as the fate of 30 million *campesinos* (small farmers), who will not be able to compete with North American grain producers (9).

References and Notes

1. The Economist Intelligence Unit (EIU), *Mexico Country Profile 1990-91* (EIU, London, 1990), p. 4.
2. Eliot Kalter and Hoe Ee Khor, "Mexico's Experience with Adjustment," *Finance and Development*, Vol. 27, No. 3 (1990), p. 22.
3. Nora Lustig, "Economic Crisis, Adjustment, and Living Standards in Mexico, 1982-85," *World Development*, Vol. 18, No. 10 (1990), pp. 1336-1338.
4. *Op. cit.* 2, pp. 24-25.
5. Secretaría de Desarrollo Urbano y Ecología (SEDUE), *Mexico: Towards a Better Environment* (SEDUE, Mexico City, 1991), pp. 12-14 and 20-21.
6. Larry Reibstein, Tim Padgett, Andrew Murr *et al.*, "A Mexican Miracle?" *Newsweek* (May 20, 1991), pp. 42-45.
7. Patricio Chirinos, "Mexican Integrated Environmental Border Plan," speech in Ciudad Juarez, Mexico (Secretaría de Desarrollo, Urbano y Ecología, Mexico City, October 23, 1991), pp. 1-13.
8. *Op. cit.* 6.
9. Aaron E. Zazueta, Senior Associate, World Resources Institute, Washington, D.C., 1991 (personal communication).

Figure 1 Gross National Product Per Capita

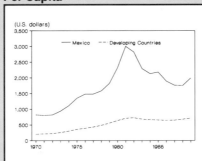

Source: The World Bank, unpublished data (The World Bank, Washington, D.C., 1991).

Figure 2 Total Fertility Rate

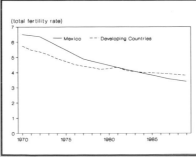

Source: The World Bank, unpublished data (The World Bank, Washington, D.C., 1991).

Figure 3 Mortality of Children Under Age 5

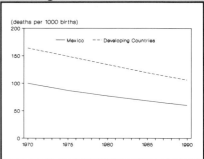

Source: United Nations (U.N.), *Mortality of Children Under 5: World Estimates and Projections* (U.N., New York, 1988), pp. 30-31.

Figure 4 Energy Consumption Per Capita

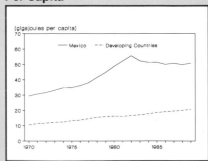

Source: United Nations Statistical Office, *U.N. Energy Tape* (United Nations, New York, May 1991).

avoiding expensive retrofits or cleanups at a later date. When a country's industrial base is expanding rapidly, policies that encourage adoption of the most efficient technologies and manufacturing systems minimize waste and pollutants and can have enormous cumulative benefits—improving a nation's economic competitiveness, sharply reducing capital needs, and protecting its environmental quality.

There is much room for improving energy efficiency in the RICs. In Indonesia, preliminary audits in plants found that 23 percent of current energy consumption could readily be saved and that energy use in new buildings in Indonesia could be reduced by 50 percent with investments that would pay for themselves in less than two years on average (79) (80). In Thailand, one assessment of potential savings found that if all industrial plants were as efficient as the best of similar plants elsewhere, the country's industries could save 24 percent of current energy consumption (81). In Brazil, which has already made considerable progress in conservation in the last five years, a study found that investing $20 billion in economy-wide efficiency improvements could cut in half the planned expansion of new generating facilities by 2010, at an estimated savings of $32 billion (82). In Chile, one assessment found that there had been little industrial investment in energy efficiency except at the very largest firms, such as copper companies, and that 70 percent of the homes in Santiago are insufficiently insulated (83).

A number of countries are making efforts to introduce efficiency standards for buildings and appliances, to require industries to have energy management programs, to provide tax reductions and low-interest loans for the purchase of more efficient equipment, and to set targets for improved efficiency (84). Yet a 1990 review of this field by the International Institute for Energy Conservation (IIEC) concluded that "most governments of developing countries, while supporting the notion of end-use energy efficiency, are more supportive of conventional energy approaches and have not made major commitments of staff or resources to end-use efficiency" (85).

In Thailand, an Energy Conservation Center was established by the government in 1988, and in late 1989 senior officials from all the agencies concerned with energy use took a study tour of the United States organized by IIEC. As a result, IIEC reported, "there has been a marked increase in interest throughout the Thai government in pursuing energy efficiency" (86). In February 1990, the Cabinet approved a conservation scheme for industry, with limits on electricity use based on the amount that is needed to produce various goods (87).

Transportation is another area where policies can have major energy and environmental impact, particularly in encouraging alternatives to automobiles and trucks such as light-rail vehicles like trams or streetcars. Commuter rail networks can also relieve congestion in central cities. In Jakarta, Indonesia, and São Paulo, Brazil, suburban rail systems that had been abandoned in recent years have been upgraded (88).

New industrial pollution control technologies can be encouraged by changes in regulatory procedures. What is needed are policies that do not entrench existing control technologies at the expense of long-term innovation and that encourage pollution and waste prevention rather than "end-of-the-pipe" cleanup technologies (89).

Growing urban pollution problems in many RICs have increasingly forced governments to confront them. Mexico, for example, is planning to spend $2.5 billion to counteract environmental deterioration in the Mexico City region over the next four years (90). President Carlos Salinas de Gortari has also strengthened enforcement of pollution control laws since 1989. (See Box 4.6, Mexico.) A new Constitutional Law for Ecological Equilibrium and Protection of the Environment has been passed, unleaded petrol has been introduced, and the huge Azcapotzalco refinery in Mexico City and other industrial plants have been closed to improve air quality. According to the air pollution coordinator of Mexico City, cleanup efforts will attempt to use the latest technologies so as to leapfrog the standards of industrial countries (91).

In Cubatão, Brazil, a city long known as the Valley of Death, state and local officials finally cracked down on industries that had been flouting pollution control regulations. Since the mid-1980s, these efforts have cut particulate emissions by 72 percent, organic waste by 93 percent, and heavy metal discharges by 97 percent (92).

NEW MARKETS, NEW PRODUCTS

South Korea, Taiwan, and other NICs followed a development path that depended on access to markets in industrialized countries, first for clothing and later for electronic equipment. For the RICs, however, the economic conditions of the 1990s and the emergence of regional trade blocks may necessitate somewhat different trade patterns. One example of the new patterns emerging is the negotiations among Canada, the United States, and Mexico for a continent-wide free trade zone (93). Several groupings of Latin American countries are seeking to liberalize trade among themselves (94).

In the past, cooperative associations of developing countries have not done much to increase trade among themselves. Even the Association of Southeast Asian Nations (ASEAN)—consisting of Malaysia, the Philippines, Singapore, Thailand, and Brunei—has been principally successful in trade negotiations with the European Community and in lobbying for greater flows of development aid (95). One theme that runs throughout the South Commission's *Challenge to the South* is the need to change this situation: "South-South co-operation can provide important new opportunities for development based on geographical proximity, on similarities in demand and tastes, on relevance of respective development experience, know-how, and skills, and on availability of complementary natural and financial resources and management and technical skills" (96).

Because of the increasing integration of global markets and the mobility of investment capital, the RICs face no shortage of industrialization options. By starting with medium-tech products and specializing in labor-intensive products and commodity production industries, industrializing countries can secure niches in global markets from which their industrial base can grow. Such an industrialization strategy may well stimulate rapid job creation, be more environmentally benign than a strategy based on heavy industry, and require lower infrastructure costs.

The bicycle industry offers a prime example of a mid-tech export product. The potential market for bicycles and motorbikes is large. Assembly is labor-intensive, and manufacturing facilities can be widely distributed within a country. The product has more than 1,000 parts. Factories producing frames thus need to be supplied by numerous smaller industries that provide seats, tires, inner tubes, lights, and so on (97). One study in Patna, India, found that $12,000 created two new jobs if invested in a conventional bus system, but six jobs in motorized rickshaw firms and 75 jobs in the cycle rickshaw industry (98). Repair shops constitute another form of local industrial development that follows logically from a greater supply of bicycles. Taiwan and China already export significant numbers of bicycles (99), and other RICs could emulate their success with similar products.

There are also likely to be many new opportunities for industrial development in the changed global environment of the 1990s, and perhaps new forms of technology cooperation and joint efforts between the RICs and industrial countries. For example:

■ Pharmaceutical companies have yet to tackle many of the diseases prevalent in developing countries. Tropical countries, which host most of the world's untapped genetic resources, could license those resources in return for revenues to support biodiversity conservation (as Costa Rica recently has) or undertake joint efforts with multinational companies to develop pharmaceuticals, cosmetics, and agricultural varieties.

■ Industrial pollution control is an area of growing concern throughout the world, and the RICs could work to develop not only state-of-the-art technologies for their own facilities but also export markets for cleanup equipment and services, building on their superior knowledge of conditions in developing countries.

■ Information technologies are spreading rapidly throughout the world, creating new business opportunities—both manufacturing and assembly plants, and new services, such as neighborhood cable television networks hooked to a satellite receiver and cellular phone- or facsimile-based message services.

CONCLUSION

Rapidly industrializing countries face extraordinarily difficult challenges. At the same time, as they explore new paths to development, they represent the hopes of the developing world—particularly if they can industrialize and improve living standards while conserving irreplaceable natural resources. Because each country varies in its resources and culture, there are likely to be a number of models and approaches to sustainable development. The countries discussed in this chapter do not exhaust the possibilities but may illustrate both the challenges and a number of creative attempts to find solutions. Nonetheless, a number of common elements stand out.

Countries such as South Korea and Taiwan have demonstrated that investing in human development—for example, by funding education and health programs and providing for equitable income distribution and land reform—is vital to combating poverty, controlling population growth, and getting development started. But as the development process gathers momentum, countries need to design policies to minimize the environmental impacts of development so clearly seen in the NICs and the industrial nations and invest in cleanup programs earlier rather than later. Efforts to install efficient, clean technologies can pay off in a big way in the future.

Governments in rapidly industrializing countries can do a great deal to steer development in a sustainable direction by adopting appropriate policies—many of which are discussed in this and preceding chapters. Governments in industrialized countries also have an important role to play by offering the necessary technical and financial assistance to support this kind of development.

An initial draft of this chapter was prepared by Linda Starke, a Washington-based editor and writer specializing in environment and development topics; additional contributions came from several senior WRI staff members

References and Notes

1. Marcus Noland, *Pacific Basin Developing Countries: Prospects for the Future* (Institute for International Economics, Washington, D.C., 1990), p. 15.

2. *Ibid.*, Table 1.1, p. 4.

3. Carl J. Dahlman, "Structural Change and Trade in the East Asian Newly Industrial Economies and Emerging Industrial Economies," in *The Newly Industrializing Countries in the World Economy*, Randall B. Purcell, ed. (Lynne Rienner Publishers, Boulder, Colorado, 1989), p. 53.

4. Steering Committee, Taiwan 2000 Study, *Taiwan 2000* (Academia Sinica, Taipei, 1989), pp. 11 and 41.

5. *Ibid.*, p. 22.

6. *Ibid.*, p. 19.

7. "Are You Really Going to Eat That?" *Bang* (Taipei, March 1988), p. 13.

8. *Op. cit.* 4, p. 20.

9. Walden Bello and Stephanie Rosenfeld, *Dragons in Distress: Asia's Miracle Economies in Crisis* (Institute for Food and Development Policy, San Francisco, 1990), p. 179.

10. "Victim of Its Own Success," *Newsweek* (June 4, 1990), p. 76, cited in Walden Bello and Stephanie Rosenfeld, *Dragons in Distress: Asia's Miracle Economies in Crisis* (Institute for Food and Development Policy, San Francisco, 1990), p. 204.

11. "'Trillions of Won' Needed for Clean-Up," *Yonhap* (August 10, 1989), reproduced in *Foreign Broadcast Information Service: East Asia* (August 10, 1989), pp. 26-27.

12. Mark Clifford, "Kicking Up a Stink," *Far Eastern Economic Review* (October 18, 1990), p. 72.

13. *Cooperative Energy Assessment* (Republic of Korea Ministry of Energy and U.S. Department of Energy, Argonne, Illinois, September 1981), p. 126, cited in Walden Bello and Stephanie Rosenfeld, *Dragons in Distress: Asia's Miracle Economies in Crisis* (Institute for Food and Development Policy, San Francisco, 1990), p. 102.

14. *Op. cit.* 9, p. 97.

15. *Op. cit.* 9, pp. 98-99.

16. Global Environment Monitoring System, *Assessment of Urban Air Quality* (United Nations Environment Programme, Nairobi, and United Nations Development Programme, Geneva, 1988), pp. 15 and 24.

17. Stephan Haggard, *Pathways from the Periphery* (Cornell University Press, Ithaca, New York, 1990), p. 240.

18. World Resources Institute and International Institute for Environment and Development, *World Resources, 1987* (Basic Books, New York, 1987), Table 16.1, p. 249.

19. Richard Grabowski, "Taiwanese Economic Development: An Alternative Interpretation," *Development and Change*, Vol. 19 (1988), p. 61.

20. *Op. cit.* 9, p. 183.

21. Pak Ki-Hyuk, "Farmland Tenure in the Republic of Korea," in *Land Tenure and Small Farmers in Asia*, FFTC Book Series, No. 24 (FFTC, Taiwan, 1983), pp. 113-116, cited in Walden Bello and Stephanie Rosenfeld, *Dragons in Distress: Asia's Miracle Economies in Crisis* (Institute for Food and Development Policy, San Francisco, 1990), p. 79.

22. Song Byung-Nak, "The Korean Economy," unpublished paper, Seoul, 1989, p. 27, cited in Walden Bello and Stephanie Rosenfeld, *Dragons in Distress: Asia's Miracle Economies in Crisis* (Institute for Food and Development Policy, San Francisco, 1990), p. 37.

23. *Op. cit.* 17, p. 227.

24. The World Bank, *Indonesia: Poverty Assessment and Strategy Report* (The World Bank, Washington, D.C., 1990), p. xiii.

25. The Economist Intelligence Unit (EIU), *Indonesia: Country Profile 1990-91* (EIU, London, 1990), p. 11.

26. The World Bank, *World Development Report 1991* (Oxford University Press, New York, 1991), Table 29, pp. 260-261.

27. Adam Schwarz, "Growth Strains Superstructure," *Far Eastern Economic Review* (April 18, 1991), p. 36.

28. *Op. cit.* 26.

29. The Economist Intelligence Unit (EIU), *Malaysia: Country Profile 1990-91* (EIU, London, 1990), p. 11.

30. The World Bank, *Trends in Developing Economies 1990* (The World Bank, Washington, D.C., 1990), p. 103.

31. The Economist Intelligence Unit (EIU), *Mexico: Country Profile 1990-91* (EIU, London, 1990), p. 8.

32. The Economist Intelligence Unit (EIU), *Thailand Burma: Country Profile 1990-91* (EIU, London, 1990), p. 6.

33. The World Resources Institute and International Institute for Environment and Development in collaboration with the United Nations Environment Programme, *World Resources 1988-89* (Basic Books, New York, 1988), Table 15.7, pp. 258-259.

34. The World Bank, unpublished data (The World Bank, Washington, D.C., 1991)

35. *Op. cit.* 25, p. 8.

36. *Op. cit.* 29, p. 8.

37. *Op. cit.* 34.

38. United Nations Fund for Population Activities (UNFPA), *The State of World Population 1991* (UNFPA, New York, 1991), p. 22.

39. *Op. cit.* 31, pp. 14 15.

40. Ben Ross Schneider, "Brazil Under Collor: Anatomy of a Crisis," *World Policy Journal* (Spring 1991), p. 339.

41. James Brooke, "Rural Union Chief is Slain in Brazil," *New York Times* (February 5, 1991), p. A8.

42. Anthony L. Hall, "Land Tenure and Land Reform in Brazil," in *Agrarian Reform and Grassroots Development*, Roy L. Prosterman, Mary N. Temple, and Timothy M. Hanstad, eds. (Lynne Rienner Publishers, Boulder, Colorado, 1990), p. 206.

43. *Ibid.*, pp. 222-223.

44. Theodore Panayotou, "Natural Resources and the Environment in the Economies of Asia and the Near East: Growth, Structural Change, and Policy," Harvard Institute for International Development, Harvard University, Cambridge, Massachusetts, July 1989, pp. 27 and 38.

45. John P. Lewis and Devesh Kapur, "An Updating Country Study: Thailand's Needs and Prospects in the 1990s," *World Development*, Vol. 18, No. 10 (1990), pp. 1364 and 1373.

46. *Op. cit.* 30, p. 275.

47. *Op. cit.* 24, p. ix.

48. *Op. cit.* 30, p. 328.

49. "The Dwindling Forest Beyond Long San," *The Economist* (August 18, 1990), p. 23.

50. *Op. cit.* 30, pp. 277 and 332.

51. The World Resources Institute, *Toward an Environmental and Natural Resources Management Strategy for ANE Countries in the 1990s* (World Resources Institute, Washington, D.C., 1990), pp. 26 and 27.

52. Robert Repetto, *Skimming the Water: Rent-Seeking and the Performance of Public Irrigation Systems* (World Resources Institute, Washington, D.C., 1986), p. 1.

53. Dhira Phantumvanit and Theodore Panayotou, *Natural Resources for a Sustainable Future: Spreading the Benefits*, Synthesis Paper No. 1, The 1990 Thailand Development Research Institute (TDRI), Year-End Conference, Industrializing Thailand and its Impact on the Environment (TDRI, Bangkok, Thailand, 1990), p. 74.

54. *Op. cit.* 51, p. 119.

55. Robert Weissman, "Rich Land, Poor People: The Economics of Indonesian Development," *Multinational Monitor* (October 1990), p. 19.

56. Peter Halesworth, "Plundering Indonesia's Rainforests," *Multinational Monitor* (October 1990), p. 8.

57. Theodore Panayotou and Chartchai Parasuk, *Land and Forest: Projecting Demand and Managing Encroachment*, Research Report No. 1, The 1990 Thailand Development Research Institute (TDRI), Year-End Conference, Industrializing Thailand and its Impact on the Environment (TDRI, Thailand, Bangkok, 1990), Appendix B, p. 75.

58. Walter Arensberg, Mary Louise Higgins, Rafael Asenjo *et al.*, "Environment and Natural Resources Strategy in Chile" (draft), prepared for United States Agency for International Development/Chile, World Resources Institute, Washington, D.C., November 8, 1989, p. 21.

59. "Logging Ban Move Described as Failure," (Bangkok) *Business Times* (August 22, 1990), p. 49.

60. *Op. cit.* 53, p. 30.

61. *Op. cit.* 56.

62. Directorate General of Forest Utilization, Ministry of Forestry; and Food and Agricultural Organization of the United Nations, *Situation and Outlook of the Forestry Sector in Indonesia*, Volume1: *Issues, Findings and Opportunities* (Government of Indonesia, Jakarta, September 1990), p. 10.

63. "Forestry: The Industry Strikes Back," *Asiaweek* (April 6, 1990), pp. 56-57.

64. *Op. cit.* 49.

65. Anthony Rowley, "Logged Out," *Far Eastern Economic Review* (December 13, 1990), p. 72.

66. James Brooks, "Brazilian Leader Acts to Protect the Amazon," *The New York Times* (June 26, 1991), p. A9.

67. *Op. cit.* 58, pp. 8-9 and 18-19.

68. World Resources Institute in cooperation with U.S. Agency for International Development, Latin America and Caribbean Bureau, "Toward an Environmental Strategy for Latin America and the Caribbean: Issues and Options Paper" (draft), World Resources Institute, Washington, D.C., November 30, 1990, p. 27.

69. Stephen J. Rothenburg, Lourdes Schnaas-Arrieta, Irving A. Pérez-Guerrero *et al.*, "Evaluación del Riesgo Potencial de la Exposición Perinatal al Plomo en el Valle de México," *Perinatologia y Reproducción Humana*, Vol. 3, No. 1 (1989), pp. 49 and 56.

70. David Scott Clark, "Mexico City Curbs Fuelish Ways," *The Christian Science Monitor* (October 29, 1990), p. 13.

71. "Malaysia: Merchants of Gloom," *Far Eastern Economic Review* (September 20, 1990), pp. 12 and 13.

72. *Op. cit.* 58, p. 33.

73. Adam Schwarz, "Power Struggle," *Far Eastern Economic Review* (November 8, 1990), p. 42.

74. *Op. cit.* 27, p. 40.

75. Howard S. Geller, "Electricity Conservation in Brazil: Status Report and Analysis," prepared for U.S. Environmental Protection Agency, U.S. Congress, Office of Technology Assessment, Electrobras, and Universidade de São Paulo, American Council for an Energy-Efficient Economy, Washington, D.C., 1990, p. 1.

76. "For the Record," *Energy Economist*, No. 106 (August 1990), p. 32.

77. Eric D. Larson, ed., *Report on the 1989 Thailand Workshop on End-Use-Oriented Energy Analysis* (International Institute for Energy Conservation, Washington, D.C., 1990), p. i.

78. *Op. cit.* 27, p. 40.

79. Office of Energy, Bureau for Science and Technology, U.S. Agency for International Development, *Energy Inefficiency in the Asia/Near East Region and Its Environmental Implications* (RCG/Hagler, Bailly, Inc., Washington, D.C., 1989), pp. 5.3 and 5.7.

80. Gregory H. Kats, "Slowing Global Warming and Sustaining Development," *Energy Policy* (January/February 1990), p. 30.

81. Deborah Lynn Bleviss and Vanessa Lide, eds., *Energy Efficiency Strategies for Thailand* (University Press of America, Lanham, Maryland, 1989), p. 49.

82. *Op. cit.* 75, pp. 144-156 and 168.

83. Michael Philips, *Energy Conservation Activities in Latin America and the Caribbean* (International Institute for Energy Conservation, Washington, D.C., 1990), p. 16.

84. U.S. Congress, Office of Technology Assessment, *Energy in Developing Countries* (U.S. Government Printing Office, Washington, D.C., 1991), p. 39.

85. Michael Philips, "Alternative Roles for the Energy Sector Management Assistance Program in End-Use Energy Efficiency" (working draft), International Institute for Energy Conservation, Washington, D.C., October 1990, p. 17.

86. Mark J. Cherniack, *Thailand Electricity Mission* (International Institute for Energy Conservation, Washington, D.C., 1989), pp. 5-6.

87. "South East Asia: Moving Too Fast for Comfort?" *Energy Economist* (August 1990), p. 18.

88. Marcia D. Lowe, *Alternatives to the Automobile: Transport for Livable Cities* (Worldwatch Institute, Washington, D.C., 1990), p. 20.

89. George Heaton, Robert Repetto, and Rodney Sobin, *Transforming Technology: An Agenda for Environmentally Sustainable Growth in the 21st Century* (World Resources Institute, Washington, D.C., 1991), p. ix.

90. "Tlatelolco Declaration: Who Pays the Bill?" *Development Forum* (May-June 1991), p. 9.

91. Robert Reinhold, "Mexico Proclaims an End to Sanctuary for Polluters," *New York Times* (April 18, 1991), p. A1.

92. James Brooke, "Signs of Life in Brazil's Industrial Valley of Death, *New York Times* (June 15, 1991), p. A2.

93. Mark A. Uhlig, "Canada is Expected to Join U.S.-Mexico Trade Talks," *New York Times* (January 30, 1991), p. D1.

94. Inter-American Development Bank (IDB) *Economic and Social Progress in Latin American 1990 Report* (IDB, Washington, D.C., 1990), pp. 10-13.

95. *Op. cit.* 1, pp. 140-141.

96. South Commission, *The Challenge to the South* (Oxford University Press, Oxford, U.K., 1990), p. 16.

97. Riccardo Navarro, Urs Heierli, and Victor Beck, "Bicycles, Intelligent Transport in Latin America," *Development* (No. 4, 1986), p. 47.

98. Michael Replogle, "Transportation Strategies for Sustainable Development," paper presented at the 5th World Conference on Transport Research, Yokahama [or Yokohama], Japan, July 10-14, 1989.

99. "Ways to Turn the Wheels of the Bicycle Industry," *China Daily* (March 14, 1990).

5. Central Europe

The industrial regions of Central Europe are so choked by pollution that the health of children is impaired and the lives of adults shortened. The most notorious example is the extensive coal belt that includes southwestern Poland, northwestern Czechoslovakia, and the southeastern part of (East) Germany. (See Box 5.1.) Within this area lies much of Central Europe's heavy industry—especially steel, cement, chemical, and petrochemical works—and a phalanx of inefficient coal-burning power plants spewing forth massive amounts of sulfur dioxide (SO_2) and soot. The region contains numerous environmental horror stories, including Katowice, Poland (1); Ústí, Czechoslovakia (2); and Most, Czechoslovakia (3). Dangerous conditions also have been reported in many other towns in Central Europe, including Copsa Mica, Romania (4); Bitterfeld, (East) Germany (5); and the Borsod County Industrial Region in Hungary (6) (7). (See Figure 5.1.)

Conditions are also serious in some large cities. During Prague's air inversions in January 1982 and February 1987, the 24-hour SO_2 concentrations exceeded 3,000 micrograms per cubic meter (8), more than 20 times the admissible 24-hour limit and comparable to the infamous London smog of December 1952.

Cleanup costs are staggering. In Poland alone, it is estimated that cleanup could cost $260 billion over the next 25–30 years. The costs of pollution abatement, excluding industrial and energy restructuring, have been estimated at $70 billion (9).

The situation is somewhat reminiscent of the industrialized areas of the Ruhr Valley in Western Europe and the steelmaking regions of Indiana and Pennsylvania in the 1950s and 1960s. Those areas, however, were favored with settled political institutions and mature market economies. The nations of Central Europe must simultaneously contend with fledgling political systems, slowly emerging market economies, underdeveloped service and technology sectors, and unsettled government bureaucracies. Unemployment is rising rapidly and most governments have very little money. Devising comprehensive and realistic environmental cleanup plans is proving difficult. Public pressure to force environmental cleanup could be easily overwhelmed by pressure to create jobs.

There are, however, important signs of hope. The emerging parliamentary democracies in Hungary, Poland, and Czechoslovakia have attracted considerable support from other industrialized governments and international lending institutions. Poland has a huge market, Czechoslovakia a well-developed industrial infrastructure, and Hungary a well-developed private sector. The region's workforce is well-educated and

Figure 5.1 Central Europe's Coal Belt

Source: Compiled by the World Resources Institute.

eager for consumer goods, better services, and a better environment. Foreign private investors, though initially cautious, are planning to invest billions of dollars in the region over the next five years. The eastern part of Germany—the former German Democratic Republic—has the unique advantage of its integration into the Federal Republic of Germany, one of the most dynamic economies in the world. (The former German Democratic Republic is here referred to as (East) Germany; the former Federal Republic of Germany as (West) Germany.)

Some other nations in the region, notably Romania, are less advanced politically and have attracted less international interest. Yugoslavia faces difficult ethnic divisions that threaten its political stability.

Although Central Europe's environmental problems are massive, they have not enveloped the entire region. In Poland, the government in 1983 designated 27 "areas of ecological hazard" that comprise about 11 percent of the country's total land area and include 35 percent of its population. Of these 27 areas, the 5 most serious "areas of ecological disaster"—Gdańsk, on the Baltic coast; Legnica-Glogow, in west-central Poland; and the linked areas of Upper Silesia, Kraków, and Rybnik in the southwest—cover about 4.4 percent of the country's total land area (10).

Many areas in the region remain relatively unpolluted and attractive, including the northeastern quarter of Poland (the "green lung of Poland"), the

Bieschady Mountains, the Tatra Mountains, Lake Balaton in Hungary, and the Carpathians in Romania. The end of the Cold War also has brought an end to the unpopulated, zealously guarded "no man's lands" along state borders, opening up many new opportunities for creating protected areas. (See Box 5.2.)

HOW DID IT HAPPEN?

Conventional wisdom says that Central Europe's environmental problems all began in the late 1940s with the establishment of socialist regimes and the imposition of the Stalinist model of industrial growth. In many areas, however, the patterns of industrial development were in evidence well before the political changes of the late 1940s. Katowice, for example, was a center of heavy industry long before World War II. Czechoslovakia was a relatively advanced industrial country after World War II.

Nor have these countries followed identical economic paths. Hungary's 1968 package of economic reforms (the "New Economic Mechanism"), which freed economic organizations from obligatory production targets, allowed cooperatives to become more genuinely independent and improved the private sector's ability to work with the state sector (11). Some East European governments—notably Poland and Czechoslovakia—began to express official concern about environmental problems by the 1970s and 1980s (12). Many

Box 5.2 New Opportunities for Nature Conservation

The political transformation of Central Europe has created a major new opportunity for the conservation of natural areas. Many lands along state borders have remained largely unpopulated for the past four decades. Some of these areas could now be preserved as parks or managed in a way that would protect their biological diversity and recreational values. This idea, originally devised in early 1990, has been embraced by about three dozen local and international conservation groups. These groups have also proposed creating a new organization—a European Trust for

Natural and Cultural Inheritance—that could spearhead the effort and facilitate financing. The region could take advantage of "debt-for-nature" swaps between West European (creditor) states and Central European (debtor) states.

A rapid initial survey identified 24 major conservation areas. Major areas include the Rhodope Mountains, Nestos Delta, and adjoining areas (Greece, Bulgaria, Yugoslavia, and Turkey); the floodplain areas of the Danube, Thaya, and March rivers (Austria, Czechoslovakia, and Hungary); the Danube Delta (Roma-

nia and the Soviet Union); the Bavarian and Bohemian forests (Germany, Czechoslovakia, and Austria); Lake Scutari (Yugoslavia and Albania); the Finnish-Russian woodland areas (Finland and the Soviet Union); and the Bialowieza virgin forest (Poland and the Soviet Union) (1).

References and Notes

1 "Ecological Bricks for Our Common House of Europe," *Politische Ökologie* (October 1990), pp. 16-17.

Figure 1 Forgotten Lands—Future Preserves?

Key

1. Finnish-Russian Woodland Area
2. Biebrza Marshes
3. Bialowieza Virgin Forest
4. Schorfheide/Chorin Area
5. Spreewald
6. Sächsische Schweiz
7. Karkonosze Area
8. Tatra Area
9. Pieniny Area
10. Bieszczady Region
11. Slovakian Karst
12. Floodplain Areas of the Danube, Thaya, and March
13. Thaya Valley
14. Trebonsko Pond Region
15. Bavarian Forest, Bohemian Forest Area
16. Lake of Neusiedel
17. Mur Floodplain
18. International Karst Park
19. Lower Reaches of the Drau and Kopacki-Rit
20. Sava Floodplain
21. Danube Delta
22. Lake Scutari
23. Prespa Area
24. Rhodope Mountains, Nestos Delta, and Adjoining Areas

Source: "Ecological Bricks for Our Common House of Europe," *Politische Ökologie* (October 1990), pp. 16-17.

of these governments also enacted environmental protection laws in the 1970s and 1980s, about the same time as their West European counterparts (13).

Nevertheless, four decades of socialist rule took a disastrous toll on the region's environment. Many explanations have been advanced for this failure.

Early theories of socialism reasoned that state ownership of the means of production would remove the motives for pollution because there was no reason for the state to contaminate itself and reduce its own wealth. In practice, however, factory managers were pressed to commit all their resources to meeting production targets, rather than reducing or cleaning up waste (14). There was also strong political support for independent, self-reliant economic systems that did not depend on international markets. Those pressures created a bias in favor of domestic resources such as coal and against imported energy from other countries.

Socialist economies used energy inefficiently. A primary reason, according to Hungarian economist Janos Kornai, was that industries operated under "soft budget constraints," which allowed cost increases to be passed on, and under which industries could rely on governments to bail them out rather than lose the firm's production or create unemployment (15) (16). Hungarian economist Gabor Hovanyi has also argued that socialist policies tended to reduce trade, limit foreign exchange, distort wages, and reduce investment, all of which critically affected innovation (17). Western nations contributed to the problem by blocking access to advanced technologies and credit (18).

Other components of socialist systems have affected the region's environmental deterioration:

■ The governments of Central Europe set prices of energy and natural resources at relatively low levels, and the prices were kept low even when the costs of mining and energy grew because of worsening mining conditions (19). Prices did not take into account the costs of controlling pollution. The same was true in the Western industrialized countries until regulations began to force industry to internalize these costs. Western industrialized countries made further dramatic improvements in energy efficiency following the oil price shocks of the 1970s.

■ Low prices led to overconsumption, both by industry and by consumers. Residents in apartment buildings, for instance, typically had no incentive (or individual means) to conserve heat or water because apartments lacked individual thermostats and water meters (20).

■ State enterprises received a bonus for increasing their output, but they bore no penalty for depleting resources and therefore had no reason to treat resources as a valuable asset. Inputs were also part of the plan target, and had to be used up to maintain the same quantity in the next five-year plan. Resources were often wasted, and there was little incentive to find substitutes or improve technology (21).

■ Most countries established elaborate systems of antipollution fees, but they were weakly enforced (22).

■ State enterprises had little incentive to control pollutants. The state owned and paid for everything, so min-

istries and industries included the cost of fines for pollution as part of the regular budgetary process (23).

■ Central control did not allow localities to devise policies based on local needs. Communities affected by pollution had no right to improve their environmental quality or to receive financial compensation from the polluter (24).

■ The emphasis on heavy industry was hampered by shortages of hard currency to invest in new machinery and technology and the necessary skills to operate new machinery properly (25). As machinery became outdated, maintenance costs increased and industrial efficiency declined. The problem was worsened by a frequent lack of spare parts.

Finally, the public was left largely uninformed and could protest environmental conditions only at great personal risk. Central Europeans did receive warning signals about the environment in the 1960s and 1970s, and there were early intellectual efforts, including papers and books published on the subject. Relatively weak environmental movements emerged in the 1970s in Hungary and Bohemia; there were even a few instances of environmental protest actions (26). But inhibitions on public discussion and speech left little room for the public expression of those concerns; instead, ecologists in the region had to become information sleuths, ferreting out data and transmitting what they learned via underground journals. The authoritarian regimes of the period, though not totally immune to popular pressures, were generally unresponsive.

This situation began to change with the political transformation of the 1980s. Recognition of the Solidarity trade union in 1980 reawakened Polish political life and sparked an environmental movement. In September 1980, the Polish Ecological Club—the first fully independent environmental group in the region—was founded in Krakow (27). The club actually formed a formal part of the "Round Table" negotiations to end communist power (28). In the early 1980s, the movement—a coalition of trade unions, scientists, local members of the Polish Ecological Club, and the press—convinced the State Ministry of Metallurgy to close down the Skawina aluminum works, a heavy emitter of toxic fluoride emissions located just nine miles southwest of Krakow (29).

Environmental movements played a significant role in the revolutions that toppled communist governments throughout the region in 1989 and 1990. There are by now numerous independent environmental advocacy groups in the region and a Green party (or parties) in each country (30). Many of these groups remain relatively weak, however (31).

Industrial Development and Energy Efficiency

Overall energy intensity—energy consumption per dollar of gross national product—has been much higher in the planned economies of Central Europe than in market economies. The energy required to make steel in Central Europe has been two to three times greater than in Western Europe. Steelmaking in the region also tends to use older, less efficient technol-

Table 5.1 Commercial Energy Consumption in Central Europe, 1989

Country	Consumption (petajoules) {a}					Consumption by Fuel Type as a Percent of Total			
	Total	Solid Fuels {b}	Liquid Fuels {c}	Gas {d}	Electricity {e}	Solid Fuels	Liquid Fuels	Gas	Electricity
Albania	119	42	50	16	11	36	43	13	9
Bulgaria	1,291	662	355	238	36	51	28	18	3
Czechoslovakia	2,733	1,702	513	403	114	62	19	15	4
Germany (Dem Rep)	3,648	2,753	539	303	53	75	15	8	1
Hungary	1,136	306	313	427	90	27	28	38	8
Poland	5,062	4,040	605	397	20	80	12	8	0
Romania	3,047	944	683	1,346	74	31	22	44	2
Yugoslavia	1,771	810	609	239	113	46	34	13	6
U.S.S.R.	54,958	14,510	16,049	22,970	1,429	26	29	42	3

Source: United Nations Statistical Office, U.N. Energy Tape (United Nations, New York, 1991).
Notes: a. Consumption is defined as domestic production plus net imports, minus net stock increases, minus aircraft and marine bunkers. b. Solid fuels include bituminous coal, lignite, peat, and oil shale burned directly. c. Liquid fuels include crude petroleum and natural gas liquids. d. Gas includes natural gas and other petroleum gases. e. Electricity includes primary production from hydro, nuclear, and geothermal sources.

ogies; for example, the open hearth process accounts for about 55–60 percent of steel production in Central Europe and the Soviet Union, while it is virtually out of use in Western Europe and accounts for only about 8 percent of U.S. output (32).

Greatly contributing to the region's environmental problems has been the general failure to maintain industrial plants and equipment, to replace or update machinery, or to introduce new technology, manufacturing processes, and operating practices (33). The continued dominance of heavy industry in Central Europe also contrasts with the typical pattern in most industrialized market economies, where the mix of economic activity eventually tends to shift from heavy industry to lighter industry and services.

Dependence on Coal

After World War II, both Western and Central Europe relied primarily on domestic coal resources. But the two regions have diverged sharply since then. Western Europe prospered with cheap oil imports in the 1950s and 1960s, while Central Europe had to wait until oil and gas became available from the Soviet Union in the early 1970s. Western Europe also developed domestic oil and gas resources, which now provide about 28 percent of total energy consumption; coal, meanwhile, has shrunk to about 14 percent of consumption (34). (See *World Resources 1988–89*, pp. 117–121.)

Domestic coal has continued to be the primary fuel in Central Europe, especially in (East) Germany, Poland, and Czechoslovakia. (See Table 5.1.) Much of the coal resource in the region is brown coal, or lignite, which has a high ash content, a sulfur content that varies considerably from region to region (0.7 percent in some power plants in East Germany (35), up to 5 percent in some other regions (36)), and an energy yield that may be only half that of hard coal. As a result, a great deal more brown coal has to be burned to meet a given energy demand. This increases emissions of sulfur dioxide (SO_2) and oxides of nitrogen (NO_x) and destroys more land because most brown coal is surface-mined (37).

THE EXTENT OF THE DAMAGE

Precisely describing the extent of environmental damage in Central Europe is difficult because the data gath-

ered over the past four decades have been either spotty or of uncertain quality. The region's political transformation has prompted much greater interest in environmental monitoring, and the availability and quality of data will probably improve over the next few years.

In general, however, environmental conditions are considered poor in the entire region. Conditions in Poland, (East) Germany, and Czechoslovakia are usually judged somewhat worse than the regional average; conditions in Hungary may be somewhat better. There is considerable evidence to suggest that environmental conditions have seriously affected the health of people living in the region. (See Box 5.3.)

Atmospheric Pollution

The region's reliance on hard and brown coal has inflicted a heavy toll on the atmosphere, especially in southern (East) Germany, the northern Bohemia region of Czechoslovakia, and the Silesian industrial region in southwest Poland. Sulfur dioxide emissions have been estimated at about 5.2 million metric tons in (East) Germany and 3.9 million metric tons in Poland in 1988. On a per capita basis, emissions in East Germany were estimated at 313.3 kilograms, compared with 24.2 kilograms in West Germany. (See Table 5.2.)

As a result of these emissions, several regions in Czechoslovakia have average annual sulfur dioxide concentrations that exceed the World Health Organization (WHO) limits. (See Table 5.3.) The Chomutov region typically exceeds the WHO daily limit of 150 cubic meters for 117 days a year (38).

Coal burning also produces large quantities of particulates. In 1985, East Germany emitted between 5 and 6 million metric tons of particulates and Poland nearly 3 million metric tons (39). Sweden, in contrast, had estimated annual emissions in 1982–84 of 40,000 metric tons (40).

The region also emits significant amounts of nitrogen dioxide. (See Table 5.4.) Other contributors to air pollution include carbon monoxide, ammonia, fluorine, chlorine, volatile hydrocarbons, phenol, hydrogen sulfide, arsenic, and lead (41).

Low Stacks: An Important Source

Although the high smokestacks of industries are commonly thought to be the principal source of air pollu-

Box 5.3 Environment and Health in Central Europe

The health prospects of people living in Central Europe are the bleakest in the industrialized world. Among 33 industrialized countries, life expectancy is the shortest in Central Europe and the Soviet Union (1). (See Figure 1.) The average Japanese man, for example, will live about a decade longer than the average Hungarian man (75.8 years, compared to 66.1 years). Infant mortality, while far less than in developing countries, nevertheless is high relative to other industrialized countries. In 1988, for example, it was 11.9 per 1,000 live births in Czechoslovakia, 15.8 in Hungary, and 16.2 in Poland; while in the same year, (West) Germany's rate was 7.5 and Japan's was 4.8 (2). Available data on morbidity suggest high rates of acute and chronic respiratory disease (3) (4), childhood lead poisoning (5), occupational injuries (6), and, among exposed workers, noise-induced hearing impairment (7).

These East-West differences began to emerge in the mid-1960s; until that time, Central Europe had approached other industrialized regions in infant mortality and life expectancy (8) (9) (10).

The leading causes of death in Central Europe are cardiovascular disease and cancer; death rates in both categories have increased in recent years. In Hungary, death rates for cardiovascular disease have increased for men 30 and older, and rates for almost all types of cancer increased substantially for both men and women between 1960 and 1986 (11).

ENVIRONMENTAL AND WORKPLACE FACTORS

To what extent are environmental factors the cause of this deteriorating health situation? The answer is not known. Environmental factors appear to be one of several important contributing factors. Others include high-fat diets (which contribute to the development of coronary artery disease and to certain types of cancer) and the high percentage of people smoking high-tar, high-nicotine cigarettes (which is associated with cancer of the lung and other body organs). Other social and occupational factors include stress (a contributing factor in coronary artery disease and

other disorders) and safety hazards in the workplace, on the road, and at home.

Serious environmental health hazards in Central Europe include the following:

■ High levels of sulfur dioxide, oxides of nitrogen, lead, and other hazardous chemicals in the ambient air, resulting mainly from power plant, factory, and automobile emissions;

■ Contamination of groundwater and soil by nitrogenous fertilizers, pesticides, and toxic metals;

■ Contamination of rivers by sewage and industrial waste; and

■ A variety of chemical, physical, biological, and psychosocial health hazards in the workplace.

Exposure to toxic and carcinogenic chemicals can lead to a variety of acute and chronic health problems. For example, childhood exposure to lead—even at levels previously regarded as safe—can retard normal intellectual development; exposure to volatile organic compounds and certain other chemicals can lead to neurotoxic effects in children and adults; and exposure to certain dusts, fumes, and gases can cause or contribute to acute and chronic respiratory disorders. What is often not known in Eastern Europe is the level and duration of human exposure to these chemicals.

The impact of environmental factors on health is particularly acute in the region's environmental "hot spots," especially in the Katowice-Krakow area of Poland, where there has been intense industrial pollution of the groundwater and soil for as much as 200 years, and in the contiguous mining and industrial district of northern Bohemia in Czechoslovakia. In parts of the Katowice area, lead levels in soil reach as high as 19,000 parts per million—about 50 times the acceptable level. Children have been exposed through soil contact, house dust, and crops grown in contaminated soil. One study in a hot-spot area showed a 13-point difference in IQ between children with the highest and lowest blood-lead levels, as well as increased rates of anemia, digestive problems, and chromosome damage consistent with long-term poisoning (12).

Although there is some seasonal variation in pollution levels in these areas, the long-term pollution of air and water is so severe that it has affected the health of people in the region. For example, a study of army inductees in Poland revealed that chronic bronchitis rates were more than three times higher at army recruitment centers in areas with high ambient sulfur dioxide levels than in those with low levels, and that asthma rates were four times higher in high-level than in low-level areas (13). Data from northern Bohemia in Czechoslovakia reveal that very high ambient levels of sulfur dioxide (SO_2) commonly occur in the air, with levels greater than 1,000 micrograms per cubic meter sustained for over a day at a time (14). The World Health Organization recommends that SO_2 exposure should not exceed 150 micrograms per cubic meter on more than seven days a year. (See *World Resources 1990–91*, p. 356.) These high SO_2 levels have been accompanied by a fivefold increase in respiratory disease among preschoolers and a threefold increase among school-age children compared to the rest of western Czechoslovakia. In both northern and central Bohemia, studies have repeatedly demonstrated that removing children from areas of heavy air pollution for three-week periods in winter will reduce rates of anemia and improve the functioning of their immune systems. One study also demonstrated increases in the children's breathing capacity after a three-week removal (15).

Studies comparing mortality among districts in Czechoslovakia have demonstrated relationships between mortality and certain parameters of air pollution. Strong relationships also exist between mortality and certain social factors, such as a low educational level, a high divorce rate, or a high percentage of Gypsies (who have poorer health status, on average) in the district (16). However, no studies have been done to adequately assess the joint effects of environmental and social factors on health status.

The policy response to date has varied from country to country. In general, government environmental protection and environmental health programs are likely to

tants, coal-burning low stacks—from households, small-scale industry, and district heating plants—are significant contributors. In Katowice, for example, low stacks contribute about 46 percent of all soot and dust emissions.

Like the London smogs of the early 1950s, the worst air pollution episodes are typically associated with temperature inversions during the winter, which tend to trap particulate emissions from low-stack sources close to ground level. The cost of particulate damage

to health and materials is estimated to be more than 10 times greater from low-stack sources than from high stacks (42).

Auto Emissions: A Growing Problem

Although not yet very numerous in the region, motor vehicles are rapidly increasing in number. As shown in Figure 5.2, motor vehicles in Poland account for about 30 to 40 percent of the country's emissions of car-

Box 5.3

be strengthened, but programs in the region that are concerned with health and safety in the workplace face an uncertain future.

NATIONAL POLICIES

National occupational health programs (such as Poland's, which places physicians in factories to provide diagnostic, curative, and preventive services) may be weakened or eliminated during the current period of political and economic transition. With increasing privatization of industry, occupational health researchers are likely to have less access to workers, workplaces, and information on chemical exposures and related health effects among workers. Privatization also may lead to less reporting of occupational disease and injury as cost-conscious private sector management styles emerge. Desperate to provide jobs and gain access to hard currency, some nations in the region may import hazardous industrial processes such as hazardous waste management from Western industrial countries. If such new processes are introduced, they may worsen environmental quality and cause environmental and occupational health problems.

The countries of the region must make choices that could lead them down different paths toward improved health status, better quality of life, and longer life expectancy or toward further deterioration of the environment and worsening health.

References and Notes

1. Mátyás Börzsönyi, "Environment and Health in Hungary," in *Environment and Health in Eastern Europe* (Management Sciences for Health, Boston, 1990), p. 2.

2. World Health Organization (WHO), *World Health Statistics Annual 1989* (WHO, Geneva, 1989), pp. 160-162, 412-428.

3. Péter Rudnai, "Environmental Epidemiology Research in Hungary," in *Environment and Health in Eastern Europe* (Management Sciences for Health, Boston, 1990), p. 125.

4. Clyde Hertzman, "Poland: Health and Environment in the Context of Socioeconomic Decline" (University of British Columbia, Vancouver, Canada, 1990), pp. 14-17.

Figure 1 Life Expectancy at Birth, 1985–90

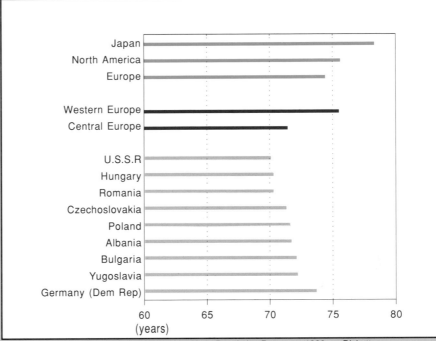

Source: Adapted from United Nations (U.N.), *World Population Prospects 1990: on Diskette* (U.N., New York, 1991).

5. *Ibid.*, pp. 13-15.

6. György Ungváry, "Occupational Health in Hungary: Occupational Safety, Hygiene, and Health Care," in *Environment and Health in Eastern Europe* (Management Sciences for Health, Boston, 1990), p. 76.

7. Danuta Koradecka, "Health, Work, and the Economy in Poland," in *Environment and Health in Eastern Europe* (Management Sciences for Health, Boston, 1990), p. 80.

8. Dhruva Nagnur, *Longevity and Historical Life Tables 1921-1981: Canada and the Provinces* (Canadian Ministry of Supply and Services, Ottawa, 1986), pp. 70-71.

9. Institute of Health Information and Statistics (IHIS), *Health Care and Health Service in Czech Republic in Statistical Data* (IHIS, Prague, 1990), p. 5.

10. Péter Józan, *Recent Mortality Trends in Eastern Europe*, unpublished manuscript

(Central Statistical Office, Budapest), pp. 22-31.

11. *Op. cit.* 1, pp. 3-4.

12. B. Hager-Malecka, paper presented at the Academy of Medicine, Zabrze, Poland, Sept. 8, 1989.

13. *Op. cit.* 4, pp. 9-10.

14. Clyde Hertzman, "Environment and Health in Czechoslovakia" (University of British Columbia, Vancouver, Canada, 1990), p. 12.

15. *Ibid.*, pp. 13-23.

16. Dagmar Dzúrova, Jan Kara, and Karel Kühnl, "Environment and Health in Czechoslovakia," paper presented at the Conference on Public Health and the Environmental Crisis in Central Europe, Woodrow Wilson International Center for Scholars, Smithsonian Institution, Washington, D.C., April 30-May 2, 1990, pp. 15-20.

bon monoxide (CO), hydrocarbons (HC), oxides of nitrogen (NOx), and lead (Pb). The number of passenger cars in Poland—currently estimated at about 5 million—is expected to double over the next 20 years, and the number of kilometers driven annually per vehicle is expected to increase from the current 7,000 kilometers per year to 8,000 by 1995, 9,000 by the year 2000, and 10,000 by 2010 (43).

Most vehicles in Poland operate on leaded petrol averaging 0.3 to 0.56 grams of lead per liter. With unleaded petrol priced about 30 to 40 percent higher than

leaded, only about 1 percent of petrol sales were unleaded in 1990 (44).

Several countries in the region have substantial numbers of automobiles—Trabants and Wartburgs—equipped with outmoded two-stroke engines that emit relatively high levels of hydrocarbons, particles, and aldehydes. About 35 percent of Hungary's autos, for example, have these engines (45).

Cities such as Budapest exhibit some of the pollution problems characteristic of Western cities with large vehicle populations. For example, carbon monoxide,

Table 5.2 Sulfur Dioxide Emissions, 1989

Country	Total Emissions (000 metric tons of SO$_2$/year)	Per Capita Emissions (kilograms)	Emissions Per Dollar GNP (grams)
Central Europe and the U.S.S.R.			
Albania {a}	50	15.6	13.2
Bulgaria	1,030	114.6	49.4
Czechoslovakia	2,800	178.9	22.7
Germany (Dem Rep)	5,210	313.3	32.7
Hungary	1,218	115.2	45.0
Poland	3,910	103.3	58.4
Romania	200	8.6	2.5
Yugoslavia	1,650	69.6	27.9
U.S.S.R. {b}	9,318	32.4	3.5
Western Europe and the United States			
Austria	124	16.3	1.1
Belgium	414	41.5	2.6
France	1,520	27.1	1.5
Germany (Fed Rep)	1,500	24.2	1.2
Italy	2,410	41.9	2.8
Sweden	220	25.9	1.2
United Kingdom	3,552	62.1	4.3
United States {c}	20,700	83.2	4.0

Sources:
1. Chapter 24, "Atmosphere and Climate," Table 24.5.
2. Chapter 15, "Basic Economic Indicators," Table 15.1.
3. The World Bank, unpublished data (The World Bank, Washington, D.C., June 1991).
Notes:
a. Estimated emissions.
b. Emissions data for European part of U.S.S.R. only. Per Capita and per dollar emissions calculated using population and GNP data for entire country.
c. 1988 emissions data.

which frequently exceeds healthy levels, tends to be highest during the morning and evening peak traffic times. Photochemical smog or ozone, which is caused in part by vehicle emissions of hydrocarbons and oxides of nitrogen, frequently exceeds acceptable levels in Budapest (46). The problem is compounded in the older cities, which have narrow, winding streets that were never intended to accommodate cars and cannot easily handle heavy traffic.

Water Pollution

Raw sewage and industrial effluents laced with heavy metals and toxic (and sometimes radioactive) chemicals are the two principal contributors to the deterioration of water quality in Central Europe's rivers. In Upper Silesia in Poland, for example, some 950,000 cubic meters of saline water is pumped daily from coal mines, of which about 650,000 cubic meters—containing about 7,000 metric tons of salt—is fed daily into the tributaries of the Oder and Vistula rivers. The impact on the ecology of these rivers has been devastating, making much of the water useless either for drinking or industrial purposes (47).

The condition of Polish surface waters has deteriorated dramatically over the last quarter-century. Class I water, defined as drinkable after disinfection, was present in 33 percent of the total length of monitored rivers in the country in 1967; by 1986, Class I water was found in only about 4 percent of the country's total river length. Unclassed water, which is virtually unusable even for industrial purposes, rose from 23 percent in 1967 to 39 percent in 1986 (48). About half of Poland's cities, including Warsaw, and 15 percent of its industrial facilities have no wastewater treatment systems, and about 32 percent of wastewater needing treatment is left untreated (49) (50).

Table 5.3 Average Annual Concentrations of Sulfur Dioxide in Selected Regions of Czechoslovakia

(micrograms per cubic meter)

Region	1970	1975	1980	1985
Chomutov	53	71	94	126
Most	57	60	102	132
Teplice	51	77	93	110
Ostrava	36	36	46	55
Prague/Karlov	100	100	128	155
Bratislava	49	67	55	60

Source: J. Vavroušek, The Environment in Czechoslovakia (State Commission for Science, Technology and Investments, Prague, 1990), p. 23.
Note: a. The admissable annual concentration limit is 40–60 micrograms per cubic meter.

In Czechoslovakia the quality of surface waters has shown a similar trend. Figure 5.3, for example, shows that the water quality of some rivers in Czechoslovakia deteriorated drastically from 1940 to 1980. Only about 27 percent of the major river lengths have been classified in the worst pollution category (incapable of sustaining fish or containing inedible fish) (51). About 40 percent of Czechoslovakia's wastewater is adequately treated. Sewage sludge, which was once sought after as a fertilizer, is now a toxic waste in many industrial areas because of contamination by heavy metals, especially cadmium. Groundwater contamination also has increased sharply: over the past 30 years, average nitrate levels in groundwater in the built-up areas of cities and towns rose from 30 to 120 milligrams per liter (52).

An analysis of five rivers in Hungary (the Kapos, Zala, Zagyva, and border sections of the Danube and Tisza) found steady deterioration in water quality over

Table 5.4 Nitrogen Dioxide Emissions, 1989

Country	Total Emissions (000 metric tons of NO₂/year)	Per Capita Emissions (kilograms)	Emissions Per Dollar GNP (grams)
Central Europe and the U.S.S.R.			
Albania {a}	9	2.8	2.4
Bulgaria	150	16.7	7.2
Czechoslovakia	950	60.7	7.7
Germany (Dem Rep)	708	42.6	4.4
Hungary	259	24.5	9.6
Poland	1,480	39.1	22.1
Romania {a}	390	16.8	4.9
Yugoslavia {a}	190	8.0	3.2
U.S.S.R. {b}	4,190	14.6	1.6
Western Europe and the United States			
Austria	211	27.7	1.8
Belgium	297	29.8	1.8
France	1,688	30.1	1.7
Germany (Fed Rep)	3,000	48.4	2.4
Italy	1,700	29.6	1.9
Sweden	301	35.4	1.6
United Kingdom	2,513	43.9	3.0
United States {c}	19,800	79.6	3.8

Sources:
1. Chapter 24, "Atmosphere and Climate," Table 24.5
2. Chapter 15, "Basic Economic Indicators," Table 15.1.
3. The World Bank, unpublished data (The World Bank, Washington, D.C., June 1991).

Notes:
a. Estimated emissions.
b. Emissions data for European part of U.S.S.R. only. Per capita and per dollar emissions calculated using population and GNP data for entire country.
c. 1988 emissions data.

Figure 5.2 Air Pollutants Contributed by Vehicles in Poland, 1989

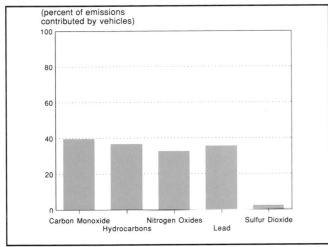

Source: Michael P. Walsh and Hans Apitz, "Motor Vehicle Pollution in Poland: The Problem at Present and a Strategy for Progress," draft paper prepared for The World Bank (October 1990), Figure 5.

Figure 5.3 Water Pollution Trends in Czechoslovakia, Selected Rivers, 1940–80

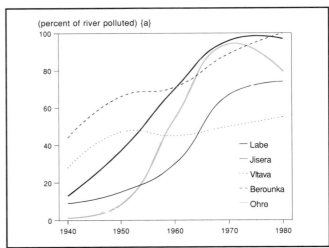

Source: Czechoslovak Academy of Science (CSAV), "State of the Development of Environment in Czechoslovakia" (CSAV, Prague, 1989), Table 2.13; cited in James R. Newman, "Draft Joint Environmental Study: Volume 2 Technical Report," prepared for the U.S. Agency for International Development and the World Bank (KBN Engineering and Applied Sciences, Gainesville, Florida, 1991), Table 5-1, p. 5-2.

Note: a. Includes rivers with water quality classifications of III and IV, defined as strong to heavy pollution.

the 1971–85 period. Budapest is responsible for the majority of the biochemical oxygen demand (BOD) in the Danube (53). (BOD, the amount of oxygen removed from the water as the organic matter in it decays, is a common water quality measurement.)

Some industries are heavy contributors of dangerous pollutants. A coal gasification plant in Espenhain, (East) Germany, discharges 4,000 cubic meters of wastewater daily, containing 20 metric tons of phenol, 2 metric tons of ammonia, and heavy metals (54). Large amounts of water pollutants in the region are carried into the Black and Baltic seas, both of which are now heavily polluted. (See Chapter 12, "Oceans and Coasts," Box 12.4.)

Agricultural Sources

Agricultural activities are a significant source of water pollution in the region. For example, in eastern Czechoslovakia, fertilizer and animal waste runoff from farms is considered the primary cause of surface and groundwater nitrate pollution. It is estimated that 80 percent of the surface water in rivers in eastern Czechoslovakia is polluted by animal waste products (55). (See Chapter 7, "Food and Agriculture," and Chapter 11, "Freshwater.")

Table 5.5 Forest Defoliation in Europe, 1989

(percent of trees affected)

Country{a}	Moderate to Severe (Classes 2-4)	No Defoliation (Class 0)
Byelorussia (R)	76.2	15.0
Kaliningrad (R)	35.0	26.9
Czechoslovakia (N)	33.0	26.0
Poland (N)	31.9	22.0
United Kingdom (N)	28.0	41.0
Denmark (N)	26.0	48.0
Bulgaria (N)	24.9	40.5
Slovenia (R)	22.6	60.3
Finland (N)	18.0	60.1
German Dem Rep (N)	16.4	45.7
Germany, Fed Rep (N)	15.9	47.1
Norway (N){b}	14.8	57.0
Sweden (N){b}	12.9	51.9
Hungary (N)	12.7	63.6
Switzerland (N)	12.0	57.0
Italy (N)	9.1	75.8
France (N)	5.6	79.3
Austria (N)	4.4	74.6
Spain (N)	3.3	78.0

Source: Christer Ågren, "Forest Decline Continues," *Acid News* (December 1990), p. 5.

Notes:

a. Based on nationwide (N) or regional (R) figures for all tree species, unless noted.

b. Conifers only.

Forest and Soil Damage

Forest damage surveys conducted in Europe in 1989 indicate that defoliation damage has increased, especially in the mountainous regions of Germany (both East and West), Czechoslovakia, and Poland. Damage to Norway spruce appears to have remained stable or even decreased slightly in most of Europe, but serious deterioration was reported in Czechoslovakia and Poland. The condition of Scots pines was generally unchanged, but older trees were deteriorating in Bulgaria, Hungary, and (East) Germany. The defoliation of oaks worsened; in Czechoslovakia, more than 60 percent of older oaks were moderately to severely damaged. Bulgaria reported that 25,000 hectares of silver firs, out of a total of 35,000 hectares, are severely damaged or dying (56).

Overall, Czechoslovakia and Poland both reported that roughly one third of their forests were moderately to severely damaged. With the exception of Byelorussia and Kaliningrad in the Soviet Union, this is the most extensive reported damage in the continent. (See Table 5.5.)

Soil degradation—caused by factors such as acid deposition, mining operations, and the dumping of industrial, residential, and agricultural waste—is a serious problem in some parts of the region. In Bulgaria, for example, 300 square kilometers of land adjacent to metallurgical plants are severely polluted by heavy metals (57). In Poland, measurements of lead

Figure 5.4 Transboundary Pollution in Central Europe, 1987

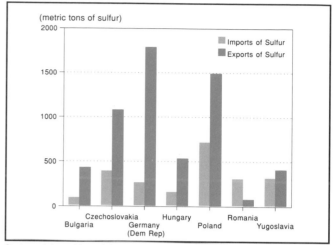

Source: Adapted from data in "Emissions are Falling...But is it Enough," *Acid Magazine* (September 8, 1989), p. 5.

and cadmium in the soil of the Upper Silesian towns of Olkusz and Slawkow are the highest ever recorded in the world (58).

The effects on the land are particularly evident in the industrial regions. In Poland, just 3 of the country's 27 identified "ecological hazard" zones account for 67 percent of the nation's stored waste and 75 percent of wastes generated annually: Upper Silesia, with 304 million metric tons stored and 55 million metric tons generated annually; Legnica-Glogow, with 203 million metric tons stored and 26 million metric tons generated; and Rybnik, with 175 million metric tons stored and 32 million metric tons generated annually (59).

Transboundary Pollution

Substantial quantities of air and water pollutants generated in one country are transmitted to others. (See Figure 5.4.) According to data compiled by the European Monitoring and Evaluation Programme (EMEP), Czechoslovakia emitted about 1 million metric tons of sulfur in 1987, but only about 36 percent of that amount was deposited in Czechoslovakia. Much of the rest came down in countries such as Poland and the Soviet Union. In Sweden, only about 12 percent of sulfur deposition is from Swedish sources (60).

Transboundary pollution—such as the chlorine emissions from a Romanian factory that blow across the Danube to Ruse, Bulgaria—has often been a politically sensitive issue in the region. Similarly, pollutants dumped into a river in one country can affect downstream users in other countries (61).

NEXT STEPS: WEIGHING THE OPTIONS

Central Europe's political and economic transformation provides an important new opportunity to assess the region's true environmental conditions and to begin tackling its problems. The region's governments face tight spending constraints and must carefully assess how to use their limited resources. Energy policy, especially as it relates to the use of coal in the northern group of countries, is a particularly critical issue. Until market systems gather momentum, government policies that manage markets effectively—requiring polluters to pay, for example, and encouraging them to reduce the quantity of pollutants, coupled with effective enforcement—could have significant long-term benefits.

For most inhabitants of the region, the question of jobs currently takes precedence over environmental protection. Nevertheless, a continuing effort to assess conditions in the region and accurately describe their impact on human health and economic growth will play a crucial role in any effort to improve environmental conditions in the coming decade. Scientists, educators, policymakers, and nongovernmental organizations all have roles to play in this effort.

For the immediate future, the most critical issues seem to be the following: managing market forces (i.e., using efficiency and market incentives to benefit the environment); devising environmental policies that provide the greatest benefits for the least cost; and building realistic, enforceable systems of laws and regulations. As Box 5.4 indicates, a variety of Western governments, lending institutions, and private organizations are eager to help the countries of the region address these problems.

Of the many environmental problems in the region, the most significant seems to be the impact of coal burning on air pollution and subsequently on public health. Many options are available to reduce emissions from coal burning. Given the region's lack of funds, the best choices seem to be the following: using higher prices to force efficiency improvements; investing in energy conservation; switching to cleaner fuels, such as natural gas; investing in relatively inexpensive pollution control devices such as electrostatic precipitators (to control particulates); and coal washing (a process in which finely ground coal is suspended in a liquid medium and denser, foreign material sinks to the bottom, thus reducing the amount of sulfur and ash).

Eventually, economic growth will bring about beneficial structural changes, but it will also substantially boost energy demand and put additional stress on the environment. For example, if Central European incomes grow to match Western levels, living area (floor space) per person could grow from the current 15 square meters to an estimated 37 square meters by 2025 (in the case of (East) Germany, to 50 square meters). Income growth will also create demand for household amenities such as appliances. Similarly, car ownership per capita could more than double by 2025 (62).

How all of this growth is regulated—what kind of fuel economy new cars will achieve, whether household appliances and new residential buildings will be energy efficient—will make a great difference in the environmental quality of the region. Environmental protection must be linked to growth through effective laws and regulations.

Many of the region's countries are beginning to tackle these problems. For example, in November 1990, Poland became the first country in the region to approve a comprehensive national environmental policy. The policy recommends the following actions:

■ Closing or restructuring the 80 worst polluting enterprises in the country, as well as 500 additional plants to be included in a list prepared by provincial governments;
■ Increasing the size of the coal washing program;
■ Noticeably reducing low and dispersed emissions of dust and gases and;
■ Improving drinking water supplies for urban areas.

By the year 2000, the plan targets reductions in air pollution (reduce SO_2 emissions by 30 percent from 1980 levels, NO_x emissions by 10 percent, and particulates by about 50 percent) and water pollution (reduce pollution loads into rivers by 50 percent) (63).

Managing Market Forces

Market forces can be brutal judges of economic efficiency. For example, Poland's 1990 stabilization program, which began to phase out energy-related budget subsidies and institute market-oriented energy prices, resulted in a substantial decrease in industrial output and thus in a reduction in emissions. The main reductions are thought to have been in water pollution (as measured by biochemical oxygen demand), which may have dropped about 33 percent, and in particulate emissions, which are down about 20–25 percent (64).

The most polluting industrial facilities are often the most inefficient, so market forces will result in the closure of many of the worst polluters. This already is the case, for example, with part of (East) Germany's chemical industry (65). Unlike other nations in the region, however, East Germany's integration with West Germany provides some economic resilience, which makes the closure of plants somewhat easier to absorb.

Market forces, however, are a mixed blessing for the environment. Competition from the European Community and the desperate need for foreign investment could make these countries pollution havens. Bronislaw Kaminski, Poland's former minister of environmental protection, has noted that "one of the first effects of relaxing the straight-jacket that hampered the spirit of entrepreneurship in Poland [was] private imports of hazardous wastes (disguised as 'raw materials') from West European countries . . . . Incidents like that have forced us to design effective policy tools as quickly as possible" (66). Such incidents apparently are not isolated: a Greenpeace International report found evidence of 64 trade schemes in which Poland was targeted to receive Western hazardous waste (67).

There are signs that the governments of the region are considering the environmental impacts of new enterprises. The Polish government stopped a contract between (West) German and Polish firms to reprocess 60,000 metric tons of zinc concentrate per year; the arrangement would have left Poland with less energy and more waste product. Hungary passed a decree in October 1990 prohibiting imports and exports based on differences in environmental standards. The envi-

Box 5.4 Building New Partnerships

Central Europe's effort to restore and manage its environment is being helped by new partnerships with Western governments and institutions.

INTERNATIONAL LENDING INSTITUTIONS

Banking institutions are actively building new bridges to the region. The new Bank for European Reconstruction and Development (BERD), with 42 charter members and an initial appropriation of $12 billion, was established in 1990 specifically to channel funds for projects to rebuild Central Europe. BERD, which began operations in 1991, is required to devote 40 percent of its loan portfolio to infrastructure projects and 60 percent to private sector initiatives. Provisions for environmental protection and sustainable development were incorporated directly into the bank's enabling legislation (1).

Other banks are also helping. The Nordic Investment Bank—jointly owned by the governments of Denmark, Finland, Iceland, Norway, and Sweden—will support commercial joint venture projects in the region that will also help clean up the Nordic environment (2). The European Investment Bank has been active in Poland, Hungary, and Yugoslavia, lending Hungary money for the modernization of their power grid and supporting improvements in domestic gas production in Poland (3).

The World Bank has provided an $18 million loan to Poland to identify and help address the highest priority environmental problems in Poland and to help establish a decentralized system of environmental management (4). Additional World Bank loans to Poland include $250 million to increase domestic production of natural gas and support energy price reform, an estimated $100 million to help the heavy chemicals and coal-mining sectors with environmentally sound restructuring, and

$150 million for modernization of district heating networks. The Bank has $398 million in loans to Hungary, primarily for three energy conservation projects, a petroleum project, and a power project. Additional environmental loans are anticipated to Czechoslovakia and Yugoslavia (5).

GOVERNMENT AID PROGRAMS

Government-to-government aid programs also are growing. A World Wildlife Fund-International survey estimated that, through 1990, Western governments had committed $728 million for environmental projects, including $123 million through the European Community (EC), $105 million from the United States, and about $500 million from other industrialized nations (6).

Activities in Europe are coordinated by the European Commission through the EC Phare Programme (Poland/Hungary Aid for Restructuring of Economies, which now also includes Bulgaria, Czechoslovakia, Yugoslavia, and (East) Germany). In July 1990, the Commission produced an "Action Plan" that attempted to give some overall direction to the diversity of aid programs of G-24 countries to the region. The EC Phare Programme also administers EC funds for the region.

TRANSBOUNDARY PROBLEMS

Many other European governments are actively assisting Central European governments with their environmental problems. Finland is interested in reducing air and water pollution in Poland and the Soviet Union. Sweden has allocated $180 million for assistance to the region, including $40 million to Poland for sewage treatment on the Vistula and Oder rivers and for air pollution control equipment (7).

The countries of the region are looking for regional and international partners to participate in the effort to reduce water pollution. For example, Germany, Czechoslo-

vakia, and the European Community have signed an international treaty to protect the 1,500-kilometer Elbe River, which rises in Czechoslovakia and flows through the German cities of Dresden and Magdeburg before emptying into the North Sea. The same model could be applied to other rivers, such as the Oder and the Danube (8).

REGIONAL INITIATIVES

The cooperative effort to clean up the Baltic Sea is being revived. The Baltic Marine Environment Protection Commission (also known as the Helsinki Commission, or HELCOM), which was originally established in 1980, met in 1988 and agreed to reduce emissions of pollutants to 50 percent of 1987 levels by 1995. That commitment was reinforced by a declaration in September 1990 that was signed by Denmark, Finland, Germany, Poland, Sweden, the Soviet Union, Norway, Czechoslovakia, and the European Commission. An action plan will identify 100 priority sites.

The declaration commits the countries to install the best available technology for all important industries (including chemical, fertilizer, and pulp and paper industries) and to promote the installation and improvement of municipal sewage treatment plants. The World Bank, European Investment Bank, European Bank for Reconstruction and Development, and Nordic Investment Bank have all taken an active role in the initiative (9).

A variety of other new relationships are springing up. For example, five countries—Austria, Czechoslovakia, Hungary, Italy, and Yugoslavia—have started the "Pentagonal Initiative." The group will be working cooperatively to harmonize environmental monitoring and data systems, waste management, and nuclear safety (10). The United Nations Development Programme and United Nations Environment Programme also have participated in projects in the region.

---

ronment ministry is preparing an act on the environmental regulation of imported technology (68).

The Impact of Higher Prices

Countries with higher energy prices generally use energy much more efficiently than those with lower energy prices. Among the industrialized (OECD) countries, roughly 50 percent of intercountry differences in energy intensity can be explained by prices. A comparative study of energy conservation in the OECD countries and Central Europe found that prices were the principal reason for Central Europe's higher energy intensity (69).

Poland, for example, has instituted higher energy prices and substantial shifts in the relative prices of various fuels. The most dramatic change should be a large increase in the price of coal relative to oil and gas. The price changes vary from industry to industry, but, in general, the price of liquid fuels relative to solid fuels should be reduced by 33–50 percent.

The changes in relative prices of fuels should create major new incentives for fuel switching, although initial responses may be slow because managers are not used to operating under hard budget constraints or responding to price signals (70).

Increased coal prices should encourage mines to produce higher quality coal, which will improve energy efficiency and reduce emissions. If pollution charges are

Box 5.4

INFORMATION EXCHANGE

Western governments also are moving rapidly to provide the information needed for improved environmental management in the region. One element of this effort is the Regional Environmental Center for Central and Eastern Europe, which is located in Budapest and opened in September 1990. Start-up funding of $12 million was provided by the United States, the European Community, Austria, Hungary, Canada, Finland, the Netherlands, and Norway. The center is operated independently and gives high priority to the role of nongovernmental organizations. It serves as a clearinghouse for the dissemination of information about Western environmental technologies and management strategies, helps area governments establish environmental institutions, and mediates between environmental groups and local governments (11).

Western environmental groups and foundations have been active in the region. The U.S. World Wildlife Fund/Conservation Foundation has started a program that includes an effort to describe the role of environmental groups in the United States. The U.S. National Academy of Sciences has held joint workshops with its Polish and Romanian counterparts on topics such as energy efficiency and natural resource management. The Institute for European Environmental Policy, Friends of the Earth International, World Environment Center, Management Sciences for Health, Environmental Law Institute, Rockefeller Brothers Fund, World Conservation Union, Ecological Studies Institute, International Institute for Applied Systems Analysis, and many other groups also are actively interested in the region (12).

TECHNOLOGY TRANSFER

The governments and industries of the region face many critical choices about the kinds of environmental technologies they should choose. In a recent study under-

written by the U.S. Environmental Protection Agency, Central Europe was singled out as an area where technology transfer could have potential impact and where there was an indigenous capability to utilize the technology. The study also recommended that U.S. policymakers encourage all nations to adopt environmental standards, both health- and performance-based, covering imports and exports of products, equipment, and processes (13).

The U.S. Environmental Protection Agency and others have provided seed money to help the government of Poland start independent, nonprofit energy efficiency centers. The centers will identify ways to increase energy efficiency, help indigenous industries develop their own energy efficiency programs, and expedite private initiatives for the introduction of energy conservation technologies (14). In May 1991, the U.S. Department of Energy awarded a $7.7 million contract to a U.S. company to supply emissions control technology to retrofit a boiler at the Skawina power plant in Krakow, Poland. The retrofit project is intended to demonstrate a U.S. technology that could be duplicated for other Central European coal-fired boilers (15). Other U.S. projects in Krakow will target reduction of low-level emissions from heating systems and small industry.

In October 1990, the European Parliament approved ECU 30 million ($36 million) from the EC Phare budget for the transfer of technology to Central Europe. The program is intended as a prelude to two larger technology transfer projects (16).

References and Notes

1. Tamara Raye Crockett and Cynthia B. Schultz, "Environmental Protection Issues in Eastern Europe," *International Environment Reporter* (June 1990), p. 261.

2. "First NIB Environmental Investments in Eastern Europe May Be Approved by Fall," *International Environment Reporter* (July 1990), p. 299.

3. World Wildlife Fund-International (WWF-I), "Who Knows Where the Money Goes? A Survey of Investments in Central and Eastern Europe" (WWF-I, Brussels, 1991), pp. 30-31.

4. "Hungary, Poland Said at Top of List For U.S. Aid to Stem Environmental Damage," *International Environment Reporter* (June 1990), p. 231.

5. Richard Ackerman, Senior Policy Analyst, Environment Division, The World Bank, Washington, D.C., 1991 (personal communication).

6. *Op. cit.* 3, p. vii.

7. *Op. cit.* 3, pp. 2, 17, 22.

8. "International Treaty to Protect Elbe Signed by Germans, Czechs, EC Official," *International Environment Reporter* (October 24, 1990), pp. 436-437.

9. Baltic Marine Environment Protection Commission, "The Ad Hoc High Level Task Force: First Meeting," press release (November 1, 1990) and Conference Document No. 1, Annex A, pp. 5-6.

10. "Five Nations Urge Regional Role in Addressing Environmental Issues," *International Environment Reporter* (August 1990), p. 337.

11. "Eastern, Central Europe To Get Help From New Center on Environmental Clean Up," *International Environment Reporter* (September 1990), p. 357.

12. World Wildlife Fund and The Conservation Foundation (WWF/CF), *Central and Eastern Europe Environmental Newsletter* (WWF/CF, Washington, D.C., January 15, 1991), pp. 1-6.

13. U.S. Environmental Protection Agency (EPA), *Final Report to the Administrator of the Environmental Protection Agency from the International Environmental Technology Transfer Board* (EPA, Washington, D.C., December 1990), pp. 13-15.

14. "Energy-Saving Center Planned To Help Solve Poland's Environmental Crisis," *International Environment Reporter* (September 1990), p. 359.

15. Peter Cover, Program Manager, Technology Exports, Office of Fossil Energy, U.S. Department of Energy, September 1991 (personal communication).

16. *Op. cit.* 3, p. 6.

increased and enforced, new incentives will be created to use high-grade coals and clean low-grade coals (71).

Effective price reform of the energy sector depends on more general changes in the structure of incentives and constraints under which all enterprises operate. Management training may be an important facet of this overall change. For example, devising a program of energy audits—designed to highlight possibilities for achieving greater fuel efficiency—could help give managers the skills to respond to the new pattern of price incentives (72).

The environmental benefits of energy price reform should be significant. Overall, it is estimated that Poland's policy of increasing energy prices to world price levels should lead to a 15 percent reduction in air

pollutants by 1993, compared to a projected increase of 22 percent without this change (73).

Managing Growth: The Case of Motor Vehicles

The rise of market economies will almost certainly create substantial new demand for automobiles.

The possibility of a major new market for auto sales in Central Europe has not escaped the attention of Western auto makers. By early 1991, Fiat had projects in Poland, Yugoslavia, and the Soviet Union totaling $8 billion and Volkswagen won a competition to acquire a substantial stake in Czechoslovakia's Skoda plant for $6.4 billion. Ford, General Motors, and Suzuki also had made investments in the region (74).

The net result may be creation of a new pan-European production base (75). The growth hasn't been trouble-free, however; automakers have often found themselves frustrated by problems with unusable plants, inadequate parts suppliers, unmotivated workers, and uncertain free-market reforms (76).

Most assessments, nevertheless, suggest that auto sales should grow rapidly in the region over the coming decades. In Poland, for example, new car sales will probably rise from the current 150,000 cars per year to over 300,000 cars in the next few years if the country's economy develops (77). This increase will likely cause a substantial increase in air pollution, especially in urban centers such as Warsaw.

Effective government policies can substantially reduce the environmental impact of new cars. For example, Poland's environment minister has decided that all new cars sold in Poland within five years will be required to meet the emission limits of the European Community (EC). EC standards require catalytic converters on virtually all new cars by the end of 1992. In addition, all new cars will be fueled with unleaded gasoline, and diesel vehicles will be required to gradually lower particulate emissions (78).

Periodic inspection and maintenance of all vehicles has proven effective in Western countries, where it eventually can reduce emissions of hydrocarbons and carbon monoxide by about 25 percent and NO_x by about 10 percent. Well-run programs in Central Europe should be able to achieve similar reductions (79).

In view of the health problems associated with lead, Central European countries may consider an aggressive program to phase out lead in petrol. Options include reducing the lead content of leaded petrol to 0.15 grams per liter as rapidly as possible, increasing the availability of unleaded petrol (either through relatively expensive adjustments in refining capacity or through increased reliance on imports), and adjusting prices so that unleaded petrol is cheaper (or no more expensive) than leaded. Several European countries have increased the tax on leaded fuel and decreased it on unleaded fuel, so that overall taxes remain the same (at least initially) but the economic incentive to use unleaded fuel increases (80).

Cars in Central Europe are now relatively energy-efficient, consuming about 8.7 liters per 100 km (27 miles per gallon) (81). That figure could easily decline in the coming years if demand for larger cars increases. Nevertheless, improvements in automobile fuel economy could yield substantial energy savings. Increasing fuel economy to 5 liters per 100 km (47 mpg), in combination with other energy saving measures, could reduce transportation energy demand in 2025 by 30 percent (about 1.5 exajoules). Even with this effort, the increased number of cars in the region could increase energy demand by 50 percent over current levels (82).

Looking for Least-Cost Solutions

In ordering priorities for environmental cleanup, the countries of the region generally are looking for the lowest-cost options that will do the most to improve public health. The options include selected pollution controls, fuel switching, and investments in energy conservation and energy efficiency, and—in a few carefully selected cases—the installation of flue gas desulfurization equipment.

Coping with Coal: Low-Cost Options

Among air pollutants from coal, particulates are usually considered at least as damaging to health as sulfur dioxide. Particulates are also relatively less expensive to remove: in the case of high stacks, cutting particulate emissions by 60 percent from 1980 levels in Poland would cost about $500 per metric ton; whereas reducing sulfur dioxide by 50 percent would cost about $1,900 per metric ton. For large energy consumers, one relatively low-cost option would be to install and/or properly operate electrostatic precipitators to remove particulates (83). About 50 percent of sulfur dioxide emissions could be removed by coal washing, a relatively low-cost option (84).

Millions of Poland's homes and buildings are heated with small stoves that burn bituminous coal; flue gases from these stoves are the predominant contributor to air pollution in towns (85). Poland and the other nations of the region could save a great deal of energy and substantially reduce emissions by expanding district heating systems and using combined heat and power (CHP) production in major urban centers. Even when burning low-quality coal, modern CHP stations—such as one built in Stockholm that uses a relatively expensive pressurized fluidized bed combustion technology—can eliminate about 90 percent of sulfur emissions, provide district heating for large urban areas and still provide the same efficiency for electricity production as a normal Polish lignite-fired plant (86). Using natural gas to power CHP plants would provide even more substantial environmental benefits. There are several obstacles to CHP development, however, including cost and a lack of practical maintenance experience (87).

Modern CHP plants in urban areas would reduce the need to transmit electricity over long distances. During long-distance transmission, Poland's national grid loses power equivalent to about 10 percent of the country's entire electricity output. Cutting losses to the (West) German level could annually save about 6 million metric tons of bituminous coal and reduce sulfur dioxide emissions by about 120,000 metric tons (88).

Flue Gas Desulfurization: A High-Cost Option.
An important but costly option for major plants in the region is to install flue gas control technologies that would substantially reduce emissions of sulfur dioxide and nitrogen oxides. This option seems realistic in (East) Germany. In 1983, the West German Bundestag passed a law requiring all large power plants to install flue gas cleaning equipment. Most major electricity suppliers have reduced their sulfur emissions by 70–75 percent from 1983 levels and have a similar goal for nitrogen oxides.

Even emissions from plants using low-quality lignite can be dramatically reduced. When one (West) German plant burning low-quality lignite was fitted with wet flue gas desulfurization equipment in 1988, the plant's sulfur dioxide emissions were cut by 85 percent, to 20,000 metric tons per year (89). Although expensive and complex, the long-term benefits of this technology could be dramatic. Eight power stations in (East) Germany emit about 2.1 million metric tons of sulfur dioxide annually (90), or about 40 percent of the total from that region (91).

Installing flue gas controls on existing plants in other countries may not be practical because of the high cost. They may be practical for new plants (or plants under construction) such as Belchatow in Poland. By mid-1991, the Polish government had signed a contract to install desulfurization equipment in 2 of the 12 blocks at Belchatow, using a Dutch wet-lime method; negotiations on other blocks were continuing. Polish officials estimate the installation will cut total SO_2 emissions from 337,000 metric tons to 277,000 metric tons, or about 18 percent from 1990 levels (92).

Adjusting the Fuel Mix

Once environmental factors are taken into account, switching to natural gas fuel appears to be a cost-effective option, especially for the hundreds of small- and medium-sized coal-fired industrial and building heating systems. The Soviet Union has been a substantial supplier of oil and gas to Central Europe in the past, but those sales were under soft-currency trading terms that are no longer available. Soviet oil and gas to Central Europe must now be paid for in hard currency and at world market prices, a major new economic burden for the region. Nevertheless, the Soviet Union has the pipelines in place and the spare capacity to export substantial volumes of gas to Central Europe (93).

Converting a boiler from coal to gas fuel eliminates all emissions of sulfur dioxide and nearly all particulates, reduces emissions of nitrogen oxides by about 45 percent, and emits about 57 percent less carbon dioxide (a major greenhouse gas) per unit of energy (94). In addition, it provides substantial savings over coal in the maintenance requirements of a power plant.

As a possible supplement to imported natural gas, Central Europe could exploit reserves of coalbed methane. Coalbed methane would be a competitively priced fuel that would benefit the environment by reducing emissions of methane (also a major greenhouse gas). Extracting coalbed methane would also increase mine safety by lowering methane concentrations in the mines (95).

Nuclear Energy: A High-Cost Option.

Nuclear energy holds the attraction of emitting few pollutants into the atmosphere; but it is costly, technically difficult to operate, creates a dangerous waste product, and—as the Chernobyl disaster vividly demonstrated—carries grave risks for the public. Over the past two decades, 23 nuclear plants—using either Soviet technology or design—were built in the region. Considerable concern has been expressed about the quality of the materials in those plants. Until recently, there was virtually no exchange of information among operators about in-

cidents or operations experiences, a process considered vital to the safety of Western reactors (96).

It was not until 1990, for example, that (East) Germany revealed that the Bruno Leuschner nuclear plant near Greifswald suffered a near-disaster in 1975, when 11 of 12 cooling pumps at the reactor failed during a fire (97). The German government has closed down all five Soviet-built reactors at Greifswald and a pilot plant in Rheinsberg; Chancellor Helmut Kohl told the German Bundestag in October 1990 that it was "irresponsible to operate them after Chernobyl" (98).

The Chernobyl disaster created great anxiety over the safety of nuclear power plants in the region. The government of Austria, for example, is seeking the closure of the Czechoslovak nuclear station at Borovnica. Austria has offered technical advice on decommissioning and compensation for the electric power that would be lost by closure of the plant (99). Nevertheless, Czechoslovakia is going ahead with the construction of two plants (Temelin 1 and 2) and probably with two more (Temelin 3 and 4) (100). In addition, the state-owned Electricité de France has also proposed the building of two 900-megawatt nuclear plants in Hungary (101).

Energy Conservation

Energy efficiency improvements hold great promise in the region. In Poland, for example, conservation options in industry include: in the iron and steel industry, replacement of the open hearth furnace with the basic oxygen furnace; and in the chemicals industry, modernizing refinery and petrochemical equipment. Opportunities in the residential sector include insulating buildings, metering individual houses and apartments, market pricing of energy, and district heating. In the public transportation area, use of mass transit could be encouraged and fuel efficiency rates maintained (102) (103).

The most cost-effective investments, according to one study of Poland, would be improving space heating management, reducing electricity transmission and distribution losses, insulating buildings, producing better automation and measurement devices, improving existing industrial equipment, and cogenerating electricity and heat. Greater energy savings could be achieved, at a net cost, through such options as railway electrification, improved coal quality, and new industrial technology (104). (See Table 5.6.)

If Poland were to aggressively implement an energy conservation strategy, it could save about 40 percent of current total energy demand by the year 2005. To do that, it would have to invest about 1.25 percent of its gross domestic product annually into energy efficiency, but that would be less than the cost of supplying the same amount of energy (105).

An effective, comprehensive effort to improve energy efficiency could hold energy demand in the region at the current annual level (about 18 exajoules) through the year 2025. Without such an effort, energy

Table 5.6 Monetary Savings/Cost of Selected Energy Saving Options in Poland, 2005

Energy Savings Options	Net Savings Per Gigajoule Saved (in 1984 zlotys)	Potential Energy Savings (petajoules)
Options That Save Money		
Heating efficiency improvements	325	56
Reduction in distribution and transmission losses	223	206
Building insulation	207	426
Automation and measurements improvement	138	562
Existing industrial equipment	68	835
Cogeneration	45	908
Options That Cost Money		
Railway electrification	(187)	968
Coal quality improvement	(427)	1,115

Source: S. Sitnicki, K. Budzinski, J. Juda, *et al.*, "Poland: Opportunities for Carbon Emissions Control," paper prepared for the U.S. Agency for International Development (Battelle Memorial Institute, Pacific Northwest Laboratories, Richland, Washington, 1990), p. 15.

Note: 1 gigajoule = 1,000,000,000 joules = 947,800 Btus; 1 petajoule = 1,000,000 gigajoules.

demand can be expected to increase by 70 percent (to about 31 exajoules annually) by 2025 (106).

Water Pollution

Cost is a daunting problem that limits efforts to reduce water pollution in the region. As part of the German government's initial attack on environmental problems in the five new eastern states, a $1.6 billion pilot program was approved in late 1990 that included 15 projects designed to improve industrial wastewater handling and sewage treatment (107).

In the short run, industrial processes could be carefully examined for opportunities to reduce the amount of waste generated. To reinforce that strategy, governments could create funding mechanisms and economic incentives for investments in pollution control equipment. Alternatively, they could impose substantial, enforceable fees on emissions, making it more cost-effective for industries (or municipalities) to invest in waste minimization or treatment facilities rather than continue to pollute.

In Poland, the discharge of saline minewater pollutes rivers. Proposals to divert the minewater through pipelines or build a desalination plant may be too expensive. Removing price subsidies, which would force inefficient mines to close, and phasing in a system of fees on discharges may prove to be the best answer (108).

Developing Effective Laws and Regulations

Led by Poland, Hungary, and Czechoslovakia, the countries of the region are slowly beginning to overhaul existing laws and regulations. For example:

■ In Hungary, 1991 laws required firms building or expanding plants to submit environmental impact assessments before receiving construction permits; required all vehicles to undergo annual emission inspections; offered tax incentives to vehicles with catalytic convert-

ers; and reequipped about 5,000 government vehicles to reduce lead emissions. The government was also planning to devise a new tax or fee system to stem the further degradation of air and water resources and a freedom-of-information act that would allow public access to government data and allow the government to publish material on polluting enterprises (109).

■ In Czechoslovakia, three environmental agencies are actively drafting new legislation, despite uncertainties about the distribution of power between the federal and republic governments. The three agencies have collectively drafted a general environmental law that anticipates command-and-control laws and environmental taxes; gives citizens the right to get information about the environment and makes companies obliged to provide it; allows citizens to claim rights under the environmental laws in court; and requires environmental impact assessments before the initiation of any construction activity, use of natural resources, or production of products. The agencies have also produced a draft air pollution law that contains both taxes and command-and-control requirements, and a draft waste law similar to the U.S. and European Community programs (110).

The drafting of new environmental laws has been difficult. For instance, the laws anticipate giving the public access to information, but there is, as yet, little experience with developing and using that information. Similarly, there is little experience in preparing environmental impact assessments and little ability on the part of local governments or private organizations to analyze and respond to such assessments (111).

■ East Germany became subject to the environmental laws of West Germany and the European Community when it formally joined West Germany in October 1990. The European Commission's waste management, water quality, and air pollution provisions will be enforced in East Germany in 1996 (112).

In addition to laws, new regulations that provide incentives to invest in pollution control equipment or stronger penalties for polluters are being developed. Poland provides incentives for environmental protection, including a three-year tax exemption for joint ventures to manufacture pollution control equipment and a 100 percent tax deduction for the purchase and installation of pollution control equipment (113).

Many of the countries in the region already have elaborate systems of fees and fines in place, but regulations have been weakly enforced or fines too small to be effective. Beginning January 1, 1991, the Polish Ministry of Environment increased fees for resource use 15-fold and fines 27-fold, with further adjustments for inflation. The success of these new fees and fines may depend on the reform of enterprises (including greater competitive pressures and the use of "hard" budgets that do not allow managers to pass on the cost of fines to customers or the state) and the creation of local governmental units with reasonably broad tax bases and the staff and legal resources to enforce the regulations (114).

This Chapter was written by World Resources Senior Editor Robert Livernash. The box on environment and health in Central Europe was written by Barry S. Levy, Director of the Program for Environment and Health at Management Sciences for Health, Boston; and Clyde Hertzman, Director, Division of Occupational and Environmental Health in the Department of Health Care and Epidemiology, The University of British Columbia, Vancouver.

References and Notes

1. Marlise Simons, "Rising Iron Curtain Exposes Haunting Veil of Polluted Air," *New York Times* (April 8, 1990), p. 14.

2. Marlise Simons, "Pollution's Toll in Eastern Europe: Stumps Where Great Trees Once Grew," *New York Times* (March 19, 1990), p. 9.

3. Marlise Simons, "Central Europe's Coal Wasteland: Progress, Yes, but at What Cost?" *New York Times* (April 1, 1990), p. 1.

4. Celestine Bohlen, "Through a Thick Veil of Soot, Romanian City Faces Future," *New York Times* (March 5, 1990), p. 1.

5. Marlise Simons, "New Taint on East German Pollution," *New York Times* (September 9, 1990), p. 20.

6. *The State of the Hungarian Environment*, Don Hinrichsen and György Enyedi, eds. (Hungarian Academy of Sciences, Ministry for Environment and Water Management, and the Hungarian Central Statistical Office, Budapest, 1990), p. 51.

7. World Wildlife Fund and The Conservation Foundation (WWF/CF), *Central and Eastern Europe Environmental Newsletter* (WWF/CF, Washington, D.C., January 15, 1991), p. 4.

8. Josef Vavroušek, *The Environment in Czechoslovakia* (State Commission for Science, Technology and Investments, Prague, May 1990), p. 22.

9. The World Bank, "Poland Environment Strategy Study," draft summary, conclusions and recommendations (The World Bank, Washington, D.C., 1991), p. iii.

10. The World Bank, "Poland—The Environment," draft (The World Bank, Washington, D.C., 1989), pp. 59, 68.

11. Stanislaw Gomulka, *Growth, Innovation and Reform in Eastern Europe* (University of Wisconsin Press, Madison, Wisconsin, 1986), pp. 34-35.

12. Jeremy Russell, "Environmental Issues in Eastern Europe: Setting an Agenda" (Royal Institute of International Affairs and World Conservation Union, London, 1990), p. 21.

13. Zbigniew Bochniarz, "Economic Instruments of Environmental Policy in East European Countries" (Hubert H. Humphrey Institute of Public Affairs, University of Minnesota, Minneapolis, Minnesota, 1989), pp. 1-4.

14. William U. Chandler, *The Changing Role of the Market in National Economies: Worldwatch Paper 72* (Worldwatch Institute, Washington, D.C., 1986), pp. 6-7.

15. *Ibid.*, p. 17.

16. Janos Kornai, *Contradictions and Dilemmas: Studies on the Socialist Economy and Society* (MIT Press, Cambridge, Mass., and London, 1986), pp. 33-51.

17. *Op. cit.* 14, p. 19.

18. Zbigniew Bochniarz, Visiting Professor, Hubert H. Humphrey Institute of Public Affairs, University of Minnesota, Minneapolis, Minnesota, 1991 (personal communication).

19. Piotr Wilczynski, "Environmental Management in Centrally-Planned Non-Market Economies of Eastern Europe," World Bank Environment Working Paper No. 35 (The World Bank, Washington, D.C., July 1990), p. 9.

20. *Ibid.*, p. 11.

21. *Ibid.*, p. 8.

22. Richard Ackerman, Senior Policy Analyst, Environment Division, The World Bank, Washington, D.C., 1991 (personal communication).

23. *Op. cit.* 12, p. 22.

24. *Op. cit.* 19, p. 39.

25. Duncan Fisher, East European Project Coordinator, The Ecological Studies Institute, London, 1991 (personal communication).

26. Miklos Persanyi, Senior Advisor, Hungarian Ministry for Environment, Budapest, 1991 (personal communication).

27. Zygmunt Fura, "Institutions: The Polish Ecological Club," *Environment*, Vol. 27, No. 9 (November 1985), pp. 4-5.

28. William U. Chandler, Senior Scientist, Battelle Memorial Institute, Pacific Northwest Laboratories, Washington, D.C., 1991 (personal communication).

29. Jean Pierre Lasota, "Darkness at Noon: Time is Running Out for Poland's Environment," *The Sciences*, Vol. 27 (New York Academy of Sciences, New York, July-August 1987), p. 28.

30. Hilary F. French, *Green Revolutions: Environmental Reconstruction in Eastern Europe and the Soviet Union: Worldwatch Paper No. 99* (Worldwatch Institute, Washington, D.C., November 1990), pp. 6, 32-33.

31. *Op. cit.* 28.

32. *Op. cit.* 10, p. 12.

33. *Op. cit.* 12, p. 22.

34. Randolf Granzer, "Perestroika in Energy: The Soviet Union and Eastern Europe," *The OECD Observer* (December 1988-January 1989), p. 27.

35. Stefan Björklund, "Big Sacrifices Needed to Cut East German Sulphur Emissions," *Acid Magazine*, No. 8 (September 1989), p. 20.

36. Bedrich Moldan, Environmental Scientist, Prague, Czechoslovakia, 1991 (personal communication)

37. *Op. cit.* 12, p. 7.

38. *Op. cit.* 8.

39. *Op. cit.* 12, p. 10.

40. World Resources Institute in collaboration with the United Nations Environment Programme and the United Nations Development Programme, *World Resources 1990-91* (Oxford University Press, New York, 1990), p. 352.

41. *Op. cit.* 12, p. 13.

42. *Op. cit.* 9, p. vi.

43. Michael P. Walsh and Hans Apitz, "Motor Vehicle Pollution in Poland: The Problem at Present and A Strategy for Progress," draft paper prepared for The World Bank (October 1990), p. 2.

44. *Ibid.*, p. 4.

45. Michael P. Walsh, "Motor Vehicle Pollution in Hungary: A Strategy for Progress," paper prepared for The World Bank (June 1990), p. 3.

46. *Ibid.*, p. 4.

47. International Union for Conservation of Nature and Natural Resources (IUCN), East European Program, *Environmental Status Reports: 1988/1989*, Vol. 1 (IUCN, Gland, Switzerland and Cambridge, U.K., 1990), p. 106.

48. *Op. cit.* 12, pp. 16-17.

49. *Op. cit.* 10, p. 48.

50. Jerzy Janota-Bzowski, Air Component Manager, Ministry of Environmental Protection, Warsaw, Poland, 1991 (personal communication).

51. James R. Newman, "Draft Joint Environmental Study: Volume 2, Technical Report," prepared for the U.S. Agency for International Development and The World Bank (KBN Engineering and Applied Sciences, Gainesville, Florida, 1991), p. 5-1.

52. *Op. cit.* 8, pp. 28, 33.

53. *Op. cit.* 6, pp. 70, 75.

54. *Op. cit.* 30, p. 17.

55. *Op. cit.* 51, p. 5-6.

56. Christer Ågren, "Forest decline continues," *Acid News* (December 1990), p. 4.

57. *Op. cit.* 12, p. 20.

58. *Op. cit.* 10, p. 87.

59. *Op. cit.* 10, p. 58.

60. "Measuring Deposition...and Calculating Where it Comes From," *Acid Magazine*, No. 8 (September 1989), pp. 7-8.

61. *Op. cit.* 30, pp. 16-17.

62. Stanislav Kolar and William U. Chandler, "Energy and Energy Conservation in Eastern Europe: Two Scenarios for the Future," paper prepared for the U.S. Agency for International Development Global Energy Efficiency Initiative (Battelle Memorial Institute, Pacific Northwest Laboratories, Washington, D.C., n.d.), pp. 12-14.

63. Ministry of Environmental Protection, Natural Resources, and Forestry, "National Environmental Policy" (Ministry of Environmental Protection, Natural Resources, and Forestry, Warsaw, 1990), pp. 12-13.

64. *Op. cit.* 9, pp. vii-viii.

65. *Op. cit.* 12, p. 30.

66. Bronislaw Kaminski, "Poland's Environmental Problems and Priorities," paper prepared for the International Environment Forum Meeting, World Environment Center, New York, March 13, 1990, p. 6.

67. "Greenpeace Says Poland Being Used As Dump for Industrialized Nations' Waste," *International Environment Reporter* (October 24, 1990), p. 438.

68. World Wildlife Fund-International (WWF-I), "Who Knows Where the Money Goes? A Survey of Investments in Central and Eastern Europe" (WWF-I, Brussels, 1991), p. 41.

69. Mark Kosmo, *Money to Burn? The High Costs of Energy Subsidies* (World Resources Institute, Washington, D.C., 1987), p. 29.

70. The World Bank, "Poland Energy Market Development," Energy and Environment Operations Division Report No. 8224-POL (The World Bank, Washington, D.C., 1991), pp. 23-24.

71. *Ibid.*, p. 26.

72. *Ibid.*, p. 19.

73. *Op. cit.* 9, p. viii.

74. *Op. cit.* 68, pp. vii, 35-39.

75. *Op. cit.* 25.

76. Bradley A. Stertz and Terence Roth, "To Western Industry, East Bloc Auto Market is Losing Some Luster," *Wall Street Journal* (November 14, 1990), p. 1.

77. *Op. cit.* 43, pp. 2-3.

78. *Op. cit.* 43, p. 13.

79. *Op. cit.* 43, pp. 14-15.

80. *Op. cit.* 45, p. 14.

81. *Op. cit.* 62, p. 14.

82. *Op. cit.* 62, p. 14.

83. *Op. cit.* 9, pp. xx-xxi.

84. American Gas Association, "An Evaluation of Alternative Control Strategies to Remove Sulfur Dioxide, Nitrogen Oxides and Carbon Dioxide at Existing Large Coal-Fired Facilities" (American Gas Association, Arlington, Virginia, 1989), pp. 3, 6.

85. *Op. cit.* 25.

86. Stefan Björklund, "Inefficient energy use at root of Poland's environmental problems," *Acid Magazine* (September 1989), p. 11.

87. *Op. cit.* 50.

88. *Op. cit.* 86.

89. Stefan Björklund, "West German coal and lignite power stations come clean," *Acid Magazine* (September 1989), pp. 12-13.

90. Bo Thunberg, "Air pollution in the GDR," *Acid Magazine* (September 1989), p. 19.

91. United Nations (U.N.) *The State of Transboundary Air Pollution: 1989 Update* (U.N., New York, 1990), p. 17.

92. *Op. cit.* 50.

93. *Op. cit.* 12, p. 28.

94. *Op. cit.* 84, p. 2.

95. Raymond C. Pilcher, "Opportunities for the Development and Utilization of Coalbed Methane in Poland," abstract of paper presented at conference on Global Perspectives on Coalbed Methane, the Coalbed Methane Forum (Lakewood, Colorado, May 9, 1991).

96. Marlise Simons, "At East Europe Nuclear Plants, Blame for Soviets," *New York Times* (June 24, 1990), p. 6.

97. *Ibid.*

98. Jeffrey H. Michel, Consulting Engineer, Schuttertal/Dörlinbach, Germany, 1991 (personal communication).

99. *Op. cit.* 68, p. 16.

100. Stanislav Kolar, President, Kolar Associates, Washington, D.C., 1991 (personal communication).

101. *Op. cit.* 68, p. 19.

102. S. Sitnicki, K. Budzinski, J. Juda, *et al.*, "Poland: Opportunities for Carbon Emissions Control," paper prepared for the U.S. Agency for International Development (Battelle Memorial Institute, Pacific Northwest Laboratories, Richland, Washington, 1990), p. 13.

103. *Op. cit.* 25.

104. *Op. cit.* 102, pp. 14-15.

105. *Op. cit.* 102, pp. 13-14.

106. *Op. cit.* 62, pp. 18, 24.

107. "Government Approves 35 Projects to Monitor, Clean Up Pollution in East," *International Environment Reporter* (November 7, 1990), p. 463.

108. *Op. cit.* 9, p. xxiii.

109. "Environment Impact Assessment, Vehicle Emission Requirements Planned," *International Environment Reporter* (December 5, 1990), pp. 503-504.

110. Margaret Bowman and David Hunter, "Environmental Law-Drafting in Czechoslovakia" (Environmental Law Institute, Washington, D.C., 1991), pp. 9-10.

111. *Ibid.*, pp. 6-7.

112. "European Community Gives East Germany Until 1996 to Comply with Regulations," *International Environment Reporter* (September 1990), p. 355.

113. *Op. cit.* 102, p. 17.

114. *Op. cit.* 9, pp. xi-xiii.

6. Population and Human Development

People are a precious, yet often neglected, resource. To a large extent this is because their sheer numbers strain the systems designed to serve them. The world population has doubled in the past 40 years and may double again in the next century, perhaps approaching stability at about 11 billion by the year 2100. Most of this increase will take place in the developing world. Without a great deal of effort and ingenuity, many of these new citizens will degrade natural resources and not be offered the health and educational resources necessary to reach their potential.

Humanitarian concerns aside, building a healthy, educated, stable population makes economic sense and is a chief component of sustainable development. (See Chapter 1, "Dimensions of Sustainable Development.") The newly industrialized countries—Asia's four tigers—made remarkable economic progress by developing an educated workforce as the basis for a manufacturing boom. Short on natural resources, South Korea, Singapore, Hong Kong, and Taiwan used their human resources to bound out of poverty. Other developing countries are following suit; ideally, they will avoid some of the environmental pitfalls experienced by Asia's tigers. (See Chapter 4, "Sustainable Development Case Study: Rapidly Industrializing Countries.")

In its recent series of *Human Development Reports*, the United Nations Development Programme has asserted that although economic development generally improves the well-being of a population, other factors are also important—specifically, increased schooling and health care. This gives hope to low-income countries and countries suffering economic stagnation that they can improve their citizens' lives by directing limited financial resources into primary education and health care programs.

Of the roughly 37 million people who died in developing countries annually in the mid-1980s, almost 37 percent were children. This shocking figure compares to developed countries where only 3 percent of the annual deaths are of children. Mortality figures—used as the most reliable measure of health—show only the most severe cases of ill-health and do not indicate a much larger population of sick, malnourished, and listless children. Most of these children are sickened by diseases that can be easily prevented or cured with proper sanitation, nutrition, and vaccines. However, these basic needs are still unavailable to many children in developing countries. Striking progress has been made in vaccinating children and in providing simple treatment for diarrhea, the biggest cause of death

Table 6.1 Estimated and Projected Population Size by Region, 1950–2025

Region	Population (millions)					Percent Share of World Population				
	1950	1970	1990	2000	2025	1950	1970	1990	2000	2025
World Total	**2,516**	**3,698**	**5,292**	**6,261**	**8,504**	**100.0**	**100.0**	**100.0**	**100.0**	**100.0**
Industrialized countries	832	1,049	1,207	1,264	1,354	33.1	28.4	22.8	20.2	15.9
Developing countries	1,684	2,649	4,086	4,997	7,150	66.9	71.6	77.2	79.8	84.1
Africa	222	362	642	867	1,597	8.8	9.8	12.1	13.8	18.8
North America	166	226	276	295	332	6.6	6.1	5.2	4.7	3.9
Latin America	166	286	448	538	757	6.6	7.7	8.5	8.6	8.9
Asia	1,377	2,102	3,113	3,713	4,912	54.7	56.8	58.8	59.3	57.8
Europe	393	460	498	510	515	15.6	12.4	9.4	8.1	6.1
Oceania	13	19	26	30	38	0.5	0.5	0.5	0.5	0.4
U.S.S.R.	180	243	289	308	352	7.2	6.6	5.5	4.9	4.1

Source: United Nations Population Division, *World Population Prospects 1990* (United Nations, New York 1991), pp. 226-233, 244-245, 252-255, 264-265, 274-275, and 582-583.

among children of the developing world. (See Focus On Children's Health, below.)

Although it might seem that reducing child mortality would increase population growth, the opposite is the case if countries also develop economically. As countries develop, they go through a process called demographic transition in which living standards are raised, child mortality is reduced, and fertility declines. This transition can be speeded by policies that promote education, health care, and use of contraceptives.

CONDITIONS AND TRENDS

Global Trends

POPULATION TRENDS

The different prospects for the industrialized and developing countries are nowhere more evident than in their respective population sizes. By 1990, of the world's 5.3 billion people, 4.1 billion—77 percent—lived in the developing world; 1.2 billion inhabited the industrialized countries. (See Table 6.1.)

The difference in growth rates of developing and industrialized countries is even more dramatic. Population growth in the industrialized countries has been relatively modest, rising about 15 percent over the 1970–90 period. In those same two decades, the population of developing countries grew by almost 55 percent, from 2.65 billion to 4.1 billion. The disparity in numbers will widen by 2025, when population in industrialized countries is projected to be 1.35 billion and 7.15 billion in developing countries (or about 84 percent of world population).

This burst of population growth in the developing world is easily explained. Before World War II, both birth rates and death rates were high in these countries, which kept growth low. Since then, rapid improvements in health care and sanitation have caused death rates to plummet, while birth rates have remained high.

Large differences in the age structure of populations in the industrialized and developing worlds help account for the projected widening of the population disparities. In the industrialized countries, the proportions of people in each age range are roughly equal,

with a slight bulge among the postwar baby-boom generation, which is now 30–45 years old. In the developing countries, far more people are in the young age groups, which will swell the number of children born each year as the increasing number of young women of childbearing age have children. (See *World Resources 1990–91*, pp. 51–55.)

Declining Growth Rates, Increasing Numbers

For several decades, population planners have focused on reducing population growth rates in developing countries. In many regions, that effort has been relatively successful, as Figure 6.1 suggests; the major exception has been Africa, where growth rates since the mid-1960s have increased.

Declining birth rates, however, belie the immense momentum already built into the system; that is, each woman is having fewer children, but many more women are giving birth. By the year 2000, over 90 million people—more than Mexico's current population—will be added annually to the population of the developing countries (1). (See Figure 6.2.) Thereafter, the number of people added each year will decrease slowly with world population probably stabilizing at a projected 11.2 billion in 2100 (2).

Fertility and Contraception Trends

As Figure 6.3 indicates, total fertility rates in the industrialized countries have remained roughly at or below 2 during the 1980s and into 1990. (The fertility rate is the average number of children women bear in their lifetime.) Within Asia, the experience has been varied. Largely because of China's strong population control programs, which resulted in a total fertility rate of 2.3, rates in East Asia have declined dramatically over the past four decades. Some countries in South and Southeast Asia—especially Singapore, Thailand, Indonesia, Sri Lanka, and India—also have made significant progress. Fertility rates in Latin America followed a similar path, but rates in Africa have remained virtually unchanged since the 1950s (3).

With large numbers of women now in or entering their reproductive ages, the downward trend in birth rates will be enormously difficult to maintain. Population assistance programs can play an important role in developing countries. Because of past investments in

Figure 6.1 Average Annual Population Growth Rates, 1960–65 and 1985–90

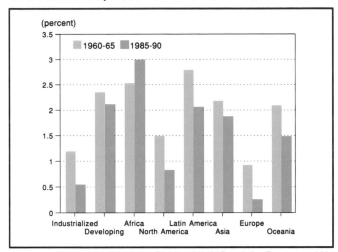

Source: United Nations Population Division, *World Population Prospects 1990* (United Nations, New York, 1991), pp. 112-115.
Note: Excludes U.S.S.R.

Figure 6.2 Projected Annual Increment to the Population, 1950–2020

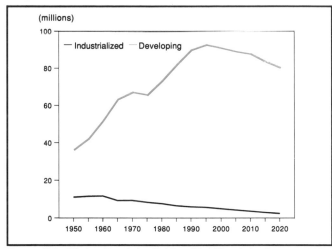

Source: United Nations Population Division, *World Population Prospects 1991* (United Nations, New York, 1991), pp. 228-231.

Figure 6.3 Total Fertility Rates, 1950–85

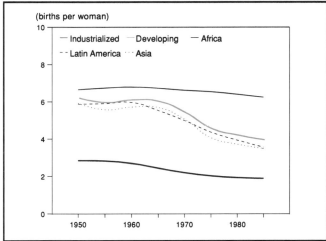

Source: United Nations Population Division, *World Population Prospects 1990* (United Nations, New York, 1991), pp. 176-193.

Figure 6.4 Trends in Contraceptive Use in Developing Regions, 1960–90

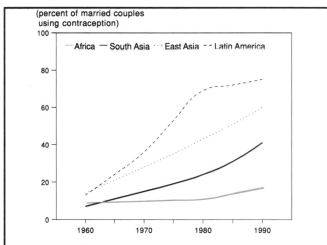

Source: Thomas Merrick, *U.S. Population Assistance: A Continued Priority for the 1990s?* (Population Reference Bureau, Washington, D.C., 1990), p. 17.
Notes: *South Asia* includes Afghanistan, Bangladesh, Bhutan, India, Iran, Maldives, Nepal, Pakistan, and Sri Lanka. *East Asia* includes China, Hong Kong, Korea (Dem. and Rep.), Macao, and Mongolia.

population programs, the world already has 400 million fewer people than it otherwise would, according to one study, and will have 4 billion fewer people during the next century than it would have had without such programs (4).

Increased access to effective contraception has been an important factor in fertility declines in developing countries, most notably in Asia and Latin America. In China, an estimated 71 percent of married women are using contraception, a figure that matches the rate in Europe and is far higher than the estimated 44 percent rate in the rest of the developing world. Contraception also is now widely used among married women in rapidly industrializing countries such as Thailand (68 percent), Republic of Korea (77 percent), Taiwan (78 percent), and Brazil (66 percent). It is still rarely used,

however, in many African countries (5). (See Figure 6.4.)

Investments in the welfare of women can have a striking impact on population and health trends. In Thailand, female literacy has reached 90 percent, while the fertility rate has declined significantly, and the population growth rate has dropped to 1.5 percent a year. (See Chapter 16, "Population and Human Development," Tables 16.1 and 16.5.) Investments in family planning and health services also can greatly benefit women: in Nicaragua, Sri Lanka, Botswana, and elsewhere, government efforts to encourage participatory, community-based health programs have helped to reduce maternal mortality substantially (6).

Table 6.2 Mortality of Children Under Age 5 by Region, 1965–90

Region	Under 5 Mortality Rate {a}					Percent Change from 1965-70 to 1985-90
	1965-70	1970-75	1975-80	1980-85	1985-90	1985-90
World Total	161	144	131	118	105	-35
Industrialized countries	32	26	24	19	17	-47
Developing countries	184	164	149	134	119	-35
Africa	261	233	203	182	163	-38
North America	26	21	17	13	11	-58
Latin America	131	115	99	88	78	-40
Asia	171	151	139	124	108	-37
Europe	35	28	22	17	15	-57
Oceania	67	52	47	40	33	-51
U.S.S.R.	36	34	37	31	27	-25

Source: United Nations (U.N.), *Mortality of Children Under Age 5: World Estimates and Projections 1950-2025* (U.N., New York, 1988), pp. 30-35.

Note: a: Under-five mortality rate is defined as the annual number of deaths of children under five years of age per 1,000 live births. Mortality rates are the annual average for each five-year period shown.

Table 6.3 Infant Mortality by Region, 1965–90

Region	Infant Mortality Rate {a}					Percent Change from 1965-70 to 1985-90
	1965-70	1970-75	1975-80	1980-85	1985-90	1985-90
World Total	102	93	86	79	70	-31
Industrialized countries	26	22	19	16	15	-42
Developing countries	116	105	97	89	78	-33
Africa	149	137	126	116	103	-31
North America	22	18	14	11	10	-55
Latin America	91	81	70	61	54	-41
Asia	110	99	91	83	72	-35
Europe	30	24	19	15	13	-57
Oceania	48	41	35	30	26	-46
U.S.S.R.	26	26	28	26	24	-8

Source: United Nations Population Division, *World Population Prospects 1990 on Diskette* (United Nations, New York, 1991).

Note: a: Infant mortality rate is defined as the annual number of deaths of infants under 1 year of age per 1,000 live births. Mortality rates are the annual average for each five-year period shown.

Some governments have begun to recognize that men are an important audience for family planning information and education. The Republic of Korea began to focus on men in the 1970s, and the number of men taking responsibility for family planning has risen dramatically since then [7].

HEALTH TRENDS

The broadest measures of human health—life expectancy at birth and mortality among children under age 5 and among infants under age 1, for example—show improvement in all developing regions (although not all countries) over the past few decades. Reductions in under-five and infant mortality have been impressive in all regions; both have dropped by about one third in developing countries as a whole. (See Tables 6.2 and 6.3.)

In absolute terms, nevertheless, stark contrasts remain in the health prospects of people living in the world's poorest and richest nations. In Africa, mortality of children under 5 is now roughly 147 per 1,000 live births, which is nearly 15 times higher than the rate in the United States and Canada [8].

Environmental pollutants pose hazards to human health. Human exposure to chemical contaminants in food, indoor air pollutants, hazardous wastes, and ionizing radiation all have significant health effects throughout the world. Moreover, in the developing world, malnutrition, inadequate water supplies and sanitation, poor hygienic practices, and overcrowded living conditions all contribute to the incidence of diarrheal and infectious diseases.

Chemical, industrial, and nuclear accidents pose potentially serious health hazards. The most tragic recent examples have been the chemical accident at Bhopal, India, and the nuclear accident at Chernobyl in the Soviet Union. Overall, it is estimated that more than 200 serious chemical accidents occur annually in the industrialized countries alone [9].

Acute pesticide poisonings are a major health problem in developing countries. The World Health Organization (WHO) estimates that worldwide each year there are more than 1 million accidental acute pesticide poisonings and more than 20,000 accidental deaths. An additional 2 million cases and 200,000 deaths are thought to be suicides rather than accidents [10].

Major Causes of Death and Disease

On a global level, about 48 million people died annually during the mid 1980s, including about 11 million in the industrial world and about 37 million in the developing world. Three fourths of all deaths in the industrial world were caused by diseases of the circulatory system (54 percent) and cancer (21 percent) [11] [12].

Statistics on causes of death in developing countries are often unavailable or unreliable. Using available data and indirect methods, WHO has estimated that of the nearly 37 million people (23.3 million adults and 13.5 million children) who died in developing countries in 1985, 44 percent (16 million) died of infectious and parasitic diseases [13]. (See Table 6.4.)

Deaths of Children

Of those who died annually in developing countries around 1985, almost 37 percent (13.5 million) were children under age 5 compared to about 3 percent in industrialized countries [14] [15]. For 1990, WHO estimated that about 12.9 million children were dying annually in developing countries. Infectious and parasitic diseases in 1990 killed about 9.8 million children before their fifth birthday. The most common causes of death in developing countries are respiratory infections, neonatal and perinatal complications, and diarrhea [16].

Cancer and AIDS

There has been less progress, and occasionally regression, in the fight against some diseases. For example, cancer, which causes more than 20 percent of the deaths in industrialized countries, is increasing primarily because of an increase in the average age of the population, improved control of other health problems, and increased use of tobacco (17).

Acquired immune deficiency syndrome (AIDS), first recognized in 1981, has rapidly become a major global health problem. AIDS is caused by the human immunodeficiency virus (HIV). Some 15–20 percent of all those infected are expected to develop AIDS within 5 years; within 10 years, about 50 percent of those infected will develop the disease. By early 1990, an estimated 5–10 million people were infected with HIV worldwide—about half in sub-Saharan Africa and half in Europe and North America—and about 600,000 clinical cases of AIDS had occurred in adults. The number of cases was expected to reach 1 million by the end of 1991 and several million by the end of the century (18).

Vector-Borne Diseases

Many vector-borne diseases—those carried by other organisms—are pervasive problems in some regions of the developing world. The most serious diseases include malaria, schistosomiasis, and other diseases such as lymphatic filariasis, and onchocerciasis.

■ Malaria occurs in some 100 countries or areas; clinical cases are estimated at 107 million a year and deaths at about 1 million a year, with about three quarters of all deaths occurring among children under 5. Data on the number of malaria cases and malaria mortality are sketchy; there appears to be an upward trend in the number of cases in the Americas and some Asian countries (19). WHO estimated that malaria claimed 800,000 children in 1990, up about 7 percent from its 750,000 estimate for 1985 (20). The increase is partially due to the growing resistance of malaria-carrying mosquitos to insecticides and of the *Plasmodium* parasites to antimalarial drugs (21).

■ Schistosomiasis is caused by schistosome parasites, which multiply in snails and are disseminated into freshwater and thence into humans, where they cause hemorrhaging and tissue damage in the bladder and intestine. The disease is endemic in 76 countries. About 200,000 people die of schistosomiasis each year; about 200 million are infected; and about 600 million are at risk (22).

■ Filariasis is a group of disorders caused by infection from a filarial worm transmitted by bloodsucking flies. The infection leads to inflammation of the lymph system. The disease affects 76 countries. About 90 million people are infected; about 900 million people are at risk (23).

■ Onchocerciasis—also known as river blindness—is caused by infection by the filarial worm *Onchocerca volvulus*. Symptoms include dermatitis and eye lesions that can lead to blindness (24). The disease is endemic in 26 countries in Africa, 2 in the eastern Mediterranean, and 6 in Latin America. An estimated 17.6–17.8

Table 6.4 Estimated Causes of Death in Industrialized and Developing Countries for Adults and Children over Age 5, mid–1980s
(in thousands)

Cause of Death	Number of Deaths	
	Industrialized	Developing
Infectious and Parasitic Diseases	506	6,500
Diarrheal diseases	X	1,000
Tuberculosis	40	2,700
Acute respiratory diseases	368	2,000
Malaria	X	250
Schistosomiasis	X	200
Chronic Obstructive Lung Diseases	385	2,300
Circulatory and Other Degenerative Diseases (heart disease, cerebrovascular disease, diabetes)	5,930	6,500
Cancer	2,293	2,500
Other	1,931	5,500
All Causes	11,045	23,300

Source: Alan D. Lopez, "Causes of Death: An Assessment of Global Patterns of Mortality Around 1985," *World Health Statistics Quarterly*, Vol. 43, No. 2 (1990), pp. 93, 98.

Note: The total for industrialized countries includes 355,000 infant-and-child deaths below age 5 (3.2 percent of the total), 275,000 of which occurred among infants. Most of these infant deaths were due to various perinatal and congenital conditions.

X = not available.

million people are infected; about 85–90 million people are at risk (25). Distribution of the drug ivermectin may be a breakthrough in the fight against this disease (26).

Key Issues

HUMAN DEVELOPMENT: A NEW MEASURE OF GROWTH

The United Nations Development Programme embarked in 1990 on a new effort to measure human development that emphasizes progress in human health and literacy. The centerpiece of the *Human Development Report 1990* and *Human Development Report 1991* is the human development index, which ranks countries using a combination of three indicators—life expectancy, literacy, and living standards as measured by gross domestic product per capita. The report asserts that while economic growth is a critical component of human development, it does not capture the broader picture of human welfare. Programs that translate economic growth into education and health care are essential to produce a better life for a nation's people (27).

The 1991 report adjusted the index slightly by broadening the literacy factor to include mean years of schooling (28). In addition, separate indexes were prepared for:

■ Women and men for 30 countries, indicating that, in areas such as life expectancy, adult literacy, wage rates, and mean years of schooling, there are wide gender disparities in many developing countries.

■ Income distribution in 53 countries, indicating that in several countries—Nepal, Brazil, and Cote D'Ivoire, for example—uneven income distribution has adversely affected overall human welfare.

Recent Developments

NEW LONG-RANGE POPULATION PROJECTIONS

In late 1991, the United Nations was expected to release new long-range population projections with a 10 percent higher mid-range scenario for global population. The new estimates vividly demonstrate the crucial role of fertility rates in estimating the ultimate size of the world's population.

Revised for the first time since 1982, the new long-range projections make a number of changes in assumptions. For example, the upper limit for life expectancy at birth was raised to 82.5 years for men (up from 73.5 years) and 87.5 years for women (up from 80 years). The forecast also made some changes in assumptions about population size in 2025, the "take-off" point for the projections, and about the pace of fertility change after 2025.

Under the medium fertility projection, which assumes fertility ultimately will stabilize at a replacement level of about 2.06, global population will reach 10 billion in 2050, 11.2 billion in 2100, 11.5 billion in 2150 and ultimately stabilize at 11.6 billion

shortly after 2200. There would be an 89 percent increase between the years 1990 and 2050, with an additional 12 percent between 2050 and 2100 and 3 percent between 2100 and 2150.

However, global population could vary greatly depending on fertility rates. Under a medium-high rate, with fertility stabilizing at 2.17 children (5 percent higher than replacement level), world population would be nearly 21 billion by 2150. At a higher fertility stabilization rate (2.5 children), world population would reach 28 billion in 2150. If fertility stabilized at 5 percent below the replacement level, population would peak at 7.8 billion in 2050 and then fall to 5.6 billion by the middle of the following century. Under an even lower fertility assumption (1.7 children), world population would peak at 7.8 billion in 2050 but then fall to 4.3 billion 100 years later. (See Figure 1.)

The U.N. medium-fertility projected population of 11.2 billion is 1 billion (10 percent) higher than that calculated by the U.N. in 1982. The new projections also have a much wider range than the 1982 fig-

ures for the highest and lowest projected outcomes. In 1982, the outcomes ranged between 7 billion and 15 billion in the year 2100; the new projections range from 6 billion to 19 billion for the same year.

The age structure of the population is projected to change dramatically. The share of the population aged 65 and over, which now stands at 6 percent, would rise to about 24 percent in 2150. The share of those aged 15 or under, now 32 percent, would drop to 18 percent by 2150. (See Figure 2.) The percentage of those aged 80 or over, now 1 percent of the total, would increase to 9 percent [1].

References and Notes

1. United Nations Population Division, *Long-Range World Population Projections: Two Centuries of Population Growth, 1950-2150* (United Nations, New York, forthcoming), executive summary.

Figure 1 Projected Population of the World, 1990–2150

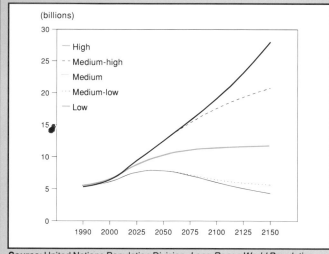

Source: United Nations Population Division, *Long-Range World Population Projections: Two Centuries of Population Growth, 1950–2150* (United Nations, New York, forthcoming), executive summary.

Figure 2 Changing Age Structure of World Population, 1990–2150

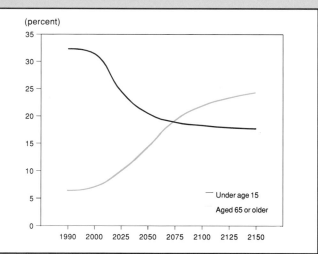

Source: United Nations Population Division, *Long-Range World Population Projections: Two Centuries of Population Growth, 1950–2150* (United Nations, New York, forthcoming), executive summary.
Note: Based on medium fertility projection in Figure 1.

■ Human freedom in 88 countries, showing that high levels of human development tend to be achieved within the framework of high levels of human freedom [29].

The index reveals that some countries—Sri Lanka, Chile, Costa Rica, Jamaica, Tanzania, and Thailand, among others—seem to have been far more successful than others in translating economic progress into broad welfare gains for their people.

In assessing the various country cases, the 1990 report came to several conclusions:

■ The most effective means of sustained human development is growth accompanied by an equitable distribution of income (as occurred in the Republic of Korea).
■ Even in the absence of rapid growth or equitable income distribution, countries can make significant improvements in human development through well-structured social spending (Botswana, Malaysia, and Sri Lanka).
■ Well-structured government social spending can generate dramatic improvements in a relatively short period, not only for countries starting from a low level of

human development but also for those starting at a moderate level (Chile and Costa Rica).
■ Setbacks in economic growth can seriously disrupt human development (Chile, Colombia, Jamaica, Kenya, and Zimbabwe).
■ Targeted government interventions can help maintain human development during recessions and natural disasters (Chile, Zimbabwe, and Botswana).
■ In countries experiencing economic growth, human development may not improve if income distribution is uneven and social expenditures are low (Nigeria and Pakistan) or most of the wealth is appropriated by those who are better off (Brazil) (30).

The 1991 report suggests ways to improve human development efficiently. In health care, for example, governments could make large savings by using the least expensive treatments rather than high-tech alternatives, buying generic rather than brand-name drugs and purchasing them through competitive bidding, improving the storage and distribution of drugs, and employing health-care personnel with fewer formal qualifications (31).

CHOLERA EPIDEMICS IN LATIN AMERICA AND AFRICA

The threat to human health posed by environmental deterioration was dramatically evident in early 1991, when, for the first time in this century, a cholera epidemic struck six countries in Latin America. Several African countries were also plagued with this disease. As of late September 1991, the World Health Organization had received reports of 300,000 cases of cholera and 3,200 deaths, primarily in Peru and to a lesser extent in Ecuador, Colombia, Mexico, Guatemala, and Brazil (32). Worldwide, the number of new cases of cholera (177,000) in the first four months of 1991 nearly equaled the total for all of 1971, when a cholera pandemic was at its peak in Africa and Asia (33). By late 1991, the epidemic in Latin America appeared to be stabilizing. However, the arrival of warmer weather could cause a resurgence in affected countries as well as the spread to countries previously unaffected (34). In Africa, the disease continued to sweep through The Gambia, Nigeria, Ghana, and other West African countries, with more than 45,000 cases and nearly 3,500 deaths reported (35).

Cholera is an acute intestinal infection caused by *Vibrio cholerae* bacterium. The first cases in Latin America were reported in Peru in January 1991, appearing almost simultaneously in communities along a 1,200 kilometer length of coastline (36). The bacterium responsible for the world's outbreak was of the same biotype (*El Tor*) that started the seventh pandemic in 1961, spreading through Asia and the Middle East in the 1960s and invading West Africa in 1970 (37).

Cholera is transmitted primarily through contaminated water and food, especially raw vegetables and seafood. It can spread rapidly, especially in overpopulated communities with poor sanitation and unsafe drinking water. Children are particularly susceptible to the disease (38).

The outbreak in Peru is a side effect of the rapid urbanization of the country together with a proliferation of crowded urban slums that lack adequate safe water and sanitation facilities. People living in these slums typically are poorly educated and poorly nourished, with little access to medical and health services. Cholera is treatable with oral rehydration salts, but the ultimate solution in countries such as Peru requires improvements in water and sanitation, health and education, and food safety (39).

FOCUS ON CHILDREN'S HEALTH

The 1.7 billion children under age 15 who inhabit the earth today represent one third (32 percent) of the planet's population; 82 percent of these children (1.4 billion) live in the developing world. Moreover, during the 1990s, the largest generation ever will be born, with nearly 90 percent of the expected 1.5 billion births to occur in developing countries (40). These are the same countries in which large numbers of children still die needlessly from malnutrition and disease caused by inadequate drinking water, poor sanitation, and other environmental ills. Nearly all deaths of children under age 5 (97 percent) and maternal deaths (99 percent) are in developing countries (41) (42) (43).

The environmental conditions in which these children live pose a serious threat to their current health and future prospects (44) (45). As the most fragile members of society, they are most vulnerable to disease and environmental stress; their long-term well-being depends on the sustained ability of the Earth's resources to support this still expanding population.

At a rhetorical level, recognition is growing that societies have responsibilities not only to their current citizens, but to future ones as well. At the World Summit for Children, held at the United Nations in September 1990, leaders from 71 countries committed themselves to "promoting the survival, protection, and development of the present generation of children and all generations to come" (46). For those concerned about sustainable development, the concept of "intergenerational equity" suggests that the welfare of future generations—including the children already born—should be an implicit consideration in today's decisionmaking (47). Despite the rhetoric, however, the economic, social, and environmental conditions in which many children live put them at serious risk for ill health, malnutrition, life-long disability (both physical and mental), and early death.

Progress has been made. Worldwide, the annual number of deaths of children under 5 declined by 4.7 million between 1965–70 and 1985–90. Developing countries have improved their children's health considerably. Between 1965–70 and 1985–90, the infant mortality rate declined by 33 percent in developing countries, from 116 per 1,000 live births to 78. (See Table 6.3.) The mortality rate of children under 5 years of age shows a similar trend: a 35 percent reduction, from 184 to 119 deaths per 1,000. Under-five mortality in industrialized countries during this time period

Figure 6.5 Estimated Causes of Death Among Children Under Age 5 in Developing Countries, 1985 and 1990

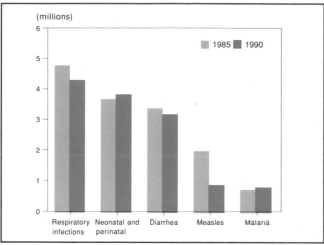

Source: Division of Epidemiological Surveillance and Health Situation and Trend Assessment, World Health Organization (WHO), *Global Estimates for Health Situation Assessment and Projections 1992* (WHO, Geneva, forthcoming).

Notes:

a. WHO attributes 400 million deaths in 1985 and 180 million deaths in 1990 to a combination of diarrhea and measles. Totals for diarrhea and measles both include deaths from combined diarrhea/measles.

b. Perinatal deaths refer to deaths from four weeks before delivery up to one month after birth; neonatal deaths refer to deaths after birth up to one month of age.

dropped 47 percent, but the number of deaths per 1,000 was already far lower, dropping from 32 to 17. (See Table 6.2.) In the developing world, 37 percent of total deaths are children under 7; in the developed, 3 percent (48) (49). A baby born in a developing country today is seven times more likely to die before its first birthday than one born in the industrialized countries. Among developing countries, disparities in child mortality have widened; in the early 1960s, the differences between the best and worst rates were 7 to 1; by the early 1980s, they had increased to 15 to 1 (50). Unfortunately, recent reports show that progress in children's health has slipped in the United States. (See Box 6.1.)

MAJOR CAUSES OF DEATH IN CHILDREN

In the developing world, 12.9 million children under age 5—more than 35,000 a day—died in 1990 of diseases, most of which were once as common in developed countries (51). In other words, these children are dying of diseases for which effective means of prevention, as well as effective treatments, are available. (See Figure 6.5.)

Acute Respiratory Infection

Respiratory infections are responsible for some 4.3 million childhood deaths annually. About 17 percent of these deaths are a consequence of pertussis (whooping cough) and measles and are thus preventable through immunization; the vast majority—roughly 75 percent—are caused by pneumonia (52).

In the developed world, most children recover from pneumonia; in developing countries, they often do

not. In Guatemala, the mortality rate among infants due to influenza and pneumonia is estimated to be 1,000 per 100,000 live births; this is 8 times higher than Argentina (120 per 100,000), 10 times higher than Cuba (97 per 100,000), and 125 times higher than Canada (8 per 100,000) (53).

One important contributing cause to acute respiratory infections (as well as to other diseases) in children are the particulates released when wood and animal dung are used to fuel traditional stoves. (See Chapter 13, "Atmosphere and Climate.") WHO estimates that 400–500 million people (including many women and young children) are affected worldwide, with rural homes having levels of particulate pollution ranging from 300 to 14,000 micrograms per cubic meter. The WHO maximum recommended level is 100–150 micrograms (54).

Bacterial pneumonia occurs far more frequently in developing countries than viral pneumonia (representing two thirds to three quarters of pneumonia cases), making oral antibiotics the treatment of choice (55). Because their administration has been considered the preserve of medical doctors, antibiotics have been difficult to dispense widely in developing countries. But as a result of a series of pilot studies, WHO estimates that deaths from acute respiratory infections can be reduced by at least 30 percent if community health workers are trained in a standard protocol that involves dispensing antibiotics when certain clear indicators are present (56) (57) (58). There already is some evidence of improvement; WHO estimated that respiratory infections claimed 4.3 million children in 1990, down about 10 percent from the 1985 estimate of 4.8 million (59).

Diarrhea

In almost every developing country, diarrhea and respiratory infection are the first and second most common causes of illness and death among children under 5 years old (60). Diarrheal disease causes about 3.2 million child deaths annually (61). In some countries, children suffer an average of eight or nine diarrheal episodes a year (compared with a global average of three per child per year) (62). As much as 13 percent of a child's life may be spent ill with diarrhea. Repeated and prolonged bouts contribute to undernourishment, which in turn increases the severity and duration of future diarrheal episodes (63).

The most serious aspect of diarrhea is the dehydration that usually accompanies it—a condition that can be prevented if parents and health care workers have access to, and know how to use, oral rehydration therapy (64). In this simple technique, vital fluids and ions lost during diarrheal episodes are restored through the administration of either a prepared packet of oral rehydration salts (ORS) or a home-prepared solution. Oral rehydration has been called one of the most important medical breakthroughs of the century in terms of numbers of lives affected, providing a less expensive and more accessible means of treatment than intravenous rehydration (65). Promoted by WHO since 1978, oral rehydration is now theoretically accessible to about 60

Box 6.1 The Troubled State of U.S. Children's Health

Despite its enormous wealth, the United States still contains a large and apparently growing number of children living in poverty and poor health. While dramatic progress was made in the 1960s in reducing child poverty, progress halted in the 1970s, and child poverty rates increased in the 1980s (1). The U.S. Census Bureau announced in late 1991 that 20.6 percent of U.S. children were living in poverty in 1990, up from 19.6 percent the previous year. The high percentage of impoverished children is driven mainly by the increasing numbers of female-headed households (2).

Poverty and illness are particularly severe problems for black children in the United States. The U.S. infant mortality rate is higher than those of 21 other industrialized countries; black babies in the U.S. are twice as likely to die as white babies. Since 1980, no progress has been made in reducing the incidence of low birthweight babies; for blacks, the rate has actually increased (3).

While developing countries have made spectacular progress in immunizing children against six major childhood diseases, with average immunization levels improving from 15 percent to about 80 percent, this has not happened in the United States. In 1990, only about 70 percent of U.S. children were immunized against measles, mumps, and rubella; in many inner cities only about one half of young children were protected. In 1990, more than 26,000 cases of measles were reported, sharply higher than the 3,000-case average in 1981—88; most cases were among children in poor, inner-city families. Cases of rubella and whooping cough also have increased. Immunization rates for diseases such as whooping cough are unknown because the federal government suspended data collection in 1985 (4).

At least 10 to 15 percent of children in the United States suffer from chronic or disabling conditions such as genetic or metabolic disorders, birth defects, trauma, premature birth, or infection. Increasingly common conditions include respiratory diseases, mental and nervous disorders (at least 10 percent of children suffer from serious mental health disorders, including autism and depression), and orthopedic and sensory impairments. An estimated 12 million American children, mostly poor children, are at risk of lead poisoning (5).

References and Notes

1. Clifford M. Johnson, Leticia Miranda, Arloc Sherman, *et al.*, *Child Poverty in America* (Children's Defense Fund, Washington, D.C., 1991), pp. 1, 4.
2. Jason DeParle, "Poverty Rate Rose Sharply Last Year as Incomes Slipped," *New York Times* (September 27, 1991), p. A1.
3. National Commission on Children, *Beyond Rhetoric: A New American Agenda for Children and Families* (Government Printing Office, Washington, D.C., 1991), p. 119.
4. *Ibid.*, pp. 119-121.
5. *Ibid.*, p. 121.

percent of the children in developing countries, but is actually used to treat about 30 percent of the children who contract diarrhea. According to UNICEF, this treatment saves an estimated 1 million young lives a year (66) (67).

Because it is important for children to continue to receive nutrients during diarrheal episodes, oral rehydration therapy is increasingly considered to involve both the administration of fluids and continued feeding. Ongoing research suggests that cereal-based oral rehydration therapy, although still somewhat controversial, may have the potential to be more effective than the standard ORS solution, which prevents dehydration, but does not actually prevent diarrhea nor reduce its duration or amount. Cereal-based therapy can reduce fluid losses by 30–50 percent as well as shorten the duration of diarrheal episodes (68).

Even more important than treatment of diarrhea, however, is its prevention. Most diarrhea is caused by bacterial, viral, and parasitic infestations transmitted through water, food, and contact with fecal matter. Preventing diarrhea requires better sanitation and more abundant, cleaner water supplies, as well as health education aimed at promoting breastfeeding, immunization, improved personal hygiene and food handling practices, and the penning of farm animals such as chickens and cattle (69) (70). Exclusive breastfeeding in the first six months of a child's life, for example, can dramatically reduce the incidence of diarrhea; the addition of even water or tea to the infant's diet has been found to double or sometimes triple the likelihood of diarrhea (71).

Vaccine-Preventable Diseases

At the end of the 1970s, the international community made a major commitment to immunizing the world's children against six major childhood diseases—measles, diphtheria, pertussis, tetanus, polio, and tuberculosis. This commitment has produced one of the most spectacular public health successes of the past decade. Today, average immunization levels of children in developing countries are at least 80 percent for all vaccine-preventable diseases except measles (78 percent) and neonatal tetanus (which requires the immunization of women, only 38 percent of whom were immunized by 1990) (72). The United Nations Children's Fund (UNICEF) estimates that these successes are preventing at least 2.5 million child deaths each year. All told, more than 12 million lives have been saved and more than 1.5 million cases of polio prevented (73).

Despite this progress, more than 2.1 million children died of vaccine-preventable diseases in 1990 (74). Expanding immunization coverage further will be more difficult, because those not yet reached tend to be from the poorest families, among whom disease and malnutrition are both more common and more likely to be fatal. The international community has committed itself to achieving 90 percent coverage by the year 2000, with a particular emphasis on reducing measles deaths by 95 percent and on eliminating tetanus and polio entirely (75).

Measles and neonatal tetanus are the biggest killers among vaccine-preventable diseases and also those for which immunization lags furthest behind. Measles accounts for some 900,000 deaths a year (76); it also causes malnutrition, further illness, and loss of vitamin A. The incidence of illness and death in the period after a measles outbreak can be 10 times greater among children who had the disease than among those who did not (77). Immunization against measles can have a significant effect on child mortality, helping to reduce deaths from all causes. In Bangladesh, for example, children who were vaccinated against measles experienced at least 40 percent lower mortality than those who were not (78).

Neonatal tetanus could be eliminated if all pregnant women were immunized and delivered their babies under hygienic conditions. Tetanus currently kills some 560,000 newborns each year and an estimated 15,000–30,000 mothers; it is an excellent barometer of the health status and well-being of mothers and newborns (79) (80) (81).

The eradication of smallpox through immunization in the 1970s provides a telling example of both the possibility and the cost-effectiveness of such efforts—approximately $1 billion a year is saved in vaccine and surveillance costs (82). Another success story is the near-total eradication of polio from the Americas. In 1985, bilateral, multilateral, and private voluntary agencies joined with the Pan American Health Organization in an intensive campaign to rid the hemisphere of polio. The campaign involved high immunization levels, enhanced surveillance to document and investigate each case, and measures to stop transmission whenever a new case occurred. In 1990, there were 18 new cases, compared with 1,050 in 1986; as of July 1991, there were only 3 confirmed cases for the year. Complete eradication is anticipated in the near future (83).

Malaria

Approximately 40 percent of the world's population is at risk of malaria, which occurs in more than 100 countries (84). It is most endemic in sub-Saharan Africa, where often more than 50 percent of the population in rural areas is infected (85). Because of widespread underreporting, the exact number of deaths due to malaria is unknown but is estimated to be about 1 million annually (86), mostly in sub-Saharan Africa and mostly in the younger age groups (an estimated 800,000 children under 5 die from malaria each year) (87). Those children who survive may acquire immunity against the most severe manifestations of the infection, but often the remnants of the disease adversely affect their growth, physical fitness, and educational achievement (88).

Environmental conditions contributing to the spread of malaria include stagnant waters around homes and construction sites; irrigation projects; industrial, hydroelectric projects requiring impoundment of water; changes in ecosystems caused by widespread deforestation, soil erosion, and flooding; overcrowding and unsanitary living conditions. Overuse of pesticides increases the mosquito's resistance and further aggravates the problem.

Combatting the disease requires controlling the mosquito population through appropriate use of chemical or biological means, preventing mortality through case management, and implementing a range of environmental management techniques depending on the predominant vector species. Malaria is transmitted through a complex of technical, political, social, cultural, environmental, and economic factors; to be successful, measures to reduce malaria mortality must be

locally and regionally specific. Simple administration of even a very effective drug such as chloroquinine is not enough to combat the disease; when used in the absence of an effective primary health care system, chloroquinine has in fact contributed to the resurgence of malaria by increasing parasite resistance. (See *World Resources 1990–91*, p. 58.) Nevertheless, when used in combination with strategies appropriate to local conditions, the drug can still provide a clinical cure in large areas of the world (89).

A ministerial level meeting to review the global malaria situation and develop new strategies is scheduled for October 1992 in Amsterdam. Organized by the World Health Organization, the meeting is to be preceded by a series of regional meetings in Africa, Asia, and Latin America.

Malnutrition

Although data are incomplete, a 1990 UNICEF survey suggests that more than one third of the developing world's children under 5 years of age (excluding China) are malnourished (90). Of these 150 million children, at least one in six—25 million—is severely malnourished. Most of the world's malnourished children reside in Asia—60 percent (91) excluding China, 80 percent including China (92). In sub-Saharan Africa, the incidence of malnutrition appears to be increasing (93).

How frequently malnutrition is an immediate cause of death is unknown (94). UNICEF, however, estimates that it is a contributing cause in approximately one third of child deaths (95). In Latin America, malnutrition was found to be the underlying or related cause in more than half of all childhood deaths (96).

Malnutrition shows up quickly in young children, acting as an early warning sign of distress, ill health, and famine. The appearance of malnutrition in young children is believed to reflect the health and nutritional situation of all members of the population (97).

Malnutrition can lower a child's immunity, making the child more susceptible to diseases such as diarrhea, measles, and respiratory infections. These in turn reduce appetite, cause nutrient loss, inhibit absorption, and alter the body's metabolism, thereby resulting in inadequate dietary intake and further malnutrition. This vicious cycle of malnutrition and infection has been termed the "most prevalent public health problem in the world today" (98).

Often the cycle begins even earlier when malnourished women give birth to babies with low birth weight (2,500 grams or less). Some 350 million women are estimated to have nutritional anemia (99). These women are more likely to die in childbirth as well as to have babies too small to thrive. Between 12 and 15 percent of all babies in developing countries are born with low birth weight and these babies account for 30–40 percent of all infant deaths (100). Low birth weight babies are seven times more likely than other babies to die of respiratory infections and three times more likely to die of diarrhea (101). In the 1980s, nearly 1 of every 10 babies in Latin America had low birth weight which was a factor in 78 percent of early neonatal deaths (i.e., those deaths that occur in the first week of life) (102). Measures to reduce low birth weight—such as improved nutritional health for women and girls, more food and rest during pregnancy, and increased spacing between births—could significantly reduce infant deaths.

The international community has committed itself to halving the incidence of severe and moderate malnutrition among children by the year 2000. If that target is to be met, parents and community health workers must be given basic nutrition information and trained to monitor children's growth. For example, exclusive breastfeeding for the first few months of life can improve child health significantly. As noted above, it reduces diarrheal morbidity and provides newborns with the best possible nourishment as well as antibodies against common infections. UNICEF estimates breastfeeding could save 1.5 million lives a year. Because breastfeeding acts as a natural contraceptive by inhibiting ovulation, it lowers fertility rates and helps lengthen birth spacing, thus improving the health of both mother and child (103).

Two other widespread nutritional problems–vitamin A and iodine deficiency—require attention. Some 40 million children under 5 suffer from vitamin A deficiency (104). Every year, 250,000 children are permanently blinded by the disease and another 250,000 have their eyesight partially impaired. At least 100,000 of these die within a few weeks of contracting the disease (105). In addition, lack of vitamin A has been associated with other diseases, including diarrhea and respiratory infection (106) (107). Vitamin A supplementation has been found to reduce measles-associated mortality by up to 50 percent (108) (109).

Improvements in vitamin A status, either through supplementation or dietary changes, are expected to save the sight of 250,000–500,000 children in developing countries each year, and the lives of 1 million children annually (110). In the longer term, adding foods rich in vitamin A such as green leafy vegetables and yellow fruits to diets is the best means of overcoming vitamin A deficiency (111). In fact, it has been argued that supplementation is a diversion of resources from the necessary task of improving diets (112). However, the mounting evidence on the benefits of adequate vitamin A consumption, combined with the difficulties in bringing about dietary changes and the seasonal or general lack of foods rich in vitamin A in many areas, is providing growing support for vitamin A supplementation for children and mothers to alleviate short-term or particularly severe deficiencies (113) (114) (115).

As a result of iodine deficiency disorder (IDD), 200–300 million people are afflicted with goiter, 20 million with mental retardation, and at least 6 million with cretinism. IDD is most prevalent in mountainous regions and flood-prone areas; when iodine is washed from the soil, whole communities may suffer, with children the most affected. Without iodine, they grow up stunted, retarded, apathetic, and incapable of normal development, speech, or hearing. Ensuring that diets include iodized salt or administering iodine in oil either orally or through injection can remedy the deficiency (116).

IMPROVING CHILDREN'S HEALTH

There is no direct measure of a population's general health, well-being, and productive potential. Although mortality figures measure only the extreme outcome of ill-health—death—they also indicate the extent of health problems in a population. Obviously, widespread health problems can affect a country's productivity and development potential.

Both infant and under-five mortality rates are considered to reflect levels of nutrition (especially among pregnant women, infants, and children), education (especially female literacy) (117), general socioeconomic status, and access to health services (118). Of the two measures, the under-five mortality rate is considered a better technical indicator, both because data collection is better and because it is one of the few social indicators for which long-run time series are available.

Reducing child mortality is possible at various levels of national income. It can be achieved through broad social and economic development or through direct targeted interventions—interventions that for a number of reasons are also direct investments in sustainable development.

First, as previously discussed, over the long run, reducing child deaths slows down the rate of population growth. In most countries, this change from high mortality-high fertility to low mortality-low fertility is not evident until under-five mortality rates fall to 150—or even 100—deaths per 1,000 live births. From initial child mortality rates of 300 or more, many countries now have reached this critical point where further declines in child mortality can be expected to be accompanied by steep declines in fertility. Where strong family planning programs exist, the decline in births is likely to take place even more quickly (119). Figure 6.6 shows a strong association between lower child death rates and the use of contraceptive measures in 67 countries for which data on both indicators are available.

Second, the environmental conditions that are both a symptom and a result of underdevelopment cause much of the ill health and disease affecting today's children. Measures that simultaneously address the related issues of poverty, ill health, and environmental degradation include providing adequate water supplies, safe sanitation facilities, and small-scale irrigation (which can increase household food supply and income as well as avoid the negative environmental and health effects of large-scale irrigation).

Third, healthy children who grow into healthy adults are more likely to make productive contributions to their communities and their countries, as well as to pass on positive health practices to the next generation. Sustainable development depends on a productive, healthy, educated population. (See Chapter 1, "Dimensions of Sustainable Development.")

Health and Poverty

A society's overall level of income is not necessarily a good indicator of its children's life chances as measured by infant and child mortality rates. Compare, for example, Sri Lanka and Brazil. At an average annual per capita income of only $430, Sri Lanka has one of the lowest child mortality rates of all developing countries (36 per 1,000). Brazil, with an average annual per capita income five times higher than Sri Lanka's ($2,550), has a child mortality rate twice as large (77 per 1,000). (See Chapter 15, "Basic Economic Indicators," Table 15.1, and Chapter 16, "Population and Human Development," Table 16.3.) With an average annual per capita income of $182, the state of Kerala in India is poorer than India as a whole; yet in 1986, the state had an infant mortality rate of 27 per 1,000, while India's was 86 per 1,000 (120).

As the *Human Development Report* points out, social programs aimed at improving literacy and health care can have a bigger effect on child mortality than simply increasing GNP. Figures 6.6 and 6.7 show that child mortality is inversely correlated with the use of contraception and with female literacy. There is only a small correlation between GNP and child mortality within developing countries (121). However, in the absence of concentrated health and education programs, poorer children do suffer more health problems than wealthier children. In the poorer Northeast of Brazil, for example, the 1986 infant mortality rate of 116 per 1,000 live births is comparable to many African countries and more than twice that in the rest of Brazil (52 per 1,000) (122). After Sri Lanka changed its food subsidy policies in the late 1970s, the infant mortality rate in 1980 was twice as high among the poorest agricultural workers (100 per 1,000) as it was for the country as a whole (50 per 1,000) (123).

In developed countries as well, it is the poorest segments of society whose children suffer most. In the United States, the Department of Health and Human Services has found that poor children are more likely both to be ill and to have many more risk factors for poor health than children in families with higher incomes. One quarter of all children under age 6 are members of families living below the government-defined poverty level. These children are more likely to suffer from prematurity, low birth weight, birth defects, and infant death. They are twice as likely, between the ages of 1 and 2, to have iron deficiency anemia. They are also at greater risk of growth retardation and impaired mental and physical development, and they experience more sickness from infectious and other debilitating conditions. In 1980, U.S. children from families with incomes under $5,000 had slightly more than nine disability days, compared with four disability days for children from families with incomes of $25,000 or more (124).

In the United Kingdom, a child born to professional parents can expect to live more than five years longer than a child born to parents who perform unskilled manual labor (125). In the Soviet Union, infant mortality rates in 1987 were 19 per 1,000 live births in urban areas and 27 per 1,000 live births in rural areas (126). Such large gaps can be found even within communities. In Guatemala City, 1976 data showed that the mortality rate for children under age 2 was 113 per 1,000 live births for poor illiterate women, compared with 33 per 1,000 live births for middle-class women with secondary education (127).

Water and Sanitation

Universal access to safe drinking water and to sanitary disposal of excreta are two of the major international targets for improving the health and well-being of children. These goals were set during the International Drinking Water Supply and Sanitation Decade of the 1980s and endorsed again at the 1990 World Summit for Children. As of 1990, 81 percent of urban areas and 58 percent of rural areas had access to safe water supplies; 71 percent of urban areas and 48 percent of rural areas had access to sanitation (128).

A 1990 review of 144 community-level studies concluded that when water and sanitation are made available to people, substantial health impacts can be achieved. In particular, the review found that water and sanitation was associated with a median reduction in child mortality of 55 percent. These community studies also suggest that, particularly for diarrheal disease, improvements in excreta disposal and water *quantity* have even greater health impacts than improvements in water quality (129).

The gains to be made from improving water supplies (both quantity and quality) and sanitation are not automatic, however. Simply installing water taps, pit latrines, hand pumps, and other hardware is not enough; their success depends as well on community participation and changes in behavior (130). Studies have found, for example, that handwashing can reduce the incidence of diarrheal disease by 14–48 percent (131).

The cumulative effect of reducing a number of water- and sanitation-related diseases may be significantly greater than the measurement of any one disease would indicate; child mortality, for example, may be reduced more than the incidence of diarrhea (132). Moreover, improvements in water and sanitation may reduce the *severity* of disease even more than the incidence.

There are also indirect benefits that follow initial improvements. Difficult to quantify, these benefits are nonetheless significant. Well-designed investments in water and sanitation bring socioeconomic, educational, and nutritional benefits. Additionally, by reducing illness they improve productivity and the ability to learn, which in turn increase general well-being, making water and sanitation measures even more cost-effective (133).

The Role of Women

An estimated three quarters of all health care takes place at home, where women—particularly in their role as mothers—generally have responsibility for promoting their families' health and nutrition (134). Much

Figure 6.6 Under-Five Mortality by Percent of Parents Using Contraception

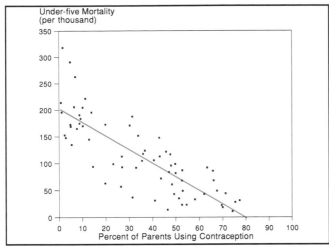

Source: Chapter 16, "Population and Human Development," Tables 16.3 and 16.6.
Note: Based on data reported by 67 developing countries. Each dot represents data from one country.

Figure 6.7 Under-Five Mortality by Degree of Adult Female Literacy

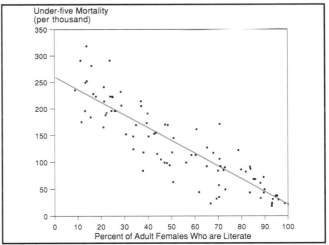

Source: Chapter 16, "Population and Human Development," Tables 16.3 and 16.6.
Note: Based on data reported by 89 developing countries. Each dot represents data from one country.

has been learned recently about which factors help or hinder women in improving their children's health.

Women's education is closely related to child health, whether health is measured in terms of infant and child mortality or children's nutritional status (135) (136). Figure 6.7 shows a high correlation between female literacy and child mortality rates. Detailed studies of 28 countries show a nearly consistent inverse relationship between child mortality and mothers' education (137).

Women's education can improve children's health through a variety of mechanisms: increased use of health services and better knowledge of nutrition; more decisionmaking power within the family and the community; and greater earning power. Women with higher levels of education are more likely to plan their families and thus to increase birth spacing, reducing a major mortality risk factor (138).

Increased education of mothers often is associated with higher education levels of fathers, higher levels of household income, the availability of water and sanitation, and the availability of other health inputs—all factors that also tend to be associated with improved child health. The net effect of either mother's or father's education on health is difficult to determine precisely (139) (140). Education of a mother is estimated to be twice as effective as education of a father in lowering infant and child mortality (141). It is not necessarily the content of the education that makes a difference in children's health but the mother's increased access to information, including health information (142).

Lack of education is not the only problem constraining mothers from protecting their children's health. Poor rural women in developing countries often work 60 to 90 hours per week gathering wood, collecting water, growing and cooking food, contributing to the family income, and caring for their children (143). For these women, steps to make immunization more acces-

sible and the administration of oral rehydration therapy easier may be key to their ability to raise healthy children (144).

Health Care

The technologies—such as immunization and oral rehydration therapy—that have made a significant difference in child health depend on a well-informed parent supported by an accessible health worker. The parent, usually the mother, must recognize the initial symptoms in time to provide home care or seek outside assistance. She must also be able to turn to someone who can immunize children, take other steps to prevent illness, and treat children who do fall ill. This person need not be an expensively educated physician; a well-trained health worker, preferably one with roots in the community and opportunities for both further education and support, can handle most situations. Access to such community health workers is essential if the opportunities for significantly reducing child deaths are to be realized.

Almost three quarters of the health expenditures of developing countries are devoted to urban hospitals that provide expensive, Western-style curative care to a minority of the population. UNICEF estimates that reducing this amount to 45 or 50 percent of total government expenditures on health would release enough funds to train the 1 million health workers needed to provide health services to the poorest 1 billion people in the developing world (145).

INDUSTRIALIZATION AND URBANIZATION

Although most environmental causes of poor health in developing-country children are related to poverty and a lack of modern development—lack of water and sanitation, poor housing, indoor air pollution resulting from the burning of wood and dung—some parts of the developing world face health hazards from industrial pollutants and urban development. Aggregate data are scarce, but evidence is mounting that industrialization and urbanization are combining to expose some populations to a variety of toxic chemicals contaminating the air, water, soil, and food. It is an area in which the need for more research and better data gathering is urgent.

Industrial Pollutants

Pollution in whatever form affects children more than adults, and poor children—who are exposed to more kinds and higher levels of pollution—are affected most of all. Children's smaller body weights and developing organs put them at greater risk. So do their habits: infants suck indiscriminately on contaminated objects; older children play on streets filled with car fumes and lead exhaust, on sewage-polluted beaches, or on open spaces that collect hazardous wastes. Malnourished and disease-prone children are even more vulnerable (146).

The fetus is perhaps most vulnerable. Methyl mercury, pesticides, polychlorinated byphenyls (PCBs), carbon monoxide, and such self-administered contaminants as alcohol and tobacco have been shown to have adverse health consequences for exposed fetuses (147). Although no aggregate data exist on the extent of the problem, selected data provide a good indication.

Mercury in seafood ingested by pregnant women has been linked to cerebral palsy in infants. On average, mercury levels in these babies' blood is 47 percent higher than those of their mothers (148). Children whose mothers ate foods contaminated with PCBs have suffered various forms of retarded growth (149). Carbon monoxide, which WHO has found regularly reaches unhealthy levels in many cities, can result in decreases in fetal weight, increases in perinatal mortality, and brain damage, depending on the length of time a pregnant woman was exposed and the concentration in the air. Here, too, the concentration in the fetus generally exceeds that in the mother (150).

Air Pollution

Air pollution—once a problem only in the industrialized world—now affects most large urban centers in developing countries; the number of vehicles, poor vehicle maintenance, industrial growth, the absence of effective air-quality regulations, and the burning of charcoal, wood, and paraffin by growing slum populations for fuel and cooking combine to create some of the dirtiest cities in the world (151) (152). Although environmental improvements there have been remarkable in recent years, the city of Cubatao, Brazil in 1980 reported grim statistics regarding health effects of air pollution. In the industrial city, 40 out of every 1,000 babies were stillborn; another 40, mostly deformed, died in the first week of life. In the same year, with a population of 80,000, Cubatao had some 10,000 medical emergencies involving tuberculosis, pneumonia, bronchitis, emphysema, asthma, and other nose and throat ailments (153). The link between air pollution

and the incidence of respiratory and pulmonary diseases in children, who inhale about twice as many pollutants per unit of body weight as do adults, is well-demonstrated (154) (155).

Lead Poisoning

Lead is a particular problem for children under 6. Excessive exposure impairs intelligence, growth, ability to hear and perceive language, and concentration (156). Even exposure to low levels seems to be associated with subsequent intellectual deficiencies (157) (158). The level of what is considered toxic has been continually reduced in the last 10 to 15 years as a result of new research showing how severe the consequences of lead exposure can be (159) (160).

Lead-based paint and exhaust fumes from leaded gasoline are two major sources of lead exposure; however, some children may be dangerously exposed from other sources as well. Lead workers bring home lead dust on their clothes, shoes, and hair (161). Painting, pottery glazing, jewelry making, stained glass work, metal sculpting, and other cottage craft industries that use lead or products that contain lead may involve the whole family; in Mexico, children whose families manufactured pottery were found to have higher blood-level concentrations and lower mental performance than children from families of similar socioeconomic background but who were employed in other occupations (162).

While airborne lead concentrations from industrial emissions and automobile exhaust are declining in most industrialized countries, they are increasing in developing-country urban areas (163). High levels of airborne lead have been found along busy roads in Delhi, Kuala Lumpur, and Zimbabwe (164) (165) (166). A survey of children living near a lead-smelting plant in Brazil found high levels of both zinc protoporphyrin and lead in their blood; the levels correlated to the children's age, their proximity to the plant, and length of residence (167). In Mexico City, 7 out of 10 newborns were found to have lead blood levels higher than the WHO norm (168).

Even in the United States, where the lead content of paint used for residential structures, toys, furniture, and eating utensils has been limited since 1971 (169) and unleaded gasoline has been required for new automobiles since 1975, 3–4 million children are estimated to have lead blood levels above the maximum threshold defined by the Environmental Protection Agency for neuropsychological impairment. Approximately 17 percent of all children living in metropolitan areas have blood levels in this range; among poor black children, the rate is 62 percent (170).

Water Pollution

In many developing countries, urban water sources used for drinking, washing, and cooking are threatened by biological pollution from human waste and chemical pollution from industrial toxic wastes. South America, for example, pollutes nearly 11 times more

Box 6.2 World Summit for Children: Declaration and Plan of Action

At the World Summit for Children, held in September 1990, the leaders of 71 countries committed themselves to taking high-level political action to assure the well-being of children (1). This commitment involves:
■ Ratifying and implementing the Convention on the Rights of the Child.
■ Promoting prenatal care and reductions in infant and child mortality.
■ Eradicating hunger, malnutrition, and famine.
■ Strengthening the role and status of women.
■ Supporting the role of the family, as well as support for children separated from their families.
■ Providing educational and training opportunities for children.
■ Addressing the plight of children in especially difficult circumstances— including victims of apartheid and foreign occupation; orphans; street children; migrant and refugee children; displaced children and victims of natural and man-made disasters; and disabled, abused, socially disadvantaged, and exploited children.
■ Protecting children from conflict.

■ Protecting the environment.
■ Alleviating poverty and revitalizing economic growth.

To achieve these broad goals, the Summit adopted a Plan of Action with a number of specific goals, many of which had previously been endorsed in a variety of international settings:
■ Reduction of the 1990 under-five mortality rates by one third or to a level of 70 per 1,000 live births, whichever is the greater reduction.
■ Reduction of maternal mortality rates to half the 1990 levels.
■ Reduction of severe and moderate malnutrition among children under 5 to half the 1990 levels.
■ Universal access to safe drinking water and to sanitary means of excreta disposal.
■ Universal access to basic education, with at least 80 percent of primary-school-age children completing primary education.
■ Reduction of the adult illiteracy rate to at least half its 1990 level, with emphasis on improving female literacy.
■ Protection of children in especially difficult circumstances.

Toward these ends, some 25 specific goals were adopted that included increasing levels of child immunization to at least 90 percent, eradicating polio by 2000, eliminating neonatal tetanus by 1995, reducing measles deaths by 95 percent by 1995, reducing by one third the deaths due to acute respiratory infection, elimination of iodine deficiency disorder and vitamin A deficiency, and access by all couples to information and services to prevent pregnancies occurring too early, too late, too close, or too often.

References and Notes

1. The "World Declaration on the Survival, Protection and Development of Children," and "Plan of Action for Implementing the World Declaration on the Survival, Protection and Development of Children," both adopted at the World Summit for Children, September 30, 1990, are reprinted in United Nations Children's Fund, *The State of the World's Children 1991* (Oxford University Press, New York, 1991), pp. 51-74.

freshwater per capita than Europe, largely because less than 10 percent of its sewage is treated (171).

Infants, who need more fluids in relation to body weight than older children and adults, are particularly vulnerable to health hazards caused by water pollution. Nitrate in groundwater is a growing cause of concern in several countries, as the use of nitrate fertilizer and manure increases. Not in itself dangerous, nitrate combines with bacteria in the mouth to become nitrite, which can induce methemoglobinemia (a reduction in the oxygen-carrying capacity of the blood), especially in infants who drink baby formula mixed with water containing nitrates (172).

Hazards of Urbanization

Although urban areas have lower infant and child mortality rates in the aggregate than rural areas, the health status of urban subpopulations varies widely. The poorest urban populations—often living in illegal squatter settlements—suffer from overcrowding, inadequate housing, contaminated water supplies, poor or nonexistent waste disposal and sanitation, and exposure to industrial pollutants. Large cities tend to have the highest concentrations of water, sanitation, and health care facilities, but as many as 30–60 percent of the poorest people do not have access to them (173).

Numerous studies show that children living in these conditions have higher rates of diarrhea, respiratory infection, tuberculosis, malnutrition, and death than children in other urban communities or even in surrounding rural areas (174). Children in squatter settlements may be 50 times as likely to die before age 5 than those born in developed countries (175).

In addition, the conditions of their poverty put these urban children at increased risk of accidents, crimes, violence, and psychological harm. A growing number of children live in the streets—without shelter, adult supervision, or income.

BUILDING A GLOBAL CONSENSUS

Dramatic declines in infant mortality took place in the industrialized countries in the early 20th Century, not primarily as a result of advances in medicine, but as a direct result of advances in overall living conditions, including better nutrition, improved hygiene and sanitation, and voluntary birth limitation (176). The question today is whether further mortality decreases must wait for overall economic development or whether they can be achieved—even in advance of overall improvements in the economy—by pursuing concerted strategies to improve food supply, water and sanitation, education, and health care.

For the last 10 years, WHO, UNICEF, and other multilateral agencies have urged the international community to pursue an aggressive "child survival" strategy. The program has focused on promoting wide-spread acceptance of several "technologies"—including oral rehydration therapy, breastfeeding, improved weaning practices, and immunization—and on providing increased access to food, family planning, and female literacy.

The strategy has had some outstanding successes. UNICEF in 1991 calculated that child survival interventions were saving 3.2 million young lives each year (177). But high mortality rates still prevail in many countries, and growing problems such as pediatric HIV and AIDS threaten the gains that have been made.

In the 10 countries of Central and East Africa, for example, HIV/AIDS could cause 250,000 to 500,000 additional deaths a year among children under age 5 by the year 2000. These children will be extremely sick before they die, putting severe strains on health care resources. Additionally, by the year 2000, HIV/AIDS is expected to orphan as many as 5.5 million children—11 percent of all the region's children under age 15 (178).

The World Summit for Children brought together representatives from 159 countries, including 71 heads of state or government. In a Declaration on the Survival, Protection and Development of Children, these representatives made a commitment to reduce child death rates by one third and malnutrition rates by one half by the end of the decade. The accompanying Plan of Action for meeting those goals contains detailed targets for specific diseases, nutrition, immunization, family planning, breastfeeding, water and sanitation, and education. (See Box 6.2.)

The world summit epitomized the growing global consensus that a commitment to children is important both in itself and as an investment in the sustainability of the planet. In November 1989, the United Nations adopted the Convention on the Rights of the Child, which sets standards for children's survival, health, and education and seeks to protect children who are exploited, abandoned, or abused. As of August 1991, 95 countries had ratified the Convention; another 45 had signed (but not yet ratified) it (179).

Meeting the goals set at the world summit will cost approximately $20 billion a year, according to UNICEF estimates, and will require commitments from both developing and developed countries (180). Developing countries will have to reallocate some military spending to social spending and divert some funding from hospitals and secondary education to primary health care and primary education. Additional support from industrialized countries will also be necessary to achieve these goals.

The status and progress of children's health and nutrition is a telling measure of society's overall development. Children must not only survive but be given the opportunity to thrive.

Conditions and Trends was written by World Resources *Senior Editor Robert Livernash. Focus On Children's Health was written by Rosemarie Philips, a writer and editor on environment and development issues in Alexandria, Virginia. Dirk Bryant,* World Resources *research assistant, contributed to this chapter.*

References and Notes

1. Thomas W. Merrick, *U.S. Population Assistance: A Continued Priority for the 1990s?* (Population Reference Bureau, Washington, D.C., April 1990), p. 16.
2. United Nations Population Division, *Long-Range World Population Projections: Two Centuries of Population Growth, 1950-2150* (United Nations, New York, 1991), p. vi.
3. Population Reference Bureau, *1991 World Population Data Sheet* (Population Reference Bureau, Washington, D.C., 1991).
4. John Bongaarts, W. Parker Mauldin, and James F. Phillips, "The Demographic Impact of Family Planning Programs," *Studies in Family Planning*, Vol. 21, No. 6 (November/December 1990), p. 305.
5. *Op. cit.* 3. Note: These rates refer to the percent of currently married or "in union" women of reproductive age (15–49) who use any form of contraception.
6. United Nations Population Fund, formally the United Nations Fund for Population Activities (UNFPA), *The State of World Population 1991* (UNFPA, New York, 1991), pp. 11-14.
7. *Ibid.*, p. 23.
8. World Resources Institute in collaboration with the United Nations Environment Programme and the United Nations Development Programme, *World Resources 1992-93* (Oxford University Press, New York, 1992), Table 16.3.
9. United Nations Environment Programme (UNEP), *Environmental Data Report*, prepared for UNEP by the GEMS Monitoring and Assessment Research Centre in collaboration with the World Resources Institute and the United Kingdom Department of the Environment (Basil Blackwell, Oxford, U.K., 1991), p. 242.
10. World Health Organization (WHO) *Public Health Impact of Pesticides Used in Agriculture* (WHO, Geneva, 1990), p. 86.

11. Alan D. Lopez, "Causes of Death: An Assessment of Global Patterns of Mortality Around 1985," *World Health Statistics Quarterly*, Vol. 43, No. 2 (1990), pp. 92-93.
12. Division of Epidemiological Surveillance and Health Situation and Trend Assessment, World Health Organization (WHO), *Global Estimates for Health Situation Assessment and Projections 1992* (WHO, Geneva, forthcoming).
13. *Ibid.*
14. *Op. cit.* 11.
15. *Op. cit.* 12.
16. *Op. cit.* 12.
17. Division of Epidemiological Surveillance and Health Situation and Trend Assessment, *Global Estimates for Health Situation Assessment and Projections 1990* (World Health Organization, Geneva, 1990), pp. 14-29.
18. *Ibid.*, p. 18.
19. *Ibid.*, p. 25.
20. *Op. cit.* 12.
21. United Nations Environment Programme (UNEP), *Environmental Data Report*, prepared for UNEP by the GEMS Monitoring and Assessment Research Centre in collaboration with the World Resources Institute and the United Kingdom Department of the Environment (Basil Blackwell, Oxford, U.K., 1989), p. 348.
22. *Op. cit.* 17, p. 27.
23. *Op. cit.* 17, p. 19.
24. *Op. cit.* 21, p. 349.
25. *Op. cit.* 17, p. 20.
26. United Nations Development Programme, *Human Development Report 1990* (Oxford University Press, New York, 1990), p. 40.
27. *Ibid.*, pp. 9-13.
28. United Nations Development Programme, *Human Development Report 1991* (Oxford University Press, Oxford, 1991), p. 2.
29. *Ibid.*, p. 3.

30. *Op. cit.* 26, p. 42.
31. *Op. cit.* 28, p. 63.
32. Pan American Health Organization (PAHO), "Update: The Cholera Situation in the Americas," *Epidemiological Bulletin*, Vol. 12, No. 3 (PAHO, Washington, D.C., 1991), Table 1, p. 11.
33. World Health Organization (WHO), "Cholera: Ancient Scourge on the Rise," *WHO Features*, No. 154 (WHO, Geneva, April 1991), p. 1.
34. Renate Plaut, Epidemiologist, Health Situation and Trend Assessment Program, Pan American Health Organization, Washington, D.C., September 1991 (personal communication).
35. Lawrence K. Altman, "'Catastrophic' Cholera Is Sweeping Africa," *New York Times*, July 23, 1991, p. C 2.
36. Pan American Health Organization (PAHO), "Cholera Situation in the Americas," *Epidemiological Bulletin*, Vol. 12, No. 1 (PAHO, Washington, D.C., 1991), p. 2.
37. *Op. cit.* 33, p. 3.
38. *Op. cit.* 33, pp. 2-3.
39. *Op. cit.* 36, pp. 18-24.
40. United Nations Department of Economic and Social Affairs, *World Population Prospects 1990* (United Nations, New York, 1991), pp. 227-231.
41. United Nations (U.N.), *Mortality of Children Under Age 5: World Estimates and Projections, 1950-2025* (U.N., New York, 1988), p. 22.
42. *Op. cit.* 17, p. 17.
43. *Op. cit.* 12.
44. United Nations Environment Program (UNEP) and United Nations Children's Fund (UNICEF), *Children and the Environment: The State of the Environment, 1990* (UNICEF and UNEP, New York and Nairobi, 1990), pp. 8-10.

45. Lloyd Timberlake and Laura Thomas, *When the Bough Breaks...Our Children, Our Environment* (Earthscan Publications, London, 1990), pp. 1-11.

46. "World Declaration on the Survival, Protection and Development of Children," in United Nations Children's Fund, *The State of the World's Children, 1991* (Oxford University Press, New York, 1991), pp. 1 and 57.

47. *Op. cit.* 44, pp. 3-4.

48. *Op. cit.* 41, p. 30.

49. United Nations Population Division, *World Population Prospects 1990* (United Nations, New York, 1991), pp. 228-230.

50. Kenneth Hill and Anne R. Pebley, "Child Mortality in the Developing World," *Population and Development Review*, Vol. 15, No. 4 (December 1989), p. 680.

51. *Op. cit.* 12.

52. *Op. cit.* 12.

53. Pan American Health Organization (PAHO), *Health Conditions in the Americas*, Vol. I, Scientific Publication No. 524 (PAHO, Washington, D.C., 1990), p. 404.

54. Global Environment Monitoring Service, *Assessment of Urban Air Quality* (United Nations Environment Programme and World Health Organization, 1988), pp. 86-88.

55. M.H. Merson, "Acute Respiratory Infections Control Programme: Summary Overview—Progress and Plans," paper presented at the Ninth Meeting of Interested Parties, Diarrhoeal Diseases Control Programme and Acute Respiratory Infections Control Program, World Health Organization, Geneva, June 29-30, 1989, pp. 2-3.

56. H.R. Hapsara, Director, Division of Epidemiological Surveillance and Health Situation and Trend Assessment, World Health Organization, Geneva, July 1991 (personal communication).

57. *Op. cit.* 55, pp. 3-4.

58. United Nations Children's Fund, *The State of the World's Children, 1991* (Oxford University Press, New York, 1991), p. 4.

59. *Op. cit.* 12.

60. United Nations Children's Fund, *The State of the World's Children, 1990* (Oxford University Press, New York, 1990), p. 21.

61. *Op. cit.* 12.

62. Programme for Control of Diarrhoeal Diseases, *Interim Programme Report 1990* (World Health Organization, Geneva, 1991), pp. 34-36.

63. Norbert Hirschhorn and William B. Greenough, III, "Progress in Oral Rehydration Therapy," *Scientific American*, Vol. 264, No. 5 (May 1991), p. 50.

64. *Op. cit.* 58.

65. "Water with Sugar and Salt," *The Lancet* (August 5, 1978), p. 300.

66. *Op. cit.* 17, p. 47.

67. *Op. cit.* 60, pp. 22-23.

68. *Cereal Based Oral Rehydration Therapy for Diarrhoea: Report of the International Symposium on Cereal Based Oral Rehydration Therapy*, Katherine Elliott and Kathy Attawell, eds. (The Aga Khan Foundation and the International Child Health Foundation, Columbia, Maryland, 1990), pp. 17-18.

69. *Op. cit.* 60.

70. Anne Gadomski and Robert E. Black, "Impact of the Direct Interventions," in *Child Survival Programs: Issues for the 1990s* (The Johns Hopkins University, School of Hygiene and Public Health, Baltimore, Maryland, 1990), p. 86.

71. Barry M. Popkin, Linda Adair, John S. Akin, *et al.*, "Breast-Feeding and Diarrheal Morbidity," *Pediatrics*, Vol. 86, No. 6 (December 1990), p. 874.

72. Expanded Programme on Immunization, "Information System," World Health Organization, Geneva, April 1991, Table 1.1.2, p. 2.

73. *Op. cit.* 58, pp. 1, 5, and 15.

74. *Op. cit.* 12.

75. "Plan of Action for Implementing the World Declaration on the Survival, Protection and Development of Children in the 1990s," in United Nations Children's Fund, *The State of the World's Children, 1991* (Oxford University Press, New York, 1991), p. 74.

76. *Op. cit.* 12.

77. *Op. cit.* 60, p. 24.

78. M.A. Koenig, M.A. Khan, B. Wojtyniak, *et al.*, "The Impact of Measles Vaccination on Childhood Mortality in Matlab, Bangladesh," Programs Division, Working Paper No. 3 (The Population Council, New York, June 1990), p. 13.

79. *Op. cit.* 12.

80. Vincent Fauveau, Robert Steinglass, Masuma Mamdani, *et al.*, "Maternal Mortality Due to Tetanus: Magnitude of the Problem and Potential Control Measures," paper presented at the National Council for International Health meeting, Arlington, Virginia, June 1991 (John Snow, Inc., Arlington, Virginia, 1991).

81. *Neonatal Tetanus Elimination: Issues and Future Directions*, Proceedings of a Meeting held January 9-11, 1990 (Resources for Child Health and MotherCare with the U.S. Agency for International Development, Alexandria, Virginia, 1990), p. 1.

82. *Op. cit.* 58, p. 14.

83. Roxane M. Eikhof, Information Officer, Expanded Program on Immunization, Pan American Health Organization, Washington, D.C., September 1991 (personal communication).

84. Division of Control of Tropical Diseases, "World Malaria Situation, 1988," *World Health Statistics Quarterly*, Vol. 43, No. 2 (World Health Organization, Geneva, 1988), p. 78.

85. J.G. Breman and C. C. Campbell, "Combatting Severe Malaria in African Children," *Bulletin of the World Health Organization*, Vol. 66, No. 5 (World Health Organization, Geneva, 1988), p. 611.

86. Division of Epidemiological Surveillance and Health Situation and Trend Assessment, "Introduction," *World Health Statistics Quarterly*, Vol. 43, No. 2 (World Health Organization, Geneva, 1990), p. 50.

87. *Op. cit.* 12.

88. *Op. cit.* 44, p. 27.

89. *Op. cit.* 84.

90. Beverley A. Carlson and Tessa M. Wardlaw, "A Global, Regional and Country Assessment of Child Malnutrition," Staff Working Paper No. 7 (United Nations Children's Fund, New York, 1990), p. 12.

91. *Ibid.*, p. 22.

92. *Op. cit.* 58, p. 29.

93. United Nations Children's Fund (UNICEF), *Strategy for Improved Nutrition of Children and Women in Developing Countries* (UNICEF, New York, 1990), p. 9.

94. Andrew Tomkins and Fiona Watson, "Malnutrition and Infection: A Review," Nutrition Policy Discussion Paper No. 5, United Nations Administrative Committee on Coordination, Subcommittee on Nutrition, New York, October 1989, p. 1.

95. *Op. cit.* 60, p. 17.

96. R.R. Puffer and C. Serrano, *Patterns of Mortality in Childhood*, Scientific Publication No. 262, Pan American Health Organization (PAHO), Washington, D.C., 1973, cited in *Health Conditions in the Americas: 1990 Edition*, Vol. I, Scientific Publication No. 524 (PAHO, Washington, D.C., 1990), Note 17, p. 116.

97. *Op. cit.* 90, pp. 15-17.

98. *Op. cit.* 94.

99. *Op. cit.* 93.

100. Jon E. Rohde, "Why the Other Half Dies: The Science and Politics of Child Mortality in the Third World," *Assignment Children*, Vol. 61-62 (1983), p. 45.

101. World Health Organization (WHO), "Infant and Young Child Nutrition," Executive Board Paper EB85/18, WHO, Geneva, December 8, 1989, cited in Timberlake and Thomas, *When the Bough Breaks*, (Earthscan Publications, London, 1990), Note 8, p. 118.

102. *Op. cit.* 53, p. 58.

103. *Op. cit.* 58, pp. 24, 43.

104. *Op. cit.* 93.

105. *Op. cit.* 60, p. 34.

106. Alfred Sommer, Ignatius Tarwotjo, and Joanne Katz, "Increased Risk of Xerophthalmia Following Diarrhea and Respiratory Disease," *American Journal of Clinical Nutrition*, Vol. 45 (1987), p. 977.

107. Richard G. Feachem, "Vitamin A Deficiency and Diarrhoea: A Review of Interrelationships and their Implications for the Control of Xerophthalmia and Diarrhoea," *Tropical Diseases Bulletin*, Vol. 84, No. 3 (1987), p. R14.

108. Gregory B. Hussey and Max Klein, "A Randomized, Controlled Trial of Vitamin A in Children with Severe Measles," *New England Journal of Medicine*, Vol. 323, No. 3 (July 19, 1990), p. 160.

109. Keith P. West, Jr., R.P. Pokhrel, Joanne Katz, *et al.*, "Efficacy of Vitamin A in Reducing Preschool Child Mortality in Nepal," *Lancet*, Vol. 338 (July 13, 1991), p. 67.

110. Alfred Sommer, Dean, School of Hygiene and Public Health, The Johns Hopkins University, September 1991 (personal communication).

111. *Op. cit.* 60, p. 38.

112. C. Gopalan, "Vitamin A and Child Mortality," *NFI Bulletin*, Vol. 11, No. 3 (Nutrition Foundation of India, New Delhi, July 1990).

113. U.S. Agency for International Development (U.S. AID), *Child Survival 1985-1990: A Sixth Report to Congress on the USAID Program* (U.S. AID, Washington, D.C., May 1991), p. 25.

114. *Op. cit.* 93, p. 29.

115. United Nations Administrative Committee on Coordination Subcommittee on Nutrition, "Malnutrition and Infection," *SCN News*, No. 4 (Late 1989), p. 10.

116. *Op. cit.* 58, p. 40.

117. *Op. cit.* 26, p. 44.

118. *Op. cit.* 53, p. 68.

119. *Op. cit.* 58, pp. 43-45.

120. Richard W. Franke and Barbara H. Chasin, *Kerala: Radical Reform as Development in an Indian State*, (Institute for Food and Development Policy, San Francisco, October 1989), p. 11.

121. Dirk Bryant, Research Assistant, World Resources Institute, unpublished data, 1991.

122. *Op. cit.* 26, pp. 56-57.

123. Bread for the World Institute on Hunger and Development, *Hunger 1990: A Report on the State of World Hunger* (Bread for the World, Washington, D.C., 1990), pp. 27-28.

124. U.S. Department of Health and Human Services, *Healthy People 2000: National Health Promotion and Disease Prevention Objectives*, Conference Edition, (Government Printing Office, Washington, D.C., September 1990), pp. 29-31.

125. "Inequalities in Health: Report of a Research Working Group," D. Black *et al.*, eds. (DHSS, London, 1980), cited in Margaret Whitehead, *The Concepts and Principles of Equity and Health*, (World Health Organization Regional Office for Europe, Copenhagen, 1990), Note 12, p. 2.

126. U.S.S.R. Government Committee for Statistics, *U.S.S.R. Demographic Yearbook: 1990* (Information Publishing Center, Moscow, 1990), p. 382.

127. H. Behm and E. Vargas, *Guatemala: Diferencias Socioeconómicas de la Mortalidad de los Menores de dos Años, 1968-1976* (Ministry of Economics, Directorate General of Statistics, Republic of Guatemala and CELADE, San José, Costa Rica, 1984), Series A/1044, cited in Pan American Health Organization (PAHO), *Health Conditions in the Americas: 1990 Edition*, Vol. I, Scientific Publication No. 524 (PAHO, Washington, D.C., 1990), p. 47.

128. *Op. cit.* 56.

129. Steven A. Esrey, James B. Potash, Leslie Roberts, *et al.*, "Effects of Improved Water Supply and Sanitation on Ascariasis, Diarrhoea, Dracunculiasis, Hookworm Infection, Schistosomiasis, and Trachoma," *Bulletin of the World Health Organization*, Vol. 69, No. 5 (World Health Organization, Geneva, forthcoming).

130. *Ibid.*

131. Richard G. Feachem, "Interventions for the Control of Diarrhoeal Diseases Among Young Children: Promotion of Personal and Domestic Hygiene," *Bulletin of the World Health Organization*, Vol. 62, No. 3 (World Health Organization, Geneva, 1984), pp. 467-476, cited in Branko Cvjetanovic, "Health Effects and Impact of Water Supply and Sanitation," *World Health Statistics Quarterly*, Vol. 39 (World Health Organization, Geneva, 1986), p. 111.

132. *Op. cit.* 129.

133. Branko Cvjetanovic, "Health Effects and Impact of Water Supply and Sanitation," *World Health Statistics Quarterly*, Vol. 39 (World Health Organization, Geneva, 1986), p. 116.

134. Joanne Leslie, Margaret Lycette, and Mayra Buvinic, "Weathering Economic Crises: The Crucial Role of Women in Health," in David E. Bell and Michael R. Reach, *Health, Nutrition, and Economic Crises: Approaches to Policy in the Third World* (Auburn House, Dover, Massachusetts, 1986), p. 307.

135. Susan H. Cochrane, Joanne Leslie, and Donald J. O'Hara, "Parental Education and Child Health: Intracountry Evidence," *Health Policy and Education*, Vol. 2 (1982), p. 213.

136. *Op. cit.* 134, p. 313.

137. Shea Oscar Rutstein, "Levels, Trends and Differentials in Infant and Child Mortality in the Less Developed Countries," paper prepared for the "Child Survival Interventions: Effectiveness and Efficiency" seminar, Institute for Resource Development, June 1991, p. 5.

138. *Op. cit.* 134, p. 313.

139. *Op. cit.* 134, p. 313.

140. *Op. cit.* 135, pp. 213-214.

141. *Op. cit.* 135, p. 247.

142. Kim Streatfield, Masri Singarimbun, and Ian Diamond, "Maternal Education and Child Immunization," *Demography*, Vol. 27, No. 3 (August 1990), pp. 454-455.

143. United Nations (U.N.), *The World's Women: 1970-1990* (U. N., New York, 1991), p. 82.

144. Joanne Leslie, "Women's Time: A Factor in the Use of Child Survival Technologies?" (International Center for Research on Women, Washington, D.C., 1988), pp. 8 and 23.

145. *Op. cit.* 60, pp. 43-44.

146. *Op. cit.* 44, p. 28.

147. *Op. cit.* 44, pp. 18-20.

148. S. Skerfvig, "Mercury in Women Exposed to Methylmercury through Fish Consumption, and in Their Newborn Babies and Breast Milk," *Bulletin of Environmental Contamination Toxicology*, No. 41 (1988), cited in United Nations Environment Program (UNEP) and United Nations Children's Fund (UNICEF), *Children and the Environment: The State of the Environment, 1990* (UNEP and UNICEF, Nairobi and New York, 1990), p. 19.

149. Walter J. Rogan, Beth C. Gladen, Kun-Long Hung, *et al.*, "Congenital Poisoning by Polychlorinated Biphenyls and their Contaminants in Taiwan," *Science*, Vol. 241 (July 15, 1988), p. 334.

150. *Op. cit.* 44, pp. 19-20.

151. *Op. cit.* 44, p. 28.

152. World Health Organization (WHO), *Urbanization and Its Implications for Child Health: Potential for Action* (WHO, in collaboration with the United Nations Environment Programme, Geneva, 1988), p. 18.

153. W. Hoge, "New Menace in Brazil's Valley of Death Strikes Unborn," *New York Times*, September 25, 1980, cited in World Health Organization (WHO), *Urbanization and Its Implications for Child Health: Potential for Action* (WHO, in collaboration with the United Nations Environment Programme, Geneva, 1988), pp. 17-18.

154. W. Dassen, B. Brunekreet, G. Hock, *et al.*, "Decline in Children's Pulmonary Function During an Air Pollution Episode," *Journal of the Air Pollution Control Association*, Vol. 36, No. 11 (1986), p. 1,223.

155. Ayana I. Goren and Sarah Hellmann, "Prevalence of Respiratory Symptoms and Diseases in Schoolchildren Living in a Polluted and in a Low Polluted Area in Israel," *Environmental Research*, Vol. 45, No. 1 (1988), p. 24.

156. Herbert L. Needleman, "The Persistent Threat of Lead: A Singular Opportunity," Commentary, *American Journal of Public Health*, Vol. 79, No. 5 (May 1989), p. 644.

157. Herbert L. Needleman, Alan Schell, David Bellinger, *et al.*, "The Long-Term Effects of Exposure to Low Doses of Lead in Childhood: An 11-Year Follow-Up Report," *New England Journal of Medicine*, Vol. 322, No. 2 (January 11, 1990), p. 83.

158. Herbert L. Needleman and Constantine A. Gatsonis, "Low-Level Lead Exposure and the IQ of Children: A Meta-Analysis of Modern Studies," *Journal of the American Medical Association*, Vol. 263, No. 5 (February 2, 1990), p. 673.

159. *Op. cit.* 156, p. 643.

160. J. S. Lin-Fu, "Historical Perspective on Health Effects of Lead," in Kathryn R. Mahaffey, ed., *Dietary and Environmental Lead: Human Health Effects* (Elsevier, Amsterdam, 1985), pp. 58-59.

161. *Ibid.*, p. 55.

162. Gilberto Molina, Miguel A. Zúñiga, Adolfo Cárdenas, *et. al.*, "Psychological Alterations in Children Exposed to a Lead Rich Home Environment," *PAHO Bulletin*, Vol. 17, No. 2 (1983), p. 191.

163. *Op. cit.* 44, p. 30.

164. *State of India's Environment, 1982: A Citizen's Report* (Centre for Science and the Environment, Delhi, 1983), cited in World Health Organization (WHO), *Urbanization and Its Implications for Child Health: Potential for Action* (WHO, in collaboration with the United Nations Environment Programme, Geneva, 1988), p. 30.

165. S. Sani, "Urbanization and the Atmospheric Environment in Southeast Asia," paper presented at the Seminar of Development, Environment and the Natural Resource Crisis in Asia and the Pacific, Penang, Malaysia (October 1983), cited in World Health Organization (WHO), *Urbanization and Its Implications for Child Health: Potential for Action* (WHO, in collaboration with the United Nations Environment Programme, Geneva, 1988), p. 30.

166. P.T. Achayo Were, "The Development of Road Transport in Africa and Its Effects on Land Use and Environment," *Industry and Environment*, Vol. 6, No. 2 (1983), pp. 25-26, cited in World Health Organization (WHO), *Urbanization and Its Implications for Child Health: Potential for Action* (WHO, in collaboration with the United Nations Environment Programme, Geneva, 1988), p. 30.

167. Fernando M. Carvalho, Annibal M. Silvany-Neto, Tania M. Tavares, *et al.*, "Lead Poisoning Among Children From Santa Amaro, Brazil," *Bulletin of the Pan American Health Organization* (PAHO), Vol. 19, No. 2 (PAHO, Washington, D.C., 1985), p. 168.

168. Hilary F. French, "Clearing the Air," *State of the World, 1990* (Worldwatch Institute, Washington, D.C., 1990), p. 103.

169. *Op. cit.* 160, pp. 53-54.

170. Paul Mushak and Annemarie F. Crocetti, *The Nature and Extent of Lead Poisoning in Children in the United States: A Report to Congress* (U.S. Department of Health and Human Services, Agency for Toxic Substances and Disease Registry, Washington, D.C., 1988), pp. I-11, I-12.

171. *Op. cit.* 53, p. 221.

172. *Op. cit.* 44, p. 26.

173. *Op. cit.* 152, p. 65.

174. *Op. cit.* 152, pp. 18-31.

175. *Op. cit.* 152, p. 7.

176. *Op. cit.* 100, p. 37.

177. United Nation's Children Fund, *The State of the World's Children, 1992* (Oxford University Press, New York, forthcoming).

178. Elizabeth A. Preble, "Impact of HIV/AIDS on African Children," *Social Science Medicine*, Vol. 31, No. 6 (June 1990), p. 679.

179. Per Miljetieg-Olssen, Public Affairs Officer, Division of Public Affairs, United Nations Children's Fund, New York, August 1991 (personal communication).

180. *Op. cit.* 58, p. 15.

7. Food and Agriculture

Global food production has increased substantially over the past two decades, but factors such as population pressures and environmental degradation are undermining agriculture's current condition and future prospects.

Measured in absolute terms, global production increases have been impressive. But in some regions, notably Africa, farmers have not been able to keep pace with rapid increases in population. Africa also is heavily burdened by poverty, which deprives people of the purchasing power to buy food, and by wars, which disrupt food production and distribution.

As population increases, how will farmers in the developing world keep up? Higher yields, not expanded area, have been responsible for most of the recent production increases. To continue that production surge will require new economic advantages such as higher prices or new physical advantages such as additional irrigated land or increased use of inputs. Yet, prices have not provided much incentive in developing countries, investment in irrigation has lagged, and in some regions water is being withdrawn at unsustainable rates. Furthermore, adding inputs such as fertilizers carries substantial environmental risks.

Farmers in the industrialized world face a different set of pressures. They are increasingly aware of the environmental toll taken by conventional farming practices, which can rapidly erode farm soils and wash fertilizers and pesticides into surface waters. To solve these problems, some farmers are using a variety of alternative practices that help reduce pollution and maintain farm resources.

Governments in industrialized countries have tended to forge agricultural policies that support conventional farming and ignore its environmental costs. But some government policies are beginning to change as awareness of environmental degradation grows, giving farmers new incentives to adopt resource-conserving alternative practices.

A change in thinking also is underway. Policymakers only now are beginning to integrate the environmental costs of farming with its economic structure. Soil erosion, for example, costs farmers money by reducing future production, yet this kind of loss never appeared on farmers' books. When such losses are quantified, resource-conserving practices can be both economically and environmentally superior to conventional practices.

CONDITIONS AND TRENDS

Global Trends

Prospects for global food and agriculture are at once promising and troubling. On the one hand, global food production has increased since 1970 and has generally been able to meet the demands of a growing world population. In addition, bumper harvests in the 1990–91 crop year exceeded global consumption and helped reverse a three-year decline in world cereal stocks (1).

It is unclear whether production increases can continue indefinitely. Some factors augur well for global production—for example, improvements in the emerging market economies of Central Europe and possibly a multilateral agreement to liberalize agricultural trade. In the longer term, improvements in the Soviet Union's farm economy are certainly possible. Better control of diseases (human and farm animal) could also open up large areas of potentially productive farming and grazing land in Africa.

On the other hand, most agricultural production in the world uses farming practices that are environmentally unsustainable. New efforts are underway in the industrialized countries to encourage more sustainable practices, but these efforts are as yet quite modest. (See Focus On Agriculture in the Industrialized World: Toward Sustainability, below.)

In developing countries, however, population growth and poverty subvert efforts to introduce sustainable practices and encourage agriculture to expand in ways detrimental to the environment. Population growth causes marginal land to be cultivated and contributes to environmental problems such as soil erosion and deforestation. Population growth also poses an immense challenge to farm productivity: it is far from certain that farmers will be able to adopt sustainable practices and still grow enough food to feed a projected world population of 10 billion or more people in the next century.

In the industrialized countries, food supplies are adequate, populations are relatively stable, incomes are relatively high, and—although poverty still exists—most people are able to buy all the food they require. Beyond a certain point, increases in income do not produce much additional demand for food. Instead, additional production—due mainly to technological innovation and farm policies—tends to generate surpluses.

In developing countries, agriculture varies considerably from region to region. In general, production is increasing in all regions. But in many regions, including Africa, Latin America, and parts of Asia, demand is severely restrained by lack of purchasing power. Shortages of foreign exchange during the recession of the 1980s further depressed food imports in Africa and Latin America.

In Africa, production increases have not kept up with population growth, and famine continues to be a serious problem in some areas. Wars—which can disrupt food production, markets, and relief efforts—

Figure 7.1 World Production of Selected Food Crops, 1970–89

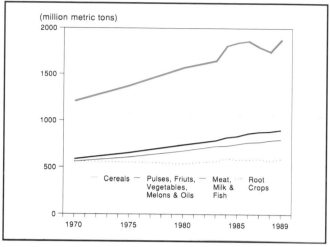

Sources:
1. Food and Agriculture Organization of the United Nations (FAO), *Quarterly Bulletin of Statistics*, Vol. 2 (1990), p. 37.
2. Food and Agriculture Organization of the United Nations (FAO), *1988 Fishery Statistics: Catches and Landings*, Vol. 66 (1990), p. 83.

Note: Data are measured in five-year intervals for 1970–80, and in single-year intervals for 1983–89.

have contributed heavily to famine in many African countries in recent years (2). Drought, poor distribution and marketing, and ineffective government policies also have been important factors. Sudan and Ethiopia are in a particularly perilous condition; famine threatens millions of people in these two countries (3). But the problem is wider than that: maintaining per capita cereal consumption in 55 low-income countries at the 1980–89 level required an estimated 16 million metric tons of food aid in 1990–91, yet only about 10 million metric tons were available (4).

Estimates of the number of people in the world who are undernourished range from about 500 million to about 1 billion. The absolute number of undernourished people may be increasing slightly, although the proportion of the population that is undernourished appears to be declining in all regions except Africa. (See *World Resources 1990–91*, p. 88.)

PRODUCTION TRENDS

The world's output of major food crops—including cereals and the main noncereal crops such as roots and tubers, pulses (peas, beans, and lentils), groundnuts, and bananas and plantains—has expanded significantly over the past 20 years. The most dramatic increase occurred in the production of cereals, which rose about 50 percent, from about 1.2 billion metric tons in 1970 to about 1.8 billion metric tons in 1989. Fruit and vegetables have also made gains, as have meat, milk, and fish; production of root crops has remained stable. (See Figure 7.1.) Much of the year-to-year variation in world production has been due to weather- or policy-induced fluctuations in the industrial countries (5).

Figure 7.2 Index of Food Production in Developing Regions, 1970–90

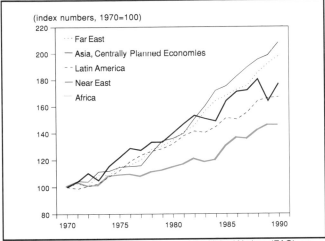

Source: Food and Agriculture Organization of the United Nations (FAO), unpublished data, March 1991.

Notes:

a. Far East = Bangladesh, Bhutan, Brunei Darussalam, East Timor, Hong Kong, India, Indonesia, Republic of Korea, Lao People's Democratic Republic, Macao, Malaysia, Maldives, Myanmar, Nepal, Pakistan, Philippines, Singapore, Sri Lanka, Thailand.

b. Asia, Centrally Planned Economies = Cambodia, China, Democratic People's Republic of Korea, Mongolia, Viet Nam.

c. Near East = *Africa*: Egypt, Libya, Sudan. *Asia*: Afghanistan, Bahrain, Cyprus, Gaza Strip (Palestine), Islamic Republic of Iran, Iraq, Jordan, Kuwait, Lebanon, Oman, Qatar, Kingdom of Saudi Arabia, Syrian Arab Republic, Turkey, United Arab Emirates, Yemen Arab Republic, Democratic Yemen.

Every region of the developing world has substantially increased its food production since 1970. Production in the Asian centrally planned economies has roughly doubled, while the Near East (Egypt, Libya, Sudan, and the Middle East) and Latin America have registered increases in the 60–80 percent range. Production in Africa is up over 40 percent. (See Figure 7.2.) Most of these production increases came from in-

Figure 7.3 Index of Grain Production, Cropland Area, and Yields in Developing Countries, 1970–90

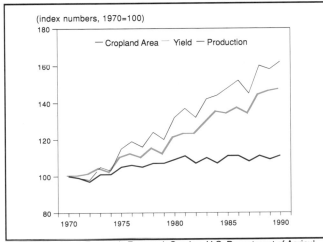

Source: Kim Hjort, Economic Research Service, U.S. Department of Agriculture, Washington, D.C., 1991 (personal communication).

Figure 7.4 Index of Food Imports into Developing Countries by Volume and Value, 1970–89

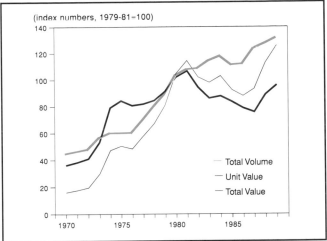

Source: Food and Agriculture Organization of the United Nations (FAO), unpublished data, March 1991.

creases in yield rather than increases in cropland. (See Figure 7.3.)

Imports of food into developing countries have also grown, helped by slight declines in prices from 1980 to 1987. (See Figure 7.4.) In some South American countries, however, both the volume and value of food imports dropped over the past decade. (See Chapter 18, "Food and Agriculture," Table 18.4.) Food exports by developing countries have also risen substantially since 1970, although the increase was primarily driven by increases in volume in the 1980s. (See Figure 7.5.)

Livestock and Fisheries

Livestock populations have risen about 18 percent over the past 20 years. India now has about 200 mil-

Figure 7.5 Index of Food Exports from Developing Countries by Volume and Value, 1970–89

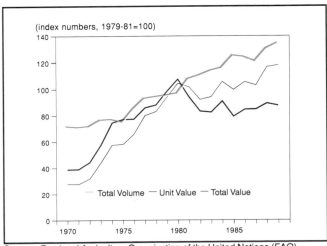

Source: Food and Agriculture Organization of the United Nations (FAO), unpublished data, March 1991.

Figure 7.6 Index of Per Capita Food Production in Developing Regions, 1970–90

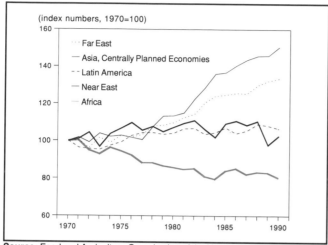

(index numbers, 1970=100)

Legend:
- Far East
- Asia, Centrally Planned Economies
- Latin America
- Near East
- Africa

Source: Food and Agriculture Organization of the United Nations (FAO), unpublished data, March 1991.

Notes:

a. Far East = Bangladesh, Bhutan, Brunei Darussalam, East Timor, Hong Kong, India, Indonesia, Republic of Korea, Lao People's Democratic Republic, Macao, Malaysia, Maldives, Myanmar, Nepal, Pakistan, Philippines, Singapore, Sri Lanka, Thailand.

b. Asia, Centrally Planned Economies = Cambodia, China, Democratic People's Republic of Korea, Mongolia, Viet Nam.

c. Near East = *Africa*: Egypt, Libyan Arab Jamahiriya, Sudan. *Asia*: Afghanistan, Bahrain, Cyprus, Gaza Strip (Palestine), Islamic Republic of Iran, Iraq, Jordan, Kuwait, Lebanon, Oman, Qatar, Kingdom of Saudi Arabia, Syrian Arab Republic, Turkey, United Arab Emirates, Yemen Arab Republic, Democratic Yemen.

lion cattle and about 12 million hectares under permanent pasture; the United States and the Soviet Union each have cattle populations of about 100 million or more. Pig populations are up about 57 percent, with much of that increase occurring in China, which, with some 340 million pigs, now has roughly 40 percent of the global total. The global population of chickens has doubled since 1970, rising from 5.2 billion to 10.4 billion [6] [7].

The average annual world catch of fish increased 67 percent from 1969 to 1989. However, preliminary data indicate that the global fish catch declined about 4 percent in 1990, the first decline in 13 years [8]. Increased catches have severely stressed many species: catches of Atlantic cod, haddock, Atlantic herring, capelin, Southern African pilchard, Pacific Ocean perch, King Crab, and Peruvian anchoveta have all declined. Aquaculture—the farming of aquatic organisms—has grown substantially and now represents about 13 percent of total fish production [9]. (See Chapter 12, "Oceans and Coasts.")

PER CAPITA PRODUCTION TRENDS

Production increases in the developing countries since 1970 are much less dramatic when population growth is taken into consideration. As Figure 7.6 indicates, the Asian centrally planned economies managed to increase production fast enough to stay well ahead of population growth. In Latin America and the Near East, however, production barely managed to stay

even with population, and in Africa population growth outstripped production increases.

In many African countries, per capita production declined significantly. The index of per capita production compiled by the Food and Agriculture Organization of the United Nations (FAO), using the 1979–81 period as a baseline of 100, shows that 35 of 47 countries dropped below 100 in 1989, with the worst declines in countries such as Angola, Botswana, Gabon, Mozambique, and Rwanda. Per capita production fluctuated dramatically in several countries during the 1980s: in Sudan, for example, the index fell to 75.87 in 1987, jumped to 94.50 in 1988, and then dropped back to 74.30 in 1989 [10]. Many factors contribute to these fluctuations, including variations in rainfall, rapidly changing prices, and civil and ethnic unrest.

Population Density and Agriculture

Largely because of population growth, per capita cropland has declined in all regions. If current population projections are accurate, the world average of 0.28 hectares of cropland per capita is expected to decline to 0.17 hectares by the year 2025. In Asia, cropland per capita is expected to decline to 0.09 hectares. There are large areas of uncultivated land in sub-Saharan Africa and Latin America, but in much of this area the soil is marginal or rainfall is unreliable. (See *World Resources 1990–91*, pp. 87–88.)

In many countries, severe population pressure on marginal lands contributes to deforestation, soil erosion, and the loss of biodiversity.

In the Philippines, for example, population growth of about 2.5 percent per year is outpacing the job-creating capacity of the Philippine economy. Unemployment has increased from below 5 percent in the early 1970s to almost 10 percent by the end of the 1980s [11]. With limited opportunities in urban areas, and with the limits of lowland agriculture now nearly reached, farmers have been moving into upland areas. By 1987, an estimated 30 percent of the country's population—18 million people—were living in upland areas. This movement into the uplands was inadvertently encouraged by government logging policies that reduced the cost of migration and settlement: logging roads made forest lands accessible, and logging cleared the land, thus saving upland farmers as much as 60 percent of the total labor associated with upland production [12]. (See Chapter 8, "Forests and Rangelands.")

ENVIRONMENTAL TRENDS

Soil Degradation

Farming activities are major contributors to soil erosion, salinization, and loss of nutrients. A global assessment of human-induced soil degradation, prepared by the International Soil Reference and Information Centre in the Netherlands, found that 1.96 billion hectares of soils were degraded to some degree, and that 300 million hectares of this total have suffered strong to extreme degradation. (See Chapter 8, "Forests and Rangelands.") Agricultural activities accounted for 28 percent of this degradation, overgrazing about 34 percent, and deforestation another 29 percent. Most of the damage has been done by wind and water erosion; other forms of degradation include salinization, loss of nutrients, compaction, and waterlogging (13). Most of the land damaged by agriculture and overgrazing is in Asia and Africa.

A study of an irrigation district in eastern Uttar Pradesh in India found that 87 percent of the farmers reported problems with alkalinity, salinity, or waterlogging that forced 29 percent of cropland out of production. The study found that rice yields decreased by more than 50 percent on salt-affected soils, and that waterlogging reduced wheat yields by about 78 percent. The study recommended two remedial actions: promoting horizontal as well as vertical drainage, and preventing canal seepage (14).

Inputs of Fertilizers, Pesticides, and Freshwater

Synthetic fertilizers are needed to take full advantage of the high-yield crop varieties developed during the Green Revolution. Global fertilizer use has increased dramatically since 1970, especially in Asia and particularly in China. (See Chapter 18, "Food and Agriculture," Table 18.2.) There is now considerable evidence that the runoff of fertilizers into rivers and estuaries is a significant source of water pollution. (See Focus On, below, and Chapters 11, "Freshwater," and 12, "Oceans and Coasts.")

Available data also indicate large increases in the use of pesticides (herbicides, insecticides, and fungicides) over the past two decades; currently, increases are mainly in developing countries. These substances enhance production, but they also pose risks to farmworkers and the general public. The incidence of unintentional pesticide poisoning is poorly documented but is considered significant, causing perhaps 20,000 deaths and 1 million illnesses per year worldwide. Pesticide poisonings occur primarily in developing countries (15).

Freshwater withdrawals—most of which are used for agriculture in developing countries—have increased steadily since the 1960s. Agriculture accounts for 86 percent of water withdrawals in Asia, with most of the water used for irrigation. In many countries—in North Africa and the Middle East, for example—water withdrawals appear to be occurring at unsustainable rates (16). (See Chapter 11, "Freshwater," Key Issues.)

ECONOMIC TRENDS

Trends in Agricultural Commodity Prices

International agricultural commodity prices have declined in real terms in recent decades. By 1989, most farm commodity prices had dropped to about 60–70 percent of their 1970 levels. Prices for cereals in the late 1980s were about half the level of the 1970s and early 1980s. Rice prices, which in real terms generally stayed above $350 per metric ton in the 1970s, collapsed in the 1980s to around $200 per metric ton (in 1980 dollars). (See Chapter 15, "Basic Economic Indicators," Table

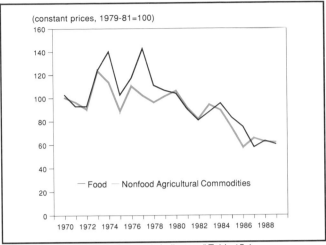

Figure 7.7 Index of International Farm Commodity Prices, 1970–89

(constant prices, 1979-81=100)

— Food — Nonfood Agricultural Commodities

Source: Chapter 15, "Basic Economic Indicators," Table 15.4.
Note: *Food commodities* include beverages (coffee, cocoa, tea), cereals (maize, rice, wheat, grain sorghum), fats and oils (palm oil, coconut oil, groundnut oil, soybeans, copra, groundnut meal, soybean meal), and other food (sugar, beef, bananas, oranges). *Nonfood agricultural commodities* include cotton, jute, rubber, and tobacco.

15.4.) This decline has significantly affected the economies of many nonindustrialized nations that depend on commodity exports.

Over a longer term, prices of nonfood agricultural commodities—e.g., cotton, jute, wool, and natural rubber—have shown a pronounced decline. The substitution of petroleum-based synthetic products in the mid-1950s depressed prices of natural rubber and natural fibers. This price decline continued through the 1960s and even through the two oil price shocks of the 1970s. (See Figure 7.7.)

Agricultural food prices have also declined, but not always uniformly. In the 1984–86 period, for example, prices of tropical beverages (coffee, tea, and cocoa) were relatively stonger than cereals, providing an advantage to countries that exported beverages. Developing countries that exported tropical beverages, especially those that were large net importers of most other foods, were helped by this difference (17). After 1986 beverage prices also dropped.

The decline in real agricultural commodity prices has complex causes that are generally thought to include the inelasticity of demand for foodstuffs in industrialized countries, increased supplies due to increases in productivity and technological innovation, prolonged protection of producers in the industrialized market economies, and slow income growth in the developing countries. Export subsidies in industrialized countries designed to dispose of these surpluses have increased the supply produced for export, thus further weakening prices (18).

Falling commodity prices have hurt some countries more than others. In Southeast Asia, which has diversified its exports into manufactured goods, the change has been less difficult than in Africa, which is increasingly dependent on traditional commodity exports. Production increases in many developing countries helped offset the decline in value of agricultural commodities (19). As Figure 7.5 indicates, the total value of food exports from developing regions has risen considerably since 1970, thanks primarily to continuing increases in export volume.

Declining Investment in Irrigation

The expansion of irrigation has slowed considerably over the past 25 years. The growth rate of irrigated area in the world has declined by about 60 percent globally and by 72 percent in Asia since the mid-1960s. Lending and assistance for irrigation by the four main financial donors—the World Bank, Asian Development Bank (ADB), U.S. Agency for International Development (U.S. AID), and the Japanese Overseas Economic Cooperation Fund (OECF)—was 50 percent lower in 1986–87 than during the 1977–79 period (20).

In Asia, this slowdown appears to be related to the decline in demand for rice, the increasing real costs per hectare of new irrigation, the debt loads carried by some countries in the region, and the declining share of undeveloped land that can be irrigated.

Some countries, such as India, have responded to the decline in international lending by increasing domestic spending; but most countries—including Indonesia, the Philippines, and Thailand—have reduced their own spending. The continuing decline in the maintenance and quality of existing irrigation infrastructure has also had an adverse effect on farm productivity (21).

World Bank Lending

World Bank lending to agriculture and rural development projects fell by almost one fifth between 1977–79 and 1986–88. The share of such projects in total World Bank lending declined from 30 to 17 percent during this period. The decline has been attributed to several factors including lower world rice prices, which have lowered the anticipated rate of return of some proposed projects below acceptable levels; the below-average rates of return of previous projects, especially in sub-Saharan Africa; and the World Bank's new emphasis on economic restructuring loans (22).

Key Issues

TRADE LIBERALIZATION AND THE GATT NEGOTIATIONS

Reluctance to reduce agricultural subsidies and import barriers nearly caused the Uruguay Round of the General Agreement on Tariffs and Trade (GATT) to founder early in 1991. Agricultural trade liberalization in a new GATT agreement could have a major impact on commodity prices and on prospects for agriculture in developing countries.

Many industrialized countries protect their agricultural sectors with price supports, thus stimulating domestic production and creating surpluses. These surpluses, shipped abroad as subsidized exports, depress international prices and reduce the trade revenues of food-exporting developing countries. The dumping of surpluses has particularly depressed the prices of highly protected commodities (dairy products and beef, for example) that have smaller international markets (23).

Most analyses argue that trade liberalization in industrialized countries would reduce food supplies and increase market prices in the short term. However, liberalization that includes developing countries could counteract price rises by stimulating increased production among developing country farmers (24). In addition, improved productivity due to technological advances could counteract higher prices.

In the short term, higher prices would redistribute wealth throughout the world. Food-exporting developing countries would benefit (25). For example, it is estimated that if industrial countries were to lift nontariff barriers, developing countries' earnings from exports of fruits and vegetables could rise by as much as 24 to 36 percent (26). In addition, farmers throughout the developing world—the vast majority of the world's poor—would benefit (27). Higher food prices would improve rural wages and slow rural-urban migration (28).

Higher food prices would hurt other groups, however, especially food-importing countries and urban consumers. Many of the world's poorest countries rely on subsidized food imports from the industrial countries. To minimize shocks to consumers, liberalization would have to be phased in slowly (29) with compensation negotiated for these countries (30). Higher prices could also hurt urban consumers in food-exporting countries, although their losses might be offset by higher national income (31).

With liberalization, food production would shift to producers with comparative advantages in land, labor, and climate. In the long term, the resulting gains in economic efficiency could produce a substantial dividend for the world economy (32). From an environmental perspective, adapting cropping patterns to the underlying productive capacities of the land would be an important step in the evolution to sustainable agriculture (33).

The impact of multilateral liberalization on three important tropical agricultural commodities—coffee, tea, and cocoa—could be quite different from that on temperate-zone commodities. Most importing nations impose low-to-moderate tariffs, which, if removed, would increase revenue to producer nations. Most producing countries, however, have imposed large taxes on producers. Removing those taxes would create a substantial incentive to increase production. Higher production, in turn, could depress international prices, and the value of trade in coffee, tea, and cocoa could decline substantially (34).

FOCUS ON AGRICULTURE IN THE INDUSTRIALIZED WORLD: TOWARD SUSTAINABILITY

Farming in the industrialized countries has successfully produced food and fiber, yet it also has caused environmental degradation, creating serious problems for farmers (such as soil erosion) and, even worse, off-farm problems (such as groundwater contamination).

These problems, epitomized by a concern that current agricultural practices are not sustainable, have led many agricultural scientists, economists, and farmers to rethink conventional farming practices. (A similar rethinking process is underway in the developing countries, but this discussion is limited to the industrialized world. Farmers in the industrialized and developing worlds face very different situations—in terms of climate, soils, size of holdings, available technologies, etc.—and space precludes considering the issue in both contexts.)

What seems to be emerging is a range of environmentally beneficial farming practices—a synthesis based on both old, proven ideas and a new understanding of natural nutrient cycles and ecological relationships.

These practices must prove themselves in the complex world of farm economics, which in all industrialized countries is a maze of incentives, subsidies, price distortions and other factors. In the end, however, farmers operate in a world of profit and loss and must consider how new practices will affect the profitability of their farms. The world of profit and loss has largely ignored the world of the environment until quite recently. For example, farm soils in many areas have been eroding, yet that erosion has often been physically subtle and offset by greater use of fertilizers. In any case, soil erosion does not show up on farmers' balance sheets, nor have farmers been held responsible for the cost of off-farm pollution, such as fertilizer runoff that pollutes rivers or bays. (See Chapter 11, "Freshwater," and Chapter 12, "Oceans and Coasts.")

Each farmer's planting and operating decisions are influenced by government policies that provide a mix of incentives and guarantees to manipulate farm production. In industrialized countries, farm policies have generally tried to maintain stable incomes for farmers by keeping farm commodity prices high. This has provided a powerful incentive for farmers to use chemical fertilizers, pesticides, and machinery to produce more crops. However, as the environmental cost of those policies becomes more evident, many governments are looking at a variety of ways to encourage farmers to adopt resource-conserving practices.

Many of these issues are being addressed by policymakers and research institutions. For example, a recent comparison of the economics of conventional and alternative systems by the World Resources Institute (discussed in more detail below) considers the impact of various U.S. government policies and incorporates the economic cost of soil erosion.

DEFINING TERMS

The complex relationship between environmental and economic considerations also shows up when defining terms such as "alternative agriculture." Different definitions emphasize different environmental factors. The

U.S. National Research Council, in an important study entitled *Alternative Agriculture,* defined alternative agriculture as any system of food or fiber production that:
■ Systematically incorporates natural processes, such as nutrient cycles, nitrogen fixation, and pest-predator relationships, into the agricultural production process;
■ Reduces the use of chemicals and fertilizers with the greatest potential to harm the environment or the health of farmers and consumers;
■ Makes greater use of the biological and genetic potential of plant and animal species;
■ Improves the match between cropping patterns and the productive potential and physical limitations of agricultural lands in order to ensure the long-term sustainability of current production levels; and
■ Emphasizes improved farm management and conservation of soil, water, energy, and biological resources (35).

Other definitions approach the issue from an economic perspective, in which the principal goal is to maintain the stock of natural resources indefinitely. In this approach, natural resources, such as soil and groundwater, are considered as forms of capital that provide a flow of economic benefits over time. Soil erosion may not affect a farmer's short-term agricultural practices or income; however, farmers should include a depreciation allowance for erosion, because it jeopardizes the future productivity of their land and thus their future income (36). Sustainability, in this approach, is concerned with measuring whether stocks of natural resources are appreciating or depreciating. (See Box 7.1.)

Different Perspectives and Open Questions

The question of definitions is further complicated by different perspectives among the industrialized countries. Much of the European discussion concentrates on organic farming, or systems that rely heavily on nutrient recycling and try to avoid all use of synthetic fertilizers and pesticides. Europeans, perhaps more than Americans, also question whether "low-input" and other alternative systems may be a short-term solution that is no more sustainable than the intensive use of agrochemicals (37). In the U.S. debate, there has been a tendency to lump reduced-input and organic systems together as resource-conserving "alternative" practices, in which the principal tests are environmental protection and long-term sustainability.

Organic farming is growing, but it remains a minor part of agriculture. In the European Community (EC), for example, organic farming accounts for less than 1 percent of the industry (38), and it will probably continue to play a small role in industrialized countries. This chapter focuses on a greater range of alternative practices that may become widespread and on how government policies encourage or discourage such practices.

The debate about alternative farming is connected to wider social issues in many countries. In the United States, some groups link alternative farming with the preservation of small farms and small towns in rural areas (39). In Japan, one large organic farming associa-

---

Box 7.1 Glossary of Terms

Traditional Agriculture. Practices such as crop rotation, returning animal manures to the soil, fully tilling the soil, and using horse- or ox-drawn cultivation.

Conventional Agriculture. Full use of chemical fertilizers and pesticides, continuous cropping or rotations, full tillage, and extensive use of machines. Conventional approaches emphasize high yields.

Alternative Agriculture. Practices such as crop rotation, reduced tillage or no-till, me-chanical/biological weed control, integration of livestock with crops, reduced use or no use of chemical fertilizers and pesticides, integrated pest management, and provision of nutrients from various organic sources (animal manures, legumes).

Low-input systems generally involve reduced use, rather than no use, of chemical fertilizers and pesticides.

Organic Agriculture. No use of chemical fertilizers and pesticides; otherwise similar to alternative practices.

Intensive Agriculture. Maximizing the amount of product per unit of land, generally with increased use of chemicals, labor, and machinery.

Extensive Agriculture. Maximizing the amount of land used in agricultural production. In Europe, extensification also implies substituting greater land area for chemicals to maintain production.

---

tion has negotiated cooperative agreements between farmers and consumers in which consumers agree to buy all the produce of a group of organic farms and to help with its distribution (40). In Europe, the preservation of rural landscapes and wildlife habitat has been an important part of the discussion (41), as have the storage and disposal of animal manure from the intensive livestock operations concentrated in northwest Europe.

Apart from different perspectives and priorities among the industrialized countries, many questions remain unsettled, including:

Is a given practice conventional or alternative? For example, crop rotation has been used for centuries and is widely regarded as a conventional practice. However, some less common rotations are specifically designed for resource conservation and thus could be considered alternative. Likewise, integrated pest management, improved methods for storing and applying livestock manures, and various types of reduced tillage could be considered conventional practices, but they are often discussed as alternative practices. All are included here as alternative practices.

If alternative practices are so good, why don't more farmers use them? First, alternative systems often require more management time to organize; many are mixed crop-animal operations, with the animals providing both a "market" for the soil-building crop and a supply of organic nutrients to further build the soil (42) (43). Second, conventional systems are commonly thought to out-yield alternative systems. Third, skeptics argue that alternative systems generate lower net returns per hectare than conventional systems (44), mainly because crop rotations force farmers to leave part of their land in a low-value "green manure" crop to restore the soil, and also because herbicides are a more effective and economical way to control weeds than alternative techniques such as mechanical cultivation and crop rotations. But recent studies have shown that net returns do not always suffer. (See The Economics of Alternative Agriculture, below.) Finally, alternative systems have an image problem: they are associated with traditional practices, such as crop rotation, whereas conventional agriculture is considered modern and scientific (45).

Is alternative agriculture merely a matter of reducing, eliminating, or changing some inputs? Switching from chemical fertilizers to animal manures is not invariably better environmentally because animal manures that are poorly stored, improperly applied, or over-applied can also cause environmental problems (46). Other changes, such as switching from pesticides to mechanical weed control (which requires additional implements and fuel), may also involve environmental trade-offs (47).

CONVENTIONAL AGRICULTURE AND ALTERNATIVE AGRICULTURE

Conventional agriculture has been a stunning production success over the past few decades. In the early 1960s, for example, farmers in Guthrie County, Iowa, could barely produce enough maize (corn) to feed local cattle herds. Maize, the principal food stock for the U.S. cattle industry and the U.S. farmers' best-paying crop, took so much nitrogen out of the soil that it could only be grown every other year. By 1963, fertilizer salesmen convinced farmers to replenish the nitrogen with chemical fertilizers such as anhydrous ammonia, which they said could allow them to grow maize every year. The chemical fertilizer worked: Guthrie County's maize production jumped 50 percent over an eight-year period (48).

However, the impact of maize "monoculture" on the health of the soil was not well understood. Soils under intensive monoculture tend to lose organic matter and their ability to retain moisture, thus becoming more susceptible to erosion and ultimately losing their fertility and productivity (49). Growing the same crop year after year also allows the pests and diseases that attack that crop to prosper (50). In 1967, maize stalks in Guthrie County began collapsing under an assault from root worms. Local farmers solved the problem with heavy doses of insecticides.

The production success also had unwelcome economic effects. By the mid-1980s, U.S. production had created huge surpluses, leading to government policies that idled millions of hectares. In Guthrie County, 25 percent of the land was idled. Environmental concerns also began to mount: traces of pesticides were found in drinking water and nitrates (a form of nitrogen) in farmers' watering troughs. Water supplies containing high levels of nitrate have been linked to methemoglobinemia (lack of oxygen in the blood) in children (51). The state of Iowa imposed a tax on fertilizers, with the proceeds used to encourage the reduced use of chemicals. By the late 1980s, farmers in areas like Guthrie County had begun to cut back on their use of chemical fertilizers (52).

The Guthrie County experience mirrors the experience of most industrialized countries, here limited to the nations belonging to the Organisation for Economic Co-operation and Development (OECD), including North America, Western Europe, Australia/New Zealand, and Japan. Agricultural production in OECD nations increased by 20–30 percent over the past decade, except in Japan, where output has been roughly constant (53). The area of land devoted to agriculture has declined about 1 percent since 1970, and the number of farms has declined (54). Average farm size has increased, accompanied by increased specialization and the substitution of machines and purchased inputs (fertilizers and pesticides) for labor and land. In Japan and to a lesser extent in Europe, farming is still relatively labor-intensive, despite the increasing number of machines used per square kilometer of arable land. The advent of machines has increased the amount of energy used by agriculture; for the OECD countries, total energy use per square kilometer rose 39 percent over the 1970–88 period (55).

OECD farmers have also relied on heavy doses of agricultural chemicals. Fertilizer consumption continued to rise slightly during most of the 1980s in Europe and Japan but may have leveled off for the industrialized countries as a whole. The use of nitrogenous fertilizer intensified in the 1970s but stabilized in most OECD countries in the 1980s (56). Pesticides are used intensively in OECD countries. Although data are scant, application rates of pesticides seem to have dropped (except for insecticides) during the 1980s (57). Declining rates may be somewhat misleading, however, because many new pesticides have higher potencies that require relatively lower application rates (58).

Alternative Approaches

In the 1970s and 1980s, a few farmers began taking a different approach. For example, at the 290-hectare crop-livestock farm of Glen and Rex Spray in Knox County, Ohio, no herbicides have been applied in over 15 years and no lime or fertilizer has been purchased since 1971. Yet in the 1981–85 period, the Sprays had yields of maize that exceeded the county average by 32 percent. Soybeans were 40 percent above average; wheat, 5 percent; and oats, 22 percent (59).

The Sprays and other farmers are achieving a synthesis of alternative farming practices. This synthesis may vary from farm to farm, but it usually includes crop rotations that conserve resources; tillage practices that conserve water and benefit soil health; legume crops or animal manures that add nutrients to the soil and reduce chemical inputs; and new ways to manage biological interactions in the soil that reduce plant diseases and increase yields. In combination, these practices help to suppress plant diseases and pests and lead to more efficient cycling of nutrients from the soil into plants and back into the soil. (See Box 7.2.)

These systems do not eliminate all use of chemical fertilizers or pesticides, nor are they simply a return to old-fashioned practices. They incorporate modern farm machinery, hybrid seeds, and the latest in plant cultivars, particularly legumes. Modern alternative systems also involve careful management of crop residues and other organic materials (60). In addition, they usually require more labor than conventional practices (61) and a greater knowledge of farm ecosystems. Higher labor costs are partially offset by lower input costs (62).

Precisely characterizing a generic "sustainable" farm is difficult, because each farm ecosystem, as each field within a farm, has different requirements. There is no recipe for sustainable farming. It is also difficult to say how many farmers now use alternative methods. Less than 1 percent of total farmland is devoted to organic farming (63), but a much greater number of farmers—in some cases, majorities or near-majorities—may be using some alternative practices (64).

PROBLEMS WITH THE CONVENTIONAL MODEL

On-Farm Impacts

Conventional agriculture can have a variety of destructive impacts on farms. The cost of these impacts is borne by the farmer. For example:

■ Conventional agricultural practices, such as deep plowing and removing crop residue, reduce the amount of organic matter in the soil. This in turn reduces soil fertility and rooting depth. Studies have found that alternative techniques can dramatically alter the loss of organic matter: for example, switching from conventional clearing to stubble-mulching, which leaves residues on the soil surface, can reduce organic matter losses by as much as 50 percent over 25 years (65). Some no-till or reduced-tillage methods are thought to require the use—often heavy use—of herbicides, but a recent study of maize production in the United States found no real difference in herbicide use between tillage systems (66).

■ Many conventional practices—growing shallow-rooted crops, using heavy machinery, or removing organic matter from the soil—encourage soil compaction, which restricts root growth, water retention, and air exchange (67). This problem may affect as much as half the intensively cultivated row-crop and small-grain cropland in North America (68) (69). Soil compaction can be reduced through reduced tillage, rotation with grasses or other crops with fibrous root systems, and the use of crop residues and manures to increase soil organic content (70).

■ Soil salinization, which is primarily caused by faulty irrigation, can lower crop yields and ultimately make land unsuitable for cultivation. Salinity is estimated to affect 1.2 million hectares of cultivated soils in Sas-

Box 7.2 Building Alternative Farming Systems

Some farmers have experimented with alternative techniques to reduce their costs, others because of growing awareness of the on- and off-farm environmental damage caused by conventional practices. They have developed a variety of alternative techniques, the most promising of which include crop rotation, improved nutrient management, and alternative ways to control pests and weeds.

ALTERNATIVE PLANTING METHODS

Crop rotation—successive planting of different crops in the same field—has a wide variety of economic and environmental benefits. From an economic perspective, rotations usually increase yields of a principal grain crop beyond yields achieved with continuous cropping, although gross returns per acre may decrease because part of the land is devoted to less valuable uses. Rotations also help improve the physical characteristics of soil and provide significant benefits in the control of weeds, insects, and diseases. Legumes in a rotation also can help fix nitrogen in the soil, thus reducing the need for additional nitrogen fertilizers (1).

Rotations that include deep-rooted crops such as alfalfa bring soil nutrients to the surface for later use by shallow-rooted crops. Rotations with hay, forage crops, or closely seeded small-grain crops can re-duce erosion, particularly when combined with contour plowing. Rotations that include rye (which contains a chemical that suppresses the growth of other plants) can reduce the need for herbicides (2).

Many other innovative cultural techniques show promise, including systems of strip intercropping using two crops; undersowing with a legume or other crop; mixtures of varieties or species to create greater crop diversity; trap crops to attract pests away from the main crop; and double-row cropping to facilitate weed control (3).

A survey of crop rotation in the United States found that the practice is relatively common except for some crops in certain areas, such as cotton in several states in the South. Farmers who plant maize commonly alternate the crop with soybeans; for example, 38 percent of land planted to maize in 1988 had grown soybeans in 1987 and maize in 1986. There is relatively little diversity in types of rotations, however (4).

TILLAGE PRACTICES

Farmers have adopted a wide range of alternative tillage practices in the past few decades. It is estimated that some sort of conservation tillage is used on about 30 million hectares of farmland in the United States (5). Nearly all these practices help prevent soil erosion; and although some are thought to increase the need for herbi-cides, recent studies have challenged this belief (6).

Ridge tillage—building seedbeds up into ridges—is a particularly promising alternative system that overcomes some of the weed control problems of untilled systems. During spring planting, ridge-till planters remove a layer of soil from the top of the ridge. This provides a relatively dry, warm seedbed that facilitates crop germination; weed germination is reduced because weed seeds are disturbed only on the top of the ridge. Soil erosion is slowed because the soil and crop residues between the ridges are not disturbed (7).

Many other alternatives to traditional deep plowing tend to reduce the number of cultivations. The alternatives include shallow plowing to a depth of 15 centimeters or less; chisel plowing, which does not invert the soil; deep subsoiling, which lifts the soil but does not invert it; shallow-tine systems, which loosen the soil; harrowing to create a seed bed; and no-till (or "one-pass") systems. All of these alternatives help reduce energy inputs, prevent soil erosion, facilitate pest and disease control, and create a more natural soil structure with better drainage and water retention (8).

PLANT NUTRIENTS

Legumes—nitrogen-fixing plants such as alfalfa, chickpeas, and various clovers—can add nitrogen to the soil for such crops

---

katchewan and 370,000 hectares in central and southern Alberta (71). In western Australia, some 440,000 hectares of land—mostly in the rain-fed wheat belt—are now salinized, a 500 percent increase since the first survey in 1955 (72).

■ Row-crop monocultures have aggravated soil erosion in many agricultural areas. Declines in soil productivity caused by erosion are difficult to measure because many other factors—management practices, new technology, new plant varieties, weather, and use of fertilizers and pesticides—also can affect crop yields (73). Nevertheless, some studies suggest that productivity losses are severe in many areas. For example, a six-year study of crop productivity in three Indiana counties found that corn yields were reduced 15 percent and soybean yields 24 percent on severely eroded sites, compared with slightly eroded sites (74). Of the roughly 171 million hectares of U.S. farmland, about 21.1 million hectares—12.3 percent—are considered so highly erodible that control measures generally require conversion to permanent vegetative cover; another 28.6 million hectares—16.7 percent—are classified as erosion-prone but can remain in production with practices such as conservation tillage (75). In Europe, it has been estimated that as much as 14 percent of the total land area is threatened by moderate to extreme human-induced water and wind erosion (76).

The problem is particularly severe in southern Mediterranean areas such as Portugal, where it is estimated that more than 20 percent of the current agricultural area is highly erodible (77). Erosion appears to be widespread in England and Wales and has increased over the past 15 years (78). In Bavaria, erosion exceeds tolerable levels on more than 50 percent of agricultural land (79).

■ Pesticides have both on- and off-farm impacts. The most worrisome problem is the possible health threat to farm workers (80). Some consumers have expressed concern about pesticide residues in food (81). In addition, pests can develop resistance to pesticides—some 504 insect and mite species are known to be resistant to some pesticides (82)—necessitating larger doses and more frequent applications or a switch to other pesticides. The chemical suppression of one pest also may allow other pests to become problems (83).

■ Excess nitrogen fertilizer runs off into surface water and leaches into groundwater, possibly contaminating farm wells, as well as water downstream. The problem has been particularly acute on crop-livestock operations, where farmers spread large quantities of animal manures but frequently continue to apply synthetic fertilizers at the same rate that would be required without manure. A survey of Iowa farmers, for example, found that about half of all farms that spread animal

Box 7.2

as corn and wheat. Under proper management, soybeans also can add nitrogen to the soil. The amount of nitrogen provided by leguminous hays—which are generally profitable only where there is a local hay market or on livestock farms—depends on management practices (9).

Animal manures can provide significant amounts of nitrogen, phosphorus, potassium, and other nutrients. Manures often are used inefficiently, however, because of poor storage, hauling, and spreading practices that can reduce the nitrogen content of manure by a substantial amount (10).

Other inputs that could substitute for inorganic chemicals include sewage sludge, composted domestic lawn clippings and leaf material, paper pulp wastes, potato processing wastes, brewery wastes, domestic organic wastes (11). Experience with sewage sludge has been mixed in Europe, where much of the sludge comes from urban sources and contains significant concentrations of heavy metals (12). Another relatively simple improvement involves more precise soil testing to determine which nutrients the soil actually needs. This may enable farmers to reduce fertilizer applications without affecting yields (13).

INTEGRATED PEST MANAGEMENT

Many management approaches offer opportunities to reduce pesticide use: disease forecasting methods to minimize use; better formulation and placement of chemicals, so that smaller amounts are effective; alternative farming systems—using crop rotations or modifying the timing of crop sowing, for example—to avoid or minimize pest attacks (14); and repeated field visits to determine whether pests have reached dangerous levels that justify spraying.

In addition, a variety of pest control strategies are increasing in importance: using biological insecticides based on insect pathogens; releasing or encouraging parasites and predators of pests; using pheromones, other allelochemicals, or repellents to keep pests away from crops; releasing sterile male insects to limit reproduction of pests; planting crop varieties that are resistant to pest attack or that produce toxins as a result of genetic engineering; and planting "trap" crops to draw pests away from the principal crop (15).

References and Notes

1. James F. Power, "Legumes: Their Potential Role in Agricultural Production," *American Journal of Alternative Agriculture*, Vol. 2, No. 2 (1987), pp. 70-71.
2. Bette Hileman, "Alternative Agriculture," *Chemical and Engineering News* (March 5, 1990), p. 33.
3. Clive A. Edwards, "The Importance of Integration in Sustainable Agricultural Systems," in *Sustainable Agricultural Systems*, Clive A. Edwards, Rattan Lal, Patrick Madden, *et al.*, eds. (Soil and Water Conservation Society, Ankeny, Iowa, 1990), p. 257.
4. Stan Daberkow and Mohinder Gill, "Common Crop Rotations Among Major Field Crops," in *Agricultural Resources: Inputs Situation and Outlook Report* (U.S. Department of Agriculture, Economic Research Service, Washington, D.C., 1989), p. 34.
5. Carmen Sandretto, Economic Research Service, U.S. Department of Agriculture, Washington, D.C., 1991 (personal communication).
6. Len Bull, "Pesticide Use by Tillage System, 1988 and 1989 Corn Production," in *Agricultural Resources: Inputs Situation and Outlook Report* (Economic Research Service, U.S. Department of Agriculture, Washington, D.C., 1991), p. 35.
7. National Research Council, *Alternative Agriculture* (National Academy Press, Washington, D.C., 1989), p. 162.
8. *Op. cit.* 3, p. 256.
9. *Op. cit.* 1, pp. 69, 72.
10. Edwin Young, Bradley M. Crowder, James S. Shortle, *et al.*, "Nutrient Management on Dairy Farms in Southeastern Pennsylvania," *Journal of Soil and Water Conservation*, Vol. 40, No. 5 (1985), p. 443.
11. *Op. cit.* 3, p. 258.
12. David Baldock, Senior Research Fellow, Institute of European Environmental Policy, London, 1991 (personal communication).
13. *Op. cit.* 2, p. 33.
14. *Op. cit.* 3, p. 255.
15. *Op. cit.* 3, p. 255.

manure did not make any adjustment in chemical fertilizer applications (84). Storage and disposal of animal manures has also been a widespread problem in Europe. In the Federal Republic of Germany, the annual nitrogen surplus on farmed land has grown tenfold, from less than 10 kilograms per hectare (kg/ha) in the 1950s to more than 100 kg/ha in the late 1980s (85).

Off-Farm Impacts

The off-farm impacts of conventional agriculture are borne by nearby residents and/or taxpayers. They appear to be even more costly than on-farm impacts (86). The most significant impacts are related to water quality, including runoff of fertilizers, pesticides, and soils into surface waters and leaching of fertilizers and pesticides into groundwater (87).

Pesticides

In the United States, various studies have found a total of 39 pesticides in groundwater in 34 states. A national survey by the U.S. Environmental Protection Agency found pesticides in about 10 percent of all community water systems and estimated that almost 1 percent contain potentially unsafe concentrations. The survey also found unsafe concentrations in many rural domestic wells—less than 1 percent, but affecting an estimated 60,900 wells (88). Percentages are higher in some areas:

surveys in Minnesota and Iowa suggest that more than 20–30 percent of community wells and 30–60 percent of private wells may contain pesticide residues (89). Pesticide runoff in surface waters may also pose a significant threat to drinking water supplies. Studies have found that conventional water supply treatment technologies are generally unable to remove pesticide residues (90).

The impact of certain pesticides on wildlife has been widely documented. High levels of DDT led to dramatic declines in predatory bird populations in the United States in the 1960s and 1970s. The banning of most organochlorines (DDT, dieldrin, aldrin, etc.) has been an important factor in the recovery of these bird populations.

Fertilizers

Overfertilization has had a major impact on water quality, primarily in the form of nitrate pollution from nitrogen fertilizers. It is estimated that 25 percent of the population in the European Community (EC) is drinking water with a nitrate level greater than the EC's recommended maximum level of 25 milligrams per liter (mg/l) (91).

Levels of nitrate contamination are generally rising in Europe (92). In Bavaria, for example, the number of catchments exceeding the maximum permitted EC standard of 50 mg/l increased by more than 30 percent within two years (1985–87). In Baden-Württemberg, the percentage of water exceeding the 25 mg/l target level increased from 17 percent in 1977 to 28 percent in 1985 (93). Rising concentrations of nitrates have been found in groundwater in parts of France, the Netherlands, and in the United Kingdom (94).

The runoff of nitrogen and phosphorous fertilizers also plays a major role in increasing nutrient levels in estuaries. A study of 78 estuaries in the United States found that agricultural runoff contributed, on average, 24 percent of all nutrient loading and 40 percent of total sediment (95). In some rural areas of Europe, agriculture causes 70 to 85 percent of the nitrogen loading and more than 30 percent of the phosphorus loading of surface waters (96). (See Chapter 11, "Freshwater," and Chapter 12, "Oceans and Coasts.")

Soil Erosion

It is estimated that approximately 880 million metric tons of eroded agricultural soils annually run into reservoirs in the United States, reducing their flood-control benefits, clogging waterways, and increasing the operating costs of water-treatment facilities (97). Suspended sediments decrease the amount of light available for submerged aquatic vegetation, which can harm fish species that depend on this vegetation for breeding and food (98). The cost of soil erosion is also substantial: in the United States, damage to the rest of the economy from waterborne sediments may exceed $10 billion per year. About 36 percent of this amount is from soil eroded from cropland (99).

Air Pollution

Agriculture also produces a variety of air pollutants. For example, fertilized soils emit 2–10 times as much nitrous oxide as unfertilized soils and pastures, with the higher emissions in temperate countries caused by ammonia and urea compounds. In the industrialized countries, livestock and fertilizers account for 80—90 percent of ammonia emissions, which in Europe may have doubled over the last 30 years (100). It is estimated that 20 percent of the acid deposition in the Netherlands currently comes from the ammonia released by animal manure (101). The burning of agricultural wastes also emits significant concentrations of carbon monoxide and dioxide, nitrogen oxides, and other gases. Finally, wet rice agriculture and livestock are significant sources of methane emissions (102).

Loss of Biodiversity and Degradation of Landscapes

Conversion of wildlife habitat and rural landscapes to agricultural use has been extensive in recent decades. Since 1945, it is estimated that England and Wales have lost 98 percent of old pasture, 70 percent of original peat lands, 58 percent of ancient forest, and 40 percent of heathland. Modern agriculture also has played a major role in the destruction of hedgerows, which provide habitat for wildlife (103).

The loss of habitat, combined with rising levels of toxic pesticides in surface waters and soils, has had a devastating effect on wildlife and biodiversity. In the Federal Republic of Germany, it is estimated 14 of 933 plant species disappeared between 1870 and 1950. In the following three decades, 130 plants became extinct, 50 more were threatened with extinction, 74 were seriously endangered, and 108 were in decline, primarily because of agricultural activities (104).

Also of concern in Europe is the loss in visual amenities caused by changes in the rural landscape, such as the elimination of hedgerows and the disappearance of grasslands (105). Many Europeans consider such scenery an important part of Europe's "cultural landscape."

AGRICULTURAL POLICIES: CREATING A NEW ENVIRONMENT

The industrialized economies have designed agricultural policies that provide adequate food supplies and maintain farmers' incomes. To do that, they have subsidized farmers at the expense of taxpayers (106). These policies have provided strong incentives for farmers to produce as much as possible, maximize their use of fertilizers and pesticides, and otherwise modify their farming practices to take advantage of distorted price structures. All of these effects have had serious environmental consequences (107).

These policies also created barriers for any transition to alternative practices; new policies developed in the last few years have tried to reduce those barriers. As shown in Figure 7.8, Japan has had the highest producer subsidies for agricultural products, largely because of high subsidies for rice (108). In North America and the EC, subsidies peaked in 1986 and have declined through 1989, although provisional estimates show increases in 1990.

U.S. Farm Law

Policies designed to promote production and stabilize farm incomes may also present formidable barriers to farmers who wish to move towards more sustainable practices. Under U.S. farm law, for example, farm program payments are determined by three factors: crop acreage bases, crop yields, and target prices. In the case of maize (corn), the crop acreage base is determined by the number of acres planted in maize during a given five-year base period. Similarly, crop yields are determined by the average number of bushels produced per acre on a farm in a five-year period before 1986. And eligible farmers are guaranteed a specific target price; if market prices fall below the target price, farmers are paid the difference.

To maximize their payments, U.S. farmers need large crop bases and high yields. The system has penalized farmers for shifting acreage out of the supported crop, because their acreage bases and government payments are lowered over the next five years. The system has also worked against yield-reducing practices such as long-term rotations or reduced chemical inputs (109). The 1990 farm law provides some flexibility by allowing farmers to plant other crops on up to 25 percent of their acreage without losing their acreage bases for the calculation of future support payments (110).

Europe's CAP

The European Community's Common Agricultural Policy (CAP) is a complex system that uses prices to regulate agricultural markets and support agricultural incomes. One of the CAP's guiding principles is market unity, which bars any restrictions on trade between member states and requires a uniform agricultural price for the whole community. Each spring, these guaranteed prices to farmers are fixed by the EC's 12 agricultural ministers. The guaranteed prices have generally been well above world market prices.

To protect against cheap imports, EC countries impose tariffs on non-EC products, ensuring their sale at the guaranteed price. The EC also uses direct market purchases (to maintain prices) or payments to farmers (to make up the difference between market and guaranteed price). In cases where there are large surpluses (sugar, milk, or wine), production quotas for individual farms are increasingly common (111). To discourage overproduction, "co-responsibility" payments require producers themselves to finance part or all of the disposal of excess supplies (112).

POLICY IMPACTS: DISTORTED PRICE STRUCTURES

Price distortions have significantly altered decisions by farmers in industrialized countries. In the European Community, for example, price policies have encouraged production of maize and sugar beets and discouraged production of root crops and pulses. High protected prices for milk and low world market prices for soya (an important input in milk production) have been an enormous incentive for milk production in the EC. This distortion has had regional impacts, shifting milk production from Europe's upland grasslands to the coastal regions of northwest Europe, where imported feed is available.

A similar shift has occurred in pig and poultry production, where farmers have substituted low-priced feed substitutes—tapioca from Thailand, or corn gluten from the United States, for example—for protected and high-priced feed cereals from EC sources. More than 15 percent of all dairy cows and 25 percent of all pigs are now concentrated on 4 percent of the EC's agricultural area in the Netherlands, Flanders, and the western part of Lower Saxony. Although mixed crop-livestock systems can be the basis for environmentally sustainable farming, distorted price structures have tended to push agriculture in the other direction, toward specialization (113).

Subsidized Inputs

Many governments subsidize agricultural inputs. A well-known example is the subsidization of irrigation water in the western United States. Subsidized water prices have encouraged the expansion of irrigated production and such relatively low-value crops as alfalfa.

Figure 7.8 Producer Subsidy Equivalents in Industrialized Countries, 1979–90

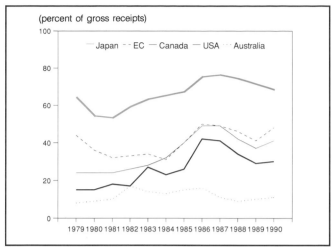

Source: Organisation for Economic Cooperation and Development (OECD), "Agricultural Policies, Markets and Trade Monitoring Outlook" (OECD, Paris, 1988, 1990, 1991).

Notes:
a. Producer Subsidy Equivalents = producer subsidies divided by the value of production plus direct payments. b. 1979–85 figures for the European Community (EC) refer to the EC-10; 1986–90 to the EC-12. c. 1989 = estimated; 1990 = provisional.

This in turn has contributed to a decline in groundwater aquifer levels and the accelerated accumulation of salts and toxic minerals in agricultural lands and adjacent bodies of water (114).

NEW POLICY OPTIONS

Industrial nations are trying a variety of new policies to encourage the transition to alternative farm practices that will reduce on-and off-farm environmental damages. Some countries are changing old programs, such as reducing or removing subsidies for inputs. Other countries are trying new programs, including land conservation programs, management agreements, taxes and fees on inputs, regulations, and subsidies to support conversion to sustainable practices.

Although the OECD countries have agreed to follow the "polluter-pays" principle, meaning that the costs of pollution control or prevention should be borne by the polluter (115), this principle is infrequently applied to agriculture. In one of the few examples, the Dutch government has imposed a tax on the production of excess manure and requires farmers to dispose of all surpluses at their own expense (116).

Reducing Input Subsidies

Austria, Australia, Finland, Portugal, New Zealand, and Sweden have all found that increasing the cost of inputs is an effective way to reduce their use, reduce on- and off-farm pollution, and internalize some of the off-site costs of agricultural pollution. In Australia, for example, the government of New South Wales has substantially increased its water charges, leading to an almost immediate adoption of more efficient farming practices and a decline in soil salinity levels (117).

Land Conservation Programs

One of the most ambitious land retirement programs established to date is the Conservation Reserve Program (CRP) in the United States, which was created by the Food Security Act of 1985. The program pays farmers to idle highly erodible land for 10 years; about 14 million hectares were enrolled as of 1991 (118). U.S. farm programs also link eligibility for federal benefits to compliance with conservation programs. For highly erodible croplands not covered by the CRP, farmers must implement an approved conservation plan by 1995 or lose eligibility for nearly all federal program benefits. Other provisions of the 1985 law deny eligibility for farm program payments to any farmers who plow previously uncultivated, highly erodible land or drain wetlands for cultivation. The effectiveness of these programs is greatest in periods of low commodity prices, when farmers rely most on government benefits (119).

Other governments have taken steps to protect environmentally fragile lands. In 1980, the government of South Australia became concerned about rapidly dwindling areas of wildlife habitat and native vegetation, which farmers were buying and clearing for crops or pasture. The government created a voluntary heritage agreement (conservation easement) program and then, in 1983, banned all future clearing without a permit. After a period of political and legal negotiations, the program now requires farmers to obtain a permit before clearing any native vegetation. If the permit is refused, farmers can be compensated for any reduction in the market value of their farm if they agree to attach a heritage agreement to the farm title, protecting the native vegetation in perpetuity. They can also receive financial aid for the cost of constructing fences or other improvements to protect vegetation. State and local land and other taxes may be waived on areas subject to a heritage agreement (120).

Management Agreements

In 1985, the European Community approved a directive for funding management agreements to protect environmentally sensitive areas (ESAs). The ESA designation, which has been used in the United Kingdom, the Federal Republic of Germany, France, and the Netherlands (121), permits agriculture ministries to pay farmers to retain traditional agricultural practices in order to maintain biologically important habitats and traditional landscapes (122). The United Kingdom has identified ESAs where farmers can be paid to maintain or improve the environment by, for example, deferring hay-making, using less fertilizer, or leaving their fields unplowed. Unlike the heritage agreements in South Australia, which are effective in perpetuity, most of the European management agreements run for five years (123).

The EC's 1975 Less-Favoured Areas Directive was partly intended to maintain agricultural activity in hilly and remote areas and to preserve the landscape and environment (124). For example, livestock farmers in the mountainous areas of Austria are paid to maintain traditional herb-rich meadows, and Swiss farmers are paid to cut hay on mountain slopes to reduce the risk of snow avalanche (125). Many other such management agreement programs are underway:

■ The U.K. Countryside Commission provides premiums to farmers who implement environmentally preferred management practices on set-aside lands.

■ In almost all German townships, farmers can receive payments to protect native plants and animals by leaving some meadows uncropped and avoiding the application of certain fertilizers and pesticides on grassland and on the edges of fields (126). Most such programs are managed by the state-level "Lander" governments (127).

■ Sweden and some other European countries provide investment aid to farmers who upgrade manure storage facilities (128).

■ Portugal, as part of its program to reduce soil erosion, offers subsidies and loans to farmers for reforestation and the establishment of permanent pastures (129).

Taxes, Fees, and Tax Incentives

Some countries are experimenting with the use of taxes and fees to encourage more efficient use of fertilizers and pesticides, with tax incentives to encourage sustainable practices. Sweden, Finland, and Austria all use taxes and input levies, with some of the revenue going to reduce pesticide and fertilizer use as well as supporting research and extension programs. Sweden, for example, imposes a 20 percent price-regulation charge and a 5 percent input tax on both the value of nitrogen and phosphorus in fertilizers and the value of each unit of active ingredient in pesticides (130). The Netherlands has introduced a modest levy on manufactured feed to help pay for research and advisory services dealing with nitrate and phosphate pollution from intensive animal husbandry (131).

Tax reduction incentives also are employed in a few countries. Australia, for example, abolished tax advantages for clearing land and now provides them for planting trees. Australia also allows accelerated depreciation and tax write-offs for investments in erosion prevention and water conservation (132).

Strengthening Regulations

In nearly all OECD countries, new pesticides and herbicides must undergo extensive government testing and evaluation before they can be sold. Some countries are also retesting older pesticides to see whether they meet current standards. Most countries also reserve the right to withdraw pesticide licenses based on new data (133). By 1993, for example, Denmark may remove from the market as many as one fourth of current pesticides, for a variety of reasons, including their toxicity (134). In 1985, Sweden announced that it intended to reduce the use of pesticides in agriculture by 50 percent over five years, using measures such as stricter review and testing procedures, alternative control methods, training courses for all farmers, and a ban on aerial application (135). Denmark has a similar program that calls for a 25 percent reduction in total pesticide application by 1990, and a 50 percent reduction by 1997, compared with average pesticide use in 1981–85. The intention of the Danish law is to reduce both the amount of active ingredients and the number of treatments (136). Some countries have also devised standards limiting the cadmium content of manufactured fertilizers (137).

In several European countries, the growth of intensive animal husbandry has created a severe excess of animal manures that are leaching nitrates into groundwater and surface waters (138). The problem has led many governments to impose restrictions on manures. To reduce runoff into surface waters, Denmark prohibits the spreading of manure and sludge on frozen ground (139). The Netherlands and Denmark now limit the amount of manure that may be spread per hectare, although the controls are proving difficult to enforce (140). Denmark also requires farmers to have adequate storage capacity for animal manure; requires fertilizer management plans for farms over 10 hectares; and requires that a 55 percent "green cover" be planted in autumn on bare fallow lands to reduce nitrate leaching. Green cover includes winter cereals and oilseeds, which can provide some income for farmers (141).

In Laholm, Sweden, nitrate pollution of groundwater became so serious in 1975 that the government restricted fertilizer applications around the recharge area of a municipal well to 100 kilograms of nitrate per hectare per year. Within two years, nitrate concentrations in the well fell from 80 to 40 milligrams per liter (142). Many other European countries, including Germany and the Netherlands, also have policies that protect groundwater recharge zones (143).

Subsidizing Conversion

Some European governments subsidize the conversion to organic farming, both as a means to alleviate environmental problems and as a way to reduce agricultural surpluses. The rationale for the subsidy is that, during their transition to organic farming, farmers must usually make some capital investments, yet they are unable to charge premium prices for their produce until it is certifiably organic, which usually takes two to five years. Yields also may decline, especially in the first few years (144).

To help farmers get through this transition period, countries such as Austria, Denmark, Finland, Germany, Norway, Sweden, and some cantons in Switzerland offer conversion subsidies, usually for three years. The Swedish subsidy program seems to have made a difference in farmers' decisions: 1,000 farmers signed up when state aid was available in 1989, but only 85 farmers started converting without aid the following year (145). Studies in the United Kingdom indicate that conversion to more sustainable farming systems could be cheaper than set-aside programs in controlling cereal surpluses (146).

THE ECONOMICS OF ALTERNATIVE AGRICULTURE

The question of the profitability of alternative farming systems remains unsettled. Some European experts have been less optimistic than their U.S. counterparts about the ability of alternative systems to maintain yields that are comparable to conventional systems (147). The difference may be partly due to Europeans' tendency to compare conventional systems with organic alone, rather than with all alternative systems. A comparison of the economic performance of organic and conventional farming in Denmark found that average crop yields on organic farms were about 40 percent below the conventional average, and that labor requirements for organic farms exceeded the conventional average by at least one third. The cost savings on fertilizer and chemicals covered only about 40 percent of the extra costs incurred by lower yields and higher labor requirements. Gross profits were comparable, however, largely because of significantly higher prices for organic produce (148).

Low-input alternative systems, by contrast, have achieved yields equivalent to conventional systems. A five-year experiment in Pennsylvania found that yields in low-input systems were 75 percent of conventional in the initial years but were comparable to conventional by the fifth year. The study found that the transition was helped by starting with crops that fix their own nitrogen or have low nitrogen requirements and compete well with weeds (149).

Accounting for Resources in Assessing Policies

A World Resources Institute analysis of alternative production systems in Pennsylvania and Nebraska attempted to assess the impact of alternative domestic and international farm policies on farmers' decisions and to account for soil erosion in comparing the economics of conventional and alternative systems. In Pennsylvania, where on- and off-site resource costs are high, organic farming rotations were found to be both economically and environmentally superior to conventional maize and maize-soybean production. Practices that conserve resources cut production costs by 25 percent, eliminated chemical fertilizer and pesticide use, reduced soil erosion by more than 50 percent, and increased yields after the five-year transition from conventional systems (150). By reducing soil erosion and improving water retention, these practices reduced off-site damages by more than $74 per hectare of farmland. They also forestalled a 30-year income loss (with a present value of $306 per hectare) by building soil productivity by 2 percent and preventing a 17 percent decline in soil productivity. When on- and off-farm soil and surface water resource costs were included, resource-conserving farming outperformed conventional approaches by almost a two-to-one margin in net economic value per hectare (including off-site environmental costs) (151).

In Nebraska, where flat land reduces the costs of erosion, alternative practices were also found to be environmentally superior to the predominant, high-input, maize-bean rotation. Alternative treatments (one using inorganic fertilizer but no herbicides, the other substituting manure and mechanical weed control for agrochemicals) proved to be slightly less competitive financially than conventional treatment using inorganic fertilizers and herbicides. However, the study also found that an organic maize-bean rotation reduced soil erosion by 20 percent compared with the chemical-intensive maize-bean rotation, and by 50 percent compared with continuous maize (152). The underlying financial calculations assumed no price premiums for produce grown in alternative systems, reasoning that widespread adoption of such systems would cause premiums to diminish or disappear altogether.

In comparing various policy options, the study found that the best option for U.S. farmers is an international policy that "decouples" commodity production and government income supports—that is, ending program constraints (thereby forcing farmers to use their resources more efficiently) and opening markets (thereby reducing supplies from high-cost producers, driving up world prices, and sending farmers undistorted market signals). Under all the different rotations and treatments in both case studies, net farm operating incomes improved under decoupling (153).

Another policy option—a 25 percent agrochemical tax—significantly discourages chemical use within any cropping system. In the Nebraska case, the study found that a 12 percent pesticide and fertilizer tax would eliminate any difference in net farm income between the chemical-intensive and organic maize-bean rotation (154).

Reforming the CAP

Multilateral decoupling may be a desirable option for U.S. farmers, but it might be less attractive financially for relatively high-cost producers in the EC nations. One study that simulated the impact of abolishing EC price supports estimated that in Germany, output would drop by 5.75 percent, employment by 11.5 percent, and exports by 86.5 percent. These losses in agriculture, however, would be more than offset by gains in other economic sectors (155).

Lower prices would probably have the greatest impact on small farms with low incomes in less productive farming areas. Some think that abandoning these farms would be desirable, because the lands would revert to natural habitat; others think it best to preserve these farms and encourage forms of farm management that also protect the environment. The best solution,

according to one assessment, may be to reduce price supports incrementally over a longer period, use taxes to reduce consumption of chemical inputs, and encourage management agreements as a form of direct payment to farmers to protect the environment (156).

FUTURE DIRECTIONS

Current farm policies in industrialized countries have created incentives for farmers to use environmentally damaging practices and, in many cases, penalized farmers for switching to more sustainable practices. Despite these disincentives, however, many farmers are finding it profitable to develop and invest in alternative systems. Removing price supports and other policy distortions could encourage this transition; policies that provide investment capital or otherwise reduce the risk for farmers could accelerate the transition.

Removing counterproductive policies may not adequately control off-site impacts, however. To control these impacts, governments could return the cost of off-site damages to the farm sector by imposing agrochemical taxes (157). Alternatively, they could provide tax incentives for sustainable practices, strengthen regulations, or pay farmers directly to adopt sustainable practices or retire land (158). Farmers, who work in a world of profit and loss, have not been forced to take adequate account of the real costs of environmental degradation. The economic attractiveness of sustainable practices becomes more apparent when these new accounting approaches are incorporated.

The context of the debate over sustainable agriculture must also encompass the food demands of a growing world population. Devising sustainable practices that are both highly productive and profitable may prove to be the challenge for agriculture in the industrial countries in the coming decades. And it also suggests that developing countries, in their search for ways to increase food production, will have models to consider other than conventional high-input farming—models that, in the long run, may provide their growing populations with a more sustainable food supply.

The Food and Agriculture chapter was written by World Resources *Senior Editor Robert Livernash.*

References and Notes

1. U.S. Department of Agriculture (USDA), *Global Food Assessment: Situation and Outlook Report* (Economic Research Service, USDA, Washington, D.C., November 1990), p. 9.

2. Bread for the World Institute on Hunger and Development, *Hunger 1990: A Report on the State of World Hunger* (Bread for the World Institute on Hunger and Development, Washington, D.C., 1990), p. 7.

3. U.S. Agency for International Development, *FEWS Bulletin*, No. 4 (June 3, 1990), p. 1.

4. *Op. cit.* 1, p. 4.

5. Leonardo A. Paulino, "World Food Trends and Projections," paper prepared for the BIFAD Task Force on Development Assistance and Cooperation (International Food Policy Research Institute, Washington, D.C., December 1990), pp. 3-4.

6. Food and Agriculture Organization of the United Nations (FAO), *Agrostat PC*, data diskette (FAO, Rome, 1991).

7. United Nations Environmental Programme (UNEP), *Environmental Data Report*, 3d edition, prepared for UNEP by the GEMS Monitoring and Assessment Research Centre in

collaboration with the World Resources Institute and the U.K. Department of the Environment (Basil Blackwell, Oxford, 1991), p. 143, and Table 3.9, pp. 176-179

8. Food and Agriculture Organization of the United Nations (FAO), *Fishery Statistics: Catches and Landings*, Vol. 68 (1989), p. 95, and unpublished data.

9. *Op. cit.* 7, p. 146.

10. Food and Agriculture Organization of the United Nations (FAO), *FAO Quarterly Bulletin of Statistics*, Vol. 3 (FAO, Rome, 1990), p. 31.

11. Wilfrido Cruz and Christopher Gibbs, "Resource Policy Reform in the Context of Population Pressure: The Philippines and Nepal," paper presented at the joint annual meeting of the American Agricultural Economics Association and the Association of Environmental and Resource Economists, Vancouver, British Columbia, 1990, p. 4.

12. *Ibid.*, pp. 3-6.

13. International Soil Reference and Information Centre (ISRIC), "Global Assessment of Soil Degradation 'GLASOD'," draft report (ISRIC, Wageningen, Netherlands, 1991), p. 6, Table 7.

14. P.K. Joshi and Dayanatha Jha, "Environmental Externalities in Surface Irrigation Systems in India," in *Environmental Aspects of Agricultural Development* (International Food Policy Research Institute, Washington, D.C., 1990), pp. 3-4.

15. World Health Organization (WHO), *Public Health Impact of Pesticides Used in Agriculture* (WHO, Geneva, 1990), p. 86.

16. *Op. cit.* 7, p. 146.

17. Enzo R. Grilli and Maw Cheng Yang, "Primary Commodity Prices, Manufactured Goods Prices, and the Terms of Trade of Developing Countries: What the Long Run Shows," *The World Bank Economic Review*, Vol. 2, No. 1 (1988), pp. 11, 18.

18. Thomas W. Hertel, "Agricultural Trade Liberalization and the Developing Countries: A Survey of the Models," in *Agricultural Trade Liberalization: Implications for Developing Countries*, Ian Goldin and Odin Knudsen, eds. (Organisation for Economic Co-operation and Development, Paris, and The World Bank, Washington, D.C., 1990), p. 19.

19. *Op. cit.* 17, pp. 24-25.

20. Mark W. Rosegrant and Prabhu L. Pingali, "Sustaining Rice Productivity Growth in Asia: A Policy Perspective" (International Food Policy Research Institute, Washington, D.C., January 1991), pp. 30-34, Table 3, and Figures 2 and 3.

21. *Ibid.*, pp. 3-4.

22. Michael Lipton, "Commentary: Agricultural Development and World Bank Lending," in *IFPRI Report*, Vol. 12, No. 4 (1990), p. 1.

23. Fred H. Sanderson, "Overview," in *Agricultural Protectionism in the Industrialized World*, Fred H. Sanderson, ed. (Resources for the Future, Washington, D.C., 1990), p. 6.

24. Ian Goldin and Odin Knudsen, "The Implications of Agricultural Trade Liberalization for Developing Countries," in *Agricultural Trade Liberalization: Implications for Developing Countries* (Organisation for Economic Co-operation and Development, Paris, and The World Bank, Washington, D.C., 1990), pp. 477-478.

25. *Op. cit.* 18, p. 22.

26. Nurul Islam, "Nontraditional Exports of Developing Countries: The Case of Horticultural Exports," in *The GATT, Agriculture, and the Developing Countries*, Nurul Islam and Alberto Valdes, eds. (International Food Policy Research Institute, Washington, D.C., 1990), p. 22.

27. Kym Anderson, "Policy Implications of Model Results," in *Agricultural Trade Liberalization: Implications for Developing Countries*, Ian Goldin and Odin Knudsen, eds. (Organisation for Economic Co-operation and Development, Paris, and The World Bank, Washington, D.C., 1990), p. 461.

28. *Op. cit.* 18, pp. 28-29.

29. *Op. cit.* 24, p. 479.

30. Panos Konandreas and Richard J. Perkins, "Some Implications of Trade Liberalization in Cereals for Low-Income Food Deficit Countries," in *Agricultural Trade Liberalization: Implications for Developing Countries*, Ian Goldin and Odin Knudsen, eds. (Organisation for Economic Co-operation and Development, Paris, and The World Bank, Washington, D.C., 1990), p. 468.

31. *Op. cit.* 18, pp. 27-28.

32. *Op. cit.* 24, pp. 475, 479.

33. John Mellor, Research Fellow, International Food Policy Research Institute, Washington, D.C., 1991 (personal communication).

34. Carl Mabbs-Zeno and Barry Krissoff, "Tropical Beverages in GATT," in *Agricultural Trade Liberalization: Implications for Developing Countries*, Ian Goldin and Odin Knudsen, eds. (Organisation for Economic Co-operation and Development, Paris, and The World Bank, Washington, D.C., 1990), pp. 188-191.

35. National Research Council, *Alternative Agriculture* (National Academy Press, Washington, D.C., 1989), p. 27.

36. Paul Faeth, Robert Repetto, Kim Kroll, *et al.*, *Paying the Farm Bill: U.S. Agricultural Policy and the Transition to Sustainable Agriculture* (World Resources Institute, Washington, D.C., 1991), p. 5.

37. Nicolas Lampkin, Development Director, Aberystwyth Centre for Organic Husbandry and Agroecology, University College of Wales, Aberystwyth, 1991 (personal communication).

38. Nicolas Lampkin, "Organic Farming and Agricultural Policy in Europe," paper presented at the Conference on Sustainable Agriculture and Agricultural Policy, Quebec Ministry of Agriculture, Fisheries, and Food, Quebec City, November, 1990, p. 2.

39. Chuck Hassebrook, "Developing a Socially Sustainable Agriculture" *American Journal of Alternative Agriculture*, Vol. 5, No. 2 (1990), p. 50.

40. Katsu Murayama, "Beyond Farming Methodology or Food Safety: Farmer-Consumer Co-Partnerships in Japan," *Soil and Health*, No. 220, (December 1990), pp. 17-21.

41. David Baldock, Senior Research Fellow, Institute for European Environmental Policy, London, 1991 (personal communication).

42. Pierre Crosson and Leonard Gianessi, "Why Do So Few Farmers Adopt Alternative Agricultural Practices?", draft (Resources for the Future, Washington, D.C., 1990), pp. 3-4.

43. Victor J. Oliveira, "Nonfarm Employment of Farm Operators, Hired Farmworkers, and Unpaid Farmworkers" (Economic Research Service, U.S. Department of Agriculture, Washington, D.C., 1990), p. 4.

44. *Op. cit.* 42, pp. 2-3.

45. *Op. cit.* 41.

46. C. Edwin Young, Bradley M. Crowder, James S. Shortle, *et al.*, "Nutrient Management on Dairy Farms in Southeastern Pennsylvania," *Journal of Soil and Water Conservation*, Vol. 40, No. 5 (1985), p. 443.

47. William Lockeretz, "Open Questions in Sustainable Agriculture," *American Journal of Alternative Agriculture*, Vol. 3, No. 4 (1988), p. 176.

48. Scott Kilman, "Farmers, Eying Costs and the Environment, Limit Use of Chemicals," *Wall Street Journal* (May 30, 1990), pp. 1, 14.

49. D.L. Karlen, D.C. Erbach, T.C. Kaspar, *et al.*, "Soil Tilth: A Review of Past Perceptions and Future Needs," *Soil Science Society of America Journal*, Vol. 54 (1990), pp. 156, 158.

50. C.A. Francis and M.D. Clegg, "Crop Rotations in Sustainable Agricultural Systems," in *Sustainable Agricultural Systems*, Clive A. Edwards, Rattan Lal, Patrick Madden, *et al.*, eds. (Soil and Water Conservation Society, Alkeny, Iowa, 1990), p. 115.

51. World Health Organization (WHO), *Guidelines for Drinking-Water Quality*, Vol. 2 (WHO, Geneva, 1984), pp. 132-133.

52. *Op. cit.* 48, pp. 1, 14.

53. *Op. cit.* 7, p. 242.

54. Organisation for Economic Co-operation and Development (OECD), *The State of the Environment* (OECD, Paris, 1991), pp. 171, 175.

55. *Ibid.*, p. 173.

56. *Ibid.*, pp. 173, 180.

57. *Ibid.*, p. 173.

58. World Resources Institute in collaboration with the United Nations Development Programme and the United Nations Environment Programme, *World Resources 1990-91* (Oxford University Press, New York, 1990), p. 289.

59. *Op. cit.* 35, p. 255.

60. U.S. Department of Agriculture (USDA), *Report and Recommendations on Organic Farming* (USDA, Washington, D.C., 1980), p. xii-xiii.

61. Alex Dubgaard, Per Olsen, and Soren Sorenson, "Profitability of Organic Farming in Denmark" (Institute of Agricultural Economics, Copenhagen, 1990), p. 65.

62. *Op. cit.* 60, pp. xiii, 11.

63. *Op. cit.* 38, p. 2.

64. American Farmland Trust, *Agriculture and the Environment: A Study of Farmer Practices and Perceptions* (American Farmland Trust, Washington, D.C., 1990), p. i.

65. David C. Coleman and Paul F. Hendrix, "Agroecosystem Processes," in *Ecological Studies 67*, L.R. Pomeroy and J.J. Alberts, eds. (Springer-Verlag, New York, 1988), pp. 156-157.

66. Len Bull, "Pesticide Use by Tillage System, 1988 and 1989 Corn Production," in *Agricultural Resources: Inputs Situation and Outlook Report* (Economic Research Service, U.S. Department of Agriculture, Washington, D.C., 1991), p. 35.

67. *Op. cit.* 49, pp. 156, 158.

68. Bette Hileman, "Alternative Agriculture," *Chemical and Engineering News* (March 5, 1990), p. 31.

69. Science Council of Canada, *A Growing Concern: Soil Degradation in Canada* (Science Council of Canada, Ottawa, 1986), p. 12.

70. *Op. cit.* 49, p. 158.

71. *Op. cit.* 69, p. 11.

72. Arthur J. Conacher, "Salt of the Earth," *Environment* (July/August 1990), p. 4.

73. *Op. cit.* 36, p. 33.

74. D.L. Schertz, W.C. Moldenhauer, S.J. Livingston, *et al.*, "Effect of Past Soil Erosion on Crop Productivity in Indiana," *Journal of Soil and Water Conservation*, Vol. 44, No. 6 (1989), p. 604.

75. Tim Osborn, Section Leader, Domestic and Agricultural Policy, Economic Research Service, U.S. Department of Agriculture, Washington, D.C., 1991 (personal communication).

76. *Op. cit.* 13, p. 12, Table 5.

77. Brian Gardner, "European Agriculture's Environmental Problems," paper presented at the First Annual Conference of the Hudson Institute, Indianapolis, Indiana, April 1990, p. 6.

78. C. Arden-Clarke and R.D. Hodges, "The Environmental Effects of Conventional and Organic/Biological Farming Systems. 1. Soil Erosion, with Special Reference to Britain,"

Biological Agriculture and Horticulture, Vol. 4 (1987), p. 322.

79. Heino von Meyer, "Agriculture and the Environment in the European Community" (Institute for Agricultural Economics, Frankfurt, Germany, 1989), p. 5.

80. Robert F. Wasserstrom and Richard Wiles, *Field Duty: U.S. Farmworkers and Pesticide Safety* (World Resources Institute, Washington, D.C., 1985), p. 4.

81. Michael J. Dover, *A Better Mousetrap: Improving Pest Management for Agriculture* (World Resources Institute, Washington, D.C., 1985), p. 4.

82. George P. Georghiou, "Overview of Pesticide Resistance," in *Managing Resistance to Agrochemicals*, Maurice B. Green, Homer M. LeBaron, and William K. Moberg, eds. (American Chemical Society, Washington, D.C., 1990), p. 18.

83. *Op. cit.* 81, pp. 5-6.

84. Michael Duffy and Leland Thompson, "The Extent and Nature of Iowa Crop Production Practices, 1989" (Iowa State University, Ames, Iowa, 1991), pp. 12, 15.

85. *Op. cit.* 79, p. 4.

86. Edwin H. Clark II, Jennifer A. Havercamp, and William Chapman, *Eroding Soils: The Off-Farm Impacts* (The Conservation Foundation, Washington, D.C., 1985), p. 7.

87. Carl F. Myers, James Meek, Stuart Tuller, *et al.*, "Nonpoint Sources of Water Pollution," *Journal of Soil and Water Conservation*, Vol. 40, No. 1 (1985), p. 10.

88. U.S. Environmental Protection Agency (EPA), "National Survey of Pesticides in Drinking Water Wells: Phase 1" (EPA, Washington, D.C., 1990), p. vii.

89. George R. Hallberg, "Pesticide Pollution of Groundwater in the Humid United States," *Agriculture, Ecosystems and Environment*, Vol. 26 (1989), p. 299.

90. *Ibid.*, p. 343.

91. *Op. cit.* 77, p. 5.

92. *Op. cit.* 77, p. 5.

93. *Op. cit.* 79, p. 5.

94. *Op. cit.* 54, p. 182.

95. Steve Crutchfield, "Controlling Farm Pollution of Coastal Waters," in *Agricultural Chemicals and the Environment* (Economic Research Service, U.S. Department of Agriculture, Washington, D.C., 1988), p. 8.

96. *Op. cit.* 54, p. 182.

97. Marc O. Ribaudo, "Water Quality Benefits from the Conservation Reserve Program" (U.S. Department of Agriculture, Washington, D.C., 1989), pp. 4, 7.

98. *Op. cit.* 86, pp. 63-64.

99. *Op. cit.* 36, p. 3.

100. Jules N. Pretty and Gordon R. Conway, "Agriculture as a Global Polluter" (International Institute for Environment and Development, London, 1988), pp. 5-7.

101. Organisation for Economic Co-operation and Development (OECD), *Agricultural and Environmental Policies: Opportunities for Integration* (OECD, Paris, 1989), p. 44.

102. *Op. cit.* 100, pp. 8-9.

103. *Op. cit.* 77, p. 7.

104. *Op. cit.* 91, p. 7.

105. *Op. cit.* 54, p. 183.

106. Katherine H. Reichelderfer, "Environmental Effects of Farm Programs in Developed Countries," in *Sustainable Agriculture: Its Policy Effects on the Future of Canada and Ontario's Agrifood System* (University of Guelph, Guelph, Ontario, May 1990), pp. 32-33.

107. *Ibid.*, pp. 36-37.

108. *Op. cit.* 41.

109. J.F. Parr, R.I. Papendick, I.G. Youngberg, *et al.*, "Sustainable Agriculture in the United States," in *Sustainable Agricultural Systems*, Clive A. Edwards, Rattan Lal, Patrick Madden, *et al.*, eds. (Soil and Water Conservation Society, Ankeny, Iowa, 1990), pp. 62-63.

110. U.S. Department of Agriculture (USDA), "The 1990 Farm Act and the 1990 Budget Reconciliation Act" (Economic Research Service, USDA, Washington, D.C., 1990), pp. 23-25.

111. Heino von Meyer, "The Common Agricultural Policy and the Environment: The Effects of Price Policy and Options for its Reform" (World Wildlife Fund International, Gland, Switzerland, n.d.), p. 5.

112. Julius Rosenblatt, Thomas Mayer, Kasper Bartholdy, *et al.*, *The Common Agricultural Policy of the European Community: Principles and Consequences* (International Monetary Fund, Washington, D.C., 1988), p. 6.

113. *Op. cit.* 111, pp. 5, 7-8.

114. *Op. cit.* 106, p. 38.

115. *Op. cit.* 101, p. 59.

116. U.S. Environmental Protection Agency (EPA), "Agriculture and the Environment: OECD Policy Experiences and American Opportunities" (EPA, Washington, D.C., 1990), p. 12.

117. *Op. cit.* 101, pp. 100-101.

118. C. Tim Osborne, Section Leader, Economic Research Service, U.S. Department of Agriculture, Washington, D.C., 1991 (personal communication).

119. *Op. cit.* 106, p. 48.

120. *Op. cit.* 116, p. 14.

121. David Ervin and James Tobey, "European Agricultural and Environmental Policies: Sorting through Incentives," paper presented at a conference entitled, "Is Environmental Quality Good for Business? Problems and Prospects in the Agricultural, Energy, and Chemical Industries," American Enterprise Institute for Public Policy Research, Washington, D.C., June 1990, pp. 6, 13.

122. *Op. cit.* 101, p. 173.

123. Michael D. Young, "Some Steps in Other Countries," *EPA Journal* (April 1988), p. 25.

124. *Op. cit.* 121, p. 11.

125. *Op. cit.* 123, p. 25.

126. *Op. cit.* 121, pp. 13-14.

127. Heino von Meyer, Institute for Agricultural Economics, Frankfurt, Germany, 1991 (personal communication).

128. *Op. cit.* 101, p. 110.

129. *Op. cit.* 121, pp. 13-14.

130. *Op. cit.* 101, p. 99.

131. *Op. cit.* 121, p. 10.

132. *Op. cit.* 101, pp. 110, 118.

133. *Op. cit.* 101, p. 103.

134. Alex Dubgaard, Professor, Department of Economics and Natural Resources, Royal Veterinary and Agricultural University, Frederiksberg, Denmark, 1991 (personal communication).

135. *Op. cit.* 121, pp. 16-17.

136. Alex Dubgaard, "Danish Policy Measures to Control Agricultural Impacts on the Environment" (Institute of Agricultural Economics, Copenhagen, 1990), p. 18.

137. *Op. cit.* 101, p. 102.

138. *Op. cit.* 54, p. 182.

139. *Op. cit.* 136, p. 14.

140. Ernst Lutz and Michael Young, "Integration of Environmental Concerns into Agricultural Policies of Industrial and Developing Countries," *World Development* (forthcoming).

141. *Op. cit.* 136, pp. 15-16.

142. *Op. cit.* 101, p. 98.

143. Glen Anderson, Ann De Bossu, and Peter Kuch, "Control of Agricultural Pollution by Regulation," in *Agriculture and Water Quality: International Perspectives*, John Braden and Steve Lovejoy, eds. (Lynne Rienner Publishers, Boulder, Colorado and London, 1990), p. 77.

144. Food and Agriculture Organization of the United Nations (FAO), "Socio-Economic Aspects of Environmental Policies in European Agriculture" (FAO, Rome, 1990), p. 25.

145. *Op. cit.* 38, p. 7.

146. *Op. cit.* 38, p. 11.

147. *Op. cit.* 61, p. 68.

148. *Op. cit.* 61, pp. 65, 68, 71.

149. W.C. Liebhardt, R.W. Andrews, M.N. Culik, *et al.*, "Crop Production During Conversion from Conventional to Low-Input Methods," *Agronomy Journal*, Vol. 81, No. 2 (1989), pp. 150, 158.

150. *Op. cit.* 36, p. 11.

151. *Op. cit.* 36, p. 11.

152. *Op. cit.* 36, pp. 11-12.

153. *Op. cit.* 36, pp. 12-13.

154. *Op. cit.* 36, pp. 18-19.

155. *Op. cit.* 112, p. 11.

156. *Op. cit.* 111, pp. 13-16.

157. Edward Barbier, Director, London Environmental Economics Centre, University College London, London, 1991 (personal communication).

158. *Op. cit.* 111, pp. 15-16.

8. Forests and Rangelands

Two new studies offer the best estimates so far on the condition of global soil resources and tropical forests. Both these resources faced heavy pressure during the past half-century, when the world population doubled. As a result, their condition is declining rapidly. Over the past 45 years, about 11 percent of the Earth's vegetated soils became degraded to the point that their original biotic functions are damaged, and reclamation may be costly or in some cases impossible. Preliminary results of a United Nations tropical deforestation assessment confirm scattered data showing that deforestation increased 50 percent during the 1980s to an average of nearly 17 million hectares per year.

The extent of soil degradation and tropical deforestation has been controversial. Environmentalists have pointed with alarm to eroding hillsides, barren drylands studded with the trunks of once-thriving trees, and burned-out tropical forests. Others have pointed to rising crop and livestock production as a sign that no problem exists. Although many researchers documented local conditions, the lack of scientific up-to-date global assessments has left policymakers without a firm information base for making decisions. The new studies are significant advances in global resource information although they have limitations and reflect funding and time constraints. Both are preliminary assessments released in advance of longer-term, more detailed studies. However, they are clearly the best estimates available and they offer urgently needed information to policymakers.

These studies can be viewed as waypoints used by a navigator in sailing a course. They assess where we are now. An old Chinese proverb warns that if we do not change the direction we are going, we will end up where we are headed.

CONDITIONS AND TRENDS

NEW SOIL DEGRADATION ESTIMATES

An area approximately the size of China and India combined has suffered moderate to extreme soil degradation caused mainly by agricultural activities, deforestation, and overgrazing in the past 45 years, accor-

Table 8.1 Human-Induced Soil Degradation, 1945–90

Region	Total Degraded Area (million hectares)	Degraded Area as a Percentage of Vegetated Land
World		
Total degraded area	1,964.4	17.0
Moderate, severe, and extreme	1,215.4	10.5
Light	749.0	6.5
Europe		
Total degraded area	218.9	23.1
Moderate, severe, and extreme	158.3	16.7
Light	60.6	6.4
Africa		
Total degraded area	494.2	22.1
Moderate, severe, and extreme	320.6	14.4
Light	173.6	7.8
Asia		
Total degraded area	747.0	19.8
Moderate, severe, and extreme	452.5	12.0
Light	294.5	7.8
Oceania		
Total degraded area	102.9	13.1
Moderate, severe, and extreme	6.2	0.8
Light	96.6	12.3
North America		
Total degraded area	95.5	5.3
Moderate, severe, and extreme	78.7	4.4
Light	16.8	0.9
Central America and Mexico		
Total degraded area	62.8	24.8
Moderate, severe, and extreme	60.9	24.1
Light	1.9	0.7
South America		
Total degraded area	243.4	14.0
Moderate, severe, and extreme	138.5	8.0
Light	104.8	6.0

Source: L.R. Oldeman, V.W.P. van Engelen, and J.H.M. Pulles, "The Extent of Human-Induced Soil Degradation," Annex 5 of L.R. Oldeman, R.T.A. Hakkeling, and W.G. Sombroek, *World Map of the Status of Human-Induced Soil Degradation: An Explanatory Note*, rev. 2d ed. (International Soil Reference and Information Centre, Wageningen, the Netherlands, 1990), Tables 1-7.
Note: Totals may not add because of rounding.

ding to a new study sponsored by the United Nations Environment Programme (UNEP). This area—1.2 billion hectares—represents almost 11 percent of the Earth's vegetated surface (1) (2) (3). (See Table 8.1.)

This degraded land has lost some of its natural productivity. Most of it suffers from "moderate" degradation, that is, its agricultural productivity is "greatly reduced," but it can still be used for agriculture. The soil's original biotic functions (its ability to process nutrients into a form usable by plants) have been partially destroyed and only with major improvements can productivity be restored. A smaller portion of vegetated land—300 million hectares, almost 3 percent of the world total—shows "severe" degradation; its original biotic functions are largely destroyed, and it is reclaimable only with major international financial and technical assistance. Degradation of less than 1 percent—9 million hectares—is classified as "extreme," defined as "unreclaimable and beyond restoration." Its original biotic functions are fully destroyed (4). (See Chapter 19, "Forests and Rangelands," Table 19.3.)

If one were to include the nearly 750 million hectares of terrain whose degradation is "light," the area with soil degraded just since World War II would be 17 per-

cent of the Earth's total vegetated land. (See Table 8.1.) Lightly degraded soils have lost some productivity but can be restored through farm conservation practices. Their biotic functions are largely intact (5).

The three-year study, the Global Assessment of Soil Degradation (GLASOD), was sponsored by UNEP and coordinated by the International Soil Reference and Information Centre (ISRIC) in the Netherlands. The GLASOD study is associated with a more detailed global soils project—the World Soils and Terrain Digital Database (SOTER), also being coordinated by ISRIC, for the International Society of Soil Science (ISSS) and targeted for completion in 15–20 years. UNEP pressed for an earlier assessment because "politically it is important to have an assessment of good quality *now* instead of having an assessment of very good quality in 15 or 20 years" (6). UNEP plans to combine elements of the GLASOD soil degradation survey with data on population, climatology, and vegetation loss in a world desertification atlas (7). Desertification encompasses soil degradation and associated changes in vegetation in arid and semiarid regions.

GLASOD asked more than 250 soil scientists and 21 regional coordinators for their expert estimates of the degree, type, and causes of the human-induced soil degradation that has occurred since World War II. They were also asked to estimate how much land area was affected in specified physiographic mapping units. After this information was compiled, it was mapped at an average scale of 1:15 million. The map was subsequently digitized and summary tables and thematic maps drawn.

GLASOD also included a pilot study in Latin America (parts of Argentina, Brazil, and Uruguay) to test a methodology for SOTER.

Trends

GLASOD is the first baseline study using a consistent methodology to estimate global soil degradation. ISRIC researchers hope to follow it with surveys every 10 years, which will enable them to estimate a rate of degradation (8).

The GLASOD results are all the more alarming because, unlike other attempts to estimate land degradation, they do not include land degraded by ancient civilizations or even by colonial expansion; nor do they include land that is naturally barren. Soil scientists were asked to categorize only soils degraded over the past 45 years because of human intervention (9). But the 45-year period masks improvements. In at least the United States, and parts of Europe and Australia, soil conditions worsened, then improved owing to government soil conservation programs (10) (11). In the United States, for example, nonfederal land suffering water-related erosion in excess of an accepted sustainable rate declined from 13.6 percent in 1982 to 12.6 percent in 1987 (12).

Degrees of Soil Degradation

GLASOD defines soil degradation as "a process that describes human-induced phenomena which lower

Box 8.1 Degrees of Soil Degradation

LIGHT DEGRADATION

About 750 million hectares are lightly degraded. In deep soils, part of the topsoil has been removed and/or shallow, widely spaced rills or hollows appear . On rangeland, 70 percent of the land is covered by native perennials. In salinized areas, salinity has increased slightly over the past 45 years.

MODERATE DEGRADATION

Most of the degraded land—910 million hectares—is moderately degraded. Manifestations of moderate degradation include:

Water and wind erosion. For deep soils, all topsoil has been removed, or the terrain shows shallow rills less than 20 meters apart, moderately deep gullies 20–50 meters apart, or shallow to moderately deep hollows. In shallow soils, part of the topsoil has been removed, or the terrain shows either shallow rills 20–50 meters apart or shallow hollows. In rangelands, the terrain has 30–70 percent of its native vegetation.

Chemical degradation due to nutrient decline. In temperate regions, on cleared and cultivated grassland or savannahs with rich soil, nutrient decline involves a marked reduction in the decomposition of organic matter into stable nutrients that can be used by plants. Decomposition of organic matter by micro- and macro-organisms not only improves soil fertility, it also increases the soil's water-holding capacity and gives it a more stable structure. The organisms convert leaves and other fresh organic matter into more stable organic components called humus. Humus adsorbs nutrients and water and "glues" soil particles together in stable clusters. If this process is disrupted, decomposition can proceed too rapidly, burning up nutrients before plants can use them. Soil with faulty decomposition is less fertile, drier, and more easily compacted (1).

In humid tropical regions, some nutrient loss often occurs in moderately rich soils that were deforested for cultivation and then not fertilized adequately. Land defined as moderately saline has increased in salinity since World War II, as indicated by a loss in productivity of crops that are not tolerant to salt or by a shift from intolerant to more tolerant species (e.g., from salt-intolerant wheat to barley) (2).

Physical degradation. Here the soil structure no longer allows good water retention and deep root penetration but allows only the development of shallow root systems. Water runoff from compacted soil can cause both further erosion and water pollution. Physical degradation is the least common of the four types of soil degradation. It is found mainly on heavily stocked pastureland and on farmland where heavy machinery is used (3).

SEVERE DEGRADATION

Worldwide, 300 million hectares have become severely degraded in the past 45 years. Soils severely degraded by wind and water erosion show deeper, more frequent gullies and hollows. Pastureland has less than 30 percent of its native vegetation (4). In tropical areas with poor soils, severe nutrient depletion occurs where all biomass has been cleared and crops grow poorly or not at all. Productivity cannot be improved by nitrogen fertilizer alone.

EXTREME DEGRADATION

Extremely degraded soils can be found where deforestation, overgrazing or other causes of degradation have occurred on soils with inherently poor parent materials. No crop growth occurs and restoration is impossible (5). About 9 million hectares fall into this category. Extreme degradation has been documented in central Italy (caused by water erosion), Somalia (wind erosion) and the Soviet Union near Iran (salinization) (6).

References and Notes

1. L.R. Oldeman, Program and Project Division, International Soil Reference and Information Centre, Wageningen, the Netherlands, 1991 (personal communication).
2. *Ibid.*
3. *Ibid.*
4. L.R. Oldeman, ed., *Guidelines for General Assessment of the Status of Human-Induced Soil Degradation* (International Soil Reference and Information Centre, Wageningen, the Netherlands, 1988), p. 6.
5. *Ibid.*, p. 5.
6. Global Assessment of Soil Degradation, *World Map on Status of Human-Induced Soil Degradation*, Sheet 2, Europe, Africa, and Western Asia (United Nations Environment Programme International Soil Reference and Information Centre, Nairobi, 1990.)

the current and/or future capacity of the soil to support human life" (13). The degrees of soil degradation used in the study (light, moderate, severe, and extreme) are described in Box 8.1. Land that is lightly degraded (about 750 million hectares) generally involves good soils that show signs of degradation but can be restored by using conservation practices. Of more concern are soils moderately, severely, and extremely degraded. Even though agricultural production may be increasing owing to increased inputs of fertilizers and pesticides, moderately degraded soils (910 million hectares) would produce even higher yields were they not degraded. Without intervention, loss of potential productivity will continue. Severely (300 million hectares) and extremely degraded (9 million hectares) soils are obviously degraded even to a nonexpert and show an actual loss of productivity (14).

Restoring Degraded Soils

Restoring lightly degraded soils can be accomplished with crop rotation, minimum tillage, and other on-farm practices. (See Chapter 7, "Food and Agriculture.")

Restoring moderately degraded land to its former productivity would take more resources than an average farmer can provide, according to GLASOD. Changes in soil conservation practices might slow the degradation but will not restore fertility. For moderately degraded soils to be restored, national programs will have to provide financial incentives and technical expertise. Restoring productivity usually requires major structural changes—draining for waterlogging or salinity or creating contour banks for eroding soil, for example.

Severely eroded land generally requires a restoration effort beyond the capacity of most developing nations; bilateral or multilateral financial and technical assistance would be needed. Restoration efforts would require similar but more extensive engineering works, such as deep ditches to drain the land and terraces to hold it in place and, for compacted land, mechanized deep plowing and reseeding. In practice, land that requires expensive restoration is often simply abandoned (15) (16).

Figure 8.1 Types of Soil Degradation

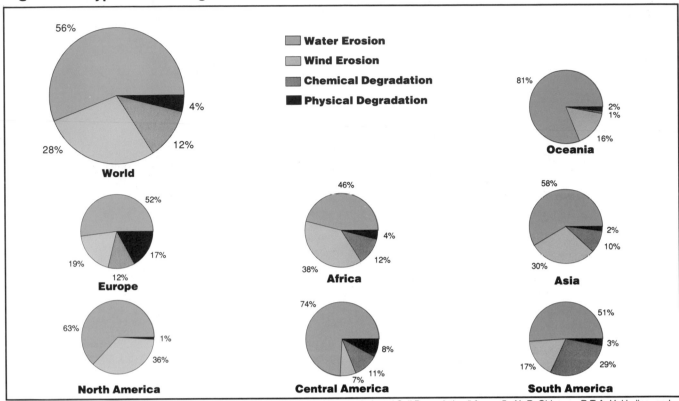

Source: L.R. Oldeman, V.W.P. van Engelen, and J.H.M. Pulles, "The Extent of Human-Induced Soil Degradation," Annex 5 of L.R. Oldeman, R.T.A. Hakkeling, and W.G. Sombroek, World Map of the Status of Human-Induced Soil Degradation: An Explanatory Note, rev. 2d ed. (International Soil Reference and Information Centre, Wageningen, the Netherlands, 1990), Figure 5. **Note:** Categories not shown in regions represent less than 1 percent.

Figure 8.2 Causes of Soil Degradation

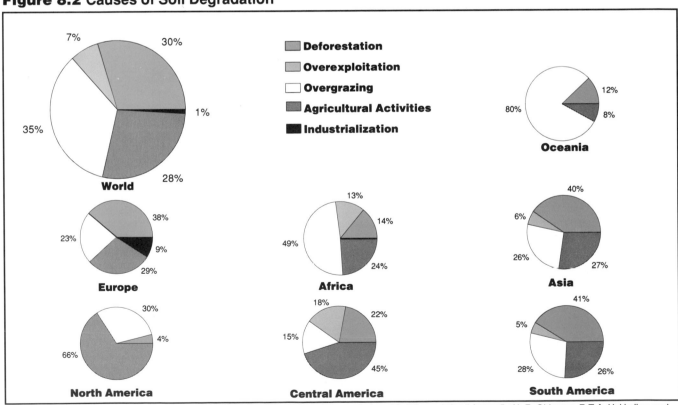

Source: L.R. Oldeman, V.W.P. van Engelen, and J.H.M. Pulles, "The Extent of Human-Induced Soil Degradation," Annex 5 of L.R. Oldeman, R.T.A. Hakkeling, and W.G. Sombroek, World Map of the Status of Human-Induced Soil Degradation: An Explanatory Note, rev. 2d ed. (International Soil Reference and Information Centre, Wageningen, the Netherlands, 1990), Figure 5. **Note:** Categories not shown in regions represent less than 1 percent.

Box 8.2 Types of Soil Degradation

Wind and water erosion strip away nutrient-rich topsoil, leaving the land less productive; whereas degradation by physical and chemical processes reduces the productivity of the soil *in situ*. The four processes of degradation defined by the Global Assessment of Soil Degradation are described below.

WATER EROSION

Loss of topsoil through water erosion is the most common type of soil degradation. Also called surface or sheet erosion, it occurs in all countries. Because topsoil is relatively rich in nutrients, its loss may impoverish the soil. Terrain deformation, such as the creation of gullies, is an extreme form of water erosion. Control of gullies is difficult and reclamation almost impossible. Water erosion that occurs naturally on steep slopes is not included in this study unless it is accelerated by human intervention.

WIND EROSION

Wind erosion is widespread in both arid and semiarid climates. In general, coarse soils are highly susceptible to wind erosion. It is nearly always caused by a decrease in the vegetative cover of the soil by overgrazing, agricultural practices, deforestation, or fuelwood removal. Terrain displaced by wind erosion forms hollows and dunes. Overblowing, the coverage of off-site land by a layer of blown soil, is a side effect of wind erosion. It affects roads, buildings, and waterways and can damage agricultural land.

CHEMICAL DETERIORATION

Nutrients can be depleted or stripped when agriculture is practiced on poor or moderately fertile soils without sufficient application of manure or other fertilizers. As soil nutrients are progressively exhausted, production drops. Loss of nutrients is widespread in countries where unsustainable agriculture is practiced. Loss of nutrients also occurs when natural forest or other vegetation is cleared.

Salinization occurs when the concentration of salts in the topsoil increases, rendering the land unfit for agriculture. It can be caused by three human activities: poorly drained irrigation systems; excessive groundwater withdrawals in coastal areas, allowing sea water to infiltrate an aquifer; and activities that lead to increased evapotranspiration in soils with salt-containing parent material or saline groundwater.

Acidification can be caused by the drainage of pyrite-containing soils in coastal areas or by overapplication of acidifying fertilizer. Acidification reduces productivity.

Pollution is most closely associated with industrial and urban wastes, excessive pesticide use, airborne pollutant acidification, excessive manuring in feedlots, and oil and chemical spills.

PHYSICAL DETERIORATION

Compaction occurs in all continents under nearly all climatic and soil conditions. Compaction is usually caused by heavy machinery, but it is also caused by cattle trampling. Soils with low organic matter levels are especially vulnerable. Compaction makes tillage more costly, impedes seedling emergence, and decreases water infiltration, causing higher runoff of rainwater and increasing water erosion.

Waterlogging includes flooding by river water and submergence by rainwater as a result of human intervention in natural drainage systems. The construction of flooded paddy fields is not included because they are considered an improvement to the soil.

Subsidence of organic soils caused by drainage and/or oxidation is recognized as a deteriorator only when the agricultural potential of the land is reduced [1].

References and Notes

1. L.R. Oldeman, R.T.A. Hakkeling, and W.G. Sombroek, *World Map of the Status of Human-Induced Soil Degradation: An Explanatory Note*, rev. 2d ed. (International Soil Reference and Information Centre, Wageningen, the Netherlands, 1990), pp. 12-14.

Types of Soil Degradation

Figure 8.1 shows the four types of soil degradation in each geographic region. Wind and water erosion sweep soil away when its vegetation is removed; chemical and physical degradation are characterized by changes in the soil rather than by its displacement. Only land that has been abandoned or forced into less intensive use is classified as chemically degraded [17]. (See Box 8.2 for a more detailed discussion of types of soil degradation.)

Causes of Soil Degradation

Figure 8.2 shows that the causes of the land degradation documented by GLASOD are about equally divided among unsustainable livestock grazing, agriculture, and forestry practices. Some degradation is caused by overexploitation for fuelwood collection. A small amount (1.5 percent) is degraded by industrial activities, such as waste disposal and excessive pesticide use.

Overgrazing

Overgrazing by livestock decreases vegetation, exposing the soil to water and wind erosion. In addition, livestock trample and thereby compact the soil, reducing its capacity to retain moisture. Overgrazing is the most pervasive cause of soil degradation, affecting 679 million hectares (35 percent of all degraded land). In Africa and Australia, overgrazing causes 49 percent and 80 percent, respectively, of soil degradation, mainly in semiarid and arid regions [18].

Agricultural Activities

Common agricultural practices such as insufficient use of fertilizers or shortening the fallow periods in shifting cultivation can lead to a loss of nutrients. But too much fertilizer can lead to soil acidification. Cultivating hillsides without adequate preventive measures leads to water erosion. Leaving soil exposed during fallow periods often results in wind erosion. Use of heavy machinery compacts soil, resulting in physical damage. Insufficient drainage of irrigation water may cause salinization. Worldwide, faulty agricultural practices account for 28 percent of the degraded soils, although North America is the region where agricultural practices cause the greatest share (57 percent) [19].

Deforestation and Land Conversion

In this category, GLASOD includes both conversion of forestland to agriculture and urban use and large-scale logging. (Deforestation statistics in "Trends in Defores-

Box 8.3 World Areas of Soil Degradation

Of the world's 1.2 billion hectares with moderate, severe, and extreme soil degradation, the largest areas are in Asia (453 million hectares) and Africa (321 million hectares). Most of this soil degradation is caused by water and wind erosion resulting from agricultural activities, overgrazing, deforestation, and fuelwood collection. Central America shows the highest percentage of vegetated land with moderate to extreme soil degradation (24 percent), followed by Europe (17 percent), Africa (14 percent), and Asia (12 percent). (See Table 8.1.)

Figure 1 is a simplified version of the Global Assessment of Soil Degradation (GLASOD) map, which indicates areas of major concern because of either severe degradation in small areas or moderate degradation over larger areas.

EUROPE
In Europe, a relatively high amount—28 percent—of degraded soils are chemically and physically degraded. More than 14 million hectares are contaminated with industrial and urban wastes, pesticides, and other pollutants. Much of the chemical degradation is found in Poland, Germany, Hungary, and southern Sweden. Almost 8 million hectares, mostly in southern Sweden and Finland, Germany, Belgium, northern Italy, Spain, and Romania are degraded by compaction from livestock and the use of heavy machinery (1) (2).

AFRICA
Areas of serious chemical soil deterioration have been reported in several areas of sub-Saharan Africa and the Nile valley. This condition is caused mainly by nutrient loss on land under low-input agriculture (25 million hectares) and by salinization resulting from poor management of irrigation systems (10 million hectares). Areas of extreme physical deterioration, mainly from cattle trampling, are found in

parts of the Sahel and southern Africa. Erosion is a major cause of Africa's soil degradation—wind erosion in the belts north and south of the Sahara and water erosion in sub-Saharan Africa (3) (4). Almost one half (49 percent) of the continent's soil degradation results from overgrazing. Other human activities that lead to soil degradation are agricultural practices (24 percent), deforestation (14 percent), and fuelwood collection (13 percent) (5).

ASIA
Severe water erosion is extensive in western India, throughout the Himalayas, in Southeast Asia, and in large areas of China. Western China and Mongolia experience serious wind erosion. Chemical deterioration (mostly loss of nutrients in agriculture, acidification, and salinization) is found in northern India, Bangladesh, Burma, Thailand, Malaysia, Indonesia, northern China, and North and South Korea. Forty percent of Asia's soil degradation is caused by deforestation, 27 percent by agriculture, 26 percent by overgrazing, 6 percent by fuelwood collection, and less than 1 percent by industrialization (6) (7).

OCEANIA
Eighty percent of the soil degradation in Australia and the South Pacific results from overgrazing. Southern Australia shows some water and wind erosion. Many Pacific islands suffer moderate to strong water erosion (8) (9).

NORTH AMERICA
North America's breadbasket, the area of rich prairie soils extending from the U.S. Midwest through the Great Plains into Canada, shows moderate degradation from wind and water erosion. Although soils here are still among the world's most fertile, they have lost some of their original productivity. They require more fertilizers and high-yielding crop varieties to

sustain outputs. In the United States, major government soil conservation programs have begun to stabilize some areas, yet unsustainable farming practices could lead to further deterioration (10). High water-related erosion rates are found in areas along the Mississippi and Missouri rivers, in California's central valley, and in the hilly Palouse of Washington state. There are areas of serious salinization in the U.S. Southwest (11). About 25 percent of U.S. cropland is eroding at a rate faster than is considered sustainable by the Soil Conservation Service (12). North America is the region with the least amount of vegetated land degraded by humans (5.3 percent).

CENTRAL AMERICA
Severe water, chemical, and physical degradation of the soil is found in Mexico and Central America, where 25 percent of the vegetated land is moderately to extremely degraded, 10 percent of it (25.5 million hectares) in the serious and extreme categories (13). Most of the soil degradation results from water erosion along the mountainous Pacific coast, but there is also serious physical and chemical deterioration in southeastern Mexico, Honduras, and Nicaragua. Most of this degradation was caused by deforestation and overgrazing, some by poor agricultural practices (14).

SOUTH AMERICA
In the Amazon region, most of the soil is stable or shows low deterioration rates except for areas of extensive deforestation, such as southwestern and northeastern Brazil and eastern Paraguay. The agricultural and grazing lands of Argentina show medium to high wind erosion degradation, and the western slopes of the Andes show medium to high water erosion degradation. Much of the coastline, which includes the majority of human settlements, shows medium to high soil degradation (15).

---

tation," below, include land conversion, but not logging.) Deforestation accounts for 579 million hectares, 30 percent of the world's degraded land area. Deforestation occurs on all continents, but it is most pronounced in Asia, where it has caused the degradation of 298 million hectares (20).

Overexploitation for Fuelwood

In dry areas, stripping land of vegetation for fuelwood also leads to wind and water erosion. Worldwide, over-exploitation accounts for 7 percent of the degraded soils. Africa has the highest percentage (13 percent) of degraded soils from this cause. (See Figure 8.2.)

Industrialization

This category includes industrial and waste accumulation and acidification by airborne pollutants. Almost

23 million hectares—more than 20 million of them in Europe—are degraded by these activities (21).

Interpretation of Results

Box 8.3 describes the location of degraded soils regionally and points to the areas of special concern. The GLASOD report concludes that if no restoration of the 910 million hectares of moderately degraded land is accomplished soon, "one may fear that at least part of it may become strongly degraded in the near future." The report further notes that the "vast majority of strongly degraded land is located in Asia and Africa," where a large fraction of the world's poor lives. "Only major investments and engineering works can restore some of [these lands'] productivity" (22). Should the moderately degraded land—an area almost the size of the United States—become seriously or extremely degraded, it could have a major impact on the produc-

Figure 1 Areas of Concern for Soil Degradation

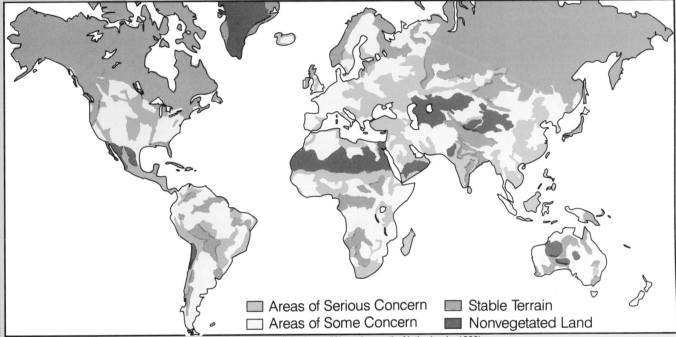

Areas of Serious Concern ☐ Stable Terrain
Areas of Some Concern ☐ Nonvegetated Land

Source: International Soil Reference and Information Centre, unpublished map (Wageningen, the Netherlands, 1990).
Note: Dark colored areas are of serious concern because of localized severe or extreme soil degradation or widespread moderate degradation. Light colored areas are of some concern because of localized moderate or severe degradation or widespread light degradation.

References and Notes

1. L.R. Oldeman, V.W.P. van Engelen, and J.H.M. Pulles, "The Extent of Human-Induced Soil Degradation," Annex 5 of L.R. Oldeman, R.T.A. Hakkeling, and W.G. Sombroek, *World Map of the Status of Human-Induced Soil Degradation: An Explanatory Note*, revised 2d ed. (International Soil Reference and Information Centre, Wageningen, the Netherlands, 1991), p. 3 and Table 7.

2. Global Assessment of Soil Degradation, *World Map on Status of Human-Induced Soil Degradation*, Sheet 2, Europe, Africa, and Western Asia (United Nations Environment Programme, International Soil Reference and Information Centre, Nairobi, 1990).

3. *Op. cit.* 1, p. 3 and Figure 4.
4. *Op. cit.* 2.
5. *Op. cit.* 1, Figure 5.
6. *Op. cit.* 1, Figure 5.
7. *Op. cit.* 1, Figure 5.
8. *Op. cit.* 1, Figure 5.
9. *Op. cit.* 1, Figure 5.
10. Richard W. Arnold, Director, Soil Survey Division, U.S. Department of Agriculture, Washington D.C., 1991 (personal communication.)

11. *Op. cit.* 1, Figure 5.
12. U.S. Department of Agriculture (USDA), Soil Conservation Service, *Summary Report: 1987 National Resources Inventory*, Statistical Bulletin No. 790 (USDA, Washington, D.C., 1989), Table 9.
13. L.R. Oldeman, Program and Project Division, International Soil Reference and Information Centre, Wageningen, the Netherlands, 1991 (personal communication).
14. *Op. cit.* 2, Sheet 1, Figure 5.
15. *Op. cit.* 2, Sheet 1.

tion of food, livestock, and forest products. Productivity losses on moderately degraded agricultural land can be mitigated by the increased application of fertilizers. But increasing chemical inputs alone will not reverse the degradation process and may in fact cause serious environmental effects associated with the contamination of surface and groundwater. (See Chapter 7, "Food and Agriculture.")

Despite massive soil degradation, agricultural yields have steadily increased since World War II owing to improved high-yielding crop varieties, irrigation, and increased chemical inputs, such as fertilizer and pesticides. Yet real economic losses have occurred. Modern agricultural technologies are more productive on good soils than on poor soils. Although technology often sustains yields, it only temporarily masks the effects of soil degradation; the yield increases might have been even greater if the soil had not been degraded. This difference between the actual and the potential yield represents a real loss of income (23). For example, as Figure 8.3 shows, farmers in the highly erodible Palouse area of Washington state are estimated to have lost the potential to produce an additional 670 kilograms of winter wheat per hectare because of soil erosion.

Why do farmers, even those with a secure title to their land and a continuing commitment to farming, allow soil degradation? Two reasons are given by soil scientists and economists. GLASOD soil scientists point out that stopping or reversing moderate soil degradation requires action beyond the scale of a farm. Watershed management, installation of catchment basins, and other soil conservation measures are typically adopted on a regional level by governments. At a certain point, then, the farmer is helpless to restore pro-

Figure 8.3 Predicted Winter Wheat Production Loss from Soil Erosion in the Palouse River Basin, 1930–80

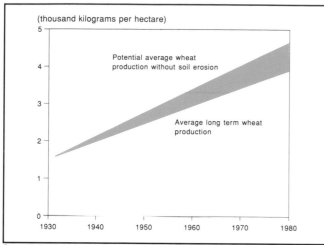

(thousand kilograms per hectare)

Potential average wheat production without soil erosion

Average long term wheat production

Source: Michael T. Jennings, Baird C. Miller, David F. Bezdicek, *et al.*, "Sustainability of Dryland Cropping in the Palouse: An Historical View," *Journal of Soil and Water Conservation* (January-February 1990), p. 79.

ductivity. Economists point out that farmers' planting decisions are usually influenced more by the current selling price of their crops than by long-term gains to be realized from land husbandry. In fact, in fertile areas, an individual farmer may not benefit from conservation practices. According to a Washington, D.C., economic institute, for U.S. farmers, "the adoption of practices that would indefinitely maintain the productivity of the land would not serve the economic interest of farmers unless their planning horizons extend over 50 years or more and they discount future earnings at a very low, or even zero, rate." Although farmers may realize short-term benefits from unsustainable agricultural practices, these practices may not serve society's long-term interests (24). Thus, because of the scale and timeline of the problem, action at the regional and national levels will be necessary to conserve soil resources and maintain productivity of agricultural, pasture, and forestlands.

TRENDS IN DEFORESTATION

Preliminary results of the Food and Agriculture Organization of the United Nations (FAO) second global assessment of deforestation confirm earlier reports that tropical deforestation has accelerated dramatically. The FAO interim report released in late 1991 found tropical deforestation to be almost 17 million hectares per year compared to an early 1980s estimate of 11.3 million—an increase of 50 percent (25). These results confirmed *World Resources 1990–91* estimates, based on recent national deforestation estimates by nine tropical countries that tropical deforestation had accelerated during the 1980s (26). Preliminary FAO figures show that temperate and boreal forests are no longer suffering acute deforestation; instead, these forest areas may have increased about 5 percent from 1980 to 1990 (27).

Tropical Deforestation

Tropical deforestation is currently a significant environment and development issue. Loss of tropical forests diminishes biodiversity (see Chapter 9, "Wildlife and Habitat"), contributes to climate change by releasing stored carbon into the atmosphere, and often results in serious soil degradation, sometimes rendering the land unfit for future agriculture. Yet poor farmers in many tropical countries have no choice but to clear forest to grow crops. Some countries offer economic incentives for establishing large ranches on tropical forestland. Efforts to offer more sustainable options are described in Focus On Policies to Manage Tropical Forests, below, and in Chapter 1, "Dimensions of Sustainable Development." This section describes efforts to document the extent of tropical deforestation.

As used here, the term deforestation describes a complete change in land use from forest to agriculture—including shifting cultivation and pasture—or urban use. It does not include forest that has been logged and left to regrow, even if it was clearcut. By opening a forest area to settlement, logging is often a precursor of deforestation. Tropical forest that has been fragmented by patches of farm or pastureland shows a greatly diminished biodiversity and is often degraded (28) (29). Although the FAO is studying fragmentation's effects on forests, statistics on fragmented areas have not been published and are not included in the deforestation data here.

According to preliminary FAO data, the annual rate of deforestation in 76 tropical countries, which contain 97 percent of the world's tropical forest, rose to 0.9 percent per year during the 1980s, compared with 0.6 percent in 1976–80, when the earlier FAO assessment was made.

To produce the preliminary data, the FAO team compiled subregional estimates based on the most recent available data from tropical countries. The data were then updated to 1990 by a computer model based on ecological data and population growth. By comparing the 1990 estimates with deforestation estimates from 1976–80, FAO calculated an annual rate of deforestation for 3 tropical regions and 12 subregions. (See Table 8.2.) These rates indicate the part of the forest area in the subregion that is deforested each year.

Of the three tropical regions, Asia's deforestation rate is the highest (1.2 percent per year for 1981–90), Latin America is second (0.9 percent), and Africa is a close third (0.8 percent). Regionally, West Africa's annual loss rate is highest (2.1 percent), followed by Central America and Mexico (1.8 percent), continental Southeast Asia (1.6 percent), and insular Southeast Asia and insular Africa (Madagascar, 1.2 percent) (30).

A comparison of the new deforestation rates with the rates for 1976–80 shows that deforestation has accelerated in some subregions and remained steady in others. Four subregions' deforestation rates increased by more than 50 percent: Central Africa, the Caribbean, continental Southeast Asia, and insular Southeast Asia. Subregions whose deforested area has increased by about 50 percent include tropical South

Table 8.2 Preliminary Estimates of Tropical Forest Area and Rate of Deforestation for 87 Tropical Countries, 1981–90
(thousand hectares)

Regions/Subregions	Number of Countries Studied	Total Land Area	Forest Area 1980	Forest Area 1990	Area Deforested Annually 1981–90	Annual Rate of Change 1981–90 (percent)
Total	**87**	**4,815,700**	**1,884,100**	**1,714,800**	**16,900**	**-0.9**
Latin America	**32**	**1,675,700**	**923,000**	**839,900**	**8,300**	**-0.9**
Central America and Mexico	7	245,300	77,000	63,500	1,400	-1.8
Caribbean Subregion	18	69,500	48,800	47,100	200	-0.4
Tropical South America	7	1,360,800	797,100	729,300	6,800	-0.8
Asia	**15**	**896,600**	**310,800**	**274,900**	**3,600**	**-1.2**
South Asia	6	445,600	70,600	66,200	400	-0.6
Continental Southeast Asia	5	192,900	83,200	69,700	1,300	-1.6
Insular Southeast Asia	4	258,100	157,000	138,900	1,800	-1.2
Africa	**40**	**2,243,400**	**650,300**	**600,100**	**5,000**	**-0.8**
West Sahelian Africa	8	528,000	41,900	38,000	400	-0.9
East Sahelian Africa	6	489,600	92,300	85,300	700	-0.8
West Africa	8	203,200	55,200	43,400	1,200	-2.1
Central Africa	7	406,400	230,100	215,400	1,500	-0.6
Tropical Southern Africa	10	557,900	217,700	206,300	1,100	-0.5
Insular Africa	1	58,200	13,200	11,700	200	-1.2

Source: Forest Resources Assessment 1990 Project, Food and Agriculture Organization of the United Nations, "Second Interim Report on the State of Tropical Forests," paper presented at the 10th World Forestry Congress, Paris, September 1991 (rev. October 15, 1991), Table 1.
Note: The major countries in each subregion are listed in Chapter 19, " Forests and Rangelands," Table 19.1. Totals may not add because of rounding.

America, Central America and Mexico, and tropical Southern Africa. The deforestation rate in five other subregions, four in Africa and one in Asia, remained about the same. (See Chapter 19, "Forests and Rangelands," Table 19.1.)

The interim 1990 FAO figure for tropical South America shows an increase in the amount of land deforested from 4.6 million hectares per year in 1981–85 to 6.8 million hectares per year in 1981–90 (31). Brazil considers the recent FAO figures too high. National satellite studies of Brazil's Legal Amazon, an area of 5 million square kilometers encompassing six states and territories and parts of three others, show a 23 percent decrease in the annual deforestation rate from 1.79 million hectares in 1988–89 to 1.38 million hectares in 1989–90 (32). Satellite studies by the National Space Research Institute of Brazil showed an average annual deforestation rate of 2.18 million hectares per year for the Legal Amazon from 1979 to 1990. The FAO used a similar estimate of 2.14 million hectares per year for the Legal Amazon during 1985–90 (33). Adding an annual loss of 1 million hectares of dry forest outside the Legal Amazon, as per the FAO 1980 assessment, would raise Brazil's total annual deforestation to 2.4–3.1 million hectares. Although the exact figures remain in dispute, most observers agree that Brazil's deforestation rate was not steady throughout the 1980s but that it peaked around 1987, then lessened because of changed government policies and an economic slowdown.

According to Brazilian studies, the *total cumulative* deforestation in the Legal Amazon as of 1990 was 41.5 million hectares (34). This figure represents an area the size of Sweden.

The FAO tropical assessment team has proposed a new, more scientific methodology for estimating the amount and rates of deforestation. This method involves comparing satellite data from two time periods in statistically selected sites. By comparing and analyzing satellite images taken at comparable time of year and confirming the data with field observations, specialists at regional centers could produce more accurate deforestation estimates. These estimates would be fed to FAO for compilation of an assessment covering all tropical regions. The FAO team has also proposed that tropical deforestation be monitored continuously rather than once every 10 years as has been the case.

Unfortunately, as of late 1991, the team has been unable to secure the satellite images from the U.S. archives nesessary to make comparative studies. And funding was uncertain for ongoing tropical forest monitoring. Nevertheless, The FAO team hopes to present its best estimates in a final report to the United Nations Conference on Environment and Development in June 1992.

Key Issues

INITIATIVES TO HALT DEFORESTATION

Delegates to the June 1992 United Nations Conference on Environment and Development are expected to consider a nonbinding statement of principles on the management, conservation and sustainable development of the world's forests.

The decision to consider a nonbinding statement of principles, rather than something more authoritative such as a forest convention, was reached at a mid-1991 preparatory meeting. It reflected a view that there was relatively little consensus about the substance of a convention and insufficient time to reach a consensus before the 1992 meeting.

The principles were in an early draft form in September 1991, with much of the language still subject to further negotiation or deletion. The September draft affirmed that states had the right to develop their forests according to their needs, but that forests should be sustainably managed and that national policies were needed to strengthen the conservation and sustainable development of forests. Each state had the responsibility to establish plans for the management, conservation, and sustainable development of all types of forests.

The draft principles attempt to acknowledge the global complexity of forest conservation by, for example, recognizing that the external indebtedness of developing countries had reduced their capacity to manage forests sustainably, that problems of poverty and food security were linked to deforestation, and that consumption of forest products in industrialized countries was an important cause of deforestation.

The principles are likely to say that the bulk of the additional costs of forest conservation and sustainable development should come from industrialized countries, perhaps through a new global fund (35).

The statement of principles may become the basis for later negotiations on a forest convention. The global forestry convention was proposed by the Group of Seven—seven of the world's top economic powers—following its annual meeting in July 1990 (36). The FAO quickly offered to take the lead in drafting a proposed convention. However, the idea lacked support in tropical countries, which saw it as an effort by northern countries to control deforestation in the name of the global environment while sidestepping the issue of their own responsibility for greenhouse gas emissions.

In particular, developing countries with major timber resources want new and additional funding from industrialized countries to pay for any requirements imposed by a convention, whereas industrial countries want more specific assurances about what developing countries will do in exchange for such assistance.

More fundamentally, there are many schisms about who should benefit from forests and general approaches to forest management. Partly this reflects the complexity of accommodating three levels of forest constituents: environmentalists concerned with global warming and loss of biodiversity, tropical countries concerned with making both short- and long-term economic benefits from their forests, and local interests such as forest dwellers, ranchers, and farmers.

These three constituencies often have dissimilar goals. For example, national plans to increase revenues from logging can result in a decline in biodiversity as natural forest is turned into plantations. On the local level, forest dwellers and local farmers are demanding a voice in forest policy, usually insisting some of the economic benefits of the forest be retained locally, rather than going to timber companies.

Agenda 21

Agenda 21, the UNCED document that will map out how to achieve global environmental objectives, also will contain an extensive section on forestry. A draft version of the section contained a long list of initiatives, including strengthening forestry laws, plans, education, and research; beginning a massive global effort to expand the area under forest cover; improving techniques to sustainably manage forests; creating a system to assess and monitor the state of forest re-

sources; and expanding mechanisms for regional and international cooperation on forestry. The draft indicated that these new programs would require about $6.18 billion in international financing on concessional terms, which is more than four times the $1.35 billion in official development assistance provided for forestry in 1990 (37).

Tropical Forestry Action Plan

The Tropical Forestry Action Plan (TFAP) was launched in June 1985 to slow tropical deforestation and serve as a blueprint for forest management at the national, regional, and global levels. The plan provides a forum for development agencies to coordinate their forestry programs and a process for tropical countries to formulate forestry plans that are then likely to be funded by the development agencies. By 1991, 74 countries were participating, but critics charged that rather than halting deforestation the plans merely channeled more money into logging projects. A 1990 evaluation of TFAP said that "most national plans, based mainly on forestry sector reviews, simply justify increased investment in the forestry sector—a focus too narrow to adequately assess the root causes of deforestation, much less to affect them significantly." The evaluation found that TFAP's effect on controlling deforestation was "modest at best," and that its controlling institutions (principally FAO) had "lost sight of these concerns as the plan has been carried out" (38).

TFAP has helped many countries analyze their forest resources in a more disciplined fashion, but the widely held criticisms of the program's objectives, structure, and impact have cast a cloud over its future. New goals and objectives have been developed, but, in late 1991, TFAP's future seemed to hinge on the uncertain prospects for creation of an independent consultative forum to guide the program.

FOCUS ON POLICIES TO MANAGE TROPICAL FORESTS

Many governments, environmental and other nongovernmental organizations, and international aid agencies insist that tropical forests must be managed on a sustainable basis if their economic, social, and ecological benefits are to continue into the future.

Much of the current discussion on tropical forest management concerns issues outside the forestry sector. Experts agree that world opinion and the forests' global and local significance have created a unique opportunity to explore the issues influencing sustainability and, ultimately, to take action. Action may be at the local and national levels or at the international level. Four major areas of discussion—areas in which actions are being proposed—are described below:
■ Reforming national policies,
■ Creating new international agreements on trade, aid, and debt relief,
■ Recognizing the rights of indigenous peoples, and

■ Coordinating overlapping areas with climate change and biodiversity.

NATIONAL POLICY REFORMS

Natural Resource Accounting

National resource management practices can promote both conservation and long-term sustainable economic development.

By undervaluing intact natural forest, many current national policies destroy forests (39) (40). Typically, the "value" of forestland is confined to its timber or its agricultural potential when cleared. Nations hard-pressed for cash and struggling with burgeoning populations are tempted almost irresistibly to mine the forest capital—its trees—or convert it to a more "valuable" use.

The value of the nontimber goods the forest provides—the fruits, nuts, resins, oils, subsistence food, and fuelwood—as well as the soil conservation, carbon storage, and other intangible environmental services the forest renders, are routinely ignored in economic assessments of forest use although studies show their value may far exceed that of timber (41). Their loss remains hidden in national accounts because replacement is not given a monetary value. Part of the reason is that many of these goods and services do not have conventional commodity value. They are either not sold in conventional markets because they are consumed for subsistence or barter—or because they are considered public goods, as are most ecological services.

In a related vein, the current and expected benefits of converting a forest for other uses are often overstated. The benefits of logging, for example, do not reflect the environmental and social costs of deforestation. In fact, researchers calculated that in a one-hectare rainforest plot near the town of Iquitos in Peru, the net value of nonwood resources is 13 times more than that of timber (42). Agriculture is often similarly unprofitable because the soils underlying 95 percent of the remaining tropical rainforests are infertile and are easily degraded (43). When the cost of infrastructure, tax credits, and production subsidies are added, the anticipated economic benefits of forest conversion may vanish (44).

A case in point is the widespread conversion of forest to rangeland in the Amazon. Studies show that preserving forests and managing their extractive resources —collecting Brazil nuts and rubber latex in the wild, for example—provides short-term economic returns per hectare that are comparable to cattle ranching. Because the number of people who benefit from a given area of extractive forest far exceeds the number of laborers who work on a cleared-land cattle ranch, extractive forests provide more widespread economic benefits (45).

The economic benefits of timber harvests may be further overstated owing to governments' undervaluing the forest ecosystem. Because royalties and taxes collected from timber concessionaires in tropical nations are set at uniformly low rates, government timber revenue is only a fraction of what it could be. For example, between 1979 and 1982, the Philippine Government earned $170 million from forest charges and export taxes. This sum represents only 11.4 percent of the potential revenues from forest exploitation. The balance accrued to concessionaires and timber operators (46).

Moreover, harvest and processing subsidies often compound the loss of government timber revenue. Subsidies have been used to encourage the development of a domestic timber processing industry in Malaysia and Ghana, among other nations, so that domestic producers of sawnwood, plywood, and finished products could capture the so-called "value added." The unfortunate result has often been the creation of inefficient facilities that require more wood per unit of production while yielding poor-quality products, bringing low prices and lower government revenues (47).

Correcting these policies involves revaluation of forest resources to recognize the full costs of their loss or replacement. By treating forest resources and services as capital assets, governments can begin realistically to account for the depreciation of these assets through deforestation. A likely result of this change is that national budgets will reflect the value of forests to the nation's well-being, abolish or modify questionable subsidies, and charge timber harvesters rates that reflect the true environmental and social costs and give credit for sustainable harvest practices.

Land Ownership

A second major area of proposed policy reform involves land ownership, tenure, and distribution. Although most forestlands may have been continuously occupied or used by local peoples for millennia, they are legally government controlled. Thus, forest residents on public domain land have no secured right of use or access (48).

To make matters worse, many governments consider their forestland "undeveloped" and will grant title to forestland to those who will "improve" it, by clearing it for pasture or plantation agriculture, for example (49). However, traditional land uses, such as shifting cultivation and collecting nontimber forest products, do not usually qualify as improvement, and local residents can face eviction from lands long used sustainably.

Changes in tenure laws to grant title or legal use rights to forest dwellers have advantages. They could help local peoples retain their self-sufficiency and provide an incentive for forest immigrants to invest in more careful husbandry of their homesteads.

A related issue is agrarian reform. One of the primary forces pushing landless migrants into the forest—where their slash-and-burn clearing for subsistence agriculture is now a leading cause of deforestation worldwide—is the inequitable distribution of agricultural land (50). In non-Amazonian Brazil, 81 percent of the land is controlled by just 4.5 percent of the landowners, whose holdings are often vast and underused. Similar patterns prevail in other parts of Latin America, Africa, and Southeast Asia (51). Land reform policies, therefore, are one of the most potent tools governments possess to stabilize forest use.

Other Policy Areas

Other areas of possible reform include removing the economic bias toward large-scale agriculture by providing credit and markets to small-scale forest farmers. Government support of agroforestry would provide timber as well as food for sustenance and commercial needs. In an effort to relieve urban crowding and overpopulation, governments have resettled large numbers of people to less densely populated areas. Such resettlement can lead to forest conversion for agriculture. Before proceeding with such schemes, governments must carefully weigh long-term environmental impacts.

INTERNATIONAL ACTIONS

Several international actions to promote sustainable tropical forests that have surfaced in the last few years are discussed below.

Adjust Trade Structures

The current price of commercially traded raw logs and processed wood rarely, if ever, includes the environmental or social costs of timber harvesting. Undervaluing the resource often leads to overuse and depletion. For prices to reflect these hidden costs accurately, governments could use export or import taxes levied on the value of the tropical wood product and other fiscal tools. In 1989, the United Kingdom Timber Trade Federation and the *Nederlandse Houtbound* jointly proposed a Tropical Timber Import Surcharge for the European Community (EC). Levied at the point of import, revenues from the surcharge would be pooled and used to fund projects that promote sustainable forest management (52). Interest in a surcharge was recently voiced by several International Tropical Timber Organization (ITTO) members, but some producer countries have resisted (53); it may lead to lower prices for producers, more waste in logging, and conversion of little-valued forests to agricultural uses (54).

There are also calls for a tropical timber commodity agreement that, in addition to mandating the above surcharge, would establish timber import restrictions based on compliance with a comprehensive conservation and management program designed to achieve no net loss of forests (55).

Aside from the difficulties in negotiating an agreement, some experts warn that imposition of quotas or export bans often has undesirable side effects. For example, when Thailand recently implemented a ban on log exports to conserve its remaining forests, the black market in illegal timber began to thrive. Legal timber operators sold their equipment to profiteers over whom no government control could be exercised (56).

Even when illegal markets do not develop in response to quotas or export bans, the economic repercussions may still be unfavorable. Log export bans, for example, artificially force local timber prices down,

thereby giving domestic processors a windfall. These profits attract new firms, resulting in overcapacity, inefficiency, and waste (57).

Creation of a labeling scheme to identify timber grown and harvested sustainably is another possible strategy to use market forces to encourage sustainable timber management. Public opinion surveys indicate that consumers in importing countries would pay a premium for sustainably produced timber. A credible certification program is requisite to success of any such labeling plan (58).

Elimination of protectionist tariffs imposed by major importers, such as Japan and the EC, on processed forest products would allow exporting countries to retain more of the value of their timber, thus possibly relieving some pressure to maintain current harvest levels (59).

Many experts warn that any manipulation of global trade structures may run afoul of the General Agreement on Tariffs and Trade (GATT), the mechanism that governs 90 percent of world trade (60) (61). Under GATT terms, many of the trade restrictions being suggested or any labeling program to certify sustainably produced timber would likely be disallowed. Legislators and environmental organizations from several countries are currently proposing that specific language allowing such mechanisms—adopted for legitimate environmental purposes—should be included in GATT (62) (63).

Decrease Demand for Tropical Timber

A potent and direct means to slow logging and deforestation is to reduce the demand for tropical wood products. A commitment by Japan, the United States, and the EC—the three main consumers of tropical timber exports—to eliminate wasteful one-time uses of tropical woods would be an important component of "demand management." Each year, for example, 25 billion pairs of chopsticks and $2 billion worth of non-reusable concrete forms are used and discarded. Substituting reusable products whenever possible would contribute to preserving tropical forests (64).

Since 1988, the EC, the United States, and other timber-importing countries have taken decisive steps to restrict wood imports. Some of these initiatives are highly prescriptive, such as a U.S. effort to ban teak from Myanmar and Prince Charles' appeal to ban the importation of unsustainably grown wood in the U.K. In Germany, however, measures are more sweeping, and in 1989, the government of the Federal Republic officially stopped using tropical timber (65). But such unilateral boycotts may have unintended negative effects. Although boycotts do indeed reduce the demand for tropical timber, they also deflate not only the value of the wood but of the forest as well. Thus forests may in fact be converted more rapidly to higher-value purposes, such as export agriculture or cattle ranching (66).

Use Debt to Finance Conservation

Tropical nations are presently struggling under a massive debt load of some $800 billion, which drains their economic vitality and encourages them to liquidate their forest capital more quickly to raise foreign exchange (67). One-half the debt of developing countries is owed by the 14 countries that account for more than two thirds of the global deforestation (68). Many conservationists have come to view this situation as a unique opportunity to fund innovative strategies for saving tropical forests while reducing tropical nations' debt burdens.

Among the proposed strategies are "debt-for-nature" swaps, in which a given amount of debt is purchased by a conservation organization from the developed country lender at a discount. The borrower then redeems the obligation at face value in local currency, and the proceeds are used to fund conservation efforts in the debtor country (69). These swaps have been endorsed by world leaders, and both the United States and the EC, whose banks hold much of the outstanding debt, have publicly advocated expanding their use (70) (71).

Although debt-for-nature swaps have so far been fairly small, their radical expansion as part of a larger North-South bargain is widely expected. Such a bargain is predicated on industrialized nations' realization that they must assume a fair, some say the major, financial burden of saving tropical forests if they expect to enjoy the global services these forests provide (72) (73).

In 1990, the United States passed legislation that will help alleviate the burden of Latin American and Caribbean countries' external debt. Under the farm bill (Food, Agriculture and Conservation Trade Act of 1990), nearly $7 billion of outstanding commercial loans made by the Agency for International Development and the Food for Peace Program (P.L. 480) can be reduced. In addition, interest that accrues on the remaining balances can be paid in local currency and used for environmental programs agreed to by the debtor country. In 1991, the first debt reductions under the farm bill were orchestrated for Bolivia, Chile, and Jamaica (74). (For a list of debt-for-nature swaps, see Chapter 20, "Wildlife and Habitat," Table 20.6.)

Expand and Reform Development Assistance

International lenders, such as the multilateral and bilateral development banks, significantly influence development decisions in the Third World and thus have an important role in ensuring that tropical nations' development is environmentally sound. But in the past, bilateral lenders have funded many projects that were responsible for massive deforestation, including construction of jungle highways and hydroelectric plants and development of plantations.

On the positive side, some of these organizations are requiring increasingly stringent environmental impact assessments for their projects and are expanding the scope of their loan portfolios to include policy and institutional reform, land use planning, research on agroforestry and silviculture, and training (75) (76). In light of the many needs, however, the level of funding for these kinds of activities must grow.

The environmental policies of these institutions have been formulated in the past several years, but there are still notable lapses, as with a road that the African De-

velopment Bank plans to fund that will run through one of the Ivory Coast's last rainforest tracts (77).

Transfer Funds from North to South

Leaders of both the industrialized and developing countries are now more often discussing global initiatives that would benefit countries in both the North and the South. Many of the proposals hinge on industrialized countries' providing new financial support to developing countries.

One such dialogue among opinion leaders from the Americas resulted in their agreement on eight new initiatives embodied in the *Compact for a New World* (78). The forestry initiative calls for the United States, Canada, Argentina, and Chile to stop overcutting their temperate forests, move quickly to sustainable forestry on public and private lands (including ending subsidized timber cutting), and protect ancient forest reserves in the Pacific Northwest region of the United States and Canada. Tropical forest countries would seek to halt, and then reverse, net forest loss by reforming policies that further deforestation, promoting afforestation and sustainable forest management, and creating economic opportunities that relieve pressures on forest resources.

Recognizing that preserving tropical forests is vital, the *Compact* proposes that the United States and Canada provide major support for national forestry plans and support research on the underlying causes of deforestation (e.g., poverty, inequitable land distribution, population growth, and the need to service international debt) (79).

RESPECTING THE RIGHTS OF LOCAL PEOPLES

Local forest dwellers are most vulnerable to the impacts of forest destruction. These people are typically unrepresented when land-use decisions are made regarding their homelands, although the results of those decisions frequently jeopardize their cultural and economic survival. Several previously proposed Amazonian hydroelectric projects, for example, would have flooded 26,000 square kilometers of pristine forest (80).

In the past few years, a surge of activism has swept many of these indigenous peoples' groups, resulting in well-publicized public actions against logging companies and development projects threatening traditional forest holdings (81) (82). (See Chapter 14, "Policies and Institutions.") In Altamira, Brazil, for example, some 600 people representing indigenous groups rallied to block Xingu River dam construction (83). And in Malaysia, native Penan have erected more than three dozen blockades in the past four years to protect their ancestral lands from logging (84). The message from these actions is clear: local peoples must be a part of any attempt to manage their forests.

Representatives of many local peoples state that they must have a predominant and substantive voice, not observer status and after-the-fact consultation, in decisions to exploit or develop their traditional domains. Often their struggle to be heard coincides with efforts to gain legal title to their ancestral lands—or to expand

Box 8.4 Peru's HIFCO Project: Sustainable Agroforestry for Cultural Survival

Located amidst abandoned farms and degraded pastures, the HIFCO project—the Family/Community Integrated Garden Project (*Huerto Integral Familiar Comunal*)—near Pucallpa in Peru's Amazon is a significant example of how sustainable forest practices can contribute to both ecological restoration and cultural preservation (1).

When a road was opened from Lima to Pucallpa in the mid-1960s, Pucallpa area forests were rapidly and extensively depleted through colonization and conversion to crop and pastureland. In the process, the indigenous peoples lost access to their traditional lands. By 1985, when HIFCO began, the area was dominated by low-productivity pastures and degraded farmlands heavily laced with pesticide residues.

The HIFCO experiment arose in response to the need for dependable food production on degraded sites and the desire of the local Shipibo Indians to restore their homeland. Under the aegis of AIDESEP, the Interethnic Association for Development of the Peruvian Jungle, the parent body representing 300,000 indigenous Amazonian peoples from 60 ethnic groups, an 11-hectare abandoned cattle pasture was leased, and a sustainable farming system using intercropping and infiltration ditches was established.

Although initial soil conditions were poor (soil pH was 3.5, too acidic for most crops), a rigorous program of soil improvement began. Organic matter, such as leaf litter and animal wastes added to special raised beds, transformed the abandoned pasture into a highly productive small farm. By 1990, 4.5 hectares had been revitalized and brought under intensive cultivation, with a soil pH of 5.2; crop yields exceeded those on surrounding "modern" farms, even without artificial fertilizers or pesticides.

HIFCO farmers use a novel combination of traditional and modern agricultural practices to work their land. Learning from natural forest species diversity, they rejected the monoculture of modern agribusiness and planted more than 40 species

of annuals and perennials, which are surrounded by a variety of tree species.

Leguminous plants and green mulches are used extensively throughout the garden as a source of nitrogen, and the trees not only produce fruits and timber but support vine crops, allowing more efficient use of garden space. The area around the garden is being replanted with some 60 species of trees.

Between the raised beds, infiltration ditches act as small reservoirs for rainwater, allowing continued crop production through the three-month dry season. In addition, fish raised in these reservoirs provide a protein supplement to the farmers' diet. This year-round production capability, which other local farms lack, provides both food and income security for HIFCO farm families; they no longer need to work off-farm during the dry season.

In addition to the raised-bed gardening used to rehabilitate degraded land, HIFCO farmers also employ a modified "slash-and-burn" system in areas where forest canopy still remains. In this traditionally based system, 1 hectare in the center of a 6-hectare forest plot is burned in a circular pattern for intensive cultivation. Intercropping, composting, and animal manures provide nutrients; in addition, some leaf litter is collected on the surrounding 5 hectares for use as mulch on the central plot when productivity begins to decline.

The burned plot is planted in concentric rings, with vegetables and household food crops in the center, then staple crops, cash crops, fruit trees, and timber trees the outermost ring. This planting arrangement creates a tiered effect that maximizes use of available light, with the lowest-growing plants in the center and the tallest on the periphery.

HIFCO's production is not limited to plants. Fish ponds and guinea pigs, geese, ducks, guinea hens, and other small farm animals provide protein and are an incidental source of fertilizer. HIFCO's holistic approach extends to pest control through interplanting insect-repellant plant varieties, such as marigolds and sesame, and

using a home-brewed organic pesticide. The HIFCO project also includes a crop improvement program, complete with a seed bank and a program of field trials.

Even while HIFCO works to develop a sustainable source of food and income within the forest setting, it also sustains indigenous culture throughout Peru's Amazon. Since its second year of operation, HIFCO has been managed and staffed by indigenous people, with outreach to the entire AIDESEP confederacy its primary goal.

The HIFCO farm is a training center for apprentices from AIDESEP's 28 member federations who take part in a comprehensive 3-month course in sustainable agroforestry based on traditional models enhanced by modern innovations. AIDESEP then pays apprentices who finish the course one year's stipend to promote the HIFCO model in their own communities.

Although HIFCO has met with considerable success so far, it faces formidable challenges, particularly with regard to outreach. Apprentices frequently find their communities reluctant to support HIFCO-style practices, and start-up funds and continued field assistance from HIFCO advisers are often limiting factors. Nonetheless, the HIFCO experiment is one model for restoring the ecological viability of denuded forest lands and the cultural integrity of those who make the forest their home.

References and Notes

1. This account is drawn from: Bruce Cabarle, "Ecofarming in the Peruvian Amazon: An Indigenous Response," World Resources Institute trip report, March 1991, pp. 1-8; Bruce Cabarle, Associate, Forestry and Land Use Program, World Resources Institute, Washington, D.C., 1990 (personal communication); and Elizabeth Darby Junkin, "The Monte: Why the Indigenous Peoples of the Amazon Basin Want to Be Part of Saving the World's Largest Rainforest," *Buzzworm: the Environmental Journal*, Vol. 2, No. 4 (1990), p. 36.

the often restricted holdings they have been granted—so that they have legal standing in their bid to prevent destruction of their forests (85) (86).

The lack of local groups participating in development decisionmaking is exemplified by their conspicuous absence from ITTO and the forest planning organized under the Tropical Forestry Action Plan (TFAP). Recent critiques of the plan signal that this major TFAP shortcoming will inevitably weaken the national forest plans that result (87) (88).

Many local groups also complain that environmental groups working to prevent deforestation and preserve biodiversity in the tropics also exclude them

from consideration in their rush to conserve. At a spring 1990 meeting in Peru between leaders of *Coordinadora de las Organizaciones Indígenas de la Cuenca Amazónica* (COICA)—the umbrella organization representing 1.2 million local peoples in the Amazon basin—and representatives of major environmental organizations, local leaders reminded environmentalists that they do not necessarily speak for the interests of all local peoples (89) (90).

Contention especially surrounded the issue of debt-for-nature swaps, which, so far, have been negotiated with little input from local groups. These swaps, the groups believe, have harmed their cause in some cases because parkland conservation often excludes traditional local groups' land uses. The groups believe they should be major participants in negotiating any future swaps and that the swaps should explicitly enhance their territorial claims and recognize their role in sustainable forest management (91).

COICA welcomed an alliance with environmental groups while making its position clear: "The most effective defense of the Amazonian Biosphere is the recognition and defense of the territories of the region's Indigenous Peoples and the promotion of their models for living within that biosphere and for managing its resources in a sustainable way" (92). (See Box 8.4.)

FORESTS, CLIMATE CHANGE, AND BIODIVERSITY

These three issues overlap; their convergence point is the forest's dual role as habitat and carbon sink.

Because tropical and temperate forests are the terrestrial biomes with the most biomass, they have the highest potential for carbon storage as wood fiber and leaf canopy. At the same time, the many levels of the forest canopy, with their varying light intensities and moisture levels, allow a multitude of habitats to coexist in a small area, creating the most favorable conditions for biodiversity.

Preserving forests thus contributes to both climate stability and biodiversity goals. Yet other forest values are independent of these—namely, as human habitat and repository of natural resources. Although all these values may be present together in the intact forest, different management strategies emphasize one over the others.

Fortunately, points for compromise may not be hard to find among these different visions of forest use. For example, it is now thought that stabilizing carbon emissions would best be served through minimization of further primary forest loss; deforestation itself may account for as much as one quarter the global carbon released each year (93). If carbon sink plantations are deemed a good option to complement this "no net loss" strategy, they could be located on degraded land. Their establishment would then also work to relieve pressure on natural forests.

Similarly, management schemes such as extractive reserves can preserve important habitat values while still providing subsistence and commodity values to human populations. Even more intensive forest uses, such as agroforestry systems, can be compatible with many biodiversity conservation goals, especially when the uses are part of an integrated land use plan that includes undisturbed land.

Conditions and Trends was written by Mary Paden, World Resources managing editor and Focus On Policies to Conserve Tropical Forests by Gregory Mock, a California-based writer. Robert Livernash, World Resources senior editor, also contributed.

References and Notes

1. L.R. Oldeman, V.W.P. van Engelen, and J.H.M. Pulles, "The Extent of Human-Induced Soil Degradation," Annex 5 of L.R. Oldeman, R.T.A. Hakkeling, and W.G. Sombroek, *World Map of the Status of Human-Induced Soil Degradation: An Explanatory Note*, rev. 2d ed. (International Soil Reference and Information Centre, Wageningen, the Netherlands, 1990), Table 7. "Vegetated surface" refers to the Earth's total land surface of 13 billion hectares less 1.5 billion hectares of "wasteland," or 11.5 billion hectares. Wasteland is defined as areas that "historic or recent natural processes have turned [into] terrains without appreciable vegetative cover or agricultural potential." Six types of wasteland are included: active dunes, salt flats, rock outcrops, deserts, ice caps, and arid mountain regions.

2. The definition of wasteland is taken from L.R. Oldeman, R.T.A. Hakkeling, and W.G. Sombroek, *World Map of the Status of Human-Induced Soil Degradation: An Explanatory Note*, rev. 2d ed. (International Soil Reference and Information Centre, Wageningen, the Netherlands, 1990), p. 14.

3. The calculations for total land and wasteland are taken from L.R. Oldeman, V.W.P. van Engelen, and J.H.M. Pulles, "The Extent of Human-Induced Soil Degradation," Annex 5 of L.R. Oldeman, R.T.A. Hakkeling, and W.G. Sombroek, *World Map of the Status of Human-Induced Soil Degradation: An Explanatory Note*, rev. 2d ed. (International Soil Reference and Information Centre,

Wageningen, the Netherlands, 1990), Table 7.

4. L.R. Oldeman, R.T.A. Hakkeling, and W.G. Sombroek, *World Map of the Status of Human-Induced Soil Degradation: An Explanatory Note*, rev. 2d ed. (International Soil Reference and Information Centre, Wageningen, the Netherlands, 1990), pp. 14-15.

5. L.R. Oldeman, V.W.P. van Engelen, and J.H.M. Pulles, "The Extent of Human-Induced Soil Degradation," Annex 5 of L.R. Oldeman, R.T.A. Hakkeling, and W.G. Sombroek, *World Map of the Status of Human-Induced Soil Degradation: An Explanatory Note*, rev. 2d ed. (International Soil Reference and Information Centre, Wageningen, the Netherlands, 1990), Table 7.

6. *Op. cit.* 4, p. 2.

7. "Ad-hoc Consultation Meeting Assessment of Global Desertification: Status and Methodologies," *Desertification Bulletin* (United Nations Environment Programme), No. 18 (1990), p. 26.

8. L.R. Oldeman, Program and Project Division, International Soil Reference and Information Centre, Wageningen, the Netherlands, 1991 (personal communication).

9. *Ibid.*

10. Richard W. Arnold, Director, Soil Survey Division, U.S. Department of Agriculture, Washington D.C., 1991 (personal communication).

11. *Op. cit.* 4, p. 20.

12. U.S. Department of Agriculture (USDA), Soil Conservation Service, *Summary Report:*

1987 National Resources Inventory, Statistical Bulletin No. 790 (USDA, Washington, D.C., 1989), Table 9.

13. L.R. Oldeman, ed., *Guidelines for General Assessment of the Status of Human-Induced Soil Degradation* (International Soil Reference and Information Centre, Wageningen, the Netherlands, 1988), p. 2.

14. *Ibid.*, p. 6.

15. *Op. cit.* 5, p. 5.

16. *Op. cit.* 8.

17. *Op. cit.* 5, pp. 1-4.

18. *Op. cit.* 5, p. 5.

19. *Op. cit.* 5, p. 6.

20. *Op. cit.* 5, p. 5.

21. *Op. cit.* 5, p. 6.

22. *Op. cit.* 5, p. 7.

23. Paul Faeth, Robert Repetto, Kim Kroll, Qi Dai, and Glenn Helmers, *Paying the Farm Bill* (World Resources Institute, Washington D.C., 1991), pp. 35-36.

24. Pierre R. Crosson, Resources for the Future, Washington, D.C., "Future Economic and Environmental Costs," in *The Cropland Crisis: Myth or Reality?* Pierre R. Crosson, ed. (Johns Hopkins University Press, Baltimore, 1982), p. 184.

25. Forest Resources Assessment 1990 Project, Food and Agriculture Organization of the United Nations, "Second Interim Report on the State of Tropical Forests," paper presented at the 10th World Forestry Congress, Paris, September 1991 (rev. October 15, 1991).

26. World Resources Institute in collaboration with the United Nations Environment Programme and United Nations Development Programme, *World Resources 1990-91* (Oxford University Press, New York, 1990), p. 102.

27. Food and Agriculture Organization of the United Nations, "Global Tropical Deforestation Accelerating: Coordinated Action Key to Control," September 8, 1991 (press release).

28. David S. Wilcove, Charles H. McLellan and Andrew P. Dobson, "Habitat Fragmentation in the Temperate Zone," in *Conservation Biology: The Science of Scarcity and Diversity*, Michael E. Sonlé , ed. (Sinauer Associates, Inc., Boston, Massachusetts, 1986), pp. 237-256.

29. T.E. Lovejoy, R.O. Bierregaard, A.B. Rylands *et al.*, "Edge and Other Effects of Isolation on Amazon Forest Fragments," in *Conservation Biology: The Science of Scarcity and Diversity*, Michael E. Sonlé , ed. (Sinauer Associates, Inc., Boston, Massachusetts, 1986), pp. 257-285.

30. *Op. cit.* 25.

31. Chapter 19, "Forests and Rangelands," Table 19.1.

32. G. Meira, Instituto Nacional de Pesquisas Espacias, São José dos Campos, São Paulo, 1991, (personal communication).

33. K.D. Singh, Project Coordinator, Forest Resources Assessment 1990 Project, Food and Agriculture Organization of the United Nations, Rome, 1991 (personal communication).

34. *Op. cit.* 32.

35. Preparatory Committee for the United Nations Conference on Environment and Development, "Land Resources: Deforestation," draft statement of principles prepared for Working Group I, Third Session, (Geneva, August 12-September 4, 1991).

36. The Office of the Press Secretary, The White House, "Proposed Global Forests Convention," July 11, 1990 (press release).

37. United Nations Conference on Environment and Development (UNCED), "Conservation and Development of Forests: Options for Agenda 21," third draft (October 29, 1991).

38. Robert Winterbottom, *Taking Stock: The Tropical Forestry Action Plan After Five Years* (World Resources Institute, Washington, D.C., 1990), pp. 21-24.

39. Kenton R. Miller, Walter V. Reid, and Charles V. Barber, "Deforestation and Species Loss: Responding to the Crisis," in *Preserving the Global Environment: The Challenge of Shared Leadership*, Jessica Tuchman Mathews, ed. (W.W. Norton & Co., New York, 1991), pp. 91-93.

40. Robert Repetto, *The Forest For the Trees? Government Policies and the Misuse of Forest Resources* (World Resources Institute, Washington, D.C., 1988), p. 13.

41. Robert Repetto, "Deforestation in the Tropics," *Scientific American*, Vol. 262, No. 4 (1990), p. 38.

42. Charles M. Peters, Alwyn H. Gentry, and Robert O. Mendelsohn, "Valuation of an Amazonian Rainforest," *Nature*, Vol. 339 (June 1989), pp. 655-656.

43. *Op. cit.* 39, pp. 92-93.

44. John O. Browder, "Public Policy and Deforestation in the Brazilian Amazon," in *Public Policies and the Misuse of Forest Resources*, Robert Repetto and Malcolm Gillis, eds. (Press Syndicate of the University of Cambridge, U.K., 1988), pp. 247-289.

45. James LaFleur, Manager, Tropic International Ltda. (Ecotec), Brazil, 1991 (personal communication).

46. Eufresina L. Boado, "Incentive Policies and Forest Use in the Philippines," in *Public Policies and the Misuse of Forest Resources*, Robert Repetto and Malcolm Gillis, eds. (Press Syndicate of the University of Cambridge, U.K., 1988), pp. 184-185.

47. Clark S. Binkley and Jeffrey R. Vincent, "Forest-Based Industrialization: A Dynamic Perspective," The World Bank Forest Policy Issues Paper, 1990, pp. 28-51.

48. Owen J. Lynch, *Whither the People?" Demographic, Tenurial, and Agricultural Aspects of the Tropical Forestry Action Plan* (World Resources Institute, Washington, D.C., 1990), p. 9.

49. Douglas Southgate, "The Causes of Land Degradation along 'Spontaneously' Expanding Agricultural Frontiers in the Third World," *Land Economics*, Vol. 66, No. 1 (1990), p. 93.

50. Norman Myers, "The World's Forests and Human Populations: The Environmental Interconnections," in *Resources, Environment, and Population: Present Knowledge, Future Options*, Kingsley Davis and Mikhail S. Bernstam, eds., Supplement to *Population and Development Review*, Vol. 16 (Oxford University Press and Population Council Inc., New York, 1991), p. 240.

51. Judith Gradwohl and Russell Greenberg, *Saving the Tropical Forests* (Earthscan Publications Ltd., London, 1988), pp. 41-42.

52. Willem Keddeman, Stef Meijs, and Koos van Dijken, *An Import Surcharge on the Import of Tropical Timber in the European Community* (Netherlands Economic Institute, The Hague, 1989).

53. Senator John Heinz, *Globe Working Group on Tropical Forests: Action Plan Report*, report given to the Plenary Session of the Global Legislators Organization for a Balanced Environment, Nov. 15, 1990, Washington, D.C., p. 4.

54. Marc J. Dourojeanni, Chief, Environmental Protection Division, Inter-American Development Bank, Washington, D.C., 1991 (personal communication).

55. Charles Arden-Clarke, "Conservation and Sustainable Management of Tropical Forests: The Role of ITTO and GATT," World Wildlife Fund Discussion Paper, Washington, D.C., 1990, p. 13.

56. *Op. cit.* 53, pp. 4-6.

57. *Op. cit.* 47, pp. 29-38.

58. *Op. cit.* 55, pp. 9-10.

59. Subgroup on International Trade and Resource Flows, "International Trade and Resource Flows Effects on Forests Policy Options for a World Forest Convention," paper prepared for the Environmental and Energy Study Institute World Forest Agreement Working Group, Washington, D.C., 1990, p. 3.

60. Steven Shrybman, "International Trade and the Environment: An Environmental Assessment of the General Agreement on Tariffs and Trade," *The Ecologist*, Vol. 20, No. 1 (1990), pp. 30-34.

61. *Op. cit.* 55, pp. 1-10.

62. *Op. cit.* 60.

63. *Op. cit.* 55, pp. 9-10.

64. Robert J.A. Goodland, Emmanuel O. Asibey, Jan C. Post *et al.*, "Tropical Moist Forest Management: The Urgency of Transition to Sustainability," *Environmental Conservation*, Vol. 17, No. 4 (1990), p. 314.

65. *Ibid.*, p. 304.

66. Andre Carothers, "Defenders of the Forest," *Greenpeace*, Vol. 15, No. 4 (1990), p. 11.

67. *Op. cit.* 50, p. 244.

68. James Gustave Speth, "Coming to Terms: Toward a North-South Bargain for the Environment," in *WRI Issues and Ideas* (World Resources Institute, Washington, D.C., 1990), p. 4.

69. J.A. McNeely, K.R. Miller, W.V. Reid, R.A. Mittermeier, and T.B. Werner, *Conserving the World's Biodiversity* (International Union for Conservation of Nature and Natural Resources, World Resources Institute, Conservation International, World Wildlife Fund-US, and The World Bank, Gland, Switzerland, 1990), p. 124.

70. Patti Petesch, "Tropical Forests: Conservation with Development?" Policy Focus, No. 4 (Overseas Development Council, 1990), p. 10.

71. Reuters News Service, "Loggers, Ranchers Ravish Rain Forests," *Environment Week*, Vol. 3, No. 27 (1990), p. 6.

72. *Op. cit.* 50, pp. 244-246.

73. *Op. cit.* 69, p. 89.

74. Nina M. Serafino and Betsy A. Cody, "The Enterprise for the Americas Initiative: Issues for Congress," *CRS Issues Brief* (Library of Congress, Washington, D.C., September 10, 1991), pp. 1-4.

75. The World Bank, Agriculture and Rural Development Department, "Forest Policy Paper," Washington, D.C., July 1991.

76. The Inter-American Development Bank, "Foreign Policy," Washington, D.C., March 1991.

77. *Op. cit.* 41, p. 42.

78. The New World Dialogue on Environment and Development in the Western Hemisphere, *Compact for a New World: An Open Letter to the Heads of State and Government and Legislators of the Americas* (World Resources Institute, Washington, D.C., 1991).

79. *Ibid.*, pp. 9-10.

80. Nicholas Hildyar, "Adios Amazonia? A Report from the Altamira Gathering," *The Ecologist*, Vol. 19, No. 2 (1989), p. 54.

81. *Op. cit.* 66, pp. 8-12.

82. Paisal Sricharatchanya, "Too Little, Too Late," *Far Eastern Economic Review* (January 12, 1989), p. 40.

83. "More Dams in the Works for Brazil?" *World Rivers Review*, Vol. 4, No. 3 (1989), p. 3.

84. *Op. cit.* 66, pp. 8-9.

85. Coordinadora de las Organizaciones Indígenas de la Cuenca Amazónica (COICA), *To the Community of Concerned Environmentalists* (COICA, Lima, 1990), pp. 1-7.

86. Douglas Foster, "No Road to Tahuanti?" *Mother Jones* (July/August, 1990), p. 44.

87. Elizabeth A. Halpin, *Indigenous Peoples and the Tropical Forestry Action Plan* (World Resources Institute, Washington, D.C., 1990), pp. 32-36.

88. *Op. cit.* 48, pp. 15-16.

89. *Op. cit.* 85.

90. Jed Horne, "Rumble in the Rain Forest: Indians and Greens Square Off in the Amazon," *Voice* (July 24, 1990, New York), p. 21.

91. *Op. cit.* 86.

92. *Op. cit.* 85, p. 2.

93. *Op. cit.* 26, p. 109.

9. Wildlife and Habitat

Biological diversity—the variety among living organisms and the ecological communities they inhabit (see Box 9.1)—is more threatened now than at any time in the past 65 million years. Tropical deforestation is the main force behind this crisis, but the destruction of wetlands, coral reefs, and temperate forests also plays an important role. Continued loss or degradation of habitats at the present rate could doom up to 15 percent of the Earth's species over the next quarter century. Besides its profound ethical and aesthetic implications, such losses have severe economic costs. As habitats are fragmented, altered, or destroyed, they also lose their ability to provide such "ecosystem services" as purifying water, regenerating soil, protecting watersheds, regulating temperature, recycling nutrients and wastes, and maintaining the atmosphere. As plants and animals disappear, or their genetic diversity is reduced, so too do potential advances in medicine and agriculture.

The genes, species, ecosystems, and human knowledge that are being lost represent a living library of options for adapting to local and global change. Not only are more species being sentenced to extinction, but the reduction and fragmentation of habitats prevents the evolution of new species. And as habitats and species are destroyed, the human cultures that have evolved as unique adaptations are often lost as well. Humans as well as other species are the losers.

A variety of techniques—including parks, refuges, zoos, and seed banks—have been used in the past with varying degrees of success to try to preserve wildlife and their habitats. Protected areas, zoos, and seed banks all have an important role in conservation. However, analysis of the root causes of biodiversity loss shows that new approaches are also needed. Because the root causes are deeply imbedded in modern economic and social development, conservation efforts must expand to political and economic arenas.

CONDITIONS AND TRENDS

Global Trends

SPECIES AND HABITAT LOSS

Species

The total number of species is not known. Biologists estimate that there are between 5 million and 30 million species, with a best estimate of about 10 million. Most of them are inconspicuous organisms such as microbes, insects, and tiny sea creatures. Only 1.4 million species

Box 9.1 The Diversity of Life

Biological diversity is an umbrella term for the degree of nature's variety. It can be divided into three hierarchical categories—genes, species, and ecosystems—that describe quite different aspects of living systems and that scientists measure in different ways.

Genetic diversity refers to the variation of genes within a species. This covers distinct populations of the same species (such as the thousands of traditional rice varieties in India) or genetic variation within a population (which is very high among Indian rhinos, for example, but very low among cheetahs). Until recently, measurements of genetic diversity were applied mainly to domesticated species and populations held in zoos or botanic gardens, but the techniques are increasingly being applied to wild species.

Species diversity refers to the variety of species within a region. There are many different ways of measuring species diversity, and scientists have not settled on a single best method. The number of species in a region—its species "richness"—is often used as a measure of species diversity, but a more precise measurement, "taxonomic diversity," takes into account how closely related species are to each other. For example, an island with two species of birds and one species of lizard has greater taxonomic diversity than an island with three species of birds but no lizards. Thus, even though there may be more species of beetles on Earth than all other species combined, they do not account for the greater part of species diversity because they are so closely related. Similarly, many more species live on land than in the sea, but terrestrial species are more closely related to each other than ocean species are, so diversity is higher in marine ecosystems than a strict count of species would suggest.

Ecosystem diversity is harder to measure than species or genetic diversity because the "boundaries" of ecosystems and communities—associations of species—are elusive. Nevertheless, as long as a consistent set of criteria are used to define communities and ecosystems, their number and distribution can be measured. Until now, such schemes have been applied mainly at national and subnational levels, although some coarse global classifications have been made.

Besides ecosystem diversity, many other expressions of biodiversity can be important. These include the relative abundance of species, the age structure of populations, the pattern of communities in a region, changes in community composition and structure through time, and even such ecological processes as predation, parasitism, and mutualism. More generally, to meet specific management or policy goals, it is often important to examine not only compositional diversity—genes, species, and ecosystems—but also diversity in ecosystem structure and function.

Human cultural diversity could also be considered part of biodiversity. Like genetic or species diversity, some attributes of human cultures (say, nomadism or shifting cultivation) represent "solutions" to the problems of survival in particular environments. And, like other aspects of biodiversity, cultural diversity helps people adapt to changing conditions. Cultural diversity is manifested by diversity in language, religious beliefs, land management practices, art, music, social structure, crop selection, diet, and any number of other attributes of human society.

Source: World Resources Institute, World Conservation Union, and United Nations Environment Programme, in consultation with the Food and Agriculture Organization of the United Nations and the United Nations Education, Scientific and Cultural Organization, *Global Biodiversity Strategy* (World Resources Institute, Washington, D.C., forthcoming).

---

have even been named by taxonomists (1) (2). Many others may have local names and uses, but this knowledge is dying out as well (3).

Because the total number of species is unknown, and because many species become extinct without being cataloged, it is difficult to calculate the exact number of species that will become extinct. Most estimates are based on "species area curves," a calculation based on the relationship between the size of an area, the number of known species it holds, and, thus, the percentage of species that will be lost if a certain amount of habitat is destroyed. A recent analysis of tropical forest habitat (which contains 50–90 percent of the world's species) concluded that at current rates of deforestation, 4 to 8 percent of rainforest species would be sentenced to extinction by 2015 and 17–35 percent by 2040. Assuming a conservative global total of 10 million species, *20 to 75 species per day* would be condemned by 2040. This rate may seem extraordinarily high, but humans are largely unaware of most species. Large, visible species of mammals, birds, and plants make up fewer than 5 percent of the world's species (4). Continued loss of species at this rate could doom up to 15 percent of Earth's species over the next 25 years (5).

Being "sentenced to extinction" is not the same as becoming extinct, but it does mean that a species is likely to lose the ability to breed and reproduce into the future. Although the species may continue for a few generations in some areas, it lacks the habitat, food sources, or breeding conditions that would ensure a viable population. However, extraordinary efforts to restore habitat and employ captive breeding programs may save some species. The Arabian oryx, for example, was reintroduced on that peninsula in the early 1980s and is showing signs of establishing and breeding healthy populations (6).

Another way to gauge the status of species is to look at the proportion that are threatened, either globally or nationally, and whose populations are decreasing. In many countries, a sizeable percentage of the bird or mammal populations are threatened at the global level, and even more are threatened at the national level. (See Table 9.1.) The status of species at the national level often has the greatest influence on actions taken in that particular country.

Habitat

Since the advent of agriculture some 12,000 years ago, more and more wildlife habitat has been cleared to provide farmland, rangeland, and human and industrial settlements. Figure 9.1 shows the percent of grasslands and savannahs lost since preagricultural times in selected countries; most habitats have been reduced to less than half their preagricultural extent (7). This trend accelerated significantly in the 20th Century as human population more than tripled (8). Some industrialized

Table 9.1 Threatened Bird and Mammal Species in Selected OECD Countries

A. Bird Species

	Number of Bird Species				Percent of Bird Species		
	Known	Globally Threatened	Nationally Threatened	With Decreasing Populations	Globally Threatened	Nationally Threatened	With Decreasing Populations
Denmark	190	16	33	66	8.4	17.4	34.7
Finland	232	12	14	24	5.2	6.0	10.3
France	342	21	136	77	6.1	39.8	22.5
Italy	419	19	60	X	4.5	14.3	X
Japan	668	31	54	X	4.6	8.1	X
Netherlands	257	13	85	52	5.1	33.1	20.2
New Zealand	282	26	16	16	9.2	5.7	5.7
Norway	225	8	23	12	3.6	10.2	5.3
Portugal	313	18	124	67	5.8	39.6	21.4
United Kingdom	233	22	35	23	9.4	15.0	9.9
United States	1,090	43	79	X	3.9	7.2	X

B. Mammal Species

	Number of Mammal Species				Percent of Mammal Species		
	Known	Globally Threatened	Nationally Threatened	With Decreasing Populations	Globally Threatened	Nationally Threatened	With Decreasing Populations
Denmark	49	1	14	16	2.0	28.6	32.7
Finland	62	3	7	11	4.8	11.3	17.7
France	113	6	59	30	5.3	52.2	26.5
Italy	97	3	13	35	3.1	13.4	36.1
Japan	188	5	14	X	2.7	7.4	X
Netherlands	60	2	29	28	3.3	48.3	46.7
New Zealand	69	1	14	21	1.4	20.3	30.4
Norway	54	3	4	3	5.6	7.4	5.6
Portugal	82	6	42	24	7.3	51.2	29.3
United Kingdom	77	2	24	9	2.6	31.2	11.7
United States	466	21	49	X	4.5	10.5	X

Sources:
1. Organisation for Economic Co-operation and Development (OECD), *Environmental Data Compendium 1991* (OECD, Paris, 1991), p. 114.
2. Chapter 20, "Wildlife and Habitat," Table 20.4.

Note: X = not available.

countries have lost substantial portions of their wetlands just in the past few decades. (See Figure 9.2.) As startling as these habitat loss figures are, they do not consider the effects of habitat fragmentation on wildlife or ecosystems, a topic of increasing interest among ecologists.

Habitat loss poses a major threat to biodiversity, but other threats include overexploitation of plant and ani-

Figure 9.1 Percentage of Grasslands and Savannah Lost Since Preagricultural Times, Selected Countries

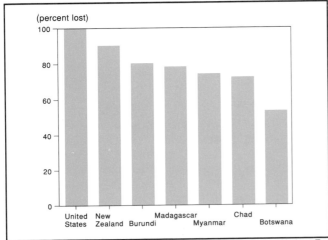

Source: World Resources Institute, in collaboration with the United Nations Environment Programme and the United Nations Development Programme, *World Resources 1990-91* (Oxford University Press, New York, 1990), Table 20.4, pp. 306-307.

Figure 9.2 Wetland Loss in Selected Industrialized Countries, 1950–80

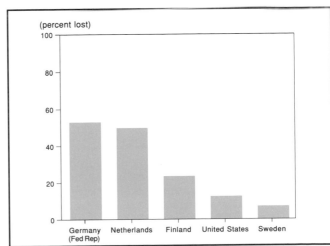

Source: Organisation for Economic Co-operation and Development (OECD), *OECD Environmental Data Compendium 1991* (OECD, Paris, 1991), p. 75.

Box 9.2 Looking at Biodiversity Through Three Lenses

Because its issues are complex and intertwined, it is useful to view biodiversity through three lenses—global, national, and local. The global perspective, for example, gives an overview of patterns around the world, as well as the "hot spots" where biodiversity is richest or most threatened. From this global point of view, biodiversity should be preserved as the common heritage of all humans, and all species therefore have a right to exist (1). The global lens is most often used by northern countries looking at biodiversity loss in tropical countries; giving funding priority to hot spots stresses the need to conserve as much biodiversity as possible with limited resources.

From the national perspective, however, it may be more important to conserve as many *native* species within a nation's borders as possible. In countries with low biotic diversity, the loss of even a few species could represent a large loss of diversity. For example, Table 9.1 shows that a large percentage of the bird and mammal

species in several European countries are threatened within national boundaries, though only a few are threatened in all regions where they are found throughout the world. Through a national lens, it would be more important to establish good conservation practices in each country, rather than focusing on a few scattered international habitats.

The national lens can also reveal more utilitarian concerns. Biodiversity can be viewed as a national asset, with economic and cultural as well as environmental value. Nations seek to benefit from biodiversity through increased living standards, crop production, and tourism revenues. Tropical countries also expect to share the profit from medicines, foods, cosmetics, or other products developed from their native plants. Nations may therefore seek to control local actions, such as poaching or freelance mining, that may adversely affect biodiversity.

The local lens provides an even more practical view of biodiversity. Local peo-

ple often derive direct benefits from plant, crop, and wildlife species. Many local cultures depend on the plants and animals they have lived with, studied, and domesticated. Yet local people must struggle with national or international forces for control of biological resources. Because the economic benefits of natural resources often accrue to influential business or government coffers without trickling down to the local level, local people not only miss the benefits of "development" but may also lose access to resources on which their health and livelihoods depend.

References and Notes

1. "The World Charter for Nature," as cited in Jeffrey A. McNeely, Kenton R. Miller, Walter V. Reid *et al.*, *Conserving the World's Biological Diversity* (International Union for Conservation of Nature and Natural Resources, Gland Switzerland, 1990), pp. 134-136.

mal species; pollution of soil, water, and atmosphere; introduction of nonnative species; industrial agriculture and forestry; and global climate change. A few examples illustrate how these threats affect biodiversity. The accidental introduction of the zebra mussel into the Great Lakes of North America from the Caspian Sea has led to fouling of municipal and industrial water intake systems, disruption of shipping, and has significantly reduced the phytoplankton population—an important link in the food chain of the Great Lakes—thereby threatening native fish species (9). In India, as in many other places, local women manage the forest as a source of food, fuel, and medicines that provide nourishment and income for their families. These "minor forest products" also provide important export earnings for the national economy. Yet when forests disappear, so too does this important component of the family and national economies (10).

AREAS OF HIGH DIVERSITY

The diversity of life, and often the threats to its survival, is not evenly distributed around the world. Some habitats have more species or greater genetic variability than others. In general, temperate regions tend to have large populations of a small number of species, while areas in or near the tropics tend to have a greater number of species with smaller individual populations. Endemic species (those that are limited to a certain area) and tropical species (which tend to have smaller, localized populations) are at greater risk of extinction from habitat destruction, pollution, overexploitation, or competition with introduced species (11).

Globally, the countries with the most species of vascular plants are in the neotropics (Central and South

America) and in Southeast Asia, where most of the world's rainforests are located (12). Africa has fewer species in the dry countries surrounding the Sahara and more species in the southern and eastern countries, which have more rainfall. Northern countries such as Canada, Norway, Sweden, Finland, and the U.S.S.R., and southern temperate countries such as Chile and Argentina, have comparatively few species.

One approach to conservation has been to identify areas as global priorities for immediate action because they are species-rich and also threatened. Fourteen of the 18 "hot spots" thus defined are in the tropics (13). This global approach—saving as many species as possible—has been criticized because of the need to encourage practices that conserve biodiversity in all countries (14). (See Box 9.2.) Various global, national, and local approaches to conservation are discussed later in this chapter.

STATUS OF SELECTED HABITATS

Tropical Forests

Tropical forests are richer in species than any other terrestrial habitat. Closed tropical forests, as mentioned above, contain at least 50 percent and perhaps 90 percent of the world's species, although they cover only 7 percent of the Earth's land surface. They include two thirds of the world's vascular plant species and about 30 percent of its terrestrial vertebrate species. Up to 96 percent of the world's arthropods may occur in tropical forests (15).

Tropical forests are important not only as the home to myriad plant and animal species, and as the source of valuable products, but also because they support di-

Figure 9.3 Global Distribution of Coral Reefs

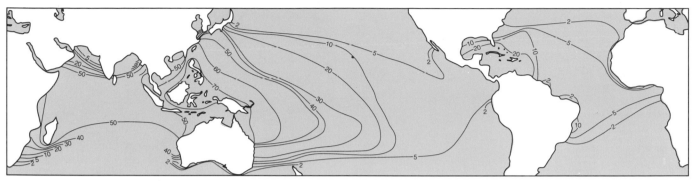

Source: J.E.N. Veron, "Distribution of Reef-Building Corals," *Oceanus* (Summer 1986), p. 29.

verse human cultures (16). Tropical forests also regulate vital biological, geological, and chemical cycles. As these forests decline, however, they cannot support the local climate necessary for their own survival (17). Between 1981 and 1990, an estimated 9 percent of the world's tropical forest was lost (18). Some types of tropical forests have been under especially high levels of threat. For example, 98 percent of the tropical dry forest along the Pacific Coast of Central America has disappeared (19).

Temperate Rainforests

The loss of temperate rainforests is only beginning to receive attention. Even the existence of areas such as the temperate rainforests of the Pacific coast of the United States and Canada and in New Zealand, Tasmania, and Chile is not widely known. Historically, temperate rainforests also occupied parts of Ireland, Scotland, Iceland, and Norway, whose climates are moderated by the Gulf Stream.

These forests were never extensive. About 30 million hectares of temperate rainforest once covered an area only 4 percent of the size of today's tropical rainforest. A recent study found that only 44 percent of the temperate rainforest remains, mostly along the Pacific coast of North America (20) (21). The areas that remain are highly productive as well as diverse, playing a critical role in maintaining the health of the coastal watersheds.

The environmental and economic impacts of the loss of temperate rainforests are widespread. As these habitats decline, so do the sectors of the economy that depend on healthy forests and fisheries.

Coral Reefs

Coral reefs are the underwater analog of tropical forests—habitats of unparalleled biotic richness. Figure 9.3 shows that the largest number of coral genera are found in the Indian and tropical western Pacific Oceans, with fewer species in the reefs of the Caribbean and Atlantic (22). While tropical terrestrial areas have a greater number of species, marine environments contain many more phylla (a higher taxonomic classification), most of which live in coastal waters (23). Unlike the rainforests, coral reefs have fewer highly lo-

calized (endemic) species—most species that occur anywhere in the Pacific and Indian Oceans are found throughout those oceans.

Coral reefs are under severe pressure from a variety of threats. By the year 2000, approximately 1 billion people will live in coastal cities. (See Chapter 23, "Oceans and Coasts," Table 23.1.) Overfishing is depleting fish stocks; burgeoning coastal populations and their associated human, agricultural, and industrial pollution are poisoning the reefs; soil erosion from upstream agricultural lands and the destruction of forests are smothering the reefs; even tourists who visit the reefs can cause damage by walking on them. There is even speculation that global climate change is a factor in recent coral-bleaching episodes (24). (See Chapter 12, "Oceans and Coasts.")

Mediterranean Climate Areas

Five areas of the world with a Mediterranean climate—cool, wet winters and warm, dry summers—have numbers of plant species and levels of endemism that rival the tropics. These areas include the Mediterranean basin of southern Europe and North Africa, parts of California and Chile, the Cape region of South Africa (the fynbos), and southwestern Australia. For example, the fynbos of South Africa is home to 8,600 species of plants, of which two-thirds are endemic (25). Because the Mediterranean climate is so agreeable to humans, however, these regions have historically been among the most extensively disturbed in the world (26).

Islands

Because their evolution takes place in relative isolation, many islands are home to species that are found nowhere else. Remote ocean islands—such as Hawaii and Ascension—have some of the world's most unique flora: only a few of the species on these islands are found anywhere else (27). However, the fixed boundaries and endemic species of islands also put them at great risk of species extinction. Indeed, the largest number of recorded extinctions has been on oceanic islands (28). About 10 percent of the vascular plant species endemic to Hawaii are extinct and 40 percent are threatened, as are 580 endemic plant species of the Canary Islands (29).

Figure 9.4 Areas with High Genetic Diversity of Crop Varieties

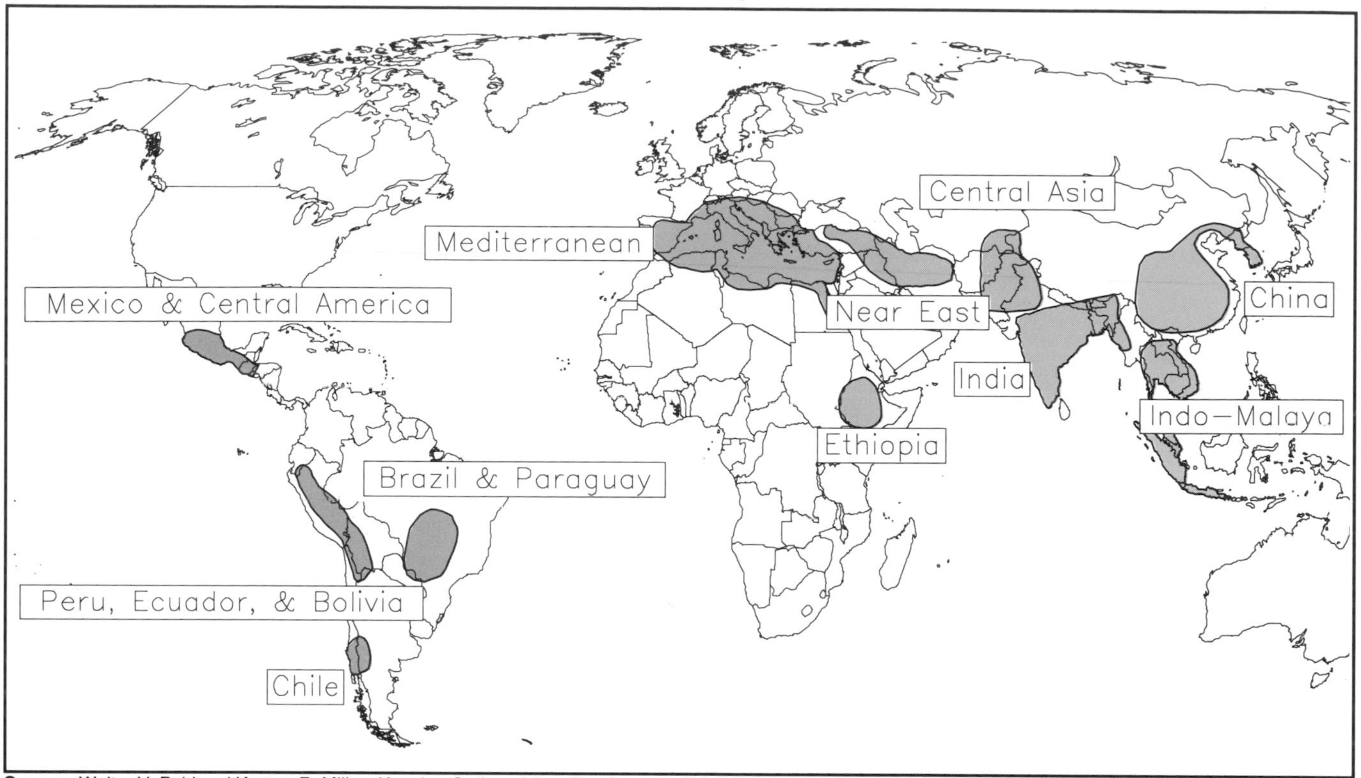

Source: Walter V. Reid and Kenton R. Miller, *Keeping Options Alive: The Scientific Basis for Conserving Biodiversity* (World Resources Institute, Washington, D.C., 1989), p. 24.

The introduction of nonnative species can be an especially serious threat to islands. On Guam, the brown tree snake has caused the extinction of three of the island's five endemic bird species and has nearly eliminated the other two. A program of captive breeding and introduction onto a nearby island free of brown snakes may save the last of Guam's unique birds (30).

Freshwater Lakes

Just as isolated islands evolve unique species, so do isolated freshwater lakes. A survey by the American Fisheries Society found that 30 percent of the native freshwater fish species found north of Mexico are endangered; of the endangered fish, 93 percent are affected by habitat loss (31). The lakes of Africa's Rift Valley contain more species than any other lakes in the world, with high levels of endemism. Lake Victoria has more than 200 endemic species, Lake Tanganyika over 140, and Lake Malawi at least 500 endemics (32). Pollution, introduction of nonnative species, and overfishing (for both subsistence and the international hobby-fish trade) all pose threats to these species (33).

Areas of High Crop Biodiversity

The loss of crop varieties, although less publicized than the loss of wild species, has severe implications for global food security. Fewer than 100 species currently provide most of the world's food supply (34), yet thousands of species and many more thousands of varieties (subspecies) have been grown since the development of agriculture 12,000 years ago (35). Not only is

genetic diversity declining on farms, but many of the areas that are home to the wild relatives of our food crops are also under serious threat. Most of these crops were domesticated in temperate and subtropical zones and in tropical highlands (36). Figure 9.4 shows areas of high diversity in crop varieties.

Domesticated varieties are also under threat as a result of the homogenization caused by large-scale agriculture and the demand for uniform varieties that can withstand the rigors of shipping and storage. For example, a recent survey of fruit and vegetable varieties revealed that up to 96 percent of the commercial vegetable varieties listed by the U.S. Department of Agriculture in 1903 are now extinct. Of more than 7,000 apple varieties in use between 1804 and 1904 in the United States, 86 percent have been lost; of 2,683 pear varieties, 88 percent are no longer available (37).

Thousands of traditional crop varieties were also dropped from cultivation with the advent of the Green Revolution, which promoted use of a limited number of high-yielding varieties (38). In developing countries, these high-yielding varieties are now used on 52 percent of the agricultural land planted in wheat, 54 percent of land planted in rice, and 51 percent of land planted in maize (39) (40). Unfortunately, most poor farmers on rainfed lands have not benefitted from these so-called miracle varieties, which require irrigation and high chemical inputs.

Crop breeders need a diversity of crop varieties in order to breed new varieties that resist evolving pests and diseases. There are many examples of crops that

Recent Developments

NEW ANTICANCER DRUG FROM TREES IN PACIFIC NORTHWEST

The potential of plants to provide new medicines has been demonstrated many times, but the issue took a new twist in the United States with the development of a highly effective anticancer drug made from the bark of trees found in the ancient forests of the Pacific Northwest.

The drug, known as taxol, was originally discovered in the early 1960s as part of a program at the U.S. National Cancer Institute to examine the cancer-fighting potential of naturally occurring compounds; however, scientists did not begin to realize its potential until 1979. The first clinical results were published in 1989 by Johns Hopkins University scientists. Among 48 women with advanced ovarian cancer that did not respond to standard chemotherapy, 30 percent responded to taxol. Other studies have found that the drug also may be effective in treating advanced cases of breast cancer and possibly lung cancer [1].

The supply of the drug raises environmental issues, however. At present, it can only be made from the bark of 100-year-old Pacific yew trees, which are scattered among the old-growth forests of the Pacific Northwest. Harvesting Pacific yews usually requires clear cutting, but many U.S. environmental groups oppose any clear cutting in the region because it would reduce the habitat of the endangered spotted owl as well as numerous other species. It takes about six mature Pacific yews to treat one patient [2].

Before its medical potential was discovered, the tree was considered commercially unimportant and was typically burned as part of logging operations. The U.S. Forest Service ordered a stop to the burning of yews in March 1991 [3].

The taxol molecule is complex, and synthesis is expected to take several years. Environmentalists, meanwhile, point to this as further evidence of the need to preserve biological diversity. Other plants, including the rosy periwinkle of Madagascar, have also proven to be sources of anticancer medicine. All told, plant-derived drugs had an estimated retail value of $43 billion in 1985 [4].

ELEPHANT IVORY BAN PROVES EFFECTIVE BUT CONTROVERSIAL

After eight years during which poaching reduced African elephant populations by roughly 50 percent, most countries participating in the Convention on International Trade in Endangered Species (CITES) agreed to a ban on ivory trade in 1989. The ban, along with other conservation efforts, seems to have been effective. Poaching has declined drastically in some (though not all) areas, and the price of ivory has dropped to a few dollars per kilogram (in 1989 the price was as high as $100 per kilogram). Elephant populations are stabilizing or increasing, and elephants are beginning to return to areas such as northern Kenya where they had been eradicated [5].

All countries have officially stopped exporting ivory, including the southern African countries that were opposed to the ban. The lower market price has made ivory more affordable for many Africans, and domestic consumption appears to have increased since the ban [6].

These countries have carried out few elephant herd culls since the ban because they are no longer economically feasible. But the pressure to thin the herds is increasing as elephant populations grow. In Botswana, for example, the elephant population has reached about 67,000, but government officials say the nation's preserves can sustain only 55,000 animals. Botswana officials say the herd is damaging water and plant resources; they want to cull 3–5 percent of the herd annually. Other southern African nations are expected to join in the effort to permit sustainable culling of herds [7]. Five states (Botswana, Namibia, Zimbabwe, Malawi, and Zambia) want to establish a Southern African Ivory Marketing Centre that will auction ivory and be exempted from the CITES ban. A new scientific technique has been developed that can be used to identify legal ivory as opposed to ivory from poached elephants. Proponents say such a market could put revenue back into the hands of African governments, which could use the money for elephant conservation [8].

References and Notes

1. Gina Kolata, "Tree Yields a Cancer Treatment, But Ecological Costs May be High," *New York Times* (May 13, 1991), p. A1.
2. *Ibid.*
3. *Ibid.*
4. Jeffrey A. McNeely, "Biological Diversity," draft chapter for the United Nations Environment Programme's State of the Environment Report, February 13, 1991, p. 8.
5. Mark Pagel and Ruth Mace, "Keeping The Ivory Trade Banned," *Nature*, Vol. 351, No. 6324 (1991), p. 265.
6. Jorgen Thomsen, Director, TRAFFIC International, World Wildlife Fund, Cambridge, United Kingdom, 1991 (personal communication).
7. Clara Germani, "Elephant Controls Urged," *Christian Science Monitor* (September 26, 1991), p. 10.
8. Michael Cherry, "African States Invoke Origin Test to Resist Ban," *Nature*, Vol. 351, No. 6321 (May 2, 1991), p. 7.

have been "rescued" with genetic material from wild relatives or traditional varieties, including wheat, rice, maize, sugar cane, potato, peanuts, chocolate, and cotton [41]. For example, a variety of wheat collected in Turkey in 1948 that showed little promise (it was thin-stemmed, lacked winter hardiness, and showed poor baking qualities) turned out to be resistant to several types of devastating wheat rust and is now used in all wheat-breeding programs in the northwestern United States [42]. Similarly, a tomato found growing on the shoreline in the Galapagos Islands could be used to introduce salt-tolerance to domesticated tomatoes, especially important to areas with salinized soils [43].

In an amazing display of genetic uniformity, nearly all the coffee trees in South America are descended from a single tree growing in an Amsterdam botanical garden 200 years ago—a serious situation when a new disease began attacking coffee trees. The origin of that *Coffea arabica* tree was the forests of southwest Ethiopia—forests that have virtually disappeared. Because there are no international agreements to guarantee that Ethiopia benefit from the use of these important genetic resources, the country has barred future collections from the forests [44].

Key Issues

GLOBAL BIODIVERSITY STRATEGY

The Global Biodiversity Strategy, scheduled for release in early 1992, is the result of a process that brought together more than 500 scientists, community leaders, and representatives of government and industry from around the world under the auspices of the World Resources Institute, the World Conservation Union (IUCN), formally known as the International Union for the Conservation of Nature and Natural Resources, and the United Nations Environment Programme (UNEP). The strategy proposes that the goal of biodiversity conservation is to support sustainable development by protecting and using biological resources in ways that do not diminish the world's variety of genes and species or destroy important habitats. The strategy emphasizes developing a national and international policy framework that fosters the sustainable and equitable use of biological resources and the maintenance of biodiversity as well as providing conditions and incentives for effective conservation by local communities (45). The draft strategy and other program materials were provided to the Secretariat of the United Nations Conference on Environment and Development (UNCED) and to governments negotiating a biodiversity convention under the auspices of UNEP (see below).

The plan sets forth basic principles to guide biodiversity planning at the local, national, and international levels and suggests actions to accomplish these principles. It suggests that if these actions are carried out within the next 10 years, the predicted species extinction crisis can be postponed and key genetic resources can be stabilized. Locally, the plan calls for community organizations, local governments, and others traditionally excluded (such as women and indigenous people) to participate in decisionmaking. Nationally, it urges biodiversity action plans, policy reforms, better management, and more investment in biodiversity conservation. Between governments, the plan calls for the adoption of a biodiversity convention (decribed below), as well as other conservation agreements, and changes in development assistance. Globally, it calls for new funding mechanisms, strengthened professional networks, and better monitoring efforts (46).

BIODIVERSITY CONVENTION

In late 1991, a convention on biodiversity was being drafted by international working groups facilitated by UNEP, but it was not clear whether the convention would be adopted at UNCED in June 1992. Negotiations have been slow because of the complexity of issues related to domesticated species, technology transfer, biotechnology, and intellectual property rights.

Much of the controversy revolves around the concept of who owns biodiversity. With advances in genetic engineering, the vast genetic resources of tropical countries could become the "oil" of the 21st Century (47). In the past, pharmaceutical and agricultural interests have had virtually unrestricted access to tropical plants and animals without providing what many developing countries consider adequate compensation. On the other hand, while developing countries know how to use wild species, they often lack the sophisticated technologies to develop their raw genetic materials into valuable commercial products.

As of early 1991, a draft convention proposed that countries give open access to genetic materials for scientific research, but that companies share the fruits of for-profit research with host countries, perhaps through joint ventures (48). The draft convention also stresses the need to transfer both technology and finances from North to South to conserve tropical biodiversity.

FOCUS ON CONSERVING BIODIVERSITY

The conventional approach to preserving biodiversity has emphasized the creation of parks and preserves, plus offsite conservation facilities such as zoos and botanical gardens. This approach has helped sustain many species, and it can mitigate some of the effects of threats such as habitat loss, overexploitation of plant and animal species, air and water pollution, the introduction of nonnative species, large-scale agriculture and forestry, and global climate change. Yet many such efforts do not address the root causes of biodiversity loss (49). The Global Biodiversity Strategy has identified several of these root causes: burgeoning human populations, increasing consumption of resources, ignorance about species and ecosystems, poorly conceived policies, and economic causes such as the effects of global trading systems, inequity in resource distribution, and the failure of economic systems to account for the value of biological resources (50). Many of these root causes occur simultaneously and are intricately connected.

ROOT CAUSES OF BIODIVERSITY LOSS

Population Growth and Increasing Resource Consumption

The world's population has more than tripled in the 20th Century, and continued growth is assured over the next 50 years, especially in the developing countries. Humankind's burgeoning numbers have an increasingly voracious appetite: people use or destroy about 40 percent of the net primary productivity of terrestrial and aquatic plants (51). At the present pace, the Earth's renewable resources are rapidly being depleted; the probable doubling of the world's population over the next 50 years will greatly increase these pressures. (See Chapter 6, "Population and Human Development," Recent Developments.)

The issue of population is not only a matter of numbers, but also of patterns and levels of resource consumption. The average resident of an industrialized nation uses 15 times as much paper, 10 times as much steel, and 12 times as much fuel as a person in a developing country (52).

Population growth and increasing resource consumption affect biodiversity in two ways: they create pressure to convert wildlife habitat into agricultural and urban land, and they produce wastes that pollute habitat and poison wildlife. These trends can be offset by stabilizing populations, using resources more efficiently, recycling, and controlling pollution.

Ignorance About Species and Ecosystems

Knowledge about the world's life forms lags surprisingly far behind other fields of scientific inquiry. While a great deal is known about individual species of birds, fishes, mammals, and plants, fewer than 1.4 million of the world's 5–30 million species have been named, let alone studied in detail (53). Knowledge about the structure and functioning of ecosystems is just as scant.

Information is also limited on the condition and value of biological resources, as well as uses and management techniques employed by traditional cultures over the centuries. For example, residents of one forest village in Thailand eat 295 different local plants and use another 119 for medicine. The World Health Organization estimates that 3,000 plant species are used for birth control by tribal people around the world (54). This knowledge is rapidly disappearing along with the indigenous tribes that possess it. Over 6 million tribal people lived in the Amazon basin 500 years ago; today there are only about 200,000 (55). Compounding the problem is the lack of trained scientists and engineers in many of the developing countries where biodiversity loss is the most severe.

Poorly Conceived Policies

Government policies designed to encourage some sectors, such as agriculture or forestry, can have the side effect of destroying biodiversity. For example, policies that award titles to settlers who "improve" or clear the land can result in the destruction of biodiversity. In Botswana, the government provides full cash subsidies for farmers to clear, plow, seed, and fence up to 10 hectares for cultivation (56). Modern land laws are generally incompatible with the few remaining community property systems, such as that of the Cree of Canada, in which hunting and gathering are strictly regulated for the long-term benefit of a group (57) (58).

Simple lack of coordination between government agencies with overlapping responsibilities may also result in loss of biodiversity. For example, an environmental agency may be charged with halting deforestation while the agriculture ministry tries to boost crop exports by subsidizing farmers to clear land. A government may embark on a program to link protected areas with rural development but not set aside funds to continue the program once the initial project money has run out (59).

Effects of Global Trading Systems

The world economy's reliance on trade has greatly increased pressures to build national economies based on comparative advantage and specialization. In developing countries, which rely heavily on agricultural commodities for export earnings, those pressures have pushed farmers toward large-scale plantations growing a relatively narrow range of crops that are in demand on world markets—coffee, cocoa, and bananas, for example. As the number of crop species declines, so too does the complex system of supporting species—pollinators, seed dispensers, etc.—that evolved with traditional agricultural systems.

The growth of such farming systems has often been at the expense of species-rich forests, wetlands, and diverse small-scale agricultural lands. In the process, the cultivation of better-adapted local varieties for more predictable local markets has been abandoned and much local knowledge lost.

Inequity of Resource Distribution

People who depend on the bounty provided by land and biotic resources have a strong interest in maintaining the productivity of those resources. But local communities often do not control such resources, have little say in their management, and must pay the costs for their unsustainable use. Inequities in who manages resources versus who receives their benefits can be found between rich and poor, men and women, and among various ethnic groups.

Globally, there are inequities between richer countries with the technological and financial capacity to develop and exploit natural resources and the poorer countries where the resources exist. For example, a successful drug for childhood leukemia has been developed from the rosy periwinkle of Madagascar, but none of the $100 million annual estimated revenue has flowed to its country of origin (60). Most developing countries also are heavily burdened by debt to industrialized countries, which limits their ability to invest in conserving their own resources (61).

Failure to Account for the Value of Biodiversity

Markets tend to undervalue biodiversity, thereby promoting (directly or indirectly) its depletion. Ironically, biodiversity produces and supports immense benefits to society, but it is almost totally ignored in national economic accounts because it is so difficult to value. When markets undervalue biodiversity, policies and subsidies may encourage unsustainable or destructive activities. For example, Indonesia has subsidized the use of pesticides in an effort to boost yields, but the resulting poisoning caused the loss of beneficial insect predators and various species of fish, in addition to the loss of human life (62). In other countries, subsidized irrigation has discouraged farmers from adopting what would otherwise be practical and economical water conservation measures (63).

When property rights are uncertain, there are few incentives for sustainable use by tenants. Research has shown that people are more likely to use land sustainably if they are confident that they will continue to have access to that land in the future. Their good land stewardship can help preserve species diversity (64).

Interaction of Root Causes

The root causes described above do not operate in isolation, but rather tend to act with and exacerbate one another. For example, the global market demand for shrimp encourages national governments to create policies and subsidies for private businessmen to invest in shrimp ponds. In Asia, the production of cultivated shrimp in 1990 was nearly seven times that of 1982 (65).

The environmental costs of this growth, particularly in the razing of coastal mangrove forests to build the ponds, have been high. The islands of the Philippines have lost about 70 percent of their coastal mangrove forests, mostly in the past 15 years. As a result, many of the valuable ecological functions provided by mangroves—as nurseries and shelters for many commercially important fish, as buffer zones against destructive wind and wave action, and as natural water purification areas—are lost. In addition, the shrimp ponds cause excessive freshwater withdrawal as well as pollution (excess lime, organic wastes, pesticides, chemicals, and disease organisms) that is flushed into adjoining mangroves. Meanwhile, the costs of this habitat loss are borne by local people who depend on the mangrove ecosystems for fish protein, revenue, and forest materials (66).

CONVENTIONAL CONSERVATION TECHNIQUES DO NOT ADDRESS ROOT CAUSES

In the past, efforts to conserve wildlife and habitats have directly addressed the threats to those species or areas. In tropical countries, conservation efforts have been largely influenced by organizations or agencies outside the country. The traditional conservation model followed by industrial countries and adopted by many developing countries emphasizes custodial management, such as parks and reserves that ban most human activities within their boundaries. Protected areas have typically been established to preserve the so-called charismatic species (e.g., elephants, tigers, or bears), spectacular vistas or geologic formations, and recreational or historic sites. Some areas have also been set aside to protect watersheds or reserve timber supplies. Until recently, however, few areas were established expressly for conserving biological diversity.

The global network of international, national, and regional protected areas remains an important tool in biodiversity conservation. These areas serve as critical repositories ensuring that at least a minimum of the world's genes, species, and ecosystems are conserved (67). However, the continued loss of biodiversity suggests that these efforts alone are inadequate.

Custodial Management

In 1861, the first protected area in the world was created–Yosemite National Park in California. Since then, 6,940 national parks, reserves, and other protected areas have been established (68). In addition to protected areas, there are more than 500 zoos (69), 1,500 botanic gardens, 60 gene banks, and a small number of scientific aquaria, collectively known as ex situ, or offsite, conservation facilities (see below) (70). Protected areas and ex situ facilities have helped sustain many species, including some in serious danger of extinction, but they have not slowed the overall rate of species or habitat loss. Between 1950 and 1990, the number and extent of protected areas increased more than fivefold (71). The average rate of species extinction, though not known with much precision, has clearly increased dramatically over the same time period (72). Why hasn't custodial management solved the global biodiversity problem?

As mentioned above, protected areas were often established for purposes other than biodiversity conservation. Furthermore, park boundaries usually follow political lines rather than ecological lines, such as the limits of a watershed (73). Many parks are also too small to effectively conserve intact ecosystems or provide for their inhabitants. For example, many park animals must range outside the boundaries during certain seasons to find enough food to survive.

A number of other obstacles prevent protected areas from making a greater contribution to biodiversity conservation. Frequently, protected areas are imposed on a community with no input from and little regard for the local people, thus creating conflict. Conflict also arises when the benefits of the areas go to society at large, or into government or business coffers, while the costs are borne by local people, whose use of the area is restricted. When the people who had managed and depended on the resources of a park are excluded, they sometimes resort to destructive activities (such as poaching) because they have no other way to provide for their families.

Numerous activities outside a park's boundaries can also have adverse effects inside the park. When land adjacent to a park is altered, for example, there may be changes in breeding and migration of park species, changes in water availability or quality, or air pollution. Sometimes the threats occur inside the boundaries from activities such as mining, logging, road building, or poaching.

Other problems that protected areas face include ineffective management and insufficient funding to carry out a mandate. In many countries, the responsibility for managing natural areas is scattered among various agencies or ministries, and in most countries, the responsible agencies are grossly underfunded and understaffed. Ironically, in many countries where parks are major sources of tourist revenue, very little is reinvested in conservation. A recent survey of threats to certain protected areas called World Heritage Sites showed that development was the most commonly reported threat in North America, Europe, and Oceania; inadequate management was the biggest threat in Asia; poaching, in Africa; and fire and natural threats, in South America. (See Chapter 20, "Wildlife and Habitat," Table 20.3.)

Ex situ forms of management have their own problems and limitations. Many zoos, botanical gardens, and aquaria began a century ago as mere menageries of exotic biological curiosities for public display. Some of them still treat plant and animal species strictly as acquisitions. In the past, seed banks have collected a limited number of species, and storage methods have sometimes failed to maintain the viability of the material. Even modern facilities with larger collections and good storage methods cannot allow for evolution.

Reorienting Old Strategies

One of the major limitations of conventional strategies is that protected areas cover relatively limited territory and ex situ collections hold relatively little genetic material. Indeed, much biodiversity exists in areas inhabited by humans (74). To respond to today's challenges, many leading zoos, botanic gardens, and other facilities have begun to reorient their missions through captive breeding, scientific research, and public education.

For example, leading zoos and botanic gardens now seek to breed and propagate rare species (75). Unfortunately, these facilities have the capacity to maintain viable populations of only a small fraction of the species threatened with extinction (76). While captive breeding and reintroduction hold some promise, they are expensive and somewhat limited in scope. More importantly, they cannot control one of the primary threats to endangered species—habitat destruction.

A number of zoos and botanic gardens have also expanded their educational efforts to inform the public about the loss of wild species and habitats. Such a biological education center would display re-creations of naturally diverse communities. The concept of a "biopark" may be the evolving role of these institutions as they enter the 21st Century (77).

Buffer Zones and Biosphere Reserves

Buffer zones and biosphere reserves are examples of a new generation of conservation techniques, although so far they have had limited application and success. Biosphere reserves are based on concentric areas zoned for different uses. In theory, they center around a "core zone" dedicated to preserving biodiversity with no human interference. Around the core is a "buffer zone," in which some settlement and resource use is allowed, surrounded in turn by an indefinite "transition area," where sustainable development activities are promoted (78). Since the first 57 biosphere reserves were designated by the Man and Biosphere Programme of the United Nations Education, Scientific and Cultural Organization in 1976, there has been a slow increase in their numbers. (See Figure 9.5.)

In practice, however, many biosphere reserves were created simply by giving the designation to an existing national park or nature reserve, without adding new land, regulations, or functions (79) (80). Nor have agencies been sufficiently funded to make the complicated zoning system work. Buffer zones along park boundaries are meant to enhance the park's conservation goals by barring human encroachment, broadening the area of natural habitat being managed, and providing economic opportunities that reconcile local people to the presence of the park. Without local involvement in design and management, however, the only way a buffer zone can work is if the park agency has the authority and ability to enforce its regulations—a situation that is rarely the case (81).

ADDRESSING ROOT CAUSES

New conservation techniques that address the root causes of biodiversity loss are being implemented in several countries. One is bioregional management, a method that goes beyond the buffer zone approach by involving local people, integrating ecological, economic, cultural, and managerial considerations at the regional scale. Another effort in Costa Rica trains local people to gather and classify specimens from the tropical forest; with an extensive inventory of species along with their descriptions and uses, the country is then in a position to sell information to pharmaceutical compa-

nies and negotiate arrangements that recover a percentage of profits from products derived from local species (82). This approach addresses the root causes of ignorance about species and ecosystems and inequity in the distribution of the benefits of biodiversity. A third effort, in Indonesia, involves local planning and management of a nature reserve.

The examples above inspire hope that regional or local efforts can effectively address the root causes of biodiversity loss. However, these efforts can only flourish if nations create a supportive political and economic framework. The final section of this chapter discusses national policy reforms proposed by the Global Biodiversity Strategy.

Bioregional Management

Perhaps the most ambitious expression of the integrative approach is the idea of managing whole regions with biodiversity in mind. Dividing government responsibility into isolated forestry, agriculture, parks, and fisheries sectors does not reflect ecological, social, or economic reality. A "bioregional" approach requires cross-sectoral and, in some cases, transboundary cooperation and integration, as well as broad participation by all affected constituencies.

Bioregions are areas with high value for biodiversity conservation in which a management regime is established to coordinate land-use planning of both public and private landowners and to define development options that will meet human needs without diminishing biodiversity (83). The success of the idea depends on eliciting cooperation among various interests. Some conservation-oriented regional management plans have had trouble gaining local acceptance; an ambitious plan for an Adirondack regional park in New York state is an example (84) (85). On the other hand, Australia's Great Barrier Reef Marine Park, in which large marine ecosystem and the adjacent mainland are managed for sustainable development, is widely recognized as a success (86). (See Box 9.3.)

Monitoring with a Purpose: Collecting Species Data in Costa Rica

Costa Rica is pioneering a new model of collecting field information and cataloguing species using local "parataxonomists." The Instituto Nacional de Biodiversidad (INBIO), founded in 1989 with the help of the national government, is a private nonprofit organization based in Heredia. It serves as a clearinghouse for information on and monitoring of Costa Rica's flora and fauna—between 500,000 and 1 million species in all—and has begun a comprehensive national survey of them. The name, location, conservation status, and potential commercial uses of each species are catalogued on computer. Using the catalogue, researchers can look for possible chemical uses among newly described wild plant species. Plants free of insect damage or fungal growth, for example, may contain natural chemicals that act as insect repellents, growth inhibitors, or antibiotics. Such finds are worth money to agrochemical, pharmaceutical, or biotechnology com-

Figure 9.5 Number of Biosphere Reserves, 1976–91

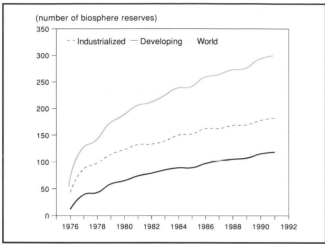

(number of biosphere reserves)

Source: World Conservation Monitoring Centre, Cambridge, U.K., March 1991 (unpublished data).

panies. For a fee, INBIO helps commercial users "prospect" in the catalogue (87) (88). INBIO's first major customer was Merck & Co., Inc., the world's largest pharmaceutical company, which has a successful history of developing pharmaceuticals from natural sources. In exchange for plant, insect, and microbe samples from INBIO, Merck agreed to pay INBIO $1 million as well as royalties on the sale of any products that Merck ultimately develops. Both Merck and INBIO hope that useful chemicals found in samples could then be synthesized in the laboratory rather than harvested from the forest. Part of the research funding will go to the Costa Rican National System of Conservation Areas to conserve biological diversity in the field (89) (90).

Costa Rica (like many tropical countries) has a shortage of taxonomists—scientists who can identify and classify species (91). INBIO's solution is innovative: it hires and trains local people to act as field collectors and do initial identification of insect specimens for the national biodiversity survey. The first class of 16 "parataxonomists" went into the field in 1989 and are now collecting 100,000 insect specimens per month. During their first six months, they collected four times as many insect specimens as had been put into Costa Rica's national collections during the previous 100 years. The parataxonomists include former housewives, farmers, ranchers, high school students, and national park guards. The specimens are sent from the field to INBIO, where apprentice curators classify them. Finally, international experts are brought in to confirm identifications and make definitive taxonomic judgments (92).

Reserve Management in Indonesia's Arfak Mountains

Including local people in the design and management of conservation programs can address several of the root causes of biodiversity loss: inequity, ignorance,

and the failure of policies and economic systems. Local involvement often results in innovative policies and a more equitable distribution of resources. A leading example is Indonesia's Arfak Mountains Nature Reserve, which covers 70 square kilometers of rainforest in the "Bird's Head" region of Irian Jaya, on the island of New Guinea (93). It lies within the territory of the Hatam tribe, who rely on forest products for housing and food. The Hatam have agreed to help protect and manage the reserve, a concept proposed by the Indonesian Directorate for Forest Protection and Nature Conservation and the World Wide Fund for Nature (94).

The objectives of the reserve are to maintain a naturally regenerating rainforest, to benefit local people by allowing traditional use of the forest, to make the reserve part of regional development planning, and to increase environmental awareness of and research in the area. All aspects of the reserve's development have come from a consensus worked out in a series of meetings between the Forest Directorate and the local Hatam government. There are now 13 village-level management committees through which local residents participate in decisions about boundaries, regulations, and future plans (95). As a result, every Hatam landholder in the reserve has agreed in writing to uphold the regulations. In fact, landholders act as a "guard force" to maintain reserve boundaries and report violations of reserve regulations. For example, people from outside the tribe wanted to establish an illegal butterfly ranch within the reserve but were thwarted after the Hatam refused to sell their traditional rights and reported the offer. Illegal forest cutting within the reserve was similarly stopped. There have been no known infringements of the regulations by the Hatam (96).

The Arfak project is promising, but it is too early to say whether it will have any lasting benefit for biodiversity. Optimism should be tempered by a 1990 World Bank review of 18 projects in the tropics that are trying to tie biodiversity conservation to sustainable local development. The review found few instances in which those benefitting from the programs were the same individuals or groups who constituted a threat to the protected areas, and little evidence that generating local benefits would lead to reduced pressure on these areas. Despite this, the authors concluded that the idea of local involvement in the management of protected areas is fundamental to conserving biodiversity (97).

NATIONAL POLICIES FOR BIODIVERSITY

Much of the innovative work in conserving biodiversity is spearheaded by nongovernmental organizations and international aid agencies. Without policy reform at the national level, however, these efforts might remain promising but isolated experiments. The Global Biodiversity Strategy identifies four major areas of policy reform that address the root causes of biodiversity loss:

■ Reforming existing policies that invite the loss of biodiversity,

■ Adopting new policies and accounting methods that promote conservation,

Box 9.3 The Great Barrier Reef: The World's Premier Marine Protected Area

The Great Barrier Reef, stretching 2,000 kilometers along the northeastern coast of Australia, is successfully managed as a $1 billion a year park that supports tourism, scientific study, fishing, and other uses in separately zoned areas. It is managed by a powerful Marine Park Authority with representatives from both the federal and state governments. The authority is advised by a Consultative Committee that includes representatives of the groups with an interest in the reef: tourism officials, fishermen, local politicians, Aboriginals, scientists, and conservationists (1). A Ministerial Council, composed of two representatives each from the federal and state governments, coordinates policy with the respective governments (2).

Although it continues to confront serious problems, including fishing-tourism conflicts, land-based pollution, and an outbreak of the crown of thorns starfish, the park is considered a model of good management and citizen involvement. The 1975 Act creating the park was the first piece of legislation in the world to apply the concept of sustainable development to the management of a large natural area. The administrative structure of the park was also designed to be sustainable. According to Graeme Kelleher, chairman of the Great Barrier Reef Marine Park Authority, "In Australia the major determinant of administrative survivability of organizations like the Authority is public support. In the long run, government support flows from it" (3).

The authority, consisting of Kelleher and representatives of the state of Queensland government and a third member, has strong powers to approve or reject proposals for development or zoning changes within the park. Its zoning power has precedence over almost all conflicting state and federal legislation (4). Technically, the authority may even have jurisdiction over land-based activities that affect the park (5)—a power possibly unprecedented in park management.

Corals have already been damaged by excess nitrogen and phosphorus runoff, and Kelleher believes that the park's greatest challenge in the next two decades will be dealing with increasing nutrient runoff from the area farmlands (6). In hopes of influencing decisions about farm practices and land use, the state and federal ministers for environment and primary industries were recently appointed to the authority's Ministerial Council (7).

Relying on public participation to sustain the park is not without its drawbacks. The authority's 1989–90 annual report notes that as the park attracts an increasing number of visitors, conflicts will inevitably increase among tourists, fishermen, and conservationists who use the park in different ways. "[The various interest groups] have developed a degree of sophistication which enables them to apply significant pressure on the zoning team, making resolution of contentious points more difficult" (8). Currently at issue is a rezoning proposal that would cluster tourism development.

The park has separate zones for preservation and scientific research, recreation, and general use, which includes fishing, collecting, cruise ships, and other activities. Bottom trawling for shrimp is allowed in certain areas. The only commercial activities prohibited throughout the park are oil drilling and mining (9).

A major effort is made to educate both locals and tourists about the fragile reef ecology. A popular, self-supporting onshore aquarium features a coral reef system with a walk-through viewing tunnel, museum displays, a cinema, and a commercial center with shops, food outlets, and charter boat services (10). The Authority also provides grants to school and nonprofit groups to develop educational materials (11).

References and Notes

1. Great Barrier Reef Marine Park Authority (GBRMPA), *Annual Report 1989-1990* (GBRMPA, Townsville, Queensland, 1990), pp. 12-14.
2. *Ibid.*, p. 10.
3. Graeme Kelleher, "Managing the Great Barrier Reef," *Oceanus*, Vol. 29, No. 2 (Summer 1986), p. 16.
4. *Ibid.*, p. 14.
5. *Op. cit.* 1, p. 60.
6. Graeme Kelleher, "Sustainable Development of the Great Barrier Reef Marine Park," unpublished paper (Great Barrier Reef Marine Park Authority, Townsville, Queensland, n.d.), p. 11.
7. *Op. cit.* 1, p. 2.
8. *Op. cit.* 1, p. 1.
9. *Op. cit.* 3.
10. *Op. cit.* 1, p. 45.
11. *Op. cit.* 1, pp. 37-39.

■ Reducing demand for biological resources, and
■ Integrating biodiversity conservation into national planning.

These policy reforms go far beyond previous conservation measures that focus more narrowly on species and habitats. Specifics in each policy category, discussed below, include changes in population planning, education, trade patterns, national income accounting, and agricultural supports. Many of these policies are controversial and will be difficult to institute. A first step is to identify and discuss government policies that have an impact on biodiversity (98).

Reforming Existing Policies

National policies identified by the Global Biodiversity Strategy as potentially harmful to biodiversity include:
■ Policies that encourage wasteful and unsustainable logging by charging low rents for short-term leases on public land; and
■ Agricultural policies that encourage monocultures and excessive use of pesticides, fertilizers, and water. These policies include subsidies for pesticides, fertilizers, and water; food price controls that prevent farmers from making an adequate return on investment; research biased toward high-input agriculture; and credit policies that discriminate against traditional crop varieties (99).

Establishing New Policies that Promote Conservation

■ Modify the national income accounting system to make it reflect the economic loss that results when biological resources are degraded and biodiversity is lost. Under current accounting systems, ecological disasters can appear profitable. For example, the *Exxon Valdez* oil spill in Alaska actually increased the U.S. gross national product: billions of dollars were spent on cleanup, but resource losses did not show up on the ledger. About 20 countries are developing national balance sheets for natural resources such as soil and timber that are more easily "monetized." This system of accounting incorporates the value of biological resources and of biodiversity itself where possible, as well as the costs of lost genetic resources, degraded watersheds, or eroded soils.

Box 9.4 Financing Biodiversity Conservation

A number of innovative financing schemes have been developed to support biodiversity conservation efforts. "*Debt-for-nature" swaps* have proved successful, for example, although most such swaps have been fairly small, relative to both the debt of many developing countries and their conservation and development needs. Chapter 20, "Wildlife and Habitat," Table 20.6, lists 17 officially sanctioned and funded debt-for-nature swaps that reduced debts by almost $100 million and provided $61 million in conservation funds. One suggestion for expanding their scope is to establish an International Debt Management Authority to purchase debt obligations on the secondary market for all areas of sustainable development, including biodiversity conservation (1).

Endowments are another mechanism for providing steady long-term financial support for conservation. One such trust fund is being established in Bhutan with a principal of more than $10 million; the interest earned will be used to fund training, inventory, protected areas management, environmental education, institutional support for government ministries, and integrated conservation and development projects (2).

The *World Parks Endowment*, created in 1989 to support conservation in the "250 environmentally richest areas of the world," solicits contributions and funnels them into protected area projects in tropical countries. The endowment is run by The World Conservation Union formally known as the International Union for the Conservation of Nature and Natural Resources (IUCN). In its first two projects, it bought 45 square kilometers of tropical rainforest in Guatemala's Sierra de las Minas and endowed a Belize watershed protection area with $200,000 (3) (4).

Over $1 million per year is given under the auspices of the *World Heritage Convention* to protect biodiversity at sites of outstanding natural importance. Another $600,000 is spent annually on conservation projects under the *Convention on Wetlands of International Importance*. Several *UNEP Regional Seas Conventions* also operate conservation trust funds (5).

The *Tropical Forest Action Plan* (TFAP), launched in 1985, and the *International Tropical Timber Organization* (ITTO), founded in 1986, have conservation components that relate to biodiversity. Although both have been criticized as being too oriented toward timber production, they can help nations obtain development assistance funds for sustainable forest management (6) (7).

An *International Fund for Plant Genetic Resources* was started in 1988. It has been esti-

mated that the Fund would require $500 million per year to be effective. Contributions are voluntary, however, and response so far has been inadequate (8).

An international financing mechanism, called the *Global Environmental Facility* (GEF), was established in 1990 by the World Bank, United Nations Environment Programme, and United Nations Development Programme. GEF is a three-year pilot project that will dispense more than $1 billion in grants and low-interest loans to developing countries (9). During the pilot phase, $250 million or more will be made available to address loss of biodiversity, one of four global problems that GEF will address(10).

An *International Fund for the Conservation of Biological Diversity* has been proposed as part of a global biodiversity convention. It would be funded by voluntary contributions and by levies on discharges into the biosphere, on trade in natural living materials or products derived from them, and on patentable new genetic material or products synthesized from wild sources (11).

Nature tourism, also called "ecotourism"—travel made to destinations specifically to enjoy their wild plants and animals, scenery, and other natural attributes (12)—has the potential to become an important source of funds for biodiversity conservation. In 1988, tourism in developing countries was valued at $55 billion; nature tourism contributed up to $12 billion of that total (13) (14). In some small countries, such as Ecuador, Rwanda, and Kenya, nature tourism is a major earner of foreign exchange (15) (16). The benefits of ecotourism may be overstated, however. The World Bank estimates that 55 percent of gross revenues leak back to developed countries in the form of repatriated earnings, advertising costs, and payments for tourism-related imports such as oil, luxury goods, and infrastructure (17). Of what remains, little goes into conserving the biodiversity that makes nature tourism possible. Each tourist authority will have to find its own best way to invest its earnings, but earmarking revenues for biodiversity conservation is one possibility (18).

Whether these financial efforts will be sufficient remains to be seen. However, they do not approach the $52 billion required to implement the forest management and biodiversity aspects of *Caring for the Earth: A Strategy for Sustainability*, world conservation strategy for the 1990s (19).

References and Notes

1. Environmental and Energy Study Institute (EESI), *Partnership for Sustainable Development: A New U.S. Agenda for International Development and Environmental Security* (EESI, Washington, D.C., 1991), pp. 15-17.
2. Royal Government of Bhutan, United Nations Development Programme, and World Wildlife Fund (WWF), "Prospectus: Trust Fund for Environmental Conservation in Bhutan" (WWF, Washington, D.C., 1991).
3. "Belize Park Endowed," *IUCN Bulletin*, Vol. 21, No. 3 (September 1990), p. 9.
4. The World Conservation Union (IUCN), "World Parks Endowment: Prospectus," unpublished paper (IUCN, Washington, D.C., 1991), pp. 1-2.
5. Jeffrey A. McNeely, Kenton R. Miller, Walter V. Reid *et al.*, *Conserving the World's Biological Diversity* (the World Conservation Union (IUCN), Gland, Switzerland, 1990), p. 123.
6. *Ibid.*, p. 111.
7. Mark Timm, "Timber Pact to Protect Tropical Forests," *Development and Cooperation* (March 1987), p. 23.
8. The Keystone Center, *Final Consensus Report of the Keystone International Dialogue Series on Plant Genetic Resources: Madras Plenary Session* (The Keystone Center, Keystone, Colorado, 1990), pp. 26-27, 29-30.
9. "The Global Environment Facility," *Our Planet* Vol. 3, No. 3 (United Nations Environment Programme, Nairobi, 1991), pp. 10-12.
10. The World Conservation Union (IUCN) Environmental Law Centre, "Legal Measures for Supporting the Conservation of Biological Diversity," paper presented at the IUCN General Assembly, Perth, Australia, November 1990, p. 11.
11. *Op. cit.* 5.
12. Hector Ceballos-Lascurain, "The Future of 'Ecotourism,'" *Mexico Journal* (January 27, 1988), p. 13.
13. "Riding the Tourist Boom," *South* (August 1989), p. 12.
14. Kreg Lindberg, *Policies for Maximizing Nature Tourism's Ecological and Economic Benefits* (World Resources Institute, Washington, D.C., 1991), p. 5.
15. Elizabeth Boo, *Ecotourism: The Potentials and Pitfalls*, Vol. 1 (World Wildlife Fund, Washington, D.C., 1990), pp. xiv and xvi.
16. *Op. cit.* 13.
17. Susanne Frueh, "Report to WWF on Tourism to Protected Areas" (World Wildlife Fund, Washington, D.C., 1988), p. xv.
18. James R. Barborak, "Innovative Funding Mechanisms Used by Costa Rica Conservation Agencies," paper presented at the IUCN General Assembly, San Jose, Costa Rica, February 1988, cited in Kreg Lindberg, *Policies for Maximizing Nature Tourism's Ecological and Economic Benefits* (World Resources Institute, Washington, D.C., 1991), p. 25.
19. The World Conservation Union (IUCN), United Nations Environment Programme, and World Wildlife Fund, *Caring for the Earth: A Strategy for Sustainable Living* (IUCN, Gland, Switzerland, 1991), p. 22.

■ Assert sovereignty over genetic resources and regulate their collection. To avoid legal complications over intellectual property rights, governments could tax companies that prospect for new species or form their own research institutes such as INBIO, described above.

■ Regulate the introduction of species. Many countries have strict regulations concerning imported plants or animals, but others leave this matter unregulated. There are numerous examples of introduced species decimating local populations.

■ Establish and enforce methods to control water pollution from both point sources and nonpoint sources, such as agricultural and urban runoff. Recent estimates show that up to 80 percent of marine pollution originates inland, yet few countries effectively control land-based sources of water pollution.

■ Formulate fisheries policies based on sustainable harvest levels.

■ Set aside key marine habitats and other sensitive areas when planning coastal development (100).

Reducing Demand for Biological Resources

■ Provide universal access to family planning services and increase funding to support their distribution.

■ Reduce resource consumption through recycling and conservation (101).

Integrating Biodiversity into National Planning

■ Incorporate biodiversity conservation into national planning to help countries define and articulate their international interests. Countries that set biodiversity priorities, assess their natural resources, and determine what they have to offer and what they want in return have an advantage at the international bargaining table (102).

FINANCIAL SUPPORT

An effective effort to conserve biodiversity must address the root causes of habitat loss; it must also involve local people and provide economic incentives to conserve diversity. But while surveys indicate that there is public support for government action to protect the natural environment (103), biodiversity conservation remains relatively underfunded. Efforts to include an economic value for biodiversity in national accounts and to tax resource use or sell information to pharmaceutical companies will help, but biodiversity conservation will likely depend on direct financial support. Box 9.4 describes a number of recent international financing schemes.

Wildlife and Habitat was authored by Janet N. Abramovitz, an associate in WRI's Forests and Biodiversity program. Contributors included Mary Paden, World Resources managing editor, David Harmon, a conservation consultant in Houghton, Michigan, Robert Livernash, World Resources senior editor, and W. James Batten.

References and Notes

1. World Resources Institute, World Conservation Union, and United Nations Environment Programme, in consultation with the Food and Agriculture Organization of the United Nations and the United Nations Education, Scientific and Cultural Organization, *Global Biodiversity Strategy* (World Resources Institute, Washington, D.C., forthcoming).

2. Edward O. Wilson, "The Current State of Biological Diversity," in *Biodiversity*, Edward O. Wilson, ed. (National Academy Press, Washington, D.C., 1988), p. 5.

3. Michael Krauss, "The World's Languages in Crisis," paper presented at the Symposium on Endangered Languages and their Preservation, meeting of the Linguistic Society of America, Chicago, January 3, 1991, p. 3.

4. Walter V. Reid, "How Many Species Will There Be?" in *Tropical Deforestation and Species Extinction*, J. Sayer and T. Whitmore, eds. (Chapman and Hall, London, forthcoming).

5. *Op. cit.* 1.

6. "Recent Developments in the Reintroduction of Arabian Oryx (*Oryx leveoryx*) to Oman," *CBSG News*, Vol. 2, No. 1 (Captive Breeding Specialist Group, Apple Valley, Minnesota, 1991), p. 8.

7. The preagricultural habitat figure is based on the expected vegetation composition in each area based on soils, climate, etc., in the absence of human disturbance.

8. Thomas W. Merrick, "World Population in Transition," *Population Bulletin*, Vol. 41, No. 2 (1986), p. 13.

9. Charles R. O'Neill, Jr. and David B. MacNeill, "Dreissena Polymorpha: An Unwelcome New Great Lakes Invader," *Sea Grant* (Cornell University, Ithaca, N.Y., February, 1990), p. 1.

10. Ravinder Kaur, "Women in Forestry in India," paper prepared for The World Bank, October 1990, pp. 17 and 43.

11. Michael E. Soul , "Conservation: Tactics for a Constant Crisis," *Science*, Vol 253, No. 5021 (August 16, 1991), p. 745.

12. Walter V. Reid and Kenton R. Miller, *Keeping Options Alive: The Scientific Basis for Conserving Biodiversity* (World Resources Institute, Washington, D.C., 1989), pp. 12-15.

13. Norman Myers, "The Biodiversity Challenge: Expanded Hot-Spots Analysis," *The Environmentalist*, Vol. 10, No. 4 (1990), pp. 253-254.

14. *Op. cit.* 1.

15. *Op. cit.* 12, p. 15.

16. Daniel H. Janzen, "Tropical Ecological and Biocultural Restoration," *Science*, Vol. 239 (January 15, 1988), p. 243.

17. Paul R. Ehrlich and Edward O. Wilson, "Biodiversity Studies: Science and Policy," *Science*, Vol. 253, No. 5021 (August 16, 1991), p. 760.

18. Food and Agriculture Organization of the United Nations, "Second Interim Report on the State of Tropical Forests," paper presented at the 10th World Forestry Congress, Paris, September 1991, Table 1.

19. Daniel H. Janzen, "Tropical Dry Forests: The Most Endangered Tropical Ecosystem," in *Biodiversity*, Edward O. Wilson, ed. (National Academy Press, Washington, D.C., 1988), p. 130.

20. J.F. Weigand, "Coastal Temperate Rain Forests: Definition and Global Distribution," a working manuscript (Ecotrust and Conservation International, Portland, Oregon, September 1991), p. 6.

21. Haisla Nation and Ecotrust, "A Cultural and Scientific Reconnaissance of the Greater Kitlope Ecosystem" (Ecotrust and Conservation International Canada, Portland, Oregon, 1991), p. 10.

22. Jeremy B.C. Jackson, "Adaption and Diversity of Coral Reefs," *Bioscience*, Vol. 41, No. 7 (1991), pp. 475-482.

23. G. Carleton Ray, "Coastal-Zone Biodiversity Patterns," *Bioscience*, Vol 41, No. 7 (1991), pp. 490-498.

24. Ernest H. Williams, Jr., and Lucy Bunkley-Williams, "Coral Reef Bleaching Alert," *Nature*, Vol. 346, No. 6281 (July 19, 1990), p. 225.

25. Jeffrey A. McNeely, Kenton R. Miller, Walter V. Reid *et al.*, *Conserving the World's Biological Diversity* (the World Conservation Union (IUCN), Gland, Switzerland, 1990), p. 46

26. Harold A. Mooney, "Lessons from Mediterranean Climate Regions," in *Biodiversity*, Edward O. Wilson, ed. (National Academy Press, Washington, D.C., 1988), p. 158.

27. *Op. cit.* 12, p. 18.

28. Peter M. Vitousek, "Diversity and Biological Invasions of Oceanic Islands," in *Biodiversity*, Edward O. Wilson, ed. (National Academy Press, Washington, D.C., 1988), p. 181.

29. Steven D. Davis, Steven J.M. Droop, Patrick Gregerson *et al.*, *Plants in Danger: What Do We Know?* (International Union for Conservation of Nature and Natural Resources, Gland, Switzerland, 1986), pp. 62 and 159.

30. John Carey, "Massacre on Guam," *National Wildlife*, Vol. 26, No. 5 (August-September 1988), pp. 13-15.

31. Larry Master, "Aquatic Animals: Endangerment Alert," *Nature Conservancy* (March-April 1991), p. 26.

32. *Op. cit.* 25.

33. Simon N. Stuart, Richard J. Adams, and Martin D. Jenkins, *Biodiversity in Sub-Saharan Africa and Its Islands: Conservation, Management and Sustainable Use* (the World Conservation Union (IUCN), Gland, Switzerland, 1990), p. 134.

34. Robert Prescott-Allen and Christine Prescott-Allen, "How Many Plants Feed the World?" *Conservation Biology*, Vol. 4, No. 4 (1990), p. 365.

35. Cary Fowler and Pat Mooney, *Shattering: Food, Politics, and the Loss of Genetic Diversity* (University of Arizona Press, Tucson, 1990), p. 19.

36. *Op. cit.* 12, p. 23.

37. *Op. cit.* 35, p. 63.

38. *Op. cit.* 35, p. 60.

39. Dana G. Dalrymple, *Development and Spread of High-Yielding Wheat Varieties in Developing Countries* (U.S. Agency for International Development, Washington, D.C., 1986), p. 86.

40. David H. Timothy, Paul H. Harvey, and Christopher R. Dowswell, *Development and Spread of Improved Maize Varieties and Hybrids in Developing Countries* (U.S. Agency for International Development, Washington, D.C., 1988), p. 55.

41. *Op. cit.* 35, pp. 51-52.

42. *Op. cit.* 35, p. 69.

43. *Op. cit.* 35, p. 51.

44. *Op. cit.* 35, p. 104.

45. *Op. cit.* 1.

46. *Op. cit.* 1.

47. Jack Kloppenburg, Jr., "A View From the North," *Panoscope*, No. 23 (March 1991), p. 17.

48. United Nations Environment Programme (UNEP), *Draft Convention on Biological Diversity* (UNEP, Nairobi, Kenya, 1991), p. 47.

49. *Op. cit.* 1.

50. *Op. cit.* 1.

51. Peter M. Vitousek, Paul R. Ehrlich, Anne H. Ehrlich *et al.*, "Human Appropriation of the Products of Photosynthesis," *BioScience*, Vol. 36, No. 6 (1986), pp. 368-373.

52. Alan Durning, "Asking How Much is Enough," in *State of the World 1991* (Worldwatch Institute, Washington, D.C., 1991), p. 161.

53. *Op. cit.* 2, p. 3.

54. Norman Myers, *The Sinking Ark* (Pergamon Press, Oxford, U.K., 1979), p. 127.

55. *Op. cit.* 35, p. 108.

56. Hans P. Binswanger, "Brazilian Policies That Encourage Deforestation in the Amazon," *World Development*, Vol. 19, No. 7 (1991), pp. 821-829.

57. Fikret Berkes, "Cooperation from the Perspective of Human Ecology," in *Common Property Resources: Ecology and Community-Based Sustainable Development*, Fikret Berkes, ed. (Belhaven, London, 1989), pp. 76- 79, 83-85.

58. Community property systems (which are not the same as open-access commons) formerly operated throughout much of the world, but the erosion of traditional local authority and population pressure on resources have made many of them unworkable in their original forms. See Agnes Kiss, ed., *Living with Wildlife: Wildlife Resource Management with Local Participation in Africa*, World Bank Technical Paper No. 130 (The World Bank, Washington, D.C., 1990), p. 12.

59. Agnes Kiss, ed., *Living with Wildlife: Wildlife Resource Management with Local Participation in Africa*, World Bank Technical Paper No. 130 (The World Bank, Washington, D.C., 1990), p. 2.

60. M.D. Jenkins, ed., *Madagascar: An Environmental Profile* (World Conservation Monitoring Centre, Cambridge, U.K., 1987).

61. World Resources Institute (WRI), *Natural Endowments: Financing Resource Conservation for Development* (WRI, Washington, D.C., 1989), p. 3.

62. Jeffrey A. McNeely, *Economics and Biological Diversity: Developing and Using Economic Incentives to Conserve Biological Resources* (International Union for Conservation of Nature and Natural Resources, Gland, Switzerland, 1988), p. 45.

63. Robert Repetto, *Promoting Environmentally Sound Progress: What the North Can Do* (World Resources Institute, Washington, D.C., 1990), p. 5.

64. *Op. cit.* 62, pp. 11-12.

65. Conner Bailey and Mike Skladany, "Aquacultural Development in Tropical Asia: A Re-evaluation," *Natural Resources Forum*, Vol. 15, No. 1 (1991), pp. 66-73.

66. J. Honculada Primavera, "Intensive Prawn Farming in the Philippines: Ecological, Social, and Economic Implications," *Ambio*, Vol. 20, No. 1 (1991), pp. 28-33.

67. *Op. cit.* 1.

68. World Conservation Monitoring Centre (WCMC), *Global Biodiversity 1992: Status of the Earth's Living Resources* (WCMC, Cambridge, U.K., forthcoming), Table 6.02B, p. 96.

69. World Resources Institute, in collaboration with the United Nations Environment Programme and the United Nations Development Programme, *World Resources 1990-91* (Oxford University Press, New York, 1990), p. 314.

70. *Ibid.*, p. 129.

71. World Conservation Monitoring Centre and the World Conservation Union (IUCN) Commission on National Parks and Protected Areas, *1990 United Nations List of National Parks and Protected Areas* (IUCN, Gland, Switzerland, 1990), p. 215.

72. *Op. cit.* 54, p. 4.

73. David Western, "Conservation without Parks: Wildlife in the Rural Landscape," in *Conservation for the Twenty-First Century*, David Western and Mary C. Pearl, eds. (Oxford University Press, New York, 1989), p. 158.

74. William Conway, "Can Technology Aid Species Preservation?" in *Biodiversity*, Edward O. Wilson, ed. (National Academy Press, Washington, D.C., 1988), pp. 263-268.

75. *Op. cit.* 69, Table 20.5, pp. 308-310.

76. *Op. cit.* 74.

77. Michel H. Robinson, "Bioscience Education through Bioparks," *BioScience*, Vol. 38, No. 9 (October 1988), pp. 630-634.

78. Michael Batisse, "Developing and Focusing the Biosphere Reserve Concept," *Nature and Resources*, Vol. 22, No. 3 (United Nations Education, Scientific and Cultural Organization, Paris, July-September 1986), pp. 2-12.

79. *Ibid.*

80. John Hough, "Biosphere Reserves: Myth and Reality," *Endangered Species Update* Vol. 6, Nos. 1-2 (University of Michigan School of Natural Resources, Ann Arbor, November/December 1988), pp. 1-4.

81. Michael Wells, Katrina Brandon, and Lee Hannah, *People and Parks: An Analysis of Projects Linking Protected Area Management with Local Communities*, draft report (The World Bank, Washington, D.C., 1990), pp. 44-46.

82. *Op. cit.* 1.

83. *Op. cit.* 1.

84. The Commission on the Adirondacks in the Twenty-First Century, *The Adirondack Park in the Twenty-First Century* (State of New York, Albany, 1990).

85. *Governor Mario M. Cuomo's Proposals for the Adirondacks* (State of New York, Albany, New York, October 1991), pp. 1-2

86. Graeme Kelleher, "Managing the Great Barrier Reef," *Oceanus*, Vol. 29, No. 2 (Summer 1986), pp. 13-19.

87. Instituto Nacional de Biodiversidad (INBIO), "National Biodiversity Institute of Costa Rica: INBIO," unpublished paper (INBIO, Heredia, Costa Rica, September 1990), pp. 1-3.

88. Laura Tangley, "Cataloging Costa Rica's Diversity," *BioScience*, Vol. 40, No. 9 (October 1990), pp. 633-636.

89. INBIO and Merck & Co., Inc., joint press release, September 19, 1991.

90. William Booth, "U.S. Drug Firm Signs Up To Farm Tropical Forests," *Washington Post* September 21, 1991, p. A3.

91. Warren Y. Brockelman, "Priorities for Biodiversity Research," *Journal of the Scientific Society of Thailand*, Vol. 15 (1989), p. 235.

92. *Op. cit.* 88.

93. Ian Craven, "Community Involvement in Management of the Arfak Mountains Nature Reserve," unpublished paper (World Wide Fund for Nature, Jayapura, Indonesia, 1990), p.1.

94. Ian Craven and Mary Ann Craven, "An Introduction to the Arfak Mountains Nature Reserve" (World Wide Fund for Nature, Jayapura, Indonesia, April 1990), n.p.

95. *Op. cit.* 93, p. 2.

96. *Op. cit.* 93, pp. 2-4.

97. *Op. cit.* 81, pp. 9-11, 16-19, and 84-85.

98. *Op. cit.* 1.

99. *Op. cit.* 1.

100. *Op. cit.* 1.

101. *Op. cit.* 1.

102. *Op. cit.* 1.

103. Louis Harris and Associates, "Public and Leadership Attitudes to the Environment in Four Continents: A Report of a Survey in Fourteen Countries" (Louis Harris and Associates, New York, 1988).

10. Energy

Energy production and use are vital to the economies and environments of all countries. Furthermore, the mix of energy sources has profound consequences for environmental quality. The burning of fossil fuels, for example, contributes to global warming.

Global energy production has increased by roughly 50 percent over the past two decades, with fossil fuels (coal, oil, and gas) together accounting for over 90 percent of production. The industrialized countries use about three times more commercial energy than developing countries and about 10 times more energy on a per capita basis. These statistics, however, do not include traditional fuels such as firewood and animal waste, which continue to be significant sources in developing countries and remain the main energy source in oil-importing African nations. (See Chapter 21, "Energy and Materials," Table 21.2.)

The western industrialized market economies, which were profoundly affected by the 1970s oil price shocks, have rapidly improved their energy efficiency and increased their use of natural gas over the past 20 years. Central Europe and the Soviet Union, in contrast, use energy much less efficiently and have a greater reliance on coal. The economic transition underway in that region is likely to bring changes in energy use and improvements in efficiency. (See Chapter 5, "Regional Focus: Central Europe.")

In the developing countries, total consumption of commercial energy has almost tripled since 1970, with coal and oil the major new sources. In the villages of the developing world, however, growing populations still must rely heavily on forests and woodlands as fuel sources.

A further tripling of energy demand in developing countries is expected between 1985 and 2025, with fossil fuels such as oil expected to be the major energy source.

Some of this energy use could be avoided with improvements in energy efficiency; many new industrial plants in developing countries could improve their energy efficiency by 30 percent or more, for example. To realize these opportunities, new efforts are needed to make available information about energy planning and available technologies, to improve the marketing of energy-efficient products for export, to improve finance and trade policies for energy-efficient products, and to facilitate joint manufacturing ventures.

CONDITIONS AND TRENDS

Global Trends

ENERGY PRODUCTION AND CONSUMPTION

Global commercial energy production has increased 52 percent over the past two decades, from 205 exajoules in 1970 to 311 exajoules in 1989 (1 exajoule equals 10^{18} joules). This trend has been interrupted only twice, when the oil price increases of 1973–75 and 1979–82 shocked the global economy and transformed the world's political and energy landscape (1).

Oil remains the principal source of commercial energy production, but its share of production has dropped from 48 to 42 percent since 1970. Coal ranks second with 31 percent of the total; gas, third, with 23 percent; and primary electricity—from nuclear, hydro, geothermal, and wind—makes up 5 percent of world production. Gas and primary electricity were responsible for 39 percent of global production growth from 1970 to 1989; oil accounted for 30 percent (2) (3). (See Table 10.1; note that gas is defined as natural gas and other petroleum gases.)

Trends in energy consumption have differed slightly between the industrialized and developing countries. In the industrialized countries, which use about three times more energy than developing countries, consumption leveled off during both oil price shocks but then resumed growing. In the developing countries, however, growth was uninterrupted. As a result, developing countries raised their share of global consumption from 14 to 26 percent. (See Figure 10.1.)

Energy consumption per capita shows striking differences between the developing and industrialized countries. Each person in the industrialized world uses as much commercial energy as 10 people in the developing world. An average U.S. citizen consumes as much energy as 2 Swedes, 3 Greeks, 33 Indians or 295 Tanzanians. (See Chapter 21, "Energy and Materials," Table 21.2.)

However, these comparisons underestimate consumption in developing countries, because traditional fuels such as firewood, animal and plant waste, and charcoal are not included in international statistics. As Figure 10.2 indicates, traditional fuels are a significant source of total consumption in oil-importing developing countries and are the primary energy source in oil-importing African nations. In most developing countries, modern commercial sources of energy are consumed mainly by the industrial and transport sectors in urban areas. In sub-Saharan Africa, traditional fuels supply nearly all the energy to the rural population. In Bangladesh, India, and Pakistan, traditional fuels provide 90 percent of the energy used by rural households. The great majority of the 2.5 billion villagers in developing countries have no energy other than their muscle power and a few domestic animals to work the fields, process crop residue, and draw water. Traditional fuels are used primarily to prepare meals; other uses include heating, lighting, and energy for rural crafts (4).

Trends in Industrialized Countries

Industrialized countries—divided here between the market economies of the Organisation for Economic

Table 10.1 Commercial Energy Production and Consumption by Region and Fuel, 1989

(petajoules) {a}

Region	Liquids {b} Production	Liquids {b} Consumption	Gas {c} Production	Gas {c} Consumption	Solids {d} Production	Solids {d} Consumption	Primary Electricity {e} Production Nuclear	Primary Electricity {e} Production Hydro {f}	Primary Electricity {e} Consumption {g}	Total Production	Total Consumption
World	130,299	116,573	70,497	70,144	95,713	97,019	6,783	7,680	14,522	310,972	298,258
Developing Countries	72,732	29,789	13,033	10,391	34,618	34,963	340	2,593	2,992	123,316	78,135
Oil-Exporting Developing	59,773	11,325	9,531	6,907	460	447	0	365	358	70,129	19,037
OPEC {h}	47,384	6,771	7,242	5,020	234	187	0	210	210	55,070	12,188
Non-OPEC Oil-Exporting{i}	12,389	4,554	2,290	1,887	226	260	0	155	148	15,060	6,849
Oil-Importing Developing{j}	12,959	18,464	3,502	3,484	34,158	34,516	340	2,228	2,634	53,187	59,098
Africa Oil-Importing	621	1,434	16	46	4,068	2,880	14	120	126	4,840	4,486
Asia and Oceania Oil-Importing	8,764	12,332	2,305	2,171	29,374	30,904	299	1,030	1,330	41,773	46,737
Latin America Oil-Importing	3,574	4,698	1,180	1,267	716	732	27	1,078	1,178	6,575	7,875
Industrialized Countries	57,567	86,784	57,464	59,753	61,095	62,056	6,443	5,087	11,530	187,656	220,123
OECD Industrialized	31,286	67,606	28,905	33,719	37,322	39,036	5,511	4,090	9,643	107,114	150,004
North America {k}	22,043	35,321	21,158	21,403	23,595	21,117	2,193	2,090	4,292	71,080	82,133
Western Europe {l}	8,108	22,486	6,859	9,621	9,457	13,000	2,660	1,505	4,197	28,589	49,304
Pacific {m}	1,134	9,799	888	2,695	4,270	4,919	658	495	1,154	7,445	18,567
Non-OECD Industrialized	26,281	19,178	28,559	26,034	23,773	23,020	932	997	1,887	80,543	70,119
Central Europe	813	3,129	1,611	3,063	8,687	8,510	165	195	458	11,471	15,160
U.S.S.R.	25,468	16,049	26,948	22,971	15,086	14,510	767	802	1,429	69,071	54,959

Source: United Nations Statistical Office, *U.N. Energy Tape* (United Nations, New York, May 1991) (on diskette).

Notes: a. 1 petajoule = 10^{15} joules = 947.8 x 10^{9} Btus. b. Includes crude petroleum and natural gas liquids. c. Includes natural gas and other petroleum gases. d. Includes bituminous coal, lignite, peat, and oil shale burned directly. e. Production and consumption of electricity assessed at the heat value of electricity (1 kilowatt-hour = 3.6 million joules), the equivalent of assuming a 100 percent efficiency. f. Includes geothermal and wind. g. World electricity production shown as less than consumption because of incomplete trade data. h. Algeria, Ecuador, Gabon, Indonesia, Iran, Iraq, Kuwait, Libya, Nigeria, Qatar, Saudi Arabia, United Arab Emirates, and Venezuela. i. Developing countries whose exports of petroleum and gas including reexports account for at least 30 percent of merchandise exports: Afghanistan, Angola, Bahrain, Bolivia, Brunei, the Congo, Egypt, Mexico, the Netherlands Antilles, Oman, Syria, Trinidad & Tobago, and Yemen. j. Also includes countries that are self sufficient in oil whose oil exports are less than 30 percent of merchandise exports. k. Canada and United States. l. Does not include Turkey, which is included in total for Asia and Oceania Oil-Importing. m. Australia, Japan, and New Zealand.
Totals may not add because of rounding.

Figure 10.1 Commercial Energy Consumption, 1970–89

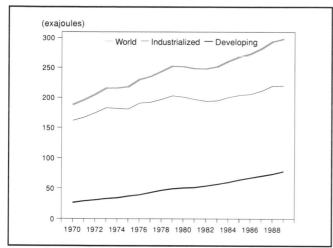

Source: United Nations Statistical Office, *Energy Statistics Yearbook* (United Nations, New York, 1991), and previous volumes.

Figure 10.2 Energy Consumption in Oil-Importing Developing Countries, by Fuel Type, 1989

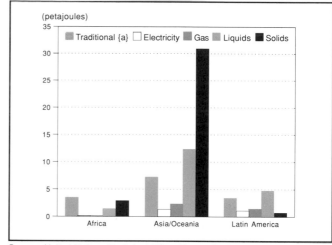

Source: United Nations Statistical Office, *Energy Statistics Yearbook* (United Nations, New York, 1991).
Note: a. Traditional fuels include firewood, animal and plant waste, and charcoal.

Co-operation and Development (OECD) and the transitional economies of Central Europe and the Soviet Union—are responsible for 53 percent of the growth in global energy consumption in the past 20 years (5). These countries produce 85 percent of the energy they consume. The remaining 15 percent, almost all of it petroleum products, is imported from developing countries. About one third of the oil consumed in industrialized countries comes from developing countries, primarily from the Persian Gulf states. (See Table 10.1.)

Patterns of fuel use have changed considerably in industrialized countries over the past two decades. As Figure 10.3A reveals, gas consumption grew steadily and by 1989 nearly equalled coal consumption. Coal consumption has increased 22 percent since 1970 and represented 28 percent of total consumption in 1989. By 1986, electricity from nuclear sources passed the combined total for hydro, geothermal, and wind power, a result of strong growth in France and the Soviet Union. Primary electricity now accounts for 5 percent of total consumption, up from 2 percent in 1970. Overall, oil consumption is down slightly since 1979, but consumption has recovered since 1985 because of a decline in real oil prices (6).

Energy Trends in OECD Countries

Energy demand in the industrialized market economies of the OECD nations was profoundly affected by the 1973 and 1979 oil price hikes. (See Figure 10.3B.) These countries responded with structural changes in their energy sectors, primarily by increasing energy efficiency and reducing dependence on imported oil.

In the past two decades, for example, energy intensity (the amount of energy required to produce a unit of gross domestic production) declined by 25 percent in OECD countries, with the steepest drop occurring after 1979. The decoupling of economic growth from energy consumption was encouraged by high energy prices, faster economic growth of the service sector,

and the relocation of energy-intensive industries to developing countries. Japan, Denmark, and the United Kingdom have reduced their energy intensities by over 30 percent in the last 20 years; Japan's energy intensity is now the lowest among OECD countries (7).

For OECD countries as a whole, net oil imports grew slowly in the 1970s and declined in the 1980s. The net decline of 6 percent from 1970 to 1988 was primarily due to a sharp drop in oil imports in Western Europe. That pattern did not hold in the United States, where net imports more than doubled (up 112 percent), or in Japan, where net imports grew 15 percent (8).

Increased domestic energy production has also helped reduce the oil dependency of the industrialized market economies. Total energy production has jumped 22 percent over the last two decades, including a 66 percent increase in Europe, primarily from North Sea oil and gas production (9). Most OECD countries also expanded nuclear energy production, with France and Japan in the lead. Expansion of nuclear capacity has slowed, however, because of cost concerns and the chilling effect of the accidents at Three Mile Island and Chernobyl. Coal production has increased in OECD countries, primarily in Australia and the United States, because of a switch from oil to coal for generating electricity (10). Finally, renewable energy sources such as geothermal, solar, biomass, or wind energy have increased their share in some OECD countries. They now provide up to 5 percent of total primary energy requirements in Australia, Austria, Canada, Denmark, Sweden, and Switzerland (11).

Energy Trends in Non-OECD Industrialized Countries

The 1973 and 1979 oil price shocks were not felt in the Soviet Union and Central Europe because of the region's self-sufficiency in energy. As a result, energy

Figure 10.3 Commercial Energy
Consumption in Industrialized Countries,
1970–1989

A. All Industrialized Countries

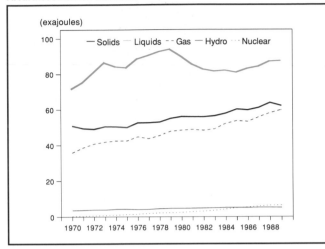

B. OECD Industrialized Countries

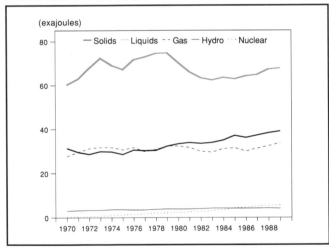

C. Central Europe and the Soviet Union

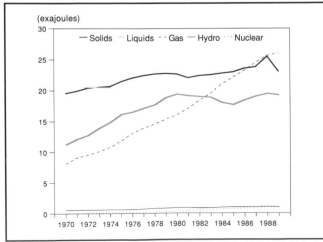

Source: United Nations Statistical Office, *Energy Statistics Yearbook* (United
Nations, New York, 1991), and previous volumes.
Note: See Notes in Table 10.1 for definitions of terms.

consumption in that region continued virtually uninterrupted until the dramatic political and economic changes of the past few years. (See Chapter 5, "Regional Focus: Central Europe.")

Energy supply and demand in the eight non-OECD industrialized nations (Albania, Bulgaria, Czechoslovakia, Hungary, Poland, Romania, the Soviet Union, and Yugoslavia) have been dominated by the Soviet Union, the world's largest producer of oil and natural gas. The U.S.S.R. is a net exporter of primary energy, with Central and Western Europe importing almost equal shares (12). However, since the breakup of the region's economic alliance—the Council for Mutual Economic Assistance (CMEA)—Central European countries are required to pay for their energy imports with hard currency, putting a heavy burden on these struggling economies (13).

Natural gas has emerged as the most important energy source in the non-OECD industrialized countries, surpassing oil in 1983 and coal in 1987. (See Figure 10.3C.) This shift was primarily due to the Soviet Union's supply-oriented energy policy, which shifted financial resources into the oil sector when coal production stagnated in the late 1970s and then into the gas sector when oil production leveled off in the 1980s (14).

In 1989, total energy production in non-OECD industrialized countries fell for the first time. Depletion of old deposits, skyrocketing capital costs to develop new energy resources in remote regions of western Siberia, and economic and political turbulence all contributed to this decline (15). The Soviet Union's ambitious nuclear program has also fallen behind its target, although it may play a greater role in the future energy supply mix (16). A growing environmental movement in Central Europe combined with high costs may curtail most nuclear expansion there.

Central Europe and the Soviet Union still rely heavily on coal, contributing to severe urban pollution problems. Coal is the most important source of energy in Poland and Czechoslovakia and it powers the industrial sector of Bulgaria. The majority of households in Bulgaria, Czechoslovakia, Hungary, and Poland burn coal to heat their homes: 47 percent of all coal consumed in Poland and 75 percent in Hungary goes to the residential sector. The U.S.S.R. differs from its Central European neighbors in this regard: 52 percent of the residential energy consumed comes from natural gas, followed by district heat and electricity (17). Unlike the OECD countries, however, these countries have not yet decoupled energy and economic growth; their economies remain among the least energy efficient of the industrialized countries.

Future Trends

In the 1990s, the trend toward higher energy efficiency and greater supply self-reliance should continue in OECD countries. The non-OECD industrialized nations will concentrate on modernizing the energy supply system and accelerating the development of new and renewable energy sources. In addition, a number of countries are beginning to adjust their energy policies to discourage the use of fuels that emit greenhouse gases. For instance, Germany has pledged to cut carbon dioxide emissions 25 percent by the year 2005, and many other countries have pledged to cut or stabilize emissions (18).

Trends in Developing Countries

Commercial energy production in developing countries grew from 35 to 40 percent of the world total between 1970 and 1979, but reduced oil production after 1979 brought the share back down to 35 percent. By 1989, developing countries' share had returned to 40 percent, a result of restored oil production and constant expansion of other fuel types: in the last 20 years, the developing countries' global share grew from 20 to 36 percent for coal production, from 6 to 18 percent for natural gas production, and from 15 to 20 percent for primary electricity production (19).

Total consumption of commercial energy almost tripled, with the demand for coal growing faster than that for oil after the 1979 oil price shock. (See Figure 10.4A.) In 1989, coal satisfied about 45 percent of total commercial energy demand, followed by oil with 38 percent. Primary electricity and gas have both increased more than fourfold but still play a less important role in the energy supply system (20). The current proven natural gas reserves could sustain six times the current production levels, but many developing countries are deterred by high development and distribution costs (21).

Developing countries as a group remain a net exporter of energy, their oil and gas fueling the economies of the industrialized countries. The total for the group is misleading, however, because energy production is concentrated in only a few developing countries. Most developing countries remain dependent on oil imports, and the changing energy markets in the last two decades have had different effects on the economies and development of oil importers and exporters.

Of the 26 major oil-exporting developing countries—for whom oil represents more than 30 percent of their merchandise exports—13 are members of the Organization of Petroleum Exporting Countries (OPEC) and 13 are unaffiliated. (See Table 10.1.) These oil exporters have suffered a significant loss of revenues since prices fell in 1986. The net oil export earnings for OPEC members was $73.5 billion in 1986, half the amount collected three years before (22). After cutting production by 45 percent from 1979 levels, OPEC has increased production steadily since 1985, yet 1990 production was still 20 percent lower than 1979 (23). This volatility has shaken the economies of oil-exporting developing countries, severely restricting economic growth, limiting debt servicing for highly indebted countries such as Nigeria and Mexico, and impeding the transition to a diversified and developed post-oil economy. Most of the growth in oil consumption by developing countries was internal consumption within oil-exporting developing countries, caused by low domestic petroleum product

Figure 10.4 Commercial Energy Consumption in Developing Countries, 1970–89

A. All Developing Countries

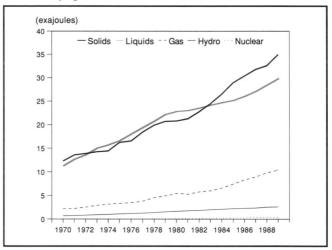

B. Oil-Exporting Developing Countries

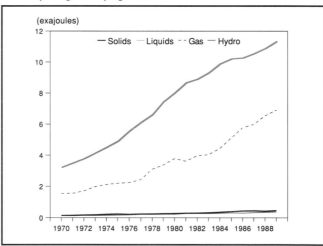

C. Oil-Importing Developing Countries

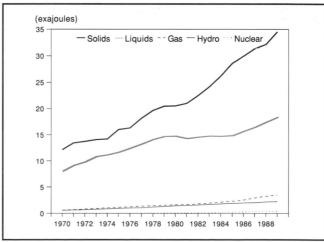

Source: United Nations Statistical Office, *Energy Statistics Yearbook* (United Nations, New York, 1991), and previous volumes.
Note: See Notes in Table 10.1 for definitions of terms.

Table 10.2 Proven Commercial Energy Reserves, 1987

(petajoules) {a}

| | Oil | | Natural Gas | | Coal | | | |
Region	Reserves	R/P {b} Years	Reserves	R/P {b} Years	Hard Coal Reserves	Soft Coal Reserves	R/P {b} Years	Total Reserves
World	**5,173,410**	**40**	**4,246,221**	**60**	**30,016,404**	**7,294,196**	**390**	**46,730,231**
Developing Countries	**4,484,707**	**62**	**2,014,035**	**155**	**20,889,320**	**1,883,035**	**658**	**29,271,097**
Oil-Exporting Developing	**4,274,759**	**72**	**1,780,387**	**187**	**83,869**	**40,008**	**269**	**6,179,023**
OPEC {c}	3,878,753	82	1,639,048	226	46,721	30,600	330	5,595,122
Non-OPEC Oil-Exporting Developing {d}	396,006	32	141,339	62	37,148	9,408	206	583,901
Oil-Importing Developing {e}	**209,948**	**16**	**233,648**	**67**	**20,805,451**	**1,843,027**	**663**	**23,092,074**
Africa Oil-Importing	16,371	26	27,732	1,699	1,745,882	977	429	1,790,962
Asia and Oceania Oil-Importing	151,414	17	166,183	72	18,762,143	1,805,405	700	20,885,145
Latin America Oil-Importing	42,163	12	39,733	34	297,426	36,645	467	415,967
Industrialized Countries	**688,703**	**12**	**2,232,186**	**39**	**9,127,084**	**5,411,161**	**238**	**17,459,134**
OECD Industrialized	**342,082**	**11**	**613,374**	**21**	**5,351,810**	**2,950,502**	**222**	**9,257,768**
North America {f}	223,795	10	322,178	15	3,259,972	1,471,440	201	5,277,385
Western Europe {g}	105,433	13	235,266	34	801,754	840,992	174	1,983,445
Pacific {h}	12,854	11	55,930	63	1,290,084	638,070	452	1,996,938
Non-OECD Industrialized	**346,621**	**13**	**1,618,812**	**57**	**3,775,274**	**2,460,659**	**262**	**8,201,366**
Central Europe	11,661	14	23,265	14	872,634	548,139	164	1,455,699
U.S.S.R.	334,960	13	1,595,547	59	2,902,640	1,912,520	319	6,745,667

Sources:

1. World Energy Conference (WEC), *1989 Survey of Energy Resources* (WEC, London, 1989).

2. United Nations Statistical Office, *Energy Statistics Yearbook* (United Nations, New York, 1991).

Notes: a. 1 petajoule (PJ) = 10^{15} joules = 947.8 x 10^9 Btus. Conversion factors: 1 million metric tons of oil equivalent = 41.87 PJ, 1 billion cubic meters natural gas = 38.84 PJ, 1 million metric tons of coal equivalent (hard coal) = 27.91 PJ, 1 million metric tons of coal equivalent (soft coal) = 13.96 PJ. b. R/P is the ratio of proven reserves to 1989 production rate. c. Algeria, Ecuador, Gabon, Indonesia, Iran, Iraq, Kuwait, Libya, Nigeria, Qatar, Saudi Arabia, United Arab Emirates, and Venezuela. d. Developing countries whose exports of petroleum and gas including reexports account for at least 30 percent of merchandise exports: Afghanistan, Angola, Bahrain, Bolivia, Brunei, the Congo, Egypt, Mexico, the Netherlands Antilles, Oman, Syria, Trinidad & Tobago, and Yemen. e. Also includes countries that are self sufficient in oil whose oil exports are less than 30 percent of merchandise exports. f. Canada and United States. g. Does not include Turkey, which is included in total for Asia and Oceania Oil-Importing. h. Australia, Japan, and New Zealand.
Totals may not add because of rounding.

prices, increased urbanization, and population growth. (See Figure 10.4B.) Natural gas plays an important supply role in only three oil-exporting developing countries: Algeria, Mexico, and Venezuela (24).

The remaining developing countries have generally benefited from lower oil prices. They include 11 countries that are self sufficient in oil and are minor exporters, 16 minor producers that still have to import a sizable share of their oil supply, and 63 nations that produce no oil and are completely dependent on imports (25). (See Chapter 21, "Energy and Materials," Table 21.2.) Oil demand for this group as a whole has followed price trends, with consumption slowing after the 1973 and 1979 price shocks and rebounding since 1986. (See Figure 10.4C.)

China, India, South Africa, and the Democratic People's Republic of Korea produce 92 percent of the coal from developing countries. These four countries are also responsible for the rapid increase in coal consumption shown in Figure 10.4C. Most of this coal is used in the industrial sector. In China, whose economy depends on coal for 73 percent of its energy needs, one quarter of all coal is burned for residential heating, contributing to severe urban air pollution (26).

Hydropower has expanded rapidly in Latin America; the region now accounts for one half of the hydro production in developing countries. (See Chapter 21, "Energy and Materials," Table 21.1.) Eight developing countries—India, Pakistan, the Republic of Korea, Taiwan, Argentina, Mexico, Brazil, and South Africa—also produce commercial electricity from nuclear

reactors. In late 1990, their total net capacity was 12,776 megawatts, or 4 percent of the world total (27).

Oil-importing developing countries face two major energy challenges. First, the cost of fuel forces countries to divert scarce funds away from the development of indigenous energy supply systems and away from urgently needed improvements in other sectors, such as health care or agriculture.

Second, because most of their people depend on traditional fuels, oil-importing developing countries must stimulate the modern sector of their economies to become less dependent on oil, while at the same time the traditional sector develops sustainable sources of traditional fuels or switches to modern fuels. An analysis of this transition in Southeast Asian nations found that the share of traditional fuels in total energy supply declined in all studied countries between 1970 and 1985. The total demand for traditional fuels, however, increased over that time period: by 30 to 40 percent in India, the Philippines, and Bangladesh; by 45 to 60 percent in Nepal, Malaysia, and Pakistan; and by 81 percent in Thailand. In a few countries—India, Nepal, the Philippines, and Malaysia—per capita consumption of traditional fuels declined, partly due to switching to other fuels, but this trend was offset by increases in population (28). These results indicate that—even in nations where per capita consumption of traditional fuels is declining and the transition to modern fuels is well underway—pressure to use forests and fragile landscape to satisfy energy needs continues, thus prolonging or exacerbating the fuelwood crisis.

ENERGY RESERVES

Proven reserves are those resources that, under existing conditions, can be extracted in the future with reasonable certainty, according to geological and engineering information. Proven *reserves* are a component of total energy *resources,* a broader measure that includes marginally economic and subeconomic reserves, either demonstrated or inferred. The following discussion is of proven reserves. (See Table 10.2.)

Coal. Coal is the most abundant of the three commercial fuel types and has a reserves-to-production ratio of 390 years. Over 60 percent of world coal reserves are found in developing countries, 50 percent in China alone. Among industrialized countries, the Soviet Union and the United States have the largest reserves, with 13 percent and 12 percent, respectively. Coal reserves in developing countries are very likely underestimated, because exploration activities have been less extensive (29).

Oil. The world's oil reserves stood at 124 billion metric tons, or 40 years at 1989 production levels. Developing countries account for over 86 percent of world reserves, with the majority found in oil-exporting countries. Proven reserves in industrialized countries were almost evenly divided between OECD and non-OECD, each group having a reserves-to-production ratio of a little over 10 years.

Gas. Developing and industrialized countries each share half of the world's natural gas reserves. The lower output level in the developing countries puts the reserves-to-production ratio at 155 years, compared to 39 years in industrialized countries. The Soviet Union has the world's largest natural gas reserve (38 percent of the total).

Hydropower. The development of large-scale hydropower projects in developing countries has been slowed by financial problems and social and environmental concerns. Only a small proportion of the potential hydropower in developing countries has been harnessed: 5 percent in Africa, 8 percent in Latin America, and 9 percent in Asia (30). China has tapped about 10 percent of its 378 gigawatt exploitable potential, the world's largest (31). A greater share of hydro potential has been developed in industrialized countries, including 26 percent in OECD countries and 52 percent in the United States. (See Chapter 22, "Freshwater," Table 22.2.)

FOCUS ON TECHNOLOGY COOPERATION IN ENERGY EFFICIENCY

ENERGY DEMAND AND ENERGY EFFICIENCY

The developing countries are expected to see the demand for energy more than triple between 1985 and 2025 (32). Rising demand for oil, particularly to meet transportation needs, will make developing countries important participants in the global demand for oil, but it will also leave them increasingly vulnerable to oil price shocks.

The capital requirements to meet these energy demands will grow correspondingly. Average annual expenditures for energy are projected to increase from $65 billion for the period 1990–2000 to $138 billion for the period 2000–25 (33). Financing for the electric sector from multilateral and bilateral agencies is expected to account for only $22.5 billion annually by 2008; total financing from these agencies is unlikely to meet more than 20 percent of the energy financing needs of developing countries (34). As energy investment crowds out productive investments in other sectors, the most likely results will be increased levels of indebtedness and a slowdown in economic expansion.

Rapid growth of the energy sector will also have substantial environmental consequences. Developing countries will experience significant increases in such regional pollutants as nitrogen oxides, hydrocarbons, carbon monoxide, and sulfur dioxide. (See Chapter 13, "Atmosphere and Climate.") Emissions of carbon dioxide (CO_2), a greenhouse gas, in developing countries are projected to at least double over the next 35 years (35). As a result, developing countries are expected to account for more than half of the global increase in CO_2 emissions by 2025 (36).

Pursuing energy development with "business-as-usual" strategies therefore offers developing countries a bleak view of the future: mounting debt, slow or stagnant economic growth, intensifying environmental pollution, and frequent oil crises to buffet their weak economies. The populations of these countries will not gain access to needed energy services such as lighting, refrigeration, and heating and cooling to the degree expected and promised. Many developing countries already face these problems, and with growing populations and greater capital constraints in the future, the problems will only increase.

Benefits of Increased Energy Efficiency

Increasing the efficiency of energy services is one mechanism for addressing these problems. This does not mean that energy supplies are reduced, nor that energy services are cut off. Rather, the energy required to provide a given service is reduced by improving the energy efficiency of that service, as for example, by providing refrigeration with more efficient compressors. This stretches energy supplies so that more people gain access to energy services.

There is room for substantial improvement in the efficiency of energy services in developing countries. The industrial sector accounted for about 50 percent of the final energy consumption in these countries in 1987; the transport sector, 22 percent; and buildings and agriculture, 29 percent (37). In the industrial sector, energy-intensive products such as steel, cement, chemicals, and paper account for much of the energy use (38). The energy efficiency of producing these materials is often much lower than in industrialized countries. For example, integrated steel plants in India and China—among the largest steel producers in the developing world—presently use, on average, 45 to 53 gigajoules per metric ton of steel produced (1 gigajoule = 10^9

Recent Developments

KUWAIT OIL FIELDS RECOVERING

The last of about 650 oil-well fires in Kuwait was extinguished on November 6, 1991, after eight months of intensive effort by firefighting crews from around the world. The fires were tamed months ahead of schedule with the help of a new technique involving liquid nitrogen (1).

Of Kuwait's 935 oil wells, 749 were damaged or sabotaged during the Persian Gulf War and 650 of those were either set ablaze or left gushing oil. The Kuwait Oil Company hired some 9,000 workers from 32 countries to get the wells back into production (2).

Before the war, Kuwait was capable of producing about 272,000 metric tons of oil per day (3). By early November 1991, production was about 44,200 metric tons per day. Kuwaiti government officials hope production will increase to about 54,000 metric tons per day by the end of 1991 and to 204,000 metric tons per day (about 75 percent of prewar capacity) by the end of 1992 (4). The war-damaged Mina al-Ahmadi refinery was nearly ready to resume production in September 1991 (5).

Kuwaiti government officials said the amount of crude oil lost could ultimately total as much as 3 percent of Kuwait's total proven reserves, or about 385 million metric tons. In January 1991, Kuwait reported estimated total reserves of about 12.8 billion metric tons (6).

Many experts initially thought it might take two to three years to put out the oil-well blazes. But the fires were extinguished far ahead of the most optimistic schedule, in part because of a new technique in which liquid nitrogen was sprayed onto the flames or pumped into metal sleeves placed atop the burning wells. The intensely cold liquid robbed the fires of oxygen (7).

The Kuwaiti government spent $1.5 billion to put out the fires, but reportedly saved $12 billion in losses by capping the wells three months ahead of schedule (8).

Though the fires were extinguished by November, much remained to be done. Kuwaiti officials said between 3.4 and 6.8 million metric tons of oil remaining in lakes around damaged wells must be drained. Residue from the oil lakes took an immense toll on the fragile desert environment, killing thousands of migratory birds, who often mistook the oil lakes for water (9).

SOVIET OIL PRODUCTION FALLS

The Soviet Union's oil industry slid perilously close to collapse during the political and economic turbulence of 1990 and 1991.

From May 1988 to March 1991, Soviet oil production dropped by about 250,000 metric tons per day, which is roughly equivalent to the entire flow of Kuwaiti oil lost after Iraq's invasion. Soviet oil exports in 1991 were expected to be less than half the level of the late 1980s. Even Soviet gas production, which experienced dramatic output gains in the late 1970s and 1980s, was eroding. Gas flow rose just 0.3 percent during the first quarter of 1991, much slower than gains registered in previous years (10).

A multitude of factors—technological, organizational, and political—have contributed to the oil and gas industry's problems. For example, ethnic unrest early in 1990 in Azerbaijan, which produces 60 percent of Soviet oil field equipment, caused equipment shortages (11). Following the breakup of the union in August and September 1991, coordination problems between republics threaten to further hurt oil and gas production.

ELECTRIC VEHICLES MOVE TOWARD COMMERCIALIZATION

Clean air laws and regulations in the United States are providing a significant new push for the commercial development of electric vehicles.

In California, the city of Los Angeles is sponsoring a competition to introduce electric vehicles. The Los Angeles Department of Water and Power and Southern California Edison are funding a $17 million effort to bring 10,000 electric vehicles into the area by 1995. The department received over 200 responses to its 1989 invitation for proposals and selected two companies to produce electric vehicles. Clean Air Transport, which is based in England and Sweden, will produce four-passenger cars with a range of 240 kilometers; Unique Mobility Inc., of Englewood, Colorado, will produce a mid-sized van with a range of 190 kilometers (12).

As many as 15 other U.S. states also are considering rules that would require the sale of low-emission and zero-emission vehicles (presumably electric vehicles) in the 1990s (13).

Meanwhile, many auto manufacturers are moving rapidly to develop electric vehicles. At least eight Japanese companies (including Nissan, Toyota, Mazda, and Suzuki) have developed intensive electric vehicle programs and introduced prototypes (14). Many European companies also are developing electric vehicles; BMW, for instance, introduced a new four-passenger electric car with a range of 250 kilometers at the 1991 Frankfurt Motor Show (15).

The principal technical problem for electric vehicles is the development of lower-cost batteries with faster recharge times, longer durability, and lower weight.

References and Notes

1. Jennifer Parmelee, "Kuwaiti Emir Snuffs Out Last Iraqi-Lit Oil Fire," *Washington Post* (November 7, 1991), p. A1.
2. Richard L. Holman, "Kuwait Dousing Halfway Done," *Wall Street Journal* (September 12, 1991, New York), p. A12.
3. "Kuwait's Last Oil-Well Fire From Gulf War is Put Out," *Wall Street Journal* (November 7, 1991, New York), p. A10.
4. *Op. cit.* 1. 4
5. "Kuwait's Oil Industry Slowly Recovering," *Oil and Gas Journal*, Vol. 89, No. 35 (September 2, 1991), p. 36.
6. "More Nations Join Kuwait Well Fire Campaign," *Oil and Gas Journal*, Vol. 89, No. 33 (August 19, 1991), p. 19.
7. *Op. cit.* 1.
8. *Op. cit.* 3.
9. *Op. cit.* 1.
10. "Soviet Oil Industry Woes May Extend Crisis," *Oil and Gas Journal*, Vol. 89, No. 22 (June 3, 1991), pp. 65-66.
11. *Ibid.*, p. 70.
12. Los Angeles Department of Water and Power (DWP), "Going Electric" (DWP, Los Angeles, June 1991), pp. 4-5.
13. "New York State EV Hearings Set," *Electric Vehicle Progress* (Sepember 1, 1991), p. 6.
14. "Japan Gears Up for EV Market With These Prototypes," *Electric Vehicle Progress* (September 1, 1991), p. 3.
15. "BMW Unveils New EV Prototype," *Electric Vehicle Progress* (September 15, 1991), p. 1.

joules) while plants in the United States and Japan generally use half as much energy (39). With proper design and operation, many new industrial plants in developing countries could reduce fuel consumption by 30 percent or more, and achieve considerably greater savings using state-of-the-art industrial processes (40).

The transport sector is generally the largest consumer of petroleum in developing countries, frequently accounting for more than 40 percent of oil consumption. Between 60 and 80 percent of transport fuel is consumed by vehicles; a major factor influencing transport fuel consumption is the growth in demand for passenger vehicles. Car ownership increased nearly 10 percent annually in developing countries in the 1970s and 5 percent annually in the 1980s (41). (See Chapter 17, "Land Cover and Settlements," Table 17.3.) These vehicles are often less energy efficient than those found in industrialized countries, however, and alternatives to individual car use—such as the mass transit systems found in Europe and Japan—have received little attention in the developing world, often because of lack of interest by funding agencies.

Buildings and agriculture are the fastest growing energy sectors, increasing by a combined rate of almost 6 percent per year during the 1973–86 period (42). Buildings in developing countries are often much less energy efficient than in industrialized countries. Opportunities to improve efficiency include better heating, cooling, and lighting equipment; appropriate use of energy controls; better insulation (particularly in cold climates); and the use of reflective roof coatings, shading, and natural lighting (particularly for warm climates).

The major uses of energy for agriculture include irrigation pumping, tractors, and post-harvest drying and curing, all of which frequently operate below efficiency levels common in industrialized countries. In Pakistan, for example, the tubewell pumps used to irrigate field crops operate at only 30 percent of the average efficiency that is technically achievable; a 20 percent improvement could be achieved in these systems through cost-effective retrofits (43).

Extrapolations show that even a modest increase in energy efficiency could have major benefits for developing countries. Conservation measures could significantly reduce projected increases in energy consumption (by 25 percent), capital expenditures on energy (by 50 percent), and CO_2 emissions (by 30 percent), by 2025 (44). However, there are major barriers to increased energy efficiency. The 1979 oil crisis prompted industrialized countries to reduce energy intensity by developing more energy-efficient products and strategies, but few of these techniques have been established effectively in developing countries. Indeed, until recently there was a prevailing belief that energy efficiency was a strategy applicable only to the relatively stable economies of the developed world rather than the rapidly growing economies of the developing world.

It should be noted that the countries of Central Europe face many of the same energy problems as developing countries. They, too, face rapidly rising energy demand, with a resultant increase in debt, constraints on capital, and growing environmental threats. The efficiency with which energy services are provided is well below that achieved in the rest of the industrialized world, and thus energy efficiency offers substantial opportunities in these countries as well. However, the economic structure of Central European countries are quite different from those of developing nations, so they will not be treated in this section. Nevertheless, many of the following options for technology cooperation in energy efficiency are also applicable to Central Europe. (See Chapter 5, "Regional Focus: Central Europe.")

Least-Cost Energy Planning

Developing countries have traditionally viewed energy conservation either as unwanted energy curtailment, or as a strategy that can make only a marginal difference in future energy demand. Rarely has conservation been viewed as a resource in itself that can be directly integrated into energy planning. This approach is gaining increasing legitimacy in industrialized countries, however, and its first widespread application in U.S. and Canadian electric sectors is resulting in dramatic reductions in the need to build new power plants.

This approach, known as "integrated resource" electric planning or least-cost utility planning, involves an effort to develop and implement a power resource acquisition strategy *at the lowest possible cost*. Conservation or demand-management resources are treated on a par with supply resources. The process involves forecasting future energy service needs (e.g., lighting or heating) for each energy end-use sector, and then estimating the costs of meeting those needs through a variety of supply or conservation resources (including improvements in the efficiency of the services needed). Finally, a "supply" curve is erected, in which the least costly options are purchased first (45).

Although this approach has been used extensively by the electric sector in North America, knowledge of least-cost utility planning is lacking in most developing countries. There are some exceptions: analyses of this type have already been done for Brazil, Costa Rica, Jamaica, Karnataka State in India, and Thailand (46) (47) (48) (49) (50). The impact of this approach can be substantial. In a preliminary analysis of Thailand, projections show that power demand in the year 2000 could be reduced significantly by a strong conservation policy that emphasizes improved efficiency of electric end-use services (51).

The integrated resource approach to energy planning is not fully developed. Even in the electric sector, differences of opinion remain on such issues as how to measure and price conserved energy. Nevertheless, the approach remains a powerful tool for integrating energy efficiency into energy planning. And because this approach inevitably requires local adaptation, analysts and planners in developing countries need only learn the general principles—how energy conservation supply curves are constructed and integrated with energy supply options—rather than highly detailed formulations for applying the approach in specific instances. This involves the development of written materials as well as training in the computer applications of this technique. A 10-day training course on end-use-oriented energy analysis, held in Thailand in 1989 for academics and government and utility officials, is a rare example of the type of transfer process required (52).

New Modes of Technology Cooperation

Technology cooperation has traditionally been viewed as a process of moving technologies developed in the industrialized world to the developing world. However, changing world conditions, the diffuse nature of energy efficiency implementation, and the structural differences between the industrialized world and the developing world render this simplistic approach outdated. In fact, successful technology cooperation involves a variety of techniques, including improved

Box 10.1 The Refrigerator Factor: A Model Technology Cooperation Issue

As demand for refrigerators, air conditioners, and similar products begins to rise in developing countries, so do concerns for the environmental effects of meeting this demand. Aside from the obvious implications for the energy sector, the rising number of cooling devices in developing countries poses a serious threat to the stratospheric ozone layer unless alternatives to present refrigerant technology—which is based on ozone-destroying chlorofluorocarbons (CFCs)—are made available (1). Refrigeration is the largest and fastest-growing use of CFCs in the developing world.

CFC alternatives pose a critical test case for the much broader issues of technology cooperation between industrialized and developing countries. If the sharply focused problem of affordable CFC alternatives for the developing world cannot be solved, there may be little hope of resolving the much thornier problems of providing energy-efficient technology to developing countries to minimize future carbon emissions (2).

THE MONTREAL PROTOCOL

The international community has taken unprecedented steps to control and ultimately ban the production of CFCs and other ozone-depleting substances (ODSs) —such as halons and carbon tetrachloride—by the year 2000. The Vienna Convention and the subsequent Montreal Protocol on Substances That Deplete the Ozone Layer, adopted in 1987 and strengthened in 1990, set strict timetables for phasing out CFCs and other ODSs by 2000 and established rules governing international trade in ODSs and products based on these materials (3). In late 1991, new scientific evidence that the ozone is thinning more quickly than predicted prompted calls to speed up the phase out (4). (See Chapter 13, "Atmosphere and Climate.")

About 70 nations (representing over 90 percent of global CFC production and consumption) had signed the convention by July 1991. Some 30 of the signatories are developing nations, several of which, including Egypt and Mexico, were among the first to ratify the treaty and take steps to comply (5) (6). In many ways, these developing nations face a more formidable task in reforming their CFC use than nations with greater financial and technological means. In recognition of their special circumstances, the Montreal Protocol allows developing nations a 10-year grace period before full compliance is required (7).

Nonetheless, many developing nations remain skeptical of the Montreal Protocol and have refused to sign the treaty. Leaders in these countries fear the expense of switching to ozone-friendly technology.

Nearly 90 percent of the cost of complying with the Montreal Protocol will derive from conversion of refrigeration equipment (8).

In response to this concern, the treaty was amended in 1990 to create a $160 million fund, financed by the largest CFC users, to compensate developing countries for the added costs they incur in following a CFC-free path. The establishment of this multilateral fund demonstrates a recognition that rapid compliance by developing countries is essential to the treaty's success, even though these countries now account for only about 16 percent of total CFC consumption (9).

Behind this recognition are several compelling facts. CFC molecules are long-lived and remarkably efficient at ozone depletion—a single CFC molecule can participate in the destruction of 100,000 ozone molecules (10). Thus, even relatively low levels of CFC emissions can have far-reaching effects. A number of developing countries are poised to boost their CFC consumption significantly in the next decade as their economies expand unless suitable alternatives are made available in the next few years.

China and India are cases in point. Between them, they represent about 40 percent of the world's population, but consume only 5 percent of all CFCs (11). That could change quickly if the goal of supplying refrigerators to their citizens is met with units that use CFC-based technology. In India, where refrigeration accounts for nearly 75 percent of all CFC use (12), the number of refrigerators is expected to reach almost 80 million units by 2010, up from just over only 6 million in 1989 (13). In China, the current total of 30 million refrigerators is expected to almost double by 1996, with production capacity reaching over 11 million units per year (14). Hence the concern that these nations' development goals be met in an environmentally sound manner.

To address this concern, Protocol signatories agreed to increase the multilateral fund to $240 million if India and China signed the Protocol, with the extra $80 million reserved for the use of the two nations and other new signatories (15). With this incentive, China declared in June 1991 that it would sign the amended Protocol, scheduled to take effect January 1, 1992 (16).

THE CHALLENGE OF TECHNOLOGY COOPERATION

Alternatives have been found for many of the major product applications of CFCs. However, instituting these alternatives in developing countries will require the direct assistance of the private sector in industrialized countries, where the ownership of these technologies and the exper-

tise to apply them often resides (17) (18). Significantly, the industrial sectors in some developing countries—Mexico, Brazil, Egypt, and China, for example—also have important technology to share, so the flow of technology between industrialized and developing regions could go both directions. However, although an unprecedented level of technical exchange is expected—some of it free of charge—no one expects the process of technology transfer to be painless or without cost (19) (20).

For example, the use of CFC-like substitutes that break down more quickly in the atmosphere is expected to be a popular strategy in industrialized nations, because it will reduce overall disruption of manufacturing processes that rely on CFCs (21). But transferring this "drop-in" technology to developing nations involves overcoming some serious obstacles. First, the immediate cost is bound to be high, because the new chemicals are likely to sell for three to five times as much as CFCs, at least initially (22). More importantly, most of these new chemicals are proprietary substances, with patent rights held by international chemical manufacturers who have invested heavily in research and development and expect a profitable return. Negotiations for licensing agreements may be contentious, with developing nations fighting to minimize or avoid royalty payments altogether (23).

India, for example, has a robust chemical industry with a tradition of supplying its domestic chemical needs, including all of its own CFCs. Patent protection has lapsed on most CFC production technology, so India currently pays no royalties to produce its CFC supply. Hoping to preserve this situation, it has pressed particularly hard for free access to the technology behind CFC substitutes. However, the international chemical producers who own the new technology view the Indian chemical industry as an able competitor and do not wish to forego access to the Indian market (24) (25).

Fortunately, the multilateral fund established under the Montreal Protocol can be used to purchase patent rights and pay royalties, although negotiating discounts for such payments will undoubtedly be important in light of the fund's limited budget. Presumably, some or all of India's share of the fund (should it sign the Convention) could be used for this purpose (26) (27). China, on the other hand, is reported to be well on its way to developing its own CFC substitute (28), so its use of the multilateral fund will probably differ markedly.

Avoiding expensive CFC substitutes may be a more attractive alternative for many developing nations. Some observers think that the chemical industry has placed too much emphasis on these exotic compounds, skewing the search for CFC alternatives away from lower-cost, less glamorous options (29). Yet such options do exist. For example, ammonia-based refrigeration systems (which predate CFC technology) offer several advantages, including an abundant and royalty-free supply of the chemical and an energy efficiency superior to CFC—a factor that may eventually weigh heavily in its favor in the years ahead (30). Disadvantages center on safety concerns: ammonia is toxic and flammable, which could make it inappropriate for domestic applications, especially in densely populated or earthquake-prone areas. Nonetheless, many large commercial ammonia refrigeration systems exist today, and commercial applications could be expanded in the future (31) (32).

Another promising alternative to CFCs for low-cost refrigeration is propane. Like ammonia, it is cheap, plentiful, and more energy efficient than CFC refrigerants. Propane can be used in standard refrigerators but performs better when installed in a specially designed unit, where as little as 10 milliliters are needed. Like ammonia, however, propane is an older technology and therefore suffers from an image problem that has kept it from being seriously reconsidered, despite technical advances that have improved its efficiency and safety (33).

Without underestimating the magnitude of the challenge or the obstacles, most observers are impressed by the progress to date and hopeful that the sense of global urgency surrounding the CFC issue—together with technical cooperation and financial aid—will lead to success (34) (35) (36). Many developing countries are already acting to phase out CFCs, rather than exercising the full 10-year grace period permitted under the Protocol (37). By 1990, for instance, the Mexican government had already negotiated agreements with both CFC producers and major CFC-consuming industries to sharply curtail CFC use (38).

Observers also believe that market forces will help the process. Over time, CFC substitutes will grow less expensive, and expertise in adapting these alternatives to local conditions will grow. The private sector will undoubtedly view the switch to CFC alternatives as an economic opportunity and will form joint ventures with developing country manufacturers, providing needed capital for equipment redesign and retooling in hopes of tapping future demand for consumer items in the developing world (39) (40). In the meantime, the Protocol's trade restrictions will make it more difficult for nonsignatory nations to import or export CFC-containing prod-

ucts. A country such as India, which hopes to expand its refrigerator exports, could find itself frozen out of lucrative markets if it does not sign the Protocol (41).

Finally, as mentioned above, developing countries themselves have already begun to provide substantial innovations in the search for alternatives to CFCs, and experts expect that they will act increasingly as the source of shared technologies rather than passive recipients (42). For example, Mexico is a recognized leader in adopting alternate propellants for use in aerosol spray cans (43), and Brazil has recently developed a more efficient refrigerator compressor (44). China has also conducted substantial research into substitute refrigerants and is currently testing refrigerators equipped with a range of substitutes, including one that is different than the compound expected to dominate the U.S. and European markets (45).

References and Notes

1. Armin Rosencranz and Reina Milligan, "CFC Abatement: The Needs of Developing Countries," *Ambio*, Vol. 19, No. 6-7 (1990), pp. 312-315.
2. "Intellectual Property and Technology Transfer: An Uneasy Relationship," *Global Environmental Change Report*, Vol. 2, No. 18 (Cutter Information Corp., Arlington, Virginia, September 28, 1990), pp. 1-2.
3. United Nations Environment Programme (UNEP), *Report of the Second Meeting of the Parties to the Montreal Protocol on Substances That Deplete the Ozone Layer* (UNEP, Nairobi, Kenya, June 1990), pp. 1-68.
4. R. Davis and B. Rosewicz, "Panel Sees Ozone Thinning, Intensifying Political Heat," *Wall Street Journal* (October 23, 1991), p. B1.
5. Arno Rosemarin, "Some Background on CFCs," *Ambio*, Vol. 19, No. 6-7 (1990), p. 280.
6. Elizabeth Crool, Project Manager, Technology Transfer and Industry Program, Division of Global Change, U. S. Environmental Protection Agency, Washington, D.C., 1991 (personal communication).
7. *Op. cit.* 3, p. 31.
8. Debora MacKenzie, "Cheaper Alternatives for CFCs," *New Scientist* (June 30, 1990), p. 39.
9. *Op. cit.* 1, pp. 312-313.
10. F. Sherwood Rowland, "Stratospheric Ozone Depletion by Chlorofluorocarbons," *Ambio*, Vol. 19, No. 6-7 (1990), p. 281.
11. *Op. cit.* 1, p. 312.
12. *Op. cit.* 8.
13. Touche Ross Management Consultants, *Reducing Consumption of Ozone Depleting Substances in India; Phase 1: The Cost of Complying With the Montreal Protocol* (Touche Ross Consultants, London, England, 1990), p. 55.

14. Ivar Isaksen, Lindsey Roke, and Michael Fergus, *Report of a United Nations Development Programme Mission to Investigate Ozone Layer Protection in China* (National Environmental Protection Agency, Beijing, 1990), Sections 4.1.3-5, and 4.4.1.
15. Bureau of National Affairs (BNA), "Parties to Montreal Protocol Agree to Phase Out CFCs, Help Developing Nations," *International Environment Reporter* (BNA, Rockville, Maryland, July 1990), p. 275.
16. Stephen Seidel, Deputy Director, Global Change Division, U.S. Environmental Protection Agency, Washington, D.C., 1991 (personal communication).
17. *Op. cit.* 10, p. 288.
18. Renee Hancher, Manager of International Trade, Air Conditioning and Refrigeration Institute, Arlington, Virginia, 1991 (personal communication).
19. *Ibid.*
20. Kevin Fay, Executive Director, Alliance for Responsible CFC Policy, Arlington, Virginia, March 1991 (personal communication).
21. John S. Hoffman, "Replacing CFCs: The Search for Alternatives," *Ambio*, Vol. 19, No. 6 (1990), pp. 329-333.
22. *Op. cit.* 8.
23. *Op. cit.* 2.
24. *Op. cit.* 2.
25. *Op. cit.* 1, p. 315.
26. *Op. cit.* 2, p. 2.
27. Alan Miller, Executive Director, Center for Global Change, College Park, Maryland, March 1991 (personal communication).
28. *Op. cit.* 14, Sections 4.8.1-3.
29. *Op. cit.* 8.
30. *Op. cit.* 14, Section 6.6.5.
31. *Op. cit.* 10, pp. 288-289.
32. *Op. cit.* 6.
33. *Op. cit.* 8, p. 40.
34. *Op. cit.* 6.
35. *Op. cit.* 6.
36. *Op. cit.* 1, p. 315.
37. *Op. cit.* 6.
38. Mexican Secretariat for Urban Development and Ecology, Mexican Chamber of Industries, and U.S. Environmental Protection Agency, *Case Study of the Cost to Mexico of Protecting the Ozone Layer* (United Nations Environment Programme, Nairobi, Kenya, 1990), pp. 12-13.
39. Guy D. Phillips, "CFCs in the Developing Nations: A Major Economic Development Opportunity. Will the Institutions Help or Hinder?" *Ambio*, Vol. 19, No. 6-7 (1990), pp. 316-319.
40. *Op. cit.* 1, p. 314.
41. *Op. cit.* 1, pp. 313-314.
42. *Op. cit.* 6.
43. Deanna Richards, Senior Program Officer, Technology and Environment, National Academy of Engineering, Washington, D.C., 1991 (personal communication).
44. Howard S. Geller, *Efficient Energy Use: A Development Strategy for Brazil* (American Council for an Energy-Efficient Economy, Washington, D.C., 1991), pp. 26-27, 129.
45. *Op. cit.* 14, Sections 4.8.1-3.

information dissemination; expanded export, licensing, and joint venture activities; joint technology development; and the establishment of model programs. (See Box 10.1.)

ENERGY EFFICIENCY DATA BASES AND CLEARINGHOUSES

Once they decide to integrate energy efficiency into energy planning, developing countries need information on the energy efficient technologies available. Many, if not most, of these technologies are not presently available in developing countries. Thus, there is a need for reliable, impartial information on available products, including a detailed description of the technology itself, real-world examples of how it is applied, projected energy savings, range of costs, how to get access to the product, and a list of further readings about the specific technology.

In response to the oil crises of the 1970s, many industrialized countries established data bases or clearinghouses that contain information on energy-efficient technologies, but their usefulness to developing countries has been very limited:

■ Most of these data bases are tailored to industrialized country users. The information they contain has limited application to other countries, and some are not even in languages that can be easily understood by developing country users.

■ Many data bases do not determine the quality of the information they provide, and some contain purely bibliographic information with little additional analysis.

■ Access to some of these data bases is limited to industrialized countries.

■ Even where access is not limited, most of the available data bases make little effort to "market" their products in developing countries.

■ Even the few data bases specifically oriented to developing country users tend to be biased in favor of "appropriate," low-technology options (e.g., wood stoves) aimed largely at the rural sector, rather than high-technology applications for the modern sectors of developing countries (53).

The International Institute for Energy Conservation has a catalogue designed for developing country users with information on specific data in existing technology data bases, how these data are reviewed, and how to access such information (54). Another effort to address the shortcomings of existing technology data bases launched by Lund University, with initial support from Vattenfall, the Swedish State Power Board, is "The Technology Menu for Efficient End Use of Energy" (55). Designed as a "first-stop" information resource for a broad range of energy decisionmakers, it presents technology descriptions, technical and cost data, and illustrative economic analyses, with an emphasis on advanced technology and advances in existing technologies. Although initially targeted to Sweden, its developers intend to orient the Technology Menu to developing country users: indeed, Princeton University is adapting and expanding the Technology Menu for application to India.

Even when information on energy-efficient technologies is available, technology dissemination will be limited unless information is also available on the policies that will create demand for the technologies. No such data base currently exists. As part of its charter, the International Energy Agency, whose membership consists largely of industrialized countries, publishes annual reports on the energy policies and programs of member countries (56). These reports include a section on energy conservation, but the descriptions lack detail and there is no independent verification of their accuracy. Many governments use the reports to publicize intentions rather than actions. Finally, there is no analysis on the effectiveness of the policies, particularly, how much energy has been saved. To address this need, the International Institute for Energy Conservation is preparing a policy data base that will focus initially on four subjects: least-cost utility planning; policies to promote energy efficiency in buildings; policies to promote energy efficiency in appliances; and policies to promote energy efficiency in motor vehicles (57).

EXPORTS, LICENSING, AND JOINT VENTURES

Energy-Efficient Imports and Exports

Even when information on technologies and policies is available, these technologies may still not be accessible in many countries. Most of these technologies have evolved in industrialized countries, and the companies that produce them have focused on domestic markets for several reasons. First, there is a widespread perception that developing countries are not interested in improving energy efficiency. Second, there is both a lack of knowledge about how to market in developing countries and a sense that exporting to them is difficult. The sizable tariffs placed on imported goods by many of these countries is often cited as an example of this difficulty. Third, potential exporters are discouraged by the small market for energy-utilizing goods (e.g., lamps and refrigerators), whether efficient or inefficient, in developing countries. Finally, many of these companies, especially the smaller ones, simply do not have the capacity to market goods in these countries.

Compared to the energy supply industry, the energy efficiency industry is diffuse, highly disaggregated, and poorly organized. In the United States, for example, the energy efficiency industry has not yet formed a consolidated trade association. Nevertheless, the potential market for energy efficiency exports to developing countries is substantial. For example, a recent study estimated that an investment of $20 billion would be required to meet the technical energy conservation potential of India, one of the largest developing countries (58).

A variety of options exist to address export problems. From the perspective of the industrialized countries, one mechanism for creating demand for energy-efficient products and services without requiring individual companies to market their products is to develop lists of product and service vendors and make them available in developing countries. In Tunisia, for example, such a list is being compiled for many European vendors (59). Briefings for companies on specific market opportunities in specific countries would also be useful, in addition to trade missions for energy efficiency vendors. Both approaches have been used to a limited extent by both the U.S. and California governments.

Another mechanism for industrialized countries would be to target assistance to meet the financing and insurance needs of energy efficiency vendors working in developing countries. Many programs assist smaller businesses in marketing overseas, but few have specifically targeted the energy efficiency industry. Finally, new institutions could be created to facilitate the marketing of energy efficiency products which go beyond the capabilities of individual companies. For example, energy efficiency export trading companies could be established. Several energy efficiency vendors have attempted to use generic export trading companies to market their products. These trading companies, the most dominant and largest of which are Japanese, were created to facilitate export activity, particularly by smaller companies that do not have the resources to market widely in other countries nor to establish relationships with local enterprises in each country that will be responsible for selling their goods. Unfortunately, the experience to date with trading companies by energy efficiency vendors has not been good. Training for the product purchasers on how to use—or even program—energy efficiency products frequently is required, particularly if system design changes are required; this is a capability most trading companies lack. Trading companies with specific expertise in energy efficiency products could potentially address this problem.

From the perspective of the developing countries, reducing tariffs for energy-efficient goods and services is an important strategy for encouraging imports. India and Thailand have both developed policies to reduce tariffs on selected energy-efficient products (60) (61). Another critical mechanism is for the governments of developing countries to indicate their interest in seeing energy-efficient imports, and to invite trade missions of companies to explore the import potential. A trade mission of U.S. companies to Thailand in April 1991, for example, resulted from a request by the Thai government to a U.S. government agency (62).

Licensing and Joint Ventures

However beneficial they might initially be, imports of energy-efficient products can only be a transitional strategy. As the internal market for these products grows, the governments of developing countries are likely to want more of the benefits to accrue to their own economies in the form of increased domestic employment and industrial capacity. For effective technology cooperation to occur, therefore, both licensing and joint venture production of those goods needs to evolve.

Many of the strategies described above to encourage exports and imports of energy-efficient products could also be used to encourage licensing and joint manufacturing ventures. Industrialized country governments could also provide investment and insurance assistance to energy efficiency companies seeking to undertake such arrangements. At the same time, developing countries could offer interested companies detailed information about how to set up joint ventures and licensing arrangements.

JOINT DEVELOPMENT

Direct export and eventual licensing or joint manufacturing of products can address many issues of energy efficiency in developing countries, but not all of them. Circumstances in developing countries can be so completely different from industrialized countries that products developed for the latter are not directly applicable to the former. For example, many developing countries have a problem maintaining the voltage levels of their power supply; voltage fluctuations can be frequent and substantial. As a result, energy-efficient electric products developed for industrialized countries, where voltage regulation is generally not a problem, may not function effectively in developing countries. Products that are affected include many motors, appliances, and lamps.

In addition, some of the most promising technologies for specific industries in developing countries are not likely to be developed in industrialized countries, regardless of their benefits (including energy efficiency), and thus will never be available for export to developing countries. In response to market demands, industrialized economies are moving away from heavy, energy-intensive industries toward more service-oriented industries. Companies in the industrialized countries may be unwilling to develop innovations that promise energy savings for heavier industries when they face declining demand and revenues in this area. Examples include the plasmasmelt process for steelmaking (which improves energy efficiency through the use of a very high temperature plasma for the final reduction of iron ore) and the use of biomass-integrated gasifiers and steam injected gas turbines for sugar processing (which convert waste residue to energy, with the potential of producing more than 600 kilowatt-hours of electricity per metric ton of cane processed) (63) (64).

A growing trend in the developing world is to import manufactured products from other developing countries. Indeed, exports of machinery and transport equipment from developing countries have increased nearly 50-fold since 1970, growing from 2 to 10 percent of total world output (65). Many of these products are unique to developing countries—the three-wheeled bajaj of India is an example. They fill an important niche for the importing countries, particularly the poorer ones that cannot afford to import similar but more expensive products from the industrialized countries. The most significant exporters of these products to other developing countries are Brazil and Mexico, although India and China are rising in importance (66) (67).

As a result, the flow is no longer just from industrialized to developing countries. Instead, several tiers of technology flows are evolving: from industrialized

Box 10.2 The Flow of Energy-Efficient Products from Developing to Developed Countries

While most of the capacity for producing energy-efficient products is in industrialized countries, there are notable exceptions where products are manufactured in developing countries almost exclusively for use in industrialized countries. Embraco, a subsidiary of the Brazilian company Brasmotor, manufactures one of the most energy-efficient compressors available in refrigerators in the United States. The Embraco compressor, which was developed in response to American energy efficiency standards, cannot be used directly in the Brazilian market because it cannot withstand the voltage fluctuations characteristic of that market. The company has not yet attempted to upgrade its compressor for use in its home market because of a perceived lack of mar-

ket demand. Nevertheless, some characteristics of the U.S.-bound compressor have been incorporated into Embraco's domestic products, with a 10 to 15 percent improvement in efficiency [1].

Another example is Philips Mexico, which produces 6 million compact fluorescent lamps annually at its Monterrey plant, mostly for the U.S. market. Only about 200,000 per year are sold in Mexico; the reason, according to Philips, is the high initial cost of the lamps. The company has not found substantial problems with voltage fluctuations, particularly in the urban regions where they would be targeted. To stimulate domestic demand for the lamps, Philips Mexico has engaged in some demonstration programs of compact fluorescents. In all cases, the demon-

strations have been small: 500 lamps in Puebla, near Mexico City; 750 in Hermosill on the Pacific coast; and 29 on a chicken farm in Culiacon, also near Mexico City. In each case, the lamps were provided to the Comision Federal de Electricidad, the national electric utility, which then gave the lamps to participants [2].

References and Notes

1. Howard S. Geller, *Efficient Energy Use: A Development Strategy for Brazil* (American Council for an Energy-Efficient Economy, Washington, D.C., 1991), pp. 26-27, 129.

2. Christine Eibs Singer, Senior Associate, La Rocco Associates, New York, 1991 (personal communication).

countries to wealthier developing countries; from wealthier to poorer developing countries; and, in some instances, from developing to developed countries. (See Box 10.2.) A strategy that focuses only on exporting, licensing, or establishing joint manufacturing ventures for products developed in industrialized countries fails to recognize this new reality.

A promising alternative is the creation of joint technology research and development efforts between developed and developing countries, with the goal of bringing the necessary products to market. Both sides bring important qualities to the table: industrialized countries tend to have more expertise in high-technology areas; developing countries have more expertise in the product needs of their regions and the conditions under which the products must operate, as well as the manufacturing experience of designing and producing technologies that meet these needs. Joint technology development programs are not appropriate for all developing countries because they require strong research capabilities and sufficient manufacturing experience for domestic and export markets. At a minimum, however, the largest developing countries—China, India, Brazil, Indonesia, and Mexico—should all be candidates for joint technology development ventures, as should many of the heavily industrialized Central European nations. Other smaller but rapidly industrializing and export-oriented countries, such as Thailand, Malaysia, and Chile, would also be appropriate candidates.

Unfortunately, there are currently very few joint technology development ventures between developed and developing countries, much less any that focus on energy efficiency needs. India has been an exception: with funding from the U.S. Agency for International Development (U.S. AID), the Program for Advancement of Commercial Technology (PACT) was established in the 1980s with the goal of accelerating the pace and quality of technological innovation in prod-

ucts and processes relevant to the economic development of India. Administered by the Industrial Credit and Investment Corporation of India, which has also provided some of the investment capital, PACT provides grants to support up to 50 percent of the costs of Indo-U.S. joint venture research and development projects aimed at producing commercially viable products or processes. If the product or process is successfully commercialized, the joint venture partners must repay 200 percent of the grant through royalty fees based on gross product sales. A total of $6.8 million has been invested in 18 projects, ranging from food processing to developing a cathode ray controller for Indian-language computer terminals [68]. Based on the positive response to the PACT program, U.S. AID helped support a second technology development program in 1987 aimed solely at the Indian energy sector. Known as the Program for Commercial Energy Research (PACER), it has a budget of $20 million [69]. Energy efficiency projects are eligible for both the PACT and PACER programs.

MODEL PROGRAMS

Because energy efficiency requires related actions from many participants, the successful initial transfer of a specific energy-efficient technology to a developing country does not automatically ensure its widespread adoption. The progress in energy efficiency achieved in industrialized countries following the oil crises of the 1970s resulted from a variety of policies and programs to spur the adoption of efficient products. These have included higher energy prices, differential pricing on products according to their energy efficiency, efficiency standards, the encouragement of energy service companies (which contract with a facility to assume its energy management, invest in energy conservation, and then draw their profits from the savings), and the establishment of electric utility-based least-cost or integrated resource planning.

At present, few of these policies have been translated into action in developing countries, nor have many of these countries had the opportunity to develop unique programs of their own. As already noted, some countries are considering the possible implementation of least-cost utility planning. Building and/or appliance energy efficiency standards are being considered by a variety of countries, including Jamaica, Thailand, Malaysia, the Philippines, Indonesia, and Brazil [70] [71] [72]. Other strategies are being pursued in Tunisia, Brazil, Pakistan, and Hungary [73]. However, in all these cases, the countries lack models in other developing countries that they can follow. The creation of such models would go far in assisting the adoption of policies that could lead to the widespread implementation of energy efficiency technologies.

In particular, models are needed in the transport sector. This sector is the largest or second-largest consumer of energy in most developing countries, and the single largest consumer of oil, yet energy efficiency efforts have lagged badly. In transportation more than any other sector, translating the experiences of industrialized countries to developing countries is problematic because the conditions are so different. One unique transportation model that has not yet been sufficiently analyzed is the experience of Curitiba, Brazil. Beginning in the 1960s, the city pursued an aggressive program of mass transit development combined with land-use planning. Five dedicated bus lanes radiate out from the city center, connecting feeder buses that move between the arteries and local buses that serve local neighborhoods. Major residential and commercial development has been limited to areas near these arteries. Seventy percent of Curitiba's population now uses the system [74], and despite the fact that per capita automobile ownership is among the highest in Brazil, fuel consumption per vehicle is among the lowest [75].

FUTURE DIRECTIONS

The United Nations Conference on Environment and Development, to be held in Brazil in 1992, will have as one of its major themes the successful transfer to developing countries of environmentally sustainable technologies. However, the traditional view of how to transfer technology between industrialized and developing countries does not really apply to technology cooperation in energy efficiency. The export of products manufactured in industrialized countries is an important factor in improving energy efficiency in developing countries, particularly in the near term. If these products are to be widely used within developing countries, however, they must eventually be manufactured there. Because so many of the technologies needed in the developing countries do not exist in the developed countries, there is also a need for joint technology development programs. Finally, there is a need for information and model programs to create widespread awareness of and demand for these technologies.

Conditions and Trends was written by Norbert Henninger, World Resources research analyst. Focus On Technology Cooperation in Energy Efficiency was written by Deborah Lynn Bleviss, executive director of the International Institute for Energy Conservation, Washington, D.C. Box 10.1 was written by Gregory Mock, a California-based author.

References and Notes

1. United Nations Statistical Office, *U.N. Energy Tape* (United Nations, New York, May 1991) (on diskette).

2. *Ibid.*

3. There are two conventions to convert primary electricity production (geothermal, hydro, nuclear, and wind) in energy balances: *conventional fuel equivalent* and *physical energy input*. Conventional fuel equivalent is defined as the quantity of fossil fuels required to generate a given quantity of electricity in a conventional thermal power plant, assuming 30 percent efficiency. Physical energy input assesses electricity production at its heat value (1 kilowatt hour = 3.6 million joules). The data in the present chapter and Chapter 21, "Energy and Materials," account for primary electricity using the physical energy input convention. Studies that use conventional fuel equivalents yield slightly different totals and production shares.

4. *Op. cit.* 1.

5. *Op. cit.* 1.

6. United Nations, *Energy Issues and Options for Developing Countries* (Taylor and Francis, New York, 1989), p. 130.

7. Organisation for Economic Co-operation and Development (OECD), *The State of the Environment* (OECD, Paris, 1991), p. 226.

8. *Ibid.*, p. 236.

9. *Op. cit.* 1.

10. *Op. cit.* 7, pp. 222 and 225.

11. World Resources Institute in collaboration with the United Nations Environment Programme and the United Nations Development Programme, *World Resources 1990-91* (Oxford University Press, New York, 1990), p. 145.

12. United Nations Conference on Trade and Development (UNCTAD), *UNCTAD Commodity Yearbook 1990* (United Nations, New York, 1990), pp. 5, 46.

13. Jeremy Russell, "Environmental Issues in Eastern Europe: Setting an Agenda" (Royal Institute of International Affairs and World Conservation Union, London, 1990), p. 28.

14. R. Caron Cooper and Lee Schipper, "Energy Use and Conservation in the U.S.S.R.: Patterns, Prospects, and Problems," *Energy* (Pergamon, Elmsford, New York, forthcoming).

15. International Energy Agency, *World Energy Outlook* (Organisation for Economic Co-operation and Development, Paris, 1982), p. 180.

16. "Moscow Plans to Triple Nuclear Energy Capacity," *Financial Times*, May 29, 1991, n.p.

17. International Energy Agency, *World Energy Statistics and Balances: 1985-1988* (Organisation for Economic Co-operation and Development, Paris, 1990), pp. 308-332.

18. Karen Schmidt, "Industrial Countries' Responses to Global Climate Change" (Environmental and Energy Study Institute, Washington, D.C., 1991), p. 7.

19. *Op. cit.* 1.

20. *Op. cit.* 1.

21. U.S. Congress, Office of Technology Assessment, *Energy in Developing Countries* (U.S. Government Printing Office, Washington, D.C., January 1991), p. 100.

22. International Energy Agency, *Energy in Non-OECD Countries: Selected Topics 1988* (OECD, Paris, 1988), p. 11.

23. British Petroleum Company (BP), *BP Statistical Review of Energy* (BP, London, June 1991), p. 5.

24. *Op. cit.* 21, p. 99.

25. United Nations Statistical Office, *Energy Statistics Yearbook* (United Nations, New York, 1991).

26. *Op. cit.* 17, pp. 260-262.

27. International Atomic Energy Agency, *IAEA Bulletin*, Vol. 32, No. 4 (1990), p. 51.

28. Institute of Energy Economics and Politics (IPEP), *International Energy 1988-1989: Annual Report on Worldwide Energy Trends* (IPEP, Paris, 1988), p. 270 (in French).

29. *Op. cit.* 11, Table 21.3, pp. 320-321.

30. *Op. cit.* 11.

31. *Op. cit.* 22, p. 43.

32. Mark D. Levine, Ashok Gadgil, Stephen Meyers, *et al.*, "Energy Efficiency, Develop-

ing Nations and Eastern Europe: A Report to the U.S. Working Group on Global Energy Efficiency" (International Institute for Energy Conservation, Washington, D.C., June 1991), p. 5.

33. *Ibid.*, Table 9, p. 34.

34. U.S. Agency for International Development (U.S. AID), "Power Shortages in Developing Countries: Magnitude, Impacts, Solutions, and the Role of the Private Sector," a report to the U.S. Congress (U.S. AID, Washington, D.C., March 1988), p. 26.

35. *Op. cit.* 32, p. 2.

36. *Op. cit.* 32, p. 33.

37. *Op. cit.* 32, p. 13.

38. *Op. cit.* 21, p. 64.

39. *Op. cit.* 21, p. 65.

40. *Op. cit.* 32, p. 18.

41. *Op. cit.* 32, p. 19.

42. *Op. cit.* 32, p. 13.

43. *Op. cit.* 32, p. 19.

44. *Op. cit.* 32, pp. 3, 16.

45. National Association of Regulatory Utility Commissioners (NARUC), *Least- Cost Utility Planning: A Handbook for Public Utility Commissioners*, 3 vols. (NARUC, Washington, D.C., 1988-89).

46. Howard S. Geller, "Electricity Conservation in Brazil: Status Report and Analysis" (American Council for an Energy-Efficient Economy, Washington, D.C., November 1990).

47. RCG/Hagler, Bailly, Inc., "Costa Rica: Power Sector Efficiency Assessment," draft, prepared for the Office of Energy, U.S. Agency for International Development, February 1991.

48. Conservation Law Foundation of New England in association with the Resources Development Foundation and Biomass Users Network, "Power by Efficiency: An Assessment of Improving Electrical Efficiency to Meet Jamaica's Power Needs," a report for the Jamaica Public Service Company, June 1990.

49. Amulya K.N. Reddy, Gladys D. Sumithra, P. Balachandra, *et al.*, "Energy Conservation in India: A Development-Focussed End-Use-Oriented Energy Scenario for Karnataka; Part 2—Electricity" (Indian Institute of Science, Bangalore, April 1990).

50. Mark Cherniack, Director of the Asia Office, International Institute for Energy Conservation, Washington, D.C., 1991 (personal communication).

51. Eric D. Larson, ed., "Report on the 1989 Thailand Workshop on End-Use Oriented Energy Analysis" (International Institute for Energy Conservation, Washington, D.C., April 1990), p. i.

52. *Ibid.*, n.p.

53. International Institute for Energy Conservation (IIEC), "Preliminary Notes on a Survey of Databases and Information Centers" (IIEC, Washington, D.C., 1989) n.p.

54. Matthew Grund, "The IIEC Technical Information Directory" (International Institute for Energy Conservation, Washington, D.C., forthcoming).

55. Eric D. Larson, Lars J. Nilsson, and Thomas B. Johansson, "The Technology Menu for Efficient End Use of Energy: Volume 1— Movement of Material" (Environmental and Energy Systems Studies, Lund University, Lund, Sweden, August 1989).

56. International Energy Agency, *Energy Policies and Programmes of IEA Countries* (Organisation for Economic Co-operation and Development, Paris, published annually).

57. The data base is being developed by the International Institute for Energy Conservation.

58. Curtis S. Felix, "Assessment of U.S. Trade and Investment Opportunities in Energy Efficiency Markets in India" (International Institute for Energy Conservation, Washington, D.C., September 1990), p. E-4.

59. Moncef Ben Abdallah, President, Energy Management Agency, Tunisia, 1990 (personal communication).

60. R. Govinda Rao, "India—A Case Study," draft (International Institute for Energy Conservation, Washington, D.C., 1990), p. 54.

61. Mark Cherniack, "Exporting Energy Efficient Technologies: Briefing to Interested U.S. Companies by the International Institute for Energy Conservation and the Alliance to Save Energy," (International Institute for Energy Conservation, Washington, D.C., June 11, 1990).

62. *Op. cit.* 50.

63. Jose Goldemberg, Thomas B. Johansson, Amulya K. N. Reddy, *et al.*, *Energy for a Sustainable World* (Wiley Eastern Limited, New Delhi, 1988), pp. 137-139, and 446.

64. Jose Goldemberg, Thomas B. Johansson, Amulya K.N. Reddy, *et al.*, "Energy for a Sustainable World: An Update, with Emphasis on Developing Countries," presented at the Bellagio Seminar on Energy for a Sustainable World, Bellagio, Italy, June 1990.

65. United Nations Conference on Trade and Development (UNCTAD), *Handbook of International Trade and Development Statistics, 1989* (United Nations, New York, 1990), p. A36.

66. *Ibid.*, pp. 223, 224.

67. United Nations Department of International Economic and Social Affairs, *1987 International Trade Statistics Yearbook* (United Nations, New York, 1989), pp. 109, 173, 421, and 575.

68. Management Systems International (MSI), "USAID/India Program for the Advancement of Commercial Technology, Midterm Evaluation, Second Phase Report" (MSI, Washington, D.C., December 1989).

69. David Jhirad, "Power Sector Innovation in Developing Countries: Implementing Multifaceted Solutions," *Annual Review of Energy 1990*, Vol. 15 (1990), pp. 390-391.

70. Michael Philips, "Energy Conservation Activities in Latin America and the Caribbean" (International Institute for Energy Conservation, Washington, D.C., 1990), p. 25.

71. *Op. cit.* 46, p. 102.

72. Mark D. Levine, Program Leader, Energy Analysis Program, Lawrence Berkeley Laboratory, Berkeley, California, 1991 (personal communication).

73. *Op. cit.* 32, pp. 37-40.

74. *Op. cit.* 70, p. 11.

75. Jaime Lerner, "Curitiba Bus System," in *Driving New Directions: Transportation Experiences and Options in Developing Countries*, Mia L. Birk and Deborah L. Bleviss, eds. (International Institute for Energy Conservation, Washington, D.C., 1991), pp. 85-89.

11. Freshwater

Freshwater resources are under severe and increasing environmental stress. About two thirds of global withdrawals are used for agriculture and about one fourth for industry. By the end of the century, withdrawals for agriculture will increase slightly and industrial withdrawals will probably double. Industrial development and population growth will also add pollutants to freshwater, unless governments boost their efforts to treat wastewater or prevent pollution.

The world's supply of freshwater is unevenly distributed and frequently unreliable. Water shortages are already acute in many regions, chronically so in areas of East and West Africa. Consumption is outstripping supplies in northern China, and shortages could reach crisis proportions in the Middle East and North Africa, where the water issue is complicated by political tensions. To cope with shortages, some countries are turning to desalination of ocean water; other options include the reuse of wastewater.

The source of most freshwater is the river basin, which in most parts of the world is under severe environmental stress. Farming, industry, and human settlements all contribute to pollution in freshwater river basins. In the developing world, more than 95 percent of urban sewage is discharged untreated into surface waters. Loaded with bacteria and viruses, these waters are a major threat to human health.

Industrial practices also are major contributors to freshwater pollution, accounting for a large share of pollution from heavy metals and toxic chemicals. Logging operations and agriculture add sediment and organic matter, which adversely affects the habitats of river organisms and can smother coastal fishing grounds hundreds of miles away. (For a discussion of how watershed pollution affects coastal areas, see Chapter 12, "Oceans and Coasts," Focus On Coastal Pollution.)

A few alternatives to conventional sewage treatment are attracting attention. For example, wetlands can be designed to serve as simple, low-cost wastewater treatment plants that use natural processes for filtration and cleaning. Partially treated sewage also can be used to raise fish. Waste reduction also offers potential: chemical companies that instituted waste reduction programs have been able to reduce regulated waste by about two thirds.

Dealing with water resources is a political as well as an economic and technical challenge. Roughly one half of the world's river basins are shared by two or more countries. International cooperation in the management of river basins has not been easy, but in a few cases, such as the management of the Rhine River in Europe, it has produced some measurable environmental benefits.

CONDITIONS AND TRENDS

Global Trends

FRESHWATER RESOURCES

Water is the most abundant resource on Earth, covering about 71 percent of the planet's surface (1). The total volume of water on the planet is immense—about 1.41 billion cubic kilometers. Spread evenly over the Earth's surface, it would form a layer nearly 3,000 meters deep. About 98 percent of this volume is in the world's oceans and inland seas and is too salty for drinking, growing crops, or for most industrial uses. About 3 percent is freshwater, but nearly all of that amount (87 percent) is locked in ice caps or glaciers, in the atmosphere or soil, or deep underground (2). In fact, if the world's total water supply were only 100 liters, the usable supply of freshwater would be only 0.003 liter, or one-half teaspoon (3).

Humankind's primary supply of freshwater is in rivers, lakes, and reservoirs. About 2,000 cubic kilometers of freshwater are flowing through the world's rivers at any one time; nearly one half the total is in South America and another one fourth is in Asia. The actual amount available for use annually is much greater, because water in rivers is replaced roughly every 18–20 days (4). Over a full year, the total amount of freshwater flowing through rivers is about 41,000 cubic kilometers, including about 28,000 cubic kilometers of surface runoff and about 13,000 cubic kilometers of "stable" underground flow into rivers (5). Only about three fourths of the stable underground flow—9,000 kilometers—is easily accessible and economically usable (6). An additional 3,000 cubic kilometers of useful capacity is available from human-made lakes and reservoirs (7).

The primary source of freshwater is precipitation. Global precipitation totals about 500,000 cubic kilometers per year, but only about one fifth of this amount—110,000 cubic kilometers—falls on land. About 65 percent of continental rainfall evaporates and is transported back to the atmosphere. The remaining precipitation either stays on the surface—in rivers, lakes, wetlands, and reservoirs—or flows into the ground, where it is stored in groundwater aquifers (8).

Global precipitation varies considerably. For example, heavy rainfall is characteristic of the Amazon Basin and parts of South and Southeast Asia; meager rains typify the Middle East, North Africa, North-Central Asia and Central Australia (9). Areas of low rainfall also tend to be areas with unreliable precipitation. Reduced precipitation is a threat in many regions; at least 80 arid and semiarid countries, with about 40 percent of the world's population, have serious periodic droughts (10). The Sahel region in Africa, for example, has experienced below-normal precipitation for two decades. (See Figure 11.1.)

Conversely, flooding is a major and apparently growing problem in some regions. Bangladesh historically suffered major floods about once every 50 years, but in the 1970s and 1980s, the average interval was

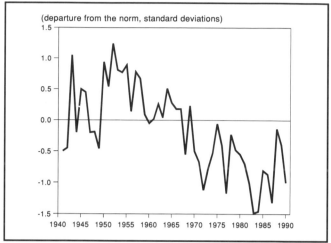

Figure 11.1 Index of Rainfall in the Sahel, 1941–90

Source: Peter J. Lamb and Randy A. Peppler, "Further Case Studies of Tropical Atlantic Surface, Atmospheric, and Oceanic Patterns Associated with Sub-Saharan Drought," *Journal of Climate*, Vol. 5, forthcoming.
Note: Norm = 1941-82 average.

only four years. Part of the problem originates in the Himalayan watershed, where rapid population growth, deforestation, and unsustainable farming on steep slopes have greatly reduced the capacity of the land to absorb water. The destruction of coastal mangrove forests (which break the impact of ocean waves) has also increased the coastal population's vulnerability to storm surges (11).

Freshwater has many critical linkages with other aspects of the environment. For example, forests play an important role in absorbing precipitation. Depending on the species and locality, trees in temperate North American forests may intercept 40 percent or more of annual precipitation, delaying runoff and greatly reducing the flow of pollutants to streams, rivers, and lakes (12). In the past two years, the importance of forests for controlling runoff has been illustrated in areas where acid rain or other factors have damaged trees. In the Black Forest in Germany, which has experienced severe tree damage, rainfall has remained fairly constant but runoff has increased considerably. Studies of a river basin in southwestern Australia have found a similar link between deforestation and surface water runoff (13).

Global warming is likely to lead to increased evaporation from the sea and hence to increased precipitation and river runoff. Global circulation models generally predict that precipitation will gradually increase 4–12 percent if carbon dioxide levels in the atmosphere double, with potentially greater increases in the higher latitudes (14).

Water Use

Human use of water has increased more than 35-fold over the past three centuries. In recent decades, water withdrawals have been increasing about 4–8 percent per year, with most of that increase occurring in the developing world. Water use is stabilizing in the industrialized countries, where the rate of increase of withdrawals is expected to decline to 2–3 percent annually in the 1990s (15). Annual average per capita water use varies widely: 1,692 cubic meters in North and Central America, 726 in Europe, 526 in Asia, 476 in South America, and 244 in Africa. (See Chapter 22, "Freshwater," Table 22.1.)

Globally, 3,240 cubic kilometers of freshwater are withdrawn and used annually. Of this total, 69 percent is used for agriculture, 23 percent for industry, and 8 percent for domestic uses. (See Table 22.1.) As Figure 11.2 shows, water use varies considerably around the world. In Africa, Asia, and South America, agriculture is the primary use; for example, Asia uses 86 percent of its water for agriculture, mainly for irrigation. About 25 percent of agricultural water is returned to streams as wastewater (16).

Industrial and domestic withdrawals are expected to increase more rapidly than agricultural withdrawals in the coming years, but agricultural withdrawals will nevertheless increase in absolute terms. By the year 2000, total irrigated area is expected to increase by about 19 percent, including increases of perhaps 30 percent in Africa and South America. To accommodate that increase, water withdrawals for irrigation are projected to increase by about 17 percent (17).

Global withdrawals for industrial purposes are currently estimated at about 745 cubic kilometers annually, or about one fourth of total withdrawals. Industrial uses account for a substantial share of water withdrawals in Europe (54 percent of total withdrawals) and North America (42 percent of total withdrawals). About 640 cubic kilometers—86 percent—is discharged back into rivers and coastal waters as wastewater. By the end of the 1990s, industrial withdrawals are expected to increase to roughly 1,200 cubic kilometers, with an accompanying global increase in industrial wastewater to nearly 1,000 cubic kilometers (18). (See Table 22.1.)

A relatively small amount of freshwater—roughly 8 percent of the global total—is withdrawn for domestic and municipal requirements. In regions experiencing rapid population growth, such as Asia, domestic use is expected to increase sharply by the end of the 1990s. About 60 percent of water used for domestic purposes is returned to rivers as wastewater (19).

Freshwater Quality

Pollution in freshwater is of three major types:
■ Excess nutrients from sewage and soil erosion, which cause algae blooms that eventually deplete the oxygen content of the water;
■ Pathogens from sewage that spread disease; and
■ Heavy metals and synthetic organic compounds from industry, mining, and agriculture, which bioaccumulate in aquatic organisms.

These types of pollution, their sources, and methods of control are discussed further in "Focus On River Basin Pollution," below.

In general, river water quality, as measured by biological oxygen demand, has improved in industrial-

Figure 11.2 Sectoral Water Withdrawal by Region

A. World, North and Central America, Europe

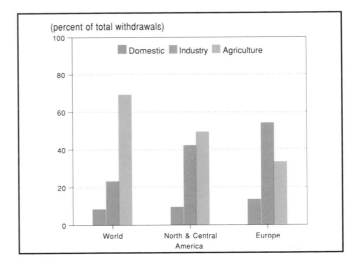

B. Africa, Asia, South America

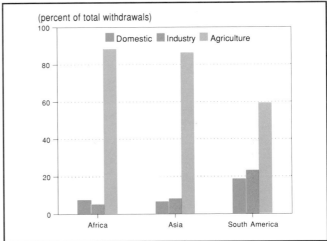

Source: Chapter 22, "Freshwater," Table 22.1.

ized countries over the past 20 years because of increased sewage treatment. Switzerland, Denmark, the Netherlands, Sweden, and the Federal Republic of Germany have achieved nearly complete sewage treatment coverage; Japan has made considerable progress but still lags behind most other industrial countries (20).

Some progress has also occurred in reducing the concentrations of heavy metals in industrialized countries. For example, lead concentrations near the mouths of rivers in Canada, Japan, Belgium, the Federal Republic of Germany, and the United Kingdom generally decreased over the 1970–85 period (21). Concentrations of metals in the Rhine River have also declined slightly after decades of increases (22). Trends in metals besides lead and in toxic substances are less encouraging.

In developing countries, water quality trends remain difficult to ascertain because of deficiencies in the assessment of pollution sources and in the monitoring of groundwater and surface waters. Water quality is gen-

Table 11.1 Sources and Impacts of Selected Pollutants

Pollutant	Source	Impact on Aquatic Organisms	Impact on Human Health and Welfare
Sediment	Agricultural fields, pastures, and livestock feed lots; logged hillsides; degraded streambanks; road construction.	Reduced plant growth and diversity; reduced prey for predators; clogging of gills and filters; reduced survival of eggs and young; smothering of habitats.	Increased water treatment costs; transport of toxics and nutrients; reduced availability of fish, shellfish, and associated species; shortened lifespan of lakes, streams, and artificial reservoirs and harbors.
Nutrients	Agricultural fields, pastures, and livestock feed lots; landscaped urban areas; raw and treated sewage discharges; industrial discharges.	Algal blooms resulting in depressed oxygen levels and reduced diversity and growth of large plants; release of toxins from sediments; reduced diversity in vertebrate and invertebrate communities; fish kills.	Increased water treatment costs; risk of reduced oxygen-carrying capacity in infant blood; possible generation of carcinogenic nitrosamines; reduced availability of fish, shellfish, and associated species; impairment of recreational uses.
Organic materials	Agricultural fields and pastures; landscaped urban areas; combined sewers; logged areas; chemical manufacturing and other industrial processes.	Reduced dissolved oxygen in affected waters; fish kills; reduced abundance and diversity of aquatic life.	Increased costs of water treatment; reduced availability of fish, shellfish, and associated species.
Disease-causing agents	Raw and partially treated sewage; animal wastes; dams that reduce water flow.	Reduced survival and reproduction in fish, shellfish, and associated species.	Increased costs of water treatment; river blindness, elephantiasis, schistosomiasis, cholera, typhoid, dysentery; reduced availability and contamination of fish, shellfish, and associated species.
Heavy metals	Atmospheric deposition; road runoff; industrial discharges; sludge and discharges from sewage treatment plants; creation of reservoirs; acidic mine effluents.	Declines in fish populations due to failed reproduction; lethal effects on invertebrates leading to reduced prey for fish.	Increased costs of water treatment; lead poisoning, itai-itai, and minamata diseases; kidney dysfunction; reduced availability and healthfulness of fish, shellfish, and associated species.
Toxic chemicals	Urban and agricultural runoff; municipal and industrial discharges; leachate from landfills.	Reduced growth and survivability of fish eggs and young; fish diseases.	Increased costs of water treatment; increased risk of rectal, bladder, and colon cancer; reduced availability and healthfulness of fish, shellfish, and associated species.
Acids	Atmospheric deposition; mine effluents; degrading plant materials.	Elimination of sensitive aquatic organisms; release of trace metals from soils, rocks, and metal surfaces such as water pipes.	Reduced availability of fish, shellfish, and associated species.
Chlorides	Roads treated for removal of ice or snow; irrigation runoff; brine produced in oil extraction; mining.	At high levels, toxic to freshwater life.	Reduced availability of drinking water supplies; reduced availability of fish, shellfish, and associated species.
Elevated temperatures	Urban landscapes; unshaded streams; impounded waters; reduced discharges from dams; discharges from power plants and industrial facilities.	Elimination of cold-water species of fish and shellfish; reduced dissolved oxygen due to increased plant growth; increased vulnerability of some fishes to toxic wastes, parasites, and diseases.	Reduced availability of fish, shellfish, and associated species.

Sources:

1. Thomas R. Schueler, *Controlling Urban Runoff: A Practical Manual for Planning and Designing Urban BMPs* (Metropolitan Washington Council of Governments, Washington, D.C., 1987), pp. 1.5-1.9.
2. G. Tyler Miller, Jr., *Environmental Science: Sustaining the Earth* (Wadsworth Publishing Company, Belmont, California, 1991), p. 248.
3. Margaret S. Petersen, *Water Resource Planning and Development* (Prentice-Hall Inc., Englewood Cliffs, New Jersey, 1984), p. 140.
4. Mark K. Mitchell and William B. Stapp, *Field Manual for Water Quality Monitoring: An Environmental Education Program for Schools*, 4th ed. (Thomson-Shore Inc., Dexter, Michigan, 1990), pp. 51 and 54.
5. U.S. Environmental Protection Agency (EPA), *Report to Congress: Water Quality of the Nation's Lakes* (EPA, Washington, D.C., 1989), pp. 9 and 11.
6. Organisation for Economic Co-operation and Development (OECD), *Water Pollution by Fertilizers and Pesticides* (OECD, Paris, 1986), pp. 50-52.
7. D.R. Nimmo, D.L. Coppage, Q.H. Pickering, *et al.*, "Assessing the Toxicity of Pesticides to Aquatic Organisms," in *Silent Spring Revisited*, Gino J. Marco, Robert M. Hollingworth, and William Durham, eds. (American Chemical Society, Washington, D.C., 1987), pp. 58-62.
8. R.C. Muirhead-Thomson, "Effects of Pesticides on the Feeding Habits of Fish," *Outlook on Agriculture*, Vol. 17, No. 2 (1988), p. 71.
9. Michel Meybeck, Deborah V. Chapman, and Richard Helmer, eds., *Global Environment Monitoring System: Global Freshwater Quality, A First Assessment* (Basil Blackwell Ltd., Oxford, U.K., 1989), pp. 107, 159, 160, 163.

erally thought to be deteriorating, especially around urban areas. Few cities have sewage treatment facilities, and municipal water supplies are often neither treated nor disinfected, greatly increasing the risk of diarrhea and other gastrointestinal illnesses that are factors in infant mortality. Industrial discharges are usually poorly controlled (23). (See Table 11.1.)

A 1991 regional review of global water quality by the World Health Organization and United Nations Environment Programme listed several areas of special concern, including the following:
■ Fecal discharge, from humans and animals, which transports a variety of bacteria and viruses and threatens human health.

■ High salinity, which can occur naturally or as part of poor irrigation practices.
■ Nitrate pollution, primarily from fertilizers and animal manures, a serious problem in North America and Europe that has begun to affect developing countries such as Brazil and India (24).

Key Issues

WATER SHORTAGES

Acute water shortages in many parts of the world require solutions that will be costly, technically difficult, and—in many regions—politically sensitive. Water scarcity contributes to the impoverishment of many countries in East and West Africa, threatening their ability to increase food production fast enough to keep pace with population growth. Many of these countries share the combination of a short growing season, which makes crops vulnerable to intermittent droughts, and a lack of water in rivers and aquifers as a result of limited freshwater recharge (25).

One of the most serious shortages is in the North China Plain, a semiarid region with a population of about 200 million people, including major cities such as Beijing and Tianjin. Consumption by industry, agriculture, and the increasing population is outstripping supplies. If present trends continue, the region will have 6 percent less water than needed by the end of the century; Beijing alone will have a daily shortfall of 550,000 cubic meters, or about two thirds of its current supply. Groundwater levels are falling drastically—as much as 80 meters in some areas—and as a result, land in Beijing has sunk as much as 0.5 meters because of the resulting subsidence.

Some experts think Beijing and other communities in the region should initiate conservation measures, reduce demand (by raising water prices), increase supplies (by recycling and reducing leakage), and reallocate water from agriculture to more efficient uses. The Chinese government is considering a massive, 1,190-kilometer diversion of water from the Yangtze River near Shanghai (26).

Water shortages have also reached serious proportions in the southwestern United States, especially in drought-stricken California. Beginning in 1987 and continuing into 1991, the drought in some parts of the state has been the worst in the last century (27). The ecological effects have been significant. Catches of coho and chinook salmon, striped bass, and herring have declined dramatically. Waterfowl populations have dropped for many reasons, but the drought has worsened their decline by drying up wetland areas. Tree mortality has been extremely high (30–80 percent are dead or dying) in some forest areas of the Sierra Nevada, and many threatened or endangered plant and animal species have been adversely affected (28).

The drought also reduced California's hydroelectric capacity. As a result, more fossil fuels were purchased and burned by California utilities, increasing utility emissions of carbon dioxide by more than 25 percent. Water quality was also affected in some regions due to low freshwater flows and increased salinity intrusion (29). To cope with the shortage, the city of Santa Barbara on the central coast is planning to build a desalination plant. Some environmentalists have criticized this strategy, arguing that conservation is a better way to deal with water shortages (30). Desalination, nevertheless, is growing rapidly around the world. (See Box 11.1.)

The Middle East: Politics and Water

Water shortages could reach crisis proportions in the Middle East and North Africa in this decade. Jordan, Israel, Algeria, Egypt, Tunisia, and the countries of the Arabian Peninsula are already reaching a point where nearly all available supplies are being used (31). The water issue is particularly difficult in this region because so many countries share common water sources. For example, Egypt relies on the Nile for 86 percent of domestic consumption, yet most of the river's waters originate in eight upstream countries (32).

Israel, the West Bank and Gaza, and Jordan are facing a combined water deficit of at least 300 million cubic meters per year. Water has many political implications in the region: for example, the Yarkon/Taninim aquifer, which provides 25–40 percent of Israel's water, lies beneath both pre-1967 Israel and the West Bank and is thus a strategic concern for Israel in negotiations over the future of the West Bank (33). Efforts to develop the Jordan and Yarmuk River basins have been stopped by Arab-Israeli or Syrian-Jordanian tensions. Turkey, Iraq, and Syria have frequently been at odds over the management of the Tigris and Euphrates river basins (34).

Egypt has started a consultative group of the Nile countries—the Undugu Group—and has proposed a long-range scheme for the development of the Nile. Turkish President Turqut Ozal was to have hosted a Middle East Water Summit in Istanbul in November 1991, although the meeting was later cancelled because of Israeli-Arab tensions (35).

WATER AND SUSTAINABLE AGRICULTURAL DEVELOPMENT

In many regions, a critical challenge will be to provide enough water for sustainable agriculture. Improved water resources management can help considerably. For example, a variety of water harvesting and water spreading techniques, such as stonelines to collect water for dryland crops, have potential. In the semiarid and subhumid regions of Africa, water harvesting could increase agricultural production on 10 million hectares in the short term and 50 million hectares in the long term.

In rainfed areas, water conservation strategies such as fallow management and runoff control have potential. Other farm practices—such as the use of drought-tolerant varieties, crop rotation, and carefully timed planting dates—can be important complements to water resource management (36).

Box 11.1 Desalination: An Increasingly Popular Option

Areas with water shortages, especially in high-income countries, are turning increasingly to desalination plants to supplement water resources. In the 1980s, the number of plants producing more than 100 cubic meters per day increased dramatically, from 3,527 plants in December 1986 to 7,536 plants operating in 120 countries in December 1989 [1] [2]. At that time, global capacity (either installed or contracted) was estimated at nearly 13.3 million cubic meters per day, roughly a 13-fold increase since 1970 [3].

Desalination plants are now common in areas that can afford the relatively high cost such as Saudi Arabia, Kuwait, and south Florida. Measured by percentage of total global capacity, Saudi Arabia is the world leader with 27 percent; followed by the United States, 12 percent; Kuwait, 11 percent; and the United Arab Emirates, 10 percent [4].

Large plants, such as the 1 million cubic meter per day Jubail plant in Saudi Arabia, usually use the distillation process, in which salt water is heated and the resulting steam condenses into freshwater. The main distillation process—the multistage flash process—has declined from 67 percent of total capacity in 1984 to about 56 percent in 1989, but it still plays a significant role in very large plants and in dual-purpose plants coupled with power generation. Smaller plants typically use reverse osmosis, which uses high pressure to force saltwater through a screen that filters out both suspended and dissolved solids. Reverse osmosis climbed to about 31 percent of total global capacity by 1989, up from 20 percent in 1984 [5].

Desalination is still three to four times more expensive than conventional sources of freshwater, costing 40–60 cents per 1,000 liters of brackish water and $1.05 to $1.60 per 1,000 liters of sea water. As the technology improves, however, and the cost of conventional freshwater increases, desalination plants are likely to become more popular and the costs are likely to continue to decline slightly. There is greatly increased interest, for example, in building distillation plants alongside electric utilities and using the waste heat from power generation to drive the desalination process [6] [7].

About 65 percent of all plants are treating sea water and 27 percent are treating brackish water. Desalination plants are increasingly being used for applications other than removing salt, such as the treatment of effluent waters, of river water to obtain water for boilers, of groundwater that has been polluted by nitrates and pesticides, and of municipal water to make ultrapure water for the electronics industry [8].

References and Notes

1. U.S. Congress, Office of Technology Assessment (OTA), *Using Desalination Technologies for Water Treatment* (U.S. Government Printing Office, Washington, D.C., 1988), p. 7.
2. Pat Burke, President, International Desalination Association, Topsfield, Massachusetts, 1991 (personal communication).
3. Klaus Wangnick, *1990 IDA Worldwide Desalting Plants Inventory Report No. 11*, prepared for the International Desalination Association (Wangnick Consulting, Gnarrenburg, Germany, 1990), pp. 17, 21.
4. *Ibid.*, p. 38.
5. *Ibid.*, p. 19.
6. Richard W. Stevenson, "Dry California Turns to the Pacific," *New York Times* (March 5, 1991), p. D1.
7. *Op. cit.* 1, pp. 25-26.
8. *Op. cit.* 3, p. 17.

WATER AND SANITATION: DECADE OF EFFORT

The conclusion of the 1981–90 International Drinking Water Supply and Sanitation Decade provides an opportunity for evaluating the world's progress in water and sanitation and for devising new strategies for the 1990s. This U.N. effort, an outgrowth of the United Nations Water Conference held in Mar del Plata, Argentina in 1977, called on countries to set realistic goals for the decade and to develop national water and sanitation plans. In addition, it called upon aid agencies to provide assistance to implement the plans.

Unfortunately, the goals of the decade were blocked by a sudden slowdown of economic growth in the developing countries. During the 1980s, many countries went through a difficult financial readjustment and were burdened with rising costs of external financing: simply keeping up with rapid population growth and urbanization was difficult [37].

Measuring progress in water and sanitation has been difficult because of a lack of adequate information. A U.N. document concluded that, with the exception of West Asia, most regions had merely kept pace with or even fallen behind population growth. In sub-Saharan Africa, for example, the number of people served roughly doubled, but the number of urban dwellers without safe water increased by 29 percent [38]. By the year 2000, the number of urban dwellers lacking adequate water supplies may increase by 83 percent, and the number lacking adequate sanitation services by nearly as much. Making substantial progress in water and sanitation by the end of the decade would require roughly a tripling of investment over the average achieved during the 1980s [39].

Work is underway to develop new strategies for water and sanitation in the 1990s. A key event is the International Conference on Water and the Environment, to be held in Dublin in January 1992, which is scheduled to focus on six major issues:

■ Knowledge of the resource and demands upon it;
■ Water for sustainable agricultural production;
■ Water for sustainable urban development;
■ Environmentally sound water management;
■ Capacity building for water resources management; and
■ Integrated water resources management.

The strategies and action plans developed at this conference will be presented to the United Nations Conference on Environment and Development in Brazil in June 1992 [40].

As the decade begins, economic issues—the gap between increasing costs and users' ability to pay, the inefficient pricing of services, the promotion of incentives to conserve water—seem to predominate, along with the problem of institutional weaknesses in water resources management and planning. But as urban areas continue to grow, the problems of water availability are likely to be increasingly important, and options such as the reuse of wastewater and desalination may become increasingly attractive.

FOCUS ON RIVER BASIN POLLUTION

The land area drained by a river and its tributaries—known as a river basin—is the basic unit for understanding the sources and effects of freshwater pollution as well as the ecological relationships between terrestrial and aquatic systems. Figure 11.3 shows the world's major river basins.

As water circulates from the atmosphere through the watershed and oceans and back into the atmosphere—a process known as the hydrological cycle—it is vulnerable to pollution from many sources. First, airborne dust, nutrients, metals, and other chemicals may fall as dry deposition or adhere to and fall with raindrops and snowflakes on both land and water. Second, as it flows over or filters through the soil, precipitation may dissolve nutrients and chemical residues or pick up nutrients, agricultural and industrial chemical residues, metals, and other pollutants. Eventually, some of the water may enter tributary streams and rivers, into which a third source of pollution—sewage and industrial wastewater—is discharged directly. At their mouths, rivers disgorge their loads of sediment and pollutants into coastal estuaries, where they may remain for many years. (See Chapter 12, "Oceans and Coasts," Focus On Coastal Pollution.)

In addition to producing chemical pollution, human activities affect aquatic ecosystems in a variety of ways. When cities are built, grasslands, forests, and wetlands are converted to impermeable surfaces such as roads, parking lots, and roofs, greatly altering streamflow patterns. In cities, on farms, and in logging operations, removal of streamside vegetation can promote streambank erosion and subsequent smothering of freshwater animals and plants by sediments. Dams

for power or irrigation impede fish migration and alter water chemistry and temperature in downstream areas.

Throughout a river system, pollution of groundwater, surface waters, and ultimately coastal waters can directly and indirectly damage human health and economic activities, as well as aquatic plant and animal communities. The health impact is particularly severe in developing countries, where waterborne infectious diseases affect more people than any other health problem (41). Once polluted, freshwater, especially groundwater, is expensive to cleanse for human use.

Waterways degraded by development or pollution suffer decreased diversity and reduced abundance of fish and the invertebrates upon which fish and other animals feed (42) (43). Furthermore, in a process known as bioaccumulation, metals and inorganic chemicals may accumulate in aquatic organisms to levels well above those in the water itself, as the contaminants are passed up the food chain from prey to predator, including humans who consume fish. Finally, erosion resulting in sedimentation of waterways can impede navigation and require expensive dredging.

Pollution by upstream users can significantly reduce the quality of water available to downstream users (and ecosystems) at little or no cost to polluters. This greatly complicates efforts to maintain or restore water quality. The resulting conflicts can have local, national, and international ramifications. Within countries, agencies responsible for water quality have little or no control over activities—such as siting of hazardous

Figure 11.3 The World's Major River Basins

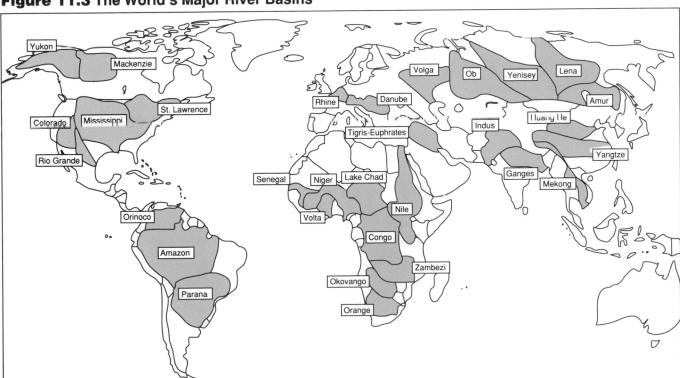

Source: Compiled by the World Resources Institute.

waste dumps, agricultural practices, or urban development—that influence the quality or quantity of available water (44) (45).

Most sources of pollution have been identified and technologies or processes have been devised to reduce each pollutant. Where watershed pollution continues, it is usually because of a lack of political will, intergovernmental coordination, or inadequate funding. Many governments are recognizing that the protection of freshwater and coastal water quality depends on integrated water resource management, which emphasizes river basin and coastal zone planning and involves agencies responsible for resource protection and for economic development (46) (47).

THE DYNAMICS OF RIVER BASINS

River basins are dominant features of the Earth's surface (48). They range in size from the tiny river basins along the mountainous Na Pali coast on Kauai in the Hawaiian islands to huge basins such as the Amazon River basin, which covers more than 7 million square kilometers, an area twice the size of India. Precipitation in a river basin can depend on continental-scale weather systems. For example, weather systems moving across the industrialized midwestern United States pick up pollutants that fall as acid precipitation in eastern Canada.

Movement of Groundwater and Surface Water

Once precipitation falls on the ground, whether as rain or snow, it either evaporates, seeps into the soil and flows to aquifers, or forms surface rills, streams, and eventually rivers. The slopes of a river basin concentrate surface runoff to form a river system leading to lakes or the sea (49) (50).

Precipitation that seeps into the ground eventually reaches the zone of saturation where it fills all available pores in soil or porous rock, forming great bodies of groundwater (51). Moving toward areas of lower pressure and elevation, groundwater may eventually discharge into wetlands, springs, lakes, geysers, or coastal waters. Groundwater provides the base flow of many rivers (52).

A river can be divided into three parts (53). The headwaters are characterized by small, steep streams that are fed by rain, snow, glaciers, or springs. Their high-velocity streamflow can carry away large amounts of sediment if the soil of surrounding slopes is not protected by vegetation. Eroded sediments (a problem not restricted to headwaters) represent the major source of pollutants in surface waters (54).

The middle sections of a river are generally less steep. Flowing through comparatively flat land, a river is often surrounded by a floodplain, which is seasonally inundated by runoff from heavy rains or rapid snowmelt. Floodplains can support productive fisheries and agriculture, which depend on nutrient-rich, riverborne sediment. However, periodic floods can cause massive destruction and loss of human life. Human activities also add pollutants—nutrients, pesticides, toxic metals, and toxic organic compounds—to rivers.

Lakes and wetlands are found mainly along the middle and lower reaches of rivers. The water stored in wetlands can recharge groundwater, maintain streamflows during dry periods, and reduce flooding. Wetlands, lakes, and artificial reservoirs often act as sinks for contaminants, which settle with suspended sediments (55). As a river approaches the sea, its freshwater mixes with saltwater. Because of slower currents and changed water chemistry, organic and inorganic matter collected from the runoff of the river basin settles to the bottom. Chapter 12, "Oceans and Coasts," Focus On Coastal Pollution, details the impact of such deposits on estuaries and other coastal waters.

On different continents, humans withdraw 1 to 16 percent of river flows for irrigation, industry, and domestic and municipal use. (See Chapter 22, "Freshwater," Table 22.1.) These withdrawals can have dramatic impacts in particular river systems. Extreme examples of rivers drained dry by withdrawal for irrigation include the Colorado in the United States and the Amu Darya and Syr Darya, which feed the Aral Sea in the Soviet Union (56) (57). Increasing demands are also being made upon groundwater; in the United States, about one half of the drinking water and 40 percent of the irrigation water is drawn from groundwater (58). Overpumping of groundwater by large coastal cities, such as Dakar, Senegal; Jakarta, Indonesia; and Lima, Peru; has led to contamination of underground freshwater by intruding coastal saltwater (59). (See Conditions and Trends, Water Use, above.).

Differences in River Basins

River basins differ greatly in size, climate, topography, geology, vegetation, and land use. Large river basins may contain different mixes of these characteristics, all of which influence the volume and quality of groundwater and surface waters moving through a river basin into the ground, lakes, and coastal waters (60).

In many river basins with extensive vegetative cover, precipitation infiltrates soils and groundwaters, which contribute to steady river flows. Although vegetation causes water loss to the atmosphere through evapotranspiration, it retards the flow of water over land and increases recharge of shallow aquifers (61).

In desert regions with little vegetation, heavy rainfall leads to higher surface runoff rates and flooding. When a river basin is stripped of its natural moisture-holding vegetation by agriculture, deforestation, or urbanization, runoff velocity and erosion increase. Geological conditions—such as soil type—also influence the dynamics of a river basin. For example, permeable soils absorb precipitation more readily, thereby reducing overland flow and runoff volume and velocity.

River basins also differ in the features that determine water flow pattern and chemical composition (62). For instance, floodplains and wetlands store floodwaters and release them slowly, reducing surges in flow following heavy rainfall. According to one study, river basins without wetlands discharge water at five times the rate of basins with 40 percent wetland cover (63).

By capturing sediments in stormwater runoff, wetlands and riparian (riverbank) forests also filter nutrients (primarily nitrogen and phosphorus) and other potential pollutants from river water (64). Such buffer zones help maintain river water quality, particularly because most pollutants enter river waters during rapid snow melt or heavy rainfall (65).

SOURCES OF MAJOR POLLUTANTS

With the exception of a few communities in desert and tundra areas, most humans live in river basins (66). Human settlements, industrial development, agriculture, and deforestation have significantly altered the physical and ecological features of many river basins. All of these human activities contribute additional nutrients, metals, and synthetic chemicals to the hydrologic cycle. Table 11.1 describes the major river basin pollutants, their sources, and their effects on aquatic organisms and humans.

Some water pollution comes from diffuse or "nonpoint" sources. For instance, airborne pollutants (from automobiles, factories, and power plants) and waterborne pollutants (from croplands, feed lots, logged forests, and urban areas) can contribute significantly to river basin pollution (67). A 1980 study showed that airborne pollutants in the Potomac River basin account for 70–95 percent of the nitrogen and 20–35 percent of the phosphorus in urban runoff (68). A 1989 study showed that 76 percent of nitrogen, phosphorus, and sediment in U.S. lakes surveyed came from nonpoint sources (69).

Pollutants from diffuse sources may behave differently than those from specific "point" sources, such as sewage treatment facilities and industrial discharge pipes. As contaminants move through aquifers, they form underground plumes that may move slowly toward areas of lower pressure (such as wells) (70). Plumes from point sources tend to be long and narrow but highly contaminated, while plumes from nonpoint sources are large, diffuse, and less contaminated (71).

Human Settlements

Urbanization greatly influences water quantity and quality because of runoff and sewage. Impermeable surfaces such as roofs and highways replace permeable soils and vegetation, increasing the volume, velocity, and temperature of urban runoff, reducing the base flow of rivers during dry periods, raising the temperature of urban streams, and collecting pollutants that range from litter and pet droppings to toxics from atmospheric deposition (72) (73) (74).

Inadequately treated sewage from human settlements introduces large quantities of nutrients, pathogens, heavy metals, and synthetic organic chemicals into surface waters. In industrial countries, much of the sewage generated in urban areas is collected by sewer systems and treated to varying degrees before being discharged into rivers, lakes, or coastal waters. (See Table 11.2.). Primary (physical) and secondary (biological) treatment of sewage may remove 35 and 85 percent of pollutants in sewage, respectively (75), but

Table 11.2 Population Served by Wastewater Treatment, OECD Countries
(percent)

Country	1970	1975	1980	1985	Late 1980s
OECD North America	**42**	**65**	**69**	**72**	**73**
Canada	X	49	56	57	66
United States	42	67	70	74	X
OECD Europe	**33**	**39**	**46**	**50**	**57**
Austria	17	27	38	65	72
Belgium	4	6	23	X	X
Denmark	54	71	80	91	98
Finland	27	50	65	72	75
France	19	31	43	49	52
(West) Germany	62	75	82	87	90
Greece	X	X	1	X	X
Ireland	X	X	11	X	X
Italy	14	22	30	X	60
Luxembourg	28	X	81	83	91
Netherlands	X	45	72	85	92
Norway	21	27	34	42	43
Portugal	3	6	9	9	11
Spain	X	14	18	29	48
Sweden	63	81	82	94	95
Switzerland	35	55	70	83	90
Turkey	X	X	X	X	1
United Kingdom	X	X	82	83	84
OECD Pacific	**X**	**X**	**X**	**X**	**X**
Australia	X	X	X	X	X
Japan	16	23	30	36	39
New Zealand	52	56	59	88	X
Total	**34**	**46**	**51**	**57**	**60**

Source: Organisation for Economic Co-operation and Development (OECD), *OECD Environmental Data Compendium 1991*, draft (OECD, Paris, 1991), Table 3.2A, p. 51.

Note: Numbers may not add due to rounding.

X = not available.

they remove only 30 percent of the phosphorus, 50 percent of the nitrogen, and 70 percent of the most toxic compounds. Advanced sewage treatment plants that can further reduce specific pollutant levels cost twice as much to build and four times as much to operate as secondary treatment plants (76). Without regular maintenance and proper operation, primary, secondary, and advanced sewage treatment plants will operate well below their intended standards.

Conventional treatment of sewage does not eliminate the problem of pathogens in sewage. To eliminate human pathogens, the water discharged from sewage treatment plants is sometimes treated with chlorine, which reacts with organic chemicals to form carcinogenic chlorinated hydrocarbons. The sludge produced by sewage treatment can also pollute water, unless it is further treated and incinerated or properly applied to land (77). Finally, where cities combine their sewer systems with storm drainage systems, storm water may overwhelm storm drainage systems and flow into sewer systems, mixing with sewage and discharging into the receiving river, lake, or coastal water body. Some cities have built storm water retaining basins to prevent such discharges (78).

The situation is much worse in the developing world, where more than 95 percent of urban sewage is discharged into surface waters without treatment (79). Many cities in developing countries lack even sewer systems, let alone sewage treatment facilities. For example Bangkok, Thailand—the capital of one of the most economically advanced developing countries—

Table 11.3 Percent of Sewage Treated in Selected Areas[a]

Area	Percent	Source
Europe	72	1
Mediterranean Sea[b]	30	2
Caribbean Basin	less than 10	3
Southeast Pacific	almost zero	3
South Asia	almost zero	4
South Pacific	almost zero	3
West and Central Africa	almost zero	5

Sources:

1. P.C. Wood, "Sewage Sludge Disposal Options," in *The Role of the Oceans as A Waste Disposal Option*, G. Kullenberg, ed. (D. Reidel Publishing Company, Dordrecht, the Netherlands, 1986), p. 111.
2. The World Bank and the European Investment Bank, *The Environmental Program for the Mediterranean* (The World Bank, Washington, D.C., 1990), p. 17.
3. Don Hinrichsen, *Our Common Seas: Coasts in Crisis* (Earthscan Publications Ltd., London, in association with the United Nations Environment Programme, Nairobi, 1990), pp. 28, 52, 67, and 86.
4. United Nations Environment Programme (UNEP), *Environmental Problems of the South Asian Seas Region: An Overview* (UNEP, Nairobi, 1987), p. 8.
5. United Nations Environment Programme (UNEP), *The Marine and Coastal Environment of the West and Central African Region and its State of Pollution* (UNEP, Nairobi, 1984), p. 54.

Notes:

a. Includes any type of sewage treatment.
b. Percent of sewage treated from 700 Mediterranean coastal towns and cities.

was considering plans for a sewage system in late 1990. The city relies on four rivers and a series of canals to dispose of an estimated 10,000 metric tons of raw sewage and municipal waste every day (80). Sanitation systems without sewage treatment may actually increase water pollution elsewhere if they merely transfer sewage to rivers and lakes that others use as a water source (81). For many developing countries, bacteria, parasites, and viruses in water supplies remain a more serious threat to human health than toxic contaminants (82). Table 11.3 illustrates the amount of water treatment in certain world regions.

Industry And Mining

Industry and mining are the principal sources of heavy metals and synthetic organic chemicals in freshwater. Industrial sources of heavy metal pollution include dust from smelting and metal processing; discharge of heavy metal solutions used in plating, galvanizing, and pickling; use of metals and metal compounds in paints, plastics, batteries, and tanning; and leaching from solid waste dumps (83) (84). A 1980 study showed that about 70 percent of anthropogenic heavy metals in the Federal Republic of Germany's Ruhr River came from industrial sources (85).

Heavy metals bioaccumulate at higher levels of the food chain and so pose special risks for people who consume crops grown with, or fish caught in, contaminated waters. More than 600 reported deaths in Japan between 1953 and 1970 were attributed to heavy metal contamination of air, drinking water, fish, and rice (86). Since the 1970s, however, improved wastewater treatment has reduced levels of heavy metals in most major rivers in the industrialized countries (87).

Most synthetic organic chemical pollution comes from industrial sources, including chemical and petrochemical refineries, pharmaceutical manufacturing, iron and steel plants, wood pulp and paper process-

ing, and food processing. Like heavy metals, synthetic organic compounds such as PCBs and certain pesticides concentrate at higher levels of the food chain. Some increase the risk of cancer and reproductive abnormalities in fish, aquatic mammals, and humans. Costs of freshwater pollution from synthetic organics include reduced productivity of fisheries (88), restrictions on consumption of fish from contaminated areas, and contamination of drinking water (89).

In general, industry accounts for a smaller share of freshwater pollution in developing than in developed countries (90). Nevertheless, it poses a serious problem in developing countries because pollution control is often lacking. Such pollution is especially severe in rapidly industrializing regions such as East Asia (91).

Mining and petroleum extraction pollute freshwater either through discharges of brine or through leaching from mine tailings into groundwater (92). Coal mining and petroleum drilling and refining discharge organic compounds (93). Coal, phosphate, and metal mines pollute freshwater with heavy metals, often at high environmental costs (94). For instance, heavy metals leaching from mine wastes contaminated rice fields in the Ichi River basin in Japan and are correlated with a high incidence of kidney failure. Heavy metal pollution from mines in the Upper Silesia area of Poland wiped out fish in the Szola River (95).

The brine discharged from oil wells (96) or salt and potash mines can also increase the salinity of freshwater bodies. Saline discharges from mines in Germany have made Rhine water unsuitable for greenhouse gardening in the Netherlands (97). Finally, water withdrawal for mine drainage can cause saltwater intrusion into freshwater aquifers (98).

In developing countries, mining can be a greater source of pollution than manufacturing or processing. For instance, mining is a major source of pollution in South America, particularly in the Andes (99).

Agriculture

Agriculture is the leading nonpoint source for water pollutants such as sediments, pesticides, and nutrients, principally nitrogen and phosphorus (100). Increasing demand for food crops has resulted in increased conversion of forests and grasslands into croplands in many countries. One result is greater soil erosion and sedimentation of streams. At the same time, farmers—especially in some developing countries—have increased production by using larger amounts of fertilizers and pesticides, some of which run off into streams or percolate into groundwater (101). Other agricultural practices, such as frequent plowing and excessive irrigation, can aggravate pollution of freshwater with sediments, salts, and pesticides (102). (See Chapter 7, "Food and Agriculture," Environmental Trends.)

Diversions of water for irrigation can dramatically affect water quality. For example, the Soviet Union's diversion of water from the Amu Darya and Syr Darya (to increase cotton production) has so altered the Aral Sea—once the fourth largest freshwater lake in the world—that even if flows into the sea were to double, the Aral would still shrink to one sixth of its 1960 area, while its salinity would increase to four times that of the oceans (103). All native fish species have disappeared, destroying the local fishing industry (104). (See *World Resources 1990–91*, Box 10.2, p. 171.)

Transport of agricultural pesticides by surface runoff and leaching into groundwater depends not only on the chemical character and solubility of a pesticide but also on soil properties, agricultural practices, and climatic conditions, particularly precipitation (105). Leaching is greatest where precipitation is high and soils have high permeability but low water-holding capacity. The chemical character of modern pesticides makes them more likely to contaminate groundwater than older pesticides, which leach more slowly through soils (106).

Livestock Farming

Over the past two decades, livestock farming has intensified, especially in Africa, Asia, and Central and South America. (See *World Resources 1990–91*, Table 18.3, pp. 282–283.) Grazing livestock remove vegetation, compact soil, and generate large quantities of manure, which affect the quality and quantity of surface runoff (107). Crop-livestock operations pose special risks for freshwater resources when farmers apply excessive amounts of manure and other nutrients to cropland. The problem is especially acute in Europe. (See Chapter 7, "Food and Agriculture," Problems with the Conventional Model.)

Logging

The clearest consequence of imprudent logging practices, particularly along streams, is an increase in erosion and sediment loads, with resulting damage to habitats for river organisms and to the water clarity necessary for aquatic plants (108). Debris from logging operations can also increase the input of organic materials, whose decomposition reduces oxygen in river waters. A recent United Nations report cites deforestation as a major cause of changes in runoff, increases in sedimentation, and downstream nutrient enrichment of rivers and lakes worldwide (109).

Deforestation along streams also allows pollutants to wash into rivers and exposes shallow nearshore waters to sunlight, raising water temperatures and fostering oxygen depletion through decomposition of aquatic plants (110). In West and Central Africa, forest clearing for grazing purposes has led to increased streambank erosion, sedimentation of streams, and loss of habitat for a wide variety of stream organisms. Increased sunlight combined with nutrient enrichment in streams has promoted the growth of filamentous algae favored by snails that host the vectors for schistosomiasis (111).

LOW-COST SOLUTIONS

Freshwater polluted by metals and industrial or agricultural chemicals requires expensive, technologically advanced treatment. Preventing pollutants from enter-

ing groundwater or surface waters can reduce treatment costs and downstream damage. Some existing, small-scale measures can also salvage nutrients for use in raising food and creating habitat for wildlife.

Treating Sewage in Wetlands and Fish Ponds

Conventional sewage treatment is expensive. In the United States, the federal government has provided $57 billion since 1972—as much as 55–75 percent of construction costs, depending on type—for sewage treatment plants (112). The United Nations has estimated that construction costs for treatment plants and submarine outfalls for the 539 Mediterranean coastal towns with populations greater than 10,000 would amount to more than $5 billion (113).

As an alternative to conventional sewage treatment, Arcata, California, a small coastal town of 15,000, has transformed a local garbage dump into 63 hectares of wetlands that serve as a simple, low-cost waste treatment plant. Sewage is collected in sewers, held in ponds where solids settle out, then released into marshes, where it is filtered and cleansed by natural processes. Some of the treated water irrigates other wetlands, the rest is pumped into the bay, where oysterbeds thrive (114).

This approach requires more land than conventional sewage treatment plants. Its cost-effectiveness depends on whether the land would produce greater value from another use, such as agriculture. One Swedish study concluded that the benefits of sewage treatment are greater than the costs of lost agricultural production on the same land (115).

In other areas of the world, partially treated sewage is used to raise fish. For example, a small fraction of the sewage generated by the 7 million inhabitants of Lima, Peru, is directed into holding ponds, where solids settle out and bacteria decompose many of the wastes. After 20–30 days, the water is clean enough to irrigate grain crops for cattle and to raise fish (116). A 1985 study for the World Bank described similar aquaculture operations relying on human excreta in Bangladesh, China, the Federal Republic of Germany, Hungary, India, Indonesia, Israel, Malaysia, Taiwan, Thailand, and Viet Nam (117).

The largest single waste-fed aquaculture system in the world is the Calcutta sewage system, where water and sewage are fed into two lakes covering an estimated 2,500 hectares. After an initial bloom of algae, fish—principally carp and tilapia—are introduced, and additional sewage is fed into the lakes once each month. The system supplies about 7,000 metric tons of fish annually to the Calcutta market, or 2.8 metric tons per hectare per year (118).

Several measures can virtually eliminate human health concerns about fish from sewage-fed fish ponds, such as detaining sewage in stabilization ponds for at least 20 days before introducing it into fish ponds, or transferring fish and shellfish to clean water before harvesting (119).

Reducing Industrial Pollution

Tighter government regulation has increased the costs of traditional "end-of-pipe" waste management, such as cleaning up spills and dumps, landfilling, incineration, and off-site recycling (120). In the United States, private business spending on pollution control and waste management increased from $28 billion in 1972 to $47 billion in 1988 (in constant dollars) (121) (122). As a result, industry has sought to reduce the amount of waste it generates in the first place.

Waste reduction is a broad management approach using a variety of technologies. It cuts the volume and toxicity of wastes by recycling them or by redesigning processes and products (123). Companies that undertake waste-reduction programs often save money by using materials and energy more efficiently or by reducing the costs of conventional pollution control and waste disposal (124). Waste reduction has been most successful for process industries such as manufacturing and chemicals. The approach does not work as well in mining or in such high-temperature operations as burning fossil fuels, smelting, and cement production.

The Institute for Local Self-Reliance in Washington, D.C., has documented a variety of waste reduction schemes that significantly reduce production of hazardous materials—and water pollution:

■ The Eaton Corporation of Humboldt, Tennessee, a manufacturer of truck axle housings, started closed-loop recycling of all metalworking fluids. The process has cut annual regulated wastewater generation from 1.8 million liters to zero, while saving the company $191,200 per year (125).

■ SKF Steel, Inc., of Hofors, Sweden, uses high-temperature "plasma gas" technology to recycle metal-bearing wastes from conventional steel smelters into usable metals and a nonhazardous slag suitable for road construction. Its SkanDust plant in Landskrona, Sweden, processes 63,500 metric tons of smelting dust a year, eliminating wastes that otherwise could leach heavy metals into groundwater, rivers, and lakes (126).

■ As part of a company-wide waste-minimization program, the 3M Corporation plant in Cordova, Illinois, a manufacturer of organic chemicals including resins and adhesives, adopted a new method for cleaning reaction tanks using high-pressure application of solvents and strippers. The new method reduced the amount of cleaning agents used by 900 metric tons per year while reducing equipment downtime, energy consumption, and the cost of pollution control (127).

According to INFORM, a New York-based environmental research organization, waste reduction probably offers the greatest potential for environmental benefit of any waste management strategy. Preliminary data show that 29 chemical manufacturers, implementing 181 individual waste reduction actions, reduced targeted waste streams by an average of 71 percent (measured by weight) at an average annual savings of $351,000 per action (128). Despite such savings, factory managers often neglect waste reduction because environmental regulations encourage them to focus on disposal or because other investments yield marginally higher returns (129) (130).

Controlling Runoff Pollution

The diffuse nature of runoff requires an emphasis on land management throughout a river basin. A variety of techniques can be used to reduce runoff pollution, including soil-conserving agricultural practices, forestry road management, land surface roughening, sedimentation traps, bank stabilization, and redesigned streets (131).

Urban Runoff

In the last two decades, several practices—including small-scale detention ponds, infiltration basins, porous pavements, and vegetative strips—have been developed that can reduce urban inputs of pollutants by up to 80 percent. Most of these practices enhance pollutant removal by detaining storm waters or enabling them to infiltrate the ground (132).

The effectiveness of these techniques depends on the mechanism used, the fraction of annual runoff that is effectively treated, and the nature of the pollutant being removed (133). Settling ponds, for instance, can be almost completely effective in removing pollutants bound to sediments, but they generally remove less than half of soluble nutrients. Biological mechanisms, such as uptake by bacteria or plants can remove more soluble nutrients. With proper planning, many techniques can also provide important wildlife habitat, groundwater recharge, and recreational benefits (134). Some techniques, such as retaining ponds, may increase downstream water temperatures, whereas others, such as infiltration systems, have little effect on temperature (135).

Agricultural Runoff

In the last 20 years, agricultural management practices have been developed to reduce runoff containing nutrients and pesticides that pollute groundwater and surface waters. Such practices include conservation tillage, crop rotation, contour planting, planting cover crops in winter, filter systems, terrace systems, and fertilizer management. These practices control sediment erosion and remove up to 60 percent of the nitrogen and phosphorous available for runoff from croplands.

One study estimated that conservation tillage alone can reduce phosphorus loads to surface waters by 30 percent, although nitrogen is unaffected (136). In combination, these practices are even more effective. They can also reduce pesticide runoff, although their effect on migration of pesticides to groundwater is undetermined (137). (See Chapter 7, "Food and Agriculture," Box 7.2.)

Other new mechanisms for reducing agricultural pollution include increasing taxes and fees on inputs such as pesticides, fertilizers, and irrigation water; incentives to leave highly erodible land uncultivated; and the removal of production subsidies. (See Chapter 7, "Food and Agriculture," New Policy Options.)

Runoff from Livestock Farms

Practices such as pond construction and permanent vegetation improvement can reduce nitrogen and phosphorus runoff from pasturelands by up to 60 percent (138). Limited use of such practices in the Potomac River basin in the United States has yielded runoff reductions of 7 percent in nitrogen and phosphorus (139). Management of manure through proper storage and application can substantially reduce nutrient runoff and the need for commercial fertilizers. Treatment lagoons and ponds can reduce the amount of nutrients in animal wastes before they are applied to fields (140).

In the Netherlands, the size and number of livestock farms are being reduced, and regional centers are being established to store surplus manure during periods when spreading these nutrients on agricultural lands would lead to runoff or leaching (141). Dairy farms near the Everglades in the United States are now required to reduce the flow of nutrients from their feed lots by using wastewater to irrigate pastures (142).

Logging Runoff

Protecting forested areas along the headwaters of a river is central to protecting the water quality of the entire river (143). Locating roads across rather than up and down slopes, allowing drainage to flow through culverts beneath roads, and locating activities away from streams can significantly reduce runoff and sedimentation from logging operations. Leaving forested buffers along streams can filter out sediments and nutrients eroded from deforested areas and reduce streambank erosion (144).

INTERNATIONAL COOPERATION

Effective water management requires a broad plan for an entire river basin (145). This is particularly challenging where a river basin is under the jurisdiction of several nations. Worldwide, 214 river or lake basins, populated by 40 percent of the world's human population and covering more than 50 percent of the Earth's land area, are shared by two or more countries (146) (147). Competition for groundwater also contributes to international tensions, especially in the Middle East (148). (See Table 11.4.).

International law regarding shared freshwater resources gives little guidance in international river basin management. For instance, current international law limits the responsibility of upstream nations to ensuring that their activities do not conflict with the rights of downstream nations (149). As a result, most downstream countries do not pursue their rights through international courts, but through diplomacy (150). The United Nations has attempted to provide guidance in this area. (See Box 11.2.)

By 1971, 286 international treaties concerning water resources had been negotiated. More than two thirds of them concerned river basins in Europe and North America, and most sought coordinated surveys and planning or regulation of navigation (151). Some of the more recent efforts involve control of land-based

Table 11.4 International Water Disputes

River	Countries in Dispute	Issues
Nile	Egypt, Ethiopia, Sudan	Siltation, flooding, water flow/diversion
Euphrates, Tigris	Iraq, Syria, Turkey	Reduced water flow, salinization
Jordan, Yarmuk Litani, West Bank aquifer	Israel, Jordan, Syria, Lebanon	Water flow/diversion
Indus, Sutlei	India, Pakistan	Irrigation
Ganges-Brahmaputra	Bangladesh, India	Siltation, flooding, water flow
Salween	Myanmar, China	Siltation, flooding
Mekong	Cambodia, Laos, Thailand, Viet Nam	Water flow, flooding
Paraná	Argentina, Brazil	Dam, land inundation
Lauca	Bolivia, Chile	Dam, salinization
Rio Grande, Colorado	Mexico, United States	Salinization, water flow, agrochemical pollution
Rhine	France, Netherlands, Switzerland, Germany	Industrial pollution
Maas, Schelde	Belgium, Netherlands	Salinization, industrial pollution
Elbe	Czechoslovakia, Germany	Industrial pollution
Szamos	Hungary, Romania	Industrial pollution

Source: Michael Renner, *National Security: The Economic and Environmental Dimensions*, Worldwatch Paper 89 (Worldwatch Institute, Washington, D.C., 1989), p. 32.

sources of pollution. In February 1991, for instance, the Economic Commission for Europe adopted a convention addressing the prevention, control, and reduction of transboundary pollution that could have an important effect on water resources (152). Countries sharing river basins flowing into the North Sea are cooperating to reduce contamination of marine waters by reducing contamination of freshwater.

International Management of the Rhine River Basin

One of the few examples of international efforts to reduce pollutants in an international river basin is a series of treaties concerning the Rhine River, the basin of which covers 225,000 square kilometers and includes eight countries (153). These treaties have had both encouraging success and spectacular failure.

At the insistence of the Netherlands, which was concerned about increased salinity in the Rhine, France, the Federal Republic of Germany, Luxembourg, the Netherlands, and Switzerland began discussing arrangements for reducing pollution in the 1950s, and formed the International Commission for the Protection of the Rhine against Pollution (ICPRP) in 1963. A technical commission, charged with monitoring pollutants, the ICPRP at first achieved few concrete results. However, to stem increasing pollution from industrial and municipal sources, the parties to the ICPRP signed the Convention for the Protection of the Rhine Against Chemical Pollution in 1976 (154) (155). In December 1986, they agreed to the Rhine Action Programme,

Box 11.2 The United Nations on Freshwater Resources

In 1972, the United Nations Conference on the Human Environment suggested the following principles in its Recommendation 51 of the Stockholm Action Plan:

■ Nations agree that when major water resource activities are contemplated that may have a significant environmental effect on another country, the other country should be notified well in advance of the activity envisaged.

■ The basic objective of all water resource use and development activities from the environmental point of view is to ensure the best use of water and to avoid its pollution in each country.

■ The net benefits of hydrologic regions common to more than one national jurisdiction are to be shared equitably by the nations affected (1).

In January 1991, a report on freshwater by the Preparatory Committee for United Nations Conference on the Environment and Development called for action in seven areas (2):

■ Environmentally sound development of freshwater resources through incorporation of environmental quality concerns in development plans, economic valuation of water resources, and preservation of ecologically sensitive water resources;

■ Managing transboundary watercourses and international lakes through establishment of multilateral commissions, adjustment of national laws to enhance intercountry cooperation, improved communication capabilities, and planning for entire watersheds;

■ Control of water pollution through land use policy, recycling and recovery, clean technology, substitution of hazardous substances and techniques, and testing of appropriate techniques for reduction and control of urban wastewater and agricultural runoff;

■ Safeguarding water supplies through integrated management of water resources and liquid and solid wastes, strengthening of local institutions in managing water and sanitation programs, and use of appropriate technologies;

■ Wise use of living freshwater resources through conservation of aquatic biological diversity, increased propagation and culture, and increased research on aquaculture;

■ Building capacity for monitoring, including development of national water quality monitoring networks, standardized monitoring techniques and measurements, and

adaptation of monitoring techniques to tropical conditions; and

■ Strengthening institutional and manpower capacities through preparation and implementation of necessary legislation, guidance on technical issues by international agencies, information exchange, development of national training plans, and special attention to specific sociocultural and linguistic groups and to the role of women in this area.

References and Notes

1. United Nations Environment Programme (UNEP), *In Defense of the Earth* (UNEP, New York, 1981), p. 47, quoted in Alexander Kiss, "The Protection of the Rhine Against Pollution," *Natural Resources Journal,* Vol. 25, No. 3 (University of New Mexico School of Law, Albuquerque, New Mexico, July 1985), p. 615.

2. Preparatory Committee for the United Nations Conference on Environment and Development (PREPCOM), "Protection of the Quality and Supply of Freshwater Resources: Application of Integrated Approaches to the Development, Management and Use of Water Resources," (PREPCOM, Geneva, 1991), pp. 17-21.

which seeks to produce drinkable water from the Rhine, reduce sediment pollution, and restore the Rhine environment so that indigenous aquatic life returns. To this end, the parties agreed to a 50-percent reduction (from 1985 levels) in the discharge of 30 priority pollutants into the river by 1995 (156). The Netherlands, the Federal Republic of Germany, France, and Switzerland agreed to share abatement costs of $136 million (157). And in the summer of 1991, the German chemical industry federation agreed to reduce the flow of toxic chemicals into the Rhine (158). These international efforts, combined with domestic pollution controls, have produced measurable benefits: since the early 1970s, concentrations of heavy metals have fallen and biological treatment of organic waste has reduced oxygen depletion and fish kills (159) (160).

These encouraging results must be measured against a spectacular and nearly catastrophic failure. The Convention for the Protection of the Rhine Against Chemical Pollution includes provisions for an international warning system that is triggered by sudden and sizable increases in pollutants. The warning system failed in November 1986, when efforts to extinguish a fire in a chemical warehouse in Basel, Switzerland, released unknown quantities of a potpourri of chemicals including organophosphates, organic mercury compounds, and various agrochemicals. Swiss authorities may have violated the Conventions' warning provisions by not informing the other parties about the release of pollutants. If winter ice had covered the river and concealed the fish killed by the toxic chemicals, withdrawals from the river for drinking water might well

have continued—with catastrophic consequences. The Rhine conventions did not provide citizens downstream from the accident with a clear basis for pursuing damages against the chemical plant or Swiss authorities (161).

So far, international agreements have failed to control some key pollutants; for example, concentrations of nitrates, mostly of agricultural origin, continue to rise; and groundwater in Germany is increasingly contaminated with nitrates and pesticides. Salmon, at the top of the food chain and therefore a key indicator of river health, have disappeared completely from the Rhine. And although chlorides were one of the pollutants originally targeted for control by the ICPRP, only one country, France, has reduced discharges (162).

Upstream Downstream

Cooperation among states and nations is usually necessary to manage watershed pollution, but upstream nations or states have little incentive to curb their pollution when they can simply pass the damage on to their downstream neighbors. The case studies in Chapter 12, "Oceans and Coasts," suggest that regional agreements have the best chance of success when there is a mediating body, a history of cooperation, a scientific basis for action—and when all parties benefit from cleaner water. When upstream polluters can see no benefit from the expense of curbing their pollution, negotiations are especially difficult.

Even within a nation, where a central government can provide economic incentives or impose regulations to protect downstream interests, there are few examples of effective watershed management. Most industrialized nations have applied discharge regulations to industrial polluters and have helped finance municipal sewage systems. Controls on runoff pollution are just emerging, however, and very little has been done to hold upstream polluters, such as farming and logging interests, responsible for downstream loss of water quality, fisheries, and habitat. A watershed "polluter pays" management scheme might involve policy tools such as regulations, penalties, compensation, or tax incentives to discourage upstream pollution.

The Conditions and Trends section was written by World Resources *Senior Editor Robert Livernash. Focus On River Basin Pollution was written by Michael Weber, a marine consultant in Washington, D.C. Daniel Seligman,* World Resources *research assistant, contributed to this chapter.*

References and Notes

1. G. Tyler Miller, Jr., *Environmental Science: Sustaining the Earth* (Wadsworth, Belmont, California, 1991), p. 232.
2. World Resources Institute in collaboration with the United Nations Environment Programme and the United Nations Development Programme, *World Resources 1990-91* (Oxford University Press, New York, 1990), p. 166.
3. *Op. cit.* 1.
4. *Op. cit.* 2.
5. M.I. L'vovich, "Ecological Foundations of Global Water Resources Conservation," in *Resources and World Development*, D.J. McLaren and B.J. Skinner, eds. (John Wiley and Sons, Chichester and New York, 1987), p. 831.
6. World Resources Institute and International Institute for Environment and Development, *World Resources 1986* (Basic Books, New York, 1986), pp. 124-125.
7. *Op. cit.* 5.
8. World Resources Institute and International Institute for Environment and Development in collaboration with the United Nations Environment Programme, *World Resources 1988-89* (Basic Books, New York, 1988), p. 128.
9. Frits van der Leeden, Fred L. Troise, and David K. Todd, *The Water Encyclopedia* (Lewis Publishers Inc., Chelsea, Michigan, 1990), p. 41.
10. *Op. cit.* 1, p. 236.
11. *Op. cit.* 1, pp. 237-238.
12. *Op. cit.* 9, p. 66.
13. United Nations Environment Programme (UNEP), *State of the Environment*, draft freshwater chapter (UNEP, Nairobi, forthcoming), February 1991, p. 14.
14. *Op. cit.* 2, pp. 174-176.
15. *Op. cit.* 2, p. 170.
16. *Op. cit.* 2, p. 172.
17. *Op. cit.* 2, p. 172.
18. *Op. cit.* 2, p. 173.
19. *Op. cit.* 2, p. 173.
20. Organisation for Economic Co-operation and Development (OECD), *The State of the Environment* (OECD, Paris, 1991), p. 60.
21. *Ibid.*
22. *Op. cit.* 2, p. 163.
23. *Op. cit.* 2, pp. 162-163.
24. World Health Organization (WHO) and United Nations Environment Programme (UNEP), *WHO/UNEP Report on Water Quality* (WHO and UNEP, Geneva and Nairobi, 1991), pp. 61-63.
25. Malin Falkenmark and Jan Lundqvist, "Water Scarcity—The Forgotten Dimension," paper presented at the IUCN Workshop on Pollution and Natural Resources, Perth, Australia, November 1990, pp. 9-11.

26. Ann Scott Tyson, "Water is Running Out in China," *Christian Science Monitor* (June 5, 1990), pp. 12-13.
27. California Department of Water Resources, "Water Conditions in California," Bulletin 120-91, Report No. 4 (State of California, Sacramento, California, 1991), reprinted in Peter H. Gleick and Linda Nash, *The Societal and Environmental Costs of the Continuing California Drought* (Pacific Institute for Studies in Development, Environment and Security, Berkeley, California, 1991), p. 5.
28. Peter H. Gleick and Linda Nash, *The Societal and Environmental Costs of the Continuing California Drought* (Pacific Institute for Studies in Development, Environment and Security, Berkeley, California, 1991), p. x.
29. *Ibid.*, pp. xii-xiv.
30. Richard W. Stevenson, "Dry California Turns to the Pacific," *New York Times* (March 5, 1991), p. D1.
31. Joyce R. Starr, "Water Wars," *Foreign Policy*, No. 82 (Spring 1991), p. 17.
32. *Ibid.*, p. 21.
33. *Ibid.*, pp. 24, 26.
34. *Ibid.*, pp. 27, 29.
35. *Ibid.*, pp. 22, 33-34.
36. Food and Agriculture Organization of the United Nations (FAO), "An International Action Programme on Water and Sustainable Agricultural Development" (FAO, Rome, 1990), p. 15.
37. United Nations Economic and Social Council, "Achievements of the International Drinking Water Supply and Sanitation Decade 1981-90" (United Nations, New York, 1990), pp. 3-6.
38. *Ibid.*, p. 21.
39. *Ibid.*, pp. 23-24.
40. Preparatory Committee for the United Nations Conference on Environment and Development (PREPCOM), "Protection of the Quality and Supply of Freshwater Resources: Application of Integrated Approaches to the Development, Management and Use of Water Resources" (PREPCOM, Geneva, 1991), pp. 7-9.
41. *Ibid.*, pp. 2-4.
42. Peter A. Kumble, *The State of the Anacostia: 1989 Status Report* (Metropolitan Washington Council of Governments, Washington, D.C., 1990), pp. 13-19.
43. Larry Master, "Aquatic Animals: Endangerment Alert," *Nature Conservancy* (March/April 1991), pp. 26-27.
44. Organisation for Economic Co-operation and Development (OECD), *Water Pollution by Fertilizers and Pesticides* (OECD, Paris, 1986), p. 65.
45. Timothy R. Henderson, "The Institutional Framework for Protecting Groundwater in the United States," in *Planning for Groundwa-*

ter Protection, G. William Page, ed. (Academic Press, San Diego, California, 1987), pp. 29-30.
46. *Op. cit.* 42, pp. 21-22.
47. *Op. cit.* 40, pp. 11-13.
48. M. Marchand and F.H. Toornstra, *Ecological Guidelines for River Basin Development* (translated from Dutch) (Commission on Ecology and Development Cooperation, Leiden, the Netherlands, 1986), p. 1.
49. *Op. cit.* 2, pp. 167-168.
50. Peter Rogers, Peter Lydon, and David Seckler, *Eastern Waters Study: Strategies to Manage Flood and Drought in the Ganges-Brahmaputra Basin*, prepared for U.S. Agency for International Development, (Irrigation Support Project for Asia and the Near East, Arlington, Virginia, 1989), pp. 9 and 12.
51. *Op. cit.* 1, pp. 232-234.
52. *Op. cit.* 1, pp. 232-234.
53. *Op. cit.* 48, p. 4.
54. A.J. Bowie and C.K. Mutchler, "Sediment Sources and Yields from Complex Watersheds," in *Proceedings of the Third International Symposium on River Sedimentation*, S.Y. Wang, H.W. Shen and L.Z. Ding, eds. (University of Mississippi, University, Mississippi, 1986), p. 1223.
55. *Op. cit.* 1, p. 250.
56. John D. Milliman, "Fluvial Sediment in Coastal Seas: Flux and Fate," *Nature and Resources*, Vol. 26, No. 4 (Parthenon, Park Ridge, New Jersey, 1990), p. 16.
57. *Op. cit.* 2, p. 171.
58. *Op. cit.* 1, p. 240.
59. Martine Allard, GEMS/Water Co-ordinator, National Water Institute, Burlington, Ontario, Canada, 1991 (personal communication).
60. P.G. Waldo, "Sediment Yields from Large Watersheds," in *Third International Symposium on River Sedimentation* (University of Mississippi, University, Mississippi, 1986), p. 1241.
61. *Op. cit.* 2, p. 168.
62. *Op. cit.* 48, pp. 12-14.
63. G. Noble and W. Wolff, "The Ecological Importance of Wetlands," paper presented at the Conference of the Contracting Parties of the Convention on Wetlands of International Importance Especially as Waterfowl Habitat, Goningen, May 1984, cited in M. Marchand and F.H. Toornstra, *Ecological Guidelines for River Basin Development* (translated from Dutch) (Commission for Ecology and Development Cooperation, Leiden, the Netherlands, 1986), p. 12.
64. Mark K. Mitchell and William B. Stapp, *Field Manual for Water Quality Monitoring: An Environmental Education Program for*

Schools, 4th ed.(Thomson-Shores, Dexter, Michigan, 1990), p. 153.

65. Robert C. Petersen, Jr., Bent Lauge Madsen, Margaret A. Wilzbach, *et al.*, "Stream Management: Emerging Global Similarities," *Ambio*, Vol. 16, No. 4 (1987), p. 16.

66. *Op. cit.* 2, p. 16.

67. *Op. cit.* 1, pp. 248-249.

68. Jon Lugbill, *Potomac River Basin Nutrient Inventory* (Metropolitan Washington Council of Governments, Washington, D.C., 1987), p. 141.

69. U.S. Environmental Protection Agency (EPA), *Report to Congress: Water Quality of the Nation's Lakes* (EPA, Washington, D.C., 1989), p. 12.

70. *Op. cit.* 1, pp. 233-234.

71. David Moody, Chief, Office of Water Summary, U.S. Geological Survey, Washington, D.C., 1991 (personal communication).

72. *Op. cit.* 64, pp. 47 and 149.

73. Bruce Newton, Chief, Watershed Branch, U.S. Environmental Protection Agency, Washington, D.C., 1991 (personal communication).

74. "Urbanization Increases Temperatures in Small Headwater Streams According to COG Study," *Waterline*, Vol. 2, No. 3 (Metropolitan Washington Council of Governments, Washington, D.C., Winter 1991), pp. 4-5.

75. *Op. cit.* 69, p. 15.

76. *Op. cit.* 1, p. 260.

77. *Op. cit.* 1, p. 261.

78. *Op. cit.* 64, p. 33.

79. *Op. cit.* 40, p. 3.

80. Don Hinrichsen, *Our Common Seas: Coasts in Crisis*, (EarthScan Publications, London, in association with the United Nations Environment Programme, Nairobi, 1990), p. 108.

81. *Op. cit.* 2, p. 69.

82. G. William Page, "Drinking Water and Health," in *Planning for Groundwater Protection*, G. William Page, ed. (Academic Press, San Diego, California, 1987), p. 69.

83. Michel Meybeck, Deborah V. Chapman, and Richard Helmer, eds., *Global Environment Monitoring System: Global Freshwater Quality, A First Assessment* (Basil Blackwell Ltd., Oxford, U.K., 1989), p. 160.

84. Rodney Sobin, Research Assistant, World Resources Institute, Washington, D.C., 1991 (personal communication).

85. *Op. cit.* 82, p. 161.

86. *Op. cit.* 82, p. 159.

87. Organisation for Economic Co-operation and Development (OECD), *OECD Environmental Data Compendium 1991* (OECD, Paris, 1991), Data Supplement, Tables 3.3 D and E, pp. 60-63.

88. *Op. cit.* 2, p. 186.

89. *Op. cit.* 83.

90. *Op. cit.* 82, p. 12.

91. *Op. cit.* 40, p. 3.

92. *Op. cit.* 82, p. 282.

93. *Op. cit.* 82, pp. 182-183.

94. *Op. cit.* 82, p. 144.

95. *Op. cit.* 82, pp. 162-163.

96. *Op. cit.* 82, p. 145.

97. *Op. cit.* 82, p. 283.

98. *Op. cit.* 82, p. 144.

99. *Op. cit.* 40, p. 3.

100. *Op. cit.* 1, p. 25.

101. *Op. cit.* 44, pp. 30-31, 33, and 131.

102. *Op. cit.* 44, pp. 25-26.

103. Kenneth D. Frederick, "The Disappearing Aral Sea," *Resources*, No. 102 (Winter 1991), p. 11.

104. *Op. cit.* 1, p. 242.

105. Robert F. Carsel and Charles N. Smith, "Impact of Pesticides on Ground Water Contamination," in *Silent Spring Revisited*, Gino J. Marco, Robert M. Hollingworth, and William Durham, eds. (American Chemical Society, Washington, D.C., 1987), p. 74.

106. *Ibid.*, p. 76.

107. *Op. cit.* 44, pp. 100-101.

108. R.L. Welcome, *River Basins* (Food and Agriculture Organization of the United Nations, Rome, 1983), p. 38.

109. *Op. cit.* 40, pp. 2-3.

110. *Op. cit.* 106, p. 38.

111. *Op. cit.* 65, p. 171-172.

112. Martin R. Lee, John Blodgett, Claudia Copeland, *et al.*, *Summaries of Environmental Laws Administered by the Environmental Protection Agency* (Congressional Research Service, Washington, D.C., 1991), p. 34.

113. Michel Grenon and Michel Batisse, eds., *Futures for the Mediterranean Basin: The Blue Plan* (Oxford University Press, Oxford, U.K., 1989), p. 255.

114. *Op. cit.* 1, p. 263.

115. *Op. cit.* 65, pp. 171-172.

116. *Op. cit.* 1, p. 26.

117. Peter Edwards, *Aquaculture: A Component of Low Cost Sanitation Technology* (The World Bank, Washington, D.C., 1985), pp. 3-14.

118. *Ibid.*, pp. 7-9.

119. *Ibid.*, pp. 37-42.

120. John Elkington and Jonathan Shopley, *Cleaning Up: U.S. Waste Management Technology and Third World Development* (World Resources Institute, Washington, D.C., 1989), p. 7.

121. Kit D. Farber and Gary L. Rutledge, "Pollution Abatement and Control Expenditures: Revised Estimates for 1972-83, Estimates for 1984," *Survey of Current Business*, Vol. 66, No. 7 (U.S. Department of Commerce, Bureau of Economic Analysis, Washington, D.C.), July 1986, p. 97.

122. David M. Bratton and Gary L. Rutledge, "Pollution Abatement and Control Expenditures, 1985-1988," *Survey of Current Business*, Vol. 70, No. 11, (U.S. Department of Commerce, Bureau of Economic Analysis, Washington, D.C., November, 1990), p. 34.

123. *Op. cit.* 118, p. 14.

124. George Heaton, Robert Repetto, and Rodney Sobin, *Transforming Technology: An Agenda for Environmentally Sustainable Growth in the 21st Century* (World Resources Institute, Washington, D.C., 1991), p. 17.

125. Larry Martin, *Proven Profits from Pollution Prevention: Volume II* (Institute for Local Self-Reliance, Washington, D.C., 1989), pp. 87-89.

126. *Ibid.*, pp. 65-69.

127. *Ibid.*, pp. 41-43.

128. Warren R. Muir, "Testimony Before the United States Senate Committee on Environment and Public Works, Subcommittee on Environmental Protection, on the Toxic Use and Source Reduction Provisions of S.976, The Resource Conservation and Recovery Act Amendments of 1991" (INFORM, New York, July 24, 1991), pp. 3 and 5.

129. Mark Dorfman, Associate Program Director, INFORM, New York, 1991 (personal communication).

130. Larry Martin, United Nations Conference on Environment and Development Liaison,

The Other Economic Summit, Washington, D.C., 1991 (personal communication).

131. *Op. cit.* 69, p. 16.

132. Thomas R. Schueler, *Controlling Urban Runoff: A Practical Manual for Planning and Designing Urban BMPs* (Metropolitan Washington Council of Governments, Washington, D.C., 1987), Figure 2.4, p. 2.13.

133. *Ibid.*, p. 2.11.

134. *Ibid.*, p. 2.12.

135. *Op. cit.* 74, p. 4.

136. *Op. cit.* 68, p. 47 and Table 4.8, p. 50.

137. *Op. cit.* 104, p. 81.

138. *Op. cit.* 68, p. 77.

139. *Op. cit.* 68, p. 85.

140. *Op. cit.* 68, p. 94.

141. *Op. cit.* 65, p. 170.

142. Keith Schneider, "Returning Part of Everglades to Nature for $700 Million," *New York Times* (March 11, 1991), p. B10.

143. *Op. cit.* 65, p. 172.

144. *Op. cit.* 68, p. 128.

145. B.M. Abbas, "River Basin Development: Keynote Address," in *Proceedings of the National Symposium on River Basin Development*, Munir Zaman, ed. (Tycooly International, Dublin, 1983), p. 6.

146. Jerome Delli Priscoli, "Epilogue," *Water International*, Vol. 15, No. 4 (International Water Resources Association, Urbana, Illinois, 1990), p. 236.

147. Asit K. Biswas, "Some Major Issues in River Basin Management for Developing Countries," in *Proceedings of the National Symposium on River Basin Development*, Munir Zaman, ed. (Tycooly International, Dublin, 1983), p. 22.

148. *Op. cit.* 31, p. 17.

149. Andrew H. Darrell, "Killing the Rhine: Immoral, But Is It Illegal?" *Virginia Journal of International Law*, Vol. 29, No. 2 (1989), pp. 441-447.

150. *Ibid.*, p. 449.

151. Margaret S. Petersen, *Water Resource Planning and Development* (Prentice-Hall, Englewood Cliffs, New Jersey, 1984), p. 164.

152. United Nations (U.N.), "Convention on Environmental Impact Assessment in a Transboundary Context" (U.N., Espoo, Finland, 1991), p. 2.

153. John Bartholomew and Son, *Times Atlas of the World*, 7th ed. (Times Books, London, 1988), p. xiv.

154. Alexander Kiss, "The Protection of the Rhine Against Pollution," *Natural Resources Journal*, Vol. 25, No. 3 (University of Mexico School of Law, Albuquerque, New Mexico, 1985), pp. 621-625.

155. A. Volker, "Integrated Development of the Delta and Upland Portions of a River Basin," in *Proceedings of the National Symposium on River Basin Development*, Munir Zaman, ed. (Tycooly International, Dublin, 1983), pp. 47-50.

156. J. de Jong, "Management of the River Rhine," *Water Environment and Technology*, Vol. 2, No. 4, (April 1990), pp. 50-51.

157. Peter H. Sand, *Lessons Learned in Global Environmental Governance* (World Resources Institute, Washington, D.C., 1990), p. 8.

158. *Op. cit.* 154, p. 46.

159. *Op. cit.* 154, p. 46.

160. Richard L. Holman, "International World Wire: Protection Pact for the Rhine," *Wall Street Journal* (August 22, 1991), p. A7.

161. *Op. cit.* 147, pp. 422 and 453.

162. *Op. cit.* 154, pp. 46, 49, and 50.

12. Oceans and Coasts

The trends of the past 20 years show increasing coastal pollution, accelerated destruction of coastal marine habitats, and, in many areas, a declining catch of marine fish species that have been affected by overfishing and pollution.

Marine pollution control efforts have shown good results in a few areas, but despite years of effort, only a small fraction of the world's wastewater is treated. In addition, new surveys show that over 50 percent of nitrogen, phosphorus, and sediment pollution comes not from sewage discharge pipes but from runoff from cities, farms, and logging and mining operations. Few governments attempt to control these pollution sources. Marine pollution is especially serious in estuaries and enclosed seas, such as the Baltic and Mediterranean, where pollutants become trapped. (See Focus On Coastal Pollution, below, and Chapter 11, "Freshwater," Focus On River Basin Pollution.)

The destruction of coastal habitat continued over the past 20 years as countries developed their coastlines for urban, commercial, and industrial uses. For example, available figures indicate that most tropical countries have lost more than one half their mangrove forests. (See Coastal Habitat Destruction, below.)

Pollution and destruction of coastal breeding and nursery grounds, combined with overfishing, have reduced the catch of many important commercial fish species. While increasing the total catch per vessel over the past several decades, improvements in electronic navigation, fish-finding instruments, and the efficiency of fishing gear may have masked declining populations in some areas. Yet, in the late 1980s, catches began declining in several major fishing areas. In 1990, the total global fish catch declined for the first time in 13 years. This situation may reflect natural fluctuations in fish stocks and a decrease in fishing effort dictated by conservation efforts, but overfishing, coastal habitat destruction, and water pollution may also be the cause.

Dealing with ocean pollution and overfishing can be hampered by the longstanding tradition of freedom of the seas and the widespread misconception that the resources there are unlimited. It is becoming increasingly clear that without cooperative international management, the oceans—like freshwater—can be seriously degraded. There is also widespread failure to connect upstream polluting activities with coastal pollution because watersheds are typically fragmented into several political jurisdictions.

Over the past 20 years, several international actions have been taken to control both dumping of hazardous and radioactive materials at sea and pollution from ships. Fishing agreements exist for a number of regions and species. Under the United Nations Environment Programme (UNEP), 10 regions have formed (and 3 more are forming) Regional Seas Programmes to protect coastal seas. More recently, nearly 1,000 marine protected areas have been established by 71 nations. However, international commissions are beginning to recognize that only a few of these efforts have even considered the major sources of land-based ocean pollution, and none has succeeded in controlling them.

Stopping land-based pollution, especially pollutants from runoff, requires entering a new political arena, contesting powerful interests in agriculture and industry, and dealing with a nearly worldwide economic framework that allows land-based pollutant sources to dispose of their wastes in waterways at no direct cost.

CONDITIONS AND TRENDS

Global Trends

POLLUTION TRENDS

Because no international body regularly monitors the oceans' health, determining trends is difficult. Many nations cooperate with the United Nations International Oceanographic Commission and the United Nations Environment Programme's Regional Seas Programmes; however, the data they gather are not yet sufficiently extensive and reliable for global assessment. Yet, periodic assessments and sporadic data indicate that pollution is worsening in most areas.

In 1990, a U.N. advisory panel, the Group of Experts on the Scientific Aspects of Marine Pollution (GESAMP), reported that coastal pollution was more widespread globally than in 1982, when GESAMP first reported on the oceans' health. (See *World Resources 1990–91*, pp. 179–188.) GESAMP also reported rapid destruction of coastal habitats worldwide, although it could not estimate the rate of loss. It concluded that "if unchecked, these trends will lead to global deterioration in the quality and productivity of the marine environment" (1).

Several recent studies reported that the percentage of pollutants coming from upstream sources is higher than previously thought—accounting for up to 70 percent of nutrient pollution in some areas. (See Focus On Coastal Pollution, below.)

Nutrient Pollution

GESAMP identified a worldwide overload of nutrients—mainly nitrogen and phosphorus from sewage, agricultural runoff, erosion, and other land-based sources—as the most widespread and serious coastal pollution problem (2). Human activities may have increased the amounts of nitrogen and phosphorus entering coastal areas by 50–200 percent. The estimated natural annual global discharge from rivers (based on measurements of unpolluted rivers) is 15 million metric tons of dissolved nitrogen and 1 million metric tons of dissolved phosphorus (3). Estimates of the global anthropogenic annual discharge into rivers range from 7

Figure 12.1 Increase in Population and Pollution in 42 Major Rivers

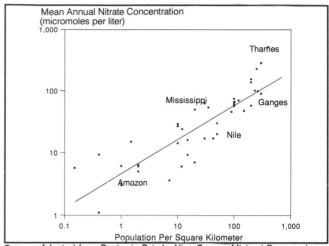

Source: Adapted from Benjamin Peierls, Nina Caraco, Michael Pace, and Jonathan Cole, "Human influence on river nitrogen," *Nature*, Vol. 350, 4 April 1991, pp. 386–387.

Note: Each dot represents one river.

million to 35 million metric tons of dissolved nitrogen and from 0.6 million to 3.75 million metric tons of dissolved phosphorus (4). Most of these nutrients do not disperse in the open ocean; instead they tend to remain in bays and along the continental shelf: only 0.44 million metric tons of nitrogen and 0.3 million metric tons of phosphorus are added to suspended sediments in the deep ocean each year (5).

Excess nutrients overfertilize a marine area, causing algal blooms that deplete oxygen as they decay. Increased algal blooms, including those of toxic algae, can lead to mass kills of fish and invertebrates, to changes in the composition of benthic communities, and to smothering of coral reefs. They are indicators of pollution caused by excessive nutrients (6). The increased algal blooms—called red, brown, or green tides, depending on the color—have been reported from coastal areas around the world, including the Baltic Sea; Kattegat and Skagerrak straits; Dutch Wadden Sea; the North Sea; the Black Sea; Tolo Harbor, Hong Kong; Seto Inland Sea, Japan; the Gulf of Mexico; off North Carolina in the United States; off Prince Edward Island in Canada (7), and the East China Sea (8).

The volume of nutrients entering coastal waters can generally be correlated with the number of people in the watershed. As the population increases, so does the pollution. In 1991, a study of 42 rivers directly linked the population density of a watershed and the amount of nitrogen pollutants in the watershed's coastal area, a relationship long understood by biologists but previously unquantified (9). (See Figure 12.1.)

Sewage treatment reduces nutrient pollution. Rivers and bays that were cleaner in 1990 than in 1970 because of new sewage treatment facilities include the Potomac River near Washington, D.C., the Singapore River and harbor, and the Hudson River and estuary (10) (11). Yet, most of the world's sewage still flows into coastal areas untreated. (See Chapter 11, "Freshwater," Tables 11.2 and 11.3.) Most industrialized countries are just beginning to consider nutrient runoff from agriculture, logging, and mining; it is ignored in most of the world. (See Focus On Coastal Pollution, below.) As population increases, so does agriculture and other activities that cause runoff pollution.

Human Health Problems

Pathogenic bacteria and viruses contained in sewage can cause gastrointestinal and other infections, such as hepatitis, cholera, and typhoid. These ailments may arise from swimming or from eating seafood caught in contaminated sea water. According to the 1990 GESAMP report, "the principal problem for human health on a world-wide scale is the existence of pathogenic organisms discharged with domestic sewage to coastal waters, estuaries or rivers and drainage canals that carry these organisms to the sea" (12).

Certain algae naturally produce toxic substances. Bivalve molluscs that feed on these algae accumulate the toxins and may cause paralytic and diarrhoeic shellfish poisoning (PSP and DSP) when eaten by humans. PSP can cause respiratory paralysis and death by asphyxia in humans. First reported in Canada in 1793, PSP has become common throughout the world in the past 20 years. DSP, which has appeared in many countries, causes severe gastrointestinal disorders, though no fatalities have been reported. Ciguatera, characterized by neurological, cardiovascular, and gastrointestinal symptoms, is caused by eating tropical fish that have bioaccumulated toxins produced naturally in certain algae. The toxin is found more commonly in algae from sewage-contaminated waters (13). Common in northeast Asian seas and the Pacific, ciguatera affects about 50,000 people a year (14). In some areas these toxins have constrained the development of fisheries.

Toxic Chemical Pollution

Heavy metals and synthetic organic compounds are taken up by marine organisms through the food web, with larger amounts of the chemicals accumulating in predatory fish. These chemicals can cause lesions and tumors in fish and accumulate in humans who eat the fish (15). A recent U.S. study shows a clear association between diseased fish and chemically polluted sites (16). High levels of chemical pollutants are found in localized "hot spots" around urban and industrialized areas (17), and traces of synthetic organic compounds, such as DDT and PCBs, are found in ocean waters from the Arctic to the Antarctic (18). High levels of synthetic organic compounds can accumulate in marine mammals feeding in polluted waters and are suspected of lowering the animals' resistance to disease (19). Outbreaks of fatal viral diseases appeared in marine mammals in the North Sea, off the coast of Spain, in the Mediterranean Sea, in the Saint Lawrence Seaway, and in the Atlantic off the United States and Canada in recent years (20) (21) (22).

For four of six heavy metals—arsenic, cadmium, lead, and tin—anthropogenic atmospheric emissions far exceed natural atmospheric emissions. Natural emission of the two other heavy metals—mercury and selenium—are higher than natural levels (23). The Mussel Watch program of the U.S. National Oceanic and Atmospheric Administration monitors bioaccumulation of heavy metals and other toxic materials in mussels and oysters along the U.S. coast. In 1990, it found that lead levels in mussels had fallen since the phaseout of leaded gasoline in the late 1970s. But levels of copper had increased (24).

The human health effects of eating fish or shellfish contaminated by synthetic organic compounds or heavy metals depend on their concentrations in the seafood and on how much seafood is consumed (25). Obviously, those most affected would be fishermen and coastal dwellers whose main source of protein is restricted to fish from polluted waters. In tropical developing countries, 60 percent of the people depend on fish for 40 percent or more of their protein (26). Unfortunately, few of these fish are tested for contamination, human health records are poorly kept, and little is known about the human health effects of long-term low-concentration exposures. Outbreaks of acute poisonings occur periodically (27). In some parts of the United States, women of childbearing age are warned not to eat trout or salmon—two predatory game fish—because they contain levels of synthetic organic compounds that could cause birth defects.

COASTAL HABITAT DESTRUCTION

Coastal habitats, especially wetlands, mangroves, salt marshes, and seagrasses, are rapidly being cleared for urban, industrial, and recreational growth as well as for aquaculture ponds. Coral reefs are being destroyed by pollutants, siltation from upstream erosion, use of dynamite and poison in fishing, and mining for construction materials.

Population pressures on coastal habitats are growing. New data on coastal population growth shows that about one third of the world's urban population lives within 60 kilometers of the coast. From 1980 to 2000, coastal urban populations are expected to increase by 380 million—about the 1990 population of Canada, the United States, and Mexico (28). Few countries have plans to manage development in coastal areas to offset the impact of this growth.

Measures of coastal habitat loss in developing countries are difficult to obtain. But indications are alarming. For example, in tropical countries where estimates have been calculated, the loss of mangroves averages well over 50 percent of the pre-agricultural area. (See Table 12.1.) Industrialized countries have cleared most of their coastal wetlands. The United States has lost over 50 percent of its coastal wetlands (29). The rate of loss has slowed since the mid-1970s, with the promulgation of state and federal regulations (30). In the Mediterranean, wetlands have been drained for development and for the prevention of malaria. As a result, Italy had lost over 95 percent of its historic wetlands by 1972 (31).

Coastal habitat loss is important because 90 percent of the world's marine fish catch (measured by weight) reproduces in these areas (32). Deep-water fish often

Table 12.1 Loss of Mangroves in Selected Countries Since Preagricultural Times

Location	Current sq km	Percentage Lost
Africa		
Angola	1,100	50
Cameroon	4,860	40
Côte d'Ivoire	640	60
Djibouti	90	70
Equatorial Guinea	120	60
Gabon	1,150	50
Gambia, The	510	70
Ghana	630	70
Guinea	1,200	60
Guinea-Bissau	3,150	70
Kenya	930	70
Liberia	360	70
Madagascar	1,302	40
Mozambique	2,760	60
Nigeria	12,200	50
Senegal	420	40
Sierra Leone	3,400	50
Somalia	540	70
South Africa	450	50
Tanzania	2,120	60
Zaire	1,250	50
Central America		
Guatemala	500	60
Asia		
Bangladesh	2,910	73
Cambodia	156	5
India	1,894	85
Indonesia	21,011	45
Malaysia	7,310	32
Pakistan	1,540	78
Philippines	777	61
Thailand	191	87
Viet Nam	1,468	62
Total	**76,939**	**56**

Source: World Resources Institute in collaboration with the United Nations Environment Programme and the United Nations Development Programme, *World Resources 1990-91* (Oxford University Press, New York, 1990), Table 20.4, pp. 306-307.

Figure 12.2 Global Fish Catch, 1950–90

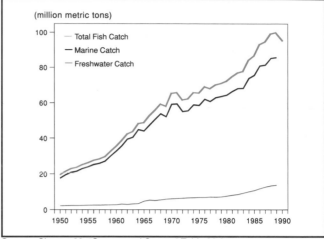

Source: Chapter 23, "Oceans and Coasts," Table 23.2.
Note: 1990 figure is preliminary.

feed on fish that spawn in coastal areas. The U.S. National Marine Fisheries Service estimates that 77 percent of the nation's commercial fish catch is from species that depend on estuarine wetlands for survival (reproduction, nursery areas, food production, or migration). In the Gulf of Mexico and the southeast Atlantic states, 98 percent of the commercial fish catch depends on estuaries (33). Degradation of coastal habitats can have long-term consequences for populations.

Coral Reef Bleaching

Of recent concern is a potential new threat to coral reefs—elevated sea temperatures that may be caused by global warming. Over the past several years, researchers in the Caribbean and eastern Pacific observed increased coral "bleaching," in which the coral's symbiotic algae, which give coral its color, abandon the coral. Without these algae, the coral will eventually die. Known causes of bleaching include pollution and sedimentation. But in some areas, researchers correlated the increased incidents of bleaching with water temperatures one or two degrees higher than normal, leading them to warn that reefs might become a casualty of global warming. Fifty scientists meeting in Miami in 1991 concluded that the incidence of bleaching has increased, much of it related to higher water temperatures, but these incidents indicate environmental stress, not global climate change. However, they warned that a 3–4° C rise in ocean temperature

predicted to be caused by global warming could seriously damage corals. The scientists strongly recommended a global program of coral reef monitoring (34) (35) (36).

Threats to The Ocean's Surface

Although the open ocean still appears relatively clean, new studies indicate possible dangers to microscopic plants and animals that live on the ocean's surface and constitute an important part of the oceanic food web. Initial reports show that increased UV-B radiation resulting from a thinning of the ozone layer can cause reduced productivity or death in several surface-dwelling organisms, phytoplankton, zooplankton, and fish larvae, for example (37). In addition, new studies indicate that pollutants tend to concentrate in the ocean's upper layer—a critical reproductive and feeding ground for many commercially important species. Heavily trafficked seas near industrialized regions are especially vulnerable. Surface waters collected 100—200 kilometers offshore in the North Sea were contaminated with enough heavy metals and other pollutants to be toxic to the embryos of various species (38) (39).

FISHERIES TRENDS

The world harvest of fish, crustaceans, and molluscs reached a record 99.6 million metric tons in 1989, then declined to 95.2 million in 1990, according to preliminary figures from the Food and Agriculture Organization of the United Nations (FAO) (40). (See Figure 12.2.) Most of the 1989 increase was attributed to increased inland aquaculture, mainly in Asia and Africa. Landings of wild marine fish decreased or remained stable in most areas in 1989. The 4 percent decline in the 1990 catch was attributed to a 12 percent decline in the catch of small pelagic fish used for animal feed in the Southeast Pacific off the coast of South America and to reduced quotas for some North Atlantic species owing to conservation measures (41).

Figure 12.3 World Fishery Catches, Increase or Decrease by Region, 1989–90

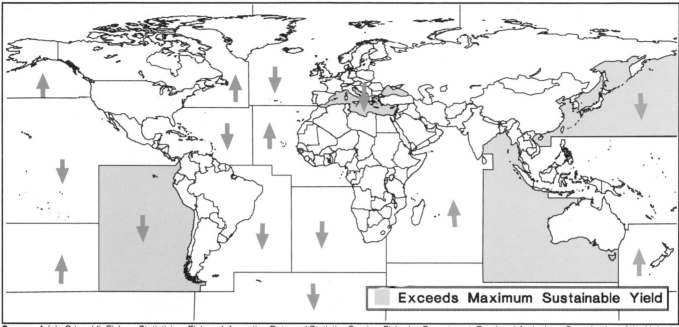

Exceeds Maximum Sustainable Yield

Source: Adele Crispoldi, Fishery Statistician, Fishery Information Data and Statistics Service, Fisheries Department, Food and Agriculture Organization of the United Nations (FAO), Rome, 1991 (personal communication).
Note: Up arrow indicates a larger fish catch in 1990 than in 1989. Down arrow indicates a smaller catch. No arrow indicates the catch remained stable. Shaded ocean areas indicate a catch that exceeds maximum sustainable yield.

Perhaps more importantly, the FAO reported that most traditional marine fish stocks have reached full exploitation; that is, an intensified fishing effort is unlikely to produce an increase in catch, and the use of any new fishing methods that did increase the catch would cause overfishing and therefore a further decline in fish populations (42). Four of FAO's 17 major marine fishing areas are overfished. They report catches over the maximum sustainable limit set by the FAO. (See Figure 12.3.)

Between 1988 and 1990, the fish catch declined in 9 fishing areas, remained stable in 3, and increased in 5. (See Figure 12.3.) In some areas, where the total catch remained stable or increased, catches of the most commercially valuable fish declined.

■ The largest decrease occurred in the Southeast Pacific, which is heavily influenced by the anchovy catch off Peru.

■ In the Northwest Pacific, the catch of pelagic fish decreased off Japan. The abundance of these fish is influenced by change in the Kuroshio current as well as by fishing pressures.

■ In the North Pacific off Alaska, landings of pollack decreased, though the overall catch of commercially valuable fish increased.

■ In the Northeast Atlantic off Europe, where most commercially valuable species are already under quota restrictions because of overfishing, the reported catch declined substantially (43).

Table 12.2 shows that 30 percent of the species, stocks, or species groups caught by U.S. fishermen have declined since 1977 (the year the United States extended its jurisdiction out to 200 nautical miles). Sixty-four percent of U.S. fish species, stocks, or species groups are fully or overexploited, with 18 percent in the overexploited category.

Table 12.2 Declines in U.S. Fisheries

A 1990 assessment of fisheries within the 200-mile U.S. exclusive economic zone by a nonprofit research institute reported the following conclusions:

A. 18 percent of U.S. fish stocks are overexploited

Level of Exploitation	Species, Stocks, or Species Groups {a}	
	Number	Percent
Not exploited	1	1
Underexploited	10	13
Moderately exploited	13	16
Fully exploited	36	46
Overexploited	14	18
Protected	4	5
Not available	3	4

B. 30 percent of U.S. fish stocks have declined since 1977

Abundance Trend	Species, Stocks, or Species Groups {b}	
	Number	Percent
Increasing	16	17
Stable	19	20
Fluctuating	4	4
Decreasing	28	30
Not available/unknown	27	29

Source: Amos Eno, The National Fish and Wildlife Foundation, *Needs Assessment of the National Marine Fisheries Service* (The National Fish and Wildlife Foundation, Washington, D.C., 1990), pp. 73-74.
Notes:
a. The statistics may represent entire fisheries management program (FMP) units, separate species, or individual stocks covered under an FMP. Percentage figures do not total 100 because two species are counted twice; Atlantic salmon and red drum were reported as both overexploited and protected. Regulated fishing continues in other overexploited fisheries.
b. Statistics may represent FMP management units, separate species, or individual stocks covered under an FMP.

Box 12.1 Global Fishery Trends Mask Changes

The steady increase in the world fish catch through 1989 is misleading. It masks declines in some species caused by overfishing and habitat loss or changes in the numbers of other species caused by natural climatic oscillations. For example, the Japanese pilchard catch increased more than sixfold between 1970 and 1989 because of favorable conditions created by the Kuroshio current (1). In the North Atlantic, when herring was overfished in the late 1970s, fishermen switched to capelin, overfishing that species by the late 1980s. The herring population, given a chance to recover by fishing restrictions, began to build up its population in the mid-1980s (2).

Figure 1 shows a situation in which overfishing may have permanently changed the composition of a fish community on Georges Bank. As high-value groundfish, such as the flounder, were depleted, skates, dogfish, and other low-value species replaced them. Because they compete with groundfish for food, the groundfish population may not recover (3).

Generally, when larger fish—mainly used as food for humans—are overexploited, they are replaced by smaller, fast-growing species more likely to be used for animal feed. In some cases, reducing the fishing pressure restores the original species composition, but not always. The Food and Agriculture Organization of the United Nations warns that overfishing may shift species dominance toward smaller species, "thereby modifying the options available for development" (4).

References and Notes

1. Food and Agriculture Organization of the United Nations (FAO), "Environment and Sustainability in Fisheries" (FAO, Rome, February 1991), p. 9.

2. Ibid.

3. Massachusetts Offshore Groundfish Task Force, New England Groundfish in Crisis—Again (Massachusetts Offshore Groundfish Task Force, Boston, 1990), pp. 9-10.

4. Food and Agricultural Organization of the United Nations (FAO), "Recent Developments," (FAO, Rome, April 1991), p. 16.

Figure 1 Changes in Species Composition Caused by Overfishing

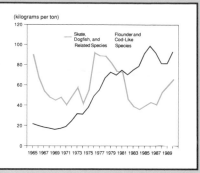

Source: Massachusetts Offshore Groundfish Task Force, New England Groundfish in Crisis—Again (Massachusetts Offshore Groundfish Task Force, Boston, 1990), p. 10.

In New England, an area with a longstanding fishery, a special task force reported in 1990 that landings of commercially valuable fish had reached their lowest reported level, causing a loss of $350 million in income and 14,000 jobs. Overfishing of commercially valuable species, such as cod, haddock, and flounder, has led to an increase in the catch of less valuable species, such as dogfish and skates. (See Box 12.1.) The task force recommended strict quotas on certain species in hopes of restoring commercial fish to their 1960 abundance in 5–10 years (44).

Other fishery issues involve the use of powerful ocean driftnets that trap most marine life in their path (see Box 12.2) and the continuing tuna-dolphin controversy (see Recent Developments, below).

AQUACULTURE

The vast majority of the world's fish, about 87 percent, comes from marine areas. About 13 percent of the catch is from inland fisheries (45). Although aquaculture production has been growing steadily and is expected to double by the end of the century, it accounts for only 12 percent of global fish production (7 million metric tons from inland aquaculture and 5 million metric tons from marine aquaculture) (46). (See Figure 12.4.)

Aquaculture has followed two paths: the traditional rural aquaculture practiced extensively in developing countries and the intensive commercial aquaculture (usually of shrimp and other high-value species) practiced in both developing and developed countries (47). The second type, growing in popularity among many Asian and Latin American countries as an export industry, could have harmful consequences. For example, shrimp aquaculture replaces coastal mangrove habitats, reducing the breeding grounds of wild stocks. The finfish that are farmed are limited to carp, tilapia, salmon, trout, striped bass, catfish, milkfish, and amberjack, and the shellfish mainly to shrimps, but oysters, mussels, and clams are farmed as well. The FAO cautions that "concern should be given to maintaining wild species diversity until more is known about a considerable number of species" (48).

Key Issues

A REGIONAL APPROACH TO PREVENTING POLLUTION

Unlike other issues—climate change, biodiversity, deforestation—for which global conventions or action plans are being formulated for the United Nations Conference on Environment and Development (UNCED) to be held in June 1992, experts meeting to discuss ocean issues are promoting a regional approach, with new emphasis on controlling land-based pollution.

Of the 15 regional seas agreements, 10 are under UNEP auspices. Agreements for the Antarctic, the North Sea, the Baltic Sea, the Northeast Atlantic, and the Nordic Area preceded UNEP's Regional Seas Programme. UNEP is developing three new Regional Seas Programmes, for the Black Sea, the Northwest Pacific, and the Southwest Atlantic (49). Table 12.3 shows the types of agreements concluded by each group. Typically, a regional seas group begins with a framework convention. This may be followed by progressive agreements to establish scientific cooperation and monitoring efforts, to respond cooperatively to oil spills or other environmental emergencies, to curb pollution

Figure 12.4 World Marine and Freshwater Fish Catch, 1989

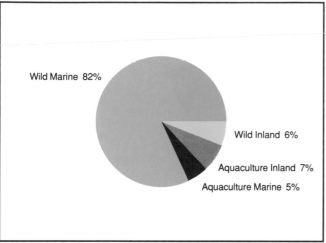

Wild Marine 82%

Wild Inland 6%

Aquaculture Inland 7%

Aquaculture Marine 5%

Source: Food and Agriculture Organization of the United Nations (FAO), "Environment and Sustainability in Fisheries" (FAO, Rome, February 1991), p. 12.

(first from ocean dumping and then from land-based sources), and possibly to protect marine species or areas. The most effective, and the rarest, agreements involve ending certain pollution by an agreed deadline.

Only six regions (the North Sea, the Baltic Sea, the Northeast Atlantic, the Mediterranean, the Persian Gulf, and the Southeast Pacific) have agreements in force that deal with land-based pollution. (See Table 12.3.) The Mediterranean Regional Seas Programme recently published a comprehensive plan dealing with land-based sources. (See Focus On Coastal Pollution, below.)

The regional seas programs may seem to move ponderously, often hampered by political and financial problems. Yet, they have overcome intense animosities among individual countries in order to form working alliances. Examples are the regional seas programs that gained cooperation between Iran and Iraq in the Persian Gulf, the United States and Cuba in the Caribbean, and Israel and Syria in the Mediterranean (50).

FOCUS ON COASTAL POLLUTION

Sophisticated methods of measuring and tracking coastal pollutants are confirming what had long been suspected by coastal scientists: pollutants carried by rivers—in runoff from inland farm fields, logged forests, and urban streets as well as municipal and industrial discharges—introduce damaging levels of

---

Box 12.2 Driftnet Fisheries

Use of large driftnets—nets that hang vertically and stretch 5–50 kilometers—by industrial fishing fleets has proven so efficient at catching targeted fish as well as nontargeted fish, marine mammals, and birds that the United Nations General Assembly and several regional associations have denounced them. In a December 1989 resolution, the United Nations urged that, unless major fishing nations implement conservation measures to mitigate the impacts of driftnets, a moratorium on high seas driftnetting should take effect in June 1992. In addition, the United Nations recommended an immediate end to fishing in the South Pacific and a cessation of the growth of driftnet fishing in other oceans. Small driftnets used by coastal fishermen would not be affected by the U.N. moratorium (1).

In November 1989, South Pacific nations agreed by a formal convention adopted at Wellington, New Zealand to restrict driftnet fishing in the region (2). Australia, Fiji, Indonesia, New Zealand, and the United States banned the use of driftnets larger than 2.5 kilometers within their waters and by their nationals on the high seas. On October 28, 1991, the European Community (EC) imposed a similar ban on the use of large driftnets by EC vessels in EC waters and on the high seas. The EC ban did not cover the Baltic Sea and, with some restrictions on the type of nets used, exempted albacore fishing vessels in the Northeast Atlantic until December 1993.

Japan, a major driftnet fishing nation, bowed to international pressure in late 1991 and agreed to curtail one half its remaining driftnet fishery by June 1992 and the other half by the end of the year (3). As of late 1991, Japan and Korea, but not Taiwan, had stopped driftnet fishing in the South Pacific. Driftnetting by Japanese, Korean, and Taiwanese fishing fleets continued in the North Pacific and, to a lesser extent, by French, British, and Irish fleets in the Atlantic and by the Taiwanese fleets in the Indian Ocean (4). Some driftnet fishing nations are urging the United Nations to postpone the moratorium while the United States, Canada, Australia, and New Zealand favor keeping the worldwide moratorium on schedule (5).

Driftnets are a type of gillnet that, hanging like curtains in the ocean, are suspended by floats at or near the surface. Fish that attempt to swim through the nets become entangled by their gills. Of concern are the huge oceanic driftnets used mainly to catch commercial species distributed in low densities over large areas, such as the albacore tuna and squid. In addition to catching target species efficiently, driftnets capture other fish, mammals, and birds. For example, the North Pacific driftnet fishery caught and discarded 100,000 metric tons of pomfret, a nontarget fish, in 1988–89 according to the Food and Agriculture Organization of the United Nations. Between 300,000 and 1 million cetaceans, mainly dolphins, were killed by driftnets worldwide during the same period (6).

In a survey of 10 percent of the Japanese squid driftnet fishing operations in the

North Pacific during the 1990 season, scientific observers reported mortality of 1,758 whales and dolphins, 30,464 seabirds, 81,956 blue sharks, 253,288 tuna, and more than 3 million pomfret (7).

References and Notes

1. Report of the Secretary-General, United Nations (U.N.), "Large Scale Pelagic Driftnet Fishing and Its Impact on the Living Marine Resources of the World's Oceans and Seas" (U.N., New York, 1990), pp. 1 and 8.

2. *Ibid.*, p. 6.

3. Steven R. Weisman, "Japan Agrees to End Use of Huge Fishing Nets," *New York Times*, November 27, 1991, p. A3.

4. Report of the Secretary General, United Nations (U.N.), "Large Scale Pelagic Driftnet Fishing and Its Impact on the Living Marine Resources of the World's Oceans and Seas" (U.N., New York, 1991), pp. 5-11 and Corr. 1.

5. "Large Scale Pelagic Driftnet Fishing and Its Impact on the Living Marine Resources of the World's Oceans and Seas," draft resolution: Australia, Canada, Federated States of Micronesia, New Zealand, Romania, Soloman Islands, Sweden, and the United States (United Nations, New York, 1991), pp. 1-3.

6. *Op. cit.* 1, pp. 14-16.

7. International North Pacific Fisheries Commission, "Final Report of 1990 Observations of the Japanese High Seas Squid Driftnet Fishery of the North Pacific Ocean," (Alaska Fisheries Science Center, Seattle, 1991) Table 24, pp. 193-195

Recent Developments

GULF OIL SPILL LEAVES MASSIVE ENVIRONMENTAL TOLL

The deliberate release of oil from Kuwait's Sea Island terminal by Iraqi soldiers on January 19, 1991 devastated hundreds of miles of shoreline and wreaked untold damage on marine life in the Persian Gulf.

Its impact was worsened by the natural characteristics of the Persian Gulf. Not only is the gulf shallow, but its current takes about three years to circulate completely. The coastline includes numerous salt marshes, lagoons, tidal flats (1), coral reefs, seagrass beds, and some coastal mangrove forests (2).

Initial estimates of the amount of oil released, primarily from the Sea Island terminal, varied widely. By mid-1991, the estimate was about 950,000 cubic meters—nearly twice the previous record spill at Ixtoc, a drilling rig blowout in the Gulf of Mexico. It was 20 times larger than the 1989 *Exxon Valdez* spill in Alaska. In June 1991, Saudi officials reported that the terminal and sunken tankers were still releasing about 400 cubic meters per day, but by August, the leaks were estimated at 75 metric tons daily (3).

Most of the oil moved south along the coast of Saudi Arabia and in March went ashore near the peninsula of Abu Ali. Relatively little reached Bahrain or Qatar, to the south. Saudi Arabia suffered extensive damage; about 350 miles of coastline, including numerous marshes and tidal flats, were inundated with oil (4). All the mangroves and over 90 percent of the salt marshes were affected. Recovery could take a decade (5).

The cleanup effort had few successes. Booms, nets, and skimmers were deployed to protect the water-intake pipes of Saudi desalination plants and refineries. In June, Aramco, the Saudi Arabian Oil Co., and the Saudi Meteorology and Environmental Protection Administration (MEPA) claimed that they had scooped up about 300,000 cubic meters of crude, which would be the most oil recovered from a major spill. But none of the bays or inlets was protected, 20,000–30,000 birds were killed, and the salt marshes were matted with oil. In addition, Kuwait's burning wells emitted large quantities of soot, some of which fell into gulf waters (6).

Assessing the long-term damage is difficult. Debate over the long-term impacts of the *Exxon Valdez* spill continues, with some studies suggesting that it may be decades before all the seabird colonies and marine organisms recover fully (7).

The value of cleanup techniques also remains unsettled. Some scientists, for example, question whether spraying hot water at high pressure to remove oil as was done in the *Exxon Valdez* cleanup may delay recovery of an ecosystem (8).

Saudi officials rejected the introduction of oil-consuming bacteria into the gulf, because it is still a relatively unproven technology. They also resisted sprinkling the shoreline with nitrogen-based fertilizers, which could help degrade the oil but could also cause algal blooms in the gulf (9).

GATT OVERRULES U.S. BAN ON MEXICO TUNA IMPORTS

An international trade panel in August 1991 ruled that the United States may not ban imports of tuna caught by Mexican boats, which use fishing techniques that incidentally kill more dolphins than U.S. tuna boats.

The panel's decision affects not only dolphins but could undermine a broad range of international environmental protections. If adopted by a majority of the 108 member nations, the decision could make it impossible for parties to the General Agreement on Tariffs and Trade (GATT) to use trade sanctions to protect natural resources outside their borders. And it could undermine efforts to regulate domestic industries to protect the environment, since such regulations would undermine the competitiveness of domestic products (10).

A U.S. law bans the import of tuna from countries that allow more dolphins to be killed during tuna fishing operations than the U.S. fleet; the ban also applies to countries that buy tuna products from the banned countries. Mexico and a half-dozen other countries protested the law before a panel of the GATT, arguing that it was an assertion of extraterritorial powers. A GATT panel found the law in violation of GATT rules that prevent a country from telling other countries how to produce goods for export (11). The United States is bound to comply with the ruling if it is approved by the member nations. However, in late September, the United States and Mexico agreed not to submit the ruling to the full membership. Given the broad implications of the ruling for international environmental protection and concern raised about Mexico's environmental record in the context of North American free trade talks, both governments prefer to pursue a bilateral solution to the conflict.

Mexican officials say that they remain committed to marine conservation and that the Mexican tuna fleet has reduced the annual dolphin kill 70 percent over the previous five years (12).

The latest estimates of dolphin deaths resulting from tuna fishing in the eastern tropical Pacific Ocean, where fishing effort is concentrated, show a significant decline. In 1990, the estimated incidental kill on non-U.S. vessels was 47,448, about 56 percent of the 1989 level. The kill on U.S. vessels is estimated at 5,083, less than one half the 1989 total (13).

References and Notes

1. John Horgan, "The Muddled Cleanup in the Persian Gulf," *Scientific American*, Vol. 265, No. 4 (1991), pp. 106-110.
2. World Conservation Monitoring Centre (WCMC), "Gulf War Environmental Information Service: Impact on the Marine Environment," WCMC, Cambridge, U.K., January 31, 1991, p. 4.
3. *Op. cit.* 1, p. 106.
4. *Op. cit.* 1, p. 106.
5. World Conservation Monitoring Centre (WCMC), "Gulf War Environmental Information Service Environmental Briefing," WCMC, Cambridge, U.K., June 7, 1991, p. 3.
6. *Op. cit.* 1.
7. John Lancaster, "Long-term Damage Seen from Exxon Valdez Spill," *Washington Post* (February 21, 1991), p. A1.
8. Marguerite Holloway, "Soiled Shores," *Scientific American*, Vol. 265, No. 4 (1991), pp. 104-105.
9. *Op. cit.* 1, p. 110.
10. Center for International Environmental Law (CIEL), "GATT Panel Rules on Tuna Trade Sanctions," press release (CIEL, Washington, D.C., 1991), p. 2.
11. Keith Bradsher, "U.S. Ban on Mexico Tuna Is Overruled," *New York Times* (August 23, 1991), p. D1.
12. *Ibid.*
13. U.S. Marine Mammal Commission, *Annual Report of the Marine Mammal Commission, Calendar Year 1990* (Marine Mammal Commission, Washington, D.C., 1991), p. 101.

sediments, nutrients, and toxins into coastal waters (51) (52). But so far, governments have focused on the more obvious causes of coastal pollution, such as coastal discharges of sewage and industrial chemicals.

Further, because coastal areas have borne such costs of pollution as the reduced fishery harvests, there has been little incentive to stop polluting activities upstream. Until these costs are recognized and agreements worked out among various interest groups or up- and downstream jurisdictions, coastal areas will likely continue to be a dumping ground.

In many major bays and seas, a large proportion of pollutants comes not from coastal sources but from the watershed. A 1991 survey of 85 coastal watersheds in the United States found that upstream sources, including agricultural and urban runoff, accounted for about 70 percent of the nitrogen and 60 percent of the phosphorus in the estuaries studied. (See Box 12.3.) In the Black Sea, the main causes of deterioration were reduced riverflow and increases in its organic and toxic pollutants. (See Box 12.4.) An exhaustive study of the Mediterranean found that at least one half the nutrient pollutants, mercury, chrome, lead, zinc, pesticides, and radioactive materials comes from rivers draining areas outside the immediate coastal zone (53). Although high levels of pollutants are being documented in major watersheds, no information has been systematically collected worldwide.

Traditional economic evaluations of freshwater and coastal resources hide the real costs of pollution imposed by upstream inhabitants on their downstream neighbors (54). But closer investigation is revealing. For example, a recent study showed that the smothering of coral reefs by sediments from logging in the watershed surrounding Bacuit Bay in the Philippines will likely reduce gross revenues $41 million over 10 years, primarily through losses in tourism and fishing (55).

Activities of governmental and nongovernmental organizations often reflect this artificial separation of terrestrial from marine coastal environments and resources. Governmental agencies responsible for marine fisheries and environments, for example, have little or no influence on damaging upland activities, and forestry agencies do not consider coastal impacts of logging. Nongovernmental organizations concerned with agricultural, forest, and urban issues seldom consider the effects of favored policies upon coastal resources. Both governmental and citizen institutions concerned with coastal water conservation have only recently looked to watersheds for the causes of deteriorating coastal water quality and resources.

TRENDS IN MARINE POLLUTION CONTROL

Early pollution control efforts began with the most obvious source, direct dumping, and progressed to controlling industrial and municipal discharge pipes (point sources).

The first efforts focused on sludge and debris. The London Dumping Convention of 1972, which 65 nations had adopted by 1990, prohibits deliberate ocean dumping of wastes, including radioactive and toxic wastes. At their November 1990 meeting, the parties to the London Dumping Convention agreed to a complete phase-out of industrial waste dumping by 1995 (56).

Some 80–90 percent of the material dumped directly at sea is dredge spoils, mostly silt from harbors, rivers, and other waterways. And about 10 percent of it is contaminated with oil, heavy metals, nutrients, and chlorinated hydrocarbons from shipping, industrial and municipal discharges, and runoff (57).

Throughout the world, ports are dredged at public expense. Toxic chemical contamination has magnified the costs of disposing of these dredge spoils safely. In 1991, a new kind of environmental agreement was negotiated between Rotterdam and the German Chemicals Manufacturers Association (VCI). The VCI agreed to reduce the levels of seven heavy metals it discharged into the Rhine River by 1995. In return, the city agreed to drop lawsuits against member companies in which it sought damages for the cost of dispos-

Table 12.3 Regional Seas Agreements, Selected Provisions

Region	Convention (C) Protocol (P)	Date and Place Adopted	Emergency Response	Control Ocean Dumping	Control Land-based Pollution Sources	Protected Areas/Species	Other
Regional Programs Predating UNEP Programs							
Antarctic	C	12/59, Washington, D.C.	•	•			
	C	5/80, Canberra				•	
North Sea	C	6/69, Bonn	•				
	C	9/83, Bonn	•				
Baltic Sea	C	9/71, Copenhagen	•				
	C	3/74, Helsinki	•	•	•	•	
Arctic and Northeast Atlantic	C	2/72, Oslo		•			
	C	6/74, Paris			•		
	P	3/83, Oslo		•			
	P	3/86, Paris*			•		
Nordic Area	C	2/74, Stockholm					{a}
UNEP Regional Seas Programs							
Mediterranean	C	2/76, Barcelona	•				
	P	2/76, Barcelona		•			
	P	2/76, Barcelona					
	P	5/80, Athens			•		
	C	1/81, Monaco				•	{b}
	P	5/82, Geneva					
Persian Gulf and Gulf of Oman	C	4/78, Kuwait	•				
	P	4/78, Kuwait					
	P	3/89, Kuwait			•		{c}
	P	2/90, Kuwait					
West and Central Africa	C	3/81, Abidjan	•				
	P	3/81, Abidjan					
Southeast Pacific	C	11/81, Lima	•				
	C	11/81, Lima	•				
	P	7/83, Quito					
	P	7/83, Quito			•		{d}
	P	9/89, Quito*					
	P	9/89, Quito*				•	
Red Sea and Gulf of Aden	C	2/82, Jeddah	•				
	P	2/82, Jeddah					
Wider Caribbean	C	3/83, Cartagena	•				
	P	3/83, Cartagena					
	P	1/90, Kingston*				•	
East Africa	C	6/85, Nairobi*	•				
	P	6/85, Nairobi*					
	P	6/85, Nairobi*				•	
South Pacific	C	11/86, Noumea	•				
	P	11/86, Noumea		•			
	P	11/86, Noumea					
East Asia	Draft Convention						
South Asia	Draft Convention						

Sources:

1. Economic Commission for Europe, "Convention on Environmental Impact Assessment in a Transboundary Context," United Nations, 1991.
2. United Nations (U.N.) Secretariat, Office of Ocean Affairs and the Law of the Sea, "International Institutions and Legal Instruments," U.N., New York, 1991, pp. 28-33.
3. "Protection of Oceans, All Kinds of Seas Including Enclosed and Semi-Enclosed Seas, Coastal Areas and the Protection, Rational Use and Development of their Living Resources," Preparatory Committee for the United Nations Conference on Environment and Development, U.N., New York, 1991, pp. 46-47.

Notes: a. Protects environment between Denmark, Norway, Sweden, and Finland. b. Protects coastal waters. c. Protects against pollution resulting from exploration and exploitation of the continental shelf. d. Protects against radioactive pollution.

* = not yet in force; • = provision

Box 12.3 Pollution of U.S. Coastal Estuaries

A surprisingly large amount of nutrients that lead to water pollution—70 percent of the notrogen and 60 percent of the phosphorus—entering U.S. coastal estuaries comes from upstream sources, both point and nonpoint, that may originate hundreds of miles from the coast. (See Figure 1.)

Figure 1 Sources of Nitrogen and Phosphorus in U.S. Coastal Waters, 1990

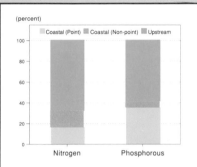

Source: National Oceanic and Atmospheric Administration (NOAA) and U.S. Environmental Protection Agency Team on Near Coastal Waters, *Strategic Assessment of Near Coastal Waters,* 4 vols. (NOAA, Washington D.C., 1989-91).

These findings from a four-part study published by the National Oceanic and Atmospheric Administration (NOAA) between 1989 and 1991 highlight the need to incorporate watershed planning into coastal management. NOAA estimated the annual nitrogen and phosphorus inputs from various sources to 85 major estuaries (1). Because actual measurements of nutrient concentrations for each estuary do not exist, the next best data were obtained by estimating these inputs and allowing for variations in each estuary's ability to cleanse itself as measured by its tendency to concentrate pollutants. For example, even a low volume of nutrients could cause a pollution problem in a small, shallow, enclosed estuary, whereas a much larger volume of nutrients could be cleansed by a large estuary with strong currents that moved pollutants out into the open ocean (2).

Figure 2 shows the sources of nitrogen and phosphorus in estuaries with low, medium, and high susceptibility to nutrient

pollution (the NOAA study makes a separate grouping for susceptibility to chemical pollution). For estuaries with the highest susceptibility to nitrogen pollution, about 20 percent of the nitrogen is from coastal point sources and 80 percent is from nonpoint (coastal) and all upstream sources. (See Figure 2A.) Nitrogen is the limiting nutrient in most marine systems; it is the additional nitrogen that often initiates algal blooms. The major sources of nitrogen are sediments, chemical fertilizers, sewage, and runoff from feedlots. Phosphorus inputs are more likely to come from coastal point sources—almost 70 percent in the most susceptible estuaries compared to about 30 percent from coastal nonpoint and upstream. (See Figure 2B.) The major sources of phosphorus are synthetic laundry detergents and water treatment chemicals (3).

The most susceptible estuaries are not necessarily currently the most polluted. The NOAA analysis of susceptibility points out the sources of major nutrients flowing into vulnerable estuaries as a tool for policymakers (4).

The study identifies point sources as wastewater treatment plants and industrial facilities that discharge directly into surface water in coastal counties. For purposes of the study, nonpoint sources were runoff from agriculture, forest, urban and other types of land in coastal counties. Upstream sources include input from all rivers in the watershed from both point and nonpoint sources (5). The study is based on inputs of pollutants and does not subtract nutrients that might settle out of the water before reaching the estuary. However, it notes that most nitrogen and phosphorus are dissolved in the water rather than attached to sediments that tend to settle. Inputs of nutrients from ocean influx, groundwater inflow, bottom sediments, wetlands, barren lands, or direct atmospheric deposition to the estuary are not included (6). NOAA plans to continue the study by collecting site-specific information on nutrient pollution.

References and Notes

1. National Oceanic and Atmospheric Administration (NOAA) and U.S. Environmental Protection Agency Team on Near Coastal Waters, *Strategic Assessment of Near Coastal*

Figure 2 Susceptibility of U.S. Coastal Waters to Nitrogen and Phosporus Pollution, 1990

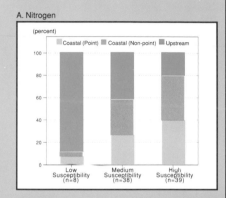

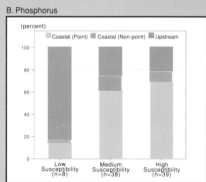

Source: National Oceanic and Atmospheric Administration (NOAA) and U.S. Environmental Protection Agency Team on Near Coastal Waters, Strategic Assessment of Near Coastal Waters, 4 vols. (Washington D.C., 1989–91).

Waters, 4 vols. (NOAA, Rockville, Maryland, 1989-1991).

2. National Oceanic and Atmospheric Administration (NOAA) and U.S. Environmental Protection Agency Team on Near Coastal Waters, *Strategic Assessment of Near Coastal Waters, Susceptibility of East Coast Estuaries to Nutrient Discharges: Passamaquoddy Bay to Chesapeake Bay* (NOAA, Rockville, Maryland, 1989), pp. 1 and 3.

3. *Ibid.,* p. 2.

4. *Ibid.,* pp. 3-4.

5. *Ibid.,* p. 3.

6. *Ibid.*

---

ing of 10 million cubic meters of contaminated sludge per year (58). This lawsuit and the subsequent agreement are an example of shifting pollution costs to the polluters upstream.

In the 1980s, especially in partially enclosed areas such as the Mediterranean and Baltic seas and the Chesapeake Bay in the United States, billions of dollars were spent to reduce the flow of sewage and in-

dustrial wastes into coastal waters. But success was limited.

Prevention measures led to significant reductions in some areas. For example, between 1980 and 1985, sewer construction and other measures more than halved levels of key pollutants in Singapore's nearshore waters (59). State governments in the Chesapeake Bay region reduced phosphorus discharges 29 percent between 1985 and 1988 by banning phosphate detergents. At the same time, despite improved sewage treatment, nitrogen discharges increased 8 percent because the population increased (60). Surveys in U.S. coastal waters indicate that the phase-out of PCBs in the 1970s has resulted in a decrease in the levels of these contaminants in mussels and oysters (61).

Yet such reductions are not widespread. Collection and conventional treatment of sewage remains an unmet need in many areas. By the late 1980s, only 72 percent of the sewage generated in Europe and less than 5 percent of that in developing regions was treated at any level. (See Chapter 11, "Freshwater," Table 11.1.)

UPSTREAM ACTIVITIES THAT POLLUTE COASTAL WATERS

Among the many upstream activities known to degrade water quality in coastal areas are logging, agriculture, and dam building for power and irrigation; urbanization and air pollution are also widespread. (See Chapter 11, "Freshwater," Focus On River Basin Pollution.)

Logging

Both tree-cutting and road construction for logging operations expose underlying soil directly to wind and rain. Sediments transported by runoff into streams and rivers smother sensitive nearshore coastal habitats, such as seagrass beds and coral reefs. In a 1986 study, erosion of logged forest was found to be 240 times greater per unit than that from uncut areas in the same watershed above Bacuit Bay in the Philippines (62). Levels of suspended sediment discharged into the bay from the Manlag River, which drains two thirds of the watershed (including the logging concession area) were 1,000–3,000 milligrams per liter, compared with 10–30 in a similar unlogged river in the same watershed (63). At the same time, sedimentation of reefs in the bay reduced live coral cover as much as 50 percent (64). These losses led to further losses in both coral species diversity and fish biomass (65).

Analysis of the harm done to fishing and tourism in Bacuit Bay indicates that a ban on logging would create net economic and environmental benefits (66).

Coral reefs and seagrass beds in other tropical countries are also at risk from sedimentation from logging operations. Excessive sedimentation in temperate regions can overwhelm communities of oysters and other filter-feeding invertebrates, block sunlight necessary for the growth of submerged aquatic vegetation (67), and damage spawning grounds of anadromous fish (68).

Agriculture

Agricultural operations can release high levels of sediments (69). Contaminants, including pesticides and fertilizers, bind to sediment particles and are carried downstream where they may be deposited in shallow estuaries (70). Pesticides and fertilizers are particularly hazardous in estuaries because they are generally not flushed out and diluted in open waters (71).

Although the effects of some pesticides on aquatic life are well understood, many have not been tested (72). One half the 128 coastal fish kills off South Carolina in the United States between 1977 and 1984 were attributed to pesticides (73). Other fish kills occur near watersheds where pesticide use is heavy (74). Some pesticides, such as mirex, are highly toxic to marine crustacea (75). But chronic exposure to one or several agricultural contaminants has been little explored (76). Studies indicate that regular consumption of fish and shellfish in heavily contaminated areas poses a high risk to fetuses and children (77).

Nitrogen from agricultural fertilizers and animal wastes enters coastal waters through runoff or from migration through groundwaters. Excessive amounts of nitrogen (generally a limiting factor on marine plant growth just as phosphorus is limiting on freshwater plant growth) has contributed to more frequent and widespread algal blooms. (See Conditions and Trends, above.)

Dam Construction and Irrigation

Dams can jeopardize living coastal resources by blocking the migration of anadromous fish, preventing an adequate supply of nutrients to estuaries, altering salinity in estuaries beyond the tolerance of estuarine species, and introducing pollution from associated irrigation (78). In the U.S.S.R., dams have reduced natural runoff from the Dniester, Dnieper, and Don rivers by 50–60 percent, aggravating the accumulation of salts and pollutants in Black Sea coastal waters (79). Dams and canals also block migratory routes of anadromous fishes, virtually eliminating the commercial Russian sturgeon fisheries in the Black, Azov, and Caspian seas— once among the most productive in the world (80).

Dams are often built to store water for the dry season. But besides eliminating flooding and reducing the release of sediments and nutrients into productive estuarine areas, dams also reduce freshwater flows into estuarine areas during dry seasons. In tropical regions, reduction of such inflows raises the salinity above tolerable levels for mangroves or marsh grasses, which provide critical habitat for commercially valuable finfish and shellfish (81). Nutrient reductions from a watershed to estuarine and coastal marine waters contribute to declines in commercial fisheries (82).

Canalization for flood control or water supply can also significantly reduce the flow of sediments, nutrients, and freshwater into estuarine areas, jeopardizing fishery resources. For example, diversion of water for agricultural and municipal uses has reduced freshwater inflow to San Francisco Bay over 62 percent (83). This change contributed to declines of 60–80 percent in adult striped bass and greatly reduced survival of young (84). Canalization of the Mississippi River has diverted riverborne sediments from productive coastal marshes and contributed to the annual loss of 142 square kilometers of wetlands in the Louisiana coastal zone (85).

Box 12.4 The Black Sea

The Black Sea ecosystem, which has been visibly deteriorating since about 1970, had reached a critical stage by 1991, especially in coastal areas. The nutrient inflows from rivers in an 11-country watershed and the coastal pollutants had overfertilized the northwestern part of the sea to such an extent that the plankton biomass increased 15-fold—from 52 to more than 800 grams per cubic meter (1)—increasing the frequency of red tides. Decay of these plankton causes oxygen depletion of shallow bottom waters every summer and fall (2).

Increasing flows of pollutants and toxic substances—oil, detergents, chlorinated organic compounds, heavy metals, and radioactive materials—have suppressed other biota. Some have accumulated in predatory fish to high levels; average DDT concentrations in Black Sea fish, for example, reached 0.15 per million by the end of the 1980s (3).

Withdrawals of freshwater for hydropower, industry, urban use, and inland shipping waterways have increased salinity in the seas. This increase reduced productivity 60 percent and anadromous fish catches in the adjacent Sea of Azov 95 percent between 1950 and 1975 (4).

The three most important causes of the decline of the Black Sea ecosystem are increases in:

■ Withdrawals of freshwater from the Black Sea watershed for irrigation and other consumptive anthropogenic purposes, leading to a 15 percent decline in runoff (projected to increase to 25 percent) within the next several decades (5).

■ The nutrients carried by river runoff: 400,000 metric tons of nitrogen and 84,000 metric tons of phosphorus (6), and

■ Toxic and pollutant inflows from upstream activities.

In recent years, however, the volume of nutrients from growing coastal communities' sewage is now comparable to that from river runoff (7). Oil spills, pollution of the straits connecting the sea to the Mediterranean, and increased trawl fishing are also contributors to this worsening situation.

References and Notes

1. Yu P. Zaitsev, G.P. Garkavaya, D.A. Nestcrova et al., "Contemporary State of the North-Western Part of the Black Sea Ecosystem," in Contemporary State of the Black Sea Ecosystem (Nauka Publishing House, Moscow, 1987), pp. 216-230, cited in A.F. Mandych, A.V. Drozdov, and S.I. Shaporenko, The Black Sea: The Contemporary Ecological State of the Coastal Water and Coasts within the Territory of the U.S.S.R. (U.S.S.R. Academy of Science, Institute of Geography, Moscow, 1991.)

2. M.E. Vonogradov and A.I. Simonov, Black Sea Ecosystem Changes," in Main Problems of the World Ocean Research (Hydrometeoizdat, Leningrad, 1989), pp. 61-75, cited in A.F. Mandych, A.V. Drozdov, and S.I.

Shaporenko, The Black Sea: The Contemporary Ecological State of the Coastal Water and Coasts within the Territory of the U.S.S.R. (U.S.S.R. Academy of Science, Institute of Geography, Moscow), 1991.

3. A.M. Bronfman and E.P. Khlebnikov, "The Azov Sea: Reconstruction Basis" (Hydrometeoizdat, Leningrad, 1985), cited in A.F. Mandych, A.V. Drozdov, and S.I. Shaporenko, The Black Sea: The Contemporary Ecological State of the Coastal Water and Coasts within the Territory of the U.S.S.R. (U.S.S.R. Academy of Science, Institute of Geography, Moscow), 1991.

4. Group of Experts on the Scientific Aspects of Marine Pollution The State of the Marine Environment, Technical Annex 1 (United Nations Environment Programme, Nairobi, 1990), p. 249.

5. A.M. Bronfman and E.P. Khlebnikov, "The Azov Sea: Reconstruction Basis" (Hydrometeoizdat, Leningrad, 1985).

6. A.M. Bronfman, L.V. Vorob'eva, G.P. Garkavaya et al., "Main Features and Trends of Anthropogenic Changes of the North-Western Black Sea Shelf's Ecosystem," cited in A.F. Mandych, A.V. Drozdov, and S.I. Shaporenko, The Black Sea: The Contemporary Ecological State of the Coastal Water and Coasts within the Territory of the U.S.S.R. (U.S.S.R. Academy of Science, Institute of Geography, Moscow, 1991.)

7. A.F. Mandych, A.V. Drozdov, and S.I. Shaporenko, The Black Sea: The Contemporary Ecological State of the Coastal Water and Coasts within the Territory of the U.S.S.R. (U.S.S.R. Academy of Science, Institute of Geography, Moscow, 1991.)

Cities and Industry

Throughout history, people settled near water for transportation and for domestic and industrial use. So long as riverfront and coastal populations remained small, coastal habitats could absorb human wastes. But, many of the world's largest cities and industrial centers are along coasts or on rivers with direct access to the coast. By the turn of the century, more than one fifth of the world's population—1 billion people—will live in coastal cities. (See Chapter 23, "Freshwater," Table 23.1.) This concentration of people and industry plus the lack of adequate waste disposal has degraded coastal waters.

A recent study of 42 rivers around the world found a significant correlation between a watershed's human population density and the amount of nitrogen discharged at the mouth of the river into a coastal ecosystem (86). (See Conditions and Trends, and Figure 12.1.) Thus, the increase in a watershed's population—without concurrent controls on wastes—may be the single most important factor in coastal pollution. Most of the world's population lives in watersheds.

Air Pollution

Another newly recognized source of coastal pollutants is deposition of airborne pollutants. For example, atmospheric deposition contributes an estimated 413,000 of the 940,000 metric tons of nitrogen entering the Baltic Sea each year; it is second only to river sources, at 449,000 metric tons (87). Atmospheric deposition of nitrogen from distant power-generating plants, industrial facilities, and agricultural activities may account for nearly 40 percent of the total nitrogen inputs into the Chesapeake Bay (88). Nearly all the lead, cadmium, copper, iron, and zinc that enter the oceans come from the atmosphere (89).

Marine pollution from atmospheric deposition can only be reduced at the source and is not often associated with cleaning up coastal waters. For example, in the United States, the phase-out of lead in gasoline during the 1970s contributed to decreased lead levels in mussels and oysters (90).

VULNERABILITY OF COASTAL WATERS TO POLLUTION

Numerous factors determine the sensitivity of estuaries and bays to pollutants. In general, estuaries with a small volume and little tidal flushing and freshwater inflow trap sediments and pollutants, and those with large volumes and river discharges transport sediments into coastal waters and dilute the pollutants (91). The likelihood of estuarine waters concentrating pollutants also depends on the size and configuration of the adjacent watershed (92).

Large watersheds often generate large riverflows with the potential for transporting great volumes of sediment, toxins, and nutrients into coastal waters. For example, the Mississippi River, whose total drainage area measures 2.9 million square kilometers, averages a daily freshwater discharge of 572,900 cubic feet per second and an estimated 463,782 metric tons of nitrogen annually (93).

Coastal areas fed by large watersheds are generally flushed out more quickly. Although these areas can be heavily polluted (many are among the most polluted areas in the world), they are easier to clean up once the sources of pollution are eliminated.

Consequently, estuaries and bays with high water turnover rates are considered less susceptible to heavy pollution than enclosed waters with low inflow and outflow, such as the Mediterranean Sea or the Chesapeake Bay. Both are highly vulnerable to pollution not only because they can be quickly degraded but also because they take a long time to recover after pollution controls are imposed. (See Box 12.3.)

COORDINATING POLLUTION CONTROL

Management of human activities in coastal areas and watersheds remains fragmented among many government units. Even within a single country, lack of coordination has allowed, even promoted, activities damaging to coastal resources. Controlling onshore and atmospheric sources of marine pollution will require new approaches that reach further into each nation's economy (94) than merely banning dumping from ships.

Linking the Land and the Water

Governments and agencies responsible for economic development seldom consider the impacts of watershed settlements on coastal resources (95). For example, only recently has the World Bank considered the offshore effects of its dam construction projects; it had focused on impacts only in the immediate area of construction and on reservoir flooding (96). Part of the reason is that the economic consequences of coastal degradation are considered too speculative to be included in the cost-benefit analysis of dam construction.

Even when agencies do evaluate the coastal impacts of inland activities, the impacts are considered secondary. In the United States, when coastal resource agencies are given the opportunity to review proposed dams and other water management projects, they can only make recommendations, which are often ignored (97). For example, fish and wildlife agencies responsible for anadromous salmon populations in the Columbia River have limited influence over the operation of the dam turbines that kill more than 90 percent of the salmon smolts migrating downstream to the ocean (98). In Ecuador, a major concern is construction of highland dams funded partly by the Inter-American Development Bank, over which the coastal conservation agencies have no control (99).

Further, national government plans and decisions are often not implemented or are ignored by local governments and citizens, who simply do not understand the situation.

UNEP has drawn up a set of guidelines on how nations might address land-based marine pollution within their boundaries and what responsibilities they have to other nations. (See Table 12.4.)

CASE STUDIES OF WATERSHED/COASTAL MANAGEMENT

The following case studies describe efforts to reduce coastal pollution from watershed sources at three geographic scales and levels of political complexity—local, interstate, and international. How can groups with diverse interests, including recreation, tourism, fishing, industry, agriculture, local government, and both upstream and downstream states or nations be brought together to reduce coastal pollution? This is the key issue. In all watersheds, the classic upstream-downstream situation exists in which upstream interests can extract or pollute water to the detriment of downstream users unless they are constrained by a higher government power or a negotiated agreement.

Internationally, the issue of watershed pollution follows water resource allocation, one of the oldest resource issues that necessity forces countries to consider. Formal mechanisms to allocate water use or control pollution include the Nile Water Agreement, the Great Lakes water quality agreements, the Indo-Bangladesh Joint Rivers Commission, and the International Commission for the Protection of the Rhine Against Pollution. An analysis of international watershed agreements found that success is more likely when all parties perceive the problem as serious, the countries or states are of relatively equal strength and share a history of cooperation, a favorable scientific and legal framework exists, and an outside mediator (e.g., a U.N. agency or another nation) can help facilitate an agreement (100).

The first case study describes a campaign sponsored by an aid agency to build local support for watershed cleanup on the resort island of Phuket, Thailand. Because Thailand's major source of foreign earnings is tourism, maintaining an attractive coast offered clear economic benefits, and the federal government agreed to enforce pollution standards upland. Local scientists, fishermen, scuba dive operators, government officials, hotel operators, and upland plantation owners worked out a plan.

The second case study is of a more complex political situation in which six states and the District of Columbia contributed pollutants to the largest U.S. estuary, the Chesapeake Bay. Following a model program of scientific study, citizen involvement, state negotiations, and federal support, local developers are slowing progress by their resistance to changes in land use.

The third case study looks at the Mediterranean, an enclosed sea bordered by 18 nations. Unlike watersheds bounded by states or provinces in which a federal government may set emission standards or settle disputes, the Mediterranean is bounded by sovereign nations. They have negotiated a cooperative agree-

Table 12.4 The Montreal Guidelines on Land-Based Pollution

The United Nations Environment Programme (UNEP) drew up a set of guidelines in 1985 to help nations develop international agreements and national legislation to protect the marine environment against pollution from land-based sources. The guidelines are intended as a checklist of basic provisions rather than a model agreement, from which nations might select or adapt elements to suit their specific needs.

The guidelines declare that nations have a responsibility to:

■ Prevent, reduce and control marine pollution and to ensure that discharges from land-based sources do not pollute the marine environment beyond their national jurisdictions.

■ Cooperate internationally, regionally and locally to limit pollution from land-based sources. Noncoastal nations should control release of pollutants in their territories that reach the seas; all nations should limit pollution of shared watercourses that drain into the sea.

■ Share scientific data and technology related to pollution control. Developed countries should provide technical, scientific, and educational assistance to developing countries for pollution control.

■ Prevent or manage pollution emergencies and inform other nations about releases of pollutants from land-based sources.

■ Develop comprehensive environmental management plans to prevent, reduce, and control pollution from land-based sources. Nations have the right to set national pollution control standards more stringent than international standards.

■ Grant foreign nationals equal access to their courts to seek compensation for damages from marine pollution.

Specific pollution control strategies include:

■ Setting pollution limits to achieve certain marine environmental quality standards. These standards may be determined by a desired level of intended use, by existing ambient pollution levels, by dilution rates for a specific site, or by loading allocations for an entire receiving environment rather than a specific site.

■ Setting emission or technology-based standards. Technology-based standards include best practicable technology, best available technology, discharge as low as reasonably achievable, and zero discharge.

■ Managing human activities to limit use of the marine environment or to control siting of activities affecting the marine environment.

The guidelines suggest that nations select strategies and control instruments appropriate to their socio-economic status and the availability of pollution control infrastructure. Strategy selection will depend on:

■ Economic conditions such as a country's over-all economic health, availability of public finance, availability of external finance, viability of implementing the polluter pays principle.

■ Scientific/technical resources such as availabilty of data on the marine environment, knowledge of waste stream constituents and control technologies, ability to monitor pollution, engineering infrastructure, knowledge of pollution trends.

■ Social/political resources such as quality of administrative infrastructure, use made of the marine environment, and public awareness of environmental problems.

Sources:

1. Group of Experts on the Scientific Aspects of Marine Pollution, *Technical Annexes to the Report on the State of the Marine Environment*, UNEP Regional Seas Reports and Studies No. 114/2 (United Nations Environment Programme, Nairobi, 1990), pp. 359-367.

2. Peter H. Sand, *Marine Environment Law in the United Nations Environment Programme* (Tycooly Publishing, London, 1988), pp. 235-254.

ment under a UNEP-sponsored Regional Seas Programme, but inspection and enforcement are much weaker than in a federal system.

Phuket Province, Thailand

Recent efforts to combat the deteriorating coastal waters of Thailand began locally with the Patong, Karon, and Kata watersheds on Phuket Island (101). (See Figure 12.5.)

Phuket's coral reefs and beaches are key to national efforts to build and increase the tourist industry (Thailand's leading source of foreign income). But the island's explosive growth of hotels and resorts brought overuse of the reefs and sewage and sediment pollution of nearshore waters. These threats to the reefs aggravated the damage from the increased sedimentation that was caused by converting more than one half the island's native forests into rubber and coconut plantations (102).

The Coastal Resources Management Project (in which the Office of the National Environment Board of Thailand, the Phuket Marine Biological Center, the University of Rhode Island, and the U.S. Agency for International Development participated) met with local scientists, fishermen, scuba dive operators, government officials, hotel operators, and upland landowners to develop a consensus that their economic prosperity depended on sustainable use of the coast (103). In 1991, the project issued a detailed action plan for three watersheds, which espoused several measures to protect water quality:

■ Modification of environmental assessment of new development in the three target watersheds to consider impacts on the reefs,

■ Protection of streambanks by developers,

■ Protection of bottomlands from filling,

■ Institution of maximum density limits,

■ Restoration of natural vegetation on public lands illegally converted to coconut plantations, and

■ Establishment of cooperative water-quality monitoring programs.

None of these actions required legislation (104).

Critical to success of the plan is the involvement of citizens, businesses, and government. To implement successful resource management projects in other threatened coastal zones, the plan calls for citizen access to information on local waters and on relevant government decisions. Instead of applying national policy locally, the Phuket Island project developed its own local policy (105). But as the plan acknowledges, effective implementation requires both political will and funding (106).

The Chesapeake Bay

Chesapeake Bay planners followed what many consider a model process. The U.S. Environmental Protection Agency spent millions of dollars and seven years studying the bay's ecology and hydrology and tracing pollution sources. Some pollutants, it was found, originated in Pennsylvania and New York—states that are in the bay's 165,760-square-kilometer watershed but that do not border on the bay. Public education programs were launched, and state governments approved an agreement on general goals. (See Figure 12.6.)

The Chesapeake Bay study was one of the first to document the coastal pollutants from upstream sources; three rivers carried 78 percent of the nitrogen and 70 percent of the phosphorus entering the bay (107). Most of the phosphorus came from point sources, primarily sewage treatment plants, and most of the ni-

Figure 12.5 Watershed and Coral Reefs of Southwestern Phuket Island

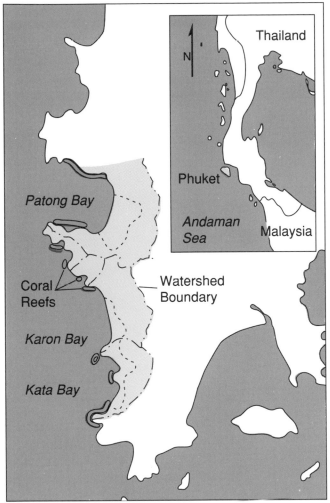

Source: Adapted from Coastal Resources Management Project, *What Future for Phuket?* (University of Rhode Island, Narragansett, February 1991), and Michele H. Lemay and Hansa Chansang, *Coral Reef Protection Strategy for Phuket and Surrounding Islands* (Thailand Coastal Resources Management Project, Bangkok, 1989).

trogen was from nonpoint sources, such as agricultural lands, of which some 45,000 square kilometers lie in the bay watershed (108).

In response to this information, the Chesapeake Bay Program proposed policies regarding upstream pollution. Among other points, the states agreed to a 40 percent reduction in the amounts of nitrogen and phosphorus reaching the bay by the year 2000 (109). This goal has been pursued largely through subsidies for improved agricultural practices, reduction of urban runoff, and treatment of sewage (110). Several states, for example, have provided millions of dollars in matching funds for measures that reduce the amounts of runoff pollutants from feedlots and croplands, including no-till and low-till techniques. National legislation passed in 1985 will also reduce runoff through the withdrawal of subsidies for crops planted on highly erodible land (111).

To meet federal requirements for stormwater runoff treatment, several communities instituted a "rain tax" on upstream property owners to pay for building settling ponds and drainage systems to clean runoff before it reaches rivers and bays (112).

Since 1987, nitrogen and phosphorus from nonpoint sources have decreased an estimated 7 percent, but goals for the year 2000 are unlikely to be met if current trends continue (113). A 1988 report on anticipated population growth and development in the Chesapeake Bay watershed to the year 2020 concluded that current development planning mechanisms were not preventing scattered, unplanned development that generates larger amounts of pollutants, additional expense, and more waste (114).

After a decade of government research and deliberation, citizens' meetings, and newspaper and magazine articles, the Chesapeake Bay region has gone far in overcoming jurisdictional division. Both government policy and programs recognize that restoration of water quality depends on changing behavior in the watershed. But it is not yet certain whether upstream landowners and governments are willing to restore the bay by restricting their own activities when downstream neighbors pay for the impacts of those activities. Planners are now recognizing that present efforts will not reverse degradation of the bay. Restoring water quality depends on withdrawing subsidies for urban sprawl (115) and preventing rather than regulating pollution (116).

Figure 12.6 Watershed of Chesapeake Bay

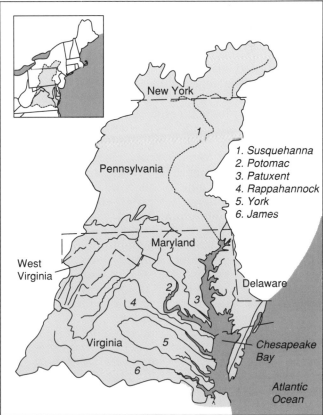

1. Susquehanna
2. Potomac
3. Patuxent
4. Rappahannock
5. York
6. James

Source: U.S. Environmental Protection Agency (EPA), *Chesapeake Bay Program: Findings and Recommendations* (EPA, Philadelphia, 1983), p. 6.

Figure 12.7 Watershed of the Mediterranean Sea

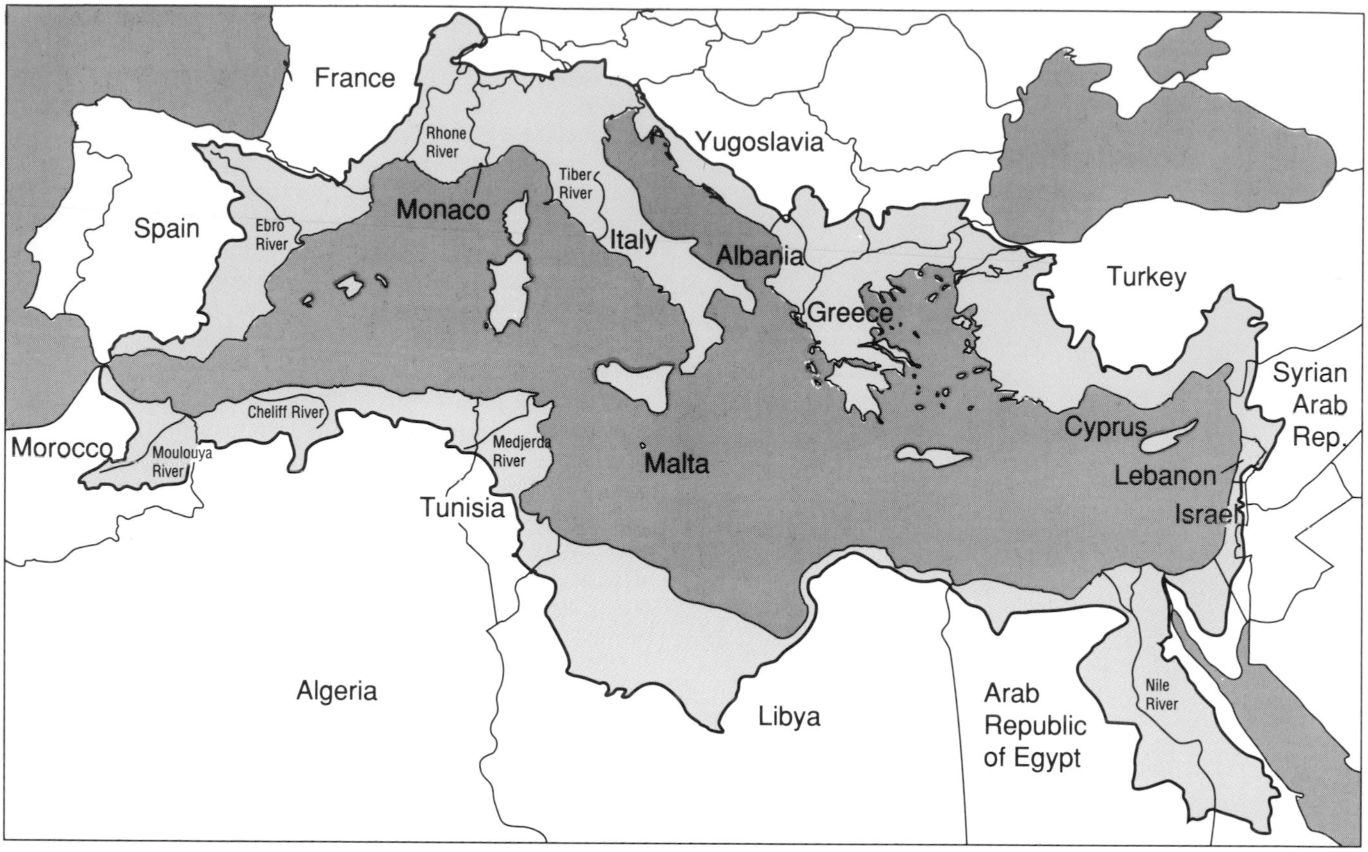

Source: United Nations Enviroment Programme (UNEP), *State of the Mediterranean Marine Environment* (UNEP, Athens, 1989), pp. 4 and 195.

The Mediterranean

The Mediterranean Sea, covering 2.5 million square kilometers and nearly 400 times larger than the Chesapeake Bay, is the subject of the oldest and most developed of the UNEP's 10 Regional Seas Programmes (117). With the 1975 adoption of the Mediterranean Action Plan (MAP), the 18 countries bordering the Mediterranean Sea initiated UNEP's regional approach to marine pollution and resource problems (118).

While newer Regional Seas Programmes are launching studies and agreeing to collaborate on oil spill cleanups, the Mediterranean program is trying a comprehensive approach to land-based watershed pollution. MAP studies suggest that at least one half the nutrient, mercury, chrome, lead, zinc, pesticide, and radioactive pollutants entering the Mediterranean Sea come from rivers draining areas outside the immediate coastal zone (119). (See Figure 12.7.) The weakness of tides in the Mediterranean Sea reduces flushing of coastal waters, worsening pollution (120).

The marine resources and environment of the region have suffered great damage (121). Industrial, domestic, and agricultural pollutants significantly degraded water quality in 20 of the 29 drainage basins discharging into the Mediterranean, causing massive algal blooms in some areas (122). In 1988, pathogens measured at 25 percent of sampled beaches in France,

Greece, Italy, and Spain exceeded safe levels (123). Airborne contaminants are also a problem; as much chromium and mercury enter the sea from the atmosphere as from rivers (124).

As the Blue Plan, part of the Mediterranean Action Plan, makes clear, the future for the coastal waters of the Mediterranean looks bad (125). The urban population of coastal Mediterranean areas is expected to increase from 81 million to as many as 170 million by 2025 (126). Most of this growth will occur from Morocco to Turkey, where the coastal population will triple; it will then account for more than one half the coastal population of the Mediterranean (127). Adding to the situation is a doubling in the number of tourists in the region to about 260 million by 2025 (128).

According to the Blue Plan, the fate of the Mediterranean marine environment depends principally on landuse planning, urban management, and pollution prevention (129). Yet the plan makes only general recommendations on how individual countries might address the discharge of industrial chemicals, soil erosion, nutrient and pesticide runoff, and coastal development while maintaining an economically competitive position in the region and globally.

To offer more specific suggestions regarding pollution problems, in 1988, the World Bank and the European Investment Bank produced an environment program for the Mediterranean. It sets priorities for action and offers technical and financial support (130). The two major priorities are to minimize public health risks and ensure sustainable growth. The banks point out the long-term economic effects of water contaminated by hazardous substances, overuse of aquifers, and enviromental degradation on all the Mediterranean countries. They recommend using economic incentives or disincentives, such as pollution charges, taxes, and subsidies to encourage water resuse, conserve energy, and prevent pollution (131). In addition to economic incentives, the banks encourage increased environmental planning and management—especially regarding water use and hazardous waste disposal, ap-

propriate land use, and preservation of environmentally sensitive areas (132). Noting that preventive programs are usually more economical than cleanup programs, the banks will help Mediterranean countries design and implement projects, strengthen or build institutions, give policy advice, and help mobilize financial resources (133).

The conditions and Trends section was written by World Resources Managing Editor Mary Paden. Focus On Coastal Pollution was written by Michael Weber, a Washington D.C. marine consultant. Information on the Black Sea was provided by the Institute of Geography, Soviet Academy of Sciences. WRI Research Assistant Daniel Seligman contributed to this Chapter.

References and Notes

1. Group of Experts on the Scientific Aspects of the Marine Environment, *The State of the Marine Environment* (United Nations Environment Programme, Nairobi, 1990), p. 1.

2. *Ibid.*

3. Group of Experts on the Scientific Aspects of Marine Pollution, *Technical Annexes to the Report on the State of the Marine Environment*, No. 114/2 (United Nations Environment Programme, Nairobi, 1990), p. 420.

4. *Ibid.*, p. 435.

5. *Op. cit.* 3, p. 422.

6. *Op. cit.* 1, p. 64.

7. Theodore J. Smayda, "Novel and Nuisance Phytoplankton Blooms in the Sea: Evidence for a Global Epidemic," *Proceedings of the Fourth International Conference on Toxic Marine Phytoplankton*, E. Granéli and L. Elder, eds. (Elsevier Science Publishing Co., New York, 1990), preprint, pp. 1-3.

8. "State of Environmental Pollution," *China Environment News*, No. 23 (June 1991), p. 7.

9. Benjamin L. Peierls, Nina F. Caraco, Michael L. Pace *et al.*, "Human Influence on River Nitrogen," *Nature*, Vol. 350 (April 4, 1991), p. 386.

10. Michael L. Pace, Aquatic Ecologist, Institute of Ecosystem Studies, The New York Botanical Gardens, Millbrook, August 1991 (personal communication).

11. Don Hinrichsen, *Our Common Seas: Coasts in Crisis* (Earthscan Publications Ltd., London, 1990), p. 118.

12. *Op. cit.* 1, pp. 53-55.

13. Stephen Olsen, Director, Coastal Resources Center, University of Rhode Island, Narragansett, 1991 (personal communication).

14. *Op. cit.* 1, pp. 56-57.

15. Carl Sinderman, "Pollution-Associated Disease Conditions in Marine Fish" in *MTS 90: Science and Technology for a New Oceans Decade*, proceedings from the 1990 Marine Technology Society (MTS) Conference (MTS, Washington, D.C., 1990), pp. 137-138.

16. National Oceanic and Atmospheric Administration (NOAA), *Coastal Environmental Quality in the United States, 1990: Chemical Contamination in Sediment and Tissues* (NOAA, U.S. Department of Commerce, Washington, D.C., 1990), p. 9.

17. *Op. cit.* 3, p. 470.

18. *Op. cit.* 1, p. 37.

19. Arthur L. Dahl, Deputy to the Director, Oceans and Coastal Areas/Programme Activity Centre, United Nations Environment Programme Regional Seas Programme, Nairobi, 1991 (personal communication).

20. Delegation of the United States to the Second Session of the Preparatory Committee for the United Nations Conference on Environment and Development, "Living Marine Resources: Background Paper for the U.S. Response to the 1991 Geneva Prep Com," Washington, D.C., March 1991, p. 22.

21. Philip Shabecoff, "Pollution Is Blamed for Killing Whales in the St. Lawrence," *New York Times* (January 12, 1988), p. C1.

22. Alan Cowell, "A Poisoned Season: Dead Dolphins, Abused Pups," *New York Times* (September 4, 1991), p. A4.

23. *Op. cit.* 3, p. 488.

24. *Op. cit.* 16, pp. 14-16.

25. *Op. cit.* 3, p. 473.

26. Food and Agriculture Organization of the United Nations (FAO), *The State of Food and Agriculture 1984* (FAO, Rome, 1985), p. 63.

27. *Op. cit.* 1, pp. 58-62.

28. Parviz S. Towfighi, Chief, Inter-Agency Affairs, United Nations Centre for Human Settlements (HABITAT), "Distribution and Trends of Growth of Urban Population in Urban Agglomerations on Sea/Ocean Coast Areas," (HABITAT, Nairobi, February 1991), Tables 1 and 2.

29. Ralph W. Tiner, Jr. *Wetlands of the United States: Current Status and Recent Trends* (U.S. Fish and Wildlife Service, Washington, D.C. 1984), p. 36.

30. Ralph W. Tiner, "Recent Changes in Estuarine Wetlands of the Coterminous United States," in H. Suzanne Bolton, ed., *Coastal Wetlands* (American Society of Civil Engineers, Long Beach, California, 1991), p. 100.

31. The World Bank and European Investment Bank, *The Environmental Program for the Mediterranean: Preserving a Shared Heritage and Managing a Common Resource* (The World Bank, Washington, D.C. 1990), p. 23.

32. Food and Agriculture Organization of the United Nations (FAO), Committee on Fisheries, "Environment and Sustainability in Fisheries," FAO, Rome, February 1991, p. 7.

33. James R. Chambers, "Coastal Degradation and Fish Population Losses," in *Stemming the Tide of Habitat Loss: Conservation of Coastal Fish Habitat* (National Coalition for Marine Conservation, Savannah, Georgia, in press).

34. National Science Foundation, U.S. Environmental Protection Agency, and National Oceanic and Atmospheric Administration, *Workshop on Coral Bleaching, Coral Reef Ecosystems and Global Change: Report of Proceedings* (University of Maryland, College Park, Maryland, 1991), p. I-7.

35. Leslie Roberts, "Greenhouse Role in Reef Stress Unproven," *Science*, Vol. 253 (July 19, 1991), pp. 258-259.

36. Thomas J. Goreau, "Written Statement to the UNCED Biodiversity Working Group," Global Coral Reef Alliance, (Chappaqua, New York, 1991), pp. 1-2.

37. John Hardy and Hermann Gucinski, "Stratospheric Ozone Depletion: Implications for Marine Ecosystems," *Oceanography* (November 1989), pp. 18-19.

38. John Hardy, "Where the Sea Meets the Sky," *Natural History* (May 1991), pp. 59-65.

39. John Hardy, Associate Professor, Huxley College of Environmental Studies, Western Washington University, Bellingham, Washington, 1991 (personal communication).

40. Adele Crispoldi, Fishery Statistician, Fishery Information, Data and Statistics Service, Fisheries Department, Food and Agriculture Organization of the United Nations, Rome, October 3, 1991 (personal communication).

41. Food and Agriculture Organization of the United Nations (FAO), "Recent Developments in World Fisheries," (FAO, Rome, April 1991), p. 1.

42. *Ibid.*

43. Adele Crispoldi, Fishery Statistician, Fishery Information, Data and Statistics Service, Fisheries Department, Food and Agriculture Organization of the United Nations, Rome, 1991 (personal communication).

44. Massachusetts Offshore Groundfish Task Force, *New England Groundfish in Crisis — Again* (Executive Office of Environmental Affairs, Boston, 1990), pp. iii-iv.

45. *Op. cit.* 32, p. 1.

46. *Op. cit.* 32, p. 12.

47. *Op. cit.* 32, p. 13.

48. *Op. cit.* 32, p. 13.

49. United Nations (U.N.) General Assembly, "Protection of Oceans, All Kinds of Seas Including Enclosed and Semi-Enclosed Seas, Coastal Areas and the Protection, Rational Use and Development of Their Living Resources," (U.N., New York, July 2, 1991), p. 2.

50. *Op. cit.* 11, pp. 26, 47-48, and 61.

51. National Oceanic and Atmospheric Administration (NOAA), *Estuaries of the United States: Vital Statistics of a National Resource Base* (NOAA, Washington, D.C., 1990), pp. 10-12.

52. Natural Resources Defense Council (NRDC) and Chesapeake Bay Foundation (CBF), *Poison Runoff in the Harrisburg Region: Stemming the Flow* (NRDC Washington D.C., and CBF, Annapolis, 1990), p. 1.

53. United Nations Environmental Programme (UNEP) *State of the Mediterranean Marine En-*

vironment, (UNEP, Athens, 1989), Table 31, p. 168.

54. Robert Repetto, *Promoting Environmentally Sound Economic Progress: What the North Can Do* (World Resources Institute, Washington, D.C., April 1990), p. 10.

55. Gregor Hodgson and John A. Dixon, *Logging Versus Fisheries and Tourism in Palawan: An Environmental and Economic Analysis* (East-West Environment and Policy Institute, Honolulu, 1988), Table 12, page 58.

56. Clifton Curtis, "Decisions of the Contracting Parties to the London Dumping Convention at Their 13th Consultative Meeting (29 October–2 November 1990)," memorandum to U.S. colleagues and others (United Nations, Economic Commission for Latin America, Santiago, Chile, November 1990), p. 1.

57. Group of Experts on the Scientific Aspects of Marine Pollution *The State of the Marine Environment* (United Nations Environment Programme, Nairobi, 1990), p. 12.

58. Rotterdam Municipal Port Management, "Rotterdam and Chemicals Manufacturers Association Conclude Environmental Agreement," press release, August 21, 1991.

59. Manuwadi Hungspreugs, "Heavy Metals and Other Non-Oil Pollutants in Southeast Asia," *Ambio*, Vol. 17, No. 3 (1988), p. 179.

60. Chesapeake Executive Council, *The Second Progress Report under the 1987 Chesapeake Bay Agreement* (U.S. Government Printing Office, Washington, D.C., 1989), pp. 12-15.

61. National Oceanic and Atmospheric Administration (NOAA), *Coastal Environmental Quality in the United States, 1990* (NOAA, Rockville, Maryland, 1990), p. 14.

62. *Op. cit.* 55, p. 30.

63. *Op. cit.* 55, p. 33-34.

64. *Op. cit.* 55, p. 37.

65. *Op. cit.* 55, p. 41.

66. *Op. cit.* 55, p. 64.

67. *Op. cit.* 57, p. 20.

68. Stephen Crutchfield, "Controlling Farm Pollution of Coastal Waters," *Agricultural Outlook* (U.S. Department of Agriculture, Economic Research Service, Washington, D.C., May 1988), p. 7.

69. National Research Council, *Coastal Resource Development and Management Needs of Developing Countries* (National Academy Press, Washington, D.C., 1982), p. 58.

70. *Op. cit.* 57, p. 20.

71. *Op. cit.* 68.

72. Anthony S. Pait, Daniel R.G. Farrow, Jamison A. Lowe, *et al.*, *Agricultural Pesticide Use in Estuarine Drainage Areas: A Preliminary Summary for Selected Pesticides* (National Oceanic and Atmospheric Administration, Rockville, Maryland 1989), p. 8 and Table 3, pp. 28-29.

73. Alan H. Trim, "Acute Toxicity of Emulsifiable Concentrations of Three Insecticides Commonly Found in Nonpoint Source Runoff into Estuarine Waters to the Mummichog, *Fundulus heteroclitus*," *Bulletin of Environmental Contamination and Toxicology*, Vol. 38 (1987), p. 681.

74. *Op. cit.* 72, p. 11.

75. Jack I. Lowe, "Mirex, Fire Ants, and Estuaries," *Proceedings of the Workshop on Agrichemicals and Estuarine Productivity* (National Oceanic and Atmospheric Administration, Washington, D.C., 1982), pp. 65-66.

76. Stephen Olsen, Lynne Zeitlin Hale, Random DuBois, *et al.*, "Integrated Resources Management for Coastal Environments in the Asia Near-East Region"(Coastal Resources Center, University of Rhode Island), 1989, p. 17.

77. Committee on Evaluation of the Safety of Fishery Products, *Seafood Safety* (National Academy Press, Washington, D.C., 1991), pp. 4-5.

78. John A. Dixon, Lee M. Talbot, and Guy J.-M. Le Moigne, *Dams and the Environment: Considerations in World Bank Projects* (The World Bank, Washington, D.C., 1989), pp. 18-19.

79. Michael A. Rozengurt, "Strategy and Ecological and Societal Results of Extensive Resources Development in the South of the USSR," in *Symposium Proceedings: Soviet Union in the Year 2010* (Georgetown University, Washington, D.C., 1991), pp. 127-128.

80. *Ibid.*, pp. 129-131.

81. International Union for the Conservation of Nature and Natural Resources, Commission on Ecology, Working Group on Mangrove Ecosystems, with United Nations Environment Programme and World Wildlife Fund, "Global Status of Mangrove Ecosystems," *The Environmentalist*, Vol. 3, Supplement 3 (1983), pp. 29-30.

82. Brent Blackwelder and Peter Carlson, *Disasters in International Water Development* (Environmental Policy Institute, Washington, D.C., 1986), p. 10.

83. Frederic H. Nichols, James E. Cloern, Samuel O. Luoma *et al.*, "The Modification of an Estuary," *Science*, Vol. 231 (February 7, 1986), Figure 5, p. 570.

84. Donald E. Stevens, David W. Kohlhurst, Lee W. Miller *et al.*, "The Decline of Striped Bass in the Sacramento—San Joaquin Estuary, California," *Transactions of the American Fish Society*, Vol. 114 (1985), cited in James R. Chambers, "Coastal Degradation and Fish Population Losses," paper presented at the National Symposium on Fish Habitat Conservation (National Coalition for Marine Conservation, Baltimore, March 1991).

85. Louisiana Wetland Protection Panel, *Saving Louisiana's Coastal Wetlands: The Need for a Long-Term Plan of Action* (U.S. Environmental Protection Agency, Washington, D.C., 1987), p. 9.

86. Benjamin L. Peierls, Nina F. Caraco, Michael L. Pace *et al.*, "Human Influence on River Nitrogen," *Nature*, Vol. 350 (April 4, 1991), pp. 386-387.

87. Bertil Haegerhaell, "Coastal Seas Damaged Worldwide by Excess Nutrients," *Acid Magazine* (Swedish Environmental Protection Agency, Solna, June 1990), p. 18.

88. Stuart Lehman, "Air Pollution," in *The Chesapeake Crisis: Turning the Tide*, (Chesapeake Bay Foundation, Annapolis, Maryland, 1990), p. 23.

89. *Op. cit.* 57, p. 36.

90. *Op. cit.* 61, pp. 14-16.

91. National Oceanic and Atmospheric Administration (NOAA), *Estuaries of the United States* (NOAA, Rockville, Maryland, 1990), p. 53.

92. *Ibid.*, pp. 5-6.

93. National Oceanic and Atmospheric Administration and U.S. Environmental Protection Agency, *Strategic Assessment of Near Coastal Waters: Susceptibility and Status of Gulf of Mexico Estuaries to Nutrient Discharges* (Department of Commerce, Washington, D.C., 1989), p. 26.

94. *Op. cit.* 54.

95. *Op. cit.* 76, p. 19.

96. *Op. cit.* 78, p. 10.

97. *Op. cit.* 33.

98. Hal Weeks, Endangered and Threatened Fish Program Leader, Oregon Department of Fish and Wildlife, 1991 (personal communication).

99. *Op. cit.* 13.

100. World Resources Institute and International Institute for Environment and Development, *World Resources 1987* (Basic Books, New York, 1987), pp. 181-189.

101. Coastal Resources Management Project, *What Future for Phuket?* (University of Rhode Island, Narragansett, February 1991), p. 6.

102. *Ibid.*, p. 39.

103. *Ibid.*, pp. 6, 18 and 19.

104. *Ibid.*, pp. 24, 34, and 49.

105. *Ibid.*, pp. 56-57.

106. *Ibid.*, pp. 50-51.

107. U.S. Environmental Protection Agency (EPA), *Chesapeake Bay Program: Findings and Recommendations* (EPA, Philadelphia, 1983), p. 30.

108. Patrick Gardner, "Agriculture and the Bay," in *The Chesapeake Crisis: Turning the Tide*, (Chesapeake Bay Foundation, Annapolis, Maryland, 1990), p. 10.

109. *Op. cit.* 60, p. 12.

110. *Op. cit.* 60, pp. 14-19.

111. *Op. cit.* 60, pp. 20-22.

112. D'Vera Cohn, "New Law Tackles Rampant Pollution Source—Rain," *Washington Post*, October 14, 1991, p. 1.

113. *Op. cit.* 60, p. 20.

114. Year 2020 Panel, "Population Growth and Development in the Chesapeake Bay Watershed to the Year 2020: Summary," report of the Year 2020 panel to the Chesapeake Executive Council (Chesapeake Bay Commission, Annapolis, Maryland, December 1988), pp. 1-2.

115. *Ibid.*, p. 1.

116. Alliance for the Chesapeake Bay, "Pollution Prevention Strategies to Get Greater Emphasis within Bay Program," *Bay Journal*, Vol. 1, No. 4 (June 1991), p. 8.

117. Regional Seas programmes have been developed for the following areas: Mediterranean, Persian Gulf and Gulf of Oman, West and Central African, Southeast Pacific, Red Sea and Gulf of Aden, Wider Caribbean, East African, South Pacific, East Asian, and South Asian regions. United Nations (U.N.) Secretariat, Office of Ocean Affairs and the law of the Sea, "International Institutions and Legal Instruments" (U.N., New York, 1991), pp. 28-33.

118. The World Bank and European Investment Bank, *The Environment Program for the Mediterranean* (World Bank, Washington, D.C., 1990), p. 13.

119. *Op. cit.* 53.

120. Michel Grenon and Michel Batisse, eds., *Futures for the Mediterranean Basin: The Blue Plan* (Oxford University Press, New York, 1989), p. 1.

121. The World Bank and European Investment Bank, *The Environmental Program for the Mediterranean: Preserving a Shared Heritage and Managing a Common Resource* (World Bank, Washington, D.C., 1990), pp. 9-11.

122. *Ibid.*, pp. 20 and 27.

123. *Ibid.*, p. 2.

124. *Op. cit.* 118, p. 31.

125. *Op. cit.* 120, pp. 231-249.

126. Michel Batisse, "Probing the Future of the Mediterranean Basin," *Environment*, Vol. 32, No. 5 (1990), p. 29.

127. *Ibid.*, p. 29.

128. *Op. cit.* 121, p. 3.

129. *Op. cit.* 120, p. viii.

130. *Op. cit.* 118, p. vii.

131. *Op. cit.* 118, pp. 51-54.

132. *Op. cit.* 118, pp. 51-54.

133. *Op. cit.* 118, p. 59.

13. Atmosphere and Climate

Seen from orbit, the Earth's atmosphere is a thin and seemingly fragile skin of air protecting the planet from the harshness of space. From the ground, this perspective is harder to appreciate. We take for granted that the atmosphere will protect us from the sun's most harmful rays, provide a moderate and stable climate, and renew and cleanse itself to provide fresh air to breathe. The persistent and growing problem of air pollution illustrates the degree to which human activities and practices have overwhelmed such natural processes. Likewise, the Antarctic ozone hole and new evidence that the degradation of the Earth's protective ozone layer is accelerating demonstrate that air pollution can have global effects.

The most threatening effect of global air pollution would be to alter the Earth's climate. Modern human societies have experienced moderate and stable climates, but earlier human societies experienced a glacial period or ice age extending until about 10,000 years ago. In still earlier periods, the Earth was ice-free and far warmer than today. These variations in climate were natural and gradual, but human activity is altering the composition of the atmosphere in ways that could bring rapid changes in climate.

Just how soon—and how much—these atmospheric alterations will translate into warmer global temperatures remains uncertain. Nonetheless, concern about the potential for global warming has stimulated efforts to impose international limits on emissions of greenhouse gases. Negotiations for a Global Climate Convention began early in 1991 under the auspices of the United Nations General Assembly, in hopes of reaching agreement prior to the United Nations Conference on Environment and Development, to be held in the summer of 1992.

This chapter reports on past and current trends in the major forms of atmospheric pollution and on the relative contributions of the countries of the world to these emissions. It also reports on emissions of carbon dioxide from industrial processes—principally the combustion of fossil fuels—which is the largest single source of greenhouse gases and an appropriate target for initial efforts to limit emissions.

CONDITIONS AND TRENDS

This section briefly reviews the sources, trends, effects, and possible solutions for a range of important urban and regional air pollutants. It also considers indoor air pollution, a relatively new area of concern but one with the potential to adversely affect much of the world's population, particularly residents of developing countries who cook and heat with "dirty" fuels such as coal, dung, or crop residues. (For a more extensive discussion of the pollution problems facing the newly democratic countries of Central Europe, see Chapter 5.) This section also reports on recent developments in global air pollution and the issues involved in trying to negotiate a global climate convention.

Global Trends

URBAN AIR POLLUTION: SOURCES, TRENDS, AND EFFECTS

Urban areas have long been a primary locus of serious air pollution because of the density of pollution sources—industries, residences, and vehicles. Since the 1970s, national air pollution policies have tended to focus on the control of six of the most serious urban pollutants: particulates (smoke and soot), sulfur dioxide (SO_2), nitrogen oxides (NO_x), ozone (photochemical smog), carbon monoxide (CO), and lead. Because these substances have known health and environmental effects, most industrialized nations—and many developing nations—have set legal air quality standards for some or all of them.

Particulates and Sulfur Dioxide

Suspended particulate matter and sulfur dioxide (SO_2) are good general indicators of urban pollution levels. Together they constitute a major portion of the pollutant load in many cities and act both separately and in concert to damage human health [1]. Both SO_2 and particulate matter can be potent respiratory irritants and can impair lung function by constricting airways and damaging lung tissue. Asthmatics and those suffering from other respiratory ailments such as emphysema are particularly susceptible [2] [3]. As one of the principal elements in acid deposition, SO_2 also has potent ecological effects, including direct damage to plant foliage and indirect disruption of ecosystems through acidification of soils and surface waters. (See Regional Air Pollution, below.)

Particulates include smoke, soot, dust, and liquid droplets emitted from fuel combustion, industrial processes, agricultural practices, or a number of natural sources [4]. Condensation of gases such as SO_2 and volatile organic compounds (VOCs) is also a significant source of particulates; roughly half of all human-caused particulates arise from conversion of SO_2 to sulfate particles in the atmosphere [5]. SO_2 emissions arise predominantly from the combustion of sulfur-containing fossil fuels—mostly coal—for electricity generation or residential heating. Metal smelting and some indus-

trial processes also create significant SO_2 emissions in some areas, as do diesel exhaust fumes in some cities.

National trends in emissions and urban ambient concentrations of SO_2 and particulates are mixed. In general, Western industrialized countries have made significant progress since the 1970s in reducing urban SO_2 and particulates, as well as national emissions of these substances. On the other hand, many developing nations with expanding industrial sectors and growing urban vehicle populations have seen increases in either SO_2 or particulate levels or both [6].

Coal washing, switching to a lower sulfur fuel, and the application of pollution reduction technologies such as stack "scrubbers" have achieved impressive results in industrialized countries like Japan, where SO_2 emissions decreased nearly 40 percent between 1974 and 1983 [7]. The use of tall stacks has further reduced urban SO_2 levels in industrialized countries by increasing the dispersion of the exhaust gases at power generation facilities and industrial sites, thus lowering pollutant concentrations nearby without decreasing overall emissions [8]. An unfortunate side effect of this practice has been the long-range transport of these emissions and their subsequent deposition in locations far from their source.

Elevated levels of particulates and SO_2 still plague a large fraction of the world's urban residents. Actual exposure levels vary considerably from city to city and from season to season, and data quantifying international urban pollution are seldom complete or timely. Nonetheless, the United Nations-sponsored Global Environmental Monitoring System estimated in 1987 that 70 percent of the world's urban population lived in cities where the level of suspended particulates exceeded World Health Organization (WHO) guidelines, and some two thirds of urban residents lived in cities where the ambient SO_2 concentration was at or above the WHO limit [9].

Smog and Its Precursors: Ozone, Nitrogen Oxides, and Organic Compounds

Photochemical smog forms when nitrogen oxides (NO_x) produced during fuel combustion react with VOCs in the presence of sunlight. The resulting mix of chemicals—containing more than 100 different compounds—is dominated by ozone. When formed at ground level, ozone is a highly reactive gas toxic to most living organisms. In the upper atmosphere, however, ozone absorbs harmful ultraviolet radiation. This "stratospheric" ozone layer is being damaged by chemical attack from chlorofluorocarbons. The control of smog—ozone—is one of the most vexing problems in modern pollution control, because smog formation is influenced by a complex interaction of pollutants, weather, and topography, and because smog precursors—NO_x and VOCs—are produced by sources that are difficult to control [10] [11] [12].

Nitrogen oxides (NO and NO_2) form when atmospheric oxygen and nitrogen, as well as the nitrogen contained in the fuel source, react at high temperatures. In industrialized countries, emission sources are

Box 13.1 Indoor Air Pollution

The problem of air pollution extends not just to the macroscale—the urban, regional, and global levels—but to the microscale as well. The indoor environment provides an intimate field of action for a host of airborne pollutants, from the exotic chemical effluent of modern technology to the more traditional byproducts of smoking, cooking, and heating. In fact, it is becoming increasingly clear that what we breathe indoors, whether at home, in the workplace, or in the car traveling between the two, may pose a greater health risk than what we breathe outdoors [1]. This is true in both industrialized and developing countries, although the sources and concentrations of pollutants in the two settings vary considerably [2].

The health risks of indoor air pollution are magnified because people the world over spend 80–90 percent of their time indoors [3]. A 1990 study by the U.S. Environmental Protection Agency ranked indoor pollution at the top of a list of 18 sources of environmental health risk in terms of the number of cancers these contaminants would cause in the general U.S. population [4]. Some health researchers believe that indoor pollution may represent one of the top ten causes of death in the United States [5].

In industrialized countries, exposure to indoor pollutants comes from a wide range of sources. Cigarettes, for instance, are potent emitters of carbon monoxide (CO), aldehydes, and a variety of carcinogens. Gas appliances and unvented kerosene heaters are a primary source of indoor nitrogen dioxide (NO_2), a respiratory irritant. Building materials such as particle board, plywood, and foam insulation give off formaldehyde, a probable carcinogen. Moreover, the recent trend toward energy efficiency has tended to make houses more airtight, a factor that tends to concentrate these pollutants, making them more of a problem than they were in the past [6]. Common consumer products that give off volatile organic compounds include dry-cleaned clothing, cleaning products, carpet adhesives, moth balls, aerosol products, and even typewriter correction fluid. Finally, molds, bacteria, fungi, asbestos, and radon are also known airborne contaminants in the home and workplace [7] [8].

In developing countries, indoor pollutants derive mainly from the everyday activities of cooking and heating with coal or biomass fuels—wood, crop wastes, or dung. The World Health Organization (WHO) estimates that approximately two thirds of the world's population, primarily in rural areas, burn these traditional fuels, often in stoves with poor or no ventilation [9]. Used in this way, biomass materials and coal emit a complex brew of hundreds of toxic substances, including particulates coated with a variety of organic compounds; NO_2; CO; sulfur dioxide (SO_2);

and a number of aromatic hydrocarbons, many of which have been identified as carcinogenic [10]. Poorly vented households can build up concentrations of these substances that sometimes exceed recommended exposure levels by two or three orders of magnitude [11]. In a field study conducted by WHO in rural Kenya, average particulate levels in houses where wood or crop residues were used for cooking were over 20 times higher than the WHO exposure guidelines; levels of aromatic hydrocarbons were also very high [12].

These extremely high exposure levels have major health impacts, including chronic lung and heart diseases, cancer, and acute respiratory infections, especially in children. An estimated 400–500 million people in the developing world are subject to such health effects, most of them women, infants, and the aged. Indeed, exposure to indoor fuel emissions is likely to be the most important occupational health hazard for women in developing countries [13].

Even in industrialized nations the health consequences of indoor air pollution are thought to be significant. For example, the NO_2 levels produced by a kerosene heater can cause respiratory problems in many asthmatics [14]. It is not surprising, therefore, that the economic impact associated with ill health caused by indoor pollution is estimated in the tens of billions of dollars per year in the United States alone [15]. Despite this fact, exposure to indoor pollutants is largely unregulated [16].

Addressing indoor pollution will require action on a number of fronts. In industrialized countries, homeowners will have to pay closer attention to their total indoor exposure, both by regulating pollution sources and by increasing household ventilation to dilute unavoidable pollutants. Smoking outdoors (if at all), airing dry-cleaned clothing outside before wearing, minimizing aerosol spray use, adjusting stoves and heaters for proper ventilation, cleaning molds and fungi out of air conditioners and humidifiers, and choosing carpeting and building materials wisely—are all ways in which the homeowner can reduce exposure [17] [18] [19].

In developing countries, efforts must focus on converting to cleaner fuels and properly vented stoves and heaters. In Chinese households, replacing coal with natural gas in urban areas and biogas in rural areas is a good example of this strategy. (Biogas is a mixture of gases—mostly methane—that comes from the decomposition of household wastes and organic materials in a special digester.) Over six million biogas digesters were built by rural Chinese households in the 1970s and more than 500,000 improved models were built in the 1980s [20]. Providing more efficient and better vented stoves, no matter what the fuel, has been a major focus of action in rural India, Africa, and elsewhere for many years, both to address health con-

cerns and the chronic fuel shortage in these regions. Over 64 million efficient cookstoves have been distributed in these areas since the early 1980s [21]. Some observers argue that, given the limited funds available for pollution control in developing nations, money spent on low-emission stoves would yield greater benefits in terms of improved human health than funds spent on expensive pollution control technology for large sources of outdoor pollution like power plants, although the environmental benefits are clearly not as great [22].

References and Notes

1. Larry B. Stammer, "Indoor Air—How Clean Is It?" *Washington Post* (January 23, 1990), p. A17.
2. Global Environmental Monitoring System, United Nations Environment Programme, and World Health Organization, *Assessment of Urban Air Quality* (United Nations, London, 1988), pp. 81-88.
3. *Ibid.*, p. 81.
4. Jonathan Bor, "Indoor Air More Polluted Than Outdoor, EPA Finds," *Baltimore Sun* (April 16, 1990), p. 1A.
5. *Op. cit.* 1.
6. *Op. cit.* 2, pp. 81-83.
7. D'Vera Cohn, "In Fight Against Pollution, the Frontier Moves Indoors," *Washington Post* (February 12, 1989), p. A1.
8. *Op. cit.* 2, pp. 82-83.
9. *Op. cit.* 2, p. 84.
10. *Op. cit.* 2, p. 84.
11. *Op. cit.* 2, pp. 86-87.
12. World Health Organization (WHO) and United Nations Environment Programme, *HEAL (Human Exposure Assessment Location) Project: Indoor Air Pollution Study, Maragua Area, Kenya* (WHO, Geneva, 1987), pp. 18-19.
13. *Op. cit.* 2, p. 88.
14. U.S. Environmental Protection Agency (EPA), *Report To Congress on Indoor Air Quality, Volume 2: Assessment and Control of Indoor Air Pollution* (EPA, Washington, D.C., 1989), pp. 3-8.
15. U.S. Environmental Protection Agency (EPA), *Report To Congress on Indoor Air Quality: Executive Summary and Recommendations* (EPA, Washington, D.C., 1989), p. 17.
16. *Op. cit.* 7.
17. U.S. Environmental Protection Agency (EPA), *The Inside Story: A Guide to Indoor Air Quality* (EPA, Washington, D.C., 1988), pp. 15-18.
18. *Op. cit.* 15.
19. *Op. cit.* 7.
20. Kirk R. Smith, "Air Pollution: Assessing Total Exposure in Developing Countries," *Environment*, Vol. 30, No. 10 (December 1988), pp. 16-20 and 28-35.
21. Jamuna Ramakrishna, M.B. Durgaprasad, and Kirk R. Smith, "Cooking in India: The Impact of Improved Stoves on Indoor Air Quality," *Environment International*, Vol. 15 (1989), pp. 341-352.
22. *Op. cit.* 20 pp. 28-29.

roughly evenly divided between vehicles and stationary sources such as power stations and industrial boilers, although vehicle emissions usually predominate in urban environments (13) (14). In terms of human exposure to NO_x, indoor sources such as unvented heating or cooking may be even more important than outside sources, especially in some developing countries (15). (See Box 13.1.)

Sources of VOCs are many and varied: vehicles, refineries, gas stations, and solvent sources such as dry cleaners, print shops, and house paints all contribute to the wide range of volatile compounds—mostly hydrocarbons—that react with NO_x in the presence of sunlight to yield smog (16).

Photochemical smog is a widespread urban problem, especially in Europe, Japan, and North America, where precursor molecules are often abundant and ambient summer ozone levels frequently exceed WHO exposure limits for hours and sometimes days at a time. In 1988, for instance, nearly half of the U.S. population lived in counties where the air did not meet the national ozone standard (17).

Cities in many developing countries also suffer from high ozone levels, but the ozone risk often takes second place to the threat posed by other pollutants. Data are not readily available to determine global trends in urban smog, but trends in NO_x emissions show increases in nearly every city monitored. Both NO_x and VOC concentrations are likely to climb in the years ahead as the vehicle populations in these cities continue to rise. Moreover, many of these cities are located in hot and sunny climates that favor ozone formation. As a result, the smog problem is likely to increase in severity in developing countries in the future (18).

The health effects of ozone are varied and severe. Because it is a reactive oxidizing agent, ozone tends to attack cells and break down biological tissues. It can be particularly damaging to lung tissue, even at low concentrations. A variety of symptoms ensue, including stinging eyes, coughing and chest discomfort, increased asthma attacks, and greater susceptibility to infection. Peroxy acetyl nitrate, another oxidant found in smog mixtures, produces or contributes to many of the same symptoms (19) (20) (21).

Ozone precursors also pose a threat to human health and the environment. NO_2 is a respiratory irritant that causes constriction of airways, reduced resistance to infection, and hypersensitivity to dust and pollen in asthmatics (22). VOCs can have a variety of effects depending upon the compound, including eye irritation, respiratory irritation, even cancer (23). Ozone is also a potent plant toxin, even at very low concentrations, and there is evidence that SO_2 and NO_x work synergistically to increase plant sensitivity to ozone leaf damage (24).

Carbon Monoxide

Global emissions of carbon monoxide (CO), created mostly by the incomplete combustion of carbon-containing fuels, exceed those of all other urban air pollutants combined. Although there are a variety of human-induced CO sources, vehicle exhaust accounts for nearly all of the CO emitted in many urban areas (25). (See Table 13.1.) Successful CO reduction strategies therefore rely chiefly on auto emission controls such as catalytic converters, which change most of the CO to carbon dioxide (CO_2) (26). Such controls have substantially lowered emissions and ambient CO concentrations in cities in the industrialized world: in Japan, ambient CO levels fell approximately 50 percent between 1973 and 1984 (27), while in the United States CO levels fell 28 percent between 1980 and 1989, in spite of a 39 percent increase in vehicle-miles traveled (28). However, most of the developing world is experiencing increases in CO levels as vehicle numbers and traffic congestion rise. Rough estimates by WHO indicate that unhealthy CO concentrations may exist in approximately half of the world's cities (29).

Table 13.1 Contribution of Road Transport to Air Pollution in Selected Cities

Region	Year	Total Pollutants From All Sources (thousand metric tons)	Percent Attributable to Road Transport					
			CO	HC	NOx	SOx	Particulates	Total
Mexico City	1987	5,027	99	89	64	2	9	80
São Paulo	1981	3,150	96	83	89 {a}	26	24	86
	1987	2,110	94	76	89 {a}	59	22	86
Ankara	1980	690	77	73	44	3	2	57
Manila	1987	500	93	82	73	12	60	71
Kuala Lumpur	1987	435	97	95	46	1	46	79
Seoul	1983	X	15	40	60	7	35	35
Hong Kong	1987	219	X	X	75	X	44	X
Athens{b}	1976	394	97	81	51	6	18	59
Gothenburg{b}	1980	124	96	89	70	2	50	78
London	1978	1,200	97	94	65	5	46	86
Los Angeles{b}	1976	4,698 {c}	99	61	71	12	X	88
	1982	3,391 {c}	99	50	64	21	X	87
Munich	1974/5	213	82	96	69	12	56	73
Osaka	1982	141	100	17	60	43	24	59
Phoenix	1986	1,240 {d}	87	64	77	91	1	28

Source: Asif Faiz, "Automotive Air Pollution: An Overview" (The World Bank, Washington, D.C., 1990), p. 12.
Notes:
a. Includes evaporation losses from storage and refueling.
b. Percent shares apply to all transport. Motor vehicles account for 75–95 percent of the transport share.
c. Excluding particulate matter.
d. Includes 490,000 metric tons of dust from unpaved roads.
X = not available.

Once inhaled, carbon monoxide binds to hemoglobin, interfering with oxygen transport by the blood. This can impair perception, slow reflexes, bring on headaches, and cause drowsiness. Among those most at risk from CO are pregnant women, infants, heart disease patients, and those with respiratory problems (30).

Although CO is not thought to have any direct ill effects on the environment, it does contribute indirectly to the formation of photochemical smog by reacting with hydroxyl radicals in the atmosphere. Hydroxyl radicals scavenge many other atmospheric pollutants, such as methane and other hydrocarbons, removing them from further smog-forming reactions. By depleting the population of hydroxyl radicals, CO increases the levels of other primary pollutants available for smog production and contributes to the buildup of methane—a potent greenhouse gas—in the atmosphere (31).

Lead and Other Pollutants

Airborne lead is derived primarily from fuel additives, metal smelters, and battery manufacturing plants; but leaded gasoline is by far the greatest source of airborne lead exposure in the industrialized world (32). Direct inhalation of airborne lead particulates from auto exhaust probably contributes only 1–2 percent of total human lead intake, but secondary exposure (from ingestion and inhalation of lead that has fallen on dust, soil, food, and water) can contribute up to 50 percent of total lead intake (33).

Lead exposure is cumulative and can result in a variety of adverse health effects in adults (including circulatory, reproductive, nervous, and kidney damage) even at low blood concentrations (34) (35). Children, especially fetuses, are susceptible to even lower levels of lead and thus comprise the most vulnerable risk group, suffering reduced birth weight, impaired mental and neurosensory development, and learning deficits in school. There may be no minimum threshold for safe exposure of children to lead (36). (See Chapter 6, "Population and Human Development.")

Prospects for global reductions in lead emissions are one of the few bright spots in the overall air pollution picture—at least in the industrialized countries, which have taken steps to reduce lead emissions from both stationary sources and vehicles. Reducing the permissible level of lead in petrol has been the primary means of reducing ambient lead concentrations (37). In the United States, the use of leaded fuel declined more than 50 percent from 1976–80 as new cars requiring unleaded fuel reached the market. During this period, blood lead levels declined 37 percent, even though the average dietary lead intake remained unchanged (38).

In spite of such progress, however, lead contamination continues to be an urban pollution problem of considerable dimensions, with the air in as many as one third of the world's cities exceeding the WHO lead standard. Many of these cities are in developing countries, where automobile traffic chokes some urban areas, lead levels in gasoline are often very high, and conversion to unleaded fuel is not yet under way (39).

Besides lead, a host of other toxic substances adds to the pollutant load in urban areas. These range from asbestos and heavy metals (such as cadmium, arsenic, manganese, nickel, and zinc), to a wide array of organic compounds (such as benzene and other hydrocarbons, and aldehydes) (40). The dimensions of the toxics problem are difficult to ascertain on a global basis because of the lack of air quality and emissions data, but the problem is known to be significant in the industrialized world. For example, industry figures show that U.S. companies emitted at least 1.2 million metric tons of air toxics in 1987 (41). The U.S. Environmental Protection Agency estimates that exposure to these pollutants causes between 1,700 and 2,700 cancers per year (42). In response, recent U.S. clean air legislation includes provisions to cut the emissions of nearly 200 toxic substances by 90 percent within a decade (43).

REGIONAL AIR POLLUTION: SOURCES, TRENDS, AND EFFECTS

Since the late 1960s, when the concept of acid rain first gained public attention, the regional aspects of pollution have come more sharply into focus as their visible toll has mounted. From the dead and dying trees in Germany's Black Forest to the depleted red spruce stands on the flanks of Mt. Mitchell in North Carolina, the effects of long-range transport of pollutants have become abundantly clear. Acid deposition and ground-level ozone are now recognized as prime contributors to widespread forest and crop declines on two continents and adverse health effects over extensive regions, with tangible human, ecological, and economic costs.

The abundant evidence that air pollutants do not respect political boundaries has stimulated a serious response in recent years among industrialized nations, sparking hopes that the atmospheric commons will at last be seen as the vulnerable resource that it is. This hope notwithstanding, most scientific projections indicate that regional pollution effects will get much worse before they get better, both in extent and intensity, particularly in view of development patterns and economic restraints in developing regions and Central Europe.

Acid Deposition

Both "wet" deposition—acid rain, snow, fog, and cloud vapors—and "dry" deposition—acidic particulates and aerosols—are formed when large volumes of SO_2 and NO_x are released from the combustion of fossil fuels. Stationary sources, such as coal-burning power plants, ore smelters, and industrial boilers, are responsible for nearly all human-caused SO_2 emissions and about 35 percent of human-caused NO_x emissions (44). Smokestacks up to 300 meters tall inject these gases high into the atmosphere, where most are converted to sulfate and nitrate particulates and distributed downwind. If captured by prevailing winds, they may be transported as much as 1,000 kilometers before being deposited (45), though dry deposition usually occurs closer to the emission source.

Vehicle traffic is another major source of acid precursors, generating 30–50 percent of total NO_x emissions in industrialized countries and many of the volatile organic compounds (VOCs) that lead to ground-level ozone. Ozone, in addition to its direct adverse effects, is an important intermediary in the transformation of SO_2 and NO_x to sulfuric and nitric acids (46).

The phenomenon of acid deposition is largely associated with highly industrialized regions of Europe and North America, where sulfur deposition in the most polluted areas is more than 10 times higher than the natural background rate (47). China—the third largest emitter of SO_2 after the Soviet Union and the United States—has also begun to experience regional acid rain problems in its southern provinces (48). More limited incidents of acid deposition have been recorded in Japan, as well (49).

Acid deposition can have severe effects on both terrestrial and aquatic ecosystems. Over time, as the soil loses its capacity to buffer the acid load, both soils and surface waters can gradually acidify, disrupting the chemical and biological processes of the organisms that live there. Sensitive aquatic species can decline rapidly as acidity disrupts their reproductive cycles. In Norway, for example, acidification of trout streams cut formerly stable brown trout populations in half by 1978, and the remaining populations fell another 40 percent by 1983 (50).

The level of soil acidification has also reached alarming levels in some locations. In the past 50 years, the soils in many of Europe's forests have become 5–10 times more acidic (51). This increased acidity can have pronounced effects on the nutrient balance available in the soil by causing the accelerated leaching of essential plant nutrients such as calcium, magnesium, and potassium ions. At the same time, higher soil acidity leads to increased levels of soluble aluminum, a plant toxin that damages fine roots and interferes with the uptake of remaining calcium and magnesium (52) (53). Excessive levels of nitrogen from acid deposition can also overstimulate plant growth and exacerbate nutrient deficiencies (54). Forests in Central Europe typically receive four to eight times as much nitrogen through acid deposition as they need for growth (55).

Acid precipitation also causes direct damage to some plant foliage, especially when it comes in the forms of fog and cloud water, which are, on average, about 10 times more acidic than acid rain. In North America, researchers have found that acid fogs can damage or kill red spruce needles, and foliar damage is enhanced when ozone is also present. The high-elevation ridgetops where red spruce grow may be covered in highly acidic (pH as low as 2.2), high-ozone clouds and fog for up to 3,000 hours per year (56) (57).

Large-scale forest decline is probably the most alarming regional manifestation of the effects of air pollution on terrestrial ecosystems, and the rapid decline of European forests since the 1970s is the most dramatic example to date. According to one recent analysis, about 75 percent of Europe's commercial forests suffer damaging levels of sulfur deposition, and 60 percent endure nitrogen depositions above their "critical loads" (the amount they can handle without harm) (58).

In concert with high levels of ozone, this acid onslaught has been instrumental in damaging a substantial percentage of the continent's conifers and deciduous trees, especially those over 60 years old (59).

In Germany, forest surveys indicate that over half of all trees suffered some defoliation damage in 1989, though the rate of forest decline there shows signs of lessening. In many parts of Central Europe and the Baltic republics, damage is even more serious and the rate of decline seems to be increasing: in Poland, more than 75 percent of all trees showed signs of some damage in 1989—up 10 percent from the figure reported in 1988. Reported damage to conifers rose a spectacular 21 percent in Lithuania between 1988 and 1989; more than 60 percent of its trees are now affected (60).

Forest dieback of such dimensions has substantial economic costs, including lost revenue from smaller timber harvests and related losses in wood processing industries, as well as reductions in recreation and other "nonwood" social benefits. A 1990 study put the cost of pollution damage to European forests at roughly $30 billion per year—about equal to the revenues from Germany's steel industry, and three times as much as Europe's current financial commitment to air pollution abatement (61). (See Table 13.2.)

Forest decline is also evident in North America, though not yet on the scale found in Europe. Recent studies have pointed to acid rain as a primary contributor to the severe dieback of red spruce at high elevations throughout the Appalachian Mountains. At elevations over 800 meters, where red spruce are a dominant species, the number of spruce has declined by 50 percent or more over the past 25 years, with the mortality rate increasing in the past several years. Acid deposition is also implicated in the recent dieback of sugar maples in Canada and the northeastern United States (62) (63).

Ecosystem damage caused by acid rain is not the only cause for concern. Corrosion of stone and metal building materials and monuments has also become a serious problem, especially in Europe, where a rich heritage of exposed art and architecture is slowly decaying under chemical attack (64). Increasing attention is being paid to the health effects of acid aerosols derived from the chemical transformation of SO_2 and NO_x in the atmosphere. Mounting evidence suggests that acid aerosols may damage human health by contributing to respiratory problems such as bronchitis and asthma (65). In the United States, some scientists have suggested that acid aerosols should be the next pollutant for which ambient air quality standards are set (66).

Ground-Level Ozone

Like acid deposition, the regional effects of ground-level ozone are profound and widespread. Elevated ozone levels are common over most of Europe and North America for days at a time during the summer (67) (68) (69). Nor is the problem restricted to urban areas: there is evidence that background levels of ozone are in-

Table 13.2 Estimated Losses of Forest Products Attributable to Air Pollution, by Volume and Value

Region/Country	Loss of Potential Harvest Attributable to Air Pollution (million cubic meters per year)	Value of Harvest Reduction {a} (million 1987 U.S. dollars per year)
Europe	**82.3**	**$23,022.9**
Nordic countries	11.1	2,925.1
Finland	4.5	1,187.6
Norway	0.8	210.4
Sweden	5.8	1,527.1
European Community	**28.6**	**9,389.1**
Belgium & Luxembourg	0.7	252.6
Denmark	0.4	117.1
France	3.5	1,173.6
Germany (West)	11.9	3,614.0
Germany (East)	4.9	1,160.8
Italy	3.1	1,830.5
Netherlands	0.2	67.4
UK & Ireland	3.7	1,173.1
Alpine countries	**5.8**	**1,573.6**
Austria	3.4	913.4
Switzerland	2.4	660.2
Southern Europe	**7.2**	**1,797.5**
Greece	0.1	23.4
Portugal	1.5	334.1
Spain {b}	X	X
Turkey	2.8	671.4
Yugoslavia	2.8	768.6
Central Europe	**29.6**	**7,337.6**
Bulgaria	2.2	520.9
Czechoslovakia	9.5	2,371.2
Hungary	3.0	789.9
Poland	11.1	2,658.5
Romania	3.8	997.1

Source: "The Price of Pollution: Acid and the Forests of Europe," *Options* (International Institute for Applied Systems Analysis, Laxenburg, Austria, September 1990), p. 6.
Notes:
a. Preliminary data; includes roundwood, industrial products, and "nonwood" benefits.
b. Data insufficient to allow calculation of pollution effects.
X = not available.

creasing over North America and Europe as a result of progressive increases in the levels of NO_2 and VOCs— the precursors of ozone. European data indicate that amounts of ground-level ozone have doubled over the continent in the past century (70). The sources of these precursors are widely distributed and somewhat difficult to regulate, including not only power plants, vehicles, and an assortment of small industries, but also residential emissions from house paints and other solvents. Natural VOC sources such as trees can also contribute to rural ozone levels, particularly when human activities such as vehicle combustion keep NO_x levels up (71).

Ozone's role as a plant toxin is well documented. It can damage cells in the leaves of a large number of tree and crop species, interfering with photosynthesis, contributing to nutrient leaching, and resulting ultimately in reduced growth and direct foliar damage (72) (73). Ozone-injured trees are also more susceptible to insect attack and root rot (74).

Ozone exposure, in combination with acid rain and other stresses, has been implicated as a prime contributor to the current European forest decline. Ozone damage to North American forests is also widespread, with extensive damage to mountain forests near Los Angeles and in the Appalachians. Ozone damage is also suspected as the primary agent in the reduced growth rate observed in the commercial yellow pine forests in the southern United States (75) (76).

Agricultural productivity losses from ozone are common in both Europe and North America. Current ozone levels in the United States are estimated to cause a 5–10 percent loss in potential crop yields (77) (78). Human and animal health effects of ozone exposure are also thought to be significant, especially when summer weather inversions lead to continuous high exposures for several days over extensive areas (79).

Reducing urban and regional ozone levels to the point where they no longer cause widespread ecological and health effects is expected to be one of the most difficult pollution abatement goals. In Europe, for example, computer simulations indicate that both VOCs and NO_x must be reduced by an estimated 75 percent from current levels to reach the critical loads that ensure the health of local ecosystems. Such a radical cut in precursor emissions is well beyond anything yet suggested by European governments (80).

Regional Responses and Emission Trends
Given the widening scope of the air pollution problem, it has become increasingly clear that there must be a coordinated, multinational response to pollution abatement. It is not surprising that the European Community became the first to act on this realization, since nowhere else are the transboundary effects of pollution so apparent.

In 1979, 35 nations from Central and Western Europe and North America signed the Convention on Long-Range Transboundary Air Pollution. What was at first a weak document has in the intervening decade become a fairly effective mechanism for reducing regional emissions. A protocol requiring a 30 percent reduction in SO_2 emissions (from 1980 levels) by 1993 was adopted in 1985 (81) (82). Although the United States did not sign the SO_2 protocol, it has subsequently passed legislation that will reduce SO_2 emissions some 35 percent by 2000 (83). A second protocol mandating a cap on NO_x emissions at 1987 levels was adopted in 1988, and the 12 members of the European Community went further by promising 30 percent NO_x reductions by 1998 (84) (85). In November 1991, 21 members of the United Nations Economic Commission for Europe signed a protocol mandating a 30 percent reduction in VOC emissions by the year 2000, with the intent of reducing ozone levels (86). The protocol includes emission controls on both vehicles and stationary sources—such as print shops and dry cleaners —that are much more difficult to control.

These international agreements could significantly reduce the most damaging pollutants in the industrialized world, but there is little reason to believe that such reductions will cut acid deposition and ozone exposure to the critical loads that ecosystems can tolerate (see below) (87). As a result, much stricter limits may be in the offing. Nevertheless, substantial declines in SO_2 emissions have already been realized in the industrialized world, especially in Europe, where overall SO_2 emissions have fallen more than 20 percent from

Recent Developments

OZONE DEPLETION ACCELERATES

A panel of international scientists said in October 1991 that about 3 percent of the Earth's protective layer of stratospheric ozone had been depleted over the United States and other temperate countries. The ozone loss could allow as much as 6 percent more ultraviolet radiation to strike the Earth's surface, which could significantly increase the incidence of skin cancer—perhaps as many as 12 million more cases in the United States over the next 50 years—and adversely affect agricultural production [1]. Moreover, the ozone loss occurs in the spring and summer, when outdoor activities and crop planting are at their peak. The depletion is expected to worsen in the 1990s, resulting in perhaps an additional 3 percent loss by the end of the century [2]. Limiting emissions of chlorofluorocarbons (CFCs) is essential to avoid still greater losses. However, recent efforts have not yet had an effect on the depletion process because CFCs take roughly 10 years to reach the stratosphere and have a life of 50 to 100 years.

The study was sponsored by the World Meteorological Organization (WMO) and the United Nations Environment Programme (UNEP) [3]. It also confirmed that the primary causes of ozone depletion are chlorine- and bromine-containing chemicals such as CFCs, which are widely used in refrigerators and air conditioners, and halons, which are used in fire extinguishers.

Meanwhile, the loss of ozone in Antarctica continued. In late September 1991, scientists with the New Zealand Meteorological Service reported a deep hole in the ozone layer over Antarctica for the third consecutive year. Measurements taken at Scott Base on Ross Island in Antarctica found a 50–60 percent loss of ozone during September (the beginning of the southern spring, which usually lasts until late November). Virtually all the ozone was depleted at altitudes of 12–20 kilometers [4]. As a result, measurements of ultraviolet radiation reaching the ground in Antarctica were the highest ever recorded.

An international agreement known as the Montreal Protocol on Substances that Deplete the Ozone Layer already calls for eliminating CFCs and other chemicals by the year 2000 in industrialized countries and by 2010 in developing countries [5]. The new findings have prompted calls by many governments and environmental groups to speed the process, eliminate some of the proposed substitutes (some of which are also detrimental to the ozone layer), and renegotiate the Montreal Protocol in 1992. The E.I. Du Pont de Nemours Co., the world's largest manufacturer of CFCs, said it would phase out CFC sales to industrialized countries by 1996 and halon sales by 1994, more rapidly than planned, and would hasten the elimination of HCFC-22 [6].

OZONE DEPLETION AND GLOBAL WARMING

The study on ozone depletion (see above) also described a hitherto unknown phenomenon with important implications for the rate of global warming. The phenomenon stems from the dual role of CFCs: in the lower atmosphere, they heat and thus contribute to global warming but in the stratosphere they become the primary source of chlorine, which degrades the Earth's ozone shield. So effective are CFCs at trapping heat that they have been credited with about 25 percent of the warming potential added to the lower atmosphere during the past decade.

Now, however, scientists have for the first time calculated the impact of ozone depletion on global warming, concluding that decreased stratospheric ozone exerts a cooling effect on the lower atmosphere of a magnitude that may offset the warming attributed to CFCs [7]. In fact, the cooling effect of ozone loss may be large enough to have offset a significant part of the heating from increases in all greenhouse gases over the past decade—a finding that, if confirmed, may partially explain why the observed temperature increases have lagged behind those predicted by climate models.

If the warming effect of CFCs are offset by the newly discovered cooling effect, then phasing out CFC use—already under way—will not decrease global warming. Methane, another major greenhouse gas with a variety of sources (including wet rice agriculture, livestock, landfills, and coal mining), is not easily controlled, but scientists are beginning to identify new control options [8]. That leaves carbon dioxide (CO_2) emissions—from combustion of fossil fuels and from deforestation—as the principal contributor to global warming and the primary candidate for significant reductions. Mostafa Tolba, executive director of UNEP, said the recent findings showed clearly that "the main emphasis should be on carbon dioxide" [9]. CO_2 emissions can be controlled by reducing demand for fossil energy, using it more efficiently, and developing alternative sources of energy.

MT. PINATUBO EMISSIONS COULD HAVE SIGNIFICANT IMPACT ON CLIMATE

The massive eruption of Mt. Pinatubo in the Philippines in June 1991 spewed an immense volume of ash and sulfur dioxide (SO_2) into the stratosphere that could have a significant short-term impact on the Earth's atmosphere.

Pinatubo, in a single episode, emitted about 18 million metric tons of SO_2 into the stratosphere [10], about twice the amount emitted by the 1982 El Chichón volcano in Mexico [11] (at the time the largest eruption in 50 years) and almost as much as the entire SO_2 emissions of the United States in one year. (See Chapter 24, "Atmosphere and Climate," Table 24.5.)

Because the gases were superhot, they raced to the stratosphere 20–30 kilometers above the earth's surface. Once aloft, the gases drifted around the equator from east to west, eventually covering the globe. The SO_2 gas turns into tiny droplets of sulfuric acid, causing a haze that will reflect and scatter sunlight. Experts think this haze might lower the average global temperature by more than 0.3° for three or four years, enough to temporarily mask global warming [12]. Some scientists also think the volcanic particles might play a role similar to that of ice crystals in the Antarctic, enabling chemical reactions to occur that would destroy ozone in the populated midlatitude regions [13].

References and Notes

1. Bob Davis and Barbara Rosewicz, "Panel Sees Ozone Thinning, Intensifying Political Heat," *Wall Street Journal* (October 13, 1991), p. B1.
2. William K. Stevens, "Summertime Harm to Shield of Ozone Detected Over U.S.," *New York Times* (October 23, 1991), p. A1.
3. World Meteorological Organization (WMO) and United Nations Environment Programme (UNEP), "Scientific Assessment of Stratospheric Ozone, 1991," executive summary (WMO, October 22, 1991).
4. "Hole in Ozone Found Over Antarctica Again," *Washington Post* (September 28, 1991), p. A3.
5. *Op. cit.* 2.
6. *Op. cit.* 1.
7. *Op. cit.* 3.
8. Kathleen B. Hogan, John S. Hoffman, and Anne M. Thompson, "Methane on the Greenhouse Agenda," *Nature*, Vol. 354, No. 6350 (November 21, 1991), pp. 181–182.
9. *Op. cit.* 2, p. A1.
10. Arlin J. Krueger, Senior Research Scientist, Laboratory for Atmosphere, U.S. National Aeronautics and Space Administration, Goddard Space Flight Center, Greenbelt, Maryland, 1991 (personal communication).
11. William K. Stevens, "Eruption of Philippines' Volcano May Counteract Global Warming," *New York Times* (June 30, 1991), p. A1.
12. *Ibid.*
13. Dianne Dumanoski, "Volcano's Blast Has Global Reach," *Boston Globe* (August 5, 1991), p. 37.

1980 to 1989 (88). In several countries where the political momentum for pollution abatement is strong, much greater reductions have been made. For instance, Germany, whose concern over forest decline runs deep, reduced SO_2 emissions by 53 percent from 1980 to 1989 (see Chapter 24, "Atmosphere and Climate," Table 24.5) and plans to reduce SO_2 emissions by 80 percent from 1983 levels by 1993 (89).

Reducing NO_x emissions has proven more difficult, and emission increases rather than declines have been the rule in all but a few nations (90). This may change in the near future—at least among nations—as NO_x controls become more stringent in an effort to combat ozone. Some nations, such as Japan and Germany, have already made substantial progress in cutting power plant NO_x emissions (91).

However, emission reductions are highly variable among nations and are largely dependent on the financial resources available (92). More importantly, overall emissions of SO_2 and NO_x on a global level are expected to increase in the years ahead as the energy demand in developing countries continues to rise and the vehicle population expands (93) (94). Inexpensive high-sulfur coal—the worst offender in terms of SO_2—is likely to make up an increasing percentage of the fossil fuels burned by power plants and industry, especially in developing nations (95). China is expected to double its coal use by 2000 (96).

There is considerable fear that, if the trend toward higher emissions in the developing world continues at its present rate, SO_2 and NO_x emissions from developing nations will outstrip those from industrialized nations in the decades ahead, creating a huge potential for acid deposition over a much wider area (97). Many of the regions at risk have soils that are very sensitive to acidification. Tropical soils, for example, are often highly weathered and already fairly acidic—conditions that predispose them to acid damage (98).

SOLUTIONS

Solving the problem of urban and regional air pollution will require a mix of technical improvements and policy initiatives, from using new combustion technologies to taxing emissions and encouraging energy conservation. Emissions from both stationary sources and vehicles must be reduced considerably in the near term. This progress must include the developing nations if the damage to ecosystems and human health is to be held in check in the face of global development. Finally, industry must join in the cleanup by recognizing that emission reduction can be a road to greater efficiency rather than a constraint on profits.

Cleaning Up Stationary Sources

Standards and Incentives

Emission standards for large stationary sources, such as power plants, smelters, and chemical manufacturers, represent the traditional first line of attack in the effort to reduce air pollution. Such standards have gotten progressively tighter over the years in most of the industrialized world. However, they must be made much tighter if real progress is to be made in reducing emissions to biologically acceptable levels.

Europe has taken positive steps toward implementing ecologically based emission standards by accepting the concept of "critical pollutant loads" and by calculating these loads for many areas of the continent (99). Such calculations, both in Europe and North America, make it plain that emission reductions much deeper than those presently proposed will be required to bring pollutants in line with natural tolerances. It is unclear whether the political will and the economic means yet exist to attain these low emission levels, but the conceptual framework has been established—an essential first step in the process of abatement (100).

Unfortunately, emission standards are by no means ubiquitous or uniform, especially in developing countries. Nor is the research base available in most of the developing world to establish realistic critical load values to use as targets for future emission controls (101). Even where emission standards have been set, the economic means to comply with them is often lacking and enforcement weak (102).

As the necessity for expensive pollution control technology has become apparent, policymakers in industrialized countries have begun to turn to the marketplace by providing economic incentives that reward polluters for developing and deploying cost-effective abatement schemes (103). Perhaps the simplest application of this principle is the pollution tax, under which emitters are taxed per unit of pollutant discharged. France became the first nation to impose a direct pollution tax in May 1990, when a tax on SO_2 emissions was established. A more comprehensive statute that will tax CO_2 and NO_x emissions in addition to SO_2 is under consideration in Sweden (104).

A more sophisticated market mechanism uses transferable emission discharge permits or credits. First, an overall emissions cap is set within a region, and permits are required for all emissions. If a facility reduces emissions further or more quickly than required, it earns emission "credits" that can be applied to future emissions or sold to others. The owners of other facilities can then opt to purchase these credits to cover their emissions or take abatement measures themselves, with whatever technology they choose. The United States was the first to adopt this flexible approach when it updated its air pollution laws in 1990 (105). A similar system has been discussed in Europe as well, although the multitude of different jurisdictions there would make its administration difficult (106).

Technological Options

Numerous technological options are available for meeting emission targets and a combination of methods may be required as emission limits become more stringent. Switching to cleaner-burning fuels—either natural gas or low-sulfur oil or coal—is one important and relatively simple option to reduce sulfur emissions. Availability and cost are the greatest obstacles.

The wider use of natural gas is almost sure to figure prominently in pollution control efforts in the industrialized world and in those developing nations where gas is plentiful. Natural gas contains virtually no sulfur, and its combustion produces far fewer NO_x emissions than coal or oil. Because it has a higher ratio of hydrogen to carbon atoms than oil or coal, its combustion also produces less CO_2, a greenhouse gas that is to assume greater international importance in the future. Natural gas can also be burned more efficiently and more cleanly: a modern combined-cycle gas turbine power plant produces less than 55 percent of the CO_2 generated by a coal-fired plant per unit of electricity produced [107] [108] [109].

Clean coal technologies will also play an important role in the years ahead, because—in spite of coal's environmental drawbacks—global coal use is expected to rise substantially. The simplest of these technologies—coal washing—can remove 20 to 50 percent of the sulfur in coal at moderate cost, making it an attractive (if only partially effective) option for many developing nations [110]. New combustion technologies can also help reduce emissions from coal-fired installations, but their costs are considerable. Advanced burners have reduced NO_x emissions by 50 percent at some facilities. Use of fluidized bed combustion or integrated gasification/combined cycle at new plants has also resulted in substantial SO_2 and NO_x control [111].

The most common technological emissions fixes to date, known as scrubbers, remove pollutants from effluent gases in the smokestack. Again, costs are high, especially for retrofitting older facilities, but results can be impressive: up to 95 percent of the SO_2 and 70–90 percent of the NO_x can be removed by available scrubber technology [112]. Unfortunately, a considerable quantity of waste products—sludge and low-grade gypsum, for example—are produced in the process, creating disposal problems [113].

Conservation

One of the least expensive and most flexible tools in reducing emissions from stationary sources is energy conservation. (See Chapter 10, "Energy.") Increasing energy efficiency both at power generating plants and at the point of energy use offers the chance to reduce emission levels without reducing economic activity or disrupting consumer services. Energy efficiency increased rapidly in industrialized countries in the 1970s and early 1980s, but it has slowed greatly in the years since, due in large part to the powerful disincentive of low energy prices. Many opportunities still remain for conservation, from increasing the thermal efficiency of coal-fired power plants to installing energy-efficient appliances [114] [115].

Experience has shown that a unit of energy can be conserved for roughly half the cost of adding equivalent new capacity at a power plant, with little environmental impact. As a result, environmental and energy planners, who have begun to make conservation a larger part of their pollution control strategy.

Alternative Sources

The replacement of fossil fuels with alternative energy —hydro, wind, solar electric, geothermal, nuclear, or hydrogen—represents the most dramatic action available to reduce emissions of nearly every major air pollutant. Although important advances have been made, more work remains before these alternatives can be applied on a large scale. Only nuclear and hydropower have been applied extensively and both have high capital costs and other adverse environmental impacts that restrict their use.

The feasibility of using hydrogen as a clean fuel source has improved recently because of developments in wind power and photovoltaic (PV) technology, which converts solar energy to electricity. Hydrogen produces only water and small amounts of NO_x when burned, and the wind- or PV-powered electrolysis of water would offer an essentially unlimited source of hydrogen without contributing to air pollution or global warming. Capital requirements for hydrogen-fired power plants are expected to be relatively low, making hydrogen use a practical option in regions where sunshine for PV arrays is abundant [116].

In the meantime, the benefits of available technologies could be increased by better distribution of the funds available for pollution control.

The Corporate Responsibility Movement

In the past decade and particularly in the past few years, many industries have begun to modify manufacturing processes to minimize toxic emissions—in other words, to address the problem of emissions at its source, not simply to clean up afterward [117]. For example, the auto industry has begun to phase out the use of solvent-based paints in favor of water-based paints that give off no hydrocarbon emissions [118].

For some companies, these actions respond to the probability of tighter emission standards, as well as the fear that being labeled a polluter will harm the company image [119]. For others, however, waste and emission reductions are a means to more efficient use of materials, adding to the bottom line as well as salving the corporate conscience. When Deere & Co. eliminated the use of solvents in its engine manufacturing facility, for example, it saved $380,000 a year in production costs while forgoing the annual release of 320 metric tons of solvent vapors [120].

The list of large multinational corporations with programs in waste and emission reduction is impressive. Monsanto Chemical Co. announced in 1988 that it would reduce its hazardous emissions 90 percent by 1992. The Dow Chemical Co. has cut its emissions by 50 percent since 1984, and plans a similar reduction from current levels by 1995. E.I. Du Pont de Nemours & Co. has pledged a 70 percent reduction of all hazardous waste by the year 2000 [121].

Companies that achieve such ambitious goals generally share some common traits: a genuine and clearly communicated commitment to pollution reduction on the part of top management; specific, publicly announced emission reduction targets; incentives within the company to generate ideas for manufacturing refinements that benefit pollution goals; and recognition for those facilities that meet or exceed these goals (122).

Reducing Vehicle Pollution

Motor vehicles cause more air pollution than any other single human activity. They are a major source of emissions for a variety of atmospheric pollutants, contributing nearly one half of the human-caused NO_x, two thirds of the carbon monoxide, and about one half of the hydrocarbons in industrialized countries, as well as most of the airborne lead in developing nations. Addressing vehicle emissions is thus an essential element in reducing both local and regional air pollution (123) (124).

Projected increases in the global vehicle population could lead to explosive growth in vehicle emissions. More than 500 million automobiles and commercial vehicles now ply the world's roads, 10 times more than in 1950 (125). And according to recent projections, the global vehicle population will double over the next 40 years to about 1 billion (126). Much of this growth will take place in developing countries, where demand for automobiles is expected to increase by over 200 percent by the end of the century (127), greatly exacerbating current pollution problems, especially in urban areas (128).

Catalytic Converters

The options for cleaning up vehicle emissions begin with tighter tailpipe emission standards. Fairly stringent tailpipe controls have allowed Japan and the United States to greatly increase the number of vehicles without a corresponding increase in emissions, and a new round of stricter limits has just been adopted in both Europe and the United States (129) (130).

The use of catalytic converters to treat exhaust gases has been the most important tool in controlling auto emissions in Japan and the United States for over a decade. A catalytic converter can reduce emissions of VOCs and carbon monoxide by about 85 percent, and NO_x by about 60 percent, over the life of a car (131). Europe's new emission limits—driven by the need to lower ozone levels—will also require use of catalytic devices by 1993 (132). Recent improvements in this technology will help auto manufacturers meet new emission limits at reduced cost (133).

In developing countries, the adoption of state-of-the-art emission controls such as catalytic devices is complicated by the use of poor-quality leaded fuel (lead poisons catalysts), the high price, and lack of public acceptance of such controls. Phasing out leaded fuel would constitute a major first step toward cleaner air, simultaneously reducing dangerous lead exposures and allowing the eventual use of catalytic devices as emission standards are tightened. A simple graduated tax on gasoline in proportion to its lead content could help encourage such a change (134).

Rigorous vehicle maintenance and inspection programs, to ensure compliance, are an important adjunct to emission standards. Tampering and poor maintenance can quickly render emission controls ineffective (135).

Age also tends to decrease the performance of pollution equipment; most current auto emission controls are designed to meet emission standards for only 50,000 miles, about half a vehicle's average lifetime mileage. Older automobiles typically generate more harmful emissions than newer models (136). Programs to retire older vehicles from the road, perhaps by offering some financial incentive, could therefore improve the emission performance of the vehicle fleet.

Emissions from diesel trucks and buses are another important target. Diesel engines without emission controls emit 30–70 times more particulates than gasoline engines equipped with catalytic converters (137). Until recently, diesel engines were virtually unregulated worldwide, but new standards adopted by the United States and Europe have spurred development of technologies that promise to greatly improve diesel emission performance (138) (139). Gradual incorporation of these technologies, which include engine modifications as well as flow-through exhaust catalysts and particulate traps, could greatly benefit urban centers in the developing world, where diesel exhaust contributes substantially to the pollution load (140).

Alternative Fuels

In addition to exhaust controls, the use of alternative fuels that burn cleaner than petrol shows great potential for reducing emissions. The simplest option is to reformulate current petrol blends to reduce both volatility—and thus VOC emissions—and the amount of toxic additives such as benzene. Addition of alcohols and ethers to create "oxygenated" fuels ("gasohol" is an example) also helps to promote a cleaner burn. In the United States, new legislation mandates the use of such reformulated fuels in areas with the worst ozone problems (141) (142). Cleaner diesel fuels with lower sulfur contents can also yield significant emissions benefits, particularly in urban settings.

Unfortunately, reformulated fuels will probably yield emission improvements of no more than about 30 percent. Petrol alternatives (such as methanol, ethanol, compressed natural gas or liquified petroleum gas, hydrogen, or electric batteries) can give much greater emission reductions—as much as 90 percent in some cases. These options are being actively considered in such problem areas as Los Angeles, where officials feel that radical steps must be taken if pollution levels are to be reduced (143) (144).

Clean-fuel vehicles suffer practical limitations—such as reduced range—and still require much refinement (145). Nonetheless, the U.S. government has established a pilot clean-fuel program in Los Angeles that will require 150,000 clean-fuel vehicles by 1996 (146). Meanwhile, the European Community has set a goal of introducing 7 million emission-free electric vehicles to the continent by the year 2000 (147). Fleet vehicles such as taxis and buses, with limited range and central refueling facilities, would be ideal candidates for conversion to alternative fuels (148). Analysts believe this strategy can reduce urban vehicle pollution in both industrialized and developing nations.

Reducing Congestion

Regardless of improvements in fuels and controls, emissions levels will not improve if increasing traffic congestion makes travel less efficient: more vehicles burning more fuel to travel shorter distances. Already, massive congestion plagues a high percentage of the world's urban areas. Better traffic management will therefore play an important part in preserving technology-based emission gains. This can range from physical methods—coordinated traffic lights, paired one-way streets, and separate carpool or bus lanes—to economic incentives—"congestion pricing" that charges motorists for driving on roadways during peak traffic periods (149) (150).

An aggressive commitment to alternative transport, from bicycles to mass transit, is another essential element in reducing vehicle pollution and highway congestion. The pollution benefits of rail and bus transit are well known, but less attention has been paid to accommodating bicycle and pedestrian traffic, which on a global basis provide two of the least expensive and most widespread alternatives to auto transport (151). Some countries have begun to provide a safer environment for bicycle and pedestrian traffic by creating separate lanes, overpasses, or spaces at intersections, or simply slowing traffic with speed bumps and diversions. Bicycle and pedestrian transport can be integrated into a city's overall transit scheme through such strategies as uninterrupted through-routes, secure bicycle parking at transit stations, and the permission to take bicycles aboard trains and buses, thus making them useful at both ends of a workday commute (152).

Vehicle-free zones in city centers is another popular strategy to solve urban pollution problems and "reclaim" urban spaces for nonvehicle traffic. Nearly every major European city and many cities in other regions have restricted vehicle use in some part of the city center. By requiring drivers to refrain from using their autos one day a week or face stiff fines and vehicle impoundment, both Mexico City and Santiago have reduced traffic by as much as 20 percent (153) (154).

Key Issues

GLOBAL CLIMATE TREATY TALKS PROCEED

The nations of the world are poised to take a historic step in mid-1992 when they will consider an international framework treaty on climate change that may include an agreement among industrialized countries limiting emissions of gases such as carbon dioxide that contribute to global warming. By October 1991, however, many crucial details of the agreement remained unsettled. The negotiations have been difficult, but the process has moved forward and there is hope that an agreement can be ready for consideration at the June 1992 United Nations Conference on Environment and Development (UNCED) in Rio de Janeiro.

The process began in the fall of 1990 when the United Nations General Assembly established an autonomous Intergovernmental Negotiating Committee (INC) for a framework convention on climate change. With the help of the United Nations Environment Programme (UNEP) and the World Meteorological Organization (WMO), INC was charged with negotiating an "effective" treaty on climate change with "appropriate commitments." The INC process was conducted separately from the preparations for UNCED, but the treaty signing was expected to be a centerpiece of the UNCED meeting (155).

The committee split into two working groups, the first dealing with substantive issues and the second with the legal and institutional mechanisms to implement provisions of an agreement.

The first three INC meetings—in February, June, and September 1991—dealt largely with organizational issues and initial discussions about the contents of the treaty. Two more meetings (December 1991, when negotiations on the text were to begin, and February 1992) are scheduled, and a sixth meeting is possible in April or May 1992 (156).

By October 1991 many major issues remained unresolved. The critical ones included:

■ All industrialized nations except the United States favored the adoption of concrete targets and timetables for stabilizing CO_2 emissions. EC nations wanted to stabilize emissions at 1990 levels by the year 2000; a few countries proposed actual cuts below 1990 levels. The United States strongly opposed such targets, arguing that the long-term climatic benefits were uncertain and that such an agreement would curtail burning of fossil fuels such as coal and oil and threaten economic growth. The United States also argued that it was already taking actions—for example, by phasing out chlorofluorocarbons (CFCs) as part of an international agreement to prevent the destruction of stratospheric ozone—that would hold its net contribution of greenhouse gases to 1990 levels in the year 2000 (157). That argument was substantially undercut, however, by new evidence that CFC-induced ozone depletion may cool the atmosphere to a degree that offsets some of the CFC warming. (See Recent Developments.)

■ Many developing countries said their willingness to make commitments—especially if the treaty includes a review mechanism that includes enforcement measures—was contingent on new financial support from the industrialized countries to help pay the costs. The United States also was the leading opponent of new funding for the developing countries.

In the fall of 1991, the biggest stumbling block to the treaty appeared to be the U.S. opposition to targets or financial assistance, which was preventing a consensus among industrialized countries. EC nations and Japan were continuing to press for a minimum agreement on targets that the United States would support, and at the same time were concerned about the competitive implications of any agreement that did not include the United States (158).

FOCUS ON GREENHOUSE GAS EMISSIONS

Human activity is altering the composition of the atmosphere in ways that could bring rapid changes in climate.

A natural greenhouse effect keeps the Earth's surface warm. Infrared radiation that would otherwise escape into space is trapped by trace constituents of the atmosphere such as water vapor, carbon dioxide, methane, and other greenhouse gases. Human activities not only increase the atmospheric concentrations of these naturally occurring greenhouse gases but also add new powerful infrared-absorbing gases—such as the industrial chemicals known as chlorofluorocarbons (CFCs) (see Table 13.3). Emissions of greenhouse gases from human activities have accelerated in recent decades.

Is the global climate getting warmer? Certainly the 1980s were the warmest decade recorded since careful weather records began being kept. Six of the 10 hottest years on record have occurred since 1980—1989, 1988, 1987, 1983, 1981, and 1980 itself. Hotter still was 1990—the warmest year yet, according to the British Meteorological Office, based on global average surface temperatures as recorded by weather stations—and the first 10 months of 1991 were nearly as warm (159) (160). But scientists cannot yet say whether this warm weather is a trend, resulting from rising concentrations of greenhouse gases, or whether it is merely a natural fluctuation.

But extensive climate change is likely, according to a major international scientific study sponsored jointly by the United Nations Environment Programme and the World Meteorological Organization and conducted under the auspices of the Intergovernmental Panel on Climate Change (IPCC). The study involved the efforts of several hundred leading atmospheric scientists from many nations, and it produced a synthesis of the best available scientific knowledge. The report of the IPCC Scientific Assessment Panel concluded that, if current emission trends continue, mean global temperatures will rise at the rate of 0.3°C per decade, based on current models. "This will result," the report states, "in a likely increase in global mean temperature during the next century of about 1°C above the present value by 2025 and 3°C before the end of the next century" (161).

Because atmospheric concentrations of long-lived greenhouse gases adjust slowly to changes in emissions, continued emissions of such gases at present rates, the report says, "would commit us to increased concentrations for centuries ahead." To stabilize atmospheric concentrations of CO_2 and CFCs at today's levels, the report calculates, "would require immediate reductions in emissions from human activities of over 60 percent . . .; methane would require a 15–20 percent reduction" (162).

Just how such drastic reductions might be achieved, and what they might cost, is hotly debated. One recent study in the United States, for example, concluded that U.S. greenhouse gas emissions could be reduced between 10 and 40 percent of 1990 levels at low cost, or even at some net economic savings, if proper policies were implemented (163).

Table 13.3 Summary of Atmospheric Growth of Greenhouse Gases

Gas	Concentration in Air		Present Annual Increase	
	Preindustrial	1989	Rate	Percent
Carbon dioxide	275.00 ppm	354.00 ppm	1.70 ppm	0.4
Methane	0.70 ppm	1.7 ppm	12.30 ppb	0.7
Chlorofluorocarbon-12	0.00	0.47 ppb	0.025 ppb	5.3
Chlorofluorocarbon-11	0.00	0.28 ppb	0.010 ppb	3.4
Nitrous Oxide	280.00 ppb	306 .00ppb	0.600 ppb	0.2 {a}
Tropospheric Ozone	X	35.00 ppb {a}	X	

Source: U.S. Environmental Protection Agency (EPA), *Potential Effects of Global Climate Change on the United States*, draft report, Joel B. Smith and Dennis A. Tirpak, eds. (EPA, Washington, D.C., 1988), Table 2.1.
Notes: a. 1986 data.
ppm = parts per million.
ppb = parts per billion.
X = not available.

GREENHOUSE GAS EMISSIONS

Any effort to stabilize or reduce greenhouse gas emissions must begin with a realistic, quantitative picture of the volume and distribution of those emissions. This task is complicated by uncertainties in emissions data. The method used to estimate methane emissions from wet rice agriculture presented here is based on the consensus of an expert panel convened by the Organisation of Economic Co-operation and Development (164). Relatively few careful studies have been conducted, however, and many of those were in Europe, while most rice is grown in tropical countries. Preliminary studies in China suggest that methane emissions from rice fields in that country may be far higher (165); comparable studies are under way but not yet completed in India. Emissions of the gases that form tropospheric ozone are believed to occur predominantly in industrial countries, but quantitative estimates are not available and these gases are thus not included in this analysis. Estimates of carbon dioxide from combustion of fossil fuels and other industrial processes, though better known, are still accurate only to within about 10 percent.

This report also calculates greenhouse gas emissions from deforestation and land clearing on the assumption that, aside from a small portion of carbon that is sequestered in the soil, all of the carbon from cleared vegetation is oxidized and released as CO_2. A significant fraction of the carbon could be released as methane, a far more potent greenhouse gas. The deliberate burning of grasslands, particularly in developing countries, has also been shown to be a significant source of methane emissions, but no estimates of the amount of burning on a national basis are available (166). Estimates of methane emissions from industrial uses in the Soviet Union also vary widely; those used here are on the lower end of the spectrum.

Even the underlying data on land use changes, including deforestation, are uncertain. The most recent data available for most tropical countries stem from the 1980 assessment of the Food and Agriculture Orga-

Figure 13.1 Cumulative Emissions of Carbon Dioxide from Fossil Fuels for 25 Countries with the Highest Emissions, 1950–89

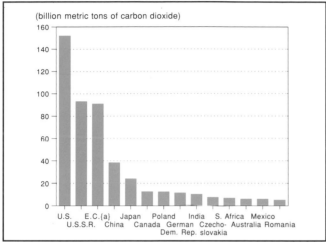

(billion metric tons of carbon dioxide)

U.S.   E.C.{a}   Japan   Poland   India   S. Africa   Mexico
U.S.S.R.   China   Canada   German   Czecho-   Australia   Romania
Dem. Rep.   slovakia

Source: Carbon Dioxide Information Analysis Center (CDIAC), Oak Ridge National Laboratory, unpublished data, (CDIAC, Oak Ridge, Tennessee, August 1989).

Note: a. The European Community (EC) comprises 12 countries: Belgium, Denmark, France, Germany, Greece, Ireland, Italy, Luxembourg, the Netherlands, Portugal, Spain, and the United Kingdom.

nization of the United Nations (FAO), which is now generally conceded to have underestimated deforestation rates. Preliminary estimates from the 1990 FAO assessment show that, on a global basis, deforestation is significantly higher than in the 1980 Assessment, but revised estimates for individual countries are not yet available. (See Chapter 8, "Forests and Rangelands.") (Brazil, which over the past three years has launched an intensive effort to monitor deforestation systematically and now compiles annual estimates of deforestation, is a notable exception.) The amount of carbon per hectare varies with the type of forest, and estimates that are both lower and higher than those used here have been published; more comprehensive studies are under way in Brazil.

The task of presenting a comprehensive picture of emissions and their impact is also complicated by lack of agreement on how to compare the heating effects of gases that have different lifetimes in the atmosphere. Accordingly, this volume of *World Resources* presents national and per capita rankings based on two methods (which nevertheless yield quite similar results) and discusses a number of other approaches.

Past Emissions

The most important greenhouse gas, CO_2, arises primarily from the burning of fossil fuels and the burning and clearing of land for agricultural purposes. An enormous quantity of CO_2 has been released through human activities, some of which can be estimated. Worldwide consumption of fossil fuels in the period 1860 to 1949 is estimated to have released 187 billion metric tons of CO_2 (167). In the past four decades, fossil

fuel use has accelerated and CO_2 emissions in the period 1950–89 totaled an additional 559 billion metric tons. (See Chapter 24, "Atmosphere and Climate," Table 24.4.) Figure 13.1 shows the relative contributions for the period 1950–89 of the 25 countries that have been the largest sources of CO_2 emissions from industrial processes (the European Community is treated as a single entity). The United States is the largest emitter, followed by the countries of the European Community and the Soviet Union.

Land use change, including deforestation for agricultural purposes, is estimated to have released about another 220 billion metric tons of CO_2 since 1860 (168). Such estimates do not take into account the accelerating deforestation in tropical forest countries in the past decade, which may account for as much as an additional 50 billion metric tons of CO_2. Data that would allow estimates of cumulative national emissions of methane or of CFCs are not available.

Current Emissions

In Chapter 24, "Atmosphere and Climate," Tables 24.1 and 24.2 provide estimates of emissions for the major greenhouse gases in 1989 (or for the most recent year prior to 1989), by source and by country. These estimates incorporate revisions in emission estimates for wet rice agriculture; the expansion of data to include methane emissions from natural gas venting, production, and transmission; and upward revisions of methane emissions from coal mining.

In all, global CO_2 emissions to the atmosphere from combustion of fossil fuels, production of cement, and land use clearing are estimated at 28 billion metric tons, 77 percent from industrial sources. Estimated emissions of methane, a far more potent gas in trapping heat but one that has a relatively short lifetime in the atmosphere, amounted to 270 million tons; the total includes emissions from solid waste, livestock, coal mining, wet rice cultivation, and natural gas production. Global emissions of CFC-11 and CFC-12, the most potent and perhaps the longest-lived greenhouse gases, are estimated at 580,000 metric tons. (See Tables 24.1 and 24.2.) Relative to 1987, CO_2 emissions from industrial processes have increased, but CO_2 emissions from land use change and deforestation have declined. Methane emissions have increased somewhat, and those of CFC-11 and CFC-12 have significantly decreased.

Other greenhouse gases include ground-level ozone (a short-lived but potent gas that is a principal constituent of smog), nitrous oxide (a very long-lived gas whose sources are poorly understood), and other CFC and CFC-replacement gases. Together, these gases are estimated to account for about 15 percent of the current warming potential attributable to human-induced emissions of greenhouse gases (warming potential means the amount of future warming that a given emission will cause). No estimates of emissions by country are available for these gases, and they are omitted in the following discussions.

Box 13.2 Calculating a Greenhouse Index

Since the publication of national and per capita Greenhouse Indexes in *World Resources 1990–91*, the work of the scientific assessment panel of the Intergovernmental Program on Climate Change (IPCC) has set a de facto standard for discussion of greenhouse gas emissions [1]. The panel adopted a conceptual unit, the "global warming potential" (GWP), for comparing the impact of gases that have different lifetimes in the atmosphere and different potencies in absorbing heat. One complication inherent in such a comparison is that the potency of a greenhouse gas depends on its concentration in the atmosphere, which in turn depends on assumptions about future emissions. A second complication is that the lifetimes of the greenhouse gases (or conversely, the rate at which they are removed from the atmosphere by natural processes) is not known with any precision, at least for carbon dioxide (CO_2), the most important greenhouse gas. Estimates of removal rates are based on models of atmospheric, oceanic, and biospheric processes that are still the subject of considerable debate.

The GWP for a given gas is determined by integrating an expression for the removal rate times an expression for the infrared absorption potency of the gas [2]. GWP values depend on the period of years over which the integration is carried out, which must be chosen arbitrarily. The IPCC panel reported values for 20, 100, and 500 years; the Greenhouse Index reported in this chapter uses an integration period of 100 years.

Values calculated by the IPCC panel are normalized so that the GWP of carbon dioxide is 1. The corresponding GWP for methane is 21 and for CFCs (the mix of CFC-11 and CFC-12 emitted in 1989), 5,873 [3]. To calculate a Greenhouse Index, national emissions of each greenhouse gas (from Chapter 24, "Atmosphere and Climate," Tables 24.1 and 24.2) are weighted by the appropriate GWP and the result is summed to obtain the impact of a country's total emissions in carbon dioxide equivalents. The IPCC panel cautions that these values are preliminary and subject to change. The GWP approach has not been universally accepted; some scientists still have strong reservations, in part because of the arbitrary integration period.

A Greenhouse Index was also calculated for this report using the method adopted in *World Resources 1990–91*, with some modifications. The method is less sophisticated than the GWP approach and is based on observational evidence rather than models of how the atmosphere behaves. It depends on the concept of the airborne fraction of a gas—the proportion of the gas emitted from human activities that is initially retained in the air rather than removed by natural processes and thus adds to the concentration levels in the atmosphere. The airborne fraction is readily determined as the (measured) increase in concentration of a greenhouse gas in a given year times the mass of the atmosphere, divided by total global emissions of that gas.

The airborne fraction is a crude but useful measure of the *effective* lifetime of a gas subject to the natural processes of the carbon cycle of the Earth; the more rapid the removal processes (i.e., the shorter the lifetime), the smaller the airborne fraction. The product of this effective lifetime and the infrared absorption potency for a given gas thus provides a weighting factor for emissions, the greenhouse forcing contribution (GFC), that is roughly equivalent but not identical to the GWP [4]. This method has been criticed as imprecise, because the gas removed from the atmosphere in a given year may have been emitted in a previous year, not the year in which the airborne fraction is calculated. In addition, this method can only be applied to periods of rising concentrations of greenhouse gases.

In calculating a Greenhouse Index with this method, earlier procedures have been modified slightly to use the same infrared potencies adopted by the IPCC scientific assessment panel, to adopt units of carbon dioxide equivalents (rather than carbon equivalents), and to determine annual concentration changes based on a three-year rolling average—thus smoothing out measurement fluctuations and short-term variations in the carbon cycle. For 1989, the airborne fraction for carbon dioxide was 0.50 and for methane, 0.13. (The airborne fraction of CFCs is assumed to be 1—i.e., all CFCs emitted to the atmosphere remain there). When combined with the potencies, the GFCs (normalized such that the GFC of carbon dioxide is 1) are 15 for methane and 10,249 for the mixture of CFC-11 and CFC-12 emitted in 1989. National emissions (from Tables 24.1 and 24.2) are weighted by the appropriate GFC and summed to obtain the impact of a country's total emissions in carbon dioxide equivalents.

The IPCC method thus weights methane emissions slightly higher and CFC emissions lower than does the *World Resources* method. Because differences in raw index scores between the two methods used here are not meaningful, Table 13.4 presents instead rank and percent share of global emissions for each country. For per capita emissions, Table 13.5 presents rank and per capita emissions relative to those of the median per capita emissions for the world.

References and Notes

1. Intergovernmental Panel on Climate Change (IPCC), *Climate Change: The IPCC Scientific Assessment*, J.T. Houghton, G.J. Jenkins, and J.J. Ephraums, eds. (Cambridge University Press, Cambridge, U.K., 1990).

2. The GWP index score is calculated as follows:

   $I = \sum_i e_i \, GWP_i$ where $\sum_i$ means to sum over all gases (i); e_i = the country's emissions of gas i; and

   $$GWP_i = \frac{\int_0^N r_i c_i \, dt}{\int_0^N r_c c_c \, dt}$$ where r_i = the radiative forcing of gas i; c_i = the atmospheric concentration of gas i; r_c = the radiative forcing of carbon dioxide; c_c = the atmospheric concentration of carbon dioxide; and N = the integration period (or time horizon).

3. Intergovernmental Panel on Climate Change (IPCC), *Climate Change: The IPCC Scientific Assessment*, J.T. Houghton, G.J. Jenkins, and J.J. Ephraums, eds. (Cambridge University Press, Cambridge, U.K., 1990), p. xxi. The combined GWP for CFC-11 and CFC-12 was calculated using IPCC data for GWPs and World Resources Institute data for emissions.

4. The GFC index score is calculated as follows:

   $I = \sum_i e_i \, GFC_i$ where $\sum_i$ means to sum over all gases (i); e_i = the country's emissions of gas i; $GFC_i = r_i Af_i$; r_i the radiative forcing of gas i; and Af_i = the airborne fraction of gas i = the net atmospheric increase of gas i over the total global emissions of gas i.

Greenhouse Indexes

The pattern of emissions of different greenhouse gases varies markedly from country to country. To describe quantitatively the effects of such emissions on the atmosphere, it is useful to calculate a Greenhouse Index that sums up each country's contribution or relative share of the warming potential for a given year. The Index and the national rankings based on it are descriptive in character and intent, apply only to the year specified, and neither imply priorities for reductions of emissions (these are considered in a following section) nor suggest responsibilities under a climate convention (which must be negotiated after taking many factors into account).

To calculate the combined impact on the atmosphere of emissions of different greenhouse gases, it is neces-

Table 13.4 Greenhouse Index Ranking and Percent Share of Global Emissions, 1989

Intergovernmental Panel on Climate Change (IPCC)		Rank	World Resources	
Percent	Country		Country	Percent
17.8	United States	1	United States	18.4
13.6	U.S.S.R.	2	U.S.S.R.	13.5
9.1	China	3	China	8.4
4.7	Japan	4	Japan	5.6
4.1	India	5	Brazil	3.8
3.9	Brazil	6	India	3.5
3.4	Germany{a}	7	Germany{a}	3.6
2.2	United Kingdom	8	United Kingdom	2.4
2.0	Mexico	9	Mexico	2.0
1.7	Indonesia	10	Italy	1.8
1.7	Canada	11	France	1.7
1.6	Italy	12	Canada	1.7
1.5	France	13	Indonesia	1.6
1.5	Thailand	14	Poland	1.4
1.5	Poland	15	Thailand	1.4
1.4	Colombia	16	Colombia	1.4
1.1	Myanmar	17	Australia	1.1
1.1	Nigeria	18	South Africa	1.1
1.1	Australia	19	Myanmar	1.1
1.1	South Africa	20	Spain	1.1
0.9	Cote d'Ivoire	21	Nigeria	1.1
0.9	Spain	22	Cote d'Ivoire	0.9
0.8	Korea, Rep	23	Korea, Rep	0.8
0.8	Philippines	24	Czechoslovakia	0.7
0.7	Czechoslovakia	25	Malaysia	0.7
0.7	Malaysia	26	Philippines	0.7
0.7	Romania	27	Romania	0.7
0.7	Viet Nam	28	Lao People's Dem Rep	0.7
0.7	Lao People's Dem Rep	29	Viet Nam	0.6
0.6	Saudi Arabia	30	Saudi Arabia	0.6
0.6	Iran, Islamic Rep	31	Iran, Islamic Rep	0.6
0.6	Argentina	32	Netherlands	0.6
0.5	Venezuela	33	Argentina	0.5
0.5	Netherlands	34	Venezuela	0.5
0.5	Ecuador	35	Yugoslavia	0.5
0.5	Korea, Dem People's Rep	36	Ecuador	0.5
0.5	Yugoslavia	37	Pakistan	0.5
0.5	Peru	38	Peru	0.5
0.5	Pakistan	39	Korea, Dem People's Rep	0.5
0.4	Bangladesh	40	Turkey	0.4
0.4	Turkey	41	Belgium	0.4
0.4	Madagascar	42	Madagascar	0.4
0.4	Zaire	43	Zaire	0.4
0.4	Belgium	44	Bulgaria	0.3
0.3	Sudan	45	Greece	0.3
0.3	Bulgaria	46	Sudan	0.3
0.3	Cameroon	47	Egypt	0.3
0.3	Egypt	48	Bangladesh	0.3
0.3	Greece	49	Cameroon	0.3
0.3	Iraq	50	Hungary	0.3

Sources:
1. Intergovernmental Panel on Climate Change (IPCC), *Climate Change: The IPCC Scientific Assessment*, J. Houghton, G.J. Jenkins, and J.J. Ephraums, eds. (Cambridge University Press, Cambridge, U.K., 1990).
2. Chapter 24, "Atmosphere and Climate," Tables 24.1 and 24.2.
Note: a. Data for Germany include both the former Federal Republic of Germany and the German Democratic Republic.

Figure 13.2 The Greenhouse Index: 25 Countries with the Highest Greenhouse Gas Emissions, 1989

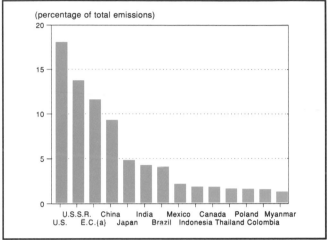

Sources:
1. Intergovernmental Panel on Climate Change (IPCC), *Climate Change: The IPCC Scientific Assessment*, J. Houghton, G.J. Jenkins, and J.J. Ephraums, eds. (Cambridge University Press, Cambridge, U.K., 1990).
2. Chapter 24, "Atmosphere and Climate," Tables 24.1 and 24.2.
Note: a. The European Community (EC) comprises 12 countries: Belgium, Denmark, France, Germany, Greece, Ireland, Italy, Luxembourg, the Netherlands, Portugal, Spain, and the United Kingdom.

National Rankings

Table 13.4 gives the national rank and percent share of the global warming potential attributable to the countries that in 1989 emitted the most CO_2, methane, and CFCs. The countries are ranked by their Greenhouse Index, as determined by the two methods given in Box 13.2 and the emissions data in Tables 24.1 and 24.2.

The United States and the Soviet Union are the largest and second largest emitters, contributing, respectively, 18 percent and 14 percent of the total atmospheric impact of current emissions. Taken as a single unit, the European Community ranks third with an 11 percent share (see Figure 13.2). The top six countries—3 industrialized and 3 developing—together account for more than 50 percent of the total atmospheric impact of current emissions. Altogether, the 50 countries listed in Table 13.4 accounted for 92 percent of 1989 total emissions.

Several countries changed their rankings by at least two places, compared with the rankings given in *World Resources 1990–91* based on 1987 emissions. Japan moved up because of increased emissions of CFCs and of CO_2 from fossil fuels. Mexico and Thailand moved higher because of increased estimates of CO_2 emissions from land use change. Brazil, India, and Indonesia moved down because of lower estimates of CO_2 emissions from land use changes. Brazil, in particular, has documented dramatic reductions in CO_2 emissions in 1988–90.

Per Capita Rankings

Table 13.5 provides per capita rank and a measure of per capita global warming potential impact attribut-

sary to combine an estimate of each gas's lifetime and its potency. The results of two methods of performing these calculations are presented here. The first method is that adopted by the IPCC Scientific Assessment Panel (see Box 13.2); the second method is that adopted in *World Resources 1990–91*, with slight refinements. Each has its advantages and disadvantages, but for the purposes of providing an overall description of the pattern of emissions, both methods give comparable results: they treat CO_2 emissions identically; the IPCC method weights methane emissions slightly higher, and CFC emissions significantly lower, than does the *World Resources* method. (For convenience, all numbers in the text are based on the IPCC method unless otherwise noted.)

Box 13.3 Alternative Indexes of Greenhouse Gas Emissions

There is vigorous debate about how to construct indexes that represent the combined effect of each nation's greenhouse emissions in a policy-relevant and appropriate fashion; no scientific consensus has yet emerged. In addition to the indexes presented in this chapter, other approaches have been proposed or are in the process of being developed.

An American researcher, Kirk Smith, has proposed an index of "natural debt" that exemplifies the cumulative approach. Natural debt arises, according to Smith, when greenhouse gases are put into the atmosphere faster than they can be naturally removed. The natural debt index is the cumulative surviving human-induced emissions of greenhouse gases per capita, taking into account the differing atmospheric lifetimes and potencies of each gas. Smith admits that calculation of such an index would be difficult in practice; as an approximation, he uses CO_2 from fossil fuel combustion over the period 1900 to the present. On that basis, he estimates that the total carbon released into the atmosphere and still present as CO_2 is about 260 metric tons per living resident of the United States, compared to about 6 metric tons for the average resident of India. Industrial nations, because of their early use of fossil fuels, have much larger cumulative emissions than developing nations. Smith argues that, because the economic status of most countries has been achieved partly by incurring natural debts, responsibility for greenhouse emissions should be measured by an index that reflects these natural debts. However, he also distinguishes between allocating responsibility for emissions—or paying for remediative measures—and setting priorities for remediative measures. Thus he suggests that the greatest responsibility for cumulative emissions lies with industrial countries, while the projects with the greatest potential for reducing emissions may occur in any country [1].

A different approach is that proposed by Yasumasa Fujii, a Japanese researcher working at the International Institute of Applied Systems Analysis in Austria. Fujii's method, based on interregional and intergenerational equity, allocates equal carbon emission rights to every person born from the year 1800 to the year 2100, regardless of when or where they lived, and permits future generations to inherit unspent carbon quotas by region. The method then establishes regional quotas designed to equalize average per capita emissions in each region over the 300-year period, assuming that CO_2 levels and world population both double from present values. Under these conditions, Fujii finds that North America's quota, because of its long history of high energy use, is about one tenth of present per capita levels. Other industrial regions where high energy use patterns are more recent have quotas only slightly smaller than at present. Developing regions would be able to increase per capita emissions substantially, but not as much as might be expected, because soaring populations overwhelm inherited balances [2] [3].

A somewhat similar approach has been developed by Anil Agarwal and Sunita Narain of the Centre for Science and Environment in New Dehli, India. Their index allocates the natural sinks for CO_2 and methane to each nation in proportion to its population, and calculates each country's excess emissions of each gas—if any—beyond what its share of the global sink can absorb. Sinks are estimated indirectly using the nonairborne fraction of global anthropogenic emissions, since the character and geographical location of sinks for carbon dioxide are not well known. The authors also suggest various schemes by which nations that exceed their emission quotas could buy emission rights from nations that do not [4].

Two other methods represent variations on the IPCC method and are intended to remove perhaps the major problem of that method, namely, the need to pick an arbitrary parameter—the integration period—in calculating global warming potentials.

One method, developed by Daniel Lashof of the Natural Resources Defense Council in Washington, D.C., employs instead a "discount rate" that at least casts the choice of such a parameter in terms commonly used by economists to make estimates about the future [5]. A second method, developed by John Reuther and his colleagues at the Pittsburgh Energy Technology Center, proposes a new model for the atmospheric lifetime of CO_2 that can be used to calculate global warming potentials without arbitrary parameters [6].

The editors of *World Resources* believe that publication of several types of indexes—total national emissions, per capita emissions, and cumulative emissions—can best serve the needs of describing physical reality and of providing measures of how countries are meeting internationally agreed-upon emission limits.

References and Notes

1. Kirk R. Smith, "Allocating Responsibility for Global Warming: The Natural Debt Index," *Ambio*, Vol. 20, No. 2 (April 1991), pp. 95-96.

2. Yasumasa Fujii, "An Assessment of the Responsibility for the Increase in the CO_2 Concentration and Inter-Generational Carbon Accounts" (International Institute for Applied Systems Analysis, Laxenburg, Austria, 1990).

3. "CO_2: A Balancing of Accounts," *Options* (International Institute for Applied Systems Analysis, Laxenburg, Austria, December 1990), pp. 10-13.

4. Anil Agarwal and Sunita Narain, "Global Warming in an Unequal World" (Centre for Science and Environment, New Dehli, India, 1991), pp. 13- 20.

5. Daniel A. Lashof and Dilip R. Ahuja, "Relative Contributions of Greenhouse Gas Emissions to Global Warming," *Nature*, Vol. 344, No. 6266 (April 5, 1990), p. 529.

6. John A. Ruether, Director, Systems Analysis Division, Pittsburgh Energy Technology Center, U.S. Department of Energy, Pittsburgh, Pennsylvania, 1991 (personal communication).

able to 1989 emissions of CO_2, methane, and CFCs. The measure given is the ratio of a country's per capita emissions to the world median per capita figure, which for 1989 is 2.96 metric tons of CO_2 heating equivalent per person. The countries are ranked by their per capita Greenhouse Index, as determined by each of two methods, and the 50 countries with the largest per capita contributions are given for each method. Some countries that ranked high on the basis of total contributions, such as China and India, disappear entirely from the 50 largest contributors on a per capita basis. The highest per capita emissions come from countries with small populations that are either oil producers (oil production also consumes energy and releases CO_2 and methane) or countries with significant deforestation.

Among the major industrial countries, the per capita warming potential impact of a U.S. resident is the highest in the world—8.7 times that of a resident of China (which happens to equal the world median) and 14.3 times that of a resident of India. The per capita impact of a resident of Japan is only 53 percent of that of a U.S. resident. Figure 13.3 displays the per capita emissions of the 15 countries ranked highest in Table 13.4, illustrating the great disparities in per capita impact on the atmosphere from greenhouse gas emissions, particularly between industrialized and developing countries.

Table 13.5 Relative Per Capita Greenhouse Emissions, 1989

Intergovernmental Panel on Climate Change (IPCC)		Rank	World Resources	
Relative Per Capita Emissions{a}	Country		Country	Relative Per Capita Emissions{a}
14.5	United Arab Emirates	1	United Arab Emirates	15.7
12.2	Qatar	2	Qatar	12.4
10.5	Brunei	3	Luxembourg	10.5
9.8	Bahrain	4	Côte d'Ivoire	10.4
9.8	Cote d'Ivoire	5	Bahrain	10.2
9.3	Luxembourg	6	United States	9.8
8.8	United States	7	Brunei	9.8
8.2	Australia	8	Australia	8.8
7.8	Canada	9	Canada	8.6
7.7	Trinidad and Tobago	10	Trinidad and Tobago	7.6
7.0	Guinea-Bissau	11	Guinea-Bissau	7.2
6.5	Kuwait	12	Kuwait	7.1
6.0	Norway	13	Czechoslovakia	6.4
5.8	Ecuador	14	U.S.S.R.	6.2
5.8	U.S.S.R.	15	Ecuador	6.2
5.7	Czechoslovakia	16	Germany {b}	6.1
5.7	Nicaragua	17	Norway	6.1
5.6	Paraguay	18	Nicaragua	6.1
5.6	New Zealand	19	Japan	6.0
5.4	Gabon	20	Paraguay	5.9
5.4	Liberia	21	Singapore	5.7
5.3	Germany {b}	22	Liberia	5.7
5.3	Colombia	23	Colombia	5.6
5.2	Malaysia	24	New Zealand	5.6
5.0	Singapore	25	Malaysia	5.6
5.0	Saudi Arabia	26	Saudi Arabia	5.5
4.7	United Kingdom	27	United Kingdom	5.5
4.7	Poland	28	Gabon	5.5
4.6	Japan	29	Belgium	5.4
4.6	Ireland	30	Ireland	5.2
4.5	Bulgaria	31	Denmark	5.2
4.5	Belgium	32	Israel	5.1
4.3	Denmark	33	Poland	5.1
4.3	Madagascar	34	Netherlands	5.0
4.3	Finland	35	Finland	4.9
4.3	Netherlands	36	Bulgaria	4.9
3.9	Israel	37	Malta	4.4
3.8	South Africa	38	Madagascar	4.4
3.7	Romania	39	Greece	4.3
3.5	Costa Rica	40	Austria	4.3
3.5	Greece	41	Italy	4.2
3.5	Iceland	42	South Africa	4.1
3.5	Austria	43	France	4.1
3.4	Myanmar	44	Romania	4.0
3.4	Venezuela	45	Iceland	3.9
3.4	Italy	46	Sweden	3.9
3.4	Libya	47	Costa Rica	3.8
3.3	France	48	Spain	3.7
3.3	Cameroon	49	Switzerland	3.7
3.3	Panama	50	Cyprus	3.7

Sources:
1. Intergovernmental Panel on Climate Change (IPCC), *Climate Change: The IPCC Scientific Assessment,* J. Houghton, G.J. Jenkins, and J.J. Ephraums, eds. (Cambridge University Press, Cambridge, U.K., 1990).
2. Chapter 24, "Atmosphere and Climate," Tables 24.1 and 24.2.

Notes:
a. 1.00 = world median.
b. Data for Germany include both the former Federal Republic of Germany and the German Democratic Republic.

A wide variety of other methods of comparing the relative impact of greenhouse gas emissions from different countries have been proposed. Several of these are summarized in Box 13.3.

TARGETS FOR LIMITING EMISSIONS

Several implications can be drawn from the description of greenhouse gas emissions and their distribution among the countries of the world given in the previous section. Clearly, the major contributors to the potential warming impact of greenhouse gas emissions include both industrialized and developing countries. At the same time, it is equally clear that both the cumulative historical impact and the per capita impact

Figure 13.3 Per Capita Greenhouse Emissions for the 15 Countries with the Highest Total Emissions, 1989

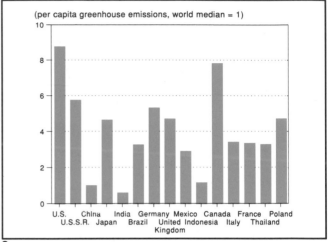

Sources:
1. Intergovernmental Panel on Climate Change (IPCC), *Climate Change: The IPCC Scientific Assessment,* J. Houghton, G.J. Jenkins, and J.J. Ephraums, eds. (Cambridge University Press, Cambridge, U.K., 1990).
2. Chapter 24, "Atmosphere and Climate," Tables 24.1 and 24.2.

are much higher in industrial countries. Equity considerations thus suggest that initial efforts at limiting emissions—and proportionately the greatest efforts—must come from industrial countries.

The largest single source of greenhouse gas emissions is CO_2 from combustion of fossil fuels and other industrial sources. These emissions are also known with far greater accuracy than emissions from any other source of greenhouse gases, making it easier to monitor compliance with emission limitation agreements. Finally, a variety of options exist for limiting such emissions. Conservation, in particular, deserves close scrutiny, because using less fossil fuel energy to accomplish the same task translates into lower CO_2 emissions. Another option would be to switch from fuels with high carbon content (such as coal) to fuels with lower carbon content (such as natural gas), or to carbon-free energy sources. Both of these options would be furthered by current proposals to tax CO_2 emissions or to establish tradable permits for CO_2 emissions.

Table 13.6 gives estimates of national industrial emissions of CO_2 for 50 countries, ranked by emissions. (Data for all countries are given in Table 24.1.) The United States is the largest emitter, followed by the U.S.S.R., China, Japan, Germany, and India. The 12 countries of the Organisation for Economic Co-operation and Development account for 47 percent of the global total; the Soviet Union plus Central Europe account for 23 percent of the global total. Figure 13.4 summarizes per capita emissions for the 15 countries ranked highest in Table 13.6.

One other option for limiting CO_2 emissions deserves early attention. Reducing the conversion of forestland to other uses could cut CO_2 emissions signif-

Table 13.6 50 Countries with the Highest Industrial Emissions of Carbon Dioxide, 1989

Rank	Country	Total CO$_2$ Emissions (million metric tons)
1	United States	4,869,005
2	U.S.S.R.	3,804,001
3	China	2,388,613
4	Japan	1,040,554
5	Germany {a}	964,028
6	India	651,936
7	United Kingdom	568,451
8	Canada	455,530
9	Poland	440,929
10	Italy	389,747
11	France	357,163
12	Mexico	319,702
13	South Africa	278,468
14	Australia	257,480
15	Czechoslovakia	226,347
16	Korea, Rep.	221,104
17	Romania	212,193
18	Brazil	206,957
19	Spain	203,227
20	Saudi Arabia	173,776
21	Iran, Islamic Rep.	166,074
22	Korea, Dem. People's	151,488
23	Indonesia	137,726
24	Yugoslavia	132,901
25	Turkey	126,078
26	Netherlands	124,990
27	Argentina	118,157
28	Bulgaria	106,989
29	Belgium	98,104
30	Venezuela	95,887
31	Egypt	79,483
32	Nigeria	79,263
33	Thailand	77,680
34	Greece	70,920
35	Iraq	68,898
36	Hungary	64,076
37	Pakistan	60,973
38	Sweden	58,888
39	Colombia	53,831
40	Austria	51,699
41	Finland	51,300
42	United Arab Emirates	50,944
43	Malaysia	49,061
44	Denmark	47,009
45	Algeria	46,492
46	Norway	46,009
47	Philippines	40,960
48	Portugal	40,912
49	Switzerland	39,326
50	Libya	37,842

Source: Chapter 24, "Atmosphere and Climate," Table 24.1.
Note: a. Data for Germany include the former Federal Republic of Germany and the German Democratic Republic.

Figure 13.4 Per Capita Carbon Dioxide Emissions for the 15 Countries with the Highest Total Emissions from Industrial Sources, 1989

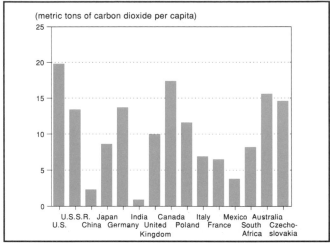

Source: Carbon Dioxide Information Analysis Center (CDIAC), Oak Ridge National Laboratory, unpublished data, (CDIAC, Oak Ridge, Tennessee, August 1989.)

icantly and would also have other local and global benefits, such as preserving biodiversity (see Chapter 9, "Wildlife and Habitat," Focus On Conserving Biodiversity.) The opportunities for such reductions occur almost entirely in developing countries. To realize these opportunities, however, will in many cases require attention to the root causes of land clearing, including local poverty, inequities of land tenure, lack of alternative employment, government incentives and subsidies, and internationally supported development schemes that promote misuse of the land. Addressing these problems on an adequate scale is likely to require expanded international goal setting, cooperation, and assistance.

The conditions and Trends section of this chapter was written by Gregory Mock, a California-based writer. The Focus On section was written by Allen Hammond, editor-in-chief of World Resources.

References and Notes

1. Global Environmental Monitoring System, World Health Organization, and United Nations Environment Programme, *Global Pollution and Health* (Yale Press, London, 1987), pp. 4-7.

2. Asif Faiz, Kumares Sinha, Michael Walsh, *et al.*, *Automotive Air Pollution: Issues and Options for Developing Countries*, Report No. 492 in the Policy, Research and External Affairs Working Paper Series, The World Bank, Washington, D.C., 1990, p. xi.

3. Claire Holman, *Air Pollution and Health* (Friends of the Earth, London, 1989), p. 9-12.

4. U.S. Environmental Protection Agency (EPA), *National Air Quality and Emission Trends Report, 1989* (EPA, Washington, D.C., 1991), p. 3-2.

5. Global Environmental Monitoring System, United Nations Environment Programme, and World Health Organization, *Assessment of Urban Air Quality* (United Nations, London, 1988), p. 25.

6. *Ibid.*, pp. 11-16 and 26-31.

7. *Ibid.*, pp. 12-14.

8. *Ibid.*, p. 15.

9. *Op. cit.* 1.

10. *Op. cit.* 4, p. 3-24.

11. *Op. cit.* 3, pp. 25-27.

12. Malcolm W. Browne, "New Tactics Emerge in Struggle Against Smog," *New York Times* (February 21, 1989), p. C1.

13. *Op. cit.* 4, p. 3-24.

14. *Op. cit.* 3, p. 27.

15. *Op. cit.* 5, p. 81.

16. United States Environmental Protection Agency (EPA), *The Clean Air Act Amendments of 1990: Summary Materials* (EPA, Washington, D.C., 1990), p.2.

17. U.S. Environmental Protection Agency (EPA), *National Air Quality and Emission Trends Report, 1988* (EPA, Washington D.C., 1990), p. 15.

18. *Op. cit.* 2, pp. viii-ix and 11-18.

19. *Op. cit.* 4, p. 3-24.

20. *Op. cit.* 2, pp 19-20.

21. *Op. cit.* 3, pp. 13-14.

22. *Op. cit.* 3, p. 16.

23. *Op. cit.* 2.

24. *Op. cit.* 3, pp. 14-15.

25. *Op. cit.* 5, p. 52.

26. *Op. cit.* 4, pp. 3-15 to 3-17.

27. *Op. cit.* 5, pp. 52-55.

28. *Op. cit.* 4, pp. 3-15 to 3-17.
29. *Op. cit.* 5, pp. 54-57.
30. *Op. cit.* 3, p. 13.
31. *Op. cit.* 3, p. 13.
32. *Op. cit.* 5, p. 58.
33. Carl M. Shy, "Lead in Petrol: The Mistake of the 20th Century," *World Health Statistics Quarterly*, Vol. 43 (1990), p. 168.
34. *Op. cit.* 2.
35. *Op. cit.* 5, p. 58.
36. *Op. cit.* 33, pp. 171, 174-175.
37. *Op. cit.* 5, p.60.
38. *Op. cit.* 33, p. 168.
39. *Op. cit.* 5, p. 64.
40. *Op. cit.* 2, pp. 22-24.
41. *Op. cit.* 16, p. 4.
42. U.S. Environmental Protection Agency (EPA), *Cancer Risk From Outdoor Exposure To Air Toxics, Volume 1* (EPA, Washington, D.C., 1990), p. ES-2.
43. Rose Gutfield and Barbara Rosewicz, "Clean-Air Accord Is Reached In Congress That May Cost Industry $25 Billion a Year," *Wall Street Journal* (October 23, 1990), p. A2.
44. *Op. cit.* 5, p. 39.
45. "The Price of Pollution," *Options* (International Institute for Applied Systems Analysis, Laxenburg, Austria, September 1990), p. 5.
46. John McCormick, *Acid Earth: The Global Threat of Acid Pollution* (Earthscan Publications, London, 1989), pp. 15 and 21.
47. Henning Rodhe, "Acidification in a Global Perspective," *Ambio*, Vol. 18, No. 3 (1989), p. 156.
48. *Ibid.*, pp. 155 and 159-160.
49. "Evidence of Acid Fog Found on Mount Ohyama," *Japan Times* (September 13, 1989, Tokyo), n.p.
50. "Working Together to Reduce Acid Rain," *Options* (International Institute for Applied Systems Analysis, Laxenburg, Austria, March 1989), p. 9.
51. *Op. cit.* 45.
52. Ursula Falkengren-Grerup, "Soil Acidification and Its Impact on Ground Vegetation," *Ambio*, Vol. 18, No. 3 (1989), pp. 179-180.
53. James J. MacKenzie and Mohamed T. El-Ashry, *Ill Winds: Airborne Pollution's Toll on Trees and Crops* (World Resources Institute, Washington, D.C., 1988), pp. 19-20.
54. *Ibid.*, p. 22.
55. *Op. cit.* 45.
56. *Op. cit.* 53, pp. 15-17.
57. William K. Stevens, "Researchers Find Acid Rain Imperils Forest Over Time," *New York Times* (December 31, 1989), p. 1.
58. *Op. cit.* 45.
59. Ellis B. Cowling, "Recent Changes in Chemical Climate and Related Effects on Forests in North America and Europe," *Ambio*, Vol. 18, No. 3 (1989), pp. 169-170.
60. United Nations Economic Commission for Europe (UNECE), *The 1989 Forest Damage Survey in Europe* (UNECE, Geneva, 1990), pp. 12-15.
61. *Op. cit.* 45, p. 4.
62. *Op. cit.* 53, pp. 8-9, 16.
63. *Op. cit.* 57.
64. *Op. cit.* 46, pp. 44-48.
65. John D. Spengler, Michael Brauer, and Petros Koutrakis, "Acid Air and Health," *Environmental Science and Technology*, Vol. 24, No. 7 (1990), pp. 946-952.
66. Frederick W. Lipfert, Samuel C. Morris, and Ronald E. Wyzga, "Acid Aerosols: The Next Criteria Air Pollutant?" *Environmental Science and Technology*, Vol. 23, No. 11 (1989), p. 1317.

67. "World Health Unit Says Pollution Remains a Serious Health Threat in Europe," *International Environment Reporter* (Bureau of National Affairs, Washington, D.C., September 26, 1990).
68. U.S. Congress, Office of Technology Assessment, *Catching Our Breath: Next Steps for Reducing Urban Ozone* (U.S. Government Printing Office, Washington, D.C., 1989), pp. 106-107.
69. *Op. cit.* 3, p. 27.
70. *Op. cit.* 3, pp. 15-16.
71. *Op. cit.* 68, p. 107.
72. *Op. cit.* 53, pp. 13-19, 25-32.
73. *Op. cit.* 59, pp. 167-171.
74. *Op. cit.* 53, p. 14.
75. *Op. cit.* 53, pp. 8-9 and 16-17.
76. *Op. cit.* 59, pp. 167-171.
77. *Op. cit.* 53, pp. 25-31.
78. James J. MacKenzie, *Breathing Easier: Taking Action on Climate Change, Air Pollution, and Energy Insecurity* (World Resources Institute, Washington, D.C., 1989), p. 13.
79. *Op. cit.* 67.
80. Christer Ågren, "With Aim on Ozone," *Acid News*, No. 4 (Swedish and Norwegian NGO Secretariats on Acid Rain, Göteborg, Sweden, December 1990), pp. 6-7.
81. C. Ian Jackson, "A Tenth Anniversary Review of the ECE Convention on Long-Range Transboundary Air Pollution," *International Environmental Affairs*, Vol. 2, No. 3 (1990), pp. 222-225.
82. *Op. cit.* 46, p. 77.
83. *Op. cit.* 16, p. 5.
84. *Op. cit.* 81, pp. 217-225.
85. *Op. cit.* 46, p. 87.
86. John C. Beale, Deputy Director, Office of Policy Analysis and Review, Air and Radiation, U.S. Environmental Protection Agency, Washington, D.C., 1991 (personal communication).
87. *Op. cit.* 45, p. 7.
88. Christer Ågren, "Unacceptable kms," *Acid News*, No. 4 (Swedish and Norwegian NGO Secretariats on Acid Rain, Göteborg, Sweden, December 1990), p. 2.
89. Anna-Karin Hjalmarsson, "What the West Germans Are Doing," *Acid News*, No. 4 (Swedish and Norwegian NGO Secretariats on Acid Rain, Göteborg, Sweden, December 1990), p. 9.
90. *Op. cit.* 88.
91. Anna-Karin Hjalmarsson, "Controlling Emissions," *Acid News*, No. 4 (Swedish and Norwegian NGO Secretariats on Acid Rain, Göteborg, Sweden, December 1990), p. 8.
92. *Op. cit.* 50.
93. Commission of the European Communities (CEC), *Energy and the Environment* (CEC, Brussels, 1990), pp. 10-12.
94. James N. Galloway, "Atmospheric Acidification: Projections for the Future," *Ambio*, Vol. 18, No. 3 (1989), p. 161.
95. *Op. cit.* 5, p. 14.
96. Anthony D. Cortese, "Clearing the Air," *Environmental Science and Technology*, Vol. 24, No. 4 (1990), p. 444.
97. *Op. cit.* 94, p. 166.
98. *Op. cit.* 47, pp. 155-160.
99. "RAINS: A Model For Negotiations," *Options* (International Institute for Applied Systems Analysis, Laxenburg, Austria, September 1990), p. 9.
100. Nigel Haigh, "New Tools for European Air Pollution Control," *International Environmental Affairs*, Vol. 1, No. 1 (Winter 1989), pp. 26-37.
101. James N. Galloway, Professor of Environmental Sciences, University of Virginia,

Charlottesville, 1991 (personal communication).
102. *Op. cit.* 46, pp. 192-212.
103. Heinz Welsch, "Cost-Effective Control Strategies for Energy-Related Transboundary Air Pollution in Western Europe," *Energy Journal*, Vol. 11, No. 2 (1990), p. 93.
104. "France Becomes First Nation To Tax Air Pollution; Approach Called Reasonable," *International Environmental Reporter* (Bureau of National Affairs, Washington, D.C., June 1990), p. 228.
105. Bryan Lee, "Highlights of the Clean Air Act Amendments of 1990," *Journal of the Air and Waste Management Association*, Vol. 41, No. 1 (January 1991), p. 16.
106. *Op. cit.* 103, p. 89.
107. "The Unfinished Business of Acid Emission Control," *ENDS Report*, No. 183 (Environmental Data Services, London, April 1990), p. 12.
108. "Decoupling Energy Consumption From Air Pollution: A First Short From Brussels," *ENDS Report*, No. 179 (Environmental Data Services, London, December 1989), p. 15.
109. James J. MacKenzie, Senior Associate, World Resources Institute, Washington, D.C., April 1991 (personal communication).
110. *Op. cit.* 46, p. 54-55.
111. *Op. cit.* 91, p. 8.
112. *Op. cit.* 91, p. 9.
113. *Op. cit.* 46, pp. 59-60.
114. *Op. cit.* 78, pp. 19-22.
115. Commission of the European Communities (CEC), *Energy and the Environment* (CEC, Brussels, 1990), pp. 18-19.
116. Joan M. Ogden and Robert H. Williams, *Solar Hydrogen: Moving Beyond Fossil Fuels* (World Resources Institute, Washington, D.C., 1989), pp. 1-3.
117. "Managing Earth's Resources" (special section), *Business Week* (June 18, 1990), pp. 6 and 31.
118. Daniel Ward, "Manufacturers Turn to Pollution-Free Production" (special section), *Financial Times* (July 27, 1990), p. 5.
119. Michael S. Baram, Patricia S. Dillon, and Betsy Ruffle, *Managing Chemical Risks: Corporate Response to SARA Title III* (Center for Environmental Management, Tufts University, Medford, Massachusetts, 1990), p. xiv.
120. *Op. cit.* 117, p. 48.
121. *Op. cit.* 117, pp. 21, 31, and 48.
122. *Op. cit.* 119, pp. xii-xiv.
123. Deborah L. Bleviss and Peter Walzer, "Energy for Motor Vehicles," *Scientific American*, Vol. 263, No. 3 (September 1990), p. 103.
124. Asif Faiz, "Automotive Air Pollution: An Overview" (The World Bank, Washington, D.C., December 1990), p. 9.
125. *Op. cit.* 2, p. 1.
126. *Op. cit.* 88.
127. *Op. cit.* 124, p. 8.
128. *Op. cit.* 2, p. viii.
129. Kevin Done, "Europe to Tighten Its Emission Standards," *Financial Times* (July 27, 1990), p. 2.
130. U.S. Environmental Protection Agency (EPA), *The Clean Air Act Amendments of 1990: Summary Materials* (EPA, Washington, D.C., 1990), pp. 3-4.
131. *Op. cit.* 96, p. 446.
132. *Op. cit.* 129.
133. *Op. cit.* 12.
134. *Op. cit.* 124, pp. 13-14.
135. *Op. cit.* 2, pp. 59-62.
136. *Op. cit.* 96, p. 446.
137. *Op. cit.* 2, p. 23.

138. Bruce Bertelsen, "Emission Control of Diesel Fueled Trucks and Buses" (Manufacturers of Emission Controls Association, Washington, D.C., December 1990), pp. 1-3.

139. European Economic Community (EEC) Spokesman's Service, "Measures To Counter Air Pollution by Emissions from Diesel-Engined Lorries" (EEC, Brussels, May 2, 1990), p. 27.

140. *Op. cit.* 2, pp. 75-77.

141. U.S. General Accounting Office (GAO), *Air Pollution: Air Quality Implications of Alternative Fuels* (GAO, Washington, D.C., 1990), pp. 17-20.

142. *Op. cit.* 130, p. 3.

143. Thomas Hayes, "Shortage of Additive Limits Clean Gasoline," *New York Times* (April 18, 1990), p. D1.

144. *Op. cit.* 141, pp. 8-18.

145. U.S. Congress, Office of Technology Assessment, *Replacing Gasoline: Alternative Fuels for Light-Duty Vehicles* (U.S. Government Printing Office, Washington, D.C., 1990), pp. 23-24.

146. *Op. cit.* 130.

147. "Environmentalists, City Representatives Debate Industry Over Cars in Urban Areas," *International Environment Reporter* (Bureau of National Affairs, Washington, D.C., July 1990).

148. *Op. cit.* 124, pp. 13-14.

149. *Op. cit.* 2, p. xiii.

150. Kenneth Small, Clifford Winston, and Carol Evans, *Road Work: A New Highway Pricing and Investment Policy* (Brookings Institution, Washington, D.C., 1989), p. 86.

151. Marcia D. Lowe, *Alternatives to the Automobile: Transport for Livable Cities*, Worldwatch Paper No. 98 (Worldwatch Institute, Washington, D.C., 1990), p. 20.

152. *Ibid.*, pp. 20-26.

153. *Ibid.*, p. 24.

154. *Op. cit.* 2, pp. 91-93.

155. Scott A. Hajost, International Counsel, Environmental Defense Fund, Washington, D.C., 1991 (personal communication).

156. Scott A. Hajost, International Counsel, Environmental Defense Fund, Washington, D.C., 1991 (personal communication).

157. William K. Stevens, "At Meeting on Global Warming, U.S. Stands Alone," *New York Times* (September 10, 1991), p. C1.

158. *Op. cit.* 156.

159. Philip D. Jones and Tom M.L. Wigley, "The Global Temperature Record for 1990," *DOE Research Summary*, No. 10 (Carbon Dioxide Information Analysis Center, Oak Ridge National Laboratory, Oak Ridge, Tennessee, April 1991).

160. Helene Wilson, Staff Scientist, Goddard Institute for Space Studies, New York, 1991 (personal communication).

161. Intergovernmental Panel on Climate Change (IPCC), *Climate Change: The IPCC Scientific Assessment*, J.T. Houghton, G.J. Jenkins, and J.J. Ephraum, eds. (Cambridge University Press, Cambridge, U.K., 1990), p. xi.

162. *Ibid.*, p. xi

163. Policy Implications of Greenhouse Warming, U.S. Committee on Science, Engineering, and Public Policy (National Academy Press, Washington, D.C., 1991), p. 73.

164. Organisation for Economic Co-operation and Development (OECD), *Estimation of Greenhouse Gases and Sinks*, final report from the OECD Experts meeting, February 18-21, 1991, prepared for the Intergovernmental Panel on Climate Change, revised August 1991, pp. 5-28.

165. M.A.K. Khalil, R.A. Rasmussen, Ming-Xing Wang, *et al.*, "Methane Emissions from Rice Fields in China," *Environmental Science and Technology*, Vol. 25, No. 5 (1991), pp. 979-981.

166. Paul J. Crutzen and Meinrat O. Andraea, "Biomass Burning in the Tropics: Impact on Atmospheric Chemistry and Biogeochemical Cycles," *Science*, Vol. 250 (1990), p. 1672.

167. Susan Subak and William C. Clark, "Accounts for Greenhouse Gases: Towards the Design of Fair Assessments," in *Usable Knowledge for Managing Climate Change*, William C. Clark, ed. (Stockholm Environmental Institute, Stockholm, 1990), p. 73.

168. *Ibid.*

14. Policies and Institutions

Nongovernmental Organizations: A Growing Force in the Developing World

An extraordinarily diverse and growing body of private organizations now dot the world's institutional landscape, working in a variety of areas such as small-scale local development, the conservation of tropical forests, and sustainable agriculture. Working at many levels, through example or advocacy these groups are influencing the direction of environment and development policy around the world.

In the industrialized countries, many of these "nongovernmental organizations" (NGOs) are small and work at the community level; some—particularly those with a broad mandate—have grown large and prosperous. In the developing world, most of these groups are community-based, relatively small, and often fragile; their chances of failure far outweigh their chances of success. For many groups in developing countries, survival depends on the courage and persistence of a few individuals. In some developing countries, members of such organizations must contend with the active hostility of the government; in a few cases, members may be risking their lives.

Nevertheless, nongovernmental organizations are growing, both in numbers and in influence, especially in the developing countries of the South. The reasons for this growth are complex: local groups often form in response to specific needs (such as the need to improve water supplies) or incentives (such as new opportunities to get bank credit) (1). National groups may form to fulfill a specific need (such as environmental protection), often with the support of Northern groups. In some cases, ineffective or nonexistent government programs create a vacuum that private organizations step into; in other cases, resource-poor governments use private organizations as an efficient way to extend their reach.

As the links among environment, development, and population become clearer, organizations devoted to a single issue see the advantages of working with other groups; development NGOs, for example, may join with NGOs advancing entrepreneurship or environmental protection or human rights. This trend is fueled by the fast-growing number of national and international NGO networks and coalitions, which in turn is helped by rapid advances in communications technology.

Most of these groups share a common vision. They want to reduce poverty, advance human development, and manage natural resources in a sustainable fashion.

They believe that local participation and/or control is important to the success of sustainable development. They put less emphasis on growth in production and more emphasis on involving local people in solving problems. (See Chapter 1, "Dimensions of Sustainable Development.")

Why are these groups important? In developing countries they can solve some pieces of the development puzzle, perhaps by taking an unusual approach to a development problem, or by listening carefully to what poor people want and working to enlist their participation and support, or by trying to simultaneously foster development and husband natural resources. NGOs can be a truly independent voice, sometimes serving as a focal point of opposition to government programs; NGO successes can become the models for new government programs.

In the North, and to some extent in the South, NGOs can bring strong pressures on governments to create and implement new policies. They can also work as partners with governments, although such alliances carry the risk of dependence on government funds.

The character and number of NGOs depend to a significant extent on the approach taken by governments. In the North, governments have learned to live with NGOs as both opponents and proponents of government programs, but many governments in the South are uncomfortable with NGOs as opponents. NGOs cannot, however, compete with governments. They cannot pass laws, and they do not have the resources to manage national programs.

The term nongovernmental organization encompasses all organizations that are neither governmental nor for-profit. What is left is a residual category that includes a vast array of organizations, many of which have little in common. They can be large or small, secular or religious, donors or recipients of grants. Some are designed only to serve their own members; others serve those who need help. Some are concerned only with local issues; others work at the national level, and still others are regional or international in scope (2).

The organizations that could fit under this giant umbrella include savings clubs, squatter associations, communal labor-sharing groups, peasant leagues, village water associations, irrigation user groups, women's associations, tribal unions, environmental advocacy groups, consumer and farmer cooperatives, human rights groups, policy analysis centers, labor unions, service clubs such as Kiwanis and Rotary, local development associations, tenants' associations, private colleges or hospitals, private relief organizations, and political action groups (3).

No classification system can capture all NGOs, but at different levels of development, a few common types emerge:

■ Grassroots organizations working in villages and urban communities in the developing world. Most of these groups are membership organizations devoted to fulfilling the needs of their members.
■ Service organizations, which support the development of grassroots groups. Some are the product of the growth of local groups into regional or national federations; other regional and national organizations promote and support local groups, but are not themselves membership organizations.
■ Regional, national, and international "thematic" organizations working in development, human rights, environment, disaster relief, family planning, and similar areas. Such organizations may have a particular emphasis, such as field work, legal defense, or policy research. Some are directly involved in supporting service organizations. Others provide financial support to grassroots and service groups.
■ Regional, national and international networks and coalitions of NGOs.

NGOs are extraordinarily diverse. This chapter provides a few examples to capture some of that diversity, but focuses mainly on the strengths and weaknesses of NGOs, on the relationship between governments and NGOs, and on some emerging trends. The chapter primarily concerns the newly emerging grassroots and service NGOs in developing countries and those Northern NGOs that work extensively in developing countries.

ORIGINS AND REGIONAL DIFFERENCES

NGOs are relatively new international actors. Only about 30 percent of Southern development NGOs are more than 15 years old, and only 50 percent are more than 10. Almost all environmental NGOs and most NGO networks and umbrella groups were started in the 1980s (4). The role of independent organizations in the developing world differs greatly from region to region and among countries within regions. Asia is generally considered to have the largest number of NGOs and the most active involvement of NGOs in policy making. Latin American NGOs are often critics of government policies. African NGOs are relatively fragile and generally do not play the same advocacy roles that many NGOs adopt in Asia and Latin America.

International NGOs have had a strong impact on the development of national NGOs in the South, especially in Africa and some parts of Asia. Indigenous NGOs in Africa are still relatively dependent on international NGOs for financial support. A few countries—India, the Philippines, and Brazil, for example—have autonomous NGO movements based in their urban middle classes.

For a variety of reasons—political, economic, and cultural—NGOs still are scarce in many parts of the world, including China, the Middle East, North Africa, northeastern India, and parts of sub-Saharan Africa (5).

Northern NGOs with a Mission in the South
Many of the early independent organizations in Europe and North America have common threads, such as missionary activity or the provision of relief to victims of war or famine.

Organizations founded before World War II—the Salvation Army, for example—were generally outgrowths of missionary activities. During and after World War II, religious and secular organizations—

Box 14.1 NGOs and the World Bank

In 1983, six U.S. environmental organizations, including the National Wildlife Federation and the Natural Resources Defense Council, began to pressure the World Bank to pay more attention to the environmental consequences of its projects. Because the World Bank needed annual appropriations and capital replenishments that required U.S. congressional approval, the groups used some two dozen congressional hearings to make their case against projects such as Brazil's Polonoreste road-building and colonization project (1).

The campaign produced notable results. In June 1986 the United States representative to the World Bank—citing environmental reasons for the first time—voted against a proposed loan to Brazil. In the same year, the World Bank announced plans to enlarge its environment office substantially. Antipoverty groups, noting the success of the environmental campaign and realizing the links between environmental degradation and poverty, joined with environmentalists to form the Development Bank Assessment Network. The network has concentrated on pushing the bank to spend more time assessing the impact of its lending on the poor and the environment and to increase its dialogue with the potential beneficiaries of bank-financed projects. Northern groups also began working more closely with Southern antipoverty and environmental groups, developing coordinated North-South critiques of World Bank projects (2).

Partially in response, the World Bank has increasingly encouraged the involvement of NGOs in Bank-financed projects. NGOs were involved in about 13 projects annually between 1973 and 1988, but that figure increased to 46 in 1989 and to 50 in 1990—nearly one quarter of all projects approved that year. The World Bank's pattern of collaboration has also changed. In the 1973–87 period, the World Bank's NGO partners tended to be international NGOs (43 percent of all projects), followed by indigenous service NGOs (31 percent) and grassroots NGOs (26 percent). In the 1988–90 period, partnerships with international NGOs had shrunk to 20 percent of the total, while projects involving intermediary NGOs increased to 35 percent and with grassroots groups to 45 percent (3). Bank-financed projects involving NGOs usually are in areas such as rural or urban development, population and health, or infrastructure. NGOs have worked primarily as implementors, but are beginning to work as consultants during the project planning stage and in the evaluation process (4).

The NGO–World Bank Committee, which is composed of senior Bank managers and 26 NGO leaders from around the world, was started in 1982 and has been increasingly active. The committees focus on how structural adjustment lending affects the poor has evolved into a discussion about an alternative vision of development that deemphasizes growth in production and stresses justice, sustainability, and democracy (5).

The World Bank's operating procedures and pace make working with NGOs difficult. In addition, NGOs are used to working with grant-giving institutions, whereas the Bank's traditional role is to lend money to governments (6). Nevertheless, NGOs and the Bank have moved through a period of conflict to develop a working—if still adversarial—relationship.

References and Notes

1. Bruce Stokes, "Storming the Bank," *National Journal* (December 31, 1988), p. 3251.
2. *Ibid.*, pp. 3251-3252.
3. David Beckmann, "The Bank and NGOs: Recent Experience and Emerging Trends," draft paper prepared for The World Bank, Washington, D.C., October 26, 1990, p. 5.
4. David Beckmann, "The World Bank and NGOs: A Growing Partnership," draft paper prepared for The World Bank, Washington, D.C., 1990, pp. 6-10.
5. *Op. cit.* 3, p. 11.
6. *Op. cit.* 3, pp. 19-22.

Catholic Relief Services (1943) and CARE (1945), for example—were started to provide relief first to people in Europe and later to those in developing nations (6). In the United Kingdom, the Oxford Committee for Famine Relief (Oxfam) was started in 1942 to aid starving civilians in Nazi-occupied Greece. In 1944, the Danish Association for International Cooperation was founded to help rebuild war-torn European countries (7). The end of the war did not bring an end to emergencies. The partitioning of India in 1947, the flight of Arabs from Palestine in 1948, and famines in Asia and Africa were among a long series of events that drew these organizations into the developing world (8).

In the 1960s, many of these agencies began to see their mission as a mix of relief and development work. Churches started to promote development projects that were unrelated to church activities. In 1958, the World Council of Churches proposed that the industrial countries transfer 1 percent of their national income to the developing countries for development assistance. The Vatican in the mid-1960s also strongly supported a strengthened commitment to eliminating poverty in the developing world. Protestant churches later were urged by the World Council of Churches to send 2 percent of their resources to developing countries (9).

The Food and Agriculture Organization's Freedom from Hunger Campaign, which began in 1960, and numerous programs that sent volunteers overseas (such as Voluntary Service Overseas in the United Kingdom and the U.S. government-sponsored Peace Corps in the United States) provided additional impetus for development-related work overseas. Oxfam pioneered direct financial support for local initiatives; by 1961, it had decided to move away from financing missionary organizations and other northern organizations and to support indigenous organizations. As the number of nongovernmental organizations grew, so too did the need for consultation among organizations. In 1962, the International Council of Voluntary Agencies (ICVA), an international liaison organization, was started by NGOs concerned with refugees and displaced persons. ICVA remains an important nondenominational structure for consultation among NGOs internationally (10).

In the 1960s and 1970s, new organizations focused on attacking the root causes of poverty in developing countries (11). The U.S. Congress created the Inter-American Foundation (IAF) in 1969, followed by the African Development Foundation in 1980. By mid-1991 IAF had provided 3,111 small grants to NGOs in Latin America and the Caribbean (12).

In the early 1970s, the World Bank began to focus on the urgent need to improve income distribution, develop affordable technologies for the poor, promote rural development, and address people's basic education, health, and family planning needs. Other official

Figure 14.1 Private and Official Financial Contributions to Northern NGOs, Selected Years, 1970–88

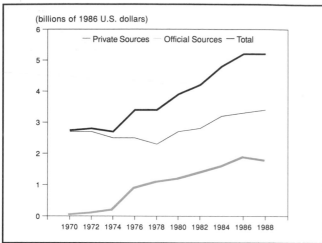

Source: John Clark, *Democratizing Development: The Role of Voluntary Organizations* (Kumarian Press, West Hartford, Connecticut, 1991), p. 40.

donors followed the World Bank's lead (13). Many NGOs, however, continued to criticize the Bank for emphasizing large development projects that did not directly benefit the poor. In the 1980s, this criticism led to increasing interaction between the institution and NGOs. (See Box 14.1.)

Earth Day in the United States in 1970 marked the beginning of a major spurt in activity and membership of environmental groups in the United States. As new reports began to surface in the 1980s about global environmental concerns such as deforestation, these groups increasingly extended their reach into environmental issues overseas.

The Worldwide Fund for Nature and its U.S. affiliate, the World Wildlife Fund (WWF), originally supported scientific missions overseas. That effort eventually developed into support for the work of local scientists. By the early 1980s, WWF began developing relationships with organizations such as Fundación Natura in Ecuador, and by the late 1980s, WWF was actively pro-viding support to projects in developing countries (14).

Interest in women's issues rose dramatically in the mid-1970s, beginning with a conference in Mexico City in 1975 marking International Women's Year and continuing with the United Nations Decade for Women (1976–85) and major conferences in Copenhagen in 1980 and Nairobi in 1985. The Decade for Women inspired the formation of many new formal and informal women's organizations. In the late 1970s and early 1980s, northern governments and multilateral agencies increasingly worked through nongovernmental organizations, particularly women's groups, in the developing countries rather than through governments. The United Nations Development Fund for Women (UNIFEM), established after the Mexico City conference, also increased its work with NGOs in the 1978–84 period (15).

By 1989, Northern independent organizations were distributing an estimated $6.4 billion to the South—about 12 percent of all development aid, public and private (16). In terms of net transfers, Northern NGOs collectively distribute more than the World Bank (17).

Roughly one third of this total now comes from government sources. Since the 1960s, the governments of the developed nations have approved partnership arrangements with nongovernmental organizations for the distribution and management of government aid (18). By 1988, $1.8 billion (in 1986 dollars) of the annual budget of all NGOs came from official sources. As Figure 14.1 indicates, government donations account for much of the increase in NGO funds in the past few decades.

United Nations agencies have increasingly promoted community development projects by supporting indigenous NGOs and cooperation between governments and NGOs. The 1992 United Nations Conference on Environment and Development is actively promoting broad NGO participation. (See Box 14.2.)

Asia

Among the regions of the developing world, South Asia has the largest number of independent organizations.

India's self-help movement has flourished since Mohandas Gandhi promoted self-reliant villages based on renewable resources. In addition, the colonial presence, competition among missionary groups, the nationalist movement, and constitutional guarantees of the right to free speech have all contributed to the proliferation of voluntary groups (19). India now has tens and probably hundreds of thousands of local groups plus an estimated 12,000 independent development organizations (20). Bombay, Maharastra, and Gujarat are the busiest centers of voluntary activity (21).

Tax incentives and a long history of religious giving also have helped support the growth of independent organizations in India. Charitable trusts such as the Tata Trusts are influential. Corporations, spurred by tax incentives, are beginning to fund voluntary organizations engaged in rural development work (22).

Foreign funding of voluntary associations has been a sensitive political issue in India; in 1976, the government passed the Foreign Contribution Act, which requires groups to obtain government approval before accepting foreign donations and to report donations from non-Indian sources (23).

Bangladesh has fostered some especially notable independent organizations such as the Bangladesh Rural Advancement Committee (BRAC) and the Grameen Bank, which provides very small loans to low-income borrowers (24). More than 10,000 national NGOs operate in Bangladesh. Most are small; about 250 receive funds from foreign sources (25).

Indonesia's independent organizations were helped by a strong indigenous tradition of community group efforts plus disillusionment with the large-scale, trickle-down development programs of the 1960s and 1970s (26). The Indonesian government has maintained

Box 14.2 NGOs and the United Nations System

The increase in links between Northern and Southern NGOs has been paralleled by similar growth between NGOs and the United Nations system. The United Nations Conference on Environment and Development (UNCED)—scheduled for June 1992 in Rio de Janeiro, Brazil—is accelerating that process.

NGOs in the past have used U.N. conferences as forums for alternative conferences. At the 1972 Stockholm conference on the environment, for example, an NGO parallel conference—under the leadership of Barbara Ward and Margaret Mead—was particularly influential and garnered major press attention (1).

The pattern of parallel conferences has continued with other U.N. conferences. Increasingly, however, the U.N. system is encouraging participation by NGOs in the preparatory process, and the 1992 conference itself may break new ground in this direction.

The United Nations has devised a system of formal relationships with NGOs. For example, about 460 NGOs have "consultative" status with the Economic and Social Council (ECOSOC). The list includes a few environmental NGOs, such as the World Conservation Union (formally the International Union for Conservation of Nature and Natural Resources), the Sierra Club, the National Audubon Society, and the World Resources Institute (2). Consultative status gives NGOs the right to attend meetings of ECOSOC and its subsidiary bodies, to submit written statements to them, to testify before ECOSOC and its committees, and in some cases to propose agenda items for ECOSOC consideration.

As preparations for the 1992 conference got under way, it appeared likely that participation in the preparatory process would be opened to a relatively broad range of "relevant" NGOs, not just those in consultative status, and that an effort would be made to achieve a balance between NGOs with an environment focus and those with a development focus (3). Conference planners hoped for an equitable representation of NGOs from developed and developing countries and from all regions, but by mid-1991, 83 percent of NGOs planning to attend were from the industrialized countries (4).

NGOs in many countries have been actively seeking a voice in their countries' preparations for the 1992 conference. For example, in Brazil NGOs are trying to build the broadest possible coalition of NGOs with a stake in the conference and are even planning to produce a "state of the environment" report on the country, which has not been attempted before in Brazil. Brazilian NGOs are also hoping to

play a major role in linking the official conference and the parallel NGO event (5). The Geneva-based Centre for Our Common Future plans to organize a worldwide series of 12 "ECO-92" public forums before the 1992 conference. The first forum, held in August 1990 in Nairobi, coincided with the 1992 Preparatory Committee's second session; members of the committee and the conference secretariat were invited to speak at the start of the ECO-92 forum and to attend the meetings (6).

The 1992 conference also will take full advantage of computerized information. The UNCED Information System includes a data base with information on the main activities under way before the conference and all documentation issued to governments. A global electronic network allows worldwide electronic access to the UNCED Information System using computers and modems. The UNCED secretariat encourages electronic conferencing during both the preparatory process and the conference itself (7).

OTHER U.N. AGENCIES

Many U.N. agencies have relatively long traditions of cooperation with NGOs. The United Nations High Commissioner for Refugees and the United Nations Fund for Population Assistance have both relied on NGOs for project implementation. During the 1969–86 period, the population fund spent about 10 percent of its budget on activities implemented by NGOs. UNICEF also works extensively with NGOs. Village and community Rotary clubs, for example, work with UNICEF on the global immunization campaign (8).

The United Nations Environment Programme (UNEP) and the United Nations Development Programme (UNDP) are increasingly working with NGOs. UNDP's "Partners in Development Programme," which operated in 60 countries in 1990, makes small grants ($25,000 per country) to NGOs and grassroots organizations to support innovative NGO projects. In Rwanda, for example, an NGO received $13,500 for a "cattle bank" to provide animals for start-up livestock projects and for training (9).

UNDP's Sustainable Development Network is an attempt to identify and link all governmental, nongovernmental, grassroots, and entrepreneurial organizations that could contribute to sustainable and environmentally sound development. The program is operating in all 152 UNDP countries (10).

In 1988, UNEP spent $8.6 million to support NGOs and other intergovernmental organizations, including the Nairobi-based Environmental Liaison Centre, the

African NGOs Environmental Network, and the Green Belt Movement. UNEP also is a key funder of NGOs in the regional assemblies on Women and the Environment, including assemblies in West Asia, Latin America and the Caribbean, and Asia and the Pacific (11). Generally taking a positive approach to NGOs, UNEP allows them to attend all UNEP meetings and works actively with them to plan and implement projects (12).

References and Notes

1. Arthur Kilgore and Curtis Roosevelt, "The Non-Governmental Organizations and the United Nations System," in Douglas Williams, *The Specialized Agencies and the United Nations: The System in Crisis* (St. Martin's Press, New York, 1987), p. 266.

2. United Nations (U.N.) Department of Public Information, *Non-Governmental Organizations Associated with the Department of Public Information* (U.N., New York, 1990).

3. United Nations Preparatory Committee for the United Nations (U.N.) Conference on Environment and Development, "Arrangements for the Effective Contributions of Relevant Non-Governmental Organizations in the Preparatory Process" (U.N., New York, August 13, 1990), pp. 1-2.

4. Sarah Burns, NGO Liaison, Policy Affairs, World Resources Institute, Washington, D.C., 1991 (personal communication).

5. "Brazilian Groups Organize for 1992," *NGO Networker* (World Resources Institute, Washington, D.C., Summer 1990), p. 3.

6. "Public Forums—ECO-92—To Be Held," *NGO Networker* (World Resources Institute, Washington, D.C., Summer 1990), p. 3.

7. United Nations Preparatory Committee for the United Nations (U.N.) Conference on Environment and Development, "The UNCED Information System," (U.N., New York, August 13, 1990), p. 2.

8. Organisation for Economic Co-operation and Development (OECD), *Voluntary Aid for Development: The Role of Non-Governmental Organizations* (OECD, Paris, 1988), pp. 95-96.

9. United Nations Development Programme (UNDP), "UNDP/NGO Partners in Development Programme" (UNDP, New York, May 15, 1990), pp. 1 and 4.

10. United Nations Development Programme (UNDP), "Subject: Sustainable Development Network," communication from the administrator (UNDP, New York, February 27, 1990), p. 1.

11. Joan Martin-Brown, Special Adviser to the Executive Director, United Nations Environment Programme, Washington, D.C., 1990 (personal communication).

12. Yusuf J. Ahmad, Senior Adviser to the Executive Director, United Nations Environment Programme, Nairobi, 1990 (personal communication).

fairly close control over independent organizations. The ORMAS (Social Organization) Law, passed in 1986, requires NGOs to register with the Ministry of Home Affairs and to get government approval for the appointment of new officers. The law allows local government officials to ban voluntary organizations without a formal explanation. Aside from the government's interest in controlling unofficial agencies, the law also reflects official concern about the high percentage of NGO funds (estimated at 95 percent) that come from foreign sources. The new law provides that all grants must have government approval (27).

In the Philippines, the current constitution recognizes the role of NGOs in the process of development, and President Corazon Aquino has encouraged their growth. Mainly because of the new political freedoms and the failure of the government to halt environmental destruction and to carry out fundamental economic changes such as land reform, NGOs have multiplied in the Philippines. Most NGOs have acted more as advocates and lobbyists for specific causes than as partners with the government. The NGOs have formed numerous networks and coalitions, including sectoral-and issue-based coalitions such as the Congress for People's Agrarian Reform (CPAR) and the Green Forum, which is working on sustainable development issues. The Caucus of Development NGOs includes 10 NGO networks with a membership of more than 1,300 NGOs (28). The Manila-based International Institute of Rural Reconstruction, founded in the early 1950s to support rural development programs, has six affiliate NGOs and has trained a large core of alumni who now work for other rural development NGOs (29).

Latin America

Until the mid-1960s, the work of the Catholic church and other NGOs in Latin America focused chiefly on charitable relief and welfare, especially transferring food surpluses from the North (30).

Independent organizations diversified in the late 1960s and 1970s, as disillusionment with conventional trickle-down development led to new groups interested in strengthening civil society and in supporting small-scale local development. Many organizations were created in reaction to the many authoritarian military regimes that held power during the period; particularly during the 1970s, NGO activity was highly politicized (31). The Catholic church—following Vatican II and a 1968 conference of bishops in Medellin, Colombia—committed itself to social justice. This move led to a massive organizational effort at the grassroots level, with priests and nuns forming NGOs to work with the poor in rural and urban areas (32). Many secular antipoverty organizations also have been started (33).

The democratization of many Latin American governments during the 1980s bolstered the creation of new popular organizations, such as peasant and neighborhood associations, as well as new movements supporting ethnic groups, women, and the environment. Progressive NGOs often are critics of government policies, but NGO-government relationships gradually are improving in many countries; cooperative projects are now relatively common (34).

As Southern NGOs have gained strength, they have insisted on greater autonomy and less dependence on Northern supporters. Latin American organizations also are eager to coordinate their work with others through national and international networks (35).

A recent survey of 1,000 groups in Brazil found that 47 percent were independent, 37 percent had church affiliations, and the rest were linked to institutions such as universities. Nearly all the organizations were started either in the 1970s (35 percent) or 1980s (55 percent). Formal regulation of these groups is minimal, nor have governments attempted to limit their freedom of speech. Their greatest institutional weakness appears to be their reliance on foreign sources of support (36).

Fundraising has proven difficult for groups in Brazil and other countries where volatile economies and fears of inflation inhibit donations by both individuals and corporations. In addition, philanthropy is not a well-established tradition in Latin America (37).

In Central America, the 1980s were a period of civil unrest and economic decline characterized by food shortages, droughts and other natural disasters, large-scale migration to cities, and drastic cuts in government-provided social services. Local NGOs survived with the help of Catholic and Protestant clergy and lay persons, international NGOs, and donor agencies. The continuing need to provide food aid tended to delay the evolution of local NGOs from relief to development agencies (38).

Africa

Though less numerous than in Asia and Latin America, independent organizations are nevertheless important in Africa. During the colonial period, churches and missionary societies were the principal providers of health and education services, especially in rural areas. Late in the colonial period, ethnic welfare groups, professional associations, and separatist churches were started, often to contest the authority of colonial rulers (39). Churches, which generally remained neutral during independence struggles and emerged from the colonial period with weak political legitimacy, have large popular followings nonetheless and have expanded their activities to include support for women's groups, environmental protection, agricultural productivity, and antipoverty efforts (40).

Community self-help has a strong tradition in many African countries, including Zimbabwe, Senegal, Kenya, and Burkina Faso (41). Since independence, local NGOs have greatly increased their involvement in environment/development work and the delivery of basic services. Much of this activity has been in response to difficulties African governments have experienced in delivering services and fighting poverty (42).

International voluntary organizations, working in areas such as food relief and the delivery of health services, have continued to maintain an active and sometimes dominant—some would argue too dominant—presence in Africa (43).

STRENGTHS AND WEAKNESSES

Strengths of Grassroots Organizations

Groups at the grassroots level can provide members with greater financial and negotiating leverage than they would have individually. Local NGOs also can provide a public voice for members' views.

Mobilizing Collective Action

An important strength of many grassroots/community groups is their ability to organize around economic goals and make economic gains for their members. Local NGOs can provide sources of credit, production inputs, marketing services, technical support, education, health, and other services in ways that are relatively efficient and accountable (44).

The dairy farmers of Durazno, Uruguay, for example, traditionally had to take their milk into the city on small wooden carts and spend the morning making deliveries. Those who did not go into the city would sell to a middleman at his price.

With the help of an Inter-American Foundation grant, the dairy farmers formed a cooperative—the Sociedad de Fomento Rural (Rural Improvement Society)—and built a milk processing plant to pasteurize and package milk in Durazno. The plant has helped provide the farmers with a stable income and easier access to credit. The society, now one of Uruguay's most successful cooperatives, also includes farmers who produce grain, wool, meat, and vegetables. The society also runs a store that sells seed and farm supplies, operates facilities for drying and milling grain, and rents farm machinery (45) (46).

The Savings Development Movement (SDM) of Zimbabwe encouraged rural villagers to save money for local investment. The approach was simple: people in a rural neighborhood deposited small amounts of household money into a joint savings account at the nearest thrift institution. Within a year the group usually had enough money to place a bulk order for seed and fertilizer. Groups organized collective work parties and some diversified into agroprocessing and consumer stores or built community wells and dams. By 1984, SDM had expanded dramatically to 5,700 clubs nationwide, with a total membership of about 250,000 and a small national staff. The overwhelming majority of members were women, who traditionally had few rights to control assets independently of their husbands (47).

Eventually the government became suspicious of the motives and accountability of the SDM leadership, however, and installed its own candidates on the board. The long-term results of this change remain to be seen (48).

The village of Wuro-Sogi in Senegal, after experiencing severe hardship following the drought of 1973, started a community development association that pooled its funds to build a community water system.

SERGIO SOLANO, INTER-AMERICAN FOUNDATION

In Costa Rica, the Asociacion de los Nuevos Alquimistas (ANAI) provides materials and assistance to villagers to establish a community tree nursery. Women and children are active participants in most tree nursery projects.

Soon other projects were undertaken: a millet mill for women, a village pharmacy, and a communal vegetable garden managed by women.

The Wuro-Sogi village association also illustrates the ability of some private organizations to make connections. The association is linked with a federation of farmers' associations of Senegal (FONGS), has a branch in Dakar that looks after relations with government service agencies, and a branch in Paris managed by emigrants (49).

A Voice for Grassroots Interests

Local organizations that grow into larger structures can become effective political and economic forces. For example:

■ The Oaxaca Food Council Coordinating Network in Mexico is a coalition of democratically run rural peasants' organizations; it represents about 1.4 million low-income rural consumers in negotiations with a state-owned food trading company and has considerable influence over the distribution of food and other resources in the area (50).

■ In India, a coalition of NGOs has worked with local organizations representing 90,000 people who were to be displaced by construction of the Narmada dams. The coalition challenged the technical analysis used by the government in support of the project, encouraged the World Bank to follow its own procedures for environmental impact analysis, testified in the U.S. Congress, and organized demonstrations of thousands of people all over India (51) (52). By mid-1991, construction was continuing, but the World Bank had appointed an independent commission to review the project (53).

■ By 1988, the National Farmers Association of Zimbabwe, which was built on village-level clubs of small farmers for the bulk ordering of farm supplies and marketing of produce, had a dues-paying membership of more than 70,000 farmers and was a powerful force in shaping Zimbabwe's farm policies (54).

Weaknesses of Grassroots Organizations

Local organizations are usually small in scale and may therefore have limited impact and little interest in scaling up their activities or influencing government strategies for poverty alleviation. Furthermore, they may have relatively weak managerial skills and little ability to provide highly technical services.

Local groups are often confronted by obstacles beyond their control. Farmers who successfully start growing vegetables may be unable to get a truck to market their produce; or squatters who have gained physical control over a piece of land may be unable to get municipal services without legal title to the land. To cope with such problems, local groups may forge alliances with service groups (55).

The survival and growth of local groups also may depend on public policies, such as laws that govern the formation and operation of grassroots organizations, the allocation of credit to the poor by the banking system, and the structure of educational opportunity (56).

Strengths of Service Organizations

Service organizations support the development of grassroots groups. Some arise from a coalition of local groups, others are regional, national, or international. Studies of successful service groups have found that they are relatively effective at reaching the poor, mobilizing local resources, delivering services, and solving problems.

Reaching the Poor

Service groups have been more effective at reaching the poor who have some assets and less effective at reaching the very poor with few or no assets. As one study points out, "the provision of credit, irrigation, or market outlets to small farmers is easier than the provision of land, farming skills, and confidence to the landless" (57).

A study of 30 successful Latin American intermediary organizations found that they generally benefited the "middle poor," those in the third and fourth quintile of the income spectrum, but that many poor households were indirect beneficiaries. Most of the programs run by these organizations involved small semicommercial agriculture that required access to some land, but the poorest rural workers generally were oc-

casional workers or squatters with no land. Such programs tended to bring forward people who were more experienced, active, and willing to take risks, which also reduced participation of the poorest. Cultural preservation, literacy, ethnic defense, and rural health programs tended to have the widest poverty reach; other activities such as marketing and small-farm diversification tended to benefit primarily the middle poor (58).

Service organizations that do not initially work with the very poor may eventually reach this group. For example, the service group Cinci wa Babili in northern Zambia developed a scheme to breed and train oxen, teach farmers how to use oxen to cultivate land, and provide credits for the purchase of oxen and equipment. The program initially appealed mostly to slightly larger farmers. The poorest farmers, including women, responded after seeing the positive experience of the larger farmers and after watching a ploughing competition Cinci organized in 1987 (59).

A few service organizations have succeeded in helping the very poor. The Society for Promotion of Area Resource Centres (SPARC) in Bombay, India, for example, was founded by a group of middle-class professionals to help the city's female pavement-dwellers gain better housing. As part of the effort to help the pavement women, SPARC arranged a workshop on housing design and construction that concluded with an exhibition of four low-cost model houses designed in large part by the women. The exhibit attracted the attention of municipal and World Bank officials. The World Bank offered some land in a distant suburb, but SPARC hesitated to accept because a move would cost families their jobs and sink them further into poverty. Despite the delays in the resettlement effort, SPARC helped build new confidence among female pavement-dwellers and enabled them to make their voices heard for the first time (60).

Participation

Effective service organizations rely on the active participation of the beneficiaries. Participation is critical to the durability of a project; for example, a project that seeks to introduce a new technology will usually get plenty of takers for the new machines. Whether these machines are used effectively and maintained properly, however, may depend on discussions with the beneficiaries to see that the technology really responds to their needs.

Another important component of participation is a commitment by beneficiaries to invest their own resources in the project. For example, the Asociacion de los Nuevos Alquimistas (ANAI) is a professionally led service organization working in one of Costa Rica's poorest and most isolated districts. Because the region's resources have been threatened by deforestation and uncontrolled settlement, ANAI has tried to promote a low-resource agriculture that requires few chemical inputs and is ecologically sustainable. In its tree nursery and other projects, ANAI has stressed the use of locally available resources, avoided the use of sophisticated concentrates or fertilizers, and chosen only tree species that can survive with local resources (61). ANAI's nursery program requires beneficiaries to contribute land, materials, and labor as a precondition to receiving seeds and technical assistance (62).

An effective strategy to build participation and confidence in the work of a service organization may be to begin with projects for which there is a clear local demand, even though the project may not fit with the service group's priorities. In one case, CIPCA, a Peruvian training organization, became active in some Peruvian villages by responding to a request for assistance in staffing and equipping some rural health clinics, even though that was not CIPCA's field of expertise (63). Such a strategy entails risks, however, because the NGO may not have the proper skills.

The participation of local groups can be critical to the success of development projects. Local groups can help provide better information about local needs, help adapt programs to local conditions, provide opportunities for better communication, help mobilize local resources, improve the odds that use and maintenance of facilities will be sustained, and improve cooperation with local people who can benefit from the innovation (64).

An examination of 25 agriculture and rural development projects financed by the World Bank found that participation by beneficiaries was a key factor for the 12 projects that achieved long-term economic sustainability. In the Muda irrigation project in Malaysia, the successful development of water users' associations proved critical for the project's long-term success. In contrast, the Hinvi Agricultural Development Project in Benin failed, largely because the network of cooperatives created to support the project was run by a parastatal (state-owned enterprise) with no self-management delegated to the farmers. Within seven years, 75 percent of the farmers had pulled out of the system (65).

Alternative Approaches to Problems

Administrative flexibility, small size, and relative freedom from political constraints make it easier for successful service organizations to try innovative solutions to problems (66).

For example, Gram Vikas in India has worked with technology centers and state banks to build more than 20,000 family and village biogas plants. The plants reduce the need for scarce fuelwood, provide fertilizer for farming and forestry, and improve the quality of life for women. Gram Vikas's costs are a fraction of government costs for similar plants (67).

In the Yatenga area of Burkina Faso, groups of farmers working with Oxfam perfected a technique to rebuild desertified soils by constructing stone lines along hill contours to retain water and increase infiltration. The technique, which has increased yields by 50 percent in some cases, is being spread by a regional federation (Naam) and has been adopted by the government as part of its land rehabilitation program (68).

The Kenya Energy and Environment Organizations (KENGO) realized in the early 1980s that forestry programs largely ignored indigenous trees in preference to exotic varieties, which in most cases were not as well suited to Kenya's ecology. KENGO began an ambitious information program on the use of indigenous tree species in Kenya, including a directory of trees and seeds in Kenya and booklets on the collection and storage of seeds. The information was published in local newspapers, distributed in workshops, and broadcast on a weekly radio program in English and Kiswahili (69).

Weaknesses of Service Groups

Most studies of NGOs have looked at successful organizations; less is known about organizations or projects that failed and the reasons for those failures.

Unlike their successful counterparts, many service NGOs that fail do not reach the poor, are not innovative, and are as rigid as government departments. In addition, some service NGOs have been criticized for having limited technical capacity for complex projects, for an inability to replicate successful projects on a larger scale, for a limited ability to sustain themselves after initial outside help is withdrawn, and for relatively weak managerial and organizational skills (70).

Service NGOs often do not benefit the very poor, and in many cases, grassroots participation, especially on the part of women, may be limited. A study of 75 NGO projects found that what was often termed participation was in practice a form of decentralized decision making still dominated by NGO staff and local elites, and that local elites often received a disproportionate share of benefits (71).

Many projects may be conceived with little thought given to what the next step should be. Long-term planning is difficult for many Southern NGOs because of their dependence on limited project grants from Northern partners (72). NGO programs may have little coordination with other projects in the same country and little relationship to state strategies (73). (Some NGOs, of course, deliberately bypass state strategies they oppose.)

NGO projects that bypass state structures may rapidly deteriorate if the donor NGO pulls out. Approaches that concentrate on local development may ignore the need to establish viable administrative structures to provide a framework for local efforts (74).

Self-Evaluation and Accountability

The documentation of NGO project experiences is often "irregular, subjective, and geared more to fundraising than to institutional learning," according to one report. Assessments made by observers in the field are rarely documented by headquarters staff and may be lost when the observers leave. Program priorities may change considerably as staff change. Northern donors, sensitive to the need to let southern NGOs run their programs, are reluctant to insist on independent monitoring and evaluation. Once a project is completed, few funding NGOs pay much attention to its impact or whether it provided any lasting benefits. Monitoring efforts rarely use nearby communities not affected by the project as a control or as baseline data (75).

Part of the evaluation problem is that NGO projects frequently have multiple, diffuse goals that may change over time. Such variables as morale and participation can also be difficult to measure (76). In addition, action-oriented NGOs may not have the time, funds, or inclination for evaluation work.

Managerial and Technical Capacity

Service NGOs frequently suffer from high staff turnover and weak managerial and technical capacity. Many Southern NGOs, for example, have little experience in financial planning and budgeting, accounting, personnel management, information systems, fundraising, and grant administration (77).

Northern donor NGOs may be concerned about the proportion of funds spent by Southern partner groups on administration, but show less concern about the competence, training, or experience of the staff. Donor NGOs may watch carefully to ensure that funds go where they are supposed to go but be less concerned about the actual effectiveness of the projects they are supporting (78).

Management training services are provided by a few NGOs, including the Asian Non-Governmental Organizations Coalition for Agrarian Reform and Rural Development (ANGOC) in Manila, Bina Swadaya in Indonesia, and the Thai Volunteer Service in Thailand (79).

KEY ORGANIZATIONAL FACTORS

Getting Started, Getting Bigger

Organizations can multiply an initial success by growing bigger and expanding beyond the community level or by creating similar organizations that work in other communities under central leadership. They can also have wider impact by being separately duplicated elsewhere.

Many factors—isolation, the uniqueness of local situations, or a lack of energy and motivation—may restrain the growth potential of small projects. Furthermore, some projects that work on a small scale may simply not work on a larger scale (80), or may be better suited to duplication than expansion. The Grameen Bank in Bangladesh expanded by duplicating the creation of small credit groups, for example (81).

At the grassroots level a few projects that were carefully matched to a regional culture have grown rapidly. In the Yatenga region of Burkina Faso, *naam* traditionally referred to a temporary sharing of tasks by young people for common activities such as feasts. Revived by a Burkina Faso sociologist, the Naam movement initially organized young people and women—but eventually entire villages—to undertake a variety of community projects, including building ditches and small dams, constructing wells, land-shaping to control erosion, maintaining communal forests, and making fuel-efficient ovens. About 100 Naam groups were operating in 1973; by 1987 the number had grown to more than 2,500 (82).

Another notable example of an NGO that now operates on a large scale is the Bangladesh Rural Advancement Committee (BRAC), which grew from a small relief organization set up in 1972 to become one of the largest NGOs in the world, with a staff of more than 2,000 (83). BRAC focuses on the poorest 50 percent of village populations. It organizes groups of 20–30 people with similar backgrounds and encourages them to analyze and seek solutions to their own problems. Landless laborers have been organized to lease land, women's groups to undertake paddy processing, and fishermen to buy boats with BRAC providing credit. Initial groups are expected to form other groups in the village. As leaders are identified, they are brought to BRAC training centers to learn organization methods (84). Realizing the need for skilled middle managers, BRAC's leadership actively recruits the most promising Bangladeshi graduates for a program of field work and training that creates a management base (85).

Some types of projects—particularly credit, marketing, and educational projects—appear to have strong potential for expansion. In Paraguay, for example, the Centro Paraguayo de Cooperativistas (CPC) has extended its rural development program from one local area to six regions. After starting with a base of local committees, CPC then builds multivillage committees and eventually regional marketing organizations with consumer stores, processing facilities, agricultural credit, and technical assistance (86).

Good projects also have a better chance of scaling up in countries or regions with active NGO networks at all levels, where promising projects can quickly receive attention. Scaling up also seems to be associated with less centralized, more democratic governments, especially when NGO staff move into government positions, as has happened in Chile, Brazil, and elsewhere (87).

The Impact of Leadership

Charismatic leadership may prove essential in the early stages of an organization's formation, when initial aspirations need to be defined (88).

The leadership qualities needed to begin an organization, however, are not always the same qualities needed to sustain it as it becomes a mature institution. For example, one Latin American organization initially confronted landlords and local politicians and later built a staff of more than 100 people providing a wide range of credit, marketing, and training services. After five years of growth, however, the organization found itself plagued by conflicts between the founder and the staff he had recruited. As it matured, the organization needed a less confrontational leader who could negotiate with other agencies, supervise the many operational details of the program, and manage the organization's personnel (89).

Such organizations often make a transition from charismatic leadership to managerial leadership. The new leaders tend to be pragmatic, concentrating on organizational stability, operating procedures, and training staff. Their first concern, according to the article, "tends to be the bottom line rather than seizure of the moral high ground" (90).

The Role of Women

Though examples abound of women organizing to advance their interests, many NGOs have not integrated women into their programs. At least three reasons explain this failure: institutional legacies, cultural constraints, and competition for scarce financial resources (91).

Both the relief agencies started in the 1940s and 1950s and the newly emerging NGOs of the past few decades have tended to view women solely in their domestic roles. In Latin America, the Catholic church played a major role in the development of grassroots efforts to fight poverty, but the Church's efforts did not envision a changed role for women. Moreover, although many NGOs have tried to work within the framework of local cultures, those cultures are often highly patriarchal and view the role of women primarily in terms of home and family. Finally, competition for scarce financial resources has often meant that funds intended for women's projects are diverted and used for other purposes (92).

NGO projects often do not sufficiently involve women in planning and decision making, may add to their workload but do little to improve their productivity, and may not address women's real economic roles or enhance their potential leadership and management skills (93).

Women's NGOs

Partly in consequence, many new NGOs exclusively for women have been started.

Like most local organizations, women's organizations tend to have limited financial resources, limited organizational and technical expertise, and limited access to the networks that allocate resources and knowhow. They may often lack institutional clout, which is reflected in the small size of projects and the difficulty of raising funds (94).

Despite these impediments, women's groups have been effective in reaching poor women, encouraging women's participation in decision making, teaching technical and managerial skills, allowing poor women to develop skills and confidence without male competition, providing access to resources, raising women's awareness of gender issues, and building their self-confidence.

Women are organizing to cope with tasks such as providing water and fuel; growing crops; and generating income from food processing, handicrafts, and similar activities (95). For example:

■ The villagers of Saye, in the Yatenga plateau in Burkina Faso, talked for years of building an earthen dam to catch the rainy season waters and hold them into the next dry season. Frustrated by the men's inaction and unwilling to continue carrying water over long distances, the village women organized and built the dam (96).

■ The Kenya Water for Health Organization (KWAHO), a consortium of NGOs established to respond to women's self-help efforts for water and sanitation improvements, organized a cooperative program in

SAM OUMA, PANOS PICTURES

With the help of the Kenya Water for Health Organization, these women operate and maintain a simple, safe water system.

the Kwale District south of Mombasa to train women to build and maintain simple water systems. Cooperation between project staff and the community was developed by five female extension workers through a process of village-level decision making. The pilot project was so successful it was extended through the entire district (97).

■ In Khirakot, a small village in Uttar Pradesh in northern India, women who collected fuelwood from the surrounding community forests also carefully managed the forests. When a Kanpur contractor obtained a lease for soapstone mining in the hills, the women in the village realized that the mining would block their access to the forests and that mine debris could kill the forests. The women protested in court, and the mines were officially closed (98).

■ The Green Belt Movement in Kenya, which was started by environmentalist and women's rights advocate Wangari Maathai, encourages people to find public areas and plant tree seedlings to form tree belts. By 1989, the movement claimed to have established 670 community tree nurseries and planted some 10 million trees in 1,000 tree belts. Some 50,000 Kenyan women have been involved in the campaign (99).

GOVERNMENT–NGO RELATIONS

Government–NGO relations are complex and vary considerably from country to country. In many cases, NGOs have had considerable impact on governments, either by offering models for new government programs, proposing reforms of existing policies, or critiquing proposed government policies. In some cases, NGOs have focused opposition to government policies, even to the point of organizing demonstrations or using more confrontational tactics.

The relationship between governments and NGOs—often determined by the degree to which governments tolerate and encourage NGOs—is a strong determinant of NGO activity in a country.

Government–NGO relations hinge on several factors, including the fitness of the government, the type of political system, and the type and location of particular NGO projects. Relations are likely to be best, according to one author, where "a confident and capable government with populist policies meets an NGO that wishes to pursue mainstream development programs in a nation's heartland." Relations are likely to be worst "where a weak and defensive government with a limited power base meets an NGO that seeks to promote community mobilization in a contested border area" (100).

The content of NGO projects also influences the response of governments. In developing countries, governments universally regard noncontroversial projects such as child immunization or clean water programs as desirable, but may not warmly welcome NGOs working in areas such as basic human rights advocacy (101).

Invariably, tension exists between the government's interest in controlling NGO activities and the NGOs interest in maintaining organizational autonomy. Governments, for example, may seek to manage the NGO sector by passing laws requiring NGOs to register and regularly report on their activities; by intervening in NGO activities in order to coordinate national development planning; by coopting NGO activity through the creation of "quangos" (quasi-NGOs, or publicly sponsored NGOs that are organizational affiliates of a government ministry), or by involving NGOs in government policymaking or other official functions; or by restricting or forcibly closing NGOs judged to be working against the government's interest. Government funding of NGO programs—or government controls on funding by external donors—can be used to reduce the autonomy of NGOs (102).

NGOs, on the other hand, can maintain autonomy by, for example, keeping a low profile and working in remote areas that are not actively monitored by government administrators or by selectively collaborating with other NGOs to increase their stature (103). Pressure from international development financing agencies to accept the work of NGOs also has provided them with some protection (104).

Many governments often are nervous about the high level of foreign support for indigenous NGOs. To control foreign donations, governments such as Indonesia require government approval for all foreign grants; requests can be turned down without explanation. In response, some NGOs have tried to bolster their independence by raising funds from local donors and finding new ways to generate income, such as selling reports or services (105).

Even governments with long histories of working with NGOs are occasionally uneasy about the relationship. India, for example, has recently debated a proposed code of conduct for NGO workers (106).

Gaining Influence

Some NGOs now play major roles in shaping public policy. For example, the National Farmers' Association of Zimbabwe has participated in annual commodity price negotiations with the government's Agricultural Marketing Authority, developed a data base on small farmers' costs of production, and been recognized by the government as the official voice for all low-income farmers in the communal and resettlement areas of the country (107).

Examples of NGOs' influence on public policy abound. In Uruguay, FUNDASOL was so effective in providing credit to rural cooperatives that changes were made in the credit practices of the Bank of the Republic. In Peru, PROTERRA's land titling activities in the Lurin Valley influenced the government to pass new laws to distribute agrarian reform lands (108). The Amul Dairy cooperative in India provided the model for the Indian government's National Dairy Development Program, known as "Operation Flood" (109). NGOs substantially revised and improved the impacts of an urban development project in the Manila area. An NGO called ZOTO initially led the challenge to the plans drawn up by Philippine government agencies and the World Bank and eventually served as part of an advisory council on the project (110).

NGOs also can build coalitions to create or implement new policies. In the Philippines, the International Institute for Rural Reconstruction worked with UNICEF, local school teachers, and officials of the Ministry of Education to create a program that trained students in biologically intensive gardening. The program helped increase the capacity of poor families to feed themselves from small plots and has become a model for school programs nationwide (111).

Many NGOs also are using the legal system successfully. In Malaysia, the local Friends of the Earth and the Consumers Association of Penang won a suit against a Japanese company that was mining rare earths and polluting the waterways. In Sri Lanka, NGOs halted the construction of a coal-powered utility in Trincomalee after showing flaws in the company's economic appraisal and proving that the team that drew up the proposal had not visited the area (112).

NGOs can be effective in demonstrating innovations on which improved policies can be based. Fundación Natura in Ecuador paved the way for a $10 million debt-for-nature program to pay for high-priority parks and reserves. The organization is also forming a regional Tropical Rainforest Network to formulate a joint policy document to present to governments and to the International Timber Trade Organization (113).

Confrontation: Risks and Rewards

When other options to effect change seem closed off, groups have used the risky strategy of confrontation with government authority to call attention to their issues. Confrontational tactics can have dramatic results and have been an important tactic in major social change movements such as Gandhianism in India and the 1960s U.S. civil rights movement. However, groups who use such tactics must be prepared to risk repression, imprisonment, and even the death of members.

One of the best-known current practitioners of confrontation tactics is Greenpeace, an international NGO that uses aggressive nonviolent tactics to protest the killing of marine mammals and the dumping of nuclear waste at sea. Protest tactics proved so effective that in 1985 the French government sent agents to New Zealand to blow up the group's flagship, the *Rainbow Warrior*.

Confrontations often continue for years, with a series of victories and defeats on both sides, before an outcome is reached. Recent examples of confrontational tactics include these:
■ From 1987 to 1989, more than 125 members of a nomadic rainforest tribe, the Penan, were arrested for blockading logging roads into their Malaysian homeland. The tribe started the Penan Association to organize Penan communities (114).
■ Ten women from North Sumatra were sentenced to six months in prison for destroying thousands of eucalyptus trees planted by a logging company in January 1989 on land the women claimed belonged to their village (115). In 1990, hundreds of villagers attempted to reoccupy lands appropriated by a state-owned logging company, PTP VII, which had failed to replace the land with similar irrigated cropland in accordance with a 1968 agreement (116).
■ In Indonesia and India, villagers have protested the flooding of their land for large dam projects. In Kedung Ombo, Indonesia, the government agreed to resettle in a nearby village 440 families who refused to move from their homes to a distant town with less fertile land (117).

Working with Governments

In recent years, many governments have increasingly welcomed the participation of environment/development NGOs. With the rise of new democracies in Latin America, for example, many new collaborative initiatives have been launched, sometimes by NGOs but mainly by the new governments seeking new approaches to development (118). Instances of NGOs acting as subcontractors for government programs or collaborating with government ministries seem to be on the upswing in many countries.

MIGUEL SAYAGO, INTER-AMERICAN FOUNDATION

A PROTERRA representative surveys land in Peru's Lurin Valley. PROTERRA has helped farmers secure land titles.

NGOs with established programs can be an effective outlet for government support. For example:
■ A program of informal education and training for street children, developed by the Undugu Society in Nairobi, has been so successful that it now receives government financial support, and the curriculum for its basic education school has been formally recognized by the government (119).
■ A program coordinated by KENGO to develop, test, and produce the Kenya Ceramic Jiko cookstove proved so effective that the Ministry of Energy became involved in organizing the training of artisans and the construction of demonstration centers (120).
■ The Fondo Nacional de Habitaciones Populares (FONHAPO), a low-income housing authority created by the Mexican government with support from the World Bank, used NGOs to help open up credit to barrio associations, cooperatives, and community groups. FONHAPO also gave local groups considerable power in the design and development of low-cost housing. FONHAPO's efforts met with mixed success but did increase the incentives for local people to become better organized (121).
■ FIDENE/UNIJUI, an NGO associated with a university in Rio Grande do Sul in Brazil, developed an effective method for organizing and educating poor peasants. Government agencies asked the group to start popular education movements in other parts of the country because the group had better outreach, and in some cases greater legitimacy, in those regions (122).

NGOs also can help extend thin government resources by organizing their clientele to receive extension services in a group setting, by training government field workers, and by integrating their programs with government programs (123). The new government of Peru, for example, asked a coalition of

Box 14.3 Political Symbolism and the Urban Popular Movement in Mexico

Aided by increasingly affordable miniaturized hardware, and greater user friendliness of data base technology, NGOs are becoming important conduits for the transmission of information to poor people. According to Sheldon Annis, formerly a fellow at the Overseas Development Council and now a professor at Boston University, the trend is especially evident in better developed and urban areas.

Annis also argues—in a paper presented to the World Conference on Education for All at Jontien, Thailand, in March 1990—that communication is increasingly decentralized and "deprofessionalized." He illustrated the point with an example from Mexico City after the 1985 earthquake, when a coalition of earthquake victims and neighborhood organizations lobbied the government and the World Bank to accelerate the rebuilding process. The following is adapted from that paper (1).

THE POWER OF INFORMATION

In general, the better developed and more urban the context, the more likely that the poor are able to incorporate and benefit from the power of information. The "urban popular movements" that are now a familiar part of the Latin American landscape function, in large measure, by their capacity to spread information, channel anger, and generate shared political purpose. During the past recessionary decade, urban popular movements have regularly mobilized thousands—even hundreds of thousands—of people in the streets of Latin America.

In one case that I have studied—the movement arising in the aftermath of the Mexico City earthquake of 1985—hundreds of thousands of earthquake victims (joined by non-poor earthquake victims, as well as nonvictim poor) joined to create a remarkable movement that forced the government and the World Bank to greatly accelerate the process of housing reconstruction.

Within days [of the quake], a coalition of organizations formed and successfully

DANIEL MENDOZA, IMAGENLATINA

Mexican NGOs created Superbarrio, a good-natured, appealing folk hero, to inspire the people to confront government officials and demand improved housing conditions. Here he leads a demonstration of mothers and children in Mexico City's central plaza.

united earthquake victims and scores of neighborhood organizations. Through deft manipulation of the media and political bartering, the coalition pressured and wrested innumerable concessions from the government—and then maintained unrelenting pressure to force compliance with

what had been promised. Whenever the Mexico government dragged its feet, renewed pressure was applied. In May 1986, for example, the coalition announced that tens of thousands of still-homeless victims would link hands around Aztec Stadium during the internationally televised

NGOs to help distribute food and medicine in rural areas (124).

In some cases, governments are themselves launching nongovernmental organizations. As part of its effort to create parks and reserves, the Costa Rican government created the Neotrópica Foundation and its sister organization, the National Parks Foundation. These organizations buy lands and transfer them to the government; pay for park rangers; channel donations for specific projects, such as saving Guanacaste National Park's dry tropical forest; and provide help in emergencies (125). More often than not, however, government-launched NGOs have lacked the resources to be effective and have failed to win allegiance from other NGOs (126).

EMERGING TRENDS

NGOs are evolving in three main directions. First, many Southern NGOs are seeking greater autonomy from their Northern partners. Second, NGOs are stepping up their efforts to make connections, both by forming networks and associations of NGOs and by using new communication technologies to stay abreast of issues and keep in touch with NGOs in other countries. Third, a few new roles for NGOs—legal defense and policy research—are emerging in the developing countries.

Evolving North-South Relations

Many Southern groups believe that their dependence on Northern groups for funds has exacted too high a

Box 14.3

World Cup Soccer championship. This action was called off only at the last minute when a crash construction program began to show visible results. Eventually, 50,000 units were constructed and another 40,000 units were repaired, more or less on time and approximately within budget.

CREATION OF A HERO

The earthquake demonstrates the galvanizing force of a natural disaster. But in the aftermath—with the relative success of the reconstruction program—the political energy of the movement waned. It was recaptured not by another natural event, but by a man-made media event: the creation of a popular hero—Superbarrio.

Superbarrio was not an identifiable individual, but a masked *lucha libre* wrestler, a good guy sworn to oppose the bureaucracy, the greedy landlord, the party political hacks, and the state. Dressed in his yellow tights, red cape, and SB-emblazoned superhero's wrestler mask, Superbarrio led tens of thousands of people in street protests over renters' rights, housing codes, credit for housing construction, and the pace and scale of the government's low-cost housing program. Superbarrio loses his superstrength when his mask is removed or when he is removed from the sight of the people. So he forced embarrassed public officials to negotiate in front of television reporters or on the street in front of cheering crowds.

Superbarrio enlivened Mexican popular politics with audaciousness and humor. In August 1987, for example, he announced he would wrestle his archenemy Catalino Creel—a takeoff of a soap opera villian, symbolizing for the tightfisted greedy landlord—in front of the National Cathedral. The government angrily rejected the unseemly location for a wrestling match. The government's willingness to allow the match (and if so, where) became a hotly disputed issue—and as a result, a media

event in itself. After suffering innumerable political lampoons, the embarrassed government finally reluctantly agreed to let the match be held *behind* the cathedral. The ring was set up; but it mysteriously disappeared in the wee hours of dawn before the scheduled match, prompting taunts, accusations of fraud, government theft, and set off new of street protests.

By creating a good-natured media hero who symbolized the popular struggle and who could not be bribed (and was therefore trusted by the people), the behind-the-scenes barrio associations managed to create considerable excitement, a shared pool of knowledge, and a formidable political force. But Superbarrio was more than street theatre. He reflected the popular movement's growing capacity to put information, not just symbolism, to use. At that time, one tactic of the barrio associations was to force the president of Mexico to negotiate publicly through open letters that appeared in the press. The letters recounted meetings and promises made by housing officials. Confronted by the barrio groups aggressively demanding a new round of low-cost housing construction and expropriations of properties belonging to landlords who evaded taxes and ignored housing regulations, the government claimed, first, that the housing needs of most victims were being successfully met, and second, that no building sites were available in the earthquake zones that would permit more low-cost construction.

ARMED WITH BANDIT

With an IBM personal computer and a simple Lotus program, the barrio groups rapidly created their own data base. I vividly recall watching a single researcher enter data supplied by a network of organizations while, in the adjoining room, Superbarrio sipped a beer, excoriated the duplicity of the government to a handful

of friendly reporters, and leaked his plans to "let the truth be known." Within a few weeks of intense negotiation, the barrio groups were backed with an up-to-date independent data base that listed the names of about 20,000 unserved earthquake victims and homeless families. They then matched this against a second data base of properties which were in violation of city codes, health standards, and paid no property taxes, and thus were eligible for expropriation under Mexican law. (In fairness, rent control laws often make it unprofitable to rent out or maintain properties.) Armed with both information and the means to convey it publicly, the barrio associations were then in a position to argue that such non-taxpaying, semi-abandoned, unsanitary properties in the central city were being held solely for speculation, were not in the "social interest," and therefore should be expropriated by the state to provide building sites for the second phase of the National Reconstruction Program.

The fact that the post-earthquake barrio associations could successfully create their own independent data base did not give them the ultimate power of decision making of course; but it did significantly affect their negotiating strength and the substance of political bartering. The media guerrilla Superbarrio generated not just jibes, but public debate over serious policy issues.

References and Notes

1. Sheldon Annis, "An Information Revolution at the Grassroots: What it Means for the Poor," paper presented at the World Conference on Education for All, Jontien, Thailand, March 1990, pp. 15-19. Note: An edited version of this paper has been published as: Sheldon Annis, "Giving Voice to the Poor," *Foreign Policy*, No. 84 (Fall 1991), pp. 93-106.

---

price in lost autonomy, compromised priorities, and reduced institutional identity (127). As Southern NGOs have raised their numbers, skills, and management capability, they are increasingly eager to set the agenda on their own terms.

Southern NGOs are pressing their Northern partners to agree that the principal responsibility for development in the South lies ultimately with the southern countries and their indigenous NGOs and that Northern financial aid should not be the controlling criterion that defines the relationship between North and South. While Northern NGOs may claim superior technical expertise, Southern NGOs maintain that they have more practical and relevant development experience in their own countries (128).

Some donors are responding to Southern NGOs efforts to assert more authority over projects by supporting Southern NGOs directly. Other donors choose to support Northern NGOs that are developing collaborative relationships with Southern colleagues or giving technical assistance to Southern NGO's on their own terms (129).

The Indonesia-Canada Twinning Project, linking two Canadian NGOs (Pollution Probe and the Canadian Institute for Law and Policy) with three counterpart organizations in Indonesia, is one example of the new ways in which Northern NGOs are transferring technical know-how to their Southern colleagues. Canadian specialists will help Indonesians use available technology to monitor water pollution in the Surabaya

People of the Penan tribe blockade a logging road in Sarawak during the Summer of 1991. Living quarters stand behind the blockade.

River in East Java and will assess how existing legislation can protect the river's environmental quality (130).

Networks and Associations: Forging Larger Alliances

A notable trend in developing countries is the creation of network organizations that link similar organizations to share information and coordinate activities. For example, the Indonesian Environmental Forum (WALHI) is an umbrella organization of more than 400 smaller environmental organizations. WALHI organizes conservation education programs, runs training programs on assessing environmental impacts or environmentally appropriate technology, provides technical assistance to its members on issues such as fundraising, and lobbies government officials. WALHI recently led several environmental groups in bringing Indonesia's first suit against a corporation for violating environmental laws (131).

Some networks are global in scope. The U.S.-based Pesticide Action Network (PAN) is an international coalition of 300 organizations in 50 countries working for sustainable pest control methods. PAN is an important source of information on pesticides for grassroots organizations in the developing world (132).

Associations can play an important role in disseminating information. The Asian NGO Coalition for Agrarian Reform and Rural Development (ANGOC), for example, disseminates research and innovations to its members and the wider development community (133). Many other environment/development networks have been formed at the international, regional, and national levels. The African Association for Literacy and Adult Communication (AALAE), the African Women's Development and Communications Network (FEMNET), and the Association of African Women for Research and Development (AAWORD) are examples of well-regarded NGO networks at the regional level (134).

Networks also can be used to bring together groups with overlapping interests. The Coordinating Body of the Indigenous Organizations of the Amazon Basin (COICA), an umbrella organization for five NGOs representing 1.2 million indigenous inhabitants of the Amazon Basin, convened a meeting with environmental NGOs in May 1990 in an effort to forge an alliance that would meld the interests of indigenous groups in the Amazon and conservationists (135).

Efforts to merge the environment and development perspectives are increasing. NGOs and NGO networks with a primary focus on environment and a secondary focus on development include Environment and Development in the Third World (ENDA-Tiers Monde), Environment Liaison Centre International (ELCI), the Haribon Foundation, the Regional Network of Energy Experts in Zimbabwe, KENGO, and WALHI (136).

The Information Explosion Global Networking:

Radio, TV, fax machines, and personal computers are technological symbols of a rapidly changing world in which information is instantly transmitted throughout an increasingly dense global network.

In Latin America, for example, radio stations blanket virtually the entire continent. Latin Americans have acquired more than 60 million television sets since the early 1950s. The number of television stations also is mushrooming. Bolivia until recently had about 7 stations but, with the advent of easily installed satellite dishes, now has about 50. One study argues that rural educators, grassroots groups, and NGOs inevitably will develop decentralized, low-cost, interconnected video systems (137). Important international news is instantly available around the world via Cable News Network correspondents with satellite video communication links.

Computers and phone-linked networks also are spreading rapidly. Brazilian NGOs routinely buy imported black market computers for as little as $1,000–2,000. Scores of larger NGOs have access to phone-linked computer systems. NGO users also are forming nonprofit user networks such as Nicarao in Central America or Alternex in Brazil, which also are linked to U.S. networks. Information sent over these networks costs about one fourth of a fax transmission or about one 40th of a telex (138).

EcoNet, a U.S.-based network, connects thousands of environmentalists, peace activists, and NGOs throughout the world. The system can be used to send documents inexpensively and instantaneously to NGOs in other countries. EcoNet also carries hundreds of electronic conferences simultaneously, allowing information to be pooled among thousands of organizations with shared interests (139).

Personal computers also allow grassroots organizations to develop their own data bases, which can significantly affect their negotiating strength. Box 14.3, a case study of the protest engendered after the 1985 earthquake in Mexico City, illustrates the point.

The communications revolution greatly facilitates international NGO partnerships. For example, the World Resources Institute, International Union for the Conservation of Nature and Natural Resources, and United Nations Environment Programme (UNEP) have organized a collaborative project to develop a biodiversity conserva-

tion strategy and a decade-long action plan for a sustained worldwide effort to use biodiversity wisely.

As part of the program, links are being established with numerous partner organizations such as WALHI in Indonesia, the National Parks Foundation in Costa Rica, Fundación Natura in Ecuador, and about two dozen other NGOs and international agencies. The program uses EcoNet to exchange drafts of the biodiversity strategy and other information, thus making the exchange of ideas easier and facilitating consensus-building among the partner organizations (140). This kind of electronic alliance is still confined mainly to large-scale NGOs.

UNEP also fostered the establishment of World-WIDE (World Women in the Environment), a worldwide network of women concerned about environmental management and protection. The organization publishes an international newsletter and a directory of women working in the environment field (141).

New Roles: Policy Research, Legal Defense

A small but growing number of Southern organizations at the regional and national levels are taking on new roles in areas such as policy research and legal defense.

Originally a birdwatching society, the Haribon Foundation in the Philippines has a legal program modeled after U.S. legal defense groups such as the Environmental Defense Fund. It works on legal issues relating to biodiversity, habitat, endangered species, and the preservation of tribal cultures. It also gives legal and research help to communities or NGOs that want to file complaints about violations of environmental law. Haribon's test case against pollution from buses in metropolitan Manila, which was designed to force the regional air pollution agency to use its authority to enforce the law, was dismissed on the ground that the foundation did not have legal standing (142).

Other national organizations are focusing on technical services or policy research. In India, the Society for Participatory Research in Asia (PRIA) provides research, training, and consulting support to grassroots organizations. PRIA staff have developed manuals and literature on community organizing and consult with NGOs to solve problems of organization and management. The society works in a wide variety of sectors, including women's development, adult literacy, and wasteland reclamation (143).

The African Center for Technology Studies (ACTS) in Nairobi is a "think tank" working on public policy issues concerning the environment and other matters. ACTS works to improve the quality of information available to policymakers and trains other NGOs in advocacy-oriented research methods (144).

CONCLUSION

NGOs in the developing world are growing quickly in numbers and in sophistication. To a large extent their potential remains unfulfilled, however, because of funding limitations, their own institutional weaknesses, and the uneasiness of many governments about the role of NGOs.

Nevertheless, NGOs are becoming increasingly important players in environment and development in the developing world, and they are likely to assume a much greater role in the coming decades.

Grassroots organizations can make numerous contributions to sustainable development.

■ They can mobilize local energies and resources to support projects over the long-run; without local participation and commitment, many projects eventually wither and die.

■ They can enable all the people of a society to improve their quality of life in ways that are sustainable and just.

■ Either through growth or building alliances with other groups, they can increase their effectiveness and potentially influence national policy making.

■ They can be used to link all the elements of sustainable development—ecological, economic, political, and cultural. Integrating women into organizations, for example, can take advantage of the linkages among women, poverty, and the environment.

■ They can enable individuals to cope with change (145).

Service organizations and national NGOs also have a significant role.

■ They can help bridge the differences in wealth, power, and culture among local organizations of poor people and government agencies or Northern institutions.

■ They can use their money, technical expertise, or persuasive powers to help solve the problems of grassroots groups or to carry a message of dissent or approval.

■ They can manage conflicts among constituencies.

■ They can span the gap between local and technical knowledge in the effort to find long-term solutions that are widely accepted by target groups.

■ They can solve problems, sometimes with new approaches, and they can disseminate what they have learned to other organizations.

■ They can provide connections to local organizations by joining networks or building links to international organizations (146).

International organizations can offer national and local groups new ideas and alert them to ongoing international policy making—trade liberalization, debt negotiations, and so forth—and its potential impact in developing countries. They can serve as international lobbyists to attack the policies of their governments, corporations, or multilateral institutions that adversely affect developing countries. Indeed, Southern NGOs are increasingly insistent that lobbying should be the primary role of Northern NGOs (147).

International NGOs also can show how otherwise disconnected communities share similar problems and can increase general awareness of global issues such as tropical deforestation, loss of biodiversity, and global warming.

NGOs are not perfect: most could be better managed, more accountable, and more professional. They could pay more attention to designing projects that can stand on their own once the original funding ceases. They need to try harder to integrate women and the very poor into projects. Northern NGOs could do more to treat their Southern counterparts as equal partners.

Political leaders who tolerate or encourage NGOs—both as critics and collaborators—will in the long term be serving their own best interests. In the many newly democratic countries, NGOs should seize the opportunity to create a dialogue with governments to strengthen the elements of political culture that are favorable to NGO growth.

NGOs have no desire to compete with or replace governments, but they can help significantly to reduce poverty on a lasting basis and to build new understanding about the links between environment and development.

This chapter was written by World Resources *Senior Editor Robert Livernash with assistance from Managing Editor Mary Paden. David Richards, a consultant to World Resources Institute, contributed to an earlier draft.*

References and Notes

1. Sheldon Annis, "Can Small-Scale Development Be a Large-Scale Policy? The Case of Latin America," *World Development*, Vol. 15, supplement (Autumn 1987), pp. 130-131.
2. L. David Brown and David C. Korten, "Understanding Voluntary Organizations: Guidelines for Donors," Policy, Planning, and Research Working Papers (Country Economics Department, The World Bank, Washington, D.C., September 1989), p. 3.
3. *Ibid.*
4. David Richards, Consultant, Brattleboro, Vermont, 1990 (personal communication).
5. Alan B. Durning, "People Power and Development," *Foreign Policy*, No. 76 (Fall 1989), p. 71.
6. Thomas H. Fox, "NGOs from the United States," *World Development*, Vol. 15, supplement (1987), pp. 11-12.
7. Organisation for Economic Co-operation and Development (OECD), *Voluntary Aid for Development: The Role of Non-Governmental Organizations* (OECD, Paris, 1988), p. 18.
8. *Op. cit.* 7, p. 19.
9. *Op. cit.* 7, p. 20.
10. *Op. cit.* 7, pp. 20-23.
11. *Op. cit.* 6.
12. Inter-American Foundation (IAF), *Annual Report 1989* (IAF, Rosslyn, Virginia, n.d.), p. 1.
13. Mayra Buvinić and Sally W. Yudelman, *Women, Poverty, and Progress in the Third World*, Foreign Policy Association Headline Series, No. 289 (Foreign Policy Association, New York, Summer 1989), pp. 35-36.
14. Diane Wood, Vice President for Latin America, World Wildlife Fund, Washington, D.C., 1990 (personal communication).
15. *Op. cit.* 13, pp. 36-39.
16. John Clark, *Democratizing Development: The Role of Voluntary Organizations* (Kumarian Press, West Hartford, Connecticut, 1991), p. 39.
17. *Ibid.* Note: Bank lending is smaller after debt service for past loans is deducted.
18. *Op. cit.* 7, p. 25.
19. Kathleen D. McCarthy, "The Voluntary Sector Overseas: Notes from the Field," Center for the Study of Philanthropy Working Papers (Graduate School of the City University of New York, New York, n.d.), p. 9.
20. *Op. cit.* 5, p. 69.
21. *Op. cit.* 19, pp. 12-13.
22. *Op. cit.* 19, pp. 10-11.
23. *Op. cit.* 19, p. 10.
24. *Op. cit.* 16, pp. 83 and 86.
25. Jacob Pfohl and Jane Yudelman, *Asian Linkages: NGO Collaboration in the 1990s* (Private Agencies Collaborating Together, New York, 1989), p. 40.
26. *Op. cit.* 19, p. 5.
27. *Op. cit.* 19, pp. 6-7.

28. Jennifer Smith, U.S. Coordinator, Philippine Development Forum, Washington, D.C., 1991 (personal communication).

29. Juan M. Flavier, President, International Institute of Rural Reconstruction, Silang, Cavite, Philippines, 1990 (personal communication).

30. David C. Korten, "NGOs and Development: An Overview," paper prepared for The World Bank under the auspices of the Institute for Development Research, Boston, 1989, p. 5.

31. Ibid.

32. Sally W. Yudelman, Senior Fellow, International Center for Research on Women, Washington, D.C., 1990 (personal communication).

33. Op. cit. 5, p. 70.

34. Op. cit. 30, p. 6.

35. Op. cit. 30, p. 6.

36. Op. cit. 19, p. 25.

37. Op. cit. 19, pp. 27-28.

38. Sally W. Yudelman, "NGOs and Social Change in Central America," paper prepared for the Off-the-Record Workshop on Peace, Development and Security in Central America, Huatulco, Mexico, May 1989, pp. 10-16.

39. Michael Bratton, "The Politics of Government-NGO Relations in Africa," World Development, Vol. 17, No. 4 (1989), pp. 570-571.

40. Op. cit. 30, p. 6.

41. Op. cit. 5.

42. Op. cit. 30, p. 6.

43. Op. cit. 30, pp. 6-7.

44. Op. cit. 2, p. 15.

45. Patrick Breslin, Development and Dignity (Inter-American Foundation, Rosslyn, Virginia, 1987), pp. 40-41.

46. Albert O. Hirschman, Getting Ahead Collectively: Grassroots Experiences in Latin America (Pergamon Press, New York, 1984), pp. 18-21.

47. Michael Bratton, "Non-governmental Organizations in Africa: Can They Influence Public Policy?" Development and Change, Vol. 21 (1990), pp. 96-97.

48. L. David Brown, "Bridging Organizations and Sustainable Development," Institute for Development Research (IDR) Working Paper No. 8 (IDR, Boston, 1990), p. 12.

49. Op. cit. 7, p. 47.

50. Betsy Aron and Jonathan Fox, Mexico's Community Food Councils, 1979-86 (The Synergos Institute, New York, 1988), p. 13.

51. Elizabeth Brubaker, "India's Greatest Planned Environmental Disaster," Ecoforum, Vol. 14, No. 2 (1989), pp. 6-7.

52. "Thousands Protest Narmada Projects," Ecoforum, Vol. 14, No. 2 (1989), p. 7.

53. Lori Udall, Attorney, Environmental Defense Fund, Washington, D.C., 1991 (personal communication).

54. Op. cit. 47, pp. 90-101.

55. Op. cit. 1, p. 131.

56. Op. cit. 1, pp. 132-133.

57. Op. cit. 16, p. 47.

58. Thomas F. Carroll, "Tending the Grassroots: Performance of Intermediary Non-Government Organizations," unpublished manuscript prepared under the sponsorship of the Inter-American Foundation, Rosslyn, Virginia, 1990, pp. IV-1-2.

59. Op. cit. 16, p. 48.

60. Darryl D'Monte, "India: The pavement dwellers of Bombay," in Against All Odds: Breaking the Poverty Trap, Donatus De Silva, ed., for The Panos Institute, Alexandria, Virginia (Seven Locks Press, Cabin John, Maryland, 1989), pp. 8-10 and 19-23.

61. Op. cit. 58, p. III-5.

62. Op. cit. 58, p. V-3.

63. Op. cit. 58, pp. V-8-9.

64. Milton J. Esman and Norman T. Uphoff, Local Organizations: Intermediaries in Rural Development (Cornell University Press, Ithaca and London, 1984), pp. 24-26.

65. Michael M. Cernea, "Farmer Organizations and Institution Building for Sustainable Development," World Bank Reprint Series (No. 414) (The World Bank, Washington, D.C., n.d.), pp. 5-6.

66. Op. cit. 2, p. 16.

67. Institute for Development Research and World Resources Institute, "NGO Contributions to Environment and Sustainable Development Policy Formulation," draft proposal, June 14, 1990, pp. 3-4.

68. Ibid., p. 40.

69. Gilbert Arum, "KENGO's Experience in Environment and Development," paper prepared for the World Resources Institute, Washington, D.C., November 1990, p. 2.

70. Op. cit. 2, pp. 16-17.

71. Judith Tendler, Turning Private Voluntary Organizations into Development Agencies: Questions for Evaluation, U.S. Agency for International Development (U.S. AID), Program Evaluation Discussion Paper No. 12 (U.S. AID, Washington, D.C., 1982), pp. 11-14.

72. Robin Sharp, Director, Southern Networks Programme, International Institute for Environment and Development, London, 1991 (personal communication).

73. Op. cit. 16, p. 59.

74. Tim Allen, "Putting People First Again: Non-Governmental Organisations and the 'New Orthodoxy' for Development," Disasters, Vol. 14, No. 1 (1990), pp. 67-68.

75. Op. cit. 16, pp. 60-61.

76. Biswajit Sen, "NGO Self-Evaluation: Issues of Concern," World Development, Vol. 15, supplement (Autumn 1987), pp. 163-164.

77. U.S. Agency for International Development (U.S. AID), Toward an Environmental and Natural Resources Management Strategy for ANE Countries in the 1990s (U.S. AID, Washington, D.C., 1990), p. 76.

78. Op. cit. 16, p. 62.

79. Op. cit. 77, pp. 76-77.

80. Diane B. Bendahmane, "New Perspectives on Evaluation," Grassroots Development, Vol. 14, No. 1 (1990), pp. 36-37.

81. Op. cit. 7, pp. 62-63.

82. Op. cit. 7, pp. 47-48.

83. Op. cit. 7, p.62. See also op. cit. 16, p. 83.

84. Op. cit. 7, p. 62.

85. Op. cit. 16, p. 83.

86. Mary Morgan, "Stretching the Development Dollar: The Potential for Scaling-Up," Grassroots Development, Vol. 14, No. 1 (1990), pp. 8-9.

87. Ibid., p. 9.

88. Jan R. Van Orman, "Leadership and Grassroots Development," Grassroots Development, Vol. 13, No. 2 (1989), p. 5.

89. Ibid.

90. Op. cit. 88, p. 6.

91. Sally W. Yudelman, "The Integration of Women into Development Projects: Observations on the NGO Experience in General and in Latin America in Particular," World Development, Vol. 15, supplement (Autumn 1987), p. 180.

92. Ibid., pp. 180-182.

93. Op. cit. 91, p. 183.

94. Op. cit. 13, pp. 44-46.

95. Irene Dankelman and Joan Davidson, Women and Environment in the Third World (Earthscan Publications, in association with

International Union for Conservation of Nature and Natural Resources, known as the World Conservation Union, London, 1988), pp. 4-5.

96. Ibid., p. 36.

97. Ibid., p. 37.

98. Ibid., p. 49.

99. Linda Starke, Signs of Hope: Working Towards Our Common Future (Oxford University Press, New York, 1990), pp. 69-70.

100. Op. cit. 39, p. 585.

101. Op. cit. 39, p. 576.

102. Rajesh Tandon, "NGO-Government Relations: A Source of Life or Kiss of Death?" paper prepared for the Society for Participatory Research, New Delhi, n.d., p. 17.

103. Op. cit. 39, pp. 576-582.

104. Op. cit. 102, p. 15.

105. Op. cit. 19, p. 7.

106. Op. cit. 19, p. 14.

107. Op. cit. 47, pp. 101-102.

108. Op. cit. 80, p. 36.

109. Samuel Paul, "Governments and Grassroots Organizations: From Co-Existence to Collaboration," in Strengthening the Poor: What Have We Learned, John P. Lewis, ed. (Transaction Books, New Brunswick, New Jersey, 1988), pp. 68-69.

110. Op. cit. 67, p. 4.

111. Op. cit. 29.

112. Op. cit. 16, p. 97.

113. Lisa Fernandez, "Private Conservation Groups on the Line in Latin America and the Caribbean," World Wildlife Fund (WWF) Letter, No. 1 (WWF, Washington, D.C., 1989), p. 4.

114. "With the Penan at the Last Blocade," Earth Island Journal, Vol. 4, No. 2 (1989), p. 28.

115. "Women Jailed for Destroying Eucalyptus," Down to Earth, No. 7 (March 1990), p. 2.

116. "Women Re-Occupy Plantation Land," Down to Earth, No. 10 (September 1990), p. 8.

117. "Kedung Ombo: Government Abandons Hard Line," Down to Earth, No. 3 (June 1989), p. 4.

118. Sarah L. Timpson, Director, and Jane Jacqz, Senior Advisor, Human Development Division, United Nations Development Programme, New York, 1990 (personal communication).

119. Dorothy Munyakho, "Kenya: The parking boys of Nairobi," in Against All Odds: Breaking the Poverty Trap, Donatus De Silva, ed. for The Panos Institute, Alexandria, Virginia (Seven Locks Press, Cabin John, Maryland, 1989), p. 80.

120. Op. cit. 69, pp. 3-4.

121. Sheldon Annis, "What is Not the Same About the Urban Poor: The Case of Mexico City," in Strengthening the Poor: What Have We Learned?, John P. Lewis, ed. (Transaction Books, New Brunswick, New Jersey, 1988), pp. 139-140.

122. Op. cit. 109, p. 66.

123. Op. cit. 39, p. 582.

124. Carlos Lopez, Ecologist, Environmental Division, Inter-American Development Bank, Washington, D.C., 1991 (personal communication).

125. Yanina Rovinski, "Costa Rica: The Private Arm of Public Interest," Panos, No. 6 (May 1988), p. 4.

126. Op. cit. 39, p. 579.

127. Anne Gordon Drabek, "Development Alternatives: The Challenge for NGOs—An Overview of the Issues," World Development, Vol. 15, supplement (Autumn 1987), p. xi.

128. Kingston Kajese, "An Agenda of Future Tasks for International and Indigenous

NGOs: Views from the South," *World Development*, Vol. 15, supplement (Autumn 1987), pp. 79-81.

129. *Op. cit.* 32.

130. *Op. cit.* 77, p. 77.

131. *Op. cit.* 77, pp. 74-75.

132. *Global Pesticide Monitor*, Vol. 1, No. 2 (May 1990), p. 2.

133. L. David Brown, "Bridging Organizations and Sustainable Development," Institute for Development Research (IDR) Working Paper No. 8 (IDR, Boston, 1990), p. 5.

134. *Op. cit.* 118.

135. Bruce Cabarle, "Indians, Environmentalists and the Fate of the Amazon," paper prepared for the World Resources Institute, Washington, D.C., 1990.

136. Sarah L. Timpson, Director, Human Development Division, United Nations Development Programme (UNDP), New York, 1990 (personal communication).

137. Sheldon Annis, "An Information Revolution at the Grassroots: What it Means for the Poor," paper presented at the World Conference on Education for All, Jontien, Thailand, March 1990, pp. 8-9. Note: An edited version of this paper has been published as: Sheldon Annis, "Giving Voice to the Poor," *Foreign Policy*, No. 84 (Fall 1991), pp. 93-106.

138. John Garrison, "Computers Link NGOs Worldwide," *Grassroots Development* (Fall 1989), cited in Sheldon Annis, "An Information Revolution at the Grassroots: What it Means for the Poor," paper presented at the World Conference on Education for all, Jontien, Thailand, March 1990, p. 12.

139. *Op. cit.* 137.

140. International Union for Conservation of Nature and Natural Resources, now the World Conservation Union, United Nations Environment Programme, and World Resources Institute (WRI), "The Biodiversity Conservation Strategy Programme," (WRI, Washington, D.C., July 1990), pp. 1 and 11, and Walt Reid, Associate, Program in Forestry and Biodiversity, World Resources Institute, Washington, D.C., 1990 (personal communication).

141. WorldWIDE, "Statement of Purpose" (WorldWIDE, Washington, D.C., n.d.).

142. Nels Johnson, Associate, Program in Environmental Planning and Management, World Resources Institute, August 1991 (personal communication).

143. *Op. cit.* 2, p. 13.

144. *Op. cit.* 67, p. 18.

145. *Op. cit.* 133, p. 2.

146. *Op. cit.* 133, pp. 2-3.

147. *Op. cit.* 16, p. 126.

15. Basic Economic Indicators

The clear value of economic data and analysis to decisionmakers has motivated them to mandate the creation of extensive global economic data sets. This chapter contains a set of these basic economic data, which provides the context for understanding the causes and the consequences of many of the decisions that affect the world's resources.

Many traditional economic indicators fail to account for the depletion or deterioration of natural resources, the long-term consequences of such depletion, the equitable distribution of income within a country, or the sustainability of current economic practices.

The type of measurement shown here, however, is still useful in showing the great differences between the wealthiest and the poorest countries. At $5.2 trillion, the economy of the United States overwhelms the economies of the other countries in the Western Hemisphere. As shown in Table 15.1, 30 countries in Africa have per capita GNPs under $500; in contrast, the per capita GNP of Switzerland is over $30,000.

Comparisons between countries based on GNP or GNP per capita must be made with care, because of variations in the exchange rate of the dollar. Comparisons of trends in GNP growth, adjusted for inflation, are not subject to this caveat. High growth rates in many Asian countries (China, India, Indonesia, the Republic of Korea, Malaysia, Pakistan, Singapore, and Thailand, among others) stand out in comparison to the relatively low growth rates in Europe and the stagnant, or even declining, economies in Latin America.

Another indicator of economic status is the provision or receipt of official development assistance (ODA), which is given to promote economic development and general welfare. The United States still gives the most overall ($8.9 billion), but Japan has increased its ODA to $8.5 billion ($73 per capita compared to $31 in the United States). India was the largest recipient of ODA ($2.1 billion), followed by Viet Nam ($1.9 billion), China ($1.7 billion), Bangladesh ($1.7 billion), and Egypt ($1.6 billion).

On a per capita basis, Mongolia receives the most ($354) ODA while Norway donates the most ($217). Saudia Arabia, Norway, and the Netherlands each give over 1 percent of their GNP to ODA. In contrast, the United States allocates only 0.2 percent of its GNP to ODA. ODA is extremely important to the economies of some countries (ODA represents over 20 percent of the GNP in 15 countries, 12 of them in Africa).

Table 15.2 shows some trends in international debt for 107 countries. The total external debt for these countries was almost $1.15 trillion in 1989 (the most recent year for which complete data are available) and is growing. In fact, many of these debt indicators show a decline in economic health over the past 10 years. Many countries pay more each year to service their existing debt than they borrow. Much of this negative capital flow is accounted for by highly indebted, middle-income countries. The poorest countries still borrow more than they pay. For many developing countries, external debt is a large proportion of GNP, and debt service takes a significant portion of the total foreign exchange earned from the export of goods and services. For example, Argentina's external long-term public debt was 95 percent of its GNP in 1989, and its debt service represented 36 percent of its total export earnings.

Table 15.3 shows how much central governments spend and how they prioritize that spending. These data come from a variety of years. In addition, the proportion of total government spending by central governments compared with local and provincial governments also varies. Therefore, comparisons of central government spending should be made with care. A country such as the United States, where many expenditures are made by state and local governments, cannot be directly compared to a country such as Singapore where all expenditures are made by the central government. For example, although only 2 percent of central government expenditures in the United States go to education, fully 14 percent of total central, state, and local government expenditures are for education—identical to Singapore's central government expenditure percentage.

Defense can account for a very high proportion of a central government's spending. For example, Sudan spends 47 percent on defense; Israel, 26 percent; and the United States, 25 percent.

Many developing countries still depend on the sale of raw materials to earn needed foreign exchange. Table 15.4 shows that price indexes for all categories of commodities (except timber) have declined over the past 15 years. Of agricultural commodity prices, only banana prices were higher in 1989 than in 1975. Most agricultural commodity prices were dramatically lower. Wood products and refined metals fared somewhat better.

Table 15.1 Gross National Product and Official Development

	Gross National Product 1989		Average Annual Change in Real GNP (percent)		Distribution of Gross Domestic Product, 1989 {a} (percent)			Average Annual Official Development Assistance (ODA) (million $US) {b}		ODA as a Percentage of GNP {b}		1989 ODA Per Capita ($US) {b}
	Total (million $US)	Per Capita ($US)	1969-79	1979-89	Agriculture	Industry	Services	1982-84	1987-89	1982-84	1987-89	
WORLD												
AFRICA												
Algeria	53,116	2,170	6.4	3.3	13.2	43.2	43.6	49	165	0.1	0.3	6
Angola	6,010	620	X	X	X	X	X	84	163	1.8	2.8	16
Benin	1,753	380	2.4	2.3	45.5	12.1	42.4	82	183	8.4	11.0	54
Botswana	1,105 c	940 c	13.5	10.8	2.9	54.8	42.3	103	155	11.2	9.0	131
Burkina Faso	2,716	310	3.2	3.8	31.8	24.3	43.8	195	287	13.8	11.0	32
Burundi	1,149	220	8.9	4.2	55.9	15.0	29.1	136	196	13.4	18.1	37
Cameroon	11,661	1,010	6.1	4.4	27.0	27.9	45.1	176	322	2.4	2.8	41
Cape Verde	281	760	X	8.9	14.4	17.1	68.5	60	83	44.6	32.2	207
Central African Rep	1,144	390	2.3	0.5	42.2	15.3	42.5	99	188	14.6	17.9	65
Chad	1,038	190	(1.5)	4.7	35.8	20.0	44.2	92	235	15.2	24.8	44
Comoros	209	460	2.1	4.5	35.8	14.1	50.1	39	50	36.0	25.1	98
Congo	2,045	930	5.4	6.1	13.7	35.5	50.8	103	110	5.2	5.6	41
Cote d'Ivoire	9,305	790	6.3	1.2	46.0	24.0	30.0	140	368	2.2	4.1	35
Djibouti	333 d	1,070 d	X	X	X	X	X	76	91	X	X	184
Egypt	32,501	630	7.1	5.6	21.2	25.0	53.9	1,577	1,639	6.0	5.4	31
Equatorial Guinea	149	430	X	X	58.7	10.3	31.0	13	43	X	30.4	103
Ethiopia	5,953	120	3.2	2.4	43.1	16.8	40.1	453	851	9.7	15.1	15
Gabon	3,060	2,770	8.0	0.8	10.3	46.5	43.2	67	107	2.1	3.5	120
Gambia, The	196	230	5.3	2.3	34.1	10.3	55.6	48	92	26.8	50.7	109
Ghana	5,503	380	1.5	1.9	50.2	17.9	31.8	157	467	3.8	9.2	38
Guinea	2,372	430	X	X	X	X	X	97	304	X	13.4	63
Guinea-Bissau	173	180	X	2.4	47.0	15.8	37.2	64	103	41.3	64.4	106
Kenya	8,785	380	7.1	4.2	30.7	19.5	49.8	432	784	7.2	10.0	41
Lesotho	816	470	12.4	2.0	24.0	29.8	46.2	101	114	14.7	16.0	74
Liberia	1,052 e	450 e	3.3	X	37.0	28.0	35.0	120	67	12.0	X	24
Libya	22,976 c	5,410 c	3.4	(4.7)	X	X	X	(63)	(92)	(0.2)	(0.4)	(27)
Madagascar	2,543	230	1.6	(0.5)	31.4	14.4	54.2	204	331	6.3	14.3	29
Malawi	1,475	180	6.0	2.2	34.8	20.1	45.1	132	349	11.6	26.5	48
Mali	2,109	260	5.1	3.4	49.6	12.2	38.2	255	419	23.2	21.8	56
Mauritania	953	490	2.1	1.6	37.6	24.1	38.3	180	204	25.3	22.8	127
Mauritius	2,068	1,950	6.4	4.2	12.6	32.0	55.3	41	61	4.0	3.1	55
Morocco	22,069	900	5.0	3.9	15.5	35.7	48.8	514	460	3.8	2.3	18
Mozambique	1,193	80	X	X	64.4	22.0	13.6	257	847	11.0	74.2	53
Namibia	1,540 f	1,245 f	X	X	X	X	X	0	33	0.0	1.9	34
Niger	2,195	290	1.5	(0.6)	36.4	12.6	51.0	198	341	11.8	16.1	40
Nigeria	28,314	250	6.3	(0.1)	30.7	44.1	25.2	39	159	0.0	0.6	3
Rwanda	2,157	310	4.5	2.2	37.1	22.8	40.1	155	244	10.3	11.0	34
Senegal	4,716	650	2.8	2.2	22.0	31.1	46.9	325	620	13.8	13.8	90
Sierra Leone	813	200	2.2	1.8	46.3	12.4	41.3	70	91	5.5	10.4	25
Somalia	1,035	170	4.7	1.2	64.8	9.6	25.7	385	478	51.7	47.6	69
South Africa	86,029	2,460	3.4	2.2	5.8	43.9	50.3	X	X	X	X	X
Sudan	13,226	540	4.1	1.7	36.0	14.6	49.4	780	864	10.3	8.9	31
Swaziland	683	900	5.6	4.0	23.2	40.3	36.5	30	38	5.8	6.1	39
Tanzania	3,079	120	3.8	1.8	65.6	7.5	26.9	616	931	10.1	31.8	39
Togo	1,364	390	3.3	2.0	33.9	22.6	43.6	100	169	13.4	13.3	52
Tunisia	10,089	1,260	7.2	3.6	13.8	32.8	53.4	203	280	2.6	3.0	30
Uganda	4,254	250	(1.8)	2.7	72.5	7.4	20.2	144	349	7.4	7.6	24
Zaire	8,841	260	(0.1)	1.6	29.6	32.1	38.3	325	614	3.1	7.5	19
Zambia	3,060	390	1.4	1.5	14.2	43.0	42.8	262	433	8.6	13.8	50
Zimbabwe	6,076	640	4.9	4.3	12.7	38.8	48.5	242	278	4.2	5.0	28
NORTH & CENTRAL AMERICA												
Barbados	1,622	6,370	3.4	1.5	6.6	20.9	72.5	13	4	1.3	0.3	9
Belize	294	1,600	6.4	4.1	22.7	22.6	54.7	14	26	8.0	9.2	156
Canada	500,337	19,020	6.9	2.9	3.3	34.8	61.8	(1,417)	(2,182)	(0.4)	(0.5)	(88)
Costa Rica	4,898	1,790	6.1	1.8	17.8	26.7	55.4	183	214	6.6	4.8	83
Cuba	20,900 g	2,000 g	X	X	X	X	X	697	800	X	X	64
Dominican Rep	5,513	790	7.6	2.3	15.2	25.5	59.3	141	131	2.3	2.5	21
El Salvador	5,356	1,040	4.5	(1.2)	21.5	23.1	55.4	257	430	7.0	8.3	86
Guatemala	8,205	920	6.0	0.8	X	X	X	68	246	0.8	3.2	29
Haiti	2,556	400	3.5	0.0	31.3	38.0	30.7	132	188	8.1	8.5	32
Honduras	4,495	900	5.6	2.1	20.6	25.1	54.3	211	274	7.4	6.5	49
Jamaica	3,011	1,260	0.6	0.5	5.6	42.0	52.4	177	208	6.6	6.9	110
Mexico	170,053	1,990	9.2	2.0	8.0	32.2	59.8	118	138	0.1	0.1	1
Nicaragua	2,803 e	800 e	(0.4)	(2.0)	21.0	34.0	46.0	198	326	8.1	X	119
Panama	4,211	1,780	4.9	0.7	10.2	14.9	74.9	53	27	1.3	0.6	7
Trinidad and Tobago	4,000	3,160	4.5	(3.4)	2.8	39.7	57.4	5	16	0.1	0.4	5
United States	5,237,707	21,100	2.8	2.6	2.0	29.3	68.7	(8,331)	(8,915)	(0.2)	(0.2)	(31)
SOUTH AMERICA												
Argentina	68,780	2,160	2.9	(1.6)	13.8	32.7	53.5	50	154	0.1	0.2	7
Bolivia	4,301	600	3.9	(0.4)	24.0	27.0	49.0	165	384	6.0	9.2	62
Brazil	375,146	2,550	8.4	2.7	8.6	42.9	48.5	159	190	0.1	0.1	1
Chile	22,910	1,770	2.0	3.2	X	X	X	(2)	43	0.0	0.2	5
Colombia	38,607	1,190	6.0	3.0	16.8	36.4	46.8	91	69	0.2	0.2	2
Ecuador	10,774	1,040	9.4	2.3	16.0	31.0	53.0	84	167	0.8	1.7	16
Guyana	248	340	2.3	(2.3)	24.5	31.2	44.3	35	34	8.5	11.7	56
Paraguay	4,299	1,030	8.1	3.6	29.5	22.4	48.1	62	83	1.2	2.1	22
Peru	23,009	1,090	3.5	0.1	7.6	30.5	61.9	272	290	1.3	1.1	14
Suriname	1,314	3,020	4.7	(2.1)	11.0	25.8	63.3	37	32	3.7	2.6	117
Uruguay	8,069	2,620	2.6	(0.2)	10.8	28.2	61.0	3	32	0.1	0.4	12
Venezuela	47,164	2,450	4.5	(0.8)	6.1	45.8	48.1	6	(25)	0.0	(0.1)	(2)

Assistance 1969–89

Table 15.1

	Gross National Product 1989		Average Annual Change in Real GNP (porcent)		Distribution of Gross Domestic Product, 1989 {a} (percent)			Average Annual Official Development Assistance (ODA) (million $US) {b}		ODA as a Percentage of GNP {b}		1989 ODA Per Capita ($US) {b}
	Total (million $US)	Per Capita ($US)	1969-79	1979-89	Agriculture	Industry	Services	1982-84	1987-89	1982-84	1987-89	
ASIA												
Afghanistan	X	X	X	X	X	X	X	258	290	X	X	17
Bahrain	3,009 c	6,360 c	X	X	1.2	43.1	55.7	170	(2)	4.7	(0.1)	(6)
Bangladesh	19,913	180	2.4	3.5	44.3	14.4	41.3	1,221	1,700	9.3	9.0	16
Bhutan	266 c	190 c	X	X	46.1	29.3	24.6	14	42	10.3	X	30
Cambodia	X	X	X	X	X	X	X	123	213	X	X	30
China	393,006	360	7.4	8.9	32.4	46.1	21.4	450	1,718	0.2	0.5	2
Cyprus	4,892	7,050	X	5.9	7.1	26.9	66.0	23	42	1.0	1.0	59
India	287,383	350	3.0	5.6	31.7	28.5	39.8	1,671	2,127	0.9	0.8	3
Indonesia	87,936	490	7.1	6.5	24.1	35.7	40.2	774	1,572	0.9	2.0	10
Iran, Islamic Rep	97,600 g	1,800 g	5.0	1.7	X	X	X	31	81	0.0	0.1	2
Iraq	35,000 g	1,940 g	X	X	X	X	X	29	113	X	X	4
Israel	44,131	9,750	5.6	3.6	X	X	X	1,145	1,211	4.3	2.9	260
Japan	2,920,310	23,730	5.3	4.1	2.6	41.2	56.2	(3,701)	(8,475)	(0.3)	(0.3)	(73)
Jordan	5,291	1,730	X	X	5.9	28.0	66.1	758	426	X	8.1	72
Korea, Dem People's Rep	28,000 g	1,240 g	X	X	X	X	X	43	88	X	X	5
Korea, Rep	186,467	4,400	9.6	8.1	10.2	44.0	45.8	2	(20)	0.0	(0.0)	(1)
Kuwait	33,082	16,380	5.3	(0.8)	1.0	55.6	43.4	5	4	0.0	0.0	2
Lao People's Dem Rep	693	170	X	X	X	X	X	109	209	X	30.7	63
Lebanon	X	X	X	X	X	X	X	130	120	X	X	44
Malaysia	37,005	2,130	7.5	5.7	X	X	X	213	202	0.7	0.6	8
Mongolia	X	X	X	X	X	X	X	611	760	23.8	21.8	354
Myanmar	X	X	4.5	2.3	X	X	X	310	334	5.1	2.6	5
Nepal	3,206	170	2.6	4.0	58.7	15.0	26.4	201	422	8.1	14.1	27
Oman	7,756	5,220	7.4	9.2	3.0	43.0	57.0	90	12	1.2	0.2	12
Pakistan	40,134	370	4.7	6.8	26.6	23.9	49.5	839	1,150	2.8	3.1	10
Philippines	34,427	700	6.3	1.8	23.5	33.3	43.3	387	823	1.1	2.1	14
Qatar	4,077 d	9,920 d	X	(0.4)	X	X	X	(55)	(1)	(0.7)	(0.0)	(0)
Saudi Arabia	89,986	6,230	13.3	0.5	7.6	42.8	49.6	(3,390)	(2,017)	(2.7)	(2.4)	(80)
Singapore	28,058	10,450	9.0	7.2	0.3	37.1	62.6	25	47	0.1	0.2	35
Sri Lanka	7,268	430	4.4	4.0	26.0	26.8	47.2	452	549	8.6	8.0	32
Syrian Arab Rep	12,812 c	1,100 c	8.5	2.4	38.3	16.0	45.6	874	392	5.1	3.5	14
Thailand	64,437	1,170	7.0	7.3	16.9	35.1	48.0	433	591	1.1	1.0	13
Turkey	74,731	1,360	5.7	4.3	16.5	35.6	47.9	420	264	0.8	0.4	3
United Arab Emirates	28,449	18,430	X	(0.4)	1.7	55.4	42.9	(277)	26	(0.9)	0.1	(4)
Viet Nam	14,200 g	215 g	X	X	X	X	X	1,279	1,899	X	6.5	26
Yemen (Arab Rep)	7,203	640	X	X	28.0	17.0	55.0	360	469	X	4.5	33
(People's Dem Rep)	1,200 h	495 h	X	X	16.0	23.0	61.0	203	X	17.7	X	X
EUROPE												
Albania	3,800 g	1,200 g	X	X	X	X	X	0	5	X	X	3
Austria	117,341	17,360	3.9	2.1	3.2	37.0	59.8	(192)	(262)	(0.3)	(0.2)	(37)
Belgium	162,026	16,390	X	X	2.0	30.8	67.2	(473)	(662)	(0.6)	(0.4)	(70)
Bulgaria	20,860	2,320	X	X	X	X	X	X	X	X	X	X
Czechoslovakia	123,200 g	7,878 g	X	X	X	X	X	X	X	X	X	X
Denmark	105,263	20,510	2.3	1.4	4.9	28.9	66.3	(420)	(906)	(0.8)	(0.9)	(183)
Finland	109,705	22,060	3.7	3.6	6.5	35.4	58.1	(158)	(582)	(0.3)	(0.6)	(142)
France	1,000,866	17,830	3.4	2.1	3.3	29.3	67.3	(3,879)	(6,947)	(0.7)	(0.7)	(133)
Germany (Fed Rep)	1,272,959	20,750	3.1	1.9	1.5	40.1	58.4	(3,037)	(4,690)	(0.5)	(0.4)	(80)
(Dem Rep)	159,500 g	9,679 g	X	X	X	X	X	X	X	X	X	X
Greece	53,626	5,340	5.3	1.2	16.2	29.2	54.6	12	34	0.0	0.1	3
Hungary	27,078	2,560	X	1.1	14.4	36.9	48.7	X	X	X	X	X
Iceland	5,351	21,240	6.4	2.4	X	X	X	X	X	X	X	X
Ireland	30,054	8,500	4.3	1.4	9.9	37.4	52.7	(38)	(52)	(0.2)	(0.2)	(14)
Italy	871,955	15,150	3.8	2.4	3.7	33.7	62.7	(926)	(1,137)	(0.2)	(0.4)	(63)
Luxembourg	9,408	24,860	7.0	4.6	2.3	35.2	62.5	X	X	X	X	X
Malta	2,041	5,820	10.7	3.7	3.9	40.5	55.6	27	(3)	2.3	(0.2)	(15)
Netherlands	237,415	16,010	3.3	1.5	4.0	30.7	65.3	(1,312)	(2,140)	(1.0)	(1.0)	(141)
Norway	72,028	21,850	4.2	3.5	3.0	34.0	63.0	(561)	(931)	(1.0)	(1.1)	(217)
Poland	66,974	1,760	X	X	X	X	X	X	X	X	X	X
Portugal	44,058	4,260	4.9	2.9	8.7	37.1	54.2	64	83	0.3	0.5	8
Romania	79,800 g	3,445 g	X	1.6	X	X	X	X	X	X	X	X
Spain	358,352	9,150	3.8	2.8	6.2	36.8	57.0	(149)	(217)	(0.1)	(0.1)	(6)
Sweden	184,230	21,710	2.4	1.8	3.3	34.8	61.9	(827)	(1,568)	(0.9)	(0.9)	(212)
Switzerland	197,984	30,270	6.8	2.4	X	X	X	(286)	(574)	(0.3)	(0.3)	(84)
United Kingdom	834,166	14,570	2.8	2.0	1.8	37.9	60.3	(1,613)	(2,368)	(0.3)	(0.3)	(45)
Yugoslavia	59,080	2,490	6.1	0.3	13.8	49.4	36.8	(1)	41	(0.0)	0.1	2
U.S.S.R.	2,659,500 g	9,211 g	X	X	X	X	X	(2,674)	(4,193)	X	X	(14)
OCEANIA												
Australia	242,131	14,440	3.5	3.0	4.2	31.5	64.3	(801)	(916)	(0.5)	(0.4)	(61)
Fiji	1,218	1,640	6.8	0.7	23.7	20.9	55.4	33	44	2.9	4.0	58
New Zealand	39,437	11,800	1.6	1.8	8.4	28.0	63.6	(60)	(93)	(0.3)	(0.2)	(26)
Papua New Guinea	3,444	900	3.7	1.2	28.4	30.6	41.0	322	347	13.5	10.6	89
Solomon Islands	181	570	X	4.9	X	X	X	25	55	18.1	33.3	158

Sources: The World Bank; Organisation for Economic Co-operation and Development; and U.S. Central Intelligence Agency.
Notes: a. Numbers in italics are from earlier years. b. For ODA, flows to recipients are shown as positive numbers; flows from donors as negative numbers (in parentheses).
c. 1988 World Bank estimate. d. 1986 Central Intelligence Agency estimate. e. 1987 World Bank estimate. f. 1987 Central Intelligence Agency estimate.
g. 1989 Central Intelligence Agency estimate. h. 1988 Central Intelligence Agency estimate. ODA data for the Yemens is combined for 1989.
0 = zero or less than half of the unit of measure; X = not available; negative numbers are shown in parentheses.
For additional information, see Sources and Technical Notes.

Table 15.2 External Debt Indicators 1979–89

	Total External Debt (million $US)			Disbursed Long-Term Public Debt (million $US)			Long-Term Public Debt as a Percentage of GNP			Debt Service as a Percentage of: Exports of Goods and Services			Current Borrowing			Current Borrowing Per Capita ($US)
	1979	1984	1989	1979	1984	1989	1979	1984	1989	1979	1984	1989	1979	1984	1989	1989
107 COUNTRIES	450,435	818,269	1,143,657	290,846	554,363	899,345										24.05
AFRICA	93,010	148,698	246,516	72,886	114,515	204,243										34.43
Algeria	18,519	15,944	26,067	16,586	14,185	23,609	52	28	52	30	38	71	69	123	128	230.67
Benin	396	674	1,177	292	576	1,046	30	61	64	3	20	8	4	121	16	34.65
Botswana	128	261	513	111	256	509	19	25	36	2	4	4	60	42	107	52.92
Burkina Faso	295	429	756	246	388	685	16	30	27	5	12	15	13	40	39	11.35
Burundi	136	344	867	93	316	810	12	32	77	4	23	33	8	29	38	18.57
Cameroon	2,117	2,722	4,743	1,652	1,700	3,708	31	23	33	10	16	19	29	99	50	63.51
Cape Verde	19	75	130	18	75	126	18	58	45	X	X	X	7	32	62	23.55
Central African Rep	150	265	716	116	216	642	16	34	59	2	16	14	29	60	46	22.38
Chad	237	158	368	207	147	317	30	23	32	4	5	5	15	72	13	16.58
Comoros	40	104	176	39	101	162	42	95	82	X	27	9	2	12	67	11.35
Congo	1,045	2,049	4,316	824	1,845	3,535	75	93	176	13	27	27	37	79	238	60.88
Cote d'Ivoire	4,755	8,107	15,412	3,680	4,842	8,155	45	79	96	20	41	41	60	84	116	99.55
Djibouti	26	86	180	21	62	133	X	18	33	X	4	X	X	15	113	32.12
Egypt	16,041	34,864	48,799	11,878	28,455	39,751	70	100	130	20	32	29	42	80	139	42.08
Equatorial Guinea	41	116	228	37	80	204	X	X	164	X	47	19	58	1,122	32	45.95
Ethiopia	729	1,524	3,013	591	1,358	2,876	15	28	48	6	20	39	17	49	94	6.00
Gabon	1,722	920	3,175	1,461	669	2,478	55	22	85	16	13	12	85	113	167	120.81
Gambia, The	81	230	342	48	152	292	21	103	148	6	11	11	20	79	48	44.64
Ghana	1,273	1,898	3,078	955	1,113	2,279	24	26	44	9	23	49	47	42	71	42.93
Guinea	1,138	1,226	2,176	992	1,104	1,967	X	X	77	25	X	15	68	137	40	50.28
Guinea-Bissau	70	240	458	65	186	427	55	135	256	X	33	45	12	26	29	42.19
Kenya	2,887	3,689	5,690	1,833	2,467	4,001	31	41	50	20	37	33	46	106	109	25.28
Lesotho	52	136	324	47	128	312	9	20	37	1	5	5	11	76	38	33.72
Liberia	595	1,076	1,761	452	774	1,091	43	79	X	14	13	X	34	47	375	0.48
Madagascar	789	2,160	3,607	598	1,839	3,345	17	66	143	8	23	52	12	59	124	17.15
Malawi	661	876	1,394	496	709	1,242	49	62	80	17	30	28	30	70	68	16.92
Mali	572	1,244	2,157	518	1,092	2,055	35	105	100	7	13	19	17	22	35	23.08
Mauritania	718	1,338	2,010	622	1,164	1,777	104	170	188	33	20	20	73	58	96	55.69
Mauritius	373	550	832	219	337	631	18	34	31	5	26	10	22	111	144	93.77
Morocco	8,495	14,027	20,851	7,354	11,642	19,507	48	96	90	35	34	41	63	73	165	50.58
Mozambique	X	X	4,737	X	X	3,885	X	X	389	X	X	24	X	X	30	13.32
Niger	629	956	1,578	256	674	1,127	13	47	57	14	27	33	33	89	68	23.95
Nigeria	6,259	18,537	32,832	3,267	11,393	31,668	4	12	115	2	34	21	27	206	118	13.40
Rwanda	156	291	652	128	244	606	12	15	28	2	7	19	13	25	43	9.81
Sao Tome and Principe	17	54	131	15	54	110	40	153	277	X	21	45	X	20	27	150.41
Senegal	1,117	2,200	4,139	814	1,688	3,508	31	77	79	18	18	29	60	68	101	51.95
Seychelles	474	71	168	13	51	133	11	35	40	0	6	12	5	46	181	198.81
Sierra Leone	369	617	1,056	267	323	512	29	30	58	21	22	X	62	87	66	1.66
Somalia	571	1,498	2,137	545	1,283	1,814	92	172	172	3	18	34	5	13	43	12.35
Sudan	4,067	8,612	12,965	3,261	6,191	8,261	35	72	53	16	18	13	15	52	41	9.66
Swaziland	181	192	281	169	171	260	40	34	40	2	6	6	14	79	155	29.30
Tanzania	2,197	3,431	4,917	1,726	2,640	4,505	39	46	170	14	24	17	25	53	55	6.61
Togo	1,019	807	1,185	907	681	946	102	100	73	9	24	19	14	129	102	25.26
Tunisia	3,399	4,096	6,899	3,007	3,705	6,085	43	48	63	15	25	25	54	80	121	117.70
Uganda	574	1,031	1,809	510	652	1,489	23	22	37	6	38	81	16	153	109	11.47
Zaire	4,838	5,150	8,843	4,136	4,160	7,571	27	61	83	11	21	21	99	137	105	14.25
Zambia	3,046	3,824	6,873	1,818	2,627	4,095	59	107	82	22	25	12	50	59	124	17.65
Zimbabwe	559	2,252	3,088	524	1,575	2,567	13	32	45	1	26	26	15	168	73	68.10
NORTH & CENTRAL AMERICA	56,425	123,276	134,382	37,891	91,836	106,908										53.18
Belize	72	97	134	34	75	126	23	41	40	X	6	8	7	83	101	96.02
Costa Rica	2,110	3,973	4,468	1,301	3,165	3,480	33	94	71	35	32	19	79	177	284	46.64
Dominican Rep	1,604	3,113	4,065	868	2,364	3,280	16	48	51	28	19	15	73	85	160	28.41
El Salvador	886	1,730	1,851	408	1,389	1,657	12	35	29	8	24	22	116	90	93	36.12
Grenada	18	50	78	13	42	68	X	42	37	5	11	X	67	102	40	65.75
Guatemala	1,040	2,353	2,601	427	1,947	2,089	6	21	26	7	22	19	45	99	159	20.34
Haiti	254	664	802	210	475	684	19	26	29	8	10	19	36	39	119	6.81
Honduras	1,182	2,284	3,350	750	1,774	2,823	36	58	61	21	23	13	64	73	95	30.76
Jamaica	1,707	3,471	4,322	1,190	2,521	3,594	52	118	111	25	32	27	71	91	158	160.79
Mexico	42,774	94,822	95,641	29,014	69,726	76,257	21	42	41	72	52	40	96	199	277	61.15
Nicaragua	1,487	5,106	9,205	1,085	4,088	7,546	73	149	511	8	18	10	33	22	11	75.64
Panama	2,604	4,369	5,800	2,072	3,185	3,575	76	74	86	16	9	0	98	114	500	0.25
St. Vincent	7	23	51	7	21	49	14	22	27	1	3	X	23	132	39	67.74
Trinidad and Tobago	681	1,222	2,012	515	1,063	1,680	12	14	46	2	8	12	30	118	159	115.77
SOUTH AMERICA	140,062	254,255	287,806	75,255	158,014	217,650										44.53
Argentina	20,950	48,857	64,745	8,600	26,700	51,429	17	37	95	23	52	36	38	633	331	41.19
Bolivia	2,551	4,317	4,359	1,888	3,372	3,605	73	139	85	33	63	31	74	255	73	54.15
Brazil	60,716	105,015	111,290	36,218	70,577	84,284	17	35	18	63	46	31	91	120	381	20.60
Chile	9,361	19,737	18,240	4,811	10,617	10,850	24	61	47	44	60	28	75	148	158	130.59
Colombia	5,869	12,039	16,887	3,384	7,734	14,001	12	21	38	14	30	49	62	79	165	69.96
Ecuador	4,525	8,305	11,311	2,602	6,557	9,421	29	70	94	45	38	36	79	128	111	91.40
Guyana	640	1,265	1,713	521	694	987	106	190	429	31	18	11	84	166	62	56.38
Paraguay	807	1,470	2,490	524	1,248	2,097	15	28	51	14	18	12	45	57	80	48.29
Peru	9,269	13,099	19,876	6,018	9,210	12,670	41	47	45	34	32	7	100	76	57	25.84
Uruguay	1,323	3,271	3,750	933	2,528	2,967	13	52	37	12	36	29	46	264	219	95.97
Venezuela	24,050	36,881	33,144	9,757	18,778	25,339	17	32	61	19	25	25	52	334	177	114.97

Table 15.2

	Total External Debt (million $US)			Disbursed Long-Term Public Debt (million $US)			Long-Term Public Debt as a Percentage of GNP			Debt Service as a Percentage of: Exports of Goods and Services			Current Borrowing			Current Borrowing Per Capita ($US)
	1979	1984	1989	1979	1984	1989	1979	1984	1989	1979	1984	1989	1979	1984	1989	1989
ASIA	**123,712**	**236,038**	**369,024**	**86,052**	**156,003**	**288,032**										**16.32**
Bangladesh	3,196	5,632	10,712	2,736	5,037	9,926	24	36	49	29	25	29	31	46	47	9.38
Bhutan	0	3	79	0	3	77	X	2	26	X	X	X	X	0	37	8.34
China	2,183	12,082	44,857	2,183	6,179	37,043	1	2	9	0	7	10	3	97	82	6.20
India	17,892	33,857	62,509	16,859	25,204	54,776	12	13	21	12	21	30	94	74	104	7.38
Indonesia	18,631	31,861	53,111	13,383	22,240	40,851	25	27	46	20	21	35	115	96	122	40.92
Jordan	1,523	3,508	7,418	1,239	2,832	6,404	X	59	148	12	21	24	44	86	53	285.80
Korea, Rep	22,885	42,099	33,111	13,766	23,833	17,351	22	27	8	15	21	11	58	104	216	91.97
Lao People's Dem Rep	255	434	949	242	422	939	X	28	151	X	10	13	31	10	9	34.80
Lebanon	271	448	520	101	188	234	X	X	X	X	X	X	17	284	236	9.16
Malaysia	4,956	18,801	18,576	3,084	13,237	14,460	15	42	40	7	14	15	73	78	197	122.80
Maldives	13	84	67	7	51	54	36	116	60	1	21	X	21	105	300	15.71
Myanmar	1,281	2,333	4,171	1,127	2,197	4,045	21	35	25	30	45	30	26	58	92	5.26
Nepal	146	470	1,359	110	430	1,290	6	16	43	3	6	17	17	21	26	13.61
Oman	660	1,633	2,974	514	1,340	2,626	15	17	34	8	5	14	89	64	114	375.84
Pakistan	8,933	12,125	18,509	7,903	9,727	14,669	41	32	37	31	33	31	72	99	73	22.07
Philippines	13,289	24,374	28,902	5,090	11,322	22,992	17	36	52	25	34	27	68	167	168	33.41
Sri Lanka	1,554	2,992	5,101	1,015	2,348	4,238	30	40	61	14	15	21	52	60	83	29.16
Syrian Arab Rep	2,336	3,463	5,202	2,022	2,838	3,934	18	18	25	13	14	22	60	91	195	20.64
Thailand	6,625	14,981	23,466	2,675	7,154	12,424	10	18	18	20	26	16	63	92	113	68.53
Turkey	15,900	21,601	41,600	11,041	16,570	34,781	16	34	45	45	33	37	29	120	149	85.67
Yemen (Arab Rep)	637	1,871	3,324	511	1,602	2,445	17	32	36	5	14	13	24	45	132	14.07
(People's Dem Rep)	546	1,387	2,505	445	1,251	2,474	60	91	194	41	46	83	28	47	59	151.26
EUROPE	**36,405**	**53,426**	**102,782**	**18,194**	**32,649**	**80,617**										**67.32**
Hungary	8,861	10,983	20,605	5,689	7,053	16,843	30	36	62	6	29	27	266	91	146	218.31
Malta	115	176	411	82	91	80	9	8	4	1	2	2	74	127	1,214	8.29
Poland	X	X	43,324	X	X	34,747	X	X	55	X	X	9	X	X	568	7.20
Portugal	7,875	14,865	18,289	5,495	10,765	14,644	27	59	33	24	43	22	63	104	101	340.25
Romania	3,583	7,758	500	3,258	6,255	0	10	16	0	1	16	13	8	525	7,485	1.12
Yugoslavia	15,970	19,644	19,651	3,670	8,485	14,303	5	19	24	32	33	19	80	259	370	42.54
OCEANIA	**821**	**2,576**	**3,147**	**567**	**1,346**	**1,895**										**117.03**
Fiji	142	413	398	110	279	286	11	25	25	4	10	12	61	123	467	27.03
Papua New Guinea	609	2,030	2,496	393	961	1,371	18	39	41	10	40	35	157	109	92	151.26
Solomon Islands	14	45	102	13	37	100	13	22	57	2	2	9	36	20	130	24.28
Tonga	X	X	45	X	X	44	X	X	43	X	X	X	X	X	250	8.16
Vanuatu	5	13	32	5	5	22	5	4	18	X	2	X	X	54	32	49.34
Western Samoa	53	75	74	46	63	72	X	65	66	18	23	15	30	45	134	30.67

Source: The World Bank.
Notes: 0 = zero or less than half of the unit of measure; X = not available.
For additional information, see Sources and Technical Notes.

Table 15.3 Central Government Expenditures

		Expenditures Total (million $US)	Expenditures Percent of GDP	Expenditures Per Capita ($US)	Defense	Education	Health	Social Security, Welfare, and Housing	Recreation, Culture, and Religion	Agriculture, Forestry, Fishing, and Hunting	Transportation and Communication
	Year										
WORLD											
AFRICA											
Algeria	1988 *	22,000	40.7	926	5	X	X	X	X	X	X
Angola	1986 *	2,700	X	301	X	X	X	X	X	X	X
Benin	1979	198	21.7	59	9	20	6	11	0	8	7
Botswana	1987	765	36.4	670	12	18	7	11	1	11	8
Burkina Faso	1987	284	15.7	34	18	14	5	X	1	5	0
Burundi	1977	118	21.5	31	11	21	5	3	3	12	10
Cameroon	1989	2,243	27.5	194	7	12	3	9	1	3	2
Cape Verde	1988 *	87	33.1	248	X	X	X	X	X	X	X
Central African Rep	1989 *	305	27.6	103	8	X	X	X	X	X	X
Chad	1988 *	85	9.4	16	X	X	X	X	X	X	X
Comoros	1986	67	43.7	164	4	22	6	X	3	14	20
Congo	1988 *	575	26.1	269	X	X	X	X	X	X	X
Cote d'Ivoire	1984	2,068	31.6	217	4	21	4	5	1	X	3
Djibouti	1986 a	137	X	374	X	X	X	X	X	X	X
Egypt	1987 a	25,844	40.0	530	19	12	2	17	7	4	4
Equatorial Guinea	1988 *	31	21.1	78	X	X	X	X	X	X	X
Ethiopia	1987 a	1,890	34.9	41	X	11 h	4 h	9 h	1 h	11 h	6 h
Gabon	1985	1,418	38.7	1,423	X	X	X	X	X	X	X
Gambia, The	1982 a	73	30.6	108	0	17	8	7	2	11	12
Ghana	1988	711	13.6	51	3	26	9	12	X	3	6
Guinea	1988 *	480	19.2	89	X	X	X	X	X	X	X
Guinea-Bissau	1987	87	72.5	95	4	5	5	17	0	20	8
Kenya	1988 a	2,356	28.6	104	12	22	6	3	4	7	3
Lesotho	1989 *	224	54.4	130	16	X	X	X	X	X	X
Liberia	1984 a	298	27.7	140	8	15	6	2	3	6	8
Libya	1986 *	11,300	54.8	2,867	20	X	X	X	X	X	X
Madagascar	1988 *	245	14.4	22	X	X	X	X	X	X	X
Malawi	1988 a	385	26.7	48	5	12	7	1	0	11	0
Mali	1988	587	29.8	73	8 h	9 h	2 h	3 h	0 h	2 h	3 h
Mauritania	1988 *	334	33.4	179	X	X	X	X	X	X	0
Mauritius	1990 a	581	26.7	541	2	15	8	18	2	7	3
Morocco	1987	5,283	28.0	226	15	17	3	7	1	5	6
Mozambique	1988 *	239	14.9	16	X	X	X	X	X	X	X
Namibia	1988 *	932	X	558	X	X	X	X	X	X	X
Niger	1988 *	510	21.3	71	4	X	X	X	X	X	X
Nigeria	1987	6,300	23.6	59	3	3 h	1	2	0	8	4
Rwanda	1988 *	522	22.7	78	X	X	X	X	X	X	X
Senegal	1984	729	30.8	117	9	15	4	7	4	7	2
Sierra Leone	1984	180	16.5	50	4	16	7	3	1	6	6
Somalia	1987 *	405	25.4	71	X	X	X	X	X	X	X
South Africa	1987 a	26,150	30.2	788	X	X	X	X	X	X	X
Sudan	1989 *	1,300	8.0	53	47	X	X	X	X	X	X
Swaziland	1989 a	172	25.4	226	6	24	9	5	1	8	13
Tanzania	1981	1,596	28.7	85	12 h	13 h	6 h	3 h	1 h	11 h	9 h
Togo	1987	390	31.3	120	11	20	5	8	3	15	7
Tunisia	1987 a	3,385	35.2	444	6	15	6	22	2	7	6
Uganda	1986	2,265	12.7	149	26	15 h	2 h	3 h	1 h	5 h	7 h
Zaire	1982 a	1,851	34.2	67	8	16	3	0	2	3	1
Zambia	1988	1,035	38.1	137	0	9	7	2	2	19	2
Zimbabwe	1988 a	2,500	46.6	270	16	22	8	4	1	11	7
NORTH & CENTRAL AMERICA											
Barbados	1988 a	533	34.0	2,094	2	16	11	27	3	3	9
Belize	1983	53	29.3	337	6	17	9	8	1	11	14
Canada	1988 f	123,198	22.2	4,748	8 h	3 h	6 h	37 h	1 h	4 h	4 h
Costa Rica	1988 a	1,131	24.5	423	2	19	25	15	1	4	6
Cuba	1989 *	13,500	X	1,283	10	X	X	X	X	X	X
Dominican Rep	1988 a	879	18.9	128	5	9	X	X	1	14	9
El Salvador	1989	664	10.3	129	28	18	7	5	1	4	8
Guatemala	1989 b	984	11.6	110	13	20	10	8	0	6	6
Haiti	1982	270	18.2	48	10	7	7	6	4	5	8
Honduras	1989 *	949	19.4	191	X	X	X	X	X	X	X
Jamaica	1984	561	32.2	246	X	X	X	X	X	X	X
Mexico	1989 c	39,535	19.8	467	2 h	12 h	2 h	10 h	0 h	3 h	2 h
Nicaragua	1988 a	575	46.9	159	X	X	X	X	X	X	X
Panama	1988 a	1,305	28.7	562	8	19	20	23	1	3	2
Trinidad and Tobago	1989	1,242	33.4	984	X	X	X	X	X	X	X
United States	1989 e	1,194,600	23.5	4,802	25	2	13	29	0	2	3
SOUTH AMERICA											
Argentina	1988 e	13,723	15.3	435	9	9	2	41	1	2	9
Bolivia	1988 c	717	14.5	104	12	21	8	12	0	1	16
Brazil	1987 d	103,413	24.1	731	4	5	10	24	0	4	4
Chile	1987 a	5,547	29.3	442	10	12	6	39	1	2	4
Colombia	1984 d	5,797	15.2	198	7	20	5	23	1	1	10
Ecuador	1988	1,368	13.3	136	4	X	X	X	X	X	X
Guyana	1981	373	65.7	487	6	10	6	3	0	17	4
Paraguay	1987 a	408	9.0	104	10	11	3	27	0	1	6
Peru	1989 c	4,754	16.6	224	X	X	X	X	X	X	X
Suriname	1986 a	519	51.7	1,267	4	18	4	7	2	4	3
Uruguay	1988	1,969	24.8	643	8	8	4	51	1	1	7
Venezuela	1986	13,014	21.5	732	6	20	10	12	1	3	5

Table 15.3

	Year		Total (million $US)	Percent of GDP	Per Capita ($US)	Defense	Education	Health	Social Security, Welfare, and Housing	Recreation, Culture, and Religion	Agriculture, Forestry, Fishing, and Hunting	Transportation and Communication
			Expenditures			**Percentage of Total Expenditures**						
ASIA												
Afghanistan	1987	*	647	X	34	X	X	X	X	X	X	X
Bahrain	1989		1,254	36.4	2,564	16	15	8	7	2	1	11
Bangladesh	1985		1,937	12.5	19	10 h	11 h	5 h	10 h	X	12 h	2 h
Bhutan	1990	a	117	41.0	82	0 h	12 h	5 h	5 h	3 h	15 h	21 h
Cambodia	X		X	X	X	X	X	X	X	X	X	X
China	X		X	X	X	X	X	X	X	X	X	X
Cyprus	1988	a	1,262	29.8	1,837	3	11	7	24	2	11	5
India	1989	e	46,202	17.6	55	17 h	3 h	2 h	X h	X h	8 h	2 h
Indonesia	1988	a	16,690	19.6	95	8	10	2	2	1	7	7
Iran, Islamic Rep	1988	b	66,495	17.5	1,292	12	19	7	17	1	3	4
Iraq	1989	*	35,000	X	1,916	X	X	X	X	X	X	X
Israel	1989	b	21,602	48.0	4,791	26 h	10 h	4 h	22 h	1 h	2 h	2 h
Japan	1988	x	471,770	16.3	3,848	X	X	X	X	X	X	X
Jordan	1988		2,164	37.0	574	26	15	4	12	2	5	6
Korea, Dem People's Rep	1989	*	15,600	X	735	X	X	X	X	X	X	X
Korea, Rep{i}	1990	c	35,409	16.7	828	26 h	20 h	2 h	12 h	1 h	8 h	1 h
Kuwait	1986	a	10,150	51.3	5,667	13	13	7	13	10	1	4
Lao People's Dem Rep	1988	*	198	X	50	X	X	X	X	X	X	X
Lebanon	1988	*	650	X	242	X	X	X	X	X	X	X
Malaysia	1989		10,843	29.0	625	9 h	0 h	0 h	5 h	X	8 h	0 h
Mongolia	1987	*	2,190	X	1,117	X	X	X	X	X	X	X
Myanmar	1989	a	1,462	13.3	36	19	14	5	15	0	21	8
Nepal	1990		625	21.8	33	6	11	5	8	0	8	13
Oman	1988	a	3,546	46.7	2,495	38	11	5	8	2	2	2
Pakistan	1986	d	7,446	23.3	75	29	3	1	9	1	1	3
Philippines	1988	b	6,109	15.6	104	13	17	4	2	1	5	10
Qatar	1988	*	3,400	X	8,395	X	X	X	X	X	X	X
Saudi Arabia	1990		38,100	X	2,557	32	X	X	X	X	X	X
Singapore	1987	a	7,362	34.5	2,817	15	14	4	11	0	X	X
Sri Lanka	1989	a	2,070	29.5	123	5	11	6	15	0	8	10
Syrian Arab Rep	1987		9,030	27.8	804	40	10	2	4	2	7	4
Thailand	1989	a	10,423	15.5	188	18	19	6	5	0	9	6
Turkey	1989		18,306	22.8	333	12	16	3	3	0	2	7
United Arab Emirates	1989		3,613	13.3	2,339	44 h	15 h	7 h	4 h	3 h	1 h	0 h
Viet Nam	1987	*	4,300	X	70	X	X	X	X	X	X	X
Yemen{i} (Arab Rep)	1990	a	1,973	29.2	170	29 h	19 h	4 h	0 h	2 h	2 h	5 h
(People's Dem Rep)	1988	*	976	X	414	X	X	X	X	X	X	X
EUROPE												
Albania	1989	*	2,300	X	719	11	X	X	X	X	X	X
Austria	1989	d	49,358	39.1	6,479	3 h	9 h	13 h	48 h	1 h	3 h	6 h
Belgium	1988	b	77,396	50.1	7,831	5 h	12 h	2 h	43 h	1 h	1 h	6 h
Bulgaria	1988	*	28,000	X	3,118	X	X	X	X	X	X	X
Czechoslovakia	1986		21,900	X	1,410	X	X	X	X	X	X	X
Denmark	1987	e	38,952	38.3	7,597	5	9	1	38	2	1	3
Finland	1988	d	31,567	30.0	6,376	5	14	11	36	2	8	8
France	1987	b	387,143	43.7	6,959	6	7	21	41	0	1	2
Germany (Fed Rep)	1987	e	339,262	30.4	5,544	9	1	18	49	0	0	4
(Dem Rep)	1986	*	123,200	X	7,411	X	X	X	X	X	X	X
Greece	1981	a	12,310	40.1	1,265	11	10	11	33	2	6	6
Hungary	1989	b	16,216	56.1	1,533	4	3	2	30	2	4	2
Iceland	1987	d	1,480	27.5	6,017	0	13	25	21	2	6	6
Ireland	1987	a	15,560	52.4	4,392	3	12	12	30	0	7	3
Italy	1988	a	387,619	46.8	6,748	4	8	11	39	1	1	7
Luxembourg	1988	a	3,139	41.3	8,380	3	0	2	49	1	2	12
Malta	1988	a	606	37.9	1,996	3	9	9	46	2	2	10
Netherlands	1989	a	120,503	53.9	8,123	5	11	12	41	1	1	3
Norway	1989	c	39,479	43.4	9,340	8	9	11	40	1	6	7
Poland	1988	c	26,612	38.7	703	X	X	X	X	X	X	X
Portugal	1987		15,409	41.9	1,503	6	10	8	27	1	X	X
Romania	1989	c	21,482	40.4	928	9	5	5	31	0	6	6
Spain	1987	c	98,304	33.6	2,532	6	5	12	37	1	2	4
Sweden	1989	d	76,222	41.3	8,969	6	9	1	56	1	1	3
Switzerland	1984	e	19,091	21.0	2,964	10	3	13	51	0	4	7
United Kingdom	1988	c	287,789	35.6	5,043	12	3	14	35	0	1	2
Yugoslavia	1989	g	3,981	5.5	168	53	0	0	6	0	4	0
U.S.S.R.	**1989**	*	**781,000**	X	**2,713**	X	X	X	X	X	X	X
OCEANIA												
Australia	1988	c	59,443	27.5	3,596	9 h	7 h	10 h	29 h	1 h	2 h	3 h
Fiji	1988		278	25.8	380	9	21	7	9	1	6	9
New Zealand	1988	b	18,352	44.7	5,575	5	13	13	34	1	2	3
Papua New Guinea	1988		1,010	28.3	271	5	15	9	3	2	7	10
Solomon Islands	1988		66	37.7	219	0 h	22 h	6 h	3 h	1 h	17 h	13 h

Sources: The International Monetary Fund and the U.S. Central Intelligence Agency.
Notes: a. The central government accounts for 95-100% of all tax revenues. b. 90-94.9%. c. 80-89.9 %. d. 70-79.9%. e. 60-69.9%. f. 50-59.9%. g. 20-49.9%.
h. Preliminary, projected, or provisional. i. Total and per capita expenditures for Korea (Rep) and Yemen (Arab Rep) are for 1989.
* = Central Intelligence Agency estimates. 0 = zero or less than half of the unit of measure; X = not available.
For additional information, see Sources and Technical Notes.

Table 15.4 World Commodity Indexes and Prices, 1975–89

Commodity Indexes (based on constant prices with 1979-81 = 100)	1975	1976	1977	1978	1979	1980	1981	1982	1983	1984	1985	1986	1987	1988	1989
33 NONFUEL COMMODITIES	101	112	123	102	105	105	91	82	89	92	81	69	63	71	70
Total Agriculture	100	116	134	108	106	104	91	81	89	94	81	71	59	63	61
Total Food	103	117	143	111	106	104	90	81	88	95	83	75	58	63	60
-Beverages	71	134	206	132	121	99	82	85	88	104	95	99	59	61	51
-Cereals	142	115	96	100	92	101	107	79	87	85	74	55	47	59	64
-Fats and Oils	104	110	112	112	114	96	92	76	92	110	76	50	53	65	59
-Other Foods	129	95	78	79	86	121	92	79	85	77	74	67	66	68	75
Nonfood Agricultural Products	89	111	103	97	102	106	92	82	95	90	75	58	65	62	62
Timber	53	70	74	68	104	110	87	88	84	99	80	75	100	98	96
Metals and Minerals	113	110	104	92	103	105	92	84	90	86	81	63	66	84	90

Commodity Prices (in constant 1980 $US per unit measure) {a}	1975	1976	1977	1978	1979	1980	1981	1982	1983	1984	1985	1986	1987	1988	1989
Cocoa (kg), New York & London	1.98	3.21	5.41	4.23	3.61	2.60	2.07	1.75	2.20	2.53	2.35	1.83	1.62	1.19	0.94
Coffee (kg), Brazil	2.94	5.17	9.70	3.97	4.26	4.58	3.85	3.20	3.26	3.48	3.49	4.50	1.90	2.02	1.66
Tea (kg), World Average	2.21	2.41	3.84	2.72	2.30	2.23	2.01	1.95	2.41	3.64	2.07	1.70	1.38	1.34	1.54
Rice (t), Thailand	578.2	399.5	388.9	456.5	363.3	433.9	480.4	295.6	286.6	265.6	225.10	185.60	186.61	226.23	243.60
Grain Sorghum (t), U.S.	178.2	165.2	126.3	116.5	118.8	128.9	125.8	109.5	133.3	124.6	107.40	72.80	58.96	73.90	80.60
Maize (t), U.S.	190.5	176.5	136.1	125.1	126.6	125.3	130.2	110.3	140.8	143.2	117.00	77.20	61.34	80.23	84.80
Wheat (t), Canada	288.7	234.1	165.4	167.5	189.0	190.8	195.4	168.0	175.5	174.3	180.70	141.60	108.19	134.74	153.00
Sugar (kg), World	0.72	0.40	0.26	0.21	0.23	0.63	0.37	0.19	0.19	0.12	0.09	0.12	0.12	0.17	0.21
Beef (kg), U.S.	2.11	2.48	2.15	2.66	3.16	2.76	2.46	2.41	2.53	2.40	2.25	1.85	1.93	1.89	1.95
Lamb (kg), New Zealand	2.27	2.42	2.36	2.70	2.60	2.89	2.73	2.40	2.00	2.02	1.92	1.90	1.75	1.81	1.77
Bananas (kg), Any Origin	0.39	0.40	0.39	0.36	0.36	0.38	0.40	0.38	0.44	0.39	0.40	0.34	0.37	0.36	0.42
Black Pepper (kg), Any Origin	3.19	3.08	3.59	2.91	2.32	1.99	1.58	1.57	1.75	2.40	3.98	4.26	4.31	X	X
Copra (t), Philippines	408.1	431.7	574.7	584.4	737.6	453.8	377.0	317.1	513.5	748.2	402.5	174.6	250.4	298.7	264.7
Coconut Oil (t), Phil. & Indonesia	626.6	656.2	826.0	848.7	1,079.5	673.8	567.1	468.6	755.6	1,216.7	615.2	261.9	358.2	424.1	393.2
Groundnut Meal (t), Any Origin	222.9	276.3	311.4	254.7	231.4	240.3	236.7	190.8	207.0	187.6	153.3	145.5	131.3	157.6	152.1
Groundnut Oil (t), Nigeria	1,364.7	1,163.3	1,217.6	1,340.6	974.5	858.8	1,037.8	590.2	735.9	1,071.3	943.7	501.8	405.2	442.8	589.5
Linseed (t), Canada	538.2	478.8	388.4	310.1	366.0	350.9	352.5	300.7	287.1	314.0	285.7	183.4	136.9	220.7	262.4
Linseed Oil (t) Any Origin	1,116.2	857.1	659.9	539.4	700.7	697.1	656.7	523.3	501.7	602.7	654.8	369.5	254.4	391.8	X
Palm Kernels (t), Nigeria	329.3	361.1	466.1	451.9	548.3	345.1	315.7	267.4	378.2	556.4	303.4	125.2	146.7	200.4	190.9
Palm Oil (t), Malaysia	691.4	638.2	757.1	745.6	716.9	583.5	567.9	449.1	519.0	768.2	522.4	226.6	277.9	328.0	266.2
Soybeans (t), U.S.	350	363	400	333	327	296	287	247	292	297	234	183	175	228	209
Soybean Oil (t), Any Origin	986	688	823	754	726	597	504	451	545	763	596	302	271	348	329
Soybean Meal (t), U.S.	247	311	329	265	267	262	251	220	246	208	164	163	164	201	187
Fish Meal (t), Peru	390	590	649	509	433	504	466	356	469	393	292	283	310	408	310
Cotton (kg), Index	1.85	2.66	2.22	1.95	1.85	2.05	1.84	1.61	1.92	1.88	1.37	0.93	1.34	1.05	1.27
Burlap (meter), U.S.	0.35	0.30	0.31	0.27	0.33	0.40	0.27	0.27	0.30	0.39	0.36	0.22	0.22	0.23	0.23
Jute (t), Bangladesh	590.8	464.1	458.4	540.0	424.8	308.0	274.6	288.4	312.8	559.3	607.8	238.2	319.2	329.9	334.7
Sisal (t), East Africa	924	736	733	609	775	765	642	598	583	615	548	453	415	413	497
Wool (kg), New Zealand	4.37	5.35	5.11	4.66	4.86	4.60	4.25	3.96	3.77	3.87	3.71	2.92	3.66	4.35	4.07
Natural Rubber (kg), New York	10.49	13.71	13.10	13.75	15.61	16.24	12.46	10.11	12.82	11.55	9.64	8.33	9.05	9.66	8.50
Logs (cubic meter), Malaysia	X	X	132.3	121.0	186.4	195.5	154.8	157.3	150.3	176.2	142.0	133.4	179.4	176.3	171.0
Plywood (sheet), Philippines	1.94	2.32	2.36	2.35	2.88	2.74	2.44	2.35	2.38	2.39	2.20	2.41	3.23	2.69	2.66
Sawnwood (cubic meter), Malaysia	265.0	263.9	220.1	255.2	371.8	365.1	312.6	304.7	315.0	323.3	288.1	234.7	223.7	230.1	320.9
Tobacco (t), India	2,416	2,215	2,386	2,099	2,336	2,300	2,338	2,432	2,324	2,097	2,034	1,688	1,499	1,466	1,441
Coal (t), U.S.	86.4	84.1	77.5	69.2	62.0	55.7	57.8	56.9	59.5	60.9	58.0	46.6	39.1	37.0	37.9
Petroleum (barrel), OPEC	16.7	18.1	17.7	15.8	19.0	29.4	33.0	34.3	30.5	30.6	29.3	12.1	13.9	10.3	12.4
Gasoline (t), Europe	191.6	216.5	188.0	198.8	367.3	358.0	352.3	326.5	293.2	271.2	266.1	128.7	138.7	119.3	146.0
Jet Fuel (t), Europe	180.3	187.8	185.0	181.6	384.1	349.3	333.7	325.3	287.4	275.7	276.1	142.3	X	X	X
Gas Oil (t), Europe	159.2	168.6	168.3	159.8	340.9	307.1	297.2	292.3	256.9	251.1	250.1	125.5	X	X	X
Fuel Oil (t), Europe	98.9	107.5	108.9	94.0	146.5	170.2	182.6	165.5	168.7	187.8	158.2	64.7	80.6	51.3	65.6
Aluminum (t), Europe	1,099	1,353	1,416	1,298	1,667	1,730	1,331	1,071	1,548	1,445	1,160	1,112	1,303	1,910	1,552
Bauxite (t), Jamaica	40.29	42.70	44.00	42.61	40.13	41.20	39.80	36.33	35.92	34.77	31.28	24.69	X	X	X
Copper (t), London	1,970	2,199	1,870	1,696	2,177	2,183	1,733	1,493	1,648	1,453	1,478	1,212	1,420	1,953	2,166
Lead (t), London	664	699	883	822	1,325	906	723	551	440	468	408	358	484	493	512
Tin (t), Malaysia	10,656	11,730	15,304	15,547	16,252	16,437	13,992	13,066	13,493	13,124	12,032	5,433	5,421	5,327	6,491
Zinc (t), New York	1,368	1,292	1,083	849	901	825	977	856	944	1,130	928	739	749	996	1,375
Iron Ore (t), Brazil	36.0	34.4	30.9	24.1	25.6	26.7	24.2	26.1	24.8	24.3	23.7	19.4	18.0	17.4	20.1
Manganese Ore (10 kg), India	2.19	2.28	2.11	1.78	1.51	1.57	1.67	1.66	1.57	1.51	1.47	1.22	1.07	1.11	1.53
Nickel (t), Canada	7,277	7,808	7,433	5,720	6,563	6,519	5,924	4,881	4,837	5,008	5,108	3,422	3,947	10,404	10,122
Steel (t), U.S.	461.9	464.2	460.9	452.1	444.4	452.8	505.4	539.5	505.3	569.1	563.2	354.8	X	X	X
Phosphate Rock (t), Morocco	106.7	56.5	43.6	36.0	36.2	46.7	49.3	42.8	38.2	40.4	35.3	30.2	25.1	27.0	31.1
Diammonium Phosphate (t), U.S.	386.9	188.4	190.0	173.7	212.0	222.2	194.0	184.5	190.0	199.3	176.2	136.0	140.3	147.5	131.4
Potassium Chloride (t), Canada	129.5	86.3	72.9	70.1	84.1	115.7	111.8	82.3	78.0	88.2	87.6	60.7	55.9	65.7	75.2
Triple Superphosphate (t), U.S.	322	143	139	122	161	180	160	139	140	138	126	107	112	119	110
Urea (t), Any Origin	315.3	175.8	182.0	179.9	189.6	222.1	214.9	160.2	140.2	140.2	180.5	142.1	94.4	94.5	101.0

Source: The World Bank.
Notes: a. Log, petroleum, and tin price series replace discontinued series for similar commodities found in previous editions.
t = metric ton; X = not available.
For additional information, see Sources and Technical Notes.

Sources and Technical Notes

Table 15.1 Gross National Product and Official Development Assistance, 1969–89

Sources: Gross national product (GNP), GNP per capita, average annual change in real GNP, distribution of gross domestic production: The World Bank, unpublished data (The World Bank, Washington, D.C., May 1991). GNP for certain centrally managed economies: U.S. Central Intelligence Agency (CIA), *The World Factbook 1990* (CIA, Washington, D.C., 1990). Official development assistance (ODA): Organisation for Economic Co-operation and Development (OECD), *Development Co-operation* (OECD, Paris, 1984, 1986, 1987, 1988, 1989, 1990); OECD, *Geographical Distribution of Financial Flows to Developing Countries 1981/84, 1983/86, 1984/87,* and *1986/89* (OECD, Paris, 1986, 1988, 1989, 1991).

Gross national product (GNP) is the sum of two components: the gross domestic product (GDP) and net factor income from abroad. GDP is the final output of goods and services produced by the domestic economy, including net exports of goods and nonfactor services. Net factor income from abroad is income in the form of overseas workers' remittances, interest on loans, profits, and other factor payments that residents receive from abroad less payments made for factor services (labor and capital). Most countries estimate GDP by the production method. This method sums the final outputs of the various sectors of the economy (agriculture, manufacturing, government services, and so on) from which the value of the inputs to production have been subtracted.

GNP is calculated as in the World Bank's *World Bank Atlas*. GNP in domestic currency was converted to U.S. dollars using a three-year average exchange rate, adjusted for domestic and U.S. inflation. However, the strong appreciation of the U.S. dollar through 1985 affected the conversion factor and may mask real growth in GNP and per capita GNP in some countries. Alternative measures of GNP exist. Of special interest are the United Nations' International Comparison Program (ICP) estimates of GDP (in U.S. dollars) using purchasing-power parity for a basket of common goods and services instead of exchange rates. These ICP GDP estimates tend to raise GNP estimates for the poorest countries and lower them slightly for most developed countries.

Traditional measures of the health of an economy, although counting the income generated by the exploitation of natural resources, do not take into account their depletion or destruction. Many believe that this oversight leads to an overestimation of economic growth and its sustainability and that these factors should be included in any calculation of GDP. Alternative measures have been calculated for a few countries. In Figures 15.1 and 15.2, an adjusted net domestic product (adjusted NDP) was esti-

Figure 15.1 Gross Domestic Product and Net Domestic Product for Indonesia, 1971–84

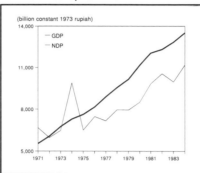

Source: Robert Repetto, William Magrath, Michael Wells, *et al., Wasting Assets: Natural Resources in the National Income Accounts* (World Resources Institute, Washington, D.C., 1989), p. 7.

Figure 15.2 Gross Domestic Product and Net Domestic Product for Costa Rica, 1970–89

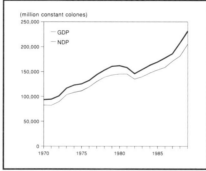

Source: R. Solórzano, R. de Camio, R. Woodward, *et al., Accounts Overdue: Natural Resource Depreciation in Costa Rica* (Tropical Science Centers, San José, Costa Rica and World Resources Institute, Washington, D.C., forthcoming), p. 16.

mated for the time series by deducting a calculated amount for natural resource depreciation from NDP (which in turn was derived from GDP) for Indonesia and Costa Rica. The adjusted NDP for Costa Rica appears to parallel GDP, whereas, in the case of Indonesia, the two lines appear to diverge.

In many centrally managed economies, such as the U.S.S.R., the net material product (NMP) is a primary economic statistic instead of GNP. The estimation of GNP in U.S. dollars for such economies is difficult and is an ongoing research project of the World Bank. Estimates of GNP for centrally managed economies are included as an attempt to show the relative magnitudes of those important economies. These GNP estimates, however, are not directly comparable to estimates made by the World Bank for other economies. Few organizations are willing to publish estimates of GNP for these countries because of these difficulties.

The *average annual change in real GNP* was obtained by using World Bank data to cal-

culate a geometric growth rate over the appropriate time period.

Distribution of gross domestic product does not always add to 100 percent because of rounding.

Net *average annual official development assistance (ODA)* is the net amount of disbursed grants and concessional loans given or received by a country. Grants include gifts in money, goods, or services, for which no repayment is required. A concessional loan has a grant element of 25 percent or more. The grant element is the amount by which the face value of the loan exceeds its present market value because of below-market interest rates, favorable maturity schedules, and repayment grace periods. Nonconcessional loans are not a component of ODA.

ODA contributions are shown as negative numbers (in parentheses); receipts are shown as positive numbers. Data for donor countries include contributions directly to developing countries and through multilateral institutions. The GNP data used to calculate *ODA as a percentage of GNP* were derived by using single-year exchange rates, not the three-year exchange rates discussed previously, since the three-year averages shown here already smooth variations in exchange rates.

Sources of ODA include the development assistance agencies of OECD and OPEC members as well as other countries. Grants and concessional loans to and from multilateral development agencies are also included in contributions and receipts.

OECD gathers ODA data through questionnaires and reports from countries and multilateral agencies. Only limited data are available on ODA flows among developing countries and from the previous members of the Council for Mutual Economic Assistance (CMEA), an association of Central European countries and the U.S.S.R. Thus, data in this table on CMEA's ODA donations are restricted to those of the U.S.S.R., which typically comprise 85–90 percent of the total. Data on net ODA from the U.S.S.R. are available for countries receiving the largest amounts. These data have been added to their net ODA receipts.

Table 15.2 External Debt Indicators, 1979–89

Source: The World Bank, *World Debt Tables 1990–91* (The World Bank, Washington, D.C., May 1990).

The World Bank operates the Debtor Reporting System (DRS), which compiles reports supplied by 107 of the Bank's member countries. Countries submit detailed reports on the annual status, transactions, and terms of the long-term external debt of public agencies and of publicly guaranteed private debt. Additional data are drawn from the World Bank, the International Monetary Fund (IMF), regional development banks, government lending agencies, and the Creditor Reporting System (CRS).

The CRS is operated by the Organisation for Economic Co-operation and Development (OECD) to compile reports from the members of its Development Assistance Committee.

Total external debt includes long-term debt, use of IMF credit, and short-term debt. Long-term debt is an obligation with a maturity of at least one year that is owed to nonresidents and is repayable in foreign currency, goods, or services. Long-term debt is divided into long-term public debt and long-term publicly guaranteed private debt. Short-term debt is public or publicly guaranteed private debt that has a maturity of one year or less. This class of debt is especially difficult for countries to monitor. Only a few countries supply these data through the DRS; the World Bank supplements these data with creditor-country reports, information from international clearinghouse banks, and other sources to derive rough estimates of short-term debt. Use of IMF credit refers to all drawings on the Fund's General Resources Account. Use of IMF credit is converted to dollars by applying the average Special Drawing Right exchange rate in effect for the year being calculated.

The World Bank reports preliminary or estimated 1989 long-term public debt data for 44 countries and shows the data as reported for the other 63 countries.

Private debt is an external obligation of a private debtor that is not guaranteed by a public entity. Data for this class of debt are less extensive than those for public debt; many countries do not report these data through the DRS. Data are currently available from 20 countries, and World Bank estimates are available for 7 others. These data are included in the total when available.

Disbursed long-term public debt is outstanding public and publicly guaranteed long-term debt. Public debt is an obligation of a national or subnational government or its agencies and autonomous bodies. Publicly guaranteed debt is an external obligation of a private debtor that is guaranteed for repayment by a public entity.

Long-term public debt as a percentage of GNP is calculated using the disbursed long-term public debt described previously. GNP is defined in the Technical Note for Table 15.1. The GNP data used to derive debt-to-GNP ratios were converted from local currencies at a single-year exchange rate, rather than the three-year average exchange rate used to determine total GNP in Table 15.1. Total *debt service* comprises actual interest payments and repayments of principal made on the disbursed long-term public debt in foreign currencies, goods, and services in the year specified. *Exports of goods and services* are the total value of goods and all services sold to the rest of the world. *Current borrowing* is the total long-term debt disbursed during the specified year. *Current borrowing per capita* was calculated using the 1989 mid-year population.

Debt data are reported to the World Bank in the units of currency in which they are payable. The World Bank converts these data to U.S. dollar figures, using the IMF par values, central rates, or the current market rates, where appropriate. Debt service data are converted to U.S. dollar figures at the average exchange rate for the given year. Comparability of data among countries and years is limited by variations in methods, definitions, and comprehensiveness of data collection and reporting. Refer to the World Bank's *World Debt Tables* for details.

Table 15.3 Central Government Expenditures

Sources: For International Monetary Fund (IMF) members: International Monetary Fund, *Government Finance Statistics Yearbook*, Vol. XIV (International Monetary Fund, Washington, D.C., 1990). For non-IMF members: U.S. Central Intelligence Agency (CIA), *The World Factbook 1990* (CIA, Washington, D.C., 1990).

The IMF staff discusses government financial information with correspondents in each government or central bank and compiles this information as available. In general, these data are shown for consolidated central government operations. There is great variability in the timeliness of data and so the *year* represented by the data is shown. There is also great variability in the extent to which central government expenditures fund all government operations. Footnote "a" shows the percentage of total tax revenue collected by the central government as a surrogate for the percentage of all expenditures made by the central government. Therefore, care should be taken in making comparisons between countries. For example, much of the expenditures of the government of the United States are made at the state and local levels and cannot be easily compared to those of a country where all expenditures are made by the central government.

Calculations of total expenditures were converted from local currency using IMF exchange rate data. *Expenditures* as a *percent of gross domestic product* (GDP) and *per capita* used IMF GDP and population estimates. Expenditures as a percentage of GDP for Burundi, Cameroon, Cape Verde, the Central African Republic, Ecuador, Equatorial Guinea, Gabon, Honduras, Libya, Myanmar, Peru, Somalia, and South Africa were derived from World Bank GDP data. WRI calculated the share of total expenditures for Burundi, France, Germany (Fed Rep), Guinea-Bissau, Italy, New Zealand, Paraguay, Sierra Leone, Tunisia, and Zimbabwe. The CIA estimated only defense spending, and its data were used only when IMF data were not available.

Expenditures are shown for only seven selected functional categories of government affairs, and therefore these seven do not

add to 100 percent. *Defense* includes military and civil defense, military aid, and relevant applied research. *Education* includes all levels from preprimary to tertiary. *Health* includes hospitals, clinics, practitioners, public health, medications and equipment, and relevant applied research. *Social security, welfare, and housing* includes social security, welfare, housing and community development, water and sanitation (including pollution abatement), and street lighting. *Recreation, culture, and religion* includes funding for those activities. *Agriculture, forestry, fishing, and hunting* includes funding for those activities as well as relevant applied research. *Transportation and communication* includes road, water, rail, and air transport, and communications. Within each category, relevant affairs and services not explicitly named are also included.

Table 15.4 World Commodity Indexes and Prices, 1975—89

Source: The World Bank, unpublished data (The World Bank, Washington, D.C., August 1991).

Price data are compiled from major international market places for standard grades of each commodity. For example, the gasoline series refers to 91/92-octane regular gasoline, in barges, f.o.b. (free on board) Rotterdam.

The 1980 U.S. constant dollar figures were derived by converting current average monthly prices in local currencies to U.S. dollars using the monthly average exchange rate. These monthly average U.S. dollar figures were then averaged to produce an annual average dollar figure, which was adjusted to 1980 constant dollars using the Manufacturing Unit Value (MUV) index. The MUV index is a composite price index of all manufactured goods traded internationally.

The aggregate price indexes have the following components:

1. *33 Nonfuel commodities*: individual items listed under items 4–10.
2. *Total agriculture*: total food and nonfood agricultural products.
3. *Total food*: beverages, cereals, fats and oils, other foods.
4. *Beverages*: coffee, cocoa, tea.
5. *Cereals*: maize, rice, wheat, grain sorghum.
6. *Fats and oils*: palm oil, coconut oil, groundnut oil, soybeans, copra, groundnut meal, soybean meal.
7. *Other food*: sugar, beef, bananas, oranges.
8. *Nonfood agricultural products*: cotton, jute, rubber, tobacco.
9. *Timber*: logs.
10. *Metals and minerals*: copper, tin, nickel, bauxite, aluminum, iron ore, manganese ore, lead, zinc, phosphate rock.

The commodity prices reported here are specific to the markets named. The commodities themselves are often defined more specifically than suggested by the table (e.g., Meranti logs Sabah SQ best quality; imported-frozen-boneless, 90-percent-visible-lean beef; Santos 4 coffee).

16. Population and Human Development

The world's population now exceeds 5.3 billion and is expected to reach 8.5 billion by 2025. Over the next 35 years, our lands, forests, and other natural resources will come under increasing pressure with the addition of 3 billion people needing food, housing, education, and jobs. This chapter contains data on population size, distribution, and growth rate, as well as health, literacy, nutrition, and contraceptive use.

The majority of people, 3.1 billion, live in Asia. That will continue to be true in 2025, according to United Nations' population projections presented in Table 16.1. Asia's share of the world's population is expected to decline slightly, however, from its current level of 59 percent of the global total. The greatest proportional increase will occur in Africa, where the population is projected to nearly triple, from a 1990 level of 642 million to 1.6 billion in 2025. In contrast, Europe is expected to show the smallest rate of population increase of all regions during this time period, growing just 3.4 percent over 1990 levels. Table 16.1 also contains data on the average annual increment to the population and the average annual growth of the labor force.

Table 16.2 shows that fertility rates have fallen for all regions over the past 20 years. But despite these declining rates, total population will continue to grow for decades to come because more people are entering their reproductive years than ever before. Average global fertility rates are expected to drop 27 percent by 1995 from 4.5 children born to a woman in her lifetime during the 1970–75 period to 3.3 children during 1990–95. All regions of the world should be at or below the 3.3 level, except Africa, where the fertility rate (6.0) will be 82 percent higher than the projected global average. Global life expectancy at birth, also shown in Table 16.2, should increase an average of seven years over this two-decade period.

Death rates of infants and children under age 5 have declined over the past two decades, as shown in Table 16.3. Under-five mortality rates have dropped in all countries for which data were available, although rates remain high in much of the world. Fifty-three countries will have levels at or exceeding 100 under-five mortality deaths per 1,000 live births during 1990–95. The European average is 13 per 1,000.

Table 16.3 also presents information on the quantity and quality of food available in each country: average calories available as a percent of need and per capita total protein consumption. Although these data do not show differential access to food within a country, they suggest that 20 countries provide less than 90 percent of their population's caloric requirement. The maldistribution of calories, and of protein, can lead to high rates of malnutrition (wasting and stunting) even when national numbers suggest that sufficient food is available. For example, although the Senegalese have food available to meet 100 percent of their daily caloric requirement, 8 percent of their children ages 12–23 months display symptoms of wasting and 28 percent ages 24–59 months are stunted.

The drop in child and infant mortality rates, and the improvement in life expectancy in general, are due to improved health and living conditions. In Tables 16.4 and 16.5, data are presented on access to health care, safe drinking water and sanitation services, numbers of trained medical personnel and percent of fully immunized 1-year-olds. Trend data are only available on safe water and sanitation and are limited to the 1980s. The World Health Organization's Expanded Program on Immunization, which seeks to protect children against six major diseases, has brought about the biggest advance in global health care of the past decade. In 1990, immunization levels of 1-year-olds averaged 80 percent or greater for countries outside North America and Europe.

Table 16.5 shows that although literacy levels increased between 1970 and 1990 in all but one country, literacy rates for women are still below 50 percent in 45 of the countries for which data are available. In contrast, literacy rates for men are below 50 percent in only 17 countries. Literacy levels are lower for women than for men in the majority of countries of the world. Table 16.5 also presents data on primary and postsecondary level educational attainment.

Although a country's investment in human resources may encourage individuals to lower fertility rates, people are unlikely to do so without access to contraception. Table 16.6 provides data on current levels of contraceptive use as well as levels of affordable access to contraceptives. All European countries reported that more than 50 percent of married couples use contraception, a level reached by less than half the Asian and American countries reporting. In contrast, only one country in Africa (Mauritius) reported that more than 50 percent of its couples used contraception.

Table 16.1 Size and Growth of Population and Labor Force,

	Population (millions)				Average Annual Population Change (percent)			Average Annual Increment to the Population (thousands)			Average Annual Growth of the Labor Force [a] (percent)		
	1950	1990	1995	2025	1975-80	1985-90	1995-2000	1975-80	1985-90	1995-2000	1975-80	1985-90	1995-2000
WORLD	2,516.44	5,292.20	5,770.29	8,504.22	1.73	1.74	1.63	73,803	88,152	98,103	2.1	1.8	1.5
AFRICA	221.98	642.11	746.82	1,596.86	2.88	2.99	2.98	12,787	17,846	23,953	2.6	2.6	2.8
Algeria	8.75	24.96	28.70	51.95	3.14	2.72	2.73	544	634	840	3.2	3.8	3.6
Angola	4.13	10.02	11.53	24.73	3.39	2.70	2.85	241	253	353	2.9	1.9	2.2
Benin	2.05	4.63	5.42	12.59	2.63	3.00	3.23	85	129	190	2.2	2.2	2.7
Botswana	0.39	1.30	1.55	3.40	3.54	3.71	3.24	29	44	55	2.9	3.2	3.5
Burkina Faso	3.65	9.00	10.40	23.71	2.30	2.66	3.02	151	224	339	1.9	2.1	2.3
Burundi	2.46	5.47	6.36	12.98	2.32	2.91	2.91	90	148	199	1.3	2.3	2.5
Cameroon	4.47	11.83	14.04	36.55	2.81	3.27	3.48	227	357	533	1.6	2.0	2.4
Cape Verde	0.15	0.37	0.44	0.92	0.00	2.65	3.21	2	9	15	1.0	3.1	2.4
Central African Rep	1.31	3.04	3.51	7.95	2.41	2.77	2.98	53	79	113	1.3	1.6	1.9
Chad	2.66	5.68	6.45	13.25	2.10	2.47	2.58	89	132	178	1.8	1.9	2.2
Comoros	0.17	0.55	0.66	1.70	4.06	3.45	3.63	14	17	26	3.1	2.5	2.7
Congo	0.81	2.27	2.68	6.57	2.85	3.16	3.35	44	66	98	2.2	1.9	2.5
Cote d'Ivoire	2.78	12.00	14.54	39.33	3.86	3.78	3.83	288	413	613	2.4	2.6	2.6
Djibouti	0.06	0.41	0.47	1.09	4.49	2.88	3.05	12	11	16	X	X	X
Egypt	20.33	52.43	58.39	90.36	2.38	2.39	1.90	917	1,183	1,164	2.4	2.6	2.8
Equatorial Guinea	0.23	0.35	0.40	0.83	(0.71)	2.42	2.60	(1)	8	11	1.2	1.4	2.0
Ethiopia	19.57	49.24	57.14	126.62	2.44	2.67	2.99	888	1,231	1,845	2.0	2.0	2.2
Gabon	0.47	1.17	1.38	2.88	4.70	3.47	3.09	34	37	46	0.9	0.7	1.2
Gambia, The	0.29	0.86	0.98	1.86	3.15	2.89	2.58	19	23	27	1.9	1.4	1.7
Ghana	4.90	15.03	17.61	35.44	1.76	3.15	3.10	181	438	591	2.7	2.8	3.1
Guinea	2.55	5.76	6.70	15.27	1.45	2.86	3.12	62	154	226	1.9	1.7	2.0
Guinea-Bissau	0.51	0.96	1.07	1.92	4.74	1.99	2.20	34	18	25	4.5	1.4	1.6
Kenya	6.27	24.03	28.98	79.11	3.82	3.58	3.81	578	787	1,217	3.7	3.6	3.7
Lesotho	0.73	1.77	2.05	4.43	2.41	2.85	2.87	30	47	63	2.1	2.1	2.2
Liberia	0.82	2.58	3.03	7.25	3.07	3.16	3.30	53	75	109	2.7	2.4	2.8
Libya	1.03	4.55	5.45	12.84	4.37	3.65	3.54	119	152	211	3.7	3.5	3.4
Madagascar	4.23	12.00	14.11	34.01	2.91	3.18	3.28	238	353	503	2.2	2.1	2.4
Malawi	2.88	8.75	10.49	24.73	3.29	3.52	3.43	188	283	393	2.6	2.6	2.7
Mali	3.52	9.21	10.80	24.77	2.13	3.04	3.22	139	260	377	1.9	2.6	2.9
Mauritania	0.83	2.02	2.34	5.12	2.46	2.73	2.92	36	52	73	1.8	2.9	3.3
Mauritius	0.49	1.08	1.14	1.42	1.59	1.17	1.01	15	12	12	3.4	2.4	1.9
Morocco	8.95	25.06	28.30	45.65	2.27	2.58	2.18	415	607	652	4.1	3.2	2.9
Mozambique	6.20	15.66	17.92	35.42	2.83	2.65	2.68	319	389	514	4.5	1.9	2.1
Namibia	0.67	1.78	2.08	4.70	2.70	3.19	3.17	33	53	71	1.8	2.4	2.9
Niger	2.40	7.73	9.10	21.48	3.15	3.14	3.33	163	225	330	2.0	2.5	2.7
Nigeria	32.94	108.54	127.69	280.89	3.35	3.30	3.17	2,417	3,305	4,385	3.2	2.7	3.0
Rwanda	2.12	7.24	8.60	18.85	3.27	3.41	3.41	156	227	320	3.3	2.8	3.1
Senegal	2.50	7.33	8.42	16.99	2.84	2.78	2.86	146	190	259	3.3	2.0	2.1
Sierra Leone	1.94	4.15	4.74	10.05	2.15	2.49	2.75	66	97	139	1.0	1.2	1.6
Somalia	2.42	7.50	8.44	18.70	5.03	3.26	2.85	238	225	259	3.6	1.4	2.1
South Africa	13.68	35.28	39.35	65.36	2.22	2.22	2.08	594	743	864	1.3	2.8	2.8
Sudan	9.19	25.20	29.13	59.61	3.08	2.88	2.87	534	676	899	2.7	2.9	3.2
Swaziland	0.26	0.79	0.94	2.25	3.12	3.44	3.47	16	25	36	2.2	2.3	2.6
Tanzania	7.89	27.32	32.97	84.92	3.42	3.66	3.68	593	914	1,334	2.9	2.9	3.1
Togo	1.33	3.53	4.14	9.84	2.70	3.07	3.22	66	101	145	2.2	2.3	2.6
Tunisia	3.53	8.18	9.08	13.63	2.58	2.38	1.79	154	184	170	3.5	3.1	2.6
Uganda	4.76	18.79	22.67	53.14	3.20	3.67	3.47	387	630	858	2.9	2.9	3.1
Zaire	12.18	35.57	41.81	99.37	2.86	3.14	3.25	700	1,034	1,475	1.9	2.3	2.6
Zambia	2.44	8.45	10.22	26.26	3.40	3.75	3.65	179	289	409	2.8	3.3	3.6
Zimbabwe	2.73	9.71	11.34	22.62	2.97	3.16	2.92	196	283	357	3.0	2.8	3.1
NORTH & CENTRAL AMERICA	220.36	427.23	453.25	595.62	1.47	1.29	1.09	5,267	5,290	5,028	2.7	1.4	1.4
Barbados	0.21	0.26	0.26	0.30	0.28	0.16	0.45	1	0	1	1.9	1.5	1.4
Belize	0.07	0.19	0.21	0.31	2.50	2.39	1.92	3	4	4	X	X	X
Canada	13.74	26.52	27.56	31.92	1.13	0.88	0.66	263	228	186	3.1	1.0	0.8
Costa Rica	0.86	3.02	3.37	5.25	2.98	2.64	1.90	63	75	67	4.0	2.5	2.4
Cuba	5.85	10.61	11.09	12.99	0.79	1.03	0.73	75	106	83	3.2	2.3	0.9
Dominican Rep	2.35	7.17	7.92	11.45	2.42	2.22	1.71	130	151	141	3.2	3.3	2.6
El Salvador	1.94	5.25	5.94	11.30	2.05	1.93	2.51	88	97	159	3.0	3.3	3.2
Guatemala	2.97	9.20	10.62	21.67	2.77	2.88	2.81	179	247	320	2.1	3.1	3.4
Haiti	3.26	6.51	7.22	13.23	1.68	2.01	2.07	87	125	158	0.9	2.1	2.3
Honduras	1.40	5.14	5.97	11.51	3.46	3.18	2.75	116	151	176	3.5	3.9	3.8
Jamaica	1.40	2.46	2.60	3.45	1.16	1.21	0.99	24	29	26	3.3	2.6	2.2
Mexico	28.01	88.60	97.97	150.06	2.57	2.20	1.81	1,699	1,844	1,853	4.4	3.2	2.7
Nicaragua	1.10	3.87	4.54	9.22	2.81	3.36	2.95	73	120	144	2.7	3.9	3.9
Panama	0.89	2.42	2.66	3.86	2.26	2.07	1.69	42	47	47	2.5	2.8	2.2
Trinidad and Tobago	0.64	1.28	1.38	1.98	1.33	1.68	1.51	14	21	22	1.8	2.1	2.0
United States	152.27	249.22	258.16	299.88	1.06	0.81	0.60	2,357	1,988	1,587	2.3	0.9	0.8
SOUTH AMERICA	111.59	296.72	325.67	493.73	2.28	2.01	1.71	5,196	5,688	5,817	2.9	2.2	2.1
Argentina	17.15	32.32	34.26	45.51	1.61	1.27	1.12	437	398	395	0.8	1.2	1.7
Bolivia	2.77	7.31	8.42	18.29	2.59	2.76	2.88	135	189	261	2.1	2.8	2.7
Brazil	53.44	150.37	165.08	245.81	2.31	2.07	1.67	2,651	2,961	2,881	3.4	2.1	2.1
Chile	6.08	13.17	14.24	19.77	1.48	1.66	1.40	159	210	207	2.5	2.1	1.4
Colombia	11.95	32.98	36.18	54.20	2.29	1.97	1.70	583	620	643	2.5	2.5	2.2
Ecuador	3.31	10.59	11.93	19.92	2.88	2.56	2.20	218	254	277	2.7	3.0	2.8
Guyana	0.42	0.80	0.83	1.16	0.68	0.15	1.44	5	1	12	4.0	2.6	2.4
Paraguay	1.35	4.28	4.89	9.18	3.20	2.93	2.48	93	117	129	3.5	2.9	2.7
Peru	7.63	21.55	23.85	37.35	2.63	2.08	1.93	427	427	484	3.4	2.8	2.7
Suriname	0.22	0.42	0.46	0.66	(0.70)	1.94	1.52	(1)	8	7	1.6	2.9	2.5
Uruguay	2.24	3.09	3.19	3.69	0.59	0.56	0.55	17	17	18	0.5	0.8	1.0
Venezuela	5.01	19.74	22.21	38.00	3.42	2.61	2.14	472	484	501	4.8	3.2	2.8

1950–2025

Table 16.1

	Population (millions)				Average Annual Population Change (percent)			Average Annual Increment to the Population (thousands)			Average Annual Growth of the Labor Force {a} (percent)		
	1950	1990	1995	2025	1975-80	1985-90	1995-2000	1975-80	1985-90	1995-2000	1975-80	1985-90	1995-2000
ASIA	**1,377.26**	**3,112.70**	**3,413.34**	**4,912.48**	**1.86**	**1.87**	**1.68**	**45,856**	**55,506**	**59,840**	**2.2**	**2.0**	**1.4**
Afghanistan	8.96	16.56	23.12	40.48	0.87	2.63	2.74	137	408	678	1.0	4.6	2.2
Bahrain	0.12	0.52	0.60	1.00	4.88	3.67	2.54	15	17	16	11.3	4.0	2.8
Bangladesh	41.78	115.59	132.22	234.99	2.83	2.67	2.60	2,328	2,889	3,674	2.2	3.0	2.9
Bhutan	0.73	1.52	1.70	3.07	1.70	2.15	2.31	20	31	42	1.8	2.0	1.9
Cambodia	4.35	8.25	9.21	13.99	(2.07)	2.48	1.75	(139)	192	168	0.6	0.8	1.7
China	554.76	1,139.06	1,222.56	1,512.59	1.43	1.45	1.22	13,773	15,908	15,324	2.6	1.9	0.9
Cyprus	0.49	0.70	0.73	0.90	0.65	1.04	0.77	4	7	6	1.2	0.9	1.3
India	357.56	853.09	946.72	1,442.39	2.08	2.07	1.91	13,631	16,782	18,965	1.7	2.0	1.7
Indonesia	79.54	184.28	201.80	285.91	2.14	1.93	1.60	3,058	3,390	3,373	2.2	2.4	2.0
Iran, Islamic Rep	16.91	54.61	60.39	113.83	3.08	2.74	2.60	1,111	1,397	1,674	3.1	3.2	3.1
Iraq	5.16	18.92	22.41	49.99	3.75	3.48	3.23	454	604	785	4.2	3.7	4.1
Israel	1.26	4.60	4.96	6.91	2.31	1.66	1.42	85	73	73	2.5	2.3	1.9
Japan	83.63	123.46	125.90	127.50	0.93	0.43	0.40	1,057	525	513	0.5	0.8	0.1
Jordan	1.24	4.01	4.74	9.88	2.34	3.25	3.19	65	120	164	0.3	4.4	4.0
Korea, Dem People's Rep	9.73	21.77	23.97	33.06	1.95	1.81	1.72	340	377	430	2.8	2.9	2.7
Korea, Rep	20.36	42.79	44.66	51.63	1.55	0.95	0.77	569	397	350	2.4	2.1	1.7
Kuwait	0.15	2.04	2.35	3.78	6.24	3.40	2.34	74	64	58	9.6	4.3	3.0
Lao People's Dem Rep	1.76	4.14	4.79	8.60	1.16	2.82	2.64	36	109	135	0.9	2.1	2.2
Lebanon	1.44	2.70	3.01	4.70	(0.72)	0.25	1.98	(19)	7	63	(0.8)	3.5	2.4
Malaysia	6.11	17.89	20.04	30.12	2.32	2.64	1.85	301	443	389	3.7	2.8	2.5
Mongolia	0.76	2.19	2.50	4.83	2.78	2.74	2.57	43	56	69	3.0	2.9	2.8
Myanmar	17.83	41.68	46.28	72.62	2.10	2.09	2.00	676	826	971	2.3	1.9	1.7
Nepal	8.18	19.14	21.52	34.97	2.67	2.48	2.25	372	446	513	1.9	2.4	2.2
Oman	0.41	1.50	1.81	4.75	5.01	3.79	3.67	44	52	73	6.3	2.3	3.0
Pakistan	39.51	122.63	141.52	267.11	2.64	3.44	2.75	2,113	3,879	4,177	3.0	2.5	3.0
Philippines	20.99	62.41	69.94	111.51	2.53	2.49	2.05	1,150	1,459	1,508	2.1	2.5	2.3
Qatar	0.03	0.37	0.44	0.86	5.84	4.16	2.70	12	14	13	5.2	5.1	2.4
Saudi Arabia	3.20	14.13	17.12	44.75	5.13	3.96	3.79	424	508	714	6.1	3.7	3.3
Singapore	1.02	2.72	2.87	3.32	1.30	1.25	0.84	30	33	25	4.2	1.1	0.5
Sri Lanka	7.68	17.22	18.34	24.57	1.71	1.33	1.14	243	221	216	2.7	1.5	1.7
Syrian Arab Rep	3.50	12.53	15.00	34.08	3.36	3.61	3.45	272	414	565	3.4	3.6	4.2
Thailand	20.01	55.70	59.61	80.91	2.44	1.53	1.32	1,072	820	813	2.8	2.1	1.4
Turkey	20.81	55.87	61.58	87.70	2.09	2.08	1.63	883	1,105	1,042	1.6	2.1	1.9
United Arab Emirates	0.07	1.59	1.78	2.65	13.97	3.26	1.87	102	48	35	14.7	2.8	1.7
Viet Nam	29.95	66.69	74.48	117.49	2.23	2.15	2.03	1,134	1,358	1,590	2.2	2.7	2.4
Yemen (Arab Rep)	3.32	9.20	11.07	28.17	3.50	3.76	3.56	204	315	431	2.0	3.1	3.6
(People's Dem Rep)	0.99	2.49	2.93	6.40	2.36	3.07	3.16	41	71	100	2.5	3.0	3.2
EUROPE	**392.52**	**498.37**	**504.25**	**515.21**	**0.45**	**0.25**	**0.23**	**2,154**	**1,233**	**1,153**	**0.7**	**0.5**	**0.2**
Albania	1.23	3.25	3.52	5.01	1.94	1.83	1.50	49	57	55	3.0	2.6	2.1
Austria	6.94	7.58	7.60	7.34	(0.08)	0.07	0.03	(5)	5	2	1.0	0.4	(0.1)
Belgium	8.64	9.85	9.85	9.37	0.11	(0.03)	(0.03)	11	(2)	(2)	0.9	0.3	(0.0)
Bulgaria	7.25	9.01	9.04	8.94	0.32	0.11	0.08	28	10	7	(0.1)	(0.0)	0.4
Czechoslovakia	12.39	15.67	15.87	17.18	0.68	0.21	0.38	102	33	61	0.8	0.5	0.7
Denmark	4.27	5.14	5.16	4.88	0.25	0.08	(0.02)	13	4	0	1.3	0.5	(0.1)
Finland	4.01	4.98	5.03	5.12	0.29	0.30	0.18	14	15	9	0.6	0.5	0.2
France	41.83	56.14	57.14	60.37	0.44	0.35	0.35	236	194	201	0.8	0.6	0.4
Germany (Fed Rep)	49.99	61.32	61.11	55.14	(0.09)	0.10	(0.12)	(53)	60	(74)	0.6	(0.1)	(0.8)
(Dem Rep)	18.39	16.25	16.22	15.77	(0.13)	(0.48)	0.00	(22)	(78)	0	0.9	0.3	0.1
Greece	7.57	10.05	10.12	10.08	1.28	0.23	0.14	119	23	14	1.2	0.4	0.2
Hungary	9.34	10.55	10.51	10.20	0.34	(0.18)	0.04	36	(18)	4	(0.8)	0.2	0.3
Iceland	0.14	0.25	0.26	0.31	0.91	0.97	0.73	2	2	2	2.7	1.3	1.2
Ireland	2.97	3.72	3.90	4.96	1.36	0.92	0.93	45	34	37	1.1	1.6	1.5
Italy	47.10	57.06	57.11	52.96	0.35	(0.03)	0.03	199	(15)	16	0.9	0.3	(0.2)
Luxembourg	0.30	0.37	0.38	0.36	0.00	0.33	0.04	0	1	0	1.1	(0.0)	(0.4)
Malta	0.31	0.35	0.36	0.35	2.09	0.49	0.35	7	2	1	1.9	0.9	1.3
Netherlands	10.11	14.95	15.41	16.82	0.71	0.63	0.54	98	93	84	1.3	1.0	0.1
Norway	3.27	4.21	4.27	4.50	0.39	0.28	0.28	16	12	12	2.0	0.9	0.4
Poland	24.82	38.42	39.37	45.07	0.89	0.65	0.50	310	244	200	0.4	0.5	0.9
Portugal	8.41	10.29	10.43	10.94	1.43	0.25	0.30	135	26	32	2.3	0.8	0.8
Romania	16.31	23.27	23.82	25.75	0.88	0.48	0.44	191	109	106	(0.1)	0.7	0.8
Spain	28.01	39.19	39.92	42.27	1.06	0.30	0.37	389	117	150	0.8	1.0	0.6
Sweden	7.01	8.44	8.51	8.58	0.29	0.22	0.12	24	19	10	1.2	0.4	0.1
Switzerland	4.69	6.61	6.68	6.79	(0.06)	0.42	0.24	(3)	28	16	0.2	0.2	(0.3)
United Kingdom	50.62	57.24	57.86	59.66	0.04	0.22	0.18	21	124	106	0.6	0.2	0.2
Yugoslavia	16.35	23.81	24.39	25.99	0.87	0.58	0.41	190	137	102	0.7	0.7	0.7
U.S.S.R.	**180.08**	**288.60**	**298.62**	**352.12**	**0.85**	**0.78**	**0.64**	**2,215**	**2,212**	**1,950**	**1.6**	**0.5**	**0.7**
OCEANIA	**12.65**	**26.48**	**28.34**	**38.21**	**1.49**	**1.48**	**1.24**	**328**	**379**	**361**	**2.2**	**1.6**	**1.1**
Australia	8.22	16.87	17.90	23.04	1.51	1.37	1.04	214	223	191	2.4	1.6	1.1
Fiji	0.29	0.76	0.82	1.12	1.91	1.78	1.40	12	13	12	2.7	1.9	2.1
New Zealand	1.91	3.39	3.53	4.12	0.19	0.87	0.71	6	29	26	X	X	X
Papua New Guinea	1.61	3.87	4.34	7.29	2.46	2.26	2.20	71	83	101	X	X	X
Solomon Islands	0.11	0.32	0.37	0.74	3.01	3.28	2.77	6	10	11	X	X	X

Sources: United Nations Population Division and International Labour Office.
Notes: a. World and regional labor force totals are totals only of countries shown.
Other world and regional totals include countries not listed here.
0 = zero or less than half the unit of measure; X = not available; negative numbers are shown in parentheses.
For additional information, see Sources and Technical Notes.

Table 16.2 Trends in Births, Life Expectancy, Fertility, and Age

	Crude Birth Rate (births per 1,000 population)		Life Expectancy at Birth (years)		Total Fertility Rate		Percentage of Population in Specific Age Groups					
							1975			1995		
	1970-75	1990-95	1970-75	1990-95	1970-75	1990-95	<15	15-65	>65	<15	15-65	>65
WORLD	31.5	26.4	58.5	65.5	4.5	3.3	36.8	57.5	5.7	32.0	61.5	6.5
AFRICA	46.6	43.5	45.9	54.1	6.6	6.0	44.8	52.1	3.1	44.9	52.1	3.0
Algeria	48.0	34.9	54.5	66.2	7.4	4.9	47.6	48.2	4.2	41.6	55.0	3.4
Angola	48.0	46.6	38.0	46.5	6.4	6.3	43.5	53.6	2.9	45.1	51.8	3.1
Benin	49.4	49.1	40.0	48.0	7.1	7.1	44.8	51.6	3.6	47.0	50.2	2.8
Botswana	52.1	43.9	51.0	61.1	6.9	6.4	50.3	47.6	2.1	48.7	48.3	3.0
Burkina Faso	49.9	47.0	41.2	49.2	6.7	6.5	44.0	53.2	2.8	44.6	52.4	3.0
Burundi	44.2	46.8	43.0	49.5	6.8	6.8	45.5	51.1	3.4	46.2	51.0	2.8
Cameroon	46.0	47.3	45.0	55.0	6.4	6.9	43.6	52.9	3.5	47.4	49.3	3.3
Cape Verde	38.8	40.9	57.5	67.8	7.0	5.3	46.7	47.9	5.4	45.3	50.8	3.9
Central African Rep	43.1	45.1	43.0	50.5	5.7	6.2	40.6	55.5	3.9	45.3	51.0	3.7
Chad	44.6	43.3	39.0	47.5	6.0	5.8	41.7	54.7	3.6	43.3	53.1	3.6
Comoros	48.6	47.3	47.5	56.0	7.0	7.0	46.7	50.7	2.6	47.9	49.7	2.4
Congo	46.1	46.1	46.7	54.7	6.3	6.3	44.4	52.2	3.4	46.6	50.2	3.2
Cote d'Ivoire	51.1	50.0	45.4	54.4	7.4	7.4	45.8	51.8	2.4	48.9	48.5	2.6
Djibouti	50.4	45.8	41.0	49.0	6.6	6.5	42.9	54.8	2.3	45.4	51.9	2.7
Egypt	38.4	30.8	52.1	61.6	5.5	4.0	40.0	55.8	4.2	37.7	58.2	4.1
Equatorial Guinea	42.4	43.5	40.5	48.0	5.7	5.9	40.1	55.6	4.3	43.2	52.8	4.0
Ethiopia	48.0	48.4	41.0	47.0	6.8	6.8	44.5	52.9	2.6	46.2	51.0	2.8
Gabon	30.9	43.4	45.0	53.5	4.3	5.3	32.4	61.8	5.8	36.1	58.2	5.7
Gambia, The	49.2	44.9	37.0	45.0	6.5	6.2	42.1	55.0	2.9	44.2	52.8	3.0
Ghana	45.8	43.5	50.0	56.0	6.6	6.3	45.4	51.9	2.7	45.8	51.3	2.9
Guinea	51.6	50.7	37.3	44.5	7.0	7.0	45.4	52.0	2.6	47.1	50.3	2.6
Guinea-Bissau	41.4	42.7	36.5	43.5	5.4	5.8	38.0	58.3	3.7	41.7	54.2	4.1
Kenya	52.9	47.0	51.0	61.0	8.1	6.8	49.1	47.2	3.7	48.9	48.3	2.8
Lesotho	42.4	40.2	48.4	58.5	5.7	5.8	41.7	54.7	3.6	43.5	52.8	3.7
Liberia	48.1	46.7	47.5	55.4	6.8	6.7	44.0	52.3	3.7	45.9	50.4	3.7
Libya	49.0	43.4	52.9	63.1	7.6	6.7	46.1	51.6	2.3	45.7	51.7	2.6
Madagascar	46.0	44.9	46.5	55.5	6.6	6.5	44.0	53.0	3.0	45.6	51.5	2.9
Malawi	56.6	55.4	41.0	49.1	7.4	7.6	47.2	50.6	2.2	49.1	48.3	2.6
Mali	51.0	50.8	38.5	46.0	7.1	7.1	46.0	51.5	2.5	47.4	50.1	2.5
Mauritania	47.0	46.0	40.0	48.0	6.5	6.5	43.3	53.7	3.0	45.0	51.9	3.1
Mauritius	26.1	17.3	62.9	70.2	3.3	1.9	39.7	57.6	2.7	25.8	68.5	5.7
Morocco	45.6	32.6	52.9	63.3	6.9	4.2	47.1	49.2	3.7	38.8	57.3	3.9
Mozambique	45.7	44.0	42.5	48.5	6.5	6.2	43.8	53.1	3.1	44.2	52.6	3.2
Namibia	45.1	41.6	48.7	58.8	6.1	5.7	43.7	53.1	3.2	45.4	51.3	3.3
Niger	52.3	51.3	39.0	46.5	7.1	7.1	46.3	51.3	2.4	48.1	49.5	2.4
Nigeria	49.3	46.5	44.5	52.5	6.9	6.6	46.5	51.1	2.4	47.3	50.1	2.6
Rwanda	52.9	50.0	44.6	50.5	8.3	8.0	48.3	49.3	2.4	48.9	48.7	2.4
Senegal	49.2	43.9	40.3	49.3	7.0	6.2	44.8	52.4	2.8	44.8	52.3	2.9
Sierra Leone	48.9	48.1	35.0	43.0	6.5	6.5	42.5	54.4	3.1	45.0	51.9	3.1
Somalia	48.3	46.8	41.0	47.1	6.6	6.6	44.3	52.6	3.1	47.7	49.6	2.7
South Africa	36.1	30.5	53.9	62.9	5.5	4.2	39.9	56.2	3.9	36.5	59.2	4.3
Sudan	47.0	43.3	42.6	51.8	6.7	6.3	44.4	52.9	2.7	44.8	52.3	2.9
Swaziland	47.5	46.7	47.3	58.0	6.5	6.5	45.7	51.4	2.9	47.8	49.3	2.9
Tanzania	51.2	50.2	46.5	55.0	7.0	7.1	47.8	49.9	2.3	49.5	48.2	2.3
Togo	45.6	44.5	45.5	55.0	6.6	6.6	44.2	52.7	3.1	45.8	51.0	3.2
Tunisia	37.1	27.2	55.6	67.8	6.2	3.4	43.8	52.7	3.5	35.8	59.9	4.3
Uganda	50.3	51.5	47.0	53.0	7.0	7.3	47.4	50.1	2.5	50.3	47.3	2.4
Zaire	46.6	45.3	46.0	54.0	6.1	6.1	44.6	52.6	2.8	46.0	51.4	2.6
Zambia	49.1	50.3	47.3	55.4	6.9	7.2	46.5	50.9	2.6	49.8	47.9	2.3
Zimbabwe	48.6	39.9	51.5	60.8	7.2	5.3	49.0	48.4	2.6	44.1	53.1	2.8
NORTH & CENTRAL AMERICA	25.0	21.3	68.6	74.0	3.1	2.4	31.4	60.3	8.3	26.3	63.9	9.8
Barbados	20.8	15.7	69.4	75.6	2.7	1.8	31.5	58.6	9.9	23.6	64.6	11.8
Belize	X	X	X	X	X	X	X	X	X	X	X	X
Canada	16.0	12.9	73.1	77.3	2.0	1.7	26.4	65.1	8.5	20.0	67.8	12.2
Costa Rica	31.5	25.5	68.1	75.2	4.3	3.0	42.2	54.4	3.4	34.5	60.9	4.6
Cuba	26.7	17.4	70.9	75.7	3.6	1.9	37.3	56.0	6.7	23.2	67.8	9.0
Dominican Rep	38.8	28.3	59.9	67.5	5.6	3.3	45.3	51.7	3.0	36.3	59.8	3.9
El Salvador	42.8	36.0	58.8	66.5	6.1	4.5	45.9	51.2	2.9	42.5	53.5	4.0
Guatemala	44.6	38.7	54.0	64.8	6.5	5.4	45.7	51.5	2.8	44.3	52.2	3.5
Haiti	38.6	35.3	48.5	56.7	5.8	4.8	41.1	54.3	4.6	40.2	55.9	3.9
Honduras	48.7	37.1	54.0	65.8	7.4	4.9	48.2	49.1	2.7	43.2	53.5	3.3
Jamaica	32.5	22.2	68.6	73.6	5.0	2.4	45.3	48.9	5.8	30.9	62.7	6.4
Mexico	42.6	26.6	62.6	70.4	6.4	3.1	46.5	50.1	3.4	35.0	60.8	4.2
Nicaragua	46.8	38.7	54.7	66.3	6.7	5.0	47.9	49.7	2.4	44.6	52.5	2.9
Panama	35.7	24.9	66.3	72.7	4.9	2.9	43.1	53.0	3.9	33.1	61.8	5.1
Trinidad and Tobago	26.4	23.1	66.5	72.2	3.5	2.7	38.1	57.0	4.9	33.3	61.2	5.5
United States	15.7	14.1	71.3	76.4	2.0	1.9	25.2	64.3	10.5	21.2	65.9	12.9
SOUTH AMERICA	33.2	26.2	61.1	67.5	4.6	3.2	39.6	56.2	4.2	33.7	61.0	5.3
Argentina	23.4	20.3	67.2	71.4	3.2	2.8	29.2	63.2	7.6	28.3	62.1	9.6
Bolivia	45.4	41.3	46.8	55.9	6.5	5.8	43.1	53.6	3.3	43.9	52.9	3.2
Brazil	33.6	26.1	59.8	66.3	4.7	3.2	40.1	56.2	3.7	33.1	61.2	5.1
Chile	27.6	22.5	63.6	72.1	3.6	2.7	36.8	57.8	5.4	30.4	63.2	6.4
Colombia	34.5	25.8	61.7	69.3	4.7	2.9	43.6	52.9	3.5	34.1	61.6	4.3
Ecuador	41.2	30.9	58.9	66.6	6.1	3.9	44.6	51.8	3.6	37.7	58.4	3.9
Guyana	35.0	23.8	60.0	65.2	4.9	2.4	44.2	52.1	3.7	31.8	64.2	4.0
Paraguay	36.6	33.0	65.6	67.3	5.7	4.3	44.3	52.2	3.5	39.6	56.8	3.6
Peru	40.5	29.0	55.5	64.6	6.0	3.6	43.2	53.3	3.5	35.5	60.4	4.1
Suriname	34.6	24.5	64.0	70.3	5.3	2.6	47.7	48.4	3.9	33.7	61.7	4.6
Uruguay	21.1	17.1	68.8	72.5	3.0	2.3	27.7	62.7	9.6	24.4	63.3	12.3
Venezuela	36.1	28.2	66.2	70.3	5.0	3.5	43.5	53.4	3.1	36.6	59.4	4.0

Structure, 1970–95

Table 16.2

	Crude Birth Rate (births per 1,000 population)		Life Expectancy at Birth (years)		Total Fertility Rate		Percentage of Population in Specific Age Groups					
							1975			1995		
	1970-75	1990-95	1970-75	1990-95	1970-75	1990-95	<15	15-65	>65	<15	15-65	>65
ASIA	**34.8**	**26.9**	**56.0**	**64.7**	**5.1**	**3.3**	**39.9**	**56.0**	**4.1**	**32.5**	**62.1**	**5.4**
Afghanistan	51.6	52.0	38.0	43.5	7.1	6.8	43.8	53.8	2.4	39.8	57.6	2.6
Bahrain	36.0	24.8	63.5	71.6	5.9	3.7	43.0	54.7	2.3	31.9	66.3	1.8
Bangladesh	48.5	40.6	44.9	52.9	7.0	5.1	45.9	50.5	3.6	42.1	55.1	2.8
Bhutan	41.0	38.2	42.3	50.0	5.7	5.5	40.4	56.4	3.2	39.7	56.8	3.5
Cambodia	39.9	36.5	40.3	51.0	5.5	4.4	41.6	55.6	2.8	41.8	55.0	3.2
China	30.6	20.8	63.2	70.9	4.8	2.3	39.4	56.2	4.4	26.3	67.4	6.3
Cyprus	18.0	16.8	71.4	76.6	2.2	2.2	25.9	64.3	9.8	25.4	64.4	10.2
India	38.2	31.0	50.3	60.4	5.4	4.1	39.8	56.4	3.8	36.0	59.2	4.8
Indonesia	38.2	26.6	49.3	62.7	5.1	3.1	42.0	54.8	3.2	33.4	62.2	4.4
Iran, Islamic Rep	44.1	33.1	55.9	67.1	6.5	4.7	45.4	51.3	3.3	41.9	54.0	4.1
Iraq	47.4	40.5	57.0	66.2	7.1	5.9	46.6	50.9	2.5	45.3	51.9	2.8
Israel	27.4	20.8	71.6	76.3	3.8	2.8	32.9	59.3	7.8	29.6	61.7	8.7
Japan	19.2	11.5	73.3	78.8	2.1	1.7	24.3	67.8	7.9	17.0	69.2	13.8
Jordan	50.0	38.8	56.6	67.9	7.8	5.5	47.2	50.0	2.8	43.4	53.9	2.7
Korea, Dem People's Rep	35.8	24.5	61.5	71.1	5.7	2.4	45.2	51.7	3.1	29.3	66.1	4.6
Korea, Rep	28.8	15.4	61.5	70.8	4.1	1.7	37.8	58.6	3.6	23.0	71.6	5.4
Kuwait	44.4	25.7	67.3	73.9	6.9	3.5	44.4	54.0	1.6	33.5	64.8	1.7
Lao People's Dem Rep	44.4	44.2	40.4	51.0	6.2	6.7	42.1	55.2	2.7	44.5	52.5	3.0
Lebanon	32.1	29.6	65.0	67.1	4.9	3.4	41.2	53.8	5.0	36.0	58.7	5.3
Malaysia	34.7	27.7	63.0	70.8	5.2	3.5	42.1	54.2	3.7	37.6	58.5	3.9
Mongolia	41.5	34.4	53.8	63.7	5.8	4.7	43.7	53.4	2.9	40.2	56.5	3.3
Myanmar	37.6	29.7	52.5	62.5	5.4	3.7	40.7	55.5	3.8	36.0	59.7	4.3
Nepal	47.1	36.3	43.3	53.5	6.5	5.5	42.9	53.8	3.3	41.4	55.4	3.2
Oman	49.6	43.2	49.0	67.9	7.2	7.1	44.6	52.7	2.7	47.2	50.1	2.7
Pakistan	47.5	41.9	49.0	59.0	7.0	5.9	45.4	51.6	3.0	46.4	50.8	2.8
Philippines	36.9	30.4	57.9	65.0	5.3	3.9	42.8	54.5	2.7	38.4	58.1	3.5
Qatar	31.3	28.4	62.5	70.0	6.8	5.3	33.4	64.6	2.0	35.7	61.8	2.5
Saudi Arabia	47.6	41.8	53.9	65.8	7.3	7.1	44.3	52.7	3.0	45.3	52.1	2.6
Singapore	21.2	16.3	69.5	74.5	2.6	1.8	32.8	63.1	4.1	23.2	70.4	6.4
Sri Lanka	28.9	20.7	65.0	71.6	4.0	2.5	39.3	56.6	4.1	30.3	63.8	5.9
Syrian Arab Rep	46.6	42.5	57.0	67.2	7.7	6.3	48.5	47.8	3.7	47.7	49.7	2.6
Thailand	35.1	20.0	59.6	67.1	5.0	2.2	44.9	52.1	3.0	29.3	66.3	4.4
Turkey	34.5	26.9	57.9	66.2	5.0	3.3	40.1	55.4	4.5	33.7	61.4	4.9
United Arab Emirates	33.0	20.3	62.5	71.0	6.4	4.3	28.2	69.8	2.0	28.6	69.1	2.3
Viet Nam	37.6	30.3	50.3	63.9	5.9	3.7	43.7	52.3	4.0	37.6	58.0	4.4
Yemen (Arab Rep)	54.8	50.8	42.5	52.6	8.0	7.6	52.0	45.4	2.6	50.6	47.1	2.3
(People's Dem Rep)	48.2	46.3	43.4	53.4	7.0	6.5	47.5	49.8	2.7	45.6	51.5	2.9
EUROPE	**15.7**	**12.8**	**71.5**	**75.3**	**2.2**	**1.7**	**23.9**	**63.8**	**12.3**	**18.9**	**66.9**	**14.2**
Albania	31.9	21.9	67.7	72.8	4.7	2.7	39.9	55.6	4.5	30.3	63.8	5.9
Austria	13.7	11.5	70.5	75.3	2.0	1.5	23.3	61.8	14.9	17.4	67.1	15.5
Belgium	13.6	11.9	71.4	75.6	1.9	1.7	22.2	63.9	13.9	17.6	66.6	15.8
Bulgaria	16.2	12.2	71.2	73.1	2.2	1.8	22.0	67.1	10.9	18.7	66.8	14.5
Czechoslovakia	18.0	13.9	70.0	72.4	2.3	2.0	23.4	64.5	12.1	21.0	67.0	12.0
Denmark	14.6	11.0	73.6	76.2	2.0	1.5	22.6	64.0	13.4	16.4	68.1	15.5
Finland	13.2	11.8	70.7	75.9	1.6	1.7	22.0	67.4	10.6	18.4	67.7	13.9
France	16.3	13.4	72.4	76.8	2.3	1.8	23.9	62.6	13.5	19.8	65.6	14.6
Germany (Fed Rep)	11.3	10.8	70.6	76.0	1.6	1.4	21.5	64.0	14.6	15.7	68.2	16.1
(Dem Rep)	11.8	11.4	71.2	74.5	1.7	1.7	21.7	62.1	16.2	19.0	67.6	13.4
Greece	15.9	11.6	72.3	76.5	2.3	1.7	23.9	63.9	12.2	18.2	66.6	15.2
Hungary	15.7	11.9	69.9	71.6	2.1	1.8	20.3	67.1	12.6	17.8	67.9	14.3
Iceland	21.0	15.3	74.3	78.1	2.8	1.9	30.0	60.8	9.2	23.6	65.5	10.9
Ireland	22.1	17.8	71.3	75.1	3.8	2.4	31.3	57.7	11.0	26.0	64.0	10.0
Italy	16.0	10.8	72.1	76.4	2.3	1.4	24.2	63.8	12.0	15.5	68.9	15.6
Luxembourg	11.8	11.6	70.4	75.3	2.0	1.5	21.6	65.3	13.1	17.3	68.5	14.2
Malta	17.5	13.4	70.0	73.9	2.1	1.9	24.7	65.7	9.6	21.4	68.2	10.4
Netherlands	15.4	12.9	74.0	77.6	2.0	1.6	25.3	63.9	10.8	18.4	68.4	13.2
Norway	16.8	12.5	74.4	77.4	2.3	1.7	23.8	62.5	13.7	18.4	65.2	16.4
Poland	17.7	14.7	70.4	72.0	2.3	2.1	24.0	66.5	9.5	23.5	65.6	10.9
Portugal	19.5	13.3	68.0	74.5	2.8	1.7	27.9	62.2	9.9	19.7	66.6	13.7
Romania	19.3	15.1	69.0	71.5	2.6	2.0	25.3	65.1	9.6	21.8	66.8	11.4
Spain	19.5	12.8	72.9	77.4	2.9	1.7	27.6	62.4	10.0	18.5	67.3	14.2
Sweden	13.6	12.6	74.7	77.8	1.9	1.9	20.7	64.2	15.1	17.7	64.6	17.7
Switzerland	14.2	11.6	73.8	77.8	1.8	1.6	22.5	64.9	12.6	16.4	68.0	15.6
United Kingdom	14.5	13.7	72.0	76.1	2.0	1.8	23.4	62.6	14.0	19.6	65.1	15.3
Yugoslavia	18.2	13.8	68.4	73.2	2.3	1.9	25.7	65.7	8.6	21.1	67.8	11.1
U.S.S.R.	**18.1**	**16.7**	**68.6**	**71.3**	**2.4**	**2.3**	**26.1**	**64.4**	**9.5**	**24.8**	**64.3**	**10.9**
OCEANIA	**23.9**	**18.6**	**66.5**	**72.5**	**3.2**	**2.4**	**31.0**	**61.5**	**7.5**	**25.9**	**64.7**	**9.4**
Australia	19.5	14.3	71.7	76.9	2.5	1.8	27.6	63.7	8.7	21.5	67.0	11.5
Fiji	31.5	24.0	58.2	65.9	3.7	2.8	39.9	57.4	2.7	34.0	62.5	3.5
New Zealand	20.8	15.8	71.7	75.6	2.8	2.0	30.0	61.3	8.7	22.4	66.4	11.2
Papua New Guinea	41.0	33.3	47.7	55.9	6.1	4.8	41.9	55.0	3.1	40.0	57.4	2.6
Solomon Islands	X	X	X	X	X	X	X	X	X	X	X	X

Source: United Nations Population Division.
Notes: World and regional totals include countries not listed here.
X = not available.
For additional information, see Sources and Technical Notes.

Table 16.3 Mortality and Nutrition, 1970–95

	Crude Death Rate (deaths per 1,000 population)		Infant Death Rate (infant deaths per 1,000 live births)		Child Deaths {a} (deaths of children < 5 years old per 1,000 live births)		Maternal Deaths (annual, from pregnancy, per 100,000 live births)	Wasting (percent of children aged 12-23 months)	Stunting (percent of children aged 24-59 months)	Per Capita Average Calories Available (as percent of need)	Per Capita Total Protein Consumption (grams/day)
	1970-75	1990-95	1970-75	1990-95	1970-75	1990-95	1980-88	1980-89	1980-89	1987-89	1987-89
WORLD	12	9	93	63	144	94					71
AFRICA	19	13	137	94	233	147					58
Algeria	15	7	132	61	200	84	130	4	14	118	76
Angola	25	19	173	127	291	214	X	X	X	77	45
Benin	26	18	136	85	255	167	X	X	X	98	55
Botswana	17	10	95	58	136	78	250	19	51	102	73
Burkina Faso	24	17	173	127	275	217	810	X	X	96	70
Burundi	21	16	143	110	228	173	X	10	60	86	61
Cameroon	20	13	119	86	200	138	300	2	43	95	52
Cape Verde	12	7	82	37	149	70	60	3	26	116	60
Central African Rep	22	16	132	95	250	205	600	X	X	89	48
Chad	25	18	166	122	281	205	960	X	X	76	55
Comoros	18	12	135	89	175	113	50	X	X	81	42
Congo	19	13	90	65	145	101	900	10	23	117	51
Cote d'Ivoire	19	13	129	87	240	133	X	17	20	112	54
Djibouti	23	16	154	112	X	X	740	19	X	X	X
Egypt	16	9	150	57	240	100	320	2	32	133	84
Equatorial Guinea	24	18	157	117	271	195	X	X	X	X	X
Ethiopia	23	18	155	122	262	233	X	19	43	70	51
Gabon	20	16	132	94	223	153	X	X	X	106	63
Gambia, The	27	20	179	132	337	261	1,100	X	35	99	56
Ghana	16	12	107	81	183	129	1,000	15	39	98	49
Guinea	27	20	177	134	305	230	X	X	X	95	51
Guinea-Bissau	27	21	183	140	276	205	X	X	X	107	51
Kenya	17	10	98	64	161	99	170	10	42	93	59
Lesotho	19	11	130	89	180	119	X	7	23	102	66
Liberia	20	14	181	126	262	187	X	3	24	104	43
Libya	15	8	117	68	180	96	80	X	X	142	81
Madagascar	19	13	172	110	X	X	240	17	56	96	51
Malawi	24	19	191	138	334	239	100	8	61	90	61
Mali	25	19	203	159	358	271	X	16	34	95	63
Mauritania	24	18	160	117	266	195	X	24	37	113	78
Mauritius	7	6	55	20	77	24	100	16	22	125	68
Morocco	16	8	122	68	190	96	300	6	34	124	81
Mozambique	22	17	168	130	289	219	300	X	X	71	28
Namibia	18	11	134	97	226	159	X	X	X	86	63
Niger	25	19	166	124	281	209	420	23	38	98	64
Nigeria	20	14	135	96	250	157	800	21	X	98	49
Rwanda	21	16	140	112	237	186	210	5	37	84	51
Senegal	24	16	122	80	275	204	600	8	28	100	68
Sierra Leone	29	22	193	143	358	271	450	14	43	80	38
Somalia	23	18	155	122	262	233	1,100	X	X	84	61
South Africa	13	9	110	62	153	80	83	X	X	127	79
Sudan	21	14	145	99	245	153	660	13	X	86	58
Swaziland	18	11	144	107	215	155	X	X	X	113	62
Tanzania	19	13	130	97	219	158	340	17	X	95	49
Togo	19	13	129	85	204	136	X	10	37	93	51
Tunisia	12	6	120	44	180	79	310	4	23	129	83
Uganda	19	14	116	94	194	153	300	4	25	92	48
Zaire	19	13	117	75	214	145	X	5	43	89	33
Zambia	18	12	100	72	164	113	150	X	X	X	53
Zimbabwe	15	9	93	55	151	99	480	2	31	96	54
NORTH & CENTRAL AMERICA	10	9	39	22	52	34					96
Barbados	9	9	33	10	38	12	69	4	7	134	103
Belize	X	X	X	X	X	X	49	X	36	118	74
Canada	7	8	16	7	20	8	3	X	X	130	100
Costa Rica	6	4	51	17	64	21	36	3	8	125	65
Cuba	7	7	36	13	45	15	29	1	X	136	74
Dominican Rep	10	6	94	57	132	72	74	3	26	104	48
El Salvador	11	7	110	53	137	69	70	X	X	102	55
Guatemala	13	8	95	48	162	82	110	3	68	102	56
Haiti	18	12	135	86	232	153	230	17	51	89	50
Honduras	14	7	110	57	171	89	50	2	34	99	54
Jamaica	8	6	42	14	48	20	110	6	7	117	65
Mexico	9	5	71	36	100	60	82	X	X	131	78
Nicaragua	13	7	100	50	150	76	47	X	22	100	54
Panama	7	5	43	21	68	30	57	7	24	110	64
Trinidad and Tobago	7	6	30	14	37	20	54	5	4	120	70
United States	9	9	18	8	21	10	8	X	X	138	111
SOUTH AMERICA	10	7	84	52	113	68					65
Argentina	9	9	49	29	58	34	69	X	X	117	101
Bolivia	19	12	151	93	244	143	480	2	51	82	54
Brazil	10	8	91	57	125	77	120	2	31	114	61
Chile	9	6	70	19	79	23	47	1	10	105	70
Colombia	9	6	73	37	102	61	110	1	27	111	58
Ecuador	11	7	95	57	136	79	190	4	39	110	52
Guyana	10	7	79	48	X	X	100	9	21	121	69
Paraguay	7	6	53	39	82	55	380	X	X	120	73
Peru	13	8	110	76	167	100	88	3	43	96	59
Suriname	8	6	49	28	63	31	89	X	X	129	70
Uruguay	10	10	46	20	52	27	38	X	16	105	82
Venezuela	7	5	49	33	67	40	59	4	7	121	65

Table 16.3

	Estimated and Projected						Maternal Deaths (annual, from pregnancy, per 100,000 live births)	Wasting (percent of children aged 12-23 months)	Stunting (percent of children aged 24-59 months)	Per Capita Average Calories Available (as percent of need)	Per Capita Total Protein Consumption (grams/day)
	Crude Death Rate (deaths per 1,000 population)		Infant Death Rate (infant deaths per 1,000 live births)		Child Deaths {a} (deaths of children < 5 years old per 1,000 live births)						
	1970-75	1990-95	1970-75	1990-95	1970-75	1990-95	1980-88	1980-89	1980-89	1987-89	1987-89
ASIA	**12**	**8**	**99**	**64**	**151**	**94**					**61**
Afghanistan	26	22	194	162	340	298	690	X	X	83	56
Bahrain	8	3	55	12	73	27	27	X	X	X	X
Bangladesh	21	14	140	108	228	168	600	28	70	86	43
Bhutan	21	16	153	118	240	178	1,710	4	56	X	X
Cambodia	23	15	181	116	271	169	X	X	X	97	51
China	9	7	61	27	83	36	44	8	41	112	63
Cyprus	10	8	29	10	33	14	X	X	X	X	X
India	16	10	135	88	218	130	340	X	X	99	53
Indonesia	17	9	114	65	173	99	450	11	46	125	60
Iran, Islamic Rep	15	7	122	40	190	138	120	23	55	132	84
Iraq	15	7	96	56	138	74	X	X	X	122	74
Israel	7	7	23	10	27	14	5	X	X	123	103
Japan	7	8	12	5	15	7	16	X	X	125	95
Jordan	14	5	82	36	116	45	X	X	X	110	74
Korea, Dem People's Rep	8	5	47	24	61	26	41	X	X	120	80
Korea, Rep	9	6	47	21	61	26	26	X	X	121	77
Kuwait	5	2	43	15	55	19	6	2	14	X	93
Lao People's Dem Rep	23	15	145	97	217	139	X	20	44	116	70
Lebanon	9	8	48	40	62	X	X	X	X	129	85
Malaysia	9	5	42	20	62	28	59	X	X	123	58
Mongolia	13	8	98	60	X	X	100	X	X	101	88
Myanmar	14	9	100	59	120	74	140	17	75	115	64
Nepal	21	13	153	118	240	178	830	14	69	94	53
Oman	20	6	145	34	271	129	X	X	X	X	X
Pakistan	18	11	140	98	226	147	500	17	42	95	60
Philippines	11	7	64	40	101	62	93	7	42	104	53
Qatar	12	4	57	26	76	32	X	X	X	X	X
Saudi Arabia	17	7	120	58	186	77	X	X	X	118	85
Singapore	5	6	19	7	23	10	5	4	11	141	90
Sri Lanka	8	6	56	24	79	36	60	19	34	104	46
Syrian Arab Rep	12	6	88	39	125	49	280	X	X	124	81
Thailand	9	7	65	24	91	39	50	10	28	104	49
Turkey	12	8	138	62	184	75	210	X	X	126	85
United Arab Emirates	10	4	57	22	76	32	X	X	X	131	101
Viet Nam	14	8	120	54	175	77	140	12	60	84	51
Yemen (Arab Rep)	22	14	168	107	290	171	X	15 b	61 b	86 b	60 b
(People's Dem Rep)	23	14	168	107	290	171	X	X b	X b	X b	X b
EUROPE	**10**	**11**	**24**	**11**	**28**	**13**					**103**
Albania	7	6	58	32	77	42	X	X	X	114	85
Austria	13	12	24	9	28	10	7	X	X	133	99
Belgium	12	12	19	8	22	10	9	X	X	150 c	104 c
Bulgaria	9	12	26	14	30	16	13	X	X	147	110
Czechoslovakia	11	11	21	13	24	14	10	X	X	146	109
Denmark	10	11	12	6	15	8	4	X	X	136	101
Finland	10	10	12	5	14	7	6	X	X	117	98
France	11	10	16	7	19	8	14	X	X	137	113
Germany (Fed Rep)	12	12	22	8	26	10	11	X	X	130	101
(Dem Rep)	14	12	17	8	20	10	16	X	X	146	114
Greece	9	10	34	13	39	15	9	X	X	152	112
Hungary	12	13	34	17	37	X	26	X	X	139	104
Iceland	7	7	12	5	15	7	X	X	X	134	105
Ireland	11	8	18	8	21	10	12	X	X	151	107
Italy	10	11	26	9	29	10	10	X	X	139	107
Luxembourg	12	11	16	9	20	9	X	X	X	X c	X c
Malta	9	9	22	9	24	11	X	X	X	131	99
Netherlands	8	9	12	7	15	8	5	X	X	118	98
Norway	10	11	12	6	15	8	2	X	X	125	104
Poland	8	10	27	17	31	X	11	X	X	132	101
Portugal	11	10	45	13	55	17	12	X	X	139	100
Romania	9	11	40	19	47	24	150	X	X	123	98
Spain	8	9	21	9	25	9	11	X	X	145	103
Sweden	10	12	10	6	12	7	5	X	X	110	94
Switzerland	9	10	13	7	16	8	5	X	X	133	99
United Kingdom	12	12	17	8	20	9	9	X	X	121	91
Yugoslavia	9	9	45	21	53	24	22	X	X	163	100
U.S.S.R.	**9**	**10**	**26**	**20**	**34**	**24**	**48**	**X**	**X**	**127**	**107**
OCEANIA	**10**	**8**	**41**	**23**	**52**	**27**					**89**
Australia	9	8	17	7	20	8	8	X	X	120	98
Fiji	9	6	45	24	58	27	X	X	X	108	69
New Zealand	8	8	16	9	20	11	6	X	X	129	104
Papua New Guinea	17	11	105	53	152	67	900	X	X	91	49
Solomon Islands	X	X	X	X	X	X	10	15	34	82	54

Sources: Food and Agriculture Organization of the United Nations, United Nations Children's Fund, United Nations Development Programme, and United Nations Population Division.

Notes: a. Data are not necessarily comparable with infant death rate numbers because of differences in methodology.
b. Data are for Yemen as a whole.
c. Data for Belgium and Luxembourg are combined under Belgium.
World and regional totals include countries not listed here.
X = not available.
For additional information, see Sources and Technical Notes.

Table 16.4 Access to Safe Drinking Water, Sanitation, and

	Percentage of Population with Access to:											Number of Trained Medical Personnel (latest year)		
	Safe Drinking Water				Sanitation Services				Health Services 1985-88				Nurses and	
	Urban		Rural		Urban		Rural								
	1980	1988	1980	1988	1980	1988	1980	1988	All	Urban	Rural	Doctors	Midwives	Other
WORLD														
AFRICA														
Algeria	X	X	X	X	X	X	X	X	88	100	80	9,056	474	67,281
Angola	85	75	10	19	40	25	15	20	30 a	X	X	481	6,518	1,910
Benin	26	66	15	46	48	42	4	31	18	X	X	238	1,640	522
Botswana	X	70	X	X	X	98	X	20	89 a	100 a	85 a	X	X	X
Burkina Faso	27	44	31	72	38	35	5	5	49 a	51 a	48 a	131	2,899	9,813
Burundi	90	100	20	34	40	80	35	5	61	X	X	216	1,503	196
Cameroon	X	100	X	96	X	X	X	X	41	44	39	X	X	X
Cape Verde	X	87	21	65	34	35	10	X	X	X	X	60	196	X
Central African Rep	X	13	X	11	X	X	X	11	45	X	X	X	X	X
Chad	X	X	X	X	X	X	X	X	30	X	X	X	X	X
Comoros	X	X	X	X	X	X	X	X	X	X	X	31	168	7
Congo	36	92	3	2	17	X	0	2	83	97	70	210	2,746	406
Cote d'Ivoire	X	100	X	75	X	69	X	20	30 a	61 a	11 a	X	X	X
Djibouti	50	50	20	21	43	94	20	50	X	X	X	77	534	161
Egypt	88	96	64	82	45	100	10	34	X	X	X	9,495	12,458	X
Equatorial Guinea	47 b	X	X	X	99 b	X	X	X	X	X	X	X	X	X
Ethiopia	X	70	X	11	X	97	X	7	46	X	X	534	1,896	5,907
Gabon	X	90	X	50	X	X	X	X	90 b	X	X	328	X	3,366
Gambia, The	85	92	X	73	X	X	X	X	X	X	X	X	X	X
Ghana	72	93	33	39	47	64	17	15	60	92	45	817	X	X
Guinea	69	55	2	24	54	65	1	X	47	100	40	X	X	X
Guinea-Bissau	18	18	8	27	21	30	13	18	X	X	X	122	785	137
Kenya	85	X	15	X	89	X	19	X	X	X	X	2,151	17,193	4,581
Lesotho	37	59	11	45	13	14	14	23	80	X	X	X	X	X
Liberia	X	93	16	22	18	4 c	5	8	39	50	30	221	1,152	350
Libya	100	100	90	80	100	100	72	85	X	X	X	5,019	5,565	1,018
Madagascar	80	62	7	10	9	X	X	X	56	X	X	X	X	X
Malawi	77	66	37	49	100	X	81	X	80	X	X	262	1,286	351
Mali	37	100	0	36	79	94	0	5	15	X	X	349	5,223	308
Mauritania	80	67	85	65	5	34	X	X	30 a	X	X	142	1,230	200
Mauritius	100	100	98	92	100	92	90	96	100	100	100	X	X	X
Morocco	100	100	X	25	X	100	X	19	70	100	50	4,908	22,207	467
Mozambique	X	44	X	17	X	61	X	11	39	100	30	X	X	X
Namibia	X	X	X	X	X	X	X	X	X	X	X	X	X	X
Niger	41	100	32	52	36	39	3	3	41	99	30	160	7,248	6,611
Nigeria	60	100	30	20	X	X	X	X	40	75	30	11,294	74,033	20,150
Rwanda	48	46	55	64	60	45	50	62	27 a	60 a	25 a	163	X	1,550
Senegal	33	79 d	25	38 d	5	87 d	2	X	40	X	X	311	1,393	2,110
Sierra Leone	50	83	2	22	31	59	6	35	X	X	X	262	2,830	478
Somalia	60	50	20	29	45	41	5	5	27 a	50 a	15 a	325	3,416	5
South Africa	X	X	X	X	X	X	X	X	X	X	X	X	X	X
Sudan	X	90 e	31	20 e	63	40 e	0	5 e	51	90	40	2,095	12,986	4,189
Swaziland	X	100 d	X	7 d	X	100 d	X	25 d	X	X	X	33	477	160
Tanzania	X	75	X	46	X	76	X	77	76 a	99 a	72 a	X	X	X
Togo	70	100	31	61	24	42	10	16	61	X	X	229	1,973	934
Tunisia	100	100	17	31	100	71	X	15	90 b	100 b	80 b	3,453	9,353	11,831
Uganda	45	45	8	12	40	40 e	10	10 e	61 a	90 a	57 a	X	X	X
Zaire	X	59	X	17	X	14	X	14	26	40	17	X	X	X
Zambia	65	76	32	43	100	77	48	34	75 a	100 a	50 a	880	5,655	2,773
Zimbabwe	X	95	X	80	X	95	X	22	71	100	62	X	X	3,238
NORTH & CENTRAL AMERICA														
Barbados	100	100 d	28	100 d	X	100 d	X	100 d	X	X	X	225	1,134	34
Belize	X	94	36	44	62	94	75	28	X	X	X	44	326	13
Canada	X	100 d	X	100 d	X	X	X	X	X	X	X	48,860	85,539	31,912
Costa Rica	100	100	68	84	93	100	82	93	80 a	100 a	63 a	2,539	5,400	1,492
Cuba	X	X	X	X	X	X	X	X	X	X	X	18,850	35,062	711
Dominican Rep	85	86	33	28	25	77	4	36	80	X	X	3,555	5,184	315
El Salvador	67	76	40	10	80	86	26	39	56	80	40	1,664	5,038	1,214
Guatemala	89	91	18	41	45	72	20	48	34	47	25	3,544	9,093	1,257
Haiti	48	55	8	36	39	X	10	15	50	X	X	810	2,537	102
Honduras	50	89	40	60	40	88	26	44	73	85	65	2,800	6,300	614
Jamaica	X	95	X	46	X	14 c	X	X	90	X	X	1,115	4,675	233
Mexico	64	79	43	49	51	100	12	12	45 a	X	X	X	87,398	3,207
Nicaragua	91	78	10	19	35	32 c	X	X	83	100	60	2,110	5,917	250
Panama	100	100	65	66	62	100	28	68	80 a	95 a	64 a	2,167	5,475	410
Trinidad and Tobago	100	100	93	87	95	100	88	97	99	X	X	1,213	4,521	238
United States	X	X	X	X	X	X	X	X	X	X	X	501,200	3,212,700	366,950
SOUTH AMERICA														
Argentina	65	73	17	17	89	100	32	29	71	80	21	80,100	30,505	7,717
Bolivia	69	77	10	15	37	55	4	13	63	90	36	4,032	1,066	349
Brazil	80	100	51	86	32	89	X	41	X	X	X	122,818	110,052	23,256
Chile	100	100	17	21	99	100	X	6	97	X	X	9,684	32,150	3,100
Colombia	X	88	79	87	100	85	4	18	60	X	X	23,520	44,520	12,208
Ecuador	82	75	16	37	39	75	14	34	75	92	40	11,033	14,794	4,403
Guyana	X	94	60	74	100	85	80	86	X	X	X	125	887	33
Paraguay	39	65	10	7	95	55	89	60	60 a	90 a	38 a	2,453	3,584	195
Peru	68	78	21	22	57	71	0	17	60	X	X	18,200	14,900	8,990
Suriname	X	82	79	56	100	64	79	36	X	X	X	306	1,400	28
Uruguay	96	85	2	5	59	60	60	65	82	X	X	5,756	3,000	2,300
Venezuela	91	89	50	89	90	97	70	70	X	X	X	24,038	15,214	4,342

Health Services, 1980s

Table 16.4

	Percentage of Population with Access to:								Health Services 1985-88			Number of Trained Medical Personnel (latest year)		
	Safe Drinking Water				Sanitation Services								Nurses and	
	Urban		Rural		Urban		Rural					Doctors	Midwives	Other
	1980	1988	1980	1988	1980	1988	1980	1988	All	Urban	Rural			
ASIA														
Afghanistan	28	39	8	17	X	20	X	X	29	80	17	2,957	2,135	329
Bahrain	X	100	X	57	X	100	X	94	X	X	X	518	1,148	19
Bangladesh	26	37	40	89	21	37	1	4	45	X	X	14,944	11,197	X
Bhutan	50	100 f	5	24 f	X	100 f	X	7 f	65	X	X	52	164	242
Cambodia	X	X	X	X	X	X	X	X	53	80	50	X	X	X
China	X	87	X	66	X	100	X	95	X	X	X	926,603	759,485	1,784,425
Cyprus	100	100	100	100	100	100	100	100	X	X	X	911	2,165	725
India	77	79	31	73	27	38	1	4	X	X	X	297,228	429,315	21,053
Indonesia	35	60	19	40	29	40	21	45	80	X	X	16,698	122,945	37,230
Iran, Islamic Rep	X	100	X	75	X	100	X	35	80	95	65	16,918	43,291	2,488
Iraq	X	100	X	72	X	92	X	18	93	97	78	9,442	9,931	1,465
Israel	X	100 f	X	97 f	X	99 f	X	95 f	X	X	X	11,895	26,895	17,010
Japan	X	X	X	X	X	X	X	X	X	X	X	181,101	651,660	X
Jordan	100	100	65	98	94	100	34	100	97	98	95	2,958	2,596	623
Korea, Dem People's Rep	X	100 f	X	100 f	X	100 f	X	100 f	X	X	X	45,120	X	X
Korea, Rep	86	91	61	49	100	99	100	100	93	97	86	35,657	70,783	X
Kuwait	X	100 f	X	X	X	100 f	X	X	100	X	X	2,804	8,831	1,134
Lao People's Dem Rep	21	61	12	17	11	X	3	6	67	X	X	551	6,753	2,088
Lebanon	100	X	100	X	94	X	18	X	X	X	X	3,953	X	X
Malaysia	90	92	49	68	100	X	55	75	X	X	X	5,394	15,902	2,932
Mongolia	X	78	X	50	X	100	X	43	X	X	X	3,881	8,083	15,384
Myanmar	38	38	15	28	38	35	15	27	33	100	11	10,031	41,590	X
Nepal	83	66	7	33	16	X	1	X	X	X	X	497	1,707	1,874
Oman	X	87	X	42	X	100	X	34	91	100	90	1,240	3,460	80
Pakistan	72	99	20	35	42	40	2	8	55	99	35	34,850	20,295	2,050
Philippines	65	100	43	75	81	98	67	85	X	X	X	8,132	19,880	X
Qatar	X	100	X	48	X	100	X	85	X	X	X	646	1,672	95
Saudi Arabia	92	100	87	74	81	100	50	30	97	100	88	17,544	37,670	1,291
Singapore	100	100	NA	NA	80	97	NA	NA	100	100	NA	1,086	4,967	890
Sri Lanka	65	87	18	40	80	74	63	44	93 a	X	X	1,914	11,346	2,204
Syrian Arab Rep	98	91 f	54	68 f	74	72 f	28	55 f	75 a	92 a	60 a	8,593	12,550	2,487
Thailand	65	67	63	76	64	84	41	X	70	85	80	8,058	62,585	13,712
Turkey	95	100 d	62	70 d	56	95 d	X	90 d	X	X	X	36,427	48,841	30,412
United Arab Emirates	95	100 f	81	100 f	93	100 f	22	77 e	90 a	X	X	1,278	3,328	97
Viet Nam	X	48	32	45	X	48	55	55	80	100	75	19,861	101,448	43,763
Yemen (Arab Rep)	100	100	18	48	60	66	X	X	38 g	X	X	1,234	2,965	159
(People's Dem Rep)	85	X	25	X	70	X	15	X	X g	X	X	492	2,022	47
EUROPE														
Albania	X	100 d	X	95 d	X	100 d	X	100 d	X	X	X	2,641	13,372	3,110
Austria	X	100 d	X	100 d	X	100 d	X	100 d	X	X	X	19,451	27,655	22,287
Belgium	X	100 f	X	100 f	X	100 f	X	100 f	X	X	X	29,776	X	17,006
Bulgaria	X	100 f	X	96 f	X	100 f	X	100 f	X	X	X	24,718	57,500	117,924
Czechoslovakia	X	100 d	X	100 d	X	100 d	X	100 d	X	X	X	55,871 h	106,968	7,435
Denmark	X	100 f	X	100 f	X	100 f	X	100 f	X	X	X	12,806	83,991	9,730
Finland	X	99 d	X	90 d	X	100 d	X	100 d	X	X	X	11,072	82,951	13,934
France	X	100 d	X	100 d	X	100 d	X	100 d	X	X	X	173,116	X	89,276
Germany (Fed Rep)	X	100 e	X	100 e	X	95 e	X	83 e	X	X	X	153,895	269,301	140,563
(Dem Rep)	X	100 e	X	100 e	X	100 e	X	100 e	X	X	X	37,943	116,600	30,240
Greece	X	100 d	X	95 d	X	100 d	X	95 d	X	X	X	28,212	21,811	8,379
Hungary	X	100 d	X	95 d	X	100 d	X	100 d	X	X	X	34,758	61,422	4,548
Iceland	X	100 d	X	100 d	X	100 d	X	100 d	X	X	X	545	2,724	293
Ireland	X	100 d	X	100 d	X	100 d	X	100 d	X	X	X	5,180	25,261	1,131
Italy	X	100 d	X	100 d	X	100 d	X	100 d	X	X	X	245,116	X	3,697
Luxembourg	X	100 e	X	100 e	X	100 e	X	100 e	X	X	X	663	102	422
Malta	100	100 d	100	100 d	100	100 d	84	100 d	X	X	X	413	3,187	453
Netherlands	X	100 d	X	100 d	X	100 d	X	100 d	X	X	X	32,193	971	9,018
Norway	X	100 f	X	100 f	X	100 d	X	100 d	X	X	X	9,176	72,448	7,403
Poland	X	94 d	X	82 d	X	100 d	X	100 d	X	X	X	73,199	198,934	36,748
Portugal	X	97 d	X	90 d	X	100 d	X	95 d	X	X	X	24,629	X	12,287
Romania	X	100 d	X	90 d	X	100 d	X	95 d	X	X	X	40,050	X	6,558
Spain	X	100 d	X	100 d	X	100 d	X	100 d	X	X	X	121,362	148,312	36,392
Sweden	X	100 f	X	100 f	X	100 f	X	100 f	X	X	X	21,596	69,261	43,704
Switzerland	X	100 f	X	100 f	X	100 e	X	100 e	X	X	X	9,298	X	3,117
United Kingdom	X	100 d	X	100 d	X	100 d	X	100 d	X	X	X	92,172	182,897	35,061
Yugoslavia	X	100 e	X	65 e	X	78 e	X	46 e	X	X	X	42,365	91,253	50,036
U.S.S.R.	X	100 d	X	100 d	X	100 d	X	100 d	X	X	X	1,170,000 h	X	587,200
OCEANIA														
Australia	X	X	X	X	X	X	X	X	X	X	X	36,610	139,434	X
Fiji	94	95 i	66	68	85	90	60	65	X	X	X	325	1,342	X
New Zealand	X	X	X	X	X	100 f	X	X	X	X	X	5,747	40,950	X
Papua New Guinea	55	93	10	23	96	54	3	56	96	X	X	269	3,941	301
Solomon Islands	91	82	20	68	82	56	10	5	X	X	X	38	301	X

Sources: World Health Organization and United Nations Children's Fund.
Notes: a. 1980 data. b. 1983 data. c. Population served by sewer connection only. d. 1985 data. e. 1986 data. f. 1987 data. g. Data are for Yemen as a whole. h. Includes dentists. i. Population served by house connection only.
0 = zero or less than 0.5 percent; X = not available; NA = not applicable.
For additional information, see Sources and Technical Notes.

Table 16.5 Education and Child Health, 1970–90

	Adult Female Literacy (percent) 1970	1990	Adult Male Literacy (percent) 1970	1990	Percentage of Population Age 25 and Over Who Have Completed Primary School Female	Male	Some Postsecondary Education Female	Male	Births Attended by Trained Personnel (percent) 1983-88	ORT Use{a} (percentage of diarrhea episodes treated) 1987-88	Low-Birth-Weight Infants (percent) 1980-88	TB	DPT	Polio	Measles
WORLD												90	83	85	80
AFRICA												80	56	55	54
Algeria	11	46	39	70	X	X	0.1	0.5	15	16	9	99	89	89	83
Angola	7	29	16	56	X	X	X	X	15	12	17	47	23	23	38
Benin	8	16	23	32	X	X	0.1	0.5	45	26	8	92	67	67	70
Botswana	44	65	37	84	21.8 b	21.6 b	0.5 b	1.4 b	77	64	8	92	86	82	78
Burkina Faso	3	9	13	28	X	X	X	X	30	16	X	84	37	37	42
Burundi	10	40	29	61	X	X	X	X	21	30	9	97	86	86	75
Cameroon	19	43	47	66	X	X	0.1	0.5	X	24	13	76	56	54	56
Cape Verde	X	X	X	X	X	X	X	X	30	X	X	97	88	87	79
Central African Rep	6	25	26	52	X	X	X	X	66	15	15	96	82	82	82
Chad	2	18	20	42	X	X	X	X	24	2	11	59 c	20 c	20 c	32 c
Comoros	X	X	X	X	X	X	X	X	24	X	14	99	94	94	87
Congo	19	44	50	70	X	X	X	X	X	6	16	90	79	79	75
Cote d'Ivoire	10	40	26	67	X	X	X	X	20	16	14	63	48	48	42
Djibouti	X	X	X	X	X	X	X	X	73	X	14	95	85	85	85
Egypt	20	34	50	63	X	X	1.3	5.5	47	83	5	88	87	87	86
Equatorial Guinea	X	37	X	64	X	X	X	X	58	X	X	97	78	75	88
Ethiopia	X	X	8	X	X	X	X	X	14	38	X	57	44	44	37
Gabon	22	49	43	74	X	X	X	X	92	10	X	96	78	78	76
Gambia, The	X	16	X	39	3.2	5.3	0.1	0.3	85	X	14	99	90	93	73
Ghana	18	51	43	70	X	X	0.1	0.7	40	21	17	81	57	56	60
Guinea	7	13	21	35	X	X	X	X	25	1	X	53	17	17	18
Guinea-Bissau	6	24	13	50	1.4 d	1.4 d	0.1 d	0.1 d	27	X	13	90	38	38	42
Kenya	19	59	44	80	X	X	X	X	28	54	15	80	74	71	59
Lesotho	74	X	49	X	13.9	13.7	0.1	0.1	40	68	11	97	76	75	76
Liberia	8	29	27	50	4.5	15.6	0.8	2.2	87	9	X	62 e	28 e	28 e	55 e
Libya	13	50	60	75	1.7	14.8	0.1	1.8	76	60	X	90 c	84 c	84 c	70 c
Madagascar	43	73	56	88	X	X	X	X	62	80	10	67	46	46	33
Malawi	18	X	42	X	2.6	12.7	0.1	0.3	45	14	20	97	81	79	80
Mali	4	24	11	41	0.7	2.6	0.1	0.3	27	3	17	82	42	42	43
Mauritania	X	21	X	47	X	X	X	X	20	23	11	75	28	28	33
Mauritius	59	X	77	X	X	X	1.9	5.5	85	7	9	94	90	90	84
Morocco	10	38	34	61	2.8	8.6	X	X	29	45	X	96	81	81	79
Mozambique	14	21	29	45	1.2 f	4.2 f	0.0 f	0.2 f	28	14	20	59	46	46	58
Namibia	X	X	X	X	X	X	X	X	X	X	X	85	53	53	41
Niger	2	17	6	40	X	X	0.0 g	0.2 g	47	35	15	50	13	13	21
Nigeria	14	40	35	62	X	X	X	X	40	35	20	96	57	57	54
Rwanda	21	37	43	64	2.9	10.2	0.1	0.5	22	24	17	92	84	83	83
Senegal	5	25	18	52	2.7 h	6.9 h	0.0 h	0.2 h	50	27	11	92	60	66	59
Sierra Leone	8	11	18	31	X	X	X	X	25	31	17	98	83	83	75
Somalia	1	14	5	36	X	X	X	X	2	12	X	31 c	18 c	18 c	30 c
South Africa	X	X	X	X	35.6	37.2	3.1	4.3	X	X	12	X	X	X	X
Sudan	6	12	28	43	X	X	X	X	20	25	X	73	62	62	57
Swaziland	X	X	X	X	17.3	25.4	X	X	50	X	X	96 c	89 c	89 c	85 c
Tanzania	18	X	48	X	10.6 i	X i	0.2 i	X i	60	14	14	93 c	85 c	82 c	83 c
Togo	7	31	27	56	X	X	0.5	2.3	15	21	20	94	61	61	57
Tunisia	17	56	44	74	X	X	1.3	4.3	68	48	8	99	90	90	87
Uganda	30	35	52	62	X	X	X	X	45	14	X	99	77	77	74
Zaire	22	61	61	84	X	X	X	X	X	18	13	65 c	32 c	31 c	31 c
Zambia	37	65	66	81	X	X	0.2	0.6	X	59	14	97	79	78	76
Zimbabwe	47	60	63	74	X	X	X	X	69	26	15	71	73	72	69
NORTH & CENTRAL AMERICA												X	X	X	X
Barbados	X	X	X	X	X	X	1.9	5.3	93	X	16	95	91	90	87
Belize	X	X	X	X	X	X	1.2	3.4	80	X	10	80	84	80	81
Canada	X	X	X	X	83.7	83.7	34.7	40.2	99	X	6	X	X	X	X
Costa Rica	87	93	88	93	34.1	35.5	5.4	6.2	96	78	10	92	95	95	90
Cuba	87	93	86	95	68.8	78.6	4.5	7.3	X	75	8	98	92	94	94
Dominican Rep	65	82	69	85	16.3	20.2	1.3	2.5	57	51	16	68	69	90	96
El Salvador	53	70	61	76	X	X	1.9 g	2.7 g	35	45	15	60	76	76	75
Guatemala	37	47	51	63	X	X	0.5	1.9	34	17	14	62	66	74	68
Haiti	17	47	26	59	X	X	0.4	X	40	35	17	72	41	40	31
Honduras	50	71	55	76	X	X	3.3	X	50	66	20	71	84	87	90
Jamaica	97	99	96	98	X	X	1.8	2.2	89	15	8	98	86	87	74
Mexico	69	85	78	90	32.2	36.5	2.7	8.0	94	72	15	70	66	96	78
Nicaragua	57	X	58	X	X	X	X	X	41	38	15	81	65	86	82
Panama	81	88	81	88	54.7	51.7	7.8	8.8	89	41	8	83	82	82	99
Trinidad and Tobago	X	X	X	X	68.8	69.6	1.9	3.9	98	60	X	X	83 j	83 j	69 j
United States	99	X	99	X	96.8	96.8	28.0	36.9	99	X	7	X	X	X	X
SOUTH AMERICA												X	X	X	X
Argentina	92	95	94	96	61.1	57.8	5.8	6.4	X	13	X	99	85	89	95
Bolivia	46	71	68	85	X	X	3.3	6.9	36	26	12	48	41	50	53
Brazil	63	80	69	83	15.9	17.7	4.1	5.9	95	39	8	78	81	93	78
Chile	88	93	90	94	X	X	5.9	8.6	98	1	7	97	99	99	98
Colombia	76	86	79	88	X	X	1.8 k	5.0 k	51	12	8	95	87	93	82
Ecuador	68	84	75	88	53.7	61.8	5.6	9.6	27	24	11	88	68	67	61
Guyana	89	95	94	98	X	X	0.9	2.7	96	X	11	85	83	79	73
Paraguay	75	88	85	92	32.6	37.0	2.5	4.3	22	36	7	90	78	76	69
Peru	60	79	81	92	41.5	56.1	7.7	12.6	44	10	9	83	72	73	64
Suriname	X	95	X	95	X	X	X	X	80	X	12	X	83	81	65
Uruguay	93	96	93	97	X	X	10.0	7.9	97	40	8	99	88	88	82
Venezuela	71	90	79	87	X	X	5.5	8.5	82	30	9	63	63	72	62

Table 16.5

	Adult Female Literacy (percent) 1970	1990	Adult Male Literacy (percent) 1970	1990	Percentage of Population Age 25 and Over Who Have — Completed Primary School Female	Male	Some Postsecondary Education Female	Male	Births Attended by Trained Personnel (percent) 1983-88	ORT Use[a] (percentage of diarrhea episodes treated) 1987-88	Low-Birth-Weight Infants (percent) 1980-88	Percentage of 1-Year-Olds Fully Immunized in 1990 Against TB	DPT	Polio	Measles
ASIA												95	90	91	88
Afghanistan	2	14	13	44	1.0	7.7	0.6	5.3	8	11	20	30	25	25	20
Bahrain	X	69	X	82	10.2	22.4	2.2	5.0	98	X	X	X	95	95	86
Bangladesh	12	22	36	47	X	X	0.3	2.2	5	32	28	86	62	62	54
Bhutan	X	25	X	51	X	X	X	X	7	40	X	99	95	95	89
Cambodia	23	22	X	48	X	X	X	X	47	6	X	54	40	40	34
China	X	62	X	84	37.7	72.2	0.5	1.5	X	30	9	99	97	98	98
Cyprus	X	X	X	X	X	X	12.0 k	X	X	X	X	X	90	90	74
India	20	34	47	62	X	X	1.1	3.8	33	23	30	97	92	93	87
Indonesia	42	68	66	84	19.6	35.1	0.4	1.2	31	56	14	93	87	91	86
Iran, Islamic Rep	17	43	40	65	X	X	X	X	82	38	5	95	93	92	83
Iraq	18	49	50	70	X	X	X	X	50	51	9	96	75	75	62
Israel	83	X	93	X	X	X	20.9	25.4	100	X	7	X	X	X	X
Japan	99	X	99	X	99.2	99.4	9.5	19.5	100	X	5	X	X	X	X
Jordan	29	70	64	89	X	X	X	X	83	53	5	X	92	92	87
Korea, Dem People's Rep	X	X	X	X	X	X	X	X	65	52	X	99	98	99	99
Korea, Rep	81	94	94	99	X	X	4.0	14.1	70	X	9	72	74	74	95
Kuwait	42	67	65	77	X	X	11.6	13.2	99	4	7	X c	94 c	94 c	98 c
Lao People's Dem Rep	28	X	37	X	X	X	X	X	X	30	39	26	18	26	13
Lebanon	58	73	79	88	21.7	30.0	1.1	5.0	X	10	10	X	82	82	39
Malaysia	48	70	71	87	21.4 l	31.5 l	X	X	82	20	10	99 c	91	90	90
Mongolia	74	X	87	X	X	X	X	X	99	59	10	92 c	84 c	85 c	86 c
Myanmar	57	72	85	89	X	X	1.5	2.5	57	21	16	75 m	69 m	69 m	73 m
Nepal	3	13	23	38	X	X	6.8 n	X n	6	28	X	97	79	78	67
Oman	X	X	X	X	X	X	X	X	60	19	7	93	96	96	96
Pakistan	11	21	30	47	X	X	0.7	3.0	24	42	25	98	96	96	97
Philippines	81	90	84	90	55.4	58.4	15.1	15.3	57	14	18	96	88	88	85
Qatar	X	X	X	X	X	X	15.3	12.7	90	X	X	97	82	82	79
Saudi Arabia	2	48	15	73	X	X	X	X	74	32	6	99	94	94	90
Singapore	55	X	82	X	X	X	2.0	4.8	100	X	7	99	85	85	87
Sri Lanka	69	84	85	93	X	X	0.8	1.4	87	77	28	88	90	90	83
Syrian Arab Rep	20	51	60	78	X	X	0.4	2.2	37	31	11	92	90	90	87
Thailand	72	90	86	96	8.3	16.1	2.4	3.4	40	30	12	99	92	92	80
Turkey	34	71	69	90	X	X	1.5	5.7	78	X	7	X	84	84	78
United Arab Emirates	7	X	24	X	X	X	4.1	6.6	96	13	7	96	85	85	75
Viet Nam	X	84	X	92	X	X	X	X	X	17	18	90	87	87	87
Yemen (Arab Rep)	1	26	9	53	X	X	X	X	12 o	7 o	X	99 o	89 o	89 o	74 o
(People's Dem Rep)	9	26	31	53	X	X	X	X	X o	X o	X	X o	X o	X o	X o
EUROPE												X	X	X	X
Albania	X	X	X	X	X	X	X	X	X	X	7	X	X	X	X
Austria	X	X	X	X	X	X	1.6	5.4	X	X	6	X	X	X	X
Belgium	99	X	99	X	X	X	5.3 p	9.9 p	100	X	5	X	X	X	X
Bulgaria	89	X	94	X	X	X	X	X	100	X	6	X	X	X	X
Czechoslovakia	X	X	X	X	X	X	4.0	8.2	100	X	6	X	X	X	X
Denmark	X	X	X	X	X	X	X	X	100	X	6	X	X	X	X
Finland	X	X	X	X	X	X	11.7	16.2	100	X	4	X	X	X	X
France	98	X	99	X	X	X	X	X	99	X	5	X	X	X	X
Germany (Fed Rep)	X	X	X	X	X	X	1.9	7.2	100	X	6	X	X	X	X
(Dem Rep)	X	X	X	X	X	X	14.1	21.3	99	X	6	X	X	X	X
Greece	76	89	93	98	63.9	80.0	4.9	10.5	97	X	6	X	X	X	X
Hungary	98	X	98	X	89.5	92.3	5.0	9.3	99	X	10	X	X	X	X
Iceland	X	X	X	X	X	X	X	X	X	X	4	X	X	X	X
Ireland	X	X	X	X	X	X	6.5	9.3	X	X	7	X	X	X	X
Italy	93	96	95	98	X	X	2.9	5.4	100	X	7	X	X	X	X
Luxembourg	X	X	X	X	X	X	X	X	X	X	X	X	X	X	X
Malta	X	X	X	X	X	X	X	X	X	X	X	X	X	X	X
Netherlands	X	X	X	X	X	X	4.8	9.6	100	X	X	X	X	X	X
Norway	X	X	X	X	X	X	8.8	15.2	100	X	4	X	X	X	X
Poland	97	X	98	X	81.5	87.9	4.4	7.2	100	X	8	X	X	X	X
Portugal	65	82	78	89	29.2	50.3	0.9	2.5	87	X	5	X	X	X	X
Romania	91	X	96	X	X	X	4.6 n	X n	100	X	6	X	X	X	X
Spain	87	93	93	97	50.7	58.7	5.8	8.3	96	X	1	X	X	X	X
Sweden	X	X	X	X	X	X	14.1 q	16.7 q	100	X	4	X	X	X	X
Switzerland	X	X	X	X	X	X	X	X	99	X	5	X	X	X	X
United Kingdom	X	X	X	X	X	X	8.0	X	100	X	7	X	X	X	X
Yugoslavia	76	88	92	97	X	X	4.8	9.0	86	X	7	X	X	X	X
U.S.S.R.	97	X	98	X	88.6	96.4	12.7	15.4	98	X	6	X	X	X	X
OCEANIA												X	X	X	X
Australia	X	X	X	X	X	X	10.0	33.2	99	X	6	X	X	X	X
Fiji	X	X	X	X	50.2	56.6	3.4	5.7	98	X	14	99	97	96	84
New Zealand	X	X	X	X	X	X	27.6	33.8	99	X	5	X	X	X	X
Papua New Guinea	24	38	39	65	5.4	12.8	X	X	34	46	25	89	69	69	67
Solomon Islands	X	X	X	X	X	X	1.0	2.1	80	X	9	87	77	75	70

Sources: United Nations Children's Fund, United Nations Development Programme, and the United Nations Educational, Scientific and Cultural Organization.
Notes: a. Oral Rehydration Therapy. b. Population age 12 and older. c. 1989 data. d. Data are for males and females combined, age 7 and over. e. 1988 data. f. Population age 5 and older. g. Population age 10 and older. h. Population age 6 and older. i. Data are for males and females combined, age 10 and older. j. 1989 data, for Trinidad only. k. Population age 20 and older. l. Data for all ages. m. Government-controlled areas only. n. Data are for males and females combined. o. Data are for Yemen as a whole. p. Population age 14 and older. q. Population age 25-74.
0 = zero or less than half the unit of measure; X = not available.
For additional information, see Sources and Technical Notes.

Table 16.6 Contraceptive Prevalence and Availability

	Date of Latest Survey	Percentage of Married Couples Currently Using									Percentage of Married Couples with Affordable Access to				
		Any Method	Sterilization Female	Male	Pill	Inject-able	IUD	Condom	Vaginal Barriers	Other Methods {a}	Female Sterilization	Pill	Condom	Abortion	Other
WORLD															
AFRICA															
Algeria	1986/87	36	1	0	27	1	2	1	0	5	X	40	25	X	X
Benin	1981/82	9	0	0	0	0	0	0	0	9	X	65	43	X	X
Botswana	1988	33	4	0	15	5	6	1	0	1	80 b	95 c,d	95	X	X
Burkina Faso	X	X	X	X	X	X	X	X	X	X	2	50 d	65	X	X
Burundi	1987	9	0	0	0	1	0	0	0	8	10 b	60	60	X	X
Cameroon	1978	2	X	X	0	X	0	0	0	2	X	X	X	X	X
Central African Rep	X	X	X	X	X	X	X	X	X	X	8	5	5	X	X
Cote d'Ivoire	1980/81	3	0	0	0	0	0	0	0	2	1	8	15	50	X
Egypt	1988/89	37	2	0	15	0	16	2	0	1	53	97	84	58	X
Ethiopia	X	X	X	X	X	X	X	X	X	X	3	30	30	X	X
Ghana	1988	13	1	0	2	0	1	0	1	8	X	X	X	X	X
Guinea	X	X	X	X	X	X	X	X	X	X	X	2 c,d	2	X	X
Kenya	1988/89	27	5	0	5	3	4	1	0	9	21	54	58	X	X
Lesotho	1977	5	1	0	1	0	0	0	0	3	6	50	16	X	X
Liberia	1986	6	1	0	3	0	1	0	0	1	X	X	X	X	X
Madagascar	X	X	X	X	X	X	X	X	X	X	2	7 d	8	X	X
Malawi	1984	7	X e	X e	1	0	0	0	X e	6	X	X	X	X	X
Mali	1987	5	0	0	1	0	0	0	0	3	1 b	45	75	X	X
Mauritania	1981	1	0	0	0	0	0	0	0	1	X	X	X	X	X
Mauritius	1985	75	5	0	21	6	2	11	1	30	X	X	X	X	X
Morocco	1987	36	2	0	23	0	3	1	0	7	40	98	80	X	X
Nigeria	1981/82	5	0	X	0	0	0	0	X	4	6	24	29	X	15 f
Rwanda	1983	10	0	0	0	0	0	0	0	9	2	X	5	X	53 g
Senegal	1986	11	0	0	1	0	1	0	0	9	X	10	15	X	X
Sierra Leone	X	X	X	X	X	X	X	X	X	X	15	23	26	15	X
South Africa	1981	48	8	0	15	14	6	3	X h	3	X	X	X	X	X
Sudan	1989	9	1	0	4	0	1	0	0	3	X	7	15	X	X
Swaziland	1988	20	3	0	6	6	2	1	0	3	X	X	X	X	X
Tanzania	X	X	X	X	X	X	X	X	X	X	3 b	X	X	3	X
Togo	1988	34	1	0	0	0	1	0	1	31	4	48	63	48	X
Tunisia	1988	50	12	X i	9	1	17	1	1	9	84	73	41	68	X
Uganda	1988/89	5	1	0	1	0	0	0	0	2	6	22	6	X	X
Zaire	X	X	X	X	X	X	X	X	X	X	X	1 c,d	5	X	X
Zambia	X	X	X	X	X	X	X	X	X	X	28	40	30	X	X
Zimbabwe	1988	43	2	0	31	0	1	1	0	7	4 b	X	50	X	38 g
NORTH & CENTRAL AMERICA															
Antigua	1988	53	11	X e	26	3	1	6	3	2	X	X	X	X	X
Barbados	1980/81	47	14	0	16	2	4	5	3	2	X	X	X	X	X
Canada	1984	73	31	13	11	X	6	8	2	4	100 b	100	100	83	X
Costa Rica	1986	70	14	1	21	1	8	13	1	11	45	90	90	X	15 f
Cuba	1987	70	22	0	10	X	X	2	0	2	98	100	100	100	X
Dominica	1981	49	15 b	0	17	10	2	4	1	2	X	X	X	X	X
Dominican Rep	1986	50	33	0	9	0	3	1	0	3	65	90	90	X	X
El Salvador	1988	47	30	1	8	1	2	2	0	3	66	89	94	7	X
Grenada	1985	31	2	0	8	3	3	8	4	4	X	X	X	X	X
Guatemala	1987	23	10	1	4	1	2	1	0	4	50	60	65	X	X
Haiti	1989	10	3	0	4	2	1	1	1	1	22 b	28	70	32	X
Honduras	1987	41	13	0	13	0	4	2	0	8	88	94	88	X	X
Jamaica	1988/89	55	14	0	20	8	2	9	0	3	32	X	100	2	100 g
Mexico	1987	53	19	1	10	3	10	2	1	8	90	97	97	X	X
Nicaragua	1981	27	7	0	11	1	2	1	1	4	X	X	X	X	X
Panama	1984	58	32	0	12	1	6	2	1	4	25	80	80	X	X
St. Lucia	1981	43	11 b	X	21	2	1	4	1	3	X	X	X	X	X
St. Vincent	1988	58	13	X e	24	7	3	7	X e	4	X	X	X	X	X
Trinidad and Tobago	1987	53	8	0	14	1	4	12	5	8	22 b	100	100	X	X
United States	1988	74	23	13	15	0	2	11	6	5	80	90	100	78	X
SOUTH AMERICA															
Argentina	X	X	X	X	X	X	X	X	X	X	2	45	50	5	X
Bolivia	1989	30	4	0	2	1	5	0	0	18	X	X	X	X	X
Brazil	1986	66	27	1	25	1	1	2	1	9	50	90	95	X	X
Chile	X	X	X	X	X	X	X	X	X	X	60	85 c	90	X	X
Colombia	1990	66	21	1	14	2	12	3	2	11	90	90	90	X	X
Ecuador	1989	53	18	0	8	1	12	1	1	11	60	90	90	50	X
Guyana	1975	31	9	0	9	0	6	3	2	3	X	X	X	X	X
Paraguay	1990	48	7	0	14	5	6	3	1	13	X	X	X	X	X
Peru	1986	46	6	0	7	1	7	1	1	23	69	90	89	X	X
Uruguay	X	X	X	X	X	X	X	X	X	X	17	94	94	X	X
Venezuela	1977	49	8	0	15	0	9	5	1	12	X	X	58	X	63 k
ASIA															
Afghanistan	1972/73	2	0	0	1	0	0	0	X e	0	X	X	X	X	X
Bangladesh	1989	31	9	1	9	1	2	2	0	7	83 b	86 c	93	X	35 f
China	1988	71	27	8	4	X e	30	2	0	1	92 b	84 c	84	92	X
India	1988	43	31 b	X	1	X	2	5	0	4	85 b	40 c	60	65	X
Indonesia	1987	48	3	0	16	10	13	2	X e	4	30	90	91	X	39 f
Iran, Islamic Rep	X	X	X	X	X	X	X	X	X	X	X	50	40	X	X
Iraq	1974	15	1	X	9	1	1	1	1	2	X	X	X	X	X
Israel	X	X	X	X	X	X	X	X	X	X	X	100 c	100	95	X
Japan	1988	56	3	1	1	X	3	43	0	14	X	X	100	100	X
Jordan	1985	27	5	0	6	0	11	0	0	4	25	30	20	X	X
Korea, Dem People's Rep	X	X	X	X	X	X	X	X	X	X	4	X	X	X	63 k
Korea, Rep	1988	77	37	11	3	X e	7	10	2	7	90 b	98	98	85	X
Lebanon	1971	53	1	0	14	X	1	7	X	35	15	29	28	X	29 f
Malaysia	1984	51	8	0	12	1	2	8	0	31	60	99	99	X	X

Table 16.6

	Date of Latest Survey	Any Method	Percentage of Married Couples Currently Using								Percentage of Married Couples with Affordable Access to				
			Sterilization		Pill	Inject-able	IUD	Condom	Vaginal Barriers	Other Methods {a}	Female Steril-ization	Pill	Condom	Abortion	Other
			Female	Male											
Myanmar	X	X	X	X	X	X	X	X	X	X	6	13	5	44	X
Nepal	1986	14	6	6	1	1	0	1	X	0	29	14	9	X	X
Pakistan	1984/85	8	2	0	1	1	1	2	0	1	3 j	30	39	X	X
Philippines	1986	44	11 b	X	6	0	2	1	X e	23	16 b	40	38	X	X
Singapore	1982	74	22	1	12	X i	X i	24	14	1	100 b	100 c,d	100	100	X
Sri Lanka	1987	62	25	5	4	3	2	2	0	22	68 b	86	86	X	56 f
Syrian Arab Rep	1978	20	0	0	12	0	1	1	1	5	X	65	45	X	X
Thailand	1987	68	22	6	20	9	7	1	0	2	74 b	95	95	X	43 f
Turkey	1988	63	2	0	6	0	14	7	2	32	22	74	74	49	X
Viet Nam	1988	53	3	0	0	X	31	1	X e	18	30	X	20	50	60 k
Yemen (Arab Rep)	1979	1	0	0	1	0	0	0	0	0	2 l	X	70 l	X	45 k,l
EUROPE															
Austria	1981/82	71	1	0	40	0	8	4	3	15	100 b	100	100	X	X
Belgium	1982/83	81	17 b	X	32	0	8	6	0	17	X	X	100	95	X
Bulgaria	1976	76	1	1	2	0	2	2	X	69	X	X	100	100	68 k
Czechoslovakia	1977	X	X	X	X	X	X	X	X	X	100 b	X	100	100	100 k
Denmark	1975	63	X	X	22	0	9	25	4	4	100 b	100	100	100	X
Finland	1977	80	4	1	11	0	29	32	1	3	100 b	90	100	90	X
France	1988	81	7	0	30	0	26	4	X e	15	X	100 c	100	98	X
Germany (Fed Rep)	1985	78	10	2	34	0	15	6	1	10	90	100 m	100 m	95 m	X
Greece	X	X	X	X	X	X	X	X	X	X	X	100	100	100	X
Hungary	1986	73	X	X	39	0	19	4	1	11	X	100	100	100	X
Ireland	X	X	X	X	X	X	X	X	X	X	87 j	88	83	X	X
Italy	1979	78	1	0	14	0	2	13	2	46	X	100	100	56	X
Netherlands	1988	76	4	11	41	X n	7	8	X e	4	100 b	100	100	100	X
Norway	1977	71	4	2	13	0	28	16	2	7	100	100	100	100	X
Poland	1977	75	X	X	7	0	2	14	3	49	X	X	X	X	X
Portugal	1979/80	66	1	0	19	2	4	6	2	34	X	100	100	X	X
Romania	1978	58	X	X	1	0	0	3	1	53	X	X	X	100	X
Spain	1985	59	4	0	16	X e	6	12	X e	22	X	80	70	30	X
Sweden	1981	78	3 b	X	23	0	20	25	X h	7	100 j	100	100	100	X
Switzerland	1980	71	16 b	X	28	0	11	8	2	6	100	100	100	90	X
United Kingdom	1983	81	12	12	29	0	9	15	2	7	100 j	100	100	100	X
Yugoslavia	1976	55	X	X	5	0	2	2	3	43	30	100	100	100	X
U.S.S.R.	X	X	X	X	X	X	X	X	X	X	X	10	20	90	X
OCEANIA															
Australia	1986	76	28	10	24	X	5	4	1	4	90	100	85	90	X
Fiji	1974	41	16	0	8	0	5	6	0	6	X	X	X	X	X
New Zealand	1976	70	11	9	29	X e	4	8	X e	10	95	95	100	95	X
Papua New Guinea	X	X	X	X	X	X	X	X	X	X	4	17	60	X	10 f

Sources: Population Crisis Committee and the United Nations Population Division.
Notes: a. Includes periodic abstinence (such as rhythm method), abstinence, withdrawal, and douche, or a combination of methods. b. Both sexes. c. Includes access to IUDs. d. Includes access to injectables. e. Included in "Other Methods." f. Access to menstrual regulation only. g. Access to injectables only. h. Included under "Condom." i. Included under "Vaginal Barriers." j. Male sterilization only. k. Access to IUDs only. l. Data for both Yemen Arab Republic and People's Democratic Republic of Yemen. m. Data for both Federal Republic of Germany and German Democratic Republic. n. Included under "Pill."
0 = zero or less than half the unit of measure; X = not covered in survey or not reported.
For additional information, see Sources and Technical Notes.

Sources and Technical Notes

Table 16.1 Size and Growth of Population and Labor Force, 1950–2025

Sources: United Nations Population Division, *World Population Prospects 1990* (U.N., New York, 1991); International Labour Office (ILO), unpublished data (ILO, Geneva, 1986).

Population refers to the midyear population. Most data are estimates based on population censuses and surveys. All projections are for the medium-case scenario (see the following discussion). The *average annual population change* takes into account the effects of international migration.

Many of the numbers in Tables 16.1–16.3 are estimated using demographic models based on several kinds of demographic parameters: a country's population size, age and sex distribution, fertility and mortality rates by age and sex groups, growth rates

of urban and rural populations, and the levels of internal and international migration.

Information collected through recent population censuses and surveys is used to calculate or estimate these parameters, but accuracy varies. The United Nations Population Division's Department of International Economic and Social Affairs (DIESA) compiles and evaluates census and survey results from all countries. These data are adjusted for overenumeration and underenumeration of certain age and sex groups (infants, female children, young males), misreporting of age and sex distributions, changes in definitions, and so forth, when necessary. These adjustments incorporate data from civil registrations, population surveys, earlier censuses, and, when necessary, population models based on information from socioeconomically similar countries. (Because the figures have been adjusted, they are not strictly comparable to the official statistics compiled by the

United Nations Statistical Office and published in the *Demographic Yearbook*.)

After the figures for population size and age/sex composition have been adjusted, the data are scaled to 1985. Similar estimates are made for each five-year period between 1950 and 1980. Historical data are used when deemed accurate, also with adjustments and scaling. However, accurate historical data do not exist for many developing countries. In these cases, the Population Division uses available information and demographic models to estimate the main demographic parameters.

Projections are based on estimates of the 1985 base-year population. Age- and sex-specific mortality rates are applied to the base-year population to determine the number of survivors at the end of each five-year period. Births are projected by applying age-specific fertility rates to the projected female population. Births are distributed by an assumed sex ratio, and the appropriate age-and sex-specific survival rates are applied. Future migration rates are also estimated on an age-and sex-specific basis. Combining future fertility, mortality, and migration rates yields the projected size and composition of the population.

Assumptions about future mortality, fertility, and migration rates are made on a country-by-country basis and, when possible, are based on historical trends. Four scenarios of population growth (high, medium, low, and constant) are created by using different assumptions about these rates. For example, the medium-case scenario assumes medium levels of fertility, mortality, and migration—assumptions that may vary among countries. Refer to the source for further details.

The labor force includes all people who produce economic goods and services. It includes all employed people (employers, the self-employed, salaried employees, wage earners, unpaid family workers, members of producer cooperatives, and members of the armed forces), and the unemployed (experienced workers and those looking for work for the first time).

The ILO determines the *average annual growth of the labor force* by multiplying the activity rates of age/sex groups (the economically active fraction of an age/sex group) by the number of people in those groups. Estimates of activity rates are based on information from national censuses and labor force surveys. ILO adjusts national labor force statistics when necessary to conform to international definitions. The growth of age/sex groups is provided to ILO by the United Nations Population Division.

Table 16.2 Trends in Births, Life Expectancy, Fertility, and Age Structure, 1970–95

Source: United Nations Population Division, *World Population Prospects 1990* (U.N., New York, 1991).

The *crude birth rate* is derived by dividing the number of live births in a given year by the midyear population. This ratio is then multiplied by 1,000.

Life expectancy at birth is the average number of years that a newborn baby is expected to live if the age-specific mortality rates effective at the year of birth apply throughout his or her lifetime.

The *total fertility rate* is an estimate of the number of children that an average woman would have if current age-specific fertility rates remained constant during her reproductive years.

The *percentage of population in specific age groups* shows a country's age structure: 0–14, 15–65, and over 65 years. It is useful for inferring dependency, needs for education and employment, potential fertility, and other age-related factors. For additional details, see sources or the Technical Note for Table 16.1.

Table 16.3 Mortality and Nutrition, 1970–95

Sources: Crude death rate and infant death rate data: United Nations Population Divi-

sion, *World Population Prospects 1990* (U.N., New York, 1991); Child deaths: United Nations Population Division, *Mortality of Children Under Age 5: World Estimates and Projections, 1950–2025* (U.N., New York, 1988); Maternal deaths, wasting, and stunting: United Nations Children's Fund (UNICEF), *State of the World's Children 1991* (UNICEF, New York, 1991); Maternal deaths for Cape Verde, Comoros, Djibouti, The Gambia, Barbados, Belize, Guyana, Suriname, Bahrain, and the Solomon Islands and wasting and stunting data for Cape Verde, Djibouti, The Gambia, Liberia, Rwanda, Sierra Leone, Zaire, Barbados, Belize, Guyana, Nepal, and the Solomon Islands: United Nations Development Programme (UNDP) *Human Development Report 1991* (Oxford University Press, Oxford, 1991). Per capita average calories available as a percentage of need and per capita total protein consumption: Food and Agriculture Organization of the United Nations (FAO), *Agrostat PC* (FAO, Rome, July 1991).

The *crude death rate* is derived by dividing the number of deaths in a year by the midyear population, and multiplying by 1,000.

The *infant death rate* is derived by dividing the number of babies who die before their first birthday by the number of live births in that year, and multiplying by 1,000.

Child deaths are derived by dividing the number of children under age 5 who die in a given year by the number of live births in that year, and multiplying by 1,000. Infant and child death rates are projected from the latest estimates available from the United Nations Population Division. These death rates are not comparable because different parameters were used in modeling projected changes.

Maternal deaths are the number of deaths from pregnancy- or childbirth-related causes per 100,000 live births. A maternal death is defined by the World Health Organization (WHO) as the death of a woman while pregnant or within 42 days of termination of pregnancy from any cause related to or aggravated by the pregnancy, including abortion. Most official maternal mortality rates are underestimated because causes of death are often incorrectly classified or unavailable. In some countries, over 60 percent of women's deaths are registered without a specified cause. Maternal deaths are highest among women of ages 10–15 years, and over 40 years, and in women with five or more children. Data are provided to UNDP and UNICEF by WHO and refer to a single year between 1980 and 1988 (1980 to 1987 for UNDP data). Data for some countries are outside the range of years indicated.

Wasting indicates current acute malnutrition and refers to the percentage of children between the ages of 12 and 23 months whose weight-for-height is less than 77 percent of the median weight-for-height of the reference population of the U.S. National Center for Health Statistics (NCHS). *Stunting*, an indicator of chronic undernutrition, refers to the percentage of children between the ages of 24 and 59 months whose height-for-age is less than 77 percent of the median. NCHS, among others, has found that healthy children under the age of 5 years

do not differ appreciably in weight or height. WHO has accepted the NCHS weight-for-age and weight-for-height standards. Children with low weight-for-age are at a high risk of mortality. Data on wasting and stunting, provided to UNDP and UNICEF by WHO, refer to a single year between 1980 and 1989 (1980 to 1988 for UNDP data). Data for some countries are outside the range of years or ages indicated.

The *per capita average calories available (as percent of need)* and the *per capita total protein consumption* are calories and protein from all food sources: domestic production, international trade, stock drawdowns, and foreign aid. Total protein is the amount provided from animal and vegetable food sources. The quantity of food available for human consumption, as estimated by FAO, is the amount that reaches the consumer. The calories and protein actually consumed may be lower than the figures shown, depending on how much is lost during home storage, preparation, and cooking, and how much is fed to pets and domestic animals or discarded. Estimates of daily caloric requirements vary for individual countries according to the age distribution and estimated level of activity of the population.

Table 16.4 Access to Safe Drinking Water, Sanitation, and Health Services, 1980s

Sources: Drinking water and sanitation: World Health Organization (WHO), *The International Drinking Water Supply and Sanitation Decade: Review of Mid-Decade Progress (as at December 1985)* (WHO, Geneva, September 1987); WHO, *The International Drinking Water Supply and Sanitation Decade: Review of National Progress (as at December 1983)*; WHO, *The International Drinking Water Supply and Sanitation Decade: Review of National Baseline Data: December 1980* (WHO, Geneva, 1984); WHO, *Global Strategy for Health for All. Monitoring 1988–1989. Detailed analysis of global indicators* (WHO, Geneva, May 1989); and unpublished data (WHO, Geneva, July 1991). Access to health services: United Nations Children's Fund (UNICEF), *State of the World's Children 1991* (UNICEF, New York, 1991). Numbers of trained medical personnel: WHO, *1988 World Health Statistics Annual* (WHO, Geneva, 1988).

WHO collected data on drinking water and sanitation from national governments in 1980, 1983, 1985, and 1988 using questionnaires completed by public health officials, WHO experts, and Resident Representatives of the United Nations Development Programme. Data for a number of countries were gathered during 1986–87. For several countries in Africa, dates were not given.

Urban and rural populations were defined by each national government.

WHO defines reasonable access to *safe drinking water* in an urban area as access to piped water or a public standpipe within 200 meters of a dwelling or housing unit. In rural areas, reasonable access implies that a family member need not spend a disproportionate part of the day fetching water. "Safe" drinking water includes treated surface water and untreated water from protected springs, boreholes, and sanitary wells.

Urban areas with access to *sanitation services* are defined as urban populations served by connections to public sewers or household systems such as pit privies, pour-flush latrines, septic tanks, communal toilets, and other such facilities. Rural populations with access were defined as those with adequate disposal such as pit privies, pour-flush latrines, and so forth. Application of these definitions may vary, and comparisons can therefore be misleading.

The population with access to *health services* is defined by UNICEF as the percentage of the population that can reach local health services by local transport in no more than one hour.

Data on *number of trained medical personnel* are the latest available to WHO regional offices at the beginning of 1988. Most are from 1983–86; however, some go back to 1977. Comparisons should be made with care, since categories and definitions vary among countries.

Health care personnel have been combined into three categories:

Doctors: all physicians or surgeons;

Nurses and midwives: all registered nurses and others in categories in which the term "nurse" or "nursing" appears; all midwives, birth attendants, and others in categories in which the term "midwife" appears;

Other: all others directly involved in diagnosis, treatment, and prevention of disease (e.g., dentists, paramedical personnel, medical assistants, acupuncturists), and all other reported categories (e.g., pharmacists, laboratory technicians, x-ray technicians, and hospital administrators).

Access to health personnel can vary substantially within a country. The degree of access in individual countries can be partly inferred from other health data (e.g., infant deaths, immunizations) presented here.

Table 16.5 Education and Child Health, 1970–90

Sources: Adult literacy for 1970: United Nations Children's Fund (UNICEF), *State of the World's Children 1989* and *State of the World's Children 1991* (UNICEF, New York, 1989 and 1991); Adult literacy for 1990: United Nations Educational, Scientific and Cultural Organization (UNESCO), *Compendium of Statistics on Illiteracy–1990 Edition* (UNESCO, Paris, 1990); The percentage of population age 25 and over who have completed primary school and who have some postsecondary education: United Nations Educational, Scientific and Cultural Organization (UNESCO) *Statistical Yearbook 1990* (UNESCO, Paris, 1990); Births attended by trained personnel, ORT use, and low-birth-weight infants: UNICEF, *State of the World's Children 1991* (UNICEF, New York, 1991); Births attended by trained personnel for Cape Verde, Comoros, Djibouti, Equatorial Guinea, The Gambia, Guinea-Bissau, Swaziland, Barbados, Belize, Guyana, Suriname, Bahrain, Yemen, Fiji and the Solomon Islands and low-birth-weight infants for Chad, Comoros, Djibouti, The Gambia, Guinea-Bissau, Barbados, Belize, Guyana,

and Suriname: United Nations Development Programme (UNDP), *Human Development Report 1991* (Oxford University Press, New York, 1991); TB, DPT, polio, and measles immunization: UNICEF, unpublished data, September 1991.

Adult female and *adult male literacy* rates refer to the percentage of people over the age of 15 who can read and write. UNESCO recommends defining as illiterate a person who cannot both read with understanding and write a short and simple statement on his or her everyday life. This concept is widely accepted, but its interpretation and application vary. It does not include people who, though familiar with the basics of reading and writing, do not have the skills to function at a reasonable level in their own society. Actual definitions of adult literacy are not strictly comparable among countries. Literacy data for 1990 are projected from past census figures, using estimates of age group size within country populations when available.

The *percentage of population age 25 and over who have completed primary school* and *who have some postsecondary education* are figures based largely on national censuses and sample surveys taken between 1970 and 1989. Primary education is defined as category 1 of the International Standard Classification of Education (ISCED). The length of primary education varies by country from three to nine years. The median length for all countries is six years for primary education, and five and a half years for secondary education. Postsecondary education consists of ISCED categories 5, 6, and 7. These categories include education at universities, technical schools, and teacher-training institutes.

The percentage of *births attended by trained personnel* includes all health personnel accepted by national authorities as part of the health system. Personnel included vary by country. Some countries include traditional birthing assistants and midwives; others, only doctors. WHO provides the data to UNICEF.

ORT (oral rehydration therapy) *use* refers to administration of oral rehydration salts to children to combat diarrheal disease leading to dehydration or malnutrition.

The percentage of *low-birth-weight infants* refers to all babies weighing 2,500 grams or less at birth. WHO has adopted the standard that healthy babies, regardless of race, should weigh more than 2,500 grams at birth. These data are provided to UNICEF by WHO, and refer to a single year between 1980 and 1988.

Immunization data show the *percentage of 1-year-olds fully immunized in 1990 against*: *TB* (tuberculosis); *DPT* (diphtheria, pertussis [whooping cough], and tetanus); *polio*; and *measles*. Data for measles immunizations include totals from countries where this vaccination is normally given to children after 1 year of age .

Table 16.6 Contraceptive Prevalence and Availability

Sources: Contraceptive prevalence: United Nations Population Division, unpublished

data (U.N., New York, March 1991). Affordable access to contraception: Population Crisis Committee (PCC), *Access to Affordable Contraception, 1991 Report on World Progress Towards Population Stabilization* (PCC, Washington, D.C., 1991).

Contraceptive prevalence is the level of current contraceptive use among couples in which the woman is of childbearing age. The data were obtained from nationally representative sample surveys of women between the ages of 15 and 49 who are married or cohabiting. The ages of women interviewed for some surveys varied slightly from this range. Many of these surveys were conducted as part of the World Fertility Survey (WFS), Contraceptive Prevalence Surveys (CPSs), or Demographic Health Surveys (DHS).

The survey procedure of determining use of a method varied: most surveys named and described each contraceptive method, but a few asked only general questions about use of family planning, without naming the methods.

Sterilization includes both female and male voluntary sterilization. Female sterilization is significantly more prevalent than male sterilization; the Netherlands is the only country where male sterilization exceeds female. *Pill* refers to oral contraceptives. *Injectable* refers to injectable hormonal contraceptives; this method is a relatively new technology and is not widely available in many countries. *Condom* use may be slightly underreported, since studies have shown that prevalence of condom use is higher when men, rather than women, are surveyed. *Vaginal barrier* methods include the diaphragm, cervical cap, and spermicides (foam, jelly, and cream). *Other methods* include traditional (also known as nonsupply) methods such as rhythm, withdrawal, abstinence, and douching. Users of folk remedies, and contraceptive users who do not identify their method, are included in *other methods.*

Affordable access is defined as ability to acquire (1) contraceptive supplies and services with, on average, no more than two hours a month of effort; and (2) one month's contraceptive supplies at a cost not exceeding 1 percent of the average monthly wage. Data represent the percentage of married couples of reproductive age in 1990 that have access to contraceptives through all sources of supply and service. Access refers only to availability, not to the actual use of contraceptives.

Female sterilization refers to voluntary female sterilization unless otherwise indicated. *Pill, condom,* and *injectable* (note d) are as defined above. *Menstrual regulation* (note f) refers to abortion performed on suspicion of pregnancy, without first determining whether the woman is pregnant.

Contraceptive accessibility and cost data were gathered through surveys of country experts, primarily family planning personnel, in 110 countries with populations over 1 million. Contraceptive accessibility data were available for 99 of these countries. The Population Council surveyed 81 developing countries. Data for a further 29 countries were collected by the PCC.

17. Land Cover and Settlements

The data for this chapter focus on the changing relationship of people to land. Also included is information on the human environment: population density, wilderness areas, urban populations, large cities, the labor force, and transportation.

Data in Table 17.1 show current levels of use and recent rates of change in how nations use their land resources. In most regions, natural and planted forest-lands have decreased over the past decade. The greatest declines have occurred in Asia (5.3 percent) and South America (4.6 percent). Worldwide, forest and woodland areas have shrunk 1.8 percent. Some of this land has been converted to cropland, which has increased globally by 2.2 percent since 1977–79. The greatest increases in cropland have occurred in Oceania (11.6 percent), South America (10.9 percent), and Africa (4.4 percent)—regions that have simultaneously experienced a net loss of forest and woodland. The world's wastelands, rangelands, and urban settlements (land categorized as "other") have registered the greatest absolute growth over the past decade, while land devoted to permanent pasture has changed little, increasing a scant 0.1 percent.

Table 17.2 shows how populations are dispersed on the land: between rural and urban areas, and between large cities of 1 million or more people and smaller settlements. In 1990, more than 75 percent of all South Americans were living in urban areas, the highest degree of urbanization of any region of the world. Europe ranked a close second, with 73.4 percent of the population in urban areas. The urban growth rate between 1960 and 1990 was highest in Africa, at 4.9 percent per year, as compared with a global annual rate of 2.8 percent. The world's rural populations have grown at a slower rate (1.3 percent per year) and, in fact, have declined over the past three decades in Europe and the U.S.S.R.

The distribution of the 1980 labor force reflects regional differences in the urban-rural population mix. Two thirds of the Asian and African labor forces worked in the agricultural sector, reflecting the importance of the rural share of total populations in those regions.

By 1990, there were 276 cities in the world with populations of 1 million or more. Although the majority of these cities (42 percent) are located in Asia, more South Americans live in large cities (about one third of the region's 1990 population) than people of any other region of the globe. In developing countries in particu-

lar, the growth of cities puts a further burden on municipal governments, which are often unable to meet demands for adequate housing, sanitation, water, and electricity. Table 17.2 also provides data on housing conditions (number of occupants and number of rooms per household, and percent of households without electricity) for many countries of the world.

The transport of people and material is essential to the successful functioning of modern economies. Governments are charged with building and maintaining transport infrastructures to promote economic activity within their borders. Countries may choose to invest in one type of infrastructure over another—for instance, rail systems over road systems—to move their people and freight. Table 17.3 describes the results of these investment decisions, which also affect a country's rate of fossil fuel consumption and emissions of greenhouse gases and other pollutants. The density of transport infrastructure, as expressed in kilometers of road, rail, and waterway network per thousand square kilometers of land, is usually in inverse proportion to the amount of wildlands left within a country. (Wilderness area, presented in Table 17.1, is defined, in part, by the absence of roads.) Road and railway construction often opens new areas to settlement, cultivation, logging, and mining.

For the majority of countries on which data are available, roads provide the most extensive transport system on a per-unit-area basis. On average, for every 1,000 square kilometers of land, the world has 170 kilometers of road compared with 9.5 kilometers of rail track and 4.7 kilometers of navigable inland waterways. Regional road density ranges from 848 kilometers per 1,000 square kilometers of land in Europe to 53 kilometers per 1,000 square kilometers in Africa.

Roads are also the primary means for transporting people, relative to rail and airline systems. Among developing countries reporting, bus lines and other public road vehicles are the dominant mode of transportation. In contrast, private vehicles (cars) are the primary means of transportation in almost all industrialized countries. This difference between developing and industrialized countries is reflected in the ratio of people to cars. The number of people per car exceeds 100 for over one half of the African countries reporting data, and for about one quarter of the developing countries of Asia, whereas there are two to three people per car in most of the industrialized world.

Table 17.1 Land Area and Use, 1977–89

	Land Area (000 hectares)	Population Density, 1990 (per 1,000 hectares)	Cropland 1987-89	Percentage Change Since 1977-79	Permanent Pasture 1987-89	Percentage Change Since 1977-79	Forest and Woodland 1987-89	Percentage Change Since 1977-79	Other Land 1987-89	Percentage Change Since 1977-79	Wilderness Area Total 1988 (000 hectares)	Percentage of Total Land Area
WORLD {a}	13,128,841	403	1,477,877	2.2	3,322,943	0.1	4,095,317	(1.8)	4,232,737	1.0	3,486,097	26
AFRICA	2,964,138	217	186,392	4.4	890,899	(0.5)	686,284	(3.6)	1,200,565	1.9	823,238	27
Algeria	238,174	105	7,613	1.1	31,168	(14.1)	4,699	11.6	194,693	2.4	140,424	59
Angola	124,670	80	3,583	2.4	29,000	0.0	53,040	(1.7)	39,047	2.1	27,049	22
Benin	11,062	419	1,853	3.5	442	0.0	3,570	(12.3)	5,197	9.2	1,209	11
Botswana	56,673	23	1,373	1.0	33,000	0.0	10,930	(0.9)	11,370	0.8	31,255	54
Burkina Faso	27,380	329	3,423	27.5	10,000	0.0	6,720	(8.2)	7,237	(1.9)	750	3
Burundi	2,565	2,133	1,334	4.0	913	2.5	65	8.3	253	(23.8)	0	0
Cameroon	46,540	254	7,004	3.9	8,300	0.0	24,760	(4.3)	6,476	14.9	1,320	3
Cape Verde	403	918	39	(1.7)	25	0.0	1	0.0	338	0.2	0	0
Central African Rep	62,298	49	2,006	4.5	3,000	0.0	35,820	(0.3)	21,472	0.0	20,917	34
Chad	125,920	45	3,205	2.3	45,000	0.0	12,890	(5.8)	64,825	1.1	61,254	48
Comoros	223	2,466	99	10.0	15	0.0	35	0.0	74	(10.8)	0	0
Congo	34,150	67	167	14.4	10,000	0.0	21,200	(0.9)	2,783	6.9	11,837	35
Cote d'Ivoire	31,800	377	3,653	20.8	13,000	0.0	7,880	(24.1)	7,267	34.7	4,268	13
Djibouti	2,318	176	0	0.0	200	0.0	6	0.0	2,112	0.0	0	0
Egypt	99,545	527	2,571	1.2	0	0.0	31	0.0	96,943	(0.0)	42,540	42
Equatorial Guinea	2,805	125	230	0.0	104	0.0	1,295	0.0	1,176	0.0	0	0
Ethiopia	110,100	447	13,930	1.0	45,000	(1.1)	27,300	(3.5)	23,870	6.1	19,716	16
Gabon	25,767	45	452	2.3	4,700	(0.7)	20,000	0.0	615	3.9	7,333	27
Gambia, The	1,000	861	174	13.7	90	0.0	168	(26.2)	568	7.3	0	0
Ghana	23,002	653	2,700	7.6	5,000	0.0	8,210	(7.9)	7,092	13.5	0	0
Guinea	24,586	234	727	3.8	6,150	0.0	14,700	(3.9)	3,009	23.5	0	0
Guinea-Bissau	2,812	343	335	17.5	1,080	0.0	1,070	0.0	327	(13.3)	0	0
Kenya	56,969	422	2,424	6.8	38,100	0.0	2,380	(7.8)	14,065	0.3	11,221	19
Lesotho	3,035	585	320	8.8	2,000	0.0	0	0.0	715	(3.5)	2,133	70
Liberia	9,632	267	372	0.4	5,700	0.0	1,780	(14.4)	1,780	20.2	1,420	13
Libya	175,954	26	2,147	3.7	13,300	5.6	678	16.6	159,829	(0.5)	65,497	37
Madagascar	58,154	206	3,079	4.3	34,000	0.0	15,830	(8.7)	5,245	35.5	691	1
Malawi	9,408	930	2,391	4.3	1,840	0.0	3,850	(19.3)	1,327	161.9	781	7
Mali	122,019	76	2,087	1.8	30,000	0.0	7,010	(4.1)	82,922	0.3	58,814	47
Mauritania	102,522	20	199	1.4	39,250	0.0	4,450	(2.2)	58,623	0.2	71,370	70
Mauritius	185	5,849	106	(0.6)	7	0.0	57	(1.1)	14	10.3	0	0
Morocco	44,630	562	8,985	14.1	20,900	5.6	7,915	2.0	6,830	(25.7)	0	0
Mozambique	78,409	200	3,097	0.5	44,000	0.0	14,500	(7.6)	16,812	7.6	6,130	8
Namibia	82,329	22	662	1.0	38,000	0.0	18,180	(1.6)	25,487	1.2	22,239	0
Niger	126,670	61	3,599	13.0	9,267	(4.0)	2,120	(22.1)	111,685	0.5	65,633	52
Nigeria	91,077	1,192	31,335	3.5	40,000	0.0	12,500	(19.4)	7,242	36.5	1,526	2
Rwanda	2,467	2,934	1,149	17.2	480	(15.8)	560	(5.1)	278	(14.9)	0	0
Senegal	19,253	381	5,226	1.5	5,700	0.0	5,942	(2.6)	2,385	3.6	1,586	8
Sierra Leone	7,162	580	1,801	4.7	2,204	0.0	2,073	(2.4)	1,084	(2.8)	0	0
Somalia	62,734	120	1,038	4.8	43,000	0.0	9,080	(1.1)	9,616	0.5	10,460	16
South Africa	122,104	289	13,172	(1.3)	81,378	(0.1)	4,515	8.8	23,039	(0.5)	0	0
Sudan	237,600	106	12,499	0.9	98,000	0.0	45,440	(6.2)	81,661	3.7	79,377	32
Swaziland	1,720	458	164	(8.4)	1,175	(1.8)	107	2.9	275	14.6	0	0
Tanzania	88,604	308	5,240	2.2	35,000	0.0	41,180	(2.8)	7,184	17.8	7,053	7
Togo	5,439	649	1,438	1.4	1,790	0.0	1,620	(5.8)	591	15.7	0	0
Tunisia	15,536	527	4,700	(5.2)	2,952	2.9	620	17.9	7,264	1.2	1,901	12
Uganda	19,955	942	6,705	20.0	1,800	0.0	5,660	(8.1)	5,790	(9.7)	530	2
Zaire	226,760	157	7,850	4.1	15,000	0.0	174,970	(1.9)	28,940	11.6	11,763	5
Zambia	74,339	114	5,238	3.9	30,000	0.0	28,990	(2.4)	10,111	5.2	15,075	20
Zimbabwe	38,667	251	2,796	10.3	4,856	0.0	19,290	(4.0)	11,725	4.8	0	0
NORTH & CENTRAL AMERICA {b}	2,137,700	184	273,816	1.1	368,631	3.1	715,415	1.0	779,838	(2.5)	907,742	41
Barbados	43	5,930	33	0.0	4	0.0	0	0.0	6	0.0	0	0
Belize	2,280	82	56	12.8	48	15.2	1,012	0.0	1,164	(1.1)	0	0
Canada	922,097	29	45,977	4.4	32,500	26.7	356,000	5.8	487,620	(5.5)	640,587	64
Costa Rica	5,106	590	527	5.5	2,310	24.0	1,640	(17.0)	629	(17.9)	0	0
Cuba	10,982	966	3,332	5.3	2,992	14.3	2,750	11.8	1,908	(30.3)	0	0
Dominican Rep	4,838	1,482	1,440	5.5	2,092	0.0	619	(3.1)	687	(7.4)	0	0
El Salvador	2,072	2,535	733	4.5	610	0.0	104	(31.6)	625	2.7	0	0
Guatemala	10,843	848	1,868	8.3	1,380	7.8	3,910	(17.0)	3,685	17.8	0	0
Haiti	2,756	2,363	904	2.7	499	(3.0)	42	(30.0)	1,311	0.8	0	0
Honduras	11,189	459	1,793	2.3	2,540	7.2	3,420	(18.8)	3,436	20.4	1,126	10
Jamaica	1,083	2,268	269	1.5	193	(7.9)	187	(5.1)	434	5.5	0	0
Mexico	190,869	464	24,700	1.9	74,499	0.0	43,540	(12.0)	48,122	12.8	3,050	2
Nicaragua	11,875	326	1,270	2.8	5,300	11.5	3,600	(23.5)	1,705	44.7	1,521	12
Panama	7,599	318	576	4.6	1,537	15.9	3,407	(19.4)	2,079	39.3	0	0
Trinidad and Tobago	513	2,497	120	3.7	11	0.0	222	(4.3)	160	3.7	0	0
United States	916,660	272	189,915	0.0	241,467	1.0	294,261	(1.1)	191,017	1.0	44,058	5
SOUTH AMERICA	1,752,926	169	141,578	10.9	477,863	4.1	895,692	(4.6)	237,792	4.7	374,597	21
Argentina	273,669	118	35,750	1.9	142,400	(0.7)	59,400	(1.3)	36,119	3.1	14,976	5
Bolivia	108,439	67	3,461	3.7	26,700	(1.5)	55,710	(1.1)	22,568	4.1	17,810	16
Brazil	845,651	178	78,233	17.1	169,000	6.3	555,560	(4.2)	42,858	7.2	202,061	24
Chile	74,880	176	4,415	5.4	13,400	3.9	8,800	1.4	48,265	(1.7)	23,086	30
Colombia	103,870	317	5,348	3.5	40,194	6.8	50,907	(5.6)	7,420	3.3	15,156	13
Ecuador	27,684	382	2,683	6.9	5,050	44.3	11,500	(21.0)	8,451	18.6	0	0
Guyana	19,685	40	495	6.2	1,230	5.9	16,369	(2.7)	1,591	29.1	12,204	57
Paraguay	39,730	108	2,203	46.7	20,420	32.6	14,967	(27.7)	2,140	0.4	7,726	19
Peru	128,000	168	3,727	8.7	27,120	0.0	68,900	(3.5)	28,253	8.5	36,660	29
Suriname	15,600	27	68	53.4	20	11.1	14,855	(0.3)	657	3.0	11,080	68
Uruguay	17,481	177	1,304	(10.0)	13,520	(0.8)	669	7.4	1,988	11.8	0	0
Venezuela	88,205	224	3,883	5.9	17,600	2.9	30,755	(8.6)	35,967	6.5	29,742	33

Table 17.1

	Land Area (000 hectares)	Population Density, 1990 (per 1,000 hectares)	Cropland 1987-89	Cropland Percentage Change Since 1977-79	Permanent Pasture 1987-89	Permanent Pasture Percentage Change Since 1977-79	Forest and Woodland 1987-89	Forest and Woodland Percentage Change Since 1977-79	Other Land 1987-89	Other Land Percentage Change Since 1977-79	Wilderness Area Total 1988 (000 hectares)	Wilderness Area Percentage of Total Land Area
ASIA	**2,731,228**	**1,140**	**454,456**	**0.8**	**694,251**	**(0.3)**	**538,855**	**(5.3)**	**1,043,666**	**2.8**	**377,586**	**13**
Afghanistan	65,209	254	8,054	0.1	30,000	0.0	1,900	0.0	25,255	(0.0)	8,740	13
Bahrain	68	7,588	2	0.0	4	0.0	0	0.0	62	0.0	0	0
Bangladesh	13,017	8,880	9,271	1.5	600	0.0	1,966	(10.4)	1,181	8.9	0	0
Bhutan	4,700	323	130	10.5	270	2.5	2,600	2.8	1,700	(5.0)	1,179	25
Cambodia	17,652	467	3,056	0.3	580	0.0	13,372	0.0	644	(1.5)	0	0
China	932,641	1,221	96,615	(3.9)	319,080	0.0	126,848	(7.7)	390,097	3.9	210,776	22
Cyprus	924	759	157	(1.5)	5	0.0	123	0.0	639	0.4	0	0
India	297,319	2,869	169,357	0.5	11,923	(3.4)	66,782	(0.7)	49,258	(0.1)	1,161	0
Indonesia	181,157	1,017	21,233	9.3	11,800	(1.9)	113,433	(5.2)	34,691	15.5	11,761	6
Iran, Islamic Rep	163,600	334	14,830	(3.6)	44,000	0.0	18,020	0.1	86,750	0.6	15,685	10
Iraq	43,737	433	5,450	1.5	4,000	0.0	1,890	(1.6)	32,397	(0.2)	6,477	15
Israel	2,033	2,263	433	4.8	148	24.0	110	(5.2)	1,342	(3.1)	0	0
Japan	37,652	3,279	4,675	(5.4)	637	15.7	25,105	0.4	7,235	1.2	0	0
Jordan	8,893	451	372	12.1	791	0.1	71	12.2	7,660	(0.6)	0	0
Korea, Dem People's Rep	12,041	1,808	1,990	5.9	50	0.0	8,970	0.0	1,031	(9.8)	0	0
Korea, Rep	9,873	4,334	2,136	(3.8)	88	116.4	6,492	(1.4)	1,157	12.2	0	0
Kuwait	1,782	1,144	4	300.0	134	0.0	2	0.0	1,642	(0.2)	0	0
Lao People's Dem Rep	23,080	179	901	4.6	800	0.0	12,900	(7.2)	8,479	12.8	437	2
Lebanon	1,023	2,640	301	(5.6)	10	0.0	80	(11.1)	632	4.6	0	0
Malaysia	32,855	545	4,880	2.5	27	0.0	19,340	(11.0)	8,698	37.5	2,844	9
Mongolia	156,650	14	1,359	19.4	123,860	(0.4)	13,914	(8.5)	17,516	10.4	24,131	15
Myanmar	65,754	634	10,035	0.3	362	0.1	32,396	0.7	22,962	(1.2)	2,547	4
Nepal	13,680	1,399	2,600	11.9	1,997	7.7	2,480	0.0	6,603	(6.0)	0	0
Oman	21,246	71	48	19.0	1,000	0.0	0	0.0	20,198	(0.0)	4,769	22
Pakistan	77,088	1,591	20,770	3.3	5,000	0.0	3,293	17.3	48,025	(2.3)	2,737	3
Philippines	29,817	2,093	7,957	4.4	1,220	23.1	10,750	(16.4)	9,890	18.6	0	0
Qatar	1,100	335	5	100.0	50	0.0	0	0.0	1,045	(0.2)	0	0
Saudi Arabia	214,969	66	1,183	7.0	85,000	0.0	1,200	(11.8)	127,586	0.1	67,889	32
Singapore	61	44,639	2	(75.0)	0	0.0	3	0.0	56	12.0	0	0
Sri Lanka	6,463	2,664	1,898	0.5	439	0.0	1,747	(1.5)	2,379	0.7	0	0
Syrian Arab Rep	18,406	681	5,564	(0.5)	8,166	(2.9)	598	31.4	4,078	3.2	0	0
Thailand	51,089	1,090	21,624	21.8	761	26.8	14,373	(15.6)	14,331	(8.8)	2,809	5
Turkey	76,963	726	27,858	(1.4)	8,633	(13.4)	20,199	0.2	20,182	8.6	0	0
United Arab Emirates	8,360	190	39	114.8	200	0.0	3	50.0	8,118	(0.3)	1,938	23
Viet Nam	32,549	2,049	6,592	2.3	330	20.5	9,356	(28.8)	16,271	28.2	0	0
Yemen (Arab Rep)	19,500	472	1,361	0.7	7,000	0.0	1,600	0.0	9,539	(0.1)	2,067	11
(People's Dem Rep)	33,297	75	119	7.5	9,065	0.0	1,520	(6.2)	22,593	0.4	9,639	29
EUROPE	**472,953**	**1,054**	**140,409**	**(1.3)**	**83,177**	**(4.0)**	**156,851**	**1.1**	**92,524**	**3.8**	**13,855**	**3**
Albania	2,740	1,184	712	2.3	401	(4.1)	1,047	3.4	581	(5.4)	0	0
Austria	8,273	917	1,526	(6.4)	2,000	(2.9)	3,200	(2.2)	1,551	18.5	0	0
Belgium {c}	3,025	3,255	744	X	626	X	617	X	1,024	X	0	0
Bulgaria	11,055	815	4,139	(3.4)	2,026	5.4	3,868	1.0	1,022	0.5	0	0
Czechoslovakia	12,537	1,250	5,120	(2.3)	1,644	(3.9)	4,608	1.8	1,165	8.2	0	0
Denmark	4,237	1,214	2,571	(3.1)	215	(20.3)	493	0.0	958	16.6	0	0
Finland	30,461	163	2,435	(6.4)	125	(27.3)	23,222	(0.4)	4,679	7.2	2,939	9
France	55,010	1,021	19,210	1.6	11,757	(9.5)	14,721	1.2	9,322	9.0	0	0
Germany (Fed Rep)	24,428	2,510	7,473	(0.7)	4,446	(8.2)	7,390	1.0	5,119	8.1	0	0
(Dem Rep)	10,519	1,545	4,924	(2.2)	1,257	0.7	2,981	1.0	1,360	(1.1)	0	0
Greece	13,085	768	3,931	0.8	5,255	0.0	2,620	0.1	1,279	(2.4)	0	0
Hungary	9,234	1,143	5,288	(1.9)	1,210	(7.3)	1,678	5.9	1,058	10.6	0	0
Iceland	10,025	25	8	0.0	2,274	(0.0)	120	0.0	7,623	0.0	2,975	29
Ireland	6,889	540	966	(16.7)	4,688	2.7	339	8.4	896	5.0	0	0
Italy	29,406	1,940	12,021	(3.1)	4,909	(5.0)	6,736	6.3	5,740	4.3	0	0
Luxembourg {c}	258	1,448	66	X	70	X	89	X	42	X	0	0
Malta	32	11,031	13	(7.1)	0	0.0	0	0.0	19	5.6	0	0
Netherlands	3,392	4,408	930	8.0	1,080	(8.9)	300	3.3	1,082	2.3	0	0
Norway	30,683	137	874	7.6	105	(0.6)	8,330	0.0	21,374	(0.3)	5,627	17
Poland	30,445	1,262	14,785	(1.6)	4,047	(0.7)	8,736	0.9	2,877	6.9	0	0
Portugal	9,195	1,119	3,771	(1.1)	761	0.0	2,968	0.0	1,695	2.6	0	0
Romania	23,034	1,010	10,581	0.6	4,406	(0.9)	6,356	0.4	1,691	(2.8)	0	0
Spain	49,944	785	20,367	(1.0)	10,210	(6.4)	15,656	1.8	3,711	19.9	0	0
Sweden	41,162	205	2,872	(4.1)	562	(22.8)	28,020	0.5	9,709	1.4	2,315	5
Switzerland	3,977	1,662	412	4.0	1,609	(1.0)	1,052	0.0	904	0.0	0	0
United Kingdom	24,160	2,369	6,888	(1.2)	11,119	(3.3)	2,353	13.8	3,800	4.4	0	0
Yugoslavia	25,540	932	7,764	(2.0)	6,352	0.2	9,344	1.3	2,080	1.5	0	0
U.S.S.R.	**2,227,200**	**130**	**231,871**	**(0.2)**	**371,500**	**(0.6)**	**945,000**	**1.7**	**678,829**	**(1.9)**	**752,022**	**34**
OCEANIA	**842,696**	**31**	**49,355**	**11.6**	**436,622**	**(3.1)**	**157,221**	**(0.6)**	**199,523**	**5.0**	**237,057**	**28**
Australia	761,793	22	47,671	11.7	422,322	(3.1)	106,000	(0.9)	185,800	5.4	229,431	30
Fiji	1,827	418	240	2.7	60	(2.7)	1,185	0.0	342	(1.3)	0	0
New Zealand	26,799	127	508	14.3	13,752	(1.5)	7,289	4.3	5,274	(2.4)	3,723	14
Papua New Guinea	45,286	86	387	7.7	85	(20.1)	38,237	(0.5)	6,577	2.9	3,903	8
Solomon Islands	2,799	116	57	10.3	39	0.0	2,560	0.0	143	(3.6)	0	0

Sources: Food and Agriculture Organization of the United Nations, Eurostat, United Nations Population Division, and J.M. McCloskey and H. Spalding.
Notes: a. Does not include Antarctica.
b. Includes Greenland.
c. Land use data are for 1987.
Regional totals include countries not listed.
0 = zero or less than half the unit of measure; X = not available; negative numbers are shown in parenthesis.
For additional information, see Sources and Technical Notes.

Table 17.2 Urban and Rural Populations, Settlements, and Labor

| | Urban Population as a Percentage of Total | | Average Annual Population Change 1960-90 (percent) | | Cities With at Least 1 Million Inhabitants | | | Average Household Size | | Percentage of Households Without Electricity | Total Labor Force 1990 | Women as a Percentage of Labor Force | Percentage of 1980 Labor Force in | | |
| | | | | | Percentage of Total Population | | Number of Cities | Number of Occupants | Number of Rooms | | | | Agri- | | |
	1960	1990	Urban	Rural	1960	1990	1990	1970-86	1970-82	1970-82	(000)	1990	culture	Industry	Services
WORLD	34.2	45.2	2.8	1.3	12.2	14.8	276				2,363,547	36.1	51	21	28
AFRICA	18.3	33.9	4.9	2.1	5.7	9.2	24				242,784	34.4	69	12	19
Algeria	30.4	51.7	4.7	1.6	8.0	12.2	1	7.2	X	X	5,819	9.6	31	27	42
Angola	10.4	28.3	5.9	1.7	4.5	17.1	1	X	X	X	4,081	38.6	74	10	17
Benin	9.2	37.7	7.4	1.2	0.0	0.0	0	5.4	X	X	2,195	47.4	70	7	23
Botswana	1.7	27.5	13.5	2.3	0.0	0.0	0	5.4	X	X	446	35.0	70	13	17
Burkina Faso	4.7	9.0	4.6	2.2	0.0	0.0	0	X	X	X	4,167	46.2	87	4	9
Burundi	2.0	5.5	5.5	2.0	0.0	0.0	0	4.5	X	X	2,820	47.3	93	2	5
Cameroon	13.9	41.2	6.5	1.4	0.0	0.0	0	5.2	4.1	94	4,365	33.3	70	8	22
Cape Verde	16.3	28.6	4.1	1.6	0.0	0.0	0	X	X	X	141	29.1	52	23	26
Central African Rep	22.7	46.7	4.8	1.0	0.0	0.0	0	5.1	X	X	1,384	45.7	72	6	21
Chad	7.0	29.5	7.1	1.1	0.0	0.0	0	X	X	X	1,971	21.1	83	5	12
Comoros	9.8	27.8	6.8	2.4	0.0	0.0	0	X	X	X	231	40.2	83	6	11
Congo	31.9	40.5	3.6	2.4	0.0	0.0	0	5.3	X	X	781	38.8	62	12	26
Côte d'Ivoire	19.3	40.4	6.5	2.9	4.7	18.1	1	X	X	X	4,599	34.2	65	8	27
Djibouti	50.0	80.7	7.3	2.3	0.0	0.0	0	X	X	X	X	X	X	X	X
Egypt	37.9	46.7	3.1	1.9	20.1	24.3	2	5.2	X	54	14,574	10.1	46	20	34
Equatorial Guinea	25.4	28.7	1.5	1.0	0.0	0.0	0	X	X	X	182	40.2	66	11	23
Ethiopia	6.4	12.9	4.8	2.2	1.7	3.8	1	X	X	X	21,225	37.4	80	8	12
Gabon	17.5	45.6	6.3	1.6	0.0	0.0	0	X	X	X	536	37.3	75	11	14
Gambia, The	12.5	23.2	5.2	2.6	0.0	0.0	0	8.3	X	X	329	40.4	84	7	9
Ghana	23.3	33.0	3.9	2.2	5.8	7.3	1	X	X	X	5,686	39.7	56	18	26
Guinea	9.9	25.6	5.3	1.4	3.6	22.5	1	6.7	X	X	3,097	39.8	81	9	10
Guinea-Bissau	13.7	19.8	3.2	1.7	0.0	0.0	0	X	X	X	458	40.8	82	4	14
Kenya	7.4	23.6	7.7	2.9	2.6	6.3	1	5.1	X	X	10,011	39.9	81	7	12
Lesotho	3.4	20.2	8.6	1.8	0.0	0.0	0	X	X	X	808	43.4	86	4	10
Liberia	18.7	45.9	6.2	1.7	0.0	0.0	0	X	X	X	912	30.3	74	9	16
Libya	22.8	70.2	8.1	0.9	12.9	45.4	1	5.8	3.3	28	1,076	9.0	18	29	53
Madagascar	10.6	23.8	5.6	2.2	0.0	0.0	0	4.5	X	X	5,004	39.2	81	6	13
Malawi	4.4	11.8	6.5	2.8	0.0	0.0	0	3.0	X	X	3,495	41.2	83	7	9
Mali	11.1	19.2	4.4	2.2	0.0	0.0	0	5.1	X	X	2,959	16.2	86	2	13
Mauritania	5.8	46.8	9.8	0.5	0.0	0.0	0	5.5	X	X	679	22.1	69	9	22
Mauritius	33.2	40.5	2.3	1.3	0.0	0.0	0	4.8	3.3	30	440	26.6	28	24	48
Morocco	29.3	48.0	4.3	1.5	11.9	17.1	2	5.9	2.1	X	7,824	20.7	46	25	29
Mozambique	3.7	26.8	9.5	1.6	2.4	10.1	1	4.3	X	X	8,437	47.4	85	7	8
Namibia	14.9	27.8	4.8	2.1	0.0	0.0	0	X	X	X	537	23.8	X	X	X
Niger	5.8	19.5	7.4	2.6	0.0	0.0	0	X	X	X	3,619	46.7	91	2	7
Nigeria	14.4	35.2	6.3	2.2	3.2	8.3	2	X	X	X	41,857	34.8	68	12	20
Rwanda	2.4	7.7	7.4	3.1	0.0	0.0	0	4.6	X	X	3,520	47.7	93	3	4
Senegal	31.9	38.4	3.5	2.5	11.5	20.4	1	X	X	X	3,192	39.3	81	6	13
Sierra Leone	13.0	32.2	5.2	1.2	0.0	0.0	0	X	X	X	1,438	32.7	70	14	16
Somalia	17.3	36.4	5.8	2.3	0.0	0.0	0	X	X	X	2,143	38.6	76	8	16
South Africa	46.6	59.5	3.2	1.4	18.9	17.6	4	X	X	X	12,434	35.6	17	35	49
Sudan	10.3	22.0	5.4	2.3	3.1	7.7	1	X	X	X	8,078	21.8	71	8	21
Swaziland	4.0	33.1	10.5	1.8	0.0	0.0	0	X	X	X	306	38.8	74	9	17
Tanzania	4.7	32.8	10.3	2.2	1.6	6.1	1	X	X	X	12,597	47.9	86	5	10
Togo	9.8	25.7	6.2	2.2	0.0	0.0	0	5.7	X	X	1,396	36.4	73	10	17
Tunisia	36.0	54.3	3.6	1.1	13.8	20.0	1	5.5	1.9	66	2,594	24.4	35	36	29
Uganda	5.1	10.4	6.1	3.4	0.0	0.0	0	X	X	X	8,129	41.0	86	4	10
Zaire	22.3	39.5	4.8	2.0	2.9	9.9	1	X	X	X	13,084	35.5	72	13	16
Zambia	17.2	49.9	7.1	1.6	0.0	0.0	0	5.0	X	X	2,644	29.0	73	10	17
Zimbabwe	12.6	27.6	5.9	2.5	0.0	0.0	0	X	X	X	3,921	34.6	73	11	17
NORTH & CENTRAL AMERICA	63.2	71.4	2.0	0.7	28.7	31.8	44				189,258	37.4	12	29	58
Barbados	35.5	44.7	1.1	(0.2)	0.0	0.0	0	3.6	3.8	41	137	47.4	10	21	69
Belize	X	X	X	X	0.0	0.0	0	5.3	X	X	X	X	X	X	X
Canada	68.9	77.1	1.7	0.3	24.5	29.8	3	2.8	5.6	X	13,360	39.8	5	29	65
Costa Rica	36.6	47.1	3.9	2.4	22.9	33.7	1	4.7	4.0	31	1,023	21.8	31	23	46
Cuba	54.9	74.9	2.5	(0.6)	20.3	19.8	1	4.1	4.0	17	4,461	31.7	24	29	48
Dominican Rep	30.2	60.4	5.1	0.8	13.8	30.7	1	5.3	3.6	63	2,187	15.0	46	15	39
El Salvador	38.3	44.4	2.9	2.1	0.0	0.0	0	5.0	1.5	66	2,155	25.1	43	19	37
Guatemala	32.4	39.4	3.5	2.5	0.0	0.0	0	5.2	2.4	72	2,628	16.4	57	17	26
Haiti	15.6	28.3	3.8	1.3	6.8	15.8	1	4.7	2.1	96	3,131	41.6	70	8	22
Honduras	22.7	43.7	5.6	2.2	0.0	0.0	0	5.7	2.4	75	1,576	18.8	61	16	23
Jamaica	33.8	52.3	2.9	0.3	0.0	0.0	0	4.2	2.4	X	1,246	45.7	31	16	52
Mexico	50.8	72.6	4.1	0.9	20.2	32.5	5	5.5	2.3	25	30,487	27.1	37	29	35
Nicaragua	39.6	59.8	4.7	1.8	13.3	26.1	1	X	2.2	59	1,204	25.2	47	16	38
Panama	41.2	53.4	3.4	1.7	0.0	0.0	0	4.6	2.6	35	873	27.2	32	18	50
Trinidad and Tobago	22.5	69.1	5.3	(1.7)	0.0	0.0	0	4.5	3.3	16	501	30.0	10	39	51
United States	70.0	75.0	1.3	0.5	34.5	36.3	30	2.7	4.7	X	122,005	41.4	4	31	66
SOUTH AMERICA	51.7	75.1	3.6	0.1	23.4	32.8	29				104,465	26.4	29	26	45
Argentina	73.6	86.3	2.0	(0.7)	39.0	42.5	3	3.9	2.8	X	11,548	28.1	13	34	53
Bolivia	39.3	51.2	3.5	1.8	10.8	16.9	1	4.3	X	66	2,283	25.8	46	20	34
Brazil	44.9	74.9	4.2	(0.2)	21.9	35.2	14	4.4	4.5	33	55,026	27.4	31	27	42
Chile	67.8	85.9	2.6	(0.9)	26.7	35.9	1	4.5	3.5	25	4,753	28.5	17	25	58
Colombia	48.2	70.0	3.7	0.6	17.8	27.3	4	5.2	3.4	42	10,394	21.9	34	24	42
Ecuador	34.4	56.0	4.6	1.6	17.3	27.5	2	5.1	2.4	59	3,287	19.3	39	20	42
Guyana	29.0	34.5	1.7	0.9	0.0	0.0	0	X	X	X	383	25.1	27	26	47
Paraguay	35.6	47.5	4.0	2.3	0.0	0.0	0	5.2	2.2	83	1,410	20.7	49	21	31
Peru	46.3	70.2	4.1	0.6	17.0	29.0	1	4.9	2.5	88	7,138	24.1	40	18	42
Suriname	47.2	47.4	1.3	1.2	0.0	0.0	0	X	X	X	135	29.6	20	20	60
Uruguay	80.1	85.5	0.9	(0.4)	45.5	38.7	1	3.3	3.5	19	1,216	31.2	16	29	55
Venezuela	66.6	90.5	4.3	(1.0)	22.5	26.6	2	5.3	3.9	23	6,860	27.6	16	28	56

Force, 1960–1990   Table 17.2

| | Urban Population as a Percentage of Total | | Average Annual Population Change 1960-90 (percent) | | Cities With at Least 1 Million Inhabitants | | | Average Household Size | | Percentage of Households Without Electricity | Total Labor Force 1990 | Women as a Percentage of Labor Force 1990 | Percentage of 1980 Labor Force in | | |
| | | | | | Percentage of Total Population | | Number of Cities | Number of Occupants | Number of Rooms | | | | Agri- | | |
	1960	1990	Urban	Rural	1960	1990	1990	1970-86	1970-82	1970-82	(000)	1990	culture	Industry	Services
ASIA	21.5	34.4	3.7	1.5	8.3	11.3	115				1,436,522	35.3	66	15	19
Afghanistan	8.0	18.2	4.3	1.0	3.3	9.5	1	6.2	X	X	6,229	8.6	X	X	X
Bahrain	82.7	82.9	4.1	4.0	0.0	0.0	0	6.6	3.0	6	220	10.5	3	35	62
Bangladesh	5.1	16.4	6.8	2.3	2.8	7.7	2	5.7	2.0	X	33,398	7.3	75	6	19
Bhutan	2.5	5.3	4.4	1.8	0.0	0.0	0	X	X	X	696	32.2	92	3	5
Cambodia	10.3	11.6	1.8	1.3	0.0	0.0	0	X	X	X	3,758	38.3	X	X	X
China	19.0	33.4	3.8	1.2	8.0	9.1	38	4.4	X	X	679,900	43.2	74	14	12
Cyprus	35.6	52.8	2.0	(0.4)	0.0	0.0	0	3.9	4.4	X	326	35.6	26	34	40
India	18.0	27.0	3.6	1.8	5.5	8.6	24	5.5	2.0	X	322,944	25.2	70	13	17
Indonesia	14.6	30.5	4.7	1.5	6.3	10.0	6	4.9	3.1	86	71,314	31.2	57	13	30
Iran, Islamic Rep	33.6	56.7	5.0	1.7	13.9	23.3	5	4.9	2.4	52	15,253	18.0	36	33	31
Iraq	42.9	71.3	5.2	1.1	14.9	21.4	1	X	X	X	5,119	21.5	30	22	48
Israel	77.0	91.6	3.2	(0.8)	34.9	40.9	1	3.5	2.9	4	1,806	33.7	6	32	62
Japan	62.5	77.0	1.6	(0.7)	22.2	27.5	6	3.1	4.3 a	X	62,202	37.9	11	34	55
Jordan	42.7	68.0	4.5	0.9	12.9	25.6	1	6.6	X	23	992	10.3	10	26	64
Korea, Dem People's Rep	40.2	59.8	3.7	1.0	6.0	10.2	1	X	X	X	10,470	45.8	43	30	27
Korea, Rep	27.7	72.0	5.1	(1.4)	20.4	49.9	6	4.5	4.1	50	18,664	33.8	36	27	37
Kuwait	72.3	95.6	7.9	0.5	86.7	52.9	1	6.5	3.5	17	835	14.6	2	32	67
Lao People's Dem Rep	7.9	18.6	5.1	1.7	0.0	0.0	0	X	X	X	2,239	44.3	76	7	17
Lebanon	39.6	83.7	3.8	(3.1)	0.0	0.0	0	X	X	X	914	27.8	X	X	X
Malaysia	25.2	43.0	4.5	1.7	4.2	9.6	1	5.2	2.3 b	36	7,071	35.1	42	19	39
Mongolia	35.7	52.3	4.1	1.8	0.0	0.0	0	X	X	X	1,029	45.5	40	21	39
Myanmar	19.3	24.8	3.0	2.0	4.5	7.9	1	5.2	X	X	18,324	36.9	53	19	28
Nepal	3.1	9.6	6.3	2.2	0.0	0.0	0	5.8	X	X	7,725	33.6	93	1	7
Oman	3.6	10.6	7.5	3.4	0.0	0.0	0	X	X	X	405	8.4	50	22	28
Pakistan	22.1	32.0	4.3	2.6	9.5	13.4	6	6.6	1.9	69	33,698	12.5	55	16	30
Philippines	30.3	42.6	3.9	2.1	8.3	13.6	1	5.6	2.4	77	22,474	31.2	52	16	33
Qatar	73.3	89.4	8.0	4.0	0.0	0.0	0	X	X	X	186	7.0	3	28	69
Saudi Arabia	29.7	77.3	7.6	0.4	5.8	22.6	2	X	X	X	4,081	7.4	48	14	37
Singapore	100.0	100.0	1.7	NA	74.7	100.0	1	4.7	X	2	1,298	32.1	2	38	61
Sri Lanka	17.9	21.4	2.5	1.7	0.0	0.0	0	5.2	2.5	85	6,367	26.7	53	14	33
Syrian Arab Rep	36.8	50.4	4.5	2.6	21.9	30.1	2	6.2	6.4	58	3,101	17.3	32	32	36
Thailand	12.5	22.6	4.6	2.1	8.2	12.8	1	5.2	1.9	76	29,534	44.6	71	10	19
Turkey	29.7	61.3	4.9	0.4	12.9	21.6	4	5.2	2.5	59	23,696	33.7	58	17	25
United Arab Emirates	40.0	77.8	12.5	6.5	0.0	0.0	0	5.2	X	X	784	6.5	5	38	57
Viet Nam	14.7	21.9	3.6	1.9	5.7	6.5	2	5.3	X	X	32,916	46.7	68	12	21
Yemen (Arab Rep)	3.4	12.0	9.9	5.0	0.0	0.0	0	5.0	1.9	95	1,954	13.6	69	9	22
(People's Dem Rep)	28.0	43.3	3.9	1.6	0.0	0.0	0	X	X	X	648	12.0	41	18	41
EUROPE	61.1	73.4	1.2	(0.7)	16.5	17.0	36				231,702	38.6	14	39	47
Albania	30.6	35.2	2.8	2.1	0.0	0.0	0	X	X	X	1,591	41.2	56	26	18
Austria	49.9	58.4	0.8	(0.4)	25.5	27.6	1	2.7	3.4 a	X	3,570	40.1	9	41	50
Belgium	92.5	96.9	0.4	(2.7)	0.0	0.0	0	2.7	5.0	0	4,151	33.7	3	36	61
Bulgaria	38.6	67.7	2.4	(1.7)	9.0	13.2	1	3.1	3.6	0	4,475	46.4	18	45	37
Czechoslovakia	47.0	77.5	2.1	(2.4)	7.8	8.3	1	2.8	3.5	0	8,386	46.6	13	49	37
Denmark	73.7	87.0	0.9	(1.9)	29.3	26.9	1	2.4	3.8 b	0	2,852	44.6	7	32	61
Finland	38.1	59.7	1.9	(1.0)	10.5	20.3	1	2.6	3.4	4	2,552	47.0	12	35	53
France	62.4	74.3	1.3	(0.6)	19.5	19.2	3	2.7	3.6	X	9,670	45.5	9	35	56
Germany (Fed Rep)	77.4	87.4	0.7	(1.6)	15.1	13.0	5	2.4	4.4	0	25,404	39.9	6	44	50
(Dem Rep)	72.3	77.2	0.0	(0.9)	6.4	7.8	1	2.5	2.7	0	29,311	37.2	11	50	39
Greece	42.9	62.5	1.9	(0.8)	27.0	34.2	1	3.1	3.5	12	3,852	26.7	31	29	40
Hungary	40.0	61.3	1.6	(1.3)	18.1	20.0	1	2.8	3.0	2	5,276	44.9	18	44	38
Iceland	80.1	90.5	1.6	(1.2)	0.0	0.0	0	X	X	X	136	42.6	10	37	53
Ireland	45.8	57.1	1.7	0.1	0.0	0.0	0	3.7	4.7	5	1,481	29.4	19	34	48
Italy	59.4	68.9	0.9	(0.5)	24.5	25.4	5	3.0	3.7 b	1	22,770	31.9	12	41	48
Luxembourg	62.1	84.2	1.6	(2.3)	0.0	0.0	0	2.8	5.3	X	155	31.6	5	35	60
Malta	69.9	87.3	1.0	(2.6)	0.0	0.0	0	3.2	X	X	146	23.3	5	42	53
Netherlands	85.0	88.5	1.0	(0.0)	15.2	14.0	2	X	5.0	X	6,153	30.9	6	32	63
Norway	49.9	75.0	1.9	(1.8)	0.0	0.0	0	2.7	3.6	X	2,128	41.2	8	29	62
Poland	47.9	61.8	1.7	(0.2)	16.0	17.5	3	3.1	3.1 b	4	19,704	45.6	29	39	33
Portugal	22.1	33.6	1.9	(0.0)	10.1	15.6	1	2.9	4.5	36	4,740	36.7	26	37	38
Romania	34.2	52.7	2.2	(0.3)	7.5	9.4	1	X	X	X	11,825	46.5	31	44	26
Spain	56.6	78.4	1.9	(1.5)	13.7	22.1	2	3.5	4.4 b	X	14,456	24.4	17	37	46
Sweden	72.6	84.0	0.9	(1.4)	10.8	19.7	1	2.2	4.1	X	4,319	44.6	6	33	62
Switzerland	51.0	59.9	1.2	0.0	0.0	0.0	0	2.5	4.8	X	3,212	36.6	6	39	55
United Kingdom	85.7	89.1	0.4	(0.6)	29.8	23.4	4	X	4.8	X	27,766	38.6	3	38	59
Yugoslavia	27.9	56.1	3.2	(0.8)	3.1	6.6	1	3.6	2.8	12	10,858	38.9	32	33	34
U.S.S.R.	48.8	65.8	2.0	(0.4)	12.4	15.3	24	4.0	X	X	146,634	48.0	20	39	41
OCEANIA	66.3	70.6	2.0	1.3	31.8	32.2	4				12,181	37.0	20	28	52
Australia	80.6	85.5	1.9	0.7	48.7	50.6	4	3.0	5.0	5	7,963	38.1	7	32	61
Fiji	29.7	39.3	3.2	1.7	0.0	0.0	0	6.0	X	X	254	20.1	46	17	37
New Zealand	76.0	84.0	1.5	(0.1)	0.0	0.0	0	2.9	5.6	X	1,570	34.9	11	33	56
Papua New Guinea	2.7	15.8	8.6	1.9	0.0	0.0	0	4.5	X	X	1,570	45.9	76	10	14
Solomon Islands	X	X	X	X	0.0	0.0	0	6.7	X	X	X	X	X	X	X

Sources: United Nations Center for Human Settlements, United Nations Population Division, and International Labour Office.
Notes: a. Excluding kitchens.
b. Includes rooms used for professional/business purposes.
World and regional totals include countries not listed.
0 = zero or less than half the unit of measurement; X = not available; NA = not applicable; negative numbers are shown in parentheses.
For additional information, see Sources and Technical Notes.

Table 17.3 Transport and Transport Infrastructure, 1980s

	Total Road	Paved Road	Rail Track	Navigable Inland Waterways	Total Number of Public Airports	Persons Per Car	Car/Bus Public	Car/Bus Private	Passenger Train	Commercial Aircraft {c}	Road	Rail	Inland Waterway	Air {c} (million)
WORLD	170	88	9.5	4.7	14,201									
AFRICA	53	12	2.8	1.9	1,521									
Algeria	30	16	1.6	X	49	34	X	X	X	37	X	X	X	23
Angola	58	7	2.4	1.0	26	151	X	X	X	8	X	X	X	52
Benin	67	7	5.2	X	8	X	X	X	2	2	X	1	X	18
Botswana	24	4	1.3	X	28	67	X	X	X	1	X	X	X	0
Burkina Faso	41	5	1.8	X	51	354	X	X	10	3	X	5	X	18
Burundi	201	14	X	X	4	X	X	X	X	0	X	X	X	0
Cameroon	112	7	2.4	4.5	43	121	70 d	X	4	5	3	9	X	32
Cape Verde	558	149	X	X	1	X	X	X	X	2	X	X	X	1
Central African Rep	33	1	X	1.3	40	2,627	X	X	X	2	0	X	X	18
Chad	25	X	X	1.6	51	X	X	X	X	2	X	X	X	18
Comoros	336	94	X	X	4	X	X	X	X	0	X	X	X	0
Congo	35	2	1.5	3.3	43	X	X	X	X	3	X	X	X	19
Cote d'Ivoire	169	12	2.1	3.1	27	52	X	X	X	3	X	X	X	18
Djibouti	125	21	4.3	X	3	36	X	X	X	1	X	X	X	0
Egypt	46	31	4.6	3.5	17	62	253	106	140	62	312	67	25	138
Equatorial Guinea	X	X	X	X	2	X	X	X	X	0	X	X	X	0
Ethiopia	19 e	4 e	0.6	X	40	1,238	X	X	X	16	X	X	X	92
Gabon	29	2	2.6	6.2	39	55	X	X	X	4	X	X	X	29
Gambia, The	236	50	0.0	40.0	1	144	X	X	X	X	X	X	X	X
Ghana	95	24	4.1	5.6	3	X	X	X	X	4	X	X	X	14
Guinea	122	5	4.3	5.3	11	X	X	X	X	0	X	X	X	0
Guinea-Bissau	114	96	X	X	10	X	X	X	X	0	X	X	X	0
Kenya	113	14	5.3	X	152	157	X	X	X	14	X	X	X	48
Lesotho	140	16	0.1	X	33	278	X	X	X	0	X	X	X	1
Liberia	84	8	5.1	X	10	327	X	X	X	0	X	X	X	0
Libya	18	14	X	X	45	X	X	X	X	17	X	X	X	5
Madagascar	25	9	1.8	X	59	394	X	X	2	4	3	2	X	29
Malawi	130	28	8.5	1.5	27	446	X	X	X	1	X	X	X	1
Mali	13	1	0.5	1.5	29	X	X	X	X	X	X	X	X	X
Mauritania	7	2	0.7	X	20	115	X	X	X	3	X	X	X	18
Mauritius	974	905	X	X	1	24	X	X	X	18	X	X	X	55
Morocco	133	65	4.2	X	29	41	X	X	14	27	12	X	38	34
Mozambique	33	7	4.2	4.8	18	X	X	X	X	5	X	X	X	10
Namibia	66	5	2.9	X	X	X	X	X	X	X	X	X	X	X
Niger	15	3	X	0.2	20	779	X	X	X	2	X	X	X	18
Nigeria	119	33	3.8	9.4	46	X	X	X	X	10	X	X	X	17
Rwanda	489	34	X	X	7	912	1	15	X	0	2	X	X	0
Senegal	78	23	4.7	4.7	16	69	23	9	1	2	X	X	X	18
Sierra Leone	103	16	1.2	11.2	13	X	X	X	X	X	X	X	X	X
Somalia	34	9	X	X	15	X	X	X	X	2	X	X	X	8
South Africa	149	43	19.3	X	156	10	X	X	X	92	X	917	X	206
Sudan	3	2	2.1	2.2	25	135	X	X	X	5	X	X	X	17
Swaziland	158	30	29.9	X	4	X	X	X	X	0	X	X	X	0
Tanzania	92	4	4.0	X	62	396	X	X	X	2	X	X	X	2
Togo	139	34	9.7	X	8	913	13	2	1	2	X	1	X	18
Tunisia	188	113	12.3	X	12	25	20	X	10	16	10	20	X	19
Uganda	142	31	6.2	X	10	457	X	X	X	3	X	X	X	22
Zaire	64	1	2.3	6.6	100	X	X	X	X	5	X	X	X	52
Zambia	50	9	2.9	3.0	70	X	X	X	X	9	X	X	X	25
Zimbabwe	202	34	7.1	X	33	33	X	X	X	8	X	X	X	63
NORTH & CENTRAL AMERICA	349	184	17.0	1.5	6,605									
Barbados	3,651	3,430	0.0	X	1	X	X	X	X	X	X	X	X	0
Belize	113	15	0.0	36.2	X	X	X	X	X	X	X	X	X	X
Canada	92	27	9.1	0.3	512	2	X	X	28	504	X	2,397	X	1,348
Costa Rica	696	102	13.7	14.3	63	19	41	40	1	9	19	1	X	33
Cuba	191	82	116.5	2.2	20	X	X	X	X	20	X	X	X	22
Dominican Rep	359	102	10.7	X	38	57	X	X	X	4	X	X	X	0
El Salvador	587	84	29.0	X	35	36	X	X	X	10	X	X	X	2
Guatemala	121	28	8.2	9.1	74	X	X	X	X	2	X	X	X	23
Haiti	145	34	1.5	X	6	X	X	X	X	X	X	X	X	4
Honduras	108	17	7.0	4.2	35	111	X	X	X	5	X	X	X	2
Jamaica	1,536	461	27.1	X	6	57	X	X	X	20	X	X	X	16
Mexico	118	53	10.6	1.5	483	14	X	X	X	161	X	X	X	114
Nicaragua	126	13	2.5	18.7	11	73	X	X	X	1	X	X	X	2
Panama	112	36	3.1	10.5	51	X	X	X	X	5	X	X	X	14
Trinidad and Tobago	1,009	X	X	X	2	5	X	X	X	27	X	X	X	14
United States	679	387	26.4	2.2 f	5,268	2	372	44,420	203	6,933	11,247	16,541	7,047	14,650
SOUTH AMERICA	135	15	4.9	6.6	2,447									
Argentina	77	21	12.5	4.0	349	8	X	X	X	93	X	X	X	201
Bolivia	38	1	3.4	9.2	590	57	X	X	6	10	17	5	1	8
Brazil	197	16	3.6	5.9	752	10	5,192 d	X	148	279	2,604	1,095	818	1,148
Chile	106	14	10.2	1.0	129	19	8	X	12	28	X	21	X	330
Colombia	102	10	2.7	13.8	197	36	672	414	2	45	98	8	28	395
Ecuador	136	23	3.5	5.4	49	36	0	0	1	12	3	82	X	68
Guyana	39	3	0.0	30.5	43	X	X	X	X	2	X	X	X	3
Paraguay	28	5	1.1	7.8	29	X	X	X	X	6	X	X	X	4
Peru	44	5	2.7	6.9	162	X	X	X	X	20	X	X	X	30
Suriname	58	15	0.0	7.7	38	12	X	X	X	4	X	X	X	15
Uruguay	285	6	17.2	9.2	27	10	X	X	3	5	X	2	X	9
Venezuela	114	38	0.4	8.0	82	8	X	X	X	54	X	0	X	161

Table 17.3

	Transport Infrastructure						Transport of Goods and Passengers							
	Total km Per 1,000 km2 of Land Area				Total Number of Public Airports	Persons Per Car	Hundred Million Passenger-km {a} Traveled per Year by:				Metric Ton-km of Freight {b} Moved Per Year by:			
	Total Road	Paved Road	Rail Track	Navigable Inland Waterways			Car/Bus		Passenger Train	Commercial Aircraft {c}	Road	Rail	Inland Waterway	Air {c}
							Public	Private			(hundred million)			(million)
ASIA	**159**	**76**	**9.9**	**8.2**	**1,180**									
Afghanistan	32	4	0.0	1.8	20	X	X	X	X	2	X	X	X	12
Bahrain	X	294	X	X	1	X	X	X	X	15	X	X	X	40
Bangladesh	56	29	21.1	61.8	15	X	X	X	X	21	X	X	X	77
Bhutan	28	9	X	X	1	X	X	X	X	0	X	X	X	0
Cambodia	76	15	3.7	21.0	6	X	X	X	X	X	X	X	X	X
China	2	1	5.8	11.8	92	X	X	X	X	179	X	X	X	683
Cyprus	1,063	460	X	X	3	4	X	X	X	17	X	X	X	33
India	520	246	41.8	5.4	179	649	X	X	X	180	X	X	X	681
Indonesia	121	75	3.6	11.9	147	159	2,750	400	68	149	250	9	250	448
Iran, Islamic Rep	83	34	2.9	0.6	34	26	X	X	47	47	683	56	X	92
Iraq	104	88	7.0	2.3	2	27	X	X	X	23	X	X	X	73
Israel	228	228	25.6	X	8	9	X	X	X	76	X	X	X	817
Japan	2,948	2,005	70.3	4.7	81	4	1,072	5,009	3,618	933	2,461	235	2,348	5,128
Jordan	84	62	8.9	X	3	22	X	X	X	37	X	X	X	206
Korea, Dem People's Rep	168	3	70.6	18.7	7	X	X	X	X	2	X	X	X	3
Korea, Rep	565	347	31.9	16.3	12	38	853	225	260	182	86	138	166	2,365
Kuwait	240	X	X	X	1	4	0	X	X	39	X	X	X	233
Lao People's Dem Rep	119	8	X	32.4	13	X	X	X	X	0	X	X	X	0
Lebanon	684	547	21.7	X	1	6	X	X	X	3	X	X	X	284
Malaysia	122	84	5.1	22.2	49	11	X	X	16	101	X	11	X	404
Mongolia	30	1	1.2	0.3	1	X	X	X	X	5	X	X	X	2
Myanmar	41	5	4.8	19.5	62	X	X	X	X	1	X	X	X	1
Nepal	44	19	0.7	X	41	X	X	X	X	7	X	X	X	11
Oman	107	18	X	X	7	X	X	X	X	15	X	X	X	40
Pakistan	144	76	11.4	X	34	205	X	X	X	91	X	X	X	419
Philippines	528	75	3.6	10.8	226	156	X	X	X	106	X	X	X	327
Qatar	136	91	X	X	1	X	X	X	X	15	X	X	X	40
Saudi Arabia	42	16	0.4	X	23	6	X	X	X	157	X	X	X	605
Singapore	4,334	4,109	59.0	X	2	11	X	X	X	305	X	X	X	1,640
Sri Lanka	394	131	22.5	6.7	3	107	X	X	X	27	X	X	X	75
Syrian Arab Rep	162	126	9.6	3.7	7	X	X	X	X	8	X	X	X	10
Thailand	143	76	7.7	7.8	31	85	X	X	X	188	X	X	X	613
Turkey	417	59	11.0	1.6	39	38	1,232	X	X	43	625	X	X	82
United Arab Emirates	24	22	X	X	5	X	X	X	X	34	X	X	X	118
Viet Nam	261	29	8.9	54.4	4	X	X	X	X	1	X	X	X	1
Yemen (Arab Rep)	205	13	X	X	19 g	X	X	X	X	8	X	X	X	8
(People's Dem Rep)	33	6	X	X	X	X	X	X	X	3	X	X	X	5
EUROPE	**848**	**705**	**52.7**	**10.0**	**1,474**									
Albania	609	X	19.8	1.6	X	X	X	X	X	2	X	X	X	X
Austria	1,295	1,295	69.5	4.3	11	3	2	3	2	30	X	34	1	42
Belgium	4,243	4,073	118.0	64.5	12	3	49	X	74	68	191	79	54	661
Bulgaria	334	305	38.9	4.3	3	7	317	X	73	23	151	149	0	8
Czechoslovakia	583	77	104.5	3.9	6	5	397	X	197	22	132	720	51	17
Denmark	1,670	1,670	47.8	9.8	45	3	89	521	48	43	106	10	18	122
Finland	252	149	19.2	20.5	73	3	85	458	32	46	242	80	41	129
France	1,464	1,350	62.6	15.5	417	2	400	5,740	740	515	1,438	516	73	3,819
Germany (Fed Rep)	2,033	2,013	119.6	18.0	182 h	X	615	5,556	418	363	1,631	620	540	3,840
(Dem Rep)	1,185	449	133.2	22.0	X	X	X	X	228	X	X	X	X	X
Greece	264	220	18.9	0.6	36	8	6	X	20	80	151	6	X	103
Hungary	1,141	569	83.4	17.6	2	6	281	X	115	14	131	211	145	6
Iceland	114	21	X	X	97	2	X	X	X	16	X	X	X	33
Ireland	1,340	1,259	28.3	X	19	4	0	X	12	43	X	6	X	118
Italy	1,026	1,026	63.9	4.6	44	2	394	1,670	438	215	1,574	183	2	1,118
Luxembourg	1,070	1,955	105.4	14.3	2	2	X	X	3	1	2	6	4	1
Malta	4,063	3,823	X	X	1	X	X	X	X	7	X	X	X	6
Netherlands	3,399	2,991	84.0	147.9	15	3	110	1,539 i	102	259	221	10	72	2,003
Norway	287	199	13.2	5.1	54	3	37	404	25	59	79	16	130	128
Poland	1,185	728	87.5	13.1	11	8	581	X	558	37	384	1,111	12	29
Portugal	565 j	488 j	39.2	1.3	30	6	85	530	59	63	X	17	X	160
Romania	316	160	48.1	7.2	17	19	X	X	X	16	51	483	31	15
Spain	307	301	28.9	2.1	39	3	354	1,330	158	228	1,242	145	X	733
Sweden	325	231	28.3	2.8	189	2	X	X	59	85	260	185	70	185
Switzerland	1,788	X	113.1	0.5	10	2	30	796	115	155	60	79	1	889
United Kingdom	1,467	1,467	69.9	9.7	141	3	410	5,170	410	923	1,302	180	609	3,447
Yugoslavia	478	287	36.6	7.8	18	8	267	370	114	51	209	254	45	136
U.S.S.R.	**72**	**54**	**6.6**	**5.5**	**38**	**20**	**4,706**	**X**	**4,022**	**2,267**	**5,080**	**39,248**	**2,512**	**2,645**
OCEANIA	**115**	**57**	**5.3**	**2.5**	**936**									
Australia	112	56	5.2	1.1	430	2	X	X	3	368	6	595	X	1,125
Fiji	235	31	35.2	11.1	17	25	X	X	X	8	X	X	X	20
New Zealand	347	191	15.8	6.0	59	2	X	X	5	106	X	32	X	317
Papua New Guinea	42	1	X	24.2	402	189	X	X	X	7	X	X	X	15
Solomon Islands	75	1	X	X	28	X	X	X	X	0	X	X	X	0

Sources: International Civil Aviation Organization, International Road Federation, Jane's Information Group Limited, United Nations Economic Commission for Europe, United States Central Intelligence Agency, and other sources.

Notes: a. Passenger-km are total passengers moved multiplied by kilometers traveled. b. Metric ton-km are total metric tons of freight moved multiplied by distance moved.
c. Country-based carriers only. Data are for 1989. d. Public and private vehicles combined. e. Excludes urban roads. f. Exclusive of Great Lakes waterways.
g. Data are for Yemen as a whole. h. Data are for Germany as a whole. i. Includes bicycles. j. Data are for continental Portugal only.
Regional totals are totals of countries with reported data only.
0 = zero or less than half the unit of measure; X = not available.
For additional information, see Sources and Technical Notes.

Sources and Technical Notes

Table 17.1 Land Area and Use, 1977–89

Sources: Land area and use: Food and Agriculture Organization of the United Nations (FAO), *Agrostat PC* (FAO, Rome, June 1991); for Belgium and Luxembourg, Eurostat, *Environmental Statistics 1989* (Statistical Office of the European Communities, Luxembourg, 1990); population density: calculated from FAO land-area data and population figures provided by United Nations Population Division, *World Population Prospects 1990* (U.N., New York, 1991); 1990 population for the Solomon Islands, The World Bank, unpublished data (The World Bank, Washington, D.C., July 1991); wilderness area: J. Michael McCloskey and Heather Spalding, "A Reconnaissance-Level Inventory of the Amount of Wilderness Remaining in the World," *Ambio,* Vol. 18, No. 4 (1989).

Land area and *land use* data are provided to FAO by national governments in response to annual questionnaires. FAO also compiles data from national agricultural censuses. When official information is lacking, FAO prepares its own estimates or relies on unofficial data. Several countries use definitions of total area and land use that differ from those used in this chapter. Refer to the sources for details.

FAO often adjusts the definitions of land-use categories and sometimes substantially revises earlier data. For example, in 1985, FAO began to exclude from the cropland category land used for shifting cultivation but currently lying fallow. Because land-use changes can reflect changes in data-reporting procedures along with actual land-use changes, apparent trends should be interpreted with caution.

Land use data are periodically revised and may change significantly from year to year. For the most recent land-use statistics, see the latest *FAO Production Yearbook.*

Land area data are for 1989. They exclude major inland water bodies, national claims to the continental shelf, and Exclusive Economic Zones. (See Chapter 23, "Oceans and Coasts," Table 23.1, Coastal Areas and Resources.)

The *population density* and *land use* figures for the world refer to the six inhabited continents. Population density was derived by using the population figures for 1990 published by the United Nations Population Division and 1989 land area data from FAO. Although the population figures were published in 1991, actual censuses and estimates were made in prior years. For additional information on population and methodology, see the Technical Notes to Table 16.1, Size and Growth of Population and Labor Force, 1950–2025, in Chapter 16, "Population and Human Development."

Cropland includes land under temporary and permanent crops, temporary meadows, market and kitchen gardens, and temporary fallow. Permanent crops are those that do not need to be replanted after each har-

vest, such as cocoa, coffee, rubber, fruit, and vines. It excludes land used to grow trees for wood or timber.

Permanent pasture is land used five or more years for forage, including natural crops and cultivated crops. This category is difficult for countries to assess because it includes wildland used for pasture. In addition, few countries regularly report data on permanent pasture. As a result, the absence of a change in permanent pasture area (e.g., 0 percent change for many African and Asian countries) may indicate differences in land classification and data reporting rather than actual conditions. Grassland not used for forage is included under *other land.*

Forest and woodland includes land under natural or planted stands of trees, as well as logged-over areas that will be reforested in the near future.

Other land includes uncultivated land, grassland not used for pasture, built-on areas, wetlands, wastelands, and roads.

Wilderness area refers to lands showing no evidence of development, such as settlements, roads, buildings, airports, railroads, pipelines, power lines, and reservoirs. The data were derived from 65 detailed, aeronautical, navigational maps published in the early and mid-1980s by the U.S. Defense Mapping Agency at scales of 1:2,000,000 and 1:1,000,000. The maps show human constructs in remote areas to provide orienting landmarks for navigators. Although the maps do not always show agricultural development or logging, these activities usually occur near roads and settlements. The minimum unit of wilderness surveyed was 4,000 square kilometers because it was impossible to identify smaller wilderness areas from these maps.

Table 17.2 Urban and Rural Populations, Settlements, and Labor Force, 1960–1990

Sources: Urban population as a percentage of total: United Nations Population Division, *World Population Prospects 1990* (U.N., New York, 1991); cities with at least 1 million inhabitants: United Nations Population Division, *Urban and Rural Areas 1990,* on diskette (U.N., New York, 1991); average household size and percentage of households without electricity: United Nations Center for Human Settlements (Habitat), *Human Settlements Basic Statistics 1990* (Habitat, Nairobi, 1990); total labor force, women as a percentage of labor force, and labor force by sector: International Labour Office (ILO), *Economically Active Population. Estimates: 1950–1980; Projections: 1985–2025* (ILO, Geneva, 1986).

Urban population as a percentage of total is the portion of the total population residing in urban areas. The rest of the population is defined as rural. Definitions of urban vary from country to country. For a list of individual country definitions, see the sources. For additional information on methods of

data collection and estimation, refer to the Technical Note for Table 16.1, Size and Growth of Population and Labor Force, 1950–2025, in Chapter 16, "Population and Human Development."

The *percentage of total population* in *cities with at least 1 million inhabitants* was calculated using figures for populations of urban agglomerations of 1 million or more residents reported in *Urban and Rural Areas 1990* and total national population estimates and projections for 1960 and 1990 in *World Population Prospects 1990.* In *Urban and Rural Areas 1990,* the United Nations provides estimates and projections of the population of 276 urban agglomerations with 1 million or more inhabitants in 1990, for each five-year period between 1950 and 2000.

The United Nations defines an "urban agglomeration" as "comprising the city or town proper and also the suburban fringe or thickly settled territory lying outside of, but adjacent to, the city boundaries. . . . For some countries or areas, the data relate to entire administrative divisions known, for example, as shi or municipos which [sic] are composed of a populated center and adjoining territory, some of which may contain other quite separate urban localities or be distinctly rural in character." For additional information, refer to the source.

Average household size refers to individuals or groups of people who share facilities for cooking and for meeting other basic needs within a housing unit. Housing units are dwellings that are either primarily intended for use as living quarters, or units that are being used for that purpose. This includes apartments and mobile homes along with hotels, rooming houses, and other group living quarters. *Number of occupants* is calculated by dividing the total number of people living in households by the number of households in existence. In estimating *number of rooms* per household, Habitat defines a room as a space at least 4 square meters, enclosed by walls at least 2 meters high, which is intended for residential use only. Examples would include bedrooms, kitchens, living and dining rooms, servants' rooms, and studies. Hallways, verandas, lobbies, bathrooms, and rooms used for work or business purposes are not included unless otherwise indicated in the table.

The *percentage of households without electricity* refers only to households not serviced by public utilities. Residences supplied by local generators or other privately owned means would be included in the percentage without electricity. Readers should be cautious in comparing figures for household size and electrification rates, because these data come from censuses taken in different years during the 1970–86 period.

All people who work or are without work but are available for and are seeking work to produce economic goods and services comprise the *total labor force,* which includes employed people and the unemployed (experienced workers who are without work as well as those looking for work for the first time). The International Labour Office provides labor force estimates and projections for men, women, and the total population. *Women as a percentage of labor force* is calculated using estimates of the total labor force and the number of women in the labor force for 1990. The data for total labor force, as well as *percentage of 1980 labor force* in *agriculture, industry,* and *services,* take into account information on the economically active population, which is obtained from national censuses of population, labor force sample surveys, and other surveys conducted through 1985. Estimates are based on midyear, medium variant population figures. (See Chapter 16, "Population and Human Development" for further information on population projections.)

Table 17.3 Transport and Transport Infrastructure, 1980s

Sources: Total road and paved road: International Road Federation (IRF), *World Road Statistics 1981–85, World Road Statistics 1985–89* (IRF, Geneva, 1986 and 1990); U.S. Central Intelligence Agency (CIA), *The World Factbook 1990* (CIA, Washington, D.C., 1990); for Cape Verde, Business International Ltd., *Senegal, The Gambia, Guinea-Bissau, Cape Verde Country Profile 1990–91* (The Economist Intelligence Unit, London, 1990); land area data: Food and Agriculture Organization of the United Nations (FAO), *Agrostat PC* (FAO, Rome, June 1991); rail track: Jane's Information Group Limited, *Jane's World Railways 1990–91* (Jane's Information Group Limited, Surrey, United Kingdom, 1990); commercial airports: International Civil Aviation Organization (ICAO), *Annual Report of the Council—1990* (ICAO, Montreal, 1991); number of passenger cars (persons per car), passenger-km traveled by car/bus and train and metric ton-km of road, rail, and waterway freight transported (primary source): IRF, *World Road Statistics 1981-85 and World Road Statistics 1985-89* (IRF, Geneva, 1986 and 1990); all non-aircraft transported freight and passenger data for Europe and the U.S.S.R. (when more recent than primary source data) and inland waterways for Europe, the U.S.S.R., and the United States: United Nations Economic Commission for Europe, *1990 Annual Bulletin of Transport Statistics for Europe* (U.N., New York, 1990); inland waterways (all other countries): CIA, *The World Factbook 1990* (CIA, Washington, D.C., 1990); air passenger and freight trans-

port: ICAO, *Civil Aviation Statistics of the World 1989* (ICAO, Montreal, 1990) and unpublished data (ICAO, Montreal, October 1991).

Definitions of *total road* and *paved road* vary from country to country. In general, they include highways, rural roads, urban streets, feeder roads, and highway on- and off-ramps. Total road for some countries includes seasonably accessible routes, agricultural roads, and rural paths. Paved road generally refers to concrete, cobblestone, bituminous-treated and asphalt- or macadam-covered road. In some cases, graded gravel roadway is included. Road data are from the latest figures provided by governments to IRF between 1981 and 1989. CIA figures are from U.S. Defense Intelligence Agency estimates, which in turn are based on information published in various country reports available as of January 1990. Estimates are of current road extent, excepting a few countries where data are for extent during the mid-1980s (1980 for the Democratic People's Republic of Korea).

Rail track generally refers to route kilometers of track, the distance covered between two termini. In a few cases (portions of the U.S. and Tanzanian networks), track kilometer distance is reported, the total amount of track between two termini (twice the route kilometers if you have double track between two points). Total rail track figures generally do not include the length of sidings. Total track is the sum of public and privately owned systems currently in use, including lines used at mines and on plantations to haul ore and agricultural produce when reported. Total track includes urban rail systems but not the below ground segments of these systems (subways).

The definition of *navigable inland waterways* varies among countries, particularly in terms of the minimum craft size that can travel a waterway in order for it to be considered navigable. Waterways for Europe, the U.S.S.R., and the United States as reported here are considered navigable if they permit passage of boats and barges with a carrying capacity of at least 50 metric tons. Canals, rivers, lakes, and in some cases, coastal routes and estuaries are included in the total. In a number of other countries, seasonally accessible waterways are also included. Waterway length of lakes is the route distance between the two farthest points traveled. Canal and river length is measured at the deepest point of the watercourse. Data reported by the United Nations Economic Commission for Europe are the waterway extent as of 1988, with the following exceptions: Portugal and Sweden, 1982; Italy and the United Kingdom, 1980; Romania, 1975; Bulgaria,

1973; and Czechoslovakia, 1969. Waterways data reported by the CIA are from country reports available as of January 1990.

Total number of public airports refers to land-based airports with permanent surface and unimproved runways. Airports served by regularly scheduled flights and other aerodromes open to the public are included. Data were compiled primarily through surveys taken by ICAO during 1989–90. Some data were taken from aeronautical publications.

Persons per car is calculated by dividing the total number of vehicles in use on December 31 of the latest census year available between 1981 and 1989 with the total population for that year. For some countries, road censuses are taken earlier in the year. In general, cars refer to privately owned vehicles with four or more wheels, which are used for noncommercial purposes. A few countries include commercial vehicles (such as taxis and rental cars) and minibuses under this category. Data for vehicles in use and other transport statistics are submitted by individual governments to IRF. Numbers for some countries have been known to vary widely from year to year, because of changes in survey methodologies and category definitions.

Passenger-kilometers traveled per year by car/bus, passenger train, and *commercial aircraft* are the total number of kilometers traveled multiplied by the total number of passengers carried for each transport category. Passenger-kilometers are generally estimated using receipts from ticket sales and do not include trips made by nonpaying passengers (e.g., military personnel, transport employees).

Metric ton-kilometers of freight moved per year is the total number of tons moved multiplied by the total distance traveled. Both passenger and freight transport data are based on the latest census results available between 1981 and 1989 for *road, rail,* and *inland waterway* transport (1980 data for waterway freight transport for Switzerland). Air freight and passenger transport data are based on 1989 figures and estimates.

Passenger-kilometers and *kilometers of freight transported by aircraft* consist of all travel on international and domestically scheduled commercial flights on carriers based within the country in question. For multinational carriers such as Air Afrique, totals are generally apportioned equally among the consortium countries. International totals for both freight and passenger transport include travel by national carriers between countries outside of the host nation. For additional information, refer to the source.

18. Food and Agriculture

Over the past 10 years, the world's food production increased by 24 percent while its population grew almost 20 percent. Food production increased, in part, because of increases in irrigation, mechanization, land used for agriculture, and inputs of fertilizers and pesticides. World trade in food, as well as food aid, also increased during this period. Physical, political, economic, and technological constraints, however, raise questions as to how long this growth can be sustained.

Even though the world's food production has outpaced population growth, regional and national data show that this increase did not occur everywhere. (See Table 18.1.) Despite a 30 percent increase in cereal production, Africa's per capita food output has dropped by 5 percent in the past decade. Per capita food production in North and Central America declined as well. In South America, Asia, Europe, and the U.S.S.R., food production grew faster than the population. However, increases in cereal production do not always represent improvements in food availability. Over 50 percent of cereal consumed in Europe, North America, and the Soviet Union is eaten by livestock.

Yield differences reflect the intensity of agricultural activity. On a global average, 1 hectare yielded about 2.6 metric tons of cereals and 11.8 metric tons of roots and tubers. However, 1 hectare in Africa yielded only 1.2 metric tons of cereals and 7.9 metric tons of roots and tubers, whereas Europe produced 4.2 and 21.2 metric tons, respectively.

Differences in yields are principally caused by differences in agricultural inputs. (See Table 18.2.) European agriculture applies 2.3 times more fertilizer per hectare of cropland than the global average, whereas Africa uses one fifth of the world average. Reasons for low rates of fertilizer use include lack of financial resources, low crop prices relative to fertilizer prices, and poor distribution systems. Geographic distribution of use rates of other inputs is similar. With only one third of the world's cropland, North American and European farmers own nearly two thirds of the world's tractors. In contrast, African farmers, with 10 percent of the world's crop area, own only 2 percent of the world's tractors, many of them out of operation because of high fuel prices and a lack of spare parts.

Livestock continues to supply traction power for cultivation and harvest in much of the world and is an important source for food, raw materials, fertilizer, and energy. Table 18.3 shows that during the past decade, the number of cattle declined slightly in Europe, North America, and Oceania but increased in South America, Asia, and Africa. The world chicken population has grown by 53 percent, with over a 100 percent increase in Asia.

The world's agricultural production systems are integrated in the world market for commodities and the flows of food aid. (See Table 18.4.) Many countries depend on agricultural trade to earn foreign exchange, but a steady decline in world commodity prices (see Chapter 15, "Basic Economic Indicators," Table 15.4) forces exporting countries to increase exports or face a decrease in export earnings. The same decrease in commodity prices, however, has made food imports more affordable for nations with agricultural trade deficits. Trade in cereals, oils, and pulses has grown by a factor of 2.5 in the past decade. The United States, Canada, and France are the largest net exporters of cereals, whereas the U.S.S.R. and Japan are the greatest net importers.

Food aid often links agricultural areas producing subsidized surpluses with countries in need. Canada, the United States, Japan, and the European Community are the world's largest donors of cereals. (See Tables 18.4 and 18.5.) Egypt and Bangladesh receive the most cereal aid in total, whereas Cape Verde and Jamaica lead the world in the amount of cereal aid received per capita. Asia's agricultural success is demonstrated by a 26 percent decline in metric tons of cereal aid received over the past decade, although that aid has risen over the past two years. The United States provides 53 percent of all cereal aid.

The inherent fertility of soils and the climatic regime together determine which crops can be grown, what inputs are required, and what outputs are possible.

Table 18.6 presents country data on the percent of soils that fall within the four climatic classes (arid, semi-arid, humid, and cold) and the three temperature zones. Also presented is the amount of land that has no inherent soil constraints and the percent of this land that falls within each of the four climate classes. To increase agricultural production, countries may need to use more intensive soil management practices to exploit lands with physical or chemical constraints. In Africa and Southwest Asia, more than 70 percent of the land that has no inherent soil constraints is located in arid areas in which growing seasons for rainfed agriculture are very short. In South America and Southeast Asia, however, most of the land without soil constraints is located in humid areas, which have longer growing seasons.

Table 18.1 Food and Agricultural Production, 1978–90

| | Index of Agricultural Production (1979-81 = 100) | | | | Index of Food Production (1979-81 = 100) | | | | Average Production of Cereals | | Average Yields of Cereals | | Average Yields of Roots and Tubers | |
| | Total | | Per Capita | | Total | | Per Capita | | (000 metric tons) | Percent Change Since | Kilograms Per Hectare | Percent Change Since | Kilograms Per Hectare | Percent Change Since |
	1978-80	1988-90	1978-80	1988-90	1978-80	1988-90	1978-80	1988-90	1988-90	1978-80	1988-90	1978-80	1988-90	1978-80
WORLD	98	122	100	104	98	122	100	104	1,859,005	18	2,638	20	11,795	(5)
AFRICA	98	124	101	95	98	125	101	96	91,102	30	1,198	11	7,889	16
Algeria	97	123	100	95	97	122	100	94	1,380	(26)	621	(3)	8,826	27
Angola	101	98	104	78	100	101	103	80	302	(30)	307	(49)	4,102	4
Benin	101	160	104	123	101	154	104	118	571	49	870	20	8,788	17
Botswana	95	110	98	79	95	110	98	79	79	178	331	51	7,000	(5)
Burkina Faso	98	146	100	116	98	144	100	114	1,947	72	691	20	6,827	(16)
Burundi	95	120	98	93	98	122	100	95	298	50	1,313	24	8,333	15
Cameroon	98	119	101	90	98	119	100	90	917	4	1,234	47	2,551	4
Cape Verde	100	153	101	124	100	154	101	124	14	126	434	(9)	3,529	(3)
Central African Rep	98	122	100	96	97	121	100	95	149	56	1,106	107	3,581	11
Chad	99	124	101	100	97	120	100	97	691	17	645	25	5,514	24
Comoros	101	123	105	90	101	123	105	90	19	4	1,629	51	5,143	39
Congo	96	121	98	92	96	121	98	92	22	43	759	24	6,826	8
Cote d'Ivoire	93	132	97	93	95	138	99	98	1,195	40	884	11	5,911	28
Djibouti	X	X	X	X	X	X	X	X	X	X	X	X	X	X
Egypt	97	142	100	114	98	154	100	123	11,024	36	5,254	31	28,330	64
Equatorial Guinea	X	X	X	X	X	X	X	X	X	X	X	X	2,788	(1)
Ethiopia	98	104	101	84	99	105	101	85	6,078	6	1,209	3	3,366	(8)
Gabon	98	115	103	81	98	114	103	81	22	109	1,558	(7)	6,242	1
Gambia, The	101	118	104	90	101	119	105	91	98	36	1,140	0	3,000	0
Ghana	97	146	100	108	97	148	100	109	1,052	58	1,029	29	6,797	4
Guinea	97	111	99	89	97	109	99	87	786	25	938	(2)	6,063	(15)
Guinea-Bissau	97	121	101	102	97	121	101	102	240	224	1,204	97	5,714	(4)
Kenya	100	146	104	105	102	149	106	107	3,322	35	1,722	31	8,663	11
Lesotho	106	105	109	82	107	104	110	81	177	(25)	765	(34)	10,000	X
Liberia	98	112	101	84	97	114	100	86	243	(1)	1,178	(5)	7,548	10
Libya	86	148	90	103	86	148	90	103	355	46	822	109	6,980	11
Madagascar	97	119	100	90	97	120	100	91	2,474	15	1,919	15	6,439	12
Malawi	99	118	102	86	99	113	102	83	1,498	5	1,107	(8)	3,153	(32)
Mali	95	130	97	100	95	127	97	98	2,138	100	962	12	8,625	4
Mauritania	98	113	100	89	98	113	100	89	154	273	896	156	2,000	(9)
Mauritius	103	114	104	103	104	114	105	103	3	167	2,667	(11)	18,333	62
Morocco	104	170	107	135	105	170	107	135	7,262	63	1,323	35	17,826	26
Mozambique	98	106	101	84	98	108	101	86	634	(3)	551	(17)	6,046	20
Namibia	99	123	102	93	99	125	101	95	135	51	591	24	8,833	(4)
Niger	98	108	101	80	98	108	101	80	1,962	19	417	(6)	7,106	(5)
Nigeria	96	151	99	113	96	151	99	113	12,907	90	1,118	10	12,288	23
Rwanda	94	107	98	79	94	103	98	76	269	2	1,107	(3)	7,801	(10)
Senegal	99	133	102	103	99	133	102	104	961	23	779	17	4,236	(3)
Sierra Leone	100	108	102	87	101	109	103	88	489	(16)	1,341	2	3,340	(14)
Somalia	97	135	102	99	97	135	102	99	612	132	729	64	9,800	(14)
South Africa	95	107	98	88	95	108	97	88	12,784	4	1,953	23	13,717	17
Sudan	96	100	99	76	94	98	97	75	3,054	10	499	(23)	2,477	(25)
Swaziland	94	124	97	92	94	125	97	93	146	56	1,833	36	3,250	66
Tanzania	97	122	101	88	97	123	101	88	4,113	38	1,391	31	7,096	(21)
Togo	98	132	101	101	99	128	101	98	492	67	894	22	7,926	(17)
Tunisia	98	118	101	94	98	117	101	94	855	(18)	851	19	12,000	6
Uganda	103	128	107	93	103	127	106	92	1,480	17	1,473	8	6,340	36
Zaire	97	127	99	97	97	127	99	97	1,267	50	758	(2)	7,562	11
Zambia	103	141	107	100	103	139	107	98	1,742	54	1,818	16	3,670	5
Zimbabwe	97	134	100	102	95	126	98	96	2,679	44	1,539	25	4,787	22
NORTH & CENTRAL AMERICA	97	103	98	92	97	104	98	92	343,656	(1)	3,565	3	19,216	7
Barbados	99	79	99	77	99	79	99	77	2	0	2,000	0	5,667	(54)
Belize	100	115	102	92	100	115	102	92	29	17	1,725	(6)	X	X
Canada	98	114	99	105	98	115	99	106	47,355	19	2,200	2	24,979	7
Costa Rica	99	123	102	96	100	117	103	91	308	(6)	2,645	6	8,484	41
Cuba	98	110	98	101	98	109	99	101	604	10	2,473	2	5,310	(11)
Dominican Rep	100	112	102	91	100	116	103	94	530	21	3,485	21	6,833	17
El Salvador	100	82	102	72	103	107	105	94	808	11	1,934	13	16,000	37
Guatemala	99	117	101	90	97	123	100	95	1,515	40	1,874	21	4,350	21
Haiti	99	108	101	91	100	110	101	93	399	(2)	954	3	4,025	1
Honduras	95	125	99	92	95	123	99	91	623	31	1,357	33	7,000	63
Jamaica	106	104	107	91	106	103	107	91	3	(63)	1,286	(20)	12,566	15
Mexico	97	117	100	95	97	118	99	96	22,700	23	2,265	11	13,896	7
Nicaragua	111	75	114	55	113	82	116	61	484	28	1,603	14	11,826	86
Panama	97	109	100	90	98	106	100	88	315	32	1,783	27	9,179	11
Trinidad and Tobago	113	84	115	72	113	86	115	74	13	(24)	2,600	(18)	10,000	(3)
United States	96	100	97	92	96	100	98	92	267,965	(5)	4,341	6	31,127	9
SOUTH AMERICA	96	124	99	103	97	126	99	105	76,356	22	2,062	22	12,121	13
Argentina	96	108	98	95	95	107	97	95	19,756	(16)	2,262	3	20,714	64
Bolivia	96	134	99	105	96	136	98	107	754	27	1,218	10	5,790	10
Brazil	94	131	96	108	95	134	97	111	39,783	41	1,878	38	12,471	8
Chile	95	130	96	112	95	131	96	112	2,976	73	3,690	85	14,536	43
Colombia	98	125	100	104	97	131	100	109	3,958	18	2,512	4	11,890	8
Ecuador	97	137	99	108	97	137	100	108	1,381	140	1,736	15	6,897	(25)
Guyana	101	74	102	70	101	74	102	71	195	(28)	2,056	(23)	7,750	17
Paraguay	94	166	97	126	93	158	96	119	1,620	166	2,047	38	16,528	16
Peru	98	120	101	98	99	122	101	100	2,200	66	2,513	38	8,336	15
Suriname	91	101	91	87	91	101	91	87	263	10	3,835	(4)	X	(100)
Uruguay	93	120	93	114	93	120	93	113	1,373	54	2,494	68	6,020	23
Venezuela	99	121	102	95	99	121	102	94	2,080	36	2,231	17	8,333	6

Table 18.1

| | Index of Agricultural Production (1979-81 = 100) | | | | Index of Food Production (1979-81 = 100) | | | | Average Production of Cereals | | Average Yields of Cereals | | Average Yields of Roots and Tubers | |
| | Total | | Per Capita | | Total | | Per Capita | | (000 metric tons) | Percent Change Since | Kilograms Per Hectare | Percent Change Since | Kilograms Per Hectare | Percent Change Since |
	1978-80	1988-90	1978-80	1988-90	1978-80	1988-90	1978-80	1988-90	1988-90	1978-80	1988-90	1978-80	1988-90	1978-80
ASIA	**97**	**139**	**99**	**118**	**97**	**139**	**99**	**117**	**833,141**	**33**	**2,713**	**32**	**12,210**	**(16)**
Afghanistan	100	84	99	85	100	84	99	85	3,463	(18)	1,338	3	15,000	5
Bahrain	X	X	X	X	X	X	X	X	X	X	X	X	X	X
Bangladesh	99	122	102	95	99	123	102	97	27,382	34	2,483	28	10,181	(0)
Bhutan	98	100	99	84	98	100	99	84	98	(37)	1,039	(28)	10,067	54
Cambodia	107	208	106	166	106	203	105	163	2,484	83	1,361	29	8,360	35
China	96	151	97	134	97	149	98	132	369,576	31	4,057	38	11,740	(32)
Cyprus	101	112	102	102	101	112	102	102	135	54	2,309	29	22,708	(8)
India	98	143	100	118	98	144	100	119	193,601	42	1,861	42	15,552	24
Indonesia	93	151	95	126	93	153	95	128	50,163	61	3,715	40	11,473	29
Iran, Islamic Rep	96	135	100	99	96	135	99	99	11,128	29	1,224	3	13,914	(4)
Iraq	102	123	106	90	102	124	106	90	2,070	21	971	23	16,556	3
Israel	102	107	104	92	104	116	106	100	223	3	1,988	16	37,278	11
Japan	104	98	105	93	104	101	105	95	14,214	(7)	5,662	3	24,599	8
Jordan	97	157	101	112	98	158	102	113	110	22	797	49	18,625	24
Korea, Dem People's Rep	97	126	99	108	97	125	99	107	10,417	21	6,598	14	13,381	5
Korea, Rep	104	106	106	95	104	108	105	97	8,708	0	5,933	20	21,579	24
Kuwait	X	X	X	X	X	X	X	X	3	X	3,000	X	X	X
Lao People's Dem Rep	88	151	89	120	88	151	89	121	1,353	49	2,177	66	8,413	(15)
Lebanon	100	142	99	141	100	145	99	145	76	50	1,876	66	17,128	12
Malaysia	95	169	97	133	92	196	94	155	1,759	(7)	2,642	(11)	9,436	5
Mongolia	101	110	104	86	101	114	104	89	752	132	1,225	115	9,610	27
Myanmar	95	120	97	99	95	122	97	101	14,112	20	2,752	22	8,553	22
Nepal	98	139	101	111	98	141	100	113	5,451	54	1,832	15	6,693	25
Oman	X	X	X	X	X	X	X	X	2	0	1,500	100	X	X
Pakistan	95	148	98	107	95	144	98	104	20,387	27	1,745	14	10,063	(3)
Philippines	96	109	99	87	96	109	99	86	13,851	28	1,936	22	6,805	(7)
Qatar	X	X	X	X	X	X	X	X	3	350	3,000	X	X	X
Saudi Arabia	135	403	140	274	135	408	141	277	3,596	1,075	4,261	502	18,500	X
Singapore	98	96	99	87	98	97	99	87	X	X	X	X	0	X
Sri Lanka	96	100	98	87	95	101	97	88	2,289	13	2,892	24	9,198	4
Syrian Arab Rep	92	116	95	85	91	114	94	83	3,156	17	1,209	18	15,338	1
Thailand	98	127	100	108	98	124	100	105	24,636	23	2,089	10	14,486	(1)
Turkey	98	120	100	97	98	120	100	97	28,125	13	2,057	11	21,926	35
United Arab Emirates	X	X	X	X	X	X	X	X	5	250	4,667	X	X	X
Viet Nam	94	148	97	122	94	145	96	119	18,971	67	2,988	55	7,653	15
Yemen (Arab Rep)	104	72	108	53	104	72	108	53	549	(28)	971	3	12,842	10
(People's Dem Rep)	98	57	100	45	98	56	100	44	30	(75)	1,085	(30)	8,000	(50)
EUROPE	**99**	**109**	**99**	**105**	**99**	**108**	**99**	**105**	**285,975**	**14**	**4,240**	**20**	**21,195**	**10**
Albania	97	112	99	94	98	112	100	94	1,023	11	2,914	15	8,818	26
Austria	99	108	99	108	99	108	99	108	5,104	14	5,407	28	26,960	9
Belgium {a}	96	96	117	117	96	96	117	117	2,313	9	6,235	29	42,643	8
Bulgaria	97	96	98	94	97	101	97	99	8,412	8	3,991	9	11,339	13
Czechoslovakia	100	126	101	123	100	126	101	123	12,149	18	4,951	25	18,317	10
Denmark	99	130	99	129	99	130	99	129	8,893	20	5,646	40	38,336	46
Finland	102	112	102	108	102	112	102	108	3,636	14	3,016	15	20,740	23
France	98	104	98	100	98	104	98	100	56,095	22	6,101	31	33,009	21
Germany (Fed Rep)	99	113	100	112	99	113	100	112	26,372	13	5,715	29	36,931	27
(Dem Rep)	98	98	115	117	98	98	115	117	10,974	16	4,507	20	23,634	20
Greece	97	98	108	104	97	98	108	104	4,697	2	3,306	13	19,573	26
Hungary	98	110	99	111	99	111	99	112	13,484	2	4,772	7	17,932	17
Iceland	100	90	101	82	100	90	101	82	X	X	X	X	10,333	(9)
Ireland	105	112	107	108	105	111	107	108	2,108	12	6,169	35	25,613	5
Italy	97	100	97	98	97	99	97	97	17,315	(3)	3,816	10	10,039	10
Luxembourg {a}	X	X	X	X	X	X	X	X	X	X	X	X	X	X
Malta	104	111	105	115	104	111	105	115	9	35	3,857	16	8,500	3
Netherlands	95	121	96	115	95	121	96	115	1,314	1	6,681	19	41,186	10
Norway	99	104	99	101	99	104	99	101	1,150	2	3,325	(8)	24,607	(7)
Poland	104	114	105	107	104	116	105	109	26,492	39	3,136	29	18,962	10
Portugal	102	113	102	107	101	113	102	107	1,535	25	1,659	59	8,205	(13)
Romania	100	100	101	96	100	100	100	96	18,320	(6)	3,115	2	11,003	(26)
Spain	101	117	102	112	101	117	102	112	20,766	27	2,669	22	18,402	19
Sweden	99	99	99	97	99	99	99	97	5,512	2	4,333	22	32,412	12
Switzerland	99	109	99	104	99	110	99	104	1,307	57	6,312	30	39,433	10
United Kingdom	98	109	98	107	98	109	98	107	22,074	22	5,792	24	37,890	13
Yugoslavia	98	99	98	94	98	100	99	94	14,923	(1)	3,550	3	7,490	(14)
U.S.S.R.	**104**	**119**	**105**	**110**	**105**	**121**	**106**	**112**	**205,449**	**5**	**1,925**	**20**	**10,995**	**(6)**
OCEANIA	**101**	**113**	**103**	**98**	**103**	**109**	**104**	**95**	**23,524**	**5**	**1,688**	**17**	**11,295**	**10**
Australia	103	117	105	102	104	109	106	95	22,693	5	1,651	17	28,043	24
Fiji	93	102	95	86	93	103	95	87	33	79	2,381	23	9,500	25
New Zealand	97	106	97	99	99	112	99	104	792	0	4,526	15	30,286	13
Papua New Guinea	98	128	100	104	98	129	100	105	3	(25)	1,800	5	7,225	3
Solomon Islands	93	122	96	89	93	122	96	89	0	(100)	0	(100)	15,611	22

Source: Food and Agriculture Organization of the United Nations.
Notes:
a. Data for Belgium and Luxembourg are combined under Belgium.
World and regional totals include some countries not listed.
0 = zero or less than half of the unit of measure; X = not available; negative numbers are shown in parentheses.
For additional information, see Sources and Technical Notes.

Table 18.2 Agricultural Inputs, 1975–89

	Cropland		Irrigated Land as a Percentage of Cropland		Average Annual Fertilizer Use (kilograms per hectare of cropland)		Average Annual Pesticide Use (metric tons of active ingredient)		Tractors		Harvesters	
	Total Hectares (000) 1989	Hectares Per Capita 1990	1977-79	1987-89	1977-79	1987-89	1975-77	1982-84	Average Number 1987-89	Percent Change Since 1977-79	Average Number 1987-89	Percent Change Since 1977-79
WORLD	1,478,190	0.28	14	16	73	97	X	X	25,896,523	26	3,964,402	22
AFRICA	186,995	0.29	5	6	14	20	X	X	569,554	30	55,714	43
Algeria	7,605	0.30	3	4	21	27	16,457	21,400	93,757	116	9,009	120
Angola	3,600	0.36	X	X	6	5	X	X	10,270	3	X	X
Benin	1,860	0.40	0	0	1	3	X	X	123	26	X	X
Botswana	1,380	1.06	0	0	1	1	X	X	4,217	111	87	25
Burkina Faso	3,564	0.40	0	0	2	5	X	X	125	23	X	X
Burundi	1,336	0.24	4	5	1	3	22	59	129	110	X	X
Cameroon	7,008	0.59	0	0	5	6	X	X	1,003	147	X	X
Cape Verde	39	0.11	5	5	0	0	X	X	16	37	X	X
Central African Rep	2,006	0.66	X	X	1	0	X	X	195	38	15	57
Chad	3,205	0.56	0	0	2	2	X	X	165	10	17	6
Comoros	100	0.18	X	X	0	0	X	X	X	X	X	X
Congo	168	0.07	2	2	0	8	X	X	695	5	50	70
Cote d'Ivoire	3,660	0.31	1	2	13	10	X	X	3,450	21	58	78
Djibouti	X	0.00	X	X	X	X	X	X	8	33	X	X
Egypt	2,585	0.05	98	99	223	384	26,970	19,567	52,497	85	2,278	7
Equatorial Guinea	230	0.65	X	X	0	0	X	X	100	3	X	X
Ethiopia	13,930	0.28	1	1	2	6	600 a	993	3,900	2	150	3
Gabon	452	0.39	X	X	1	3	X	X	1,427	24	X	X
Gambia, The	178	0.21	6	7	15	17	X	101 b	43	(7)	5	50
Ghana	2,720	0.18	0	0	8	4	X	X	3,900	16	480	89
Guinea	728	0.13	1	3	2	1	X	X	250	108	X	X
Guinea-Bissau	335	0.35	X	X	1	1	X	X	48	11	X	X
Kenya	2,428	0.10	2	2	19	47	935 b	1,307	9,538	51	703	85
Lesotho	320	0.18	X	X	10	15	X	X	1,750	37	32	20
Liberia	373	0.14	1	1	13	10	1,223	310	324	16	X	X
Libya	2,150	0.47	10	11	23	40	2,610 a	2,017	31,367	61	X	X
Madagascar	3,092	0.26	19	29	3	3	X	1,630	2,847	12	142	33
Malawi	2,409	0.28	1	1	11	21	X	X	1,380	25	X	X
Mali	2,093	0.23	7	10	7	6	X	683	835	3	48	20
Mauritania	199	0.10	6	6	10	10	11 b	X	332	29	X	X
Mauritius	106	0.10	14	16	245	302	753 a	981 a	350	11	X	X
Morocco	9,241	0.37	12	14	21	34	2,225 b	3,350	34,067	42	4,736	47
Mozambique	3,100	0.20	2	4	6	1	X	X	5,750	2	X	X
Namibia	662	0.40	1	1	X	X	X	X	2,950	20	X	X
Niger	3,605	0.47	1	1	1	1	451	159 b	179	31	X	X
Nigeria	31,335	0.29	3	3	3	10	X	4,000 b	11,033	36	X	X
Rwanda	1,153	0.16	0	0	0	1	X	X	88	8	X	X
Senegal	5,226	0.71	3	3	7	5	X	X	477	13	150	15
Sierra Leone	1,801	0.43	1	2	1	0	X	X	510	320	6	500
Somalia	1,039	0.14	10	11	0	3	X	X	2,100	39	X	X
South Africa	13,174	0.37	8	9	70	58	19,292	11,053	183,233	2	33,000	37
Sudan	12,510	0.50	14	15	2	4	X	X	21,000	108	1,220	16
Swaziland	164	0.21	35	38	83	47	16 a	X	3,293	15	X	X
Tanzania	5,250	0.19	2	3	6	9	2,992 c	5,733 c	18,550	1	X	X
Togo	1,444	0.41	0	0	1	8	X	X	353	126	X	X
Tunisia	4,700	0.57	3	6	11	22	X	1,330	25,967	3	2,637	9
Uganda	6,705	0.36	0	0	0	0	X	23 c	4,200	89	14	50
Zaire	7,850	0.22	0	0	1	1	X	X	2,333	37	X	X
Zambia	5,268	0.62	0	1	11	17	X	X	5,709	30	281	8
Zimbabwe	2,810	0.29	5	8	38	56	865 b	207 a	20,367	3	590	9
NORTH & CENTRAL AMERICA	273,834	0.64	10	9	87	85	X	X	5,709,463	(2)	828,610	(0)
Barbados	33	0.13	X	X	162	91	X	X	608	15	X	X
Belize	56	0.30	2	4	36	71	X	X	1,050	39	40	52
Canada	45,960	1.73	1	2	38	47	26,928	54,767	756,300	16	156,700	(3)
Costa Rica	528	0.18	10	22	143	191	3,027	3,667	6,350	9	1,120	15
Cuba	3,329	0.31	22	26	133	192	7,817	9,567	75,368	12	7,202	45
Dominican Rep	1,446	0.20	11	16	41	50	1,961	3,297	2,307	9	X	X
El Salvador	733	0.14	9	16	133	121	1,310	2,838 a	3,407	8	385	33
Guatemala	1,875	0.20	3	4	53	69	4,627	5,117	4,160	7	2,973	19
Haiti	905	0.14	8	8	4	3	156 d	X	215	30	X	X
Honduras	1,810	0.35	4	5	13	20	940	859	3,420	11	X	X
Jamaica	269	0.11	12	13	55	105	861	1,420	3,037	12	X	X
Mexico	24,710	0.28	20	21	44	73	19,148	27,630	165,333	53	18,233	30
Nicaragua	1,273	0.33	6	7	31	55	2,943	2,003	2,510	34	X	X
Panama	577	0.24	5	5	44	62	1,542	2,393	6,230	29	1,950	61
Trinidad and Tobago	120	0.09	17	18	61	28	X	X	2,620	16	X	X
United States	189,915	0.76	10	10	105	95	459,400	373,333	4,670,000	(6)	640,000	(1)
SOUTH AMERICA	142,134	0.48	5	6	31	40	X	X	1,089,234	43	114,046	19
Argentina	35,750	1.11	4	5	3	5	7,448	14,313	209,333	20	47,500	11
Bolivia	3,460	0.47	4	5	1	2	612	833	4,690	30	120	11
Brazil	78,650	0.52	2	3	42	46	59,292	46,698	680,000	59	44,000	29
Chile	4,525	0.34	28	28	27	73	1,838	1,800	38,447	12	8,600	8
Colombia	5,380	0.16	7	9	55	90	19,344	16,100	34,711	31	2,567	28
Ecuador	2,653	0.25	19	21	30	30	5,445	3,110	8,400	49	737	20
Guyana	495	0.62	25	26	22	29	705	658	3,580	5	423	4
Paraguay	2,216	0.52	2	3	2	6	2,957	3,423	10,500	107	X	X
Peru	3,730	0.17	31	33	35	54	2,370	2,753	16,000	26	X	X
Suriname	68	0.16	56	85	49	74	974 b	1,720 a	1,250	17	255	42
Uruguay	1,304	0.42	5	8	54	48	1,390	1,517	35,200	9	4,640	(2)
Venezuela	3,895	0.20	6	7	51	162	6,923	8,143	46,833	33	5,200	86

Table 18.2

	Cropland Total Hectares (000) 1989	Cropland Hectares Per Capita 1990	Irrigated Land as a Percentage of Cropland 1977-79	Irrigated Land as a Percentage of Cropland 1987-89	Average Annual Fertilizer Use (kilograms per hectare of cropland) 1977-79	Average Annual Fertilizer Use 1987-89	Average Annual Pesticide Use (metric tons of active ingredient) 1975-77	Average Annual Pesticide Use 1982-84	Tractors Average Number 1987-89	Tractors Percent Change Since 1977-79	Harvesters Average Number 1987-89	Harvesters Percent Change Since 1977-79
ASIA	**454,115**	**0.15**	**29**	**32**	**56**	**111**	**X**	**X**	**5,122,884**	**87**	**1,341,084**	**82**
Afghanistan	8,054	0.49	32	33	7	8	1,000 a	605 b	770	3	X	X
Bahrain	2	0.00	50	50	0	333	X	X	X	X	X	X
Bangladesh	9,292	0.08	15	26	40	86	X	234	5,083	39	X	X
Bhutan	131	0.09	20	26	0	0	X	X	X	X	X	X
Cambodia	3,056	0.37	3	3	0	0	1,593	833	1,363	1	20	0
China	96,115	0.08	47	47	115	255	150,467	159,267	878,453	54	35,129	79
Cyprus	156	0.22	19	21	94	141	X	X	13,583	30	560	56
India	168,990	0.20	22	25	29	62	52,506	53,087	791,289	136	2,850	262
Indonesia	21,260	0.12	25	35	35	113	18,687	16,344	16,100	75	17,100	28
Iran, Islamic Rep	14,830	0.27	37	39	27	72	X	X	112,667	77	2,850	(4)
Iraq	5,450	0.29	31	42	13	39	X	X	39,062	95	2,671	(31)
Israel	433	0.09	47	49	186	234	600	847	28,502	18	280	(8)
Japan	4,637	0.04	67	62	481	425	33,960	32,000	1,979,260	89	1,234,257	83
Jordan	376	0.11	10	15	26	63	X	X	5,682	35	69	14
Korea, Dem People's Rep	2,000	0.09	53	68	355	396	4,000 a	X	71,000	116	X	X
Korea, Rep	2,127	0.05	62	64	385	411	4,675	12,273	25,269	1,494	26,138	10,852
Kuwait	4	0.00	25	50	83	167	X	X	117	343	X	X
Lao People's Dem Rep	901	0.22	9	13	0	0	X	X	840	92	X	X
Lebanon	301	0.11	29	29	116	79	X	X	3,000	0	95	6
Malaysia	4,880	0.27	7	7	77	150	X	9,730 a	11,833	57	X	X
Mongolia	1,375	0.63	2	5	5	15	X	X	11,681	23	2,632	10
Myanmar	10,034	0.24	10	10	8	11	3,721	15,300	10,872	30	42	85
Nepal	2,641	0.14	15	34	7	23	X	X	2,870	50	X	X
Oman	48	0.03	78	85	14	83	X	X	136	54	35	215
Pakistan	20,730	0.17	69	78	42	85	2,120	1,856	176,000	136	823	82
Philippines	7,970	0.13	14	20	38	64	3,547 b	4,415	8,077	(25)	620	54
Qatar	5	0.01	X	X	67	200	X	X	90	79	X	X
Saudi Arabia	1,185	0.08	32	36	12	398	X	X	1,850	85	600	71
Singapore	1	0.00	X	X	3,333	6,000	X	X	59	49	X	X
Sri Lanka	1,901	0.11	27	29	69	107	X	697	29,000	54	5	67
Syrian Arab Rep	5,503	0.44	10	12	20	46	X	4,892 b,c	54,767	137	2,616	14
Thailand	22,126	0.40	12	19	13	33	13,120	22,289	142,667	206	X	X
Turkey	27,885	0.50	7	8	49	62	X	9,000 a	654,336	80	11,608	(21)
United Arab Emirates	39	0.02	13	13	60	120	X	X	X	X	5	150
Viet Nam	6,600	0.10	21	28	47	79	1,693	883 b	35,533	30	X	X
Yemen (Arab Rep)	1,362	0.15	17	18	6	6	325 c,d	1,614 b,c,d	2,257	28	X	X
(People's Dem Rep)	119	0.05	41	49	6	3	X	X	3,047	40	20	50
EUROPE	**139,865**	**0.27**	**10**	**12**	**225**	**227**	**X**	**X**	**10,244,872**	**30**	**831,801**	**2**
Albania	707	0.22	51	59	131	141	4,510	5,183	11,443	14	1,654	22
Austria	1,533	0.20	0	0	255	210	3,449	4,548	339,168	8	28,621	(10)
Belgium {e}	822 f	0.08 f	0	0	555	505	8,847	13,263	121,896	10	8,473	(15)
Bulgaria	4,146	0.46	28	30	185	199	28,287	32,400	53,510	(17)	7,811	(25)
Czechoslovakia	5,108	0.33	3	6	335	313	13,967	14,970	140,494	1	21,357	14
Denmark	2,555	0.50	13	17	271	243	4,998	7,729	166,210	(13)	33,913	(16)
Finland	2,453	0.49	2	3	190	205	1,768	2,639	242,667	21	44,333	3
France	19,119	0.34	4	6	292	312	83,017	98,733	1,511,711	7	145,989	(1)
Germany (Fed Rep)	7,478	0.12	4	4	464	405	11,900	14,133	1,447,768	(1)	140,667	(18)
(Dem Rep)	4,913	0.30	3	3	343	352	23,693	29,836	167,669	20	18,156	37
Greece	3,924	0.39	24	30	141	165	30,570	29,240	187,000	53	6,600	16
Hungary	5,287	0.50	5	3	287	258	26,267	27,595	52,220	(10)	10,759	(26)
Iceland	8	0.03	X	X	3,750	2,792	3 g,c	5 g,c	13,067	6	17	16
Ireland	953	0.27	X	X	655	717	1,721	2,250	163,667	26	5,140	(5)
Italy	12,033	0.21	23	26	177	172	83,724	98,496	1,362,786	43	45,045	17
Luxembourg {e}	X f	X f	X	X	X	X	X	X	X	X	X	X
Malta	10	0.04	8	8	77	77	X	X	448	11	10	(23)
Netherlands	934	0.06	49	58	703	662	6,593	9,670	194,000	15	5,647	(9)
Norway	878	0.21	8	11	290	252	1,494	1,508	153,491	27	18,633	20
Poland	14,759	0.39	1	1	244	224	11,360	15,277	1,099,139	111	72,162	137
Portugal	3,771	0.37	17	17	70	75	24,375	16,016	77,173	25	4,750	10
Romania	10,350	0.44	20	33	130	135	29,397	17,237	166,883	20	48,355	6
Spain	20,345	0.52	14	16	77	101	55,267	71,533	700,869	54	48,318	11
Sweden	2,853	0.33	2	4	182	134	5,454	5,736	183,000	(2)	47,000	(8)
Switzerland	412	0.06	6	6	417	430	1,945	1,699	109,000	25	4,200	(22)
United Kingdom	6,736	0.12	2	2	313	359	25,137	34,147	518,165	6	54,333	(6)
Yugoslavia	7,766	0.33	2	2	108	126	19,091	31,567	1,061,000	211	9,856	(6)
U.S.S.R.	**230,630**	**0.80**	**7**	**9**	**78**	**114**	**348,767**	**535,400**	**2,742,667**	**11**	**732,667**	**9**
OCEANIA	**50,617**	**1.90**	**3**	**4**	**33**	**33**	**X**	**X**	**417,858**	**(2)**	**60,480**	**(4)**
Australia	48,934	2.87	3	4	23	26	60,638	65,200	332,000	0	56,900	(2)
Fiji	240	0.31	0	0	57	97	X	X	4,290	13	X	X
New Zealand	507	0.15	33	54	1,110	670	1,651	1,793	78,433	(11)	3,103	(29)
Papua New Guinea	388	0.10	X	X	21	39	X	X	1,150	(7)	464	33
Solomon Islands	57	0.18	X	X	0	0	X	X	X	X	X	X

Sources: Food and Agriculture Organization of the United Nations, United Nations Industrial Development Organization, and other sources.

Notes: a. One year of data. b. Two years of data. c. May not be active ingredient. d. Imports of pesticides. e. Data for Belgium and Luxembourg are combined under Belgium. f. Cropland data for Belgium and Luxembourg are for 1987. g. Sales of pesticides.
World and regional totals include some countries not listed.
0 = zero or less than half of the unit of measure; X = not available; negative numbers are shown in parentheses.
For additional information, see Sources and Technical Notes.

Table 18.3 Livestock Populations and Grain Consumed as

	Cattle		Sheep and Goats		Pigs		Equines		Buffaloes and Camels		Chickens		Grain Fed to Livestock as Percentage of Total Grain Consumption	
	Annual Average (000) 1988-90	Percent Change Since 1978-80	Annual Average (000) 1988-90	Percent Change Since 1978-80	Annual Average (000) 1988-90	Percent Change Since 1978-80	Annual Average (000) 1988-90	Percent Change Since 1978-80	Annual Average (000) 1988-90	Percent Change Since 1978-80	Annual Average (millions) 1988-90	Percent Change Since 1978-80	1970	1990
WORLD	1,271,279	5	1,716,749	13	845,108	10	118,602	7	157,967	15	10,399	53	38	38
AFRICA	183,715	8	372,038	14	13,145	37	19,094	12	16,877	16	838	46	4	18
Algeria	1,452	12	17,015	14	5	15	624	(29)	128	(12)	23	32	0	36
Angola	3,133	4	1,250	9	486	27	6	0	X	X	6	20	0	0
Benin	932	20	1,884	2	681	56	7	0	X	X	24	132	0	0
Botswana	2,522	(13)	2,176	199	15	110	184	27	X	X	2	100	0	0
Burkina Faso	2,853	5	8,473	88	497	194	464	72	5	(6)	22	97	0	2
Burundi	432	(42)	1,208	34	84	119	X	X	X	X	4	33	0	0
Cameroon	4,583	41	6,402	40	1,300	17	65	35	X	X	17	79	0	0
Cape Verde	17	46	104	54	80	128	11	19	X	X	X	X	0	0
Central African Rep	2,493	70	1,331	35	397	89	0	0	X	X	3	125	0	0
Chad	4,156	(2)	4,604	(9)	13	56	425	2	530	26	4	33	0	0
Comoros	46	(30)	132	40	X	X	4	20	X	X	X	X	X	X
Congo	65	(2)	367	84	48	31	X	X	X	X	2	67	0	0
Cote d'Ivoire	1,022	62	1,978	3	351	14	2	0	X	X	25	61	8	4
Djibouti	72	76	916	(2)	X	X	8	14	58	17	X	X	X	X
Egypt	3,402	58	8,039	138	92	177	1,974	17	2,664	7	34	24	0	36
Equatorial Guinea	5	25	43	8	5	25	X	X	X	X	X	X	X	X
Ethiopia	28,633	10	41,387	3	20	11	8,070	24	1,070	10	57	10	0	0
Gabon	26	550	236	29	155	19	X	X	X	X	2	0	0	0
Gambia, The	392	34	361	24	11	10	20	0	X	X	X	X	0	0
Ghana	1,177	52	4,548	17	550	47	12	(59)	X	X	9	(27)	0	5
Guinea	1,800	6	965	17	34	(10)	3	(25)	X	X	13	105	0	0
Guinea-Bissau	340	20	415	20	290	18	4	0	X	X	1	0	0	0
Kenya	13,433	27	13,886	11	101	20	2	0	800	32	24	44	1	3
Lesotho	530	(9)	2,500	40	73	(9)	249	27	X	X	1	0	0	21
Liberia	42	11	475	24	140	40	X	X	X	X	4	100	0	0
Libya	240	32	6,770	4	X	X	109	38	189	67	37	600	0	41
Madagascar	10,259	5	1,916	2	1,419	71	0	(100)	X	X	19	14	0	0
Malawi	987	27	1,107	41	260	35	2	67	X	X	9	8	0	2
Mali	4,873	(3)	11,333	(10)	59	35	589	4	236	6	22	78	0	2
Mauritania	1,258	7	7,440	(2)	X	X	167	5	813	11	4	33	0	0
Mauritius	33	32	102	28	10	58	X	X	X	X	2	50	0	0
Morocco	3,287	(6)	23,310	13	9	23	1,626	(15)	39	(80)	38	65	0	29
Mozambique	1,367	(1)	500	15	165	43	20	0	X	X	22	35	0	0
Namibia	2,061	(23)	9079	14	49	36	124	7	X	X	1	X	X	X
Niger	3,570	12	11,092	15	37	24	811	18	419	8	17	79	0	0
Nigeria	12,000	(0)	31,000	0	1,067	7	950	0	18	6	160	45	0	1
Rwanda	613	(4)	1,456	31	109	(2)	X	X	X	X	1	0	0	13
Senegal	2,674	6	5,049	77	487	182	680	49	15	114	14	86	0	1
Sierra Leone	330	(3)	510	29	50	44	X	X	X	X	6	50	0	3
Somalia	5,028	29	34,583	26	10	11	50	10	6,849	26	3	0	73	2
South Africa	11,857	(13)	36,914	(1)	1,470	7	454	1	X	X	38	31	29	41
Sudan	20,556	19	34,583	18	X	X	687	(2)	2,761	9	32	22	0	0
Swaziland	654	(0)	356	13	23	33	16	(2)	X	X	1	0	0	0
Tanzania	12,956	5	13,230	43	280	81	173	7	X	X	31	90	0	3
Togo	245	8	2,624	98	389	62	5	114	X	X	6	143	0	16
Tunisia	547	(15)	6,443	13	4	33	355	10	185	8	35	62	13	27
Uganda	4,215	(19)	4,003	12	461	124	17	6	X	X	17	28	0	0
Zaire	1,500	31	3,944	17	810	19	0	0	X	X	20	40	0	7
Zambia	2,772	27	606	85	193	(10)	2	100	X	X	15	(22)	0	4
Zimbabwe	6,252	11	3,146	59	240	47	126	11	X	X	10	11	14	16
NORTH & CENTRAL AMERICA	161,050	(7)	33,566	(1)	88,730	(5)	21,449	1	9	13	1,861	33	74	65
Barbados	18	(5)	90	14	49	8	5	0	X	X	1	33	X	X
Belize	50	1	5	25	26	56	9	0	X	X	1	X	X	X
Canada	12,187	(9)	755	11	10,728	21	416	15	X	X	108	14	78	79
Costa Rica	1,750	(16)	5	67	223	4	126	2	X	X	4	(33)	16	24
Cuba	4,944	(6)	494	10	1,817	28	690	(18)	X	X	28	24	0	4
Dominican Rep	2,205	14	651	44	423	(19)	586	40	X	X	24	121	22	50
El Salvador	1,171	(11)	20	11	447	(10)	118	5	X	X	5	0	25	26
Guatemala	1,930	14	742	10	807	12	159	8	X	X	10	(29)	13	25
Haiti	1,567	68	1,336	25	933	(48)	735	7	X	X	14	180	0	9
Honduras	2,240	16	34	15	687	50	261	3	X	X	8	85	16	35
Jamaica	290	4	443	19	233	17	37	(7)	X	X	6	13	0	34
Mexico	30,100	12	15,512	(2)	16,447	1	12,523	(1)	X	X	235	42	18	31
Nicaragua	1,677	(34)	10	7	690	2	303	(8)	X	X	7	62	19	0
Panama	1,447	2	7	17	218	8	176	4	X	X	7	33	13	30
Trinidad and Tobago	79	4	63	15	72	23	5	0	9	13	9	24	0	33
United States	98,616	(13)	12,935	(7)	54,771	(11)	5,260	4	X	X	1,391	33	80	70
SOUTH AMERICA	262,254	12	134,759	10	54,803	6	21,443	11	1,190	162	877	43	38	46
Argentina	50,715	(11)	32,261	(9)	4,233	16	3,193	(2)	X	X	44	24	46	42
Bolivia	5,609	25	14,650	28	2,122	46	1,025	(9)	X	X	14	91	22	35
Brazil	138,804	24	32,333	25	32,340	(6)	9,346	19	1,190	162	543	39	44	55
Chile	3,351	(6)	7,160	10	1,403	37	541	10	X	X	27	58	29	33
Colombia	24,464	1	3,631	22	2,607	34	3,277	16	X	X	40	48	13	20
Ecuador	4,181	45	1,659	(34)	4,167	24	824	36	X	X	51	83	8	22
Guyana	210	(1)	197	9	185	39	3	0	X	X	15	22	0	3
Paraguay	8,036	39	589	13	2,286	98	377	4	X	X	17	46	0	0
Peru	4,022	1	14,564	(12)	2,304	14	1,368	1	X	X	57	55	16	28
Suriname	88	116	15	73	24	22	X	X	X	X	6	27	0	0
Uruguay	9,500	(9)	24,941	40	215	(41)	477	(4)	X	X	7	22	37	12
Venezuela	13,250	29	2,042	23	2,909	40	1,007	0	X	X	55	51	16	35

Feed, 1978–90

Table 18.3

	Cattle		Sheep and Goats		Pigs		Equines		Buffaloes and Camels		Chickens		Grain Fed to Livestock as Percentage of Total Grain Consumption	
	Annual Average (000) 1988-90	Percent Change Since 1978-80	Annual Average (000) 1988-90	Percent Change Since 1978-80	Annual Average (000) 1988-90	Percent Change Since 1978-80	Annual Average (000) 1988-90	Percent Change Since 1978-80	Annual Average (000) 1988-90	Percent Change Since 1978-80	Annual Average (millions) 1988-90	Percent Change Since 1978-80	1970	1990
ASIA	389,730	11	640,938	14	419,279	16	44,171	12	138,814	15	4,293	107	7	16
Afghanistan	1,600	(57)	14,600	(33)	X	X	1,730	(0)	265	(5)	7	17	0	0
Bahrain	6	6	24	18	X	X	X	X	1	0	1	0	X	X
Bangladesh	23,102	(17)	12,083	16	X	X	45	4	1,757	20	85	35	0	0
Bhutan	408	39	86	228	70	29	53	37	4	(20)	X	X	0	0
Cambodia	2,017	153	0	0	1,545	737	16	85	727	92	7	100	0	0
China	75,243	43	198,031	15	348,209	13	26,855	18	21,602	17	1,920	141	8	20
Cyprus	47	130	523	2	277	69	8	(51)	X	X	3	33	0	68
India	195,267	6	160,586	31	10,333	15	2,486	23	74,980	14	290	92	1	2
Indonesia	10,417	61	16,252	37	6,551	113	709	16	3,347	39	464	220	1	6
Iran, Islamic Rep	8,117	8	47,707	1	0	(100)	2,136	(9)	257	4	115	71	16	20
Iraq	1,642	(4)	10,967	(6)	X	X	498	(5)	202	(20)	78	324	0	27
Israel	357	17	509	30	125	35	11	0	10	(9)	23	(8)	62	58
Japan	4,703	14	68	(19)	11,802	25	21	(9)	X	X	334	19	34	48
Jordan	29	(1)	1,758	30	X	X	25	(8)	16	45	60	123	16	31
Korea, Dem People's Rep	1,277	38	669	30	3,148	57	47	20	X	X	20	13	0	0
Korea, Rep	2,159	25	157	(33)	4,645	123	4	(20)	X	X	60	54	6	39
Kuwait	22	57	266	(44)	X	X	3	0	7	47	27	264	0	77
Lao People's Dem Rep	808	94	111	169	1,330	33	43	43	1,046	37	8	64	0	0
Lebanon	59	(25)	614	30	48	184	18	13	0	X	12	71	22	34
Malaysia	651	25	467	13	2,388	41	5	0	197	(32)	142	189	3	41
Mongolia	2,549	4	18,116	(3)	157	454	2,117	1	553	(9)	X	X	0	0
Myanmar	9,451	14	1,375	68	2,750	34	135	14	2,095	15	28	42	0	0
Nepal	6,303	(8)	6,171	16	546	48	X	X	2,989	26	7	17	0	0
Oman	136	1	945	176	X	X	25	0	84	157	2	0	0	20
Pakistan	17,364	16	62,562	28	X	X	3,633	25	15,325	26	166	237	1	3
Philippines	1,670	(9)	2,205	45	7,793	5	300	(1)	2,832	(2)	65	22	11	21
Qatar	10	25	204	116	X	X	1	(50)	22	109	1	300	0	71
Saudi Arabia	253	(33)	11,401	128	X	X	119	5	405	51	70	380	0	75
Singapore	0	(100)	2	(25)	350	(68)	X	X	0	(100)	4	(70)	0	37
Sri Lanka	1,816	13	546	11	96	80	1	(50)	971	16	9	65	0	0
Syrian Arab Rep	773	4	15,055	63	1	50	249	(25)	6	(45)	13	(9)	0	17
Thailand	5,342	27	252	192	4,755	21	18	(42)	5,500	(6)	95	56	1	26
Turkey	11,800	(21)	48,550	(23)	10	(25)	2,030	(19)	543	(48)	58	14	26	33
United Arab Emirates	48	95	820	82	X	X	X	X	105	94	7	567	0	0
Viet Nam	3,101	89	413	106	11,972	33	137	4	2,810	22	73	27	0	0
Yemen (Arab Rep)	712	(17)	2,951	(19)	X	X	349	(37)	42	(30)	16	336	0	0
(People's Dem Rep)	64	(30)	1,557	(25)	X	X	43	(30)	54	(47)	1	0	0	0
EUROPE	124,900	(7)	166,023	24	185,696	8	5,729	(23)	370	(17)	1,289	7	60	60
Albania	699	18	2,710	41	187	16	177	50	2	0	6	89	0	0
Austria	2,564	0	303	34	3,865	(1)	46	5	X	X	14	0	62	72
Belgium {a}	3,134	2	198	74	6,155	22	23	(48)	X	X	35	17	62	28
Bulgaria	1,612	(8)	8,974	(16)	4,168	14	475	(3)	23	(59)	40	4	55	58
Czechoslovakia	5,083	5	1,108	19	7,372	(3)	44	(12)	X	X	47	4	64	63
Denmark	2,248	(26)	86	56	9,156	(2)	35	(37)	X	X	16	7	86	82
Finland	1,392	(21)	64	(42)	1,322	(3)	40	21	X	X	6	(33)	71	62
France	21,723	(9)	13,123	3	12,418	9	304	(26)	X	X	204	19	66	62
Germany (Fed Rep)	14,703	(2)	1,523	30	22,808	3	372	(1)	X	X	72	(18)	60	59
(Dem Rep)	5,718	3	2,650	33	12,327	4	104	58	X	X	50	0	71	62
Greece	729	(26)	16,432	31	1,175	30	311	(38)	1	(57)	27	(7)	45	58
Hungary	1,651	(15)	2,222	(21)	8,068	(0)	84	(39)	X	X	57	(9)	74	70
Iceland	73	19	700	(19)	12	24	56	12	X	X	X	X	X	X
Ireland	5,705	(8)	5,034	106	972	(11)	75	(28)	X	X	8	(8)	68	61
Italy	8,759	2	12,772	29	9,332	3	386	(25)	107	26	136	(0)	40	49
Luxembourg {a}	X	X	X	X	X	X	X	X	X	X	X	X	X	X
Malta	20	45	11	(3)	100	582	2	(25)	X	X	1	0	7	0
Netherlands	4,628	(6)	1,460	63	13,893	44	64	(9)	X	X	100	29	62	39
Norway	945	(3)	2,293	14	717	5	18	(10)	X	X	4	(8)	75	65
Poland	10,368	(20)	4,325	2	19,301	(10)	988	(46)	X	X	60	(22)	54	66
Portugal	1,345	3	6,110	14	2,425	(17)	276	(9)	X	X	18	8	37	42
Romania	6,402	3	17,869	14	13,749	33	722	21	211	(7)	126	47	51	67
Spain	5,190	11	28,646	68	16,746	66	478	(28)	X	X	51	1	62	69
Sweden	1,676	(12)	397	2	2,238	(17)	50	2	X	X	11	(13)	74	77
Switzerland	1,845	(9)	440	(1)	1,889	(11)	51	8	X	X	6	(5)	59	64
United Kingdom	11,897	(12)	28,837	35	7,641	(3)	173	16	X	X	122	2	59	50
Yugoslavia	4,782	(13)	7,661	3	7,650	(3)	368	(50)	25	(67)	74	30	56	59
U.S.S.R.	118,767	4	145,588	(2)	78,134	8	6,204	1	707	18	1,163	32	49	55
OCEANIA	30,862	(15)	223,838	12	5,321	17	511	(18)	X	X	79	42	46	50
Australia	22,296	(19)	161,292	20	2,662	14	324	(32)	X	X	62	39	44	51
Fiji	160	2	75	70	11	(13)	42	14	X	X	3	200	0	0
New Zealand	7,986	(2)	62,378	(4)	412	(8)	98	50	X	X	9	42	59	49
Papua New Guinea	102	(22)	16	81	1,776	30	1	0	X	X	3	125	0	0
Solomon Islands	13	(45)	X	X	52	19	X	X	X	X	X	X	X	X

Sources: Food and Agriculture Organization of the United Nations and the United States Department of Agriculture.
Notes: a. Data for Belgium and Luxembourg are combined under Belgium.
World and regional totals for livestock populations include data for countries not listed.
0 = zero or less than half of the unit of measure; X = not available; negative numbers are shown in parentheses.
For additional information, see Sources and Technical Notes.

Table 18.4 Food Trade and Aid, 1977–89

	Average Annual Net Trade in Food						Average Annual Donations or Receipts of Food Aid					
	Cereals		Oils		Pulses		Cereals		Kg Per Capita		Oils	Milk
	(000 metric tons)		(metric tons)		(metric tons)		(000 metric tons)				(metric tons)	(metric tons)
	1977-79	1987-89	1977-79	1987-89	1977-79	1987-89	1977-79	1987-89	1977-79	1987-89	1986-88	1986-88
WORLD												
AFRICA	13,868	23,295	760,698	1,752,130	30,112	189,845	3,360	5,723	7	9	185,972	92,097
Algeria	2,740	5,565	216,492	344,217	64,676	109,936	10	16	1	1	329	280
Angola	283	273	47,269	28,048	30,845	26,901	12	86	2	9	4,437	3,490
Benin	43	104	(11,574)	(12,584)	65	167	8	12	2	3	697	1,032
Botswana	47	90	(790)	(3,582)	(583)	2,345	7	43	8	36	2,945	3,282
Burkina Faso	68	111	2,196	3,539	(3,645)	(2,069)	41	38	6	4	2,923	4,986
Burundi	13	7	1,125	1,735	0	0	9	4	2	1	134	264
Cameroon	133	320	(4,322)	(16,245)	(478)	1	6	5	1	0	277	85
Cape Verde	61	44	2,282	3,893	3,118	1,517	34	54	120	155	812	935
Central African Rep	8	34	385	313	8	0	1	4	1	1	154	87
Chad	20	50	0	(867)	0	0	35	22	8	4	741	1,251
Comoros	17	31	0	117	0	3	5	8	13	15	243	133
Congo	56	91	1,251	8,173	38	520	4	1	2	0	86	18
Cote d'Ivoire	314	648	(76,760)	(116,726)	211	927	0	7	0	1	21	49
Djibouti	23	45	29	4,746	269	333	3	13	10	33	304	2,378
Egypt	5,242	8,727	360,158	599,293	66,810	51,976	1,953	1,683	50	34	41,523	8,843
Equatorial Guinea	2	12	0	1,750	0	0	0	2	0	7	0	0
Ethiopia	220	798	1,210	24,810	(41,559)	13,433	104	656	3	14	18,961	13,903
Gabon	32	55	3,477	(2,752)	45	23	1	0	1	0	0	1
Gambia, The	47	82	(12,748)	(2,459)	0	0	9	14	15	17	526	698
Ghana	221	241	12,326	11,133	1,672	183	71	74	7	5	5,322	2,012
Guinea	86	178	4,116	6,933	X	X	26	53	6	10	280	358
Guinea-Bissau	41	57	144	553	31	72	18	10	25	11	413	279
Kenya	(2)	(96)	59,860	130,288	(15,369)	(41,680)	9	112	1	5	995	97
Lesotho	91	122	X	X	258	4,300	24	41	19	25	2,310	2,651
Liberia	79	120	(2,683)	(1,003)	185	100	1	28	1	12	171	2
Libya	619	1,458	41,906	68,933	8,825	10,333	0	0	0	0	X	0
Madagascar	181	107	13,844	11,601	(10,140)	(4,236)	10	103	1	9	9,657	1,967
Malawi	9	59	3,807	5,980	(9,542)	(21,216)	2	111	0	14	76	164
Mali	48	92	(7,308)	(2,417)	(46)	(470)	18	55	3	6	1,205	1,363
Mauritania	148	203	3,731	23,217	2	150	37	54	25	28	2,092	2,379
Mauritius	150	188	15,413	25,931	6,978	9,872	9	22	9	21	28	191
Morocco	1,572	1,643	158,971	216,045	(52,308)	(32,538)	140	396	8	17	32,606	3,863
Mozambique	247	434	4,150	46,282	(3,007)	29,612	118	423	10	28	10,855	4,137
Namibia	X	X	X	X	7,667	9,333	0	0	0	0	X	X
Niger	35	107	2,534	6,283	(14,509)	(9,960)	30	41	6	6	1,156	2,574
Nigeria	1,654	391	95,710	39,758	5,520	8,333	0	0	0	0	X	37
Rwanda	11	10	1,355	9,960	0	(61)	12	9	3	1	1,896	2,292
Senegal	444	464	(126,965)	(93,841)	528	317	86	81	16	12	752	3,028
Sierra Leone	74	137	(6,712)	4,576	94	0	5	46	2	12	686	849
Somalia	130	233	7,470	18,883	294	7,357	80	129	16	18	16,713	6,537
South Africa	(2,469)	(2,612)	(6,812)	166,207	(1,571)	1,718	0	0	0	0	0	X
Sudan	42	311	(22,951)	31,678	3,050	18,500	86	568	5	24	4,931	3,859
Swaziland	16	43	0	400	0	0	0	9	1	12	427	718
Tanzania	52	73	11,623	33,603	(16,430)	(20,000)	97	69	5	3	1,371	4,542
Togo	37	92	609	4,094	(43)	348	12	11	5	3	1,132	1,268
Tunisia	803	1,646	(24,436)	80,334	(10,104)	6,374	158	365	26	47	1,560	2,919
Uganda	3	19	33	9,700	0	0	0	20	0	1	3,842	1,113
Zaire	308	405	(26,551)	(7,982)	644	500	40	96	2	3	0	820
Zambia	115	125	13,075	8,034	659	226	31	109	6	14	10,162	223
Zimbabwe	(375)	(235)	(7,687)	20,320	(1,096)	(1,484)	0	21	0	2	220	141
NORTH & CENTRAL AMERICA	(101,874)	(107,247)	(1,129,722)	(420,211)	(350,990)	(684,650)	(6,825)	(6,696)	(19)	(16)	(443,672)	(158,060)
Barbados	49	66	1,059	1,957	1,364	1,234	0	0	1	0	0	5
Belize	9	12	1,403	1,330	366	(164)	0	2	0	12	X	5
Canada	(17,812)	(22,469)	(129,233)	(341,699)	(74,027)	(392,909)	(932)	(1,157)	(40)	(45)	(74,043)	(9,102)
Costa Rica	62	275	6,930	(173)	2,270	(131)	1	124	0	43	131	266
Cuba	1,832	2,347	172,460	217,828	103,046	125,593	0	0	0	0	1,573	2,378
Dominican Rep	266	626	46,799	102,560	2,924	13,237	27	208	5	30	32,439	3,188
El Salvador	168	191	22,698	40,728	60	4,968	6	200	1	40	24,173	6,365
Guatemala	176	231	9,650	58,273	2,177	1,189	9	263	1	30	17,650	9,204
Haiti	163	211	28,648	68,800	407	8,033	61	97	12	16	8,242	5,448
Honduras	92	143	11,169	(11,553)	(575)	4,136	17	117	5	24	2,145	5,184
Jamaica	319	374	13,421	22,692	487	1,710	77	302	37	126	586	3,559
Mexico	2,958	5,695	90,122	490,720	(117,834)	7,634	0	109	0	1	6,172	25,630
Nicaragua	66	161	10,022	32,731	(1,198)	13,058	4	70	1	19	6,543	2,743
Panama	60	96	19,459	21,610	4,191	5,486	2	0	1	0	13	10
Trinidad and Tobago	216	267	12,924	6,432	10,291	12,135	0	0	0	0	X	0
United States	(90,701)	(95,693)	(1,456,504)	(1,145,498)	(292,587)	(497,316)	(6,097)	(7,031)	(27)	(29)	(469,296)	(212,944)
SOUTH AMERICA	(5,743)	(1,201)	(780,927)	(2,146,080)	(118,177)	(34,139)	175	604	1	2	22,676	41,191
Argentina	(14,590)	(8,771)	(649,935)	(1,860,129)	(192,473)	(145,479)	(25)	(24)	(1)	(1)	X	1
Bolivia	292	261	23,683	4,521	185	799	64	201	12	29	5,234	7,581
Brazil	4,079	2,392	(619,942)	(789,239)	49,056	35,802	3	14	0	0	0	14,468
Chile	945	232	58,327	48,596	(66,903)	(65,276)	30	15	3	1	246	4,432
Colombia	559	789	108,080	113,584	13,209	63,619	13	34	0	1	6	38
Ecuador	233	493	43,136	34,537	1,727	368	7	58	1	6	3,074	1,642
Guyana	(37)	2	6,009	2,983	3,119	4,000	1	43	1	54	2,636	942
Paraguay	54	1	(8,220)	(11,033)	0	63	12	2	4	0	22	284
Peru	1,049	1,411	68,485	67,852	(1,470)	7,610	71	259	4	13	7,739	11,798
Suriname	(28)	(39)	771	3,328	1,201	4,067	0	0	0	0	32	X
Uruguay	(50)	(264)	(6,460)	(8,338)	1,811	2,326	0	0	0	0	3,686	5
Venezuela	1,746	2,286	194,470	245,904	72,064	57,402	0	0	0	0	X	0

Table 18.4

	Average Annual Net Trade in Food						Average Annual Donations or Receipts of Food Aid					
	Cereals (000 metric tons)		Oils (metric tons)		Pulses (metric tons)		Cereals (000 metric tons)		Cereals (kg per capita)		Oils (metric tons)	Milk (metric tons)
	1977-79	1987-89	1977-79	1987-89	1977-79	1987-89	1977-79	1987-89	1977-79	1987-89	1986-88	1986-88
ASIA	**53,242**	**79,441**	**151,900**	**(142,557)**	**(12,694)**	**(91,634)**	**4,652**	**3,465**	**2**	**1**	**305,461**	**78,692**
Afghanistan	88	256	2,167	4,233	(3,000)	(8,000)	57	190	4	12	0	0
Bahrain	69	74	1,519	6,548	1,728	4,673	0	0	0	0	X	X
Bangladesh	1,068	2,328	95,966	372,533	1,489	23,816	1,259	1,382	15	13	28,464	117
Bhutan	3	19	X	X	X	X	1	2	0	2	308	380
Cambodia	54	78	775	0	176	0	3	13	0	2	800	0
China	11,386	16,375	336,463	1,227,447	(26,804)	(409,351)	(28)	385	(0)	0	1,861	3,383
Cyprus	244	435	8,359	12,112	689	1,036	17	1	27	1	0	109
India	(59)	875	1,050,510	1,311,227	59,144	656,900	579	221	1	0	97,682	31,254
Indonesia	2,717	1,862	(361,558)	(840,777)	976	40,002	847	256	6	1	572	4,257
Iran, Islamic Rep	2,109	5,085	254,910	390,383	26,705	(2,418)	0	12	0	0	X	X
Iraq	1,794	4,468	135,900	319,959	23,350	74,505	4	33	0	2	X	0
Israel	1,698	1,873	10,401	29,848	13,054	31,784	52	2	14	0	X	68
Japan	22,981	27,323	383,567	447,520	185,182	177,653	(185)	(510)	(2)	(4)	(267)	0
Jordan	467	779	12,542	40,033	1,718	22,428	114	25	55	8	787	374
Korea, Dem People's Rep	(85)	473	11,811	13,350	0	0	10	0	1	0	X	X
Korea, Rep	4,031	9,459	178,954	297,204	4,621	10,084	553	0	15	0	X	X
Kuwait	255	494	3,870	19,923	7,674	10,216	0	0	0	0	X	X
Lao People's Dem Rep	133	64	0	0	0	0	30	13	10	3	35	X
Lebanon	548	519	15,454	50,833	19,584	27,000	94	48	34	18	4,351	2,930
Malaysia	1,378	2,246	(1,722,366)	(4,870,759)	31,230	52,456	0	3	0	0	0	X
Mongolia	97	(42)	1,071	1,240	X	X	0	0	0	0	X	X
Myanmar	(539)	(249)	16,089	16,200	(36,796)	(43,398)	9	0	0	0	0	3
Nepal	(53)	40	40	15,213	(2,206)	(13,073)	5	17	0	1	628	1,546
Oman	79	244	565	13,131	7,093	8,322	0	0	0	0	X	X
Pakistan	329	(62)	373,041	981,872	(1,122)	136,838	324	515	4	4	162,305	4,268
Philippines	731	1,243	(843,207)	(832,933)	2,163	23,055	80	320	2	5	1,083	20,885
Qatar	58	98	711	4,325	840	2,133	0	0	0	0	X	X
Saudi Arabia	1,511	4,576	64,219	113,228	16,691	50,259	(9)	(97)	(1)	(7)	(100)	(100)
Singapore	681	616	13,551	86,058	9,384	12,568	0	0	0	0	X	X
Sri Lanka	1,182	883	(19,473)	(833)	6,795	28,675	390	307	27	18	273	5,701
Syrian Arab Rep	455	1,211	13,112	26,053	(93,960)	(53,909)	73	51	9	4	1,165	1,506
Thailand	(4,294)	(6,457)	21,850	9,299	(176,976)	(199,556)	2	70	0	1	1,344	182
Turkey	(1,239)	(127)	29,481	380,534	(121,397)	(804,485)	(13)	2	(0)	0	195	0
United Arab Emirates	186	403	8,715	46,203	8,746	12,633	0	0	0	0	X	X
Viet Nam	1,663	(174)	3,652	1,627	44	(6,167)	345	80	7	1	2,516	1,313
Yemen *(Arab Rep)*	415	936	2,983	62,717	1,553	10,184	25	95	4	11	350	472
(People's Dem Rep)	151	321	107	16,668	1,640	2,367	13	28	8	12	1,108	43
EUROPE	**31,858**	**(16,265)**	**1,494,716**	**620,403**	**536,267**	**1,037,787**	**(1,093) a**	**(2,408) a**	**(2)**	**(5)**	**(85,323) a**	**(113,201) a**
Albania	(25)	49	7,307	13,700	67	217	0	0	0	0	X	X
Austria	(73)	(916)	79,039	82,440	5,794	9,599	0	(21)	0	(3)	X	(200)
Belgium {b}	2,811	2,567	50,354	(143,023)	54,125	345,556	(48)	(31)	(5)	(3)	X	0
Bulgaria	225	907	(33,146)	8,478	(7,409)	(2,216)	0	0	0	0	X	X
Czechoslovakia	1,487	408	39,126	33,090	1,097	(5,167)	0	0	0	0	X	X
Denmark	(574)	(1,775)	146	19,711	(3,016)	(158,833)	(34)	(43)	(7)	(8)	(255)	(142)
Finland	(64)	(35)	3,901	(5,963)	3,946	2,509	(29)	(23)	(6)	(5)	(4,460)	(2,159)
France	(12,362)	(27,202)	297,578	22,876	8,561	(608,287)	(149)	(245)	(3)	(4)	X	X
Germany *(Fed Rep)*	4,024	(1,045)	(71,263)	(206,378)	79,534	674,992	(152)	(252)	(2)	(4)	(6,759)	(2,818)
(Dem Rep)	2,988	2,295	102,091	51,149	4,767	2,463	0	0	0	0	X	X
Greece	453	140	(29,070)	(90,693)	11,128	23,935	0	(8)	0	(1)	0	X
Hungary	(505)	(1,442)	(91,474)	(271,777)	(44,780)	(208,756)	0	0	0	0	X	X
Iceland	25	24	1,013	1,981	341	289	0	0	0	0	X	X
Ireland	318	(38)	6,117	24,017	9,066	24,086	(4)	(4)	(1)	(1)	0	(958)
Italy	7,486	4,030	383,844	296,186	110,060	651,000	(42)	(146)	(1)	(3)	0	0
Luxembourg {b}	X	X	X	X	X	X	X	X	X	X	X	X
Malta	131	142	4,761	5,533	914	1,286	1	0	3	0	X	X
Netherlands	3,421	3,792	159,063	(2,334)	160,608	680,494	(98)	(137)	(7)	(9)	(4,696)	(6,409)
Norway	609	480	6,960	9,462	5,997	4,781	(10)	(43)	(2)	(10)	(841)	0
Poland	6,789	2,967	68,065	90,902	1,152	(122,032)	0	0	0	0	2,514	3,652
Portugal	2,787	1,308	19,814	(6,781)	9,358	42,969	309	0	32	0	44	503
Romania	4	(144)	(159,000)	(13,133)	0	(3,733)	0	0	0	0	0	X
Spain	4,888	208	(191,772)	(249,116)	57,205	128,522	0	(33)	0	(1)	0	X
Sweden	(990)	(678)	38,003	33,972	2,153	11,594	(110)	(107)	(13)	(13)	(19,612)	0
Switzerland	1,239	782	39,812	30,205	7,068	13,365	(32)	(64)	(5)	(10)	(445)	(3,269)
United Kingdom	6,149	(2,885)	761,268	790,425	38,128	(165,302)	(70)	(168)	(1)	(3)	0	0
Yugoslavia	613	(533)	1,955	(3,679)	10,641	(5,978)	0	0	0	0	X	0
U.S.S.R.	**17,051**	**33,350**	**839,751**	**1,830,665**	**(49,640)**	**(46,572)**	**0**	**0**	**0**	**0**	**X**	**0**
OCEANIA	**(11,423)**	**(14,911)**	**(350,086)**	**(357,744)**	**(24,666)**	**(434,018)**	**(261)**	**(355)**	**(12)**	**(14)**	**(2,206)**	**(681)**
Australia	(11,643)	(15,350)	(166,032)	(89,238)	5,741	(384,349)	(270)	(357)	(19)	(22)	(2,127)	(331)
Fiji	73	87	(10,271)	4,495	3,137	5,971	10	2	16	3	0	11
New Zealand	(67)	(9)	(81,706)	(93,856)	(34,247)	(56,424)	0	0	0	0	(83)	(361)
Papua New Guinea	121	215	(56,280)	(147,267)	50	86	0	0	0	0	4	X
Solomon Islands	6	17	(9,784)	(14,717)	8	10	0	0	0	1	X	X

Source: Food and Agriculture Organization of the United Nations.
Notes: a. Total includes EC community action. b. Data for Belgium and Luxembourg are combined under Belgium.
World and regional totals for Net Trade include some countries not listed. Totals for Food Aid do not add because of rounding.
Imports and food aid receipts are shown as positive numbers; exports and food aid donations are represented by negative numbers in parentheses.
0 = zero or less than half of the unit of measure; X = not available; negative numbers are shown in parentheses.
For additional information, see Sources and Technical Notes.

Table 18.5 Flow of Cereal Aid from Major Donors to Major Recipients, 1989

Major Recipients	Total Cereal Aid (000 metric tons)	Canada Total Aid (000 metric tons)	Canada Percent of Total Aid	Canada Percent of Recipient's Total Aid	USA Total Aid (000 metric tons)	USA Percent of Total Aid	USA Percent of Recipient's Total Aid	Japan Total Aid (000 metric tons)	Japan Percent of Total Aid	Japan Percent of Recipient's Total Aid	EC Total Aid (000 metric tons)	EC Percent of Total Aid	EC Percent of Recipient's Total Aid	Others Total Aid (000 metric tons)	Others Percent of Total Aid	Others Percent of Recipient's Total Aid
TOTAL	10,044	1,170	100	12	5,286	100	53	441	100	4	1,980	100	20	1,167	100	12
% Triangular Aid	12	7			0			54			32			17		
AFRICA	4,700	397	34	8	2,286	43	49	169	38	4	1,270	64	27	576	49	12
Algeria	39	11	1	29	0	0	0	0	0	0	21	1	55	6	1	16
Angola	79	9	1	12	13	0	16	2	0	2	53	3	67	2	0	3
Benin	16	0	0	0	7	0	45	5	1	30	4	0	26	0	0	0
Botswana	33	0	0	0	30	1	91	0	0	0	2	0	7	1	0	2
Burkina Faso	49	0	0	0	31	1	62	3	1	5	9	0	18	7	1	14
Cape Verde	49	0	0	0	7	0	13	6	1	13	21	1	44	15	1	31
Chad	15	0	0	0	0	0	0	8	2	52	6	0	40	1	0	9
Cote d'Ivoire	19	0	0	0	19	0	97	1	0	3	0	0	0	0	0	0
Djibouti	12	0	0	0	0	0	0	2	0	16	10	1	83	0	0	2
Egypt	1,427	7	1	1	1,226	23	86	5	1	0	135	7	9	54	5	4
Ethiopia	573	59	5	10	112	2	19	7	2	1	158	8	28	237	20	41
Gambia, The	10	0	0	2	6	0	56	0	0	0	2	0	19	3	0	24
Ghana	46	16	1	35	17	0	37	3	1	6	0	0	0	10	1	21
Guinea	42	7	1	17	34	1	81	1	0	1	0	0	0	0	0	1
Kenya	112	0	0	0	75	1	67	0	0	0	37	2	33	0	0	0
Lesotho	34	0	0	0	11	0	33	2	0	5	17	1	49	5	0	13
Liberia	28	0	0	0	22	0	78	1	0	3	0	0	1	5	0	18
Madagascar	76		0	0	0	0	0	2	0	3	32	2	42	42	4	55
Malawi	217	13	1	6	42	1	19	9	2	4	94	5	44	58	5	27
Mali	65	9	1	14	34	1	52	2	0	3	16	1	25	1	0	2
Mauritania	70	0	0	0	22	0	31	0	0	0	48	2	69	0	0	0
Mauritius	21	1	0	6	11	0	52	0	0	0	3	0	14	6	0	27
Morocco	237	62	5	26	169	3	71	0	0	0	6	0	2	0	0	0
Mozambique	424	64	5	15	59	1	14	13	3	3	247	12	58	41	4	10
Niger	83	16	1	20	23	0	27	3	1	4	31	2	37	10	1	12
Senegal	53	7	1	13	34	1	64	10	2	19	2	0	4	1	0	1
Sierra Leone	38	0	0	0	34	1	88	1	0	1	4	0	11	0	0	0
Somalia	73	1	0	1	12	0	17	21	5	29	34	2	46	5	0	7
Sudan	198	45	4	23	18	0	9	33	7	16	83	4	42	20	2	10
Swaziland	15	0	0	0	10	0	71	0	0	0	2	0	12	2	0	16
Tanzania	76	20	2	26	22	0	29	8	2	11	13	1	18	12	1	16
Togo	11	0	0	4	4	0	36	4	1	39	0	0	4	2	0	18
Tunisia	284	33	3	12	119	2	42	0	0	0	126	6	44	6	1	2
Uganda	17	0	0	0	7	0	41	0	0	0	7	0	43	3	0	15
Zaire	55	0	0	0	35	1	64	0	0	0	17	1	32	2	0	4
Zambia	66	14	1	21	19	0	28	11	2	16	18	1	27	5	0	7
Zimbabwe	10	0	0	0	0	0	0	4	1	44	0	0	0	6	0	56
LATIN AMERICA	1,984	76	7	4	1,775	34	89	28	6	1	90	5	5	1	0	0
Bolivia	95	21	2	22	61	1	64	0	0	0	13	1	14	0	0	0
Brazil	15	14	1	99	0	0	0	0	0	0	0	0	1	0	0	0
Chile	14	0	0	0	14	0	100	0	0	0	0	0	0	0	0	0
Colombia	12	12	1	95	0	0	2	0	0	0	0	0	2	0	0	0
Costa Rica	84	1	0	1	82	2	98	0	0	0	0	0	0	1	0	1
Dominican Rep	228	0	0	0	227	4	100	0	0	0	1	0	0	0	0	0
Ecuador	89	3	0	3	86	2	96	0	0	0	1	0	1	0	0	0
El Salvador	197	2	0	1	194	4	98	0	0	0	2	0	1	0	0	0
Guatemala	277	2	0	1	270	5	98	0	0	0	5	0	2	0	0	0
Guyana	19	0	0	0	18	0	97	0	0	0	1	0	3	0	0	0
Haiti	49	0	0	0	14	0	29	28	6	58	6	0	13	0	0	0
Honduras	67	5	0	7	52	1	77	0	0	0	10	1	15	1	0	1
Jamaica	365	11	1	3	354	7	97	0	0	0	0	0	0	0	0	0
Mexico	291	0	0	0	291	5	100	0	0	0	0	0	0	0	0	0
Nicaragua	32	5	0	16	0	0	0	0	0	0	17	1	53	10	1	31
Peru	146	0	0	0	107	2	74	0	0	0	33	2	23	5	0	3
ASIA	3,235	678	58	21	1,219	23	38	193	44	6	580	29	18	564	48	17
Afghanistan	208	0	0	0	0	0	0	0	0	0	0	0	0	208	18	100
Bangladesh	1,161	317	27	27	414	8	36	60	14	5	221	11	19	149	13	13
Cambodia	11	0	0	0	0	0	0	11	2	92	0	0	0	1	0	8
China	223	178	15	80	0	0	0	0	0	0	43	2	19	2	0	1
India	308	15	1	5	286	5	93	0	0	0	0	0	0	8	1	2
Indonesia	69	7	1	10	61	1	89	0	0	0	0	0	0	0	0	0
Iran, Islamic Rep	23	0	0	0	0	0	0	22	5	93	0	0	0	2	0	7
Jordan	25	14	1	55	5	0	18	0	0	0	3	0	13	3	0	13
Lao People's Dem Rep	20	0	0	0	0	0	0	3	1	16	5	0	25	12	1	59
Lebanon	32	2	0	6	9	0	29	0	0	0	21	1	65	0	0	1
Malaysia	10	0	0	0	10	0	100	0	0	0	0	0	0	0	0	0
Pakistan	416	78	7	19	84	2	20	35	8	8	168	8	40	51	4	12
Philippines	135	7	1	5	110	2	81	0	0	0	2	0	1	16	1	12
Sri Lanka	272	21	2	8	206	4	76	0	0	0	40	2	15	5	0	2
Syrian Arab Rep	31	7	1	23	0	0	0	0	0	0	24	1	77	0	0	0
Thailand	83	0	0	0	0	0	0	62	14	75	18	1	22	3	0	3
Viet Nam	100	0	0	0	0	0	0	0	0	0	10	1	10	90	8	90
Yemen (Arab Rep)	41	9	1	22	28	1	67	0	0	0	5	0	11	0	0	0
(People's Dem Rep)	43	21	2	48	0	0	0	0	0	0	15	1	34	8	1	18
Unspecified	92	0	0	0	0	0	0	50	11	54	35	2	38	7	1	7

Source: Food and Agriculture Organization of the United Nations.
Notes: Totals do not add because of rounding. World and regional totals include countries not listed. 0 = zero or less than half the unit of measure.
For additional information, see Sources and Technical Notes.

Table 18.6 Climatic Classes and Soil Constraints in Selected Countries

	Total Land Area {a} (000 hectares)	Percent of Total Land Area				Land with No Inherent Soil Constraints {b}					Percent of Total Land Area		
		Arid	Semi-arid	Humid	Cold	(000 hectares)	Percent Arid	Percent Semi-arid	Percent Humid	Percent Cold	Tropical	Sub-tropical	Temperat
WORLD													
AFRICA	3,011,330	47	8	44	0	554,862	78	6	16	0	71	29	0
Algeria	238,174	92	3	5	0	96,958	99	0	1	0	2	98	0
Angola	124,670	4	8	87	0	15,726	17	15	68	0	99	1	0
Benin	11,062	0	1	99	0	360	0	6	94	0	100	0	0
Botswana	56,673	62	38	0	0	4,792	72	27	1	0	87	13	0
Burkina Faso	27,380	1	15	84	0	6,899	1	19	80	0	100	0	0
Burundi	2,565	0	0	100	0	66	0	0	100	0	100	0	0
Cameroon	46,540	0	1	99	0	1,949	0	2	98	0	100	0	0
Cape Verde	403	100	0	0	0	84	100	0	0	0	100	0	0
Central African Rep	62,298	0	0	100	0	800	0	0	100	0	100	0	0
Chad	125,920	67	7	27	0	34,160	81	1	17	0	84	16	0
Comoros	223	0	0	100	0	43	0	0	100	0	100	0	0
Congo	34,150	0	0	100	0	0	0	0	0	0	100	0	0
Cote d'Ivoire	31,800	0	0	100	0	730	0	0	100	0	100	0	0
Djibouti	2,318	100	0	0	0	757	100	0	0	0	0	0	0
Egypt	99,545	100	0	0	0	24,633	100	0	0	0	3	97	0
Equatorial Guinea	2,805	0	0	100	0	21	0	0	100	0	100	0	0
Ethiopia	110,100	38	16	44	2	30,079	38	21	38	3	100	0	0
Gabon	25,767	0	0	100	0	0	0	0	0	0	100	0	0
Gambia, The	1,000	0	0	100	0	355	0	0	100	0	100	0	0
Ghana	23,002	0	0	100	0	878	0	0	100	0	100	0	0
Guinea	24,586	0	0	100	0	479	0	0	100	0	100	0	0
Guinea-Bissau	2,812	0	0	100	0	0	0	0	0	0	100	0	0
Kenya	56,697	71	14	15	0	7,342	79	11	10	0	100	0	0
Lesotho	3,035	15	13	66	6	1	100	0	0	0	100	0	0
Liberia	9,632	0	0	100	0	348	0	0	100	0	100	0	0
Libya	175,954	98	1	0	0	54,004	100	0	0	0	0	100	0
Madagascar	58,154	5	8	87	0	2,273	7	30	62	0	100	0	0
Malawi	9,408	0	0	100	0	1,097	0	0	100	0	100	0	0
Mali	122,019	64	15	21	0	40,865	81	8	10	0	77	23	0
Mauritania	102,522	94	5	1	0	58,867	99	1	0	0	60	40	0
Mauritius	185	0	0	100	0	7	0	0	100	0	100	0	0
Morocco	44,630	54	10	23	13	12,968	70	10	11	9	0	100	0
Mozambique	78,409	8	9	82	0	4,952	7	7	86	0	100	0	0
Namibia	82,329	78	21	1	0	9308	81	18	1	0	59	41	0
Niger	126,670	86	13	1	0	41,388	94	5	0	0	77	23	0
Nigeria	91,077	0	8	92	0	7,797	0	6	94	0	100	0	0
Rwanda	2,495	0	0	100	0	91	0	0	100	0	100	0	0
Senegal	19,253	7	14	80	0	2,957	10	20	71	0	100	0	0
Sierra Leone	7,162	0	0	100	0	187	0	0	100	0	100	0	0
Somalia	62,734	93	7	0	0	4,519	98	2	0	0	100	0	0
South Africa	122,104	55	13	32	0	7,482	47	18	34	2	5	95	0
Sudan	237,600	55	11	34	0	50,390	77	8	15	0	99	1	0
Swaziland	1,720	0	26	74	0	178	0	7	93	0	14	86	0
Tanzania	88,604	7	15	78	0	5,052	6	21	74	0	100	0	0
Togo	5,439	0	0	100	0	319	0	0	100	0	100	0	0
Tunisia	15,536	66	16	19	0	4,303	86	9	6	0	0	100	0
Uganda	19,955	0	5	95	0	1,210	0	8	92	0	100	0	0
Zaire	226,760	0	0	100	0	5,079	0	0	100	0	100	0	0
Zambia	74,072	0	2	98	0	2,426	0	0	100	0	100	0	0
Zimbabwe	38,667	8	41	51	0	958	12	65	23	0	100	0	0
CENTRAL AMERICA	273,999	36	5	59	0	62,159	61	6	33	0	62	38	0
Barbados	43	0	0	100	0	4	0	0	100	0	100	0	0
Belize	2,280	0	0	100	0	108	0	0	100	0	100	0	0
Costa Rica	5,106	0	0	99	1	263	0	0	100	0	100	0	0
Cuba	11,086	0	0	100	0	888	0	0	100	0	100	0	0
Dominican Rep	4,838	0	12	87	1	669	0	17	81	1	100	0	0
El Salvador	2,072	0	0	100	0	376	0	0	100	0	100	0	0
Guatemala	10,843	0	0	98	2	862	0	0	99	1	100	0	0
Haiti	2,756	0	12	88	0	310	0	11	89	0	100	0	0
Honduras	11,189	0	0	100	0	1,320	0	0	100	0	100	0	0
Jamaica	1,083	0	17	83	0	164	0	28	72	0	100	0	0
Mexico	190,869	50	6	44	0	55,930	68	6	26	0	48	52	0
Nicaragua	11,875	0	0	100	0	706	0	0	100	0	100	0	0
Panama	7,599	0	0	100	0	211	0	0	100	0	100	0	0
Trinidad and Tobago	513	0	0	100	0	79	0	0	100	0	100	0	0
SOUTH AMERICA	1,898,326	11	7	79	3	191,417	28	14	54	4	72	24	4
Argentina	273,669	40	14	41	5	111,781	34	14	51	1	0	83	16
Bolivia	108,439	6	19	63	11	15,415	21	27	29	23	97	3	0
Brazil	845,651	0	3	96	0	17,081	0	8	92	0	88	12	0
Chile	74,880	51	13	16	20	7,836	44	22	8	25	2	66	33
Colombia	103,870	4	2	92	2	5,323	12	7	80	1	100	0	0
Ecuador	27,684	5	13	73	9	2,239	10	36	52	1	100	0	0
Guyana	19,685	0	0	100	0	947	0	0	100	0	100	0	0
Paraguay	39,730	0	9	90	0	3,427	0	9	91	0	61	39	0
Peru	128,000	16	5	66	13	15,264	44	18	36	2	94	6	0
Suriname	16,147	0	0	100	0	698	0	0	100	0	100	0	0
Uruguay	17,481	0	0	100	0	6,100	0	0	100	0	100	0	0
Venezuela	88,205	9	3	87	0	5,109	30	7	63	0	100	0	0

Table 18.6 Climatic Classes and Soil Constraints (continued)

	Total Land Area {a} (000 ha)	Percent of Total Land Area				Land with No Inherent Soil Constraints {b}					Percent of Total Land Area		
		Arid	Semi-arid	Humid	Cold	(000 hectares)	Percent Arid	Percent Semi-arid	Percent Humid	Percent Cold	Tropical	Sub-tropical	Temperat
ASIA, SOUTHEAST	897,615	10	6	78	5	62,495	4	10	72	14	76	24	0
Bangladesh	13,391	0	0	100	0	1,719	0	0	100	0	100	0	0
Bhutan	4,700	0	0	51	49	133	0	0	21	79	0	100	0
Cambodia	17,652	0	0	100	0	695	0	0	100	0	100	0	0
India	297,319	10	15	69	6	33,232	4	16	66	14	67	33	0
Indonesia	181,157	0	0	99	1	10,550	0	0	99	1	100	0	0
Lao People's Dem Rep	23,080	0	0	100	0	37	0	0	100	0	100	0	0
Malaysia	32,855	0	0	100	0	196	0	0	100	0	100	0	0
Myanmar	65,754	0	3	96	1	3,436	0	9	91	0	83	17	0
Nepal	13,680	0	0	67	33	1,917	0	0	56	44	0	100	0
Pakistan	77,088	71	4	3	22	5,250	18	13	4	64	10	90	0
Philippines	29,817	0	0	100	0	2,717	0	0	100	0	100	0	0
Singapore	61	0	0	100	0	0	0	0	0	0	100	0	0
Sri Lanka	6,474	0	1	99	0	624	0	0	100	0	100	0	0
Thailand	51,089	0	0	100	0	983	0	0	100	0	100	0	0
Viet Nam	32,536	0	0	100	0	989	0	0	100	0	100	0	0
ASIA, SOUTHWEST	678,017	75	15	10	0	79,750	73	19	7	1	22	76	3
Afghanistan	65,209	87	9	3	1	6,229	71	13	6	9	0	100	0
Bahrain	68	100	0	0	0	12	100	0	0	0	0	100	0
Iran, Islamic Rep	163,600	76	17	7	0	14,785	62	28	9	0	2	95	2
Iraq	43,737	73	9	18	0	2,783	100	0	0	0	0	100	0
Israel	2,033	53	11	36	0	122	65	25	10	0	0	100	0
Jordan	8,893	85	7	9	0	401	96	2	2	0	0	100	0
Kuwait	1,782	100	0	0	0	31	100	0	0	0	0	100	0
Lebanon	1,023	0	2	98	0	59	0	0	100	0	0	100	0
Oman	21,246	100	0	0	0	3,897	100	0	0	0	0	100	0
Qatar	1,100	100	0	0	0	290	100	0	0	0	0	100	0
Saudi Arabia	214,969	97	2	0	0	30,579	96	3	0	0	31	69	0
Syrian Arab Rep	18,406	49	34	16	0	643	2	68	29	0	0	100	0
Turkey	76,963	0	51	49	0	10,135	0	70	30	0	0	82	18
United Arab Emirates	8,360	100	0	0	0	3,707	100	0	0	0	91	9	0
Yemen (Arab Rep)	19,500	38	44	18	0	2,207	11	60	29	0	100	0	0
(People's Dem)	33,297	93	7	0	0	3,870	90	10	0	0	100	0	0

Source: Food and Agriculture Organization of the United Nations.
Notes: a. Regional totals differ from those in Table 17.1 because these include only the countries listed. b. No inherent soil constraints means soil that is not affected by the following constraints: steep slopes, shallow soil, poor drainage, low nutrient retention, aluminum toxicity, acid soils, phospherous fixation, amorphous material, vertic properties, low potassium reserves, calcareous soil, soil salinity, excess sodium, acid sulfate soil, and gravel.
0 = zero or less than half of the unit of measure. Totals may not add because of rounding.
For additional information, see Sources and Technical Notes.

Sources and Technical Notes

Table 18.1 Food and Agricultural Production, 1978–90

Source: Food and Agriculture Organization of the United Nations (FAO), *Agrostat PC* (FAO, Rome, July 1991).

Indexes of agricultural and food production portray the disposable output (after deduction for feed and seed) of a country's agriculture sector relative to the base period 1979–81. For a given year and country, the index is calculated as follows: the disposable average output of a commodity in terms of weight or volume during the period of interest is multiplied by the 1979–81 average national producer price per unit. The product of this equation represents the total value of the commodity for that period in terms of the 1979–81 price. The values of all crop and livestock products are totaled to an aggregated value of agricultural production in 1979–81 prices. The ratio of this aggregate for a given year to that for 1979–81 is multiplied by 100 to obtain the index number.

The multiplication of disposable outputs with the 1979–81 unit value eliminates inflationary or deflationary distortion. However, the base period's relative prices among the individual commodities are also preserved. Especially in economies with high inflation, price patterns among agricultural commodities can change dramatically over time. To overcome the latter problem, FAO generally shifts the base period every five years.

The continental and world index numbers for a given year are calculated by totaling the disposable outputs of all relevant countries for each agricultural commodity. Each of these aggregates is multiplied by a respective 1979–81 average "international" producer price and summed in a total agricultural output value for that region or the world in terms of 1979–81 prices. The total agricultural output value for a given year is then divided by the "international" 1979–81 output value and multiplied by 100 to obtain the continental and world index numbers. This method avoids distortion caused by the use of international exchange rates.

The agricultural production index includes all crop and livestock products originating in each country. The food production index covers all edible agricultural products that contain nutrients. Coffee and tea have virtually no nutritive value and thus are excluded.

Crop yields (*average yields of cereals* and *average yields of roots and tubers*) are calculated from production and area data. *Average production of cereals* includes cereal production for feed and seed. Area refers to the area harvested. Cereals comprise all cereals harvested for dry grain, exclusive of crops cut for hay or harvested green. Roots and tubers cover all root crops grown principally for human consumption; root crops grown principally for feed are excluded.

Most of the data in Tables 18.1–18.5 are supplied by national agriculture ministries in response to annual FAO questionnaires or are derived from decennial agricultural censuses. FAO compiles data from more than 200 country reports and from many other sources and enters them into a computerized data base. FAO fills gaps in the data by preparing its own estimates. As better information becomes available, FAO corrects its estimates and recalculates the entire time series when necessary.

Table 18.2 Agricultural Inputs, 1975–89

Source: Food and Agriculture Organization of the United Nations (FAO), *Agrostat PC* (FAO, Rome, July 1991). Pesticide use: United Nations Industrial Development Organization (UNIDO) Industrial Statistics and Sectoral Surveys Branch, Policy and Perspectives Division, pesticide data base specifically prepared for UNIDO's study *Global Overview of the Pesticide Industry Sub-Sector*, Sectoral Working Paper PPD.98, (UNIDO, Vienna, December 2, 1988). Pesticide use by Mauritius, Tanzania, Uganda: Environment Liaison Centre, *Africa Seminar on the Use and Handling of Agricultural and Other Pest Control Chemicals* (October 30 to November 4, 1983, Nairobi, Kenya). Pesticide use by Haiti: Data are 1972–74 pesticide imports; U.S. Agency for International Development (U.S. AID), *Draft Environmental Profile of Haiti* (U.S. AID, Washington, D.C., 1979). Pesticide use by El Salvador (1975–77 data are for 1974–76; 1982–84 data are for 1979) and by Suriname (1975–77 data are for 1979–80; 1982–84 data are for 1981): David K. Burton and Bernard J.R. Philogene, *An Overview of Pesticide Usage in Latin America* (Canadian Wildlife Service Latin American Program, Ottawa, undated). Pesticide use by Afghanistan (1975–77 data are for 1980; 1982–84 data are for 1981–82) and by the Philippines (1975–77 data are for 1980–81): Regional Network for the Production, Marketing, and Control of Pesticides in Asia and the Pacific (RENPAP), formerly Regional Network for the Production, Marketing, and Control of Pesticides in Asia and the Far East (RENPAF), *RENPAF Gazette: Supply of Pesticides in Nine Countries* (RENPAF, Bangkok, July 1985) and *RENPAP Gazette: Pesticide Data Collection System—Second Report* (RENPAP, Bangkok, October 1988). Pesticide use by Malaysia: Data are 1988 estimate by Malaysian Agrochemical Association (MACA) provided by the Ministry of Science, Technology and Environment (Kuala Lumpur, Malaysia, 1989). Pesticide use by the Syrian Arab Republic (1982–84 data are for 1983–84): L'Office Arabe de Presse et de Documentation, *Rapport Economique Syrien 1983–84* (L'Office Arabe de Presse et de Documentation, Damascus, 1984). Pesticide use by Yemen (1975–77 data are for 1972–74; 1982–84 data are for 1975–76): U.S. AID, *Draft Environmental Report on Yemen* (U.S. AID, Washington, D.C., 1982). Pesticide use by Iceland: Nordic Council and the Nordic Statistical Secretariat, *Yearbook of Nordic Statistics 1985* (Nordic Council and Nordic Statistical Secretariat, Oslo, 1986).

Cropland refers to land under temporary and permanent crops, temporary meadows, market and kitchen gardens, and temporarily fallow land. Permanent cropland is land under crops that do not need to be re-planted after each harvest, such as cocoa, coffee, rubber, fruit trees, and vines. Human population data used to calculate *hectares per capita* are for 1990. For trends in cropland area, see Chapter 17, "Land Cover and Settlements," Table 17.1.

Irrigated land as a percentage of cropland refers to areas purposely provided with water, including land flooded by river water for crop production or pasture improvement, whether this area is irrigated several times or only once during the year.

Average annual fertilizer use refers to application of nutrients in terms of nitrogen (N), phosphate (P_2O_5), and potash (K_2O). The fertilizer year is July 1–June 30; data refer to the year beginning in July.

Data on *average annual pesticide use* were compiled by UNIDO. In their study, UNIDO assessed production, trade, and use of pesticides for 119 countries and 14 geographical subgroups. The calculations were based on trade statistics of pesticide finished products. These statistics were published by the United Nations Statistical Office (UNSO), and use and trade data were compiled by FAO. For one third of the countries, UNIDO had to estimate net weight of active ingredient in the pesticides used, because country-level data were only quantified for finished products or not available at all. Time series were completed by interpolation and extrapolation or, in some cases, by an econometric need model. Parameters in this model included country-specific factors such as climatic zone, degree of development of agriculture, area under crop production, crop structure, and the frequency of pesticide applications. For additional information, refer to UNIDO's *Global Overview of the Pesticide Industry Sub-Sector.*

Data are expressed in net weight of active ingredients in the pesticides used. The active ingredients in a pesticide are the chemicals with pesticidal properties. In a pesticide formulation, active ingredients are often mixed with inert ingredients, which dilute or deliver the active ingredients. Inert ingredients can exert toxic effects of their own in the environment.

Active ingredients vary widely in potency; information on the ingredients of pesticides is necessary to ensure accurate application and to minimize harmful environmental effects. For example, 1 metric ton of the modern synthetic pyrethroid insecticide permethrin is as potent a pesticide as 3–5 metric tons of a carbamate or an organophosphate or 10–30 metric tons of DDT. The data shown in this table do not describe the potency of the active ingredients used. As a result, two countries with similar levels of pesticide use may be treating different amounts of land and getting very different results. Increasingly potent pesticides have been developed in recent years; thus, a decline in the amount of active ingredients used may not indicate a reduction in the amount of toxic materials introduced into the environment.

For additional information on pesticides, see E.J. Tait and A.B. Lane, "Insecticide Production, Distribution and Use: Analyzing National and International Statistics" in *Management of Pests and Pesticides: Farmers' Perceptions and Practices,* Joyce Tait and Banpot Napompeth, eds. (Westview Press, Boulder, Colorado, 1987).

Tractors generally refer to wheel and crawler tractors used in agriculture. Garden tractors are excluded. *Harvesters* refer to harvesters and threshers.

Table 18.3 Livestock Populations and Grain Consumed as Feed, 1978–90

Sources: Livestock data: Food and Agriculture Organization of the United Nations (FAO), *Agrostat PC* (FAO, Rome, June 1991). Feed data: Economic Research Service, United States Department of Agriculture (USDA), *PS&D View PC* (USDA, Washington, D.C., 1990).

Data on livestock include all animals in the country, regardless of place or purpose of their breeding. Data on livestock numbers are collected annually by FAO; estimates are made by FAO for countries that either do not report data or only partially report data. *Equines* include horses, mules, and asses. FAO notes that the reported number of *chickens* in some countries does not seem accurate. For some countries, data on chickens include all poultry.

Grain fed to livestock as percentage of total grain consumption was calculated using USDA grain consumption and feed numbers. Grains include wheat, rice (milled weight), corn, barley, sorghum, millet, rye, oats, and mixed grains. Grain consumption is the total domestic use during the local marketing year of the individual country. It is the sum of feed, food, seed, and industrial uses.

Table 18.4 Food Trade and Aid, 1977–89

Sources: Trade and population data: Food and Agriculture Organization of the United Nations (FAO), *Agrostat PC* (FAO, Rome, July 1991). Food aid data: FAO, *Food Aid in Figures*, No. 8/1 (FAO, Rome, 1990).

Figures shown for food trade are *net imports or exports:* exports were subtracted from imports.

Two definitions of trade are used by countries reporting trade data. "Special trade" refers only to imports for domestic consumption and exports of domestic goods. "General trade" encompasses total imports and total exports, including reexports. Trade figures for Czechoslovakia, the German Democratic Republic, Hungary, Poland, Romania, and the U.S.S.R. include goods purchased by the country that are reexported to a third country without ever entering the purchasing country. For information on the definition used by a particular country, see *FAO Trade Yearbook 1989* (FAO, Rome, 1990).

Average annual donations or receipts of food aid are shown as either positive or negative numbers: Receipts are shown as positive numbers; donations are expressed in negative figures. For some countries that are both recipients and donors of food aid, donations were subtracted from receipts.

Trade in *cereals* includes wheat and wheat flour, rice, barley, maize, rye, and oats. Trade in *oils* includes oils from soybeans, groundnuts (peanuts), olives, cottonseeds, sunflower seeds, rape/mustard seeds, linseeds, palms, coconuts, palm-kernels, castor beans, and maize, as well as animal oils, fats, and greases (including lard). Trade in *pulses* includes all kinds of dried leguminous vegetables, with the exception of vetches and lupins.

Food aid refers to the donation or concessional sale of food commodities. *Cereals* include wheat, rice, coarse grains, bulgur wheat, wheat flour, and the cereal component of blended foods. Cereal donations or receipts *(kilograms per capita)* are the result of dividing the three-year averages by the respective 1978 and 1988 populations. *Oils* include vegetable oil and butter oil. *Milk* includes skimmed milk powder and other dairy products (mainly cheese). Regional totals include only countries listed and do not reflect donations by the Organization of Petroleum Exporting Countries (OPEC) and the World Food Program. European regional totals, however, include European Community donations as well.

Food aid data are reported by donor countries and international organizations.

Table 18.5 Flow of Cereal Aid from Major Donors to Major Recipients, 1989

Source: Food and Agricultural Organization of the United Nations (FAO), *Food Aid in Figures*, Volume 8/1 (FAO, Rome, 1990).

Cereals include wheat, rice, coarse grains, bulgur wheat, wheat flour, and the cereal component of blended foods. *Major recipients* include countries that received 10,000 tons of cereal aid or more. *EC* aid includes aid from the separate European Community member countries as well as community action. Other donors include Argentina, Australia, Austria, Finland, Norway, Saudi Arabia, Sweden, Switzerland, World Food Program purchases, and others.

Triangular aid is a system of aid whereby donors pay for food to be shipped to a country in need from one of its neighbors.

Cereal aid data are reported by donor countries and international organizations.

Table 18.6 Climatic Classes and Soil Constraints in Selected Countries

Source: Food and Agricultural Organization of the United Nations (FAO), unpublished data (FAO, Rome, 1991). Data were developed by José Benites (Technical Officer, Soil Resources, Management and Conservation Service, Land and Water Development Division, FAO) and K. Groody (Consultant to FAO), based on a Fertility Capability Classification (FCC) system developed by P.A. Sanchez, W. Couto, and

S.W. Buol (North Carolina State University, Raleigh, North Carolina).

Climatic classes are calculated by length of growing period. Length of growing period is defined as the number of days when both temperature and moisture permit crop growth. Days with mean temperatures above 5°C and with soil moisture resulting from rainfall at least equivalent to half potential evapotranspiration are considered favorable to growth. A "normal" growing period includes a humid period, during which precipitation exceeds full potential evapotranspiration. Lengths of growing periods are: *arid* in the range of 75 days or less; *semi-arid* in the range of 75 to 120 days; *humid* in the range of 180 to 365 days; *cold* = 0 days (mean temperature is below 5°C while moisture is available).

Land with no inherent soil constraints includes land whose soil has no chemical and physical constraints that will significantly affect agronomic management and agricultural productivity. The extent of land with no soil constraints is also an important indicator of agricultural costs, the potential and success of future expansion, and the comparative advantage of a nation's agricultural productivity.

The FCC system groups soils according to their fertility and management of relevant chemical and physical properties. It emphasizes quantifiable topsoil parameters as well as subsoil properties directly relevant to plant growth. The system interprets three categories: topsoil texture (sandy, loamy, clayey, or organic), subsoil texture (sandy, loamy, clayey, or rock or other hard root-restricting layer), and 15 modifiers that describe chemical and physical properties of the soils. In the past 10 years, the FCC system has proven a meaningful tool for describing fertility limitations on crop yields.

The no-inherent-soil-constraints data in Table 18.6 are an addendum to the major soil constraints table that was published in *World Resources 1990-91* (Table 18.5), although some data adjustments have been made since then. The following 15 physical and chemical soil constraints are absent in soils with no inherent constraints.

Steep slopes are classified from steeply dissected to mountainous. Dominant slopes are over 30 percent.

Shallow soils are mostly lithosoils and other soils that restrict deep root penetration or mechanized tillage. High priority should be given to erosion control where such soils occur on steep slopes.

Soils with *poor drainage* are mostly gley soils (sticky, organic-rich soils) and other soils saturated with water during part of the year or prone to waterlogging. These soils require drainage to improve crop growth and generally provide a good soil for rice production in tropical and subtropical environments.

Low nutrient retention occurs in soils with a low inherent fertility. In addition, leaching causes high nutrient losses when lime or fertilizers are applied.

Aluminum toxicity is prevalent mostly in soils of the subhumid and humid tropics.

Limitations exist for growing common crops unless lime is applied. Even then, aluminum toxicity in the subsoil may restrict root development, affecting the use of soil moisture by crops.

Low to medium soil *acidity* may affect sensitive crops such as alfalfa or cotton, but acid soils that have a high percentage of aluminum saturation can be very productive for adapted crops, pastures, and trees.

Soils with *phosphorus fixation* result in crop phosphorus deficiency. These soils can produce a satisfying yield for subsistence farmers; but when used for commercial agriculture, they require high levels of phosphate applications and special management practices to increase productivity.

Amorphous material usually occurs in soils of volcanic origin. High levels of phosphate and nitrogen fertilizers are required despite high content of organic nitrogen in the soils.

Vertic properties exist in soils with a high content of clay with shrinking and swelling properties. Tillage is difficult when topsoils are too dry or too moist. These soils can be highly productive, but only with improved soil tillage practices.

Soils with *low potassium reserves* constrain crop growth because of potassium deficiency. This can be overcome by application of potassium fertilizers.

Calcareous soils, although among the most fertile, may develop micronutrient deficiencies. They also impose limitations on sources of phosphate.

Soil salinity requires special management and in some cases expensive and lengthy treatment to avoid damage to salt-sensitive crops. Salt-tolerant species and cultivars may be grown when salinity is not excessive.

Soils with *excess sodium* demand special soil management practices for alkaline soils. Drainage and gypsum application can help to reduce this constraint.

Acid sulfate soils are usually water saturated or flooded and may generate sulfuric acid when drained. This type of soil should be kept saturated or should be reclaimed by shallow, intensive drainage and managed with plants tolerant of high water table or flooding.

Soils with *gravel* (< 7.5 cm), stony phase, or rocks (> 7.5 cm) prevent mechanized agricultural operations and also present high erosion risk if occurring on steep slopes.

To calculate the *percent of land with no inherent soil constraints* within each climatic class, the land area in the specific climatic class that has no soil constraints was divided by the total land area with no soil constraints.

The three temperature zone definitions corrected to sea level, of each soil-plant nutrient and management constraint identified in this table include: tropics, where the monthly mean temperature is above 18°C; subtropics, where the monthly mean temperature is below 18°C for one or more months; and temperate, where the monthly mean temperature is below 5°C for one or more months.

19. Forests and Rangelands

Since the publication of *World Resources 1990–91*, which suggested an acceleration in the rate of deforestation in tropical countries, two interim reports have been published by the Forest Resources Assessment 1990 Project of the Food and Agriculture Organization of the United Nations (FAO) confirming this trend. FAO's most recent preliminary estimate, presented at the World Forestry Congress in September 1991, put the world's average annual tropical deforestation rate during 1981–90 at 16.9 million hectares. Compared with the previous 1980 Tropical Forest Resources Assessment, this is a 50 percent increase in the aggregate estimate for 76 tropical countries, which were identical in both appraisals and hold about 97 percent of the world's tropical forests.

Table 19.1 presents the new FAO data for the world and 12 tropical subregions. If these provisional deforestation estimates are confirmed by the final results of the 1990 assessment, they will indicate important shifts in regional deforestation: in four subregions— Central Africa, Caribbean Subregion, Continental South East Asia, and Insular South East Asia— deforestation accelerated faster than the global average; in three subregions— Tropical Southern Africa, Central America and Mexico, and Tropical Latin America—deforestation increased about 50 percent, comparable to the world average; in five subregions, four in Africa and one in Asia, deforestation did not change significantly from the 1980 assessment.

Table 19.1 also lists recent country estimates, compiled in various years by various methods. In some cases, these estimates do not agree with the FAO data. The biggest discrepancy appears between the most recent country deforestation estimate for Brazil and the FAO aggregate for Tropical South America. The FAO estimate shows an increase in the amount of land deforested from 4.6 million hectares per year during 1981–85 to 6.8 million hectares per year during 1981–90. Yet Brazil reports a decline in the amount of land deforested in its Legal Amazon (a political boundary encompassing six states and territories and parts of three others). Since no recent deforestation studies have been conducted outside the Legal Amazon, it is not known whether this difference might be accounted for by increasing deforestation elsewhere or whether one of the estimates is inaccurate. A reconciliation of these data can only come with the final results from the 1990 assessment. They are expected to be pub-

lished by mid-1992, with estimates of the forest area and the rates of deforestation at global, subregional, and country levels.

By mid-1992, the Agriculture and Timber Division of FAO and the United Nations Economic Commission for Europe (UNECE) in Geneva will release the final results of their assessment of forests in the temperate zone. It is believed that the temperate forest area has increased by 5 percent during 1981–90. Some of this increase is the result of afforestation and recolonization of nonforest land, but in some cases, it may be a statistical increase from improved survey coverage, for example of the boreal forests in the Soviet Union.

Wood is still the primary product removed from the world's forests and woodlands. Table 19.2 shows that in Africa, South America, and Asia, most wood is used for fuel, whereas in North America, Europe, Oceania, and the U.S.S.R., it is produced for industrial use. This difference can also be observed for the top six roundwood producers: the United States, the U.S.S.R., China, India, Brazil, and Canada, which together remove roughly half of the world's timber from their own territory. Canada, the United States, and the U.S.S.R. harvest most of their wood for industrial purposes and were net exporters of roundwood in 1987–89. China, Brazil and India, each cutting roughly the same quantities of roundwood as Western Europe, used most of their wood for fuel.

The production of processed wood—sawnwood and panels—is concentrated in developed countries and in the wood-rich and most industrialized developing countries. For example, during the past decade, production of panels grew most in China, India, and Brazil. In 1987–89, Indonesia was the largest producer of wood-based panels in the developing countries, following the United States, the U.S.S.R., Japan, and the Federal Republic of Germany among the developed countries.

Data on the impact of human use of land resources have been lacking. A 1991 study by the United Nations Environment Programme and the International Soil Reference and Information Centre found that the soils of 17 percent of the earth's vegetated land are degraded, as a result of vegetation removal, overgrazing, poor agricultural practices, and contamination by industrial chemicals. Table 19.3 presents data on soil degradation by severity and degradation type for six regions, and Table 19.4 specifies the causes of human-induced soil degradation.

Table 19.1 Forest Resources

	Extent of Forest and Woodland 1980 (000 ha)				Average Annual Deforestation						Average Annual Reforestation 1981-85 (000 ha)	Managed Closed Forest 1980 (000 ha)	Protected Closed Forest 1980 (000 ha)
	Natural Forest		Planta-tion	Other Wooded Area	1981-85				Most Recent Estimate {a}				
					Closed Forest Extent		Total Forest Extent						
	Closed	Open			(000 ha)	(%)	(000 ha)	(%)	Year of Data	Extent (000 ha)			
WORLD	2,822,560	742,148	28,830	1,695,017	7,501	0.3	11,502	0.3	1981-90 b	16,900	10,538	968,444	118,019
AFRICA	222,278	483,911	2,971	629,900	1,339	0.6	3,772	0.5	1981-90 c	5,000	296	2,327	9,635
North Africa	3,371	2,119	1,062	3,775	0	0.0	58	1.1	X	X	101	584	15
Algeria	1,518	249	431	2,168	X	X	40	2.3	X	X	52	X	8
Egypt	X	X	40	X	X	X	X	X	X	X	2	X	X
Libya	134	56	143	446	X	X	X	X	X	X	31	X	X
Morocco	1,533	1,703	321	1,161	X	X	13	0.4	X	X	13	421	7
Tunisia	186	111	127	X	X	X	5	1.7	X	X	3	163	X
West Sahelian Africa	2,345	39,609	47	51,123	25	1.1	388	0.9	1981-90 d	400	10	0	63
Burkina Faso	271	4,464	12	9,360	3	1.1	80	1.7	X	X	2	X	X
Cape Verde	X	X	4	1	X	X	X	X	X	X	1	X	X
Chad	500	13,000	3	10,550	X	X	80	0.6	X	X	0	X	0
Gambia, The	65	150	1	560	2	3.4	5	2.4	X	X	0	X	X
Guinea-Bissau	660	1,445	0	577	17	2.6	57	2.7	X	X	0	X	X
Mali	500	6,750	5	15,100	X	X	36	0.5	X	X	1	X	X
Mauritania	29	525	0	3,980	1	2.4	13	2.4	X	X	0	X	X
Niger	100	2,450	9	7,880	3	2.5	67	2.6	X	X	2	X	X
Senegal	220	10,825	13	3,115	X	X	50	0.5	X	X	3	0	63
East Sahelian Africa	8,412	83,883	524	226,799	45	0.5	695	0.8	1981-90	700	37	560	628
Djibouti	2	68	X	44	X	X	X	X	X	X	X	X	X
Ethiopia	4,350	22,800	98	35,300	8	0.2	88	0.3	X	X	10	X	X
Kenya	1,105	1,255	181	38,105	19	1.7	39	1.7	X	X	10	70	570
Somalia	1,540	7,510	11	53,050	4	0.2	14	0.1	X	X	1	X	X
Sudan	650	47,000	188	98,600	4	0.6	504	1.1	X	X	13	50	X
Uganda	765	5,250	46	1,700	10	1.3	50	0.8	X	X	2	440	58
West Africa	17,267	36,306	327	104,690	703	4.1	1,199	2.2	1981-90	1,200	36	1,168	1,045
Benin	47	3,820	19	6,832	1	2.6	67	1.7	X	X	X	X	X
Cote d'Ivoire	4,458	5,376	45	15,390	290	6.5	510	5.2	1981-85	260	6	1	648
Ghana	1,718	6,975	75	9,480	22	1.3	72	0.8	X	X	2	1,167	397
Guinea	2,050	8,600	2	9,900	36	1.8	86	0.8	X	X	0	X	0
Liberia	2,000	40	6	5,640	46	2.3	46	2.3	X	X	2	X	X
Nigeria	5,950	8,800	163	49,450	300	5.0	400	2.7	X	X	26	0	X
Sierra Leone	740	1,315	6	4,278	6	0.8	6	0.3	X	X	0	X	X
Togo	304	1,380	11	3,720	2	0.7	12	0.7	X	X	0	X	X
Central Africa	170,395	111,915	76	71,575	307	0.2	575	0.2	1981-90	1,500	3	0	5,830
Cameroon	17,920	7,700	18	15,600	80	0.4	110	0.4	1976-86	190	1	X	X
Central African Rep	3,590	32,300	0	21,100	5	0.1	55	0.2	X	X	X	X	X
Congo	21,340	X	17	2,500	22	0.1	22	0.1	X	X	0	X	130
Equatorial Guinea	1,295	X	X	1,175	3	0.2	3	0.2	X	X	X	X	X
Gabon	20,500	75	19	1,500	15	0.1	15	0.1	X	X	1	X	X
Zaire	105,750	71,840	22	29,700	182	0.2	370	0.2	X	X	0	X	5,700
Tropical Southern Africa	8,818	207,109	556	161,574	108	1.2	700	0.3	1981-90	1,100	29	5	834
Angola	2,900	50,700	157	28,400	44	1.5	94	0.2	X	X	3	X	X
Botswana	X	32,560	X	20,000	X	X	20	0.1	X	X	X	X	X
Burundi	27	14	19	24	1	2.6	1	2.7	X	X	3	X	17
Malawi	186	4,085	80	380	X	X	150	3.5	X	X	1	X	146
Mozambique	935	14,500	25	42,700	10	1.1	120	0.8	X	X	4	X	25
Namibia	X	18,420	0	37,645	X	X	30	0.2	X	X	X	X	X
Rwanda	120	110	29	155	3	2.6	5	2.2	X	X	3	X	16
Tanzania	1,440	40,600	98	17,900	10	0.7	130	0.3	X	X	9	0	410
Zambia	3,010	26,500	38	10,800	40	1.3	70	0.2	X	X	2	5	220
Zimbabwe	200	19,620	110	3,570	0	0.0	80	0.4	X	X	4	X	X
Temperate Southern Africa	1,351	70	102	2,803	X	X	X	X	X	X	68	10	290
South Africa	1,347	X	X	2,803	X	X	X	X	X	X	63	10	290
Swaziland	4	70	102	X	X	X	0	X	X	X	5	X	X
Insular Africa	10,319	2,900	277	7,561	151	1.5	157	1.2	1981-90 e	200	12	X	930
Comoros	16	X	0	29	1	3.1	1	3.1	X	X	0	X	X
Madagascar	10,300	2,900	266	7,500	150	1.5	156	1.2	X	X	12	X	930
Mauritius	3	X	11	32	0	3.3	0	3.3	X	X	0	X	X
THE AMERICAS	1,212,849	207,172	6,175	590,871	4,339	0.4	5,702	0.4	X	X	3,148	102,884	53,573
Temperate North America	490,554	X	X	243,922	X	X	X	X	X	X	2,495	102,362	36,068
Canada	264,100	X	X	172,300	X	X	X	X	X	X	720	X	4,870
United States	226,454	X	X	71,622	X	X	X	X	1977-87	159	1,775	102,362	31,198
Central America and Mexico	64,929	2,560	183	91,524	1,002	1.5	1,022	1.5	1981-90	1,400	32	308	742
Costa Rica	1,638	160	3	240	65	4.0	65	3.6	1973-89	42	0	X	320
El Salvador	141	X	1	315	5	3.2	5	3.2	X	X	0	X	X
Guatemala	4,442	100	15	1,865	90	2.0	90	2.0	X	X	8	X	62
Honduras	3,797	200	X	1,900	90	2.3	90	2.3	X	X	X	58	X
Mexico	46,250	2,100	159	85,500	595	1.3	615	1.3	1981-83	1,000	22	X	360
Nicaragua	4,496	X	1	1,580	121	2.7	121	2.7	X	X	1	250	X
Panama	4,165	X	4	124	36	0.9	36	0.9	X	X	0	X	X
Caribbean Subregion	37,066	482	205	3,055	25	0.1	26	0.1	1981-90 f	200	13	214	594
Belize	1,354	92	3	574	9	0.7	9	0.6	X	X	0	X	X
Cuba	1,455	X	157	1,005	2	0.1	2	0.1	X	X	11	200	X
Dominican Rep	629	X	6	321	4	0.6	4	0.6	X	X	1	X	X
Guyana	18,475	220	1	315	2	0.0	3	0.0	X	X	0	X	12
Haiti	48	X	1	96	2	3.8	2	3.7	X	X	0	X	X
Jamaica	67	X	13	386	2	3.0	2	3.0	X	X	1	X	2
Suriname	14,830	170	8	295	3	0.0	3	0.0	X	X	0	X	580
Trinidad and Tobago	208	X	16	63	1	0.4	1	0.4	X	X	1	14	X
Nontropical South America	52,540	X	1,557	25,170	X	X	50	0.1	X	X	119	X	3,439
Argentina	44,500	X	600	16,500	X	X	X	X	1980-89	105	40	X	2,594
Chile	7,550	X	817	8,550	X	X	50	0.7	X	X	74	X	845
Uruguay	490	X	140	120	X	X	X	X	X	X	5	X	X

Table 19.1

| | Extent of Forest and Woodland 1980 (000 ha) | | | | Average Annual Deforestation | | | | | | Average Annual Reforestation 1981-85 (000 ha) | Managed Closed Forest 1980 (000 ha) | Protected Closed Forest 1980 (000 ha) |
	Natural Forest Closed	Natural Forest Open	Planta-tion	Other Wooded Area	1981-85 Closed Forest Extent (000 ha)	(%)	1981-85 Total Forest Extent (000 ha)	(%)	Most Recent Estimate {a} Year of Data	Extent (000 ha)			
Tropical South America	567,760	204,130	4,230	227,200	3,312	0.6	4,604	0.6	1981-90	6,800	489	0	12,730
Bolivia	44,010	22,750	26	12,050	87	0.2	117	0.2	X	X	1	X	X
Brazil	357,480	157,000	3,855	161,820	1,480	0.4	2,530	0.5	1989-90 g	1,380	449	0	4,660
Colombia	46,400	5,300	95	14,400	820	1.8	890	1.7	X	X	8	X	2,280
Ecuador	14,250	480	43	3,470	340	2.4	340	2.3	X	X	4	X	350
Paraguay	4,070	15,640	3	12,730	190	4.7	212	1.1	1989-90	450	1	X	90
Peru	69,680	960	84	8,660	270	0.4	270	0.4	X	X	6	X	850
Venezuela	31,870	2,000	124	14,070	125	0.4	245	0.7	X	X	19	X	4,500
ASIA	424,713	47,103	19,605	176,994	1,799	0.4	2,003	0.4	1981-90 h	3,600	1,408	48,705	25,050
Temperate and Middle East Asia	153,755	20,100	14,515	70,040	X	X	20	0.0	X	X	972	9,625	7,523
Afghanistan	810	400	11	690	X	X	X	X	X	X	X	100	X
China	97,847	17,200	12,733	27,730	X	X	X	X	X	X	378	X	1,635
Cyprus	153	X	X	40	X	X	X	X	X	X	X	153	28
Iran, Islamic Rep	2,750	1,000	43	14,250	X	X	20	0.5	X	X	X	400	120
Iraq	70	1,160	20	300	X	X	X	X	X	X	X	X	X
Israel	75	X	X	34	X	X	X	X	X	X	2	56	2
Japan	23,889	X	X	1,309	X	X	X	X	X	X	240	X	490
Jordan	X	50	21	75	X	X	X	X	X	X	3	X	X
Korea, Dem People's Rep	4,800	X	X	4,200	X	X	X	X	X	X	200	X	X
Korea, Rep	4,887	X	1,628	X	X	X	X	X	X	X	67	X	437
Lebanon	X	20	18	45	X	X	X	X	X	X	X	X	X
Mongolia	9,528	X	X	4,335	X	X	X	X	X	X	X	X	4,672
Saudi Arabia	30	170	1	1,400	X	X	X	X	X	X	X	X	X
Syrian Arab Rep	60	90	40	239	X	X	X	X	X	X	X	60	X
Turkey	8,856	X	X	11,343	X	X	X	X	X	X	82	8,856	139
Yemen (Arab Rep)	X	10	0	1,590	X	X	X	X	X	X	X	X	X
Yemen (People's Dem Rep)	X	X	0	2,460	X	X	X	X	X	X	X	X	X
South Asia	60,653	5,908	2,494	17,906	305	0.5	307	0.5	1981-90	400	179	33,122	7,369
Bangladesh	927	X	128	315	8	0.9	8	0.9	X	X	17	795	52
Bhutan	2,100	40	7	230	1	0.1	1	0.1	X	X	1	0	X
India	51,841	5,393	2,068	14,848	147	0.3	147	0.3	1983-87	48	138	31,917	6,779
Nepal	1,941	180	19	340	84	4.3	84	4.0	X	X	4	X	330
Pakistan	2,185	295	160	1,105	7	0.3	9	0.4	X	X	7	410	15
Sri Lanka	1,659	X	112	1,068	58	3.5	58	3.5	X	X	13	X	193
Continental South East Asia	65,904	18,095	352	39,440	547	0.8	709	0.8	1981-90	1,400	55	3,419	3,079
Cambodia	7,548	5,100	7	625	25	0.3	30	0.2	X	X	0	X	X
Lao People's Dem Rep	8,410	5,215	11	5,735	100	1.2	130	1.0	X	X	1	X	X
Myanmar	31,941	X	16	20,700	105	0.3	105	0.3	1984	600	0	3,419	299
Thailand	9,235	6,440	114	1,300	252	2.7	379	2.4	1985-88	235	24	X	2,220
Viet Nam	8,770	1,340	204	11,080	65	0.7	65	0.6	1985	200	29	X	560
Insular South East Asia	144,401	3,000	2,244	49,608	947	0.7	967	0.7	1981-90	1,800	201	2,539	7,079
Indonesia	113,895	3,000	1,918	41,260	600	0.5	620	0.5	1982-90	1,000	131	40	5,430
Malaysia	20,996	X	26	4,825	255	1.2	255	1.2	1979-89	270	20	2,499	959
Philippines	9,510	X	300	3,520	92	1.0	92	1.0	1980-87	150	50	X	690
Singapore	X	X	X	3	X	X	X	X	X	X	X	X	X
EUROPE	136,652	X	X	41,688	X	X	X	X	X	X	1,031	74,628	1,752
Albania	930	X	X	312	X	X	X	X	X	X	X	X	X
Austria	3,754	X	X	0	X	X	X	X	X	X	21	1,489	X
Belgium	600	X	X	160	X	X	X	X	X	X	19	272	X
Bulgaria	3,400	X	X	400	X	X	X	X	X	X	50	3,600	100
Czechoslovakia	4,435	X	X	143	X	X	X	X	X	X	37	4,435	X
Denmark	466	X	X	18	X	X	X	X	X	X	X	330	56
Finland	19,885	X	X	3,340	X	X	X	X	X	X	158	10,578	294
France	13,875	X	X	1,200	X	X	X	X	X	X	51	2,057	92
Germany (Fed Rep)	6,989	X	X	218	X	X	X	X	X	X	62	5,886	X
Germany (Dem Rep)	2,700	X	X	155	X	X	X	X	X	X	X	2,697	85
Greece	2,512	X	X	3,242	X	X	X	X	X	X	X	1,603	75
Hungary	1,612	X	X	37	X	X	X	X	X	X	19	1,612	41
Iceland	X	X	X	100	X	X	X	X	X	X	X	X	X
Ireland	347	X	X	33	X	X	X	X	X	X	9	298	0
Italy	6,363	X	X	1,700	X	X	X	X	X	X	15	699	162
Luxembourg	82	X	X	0	X	X	X	X	X	X	2	38	0
Netherlands	294	X	X	61	X	X	X	X	X	X	79	225	0
Norway	7,635	X	X	1,066	X	X	X	X	X	X	106	1,130	60
Poland	8,588	X	X	138	X	X	X	X	X	X	4	8,099	103
Portugal	2,627	X	X	349	X	X	X	X	X	X	X	X	7
Romania	6,190	X	X	150	X	X	X	X	X	X	92	5,940	X
Spain	6,906	X	X	23,584	X	X	X	X	X	X	207	2,007	40
Sweden	24,400	X	X	3,442	X	X	X	X	X	X	7	14,301	230
Switzerland	935	X	X	189	X	X	X	X	X	X	40	627	7
United Kingdom	2,027	X	X	151	X	X	X	X	X	X	53	1,505	X
Yugoslavia	9,100	X	X	1,400	X	X	X	X	X	X		6,300	400
U.S.S.R.	739,900	X	X	189,700	X	X	X	X	X	X	4,540	739,900	20,000
OCEANIA	86,168	3,962	79	65,864	25	0.0	26	0.0	X	X	115	0	8,009
Australia	41,658	X	X	64,242	X	X	X	X	X	X	62	X	3,817
Fiji	811	0	40	6	2	0.2	2	0.2	X	X	7	X	X
New Zealand	7,046	X	X	46	X	X	X	X	X	X	43	X	4,137
Papua New Guinea	34,230	3,945	22	1,530	22	0.1	23	0.1	X	X	2	0	55
Solomon Islands	2,423	17	17	40	1	0.0	1	0.0	X	X	0	X	X

Sources: Food and Agriculture Organization of the United Nations, United Nations Economic Commission for Europe, and other sources.

Notes: a. Deforestation estimates are for total forest area, unless otherwise noted. World and subregional totals are provisional estimates for tropical countries; numbers are rounded to the nearest 100,000 hectares; data are not directly comparable to 1981-85 rates because only a limited number of countries are included. Country estimates in this column are from many dates and have differing reliability and thus are not necessarily comparable; country deforestation estimates are to be taken purely as indicator of order of magnitude. b. 87 tropical countries. c. 40 tropical countries. d. Only 8 countries of subregion. e. Only one country of subregion. f. 18 tropical countries. g. Legal Amazon only. h. 15 tropical countries.
0 = zero or less than half the unit of measure; X = not available.
For additional information, see Sources and Technical Notes.

Table 19.2 Wood Production and Trade, 1977–89

| | Roundwood Production | | | | | | Processed Wood Production | | | | Paper Production | | Average Annual Net Trade in Roundwood {a} | |
| | Total | | Fuel and Charcoal | | Industrial Roundwood | | Sawnwood | | Panels | | | | | |
	(000 cubic meters) 1987-89	Percent Change Since 1977-79	(000 cubic meters) 1987-89	Percent Change Since 1977-79	(000 cubic meters) 1987-89	Percent Change Since 1977-79	(000 cubic meters) 1987-89	Percent Change Since 1977-79	(000 cubic meters) 1987-89	Percent Change Since 1977-79	(000 metric tons) 1987-89	Percent Change Since 1977-79	(000 cubic meters) 1977-79	1987-89
WORLD	3,425,613	23	1,760,475	28	1,665,139	17	504,256	10	125,985	21	223,012	39		
AFRICA	485,487	34	429,829	36	55,657	19	8,714	38	1,891	46	2,427	65	(6,107)	(4,128)
Algeria	2,066	35	1,816	36	250	32	13	0	50	0	120	163	63	210
Angola	5,262	26	4,217	31	1,045	8	5	(88)	2	(74)	15	15	0	0
Benin	4,845	35	4,591	35	254	35	11	22	0	X	0	X	0	0
Botswana	1,276	43	1,197	42	79	44	0	X	0	X	0	X	X	X
Burkina Faso	8,300	29	7,925	29	375	28	1	0	0	X	0	X	0	0
Burundi	3,969	31	3,921	31	48	43	3	200	0	X	0	X	X	X
Cameroon	12,615	31	9,886	31	2,730	31	652	58	80	10	5	0	(631)	(479)
Cape Verde	X	X	X	X	X	X	X	X	X	X	X	X	X	X
Central African Rep	3,449	19	3,055	29	394	(24)	52	(40)	4	(20)	0	X	(121)	(32)
Chad	3,837	26	3,294	26	542	26	1	0	0	X	0	X	X	X
Comoros	X	X	X	X	X	X	X	X	X	X	X	X	X	X
Congo	3,119	59	1,729	31	1,390	118	54	12	56	(26)	0	X	(165)	(803)
Cote d'Ivoire	12,799	10	9,437	52	3,362	(38)	775	15	260	133	0	X	(3,043)	(572)
Djibouti	0	X	0	X	0	X	0	X	0	X	0	X	X	X
Egypt	2,210	31	2,108	31	103	32	0	X	74	66	160	32	86	200
Equatorial Guinea	607	46	447	10	160	1,614	51	993	10	2,900	0	X	(6)	(120)
Ethiopia	38,859	21	37,100	21	1,759	26	39	(46)	15	10	10	25	0	0
Gabon	3,618	24	2,396	49	1,222	(6)	126	17	228	75	0	X	(1,565)	(1,018)
Gambia, The	912	7	891	6	21	110	1	0	0	X	0	X	X	X
Ghana	17,006	56	15,905	71	1,101	(31)	482	10	60	(11)	0	X	(321)	(286)
Guinea	4,560	25	3,924	26	636	18	90	0	0	(100)	0	X	0	(8)
Guinea-Bissau	565	6	422	2	143	19	16	0	0	X	0	X	0	0
Kenya	34,206	46	32,495	47	1,711	23	189	25	45	172	99	71	(52)	0
Lesotho	579	32	579	32	0	X	0	X	0	X	0	X	0	33
Liberia	5,825	31	4,736	30	1,089	33	411	129	5	(44)	0	X	(348)	(544)
Libya	640	4	536	1	104	26	31	12	0	X	6	20	111	30
Madagascar	7,637	31	6,830	36	807	0	234	0	6	467	7	67	(1)	(2)
Malawi	7,366	36	7,016	37	351	19	31	(27)	6	13	0	X	0	0
Mali	5,359	32	5,016	32	342	32	12	106	0	X	0	X	X	X
Mauritania	12	33	7	40	5	25	0	X	0	X	0	X	X	X
Mauritius	32	(27)	20	(14)	13	(38)	4	(19)	0	X	0	X	2	1
Morocco	2,008	32	1,343	36	665	25	72	(3)	142	61	109	43	226	471
Mozambique	16,001	31	15,022	33	979	9	38	(59)	6	113	2	0	(8)	(3)
Namibia	X	X	X	X	X	X	X	X	0	X	X	X	X	X
Niger	4,287	33	4,023	33	264	33	0	X	0	X	0	X	X	X
Nigeria	104,926	41	97,058	40	7,868	48	2,712	70	233	102	81	419	(5)	(15)
Rwanda	5,842	14	5,602	12	240	87	13	550	2	500	0	X	X	X
Senegal	4,286	25	3,697	24	589	32	11	32	0	X	0	X	27	25
Sierra Leone	2,941	23	2,801	26	140	(18)	12	(37)	0	X	0	X	1	0
Somalia	6,757	47	6,669	47	88	28	14	0	1	(33)	0	X	2	0
South Africa	19,246	14	7,078	0	12,168	23	1,827	18	398	10	1,614	55	(117)	(899)
Sudan	21,584	36	19,554	36	2,030	35	13	(7)	2	(40)	10	43	X	X
Swaziland	2,223	(6)	560	10	1,663	(10)	136	27	8	118	0	X	(232)	(198)
Tanzania	31,966	46	30,019	44	1,947	87	156	78	13	39	28	X	(5)	0
Togo	840	33	662	34	178	30	5	0	0	X	0	X	X	X
Tunisia	3,088	30	2,947	29	141	50	14	378	93	172	71	240	40	27
Uganda	13,880	40	12,080	40	1,800	36	26	10	3	233	2	500	0	0
Zaire	34,255	36	31,540	37	2,715	34	121	4	53	109	2	0	(49)	(135)
Zambia	12,030	43	11,424	44	606	38	68	61	8	92	3	X	4	0
Zimbabwe	7,755	32	6,226	31	1,530	36	185	22	28	(11)	82	74	1	(9)
NORTH & CENTRAL AMERICA	769,323	30	171,189	89	598,134	19	170,866	20	41,302	10	88,639	27	(19,561)	(23,934)
Barbados	X	X	X	X	X	X	X	X	X	X	X	X	2	1
Belize	188	71	126	64	62	88	14	(18)	0	X	0	X	(2)	(8)
Canada	178,010	14	6,834	66	171,176	13	60,814	39	6,572	30	16,417	27	98	(1,220)
Costa Rica	3,953	9	2,815	33	1,138	(24)	511	(12)	55	(18)	16	78	(1)	(21)
Cuba	3,210	21	2,617	21	594	22	121	16	137	2,189	152	112	3	16
Dominican Rep	982	106	976	106	6	64	0	X	0	X	10	11	0	41
El Salvador	4,341	16	4,234	15	107	29	52	49	0	X	17	96	X	X
Guatemala	7,392	26	7,278	33	114	(71)	83	(70)	6	(42)	17	(35)	1	(10)
Haiti	5,628	19	5,389	20	239	0	14	0	0	X	0	X	6	0
Honduras	5,948	27	5,015	41	933	(17)	456	(27)	9	(32)	0	X	(22)	(21)
Jamaica	218	361	13	86	205	409	38	46	1	(75)	3	(61)	5	1
Mexico	22,303	25	14,878	27	7,425	23	2,410	8	722	79	3,108	97	12	13
Nicaragua	3,871	27	2,991	38	880	0	222	(45)	4	(64)	0	X	5	0
Panama	2,047	24	1,708	8	339	484	20	7	12	(18)	22	10	2	2
Trinidad and Tobago	64	(24)	22	38	42	(38)	21	(34)	0	X	0	X	2	1
United States	531,022	36	116,268	137	414,754	22	106,086	12	33,783	6	68,878	25	(19,662)	(22,730)
SOUTH AMERICA	330,453	31	229,847	23	100,606	51	26,436	37	4,028	34	7,646	67	(729)	(3,832)
Argentina	10,819	9	4,332	(25)	6,487	56	1,446	80	356	13	973	48	7	2
Bolivia	1,514	14	1,266	31	248	(31)	95	(44)	4	(76)	2	100	(1)	0
Brazil	251,125	33	179,116	25	72,009	59	18,140	36	2,832	29	4,734	83	(86)	2
Chile	16,727	34	6,435	18	10,292	47	2,702	64	265	182	445	54	(598)	(3,814)
Colombia	18,163	16	15,490	24	2,673	(14)	721	(24)	113	3	497	63	(5)	0
Ecuador	9,539	46	6,544	39	2,995	64	1,346	65	137	114	35	15	0	0
Guyana	228	40	19	51	209	39	57	(9)	0	X	0	X	(30)	(22)
Paraguay	8,401	48	5,213	26	3,188	106	891	120	105	253	11	52	(1)	0
Peru	8,760	17	7,590	30	1,170	(28)	571	14	43	(27)	243	42	1	0
Suriname	206	(38)	18	(43)	188	(37)	63	(15)	9	(61)	0	X	(15)	(9)
Uruguay	3,293	17	3,036	24	257	(31)	57	(45)	10	(33)	70	64	8	0
Venezuela	1,425	21	722	33	703	11	329	(6)	154	89	635	30	26	12

Table 19.2

| | Roundwood Production | | | | | | Processed Wood Production | | | | | | Average Annual Net Trade in Roundwood {a} | |
| | Total | | Fuel and Charcoal | | Industrial Roundwood | | Sawnwood | | Panels | | Paper Production | | | |
	(000 cubic meters) 1987-89	Percent Change Since 1977-79	(000 cubic meters) 1987-89	Percent Change Since 1977-79	(000 cubic meters) 1987-89	Percent Change Since 1977-79	(000 cubic meters) 1987-89	Percent Change Since 1977-79	(000 cubic meters) 1987-89	Percent Change Since 1977-79	(000 metric tons) 1987-89	Percent Change Since 1977-79	(000 cubic meters) 1977-79	1987-89
ASIA	**1,053,425**	**21**	**781,840**	**21**	**271,586**	**21**	**105,538**	**15**	**26,641**	**44**	**47,390**	**82**	**37,628**	**52,132**
Afghanistan	5,939	(5)	4,464	(6)	1,475	(3)	400	0	1	0	0	X	X	X
Bahrain	X	X	X	X	X	X	X	X	X	X	X	X	14	36
Bangladesh	29,374	30	28,509	31	864	(3)	79	(54)	8	(75)	102	60	X	X
Bhutan	3,224	6	2,946	7	278	(3)	5	50	0	X	0	X	(5)	(7)
Cambodia	5,677	20	5,110	22	567	2	43	0	2	0	0	X	(6)	0
China	275,723	24	177,610	19	98,113	32	25,861	35	3,626	88	14,159	168	7,785	13,456
Cyprus	77	(32)	22	(24)	55	(34)	57	(26)	23	X	0	X	3	18
India	264,421	25	240,193	24	24,228	33	17,460	93	442	98	1,930	91	(39)	859
Indonesia	173,580	25	133,971	21	39,608	42	10,118	191	7,693	1,635	920	522	(20,378)	(1,099)
Iran, Islamic Rep	6,815	2	2,439	6	4,376	0	163	0	54	(65)	78	1	151	117
Iraq	147	21	97	37	50	0	8	0	3	50	28	0	50	1
Israel	118	0	11	0	107	0	0	X	148	7	170	50	169	213
Japan	31,855	(5)	574	(9)	31,281	(5)	30,280	(24)	9,360	(6)	24,657	48	57,651	51,415
Jordan	8	19	4	44	4	0	0	X	0	X	11	78	2	17
Korea, Dem People's Rep	4,705	13	4,105	16	600	0	280	0	0	X	80	0	21	71
Korea, Rep	6,848	(25)	4,489	(34)	2,359	2	4,058	28	1,444	(41)	3,613	165	8,767	7,088
Kuwait	X	X	X	X	X	X	X	X	X	X	X	X	9	54
Lao People's Dem Rep	3,881	25	3,572	23	309	55	16	(66)	9	800	0	X	(11)	(34)
Lebanon	491	2	470	2	21	7	28	(16)	46	0	39	(14)	31	16
Malaysia	47,691	33	8,070	26	39,621	35	7,074	20	1,521	66	70	102	(16,749)	(21,482)
Mongolia	2,390	0	1,350	0	1,040	0	470	0	4	0	0	X	0	0
Myanmar	21,038	27	17,050	23	3,989	49	380	(20)	15	25	8	(17)	(94)	(498)
Nepal	17,389	28	16,829	29	560	0	220	0	0	X	2	0	(132)	0
Oman	X	X	X	X	X	X	X	X	X	X	X	X	0	24
Pakistan	23,646	45	22,474	43	1,171	123	478	1,085	87	113	131	156	63	34
Philippines	38,158	11	32,147	31	6,011	(39)	1,072	(35)	543	(21)	328	(1)	(1,989)	(198)
Qatar	X	X	X	X	X	X	X	X	X	X	X	X	10	36
Saudi Arabia	X	X	X	X	X	X	X	X	X	X	X	X	144	221
Singapore	X	X	X	X	X	X	206	(46)	489	(34)	10	67	1,485	(68)
Sri Lanka	8,879	18	8,199	18	680	24	20	(42)	10	(30)	27	25	0	(33)
Syrian Arab Rep	48	33	15	(4)	34	62	9	125	27	50	16	433	42	18
Thailand	38,239	17	33,624	21	4,615	(10)	1,139	(30)	252	82	500	74	(60)	423
Turkey	15,957	(27)	9,976	(31)	5,981	(19)	4,923	18	781	51	413	18	16	742
United Arab Emirates	X	X	X	X	X	X	X	X	X	X	X	X	X	X
Viet Nam	26,626	23	23,253	25	3,372	8	354	(40)	40	58	57	10	24	41
Yemen (Arab Rep)	X	X	X	X	X	X	X	X	X	X	X	X	X	X
(People's Dem Rep)	314	31	314	31	0	X	0	X	0	X	0	X	(0)	4
EUROPE	**359,018**	**12**	**55,306**	**13**	**303,712**	**12**	**85,423**	**(1)**	**36,122**	**11**	**63,941**	**35**	**16,618**	**19,031**
Albania	2,330	0	1,608	0	722	0	200	0	12	0	19	142	X	X
Austria	14,826	10	1,413	26	13,413	9	6,447	3	1,512	20	2,600	76	2,075	3,872
Belgium {b}	4,164	57	561	118	3,603	50	1,021	37	2,167	24	X	X	2,529	2,326
Bulgaria	4,449	2	1,795	92	2,654	(22)	1,410	(11)	520	(3)	457	9	303	131
Czechoslovakia	18,144	(1)	1,461	(23)	16,683	2	5,301	14	1,437	33	1,283	12	(2,903)	(725)
Denmark	2,139	13	451	327	1,688	(6)	861	7	332	(17)	326	23	(487)	(540)
Finland	44,129	13	3,243	(31)	40,886	19	7,756	(5)	1,434	(4)	8,472	64	3,046	5,098
France	43,356	14	10,434	0	32,922	19	10,205	8	2,813	(5)	6,216	25	(220)	(3,997)
Germany (Fed Rep)	32,948	7	3,656	17	29,292	5	10,517	1	7,768	6	10,591	52	1,110	(1,203)
(Dem Rep)	10,800	20	635	22	10,165	20	2,513	8	1,199	18	1,351	13	541	(94)
Greece	3,267	29	2,320	32	947	23	398	(3)	399	25	281	17	360	242
Hungary	6,653	12	2,972	20	3,681	6	1,240	(1)	390	7	520	20	919	(342)
Iceland	X	X	X	X	X	X	X	X	X	X	X	X	10	2
Ireland	1,350	222	49	121	1,301	228	319	171	327	141	32	(70)	(83)	(307)
Italy	9,009	22	4,360	59	4,640	9	1,999	(10)	3,852	47	5,316	14	5,820	5,617
Luxembourg {c}	X	X	X	X	X	X	X	X	X	X	X	X	X	X
Malta	X	X	X	X	X	X	X	X	X	X	X	X	1	0
Netherlands	1,201	31	111	86	1,090	27	407	45	90	(52)	2,399	43	517	272
Norway	10,973	37	924	79	10,049	34	2,404	11	635	14	1,683	32	604	1,240
Poland	23,213	8	3,254	97	19,959	1	5,661	(29)	2,086	4	1,411	8	(836)	(829)
Portugal	9,833	12	598	6	9,235	12	1,702	(17)	915	128	679	48	(312)	(81)
Romania	20,056	(1)	3,816	(20)	16,239	5	2,822	(38)	1,379	(15)	818	4	(26)	(59)
Spain	16,131	33	2,320	61	13,811	29	2,598	3	2,065	16	3,368	47	1,146	968
Sweden	54,301	9	4,424	30	49,877	8	11,426	3	1,324	(35)	8,111	43	1,725	7,236
Switzerland	4,598	11	861	20	3,737	9	1,681	5	765	10	1,207	46	(26)	146
United Kingdom	5,974	51	193	38	5,780	51	1,978	17	1,532	129	4,318	3	405	20
Yugoslavia	15,175	8	3,837	7	11,338	8	4,558	11	1,260	7	1,347	44	401	39
U.S.S.R.	**388,533**	**7**	**83,733**	**6**	**304,800**	**7**	**101,667**	**(3)**	**14,347**	**40**	**10,547**	**17**	**(17,781)**	**(19,407)**
OCEANIA	**39,375**	**25**	**8,732**	**27**	**30,644**	**24**	**5,612**	**4**	**1,654**	**51**	**2,422**	**28**	**(7,155)**	**(11,232)**
Australia	20,136	32	2,884	108	17,252	24	3,390	3	1,024	36	1,729	37	(4,775)	(7,531)
Fiji	310	66	37	118	273	61	95	5	16	60	0	X	0	(127)
New Zealand	10,048	9	50	(73)	9,998	11	1,963	8	595	96	693	9	(1,522)	(1,772)
Papua New Guinea	8,231	29	5,533	8	2,698	114	117	(15)	19	(22)	0	X	(601)	(1,503)
Solomon Islands	439	21	134	39	306	14	14	11	0	(100)	0	X	(259)	(276)

Source: Food and Agriculture Organization of the United Nations.
Notes: a. Imports of roundwood are shown as positive numbers; exports are represented by negative numbers. b. Data are for Belgium and Luxembourg. c. Included under Belgium.
World and regional totals include countries not listed.
0 = zero or less than half of the unit of measure; X = not available; negative numbers are shown in parentheses.
For additional information, see Sources and Technical Notes.

Table 19.3 Human-Induced Soil Degradation, 1945 to Late 1980s

	Total Degraded Area (million hectares)	Degraded Area as a Percentage of all Vegetated Land {a}	Water Erosion				Wind Erosion				
			Total (million hectares)	As a Percentage of Degraded Area	Types (million hectares) Topsoil Loss	Terrain Deformation	Total (million hectares)	As a Percentage of Degraded Area	Types (million hectares) Topsoil Loss	Terrain Deformation	Overblowing
WORLD	**1,964.4**	**17**	**1,093.7**	**56**	**920.3**	**173.3**	**548.3**	**28**	**454.2**	**82.5**	**11.6**
Light Degradation	749.0	6	343.2	17	301.2	42.0	268.6	14	230.5	38.1	0.0
Moderate Degradation	910.5	8	526.7	27	454.5	72.2	253.6	13	213.5	30.0	10.1
Strong Degradation	295.7	3	217.2	11	161.2	56.0	24.3	1	9.4	14.4	0.5
Extreme Degradation	9.3	0	6.6	0	3.8	2.8	1.9	0	0.9	0.0	1.0
AFRICA	**494.2**	**22**	**227.4**	**46**	**204.9**	**22.5**	**186.5**	**38**	**170.7**	**14.3**	**1.5**
Light Degradation	173.6	8	57.5	12	53.9	3.6	88.3	18	79.1	9.2	0.0
Moderate Degradation	191.8	9	67.4	14	60.5	6.9	89.3	18	84.2	5.1	0.0
Strong Degradation	123.6	6	98.3	20	86.6	11.7	7.9	2	7.4	0.0	0.5
Extreme Degradation	5.2	0	4.2	1	3.8	0.4	1.0	0	0.0	0.0	1.0
NORTH & CENTRAL AMERICA	**158.1**	**8**	**106.1**	**67**	**80.9**	**25.2**	**39.2**	**25**	**37.5**	**1.7**	**0.0**
Light Degradation	18.9	1	14.5	9	14.2	0.2	2.6	2	2.5	0.1	0.0
Moderate Degradation	112.5	5	68.2	43	60.1	8.1	34.9	22	33.3	1.6	0.0
Strong Degradation	26.7	1	23.4	15	6.5	16.9	1.7	1	1.7	0.0	0.0
Extreme Degradation	0.0	0	0.0	0	0.0	0.0	0.0	0	0.0	0.0	0.0
SOUTH AMERICA	**243.4**	**14**	**123.2**	**51**	**95.1**	**28.1**	**41.9**	**17**	**22.7**	**18.4**	**0.8**
Light Degradation	104.8	6	45.9	19	34.9	11.0	25.8	11	12.7	13.1	0.0
Moderate Degradation	113.5	7	65.1	27	51.9	13.2	16.1	7	10.0	5.3	0.8
Strong Degradation	25.0	1	12.1	5	8.3	3.8	0.0	0	0.0	0.0	0.0
Extreme Degradation	0.0	0	0.0	0	0.0	0.0	0.0	0	0.0	0.0	0.0
ASIA {b}	**748.0**	**20**	**440.6**	**59**	**365.2**	**74.4**	**222.2**	**30**	**165.8**	**47.5**	**8.9**
Light Degradation	294.5	8	124.5	17	99.8	24.7	132.4	18	116.7	15.7	0.0
Moderate Degradation	344.3	9	241.7	32	215.0	26.7	75.1	10	48.9	17.3	8.9
Strong Degradation	107.7	3	73.4	10	50.5	22.9	14.5	2	0.0	14.5	0.0
Extreme Degradation	0.5	0	0.0	0	0.0	0.0	0.2	0	0.2	0.0	0.0
EUROPE {b}	**218.9**	**23**	**114.5**	**52**	**92.8**	**21.8**	**42.2**	**19**	**42.2**	**0.0**	**0.0**
Light Degradation	60.6	6	21.4	10	18.9	2.5	3.2	1	3.2	0.0	0.0
Moderate Degradation	144.4	15	81.0	37	64.7	16.3	38.2	17	38.2	0.0	0.0
Strong Degradation	10.7	1	9.8	4	9.2	0.6	0.0	0	0.0	0.0	0.0
Extreme Degradation	3.1	0	2.4	1	0.0	2.4	0.7	0	0.7	0.0	0.0
OCEANIA	**102.9**	**13**	**82.8**	**81**	**81.7**	**1.1**	**16.4**	**16**	**16.4**	**0.0**	**0.0**
Light Degradation	96.6	12	79.4	77	79.4	0.0	16.3	16	16.3	0.0	0.0
Moderate Degradation	3.9	0	3.2	3	2.2	1.0	0.0	0	0.0	0.0	0.0
Strong Degradation	1.9	0	0.2	0	0.1	0.1	0.1	0	0.1	0.0	0.0
Extreme Degradation	0.4	0	0.0	0	0.0	0.0	0.0	0	0.0	0.0	0.0

Sources: United Nations Environment Programme and International Soil Reference and Information Centre.
Notes: a. Vegetated land is the total of agricultural land and vegetated natural areas.
b. U.S.S.R. east of the Ural Mountains is included under Europe. U.S.S.R. west of the Ural Mountains is included under Asia.
Land surface covered encompasses area between latitudes 72 degrees north and 57 degrees south.
Totals may not add because of rounding.
0 = zero or less than half the unit of measure.
For additional information, see Sources and Technical Notes.

Table 19.4 Causes of Human-Induced Soil Degradation

	Degraded Area {a} (million hectares)	Undegraded Area (million hectares) Permanent Agriculture and Stabilized Terrain	Natural Area	Non-vegetated Land	Vegetation Removal Total Area (million hectares)	As a % of Degraded Area	Overexploitation Total Area (million hectares)	As a % of Degraded Area	Overgrazing Total Area (million hectares)	As a % of Degraded Area	Agricultural Activities Total Area (million hectares)	As a % of Degraded Area	Industrial and Bioindustrial Total Area (million hectares)	As a % of Degraded Area
World	**1,964**	**6,092**	**3,486**	**1,469**	**579**	**30**	**133**	**7**	**679**	**35**	**552**	**28**	**23**	**1**
Africa	494	1,305	435	732	67	14	63	13	243	49	121	24	0	0
North & Central America	158	886	1,019	128	18	11	11	7	38	24	91	57	0	0
South America	243	1,143	354	28	100	41	12	5	68	28	64	26	0	0
Asia {b}	748	1,692	1,329	485	298	40	46	6	197	26	204	27	1	0
Europe {b}	219	624	106	1	84	38	1	0	50	23	64	29	1	0
Oceania	103	441	243	95	12	12	0	0	83	80	8	8	21	9

Sources: United Nations Environment Programme and International Soil Reference and Information Centre.
Notes: a. Refers to area degraded between 1945 and late 1980s.
b. U.S.S.R. east of the Ural Mountains is included under Europe. U.S.S.R. west of the Ural Mountains is included under Asia.
Land surface covered encompasses area between latitudes 72 degrees north and 57 degrees south.
Totals may not add because of rounding.
0 = zero or less than half the unit of measure.
For additional information, see Sources and Technical Notes.

World Resources 1992–93

Table 19.3

Chemical Degradation						Physical Degradation				
Total (million hectares)	As a Percentage of Degraded Area	Types (million hectares)				Total (million hectares)	As a Percentage of Degraded Area	Types (million hectares)		
		Nutrient Loss	Salinization	Pollution	Acidification			Compaction	Waterlogging	Subsidence of Organic Soils
239.1	12	135.3	76.3	21.8	5.7	83.3	4	68.2	10.5	4.6
93.0	5	52.4	34.8	4.1	1.7	44.2	2	34.8	6.0	3.4
103.3	5	63.1	20.4	17.1	2.7	26.8	1	22.1	3.7	1.0
41.9	2	19.8	20.3	0.5	1.3	12.3	1	11.3	0.8	0.2
0.8	0	0.0	0.8	0.0	0.0	0.0	0	0.0	0.0	0.0
61.5	12	45.1	14.8	0.2	1.4	18.7	4	18.2	0.5	0.0
26.0	5	20.4	4.7	0.0	1.1	1.8	0	1.4	0.4	0.0
27.0	5	18.8	7.7	0.2	0.3	8.1	2	8.0	0.1	0.0
8.6	2	6.2	2.4	0.0	0.0	8.8	2	8.8	0.0	0.0
0.0	0	0.0	0.0	0.0	0.0	0.0	0	0.0	0.0	0.0
7.0	4	4.2	2.3	0.4	0.1	5.9	4	1.0	4.9	0.0
0.5	0	0.1	0.3	0.0	0.1	1.3	1	0.5	0.8	0.0
5.7	4	4.0	1.5	0.2	0.0	3.8	2	0.5	3.3	0.0
0.8	1	0.1	0.5	0.2	0.0	0.8	1	0.0	0.8	0.0
0.0	0	0.0	0.0	0.0	0.0	0.0	0	0.0	0.0	0.0
70.3	29	68.2	2.1	0.0	0.0	7.9	3	4.0	3.9	0.0
26.3	11	24.5	1.8	0.0	0.0	6.8	3	2.9	3.9	0.0
31.4	13	31.1	0.3	0.0	0.0	0.8	0	0.8	0.0	0.0
12.6	5	12.6	0.0	0.0	0.0	0.3	0	0.3	0.0	0.0
0.0	0	0.0	0.0	0.0	0.0	0.0	0	0.0	0.0	0.0
73.2	10	14.6	52.7	1.8	4.1	12.1	2	9.8	0.4	1.9
31.8	4	4.6	26.8	0.0	0.4	5.7	1	4.6	0.4	0.7
21.5	3	9.0	8.5	1.5	2.5	6.0	1	5.0	0.0	1.0
19.5	3	1.0	17.0	0.3	1.2	0.4	0	0.2	0.0	0.2
0.4	0	0.0	0.4	0.0	0.0	0.0	0	0.0	0.0	0.0
25.8	12	3.2	3.8	18.6	0.2	36.4	17	33.0	0.8	2.6
8.1	4	2.9	1.0	4.1	0.1	27.9	13	24.8	0.5	2.6
17.1	8	0.3	2.3	14.3	0.1	8.1	4	7.8	0.3	0.0
0.6	0	0.0	0.5	0.1	0.0	0.4	0	0.4	0.0	0.0
0.0	0	0.0	0.0	0.0	0.0	0.0	0	0.0	0.0	0.0
1.3	1	0.4	0.9	0.0	0.0	2.3	2	2.3	0.0	0.0
0.2	0	0.2	0.0	0.0	0.0	0.7	1	0.7	0.0	0.0
0.7	1	0.2	0.5	0.0	0.0	0.0	0	0.0	0.0	0.0
0.0	0	0.0	0.0	0.0	0.0	1.6	2	1.6	0.0	0.0
0.4	0	0.0	0.4	0.0	0.0	0.0	0	0.0	0.0	0.0

Sources and Technical Notes

Table 19.1 Forest Resources

Sources: Food and Agriculture Organization of the United Nations (FAO), Forest Resources Division, *An Interim Report on the State of the Forest Resources in the Developing Countries* (FAO, Rome, 1988); United Nations Economic Commission for Europe and FAO (UNECE/FAO), *The Forest Resources of the ECE Region* (UNECE/FAO, Geneva, 1985); FAO and United Nations Environment Programme (UNEP), *Tropical Forest Resources Assessment Project* (in the framework of GEMS), *Forest Resources of Tropical Africa, Part II: Country Briefs* (FAO/UNEP, Rome, 1981); FAO, Committee on Forestry, Tenth Session, *Interim Report on Forest Resources Assessment 1990 Project* (FAO, Rome, September 1990); FAO, Forest Resources Assessment 1990 Project, *Second Interim Report on the State of Tropical Forests* (10th World Forestry Congress, Paris, September 1991—revised October 15, 1991).

Deforestation data (1981–85) for Algeria, Chile, Islamic Republic of Iran, Morocco, and Tunisia: FAO, unpublished data (FAO, Rome, March 1988); Deforestation data (1980–89) for Argentina: Manuel Winograd, *Deforestación en América Latina (I)*: Magnitud y Causas (Ecological Systems Analysis Group, Fundación Bariloche, Bariloche, Argentina, June 1991). Deforestation data (1989–90) for Brazil: G. Meira, Instituto Nacional de Pesquisas Espaciais (INPE), personal communication (INPE, Saõ José dos Campos, Saõ Paulo, October 1991). Deforestation data (1976–86) for Cameroon. Joint Interagency Planning and Review Mission for the Forestry Sector, *Cameroon Tropical Forestry Action Plan* (Joint Interagency, Rome, 1988). Deforestation data (1973–89) for Costa Rica: Robert Repetto, Wilfrido Cruz, Raúl Solórzano, *et al.*, *Accounts Overdue: Natural Resource Depreciation in Costa Rica* (Tropical Science Center and World Resources Institute, San José, Costa Rica and Washington, D.C., November 1991). Deforestation data (1981–85) for Côte d'Ivoire: Egnankou Wadja Mathieu, personal communication (Institut de la Carte International de la Végétation, Toulouse Cedex, France, March 1991). Deforestation data (1983–87) for India: Forest Survey of India, Ministry of Environment and Forest, *The State of Forest Report 1989* (Government of India, Dehra Dun, India, 1990). Deforestation data (1982–90) for Indonesia: Directorate General of Forest Utilization, Ministry of Forestry, FAO, *Situation and Outlook of the Forestry Sector in Indonesia, Volume 2: Forest Resource Base* (Government of Indonesia, Jakarta, September 1990); Regional Physical Planning Programme for Transmigration (RePPProT) Government of Indonesia, Overseas Development Administration (United Kingdom), *The Land Resources of Indonesia: A National Overview, Main Report* (Government of Indonesia, Jakarta, May 1990). Deforestation data (1979–89) for Malaysia: Forestry Department Headquarters, personal communication (Forestry Department Headquarters, Kuala Lumpur, February 1991). Deforestation data (1981–83) for Mexico: Victor M. Toledo, Julia Carabias, Carlos Toledo, *et al.*, *La Producción Rural en México: Alternativas Ecológicas* (Fundación Universo Veintiuno, Mexico City, 1989). Deforestation data (1984) for Myanmar: U.S. Kyaw, "National Report: Burma," in *Proceedings of Ad Hoc FAO/ECE/FINNIDA Meeting of Experts on Forest Resource Assessment, Kotka, Finland, 26–30 October 1987* (Finnish International Development Agency, Helsinki, 1987); P.E.T. Allen, *A Quick New Appraisal of the Forest Cover of Burma Using LANDSAT Satellite Imagery at 1:1,000,000 scale*, Technical Note 11, FAO/UNEP National Forest Survey and Inventory (FAO/UNEP, n.p., June 1984). Deforestation data (1989–90) for Paraguay: Jörg Henninger and Hugo Huespe Fatecha, "Reforestación y Deforestación en el Paraguay—

Un Análisis," *Revista Forestal,* Vol. VI, No. 3 (December 1990), pp. 4–12. Deforestation data (1980–87) for the Philippines: Republic of the Philippines, *Masterplan for Forestry Development* (Government of the Philippines, Manila, July 1989); David Kummer, *Deforestation in the Post-War Philippines* (University of Chicago Press, Chicago, 1992). Deforestation data (1985–88) for Thailand: Royal Forestry Department of Thailand, Forest Management Division, Ministry of Agriculture and Cooperatives, *The Area of Forest in Thailand in 1988 from LANDSAT Data* (in Thai) (Ministry of Agriculture and Cooperatives, Bangkok, January 1989). Deforestation data (1985) for Viet Nam: Vo Quy, University of Hanoi, "Vietnam's Ecological Situation Today," in *ESCAP Environment News,* Vol. 6, No. 4 (October—December 1988), p. 5; Committee for Rational Utilisation of Natural Resources and Environmental Protection (Programme 5202) with the assistance from the International Union for Conservation of Nature and Natural Resources (IUCN), *Viet Nam National Conservation Strategy* (Draft) (Environmental Services Group, World Wildlife Fund—India, New Delhi, June 1985). Deforestation data (1977–87) for the United States: personal communication (Forest Service, U.S. Department of Agriculture, December 1989).

Reforestation data for Australia, Canada, Democratic People's Republic of Korea, Israel, Japan, New Zealand, Turkey, United States, U.S.S.R. and Europe: FAO, *Forest Resources 1980* (FAO, Rome, 1985).

Reforestation data for China: Stanley D. Richardson, *Forests and Forestry in China: Changing Patterns in Resource Development* (Island Press, Washington, D.C., 1990). Reforestation data for Jordan: Library of Congress, Science and Technology Division, *Draft Environmental Report on Jordan* (Library of Congress, Washington, D.C., August 1979). Reforestation data for South Africa: FAO, unpublished data (FAO, Rome, March 1988). Reforestation data for Yugoslavia: Socijalisticka Federativna Republika Jugoslavija Savenzi Zavod Za Statistiku, *Statisticki Godisnjak Jugoslavija 1983, 1984, 1985* (Savenzi Zavod Za Statistiku, Belgrade, 1984, 1985, 1986).

FAO and UNECE/FAO use slightly different definitions in their assessments, each adapting their definitions to the respective forest ecosystem (tropical and temperate). FAO defines *closed forest* as land where trees cover a high proportion of the ground and where grass does not form a continuous layer on the forest floor. Closed forest in Table 19.1 includes broadleaved forests, coniferous forests, and bamboo forests. UNECE/FAO defines a forest as closed when tree crowns cover more than 20 percent of the area and when the area is used primarily for forestry. *Open forest,* as defined by FAO, consists of mixed forest/grasslands with at least 10 percent tree cover and a continuous grass layer. *Plantation* refers to forest stands established artificially by afforestation and reforestation for industrial and non-industrial usage. The category *other wooded area* encompasses forest fallows (closed and open forests) and shrubs in tropical countries. In the temper-

ate zone, *other wooded area* are forests that are not used for agricultural purposes, have 5—20 percent of their area covered by tree crowns, or have shrubs or stunted trees covering more than 20 percent of their area.

In FAO definitions for tropical forest, "natural" means all stands except plantations and includes stands that have been degraded to some degree by catastrophic fire, logging, agriculture, or acid precipitation. For all regions, trees are distinguished from shrubs on the basis of height: a mature tree has a single well-defined stem and is taller than 7 meters, and a mature shrub is usually less than 7 meters tall.

Average annual deforestation refers to the permanent clearing of forestlands for use in shifting cultivation, permanent agriculture, or settlements. As defined here, deforestation does not include other alterations, such as selective logging (unless the forest cover is permanently reduced to less than 10 percent) that can substantially affect forests, forest soil, wildlife and its habitat, and the global carbon cycle.

Average annual reforestation refers to the establishment of plantations in tropical regions for industrial and nonindustrial uses. Reforestation does not include regeneration of old tree crops (through either natural regeneration or forest management), although some countries may report regeneration as reforestation. Many trees are also planted for nonindustrial uses, such as village wood lots. Reforestation data often exclude this component.

Managed closed forests are those that are managed on the basis of a plan drawn up by professionally qualified foresters or that have some control of use such as harvesting regulations and/or silvicultural treatments.

Protected closed forests include forests used for protection (e.g., watershed management, soil stabilization, avalanche prevention) or conservation in national parks or wilderness areas.

Data for developing countries are based on the 1980 Tropical Forest Resources Assessment, a joint project of FAO and UNEP. The survey assessed the tropical forests of 76 tropical developing countries, covering 97 percent of the total area of developing countries in the tropics. Data for the study were collected from research institutes; correspondence with national forestry services; visits to national forestry, land use, and survey institutions; visits to FAO regional offices; photographic surveys of all or part of five countries; satellite imagery of all or part of 19 countries; and side-looking airborne radar surveys of four additional countries. Three countries—Myanmar, India, and Peru—prepared their own national reports. In many cases, FAO adjusted data to fit common definitions and to correspond to the baseline year of 1980.

The FAO *1988 Interim Report* expanded the country coverage of the 1980 assessment to 129 developing countries. In that document, FAO evaluated the overall reliability of data on closed forest areas and deforestation rates for the original 76 developing countries. FAO classified their estimates on closed forest areas and deforestation as very good or good for 15 countries or parts

of countries (containing 40 percent of the closed forest areas of the 76 tropical countries). These countries or parts of countries are Benin, Brazil (north), Cameroon (south), Colombia, Côte d'Ivoire, The Gambia, Haiti, Liberia, Malaysia (peninsular), Nepal, Paraguay (east), Sierra Leone, Togo, Trinidad and Tobago, and Venezuela. For 40 countries or parts of countries (covering an additional 40 percent of closed forest area), FAO assessed their data on forest cover as very good or good and their data on deforestation as satisfactory or poor. These countries or parts of countries are Angola, Bangladesh, Belize, Bhutan, Bolivia, Burkina Faso, Burundi, Congo (north), Congo (south), Costa Rica, Dominican Republic, El Salvador, French Guiana, Guatemala, Guinea, Guinea Bissau, Guyana, Honduras, India (15%), Jamaica, Kampuchea, Laos, Madagascar, Malaysia (Sabah), Malaysia (Sarawak), Mexico, Mozambique, Myanmar, Namibia (northwest), Nigeria, Panama, Papua New Guinea, Peru, Philippines, Senegal, Sri Lanka, Sudan, Thailand, Viet Nam, and Zaire. Estimates on the forest cover and rate of deforestation in the remaining 21 countries or parts of countries (comprising about 20 percent of the total forest area and 29 percent of the total area of open forest) were judged as satifactory or poor.

More recent or better deforestation estimates are presented to provide the reader with a more current picture. Table 19.1 presents alternative deforestation data for 15 countries, estimates for 12 tropical subregions, and a preliminary global deforestation rate. However, these data must be interpreted with caution because definitions and time period covered vary among the estimates.

Brazil's INPE is currently building a georeferenced data base of the extent of the Brazilian Amazonian forest, including the transitional forests and the forest-like portion of the highland savannah ("cerradão"). This project is scheduled to be completed in 1992. Forest area estimates in this data base are based on satellite imagery taken in 1985, 1988, 1989, 1990, and 1991, include data from two previous surveys in 1975 and 1978 by the Instituto Brazileiro de Desenvolvimento Florestal (IBDF) and INPE, and a vegetation map derived from a synthetic-aperture-radar survey during the 1970s. Additional layers in the data base contain the basic cartography and political subdivision of the Legal Amazon at the county level. Forest coverage data are obtained from visual analysis and digitization of LANDSAT thematic mapper color-composite images on the scale of 1:250,000, with a final effective resolution after digitization of the order of a few hundred meters. Such a data base, combined with information on the date of images and their relationship to the intra-annual seasonal forest felling cycle, and estimates for areas under cloud cover, will yield better estimates of the change in forest cover over the past 17 years in the Legal Amazon of Brazil.

Some results of INPE's LANDSAT surveys are already available, indicating a mean deforestation rate for the Legal Amazon of 2.18 million hectares per year for 1979–90, an annual rate of 1.79 million hectares for 1988–89, and an annual rate of 1.38 million hectares for 1989–90. Although only the completion of the georeferenced data base will reveal the detailed geographical patterns of forest change, it is already known that the 23 percent decrease from 1989 to 1990 was not uniform in the Legal Amazon. The deforestation rate for Rondonia, a state for which deforestation data exist for 1980, 1983, and 1986, is known to have reached a maximum in the mid-1980s, to have decreased toward 1989, and to have increased from 144,000 hectares per year in 1989 to 167,000 hectares per year in 1990. However, in view of the observational uncertainties, such a change is hard to distinguish from a constant rate. In the state of Amapa, cumulative deforestation, although very small, increased from 139,000 hectares to 252,000 hectares per year during the same period.

Available results also indicate that cumulative gross deforestation in the Legal Amazon stood at 41.5 million hectares. Of this total, 0.5 million hectares correspond to the area flooded by hydroelectric dams, an undetermined fraction (which nevertheless is known to be significant in some areas) corresponds to forest regrowth, and about 9.7 million hectares correspond to an area classified as "degraded forest" in the vegetation maps of Brazil (primarily secondary or degraded forest in the states of Pará and Maranhão; also referred to as "old deforestation" by some authors).

The mean rate of 2.18 million hectares per year for the period 1979–90 masks the acceleration of deforestation during the mid-1980s, a climax in the second half of the decade, and a decline since 1988.

The magnitude of the peak rate and the year it occurred remain in doubt. The only published estimate for 1987 (8 million hectares—Alberto Waingort Setzer, Marcos da Costa Pereira, Alfred da Costa Pereira, Jr., and Sérgio Alberto de Oliveira Almeida, "Relatório de Atividades do Projeto IBDF-INPE "SEQE"— Anno 1987," Saõ José dos Campos, Saõ Paulo, Brazil, May 1988) printed in World Resources 1990–91 (along with a lower estimate by INPE for the decade, and a lower estimate by Setzer for 1988) is commonly thought to be an overestimate. That estimate, obtained by correlating the annual rate of deforestation to the number of Advanced Very High Resolution Radiometer (AVHRR) thermal infrared pixels saturated by the presence of surface fires, suffered from three problems. The system could not distinguish between a fire in an area as small as 50 by 50 meters and a fire in an area of 1,100 by 1,100 meters. As many as two thirds of the "fire" pixels assigned to Rondonia were later found to be actually outside Brazil—and Rondonia accounted for 56 percent of the total in that estimate. There is no necessary correlation between new forest clearings and the use of fires (a means of clearing dry biomass of the felled forest as much as recurring agricultural practice). The first two problems also imply that the cataclysmic estimate of

20 million hectares burning in 1987 was an overestimate.

For some states, partial data from comprehensive LANDSAT surveys are available in three-year intervals during the 1980s. Together, they account for about half of the deforestation in the Legal Amazon during that period. If the same general curve shown by those data apply to the rest of the Legal Amazon, the maximum rate of deforestation occurred sometime in the second half of the decade. The same partial data also show that the peak cannot have reached a value as high as 8 million hectares per year in any year, as previously thought.

It is generally believed that there was a peak in the rate of deforestation in 1987, spurred by a constitutional debate about agrarian reform, land speculation, ranching subsidies, and an especially long dry season.

Whatever the exact magnitude of the peak and the exact year it took place, the rate of deforestation in the Legal Amazon has since decreased steadily, if not uniformly, throughout the region. Measures to control the causes of deforestation have been undertaken. They include the suspension of tax credits for new ranching schemes, a more systematic campaign to police illegal forest clearings, the issuance of fines, and a public information campaign. Superimposed upon this downward trend will likely be year-to-year modulations due to varying climatic and economic conditions.

Deforestation occurs also outside the Legal Amazon of Brazil. The most recent estimate, available from FAO, pertains to the period of 1981–85 and puts open forest deforestation at an annual rate of 1.05 million hectares.

In addition, Brazil's National Institute for Amazonian Research is working jointly with INPE to measure biomass and carbon density of the forest, sampled in the areas with high deforestation rates. These new data, expected in 1992, will improve current estimates of carbon density reported, which mostly have referred to areas of dense forest.

The Cameroon study estimated the 1986 area of closed and open forests by extrapolation from 1975 satellite images. It found that between 1.8 million and 2 million hectares had been deforested between 1976 and 1986.

Costa Rica's deforestation rate is based on digital analysis of maps of life zones, soil groups, slopes, geomorphology, and land use, which laid the foundation for a more detailed accounting of Costa Rica's natural resources. The annual deforestation rate of 41,500 hectares depicts changes in Costa Rica's forest cover from 1972–89 more accurately than the previously published rate of 124,000 hectares, which covered the period from 1977–83 and used satellite (LANDSAT) multispectral scanner images.

The Côte d'Ivoire's deforestation estimate is based on government statistics.

The Indian government established the Forest Survey of India to monitor India's

forest cover on a biennial cycle. The latest data from the 1985–87 assessment is based on visual interpretation of images from LANDSAT satellites and puts India's forest cover as follows: forest with a crown density greater than 40 percent extends over 37.85 million hectares; forest with crown density between 10 and 40 percent covers 25.74 million hectares; mangrove forest equals 0.42 million hectares. India's total forest area comes to 64.01 million hectares, equivalent to 19.5 percent of its geographical area.

Reconciliation of the data from a previous 1981–83 assessment by the Forest Survey of India and a 1980–82 assessment by India's National Remote Sensing Agency produced an estimate of 64.2 million hectares, 190,000 hectares more than the 1985–87 number. This computes to an annual loss of 47,500 hectares for the four-year period between the two assessments.

A comparison of these two assessments, however, is only partially valid because of differing scales (1:1 million versus 1:250,000) and different spatial resolution of the satellite scanners (79 meters versus 30 meters). The new deforestation rate contrasts drastically with the rate obtained by comparing the reconciled forest area from 1981–83 with satellite imagery from 1972–75 by the National Remote Sensing Agency. In that period, 10.4 million hectares of dense forest (crown density greater than 40 percent) were lost, equivalent to an annual rate of 1.5 million hectares. However, such sudden changes in the deforestation rate seem to be very unlikely. It can be concluded that all previous assessments have been of very limited value to estimate forest change and have greatly distorted deforestation estimates.

Nevertheless, the data on forest extent from the latest assessment can be used as a baseline since they have been verified by extensive ground truthing. Hence, future estimates of forest change in India will become more accurate, and a true monitoring of forest change on a national scale will be possible.

Indonesia's latest assessment on deforestation used records of the Directorate General of Reforestation and Land Rehabilitation and the Ministry of Forestry. They put the annual rate of deforestation on the Outer Islands at 906,400 hectares for the period 1982–90. If the entire area burned by the fire in Kalimantan is incorporated, Indonesia's annual deforestation reached 1.3 million hectares.

Malaysia's deforestation rate is the latest estimate by the Forestry Departments of Peninsular Malaysia, Sabah and Sarawak.

Mexico's deforestation estimate draws on the work of Toledo, who used information from agricultural censuses, cattle population, and inventories on land use. Toledo calculated an annual deforestation of 1.1 million hectares. The annual deforestation rate could be as high as 1.5 million hectares if additional clearing of forests for agricultural, urban expansion, and forest fires are included.

The deforestation rate for Myanmar is based on aerial photographs, field studies, and satellite imagery.

Paraguay's annual deforestation was estimated at 168,000 hectares for the period from 1985–90 and has soared to an annual rate of 450,000 hectares in the past year. The authors used Paraguay's total harvest of wood—official production statistics and estimates of illegal exports to Brazil—to calculate the extent of deforestation.

Philippine deforestation is derived by comparing 1980 LANDSAT data with land cover statistics that had been prepared by the Swedish Space Corporation using remote sensing.

The estimate for the average annual deforestation of Thailand's total forest area was provided by the Royal Forestry Department and is based on LANDSAT imagery.

The University of Hanoi data came from the Forest Inventory and Planning Institute (FIPI) of the Ministry of Forestry in Hanoi. It estimates that, between 1976 and 1981, Viet Nam's area of rich broadleaf forest was reduced by 865,000 hectares. Current forest loss is estimated at about 200,000 hectares annually.

Please refer to the country sources for additional information.

The deforestation estimates for 12 tropical subregions and the global rate for 1981–90 came from the Forest Resources Assessment 1990 Project, FAO's ongoing appraisal of the world's forest cover and recent trends in deforestation.

In the past two years, FAO developed a consistent methodology to estimate forest cover and change. It uses subnational statistical data on population and socioeconomic variables, maps on vegetation and ecofloristic zones, forest survey data, and images from remote sensing. On the basis of these data, FAO calculated the global and subregional rates of deforestation that include 87 countries. The area deforested annually between 1981 and 1990 is estimated at 16.9 million hectares. A comparison with FAO's previous assessment is possible for 76 countries that were identical in both assessments. It shows that the annual deforestation rate for 1976–80 jumped from 11.3 million hectares (0.6 percent) to 16.9 million hectares (0.9 percent) for the period 1981–90. Two factors were responsible for this 50 percent increase: The 1980 assessment underestimated the rate of deforestation for the period 1976–80, especially in Asia; and conversion of tropical moist forest has accelerated significantly. Not enough data are yet available to estimate the contribution of each factor.

The UNECE/FAO survey covered all types of forests in the 32 member countries of the ECE region (Europe, North America, and the U.S.S.R.). Data for this study were drawn from four types of sources: official data supplied in response to questionnaires; estimates by experts in some countries; recent ECE and FAO publications, country reports, and official articles; and estimates by the professional staff conducting the study. Most data refer to the period around 1980, but no attempt was made to adjust the data to a baseline year.

The UNECE/FAO 1990 survey of temperate-zone countries covers all forests in the 32 countries of the ECE region, as well as forests in Japan, Australia, and New Zealand. Data are being obtained mainly from official sources in response to a questionnaire and are augmented by other sources. It consists of two parts: general forestry inventory data, and the role of forests in supplying environmental and other nonwood goods and services. Preliminary results for Europe point to a continuation during the 1980s of modest growth in the area of forest and other wooded land, and somewhat stronger growth in growing stock and increment, partly as a result of fuller and more accurate inventory coverage. Because of a lack of firm data, the part dealing with nonwood benefits follows a more qualitative approach.

Table 19.2 Wood Production and Trade, 1977–89

Source: Food and Agriculture Organization of the United Nations (FAO), *Agrostat PC* (FAO, Rome, April 1991).

Total roundwood production refers to all wood in the rough, whether destined for industrial or fuelwood uses. All wood felled or harvested from forests and trees outside the forest, with or without bark, round, split, roughly squared, or other forms such as roots and stumps, is included.

Fuel and charcoal production covers all rough wood used for cooking, heating, and power production. Wood intended for charcoal production, pit kilns, and portable ovens is included.

Industrial roundwood production comprises all roundwood products other than fuelwood and charcoal: sawlogs, veneer logs, sleepers, pitprops, pulpwood, and other industrial products.

Processed wood production includes sawnwood and panels. *Sawnwood* is wood that has been sawn, planed, or shaped into products such as planks, beams, boards, rafters, or railroad ties. Wood flooring is excluded. Sawnwood generally is thicker than 5 millimeters. *Panels* include all wood-based panel commodities such as veneer sheets, plywood, particle board, and compressed or noncompressed fiberboard.

Paper production includes newsprint, printing and writing paper, and other paper and paperboard.

Average annual net trade in roundwood is the balance of imports minus exports. Trade in roundwood includes sawlogs and veneer logs, fuelwood, pulpwood, other industrial roundwood, and the roundwood equivalent of trade in charcoal, wood residues, and chips and particles. All trade data refer to both coniferous and nonconiferous wood. Imports are usually on a cost, insurance, freight basis. Exports are generally on a free-on-board basis.

FAO compiles forest products data from responses to annual questionnaires sent to national governments. Data from other sources, such as national statistical yearbooks, are also used. In some cases, FAO prepares its own estimates. FAO continu-

ally revises its data using new information; the latest figures are subject to revision.

Statistics on the production of fuelwood and charcoal are lacking for many countries. FAO uses population data and country-specific, per capita consumption figures to estimate fuelwood and charcoal production. Consumption of nonconiferous fuelwood ranges from a low of 0.0016 cubic meter per capita per year in Jordan to a high of 0.9783 cubic meter per capita per year in Benin. Consumption was also estimated for coniferous fuelwood. For both coniferous and nonconiferous fuelwood, the per capita consumption estimates were multiplied by the number of people in the country to determine national totals.

Table 19.3 Human-Induced Soil Degradation, 1945 to Late 1980s

Sources: L.R. Oldeman, R.T.A. Hakkeling, and W.G. Sombroek, *World Map of the Status of Human-Induced Soil Degradation, an Explanatory Note* (International Soil Reference and Information Centre (ISRIC) and United Nations Environment Programme (UNEP), (ISRIC/UNEP, Wageningen, Netherlands, 1990), and unpublished data (ISRIC, Wageningen, Netherlands, November 1991).

Data presented here are from a series of three digitized soil degradation maps of the world published by ISRIC in 1990. Under the sponsorship of the United Nations Environment Programme, ISRIC brought together some 250 soil scientists and environmental experts to participate in the Global Assessment of Soil Degradation (GLASOD) project. These experts used their knowledge of specific geographic regions to estimate the status of human-induced soil degradation since 1945. Because of the low resolution of the maps (scale 1:15 million) the information derived from these maps is not intended for use at the national level.

GLASOD considers *human-induced soil degradation* to be activities that "lower the current and/or future capability of the soils to produce goods or services." *Degraded area as a percentage of all vegetated land* is the proportion of degraded land to the total of land classified as "degraded", "permanent agriculture and stabilized terrain", and "natural area" (as defined in the technical note for Table 19.4).

The four broad categories of degradation are defined as follows:

Water erosion and *wind erosion* take place through *topsoil loss,* the removal of soil by wind action, or surface wash or sheet erosion caused by water; and *terrain deformation,* which is the uneven displacement of soil. Terrain deformation by wind creates dunes and hollows, whereas deformation by water results in rill and gully formation, landslides, and riverbank destruction. Wind erosion can also take the form of *overblowing,* in which wind-borne soil is deposited on the land surface.

There are four types of *chemical degradation. Nutrient loss* is caused by insufficient manuring or fertilizing of fields in poor or moderately fertile areas. It also occurs when organic matter is lost following the clearing of vegetation. Nutrient loss resulting from the displacement of fertile topsoil by wind or water erosion is counted separately under the "wind erosion" and "water erosion" categories. *Salinization* is an increase in the salt content of soils as a result of three processes: poorly managed irrigation schemes in the semi-arid zones (e.g., using irrigation water with a high salt content, improper drainage of irrigated fields), saltwater intrusion into the groundwater, and the accumulation of salts from saline groundwater or parent rock in the soil because of high moisture evaporation in intensively cultivated agricultural areas. *Pollution* takes place when soils are contaminated by pesticides, urban and industrial wastes, acids from air pollution, oil, and other substances. *Acidification* is the lowering of soil pH through the overapplication of fertilizers or from drainage of pyrite-containing soils (which causes the pyrite to oxidize into sulfuric and other acids).

Physical degradation can take place in three ways: through *compaction*, whereby soil structure deteriorates because of trampling by cattle or heavy machinery, resulting in soil crusting and sealing when it rains; *waterlogging*, which is the flooding or inundation of soils as a result of human interference with natural drainage systems (land flooded to make rice paddies is not included); and *subsidence of organic soils*, which occurs when the agricultural potential of the land is adversely effected by drainage and/or oxidation.

Experts in the GLASOD project made qualitative evaluations of the degree of degradation resulting from the activities listed above. They considered the agricultural suitability of the soil, its biotic functions,

and any decline in productivity as a basis for defining four degrees of degradation:

■ *Light degradation* has occurred where there has been only a small decline in agricultural productivity, where biotic functions are largely intact, and where soils can be fully restored, given changes in ongoing land-use practices

■ *Moderate degradation* still permits continuing agricultural use of an area, but with greatly reduced productivity. Biotic functions are only partly destroyed. Restoration is possible given major changes in land-use practices.

■ *Strong degradation* has occurred when agricultural use under local land use management is no longer possible and most biotic functions have been destroyed. Restoration is possible, at a high cost.

■ *Extreme degradation* has occurred when the area has become unsuitable for agriculture and is beyond restoration. Biotic functions are completely destroyed.

Table 19.4 Causes of Human-Induced Soil Degradation

Sources: L.R. Oldeman, R.T.A. Hakkeling, and W.G. Sombroek, *World Map of the Status of Human-Induced Soil Degradation, an Explanatory Note* (International Soil Reference and Information Centre (ISRIC) and United Nations Environment Programme (UNEP), (ISRIC/UNEP, Wageningen, Netherlands, 1990), and unpublished data (ISRIC, Wageningen, Netherlands, November, 1991).

Data presented here are from a series of 3 digitized soil degradation maps of the world published by ISRIC in 1990. For details on this project, the Global Assessment

of Soil Degradation (GLASOD) project, refer to the technical note for Table 19.3.

Degraded area refers to land affected by all degrees of human-induced soil degradation, as described in the technical note for Table 19.3. *Permanent agriculture and stabilized terrain* consist of undegraded land under permanent agriculture and land stabilized through reforestation, terracing, gully control, and other conservation practices. *Natural area* is land where few human activities take place, that is where the land is unsuitable for agriculture because of low temperatures, steep slopes, poor drainage, and poor soils, or because the areas in question are remotely located. This category includes rainforest areas, parks and other protected areas, and semidesert regions. *Nonvegetated land* consists of active dunes, salt flats, rock outcrops, deserts, ice caps, and arid mountain regions.

GLASOD identifies five causes of soil degradation:

■ *Vegetation removal* entails the removal of vegetative cover through agricultural clearing, logging, or development.

■ *Overexploitation* is the decrease in soil cover through removal of vegetation for fuelwood, sfencing, and so on.

■ *Overgrazing* by livestock leads to a decrease in vegetative cover and trampling of soil.

■ *Agricultural activities* include insufficient or excessive use of manure and fertilizers; cultivation on steep slopes or in arid areas without proper anti-erosion measures; improper irrigation; and use of heavy machinery on soils with weak structural stability.

■ *Industrial and bioindustrial activities* result in soils contaminated with pollutants, for example, through waste discharge, overuse of pesticides, and excessive fertilization.

20. Wildlife and Habitat

The world's biological resources—its species, habitats, and ecosystems—are under threat from growing populations, unsustainable consumption patterns, pollution, wasteful resource use, and global change. By damaging the highly diverse ecosystems that support the world's species, we alter hydrological cycles and climate and degrade soil-building and pollutant-absorbing mechanisms.

One traditional approach to protecting the world's biodiversity has been to establish parks and reserves that protect selected lands—often representative ecosystems—from development. Table 20.1 lists the amount of land contained in national and international protected areas by categories of protection for countries and regions. As Table 20.1 shows, almost 5 percent of the world's land mass is now either totally or partially protected as parks and reserves, not including Antarctica. For many countries, little natural habitat remains outside protected areas. (For information on habitat extent and loss, see Table 20.4 in *World Resources 1990–91*.) Of the continents, Europe has the second highest percentage of land (7.5 percent) under a park and reserve system; 7.9 million hectares of this (21 percent) are fully protected, representing virtually all the available natural habitat left in the region.

Other regions have significant amounts of unprotected natural areas remaining. Although Asia has one of the lowest percentages of land protected (3.2 percent), 13 percent of its land mass is considered wilderness. (See Chapter 17, "Land Cover and Settlements.")

Table 20.2 presents data on trade in plants, animals, and animal products. To prevent the wholesale loss of species in the face of world demand, parties to the Convention on International Trade in Endangered Species of Wild Flora and Fauna (CITES) pledge to abide by certain regulations and to report trade in designated animals and animal products to the Secretariat of CITES.

Table 20.3 gives the results of a survey of threats to World Heritage Sites, the most recent global survey of a protected area system. Regional tallies show that development is the most commonly reported threat in North and Central America (57 percent of sites), Europe (45 percent of sites), and Oceania (70 percent of sites). Inadequate or insufficient management was the most commonly reported problem in Asia, as was illegal or overharvest of wildlife in Africa, and fire and natural threats in South American sites.

Tables 20.4 and 20.5 present current data on the status of the world's rare and threatened wildlife and plant species. Data are most complete for plants; whereas very little is known about the total and threatened numbers of reptiles, amphibians, and fish.

Table 20.5 includes three measures of threats to countries' plant diversity. The numbers of threatened species reflect both the degree of biological diversity and the size of the country. Over 70 percent of South American countries and territories report a minimum of 50 threatened taxa, the highest percentage of any region. When the number of threatened species is compared on a per-unit-area basis, 56 percent of countries in Oceania report at least 40 threatened plant taxa per 10,000 square kilometers as contrasted with only 31 percent of countries in South America. Oceania also has the greatest number of countries with over 5 percent of their known plant species considered to be threatened. In part, this reflects the vulnerability of endemic island species in Oceania to introductions of exotic plants and animals as well as habitat loss. National totals also reflect differences in how thoroughly taxa have been catalogued and monitored.

Table 20.6 presents a list of officially sanctioned and funded debt-for-nature swaps. The debt-for-nature swap is an innovative conservation financing instrument developed in response to environmental problems as well as the debt crisis in the developing world. In a swap, a country's foreign debt is purchased by an outside organization. In exchange, the debtor nation pays off this loan in local currency by funding a previously determined local conservation program.

So far, debt-for-nature swaps have reduced external debt by approximately $100 million. Although these swaps have added significantly to participating countries' conservation funds, their effect on the developing countries' total external debt of approximately $1.2 trillion has been negligible.

Costa Rica has had the largest volume of debt-for-nature swaps. As shown in Table 20.6, $12.5 million in grants and donations were used to purchase Costa Rican debt nominally worth some $80 million. This debt has been exchanged for nearly $43 million in local currency bonds, which have been used to support various local conservation initiatives, including training, research, public awareness, land acquisition, and protection.

Table 20.1 National and International Protection of Natural

	All Protected Areas		Totally Protected Areas (IUCN categories I-III)		Partially Protected Areas (IUCN categories IV, V)		Percent of National Land Area Protected	Marine and Coastal Protected Areas {b}		Biosphere Reserves		Number of Natural World Heritage Sites	Wetlands of International Importance	
	Number	Area (000 ha)	Number	Area (000 ha)	Number	Area (000 ha)		Number	Area (000 ha)	Number	Area (000 ha)		Number	Area (000 ha)
WORLD	6,931	651,290	2,357	378,505	4,574	272,785	4.8	977	211,406	283	152,520	92	503	30,217
AFRICA	601	117,088	241	86,294	360	30,794	3.9	43	9,570	40	20,056	26	33	3,190
Algeria	19	11,898	12	11,787	7	110	5.0	1	2	1	7,200	1 c	2	5
Angola	6	2,692	1	790	5	1,902	2.2	2	62	--	--	--	--	--
Benin	2	844	2	844	0	0	7.5	0	0	1	880	0	--	--
Botswana	9	10,025	4	8,787	5	1,238	17.2	NA	NA	--	--	--	--	--
Burkina Faso	7	739	3	440	4	299	2.7	NA	NA	1	16	0	3	X
Burundi	1	38	0	0	1	38	1.4	NA	NA	--	--	0	--	--
Cameroon	13	2,100	8	1,558	5	542	4.4	1	160	3	850	1	--	--
Cape Verde	0	0	0	0	0	0	0.0	0	0	--	--	0	--	--
Central African Rep	7	3,904	3	2,896	4	1,008	6.3	NA	NA	2	1,640	1	--	--
Chad	1	114	1	114	0	0	0.1	NA	NA	--	--	--	1	195
Comoros	0	0	0	0	0	0	0.0	0	0	--	--	--	--	--
Congo	10	1,333	1	127	9	1,207	3.9	1	300	2	172	0	--	--
Cote d'Ivoire	12	2,020	10	1,918	2	102	6.3	1	30	2	1,480	3 d	--	--
Djibouti	1	10	1	10	0	0	0.4	0	0	--	--	--	--	--
Egypt	9	685	3	38	6	647	0.7	3	62	1	1	0	2	106
Equatorial Guinea	0	0	0	0	0	0	0.0	0	0	--	--	--	--	--
Ethiopia	24	6,223	13	3,240	11	2,982	5.1	1	200	--	--	1	--	--
Gabon	5	1,790	1	480	4	1,310	6.7	2	1,058	1	15	0	3	1,080
Gambia, The	2	12	2	12	0	0	1.1	0	0	--	--	--	--	--
Ghana	8	1,075	6	1,062	2	12	4.5	0	0	1	8	0	1	7
Guinea	2	129	2	129	0	0	0.5	0	0	2	133	1 d	--	--
Guinea-Bissau	0	0	0	0	0	0	0.0	0	0	--	--	--	1	39
Kenya	36	3,347	30	3,277	6	70	5.8	3	7	4	851	0	1	19
Lesotho	1	7	0	0	1	7	0.2	NA	NA	--	--	--	--	--
Liberia	1	131	1	131	0	0	1.2	0	0	--	--	--	--	--
Libya	3	155	1	35	2	120	0.1	0	0	--	--	0	--	--
Madagascar	36	1,078	15	703	21	375	1.8	1	2	1	140	1	--	--
Malawi	9	1,067	5	698	4	369	9.0	NA	NA	--	--	1	--	--
Mali	7	889	1	350	6	539	0.7	NA	NA	1	771	1 c	1	1,173
Mauritania	3	1,733	2	1,483	1	250	1.7	0	0	--	--	1	1	1,173
Mauritius	3	4	0	0	3	4	2.2	1	4	--	--	--	--	--
Morocco	11	368	6	88	5	280	0.8	2	13	--	--	0	4	11
Mozambique	1	2	0	0	1	2	0.0	0	0	--	--	0	--	--
Namibia	9	10,346	4	8,926	5	1,420	12.6	X	X	--	--	--	--	--
Niger	4	1,654	2	1,501	2	154	1.3	NA	NA	--	--	0	1	220
Nigeria	15	1,547	1	534	14	1,013	1.7	0	0	1	0	0	--	--
Rwanda	2	327	2	327	0	0	12.4	NA	NA	1	15	0	--	--
Senegal	10	2,181	6	1,012	4	1,168	11.1	4	81	3	1,094	2	4	100
Sierra Leone	3	101	0	0	3	101	1.4	0	0	--	--	--	--	--
Somalia	0	0	0	0	0	0	0.0	0	0	--	--	--	--	--
South Africa	178	6,310	14	3,094	164	3,215	5.2	13	152	--	--	--	7	208
Sudan	13	7,732	7	6,873	6	859	3.1	0	0	2	1,901	0	--	--
Swaziland	3	40	0	0	3	40	2.3	NA	NA	--	--	--	--	--
Tanzania	20	11,913	11	3,913	9	8,000	12.6	0	0	2	2,338	4	--	--
Togo	11	647	3	357	8	290	11.4	0	0	--	--	--	--	--
Tunisia	7	45	6	42	1	3	0.3	1	4	4	32	1	1	13
Uganda	19	1,756	4	770	15	986	7.4	0	0	1	220	0	1	15
Zaire	9	8,827	8	8,794	1	33	3.8	0	0	3	298	4	--	--
Zambia	20	6,361	20	6,361	0	0	8.5	NA	NA	--	--	1 d	--	--
Zimbabwe	21	2,831	13	2,737	8	94	7.2	NA	NA	--	--	2 d	--	--
NORTH & CENTRAL AMERICA {e}	1,640	232,689	590	142,050	1,050	90,638	10.4	214	135,781	67	93,618	20	58	15,147
Barbados	0	0	0	0	0	0	0.0	0	0	--	--	--	--	--
Belize	8	74	1	4	7	70	3.2	X	X	--	--	--	--	--
Canada	426	49,452	138	26,813	288	22,639	5.0	48	7,106	6	1,050	6 d	30	12,938
Costa Rica	28	606	17	476	11	130	11.9	7	194	2	729	1 d	--	--
Cuba	29	714	18	443	11	272	6.4	6	227	4	324	0	--	--
Dominican Rep	1	7	1	7	0	0	0.1	7	270	--	--	0	--	--
El Salvador	9	26	6	21	3	6	1.2	0	0	--	--	--	--	--
Guatemala	9	88	3	69	6	19	0.8	3	13	--	--	1 c	1	X
Haiti	2	8	2	8	0	0	0.3	0	0	--	--	--	--	--
Honduras	34	709	14	589	20	121	6.3	1	350	1	500	1	--	--
Jamaica	0	0	0	0	0	0	0.0	0	0	--	--	0	--	--
Mexico	61	9,420	47	2,223	14	7,197	4.8	11	1,119	6	1,288	1	1	47
Nicaragua	6	43	3	27	3	16	0.3	1	4	--	--	0	--	--
Panama	16	1,326	13	1,195	3	131	17.2	6	898	1	597	2 d	--	--
Trinidad and Tobago	6	15	0	0	6	15	3.0	2	3	--	--	--	--	--
United States	968	98,342	304	38,471	664	59,871	10.5	107	54,317	43	19,108	9 d	8	1,116
SOUTH AMERICA	552	101,351	280	52,278	272	49,072	5.7	94	24,717	24	11,919	9	5	232
Argentina	113	12,639	34	2,269	79	10,370	4.6	7	1,499	5	2,410	2	--	--
Bolivia	23	6,774	8	2,678	15	4,097	6.2	NA	NA	3	435	0	1	5
Brazil	162	20,525	90	13,906	72	6,619	2.4	20	2,032	--	--	1	--	--
Chile	65	13,650	32	8,378	33	5,271	18.0	32	10,050	7	2,407	0	1	5
Colombia	42	9,302	36	9,254	6	47	8.2	9	615	3	2,514	0	--	--
Ecuador	14	10,686	9	2,657	5	8,028	37.7	5	8,975	2	1,446	2	--	--
Guyana	1	12	1	12	0	0	0.1	0	0	--	--	--	--	--
Paraguay	12	1,186	8	1,157	4	29	2.9	NA	NA	--	--	0	--	--
Peru	24	5,518	13	2,531	11	2,987	4.3	4	710	3	2,507	4 c	--	--
Suriname	14	763	6	553	8	210	4.7	5	128	--	--	--	1	12
Uruguay	8	32	2	15	6	16	0.2	1	3	1	200	0	1	200
Venezuela	74	20,265	41	8,869	33	11,396	22.2	11	704	--	--	--	1	10

Areas, 1990

Table 20.1

	National Protection Systems							Marine and Coastal Protected Areas {b}		International Protection Systems {a}				
	All Protected Areas		Totally Protected Areas (IUCN categories I-III)		Partially Protected Areas (IUCN categories IV, V)		Percent of National Land Area Protected			Biosphere Reserves		Number of Natural World Heritage Sites	Wetlands of International Importance	
	Number	Area (000 ha)	Number	Area (000 ha)	Number	Area (000 ha)		Number	Area (000 ha)	Number	Area (000 ha)		Number	Area (000 ha)
ASIA	1,392	90,607	389	34,021	1,003	56,587	3.2	189	13,987	36	7,438	12	40	1,354
Afghanistan	4	142	0	0	4	142	0.2	NA	NA	--	--	0	--	--
Bahrain	0	0	0	0	0	0	0.0	0	0	--	--	--	--	--
Bangladesh	8	97	0	0	8	97	0.7	3	32	--	--	0	--	--
Bhutan	7	924	2	68	5	856	19.7	NA	NA	--	--	--	--	--
Cambodia	0	0	0	0	0	0	0.0	0	0	--	--	--	--	--
China	289	21,947	4	101	285	21,846	2.3	20	1,184	7	1,819	2 c	--	--
Cyprus	0	0	0	0	0	0	0.0	0	0	--	--	0	--	--
India	359	13,481	59	3,525	300	9,956	4.1	14	474	--	--	5	6	193
Indonesia	169	17,800	98	13,133	71	4,667	9.3	68	8,941	6	1,482	0	--	--
Iran, Islamic Rep	60	7,529	27	2,986	33	4,543	4.6	3	725	9	2,610	0	18	1,088
Iraq	0	0	0	0	0	0	0.0	0	0	--	--	0	--	--
Israel	18	226	1	31	17	195	10.9	1	31	--	--	--	--	--
Japan	65	2,402	21	1,308	44	1,094	6.4	30	637	4	116	--	3	10
Jordan	7	93	1	1	6	92	1.0	0	0	--	--	0	1	7
Korea, Dem People's Rep	2	58	1	44	1	14	0.5	0	0	1	132	--	--	--
Korea, Rep	17	578	0	0	17	578	5.8	3	285	1	37	0	--	--
Kuwait	0	0	0	0	0	0	0.0	0	0	--	--	0	--	--
Lao People's Dem Rep	0	0	0	0	0	0	0.0	NA	NA	--	--	0	--	--
Lebanon	1	4	1	4	0	0	0.3	0	0	--	--	0	--	--
Malaysia	45	1,162	39	864	6	298	3.5	9	52	--	--	0	--	--
Mongolia	14	5,618	14	5,618	0	0	3.6	NA	NA	--	--	0	--	--
Myanmar	2	173	1	161	1	13	0.3	0	0	--	--	--	--	--
Nepal	11	959	7	864	4	94	6.8	NA	NA	--	--	2	1	18
Oman	2	54	0	0	2	54	0.3	1	1	--	--	0	--	--
Pakistan	53	3,655	6	882	47	2,773	4.6	1	16	1	31	0	9	21
Philippines	28	584	15	237	13	347	1.9	5	31	2	1,174	0	--	--
Qatar	0	0	0	0	0	0	0.0	0	0	--	--	0	--	--
Saudi Arabia	7	5,619	2	325	5	5,294	2.6	2	475	--	--	0	--	--
Singapore	1	3	0	0	1	3	4.4	0	0	--	--	--	--	--
Sri Lanka	43	784	14	492	29	292	11.9	6	303	2	9	1	1	6
Syrian Arab Rep	0	0	0	0	0	0	0.0	0	0	--	--	0	--	--
Thailand	83	5,106	55	2,842	28	2,264	10.0	10	625	3	26	0	--	--
Turkey	18	269	12	196	6	73	0.3	3	114	--	--	2 c	--	--
United Arab Emirates	0	0	0	0	0	0	0.0	0	0	--	--	--	--	--
Viet Nam	58	892	7	142	51	750	2.7	2	34	--	--	0	1	12
Yemen (Arab Rep)	0	0	0	0	0	0	0.0	0	0	--	--	0	--	--
(People's Dem Rep)	0	0	0	0	0	0	0.0	0	0	--	--	0	--	--
EUROPE	1,658	36,813	266	7,909	1,392	28,904	7.5	180	7,700	83	3,853	14	311	2,790
Albania	13	55	6	23	7	32	1.9	5	28	--	--	0	--	--
Austria	129	1,594	0	0	129	1,594	19.0	NA	NA	4	28	--	5	102
Belgium	2	72	0	0	2	72	2.4	0	0	--	--	--	6	10
Bulgaria	39	129	29	113	10	16	1.2	0	0	17	25	2	4	2
Czechoslovakia	61	1,964	11	215	50	1,748	15.4	NA	NA	6	364	--	8	17
Denmark	65	423	6	15	59	407	9.8	3	12	--	--	0	27	734
Finland	35	807	33	505	2	302	2.4	0	0	--	--	0	11	101
France	81	4,779	9	278	72	4,501	8.7	27	849	5	503	1	1	85
German (Fed Rep)	54	2,956	1	13	53	2,943	27.3	9	725	1	13	0	21	315
(Dem Rep)	225	1,998	0	0	225	1,998	8.0	5	8	2	25	0	8	46
Greece	20	104	10	71	10	33	0.8	13	84	2	9	2 c	11	107
Hungary	46	511	0	0	46	511	5.5	0	0	5	129	0	13	110
Iceland	22	916	9	219	13	697	8.9	5	509	--	--	--	2	58
Ireland	6	27	3	22	3	4	0.4	0	0	2	9	--	21	13
Italy	108	1,301	3	126	105	1,175	4.0	18	411	3	4	0	45	54
Luxembourg	0	0	0	0	0	0	0.0	NA	NA	--	--	0	--	--
Malta	0	0	0	0	0	0	0.0	0	0	--	--	0	1	0
Netherlands	68	355	26	230	42	125	9.5	10	54	--	--	--	11	306
Norway	68	4,767	42	4,552	26	215	14.7	12	3,508	1	1,555	0	14	16
Poland	78	2,230	13	135	65	2,095	7.1	4	73	4	26	1	5	7
Portugal	21	454	4	103	17	350	4.9	8	132	1	0	0	2	31
Romania	36	562	2	69	34	493	2.4	0	0	3	41	--	--	--
Spain	161	3,511	9	123	152	3,388	7.0	9	75	10	615	1	17	99
Sweden	99	1,758	15	589	84	1,169	3.9	5	12	1	97	0	30	383
Switzerland	15	111	1	17	14	94	2.7	NA	NA	1	17	0	2	2
United Kingdom	138	4,639	1	4	137	4,635	18.9	35	1,194	13	44	3	44	173
Yugoslavia	68	791	33	485	35	307	3.1	12	227	2	350	4	2	18
U.S.S.R.	176	24,074	170	23,802	6	272	1.1	22	4,925	20	10,891	0	12	2,987
OCEANIA	911	48,632	421	32,151	490	16,481	5.7	229	14,547	13	4,745	11	44	4,516
Australia	728	45,654	355	29,575	373	16,079	5.9	184	13,035	12	4,743	8 c	39	4,478
Fiji	2	5	2	5	0	0	0.3	1	4	--	--	--	--	--
New Zealand	152	2,839	52	2,517	100	322	10.5	32	1,386	--	--	3	5	38
Papua New Guinea	5	29	3	7	2	22	0.1	0	0	--	--	--	--	--
Solomon Islands	0	0	0	0	0	0	0.0	0	0	--	--	--	--	--

Sources: United Nations Educational, Scientific and Cultural Organization and World Conservation Monitoring Centre.
Notes: a. Areas listed often include nationally protected systems. b. 1989 data. c. Includes one or more mixed natural/cultural sites. d. Includes one international heritage site.
e. Regional totals include Greenland.
World totals for national and international protection systems exclude Antarctica. World and regional totals include countries not listed.
0 = zero or less than half the unit of measurement; NA = not applicable; -- = country is not a party to the convention.
For additional information, see Sources and Technical Notes.

Table 20.2 Trade in Wildlife and Wildlife Products Reported

	CITES Reporting Requirement Met {a} (percent)	Mammals Live Primates (number) Imports	Exports	Cat Skins (number) Imports	Exports	Birds Live Parrots (number) Imports	Exports	Reptiles Reptile Skins {b} (number) Imports	Exports	Plants Live Cacti (hundreds) Imports	Exports	Live Orchids (hundreds) Imports	Exports
WORLD {c}		41,644	41,644	136,825	136,825	625,595	625,595	6,634,678	6,634,678	79,120	79,120	68,542	68,542
AFRICA		30	9,051	217	1,109	30,233	177,363	15,661	775,117	4	552	501	6
Algeria	50	X	X	X	X	4	0	X	X	X	X	X	X
Angola {d}	NA	X	X	X	X	0	6	X	X	X	X	X	X
Benin	0	X	X	X	X	X	X	0	3,469	X	X	X	X
Botswana	83	X	X	193	0	1	0	363	0	X	X	X	X
Burkina Faso	X	X	X	X	X	0	9	X	X	X	X	X	X
Burundi	0	X	X	X	X	0	1	X	X	X	X	1	0
Cameroon	91	0	129	11	0	0	14,191	0	148,510	1	0	X	X
Cape Verde {d}	NA	X	X	X	X	X	X	X	X	X	X	X	X
Central African Rep	60	X	X	0	43	0	465	X	X	X	X	X	X
Chad	0	X	X	X	X	X	X	0	35,710	X	X	X	X
Comoros {d}	NA	X	X	X	X	1	0	X	X	X	X	2	0
Congo	100	0	1	0	1	0	36	0	1,358	X	X	X	X
Cote d'Ivoire {d}	NA	X	X	X	X	0	1,053	0	46	X	X	0	0
Djibouti {d}	NA	X	X	X	X	X	X	X	X	X	X	X	X
Egypt	0	16	0	1	0	1,412	0	X	X	X	X	X	X
Equatorial Guinea {d}	NA	0	6	X	X	0	50	X	X	X	X	X	X
Ethiopia	0	0	1,084	0	7	3	0	X	X	X	X	X	X
Gabon	100	X	X	10	0	2	0	0	1	X	X	X	X
Gambia, The	30	X	X	X	X	X	X	X	X	X	X	X	X
Ghana	85	0	147	X	X	0	4,141	0	345	X	X	0	0
Guinea	56	0	7	0	1	0	29,878	0	18,434	X	X	X	X
Guinea-Bissau	X	X	X	0	59	0	1	0	932	X	X	X	X
Kenya	36	0	3,291	0	5	0	7	0	1,400	X	X	18	0
Lesotho {d}	NA	X	X	X	X	X	X	X	X	X	X	X	X
Liberia	89	0	3	0	1	0	7,693	0	5	X	X	0	0
Libya {d}	NA	12	0	X	X	8	0	X	X	X	X	X	X
Madagascar	93	X	X	X	X	0	12,657	0	3,177	X	X	0	5
Malawi	88	X	X	0	7	X	X	0	1,830	X	X	X	X
Mali {d}	NA	X	X	X	X	0	996	0	406,312	X	X	X	X
Mauritania {d}	NA	X	X	X	X	X	X	X	X	X	X	X	X
Mauritius	81	0	1,436	X	X	304	0	16	0	X	X	2	0
Morocco	36	0	33	X	X	26	0	342	0	0	496	X	X
Mozambique	44	0	2	1	0	X	X	0	795	X	X	X	X
Namibia	X	X	X	0	84	58	0	0	4	X	X	X	X
Niger	47	1	0	X	X	X	X	X	X	X	X	X	X
Nigeria	20	1	0	0	14	0	20	0	2,384	X	X	0	0
Rwanda	11	X	X	X	X	X	X	X	X	X	X	X	X
Senegal	92	0	645	1	0	0	33,729	0	9,200	X	X	X	X
Sierra Leone {d}	NA	X	X	X	X	0	1	0	5	X	X	X	X
Somalia	25	X	X	X	X	X	X	X	X	X	X	X	X
South Africa	93	0	23	0	634	26,165	0	14,940	0	0	55	476	0
Sudan	29	X	X	X	X	5	0	0	106,702	X	X	X	X
Swaziland {d}	NA	X	X	X	X	1,755	0	X	X	X	X	X	X
Tanzania	80	0	2,160	0	70	0	65,091	0	2,318	X	X	X	X
Togo	73	0	504	X	X	0	5,985	0	16,415	X	X	X	X
Tunisia	100	X	X	0	70	10	0	0	399	X	X	X	X
Uganda	X	X	X	X	X	0	3	0	1	X	X	X	X
Zaire	64	0	83	0	11	0	348	0	8	X	X	X	X
Zambia	56	X	X	0	38	0	1,002	0	3,754	X	X	X	X
Zimbabwe	78	0	1	0	148	537	0	0	11,607	3	0	2	0
NORTH & CENTRAL AMERICA		14,931	1,672	740	28,763	287,655	29,813	1,867,491	22,723	27,824	12,638	2,235	316
Barbados {d}	NA	0	625	X	X	58	0	X	X	6	0	8	0
Belize	67	X	X	X	X	0	10	X	X	X	X	0	73
Canada	100	864	0	0	9,160	6,191	0	119,726	0	0	8,019	632	0
Costa Rica	73	5	0	0	1	0	4,632	X	X	0	0	0	26
Cuba	X	5	0	X	X	0	181	X	X	0	0	0	0
Dominican Rep	0	X	X	X	X	444	0	X	X	0	4,578	43	0
El Salvador	0	X	X	0	2	81	0	X	X	X	X	2	0
Guatemala	70	1	0	0	1	116	0	X	X	0	0	2	0
Haiti {d}	NA	X	X	X	X	0	3	X	X	0	20	7	0
Honduras	40	0	532	0	3	0	24,515	0	15,253	X	X	0	123
Jamaica {d}	NA	X	X	X	X	0	3	X	X	0	0	0	14
Mexico	X	244	0	0	56	3,111	0	106,457	0	0	20	0	151
Nicaragua	85	0	11	X	X	0	479	X	X	X	X	X	X
Panama	83	X	X	740	0	120	0	0	7,470	X	X	0	2
Trinidad and Tobago	50	1	0	X	X	102	0	X	X	1	0	20	0
United States	87	13,811	0	0	19,540	277,432	0	1,641,308	0	27,817	0	1,520	0
SOUTH AMERICA		7	4,335	4	15,032	84	274,577	12,341	2,378,707	0	17,375	8	1,469
Argentina	100	0	25	0	15,015	0	179,762	0	1,747,153	0	10	0	0
Bolivia	55	X	X	0	1	0	4	0	93,708	0	30	0	0
Brazil	27	0	61	2	0	58	0	8,984	0	0	17,326	0	1,044
Chile	60	7	0	0	1	0	826	3,350	0	0	0	0	0
Colombia	67	0	7	0	5	0	21	0	74,173	X	X	0	85
Ecuador	71	0	1	0	1	0	10	X	X	0	0	7	0
Guyana	62	0	3,694	0	3	0	26,935	0	72,521	X	X	0	1
Paraguay	54	X	X	0	4	0	3	0	20	0	8	0	29
Peru	67	0	543	X	X	0	16,760	7	0	0	0	0	274
Suriname	100	X	X	2	0	0	9,719	X	X	X	X	0	1
Uruguay	67	X	X	X	X	0	40,537	0	29,838	0	0	0	0
Venezuela	67	0	4	0	2	26	0	0	92,294	0	0	0	34

by CITES, 1988 — Table 20.2

	CITES Reporting Requirement Met {a} (percent)	Mammals — Live Primates (number) Imports	Live Primates Exports	Cat Skins (number) Imports	Cat Skins Exports	Birds — Live Parrots (number) Imports	Live Parrots Exports	Reptiles — Reptile Skins {b} (number) Imports	Reptile Skins Exports	Plants — Live Cacti (hundreds) Imports	Live Cacti Exports	Live Orchids (hundreds) Imports	Live Orchids Exports
ASIA		10,584	25,968	39,507	89,656	76,301	135,210	1,903,216	3,704,116	166,418	27,586	51,923	65,694
Afghanistan	0	X	X	X	X	X	X	X	X	X	X	X	X
Bahrain {d}	NA	X	X	X	X	373	0	X	X	X	X	X	X
Bangladesh	100	2	0	X	X	1,238	0	X	X	X	X	X	X
Bhutan {d}	NA	X	X	X	X	X	X	X	X	X	X	X	X
Cambodia {d}	NA	0	5	X	X	X	X	X	X	X	X	X	X
China	100	0	2,199	0	89,650	118	0	0	65,665	15	0	0	1,056
Cyprus	33	X	X	7	0	451	0	0	1	4	0	0	0
Hong Kong	100	0	37	1,772	0	8,441	0	267,393	0	350	0	232	0
India	100	0	4	X	X	0	8,781	0	3,821	1	0	0	24
Indonesia	91	0	11,851	X	X	0	87,830	0	3,032,189	0	9	109	0
Iran, Islamic Rep	29	X	X	X	X	X	X	X	X	X	X	X	X
Iraq {d}	NA	X	X	X	X	8	0	X	X	20	0	X	X
Israel	0	82	0	X	X	2,242	0	8,064	0	X	X	X	X
Japan	100	7,133	0	34,696	0	35,097	0	950,047	0	0	20,589	47,426	0
Jordan	27	X	X	1	0	10,248	0	X	X	X	X	X	X
Korea, Dem People's Rep {d}	NA	2	0	X	X	X	X	X	X	X	X	11	0
Korea, Rep {d}	NA	5	0	2,861	0	363	0	25,199	0	0	6,988	4,139	0
Kuwait {d}	NA	2	0	1	0	1,127	0	X	X	3	0	X	X
Lao People's Dem Rep {d}	NA	0	201	X	X	X	X	X	X	X	X	X	X
Lebanon {d}	NA	1	0	14	0	51	0	346	0	0	0	0	0
Malaysia	83	45	0	0	1	0	6,818	0	238,205	170	0	0	323
Mongolia {d}	NA	X	X	X	X	X	X	X	X	X	X	X	X
Myanmar {d}	NA	0	52	X	X	0	597	X	X	X	X	X	X
Nepal	80	X	X	0	2	35	0	X	X	X	X	0	0
Oman {d}	NA	3	0	X	X	72	0	X	X	8	0	0	0
Pakistan	100	X	X	2	0	0	6,394	0	4	0	0	X	X
Philippines	89	0	11,386	X	X	0	661	0	35,401	0	0	0	290
Qatar {d}	NA	150	0	X	X	910	0	X	X	X	X	X	X
Saudi Arabia {d}	NA	7	0	13	0	2,456	0	8,839	0	412	0	0	0
Singapore	100	0	220	1	0	12,130	0	445,873	0	10	0	0	65
Sri Lanka	55	0	2	0	2	157	0	X	X	X	X	0	105
Syrian Arab Rep {d}	NA	X	X	X	X	2	0	1	0	X	X	X	X
Taiwan {d}	NA	3,125	0	15	0	0	21,541	162,888	0	419	0	0	12,440
Thailand	43	0	11	X	X	0	319	0	260,080	21	0	0	51,392
Turkey {d}	NA	X	X	127	0	23	0	34,566	0	218	0	X	X
United Arab Emirates	0	27	0	X	X	759	0	0	67,750	9	0	X	X
Viet Nam {d}	NA	X	X	0	1	0	2,269	0	1,000	X	X	6	0
Yemen (Arab Rep) {d}	NA	X	X	X	X	X	X	X	X	X	X	X	X
(People's Dem Rep) {d}	NA	X	X	X	X	X	X	X	X	X	X	X	X
EUROPE		13,985	11	84,622	2,179	222,942	7,458	2,818,588	0	49,435	20,970	10,595	4
Albania {d}	NA	X	X	X	X	X	X	X	X	X	X	X	X
Austria	100	164	0	1,157	0	4,472	0	96,521	0	9,468	0	240	0
Belgium	100	1,092	0	328	0	0	1,801	71,751	0	317	0	337	0
Bulgaria	X	8	0	X	X	3	0	X	X	X	X	X	X
Czechoslovakia {d}	NA	50	0	0	1	0	1,616	X	X	0	3	3	0
Denmark	100	30	0	957	0	5,205	0	546	0	1,752	0	384	0
Finland	71	3	0	0	348	4	0	2,548	0	496	0	10	0
France	100	2,091	0	3,441	0	30,120	0	883,971	0	2,796	0	297	0
Germany (Fed Rep)	100	255	0	21,637	0	54,906	0	8,381	0	12,270	0	2,837	0
(Dem Rep)	54	1	0	0	521	0	2,102	14	0	4	0	11	0
Greece {d}	NA	1	0	1,448	0	4,064	0	196	0	91	0	30	0
Hungary	80	99	0	5	0	51	0	25	0	0	53	X	X
Iceland {d}	NA	X	X	1	0	0	5	X	X	X	X	X	X
Ireland {d}	NA	0	11	1	0	17	0	X	X	X	X	12	0
Italy	100	971	0	7,978	0	29,723	0	426,546	0	5,612	0	923	0
Luxembourg	100	X	X	X	X	2	0	X	X	104	0	14	0
Malta	100	X	X	X	X	1,131	0	1,470	0	0	3	0	0
Netherlands	100	1,253	0	3	0	0	1,934	3,444	0	0	14,736	2,497	0
Norway	100	10	0	122	0	12	0	X	X	1,865	0	2	0
Poland	X	45	0	30,299	0	X	X	X	X	X	X	3	0
Portugal	44	30	0	3	0	9,019	0	1,323	0	541	0	26	0
Romania {d}	NA	34	0	X	X	16	0	X	X	0	0	X	X
Spain	100	43	0	6,956	0	30,937	0	625,457	0	0	6,175	122	0
Sweden	100	389	0	16	0	8,808	0	1,240	0	2,344	0	0	4
Switzerland	100	65	0	10,270	0	3,402	0	111,570	0	7,328	0	636	0
United Kingdom	100	5,717	0	0	1,309	40,771	0	583,585	0	4,448	0	2,212	0
Yugoslavia {d}	NA	1,634	0	X	X	279	0	X	X	X	X	X	X
U.S.S.R.	86	1,729	0	11,434	0	1,137	0	X	X	X	X	X	X
OCEANIA		1	17	14	2	288	1,133	694	23,011	165	0	1,907	978
Australia	100	0	17	13	0	0	1,129	691	0	115	0	1,635	0
Fiji {d}	NA	X	X	X	X	133	0	X	X	X	X	272	0
New Zealand	100	1	0	1	0	155	0	3	0	50	0	0	955
Papua New Guinea	71	X	X	0	2	0	4	0	23,011	X	X	0	23
Solomon Islands {d}	NA	X	X	X	X	X	X	X	X	X	X	X	X

Source: World Conservation Monitoring Centre.
Notes:
a. Includes all trade reported by members of the Convention on International Trade in Endangered Species of Wild Flora and Fauna (CITES) through 1989.
b. Reptile skins include skins of snakes, lizards, and crocodilians. c. World totals include countries not listed; regional totals include only countries listed, but totals may not add because of rounding. d. Not a member of CITES as of October 1991.
0 = zero or less than half the unit of measurement; X = not available; NA = not applicable.
For additional information, see Sources and Technical Notes.

Table 20.3 Management Problems at World Heritage Sites

Name of Area	Total Size (000 ha)	IUCN Protected Area Classes Included	Development	Tourism	Pollution	External Threats	Threats to Local Cultures	Grazing and Cultivation	Illegal or Overharvest of Wildlife	Illegal or Overharvest of Trees/Plants	Fire and Natural Threats	Introduced Plant and Animal Species	Inadequate or Insufficient Legal Protection	Inadequate or Insufficient Management	Other
AFRICA {a}	**20,077**		**48%**	**16%**	**16%**	**36%**	**8%**	**56%**	**68%**	**32%**	**52%**	**8%**	**12%**	**52%**	**20%**
Cameroon															
Dja	526	I,IX	P				S	S	S	P					
Central African Rep															
Manovo-Gounda-St. Floris	1,740	II						S	S		S			S	
Cote d'Ivoire															
Comoe	1,150	II,IX						S	S		S				
Tai	350	II	S					S	S	S			S	S	
Mt. Nimba {b}	5	I,IX	S		S	S		S							
Ethiopia															
Simien	22	II					S				S				S
Guinea															
Mt. Nimba {b}	X	II,IX	S			S	S		S						
Malawi															
Lake Malawi	9	II	S			S	S		S		S		S		
Mali															
Bandiagara {c}	400	VII		S			S				S	S			
Mauritania															
Banc d'Arguin	1,200	I,II	S					S	S		S			S	
Senegal															
Niokolo-Koba	913	II,IX	P						S			S			
Djoudj	16	II	S						S			S			
Seychelles															
Aldabra	35	I							S		S	S		S	
Vallee de Mai	0	IV									P	M	S	S	S
Tanzania															
Selous	5,000	IV	S						S					S	
Serengeti	2,305	II,IX						S	S	S	S			S	
Ngorongoro	829	VIII,IX		S		S		S	S	S	S			S	S
Mt. Kilimanjaro	76	II		S				S	S	S	S			S	S
Tunisia															
Ichkeul	13	II,IX	S	S	S	S		S	S					S	
Zaire															
Salonga	3,600	II	S			S		S	S	S	S			S	S
Virunga	790	II	P			P			S						
Kahuzi-Biega	600	II	S			S			S					S	
Garamba	492	II							M					S	
Zambia															
Victoria Falls/Mosi-oa-Tunya	7	II	S			S		S						S	
Zimbabwe															
Mana Pools	X	II,XIII	S						S		S				
NORTH & CENTRAL AMERICA {a}	**21,305**		**57%**	**33%**	**29%**	**43%**	**14%**	**29%**	**33%**	**19%**	**24%**	**43%**	**10%**	**10%**	**19%**
Canada															
Canadian Rocky Mts. {d}	X	II	S	S	S	S			S						S
Kluane {b}	5,440	II	S						S						
Wood Buffalo	4,480	II	S		P						S	S	P		
Nahanni	477	II	P		P										
Gros Morne	181	II		M		S						S			
Dinosaur	7	II,IX	S					S							
Costa Rica															
Talamanca-La Amistad {b}	585	I,II,VII, VIII,IX	S			S	S	S	S	S				S	S
Guatemala															
Tikal {c}	58	II					S		S						
Honduras															
Rio Platano	500	II,IX	P			P	S	S	S	S					
Mexico															
Sian Ka'an	528	II,IX		S	S	S						S			
Panama															
Darien	597	II,IX	P			S		S	P	P					P
United States															
Kluane {b}	5,440	II	S						S						
Yellowstone	898	II,IX	P		P	S						S			
Everglades	586	II,III,IX	S		S	S					P	S	S		
Grand Canyon	493	II	S	S	S			S				S			
Olympic	363	II,IX	S	S	S	S						S			
Yosemite	308	II	S	S								S			S
Great Smoky Mts.	209	II,IX	S	S	S				S		S	S		S	S
Hawaii Volcanoes	93	II,IX	S					S	S	S	S	S	S		
Redwood	42	II	P									S	S		
Mammoth Cave	21	II			P										

Table 20.3

Name of Area	Total Size (000 ha)	IUCN Protected Area Classes Included	Development	Tourism	Pollution	External Threats	Threats to Local Cultures	Grazing and Cultivation	Illegal or Overharvest of Wildlife	Illegal or Overharvest of Trees/Plants	Fire and Natural Threats	Introduced Plant and Animal Species	Inadequate or Insufficient Legal Protection	Inadequate or Insufficient Management	Other
SOUTH AMERICA {a}	**4,117**		**38%**	**63%**	**25%**	**63%**	**13%**	**75%**	**63%**	**25%**	**88%**	**25%**	**0%**	**63%**	**38%**
Argentina															
Los Glaciares	600	II,IV		S				S	M		S	S			
Iguazu	55	II,IV	S	S											S
Brazil															
Iguacu	170	II	S			S			S	S	S			S	
Ecuador															
Galapagos	767	II,IX		S		S		S	P		S	S			
Sangay	272	II	P			S		S	S		S			S	
Peru															
Manu	1,881	II	P			S		S	S	S	S			S	S
Huascaran	340	II,IX	S	S	S	S		S	S		S			S	S
Machu Picchu {c}	33	II		S	S		S	S			S			S	
ASIA {a}	**520**		**40%**	**50%**	**20%**	**50%**	**30%**	**40%**	**40%**	**40%**	**40%**	**10%**	**20%**	**70%**	**20%**
China															
Mt. Taishan {c}	X	V	S	S			S				S			S	S
India															
Sunderbans	133	I			P	P								S	S
Nanda Devi	63	I							S					S	
Manas	39	IV	S				S		S	S	S		S	S	
Kaziranga	38	II					S	S	S	S	S		S		
Keoladeo	3	II		S	S	S						S		S	
Nepal															
Sagarmatha	115	II		S	S		S	S	S		S				
Royal Chitwan	93	II	S	S	P	S		S			S			S	
Sri Lanka															
Sinharaja	27	IX	S			S		S			S		P	S	
Turkey															
Goreme {c}	10	V		S			S				S				
EUROPE {a}	**122**		**45%**	**18%**	**27%**	**18%**	**0%**	**27%**	**9%**	**27%**	**18%**	**27%**	**9%**	**0%**	**9%**
Bulgaria															
Pirin	40	I,II	S			S									
Srebarna	1	I,IX									S				
France															
Cape Girolata	16	V			P			M	S						
Poland															
Bialowieza	5	II,IX	S	S	S	S								S	
Spain															
Garajonay	4	II				S		S			S	S	M		
United Kingdom															
Henderson {e}	4											S			
St. Kilda	1	IV,IX	S		P						S	S			M
Giant's Causeway	0	IV													
Yugoslavia															
Durmitor	32	II,IX	S		P			S			S				
Plitvice Lakes	19	V	S	S											
Skocjan Caves	0	III				S									
OCEANIA {a}	**40,448**		**70%**	**30%**	**20%**	**10%**	**30%**	**40%**	**10%**	**20%**	**40%**	**60%**	**30%**	**10%**	**40%**
Australia															
Great Barrier Reef	34,870	II	P	S	S				S		S				
Kakadu {c}	1,307	II	S	M			S					S			
Tasmania Wilderness {c}	1,082	I,II,VIII	S	S							S				
Wet Tropics of Queensland	920	II,III	S					S		S		S	S		
Willandra Lakes {c}	600	II					S	S					S		S
East Coast Rain Forest Parks	165	II,I				S		S			S	S			S
Uluru	133	II	S	P	S		S				S	S			S
Lord Howe	2	II	S					S				S			S
New Zealand															
Fiordland	1,252	II	M						P			S	S		
Westland/Mt. Cook	118	II	M							S		S			

Sources: World Conservation Monitoring Centre and United Nations Educational, Scientific and Cultural Organization.

Notes: a. Percentages shown are the proportion of world heritage sites within a region reporting each category of threat (e.g., for Africa: 48% of the heritage sites report threats from development, 16% report threats from tourism, etc). b. International heritage site. Management problems described here generally refer to problems within this country's sector only. c. Mixed natural/cultural heritage site nominated on basis of human/nature interaction rather than natural features alone. d. Data are incomplete. e. Located on the Pitcairn Islands, a British dependency in the Pacific.
S = significant threat, M = minor threat, P = potential threat.
0 = less than half the unit of measure; X = not available.
For additional information, see Sources and Technical Notes

Table 20.4 Globally Threatened Animal Species, 1990

	Mammals (number)			Birds (number)			Reptiles (number)			Amphibians (number)			Freshwater Fish (number)	
	Known Species	Threat-ened Species	Threatened Species per 10,000 km2 {a}	Known Species	Threat-ened Species	Threatened Species per 10,000 km2 {a}	Known Species	Threat-ened Species	Threatened Species per 10,000 km2 {a}	Known Species	Threat-ened Species	Threatened Species per 10,000 km2 {a}	Known Species	Threat-ened Species
WORLD														
AFRICA														
Algeria	97	12	2	X	15	2	X	0	0	X	0	0	X	1
Angola	275	14	3	872	12	2	X	2	0	X	0	0	268	0
Benin	187	11	5	630	1	0	X	2	1	X	0	0	150	0
Botswana	154	9	2	549	6	2	158	1	0	38	0	0	81	0
Burkina Faso	147	10	3	497	1	0	X	2	1	X	0	0	120	0
Burundi	103	4	3	633	5	4	X	1	1	X	0	0	X	0
Cameroon	297	27	8	848	17	5	X	2	1	X	1	0	X	11
Cape Verde	9	0	0	103	3	4	X	1	1	X	0	0	X	0
Central African Rep	208	12	3	668	2	1	X	2	1	X	0	0	400	0
Chad	131	18	4	496	4	1	X	2	0	X	0	0	130	0
Comoros	17	3	5	99	5	8	26	0	0	2	0	0	16	0
Congo	198	12	4	500	3	1	X	2	1	X	0	0	500	0
Cote d'Ivoire	226	18	6	683	9	3	X	1	0	X	1	0	200	0
Djibouti	22	6	5	311	3	2	X	0	0	X	0	0	X	0
Egypt	105	9	2	X	16	3	X	2	0	X	0	0	X	1
Equatorial Guinea	141	15	11	392	3	2	X	2	1	X	1	1	X	0
Ethiopia	265	25	5	836	14	3	6	1	0	X	0	0	100	0
Gabon	190	14	5	617	4	1	X	2	1	X	0	0	200	0
Gambia, The	108	7	7	489	1	1	X	2	2	X	0	0	80	0
Ghana	222	13	5	721	8	3	X	2	1	X	0	0	180	0
Guinea	188	17	6	529	6	2	X	1	0	X	1	0	250	0
Guinea-Bissau	109	5	3	376	2	1	X	2	1	X	0	0	90	0
Kenya	314	15	4	1,067	18	5	191	2	1	88	0	0	180	0
Lesotho	54	2	1	288	7	5	X	0	0	X	0	0	8	0
Liberia	193	18	8	590	10	5	X	2	1	X	0	0	130	0
Libya	76	12	2	X	9	2	X	1	0	X	0	0	X	0
Madagascar	105	53	14	250	28	7	259	10	3	144	0	0	X	0
Malawi	187	10	4	630	7	3	124	1	0	69	0	0	600	0
Mali	136	16	3	647	4	1	16	2	0	X	0	0	160	0
Mauritania	61	14	3	550	5	1	X	1	0	X	0	0	15	0
Mauritius	4	3	5	102	10	17	19	6	10	2	0	0	X	0
Morocco	108	9	3	X	14	4	X	0	0	32	0	0	X	1
Mozambique	205	10	2	666	11	3	170	1	0	X	0	0	X	1
Namibia	190	11	3	640	7	2	X	2	0	X	0	0	97	4
Niger	131	15	3	473	1	0	X	1	0	X	0	0	140	0
Nigeria	274	25	6	831	10	2	114	2	0	19	0	0	200	0
Reunion	2	0	0	33	1	2	6	0	0	X	0	0	X	0
Rwanda	147	11	8	669	7	5	X	2	1	X	0	0	X	0
Sao Tome and Principe	7	1	2	124	7	15	X	0	0	X	0	0	X	0
Senegal	166	11	4	625	5	2	X	2	1	X	0	0	140	0
Seychelles	2	1	3	126	9	29	X	2	7	12	3	10	X	0
Sierra Leone	178	13	7	614	7	4	X	2	1	X	0	0	130	0
Somalia	173	16	4	639	7	2	X	1	0	X	0	0	X	0
South Africa	283	26	5	774	13	3	301	3	1	95	1	0	220	28
Sudan	266	17	3	938	8	1	X	1	0	X	0	0	120	0
Swaziland	46	0	0	477	5	4	X	1	1	X	0	0	45	0
Tanzania	310	30	7	1,016	26	6	273	3	1	X	0	0	X	0
Togo	196	9	5	630	1	1	X	2	1	X	0	0	160	0
Tunisia	77	6	2	X	14	6	X	1	0	X	0	0	X	0
Uganda	311	16	6	989	12	4	X	1	0	X	0	0	300	0
Western Sahara	15	5	2	X	5	2	X	0	0	X	0	0	X	0
Zaire	409	22	4	1,086	27	4	X	2	0	X	0	0	700	1
Zambia	228	10	2	732	10	2	152	2	0	83	0	0	156	0
Zimbabwe	194	9	3	635	6	2	155	1	0	120	0	0	132	0
THE AMERICAS														
Argentina	255	25	4	927	53	8	204	4	1	124	1	0	X	1
Bahamas	17	2	2	218	4	4	39	3	3	6	0	0	X	0
Barbados	X	1	3	X	1	3	X	0	0	X	0	0	X	0
Belize	121	8	6	504	4	3	107	3	2	26	0	0	X	0
Bermuda	X	0	0	X	2	11	X	0	0	X	0	0	X	0
Bolivia	267	21	4	1,177	34	7	180	4	1	96	0	0	X	1
Brazil	394	24	3	1,567	123	13	467	11	1	487	0	0	X	9
Canada	197	5	1	426	6	1	42	0	0	41	0	0	1,132 b	15
Cayman Islands	X	0	0	X	2	7	X	2	7	X	0	0	X	0
Chile	90	9	2	393	18	4	82	0	0	30	0	0	X	1
Colombia	358	25	5	1,665	69	14	383	10	2	375	0	0	X	0
Costa Rica	203	10	6	796	14	8	218	2	1	151	0	0	X	0
Cuba	39	2	1	286	15	7	100	4	2	40	0	0	X	0
Dominican Rep	X	1	1	X	5	3	X	4	2	X	0	0	X	0
Ecuador {c}	280	21	7	1,447	64	21	345	8	3	350	0	0	X	0
El Salvador	129	6	5	432	2	2	92	1	1	38	0	0	X	0
French Guiana	142	10	5	628	5	2	136	2	1	89	0	0	X	0
Greenland (Denmark)	26	2	1	X	1	0	X	0	0	X	0	0	X	0
Guatemala	174	10	5	666	10	5	204	4	2	99	0	0	X	0
Guyana	198	12	4	728	9	3	137	3	1	105	0	0	X	1
Haiti	X	1	1	X	4	3	X	4	3	X	0	0	X	0
Honduras	179	7	3	672	11	5	161	3	1	57	0	0	X	0
Jamaica	29	6	6	223	2	2	38	3	3	20	0	0	X	0
Mexico	439	26	5	961	35	6	717	16	3	284	4	1	X	98
Netherlands Antilles	9	0	0	171	3	6	22	2	4	X	0	0	X	0
Nicaragua	177	8	3	610	7	3	162	2	1	59	0	0	X	0

	Mammals (number)			Birds (number)			Reptiles (number)			Amphibians (number)			Freshwater Fish (number)	
	Known Species	Threatened Species	Threatened Species per 10,000 km2 {a}	Known Species	Threatened Species	Threatened Species per 10,000 km2 {a}	Known Species	Threatened Species	Threatened Species per 10,000 km2 {a}	Known Species	Threatened Species	Threatened Species per 10,000 km2 {a}	Known Species	Threatened Species
Panama	217	13	7	920	14	7	212	2	1	155	0	0	X	0
Paraguay	157	14	4	630	24	7	110	4	1	69	0	0	X	0
Peru	359	29	6	1,642	65	13	297	6	1	235	1	0	X	1
Puerto Rico	17	2	2	220	4	4	46	5	5	26	1	1	X	0
Suriname	200	11	4	670	6	2	131	1	0	99	0	0	X	0
Trinidad and Tobago	85	1	1	347	3	4	76	0	0	15	0	0	X	0
United States	466	21	2	1,090	43	4	368	25	3	222	22	2	2,640 b	164
Uruguay	77	5	2	367	11	4	66	2	1	37	0	0	X	0
Venezuela	305	19	4	1,295	34	8	246	2	0	183	0	0	X	0
ASIA														
Afghanistan	X	13	3	X	13	3	X	1	0	X	1	0	X	0
Bahrain	X	1	2	X	4	10	X	0	0	X	0	0	X	1
Bangladesh	X	15	6	X	27	11	X	14	6	X	0	0	X	0
Bhutan	X	15	9	X	10	6	X	1	1	X	0	0	X	0
Brunei	X	9	11	X	10	12	X	3	4	X	0	0	X	2
Cambodia	X	21	8	X	13	5	X	6	2	X	0	0	X	5
China	394	30	3	1,195	83	9	X	7	1	X	1	0	X	7
India	341	38	6	1,178	72	11	400	17	3	181	3	0	X	2
Indonesia	479	50	9	1,500	135	24	X	13	2	X	0	0	X	29
Iran, Islamic Rep	X	15	3	X	20	4	X	4	1	X	0	0	X	2
Iraq	X	9	3	X	17	5	X	0	0	X	0	0	X	2
Israel	X	8	6	X	15	12	X	1	1	X	1	1	X	0
Japan	188	5	2	668	31	9	86	0	0	95	1	0	207	3
Jordan	X	5	2	X	11	5	X	0	0	X	0	0	X	0
Korea, Dem People's Rep	X	5	2	X	25	11	X	0	0	X	0	0	X	0
Korea, Rep	X	6	3	X	22	10	X	0	0	X	0	0	X	0
Kuwait	X	5	4	X	7	6	X	0	0	X	0	0	X	0
Lao People's Dem Rep	X	23	8	X	18	6	X	5	2	X	0	0	X	5
Lebanon	X	4	4	X	15	15	X	1	1	X	0	0	X	0
Malaysia	X	23	7	X	35	11	X	12	4	X	0	0	X	6
Mongolia	X	9	2	X	13	2	X	0	0	X	0	0	X	0
Myanmar	300	23	6	1,000	42	10	360	10	2	X	0	0	X	2
Nepal	X	22	9	X	20	8	X	9	4	X	0	0	X	0
Oman	X	5	2	X	8	3	X	0	0	X	0	0	X	2
Pakistan	X	15	4	X	25	6	X	6	1	X	0	0	X	0
Philippines	96	12	4	541	39	13	197	6	2	60	0	0	X	21
Saudi Arabia	X	9	2	X	12	2	X	0	0	X	0	0	X	0
Sri Lanka	X	7	4	X	8	4	X	3	2	X	0	0	X	12
Syrian Arab Rep	X	4	2	X	15	6	X	1	0	X	0	0	X	0
Thailand	X	26	7	X	34	9	X	9	2	X	0	0	X	13
Turkey	118	5	1	426	18	4	93	5	1	18	1	0	555 b	5
United Arab Emirates	X	4	2	X	7	3	X	0	0	X	0	0	X	0
Viet Nam	273	28	9	774	34	11	180	8	3	80	1	0	X	4
EUROPE														
Albania	X	2	1	X	14	10	X	1	1	X	0	0	X	1
Austria	85	2	1	201	13	6	13	0	0	19	0	0	71	2
Belgium	X	2	1	X	13	9	X	0	0	X	0	0	X	1
Bulgaria	X	3	1	X	15	7	X	1	0	X	0	0	X	3
Czechoslovakia	X	2	1	390	18	8	X	0	0	X	0	0	X	2
Denmark	49	1	1	190	16	10	5	0	0	14	0	0	166 b	0
Finland	62	3	1	232	12	4	5	0	0	5	0	0	58 b	1
France	113	6	2	342	21	6	36	2	1	29	1	0	70	3
Germany	94	2	1	305	17	5	12	0	0	19	0	0	70 h	3
Greece	X	4	2	X	19	8	X	0	I	X	0	0	X	6
Hungary	X	2	1	X	16	8	X	0	0	X	0	0	X	2
Iceland	X	1	0	X	2	1	X	0	0	X	0	0	X	1
Ireland	31	0	0	139	10	5	1	0	0	3	0	0	X	1
Italy	97	3	1	419	19	6	46	2	1	28	7	2	503 b	3
Luxembourg	60	1	2	140	8	13	8	0	0	16	0	0	40	0
Netherlands	60	2	1	257	13	8	7	0	0	15	0	0	49 b	1
Norway	54	3	1	225	8	3	5	0	0	5	0	0	172	1
Poland	X	4	1	X	16	5	X	0	0	X	0	0	X	1
Portugal	82	6	3	313	18	9	35	0	0	17	1	0	39	0
Romania	X	2	1	X	18	6	X	1	0	X	0	0	X	4
Spain	108	6	2	344	23	6	64	5	1	24	3	1	55	2
Sweden	65	1	0	250	14	4	6	0	0	13	0	0	130 b	1
Switzerland	76	2	1	196	15	9	15	0	0	19	1	1	52	3
United Kingdom	77	2	1	233	22	8	11	0	0	6	0	0	377 b	1
Yugoslavia	X	3	1	X	17	6	X	1	0	X	2	1	X	5
U.S.S.R.	357	20	2	765	38	3	144	3	0	34	0	0	X	5
OCEANIA														
Australia	320	35	4	700	39	4	550	9	1	150	3	0	3,200 b	16
Fiji	X	1	1	X	5	4	X	4	3	X	1	1	X	0
New Caledonia	X	1	1	X	5	4	X	0	0	X	0	0	X	0
New Zealand	69	1	0	282	26	9	39	1	0	5	3	1	777 b	2
Papua New Guinea	X	4	1	X	25	7	X	1	0	X	0	0	X	0
Solomon Islands	X	2	1	X	20	14	X	3	2	X	0	0	X	0
Vanuatu	X	1	1	X	3	3	X	1	1	X	0	0	X	0
Western Samoa	X	1	2	X	2	3	X	0	0	X	0	0	X	0

Sources: World Conservation Monitoring Centre, World Conservation Union, Organisation for Economic Co-operation and Development, and other sources.
Notes: a. Number is standardized using a species area curve. b. Both fresh- and saltwater species. c. Includes the Galapagos Islands.
X = not available; 0 = no species listed as threatened at present.
For additional information, see Sources and Technical Notes.

Table 20.5 Rare and Threatened Plants, 1991

	Number of Plant Taxa	Endemic Flora as Percentage of Total	Number of Rare and Threatened Plant Taxa	Rare and Threatened Plant Taxa per 1,000 Existing Taxa	Rare and Threatened Plant Taxa per 10,000 Square Kilometers {a}	Red Data Book or List	Number of Botanical Gardens {b}	Members of BGCI (number) {b}
WORLD							1,553	316
AFRICA							82	31
Algeria	3,139-3,150	8	144	46	24	Yes	3	0
Angola	5,000	25	19	4	4	No	1	0
Benin	2,000	1	3	2	1	Yes	1	0
Botswana	2,600-2,800	17	4	1-2	1	Yes	0	0
Burkina Faso	1,096	X	0	0	0	No	0	0
Burundi	2,500	X	0	0	0	Yes	1	0
Cameroon	8,000	2	74	9	21	Yes	2	1
Cape Verde	659	14	1	2	1	No	1	0
Central African Rep	3,600	4	0	0	0	No	0	0
Chad	1,600	X	14	9	3	No	0	0
Comoros	416	33	3	7	5	No	0	0
Congo	4,000	22	4	1	1	No	0	0
Cote d'Ivoire	3,660	2	70	19	22	No	1	0
Djibouti	534	X	3	6	2	No	0	0
Equatorial Guinea	X	X	X	X	X	X	0	0
Bioko	1,150	4	8	7	14 c	No	X	0
Pagula	208	8	2	10	16 c	No	X	0
Egypt	2,085	4	93	45	20	Yes	5	1
Ethiopia	6,283	8	44	7	9	No	1	0
Gabon	8,000	22	80	10	27	No	1	1
Gambia, The	530	1	0	0	0	No	0	0
Ghana	3,600	1	34	9	12	Yes	3	1
Guinea	X	88 d	36	X	13	No	0	0
Guinea-Bissau	1,000	X	0	0	0	No	0	0
Kenya	6,500	4	144	22	38	Yes	5	0
Lesotho	1,591	X	7	4	5	No	0	0
Liberia	X	59 d	1	X	0	Yes	0	0
Libya	1,600-1,800	8	58	32-36	11	Yes	1	0
Madagascar	10,000-12,000	80	193	16-19	50	No	1	1
Malawi	3,600	2	61	17	29	No	3	3
Mali	1,600	1	15	9	3	No	0	0
Mauritania	1,100	X	3	3	1	No	0	0
Mauritius	800-900	33	240	267-300	419	Yes	2	2
Morocco	3,500-3,600	18	194	54-55	55	Yes	2	0
Mozambique	5,500	4	84	15	20	No	2	0
Namibia	3,159	11 d	18	6	4	No	1	1
Niger	1,178	X	1	1	0	Yes	0	0
Nigeria	4,614	5	9	2	2	Yes	5	1
Principe	314	11	1	3	2 e	No	0	0
Reunion	720	30	99	138	156	Yes	4	2
Rwanda	2,150	X	0	0	0	No	1	0
Sao Tome	601	18	0	0	2 e	No	0	0
Senegal	2,100	1	32	15	12	No	3	0
Seychelles	274	15	73	266	240	No	1	0
Sierra Leone	2,480	3	12	5	6	No	1	0
Somalia	3,000	17	51	17	13	No	0	0
South Africa	23,000	80	1,145	50	235	Yes	17	11
Sudan	3,200	2	9	3	1	Yes	1	0
Swaziland	2,715	X	25	9	21	Yes	0	0
Tanzania	10,000	11	158	16	36	Yes	2	1
Togo	2,302 f	1	0	0	0	No	1	1
Tunisia	2,120-2,200	X	26	12	11	Yes	1	0
Uganda	5,000	1	11	2	4	No	2	0
Western Sahara	300	X	0	0	0	No	0	0
Zaire	11,000	29	3	0	1	Yes	2	2
Zambia	4,600	5	1	0	0	No	0	0
Zimbabwe	5,428 g	2	96	18	29	Yes	4	2
NORTH & CENTRAL AMERICA							355	79
Antigua and Barbuda	724 f	1	1	1	3	No	0	0
Bahamas	1,350	9	23	17	23	Yes	0	0
Bermuda	165	10	14	85	80	No	1	0
Barbados	700	1	1	1	3	No	2	0
Belize	3,240	5	38	12	29	IP	1	0
British Virgin Islands	X	X	1	X	4	Yes	1	1
Canada	3,220	X	13	4	1	Yes	18	7
Costa Rica	8,000	X	456	57	266	No	2	2
Cuba	7,000	50	874	125	396	Yes	8	3
Dominica	1,600	1	62	39	146	No	1	1
El Salvador	2,500	19 d	24	10	19	Yes	1	1
Grenada	X	X	4	X	12	No	1	0
Guadeloupe	2,800 f	45	14	5	25	Yes	2	1
Guatemala	8,000	15	305	38	139	Yes	1	1
Hispaniola	5,000	X	0	0	0	IP	1	0
Honduras	5,000	3	48	10	22	No	2	1
Jamaica	3,582	30	8	2	8	Yes	4	0
Martinique	X	X	12	X	25	Yes	3	0
Mexico	20,000	17	1,111	56	196	Yes	30	6
Montserrat	X	X	1	X	5	No	0	0
Nicaragua	5,000	1	72	14	32	No	1	0
Panama	8,000-9,000	15	344	38-43	176	No	1	0

Table 20.5

	Number of Plant Taxa	Endemic Flora as Percentage of Total	Number of Rare and Threatened Plant Taxa	Rare and Threatened Plant Taxa per 1,000 Existing Taxa	Rare and Threatened Plant Taxa per 10,000 Square Kilometers {a}	Red Data Book or List	Number of Botanical Gardens {b}	Members of BGCI (number) {b}
Saint Lucia	X	X	3	X	8	No	0	0
Saint Vincent and the Grenadines	X	12 d	4	X	12	No	1	1
Trinidad and Tobago	2,281	9	4	2	5	Yes	1	0
United States	20,000 h	X	2,476	124	261	Yes	247	47
Hawaii	1,145	90	X	X	X	Yes	19	6
Puerto Rico	3,000	8	85	28	88	Yes	4	0
Virgin Islands	X	X	10	X	31	Yes	1	0
SOUTH AMERICA							67	19
Argentina	9,000	25-30	157	17	25	No	9	1
Bolivia	15,000-18,000	X	31	2	7	No	3	1
Brazil	55,000	X	240	4	26	No	11	4
Chile	5,500	50	192	35	46	Yes	9	4
Juan Fernandez	147	X	96	653	X	Yes	1	0
Colombia	45,000	33	316	7	68	IP	13	4
Ecuador	10,000-20,000	X	121	6-12	40	No	2	1
Galapagos Islands	543 g	X	130	239	X	Yes	X	0
French Guiana	6,000-8,000	X	47	6-8	23	Yes	2	0
Guyana	6,000-8,000	X	68	9-11	25	No	2	1
Paraguay	7,000-8,000	X	12	2	4	No	1	0
Peru	20,000	X	353	18	71	No	5	1
Suriname	4,500	X	68	15	27	No	1	0
Uruguay	X	X	11	X	4	No	1	0
Venezuela	15,000-20,000	29	105	5-7	24	No	7	2
ASIA							271	37
Afghanistan	3,000	25-30	2	1	1	No	0	0
Bangladesh	5,000 h	X	6	1	3	No	2	0
Bhutan	5,000	10-15	6	1	4	No	0	0
Borneo	10,000-15,000	40-50	47	3-5	X	No	0	0
Brunei	X i	X i	38	X	47	No	0	0
Cambodia	X	X	11	X	4	No	0	0
China	30,000	10	841	28	88	Yes	66	4
Cyprus	2,000	X	44	22	45	No	0	0
India	15,000	30	1,349	90	206	Yes	68	7
Andaman and Nicobar Islands	2,270 h	10	120	53	128 c	Yes	0	0
Indonesia	X	X	X	X	X	X	5	4
Irian Jaya	X j	X j	23	X	X	X	X	0
Java	4,600	X	92	20	39 c	No	X	0
Kalimantan	X i	X i	36	X	10 c	X	X	0
Lesser Sunda Islands	X	12	10	X	X	No	X	0
Moluccas	3,000	X	12	4	X	No	X	0
Sulawesi	5,000	X	16	3	6 c	No	X	0
Sumatra	8,000-10,000	12	92	9-12	26 c	No	X	0
Iran, Islamic Rep	7,000	20	1	0	0	No	3	0
Iraq	2,937	7	3	1	1	No	1	0
Israel	2,317	7	39	17	31	Yes	7	3
Japan	4,022	34	687	171	207	IP	59	0
Bonin Islands	369	41	83	225	X	Yes	0	0
Jordan	2,200	X	13	6	6	No	0	0
Korea, Rep	2,838 k	14 k	0	0	0	Yes	5	0
Kuwait	350	X	1	3	1	No	0	0
Lao People's Dem Rep	X	X	3	X	1	No	0	0
Lebanon {l}	3,000	11	6	2	6	Yes	0	0
Malaysia	X	X	X	X	X	X	9	5
Peninsular Malaysia	8,500	X	318	37	100 c	No	X	0
Sabah	X l	X l	43	X	22 c	No	X	0
Sarawak	X i	X i	108	X	47 c	No	X	0
Myanmar	7,000 h	5	23	3	6	Yes m	2	0
Nepal	6,500 h	5	21	3	9	IP	1	1
Oman	1,100	5	2	2	1	No	0	0
Pakistan	5,500-6,000	6	8	1	2	IP	5	0
Philippines	8,900	25	106	12	35	Yes m	9	2
Saudi Arabia	3,500	23 d	1	0	0	IP	2	0
Singapore	2,030	X	16	8	40	No	1	1
Sri Lanka	3,700	23	209	56	113	Yes m	5	5
Syrian Arab Rep {l}	3,000	11	13	4	5	No	0	0
Taiwan	4,300	40	94	22	132 c	Yes	2	1
Thailand	12,000	X	63	5	17	Yes	5	0
Turkey	10,150	32	1,952	192	466	Yes	6	1
Viet Nam	8,000	10	388	49	123	Yes i	2	0
Yemen (Arab Rep)	1,000	3	1	1	0	No	0	0
(People's Dem Rep)	1,700	5-10	2	1	1	No	0	0
Socotra	680	32	132	194	X	No	X	0
EUROPE							533	119
Albania	3,100-3,300	1	76	23-25	54	X	1	0
Austria	2,900-3,100	1	25	8-9	12	Yes	11	0
Belgium	1,600-1,800	0	11	6-7	8 c	Yes	15	3
Bulgaria	3,500-3,650	2	89	24-25	40	Yes	9	0
Czechoslovakia	2,600-2,750	1	29	11	13	Yes	34	1
Denmark	1,000	1	7	7	4	Yes	7	2
Finland	1,150-1,450	0	7	5-6	2	Yes	8	3
France	4,300-4,450	2	112	25-26	30	Yes	66	18
Corsica	2,516 n	5	35	14	37 c	Yes	0	0

Table 20.5 Rare and Threatened Plants, 1991 (continued)

	Number of Plant Taxa	Endemic Flora as Percentage of Total	Number of Rare and Threatened Plant Taxa	Rare and Threatened Plant Taxa per 1,000 Existing Taxa	Rare and Threatened Plant Taxa per 10,000 Square Kilometers {a}		Red Data Book or List	Number of Botanical Gardens {b}	Members of BGCI (number) {b}
Germany (Fed Rep)	2,476	1	16	6	6		Yes	59	12
(Dem Rep)	1,842	1	12	7	6		Yes	14	X
Greece	5,000	20	531	106	227		Yes	4	3
Hungary	2,400	1	21	9	10		No	17	0
Iceland	470	1	2	4	1		Yes	2	0
Ireland	1,000-1,150	0	4	4	2		Yes	8	5
Italy	4,750-4,900	11	151	31-32	49		Yes	48	10
Sardinia	1,900-2,000	2	34	17-18	25	c	No	X	0
Sicily	2,250-2,450	2	48	20-21	35	c	No	X	0
Luxembourg	1,000	0	2	2	3	c	IP	0	0
Malta	900	0	4	4	12		Yes	1	0
Netherlands	1,400	0	7	5	5		Yes	39	5
Norway	1,600-1,800	1	12	7-8	4		Yes	6	3
Poland	2,250-2,450	1	16	7	5		Yes	25	1
Portugal	2,400-2,600	4-5	90	35-38	43		Yes	6	1
Azores	600	9	36	60	X		Yes	3	2
Madeira Islands	760	17	114	150	X		No	2	0
Romania	3,300-3,400	1	68	20-21	24		Yes	10	0
Spain	4,750-4,900	15	449	92-95	124		Yes	8	5
Balearic Islands	1,250-1,450	6-8	69	48-55	87	c	Yes	1	0
Canary Islands	2,000	X	431	216	X		Yes	3	1
Gibraltar	587	1	1	2	12	c	No	1	0
Sweden	1,600-1,800	1	9	5-6	3		Yes	9	3
Switzerland	2,600-2,750	1	19	7	12		Yes	22	9
United Kingdom	1,700-1,850	1	22	12-13	8	c	Yes	60	31
Ascension Island	25	44	11	440	52	c	Yes	X	0
Channel Islands	1,800 f	0	3	2	11	c	Yes	0	0
Saint Helena	320	16	49	153	154		Yes	1	0
Tristan da Cunha Islands	74	60	18	243	83	c	No	0	0
Yugoslavia	4,750-4,900	3-4	191	39-40	66		No	32	0
U.S.S.R.	**21,000**	**7**	**531**	**25**	**42**		**Yes**	**160**	**1**
OCEANIA								**85**	**30**
Australia	18,000	80	2,133	119	239		Yes	60	22
Campbell Island	223 g	1	1	4	X		Yes	X	X
Christmas Island	280 g	5	14	50	59		Yes	X	X
Fiji	1,500 g	40-50	25	17	20		No	1	0
Guam	331 g	X	12	36	31		No	X	X
Kermadec Island	195 g	12	9	46	X		Yes	X	X
Lord Howe Island	219 g	33	19	87	X		Yes	X	X
Marquesas Islands	247 g	X	62	251	X		Yes	0	0
New Caledonia	3,250	76	169	52	138		No	0	0
New Guinea	11,000	90	X	0	X		No	X	0
New Zealand	2,000	81	254	127	86		Yes	17	5
Norfolk Island	177 g	29	48	271	297		Yes	1	X
Papua New Guinea	X j	55	68	X	19		No	4	2
Solomon Islands	2,150	X	3	1	2		No	1	1

Sources: World Conservation Monitoring Centre, Botanic Gardens Conservation International, The Europa World Yearbook 1990, and Food and Agriculture Organization of the United Nations.

Notes: a. Per unit area number is standardized using a species area curve. b. BGCI = Botanic Gardens Conservation International. World and regional totals include countries not listed. c. Calculated using total land area (including inland water bodies) instead of land area alone. d. Number of endemic taxa (includes species, subspecies, and varieties). e. Number refers to both Sao Tome and Principe. f. Number of vascular taxa (includes species, subspecies, and varieties). g. Number of seed plants. h. Number of flowering plants. i. Number included under Borneo. j. Number included under New Guinea. k. Refers to entire Korean peninsula. l. Size of flora and endemicity data refer to both Syrian Arab Rep and Lebanon. m. Preliminary. n. Number of endemic vascular plant species.
Data for mainland countries do not include island states or territories.
0 = zero or less than half the unit of measure; X = not available; IP = in preparation as of September 1991.
For additional information, see Sources and Technical Notes.

Table 20.6 Debt-for-Nature Swaps

	Purchaser/ Fundraiser	Date		Face Value of Debt {a}	Cost	Conservation Funds Generated {b}	Purpose
AFRICA							
Madagascar	WWF		Total	$3,030,476			To utilize conservation, education, and sustainable
		7/89	Transaction 1	$2,111,112	$950,000	$2,111,112	development methods in 30 designated sites and train
		8/90	Transaction 2	$919,364	$445,891	$919,363	600 conservation agents.
	CI		Total	$5,000,000			To provide ecosystem management programs for four
		1/91	Transaction 1	$118,754	$59,377	$118,754	protected areas--Zahameana, Midongy-Sud, Manongarivo, and Namoroko Reserves; to develop a university-level training and education program; to fund conservation based development; to create a trust fund.
Zambia	WWF	8/89	Total	$2,270,000	$454,000	$2,270,000	To help conserve and manage the Kafue Flats and Bangweulu Basin wetlands; to support conservation education activities; to alleviate soil erosion and habitat degradation; to protect rhino and elephant populations; to strengthen local conservation institutions.
LATIN AMERICA							
Bolivia	CI	8/87	Total	$650,000	$100,000	$250,000	To establish a local currency endowment fund to pay for the operating costs of managing the Beni Biosphere Reserve; to create three conservation and sustainable-use areas totaling 1.5 million hectares adjacent to the Beni.
Costa Rica	FPN {c}	2/88	Total	$5,400,000	$918,000	$4,050,000	To expand, manage, and protect three of Costa Rica's national parks: Guanacaste, Monteverde (C.F.), and Corcovado. The program in Guanacaste will purchase and annex land located between existing parks and reserves. Monteverde will receive administrative support.
	the Netherlands	7/88	Total	$33,000,000	$5,000,000	$9,900,000	To finance forestry development activities with the objective of protecting and managing natural resources; to fund ongoing programs in forestry and institutional strengthening.
	TNC	1/89	Total	$5,600,000	$784,000	$1,680,000	To help meet management costs and land purchases at four parks/reserves. To fund five other projects and organizations involved in park and species protection.
	Sweden	4/89	Total	$24,500,000	$3,500,000	$17,100,000	To complete the management endowment and infrastructure of Guanacaste National Park; to restore the habitat of this park.
	Sweden/WWF/TNC	3/90	Total	$10,753,631	$1,953,473	$9,602,904	To support land compensation payments of La Amistad Regional Conservation Unit; to fund education, protection, research, ecotourism, and other management programs; to set up a trust fund structure for the National Biodiversity Institute (INBio).
	Rainforest Alliance MCL/TNC	1/91	Total	$600,000 (CABEI debt)	$360,000	$540,000	To purchase an additional 2,023 hectares of land for Monteverde Cloud Forest Reserve and to improve local protection.
Dominican Republic	PRCT/TNC	3/90	Total	$582,000	$116,400	$582,000	To support the protection and reforestation of two watersheds; to establish a new nature reserve and fund staff and equipment; to support community outreach for Isla Cabritos National Park.
Ecuador	WWF/TNC/MBG		Total	$10,000,000			To support management plans for protected areas; to
		12/87	Transaction 1	$1,000,000	$354,000	$1,000,000	develop park infrastructure; to identify and acquire
		4/89	Transaction 2	$9,000,000	$1,068,750	$9,000,000	small nature reserves; to fund species inventories through a Conservation Data Center. Priority target areas are six Andean and Amazonian national parks.
Guatemala	TNC	10/91	Total	$100,000 (CABEI debt)	$75,000	$90,000	To support Sierra de las Minas Biosphere Reserve through land acquisition and protection.
Jamaica	TNC/USAID/PRCT		Total	$600,000			To fund and protect Montego Marine Park, Blue Mountain/
		10/91	Transaction 1	$437,000	$200,000	$437,000	John Crow Mountain.
Mexico	CI		Total	$4,000,000			To fund ecosystem conservation data centers to assess
		2/91	Transaction 1	$250,000	$182,000	$250,000	the distribution, status, and conservation priority of
		8/91	Transaction 2	$250,000	Debt donation	$250,000	Mexico's key species and habitats; to fund communication and education campaigns on the national and grassroots level.
ASIA							
Philippines	WWF		Total	$2,000,000			To provide for management plans, community development
		1/89	Transaction 1	$390,000	$200,000	$390,000	work in buffer zones, and infrastructure for four parks;
		8/90	Transaction 2	$900,000	$438,750	$900,000	to support research and environmental education activities, and training for community-level resource managers.
EUROPE							
Poland	WWF	1/90	Total	$50,000	$11,500	$50,000	To support project study on the Vistula River Basin program.
TOTAL TO DATE				$98,881,860 {d}	$17,271,141	$61,491,133	

Sources: Conservation International, World Wildlife Fund, The Nature Conservancy, and other sources.

Notes: a. In some swaps the agreed-upon amount of debt is swapped through several transactions over a period of time. This column identifies the total agreed-upon sum, including pending transactions, and which transactions have been approved. b. In the case of bonds, this figure does not include interest earned over the life of the bonds. c. Many organizations contributed to this deal including: WWF, CI, TNC, The Pew Charitable Trust, Jessie Smith Noyes Foundation, Asociacion Ecologica La Pacifica, John D. and Catherine T. MacArthur Foundation, Swedish Society for the Conservation of Nature, W. Alton Jones Foundation, Organization for Tropical Studies. d. Includes only approved transactions.
CI = Conservation International, MCL = Monteverde Conservation League, TNC = The Nature Conservancy, CABEI = Central American Bank for Economic Integration, WWF = World Wildlife Fund, PRCT = Puerto Rican Conservation Trust, MGB = Missouri Botanical Garden, FPN = National Parks Foundation of Costa Rica. All figures are in US$.
For additional information, see Sources and Technical Notes.

Sources and Technical Notes

Table 20.1 National and International Protection of Natural Areas, 1990

Sources: Protected Areas Data Unit of the World Conservation Monitoring Centre (WCMC), unpublished data (WCMC, Cambridge, United Kingdom, September 1991); heritage site numbers only: United Nations Educational, Scientific and Cultural Organization (UNESCO), *List of Properties Included in the World Heritage List* (UNESCO-ICOMOS Documentation Centre, Paris, December 1990).

National protection systems combine natural areas in five World Conservation Union (IUCN) management categories (areas are at least 1,000 hectares). *Totally protected areas* are maintained in a natural state and are closed to extractive uses. They encompass the following three management categories:

■ Category I. Scientific reserves and strict nature reserves possess outstanding, representative ecosystems. Public access is generally limited, with only scientific research and educational use permitted.

■ Category II. National parks and provincial parks are relatively large areas of national or international significance not materially altered by humans. Visitors may use them for recreation and study.

■ Category III. Natural monuments and natural landmarks contain unique geological formations, special animals or plants, or unusual habitats.

Partially protected areas are areas that may be managed for specific uses, such as recreation or tourism, or areas that provide optimum conditions for certain species or communities of wildlife. Some extractive use within these areas is allowed. They encompass two management categories:

■ Category IV. Managed nature reserves and wildlife sanctuaries are protected for specific purposes, such as conservation of a significant plant or animal species.

■ Category V. Protected landscapes and seascapes may be entirely natural or may include cultural landscapes (e.g., scenically attractive agricultural areas).

Marine and coastal protected areas only refer to all protected areas with littoral, coral, island, marine, or estuarine components. The area given is the whole protected area.

The figures in Table 20.1 do not include locally or provincially protected sites, privately owned areas, or areas managed primarily for the extraction of natural resources. National lists usually include sites that are listed under *international protection systems*.

Biosphere reserves are representative of terrestrial and coastal environments that have been internationally recognized under the Man and the Biosphere Programme of the United Nations Educational, Scientific, and Cultural Organization. They have been selected for their value to conservation and are intended to foster the scientific knowledge, skills, and human values necessary to

support sustainable development. Each reserve must contain a diverse, natural ecosystem of a specific biogeographical province, large enough to be an effective conservation unit. For further details, refer to M. Udvardy, *A Classification of the Biogeographical Provinces of the World* (IUCN, Morges, Switzerland, 1975), and to *World Resources 1986,* Chapter 6. Each reserve also must include a minimally disturbed core area for conservation and research and may be surrounded by buffer zones where traditional land uses, experimental ecosystem research, and ecosystem rehabilitation may be permitted.

Number of natural world heritage sites represents areas of "outstanding universal value" so called either for their natural features, for their cultural value, or for both natural and cultural values. The table includes only natural and mixed natural and cultural sites. Any party to the World Heritage Convention may nominate natural sites that contain examples of a major stage of the earth's evolutionary history; a significant ongoing geological process; a unique or superlative natural phenomenon, formation, or feature; or habitat for threatened species. Guinea and Cote d'Ivoire share one world heritage site, as do Zambia and Zimbabwe, Canada and the United States, and Costa Rica and Panama. These sites, referred to as international heritage sites, are counted only once in continental and world totals.

Any party to the Convention on Wetlands of International Importance Especially as Waterfowl Habitat (Ramsar, Iran, 1971) who agrees to respect the site's integrity and to establish wetland reserves, can designate *wetlands of international importance.*

Because categories overlap, the total number of protected sites is less than the sum of all the categories.

Table 20.2 Trade in Wildlife and Wildlife Products Reported by CITES, 1988

Source: World Conservation Monitoring Centre (WCMC), unpublished data (WCMC, Cambridge, United Kingdom, September 1991).

CITES members agree to prohibit commercial international trade in endangered species and to closely monitor trade in species that may become depleted by trade. Species are listed in the appendixes to CITES on the basis of the degree of rarity and of threat from trade. Trade is prohibited for species in Appendix I (a list of species threatened with extinction) and is regulated for species in Appendix II (a list of species not yet threatened but which could become endangered if trade is not controlled). Parties to the Convention are required to submit annual reports, including trade records, to the CITES Secretariat in Switzerland. WCMC compiles these data from those reports. Figures refer primarily

to legal trade, though illegal trade is included when known. (For a listing of CITES member states and signatories, see Chapter 25, "Policies and Institutions," Table 25.1.)

CITES reporting requirement met refers to the percentage of years for which a country has submitted an annual report to the CITES Secretariat since it became a party to the Convention, through 1989. Countries that had ratified the CITES by October 30, 1991, are listed as members.

Live primates include all species of monkeys, apes, and prosimions.

Cat skins include skins of all species of Felidae, excluding a small number of skins reported only by weight or length.

Live parrots include all psittacine species (e.g., parrots, macaws, cockatoos) except the budgerigar and the cockatiel.

Reptile skins include whole skins, reported by number, of all crocodilians and many commonly traded lizard and snake species.

Live cacti include wild and artificially propagated Cactaceae plants.

Live orchids include wild and artificially propagated Orchidaceae plants.

This table shows net trade in wild and captive bred species. The totals can be overestimates of the actual number of specimens legally traded because the same specimen could be imported and reexported by a number of countries in a single year. However, the impact of international trade on a particular species can be greater than the numbers reported because of mortality (during capture or collection, transit, and quarantine), illegal trade, trade to or from countries that are not CITES members, and omission of domestic trade data.

Ivory trade is currently prohibited. For information on 1988 ivory trade, see *World Resources 1990–91,* Table 20.3.

Table 20.3 Management Problems at World Heritage Sites

Sources: Protected Areas Data Unit (PADU) of the World Conservation Monitoring Centre (WCMC), *World Heritage at Risk* unpublished draft report (WCMC, Cambridge, United Kingdom, November 1990); reference to parks and reserves encompassed by heritage sites: World Conservation Union (IUCN), *1990 United Nations List of National Parks and Protected Areas* (IUCN, Gland, Switzerland and Cambridge, United Kingdom, 1990); total heritage site numbers (in technical note): Jim Thorsell, Senior Advisor, Natural Heritage, IUCN, September 25,1991 (personal communication); natural vs. natural/cultural listings: United Nations Educational, Scientific and Cultural Organization (UNESCO), *List of Properties Included in the World Heritage List* (UNESCO- ICOMOS Documentation Centre, Paris, December 1990).

The 337 world heritage sites established as of January 1991 are areas of "outstanding universal value," inscribed either for their natural features, for their cultural value, or for both natural and cultural values. Recreational, educational, and scientific activities are generally permitted. Cultivation, grazing, settlements, mining, and other commercial activities are allowed within specific zones of some sites on a limited basis. The scope of activities permitted is indicated by the types of IUCN protected areas included within individual heritage site boundaries (see below).

Management problems reported here are based on all PADU information sheets for natural or natural/cultural sites available as of November 1990 (83 sites, or 90 percent of the 92 site total reported in Table 20.1). These standard format sheets are compiled by PADU on the basis of reviews, reports, and management plans provided by relevant country authorities. Threats listed by PADU are both those applying to protected area values and those applying to natural heritage values (for example, poaching would be listed at a heritage site inscribed for outstanding geological formations even though this activity does not affect its heritage values). Because they are compiled from a variety of sources and rely to a great extent on self-reporting, information sheets vary in quality and detail. Conditions described date as far back as 1986 for some sites. For these reasons, readers should be cautious in comparing data between sites.

All activities described under the "Management Problems" section of each PADU information sheet were assigned to a management problem category, as described below. Threats were considered *potential* if the activity described had yet to take place. Threats were considered *minor* if they were described as a "minor" or "slight" threat, if the activity described was "almost under" control, or if associated problems from these activities were described as "few" or "negligible." All other threats described were classed as *significant*.

The 13 management problem categories presented here are based on a broader range of categories described in the draft *World Heritage at Risk*. They were selected as best representing the root causes of the full range of threats described in the PADU information sheets for each site. For example, rather than listing erosion resulting from overgrazing at a site as both a "grazing" and "erosion" problem, the former category has been chosen as best describing this type of management problem.

In some instances, one activity described in an information sheet constitutes several management problems.

IUCN protected area classes included describes some of the types of protected areas included within the boundaries of the heritage site. For descriptions of categories I–V, and biosphere reserves (category IX), refer to the Technical Notes for Table 20.1. IUCN categories VI–VIII refer to areas where limited resource use is permitted, as described below:

■ Category VI. Resource reserves/interim conservation units are undeveloped regions where access is restricted to "ongoing ecologically sound activities." This category is established for areas where governments want to control development, or areas where protective legislation has been established, but not yet implemented.

■ Category VII. Natural biotic areas/anthropological reserves are areas where use is limited to traditional activities by local cultures.

■ Category VIII. Multiple use management areas/managed resource areas are government-owned areas managed for recreation, grazing, and sustainable use of natural resources. A limited amount of land that has been settled and otherwise "altered by humans" may be included.

Management problems consist of activities that are either negatively affecting a protected area or natural heritage values or that are occurring in violation of laws protecting protected areas within the site, or the site as a whole.

Development includes all development occurring within the heritage site, such as mining (oil and natural gas drilling, peat cutting, and quarrying for minerals), water development projects, public and logging roads, settlements, military bases, ski areas, railroads, tourist accommodations, and other infrastructure not directly related to the housing of researchers and protected area staff. Mining and water development projects occurring outside the site are included under this category if they affect protected area ecosystems within the site.

Tourism includes the negative effects from recreational and tourism-related activities occurring within the site.

Pollution encompasses air and water pollution, noise pollution, and littering.

External threats include all development (except water projects and mining), logging, agriculture, hunting, and other activities in areas outside the heritage site that are having an adverse effect on the site. Sites where there is a stated risk of a growing population encroaching onto protected lands are also considered to be threatened by external causes.

Threats to local cultures come from activities adversely affecting resident indigenous cultures, and threats to archaeological remains within these sites.

Grazing and cultivation encompasses illegal or problem cultivation and grazing by domestic animals within the heritage site.

Illegal or overharvest of wildlife includes poaching or overharvest of all nonplant species.

Illegal or overharvest of trees/plants includes illegal cutting or vegetation removal, and cutting/vegetation removal that either exceeds natural replacement or has other negative effects on the ecosystem.

Fire and natural threats consist of human-caused fires, natural fires, drought and vulnerability to natural catastrophes, and effects of overbrowsing by elephants.

Introduced plant and animal species means the presence of exotic plants and animals, as well as feral livestock.

Inadequate or insufficient legal protection encompasses threats to protected area integrity from land claims, the temporary ceding of land to logging companies, or sites judged not large enough or with inadequate legal status to protect vital components of an ecosystem, or to ensure protection of key species within the heritage site. *Inadequate or insufficient management* includes insufficient staffing; lack of funding or equipment; poor staff morale; an inadequate management plan for the area; poor coordination between agencies responsible for managing the site; conflicts between management and local communities, and/or need for local extension; and the periodic attacks on people by wild animals.

Other consists of war and civil unrest; unspecified problems with soil degradation and erosion; honey gathering; risk of disease and other threats to livestock in areas adjacent to park; fish stocking; effects on black bear behavior; vandalism; alteration of marginal areas; ice collection; lack of water; siltation; isolation of forest patches in the ecosystem; and unspecified loss of species and declining populations.

Table 20.4 Globally Threatened Animal Species, 1990

Sources: International Union for Conservation of Nature and Natural Resources (IUCN), *The IUCN Mammal Red Data Book, Part I* (IUCN, Gland, Switzerland, 1982); International Council for Bird Preservation (ICBP)/IUCN, *Threatened Birds of Africa and Related Islands* (ICBP/IUCN, Cambridge, United Kingdom, 1985); World Conservation Monitoring Centre (WCMC), series of reports on *Conservation of Biological Diversity* (for some data on Botswana, Cote d'Ivoire, Ethiopia, Guinea-Bissau, Kenya, Nigeria, Senegal, India, Myanmar, and the Philippines) (WCMC, Cambridge, 1988 and 1989); unpublished data (WCMC, Cambridge, United Kingdom, 1991).

Sub-Saharan Africa (all species known): Richard Adams, Simon Stuart, IUCN, *Biodiversity in Sub-Saharan Africa and Its Islands* (IUCN, Gland, Switzerland, 1990); North Africa (bird species known): Jeffery A. Sayer, Simon Stuart, IUCN, *Environmental Conservation*, Vol. 15, No. 3 (Autumn 1988); China and Indonesia (mammal and bird species known): Regional Physical Planning Programme for Transmigration, *The Land Resources of Indonesia: A National Overview* (Department of Transmigration, Jakarta, Indonesia, 1990); Mexico: Conservation International (CI), *Mexico's Living Endowment: An Overview of Biological Diversity* (CI, n.p., April 1989); Panama (bird species known): James R. Karr, Acting Director, Smithsonian Tropical Research Institute, September 25, 1987 (personal communication); Canada, United States including Caribbean and Pacific islands, Europe, Turkey, Japan, and New Zealand (all species known), and Australia (birds, reptile, fish, and amphibian species known): Organisation for Economic Co-operation and Development (OECD), *OECD Environmental Data Compendium 1991* (OECD, Paris, 1991); Viet Nam: Vo Quy, "Viet Nam's Ecological Situation Today," *ESCAP Environment News*, Vol. 6, No. 4 (October–December 1988); Czechoslovakia (bird species known): *CSSR Red Data Book*, 1988; U.S.S.R.: A.V. Yablokov, Ostroumov, *Okhrana Zhivoi Prirody (The Conservation of Living Nature)* (Moscow, 1983).

The World Conservation Union classifies threatened and endangered species in six categories:

■ Endangered. "Taxa in danger of extinction and whose survival is unlikely if the causal factors continue operating."

■ Vulnerable. "Taxa believed likely to move into the Endangered category in the near future if the causal factors continue operating."

■ Rare. "Taxa with world populations that are not at present Endangered or Vulnerable, but are at risk."

■ Indeterminate. "Taxa known to be Endangered, Vulnerable, or Rare but where there is not enough information to say which of the three categories is appropriate."

■ Out of Danger. "Taxa formerly included in one of the above categories, but which are now considered relatively secure because effective conservation measures have been taken or the previous threat to their survival has been removed."

■ Insufficiently Known. "Taxa that are suspected but not definitely known to belong to any of the above categories."

The number of threatened species listed for all countries includes full species that are endangered, vulnerable, rare, indeterminate, and insufficiently known, but excludes introduced species or those known to be extinct. The total number of species includes introductions. Data on mammals exclude cetaceans (whales and porpoises). Threatened bird species are listed for countries included within their breeding and/or wintering ranges. Threatened marine turtles and marine fish are excluded from country totals. Endangered fish species numbers do not include approximately 250 haplochromine and 2 tilapiine species of Lake Victoria cichlids, since the ranges of these species are undetermined. *Threatened species per 10,000 km²* provides a relative estimate for comparing numbers of threatened species between countries of differing size. Because the relationship between area and species number is nonlinear (as increasingly large areas are sampled, the number of new species located decreases), a species-area curve has been used to standardize these species numbers. The curve predicts how many threatened species a country would have, given its current number of threatened species, if it was a uniform 10,000 square kilometers. It is calculated using the formula: $S = cA^z$ where S = the number of endangered species, A = area, and c and z are constants. The slope of the species-area curve is determined by the constant z, which is approximately 0.33 for large areas containing many habitats. This constant is based on data from previous studies of species-area relationships. In reality, the constant z would differ among regions and countries, because of differences in species' range size (which tends to be smaller in the tropics) and differences in varieties of habitats present. A tropical country with a broad variety of habitats would be expected to have a steeper species-area curve than a temperate, homogenous country because one would predict a greater number of both species and threatened species per unit area. Species-area curves are

also steeper for islands than for mainland countries. At present, there are insufficient regional data to estimate separate slopes for each country.

Table 20.5 Rare and Threatened Plants, 1991

Sources: Number of plant taxa: World Conservation Monitoring Centre (WCMC), Threatened Plants Unit (TPU), unpublished data (WCMC, United Kingdom, September 1991). Land area data: Food and Agriculture Organization of the United Nations (FAO), unpublished data (Agrostat PC, FAO, Rome, 1991); *Europa World Yearbook 1990* (Europa Publications Limited, London, 1990). Numbers of botanical gardens: Botanic Gardens Conservation International (BGCI), unpublished information (BGCI, Kew, United Kingdom, September 1991); C.A. Heywood, V.H. Heywood, and P.S. Wyse Jackson, *1990 International Directory of Botanical Gardens*, 5th Ed., (Koeltz Scientific Books, Koenigstein, Germany, 1991).

Unless otherwise noted, the *Number of plant taxa* refers to the number of native vascular plant species found in the country.

Endemic flora as percentage of total includes plants that occur only in a single geopolitical area or island group.

The number of *rare and threatened plant taxa* includes all plants classified as Endangered, Vulnerable, Rare, or Indeterminate. See the Technical Note for Table 20.4.

Most plant data were compiled by WCMC from the floristic literature, national *Red Data Books*, national lists of threatened species, scientific journals, and papers. *Red Data Books*, prepared for over 70 countries or islands, generally use the IUCN classification system to indicate the degree of threats to individual species of endemic and nonendemic plants.

Table 20.5 usually lists the total recorded species, but it sometimes includes estimates. Figures are not comparable between countries because taxonomic concepts and the extent of knowledge vary. For additional information, see Stephen D. Davis, *et al.*, *Plants in Danger: What Do We Know?* (IUCN, Gland, Switzerland, 1986).

Rare and threatened plant taxa per 10,000 km² provides a relative estimate for comparing numbers of threatened plant taxa between countries of differing size. Refer to the Technical Notes for Table 20.4.

Number of botanical gardens shows the number of gardens that are known to exist in the world and *members of BGCI* shows which of these were members of Botanic Gardens Conservation International at the end of August 1991. BGCI, which has records of approximately 60,000 rare plants in cultivation, estimates that botanical gardens throughout the world contain about 90,000 plant taxa.

Table 20.6 Debt-for-Nature Swaps

Sources: World Wide Fund for Nature (WWF); Conservation International (CI); The Nature Conservancy (TNC); *Convenio sobre cooperacion financiera entre el gobierno de*

Costa Rica y el gobierno de los paises bajos con el fin de apoyar el desarrollo forestal, July 1988 (financial agreement); Swedish Embassy *Completion of the purchase of $24.5 million worth of Costa Rican commercial foreign debt*, May 6, 1989 (press release). This table lists officially sanctioned and funded debt-for-nature swaps as of November 1991.

Debt-for-nature swaps involve the purchase of developing country debt at a discounted value in the secondary debt market, and the subsequent exchange of the foreign debt in return for a newly created obligation on the part of the debtor nation. The payments on the new obligation are made in domestic currency to fund an agreed-upon conservation program.

Debt-for-nature swaps are generally favorable for all parties involved. First, the developing country services a smaller amount of domestic debt. Instead of having to pay a foreign source in hard currency, local currency is used for investment inside the country for nature conservation. The local conservation agencies receive substantial funds for natural resource conservation. The funds of the conservation organization that purchased the debt from the lending institution are in effect converted at a more favorable exchange rate. And the lending institution reduces the amount of doubtful loans on its books.

Since 1987, debt-for-nature swaps have generated more than $60 million for conservation efforts while relieving close to $100 million in foreign debt. As of November 1991, 17 such swaps and 21 transactions have taken place in Bolivia, Costa Rica, the Dominican Republic, Ecuador, Guatemala, Jamaica, Madagascar, Mexico, the Philippines, Poland, and Zambia.

Country refers to the less-developed country that has agreed to put local currency toward environmental protection in exchange for a portion of its foreign debt.

Purchaser/fundraiser refers to the conservation organization(s) or government that acquired the less-developed country's debt on the secondary market and exchanged it for money to be put toward environmental protection in the developing country.

Date is the date that the actual transaction for the debt-for-nature swap was approved.

Face value of debt refers to the contracted amount of debt that the less-developed nation owed to the commercial bank. In some swaps, the agreed-upon amount of debt is swapped through several transactions over a period of time. This column identifies the total agreed-upon sum, including pending transactions, and which transactions have been approved.

Cost is the price the conservation organization(s) or government paid for the debt.

Conservation funds generated refers to the money that the less-developed country has agreed to allocate to local environmental protection, in exchange for its foreign debt.

Purpose describes types of projects that the conservation funds are supporting.

21. Energy and Materials

The world's production of commercial energy (see Table 21.1) has grown by 14 percent in the past decade. Liquid fuels are still the dominant commercial fuel, accounting for 42 percent of the world's commercial energy production. At 130 exajoules (equivalent to the energy content of 21.2 billion barrels of oil), 1989 production was only 4 percent lower than its all time high in 1979. Gaseous fuel production grew faster than any other fossil fuel during the same period. Of all commercial energy sources, primary electricity production increased the most (73 percent) from 1979 to 1989, mainly a result of expanding nuclear power generation. In 1989, industrialized countries produced 95 percent of the world's nuclear and 66 percent of its hydroelectric energy.

Table 21.2 presents two indicators of energy use: commercial energy consumption and energy requirements in conventional fuel equivalent. Commercial energy consumption is defined as the apparent consumption of commercial fuels using the heat value of electricity (100 percent efficiency) as a conversion for primary electricity. Energy requirements in conventional fuel equivalent include not only commercial energy consumption but also consumption of traditional fuels (fuelwood, animal and vegetal waste, and charcoal). In calculating conventional fuel equivalent, primary electricity is valued on a fossil-fuel-avoided basis rather than an energy-output basis.

Table 21.2 shows the wide disparities in energy consumption between regions and countries. Each person in the industrialized world consumed as much commercial energy as 10 people in the developing world. Industrialized countries used 2.8 times as much commercial energy as developing countries. Even if estimates for the use of traditional fuels are included, the energy requirements of industrialized countries are 2.4 times greater than those of developing countries.

The global consumption of traditional fuels is estimated at 20 exajoules–equivalent to the total U.S. coal production in 1989. Such a comparison, however, underestimates the critical role that traditional fuels play for the great majority of people living in developing countries. For example, most countries in sub-Saharan Africa are completely dependent on imports for their commercial fuels, and over 70 percent of their total energy requirements usually come from traditional fuels.

Table 21.2 presents a ratio of the amount of energy consumed for each dollar of gross national product, which is defined as energy intensity. A decline in national energy intensity indicates energy efficiency im-

provements, or a structural shift to a less energy-intensive economy (e.g., a more service-based economy), or a combination of the two. For most industrialized countries and many developing countries, energy intensities have declined over the past decade. Japan and most countries of the European Community are among the industrialized countries with the world's lowest energy intensities. In comparison, energy intensities are still much higher for the majority of Central European countries, and slightly higher for most developing countries.

Table 21.3 shows the relative shares of a country's total commercial energy consumption used by each major economic sector. Industry is the primary consumer of commercial energy in most European and Asian countries. Transportation accounts for the largest share in the majority of countries on the American and African continents. Data in Table 21.3 should be interpreted with care, because countries use different sectoral definitions.

With the development of industrialized economies, the quantities of wastes, both in the industrial and the consumer sector, have increased steadily. A comparison of municipal waste generation (see Table 21.4) shows the United States as the biggest waste generator in the Organisation for Economic Co-operation and Development (OECD), generating 864 kilograms per person per year. Most municipalities in OECD member countries provide waste collection services to the whole population and are responsible for waste disposal. The United States and the countries of the European Community discard about 60 and 70 percent, respectively, of their municipal waste in landfills, whereas Japan, Sweden, and Switzerland incinerate more than 50 percent of their municipal waste. Composting, systematic sorting, and other disposal methods play only a limited role in selected countries.

The production and consumption of metals (see Table 21.5) are central to many modern industrial processes. The United States, the U.S.S.R., Japan, and countries of the European Community consume the majority of the world's metals. Only six developing nations—Algeria, Brazil, China, India, the Republic of Korea, and Mexico—make it into the top 10 consumers of selected metals.

A greater number of producers and more developing economies can be found in data on reserves of major metals. Five countries—the U.S.S.R., South Africa, the United States, China, and Australia—hold over half of the world's reserves of the 15 metals listed in Table 21.6.

Table 21.1 Commercial Energy Production, 1979–89

| | Total | | Solid | | Liquid | | Gas | | Primary Electricity {a} | | | | | |
| | | | | | | | | | Geothermal & Wind | | Hydro | | Nuclear | |
	Peta-joules 1989	Percent Change Since 1979	Peta-joules 1989	Percent Change Since 1979	Peta-joules 1989	Percent Change Since 1979	Peta-joules 1989	Percent Change Since 1979	Peta-joules 1989	Percent Change Since 1979	Peta-joules 1989	Percent Change Since 1979	Peta-joules 1989	Percent Change Since 1979
WORLD	310,972	14	95,713	26	130,299	(4)	70,497	33	141	244	7,539	23	6,783	201
AFRICA	18,926	6	4,072	50	12,461	(11)	2,218	127	0	X	159	(22)	14	X
Algeria	3,869	20	0	114	2,378	(10)	1,489	145	0	X	1	(20)	0	X
Angola	959	212	0	X	948	214	7	136	0	X	5	34	0	X
Benin	12	X	0	X	12	X	0	X	0	X	0	X	0	X
Botswana	19	78	19	78	0	X	0	X	0	X	0	X	0	X
Burkina Faso	0	X	0	X	0	X	0	X	0	X	0	X	0	X
Burundi	1	900	0	250	0	X	0	X	0	X	0	X	0	X
Cameroon	345	290	0	X	336	300	0	X	0	X	9	110	0	X
Cape Verde	0	X	0	X	0	X	0	X	0	X	0	X	0	X
Central African Rep	0	13	0	X	0	X	0	X	0	X	0	13	0	X
Chad	0	X	0	X	0	X	0	X	0	X	0	X	0	X
Comoros	0	X	0	X	0	X	0	X	0	X	0	X	0	X
Congo	310	165	0	X	309	165	0	0	0	X	1	600	0	X
Cote d'Ivoire	12	40	0	X	8	27	0	X	0	X	5	73	0	X
Djibouti	0	X	0	X	0	X	0	X	0	X	0	X	0	X
Egypt	2,142	76	0	X	1,868	75	251	123	0	X	23	(33)	0	X
Equatorial Guinea	0	X	0	X	0	X	0	X	0	X	0	X	0	X
Ethiopia	2	45	0	X	0	X	0	X	0	X	2	45	0	X
Gabon	462	6	0	X	449	4	11	846	0	X	2	118	0	X
Gambia, The	0	X	0	X	0	X	0	X	0	X	0	X	0	X
Ghana	17	(12)	0	X	0	(100)	0	X	0	X	17	4	0	X
Guinea	1	17	0	X	0	X	0	X	0	X	1	17	0	X
Guinea-Bissau	0	X	0	X	0	X	0	X	0	X	0	X	0	X
Kenya	10	113	0	X	0	X	0	X	1	X	9	88	0	X
Lesotho	0	X	X	X	0	X	0	X	0	X	0	X	0	X
Liberia	1	(9)	0	X	0	X	0	X	0	X	1	(9)	0	X
Libya	2,597	(42)	0	X	2,322	(46)	275	50	0	X	0	X	0	X
Madagascar	1	179	0	X	0	X	0	X	0	X	1	179	0	X
Malawi	2	59	0	X	0	X	0	X	0	X	2	59	0	X
Mali	1	133	0	X	0	X	0	X	0	X	1	133	0	X
Mauritania	0	X	0	X	0	X	0	X	0	X	0	X	0	X
Mauritius	0	86	0	X	0	X	0	X	0	X	0	86	0	X
Morocco	23	(23)	16	(23)	1	(30)	2	(16)	0	X	4	(26)	0	X
Mozambique	1	(97)	1	(79)	0	X	0	X	0	X	0	(100)	0	X
Namibia	0	X	X	X	0	X	0	X	0	X	0	X	0	X
Niger	5	X	5	X	0	X	0	X	0	X	0	X	0	X
Nigeria	3,747	(23)	4	(24)	3,566	(26)	169	229	0	X	8	(43)	0	X
Rwanda	1	10	0	X	0	X	0	0	0	X	1	11	0	X
Senegal	0	X	0	X	0	X	0	X	0	X	0	X	0	X
Sierra Leone	0	X	0	X	0	X	0	X	0	X	0	X	0	X
Somalia	0	X	0	X	0	X	0	X	0	X	0	X	0	X
South Africa	3,875	51	3,859	51	0	X	0	X	0	X	2	(48)	14	X
Sudan	2	5	0	X	0	X	0	X	0	X	2	5	0	X
Swaziland	6	5	5	(2)	0	X	0	X	0	X	1	86	0	X
Tanzania	2	20	0	200	0	X	0	X	0	X	2	17	0	X
Togo	0	X	0	X	0	X	0	X	0	X	0	X	0	X
Tunisia	224	(9)	0	X	211	(9)	14	(11)	0	X	0	(20)	0	X
Uganda	2	13	0	X	0	X	0	X	0	X	2	13	0	X
Zaire	77	26	4	25	54	24	0	X	0	X	19	32	0	X
Zambia	34	(27)	10	(34)	0	X	0	X	0	X	24	(23)	0	X
Zimbabwe	159	50	150	60	0	X	0	X	0	X	10	(25)	0	X
NORTH & CENTRAL AMERICA	78,990	10	23,816	31	28,453	4	22,292	(5)	81	286	2,154	8	2,193	109
Barbados	3	58	0	X	2	36	1	138	0	X	0	X	0	X
Belize	0	X	0	X	0	X	0	X	0	X	0	X	0	X
Canada	10,830	28	1,717	112	3,794	6	3,981	31	0	X	1,049	19	288	124
Costa Rica	12	105	0	X	0	X	0	X	0	X	12	105	0	X
Cuba	32	141	0	X	30	150	1	75	0	X	0	(23)	0	X
Dominican Rep	3	72	0	X	0	X	0	X	0	X	3	72	0	X
El Salvador	7	27	0	X	0	X	0	X	2	20	5	29	0	X
Guatemala	15	245	0	X	8	132	0	X	0	X	8	576	0	X
Haiti	1	50	0	X	0	X	0	X	0	X	1	50	0	X
Honduras	3	19	0	X	0	X	0	X	0	X	3	19	0	X
Jamaica	0	0	0	X	0	X	0	X	0	X	0	0	0	X
Mexico	7,353	65	221	44	6,046	78	984	18	18	402	83	27	0	X
Nicaragua	2	49	0	X	0	X	0	X	1	X	1	(30)	0	X
Panama	8	171	0	X	0	X	0	X	0	X	8	171	0	X
Trinidad and Tobago	471	(21)	0	X	323	(30)	147	15	0	X	0	X	0	X
United States	60,249	3	21,878	27	18,249	(9)	17,177	(12)	60	282	979	(3)	1,906	107
SOUTH AMERICA	12,610	25	777	177	8,540	7	2,088	73	0	X	1,179	90	27	170
Argentina	1,905	36	13	(28)	1,032	(0)	785	159	0	X	55	42	20	106
Bolivia	165	22	0	X	46	(20)	114	55	0	X	5	26	0	X
Brazil	2,318	156	126	23	1,281	262	133	276	0	X	771	86	7	X
Chile	215	38	57	108	58	(8)	66	63	0	X	35	38	0	X
Colombia	1,657	186	516	294	860	210	174	43	0	X	108	123	0	X
Ecuador	633	38	0	X	612	34	4	128	0	X	18	571	0	X
Guyana	0	X	0	X	0	X	0	X	0	X	0	X	0	X
Paraguay	10	434	0	X	0	X	0	X	0	X	10	434	0	X
Peru	355	(20)	3	333	293	(26)	20	8	0	X	38	57	0	X
Suriname	13	285	0	X	9	X	0	X	0	X	3	0	0	X
Uruguay	14	199	0	X	0	X	0	X	0	X	14	199	0	X
Venezuela	5,325	(11)	61	3,713	4,349	(18)	792	30	0	X	123	128	0	X

Table 21.1

| | Total | | Solid | | Liquid | | Gas | | Primary Electricity {a} | | | | | |
| | | | | | | | | | Geothermal & Wind | | Hydro | | Nuclear | |
	Peta-joules 1989	Percent Change Since 1979	Peta-joules 1989	Percent Change Since 1979	Peta-joules 1989	Percent Change Since 1979	Peta-joules 1989	Percent Change Since 1979	Peta-joules 1989	Percent Change Since 1979	Peta-joules 1989	Percent Change Since 1979	Peta-joules 1989	Percent Change Since 1979
ASIA	85,244	8	29,810	63	45,345	(19)	7,673	122	25	317	1,434	59	957	221
Afghanistan	123	34	4	10	0	200	115	35	0	X	3	11	0	X
Bahrain	292	34	0	X	97	(11)	195	78	0	X	0	X	0	X
Bangladesh	159	283	0	X	5	1,710	151	287	0	X	3	25	0	X
Bhutan	2	7,900	0	X	0	X	0	X	0	X	2	7,900	0	X
Cambodia	0	X	0	X	0	X	0	X	0	X	0	X	0	X
China	28,484	56	21,750	67	5,755	29	586	4	0	X	394	118	0	X
Cyprus	0	X	0	X	0	X	0	X	0	X	0	X	0	X
India	6,920	106	4,920	90	1,428	166	316	412	0	X	230	40	26	156
Indonesia	4,065	7	133	1,532	2,685	(18)	1,215	135	1	X	31	497	0	X
Iran, Islamic Rep	6,895	(14)	35	33	5,970	(18)	866	24	0	X	24	24	0	X
Iraq	5,993	(17)	0	X	5,800	(19)	191	179	0	X	2	(14)	0	X
Israel	2	(36)	0	X	1	(23)	2	(40)	0	X	0	X	0	X
Japan	1,381	20	263	(44)	23	9	80	(22)	5	25	352	15	658	160
Jordan	1	X	0	X	1	X	0	X	0	X	0	X	0	X
Korea, Dem People's Rep	1,530	21	1,416	19	0	X	0	X	0	X	114	55	0	X
Korea, Rep	579	54	392	10	0	X	212	58	0	X	16	96	171	1,403
Kuwait	3,470	(38)	0	X	3,257	(40)	212	58	0	X	0	X	0	X
Lao People's Dem Rep	4	4	0	X	0	X	0	X	0	X	4	4	0	X
Lebanon	2	(41)	0	X	0	X	0	X	0	X	2	(41)	0	X
Malaysia	1,769	202	0	X	1,187	105	559	20,184	0	X	23	474	0	X
Mongolia	91	93	91	93	0	X	0	X	0	X	0	X	0	X
Myanmar	85	16	2	100	37	(37)	42	286	0	X	4	60	0	X
Nepal	2	219	0	X	0	X	0	X	0	X	2	219	0	X
Oman	1,435	125	0	X	1,344	119	91	251	0	X	0	X	0	X
Pakistan	600	117	52	89	96	360	391	97	0	X	61	106	0	(69)
Philippines	81	27	27	419	11	(76)	0	X	19	705	24	127	0	X
Qatar	1,076	(10)	0	X	862	(16)	214	26	0	X	0	X	0	X
Saudi Arabia	12,224	(40)	0	X	11,182	(45)	1,042	4,069	0	X	0	X	0	X
Singapore	0	X	0	X	0	X	0	X	0	X	0	X	0	X
Sri Lanka	10	81	0	X	0	X	0	X	0	X	10	81	0	X
Syrian Arab Rep	793	112	0	X	767	111	9	553	0	X	17	100	0	X
Thailand	416	1,420	97	537	98	25,508	202	X	0	X	20	71	0	X
Turkey	642	44	450	55	120	2	7	7,467	0	X	65	74	0	X
United Arab Emirates	4,714	18	0	X	3,952	4	762	260	0	X	0	X	0	X
Viet Nam	185	12	158	(2)	19	X	0	X	0	X	8	124	0	X
Yemen (Arab Rep)	0	X	0	X	0	X	0	X	0	X	0	X	0	X
(People's Dem Rep)	353	X	0	X	353	X	0	X	0	X	0	X	0	X
EUROPE	40,061	9	18,145	(5)	8,921	59	8,470	(12)	26	189	1,674	(1)	2,825	289
Albania	185	9	35	71	121	(3)	16	8	0	X	13	33	0	X
Austria	250	(18)	23	(36)	51	(31)	46	(52)	0	X	130	31	0	X
Belgium	248	19	97	(41)	0	X	0	(64)	0	X	1	45	148	261
Bulgaria	528	13	505	21	3	(72)	0	(93)	0	X	10	(19)	10	(56)
Czechoslovakia	1,871	(6)	1,734	(10)	6	31	27	(6)	0	X	15	2	88	1,044
Denmark	338	1,761	0	X	232	1,181	105	X	2	X	0	0	0	X
Finland	171	128	56	312	0	X	0	X	0	X	47	20	69	200
France	1,938	38	385	(39)	153	77	121	(60)	0	X	184	(22)	1,094	661
Germany (Fed Rep)	4,351	(9)	3,034	(17)	226	14	493	(32)	0	X	61	(0)	536	252
(Dem Rep)	2,773	16	2,655	17	2	(22)	66	(19)	0	X	6	18	44	26
Greece	335	134	283	117	39	X	6	X	0	X	8	(40)	0	X
Hungary	608	(7)	222	(25)	104	(12)	232	(5)	0	X	1	6	50	X
Iceland	16	58	0	X	0	X	0	X	1	450	15	51	0	X
Ireland	139	132	50	41	0	X	85	297	0	X	4	21	0	X
Italy	938	23	12	(45)	197	173	594	33	11	20	123	(26)	0	(100)
Luxembourg	3	818	0	X	0	X	0	X	0	X	3	818	0	X
Malta	0	X	0	X	0	X	0	X	0	X	0	X	0	X
Netherlands	2,440	(32)	0	X	161	140	2,264	(35)	0	X	0	X	14	15
Norway	4,873	143	10	33	3,145	299	1,292	45	0	X	426	34	0	X
Poland	4,913	(8)	4,748	(7)	8	(43)	143	(36)	0	X	14	53	0	X
Portugal	25	(47)	4	(16)	0	X	0	X	0	X	21	(51)	0	X
Romania	2,308	(8)	748	57	407	(24)	1,108	(24)	0	X	45	11	0	X
Spain	854	27	477	10	43	(10)	61	207,000	0	X	70	(58)	202	738
Sweden	497	68	0	(100)	0	(100)	0	X	0	X	260	18	237	213
Switzerland	190	24	0	X	0	X	0	X	0	X	107	(5)	82	103
United Kingdom	8,211	5	2,371	(20)	3,858	18	1,725	17	0	X	25	62	233	69
Yugoslavia	1,058	35	695	58	164	(6)	85	10	12	X	85	(11)	17	X
U.S.S.R.	69,071	26	15,086	(1)	25,468	4	26,948	90	0	X	802	30	767	344
OCEANIA	6,070	76	4,007	95	1,111	20	808	130	7	75	136	17	0	X
Australia	5,656	72	3,945	97	1,035	14	621	100	3	X	52	(10)	0	X
Fiji	1	X	0	X	0	X	0	X	0	X	1	X	0	X
New Zealand	409	151	62	35	76	370	187	359	4	5	79	41	0	X
Papua New Guinea	2	30	0	X	0	X	0	X	0	X	2	30	0	X
Solomon Islands	0	X	0	X	0	X	0	X	0	X	0	X	0	X

Source: United Nations Statistical Office.
Notes:
a. The production of primary electricity was assessed at the heat value of electricity (1 kilowatt hour = 3.6 million joules), the equivalent of assuming a 100 percent efficiency.
1 petajoule = 1,000,000,000,000,000 joules = 947,800,000,000 Btus = 163,400 "U.N. standard" barrels of oil = 34,140 "U.N. standard" metric tons of coal.
World and regional totals include countries not listed.
0 = zero or less than half of the unit of measure; X = not available; negative numbers are shown in parentheses.
For additional information, see Sources and Technical Notes.

Table 21.2 Energy Consumption and Requirements, 1979–89

	Commercial Energy Consumption								Energy Requirements in Conventional Fuel Equivalent							
	Total		Per Capita		Per Constant 1987 $US of GNP		Imports as Percentage of Consumption		Total		Per Capita		Per Constant 1987 $US of GNP		Traditional Fuels as Percentage of Total Requirements	
	Petajoules 1989	Percent Change Since 1979	Gigajoules 1989	Percent Change Since 1979	Megajoules 1989	Percent Change Since 1979	1979	1989	Petajoules 1989	Percent Change Since 1979	Gigajoules 1989	Percent Change Since 1979	Megajoules 1989	Percent Change Since 1979	1979	1989
WORLD	298,258	18	57	(1)	X	X	X	X	346,931	22	67	2	X	X	6	6
AFRICA	7,472	52	12	13	X	X	(265)	(153)	12,363	42	20	6	X	X	39	37
Algeria	666	90	27	41	10	38	(823)	(481)	686	87	28	39	11	36	4	3
Angola	25	(10)	3	(31)	4	X	(982)	(3,663)	78	13	8	(13)	14	X	49	55
Benin	6	15	1	(16)	4	(9)	99	(91)	54	32	12	(3)	32	6	84	86
Botswana	X	X	X	X	X	X	X	X	X	X	X	X	X	X	X	X
Burkina Faso	7	28	1	(1)	3	(12)	100	100	87	28	10	(1)	33	(11)	92	92
Burundi	3	109	1	58	2	38	96	79	43	38	8	4	37	(9)	95	92
Cameroon	85	220	7	134	8	108	(234)	(307)	204	81	18	32	19	18	68	49
Cape Verde	1	(68)	3	(75)	4	(87)	100	100	1	(68)	3	(75)	4	(87)	0	0
Central African Rep	4	133	1	78	4	121	86	93	38	48	13	13	36	40	92	88
Chad	3	(2)	1	(22)	3	(38)	100	99	36	24	7	(2)	38	(21)	90	92
Comoros	1	178	2	97	4	79	100	100	1	178	2	97	4	79	0	0
Congo	23	548	10	363	11	259	(3,196)	(1,249)	44	153	20	81	22	40	76	41
Cote d'Ivoire	60	11	5	(26)	6	(1)	83	79	169	36	14	(9)	18	21	52	59
Djibouti	4	3	11	(27)	X	X	100	100	4	3	11	(27)	X	X	0	0
Egypt	1,122	94	22	52	32	13	(110)	(91)	1,211	78	24	39	35	3	5	4
Equatorial Guinea	1	82	4	50	11	X	96	100	6	20	14	(1)	42	X	83	75
Ethiopia	34	40	1	4	6	11	93	93	413	22	8	(9)	73	(4)	92	91
Gabon	42	71	38	18	13	58	(1,685)	(1,013)	71	64	64	13	22	52	39	35
Gambia, The	3	24	3	(11)	14	(2)	99	100	11	7	13	(23)	61	(15)	80	77
Ghana	46	(3)	3	(30)	8	(20)	59	63	236	37	16	(0)	43	14	54	67
Guinea	14	9	3	(14)	7	X	96	96	55	21	10	(4)	25	X	69	72
Guinea-Bissau	2	56	2	26	11	23	100	100	6	13	6	(8)	34	(10)	76	67
Kenya	72	13	3	(23)	9	(25)	93	86	434	37	18	(7)	52	(9)	77	79
Lesotho	X	X	X	X	X	X	X	X	X	X	X	X	X	X	X	X
Liberia	11	(57)	5	(69)	X	X	95	89	61	(9)	24	(33)	X	X	56	78
Libya	516	170	117	79	22	339	(2,252)	(404)	521	166	119	76	22	331	3	1
Madagascar	13	(11)	1	(33)	5	(6)	97	92	87	27	8	(5)	34	33	78	82
Malawi	10	8	1	(23)	8	(13)	86	79	146	22	18	(12)	117	(1)	90	90
Mali	6	6	1	(17)	3	(24)	96	90	59	30	7	2	28	(6)	85	87
Mauritania	41	406	22	300	46	333	100	100	42	405	22	300	46	333	1	0
Mauritius	14	47	13	31	7	(2)	98	97	30	6	28	(5)	15	(29)	66	52
Morocco	264	35	11	5	13	(7)	84	91	285	32	12	2	14	(10)	5	5
Mozambique	15	(56)	1	(67)	10	(68) a	(32)	91	165	5	11	(19)	112	(8) a	76	89
Namibia	X	X	X	X	X	X	X	X	X	X	X	X	X	X	X	X
Niger	13	97	2	41	6	110	100	65	55	46	7	5	26	56	81	73
Nigeria	592	139	5	73	23	141	(1,864)	(533)	1,589	63	14	18	63	64	72	62
Rwanda	6	140	1	74	3	92	77	89	62	34	9	(3)	31	7	92	88
Senegal	41	12	6	(16)	9	(10)	100	100	83	16	12	(13)	18	(6)	49	51
Sierra Leone	9	0	2	(21)	14	(16)	100	100	37	19	9	(6)	58	(0)	71	76
Somalia	12	171	2	103	13	141	99	100	81	56	13	17	84	39	91	85
South Africa {b}	3,098	30	77	2	36	5 a	(9)	(25)	3,272	25	81	(2)	38	7 a	5	6
Sudan	45	(3)	2	(27)	4	(19)	96	96	254	29	10	(2)	25	9	75	81
Swaziland	X	X	X	X	X	X	X	X	X	X	X	X	X	X	X	X
Tanzania	28	(3)	1	(28)	8	(18)	93	92	339	38	14	1	98	16	87	90
Togo	7	(63)	2	(73)	5	(70)	100	100	16	(37)	4	(55)	12	(48)	20	43
Tunisia	167	49	21	16	17	4	(120)	(34)	197	45	25	13	20	1	17	15
Uganda	14	44	1	6	3	10	78	83	144	42	9	4	30	8	87	87
Zaire	65	10	2	(19)	9	(7)	(3)	(19)	422	31	12	(3)	57	12	73	76
Zambia	47	(28)	6	(50)	23	(38)	30	28	201	5	26	(27)	100	(10)	42	58
Zimbabwe	192	50	20	7	33	(2)	17	17	295	29	31	(8)	51	(15)	25	25
NORTH & CENTRAL AMERICA	87,638	5	207	(9)	X	X	14	10	98,570	8	233	(6)	X	X	2	2
Barbados	12	47	47	42	8	27	75	72	14	23	54	19	9	6	26	12
Belize	3	(14)	14	(35)	9	(42)	100	100	6	(11)	31	(32)	19	(40)	54	55
Canada	8,414	14	321	4	20	(14)	(15)	(29)	11,087	20	422	9	26	(9)	0	1
Costa Rica	43	8	16	(14)	9	(9)	85	72	101	30	37	3	22	9	34	33
Cuba	471	18	45	9	X	X	97	93	650	13	62	4	X	X	30	27
Dominican Rep	81	1	12	(19)	16	(19)	98	96	115	(6)	16	(25)	23	(24)	31	23
El Salvador	34	0	7	(13)	7	13	84	80	87	(1)	17	(14)	18	12	49	46
Guatemala	52	(14)	6	(35)	7	(21)	93	71	156	22	17	(8)	21	12	51	57
Haiti	10	1	2	(16)	5	0	92	88	66	18	10	(2)	32	17	80	82
Honduras	26	2	5	(27)	6	(17)	90	88	89	25	18	(11)	21	1	56	62
Jamaica	61	(45)	25	(52)	21	(48)	100	99	67	(44)	28	(50)	23	(47)	6	8
Mexico	4,293	39	51	13	30	15	(44)	(71)	4,720	38	56	12	33	14	6	5
Nicaragua	31	27	8	(8)	12	55	94	93	71	26	19	(9)	28	54	52	49
Panama	41	(5)	17	(24)	10	(11)	95	81	76	7	32	(13)	19	0	31	26
Trinidad and Tobago	209	(5)	165	(20)	50	34	(169)	(125)	212	(6)	168	(20)	51	33	2	1
United States	73,370	3	295	(7)	15	(20)	18	18	80,560	6	324	(4)	17	(18)	1	2
SOUTH AMERICA	8,803	24	30	1	X	X	(42)	(43)	14,240	31	49	6	X	X	23	20
Argentina	1,813	24	57	8	27	46	4	(5)	2,070	25	65	9	31	47	6	5
Bolivia	79	24	11	(5)	18	29	(112)	(108)	105	20	15	(8)	24	25	19	16
Brazil	3,445	28	23	3	11	(3)	66	33	7,362	34	50	8	25	2	36	30
Chile	458	44	35	22	22	5	51	53	598	41	46	20	29	3	13	12
Colombia	775	33	24	8	21	(2)	1	(114)	1,199	44	37	17	32	7	18	17
Ecuador	200	33	19	2	18	6	(205)	(216)	308	41	30	8	27	12	29	24
Guyana	9	(56)	11	(58)	29	(44)	100	100	14	(52)	17	(55)	44	(40)	28	33
Paraguay	27	40	6	2	6	(1)	90	63	93	41	22	3	22	(1)	66	59
Peru	312	3	15	(18)	15	2	(47)	(14)	484	12	23	(11)	23	11	19	20
Suriname	15	(55)	35	(62)	13	(44)	90	18	22	(46)	51	(55)	19	(33)	1	2
Uruguay	71	(15)	23	(20)	10	(14)	94	80	119	2	39	(4)	17	4	20	24
Venezuela	1,592	19	83	(10)	36	29	(347)	(234)	1,860	27	97	(4)	42	38	1	1

	Energy Consumption								Energy Requirements in Conventional Fuel Equivalent							
	Total		Per Capita		Per Constant 1987 $US of GNP		Imports as Percentage of Consumption		Total		Per Capita		Per Constant 1987 $US of GNP		Traditional Fuels as Percentage of Total Requirements	
	Peta-joules 1989	Percent Change Since 1979	Giga-joules 1989	Percent Change Since 1979	Mega-joules 1989	Percent Change Since 1979	1979	1989	Peta-joules 1989	Percent Change Since 1979	Giga-joules 1989	Percent Change Since 1979	Mega joules 1989	Percent Change Since 1979	1979	1989
ASIA	70,778	54	23	28	X	X	(72)	(194)	84,136	52	28	26	X	X	13	10
Afghanistan	107	258	5	179	X	X	(208)	(15)	157	93	8	50	X	X	57	29
Bahrain	228	90	467	24	76	82 a	(81)	(28)	228	90	467	24	76	82 a	0	0
Bangladesh	227	125	2	73	12	59	59	30	502	38	5	6	27	(2)	71	54
Bhutan	1	155	1	107	2 c	(5) a	91	(189)	30	9	22	(12)	114 c	(50) a	99	95
Cambodia	6	1,353	1	1,063	X	X	100	98	58	41	7	13	X	X	99	89
China	26,156	61	23	40	76	(31)	(12)	(9)	28,805	58	26	38	84	(32)	8	6
Cyprus	51	53	74	38	12	(14)	100	100	52	54	75	38	12	(13)	1	1
India	7,528	94	9	57	26	13	13	8	10,693	70	13	37	37	(1)	33	25
Indonesia	1,453	44	8	17	17	(23)	(276)	(180)	2,852	32	16	8	34	(29)	53	47
Iran, Islamic Rep	2,399	36	45	(4)	15	15	(352)	(187)	2,474	35	46	(4)	16	14	1	1
Iraq	567	102	31	42	X	X	(2,478)	(956)	572	100	31	40	X	X	0	0
Israel	402	61	89	35	11	13	99	99	399	61	89	35	10	13	0	0
Japan	14,533	12	118	5	5	(26)	91	90	16,573	17	135	10	6	(22)	0	0
Jordan	115	137	29	73	21	X	100	99	115	138	29	73	21	X	0	0
Korea, Dem People's Rep	1,756	28	83	8	X	X	7	13	2,025	30	95	10	X	X	2	2
Korea, Rep	2,748	83	65	62	18	(16)	75	79	3,165	91	75	69	21	(12)	7	1
Kuwait	480	148	234	57	14	169	(2,789)	(624)	480	148	234	57	14	169	0	0
Lao People's Dem Rep	5	12	1	(13)	4	X	7	15	43	25	11	(3)	42	X	82	83
Lebanon	114	53	42	54	X	X	96	98	122	42	46	43	X	X	5	4
Malaysia	705	128	41	77	20	31	(89)	(151)	834	117	48	68	23	25	17	10
Mongolia	117	62	57	23	32	(14) a	34	22	131	51	63	14	36	(19) a	15	10
Myanmar	74	36	2	10	7	8	(35)	(15)	268	27	7	3	27	2	71	69
Nepal	13	80	1	39	4	21	91	85	226	67	12	29	74	13	94	92
Oman	146	228	98	107	20	37	(1,338)	(886)	146	228	98	107	20	37	0	0
Pakistan	930	119	8	60	25	14	35	36	1,330	102	12	48	36	5	26	21
Philippines	527	9	9	(14)	14	(8)	87	85	983	21	16	(5)	25	1	38	38
Qatar	250	35	593	(18)	42	41	(546)	(330)	250	35	593	(18)	42	41	0	0
Saudi Arabia	2,535	299	176	145	30	281	(3,131)	(382)	2,535	299	176	145	30	281	0	0
Singapore	393	(2)	146	(13)	16	(51)	100	100	393	(2)	146	(13)	16	(51)	0	0
Sri Lanka	55	17	3	1	8	(21)	89	83	153	21	9	5	22	(18)	54	52
Syrian Arab Rep	340	32	28	(7)	27	4	(45)	(134)	374	36	31	(4)	30	8	0	0
Thailand	1,026	117	18	79	17	7	94	59	1,631	90	29	57	27	(6)	41	34
Turkey	1,539	69	28	34	22	11	51	58	1,766	40	32	11	25	(8)	22	5
United Arab Emirates	897	268	581	119	33	282	(1,542)	(425)	897	268	581	119	33	282	0	0
Viet Nam	210	13	3	(9)	4	X	12	12	465	22	7	(1)	8	X	49	51
Yemen (Arab Rep)	42	204	4	117	X	X	100	(734)	42	204	4	117	X	X	0	0
(People's Dem Rep)	70	151	29	87	59	X	100	100	74	142	30	80	62	X	8	4
EUROPE	64,465	(1)	127	(4)	X	X	43	38	74,398	6	146	2	X	X	1	1
Albania	119	29	37	6	X	X	(84)	(55)	156	26	49	3	X	X	13	10
Austria	892	(3)	117	(4)	7	(21)	67	72	1,153	4	151	3	9	(15)	1	1
Belgium	1,676	(12)	168	(13)	11	(22) a	89	85	1,964	(1)	197	(2)	13	(12) a	0	0
Bulgaria	1,291	(1)	144	(3)	47	(28) a	64	59	1,381	(2)	154	(4)	50	(28) a	1	1
Czechoslovakia	2,733	(4)	175	(7)	51	(17) a	30	32	2,975	1	190	(2)	55	(13) a	1	1
Denmark	665	(22)	130	(23)	7	(33)	98	49	747	(15)	146	(16)	8	(27)	0	2
Finland	840	12	169	7	9	(22)	90	80	1,164	26	235	21	12	(12)	5	3
France	6,460	(9)	115	(14)	7	(26)	80	70	8,815	10	157	5	9	(11)	1	1
Germany (Fed Rep)	9,656	(12)	156	(13)	8	(27)	56	55	10,885	(5)	176	(6)	9	(21)	0	0
(Dem Rep)	3,648	5	219	5	X	X	31	24	3,760	5	226	6	X	X	0	0
Greece	918	55	91	47	19	38	76	64	959	51	96	44	20	34	2	2
Hungary	1,136	(8)	107	(7)	46	(18)	47	46	1,344	3	127	4	54	(8)	2	2
Iceland	42	14	165	1	9	(10)	72	61	74	29	293	15	15	2	0	0
Ireland	392	15	112	10	14	(0)	82	65	400	15	114	10	14	(0)	0	0
Italy	6,384	14	111	12	0	(10)	80	83	6,942	15	121	13	9	(9)	1	1
Luxembourg	136	(13)	361	(16)	15	(44)	100	98	170	(3)	451	(7)	18	(38)	0	0
Malta	21	73	60	78	11	20	100	100	21	73	60	78	11	20	0	0
Netherlands	2,890	(3)	195	(8)	13	(17)	(20)	16	2,957	(2)	199	(7)	13	(15)	0	1
Norway	884	19	209	15	10	(15)	(171)	(451)	1,638	21	388	17	19	(14)	0	1
Poland	5,062	2	134	(5)	79	(12) a	(8)	3	5,133	3	136	(5)	81	(12) a	0	1
Portugal	543	68	53	58	14	27	85	95	598	46	58	36	15	10	1	1
Romania	3,047	2	132	(3)	56	(13)	16	24	3,228	4	139	(1)	59	(12)	1	1
Spain	2,846	10	73	5	9	(17)	74	70	3,399	14	88	9	11	(14)	0	1
Sweden	1,253	(11)	147	(13)	8	(26)	79	60	2,363	8	278	6	14	(9)	8	5
Switzerland	710	5	107	1	4	(16)	77	73	1,079	15	162	10	6	(9)	1	1
United Kingdom	8,436	(1)	147	(3)	11	(19)	8	3	9,047	2	158	0	12	(16)	0	0
Yugoslavia	1,771	31	75	23	27	27	42	40	2,034	30	86	22	31	26	2	2
U.S.S.R.	54,958	27	191	16	X	X	(27)	(25)	58,599	29	204	18	X	X	2	1
OCEANIA	4,141	40	158	20	X	X	(16)	(47)	4,624	39	176	19	X	X	4	4
Australia	3,534	38	211	19	18	3	(28)	(60)	3,770	37	225	19	20	2	2	3
Fiji	11	(1)	14	(17)	9	(8)	100	89	25	34	34	13	20	25	43	48
New Zealand	499	73	151	63	14	45	43	18	666	63	201	53	19	36	0	0
Papua New Guinea	33	25	9	(2)	11	11	95	95	91	14	24	(11)	30	(11)	64	60
Solomon Islands	2	43	7	2	14	(11)	100	100	4	(16)	11	(41)	22	(48)	64	38

Sources: United Nations Statistical Office and The World Bank.
Notes: a. Change since 1980. b. Data are for South Africa Customs Union (Botswana, Lesotho, Namibia, South Africa, and Swaziland). c. 1988 data.
1 petajoule = 1,000,000,000,000,000 joules = 947,800,000,000 Btus = 163,400 "U.N. standard" barrels of oil = 34,140 "U.N. standard" metric tons of coal.
1 gigajoule = 1,000,000,000 joules = 947,800 Btus; 1 megajoule = 1,000,000 joules = 947.8 Btus.
World and regional totals include countries not listed.
0 = zero or less than half of the unit of measure; X = not available; negative numbers are shown in parentheses; GNP = gross national product.
For additional information, see Sources and Technical Notes.

Table 21.3 Commercial Energy Use by Sector, 1979–89

	Industry 1979	Industry 1989	Transport 1979	Transport 1989	Agriculture 1979	Agriculture 1989	Commercial 1979	Commercial 1989	Residential 1979	Residential 1989	Other 1979	Other 1989	Energy Intensity 1989 Industry (megajoules per $US Industrial GDP)	Energy Intensity 1989 Agriculture (megajoules per $US Agriculture GDP)
WORLD														
AFRICA														
Algeria	28	22 a	36	40 a	5	3 a	6	6 a	21	24 a	5	5 a	6	2
Angola	21	24	59	46	0	0	0	0	5	11	14	19	X	X
Benin	6	9	72	79	0	0	1	1	21	11	1	1	3	0
Cameroon	21 b	19	61 b	53	0 b	0	1 b	1	11 b	15	6 b	13	3	0
Congo	9	10	80	79	0	0	0	0	11	11	0	0	1	0
Cote d'Ivoire	19	20	53	47	6	3	8	6	9	17	6	7	6	1
Egypt	49	47 c	22	24 c	3	3 c	2	2 c	19	18 c	4	5 c	38	4
Ethiopia	19	17	64	61	4	4	3	1	3	7	6	9	6	1
Gabon	26	27 a	53	48 a	5	1 a	6	4 a	7	12 a	3	9 a	3	0
Ghana	34	38 a	42	42 a	3	3 a	3	2 a	15	11 a	3	4 a	19	1
Kenya	21	24	53	50	5	1	10	5	8	13	3	7	15	1
Libya	44	62	45	31	2	X	0	0	6	2	3	5	22	0
Morocco	40	30 d	32	32 d	5	6 d	6	7 d	14	21 d	3	4 d	6	2
Mozambique	25	10	17	19	0	0	0	0	11	2	48	69	8	0
Nigeria	15	16 a	56	56 a	3	0 a	2	1 a	12	23 a	12	5 a	5	0
Senegal	28	31 a	62	54 a	3	3 a	1	1 a	5	8 a	2	2 a	5	1
South Africa	64	62 a	22	23 a	0	1 a	5	5 a	5	6 a	3	3 a	32	3
Sudan	27	36	50	46	12	11	3	2	4	4	4	2	X	X
Tanzania	29	34 a	44	40 a	6	7 a	3	3 a	13	14 a	5	3 a	46	1
Tunisia	33	33 a	36	31 a	5	5 a	7	7 a	16	20 a	3	3 a	14	5
Zambia	69	65 c	17	19 c	2	2 c	6	6 c	4	5 c	2	2 c	16	2
Zimbabwe	50	55 d	24	22 d	13	12 d	7	6 d	5	5 d	2	1 d	35	23
THE AMERICAS														
Argentina	29	25	37	31	5	5	2	1	19	20	8	18	18	8
Bolivia	17 b	21 d	57 b	53 d	0 b	1 d	0 b	0 d	23 b	23 d	2 b	2 d	8	0
Brazil	40	39	40	37	3	5	4	5	7	10	6	4	10	6
Canada	36	37	28	26	2	2	12	14	18	18	4	3	15	9
Chile	41	42 a	38	39 a	0	0 a	2	2 a	15	12 a	5	4 a	X	X
Colombia	34	33	38	40	2	2	3	4	13	14	10	7	14	2
Cuba	48	41	23	23	4	4	0	0	12	14	13	19	X	X
Ecuador	18	19	47	53	5	5	3	1	11	10	16	13	8	5
Guatemala	30	10	48	58	4	4	0	0	12	18	6	9	2	1
Jamaica	58	41 a	21	37 a	2	3 a	0	0 a	6	11 a	13	8 a	13	9
Mexico	40	42	37	34	4	3	0	0	11	12	8	9	23	5
Netherlands Antilles	32	20	50	55	0	0	0	0	11	15	7	11	X	X
Panama	12	22	62	48	0	0	6	14	15	14	5	1	10	0
Paraguay	8	14	77	63	0	0	0	1	12	19	3	3	5	0
Peru	35	34 d	36	36 d	7	4 d	2	2 d	17	19 d	4	4 d	12	5
Trinidad and Tobago	60	75 a	30	18 a	0	0 a	1	1 a	6	6 a	3	1 a	54	0
United States	33	30	32	35	1	1	11	12	18	18	5	4	12	6
Uruguay	32	23 a	37	35 a	5	10 a	2	7 a	17	21 a	7	5 a	7	8
Venezuela	32	39 a	46	40 a	0	0 a	1	4 a	9	10 a	11	6 a	21	0
ASIA														
Bangladesh	50	54	17	15	5	6	1	2	25	19	2	3	32	1
Bahrain	57	69	34	22	0	0	0	0	1	1	8	8	X	X
Brunei	21	22	47	51	0	0	0	0	30	27	2	1	X	X
China	64 b	64 a	5 b	5 a	6 b	5 a	3 b	3 a	19 b	19 a	3 b	3 a	66	8
Cyprus	38	29	43	52	0	0	0	4	9	9	10	6	X	X
Hong Kong	44	37	32	36	0	0	12	16	10	10	2	2	7	X
India	56	53 a	27	25 a	2	3 a	2	1 a	10	13 a	3	4 a	33	2
Indonesia	33	37 d	32	34 d	0	0 d	0	0 d	31	23 d	3	5 d	11	0
Iran, Islamic Rep	41	42 a	16	23 a	0	7 a	1	8 a	20	15 a	22	6 a	40	4
Iraq	23	20 a	46	46 a	0	0 a	0	0 a	21	13 a	10	21 a	X	X
Israel	34 b	31	48 b	48	1 b	1	3 b	6	7 b	9	7 b	5	X	X
Japan	53	46	20	24	1	2	7	9	10	12	8	7	5	3
Jordan	11	20	61	55	0	2	0	1	19	18	8	4	17	7
Korea, Dem People's Rep	88	85	6	8	0	0	0	0	1	1	5	6	X	X
Korea, Rep	43	43	18	20	0	3	4	3	33	29	1	2	12	3
Kuwait	56	45 c	30	30 c	0	0 c	0	0 c	9	19 c	5	6 c	10	0
Lebanon	30	4	54	70	0	0	0	0	6	10	10	16	X	X
Malaysia	45	44 a	37	40 a	0	0 a	4	4 a	10	9 a	4	4 a	X	X
Myanmar	49	68	41	27	0	0	0	1	8	4	2	0	X	X
Nepal	31	28	34	26	6	11	2	3	27	30	0	2	8	1
Oman	2	23 c	45	25 c	0	0 c	0	0 c	16	27 c	38	25 c	4	0
Pakistan	42	46 c	28	26 c	4	3 c	11	6 c	12	16 c	3	2 c	34	2
Philippines	41	32	27	23	12	8	3	4	12	28	5	5	9	3
Qatar	50	47 a	38	14 a	0	0 a	0	0 a	1	1 a	11	38 a	X	X
Saudi Arabia	38 b	35 c	45 b	32 c	2 b	9 c	1 b	13 c	3 b	8 c	11 b	4 c	16	23
Singapore	17	37	67	48	0	0	6	8	7	5	3	2	8	X
Sri Lanka	19	13 a	54	61 a	0	0 a	3	7 a	21	17 a	3	3 a	4	0
Syrian Arab Rep	46	34 a	35	44 a	3	4 a	0	0 a	10	13 a	6	6 a	33	4
Taiwan	62	56	17	21	5	3	5	6	9	10	4	5	X	X
Thailand	27	24	45	54	11	9	7	5	7	8	3	1	7	7
Turkey	26	32	22	22	3	5	1	1	45	38	2	2	21	6
United Arab Emirates	1	16	83	68	0	0	0	0	1	2	14	15	3	0
Viet Nam	70 b	65 e	19 b	20 e	1 b	1 e	0 b	0 e	4 b	5 e	6 b	8 e	X	X
Yemen	7 b	14 a	75 b	64 a	0 b	0 a	0 b	0 a	15 b	15 a	3 b	7 a	X	X

Table 21.3

	Industry 1979	Industry 1989	Transport 1979	Transport 1989	Agriculture 1979	Agriculture 1989	Commercial 1979	Commercial 1989	Residential 1979	Residential 1989	Other 1979	Other 1989	Energy Intensity, 1989 Industry (megajoules per $US Industrial GDP)	Energy Intensity, 1989 Agriculture (megajoules per $US Agriculture GDP)
EUROPE														
Albania	28	27	17	20	0	0	0	0	3	3	52	50	X	X
Austria	33	30	23	27	0	1	3	4	35	33	7	6	5	1
Belgium	43	41	16	23	2	2	9	8	27	23	2	3	12	7
Bulgaria	29	24	31	37	1	1	0	0	11	10	27	28	26	6
Czechoslovakia	62	56 a	11	7 a	1	5 a	0	1 a	10	18 a	17	13 a	40	33
Denmark	20	20	23	32	9	6	8	9	38	27	3	5	4	10
Finland	43	44	15	19	4	4	2	4	29	21	6	9	11	7
France	38	31	22	29	2	2	22	20	12	15	3	3	7	5
Germany (Fed Rep)	36	35	19	26	1	1	11	11	20	21	13	5	6	4
(Dem Rep)	41	38	11	10	0	0	0	0	40	42	9	9	X	X
Gibraltar	0	0	53	65	0	0	0	0	6	6	41	29	X	X
Greece	35	28	33	37	6	7	3	5	18	19	4	4	15	7
Hungary	44	39	10	13	8	6	0	7	21	29	17	5	34	14
Iceland	36	32	41	50	0	2	2	6	18	7	4	4	X	X
Ireland	31	33	27	26	1	3	9	9	29	27	4	2	34	3
Italy	41	36	23	28	2	3	3	4	27	26	3	3	6	4
Luxembourg	67	54	14	27	0	0	3	7	14	11	2	1	X	X
Malta	0	0	66	56	0	0	0	0	15	8	20	36	X	X
Netherlands	41	38	15	20	1	6	2	3	25	19	16	13	12	14
Norway	44	41	20	22	2	2	10	11	19	19	4	5	9	5
Poland	48	38	10	12	4	4	0	0	25	13	15	33	X	X
Portugal	45	46	30	30	4	4	5	5	12	12	3	4	14	5
Romania	62	40	5	4	0	1	0	0	11	17	21	38	X	X
Spain	45	38	32	37	5	4	4	6	10	11	4	5	27	5
Sweden	39	39	17	24	2	2	4	10	29	21	9	4	10	4
Switzerland	23	18	25	30	1	1	16	19	31	29	5	3	X	X
United Kingdom	37	29	22	31	1	1	9	9	25	25	6	6	7	4
Yugoslavia	51 f	45 a	23 f	24 a	2 f	1 a	2 f	0 a	10 f	16 a	12 f	14 a	15	2
U.S.S.R.	54	46	15	15	9	10	11	10	4	14	7	5	X	X
OCEANIA														
Australia	39	37	37	39	2	2	5	6	13	12	4	4	10	5
New Zealand	31	38	37	38	4	2	9	6	15	11	3	5	13	3

Sources: International Energy Agency and The World Bank.
Notes: a. Refers to 1988. b. Refers to 1980. c. Refers to 1986. d. Refers to 1987. e. Refers to 1985. f. Refers to 1981.
Totals may not add to 100 percent because of independent rounding.
0 = zero or less than half the unit of measure; X = not available; GDP = gross domestic product.
For additional information, see Sources and Technical Notes.

Table 21.4 Municipal Waste in OECD Countries

	Annual Municipal Waste Generation Year of Estimate	(000 metric tons)	Per Capita (kg)	Composition of Municipal Waste (percent of total weight) Year of Estimate	Paper and Cardboard	Plastic	Glass	Metals	Other	Organic as Percentage of Inorganic	Disposal of Municipal Waste (000 metric tons) Year of Estimate	Landfill	Incineration Total	Incineration With Energy Recovery	Other
Australia	1980	10,000	681	1980	26.0	6.1	15.1	7.0	45.8	41.4	1980	9,800	200	X	X
Austria	1988	2,700	355	1985	33.6	7.0	10.4	3.7	45.3	60.5	1987	1,836	222	20	730 a
Belgium	1989	3,470 b	349	1989	28.3	7.7	7.6	3.7	52.7	47.6	1980	1,530	720	215	832
Canada	1989	16,000	625	1989	36.5	4.7	6.6	6.6	45.6	74.3 c	1989	13,448	1,416 c	101	242 c
Denmark	1985	2,400	469	1985	38.6	3.4	5.4	5.0	47.6	81.3	1985	1,260	540	X	600
Finland	1989	2,500	504	1985 d	40.0	8.0	4.0	3.0	45.0	85.0	1987	2,000	50	50	450
France	1989	17,000	303	1989	27.5	4.5	7.5	6.5	54.0	59.0 e	1989	7,684	6,970	4,670	2,346 f
Germany (Fed Rep)	1987	19,483	318	1985	17.9	5.4	9.2	3.2	64.3	63.4 e	1987	12,917	5,942	X	624
Greece	1989	3,147	259	1989	20.0	7.0	3.0	4.0	66.0	57.0	1989	3,084	1 c	X	X
Iceland	1985	93	386	X	X	X	X	X	X	X	X	X	X	X	X
Ireland	1984	1,100	311	1984	24.5	14.0	7.5	3.0	51.0	56.0	1984	1,100	X	X	X
Italy	1989	17,300	301	1986	22.3	7.2	6.2	3.1	61.2	64.4	1989	5,286	2,794	595	5,886
Japan	1988	48,283	394	1989	45.5	8.3	1.0	1.3	43.9	77.2	1987	16,486	32,616	8,937	1,507
Luxembourg	1990	170	466	1985	17.2	6.4	7.2	2.6	66.6	44.0	1990	51	117	117	2 g
Netherlands	1988	6,900	465	1988	24.2	7.1	7.2	3.2	58.3	88.3	1988	3,790	2,555	1,840	555
New Zealand	1982	2,106	670	1980	33.6	3.0	2.5	7.6	53.3	37.0	1982	2,005	X	X	35
Norway	1989	2,000	473	1988	30.0	5.0	3.0	7.0	55.0	77.0	1989	1,500	400	76	100 g
Portugal	1985	2,350	231	1985	19.0	3.0	3.0	3.5	71.5	74.5	1989	742	X	X	1,936
Spain	1988	12,546	322	1989	20.0	7.0	6.0	4.0	63.0	49.0	1988	9,713	604	367	2,229 g
Sweden	1985	2,650	317	1980	43.0	10.0	5.0	6.0	36.0	89.0	1985	1,100	1,400	1,204	250 a
Switzerland	1989	2,850	424	1989	32.0	13.0	7.0	6.0	42.0	70.0	1989	460	2,270	1,816	120 a
Turkey	1989	19,500	353	X	X	X	X	X	X	X	X	X	X	X	X
United Kingdom	1989 h	18,000	357	1980 h	29.0	7.0	10.0	8.0	46.0	58.0	1989	14,000 i	2,500 j	1,250 j	3,500 j
United States	1986	208,760	864	1984	34.7	6.7	9.0	8.8	40.8	37.5	1986	138,705	15,000 k	X	X

Sources: Organisation for Economic Co-operation and Development and United Nations Statistical Commission and Economic Commission for Europe (ECE).
Notes: a. Composting and mechanical sorting, only. b. Total is sum from different years and regions: 1982 for Brussels region, 1987 for Flanders region, and 1989 for Wallon region. c. Refers to 1985. d. Household wastes only. e. Refers to 1980. f. Includes methanation and holding area. g. Composting only. h. England and Wales only. i. Direct landfill. j. Includes some industrial and commercial waste. k. Refers to 1984.
0 = zero or less than half the unit of measure; X = not available.
For additional information, see Sources and Technical Notes.

Table 21.5 Production, Consumption, and Reserves of Selected

	Annual Production (000 metric tons)					Annual Consumption (000 metric tons)			
	1975	1980	1985	1990		1975	1980	1985	1990
ALUMINUM {a}									
Australia	21,004.0	27,179.0	31,838.9	40,697.0	United States	3,265.0	4,453.5	4,282.0	4,352.3
Guinea	8,406.0	11,862.0	11,790.0	16,500.0	Japan	1,170.8	1,639.0	1,694.8	2,414.3
Jamaica	11,571.0	12,054.0	6,239.0	10,921.0	U.S.S.R.	1,580.0	1,850.0	1,750.0	1,700.0
Brazil	969.3	5,538.0	5,846.0	8,750.0	Germany {b}	903.7	1,272.3	1,390.9	1,378.5
India	1,273.0	1,785.0	2,281.0	5,000.0	France	399.2	600.9	586.1	720.9
U.S.S.R.	4,368.8	4,600.0	4,600.0	4,200.0	Italy	270.0	458.0	470.0	652.0
China	985.5	1,500.0	1,650.0	4,000.0	China	320.0	550.0	630.0	650.0
Suriname	4,927.6	4,646.0	3,738.0	3,267.0	United Kingdom	392.7	409.3	350.4	453.7
Yugoslavia	2,306.3	3,138.0	3,538.0	2,952.0	India	145.0	233.8	297.6	420.0
Greece	3,005.3	3,286.0	2,453.0	2,700.0	Canada	293.3	311.9	345.0	415.7
Ten Countries Total	58,816.9	75,588.0	73,973.9	98,987.0	**Ten Countries Total**	8,739.7	11,778.7	11,796.8	13,157.4
World Total	74,927.0	89,220.0	84,189.0	109,118.0	**World Total**	11,349.8	15,297.9	15,861.5	17,877.9
Bauxite, World Reserves 1990 (000 metric tons)				21,800,000	World Reserves Life Index (years)				200
Bauxite, World Reserve Base 1990 (000 metric tons)				24,500,000	World Reserve Base Life Index (years)				225
CADMIUM									
U.S.S.R.	2.6	2.9	3.0	2.8	Japan	0.4	1.1	1.9	4.8
Japan	2.7	2.2	2.5	2.4	United States	3.0	3.9	3.7	3.1
Belgium	0.9	1.5	1.3	1.8	Belgium	1.0	1.7	1.9	2.7
United States	2.0	1.6	1.6	1.7	U.S.S.R.	2.2	2.4	2.9	2.3 c
Canada	1.2	1.3	1.7	1.4	France	0.8	1.2	1.1	1.8
Germany {b}	1.0	1.2	1.1	1.2	United Kingdom	1.0	1.3	1.4	0.9
Mexico	0.6	0.8	0.9	1.0	Germany {b}	1.6	2.2	1.6	0.9
China	0.1	0.3	0.5	0.8	Mexico	X	0.3	0.2	0.5
Italy	0.4	0.6	0.5	0.7	China	X	0.3	0.4	0.4 c
Australia	0.5	1.0	0.9	0.7	Korea, Rep	X	0.2	0.3	0.4
Ten Countries Total	12.1	13.3	14.1	14.5	**Ten Countries Total**	10.2	14.5	15.4	17.8
World Total	15.2	18.2	19.1	20.2	**World Total**	12.6	17.0	17.6	20.7 c
World Reserves 1990 (000 metric tons)				535	World Reserves Life Index (years)				X d
World Reserve Base 1990 (000 metric tons)				970	World Reserve Base Life Index (years)				X d
COPPER									
Chile	831.0	1,063.0	1,359.8	1,603.2	United States	1,396.5	1,867.7	1,958.0	2,142.5
United States	1,282.2	1,181.1	1,104.8	1,587.2	Japan	827.4	1,158.3	1,226.3	1,576.5
Canada	733.8	716.4	738.6	779.6	Germany {b}	746.6	870.8	886.8	1,027.8
U.S.S.R.	580.0	590.0	600.0	600.0	U.S.S.R.	1,220.0	1,300.0	1,305.0	1,000.0
Zambia	676.9	595.8	452.6	445.0	China	316.0	386.0	420.0	512.0
Poland	230.4	343.0	431.3	380.0	France	364.5	433.4	397.8	477.6
China	99.8	115.0	185.0	375.0	Italy	290.0	388.0	362.0	474.8
Zaire	462.6	425.7	470.0	370.0	Belgium	177.4	303.9	309.6	389.5
Peru	165.8	336.1	391.3	334.0	Korea, Rep	28.0	84.0	206.6	324.2
Australia	219.0	243.5	259.8	316.0	United Kingdom	450.5	409.2	346.5	317.2
Ten Countries Total	5,281.6	5,609.6	5,993.2	6,790.0	**Ten Countries Total**	5,816.9	7,201.3	7,418.6	8,242.1
World Total	6,739.0	7,204.0	7,870.0	8,814.0	**World Total**	7,457.5	9,374.6	9,699.9	10,773.2
World Reserves 1990 (000 metric tons)				321,000	World Reserves Life Index (years)				36
World Reserve Base 1990 (000 metric tons)				549,000	World Reserve Base Life Index (years)				62
LEAD									
Australia	407.8	397.5	498.0	563.0	United States	1,120.2	1,094.0	1,141.7	1,288.4
United States	563.8	550.4	424.4	495.2	U.S.S.R.	620.0	800.0	800.0	650.0
U.S.S.R.	480.8	420.0	440.0	450.0	Germany {b}	373.5	433.1	440.0	447.5
China	99.8	160.0	200.0	315.0	Japan	189.4	392.5	394.9	416.9
Canada	349.1	296.6	268.3	236.2	United Kingdom	306.0	295.5	274.3	301.6
Peru	184.5	189.1	201.5	189.0	Italy	192.0	275.0	235.0	258.0
Mexico	178.6	145.5	206.7	179.9	France	190.3	212.8	208.0	254.5
Korea, Dem People's Rep	117.9	125.0	110.0	120.0	China	185.0	210.0	220.0	250.0
Sweden	70.4	72.2	75.9	90.0	Korea, Rep	10.2	33.0	63.2	150.0
Yugoslavia	126.9	121.5	115.1	73.0	Spain	111.0	110.7	103.1	114.6
Ten Countries Total	2,579.7	2,477.8	2,539.9	2,711.3	**Ten Countries Total**	3,297.6	3,856.6	3,880.2	4,131.5
World Total	3,432.2	3,448.2	3,431.2	3,367.2	**World Total**	4,526.2	5,348.3	5,440.7	5,544.5
World Reserves 1990 (000 metric tons)				70,000	World Reserves Life Index (years)				21
World Reserve Base 1990 (000 metric tons)				120,000	World Reserve Base Life Index (years)				36
MERCURY									
U.S.S.R.	1.9	2.1	2.2	2.1	United States	1.8	2.0	1.7	1.2 c
Spain	1.5	1.5	0.9	1.5	Spain	0.2	0.2 e	0.6	0.8 f
China	0.9	0.7	0.7	0.8	Algeria	X	X	0.2	0.7 f
Algeria	1.0	0.8	0.8	0.6	United Kingdom	0.7	0.4 e	0.3	0.4 f
Mexico	0.5	0.1	0.4	0.3	China	0.5	0.5 e	0.4	0.3 g
Finland	0.0	0.1	0.1	0.2	Brazil	X	X	0.2	0.3 f
Czechoslovakia	0.2	0.2	0.2	0.1	Germany (Fed Rep)	0.4	0.5 h	0.3	0.2 f
Turkey	0.2	0.2	0.2	0.1	Mexico	X	X	0.2	0.2 f
Yugoslavia	0.6	0.0	0.1	0.1	Belgium	0.2	0.1 h	0.3	0.1 f
United States	0.3	1.1	0.6	X	U.S.S.R.	0.9	1.8 e	X	X
Ten Countries Total	7.0	6.7	6.1	5.8	**Ten Countries Total**	4.6	5.4	4.2	4.3
World Total	8.7	6.8	6.1	5.8	**World Total**	7.3	7.7 e	7.4	6.6 f
World Reserves 1990 (000 metric tons)				130	World Reserves Life Index (years)				22
World Reserve Base 1990 (000 metric tons)				240	World Reserve Base Life Index (years)				41

Metals, 1975–90

Table 21.5

NICKEL

Annual Production (000 metric tons)

	1975	1980	1985	1990
U.S.S.R.	152.4	154.2	185.1	259.0
Canada	242.2	184.8	170.0	201.9
New Caledonia	133.3	86.6	72.4	88.0
Australia	75.8	74.3	85.8	70.0
Indonesia	19.2	53.3	40.3	58.0
Cuba	36.6	36.6	32.1	41.0
South Africa	20.8	25.7	25.0	36.0
Dominican Rep	26.9	16.3	25.4	33.0
Botswana	16.6	15.4	26.3	25.0
China	X	10.9	25.0	25.0
Ten Countries Total	723.8	658.2	687.3	836.9
World Total	807.9	779.7	812.6	937.1
World Reserves 1990 (000 metric tons)				48,988
World Reserve Base 1990 (000 metric tons)				108,862

Annual Consumption (000 metric tons)

	1975	1980	1985	1990
Japan	90.0	122.0	136.1	159.3
United States	132.9	143.1	143.1	124.6
U.S.S.R.	115.0	132.0	138.0	115.0
Germany {b}	51.8	78.1	87.0	93.3
France	31.9	38.4	31.9	44.8
United Kingdom	20.8	22.8	24.8	32.6
China	18.0	18.0	21.0	27.5
Italy	17.0	27.1	29.0	27.3
Belgium	3.2	3.6	6.6	21.3
Spain	5.0	8.6	8.2	20.6
Ten Countries Total	485.6	593.7	625.7	666.3
World Total	576.2	716.7	775.2	842.6
World Reserves Life Index (years)				52
World Reserve Base Life Index (years)				116

TIN

Annual Production (000 metric tons)

	1975	1980	1985	1990
China	22.0	14.6	15.0	40.0
Brazil	5.0	6.9	26.5	39.1
Indonesia	25.3	32.5	21.7	30.2
Malaysia	64.4	61.4	36.9	28.5
Bolivia	24.3	27.3	16.1	18.0
U.S.S.R.	30.0	36.0	13.5	15.0
Thailand	16.4	33.7	16.9	14.6
Australia	9.6	11.6	6.4	7.4
Peru	0.2	1.1	3.8	5.1
United Kingdom	4.1	3.0	5.2	4.2
Ten Countries Total	201.3	228.1	162.0	202.2
World Total	222.3	247.3	180.7	219.3
World Reserves 1990 (000 metric tons)				5,920
World Reserve Base 1990 (000 metric tons)				6,050

Annual Consumption (000 metric tons)

	1975	1980	1985	1990
United States	55.8	56.4	37.8	36.8
Japan	28.1	30.9	31.6	34.8
Germany {b}	15.6	19.0	17.8	21.7
U.S.S.R.	23.0	25.0	31.5	20.0
China	14.0	12.5	11.5	18.0
United Kingdom	14.4	9.9	9.4	10.4
France	10.0	10.1	6.9	8.3
Korea, Rep	0.6	1.8	2.6	7.8
Netherlands	3.9	5.0	4.5	6.9
Brazil	3.3	5.0	4.6	6.1
Ten Countries Total	168.7	175.6	158.2	170.8
World Total	230.5	234.6	214.6	229.7
World Reserves Life Index (years)				27
World Reserve Base Life Index (years)				28

ZINC

Annual Production (000 metric tons)

	1975	1980	1985	1990
Canada	1,229.5	1,059.0	1,172.2	1,177.0
Australia	500.9	495.3	759.1	937.0
U.S.S.R.	689.5	785.0	810.0	750.0
China	99.8	160.0	300.0	619.0
Peru	384.8	487.6	523.4	576.8
United States	425.8	317.1	251.9	543.2
Mexico	288.9	235.8	275.4	322.5
Spain	85.3	183.1	234.7	258.0
Korea, Dem People's Rep	159.7	140.0	180.0	230.0
Sweden	111.3	167.4	216.4	157.4
Ten Countries Total	3,975.4	4,030.3	4,723.1	5,570.9
World Total	5,849.7	5,961.6	6,758.3	7,325.0
World Reserves 1990 (000 metric tons)				144,000
World Reserve Base 1990 (000 metric tons)				295,000

Annual Consumption (000 metric tons)

	1975	1980	1985	1990
United States	839.0	879.0	962.0	991.0
U.S.S.R.	900.0	1,030.0	1,000.0	920.0
Japan	563.0	752.0	780.0	814.3
Germany {b}	360.0	474.0	480.0	529.5
China	180.0	259.0	349.0	500.0
France	223.0	330.0	247.0	284.0
Italy	150.0	236.0	218.0	270.0
Korea, Rep	35.0	68.0	120.0	227.2
United Kingdom	207.0	181.0	189.0	189.0
Belgium	103.0	155.0	169.0	177.6
Ten Countries Total	3,560.0	4,364.0	4,514.0	4,902.6
World Total	5,062.0	6,283.0	6,552.0	6,972.9
World Reserves Life Index (years)				20
World Reserve Base Life Index (years)				40

IRON ORE

Annual Production (000 metric tons)

	1975	1980	1985	1990
U.S.S.R.	232,792.0	244,702.6	247,639.0	236,000.0
Brazil	89,889.6	114,726.7	128,251.0	150,000.0
China	65,024.0	68,072.0	80,000.0	118,000.0
Australia	97,646.7	95,529.4	97,447.0	110,000.0
United States	80,127.9	70,726.8	49,533.0	59,032.0
India	41,403.0	41,934.4	42,545.0	52,000.0
Canada	46,866.0	48,751.7	39,502.0	36,443.0
South Africa	12,297.7	26,310.3	24,414.0	30,347.0
Venezuela	24,771.1	16,101.6	14,710.0	20,365.0
Sweden	30,865.1	27,183.1	20,454.0	19,890.0
Ten Countries Total	721,683.1	754,038.6	744,495.0	832,077.0
World Total	902,388.8	890,924.3	860,640.0	864,370.0
World Reserves 1990 (000 metric tons)				151,000,000
World Reserve Base 1990 (000 metric tons)				229,000,000

Annual Consumption (000 metric tons)

	1975	1980	1985	1990
U.S.S.R.	189,177.0	197,840.0	203,760.0	199,700.0
China	66,436.0	120,394.0	140,354.0	183,963.0
Japan	132,689.0	108,693.0	102,215.0	107,395.0 c
United States	127,531.0	90,832.0	64,679.0	73,002.0 c
Germany (Fed Rep)	48,193.0 i	50,072.0	45,204.0	46,867.0 c
Brazil	21,453.0	18,383.0	36,419.0	40,079.0
France	42,094.0 i	37,070.0	26,608.0	25,750.0 c
Korea, Rep	1,241.0	9,675.0	11,709.0	22,870.0
United Kingdom	23,696.0 i	9,326.0	15,176.0	18,663.0 c
Belgium	16,871.0 i	15,756.0	13,353.0	13,479.0 c
Ten Countries Total	669,381.0	658,846.0	659,475.0	731,768.0
World Total	902,388.8	890,924.3	860,640.0	924,869.0 c
World Reserves Life Index (years)				175
World Reserve Base Life Index (years)				265

STEEL, CRUDE

Annual Production (000 metric tons)

	1975	1980	1985	1990
U.S.S.R.	141,327.2	147,943.5	154,670.0	154,000.0
Japan	102,314.0	111,396.9	105,281.0	110,339.0
United States	105,817.6	101,456.7	80,069.0	89,726.0
China	25,401.6	37,120.8	46,721.0	66,000.0
Germany {b}	46,888.6	51,147.0	48,350.0	44,022.0
Italy	21,836.3	26,501.1	23,789.0	25,439.0
Korea, Rep	2,009.4	8,558.5	13,539.0	23,125.0
Brazil	8,308.1	15,338.9	20,456.0	20,572.0
France	21,530.6	23,176.2	18,833.0	19,017.0
United Kingdom	20,197.9	11,278.3	15,723.0	17,908.0
Ten Countries Total	495,631.5	533,918.0	527,431.0	570,148.0
World Total	644,208.2	713,813.1	718,131.0	771,979.0

Annual Consumption (000 metric tons)

	1975	1980	1985	1990
U.S.S.R.	141,031.0	150,330.0	157,161.0	166,319.0 c
United States	116,821.0	114,433.0	105,593.0	102,351.0 c
Japan	68,080.0	79,007.0	73,377.0	93,278.0 c
China	29,110.0	43,005.0	71,428.0	69,504.0 c
Germany {b}	39,793.0	44,631.0	39,995.0	44,269.0 c
Italy	17,778.0	26,764.0	21,880.0	27,994.0 c
India	8,086.0	10,900.0	14,400.0	20,036.0 c
Korea, Rep	2,964.0	6,100.0	11,310.0	18,300.0 c
France	19,261.0	20,159.0	14,812.0	17,565.0 c
United Kingdom	20,903.0	16,050.0	14,350.0	17,400.0 c
Ten Countries Total	463,827.0	511,379.0	524,306.0	577,016.0 c
World Total	644,153.0	718,921.0	720,568.0	794,470.0 c

Sources: U.S. Bureau of Mines, World Bureau of Metal Statistics (Ware, United Kingdom), and other sources.

Notes: a. Production refers to bauxite, consumption data to aluminum. b. Data are for both, Federal Republic of Germany and German Democratic Republic. c. Data refer to 1989. d. A production/reserve ratio would be misleading because production data include secondary metal. e. Data refer to 1978. f. Data refer to 1987. g. Data refer to 1986. h. Data refer to 1979. i. Data refer to 1976.
World reserves life index equals 1990 world reserves divided by 1990 world production.
World reserve base life index equals 1990 world reserve base divided by 1990 world production.
0 = zero or less than half the unit of measure; X = not available.
For additional information, see Sources and Technical Notes.

Table 21.6 World Reserves of Major Metals, 1990

	Base Metals (million metric tons of metal content)				Iron and Ferro Alloys (million metric tons of metal content)								Light Metals (million metric tons)			Metal Reserves Index {a} (%)
	Copper	Lead	Tin	Zinc	Iron Ore	Manganese	Nickel	Chromium	Cobalt	Molybdenum	Tungsten	Vanadium	Bauxite {b}	Titanium {c}	Lithium {d}	
WORLD	321.00	70.44	5.93	143.91	64,648	812.8	48.66	418.90	3.31	6.10	2.35	4.27	21,559	288.6	2.21	100.00
AFRICA	42.00	4.03	0.15	8.99	3,454	422.8	2.97	341.30	1.78	0.00	0.02	0.86	6,874	45.00	0.02	19.72
Algeria	0.00	0.10 e	0.00	0.10 f	65	0.0	0.00	0.00	0.00	0.00	0.00	0.00	0	0.0	0.00	0.02
Angola	0.00	0.00	0.00	0.00	15	0.0	0.00	0.00	0.00	0.00	0.00	0.00	0	0.0	0.00	0.00
Botswana	0.43 f	0.00	0.00	0.00	X	0.0	0.35	0.00	0.00 e	0.00	0.00	0.00	0	0.0	0.00	0.06
Burkina Faso	0.00	0.00	0.00	0.00	X	0.0	0.00	0.00	0.00	0.00	0.00	0.00	0	0.0	0.00	0.00
Cameroon	0.00	0.00	X	0.00	0	0.0	0.00	0.00	0.00	0.00	0.00	0.00	680	0.0	0.00	0.21
Congo	0.02 f	0.02 f	0.00	0.02 f	0	0.0	0.00	0.00	0.00	0.00	0.00	0.00	0	0.0	0.00	0.00
Egypt	0.00	0.00	0.00	0.00	90	0.0	0.00	X	0.00	0.00	0.00	0.00	0	0.0	0.00	0.01
Ethiopia	0.00	0.00	0.00	0.00	X	0.0	0.00	0.00	0.00	0.00	0.00	0.00	0	0.0	0.00	0.00
Gabon	0.00	0.00	0.00	0.00	0	52.6	0.00	0.00	0.00	0.00	0.00	0.00	X	0.0	0.00	0.43
Ghana	0.00	0.00	0.00	0.00	0	0.9	0.00	0.00	0.00	0.00	0.00	0.00	450	0.0	0.00	0.15
Guinea	0.00	0.00	0.00	0.00	0	0.0	0.00	0.00	0.00	0.00	0.00	0.00	5,600	0.0	0.00	1.73
Kenya	0.00	0.01 f	0.00	0.00	0	0.0	0.00	0.00	0.00	0.00	0.00	0.00	0	0.0	0.00	0.00
Liberia	0.00	0.00	0.00	0.00	500	0.0	0.00	0.00	0.00	0.00	0.00	0.00	0	0.0	0.00	0.05
Libya	0.00	0.00	0.00	0.00	X	0.0	0.00	0.00	0.00	0.00	0.00	0.00	22	0.0	0.00	0.01
Madagascar	0.00	0.00	0.00	0.00	0	0.0	0.00	2.10	0.00	0.00	0.00	0.00	0	0.0	0.00	0.03
Mauritania	0.00	0.00	0.00	0.00	200	0.0	0.00	0.00	0.00	0.00	0.00	0.00	0	0.0	0.00	0.02
Morocco	0.25 f	1.00 e	0.00	0.16 f	30	X	0.00	0.00	X	0.00	0.00	0.00	0	0.0	0.00	0.11
Mozambique	X	0.00	0.00	0.00	0	0.0	0.00	0.00	0.00	0.00	0.00	0.00	2	2.4	0.00	0.06
Namibia	1.00	0.15 e	0.06 e	0.33 f	0	0.0	0.00	0.00	0.00	0.00	0.01 g	0.00	0	0.0	X	0.14
Niger	0.00	0.00	0.01 e	0.00	0	0.0	0.00	0.00	0.00	X	0.00	0.00	0	0.0	0.00	0.01
Nigeria	0.00	0.00 f	0.02	0.00	0	0.0	0.00	0.00	0.00	0.00	0.00	0.00	0	0.0	0.00	0.02
Sierra Leone	0.00	0.00	0.00	0.00	11	0.0	0.00	0.00	0.00	0.00	0.00	X	140	3.0	0.00	0.11
South Africa	2.00	2.00	0.03 e	3.00	2,500	369.2	2.54	295.20	0.05 e	0.00	0.00	0.86	0	39.6	0.00	11.10
Sudan	0.00	0.00	0.00	0.00	0	0.0	0.00	0.50	0.00	0.00	0.00	0.00	0	0.0	0.00	0.01
Tanzania	0.00	0.00	X	0.00	X	0.0	0.00	0.00	0.00	0.00	0.00	0.00	0	0.0	0.00	0.00
Tunisia	0.00	0.60 e	0.00	0.08 f	13	0.0	0.00	0.00	0.00	0.00	0.00	0.00	0	0.0	0.00	0.06
Uganda	0.00	X	X	X	0	0.0	0.00	0.00	0.00 e	0.00	0.00 f	0.00	0	0.0	0.00	0.01
Zaire	26.00	0.00	0.02	5.00	0	0.0	0.00	0.00	1.36	0.00	0.00 g	0.00	0	0.0	0.00	3.55
Zambia	12.00	0.15 e	X	0.30 f	X	0.0	0.00	0.00	0.36	0.00	0.00	0.00	0	0.0	0.00	1.00
Zimbabwe	0.30 f	0.00	0.01 e	0.00	30	0.0	0.08	43.50	0.00 e	0.00	0.01 g	0.00	2	0.0	0.02	0.82
NORTH & CENTRAL AMERICA	81.00	21.38	0.08	47.00	8,580	3.6	26.82	0.70	1.09	3.60	0.42	0.14	2,156	35.1	0.54	21.21
Canada	12.00	7.00	0.06	21.00	4,600	0.0	8.13	0.00	0.05	0.50	0.26	0.00	0	27.0	0.18	6.08
Costa Rica	0.00	0.00	0.00	0.00	0	0.0	0.00	0.00	0.00	0.00	0.00	0.00	78	0.0	0.00	0.02
Cuba	X	0.00	0.00	0.00	X	0.0	18.14	0.70	1.04	0.00	0.00	0.00	0	0.0	0.00	4.59
Dominican Rep	0.00	0.00	0.00	0.00	0	0.0	0.52	0.00	0.00	0.00	0.00	0.00	30	0.0	0.00	0.08
Greenland	0.00	0.28 f	0.00	X	X	0.0	0.00	0.00	0.00	0.00	0.00	0.00	0	0.0	0.00	0.03
Haiti	0.00	0.00	0.00	0.00	0	0.0	0.00	0.00	0.00	0.00	0.00	0.00	10	0.0	0.00	0.00
Honduras	X	0.10 e	0.00	X	0	0.0	0.00	0.00	0.00	0.00	0.00	0.00	0	0.0	0.00	0.01
Jamaica	0.00	0.00	0.00	0.00	0	0.0	0.00	0.00	0.00	0.00	0.00	0.00	2,000	0.0	0.00	0.62
Mexico	14.00	3.00	X	6.00	180	3.6	0.00	0.00	0.00	0.10	0.01 h	0.00	0	0.0	0.00	1.03
Panama	X	0.00	0.00	0.00	X	0.0	0.00	0.00	0.00	0.00	0.00	0.00	0	0.0	0.00	0.00
United States	55.00	11.00	0.02	20.00	3,800	0.0	0.03	0.00	0.00	3.00	0.15	0.14	38	8.1	0.36	8.74
SOUTH AMERICA	94.00	2.75	1.38	9.92	8,213	20.9	1.22	2.30	0.01	1.40	0.09	0.00	4,437	67.6	1.27	14.03
Argentina	X	0.18 e	0.00 e	0.31 f	60	0.0	0.00	0.00	0.00	0.00	0.01 h	0.00	0	0.0	X	0.06
Bolivia	X	0.05 e	0.14	0.55 f	0	0.0	0.00	0.00	0.00	0.00	0.06	0.00	0	0.0	0.00	0.36
Brazil	1.00	0.50 e	1.20	2.00	6,500	20.9	0.67	2.30	0.01 e	0.00	0.02	0.00	2,800	67.6	0.00	4.99
Chile	85.00	0.02 f	0.00	0.06 f	220	0.0	0.00	0.00	0.00	1.25	0.00	0.00	0	0.0	1.27	6.99
Colombia	0.00	0.00 f	0.00	0.00 f	33	0.0	0.56	0.00	0.00	0.00	0.00	0.00	0	0.0	0.00	0.08
French Guiana	0.00	0.00	0.00	0.00	0	0.0	0.00	0.00	0.00	0.00	0.00	0.00	42	0.0	0.00	0.01
Guyana	0.00	0.00	0.00	0.00	0	0.0	0.00	0.00	0.00	0.00	0.00	0.00	700	0.0	0.00	0.22
Peru	8.00	2.00	0.04 e	7.00	200	0.0	0.00	0.00	0.00	0.15	0.01 g	0.00	0	0.0	0.00	0.93
Suriname	0.00	0.00	0.00	0.00	0	0.0	0.00	0.00	0.00	0.00	0.00	0.00	575	0.0	0.00	0.18
Venezuela	0.00	0.00	0.00	0.00	1,200	0.0	0.00	0.00	0.00	0.00	0.00	0.00	320	0.0	0.00	0.22
ASIA	30.00	9.58	3.66	23.00	7,207	30.8	4.34	23.80	0.02	0.60	1.39	0.61	1,960	69.8	0.00	16.48
China	3.00	6.00	1.50	5.00	3,500	13.6	0.73	X	0.00	0.55	1.05	0.61	150	30.0	X	8.39
Cyprus	0.01 f	0.00	0.00	0.00	0	0.0	0.00	0.00	0.00	0.00	0.00	0.00	0	0.0	0.00	0.00
India	3.00	0.10 e	0.00	5.00	3,300	17.2	0.00	18.10	0.00	0.00	0.01 g	0.00	1,000	35.4	0.00	2.23
Indonesia	3.00	0.00	0.68	0.00	16	0.0	3.20	0.20	0.02 e	0.00	0.00	0.00	750	0.0	0.00	1.54
Iran, Islamic Rep	3.00	0.00	0.00	2.00	27	X	0.00	0.70	0.00	0.05	0.00	0.00	0	0.0	0.00	0.22
Iraq	0.00	0.00	0.00	0.00	X	0.0	0.00	0.00	0.00	0.00	0.00	0.00	0	0.0	0.00	0.00
Japan	1.00	0.80 e	0.09 e	4.00	13	0.0	0.00	0.00	0.00	0.00	0.01 g	X	0	0.0	0.00	0.42
Korea, Dem People's Rep	0.72 f	2.00	0.00	4.00	140	0.0	0.00	0.00	0.00	0.00	0.08 h	0.00	0	0.0	0.00	0.63
Korea, Rep	0.00	0.18 e	X	0.68 f	17	0.0	0.00	0.00	0.00	X	0.06	0.00	0	0.0	0.00	0.21
Lao People's Dem Rep	0.00	0.00	X	X	X	0.0	0.00	0.00	0.00	0.00	0.00	0.00	0	0.0	0.00	0.00
Malaysia	1.21 f	0.00	1.10	0.00	34	0.0	0.00	0.00	0.00	0.00	0.02 h	0.00	15	X	0.00	1.32
Mongolia	3.00	0.00	0.00	0.00	0	0.0	0.00	0.00	0.00	X	0.05 f	0.00	0	0.0	0.00	0.20
Myanmar	0.24 f	0.10 e	0.02	0.06 f	0	0.0	X	0.00	0.00	0.00	0.02	0.00	0	0.0	0.00	0.08
Oman	0.79 f	0.00	0.00	0.00	0	0.0	0.00	X	0.00	0.00	0.00	0.00	0	0.0	0.00	0.02
Pakistan	0.00	0.00	0.00	0.00	0	0.0	0.00	X	0.00	0.00	0.00	0.00	20	0.0	0.00	0.01
Philippines	10.00	0.00	0.00	0.04 f	0	0.0	0.41	2.30	0.00	0.00	0.00	0.00	0	0.0	0.00	0.30
Saudi Arabia	0.03 f	0.00	0.00	0.06 f	X	0.0	0.00	0.00	0.00	0.00	0.00	0.00	0	0.0	0.00	0.00
Sri Lanka	0.00	0.00	0.00	0.00	0	0.0	0.00	0.00	0.00	0.00	0.00	0.00	0	4.4	0.00	0.10
Thailand	0.00	0.40 f	0.27	1.00	X	X	0.00	X	0.00	0.00	0.03	0.00	0	0.0	0.00	0.47
Turkey	1.00	0.00 e	0.00	1.00	160	X	0.00	2.50	0.00	0.00	0.07 h	0.00	25	0.0	0.00	0.32
Viet Nam	0.00	0.00	X	0.16 f	X	0.0	0.00	X	0.00	0.00	0.00	0.00	0	0.0	0.00	0.01

Table 21.6

	Base Metals (million metric tons of metal content)				Iron and Ferro Alloys (million metric tons of metal content)								Light Metals (million metric tons)			Metal Reserves Index {a} (%)
	Copper	Lead	Tin	Zinc	Iron Ore	Manganese	Nickel	Chromium	Cobalt	Molybdenum	Tungsten	Vanadium	Bauxite {b}	Titanium {c}	Lithium {d}	
EUROPE	23.00	9.69	0.16	26.00	3,214	0.0	0.87	11.20	0.02	0.00	0.09	0.00	1,342	33.4	0.00	4.91
Albania	0.50	0.00	0.00	0.00	X	0.0	0.18	1.90	X	0.00	0.00	0.00	0	0.0	0.00	0.07
Austria	0.00	0.02 e	0.00	0.19 f	30	0.0	0.00	0.00	0.00	0.00	0.01	0.00	0	0.0	0.00	0.04
Bulgaria	1.50	2.00	0.00	0.83 f	30	X	0.00	0.00	0.00	0.00	0.00	0.00	0	0.0	0.00	0.27
Czechoslovakia	0.00	0.04 f	X	0.09 f	30	0.0	0.00	0.00	0.00	0.00	0.00 f	0.00	0	0.0	0.00	0.02
Finland	1.00	0.01 e	0.00	1.00	27	0.0	0.08	8.90	0.02	0.00	0.00	0.00	0	1.4	0.00	0.30
France	X	0.10 e	0.00	1.00	900	0.0	0.00	0.00	0.00	0.00	0.02	0.00	30	0.0	0.00	0.21
Germany (Fed Rep)	X	0.10 e	0.00	1.00	32	0.0	0.00	0.00	0.00	0.00	0.00	0.00	2	0.0	0.00	0.06
Germany (Dem Rep)	X	0.00	X	0.00	3	0.0	X	0.00	0.00	0.00	0.00	0.00	0	0.0	0.00	0.00
Greece	0.00	0.50 e	0.00	1.00	12	0.0	0.45	0.40	0.00	0.00	0.00	0.00	600	0.0	0.00	0.35
Hungary	0.00	0.00	0.00	0.00	13	X	0.00	0.00	0.00	0.00	0.00	0.00	300	0.0	0.00	0.09
Ireland	0.00	0.70 e	0.00	5.00	0	0.0	0.00	0.00	0.00	0.00	0.00	0.00	0	0.0	0.00	0.30
Italy	0.00	0.25 e	0.00	2.00	3	0.0	0.00	0.00	0.00	0.00	0.00	0.00	5	0.0	0.00	0.12
Norway	1.00	0.04 e	0.00	0.18 f	200	0.0	X	0.00	0.00	0.00	0.00	0.00	0	32.0	0.00	0.79
Poland	10.00	0.60 f	0.00	3.00	25	0.0	X	0.00	0.00	0.00	0.00	0.00	0	0.0	X	0.41
Portugal	3.00	0.00	0.07	2.00	0	0.0	0.00	0.00	0.00	0.00	0.03	0.00	0	0.0	0.00	0.31
Romania	X	0.50 f	0.00	0.64 f	25	X	0.00	0.00	0.00	0.00	0.00	0.00	50	0.0	0.00	0.10
Spain	1.00	1.70 e	X	5.00	230	0.0	0.00	0.00	0.00	0.00	0.02 g	0.00	5	0.0	0.00	0.50
Sweden	1.00	1.00 e	0.00	1.00	1,600	0.0	0.00	0.00	0.00	0.00	0.00 g	0.00	0	0.0	0.00	0.34
United Kingdom	X	0.13 e	0.09	0.07 f	14	0.0	0.00	0.00	0.00	0.00	0.01 g	0.00	0	0.0	0.00	0.14
Yugoslavia	4.00	2.00	0.00	2.00	40	X	0.16	X	0.00	0.00	0.00	0.00	350	0.0	0.00	0.50
U.S.S.R.	37.00	9.00	0.30	10.00	23,500	294.8	6.62	39.60	0.14	0.50	0.28	2.63	300	8.4	X	14.82
OCEANIA	14.00	14.00	0.20	19.00	10,480	39.9	5.81	0.00	0.25	0.00	0.06	0.03	4,490	29.3	0.37	8.84
Australia	7.00	14.00	0.20	19.00	10,200	39.9	1.27	0.00	0.02	0.00	0.06	0.03	4,440	29.3	0.37	7.57
New Caledonia	0.00	0.00	0.00	0.00	0	0.0	4.54	0.00	0.23	0.00	0.00	0.00	0	0.0	0.00	1.09
New Zealand	0.00	0.00	0.00	0.00	280	0.0	0.00	0.00	0.00	0.00	0.00 f	0.00	0	0.0	0.00	0.03
Papua New Guinea	7.00	0.00	0.00	0.00	0	0.0	0.00	0.00	0.00	0.00	0.00	0.00	0	0.0	0.00	0.15
Solomon Islands	0.00	0.00	0.00	0.00	0	0.0	0.00	0.00	0.00	0.00	0.00	0.00	50	0.0	0.00	0.02

Sources: U.S. Bureau of Mines and United Nations Educational, Scientific and Cultural Organization (UNESCO).
Notes: a. Each country's metal reserves index is the mean of its 15 global shares calculated for each of the metals in the index; for example, a country with 30 percent of the world nickel reserves, 15 percent of the world lead reserves, and no other metal reserves has a metal reserve index of (30 + 15) / 15 = 3 percent. b. Dry weight. c. Sum of the two major mineral sources for titanium: rutile and ilmenite; data are expressed in contained titanium dioxide. d. Metal content; world total excludes Argentina, China, Namibia, Portugal, and the U.S.S.R., because data are not available. e. WRI estimate based on U.S. Bureau of Mines, Minerals Availability Program data. f. WRI estimate; the total of reserves for "other countries" was allocated to other producing countries, using production share as weight. g. UNESCO. h. U.S. Bureau of Mines, Mineral Facts and Problems 1985.
0 = zero or less than half the unit of measure; X = not available.
For additional information, see Sources and Technical Notes.

Sources and Technical Notes

Table 21.1 Commercial Energy Production, 1979–89

Source: United Nations Statistical Office (UNSO) *U.N. Energy Tape* (UNSO, New York, May 1991).

Energy data are compiled by the United Nations Statistical Office, primarily from responses to questionnaires sent to national governments, supplemented by official national statistical publications and data from intergovernmental organizations. When official numbers are not available, UNSO prepares estimates based on the professional and commercial literature.

Total production of commercially traded fuels includes solid, liquid, and gaseous fuels and primary electricity production. *Solid* fuels include bituminous coal, lignite, peat, and oil shale burned directly. *Liquid* fuels include crude petroleum and natural gas liquids. *Gas* includes natural gas and other petroleum gases. *Primary electricity* includes hydro, geothermal, wind, and nuclear power generation expressed at the energy value of electricity (1 kilowatt hour = 3.6 million joules). Electricity production data generally refer to gross production. Data for the Dominican Republic, Finland, France (including Monaco), Iceland, Mexico, Switzerland, the United States, Zambia, and Zimbabwe refer to net production. Gross production is the amount of electricity produced by a generating station before consumption by station auxiliaries and transformer losses within the station are deducted. Net production is the amount of electricity remaining after these deductions. Typically, net production is 5–10 percent less than gross production. Energy production from pumped storage is not included in gross or net electricity generation.

Electricity production includes both public and self-producer power plants. Public power plants produce electricity for many users. They may be operated by private, cooperative, or governmental organizations. Self-producer power plants are operated by organizations or companies to produce electricity for internal applications, such as factory operations.

Fuelwood, charcoal, bagasse, animal and vegetal wastes, and all forms of solar energy are excluded from production figures, even when traded commercially.

One petajoule (10^{15} joules) is the same as 0.0009478 Quads (10^{15} British Thermal Units) and is the equivalent of 163,400 "U.N. standard" barrels of oil or 34,140 "U.N. standard" metric tons of coal. The heat content of various fuels has been converted to coal-equivalent and then petajoule-equivalent values using country- and year-specific conversion factors. For example, a metric ton of bituminous coal produced in Argentina has an energy value of 0.843 metric ton of standard coal equivalent (7 million kilocalories). A metric ton of bituminous coal produced in Turkey has an energy value of 0.871 metric ton of standard coal equivalent. The original national production data for bituminous coal were multiplied by these conversion factors and then by 29.3076×10^{-6} to yield petajoule equivalents. Other fuels were converted to coal-equivalent and petajoule-equivalent terms in a similar manner.

South Africa refers to the South Africa Customs Union: Botswana, Lesotho, Namibia, South Africa, and Swaziland.

For additional information refer to the United Nations *Energy Statistics Yearbook 1989*.

Table 21.2 Energy Consumption and Requirements, 1979–89

Sources: United Nations Statistical Office (UNSO), *U.N. Energy Tape* (UNSO, New York, May 1991); The World Bank, unpublished data (The World Bank, Washington, D.C., April 1991).

Commercial energy consumption refers to "apparent consumption" and is defined as domestic production plus net imports, minus net stock increases, minus aircraft and marine bunkers, minus unallocated quantities. *Total* consumption includes energy from solid, liquid, and gaseous fuels, plus primary electricity. Included under *imports as percentage of consumption* are net imports, minus stock increases, minus aircraft and marine bunkers, minus unallocated quantities. A negative value (in parentheses) indicates that exports are greater than imports.

Total energy requirements in conventional fuel equivalent is an estimate of the total amount of energy that a nation requires in a given year. It differs from total commercial energy consumption by the inclusion of traditional fuels (fuelwood, charcoal, bagasse, animal and vegetal wastes) and by the treatment of primary electricity.

To calculate total requirements, primary electricity is valued on a fossil-fuel-avoided basis rather than an energy-output basis. For example, a hydroelectric power plant that produces 1,000 kilowatt hours of electricity provides the equivalent heat of 0.123 metric ton of coal. However, more than 0.123 metric ton of coal would be required to produce 1,000 kilowatt hours of electricity. Much of the energy released from coal combustion in a power plant is used in the mechanical work of turning dynamos or is lost in waste heat, so less energy is embodied in the final electricity than in the initial coal. The efficiency of a thermal electric plant is the ratio between final electricity produced and initial energy supplied. Although this rating varies widely from country to country and from plant to plant, the United Nations Statistical Office uses a standard factor of 30 percent efficiency to estimate the fossil fuel value of hydro, geothermal, wind, and nuclear electricity.

Fuelwood and charcoal consumption data are estimated from population data and country-specific per capita consumption figures. These per capita estimates were prepared by the Food and Agriculture Organization of the United Nations (FAO) after an assessment of the available consumption data. Specific consumption of nonconiferous fuelwood ranges from 0.0016 cubic meter per capita per year in Jordan to 0.9783 cubic meter per capita per year in Benin.

Similar estimates were prepared for coniferous fuelwood and for charcoal. Although the energy values of fuelwood and charcoal vary widely, the United Nations Statistical Office uses standard factors of 0.33 metric ton of coal equivalent per cubic meter of fuelwood and 0.986 metric ton of coal equivalent per metric ton of charcoal.

Bagasse production is based on sugar production data in the *Sugar Yearbook* of the International Sugar Organization. It is assumed that 3.26 metric tons of fuel bagasse at 50 percent moisture are produced per metric ton of extracted cane sugar. The energy of a metric ton of bagasse is valued at 0.264 metric ton of coal equivalent.

A petajoule is one quadrillion (10^{15}) joules. A gigajoule is one billion (10^9) joules. A megajoule is one million (10^6) joules.

Table 21.3 Commercial Energy Use by Sector, 1979–89

Sources: International Energy Agency (IEA), World Energy Statistics and Balances, Diskette Service (Organisation for Economic Co-operation and Development/IEA, Paris, June 1991); The World Bank, *World Development Report 1991, The Challenge of Development* (The World Bank, Washington, D.C., 1991).

Use by *industry* includes all use of commercial energy by industry: iron and steel; chemical; nonferrous metals; nonmetallic mineral products such as glass, ceramic, and cement; paper, pulp, and printing; wood and wood products; food processing; textiles and leather; transport equipment; construction; machinery; nonenergy mining; and nonspecified. The *transport* sector includes transport in the industrial sector and covers road, railway, air internal navigation, and nonspecified transport. It excludes international marine bunkers. *Agriculture* includes all uses of commercial energy in agriculture. The *commercial* sector includes energy used in commercial and public services. *Residential* includes all energy for private homes. For some countries that have difficulty providing a realistic breakdown by fuel for industrial and other sectors, *other* may include energy used in the agricultural and/or commercial and domestic sectors. It also includes nonenergy uses, military uses, and nonspecified uses.

Table 21.4 Municipal Waste in OECD Countries

Sources: Organisation for Economic Co-operation and Development (OECD), *Environmental Data Compendium 1991* (OECD, Paris, 1991); United Nations Statistical Commission and Economic Commission for Europe (ECE), *Environment Statistics in Europe and North America* (United Nations, New York, 1987).

Waste data were collected by various means and are not strictly comparable among countries. OECD collects data using questionnaires completed by government representatives.

Annual municipal waste generation refers to the household waste and bulky waste, as well as comparable wastes from small commercial or industrial enterprises, and market and garden residuals that are collected and treated by or for municipalities.

Landfill includes adequately managed and nonmanaged sites. *Other* includes mechanical sorting, composting, and other nonspecified methods. The sum of the different disposal methods may not equal annual waste generation, because treatment methods are not always mutually exclusive and because recycling may be included.

Table 21.5 Production, Consumption, and Reserves of Selected Metals, 1975–90

Sources: Production data for 1975, 1980, and 1985: U.S. Bureau of Mines (U.S.

BOM), *Minerals Yearbook 1977, 1983,* and *1989* (U.S. Government Printing Office, Washington, D.C., 1980, 1984, and 1991). Production data for 1990: U.S. BOM, unpublished data (U.S. BOM, August 1991).

Consumption data for aluminum, cadmium, copper, lead, nickel, tin, and zinc: World Bureau of Metal Statistics, *World Metal Statistics* (World Bureau of Metal Statistics, Ware, United Kingdom, December 1979, December 1980, December 1985, July 1990, August 1991, September 1991, October 1991). Consumption data for zinc: International Lead and Zinc Study Group (ILZSG), *Lead and Zinc Statistics 1960–1988 (ILZSG, London, 1990).* Consumption data for mercury: Roskill Information Services Ltd., *Roskill's Metals Databook, 5th Edition 1984* (Roskill, London, March 1984); Roskill Information Services Ltd., *Statistical Supplement to the Economics of Mercury, 4th Edition 1978* (Roskill, London, 1980); Roskill Information Services Ltd., *The Economics of Mercury, 7th Edition 1990* (Roskill, London, 1990); U.S. BOM, *Mineral Industry Surveys, Mercury in 1989* (U.S. Government Printing Office, Washington, D.C., 1989). Consumption data for iron ore: United Nations Conference on Trade and Development (UNCTAD), Intergovernmental Group of Experts on Iron Ore, *Iron Ore Statistics 1981–1990* (UNCTAD, Geneva, 1991); Statistical Office of the European Community (EUROSTAT), *Iron and Steel Statistical Yearbook 1980, 1981,* and *1990* (EUROSTAT, Luxembourg, 1980, 1981, and 1990); Organisation for Economic Co-operation and Development (OECD), *The Iron and Steel Industry in 1981, 1985,* and *1989* (OECD, Paris, 1983, 1987, and 1991); International Iron and Steel Institute, *Steel Statistical Yearbook 1985* and *1989* (International Iron and Steel Institute, Brussels, 1985 and 1989). Consumption data for crude steel: International Iron and Steel Institute, *Steel Statistical Yearbook 1985* and *1989* (International Iron and Steel Institute, Brussels, 1985 and 1989).

Reserves and reserve base data: U.S. BOM, *Mineral Commodity Summaries 1991* (U.S. Government Printing Office, Washington, D.C., 1991).

The U.S. BOM publishes production, trade, consumption, and other data on commodities for the United States as well as for all other countries of the world (depending on availability of reliable data). The data are based on information from government mineral and statistical agencies, the United Nations, and U.S. and foreign technical and trade literature.

The World Bureau of Metal Statistics publishes consumption data on the metals presented, excluding mercury, iron, and steel. Data on the metals included were supplied by metal companies, government agencies, trade groups, and statistical bureaus. Obviously incorrect data have been revised, but most data were compiled and reported without adjustment or retrospective revisions.

The countries listed represent the top 10 producers and the top 10 consumers of each material in 1990.

The *annual production* data are the metal content of the ore mined for *copper, lead,* mercury, nickel, tin, and zinc. Aluminum (bauxite) and iron ore production are expressed in gross weight of ore mined (marketable product). Iron ore production refers to iron ore, iron ore concentrates, and iron ore agglomerates (sinter and pellets). Cadmium is the production of the refined metal. Crude steel production is defined as the total of usable ingots, continuously cast semifinished products, and liquid steel for castings. The United Nations' definition of crude steel is the equivalent of the term "raw steel" as used by the United States.

Annual consumption of metal refers to the domestic use of refined metals, which include metals refined from either primary (raw) or secondary (recovered) materials. Metal used in a product that is then exported is considered to be consumed by the producing country rather than by the importing country. Data on mercury consumption must be viewed with caution; they include estimates on consumption of secondary materials, which are generally not reported. Consumption of iron ore is the quantity of iron ore and concentrates reported as delivered to consuming industries. Data for Brazil, China, the Republic of Korea, and the U.S.S.R. are calculated as apparent consumption, the net of production plus imports minus exports. Such a consumption number makes no allowance for stock inventories. This can lead to discrepancies in the published consumption data evident in the latest report by the UNCTAD Intergovernmental Group of Experts on Iron Ore. For example, Brazil had a "reported consumption" (domestic and imported ores consumed in iron and steel plants, as well as ores consumed for non-metallurgical uses) of 23.7 million metric tons in 1990, compared to 40 million metric tons apparent consumption. Apparent consumption of iron ore was chosen in Table 21.5, because "reported consumption" data were only available for a limited number of countries and years. Because different countries report different grades of iron ore, consumption data are not strictly comparable among countries. Because world consumption of iron ore is roughly equal to world production, world production data were used for world consumption totals. World-

wide stock inventories are assumed to be negligible. Crude steel consumption is calculated as apparent consumption. The International Iron and Steel Institute converted imports and exports into crude steel equivalent by using a factor of $1.3/(1 + 0.175c)$, where c is the domestic proportion of crude steel that is continuously cast. Such an adjustment avoids distortion of the export or import share relative to domestic production.

The world reserve base life index and the world reserves life index are expressed in years remaining. They were computed by dividing the 1990 world reserve base and world reserves by the respective world production rate of 1990. The underlying assumption is a constant world production at the 1990 level and capacity.

The reserve base is the portion of the mineral resource that meets grade, quality, thickness, and depth criteria defined by current mining and production practices. It includes both measured and indicated reserves and refers to those resources that are both currently economic and marginally economic, as well as some of those that are currently subeconomic.

Mineral reserves are those deposits whose quantity and grade have been determined by samples and measurements and can be profitably recovered at the time of the assessment. Changes in geologic information, technology, costs of extraction and production, and prices of mined product can affect the reserve estimates. Reserves do not signify that extraction facilities are in place and operative.

Table 21.6 World Reserves of Major Metals, 1990

Sources: U.S. Bureau of Mines (U.S. BOM), Mineral Commodity Summaries 1991 (U.S. BOM, Washington, D.C., 1991); U.S. BOM, Minerals Yearbook 1985 and 1989 (U.S. BOM, Washington, D.C., 1987 and 1991); U.S. BOM, Mineral Facts and Problems 1985 (U.S. BOM, Washington, D.C., 1985); U.S. BOM, Minerals Availability Program, unpublished data, (U.S. BOM, Washington, D.C., January 1991); Sam H. Patterson, Horace F.

Kurtz, Jane C. Olson, et al., World Bauxite Resources (U.S. Geological Survey Paper 1076-B, Washington, D.C., 1986); United Nations Educational, Scientific and Cultural Organization (UNESCO), Geology of Tungsten (UNESCO, Paris, 1986).

Mineral reserves are those deposits whose quantity and grade have been determined by samples and measurements and can be profitably recovered at the time of the assessment. Changes in geologic information, technology, costs of extraction and production, and prices of mined product can affect the reserve estimates. Reserves do not signify that extraction facilities are in place and operative.

Estimates for the countries holding the largest reserves came from the most recent U.S. BOM Mineral Commodity Summaries 1991. It usually aggregates estimates for countries with minor reserves under the category "other countries" (2 to 20 percent of world total). Other published information or unpublished data from mineral specialists of the U.S. BOM were used to fill in the data for these missing countries. In cases where no published or unpublished data were available to disaggregate the "other countries" category, WRI allocated the total reserve estimate of "other countries" by using reserve estimates of the U.S. BOM's Minerals Availability Program or production data as weights. This assumes that all countries with reserves are extracting the metal. In cases where there is a nonproducer with significant reserves, it will not be reflected in the table and the disaggregated reserves for the "other countries" will be an overestimate. WRI estimates have to be seen as preliminary and must be interpreted with caution.

World reserves total may differ slightly from those in Table 21.5 because of differences in rounding procedures.

Each country's metal reserves index is the mean of its 15 global shares calculated for each of the metals in the index. For example, a country with 30 percent of the world nickel reserves, 15 percent of the world lead reserves, and no other metal reserves has a metal reserve index of $(30 + 15)/15 = 3$ percent.

22. Freshwater

Freshwater is essential not only to the maintenance of human life, but also to the development and function of modern industry and agriculture. Freshwater resources are unequally distributed around the world, however, and people routinely impact the supply and quality. They control, dam, capture, and channel freshwater for power generation, irrigation, and industrial and domestic uses. Freshwater streams carry many urban and industrial wastes as well as eroded soil from wastelands, croplands, and urban development.

The freshwater resource easiest to access is the renewable component (precipitation minus evapotranspiration, see Table 22.1), which flows through aquifers, streams, and lakes. The global renewable resources total over 40,000 cubic kilometers, of which about 3,200 is withdrawn for domestic, industrial, and agricultural uses. Many countries, particularly those in Southwest Asia and Northern Africa, rely on river flows from neighboring countries, and governments resort to international agreements (such as that between Sudan and Egypt regulating the flow of the Nile) to protect their water supplies. Additional sources of freshwater are ancient, nonrenewable aquifers that can be tapped to fuel intensive irrigated agriculture and urban life (e.g., the Ogallala Aquifer in the United States and the Nubian Aquifer in Libya). These aquifers can be permanently depleted.

Desalinization of salt or brackish water is a capital- and energy-intensive source of freshwater but one that has become a significant portion of total supply on the Arabian peninsula. Many arid countries, such as Afghanistan, Sudan, Egypt, the former People's Democratic Republic of Yemen, the Islamic Republic of Iran, and Iraq, annually withdraw over 1,000 cubic meters of freshwater per capita; most of this water is used in irrigation. Some countries (Egypt, Libya, Israel, Qatar, Saudi Arabia, the United Arab Emirates, the former Arab Republic of Yemen, and Malta) use almost all or even more than their total renewable resources—tapping nonrecharging aquifers and desalinization plants. Some countries in the more humid and temperate zones also use large amounts of freshwater. The United States, for example, used 2,162 cubic meters per capita in 1985, and its total use is higher than that of any other country. Canada, Bulgaria, the Netherlands, Portugal, Romania, the U.S.S.R., and Australia also use over 1,000 cubic meters per capita.

Table 22.2 provides data on the numbers of large dams, their construction rates, and hydroelectric resources. The number of dams over 15 meters in height increased almost sevenfold since 1950. Half of all large dams are in China. These structures provide for the massive storage of water to control flooding, redistribute uneven river flows, generate power, irrigate new lands, and ensure the supply of water for a variety of domestic and industrial uses. There are, however, potential environmental costs to large dams. Large dams change the flow, temperature, and nutrient character of rivers. They interrupt the movement of aquatic animals and interrupt freshwater flows to coastal estuarine environments. They can flood the lands and homes of people and the habitat of wildlife.

Table 22.2 also shows the hydropower potential and current state of its exploitation for many countries of the world. Hydropower resources are exploited differently in each country, depending on inherent energy requirements, climatic variables, and maintainance requirements. In addition, countries often use only a fraction of their installed capacity over the course of a year. The importance of hydropower to total energy production also varies widely. Canada was the largest producer of hydropower in 1989 with over 290,000 gigawatt-hours, followed by the United States, U.S.S.R., Brazil, Norway, and China.

Dams permanently change the normal hydrology of a region. They interrupt the flow of sediments to the sea, and the buildup of those sediments behind dams can quickly diminish the storage capacity of reservoirs. Sediment loads are important for the agricultural fertility of many floodplains, as indicators of the relative magnitude of upstream erosion, and for maintaining the integrity of delta lands. Table 22.3 provides information on materials transport, total river flows, and basin area for 260 gauging stations.

Some large rivers, such as the Mississippi, today transport relatively low amounts of sediments and other materials for the size of their basins (0.64 metric tons per hectare). The Mississippi earned its nickname, "the Big Muddy," long before its basin was heavily dammed for power, flood control, and irrigation. Other major rivers transport considerably more material from each hectare of their watersheds. The Hwang Ho (at its mouth) transports about 14 metric tons of materials for each hectare of its watershed, and the Brahmaputra transports only slightly more. Much of these high loads is due to human activity, but soil type and typography play a large role.

Table 22.1 Freshwater Resources and Withdrawals

	Annual Internal Renewable Water Resources		Annual River Flows		Annual Withdrawals				Sectoral Withdrawals (percent) {b}		
	Total (cubic km)	1990 Per Capita (000 cubic meters)	From Other Countries (cubic km)	To Other Countries (cubic km)	Year of Data	Total (cubic km)	Percentage of Water Resources {a}	Per Capita (cubic meters)	Domestic	Industry	Agriculture
WORLD	40,673.00 c	7.69			1987 c	3,240.00	8	660	8	23	69
AFRICA	4,184.00 c	6.46			1987 c	144.00	3	244	7	5	88
Algeria	18.90	0.75	0.20	0.70	1980	3.00	16	161	22	4	74
Angola	158.00 c	15.77	X	X	1987 c	0.48	0	43	14	10	76
Benin	26.00	5.48	X	X	1987 c	0.11	0	26	28	14	58
Botswana	1.00	0.78	17.00	X	1980	0.09	1	98	5	10	85
Burkina Faso	28.00 c	3.11	X	X	1987 c	0.15	1	20	28	5	67
Burundi	3.60 c	0.66	X	X	1987 c	0.10	3	20	36	0	64
Cameroon	208.00	18.50	X	X	1987 c	0.40	0	30	46	19	35
Cape Verde	0.20	0.53	0.00	0.00	1972	0.04	20	148	9	2	89
Central African Rep	141.00 c	48.40	X	X	1987 c	0.07	0	27	21	5	74
Chad	38.40 c	6.76	X	X	1987 c	0.18	0	35	16	2	82
Comoros	1.02	1.97	0.00	0.00	1987 c	0.01	1	15	48	5	47
Congo	181.00 c	90.77	621.00	X	1987 c	0.04	0	20	62	27	11
Cote d'Ivoire	74.00	5.87	X	X	1987 c	0.71	1	68	22	11	67
Djibouti	0.30	0.74	0.00	X	1973 c	0.01	2	28	28	21	51
Egypt	1.80	0.03	56.50	0.00	1985	56.40	97	1,202	7 d	5 d	88 d
Equatorial Guinea	30.00 c	68.18	X	X	1987 c	0.01	0	11	81	13	6
Ethiopia	110.00	2.35	X	X	1987 c	2.21	2	48	11	3	86
Gabon	164.00 c	140.05	X	X	1987 c	0.06	0	51	72	22	6
Gambia, The	3.00	3.50	19.00	X	1982	0.02	0	33	7	2	91
Ghana	53.00	3.53	X	X	1970	0.30	1	35	35	13	52
Guinea	226.00	32.87	X	X	1987 c	0.74	0	115	10	3	87
Guinea-Bissau	31.00 c	31.41	X	X	1987 c	0.01	0	18	31	6	63
Kenya	14.80	0.59	X	X	1987 c	1.09	7	48	27	11	62
Lesotho	4.00	2.25	X	X	1987 c	0.05	1	34	22	22	56
Liberia	232.00 c	90.84	X	X	1987 c	0.13	0	54	27	13	60
Libya	0.70	0.15	0.00	0.00	1985 e	2.83	404	623	15	10	75
Madagascar	40.00	3.34	0.00	0.00	1984	16.30	41	1,675	1	0	99
Malawi	9.00 c	1.07	X	X	1987 c	0.16	2	22	34	17	49
Mali	62.00 c	6.62	X	X	1987 c	1.36	2	159	2	1	97
Mauritania	0.40	0.20	7.00	X	1978	0.73	10	473	12	4	84
Mauritius	2.20	1.99	0.00	0.00	1974	0.36	16	415	16	7	77
Morocco	30.00	1.19	0.00	0.30	1985	11.00	37	501	6 d	3 d	91 d
Mozambique	58.00 c	3.70	X	X	1987 c	0.76	1	53	24	10	66
Namibia	9.00 c	X	X	X	1987 c	0.14	2	77	6	12	82
Niger	14.00 c	1.97	30.00	X	1987 c	0.29	1	44	21	5	74
Nigeria	261.00 c	2.31	47.00	X	1987 c	3.63	1	44	31	15	54
Rwanda	6.30 c	0.87	X	X	1987 c	0.15	2	23	24	8	68
Senegal	23.20 c	3.15	12.00	X	1987 c	1.36	4	201	5	3	92
Sierra Leone	160.00 c	38.54	X	X	1987 c	0.37	0	99	7	4	89
Somalia	11.50	1.52	0.00	X	1987 c	0.81	7	167	3	0	97
South Africa	50.00	1.42	X	X	1970	9.20	18	404	16	17	67
Sudan	30.00	1.19	100.00	56.50	1977	18.60	14	1,089	1	0	99
Swaziland	6.96 c	8.82	X	X	1987 c	0.29	4	414	5	2	93
Tanzania	76.00 c	2.78	X	X	1970	0.48	1	36	21	5	74
Togo	11.50	3.33	X	X	1987 c	0.09	1	40	62	13	25
Tunisia	3.75	0.46	0.60	0.00	1985	2.30	53	325	13	7	80
Uganda	66.00 c	3.58	X	X	1970	0.20	0	20	32	8	60
Zaire	1,019.00 c	28.31	X	X	1987 c	0.70	0	22	58	25	17
Zambia	96.00 c	11.35	X	X	1970	0.36	0	86	63	11	26
Zimbabwe	23.00 c	2.37	X	X	1987 c	1.22	5	129	14	7	79
NORTH & CENTRAL AMERICA	6,945.00 c	16.26			1987 c	697.00	10	1,692	9	42	49
Barbados	0.05	0.20	0.00	0.00	1962	0.03	51	117	52	41	7
Belize	16.00	X	X	X	1987 c	0.02	0	X	10	0	90
Canada	2,901.00	109.37	X	X	1986	42.20	1	1,752	11	80	8
Costa Rica	95.00	31.51	X	X	1970	1.35	1	779	4	7	89
Cuba	34.50	3.34	0.00	0.00	1975	8.10	23	868	9	2	89
Dominican Rep	20.00	2.79	X	X	1987 c	2.97	15	453	5	6	89
El Salvador	18.95	3.61	X	X	1975	1.00	5	241	7	4	89
Guatemala	116.00	12.61	X	X	1970	0.73	1	139	9	17	74
Haiti	11.00	1.69	X	X	1987 c	0.04	0	46	24	8	68
Honduras	102.00	19.85	X	X	1970	1.34	1	508	4	5	91
Jamaica	8.30	3.29	0.00	0.00	1975	0.32	4	157	7	7	86
Mexico	357.40	4.03	X	X	1975	54.20	15	901	6	8	86
Nicaragua	175.00	45.21	X	X	1975	0.89	1	370	25	21	54
Panama	144.00	59.55	X	X	1975	1.30	1	744	12	11	77
Trinidad and Tobago	5.10 c	3.98	0.00	0.00	1975	0.15	3	149	27	38	35
United States	2,478.00	9.94	X	X	1985	467.00	19	2,162	12 d	46 d	42 d
SOUTH AMERICA	10,377.00 c	34.96			1987 c	133.00	1	476	18	23	59
Argentina	694.00	21.47	300.00	X	1976	27.60	3	1,059	9	18	73
Bolivia	300.00 c	41.02	X	X	1987 c	1.24	0	184	10	5	85
Brazil	5,190.00	34.52	1760.00	X	1987 c	35.04	1	212	43	17	40
Chile	468.00 c	35.53	X	X	1975	16.80	4	1,625	6	5	89
Colombia	1,070.00	33.63	X	X	1987 c	5.34	0	179	41	16	43
Ecuador	314.00	29.12	X	X	1987 c	5.56	2	561	7	3	90
Guyana	241.00 c	231.73	X	X	1971	5.40	2	7,616	1	0	99
Paraguay	94.00 c	21.98	220.00	X	1987 c	0.43	0	111	15	7	78
Peru	40.00	1.79	X	X	1987 c	6.10	15	294	19	9	72
Suriname	200.00	496.28	X	X	1987 c	0.46	0	1,181	6	5	89
Uruguay	59.00 c	18.86	65.00	X	1965	0.65	1	241	6	3	91
Venezuela	856.00	43.37	461.00	X	1970	4.10	0	387	43	11	46

Table 22.1

	Annual Internal Renewable Water Resources		Annual River Flows			Annual Withdrawals			Sectoral Withdrawals (percent) {b}		
	Total (cubic km)	1990 Per Capita (000 cubic meters)	From Other Countries (cubic km)	To Other Countries (cubic km)	Year of Data	Total (cubic km)	Percentage of Water Resources {a}	Per Capita (cubic meters)	Domestic	Industry	Agriculture
ASIA	**10,485.00**	**3.37**			**1987 c**	**1,531.00**	**15**	**526**	**6**	**8**	**86**
Afghanistan	50.00	3.02	X	X	1987 c	26.11	52	1,436	1	0	99
Bahrain	0.00	0.00	X	X	1975 e	0.31	X	609	60	36	4
Bangladesh	1,357.00	11.74	1000.00	X	1987 c	22.50	1	211	3	1	96
Bhutan	95.00 c	62.66	X	X	1987 c	0.02	0	15	36	10	54
Cambodia	88.10	10.68	410.00	X	1987 c	0.52	0	69	5	1	94
China	2,800.00	2.47	0.00	X	1980	460.00	16	462	6 d	7 d	87 d
Cyprus	0.90	1.28	0.00	0.00	1985	0.54	60	807	7 d	2 d	91 d
India	1,850.00	2.17	235.00	X	1975	380.00	18	612	3	4	93
Indonesia	2,530.00	14.02	X	X	1987 c	16.59	1	96	13	11	76
Iran, Islamic Rep	117.50	2.08	X	X	1975	45.40	39	1,362	4	9	87
Iraq	34.00	1.80	66.00	X	1970	42.80	43	4,575	3	5	92
Israel	1.70	0.37	0.45	0.00	1986	1.90	88	447	16 d	5 d	79 d
Japan	547.00	4.43	0.00	0.00	1980	107.80	20	923	17	33	50
Jordan	0.70	0.16	0.40	X	1975	0.45	41	173	29	6	65
Korea, Dem People's Rep	67.00 c	2.92	X	X	1987 c	14.16	21	1,649	11	16	73
Korea, Rep	63.00	1.45	X	X	1976	10.70	17	298	11	14	75
Kuwait	0.00	0.00	0.00	X	1974 e	0.50	X	238	64	32	4
Lao People's Dem Rep	270.00	66.32	X	X	1987 c	0.99	0	228	8	10	82
Lebanon	4.80	1.62	0.00	0.86	1975	0.75	16	271	11	4	85
Malaysia	456.00	26.30	X	X	1975	9.42	2	765	23	30	47
Mongolia	24.60	11.05	X	X	1987 c	0.55	2	272	11	27	62
Myanmar	1,082.00	25.96	X	X	1987 c	3.96	0	103	7	3	90
Nepal	170.00	8.88	X	X	1987 c	2.68	2	155	4	1	95
Oman	2.00	1.36	0.00	X	1975 e	0.48	24	325	3	3	94
Pakistan	298.00	2.43	170.00	X	1975	153.40	33	2,053	1	1	98
Philippines	323.00	5.18	0.00	0.00	1975	29.50	9	693	18	21	61
Qatar	0.02	0.06	0.00	X	1975 e	0.15	663	415	36	26	38
Saudi Arabia	2.20	0.16	0.00	X	1975	3.60	164	255	45	8	47
Singapore	0.60	0.22	0.00	0.00	1975	0.19	32	84	45	51	4
Sri Lanka	43.20	2.51	0.00	0.00	1970	6.30	15	503	2	2	96
Syrian Arab Rep	7.60	0.61	27.90	30.00	1976 e	3.34	9	449	7	10	83
Thailand	110.00	1.97	69.00	X	1987 c	31.90	18	599	4	6	90
Turkey	196.00	3.52	7.00	69.00	1985	15.60	8	317	24 d	19 d	57 d
United Arab Emirates	0.30	0.19	0.00	X	1980 e	0.90	299	565	11	9	80
Viet Nam	376.00 c	5.60	X	X	1987 c	5.07	1	81	13	9	78
Yemen (Arab Rep)	1.00	0.12	0.00	X	1987 c	1.47	147	X	4	2	94
(People's Dem Rep)	1.50	0.60	0.00	X	1975	1.93	129	1,167	5	2	93
EUROPE	**2,321.00 c**	**4.66**			**1987 c**	**359.00**	**15**	**726**	**13**	**54**	**33**
Albania	10.00	3.08	11.30	X	1970	0.20	1	94	6	18	76
Austria	56.30	7.51	34.00	X	1980	3.13	3	417	19	73	8
Belgium	8.40	0.85	4.10	X	1980	9.03	72	917	11	85	4
Bulgaria	18.00	2.00	187.00	X	1980	14.18	7	1,600	7	38	55
Czechoslovakia	28.00	1.79	62.60	X	1980	5.80	6	379	23	68	9
Denmark	11.00	2.15	2.00	X	1985 f	1.46	11	289	30	27	43
Finland	110.00	22.11	3.00	X	1980	3.70	3	774	12	85	3
France	170.00	3.03	15.00	20.50	1985 f	40.00	22	728	16	69	15
Germany (Fed Rep)	79.00	1.30	82.00	X	1983 f	41.22	26	668	10	70	20
(Dem Rep)	17.00	1.02	17.00	X	1980	9.13	27	545	14	68	18
Greece	45.15	4.49	13.50	3.00	1980 f	6.95	12	721	8	29	63
Hungary	6.00	0.57	109.00	X	1980	5.38	5	502	9	55	36
Iceland	170.00	671.94	0.00	0.00	1987 c	0.09	0	340	31	63	6
Ireland	50.00	13.44	0.00	X	1979 f	0.79	2	267	16	74	10
Italy	179.40	3.13	7.60	0.00	1980 f	56.20	30	983	14	27	59
Luxembourg	1.00	2.72	4.00	X	1985	0.04	1	119	42	45	13
Malta	0.03	0.07	0.00	0.00	1978	0.02	92	68	76	8	16
Netherlands	10.00	0.68	80.00	X	1985 f	14.47	16	1,023	5	61	34
Norway	405.00	96.15	8.00	X	1980	2.00	0	489	20	72	8
Poland	49.40	1.29	6.80	X	1980	16.80	30	472	16	60	24
Portugal	34.00	3.31	31.60	X	1980	10.50	16	1,062	15	37	48
Romania	37.00	1.59	171.00	X	1980	25.40	12	1,144	8	33	59
Spain	110.30	2.80	1.00	17.00	1985 f	45.25	41	1,174	12	26	62
Sweden	176.00	21.11	4.00	X	1980	3.98	2	479	36	55	9
Switzerland	42.50	6.52	7.50	X	1985	3.20	6	502	23	73	4
United Kingdom	120.00	2.11	0.00	X	1980	28.35	24	507	20	77	3
Yugoslavia	150.00	6.29	115.00	200.00	1980	8.77	3	393	16	72	12
U.S.S.R.	**4,384.00**	**15.22**	**300.00**	**X**	**1980**	**353.00**	**8**	**1,330**	**6**	**29**	**65**
OCEANIA	**2,011.00 c**	**75.96**			**1987 c**	**23.00**	**1**	**907**	**64**	**2**	**34**
Australia	343.00	20.48	0.00	0.00	1975	17.80	5	1,306	65	2	33
Fiji	28.55 c	38.12	0.00	0.00	1987 c	0.03	0	37	20	20	60
New Zealand	397.00	117.49	0.00	0.00	1980	1.20	0	379	46	10	44
Papua New Guinea	801.00 c	199.70	X	X	1987 c	0.10	0	25	29	22	49
Solomon Islands	44.70 c	149.00	0.00	0.00	1987 c	0.00	0	18	40	20	40

Sources: Bureau of Geological and Mining Research, National Geological Survey, France; Institute of Geography, National Academy of Sciences, U.S.S.R.; Eurostat; and the International Desalination Association.

Notes: a. Water resources include both internal renewable resources and river flows from other countries. b. Unless otherwise noted, sectoral withdrawal percentages are estimated for 1987. c. Estimated by the Institute of Geography, U.S.S.R. d. Sectoral percentages date from the year of other annual withdrawal data. e. Withdrawal quantities include desalination capacities as of June 1988. f. Reported to Eurostat.
Regional and world totals may include countries not listed.
0 = zero or less than half the unit of measure; X = not available.
For additional information, see Sources and Technical Notes.

Table 22.2 Large Dams and Hydroelectric Resources

	Large Dams, 1986				Hydropower Potential (gigawatt-hours/year)		Installed Hydropower Capacity, 1989 (gigawatts)		Hydropower Generation, 1989	
	Total Over 15 Meters In Height	Percent Change Since 1977	Total Over 30 Meters In Height	Total Under Construction	Gross Theoretical	Exploit-able	Total	Micro-hydro	Total (gigawatt-hours)	Percent of Capacity
WORLD	36,562		7,685	1,026			617.101		2,094,009	38.7
AFRICA	885		256	58			18.884		44,156	26.7
Algeria	30	50	26	13	12,000	X	0.285	X	226	9.1
Angola	10	X	X	X	150,000	100,000 a	0.412	X	1,355	37.5
Benin	1	X	X	X	X	X	X	X	X	X
Botswana	3	X	X	X	X	X	X	X	X	X
Burkina Faso	1	X	X	X	X	800 a	0.014	0.000	2	1.4
Burundi	X	X	X	X	6,605	1,445	0.032	0.012 b	103	36.7
Cameroon	8	X	X	X	172,572	115,000 a	0.528	0.003 b	2,629	56.8
Cape Verde	X	X	X	X	X	X	X	X	X	X
Central African Rep	0	X	0	X	X	X	0.022	X	74	38.4
Chad	0	X	0	X	X	X	X	X	X	X
Comoros	X	X	X	X	X	X	0.001	X	2	22.8
Congo	1	X	X	X	X	50,000 a	0.120	X	397	37.8
Cote d'Ivoire	22	57	5	0	68,000	14,000 a	0.895	X	1,250	15.9
Djibouti	X	X	X	X	X	X	X	X	X	X
Egypt	5	0	2	0	X	X	2.445	X	6,400	29.9
Equatorial Guinea	X	X	X	X	X	X	0.001	0.001	2	22.8
Ethiopia	8	X	X	X	650,000	162,000	0.230	0.001	655	32.5
Gabon	1	X	X	X	X	32,500	0.125	0.160	675	61.6
Gambia, The	X	X	X	X	X	X	X	X	X	X
Ghana	5	67	2	0	12,782	10,000	1.072	X	4,820	51.3
Guinea	2	X	X	X	X	26,000 a	0.047	X	172	41.8
Guinea-Bissau	X	X	X	X	X	300	X	X	X	X
Kenya	10	150	5	4	X	30,000 a	0.498	0.008	2,469	56.6
Lesotho	3	X	X	X	X	2,000	0.002	0.002	X	X
Liberia	1	X	X	X	X	11,000 a	0.081	0.000	320	45.1
Libya	12	X	10	0	X	X	X	X	X	X
Madagascar	10	0	0	0	400,000	23,061	0.106	0.002	317	34.1
Malawi	3	X	X	X	X	6,000 a	0.146	X	572	44.7
Mali	1	X	X	X	X	10,000 a	0.045	X	170	43.1
Mauritania	X	X	X	X	X	X	X	X	25	X
Mauritius	8	X	X	X	200	110	0.059	0.012	102	19.7
Morocco	39	70	25	23	X	4,500	0.622	0.006	1,157	21.2
Mozambique	5	X	X	X	X	72,000 a	2.078	0.003	50	0.3
Namibia	10	X	X	X	X	X	X	X	X	X
Niger	0	X	0	X	X	X	X	X	X	X
Nigeria	44	76	7	1	X	40,000 a	1.900	0.000	2,210	13.3
Rwanda	X	X	X	X	X	3,000 a	0.056	0.004 b	171	34.9
Senegal	1	X	X	X	X	2,500 a	0.000	0.000	X	X
Sierra Leone	1	X	X	X	X	6,800 a	0.002	0.002	X	X
Somalia	X	X	X	X	X	X	0.005	0.000	0	0.1
South Africa	482 c	43	127	6	X	X	0.550	0.000	600	12.5
Sudan	4	X	3	0	X	1,900	0.225	X	517	26.2
Swaziland	6	50	X	X	1,200	400	0.042	0.003	215	58.4
Tanzania	2	X	X	X	X	20,000	0.259	0.003	615	27.1
Togo	1	X	X	X	X	X	0.004	0.004	5	14.3
Tunisia	32	52	16	4	62	53	0.064	0.003	36	6.4
Uganda	1	X	X	X	X	10,200	0.155	X	691	50.9
Zaire	13	X	X	X	X	530,000	2.772	0.001	5,252	21.6
Zambia	4	33	4	0	33,500	30,900	2.245	X	6,702	34.1
Zimbabwe	94	24	24	7	18,500	16,000	0.633	0.000	2,660	48.0
NORTH & CENTRAL AMERICA	6,663		1,530	39			157.256		598,405	43.4
Barbados	X	X	X	X	X	X	X	X	X	X
Belize	X	X	X	X	X	X	X	X	X	X
Canada	608	23	162	5	1,239,777	592,982	57.924	<0.050	291,447	57.4
Costa Rica	4	33	2	0	222,953	37,000	0.735	0.030	3,328	51.7
Cuba	49	X	X	X	X	X	0.049	X	82	19.1
Dominican Rep	9	350	7	3	X	2,517	0.165	X	950	65.7
El Salvador	4	X	X	X	4,737	3,319	0.405	0.001 b	1,452	40.9
Guatemala	4	300	2	0	95,405	43,370	0.438	0.005	2,089	54.4
Haiti	1	X	X	X	548	430	0.070	0.007	320	52.2
Honduras	8	X	4	0	196,000	240,000	0.130	0.001	880	77.3
Jamaica	2	X	X	X	455	335	0.020	0.001	110	62.8
Mexico	503	16	168	17	500,000	159,624	7.825	X	22,950	33.5
Nicaragua	2	X	X	X	X	17,277 a	0.103	X	268	29.7
Panama	5	X	X	X	X	16,233 a	0.551	X	2,181	45.2
Trinidad and Tobago	4	X	X	X	X	X	X	X	X	X
United States	5,459	8	1,185	14 d	528,500	376,000	88.746	0.737	272,021	35.0
SOUTH AMERICA	885		333	69			77.175		327,373	48.4
Argentina	94	31	63	5	535,000	390,000	6.594	0.040	15,150	26.2
Bolivia	5	25	2	1	173,000	90,000 a	0.342	0.055 b	1,270	42.4
Brazil	516	16	148	47	3,020,400	1,194,900	44.622	0.100	214,238	54.8
Chile	74	17	26	5	181,000	132,433	2.290	0.011	9,603	47.9
Colombia	40	43	28	1	1,290,000	418,200	6.317	0.100	29,875	54.0
Ecuador	5	25	3	6	491,000	115,000	0.908	0.017	4,918	61.8
Guyana	0	X	0	X	67,500	63,100	0.002	0.000	5	28.5
Paraguay	3	50	3	0	X	78,000	5.440	X	2,784	5.8
Peru	66	6	13	2	1,839,600	412,000	2.275	0.050	10,518	52.8
Suriname	1	X	X	X	X	12,840	0.189	X	910	55.0
Uruguay	5	33	4	1	32,000	4,880	1.196	0.000	3,902	37.2
Venezuela	76	49	43	1	335,000	250,000	7.000	0.007	34,200	55.8

Table 22.2

	Large Dams, 1986				Hydropower Potential (gigawatt hours/year)		Installed Hydropower Capacity, 1989 (gigawatts)		Hydropower Generation, 1989	
	Total Over 15 Meters In Height	Percent Change Since 1977	Total Over 30 Meters In Height	Total Under Construction	Gross Theoretical	Exploit-able	Total	Micro-hydro	Total (gigawatt-hours)	Percent of Capacity
ASIA	**23,555**		**3,568**	**615**			**118.846**		**398,440**	**38.3**
Afghanistan	2	X	X	X	X	X	0.290	X	758	29.8
Bahrain	X	X	X	X	X	X	X	X	X	X
Bangladesh	1	0	1	0	X	X	0.230	X	735	36.5
Bhutan	X	X	X	X	X	X	0.334	0.006	654	22.4
Cambodia	1	X	X	X	X	83,000	0.010	X	30	34.2
China	18,820	14	2,287	183 d	5,922,180	1,923,304	30.000	3.875	109,500	41.7
Cyprus	46	70	18	2	X	X	0.001	0.001	X	X
India	1,137	14	220	160 d	2,637,800	600,100	18.504	0.207	63,760	39.3
Indonesia	44	69	25	8	338,800	709,000	1.850	0.013 b	8,600	53.1
Iran, Islamic Rep	21	24	15	7	36,286	6,784	1.804	X	6,700	42.4
Iraq	8	60	5	5	X	70,000	0.120	X	590	56.1
Israel	X	X	X	X	1,600	1,600	0.000	0.000	0	X
Japan	2,228	11	741	71 d	717,600	130,524	37.409	X	97,825	29.9
Jordan	4	0	4	1	87	87	0.011	X	29	30.1
Korea, Dem People's Rep	66	X	23	4	X	X	5.000	X	31,750	72.5
Korea, Rep	690	23	52	75	77,201	3,290	2.339	0.010	4,558	22.2
Kuwait	X	X	X	X	X	X	X	X	X	X
Lao People's Dem Rep	1	X	X	X	150,227	22,638	0.200	0.003	1,095	62.5
Lebanon	5	0	2	0	1,000	1,000	0.246	0.003 b	500	23.2
Malaysia	36	227	19	2	219,900	108,600	1.437	0.009	6,256	49.7
Mongolia	X	X	X	X	X	X	X	X	X	X
Myanmar	3	X	X	X	336,000	160,000 a	0.258	X	1,240	54.9
Nepal	2	X	1	1	729,500	144,000	0.160	0.009	542	38.7
Oman	X	X	X	X	X	X	X	X	X	X
Pakistan	40	21	17	0	25,443	15,531	2.897	0.109	16,974	66.9
Philippines	14	133	9	1	36,654	11,877	2.154	0.006	6,546	34.7
Qatar	X	X	X	X	X	X	X	X	X	X
Saudi Arabia	30	X	X	X	X	X	X	X	X	X
Singapore	3	X	X	X	X	X	X	X	X	X
Sri Lanka	77	20	13	2	8,000	7,255	0.940	0.009	2,650	32.2
Syrian Arab Rep	12	0	3	0	5,000	4,500	0.898	X	4,707	59.8
Thailand	81	286	25	28	19,782	5,571	2.268	0.003	5,571	28.0
Turkey	103	61	88	65	432,986	215,000	6.598	0.012	17,939	31.0
United Arab Emirates	X	X	X	X	X	X	X	X	X	X
Viet Nam	1	X	X	X	X	X	0.325	0.030	2,250	79.0
Yemen (Arab Rep)	X	X	X	X	X	X	X	X	X	X
(People's Dem Rep)	X	X	X	X	X	X	X	X	X	X
EUROPE	**3,945**		**1,680**	**202**			**168.949**		**465,016**	**31.4**
Albania	98	44	48	2	20,000	17,000	0.690	X	3,600	59.6
Austria	123	27	66	7	75,000	53,700	10.838	0.320	36,137	38.1
Belgium	15	36	9	0	798	X	1.402	0.014	362	2.9
Bulgaria	108	2	37	0	26,410	15,000	1.975	X	2,690	15.5
Czechoslovakia	146	11	52	8	28,600	10,826	2.920	0.230	4,273	16.7
Denmark	6	0	0	0	120	70	0.010	X	27	30.8
Finland	50	0	7	0	47,000	20,000	2.586	0.110	12,948	57.2
France	468	21	167	5	266,000	72,000	24.815	<0.800	51,160	23.5
Germany (Fed Rep)	191	21	60	8	99,000	24,000	6.861	0.420 b	17,000	28.3
(Dem Rep)	70	X	28	1	X	700	1.844	0.053	1,567	9.7
Greece	13	44	12	8	25,000	16,000	2.301	0.005	2,147	10.7
Hungary	11	X	X	X	7,446	4,950	0.048	0.008	88	20.9
Iceland	14	75	4	0	64,000	31,000	0.756	0.008	4,259	64.3
Ireland	15	0	4	0	X	1,180	0.512	0.001	991	22.1
Italy	440	9	274	19	341,000	66,000	10.207	0.001	34,184	21.4
Luxembourg	3	0	3	0	125	120	1.132	0.001	X	X
Malta	X	X	X	X	X	X	X	X	X	X
Netherlands	10	11	2	0	X	500	0.025	0.002	37	16.9
Norway	245	20	89	10	556,000	172,000	26.465	0.119 e	118,271	51.0
Poland	25	14	11	6	23,000	121,000	1.976	0.100	3,757	21.7
Portugal	81	33	52	6	32,000	24,000	3.360	0.040	5,819	19.8
Romania	133	64	53	37	70,000	38,000	5.583	X	12,628	25.8
Spain	737	17	381	66	162,369	67,220	16.223	0.337	19,530	13.7
Sweden	141	7	34	1	200,000	99,000	15.616	0.320	72,102	52.7
Switzerland	144	13	80	3	144,000	41,000	11.580	0.194	29,772	29.3
United Kingdom	535	3	130	4	9,300	5,200	4.163	0.036	6,970	19.1
Yugoslavia	123	32	77	11	118,000	71,000	7.000	0.119	23,730	38.7
U.S.S.R.	**132**	**81**	**101**	**18**	**3,942,000**	**3,831,000**	**64.100**	**0.400**	**222,800**	**39.7**
OCEANIA	**497**		**217**	**25**			**11.891**		**37,819**	**36.3**
Australia	409	28	179	22	264,000	30,000	7.268	0.035	14,498	22.8
Fiji	2	X	X	X	1,261	515	0.080	0.000	330	47.1
New Zealand	83	26	38	3	X	74,000	4.287	0.018	21,900	58.3
Papua New Guinea	3	X	X	X	175,000	98,000	0.155	0.012	455	33.5
Solomon Islands	X	X	X	X	X	X	0.000	0.000	0	15.2

Sources: The International Commission on Large Dams; International Water Power and Dam Construction Handbook, 1991; and the United Nations Statistical Office.
Notes: a. Technical capability. b. Installations less than 1 megawatt in capacity. c. Includes 30 dams over 15 meters in height in "homeland" areas.
d. Includes only dams over 30 meters in height. e. Installations between 1 and 2 megawatts in capacity.
Regional and world totals include countries not listed.
For additional information, see Sources and Technical Notes.

Table 22.3 Sediment Loads of Selected Rivers

• Catchment	Station	Basin Area (km2)	Rainfall (mm/yr)	Annual Discharge (cubic km)	Annual Materials Transport (metric tons/ha)	• Catchment	Station	Basin Area (km2)	Rainfall (mm/yr)	Annual Discharge (cubic km)	Annual Materials Transport (metric tons/ha)
AFRICA											
Cameroon • Mbam	Goura	42,300	X	18.1	0.67	• Tsanaga	Bogo	1,535	X	0.3	2.01
• Sanaga	Nachtigal	77,000	X	37.1	0.28						
Chad • Chari	Sarh	193,000	X	10.2	0.01	• Logone	Moundou	33,970	X	12.5	0.65
• Chari	Chagona	515,000	X	28.3	0.03	• Pende	Doba	14,300	X	4.4	0.25
• Logone	Kousseri	85,000	X	12.0	0.15						
Egypt • Nile	Delta	2,977,235	X	30.0	0.00						
Kenya • Ewaso Ngiro		15,300	X	X	1.92	• Tana	Garissa	31,700	X	X	3.81
• Tana	Kamburu	9,520	1,200	3.2	2.34	• Thiba	4DD1	1,970	X	0.8	0.77
• Tana	Grand Falls	17,400	X	X	21.03	• Thika		331	X	X	3.88
Lesotho • Sengu	White Hill	10,900	X	X	1.40	• Sengu	Seaka	19,875	X	X	2.10
Morocco • Grou	Dam	5,550	500	0.3	1.62	• N'Fiss	L. Takerkoust	1,796	560	0.2	5.30
• Lakhdar	S. Driss	3,000	661	0.5	3.66	• Oum Er Rbia	Imfout	30,000	546	3.3	2.20
• Moulouya	Mechra Homadi	51,500	306	1.5	1.30	• Tessaout	M. Youssef	1,441	656	0.4	11.60
• Nekor	MB Abdelkrim	780	X	0.1	79.00						
Madagascar • Shahamalato	Dam	316	1,800	0.2	9.00						
Mozambique • Limpopo	Mouth	410,000	X	5.0	0.80	• Zambesi	Mouth	1,200,000	X	223.0	0.17
Nigeria • Benue	Makurdi	304,300	1,525	100.4	0.43	• Niger	Baro	730,400	1,100	144.6	0.13
• Bunsuru	Zurmi	5,900	818	1.4	4.38	• Niger	Koji	1,080,900	1,380	154.6	0.19
• Cross	Ikom	16,900	3,320	34.0	0.72	• Niger	Baro	1,113,227	1,000	191.5	0.05
• Gagere	Kaura Namoda	5,670	956	1.6	2.92	• Niger	Mouth	1,210,000	X	192.0	0.33
• Gongola	Bare	55,500	1,028	6.4	0.77	• Rima	Wamako	35,370	778	1.6	1.55
• Hadejia	Wudil	1,740	918	0.2	3.55	• Sokoto	Gidan Doka	12,590	852	1.6	3.92
• Jamari	Bunga	7,980	1,001	2.1	4.59	• Taraba	Gassol	21,300	1,630	12.0	0.80
• Kaduna	Kaduna	18,420	1,213	5.3	0.52	• Watari	Gwarzo Rd.	1,450	852	0.1	4.83
• Kano	Chiromawa	6,980	1,000	1.2	2.19	• Yobe	Gashua	62,400	765	15.6	1.41
• Misare	Kari	5,600	950	0.7	0.09						
South Africa • Orange	Mouth	1,020,000	X	11.0	0.17						
Tanzania • Rufiji	Mouth	180,000	X	9.0	0.94						
Zaire • Congo	Mouth	4,012,795	1,750	1,252.0	0.18						
Zimbabwe • Austral	Dam	4,250	X	0.5	3.50	• Jotsholo	Dam	14,860	X	0.3	1.10
• Glen Avilin	Dam	1,000	X	0.2	3.20	• Rinette	Dam	6,000	X	0.2	2.70
• Gwai	Bembezi	14,400	X	0.2	0.14	• Umsweswe	Upper Claw	1,990	750	0.1	0.24
NORTH AND CENTRAL AMERICA											
Canada • Fraser	Mouth	220,000	X	112.0	0.91	• Nelson	Mouth	1,150,000	X	110.4	0.00
• Mackenzie	Mouth	1,800,000	X	302.7	1.04	• St. Lawrence	Mouth	1,025,000	X	337.4	0.58
El Salvador • Lempa	San Marcos	18,176	X	X	3.79						
Guatemala • Motagua	Morales	14,452	X	X	5.04						
Haiti • Peligre	Dam	6,615	1,780	2.5	15.00						
Mexico • Colorado	Mouth	635,000	X	20.2	0.00						
United States • Brazos	Mouth	110,000	X	7.0	1.45	• Mississippi	Mouth	3,267,000	X	580.3	0.64
• Columbia	Mouth	670,000	X	251.3	0.12	• Rio Grande	Mouth	670,000	X	3.2	X
• Copper	Mouth	60,000	X	39.0	11.67	• Susitna	Mouth	50,000	X	40.0	5.00
• Eel	Mouth	8,000	X	X	17.50	• Yukon	Mouth	770,000	X	195.5	1.47
• Hudson	Mouth	20,000	X	12.0	0.50						
SOUTH AMERICA											
Argentina • Parana	Mouth	2,304,121	1,750	470.0	0.39	• Uruguay	Concordia	388,335	1,500	125.0	0.39
• Negro	Mouth	100,000	X	30.0	1.30						
Bolivia • Cachi-Mayu		1,680	600	0.5	72.50	• Pilcomayo	Talula	6,340	428	0.6	19.87
• Matacu		3,300	407	0.3	15.75	• Pilcomayo	Icla	13,200	458	2.0	34.92
Brazil • Amazon	Obidos	4,640,000	X	X	2.00	• San Francisco	Mouth	640,000	X	97.0	0.09
• Amazon	Mouth	6,150,000	X	6,300.0	1.46	• Tocantins	Itupiranga	744,600	X	X	0.77
• Araguaia	Santa-Isabel	372,000	X	X	0.88						
Colombia • Magdalena	Mouth	240,000	X	237.0	9.17						
Peru • Chancay		2,325	X	0.7	2.06	• Jeguetepegue		3,625	X	0.5	6.95
• Chira		16,530	X	4.8	23.79						
Venezuela • Orinoco	Mouth	938,752	X	567.9	4.15	• Tuy	P. San Juan	6,610	1,250	1.5	2.38
ASIA											
Bangladesh • Brahmaputra	Delta	559,200	1,750	630.2	14.29	• Ganges/ Brahmaputra	Mouths	1,480,000	X	971.0	11.28
Burma • Irrawaddy	Prome	367,000	1,750	427.9	9.03						
China • Bailong	Bikou dam	27,600	X	X	3.38	• Mihe	Yeyuan dam	786	X	0.2	14.69
• Dadu	Gongzui	76,400	X	49.5	4.77	• Min Chiang	Yingxinwan	18,900	X	12.0	4.97
• Daling	Dalinghe	23,200	X	2.1	14.90	• Nanya	Inlake Gate	896	X	1.5	15.40
• Han Shui	Danjiangkou	95,217	X	38.2	8.39	• Shangyou	Dam	2,750	X	3.0	1.55
• Huai	Bangbu	261,500	X	26.2	1.53	• Wuki	Huangtankou	2,484	X	2.9	2.42
• Hutuo	Gangnan dam	15,900	X	X	8.69	• Xi Jiang	Wuzhou	355,000	X	252.8	2.60
• Hwang Ho	Liujiaxia dam	181,700	X	X	2.90	• Xiliao	Hongshan	24,486	X	X	10.78
• Hwang Ho	Lanzhou	222,551	X	X	4.35	• Yalong	Ertan	110,750	X	50.2	2.18
• Hwang Ho	Longmen	497,559	X	X	20.71	• Yangtze	Fengjie	987,711	X	419.8	5.31
• Hwang Ho	Xiaolangdi	694,155	470	X	22.45	• Yangtze	Datong	1,807,200	X	921.7	2.80
• Hwang Ho	Sanmenxia	752,400	X	42.9	24.80	• Yongding	Guanting dam	47,600	X	X	4.64
• Hwang Ho	Mouth	770,000	X	49.0	14.03	• Yongding	Guanting	50,800	X	4.4	19.44
• Liao	Tieling	166,300	X	5.7	2.40						
India • Batra	Marol	4,901	X	2.5	1.35	• Krishna	Srisaikam	206,041	X	69.8	5.67
• Bhakra	Sutlej	56,876	X	16.1	7.98	• Mahanadi	Naraj	132,034	1,250	90.2	5.14
• Bhakra	Gobindsagar	57,000	X	14.6	7.73	• Maithon		6,294	1,300	2.3	17.03
• Bhima	Takali	33,196	X	11.2	4.24	• Mata Tila	Betwa	20,720	1,140	6.0	5.77
• Bhima	Yedgir	69,863	X	20.5	6.59	• Nira	Sarati	7,200	X	18.5	1.43
• Damodar	Rhondie	20,000	X	9.8	15.64	• Nizam Sagar	Manjira	21,694	800	4.1	8.97
• Gandhi Sagar	Chambal	23,025	864	4.8	12.53	• Panchet Hill	Damodar	10,690	1,300	4.0	13.62

Table 22.3

• Catchment	Station	Basin Area (km2)	Rainfall (mm/yr)	Annual Discharge (cubic km)	Annual Materials Transport (metric tons/ha)	• Catchment	Station	Basin Area (km2)	Rainfall (mm/yr)	Annual Discharge (cubic km)	Annual Materials Transport (metric tons/ha)
ASIA (continued)											
India (continued) • Ganges	Calcutta	748,634	X	314.4	5.49	• Sina	Wadakal	12,092	X	2.2	7.55
• Godavari	Mouth	310,000	X	X	3.10	• Tunga	Shimoga	3,283	X	6.7	1.64
• Hayurakshi		1,860	1,321	0.8	21.42	• Tungabhadra	Marabatti	14,582	X	10.5	1.46
• Hirakud	Mahanadi	82,621	1,369	40.5	4.71	• Tungabhadra		28,180	X	9.4	7.81
• Kosi	Chatra	62,000	X	57.2	30.81	• Tungabhadra	Bharapuram	67,180	X	14.9	2.22
• Koyna	Koyna	1,890	5,080	2.8	4.02	• Ukai		62,225	X	X	6.46
• Krishna	Karod	5,462	X	5.3	2.89						
Indonesia • Cimanuk	Jatigede	1,460	2,700	2.0	54.79	• Selorejo		238	2,300	0.3	43.29
• Karangkates		2,050	2,032	2.1	44.33						
Iran • Araks	Araxe	43,500	X	5.0	4.15	• Karaj	Amir Kabir	860	X	0.5	3.76
• Dez	M. Reza Chah P	17,245	X	9.5	10.08	• Safid Rud	Mandjil	56,700	450	4.4	10.80
• Jajerud	Farahnazi P.	692	X	0.4	4.45						
Iraq • Tigris	Baghdad	471,606	800	126.9	0.34	• Tigris/Euphrates	Mouth	1,050,000	X	46.0	X
Japan • Ishikari	Ebestu	13,000	X	X	1.52	• Yodo	Hirakata	7,120	1,500	6.4	0.20
• Tone	Matsudo	12,000	1,500	15.0	2.73						
Nepal • Gandak		45,312	X	X	43.25						
Pakistan • Chenab	Alexandria	33,000	X	X	16.91	• Indus	Kalabagh	305,000	X	X	24.60
• Ghambir	Danda Shah B.	518	X	0.1	37.30	• Indus	Kotri	958,000	X	213.6	5.02
• Gilgit	Alam B.	26,148	X	21.5	24.77	• Indus	Mouth	970,000	X	238.0	1.03
• Gorband	Karora	634	X	0.7	32.20	• Kabul	Nowshera	90,000	X	21.4	2.88
• Haro	Khanpur	777	X	0.3	21.25	• Poonch	Kotli	3,236	X	3.8	41.86
• Haro	Sanjwal	1,799	X	0.6	22.89	• Soan	Chirah	326	X	0.2	49.25
• Haro	Gariala	3,055	X	0.8	14.79	• Soan	Dhok Pathan	6,472	X	1.4	34.48
• Hunza	Dainyor B.	13,152	X	12.1	42.49						
Syrian Arab Rep • Euphrates	Tabga	120,650	500	30.5	0.36						
Thailand • Chao Phraya	Nakornsawan	103,470	X	X	1.06	• Nan	Tha Pla	12,790	1,250	6.0	3.91
• Klong	Ban Tham	25,466	X	X	3.18	• Ping	Wang Kra Chao	26,386	1,750	6.1	0.88
• Lam Pao	Lower Lam Pao	5,130	1,250	1.4	1.25	• Ping	Kam Pan Petch	42,300	1,750	7.6	0.36
• Mekong	Mukdaham	391,000	X	473.5	4.79	• Wang	Wang Krai	10,204	1,750	1.4	1.51
• Nan	Phitsanuloke	25,191	1,250	8.7	1.28	• Yom	Kuang Luang	13,214	1,250	2.6	1.66
Turkey • Euphrates	Keban	63,836	500	20.0	5.17	• Yesil Irmak	Ayvacik	36,000	500	X	12.28
Viet Nam • Red	Hanoi	119,866	1,750	123.2	11.90						
EUROPE											
Albania • Drin	Can Deje	12,368	1,750	11.8	11.90	• Seman	Uraque Koit	5,288	1,250	3.6	41.50
Austria • Durrache	Bachental	55	X	0.1	6.73						
France • Drac	Sautet	990	1,300	0.9	7.00	• Rhone	Pierre Benite	50,200	X	X	0.23
• Durance	Serre-Poncon	3,500	X	2.6	4.09	• Rhone	Chateauneuf	71,300	X	X	0.61
• Durance	Cadarache	11,920	X	6.5	1.20	• Seine	Paris	43,878	X	X	0.28
• Loire	Nantes	121,005	750	26.7	0.04	• Verdon	Greoux	1,819	X	1.1	1.63
Germany • Inn	Reisach	9,760	1,250	9.7	3.27	• Main	Marktbreit	27,225	750	3.7	0.20
• Isar	Plattling	8,964	1,000	4.8	0.29						
Hungary • Danube	Nagymaros	183,262	750	74.4	0.28	• Tisza	Tivador	12,540	1,000	6.6	0.44
• Raba	Arpas	6,610	750	1.2	0.24	• Tisza	Szeged	138,408	750	27.3	0.49
Italy • Adige	Pescantina	10,954	X	X	1.07	• Po	Pontilagoscuro	54,290	1,250	48.9	2.80
• Adige	Boara Pisani	11,954	X	X	0.91	• Tiber	Roma	16,545	X	X	3.70
• Po	Piacenza	42,030	X	X	2.48						
Netherlands • Rhine		143,360	X	X	0.04	• Rhine	Lobith	160,000	750	69.4	0.17
Poland • Oder	Gozdowice	109,400	750	14.4	0.01	• Vistula	Tezew	193,900	750	30.1	0.07
Romania • Danube	Mouth	810,000	X	206.0	0.83						
Spain • Aragón	Yesa	2,191	672	1.2	7.72	• Tajo	Entrepenas	3,829	683	0.7	13.08
• Cacin	Bermejales	300	740	0.1	17.29	• Tormes	Santa Teresa	1,988	849	1.1	7.23
• Cañamares	Palmaces	275	567	0.1	7.85	• Varas	Guadalmellato	1,195	630	0.2	12.58
• Cardoner	San Pons	292	1,020	0.1	9.22	•	Barasona	1,511	1,098	0.9	3.43
• Guadalete	Bornos	1,361	1,025	0.4	18.04	•	Cabillas	647	577	0.1	3.90
• Guadalquivir	Pedro Marin	6,300	612	1.1	2.32	•	Camarillas	2,390	373	0.7	3.27
• Guadalquivir	Tranco d. Beas	558	1,050	0.2	18.45	•	Dona Aldonza	6,000	597	1.1	3.25
• Jarama	El Vado	426	962	0.2	12.11	•	La Pena	1,728	701	0.9	1.19
• Lozoya	Rio Sequillo	385	849	0.2	17.19	•	Las Tranquesa	1,478	455	0.1	3.30
• Majaceite	Guadalcacin	680	1,253	0.2	11.70	•	Los Hasones	348	1,102	0.2	7.84
• Mundo	Talave	754	495	0.1	4.17	•	Tor. d. Aquila	432	750	0.1	12.09
• Riaza	Lin. d. Arroyo	756	648	0.1	9.27						
Switzerland • Linth	Walensee	600	X	0.8	3.50						
U.S.S.R. • Amur	Mouth	1,850,000	X	325.0	0.28	• Severnay Dvina	Mouth	350,000	X	106.0	0.13
• Dnieper	Verkhned.	428,851	X	X	0.03	• Ural	Topolinski	191,462	X	X	0.09
• Don	Razdorskaya	373,811	X	X	0.14	• Volga	Dubovka	1,335,014	X	X	0.26
• Kolyma	Mouth	640,000	X	71.0	0.09	• Volga	Dubovka	1,350,085	750	252.5	0.16
• Lena	Mouth	2,500,000	X	514.0	0.05	• Yana	Mouth	220,000	X	29.0	0.14
• Ob	Mouth	2,500,000	X	385.0	0.01	• Yenisei	Mouth	2,580,000	X	560.0	0.05
• Indigirka	Mouth	360,000	X	55.0	0.39						
OCEANIA											
Australia • Burdekin	Clare	129,660	640	X	0.27	• Murrumbidgee		15,360	X	X	0.50
• Murray	Mouth	1,060,000	X	22.0	0.28	• Nogoa Qld.	Fairbairn Dam	22,344	650	X	8.00
New Zealand • Haast		1,020	6,500	6.0	127.30						
Papua New Guinea • Fly	Mouth	61,000	X	77.0	4.92	• Purari		31,000	X	77.0	25.81

Sources: B. Heusch, J. Milliman and R. Meade, and United Nations Environment Programme.
Notes: The basin area is the part of the watershed upstream of the station. Materials transport includes the movement of both dissolved and solid materials.
0 = zero or less than one half the unit of measure; X = not available.

Sources and Technical Notes

Table 22.1 Freshwater Resources and Withdrawals

Sources: Water resources and withdrawal data: J. Forkasiewicz and J. Margat, *Tableau Mondial de Données Nationales d'Economie de l'Eau, Ressources et Utilisation* (Departement Hydrogéologie, Orléans, France, 1980). Data for Algeria, Egypt, Libya, Morocco, Tunisia, Cyprus, Israel, Lebanon, Syrian Arab Republic, Turkey, Albania, France, Greece, Italy, Malta, Spain, and Yugoslavia: J. Margat, Bureau de Recherches Géologiques et Minières, Orléans, France, April 1988 (personal communication). Alexander V. Belyaev, Institute of Geography, U.S.S.R. National Academy of Sciences, Moscow, September 1989 and January 1990 (personal communication); withdrawal and sectoral use data for the United States: W.B. Solley, C.F. Merk, and R.R. Pierce, "Estimated Use of Water in the United States, in 1985," *U.S. Geological Survey Circular*, No. 1004 (U.S. Geological Survey, Reston, Virginia, 1988); withdrawal data as footnoted: European Communities—Commission, *Environment Statistics 1989* (Office des Publications Officielles des Communautés Européennes, Luxembourg, 1990), p. 130; desalination data as footnoted: O.K. Buros for the International Desalination Association, *The Desalting ABC's* (Saline Water Conversion Corporation, Riyadh, Saudi Arabia, 1990), p. 5; population: United Nations Population Division, *World Population Prospects 1990* (United Nations, New York, 1991).

Data are compiled from published documents (including national, United Nations, and professional literature) and estimates of resources and consumption from models using other data, such as area under irrigated agriculture, livestock populations, and precipitation, when necessary.

Annual internal renewable water resources refers to the average annual flow of rivers and groundwater generated from endogenous precipitation. Caution should be used when comparing different countries because these estimates are based on differing sources and dates. These annual averages also disguise large seasonal, interannual, and long-term variations. When data for *annual river flows to* and *from other countries* are not shown, the internal renewable water resources figure *may* include these flows. *Per capita annual internal renewable water resources* data were created using 1990 population estimates.

Annual withdrawals as a *percentage of water resources* refer to *total* water withdrawals, not counting evaporative losses from storage basins, as a percentage of internal renewable water resources and river flows from other countries. Water withdrawals also include water from desalination plants in countries where that source is a significant part of all water withdrawals.

Per capita annual withdrawals were calculated using national population data for the year of data shown for withdrawal.

Sectoral withdrawals are classified as *domestic* (drinking water, homes, commercial establishments, public services [e.g., hospitals], and municipal use or provision); *industry* (including water withdrawn to cool thermoelectric plants); and *agriculture* (irrigation and livestock).

Totals may not add because of rounding.

Table 22.2 Large Dams and Hydroelectric Resources

Sources: Large dam data: The International Commission on Large Dams (ICOLD), *World Register of Dams, 1984 Full Edition* and *World Register of Dams, 1988 Updating*, (ICOLD, Paris, 1985 and 1989); data on hydropower potential and micro-hydro: *International Water Power and Dam Construction Handbook, 1991* (Reed Enterprise, Sutton, Surrey, United Kingdom, 1991); data on installed hydropower capacity and generation: United Nations Statistical Office (U.N.), *Energy Statistics Yearbook 1989*, (U.N., New York, 1991).

ICOLD obtains data on individual large dams (over 15 meters in height, measured from the lowest portion of the general foundation to the crest) from its 78 member countries as well as general statistical data on large dams in nonmember countries. Known inadequacies include the absence of statistics on large dams constructed by the Ministry of Agriculture and local authorities in the U.S.S.R. (these entities might add 2,000–3,000 dams) and incomplete data on dam capacity and reservoir area. In 1950, there were only 5,270 large dams in the world, only two of them in China. Today, China accounts for over half of all large dams, which numbered 36,562 in 1986.

Gross theoretical hydropower potential is the electrical energy that would be produced if all runoff, on its way to the sea, were run through turbines with 100 percent efficiency. *Exploitable hydropower potential* is the most conservative measure of a country's hydroelectric resources and is the energy that is exploitable under existing technical limitations and economic constraints. Technical capability is provided for a few countries (as footnoted) and refers to the estimate of the sum of the energy potential from sites where it is physically possible to install dams, ignoring any economic, environmental, or social constraints.

Installed hydropower capacity is the combined generating capacity of all hydroelectric plants as of the end of 1989. It does not include pumped-storage schemes. *Micro-hydro* is the sum of the generating capacity, where known, of small hydroelectric plants (except as footnoted, each under 1-megawatt capacity). Small hydroelectric plants are of special interest because of their relatively benign (compared to large projects) social and environmental impacts.

Total hydropower generation, as a *percentage of [installed] capacity*, refers to actual electrical production during 1989 from hydroelectric generating plants, again excluding pumped-storage schemes. Many countries generate only a small fraction of their installed capacity because of considerations of need, water supply, and peak load.

Table 22.3 Sediment Loads of Selected Rivers

Sources: Bernard Heusch, unpublished data (Saint Mury-La Tour, Meylan, France, 1988); John D. Milliman and Robert H. Meade, "World-Wide Delivery of River Sediment to the Oceans," *The Journal of Geology*, Vol. 91 (1983), pp. 1-21; J.M.L. Jansen and R.B. Painter, "Predicting Sediment Yield from Climate and Topography," *Journal of Hydrology*, Vol. 21(4) (1974), pp. 371-380; J.M. Holeman, "The Sediment Yield of Major Rivers of the World," *Water Resources Research*, Vol. 4(4) (1968), pp. 737-747; United Nations Environment Programme, *Environmental Data Report* (Basil Blackwell Ltd., Oxford, 1989), pp. 121-126.

Rivers carry sediment and dissolved solids transported by rainfall and stream erosion. This material transport can be measured and stands as an indicator of the degree of land erosion upstream of the measurement station. Because sediment is deposited along the length of a stream, and in reservoirs and lakes, the measured material transport is not a direct measurement of erosion.

Transport would occur in the absence of human activity, as evidenced by the existence of the major deltas of the Nile, Amazon, Yellow, Mississippi, Orinoco, Po, Tigris/Euphrates, and Ganges/Brahmaputra. Sediment flows in themselves have been beneficial—the fertility-enhancing effects of the annual Nile flood in pre-Aswan days being the type example—and are essential to the maintenance of shoreline and even of marine life. Dam building has limited the flow of sediment in many of the world's rivers. This, in turn, has limited the lifetimes and storage capacities of dams. High levels of materials transport can indicate poor management of upstream land resources. Low levels of materials transport, on the other hand, can indicate sediment interception by dams and the subsequent need for management of floodplains and coastal land resources.

The *catchment* is the named hydrological basin for which data are available, and the *station* is the place where sediment transport and flow measurements or estimates are made. The *basin area* is the area drained by the river and its tributaries upstream of the measurement station. The *annual discharge* is the amount of water passing the gauging station and is the average of multiyear monitoring. *Annual materials transport* is the average weight of solid and dissolved materials passing by the measurement station, divided by the total area of the basin in hectares. Rivers for which sediment data were available were included in this table if annual discharge data were also available or if the basin area was greater than 10,000 square kilometers.

23. Oceans and Coasts

This chapter presents data on activities that put pressures on coastal and ocean resources, and it documents some of their effects.

Table 23.1 provides basic information on the extent of national coastal resources and the pressures on coastal zones caused by human population growth, maritime trade, and offshore oil and gas exploration.

Increasing numbers of people are settling along the world's coastlines. In 1980, over 600 million people lived in coastal urban agglomerations. This number is forecast to swell to almost 1 billion by the turn of the century, multiplying adverse effects on productive coastal ecosystems. Projections for the year 2000 concentrate nearly half of the world's coastal population along the shores of Asia. Africa's coastal population is projected to grow at the fastest regional rate, rising by a factor of over 2.5. National and city planners face a tremendous challenge in balancing the needs of millions for housing, sanitation, and employment against appropriate coastal zone management.

Maritime trade connects the economies of the world through the transfer of vital materials such as crude petroleum and other petroleum products, ores, and cereals, as well as manufactured goods. Maritime trade requires extensive investment in infrastructure and puts coastal zone areas at high risk of accidents and environmental damage. Routine operational discharges of wastes and ballast from ships account for a far greater share of vessel source pollution and have led to increased efforts to finance waste reception facilities in ports. Japan and the United States lead the world in the total volume of goods loaded and unloaded, each handling about 10 percent of the volume.

The extraction of offshore oil and gas contributes to the economic value of the coastal zone but creates waste and poses the risk of major oil spills. Roughly one fourth of the world's oil production comes from offshore areas. World offshore crude oil output increased by 11 percent in the past decade. The greatest regional increase occurred along Europe's coastal zone, expanding its global share from 17 to 25 percent. The world's offshore gas production rose 21 percent in the past decade, with India, Mexico, and Brazil having the fastest growth rates. These three countries contributed one fourth of the global increase from 1980 to 1990. However, their share still constitutes a small proportion of the world's offshore gas production.

In its 1990 report, the Group of Experts on the Scientific Aspects of Marine Pollution (GESAMP) of the United Nations Environment Programme named nutrient pollution as the gravest and most prevalent problem of ocean health. Data on the discharge of toxic pollutants into coastal waters and measurements of marine pollutants have been collected in a variety of coastal areas. However, few countries have prepared reliable estimates on the discharge of nutrients into coastal waters and the eutrophication potential of estuaries. A first comprehensive attempt to estimate nutrient loadings and predict phosphorus and nitrogen concentrations was undertaken for 85 estuaries in the United States. Table 23.2 indicates the kinds of physical and hydrological data needed to assess the vulnerability of individual estuaries to nutrient inputs. It shows that upstream areas and nonpoint sources contribute the majority of nutrients discharged.

The continued health of the oceans and the long-term livelihood of the millions employed in fishing depend on harvests that do not exceed the potential of the resource base. Many regional fisheries show signs of drastic overfishing. Table 23.3 indicates that in fishing areas such as the Northwest Pacific, the Southeast Pacific, and the Mediterranean and Black Sea, the average annual catch exceeds the estimated potential long-term yield of marine fish. Recent enormous catches of pollock, sardine, and anchoveta have pushed actual catches in the Northwest and Southeast Pacific above the estimated sustainable maxima.

Table 23.4 shows that the global marine catch increased by 35 percent and inland catch by 85 percent over the past decade. The growth rate of the world marine catch is almost entirely due to increases in the catches of four species that, combined, make up nearly one quarter of the marine harvest: Alaskan pollock, Peruvian anchovy (anchoveta), Japanese sardine (Japanese pilchard), and Chilean sardine (South American pilchard). The rate of increase of these catches, 5–25 percent annually, cannot be maintained indefinitely. Indeed preliminary figures for 1990 show a decline in their catches. (See Chapter 12, "Oceans and Coasts.")

The amount of fish produced by inland waters, including aquaculture, has expanded to 14 percent of the total world catch in 1987–89. World per capita food supply from fish and fishery products increased from 11.4 kilograms per year in 1977–79 to 13.1 kilograms in 1986–88. Aquaculture is partly responsible for this boost in the supply of fish for human consumption.

Table 23.1 Coastal Areas and Resources

	Length of Coastline (kilometers)	Maritime Area (thousand square kilometers) Shelf to 200-m Depth	Maritime Area Exclusive Economic Zone	Population in Coastal Urban Agglomerations (thousands) 1980	2000	Average Annual Volume of Goods Loaded and Unloaded 1986-88 (thousand metric tons) Petroleum Crude	Products	Dry Cargo	Offshore Oil and Gas Resources Annual Production Oil (thousand metric tons) 1980	1990	Gas (million cubic meters) 1980	1990	Proven Reserves Oil (million metric tons) 1990	Gas (billion cubic meters) 1990
WORLD	594,008	21,426.5	108,714.3	617,081	996,855	2,213,718	838,692	4,075,198	681,637	755,267	287,756	347,949	29,699	19,087
AFRICA	37,908	1,325.7	11,981.1	43,213	111,643	341,889	43,224	273,642	66,936	97,880	5,849	2,931	4,229	3,131
Algeria	1,183	13.7	137.2	3,493	7,613	28,100 a	23,739	15,507	0	0	0	0	0	0
Angola	1,600	66.9	605.7	1,132	3,603	13,435	368	2,365	4,829	19,900	0	456	249	42
Benin	121	X	27.1	585	2,527	X	441 b	978	0	204	0	0	117	X
Cameroon	402	10.6	15.4	854	2,802	10,268 a	1,211	3,388	0	6,549	0	32	714	54
Cape Verde	965	X	789.4	125	360	X	101 b	369	0	0	0	0	0	0
Comoros	340	X	249.0	89	240	X	X	105	0	0	0	0	0	0
Congo	169	8.9	24.7	217	571	6,048 a	254	3,841	1,345	7,355	0	52	514	59
Cote d'Ivoire	515	10.3	104.6	1,495	4,125	1,790	1,462	6,591	289	388	0	0	3	6
Djibouti	314	X	6.2	211	455	X	761	653	0	0	0	0	0	0
Egypt	2,450	37.4	173.5	4,246	8,020	131,332	4,123	24,583	19,437	26,927	598	1,354	299	130
Equatorial Guinea	296	X	283.2	181	392	X	X	144	0	0	0	0	0	0
Ethiopia	1,094	47.7	75.8	760	1,909	715 b	503	2,104	0	0	0	0	0	0
Gabon	885	46.0	213.6	155	498	8,170 a	218	803	8,859	4,880	0	0	435	X
Gambia, The	80	X	19.5	109	293	X	21 b	277	0	0	0	0	0	0
Ghana	539	20.9	218.1	1,336	3,139	1,067 b	235	2,400	100	0	83	0	4	X
Guinea	346	38.4	71.0	696	2,025	X	124	10,528	0	0	0	0	0	0
Guinea-Bissau	274	X	150.5	174	353	X	27 b	203	0	0	0	0	0	0
Kenya	536	14.4	118.0	489	2,020	1,922 b	94	4,117	0	0	0	0	0	0
Liberia	579	19.6	229.7	465	1,195	689 b	90 b	17,308	0	0	0	0	0	0
Libya	1,770	83.7	338.1	1,496	4,322	43,414 a	4,788	6,839	0	4,133	0	0	27	38
Madagascar	4,828	180.4	1,292.0	570	2,032	X	347	909	0	0	0	0	0	0
Mauritania	754	44.2	154.3	238	1,177	X	96 b	10,641	0	0	0	0	0	0
Mauritius	177	91.6	1,183.0	410	565	X	309 b	1,597	0	0	0	0	0	0
Morocco	1,835	62.1	278.1	5,543	11,472	4,671	144	36,137	0	0	0	0	0	0
Mozambique	2,470	104.3	562.0	1,109	5,240	449 b	115	3,904	0	0	0	0	0	0
Namibia	1,489	X	X	76	290	X	X	X	0	0	0	0	0	0
Nigeria	853	46.3	210.9	4,383	14,135	62,701 a	911	9,567	28,837	25,923	5,168	1,038	1,822	2,719
Reunion	201	X	X	279	479	X	217 b	1,168	0	0	0	0	0	0
Senegal	531	31.6	205.7	1,378	3,077	218 b	347 b	4,728	0	0	0	0	7	X
Seychelles	491	X	1,349.3	X	X	X	114 b	139	0	0	0	0	0	0
Sierra Leone	402	26.4	155.7	453	1,175	225 b	14 b	1,541	0	0	0	0	0	0
Somalia	3,025	60.7	782.8	1,186	3,308	478 b	45	951	0	0	0	0	0	0
South Africa	2,881	143.4	1,553.4	4,272	8,294	18,595 b	252 b	81,009	0	0	0	0	2	26
Sudan	853	22.3	91.6	356	1,193	1,181 b	81	2,297	0	0	0	0	0	0
Tanzania	1,424	41.2	223.2	1,750	6,945	615 b	673	2,172	0	0	0	0	X	57
Togo	56	1.0	2.1	324	983	X	127 b	1,104	0	0	0	0	0	0
Tunisia	1,143	50.8	85.7	2,476	4,540	3,854 a	836	11,307	2,170	1,107	0	0	35	X
Zaire	37	1.0	1.0	102	276	1,918 a	35 b	1,366	1,071	513	0	0	X	X
NORTH & CENTRAL AMERICA	183,950	5,632.2	18,759.1	88,896	121,410	308,744	133,276	728,887	84,901	125,307	156,585	131,522	5,681	2,992
Antigua and Barbuda	153	X	X	X	X	X	60 b	79	0	0	0	0	0	0
Bahamas	3,542	85.7	759.2	X	X	12,818	4,183	3,191	0	0	0	0	0	0
Barbados	97	0.3	167.3	100	146	111 b	37 b	561	0	0	0	0	0	0
Belize	386	X	X	X	X	X	86 b	268	0	0	0	0	0	0
Bermuda	103	X	X	X	X	X	363	237	0	0	0	0	0	0
Canada	90,908	2,903.4	2,939.4	3,066	3,852	13,267	9,101	193,556	0	0	0	0	276	298
Cayman Islands	160	X	X	X	X	1,297	35 b	106	0	0	0	0	0	0
Costa Rica	1,290	15.8	258.9	1,050	2,258	436 b	344 b	2,648	0	0	0	0	0	0
Cuba	3,735	X	362.8	6,628	8,942	6,033 b	4,263	15,020	0	0	0	0	0	0
Dominica	148	X	20.0	X	X	X	5 b	85	0	0	0	0	0	0
Dominican Rep	1,288	18.2	268.8	2,787	5,797	1,560 b	792 b	4,216	0	0	0	0	0	0
El Salvador	307	17.8	91.9	1,680	3,049	634 b	16 b	1,123	0	0	0	0	0	0
Greenland	44,087	X	X	X	X	X	184	386	0	0	0	0	0	0
Grenada	121	X	27.0	X	X	X	21 b	67	0	0	0	0	0	0
Guadeloupe	306	X	X	142	196	X	363 b	1,117	0	0	0	0	0	0
Guatemala	400	12.3	99.1	780	932	594 b	197 b	4,376	0	0	0	0	0	0
Haiti	1,771	10.6	160.5	1,216	2,845	X	8 b	843	0	0	0	0	0	0
Honduras	820	53.5	200.9	583	1,923	349 b	272	1,851	0	0	0	0	0	0
Jamaica	1,022	40.1	297.6	1,016	1,689	1,125 b	1,310	7,274	0	0	0	0	0	0
Martinique	290	2.4	X	217	279	213 b	264	830	0	0	0	0	0	0
Mexico	9,330	442.1	2,851.2	6,529	9,501	69,767 a	7,191	17,462	24,911	78,833	258	2,948	4,488	1,104
Nicaragua	910	72.7	159.8	1,166	2,837	466 b	179 b	1,255	0	0	0	0	0	0
Panama	2,490	57.3	306.5	989	1,749	1,155 b	467	1,768	0	0	0	0	0	0
Trinidad and Tobago	362	29.2	76.8	623	1,110	4,424	1,656	5,563	8,292	4,890	4,341	3,312	73	229
United States	19,924	1,870.7	9,711.4	60,324	74,305	194,496	101,878	465,003	51,697	41,583	151,985	125,262	843	1,359
SOUTH AMERICA	30,663	1,984.9	10,124.8	59,553	104,628	92,383	38,448	286,341	59,682	85,205	1,703	12,296	1,973	1,069
Argentina	4,989	796.4	1,164.5	12,273	16,643	225	3,662	32,920	0	1,743	0	91	7	4
Brazil	7,491	768.6	3,168.4	25,616	49,160	25,223 b	3,638	174,681	3,635	32,551	1,034	6,227	870	136
Chile	6,435	27.4	2,288.2	3,212	4,856	2,358 b	218	15,538	0	1,001	0	592	57	65
Colombia	2,414	67.9	603.2	2,926	3,926	9,100 c	6,536	12,387	0	0	669	0	10	40
Ecuador	2,237	47.0	1,159.0	1,529	3,877	9,344 a	1,271	3,387	0	0	0	0	5	20
French Guiana	378	X	X	X	X	X	123 b	234	0	0	0	0	0	0
Guyana	459	50.1	130.3	213	425	X	470 b	1,914	0	0	0	0	0	0
Peru	2,414	82.7	1,026.9	6,975	14,339	1,209 a	1,329	12,250	1,487	4,442	0	0	31	3
Suriname	386	X	101.2	140	216	X	661 b	6,283	0	0	0	0	0	0
Uruguay	660	56.6	119.3	1,511	1,862	968 b	7 b	1,072	0	0	0	0	0	0
Venezuela	2,800	88.1	363.8	5,158	9,324	46,719 a	20,533	25,675	54,560	45,467	0	5,385	993	801

Table 23.1

	Length of Coastline (kilometers)	Maritime Area (thousand square kilometers) Shelf to 200-m Depth	Exclusive Economic Zone	Population in Coastal Urban Agglomerations (thousands) 1980	2000	Average Annual Volume of Goods Loaded and Unloaded 1986-88 (thousand metric tons) Petroleum Crude	Products	Dry Cargo	Offshore Oil and Gas Resources Annual Production Oil (thousand metric tons) 1980	1990	Gas (million cubic meters) 1980	1990	Proven Reserves Oil (million metric tons) 1990	Gas (billion cubic meters) 1990
ASIA	163,609	6,768.6	20,258.5	281,828	487,093	853,821	274,183	1,165,154	328,221	227,758	30,072	62,650	14,698	7,383
Bahrain	161	5.1	5.1	279	582	X	12,178	4,010	0	0	0	0	61	X
Bangladesh	580	54.9	76.8	1,809	5,053	1,086 b	830	7,409	0	0	0	0	0	0
Brunei	161	X	X	X	X	8,599 a	4,861	1,179	9,574	4,709	10,180	8,063	180	198
Cambodia	443	X	55.6	50	287	X	X	110	0	0	0	0	0	0
China	14,500	869.8	1,355.8	38,936	66,510	40,294	7,654	97,518	100	1,147	0	403	153	538
Cyprus	648	6.5	99.4	291	457	532 b	474 b	4,168	0	0	0	0	0	0
Hong Kong	733	X	X	4,614	6,088	X	5,361	62,889	0	0	0	0	0	0
India	12,700	452.1	2,014.9	37,317	78,255	17,153	5,645	41,136	7,079	32,918	28	6,002	435	470
Indonesia	54,716	2,776.9	5,408.6	29,166	58,303	53,320	23,806	31,622	26,546	22,669	4,548	7,474	332	1,589
Iran, Islamic Rep	3,180	107.0	155.7	872	1,480	82,453 a	3,120	10,688	7,470	16,997	0	355	435	453
Iraq	58	0.7	0.7	0	0	X	X	X	0	0	0	0	0	0
Israel	273	4.5	23.3	2,826	4,110	5,669 b	975	17,622	0	0	0	0	0	0
Japan	13,685	480.5	3,861.1	78,349	88,798	179,670 b	72,826	454,578	76	294	493	155	1	X
Jordan	26	X	0.7	70	146	X	X	18,272	0	0	0	0	0	0
Korea, Dem People's Rep	2,495	X	129.6	5,973	14,233	3,066 b	1,027 b	1,731	0	0	0	0	0	0
Korea, Rep	2,413	244.6	X	16,911	29,292	30,644 b	8,790	126,510	0	0	0	0	0	0
Kuwait	499	12.0	12.0	1,190	2,660	39,649 a	18,305	8,927	0	0	0	0	0	0
Lebanon	225	4.5	22.6	2,016	3,135	19 b	206 b	1,030	0	0	0	0	0	0
Macao	40	X	X	X	X	X	280 b	3,083	0	0	0	0	0	0
Malaysia	4,675	373.5	475.6	3,997	9,158	20,971	12,968	44,926	13,960	29,915	0	19,288	367	1,475
Maldives	644	X	959.1	X	X	X	5 b	87	0	0	0	0	0	0
Myanmar	3,060	229.5	509.5	3,923	7,695	X	48	1,760	0	0	0	0	X	X
Oman	2,092	61.1	561.7	62	302	27,738 a	154 b	2,975	0	0	0	0	0	45
Pakistan	1,046	58.3	318.5	5,215	12,350	4,359 b	2,709	13,394	0	0	0	0	0	0
Philippines	22,540	178.4	1,786.0	17,736	37,181	8,200 b	929	21,300	199	386	0	0	11	6
Qatar	563	24.0	24.0	197	455	13,422 a	729	2,470	12,328	9,163	0	1,147	258	396
Saudi Arabia	2,510	77.9	186.2	1,954	4,201	110,873 a	35,330	41,795	167,378	73,709	0	5,995	8,538	1,450
Singapore	193	0.3	0.3	2,414	2,950	38,100	39,080	46,782	0	0	0	0	0	0
Sri Lanka	1,340	26.8	517.4	2,433	3,496	1,368 b	460	8,694	0	0	0	0	0	0
Syrian Arab Rep	193	X	10.3	266	853	15,115	3,197	5,731	0	0	0	0	0	0
Thailand	3,219	257.6	85.8	5,698	13,541	6,596 b	2,138	32,852	0	948	0	6,326	28	405
Turkey	7,200	50.4	236.6	9,928	17,028	87,734	3,497	32,614	0	0	0	0	X	7
United Arab Emirates	1,448	59.3	59.3	824	1,517	53,158 a	4,601	12,356	83,513	34,904	14,823	7,442	3,884	341
Viet Nam	3,444	327.9	722.1	5,585	14,317	X	321 b	1,431	0	0	0	0	13	8
Yemen (Arab Rep)	523	24.7	33.9	278	1,088	4,034	1,678	3,505	0	0	0	0	0	0
(People's Dem Rep)	1,383	X	550.3	649	1,572	X	X	X	0	0	0	0	0	0
EUROPE	69,643	1,951.5	14,680.9	111,806	129,989	532,592	287,004	1,240,461	115,683	187,780	76,006	110,123	2,188	1,282
Albania	418	5.5	12.3	622	1,140	X	74	1,633	0	0	0	0	0	0
Belgium	64	2.7	2.7	1,968	2,097	9,774 b	20,044	103,856	0	0	0	0	0	0
Bulgaria	354	12.3	32.9	857	1,182	12,069 b	888	16,311	0	0	0	0	0	0
Denmark	3,379	68.6	1,464.2	3,980	4,201	6,094	5,994	32,430	330	6,340	0	2,969	45	91
Finland	1,126	98.1	98.1	1,539	1,998	9,655 b	6,311	37,083	0	0	0	0	0	0
France	3,427	147.8	3,493.1 d	9,380	10,692	67,056	36,676	105,128	0	0	0	0	0	0
Germany (Fed Rep)	1,488	40.8	40.8	2,845	3,052	19,300 b	13,634	104,559	0	553	0	0	14	5
(Dem Rep)	901	X	9.6	1,099	1,249	X	3,634	22,167	0	0	0	0	0	0
Greece	13,676	24.7	505.1	5,252	6,559	14,411	4,245	27,389	0	669	0	32	5	12
Iceland	4,988	133.8	866.9	186	231	X	553 b	2,306	0	0	0	0	0	0
Ireland	1,448	125.9	380.3	1,766	2,469	3,349	1,799	16,483	0	0	1,292	2,407	X	23
Italy	4,996	144.1	552.1	21,232	23,721	87,442	43,952	91,825	312	4,143	227	4,062	7	246
Malta	140	13.0	66.2	303	327	X	519	1,488	0	0	0	0	0	0
Netherlands	451	84.7	84.7	7,764	9,032	81,659	49,002	208,919	0	2,355	12,094	17,962	21	603
Norway	5,832	102.0	2,024.0	2,024	3,033	27,188	7,108	47,439	31,315	83,704	25,077	32,044	1,540	329
Poland	491	28.5	28.5	1,842	2,853	758 b	3,663	46,160	0	0	0	0	0	0
Portugal	1,693	39.1	1,774.2	2,352	3,499	7,056 b	2,491	16,216	0	0	0	0	0	0
Romania	225	24.4	31.9	573	866	16,085 b	8,761	21,713	0	155	0	0	4	0
Spain	4,964	170.5	1,219.4	13,903	17,925	43,865 b	17,038	78,371	1,556	777	0	1,261	2	8
Sweden	3,218	155.3	155.3	4,018	4,306	13,574 b	15,128	76,410	0	0	0	0	0	0
United Kingdom	12,429	492.2	1,785.3	26,765	27,790	105,023	42,625	159,867	82,170	89,085	37,316	49,486	546	234
Yugoslavia	3,935	36.7	52.5	1,236	1,767	8,069 b	2,868	22,707	0	0	0	0	5	1
U.S.S.R.	46,670	1,249.5	4,490.3	18,372	23,975	72,346	52,092	116,614	9,960	7,157	12,663	13,024	517	2,379
OCEANIA	61,565	2,514.1	28,419.6	13,413	18,117	11,942	10,464	264,099	16,253	24,180	4,879	15,402	414	852
Australia	25,760	2,269.2	4,496.3	10,568	13,902	10,484	7,259	243,060	16,096	22,620	4,011	12,714	367	425
Cook Islands	120	X	1,830.0	X	X	X	8 b	34	0	0	0	0	0	0
Fiji	1,129	2.1	1,135.3	244	423	X	483	639	0	0	0	0	0	0
French Polynesia	2,525	X	5,030.0	X	X	X	259 b	364	0	0	0	0	0	0
Kiribati	1,143	X	3,550.0	X	X	X	5 b	32	0	0	0	0	0	0
New Caledonia	2,254	X	1,740.0	X	X	X	358 b	1,991	0	0	0	0	0	0
New Zealand	15,134	242.8	4,833.2	2,279	2,832	1,283 b	1,166	14,022	157	1,560	869	2,688	10	113
Niue	64	X	390.0	X	X	X	X	X	0	0	0	0	0	0
Papua New Guinea	5,152	X	2,366.6	322	960	X	856 b	3,172	0	0	0	0	37	314
Solomon Islands	5,313	X	1,340.0	X	X	X	34 b	574	0	0	0	0	0	0
Tonga	419	X	700.0	X	X	X	19 b	85	0	0	0	0	0	0
Tuvalu	24	X	328.2	X	X	X	X	X	0	0	0	0	0	0
Vanuatu	2,528	X	680.0	X	X	X	17 b	126	0	0	0	0	0	0

Sources: United Nations Statistical Office, United Nations Office for Ocean Affairs and the Law of the Sea, Offshore Magazine, and other sources.
Notes: a. Goods loaded. b. Goods unloaded. c. Two years of data. d. Includes overseas territory except French Polynesia and New Caledonia.
World and regional totals include countries not listed.
0 = zero or less than half the unit of measure; X = not available; billion = thousand million.
For additional information, see Sources and Technical Notes.

Table 23.2 Nutrient Discharges and Predicted Concentrations

	Physical Characteristics (thousand hectares)					Nitrogen					Phosphorus				
	Total Drainage Area	Fluvial Drainage Area	Estuarine Drainage Area Total	Estuarine Drainage Area Coastal	Up-stream	Predicted Concentration (mg/l)	Estimated Loadings (metric tons per year) Total	Coastal Point	Coastal Non-point	Up-stream	Predicted Concentration (mg/l)	Estimated Loadings (metric tons per year) Total	Coastal Point	Coastal Non-point	Up-stream
TOTAL (85 ESTUARIES)	572,332	509,906	62,425	43,920	528,411		1,712,644	267,976	266,603	1,178,065		355,514	124,172	21,116	210,226
ATLANTIC OCEAN	77,508	46,655	30,853	20,459	57,049		419,829	121,480	61,159	237,190		91,145	65,942	6,770	18,433
Passamaquoddy Bay	829	NA	829	356	472	<0.1	266	93	173	0	<0.01	25	11	15	0
Englishman Bay	229	NA	229	229	0	<0.1	136	23	113	0	<0.01	20	11	9	0
Narraguagus Bay	108	NA	108	108	0	<0.1	94	12	83	0	<0.01	10	4	6	0
Blue Hill Bay	214	NA	214	207	6	<0.1	140	44	96	0	<0.01	32	20	12	0
Penobscot Bay	2,437	1,619	818	286	2,151	0.1-1	7,083	157	318	6,609	0.01-0.1	699	53	25	621
Muscongus Bay	90	NA	90	90	0	<0.1	51	12	39	0	<0.01	15	10	5	0
Sheepscot Bay	2,608	1,015	1,593	255	2,353	<0.1	7,933	71	428	7,435	<0.01	582	48	40	494
Casco Bay	300	NA	300	252	48	<0.1	1,281	675	606	0	0.01-0.1	422	370	52	0
Saco Bay	459	NA	459	142	316	<0.1	1,140	170	177	794	<0.01	175	106	19	50
Great Bay	246	NA	246	234	12	<0.1	577	220	357	0	0.01-0.1	185	146	39	0
Merrimack River	1,290	694	596	179	1,111	>1	9,173	1,218	557	7,397	>0.1	1,474	738	82	655
Massachusetts Bay	311	NA	311	305	6	0.1-1	7,253	5,607	1,646	0	>0.1	3,711	3,488	223	0
Cape Cod Bay	200	NA	200	200	0	<0.1	342	243	99	0	0.01-0.1	170	153	16	0
Buzzards Bay	149	NA	149	149	0	<0.1	426	278	149	0	0.01-0.1	195	175	20	0
Narragansett Bay	461	117	344	344	117	0.1-1	4,147	2,589	1,558	0	0.01-0.1	1,611	1,398	213	0
Gardiners Bay	104	NA	104	104	0	0.1-1	893	583	309	0	0.01-0.1	400	369	31	0
Long Island Sound	4,465	2,593	1,873	918	3,548	0.1-1	45,509	18,126	5,019	22,364	0.01-0.1	6,819	4,524	572	1,723
Great South Bay	219	NA	219	219	0	>1	7,352	5,547	1,805	0	>0.1	3,767	3,509	258	0
Hudson River & Raritan Bay	4,275	2,082	2,193	1,732	2,542	>1	62,313	31,322	11,940	19,051	>0.1	20,975	18,768	1,054	1,153
Barnegat Bay	350	NA	350	350	0	0.1-1	1,840	740	1,100	0	0.01-0.1	445	283	162	0
Delaware Bay	3,484	2,253	1,230	972	2,512	0.1-1	45,468	16,942	3,832	24,694	>0.1	11,892	9,811	541	1,540
Chincoteague Bay	78	NA	78	78	0	<0.1	265	100	165	0	0.01-0.1	76	56	20	0
Chesapeake Bay	17,944	12,257	5,686	4,549	13,394	0.1-1	108,800	19,693	9,955	79,152	>0.1	15,253	10,113	1,300	3,840
Albemarle & Pamlico Sounds	7,660	4,657	3,003	2,282	5,378	0.1-1	25,605	816	8,254	16,536	0.01-0.1	3,234	546	504	2,184
Bogue Sound	176	NA	176	176	0	0.1-1	644	58	586	0	<0.01	51	24	26	0
New River	122	NA	122	122	0	0.1-1	559	79	480	0	0.01-0.1	102	46	55	0
Cape Fear River	2,354	1,230	1,124	382	1,972	0.1-1	7,350	158	608	6,584	0.01-0.1	1,348	91	69	1,188
Winyah Bay	4,685	2,222	2,463	714	3,971	0.1-1	20,639	103	583	19,952	0.01-0.1	2,186	65	64	2,057
Charleston Harbor	4,088	3,777	311	311	3,777	0.1-1	2,731	2,116	615	0	0.01-0.1	1,348	1,255	93	0
North & South Santee Rivers	3,963	3,777	186	171	3,792	>1	6,098	0	67	6,031	>0.1	455	0	8	447
St. Helena Sound	1,238	840	398	303	935	0.1-1	2,229	46	420	1,763	0.01-0.1	328	28	49	251
Broad River	259	NA	259	150	109	0.1-1	327	60	268	0	0.01-0.1	67	34	33	0
Savannah River	2,694	2,456	237	95	2,599	0.1-1	7,883	595	293	6,995	0.01-0.1	1,070	231	49	790
Ossabaw Sound	1,225	839	386	100	1,125	0.1-1	1,480	288	221	971	0.01-0.1	239	112	37	90
St. Catherines & Sapelo Sounds	250	NA	250	232	17	0.1-1	181	32	150	0	0.01-0.1	41	18	23	0
Altamaha River	3,678	3,287	391	27	3,650	0.1-1	6,122	0	1	6,121	0.01-0.1	831	0	0	831
St. Andrew & St. Simon Sounds	1,045	200	844	650	394	>1	4,989	179	68	4,742	>0.1	571	43	9	519
St. Johns River	2,424	741	1,684	1,684	741	0.1-1	9,870	5,871	3,999	0	>0.1	5,636	5,148	487	0
Indian River	323	NA	323	323	0	0.1-1	2,060	1,001	1,060	0	0.01-0.1	822	634	188	0
Biscayne Bay	479	NA	479	479	0	0.1-1	8,581	5,617	2,964	0	>0.1	3,862	3,501	361	0
GULF OF MEXICO	401,602	379,214	22,388	15,490	386,112		809,199	97,463	66,692	645,044		200,977	24,653	11,497	164,827
Ten Thousand Islands	1,088	NA	1,088	816	272	0.1-1	560	222	337	0	0.01-0.1	64	28	35	0
Charlotte Harbor	1,303	NA	1,303	1,186	117	0.1-1	2,267	699	1,568	0	0.01-0.1	907	771	136	0
Tampa Bay	673	NA	673	673	0	0.1-1	4,487	3,037	1,450	0	>0.1	1,380	1,248	132	0
Suwannee River	2,642	2,160	482	482	2,160	0.1-1	3,390	87	760	2,543	0.01-0.1	1,211	7	306	898
Apalachee River	1,203	240	963	809	394	0.1-1	4,567	1,270	2,533	764	0.01-0.1	666	156	240	269
Apalachicola Bay	5,310	4,541	769	746	4,564	0.1-1	10,055	47	957	9,051	0.01-0.1	1,201	7	68	1,126
St. Andrew Bay	293	NA	293	293	0	<0.1	1,037	246	791	0	<0.01	93	38	55	0
Choctawhatchee Bay	1,391	805	585	538	852	0.1-1	4,991	105	2,742	2,144	0.01-0.1	462	18	221	222
Pensacola Bay	1,810	909	901	622	1,188	0.1-1	4,443	1,419	2,643	381	0.01-0.1	595	345	215	35
Perdido Bay	312	NA	312	300	12	0.1-1	1,734	203	1,475	55	0.01-0.1	288	167	116	5
Mobile Bay	11,551	10,289	1,263	518	11,034	0.1-1	38,661	2,671	2,944	33,047	0.01-0.1	7,175	762	239	6,174
Mississippi Sound	6,967	3,844	3,124	1,749	5,218	0.1-1	30,915	4,500	5,451	20,964	0.01-0.1	4,315	1,009	631	2,674
Mississippi River	293,005	292,618	387	135	292,870	0.1-1	420,743	21,587	276	398,880	>0.1	109,156	7,166	47	101,943
Atchafalaya & Vermilion Bays	25,512	23,983	1,528	1,528	23,983	0.1-1	161,531	6,408	4,616	150,507	>0.1	39,289	562	875	37,852
Calcasieu Lake	1,122	842	280	280	842	>1	9,135	6,162	728	2,244	>0.1	1,312	802	290	220
Sabine Lake	5,413	4,167	1,246	399	5,014	0.1-1	12,547	2,794	1,028	8,725	0.01-0.1	1,732	795	271	666
Galveston Bay	6,294	5,189	1,105	1,083	5,211	>1	45,850	36,729	4,645	4,476	>0.1	11,419	9,309	1,103	1,007
Brazos River	11,836	11,409	427	179	11,657	>1	12,362	4,897	920	6,545	>0.1	7,648	388	219	7,041
Matagorda	12,865	11,500	1,365	819	12,046	>1	12,132	247	8,872	3,014	>0.1	5,577	127	2,188	3,262
San Antonio Bay	2,812	2,670	142	142	2,670	0.1-1	723	7	716	0	0.01-0.1	172	0	172	0
Aransas Bay	717	NA	717	394	323	>1	3,543	156	3,324	63	>0.1	806	18	717	71
Corpus Christi Bay	4,564	4,048	516	516	4,048	>1	6,217	3,457	2,033	727	>0.1	1,950	744	425	781
Laguna Madre	2,922	NA	2,922	1,285	1,636	0.1-1	17,311	512	15,884	915	>0.1	3,560	185	2,795	580
PACIFIC OCEAN	93,221	84,037	9,184	7,971	85,251		483,616	49,032	138,753	295,831		63,392	33,577	2,850	26,966
San Diego Bay	196	77	120	120	77	>1	3,047	2,821	226	0	>0.1	2,390	2,371	20	0
San Pedro Bay	447	NA	447	438	9	>1	9,720	8,559	1,161	0	>0.1	5,991	5,835	156	0
Santa Monica Bay	137	NA	137	137	0	>1	16,690	15,856	834	0	>0.1	11,615	11,571	44	0
Monterey Bay	1,549	1,417	132	129	1,419	>1	24,727	1,363	23,232	132	>0.1	1,077	621	451	5
San Francisco Bay	11,434	9,742	1,691	1,607	9,827	0.1-1	83,634	10,094	45,316	28,223	>0.1	11,880	6,731	1,078	4,071
Eel River	941	550	391	297	643	0.1-1	10,563	41	9,850	671	0.01-0.1	495	25	108	362
Humboldt Bay	57	NA	57	57	0	0.1-1	540	202	200	138	0.01-0.1	161	112	15	34
Klamath River	4,015	3,621	394	197	3,818	0.1-1	10,984	1	2,374	8,609	0.01-0.1	496	0	24	473
Rogue River	1,329	1,097	233	86	1,243	0.1-1	11,915	5	2,693	9,217	0.01-0.1	868	3	27	838
Coos Bay	153	NA	153	153	0	0.1-1	2,771	100	2,671	0	0.01-0.1	86	54	33	0

World Resources 1992–93

in U.S. Estuaries

Table 23.2

	Physical Characteristics (thousand hectares)					Nitrogen					Phosphorus				
			Estuarine Drainage Area			Pre-dicted Concen-tration (mg/l)	Estimated Loadings (metric tons per year)				Pre-dicted Concen-tration (mg/l)	Estimated Loadings (metric tons per year)			
	Total Drainage Area	Fluvial Drainage Area			Up-stream			Coastal		Up-stream			Coastal		Up-stream
			Total	Coastal			Total	Point	Non-point			Total	Point	Non-point	
Umpqua River	1,202	813	389	389	813	0.1-1	8,047	116	7,931	0	0.01-0.1	148	54	93	0
Siuslaw River	199	NA	199	199	0	0.1-1	3,501	21	3,480	0	<0.01	44	8	36	0
Alsea River	124	0	124	80	45	0.1-1	3,515	4	1,706	1,805	0.01-0.1	55	2	17	36
Yaquina Bay	66	NA	66	66	0	0.1-1	893	98	795	0	0.01-0.1	44	34	10	0
Siletz Bay	96	NA	96	69	27	0.1-1	1,375	28	993	354	0.01-0.1	41	12	12	17
Netarts Bay	4	NA	4	4	0	0.1-1	133	3	131	0	<0.01	3	2	1	0
Tillamook Bay	148	NA	148	138	10	0.1-1	3,915	59	3,856	0	<0.01	66	27	39	0
Nehalem River	223	NA	223	212	11	0.1-1	2,637	17	2,620	0	<0.01	32	5	26	0
Columbia River	66,733	65,276	1,457	933	65,800	0.1-1	255,150	3,063	8,350	243,737	0.01-0.1	22,642	1,488	181	20,973
Willapa Bay	285	NA	285	285	0	0.1-1	3,406	62	3,344	0	<0.01	65	30	35	0
Grays Harbor	703	339	364	364	339	0.1-1	7,320	384	4,315	2,622	<0.01	288	95	75	117
Puget Sound	3,181	1,106	2,075	2,013	1,168	<0.1	19,134	6,137	12,674	322	0.01-0.1	4,905	4,497	367	41

Source: U.S. National Oceanic and Atmospheric Administration, Strategic Environmental Assessments Division.
Notes: Totals may not match because of independent rounding.
Estuaries are sorted geographically, starting at the U.S.-Canadian border in the northeast and following the U.S. coastline in a clockwise pattern.
0 = zero or less than half the unit of measure; NA = not applicable; mg/l = milligram per liter.

Table 23.3 Marine Fisheries, Yield and Estimated Potential

| | Marine Fish (million metric tons) | | | Cephalopods (million metric tons) | | | Crustaceans (million metric tons) | | | Total Marine Catch {a} (million metric tons) | | |
| | Average Annual Catch | | | Average Annual Catch | | | Average Annual Catch | | | Average Annual Catch | | |
	1977-79	1987-89	Potential	1977-79	1987-89	Potential	1977-79	1987-89	Potential	1977-79	1987-89	Potential
WORLD	54.34	71.14	62.29-86.91	1.35	2.37	4.09-6.09	2.65	4.04	2.44-3.23	58.34	77.55	68.82-96.23
ATLANTIC OCEAN	21.42	19.66	25.50-33.30 b	0.39	1.00	2.01-2.97	0.54	0.89	0.72-0.94	22.35	21.55	28.23-37.21
Northwest	1.98	2.10	3.40-4.30 c	0.14	0.03	X	0.00	0.24	0.14-0.18	2.12	2.37	
Northeast	11.27	9.09	10.10-12.30 c	0.02	0.04	0.60-1.00	0.16	0.23	0.15-0.19	11.46	9.36	
Western Central	1.23	1.35	3.20-5.10 c	0.01	0.01	0.40-0.60	0.24	0.26	0.29-0.35	1.48	1.62	
Eastern Central	3.01	3.22	2.90-3.70 c	0.15	0.17	0.18-0.22	0.04	0.05	0.02-0.04	3.19	3.45	
Southwest	1.12	1.49	2.60-3.80 c	0.07	0.73	0.80-1.10	0.08	0.09	0.09-0.13	1.27	2.31	
Southeast	2.81	2.40	2.50-3.10 c	0.01	0.02	0.03-0.05	0.02	0.02	0.03-0.05	2.83	2.44	
PACIFIC OCEAN	28.52	45.00	31.00-45.10 d	0.88	1.20	1.71-2.57	1.56	2.24	1.40-1.81	30.96	48.44	34.11-49.48
Northwest	15.18	20.94	13.50-16.50 c	0.67	0.77	0.70-0.90	0.75	1.41	0.36-0.44	16.60	23.12	
Northeast	1.38	2.75	2.60-3.20 c	0.00	0.05	0.06-0.10	0.21	0.10	0.22-0.28	1.59	2.93	
Western Central	4.59	6.01	5.00-7.80 c	0.15	0.19	0.13-0.19	0.47	0.49	0.43-0.53	5.21	6.69	
Eastern Central	1.76	1.49	2.20-3.00 c	0.02	0.07	0.40-0.80	0.08	0.09	0.32-0.48	1.85	1.65	
Southwest	0.32	0.79	1.20-2.00 c	0.04	0.12	0.10-0.14	0.01	0.01	0.01-0.02	0.37	0.92	
Southeast	5.29	13.02	3.70-10.20 c	0.00	0.01	0.32-0.44	0.05	0.12	0.06-0.08	5.34	13.14	
INDIAN OCEAN	3.02	4.85	4.70-7.10 e	0.03	0.10	0.32-0.48	0.33	0.48	0.29-0.43	3.38	5.44	5.31-8.01
Western	1.78	2.68	2.70-4.20 c	0.02	0.05	0.19-0.29	0.24	0.26	0.20-0.30	2.04	2.99	
Eastern	1.24	2.17	1.50-2.20 c	0.01	0.05	0.13-0.19	0.09	0.22	0.09-0.13	1.34	2.45	
MEDITERRANEAN AND BLACK SEA	1.13	1.53	1.09-1.41	0.05	0.07	0.05-0.07	0.03	0.05	0.03-0.05	1.21	1.65	1.17-1.53
ANTARCTIC	0.25	0.10	X	0.00	0.00	X	0.20	0.38	X	0.45	0.48	
ARCTIC	0.00	0.00	X	0.00	0.00	X	0.00	0.00	X	0.00	0.00	

Source: Food and Agriculture Organization of the United Nations.
Notes: a. Total marine catch includes marine fish, cephalopods, and crustaceans only. b. Includes oceanic perlagic fish whose estimated potential is 0.8-1.0 million metric tons for the whole Atlantic Ocean. c. Does not include oceanic pelagic fish. d. Includes oceanic pelagic fish whose estimated potential is 2.0-2.4 million metric tons for the whole Pacific Ocean. e. Includes oceanic pelagic fish whose estimated potential is 0.5-0.7 million metric tons for the whole Indian Ocean.
0 = zero or less than half the unit of measure; X = not available.

Table 23.4 Marine and Freshwater Catches, Aquaculture, and

	Average Annual Marine Catch		Average Annual Freshwater Catch		Average Annual Aquaculture Production 1987-89 (000 metric tons)							Average Annual Food Supply from Fish and Fishery Products 1986-88	
	(000 metric tons) 1987-89	Percent Change Since 1977-79	(000 metric tons) 1987-89	Percent Change Since 1977-79	Fresh-water Fish	Diad-romous Fish	Marine Fish	Crus-taceans	Molluscs	Total Fish and Shellfish	Other {a}	(000 metric tons)	Per Capita (kilo-grams)
WORLD	84,220.3	35	13,303.2	85	5,829.2	908.5	271.5	613.9	2,952.7	10,575.8	3,160.3	65,488.9	13.1
AFRICA	3,439.0	21	1,820.2	27	73.7	1.6	0.8	0.1	2.1	78.2	0.1	4,747.5	8.1
Algeria	99.9	158	0.4	X	0.0	X	X	0.0	0.0	0.0	X	101.3	4.4
Angola	90.6	(20)	8.0	0	X	X	X	X	X	X	X	218.0	23.6
Benin	9.3	126	31.2	53	0.0	X	X	X	X	0.0	X	47.0	11.1
Botswana	X	X	1.9	63	X	X	X	X	X	X	X	3.6	3.1
Burkina Faso	X	X	7.9	19	0.0	X	X	X	X	0.0	X	17.6 b	2.1 b
Burundi	X	X	11.8	(23)	0.0	X	X	X	X	0.0	X	11.9 b	2.3 b
Cameroon	60.9	20	20.0	0	0.2	X	X	X	X	0.2	X	154.0	14.4
Cape Verde	6.5	(5)	0.0	X	0.1	X	X	X	X	0.1	X	4.2	12.3
Central African Rep	X	X	13.0	0	X	X	X	X	X	X	X	14.5	5.2
Chad	X	X	110.0	(1)	X	X	X	X	X	X	X	92.2	17.5
Comoros	5.4	34	0.0	X	X	X	X	X	X	X	X	5.6	11.4
Congo	21.3	25	17.5	119	0.2	X	X	X	X	0.2	X	75.0	36.3
Cote d'Ivoire	67.9	(10)	30.1	289	1.1	X	X	X	X	1.1	X	177.7 b	16.0 b
Djibouti	0.5	96	0.0	X	X	X	X	X	X	0.0	X	1.3	3.5
Egypt	49.5	69	201.8	138	55.1	X	X	X	X	55.1	X	361.7	7.4
Equatorial Guinea	3.6	(10)	0.4	X	X	X	X	X	X	X	X	7.1	21.5
Ethiopia	0.9	X	3.2	26	0.0 c	X	X	X	X	0.0	X	4.8 b	0.1 b
Gabon	20.7	31	1.9	6	0.0	X	X	X	X	0.0	X	32.9	31.2
Gambia, The	11.6	(3)	2.7	0	0.0	X	X	X	X	0.0	X	12.6	16.0
Ghana	311.8	40	56.4	46	X	0.4	X	X	X	0.4	X	355.6	25.9
Guinea	31.0	169	3.0	200	0.0	X	X	X	X	0.0	X	44.5	8.4
Guinea-Bissau	3.5	9	0.0	X	X	X	X	X	X	X	X	3.3	3.6
Kenya	7.5	73	130.4	206	0.3	0.2	0.0	X	X	0.6	X	122.9	5.7
Lesotho	X	X	0.0	18	0.0	0.0	X	X	X	0.0	X	2.9	1.8
Liberia	13.3	77	4.0	0	0.0	X	X	X	X	0.0	X	34.2	14.6
Libya	8.7	139	0.0	X	X	X	X	X	X	X	X	16.2	4.0
Madagascar	61.0	368	36.7	(11)	0.2	0.0	X	X	X	0.2	X	90.3 b	8.0 b
Malawi	X	X	88.1	35	0.1	X	X	0.0	X	0.1	X	82.9	10.5
Mali	X	X	61.1	(29)	0.0	X	X	X	X	0.0	X	61.1 b	7.0 b
Mauritania	90.5	270	6.0	0	X	X	X	X	X	X	X	17.9	9.6
Mauritius	17.5	146	0.1	681	0.0	X	0.0	0.1	0.0	0.1	X	19.2 b	18.2 b
Morocco	520.5	87	1.5	159	0.0	0.0	X	X	0.1	0.2	X	176.7	7.6
Mozambique	34.2	42	0.3	(95)	0.0	X	X	X	X	0.0	X	44.0	3.1
Namibia	28.0	(93)	0.2	233	X	X	X	X	X	X	X	15.2 b	9.1 b
Niger	X	X	3.2	(62)	0.1	X	X	X	X	0.1	X	3.0	0.4
Nigeria	154.9	(43)	105.6	(58)	13.8	X	0.3	X	X	14.2	X	658.4	6.7
Rwanda	X	X	1.5	47	0.0	X	X	X	X	0.0	X	1.6	0.3
Senegal	244.5	19	16.3	9	0.0	X	0.0	0.0	X	0.0	X	143.8	21.3
Sierra Leone	37.2	(23)	16.0	219	0.0	X	X	X	X	0.0	X	56.5	14.7
Somalia	17.5	79	0.5	X	X	X	X	X	X	X	X	1.8	2.3
South Africa	1,199.0	102	1.3	X	0.2	0.8	0.0	X	1.6	2.7	0.0	345.1 b	10.2 b
Sudan	1.2	76	22.8	(11)	0.0	X	X	X	X	0.0	X	23.7	1.0
Swaziland	X	X	0.1	127	0.0	X	X	X	X	0.0	X	0.1	0.1
Tanzania	46.0	7	328.1	84	0.0	X	X	X	X	0.0	X	348.2	14.2
Togo	15.1	39	0.6	2	0.0	X	X	X	X	0.0	X	43.2	13.4
Tunisia	99.0	76	0.0	X	X	X	0.4	X	0.3	0.7	X	83.6	11.0
Uganda	X	X	227.0	9	0.0	X	X	X	X	0.0	X	212.9	12.6
Zaire	2.0	34	161.3	48	0.7	X	X	X	X	0.7	X	296.0	9.2
Zambia	X	X	68.0	35	1.1	X	X	X	X	1.1	X	67.1	8.9
Zimbabwe	X	X	18.3	145	0.0	0.1	0.0	X	X	0.2	X	18.3	2.1
NORTH & CENTRAL AMERICA	8,980.2	54	545.6	310	209.6	96.1	0.6	43.8	184.2	534.4	0.1	6,887.0	16.7
Barbados	5.1	30	0.0	X	X	X	X	X	X	X	X	8.1	32.0
Belize	1.4	(5)	0.0	(93)	X	X	X	0.3	X	0.3	X	1.2	7.2
Canada	1,521.1	18	50.1	4	X	10.0	X	X	7.2	17.1	X	632.2 b	24.4 b
Costa Rica	19.9	9	0.5	548	0.1	0.1	0.0	0.2	0.0	0.4	X	14.7	5.3
Cuba	195.9	9	16.8	381	15.8	X	0.1 c	0.4	1.2	17.5	X	219.0 b	21.1 b
Dominican Rep	16.7	219	1.7	160	0.0	0.0 c	X	0.3	X	0.3	X	39.7	5.9
El Salvador	12.8	62	2.1	33	0.0	X	0.5	0.2	X	0.7	X	13.9	2.8
Guatemala	2.3	(40)	0.5	(15)	0.1	X	X	0.7	X	0.9	X	3.9 b	0.4 b
Haiti	7.8	93	0.3	0	X	X	X	X	X	0.0	X	28.1	4.6
Honduras	18.8	193	1.7	X	0.2	X	X	1.9	X	2.2	X	17.6 b	3.7 b
Jamaica	7.6	(22)	2.7	X	2.1	X	X	0.0	0.0	2.1	X	44.1	18.6
Mexico	1,225.9	65	176.8	X	7.3	0.7	X	0.6	51.6	60.2	X	852.1 b	10.0 b
Nicaragua	4.6	(49)	0.1	(43)	0.0	X	X	0.1	X	0.1	X	3.1 h	0.8 b
Panama	155.5	(14)	0.6	X	0.5	X	X	3.3	X	3.8	X	27.9 b	12.0 b
Trinidad and Tobago	3.2	(26)	0.0	X	X	X	X	X	X	X	X	13.2	10.9
United States	5,597.6	73	291.5	310	183.3	85.5	X	35.5	123.9	428.1	X	5,245.7 b	21.3 b
SOUTH AMERICA	13,841.1	94	354.8	44	14.8	8.8	0.0	81.9	3.5	109.0	22.8	2,382.5	8.5
Argentina	503.2	6	10.1	(27)	0.3	X	X	X	0.0	0.3	X	205.7	6.6
Bolivia	X	X	4.9	118	0.2	0.1	0.0 d	X	X	0.4	X	6.3	0.9
Brazil	655.3	9	215.8	39	12.0	X	X	1.7	0.1	13.8	X	936.3	6.6
Chile	5,491.5	180	1.4	X	X	6.7	X	X	3.2	9.8	22.8	281.8 b	22.1 b
Colombia	36.8	85	50.6	3	1.3	0.6	0.0	2.9	X	4.8	X	94.5 b	3.0 b
Ecuador	723.3	31	1.7	X	0.1	0.3	X	73.9	0.0	74.2	X	107.4 b	10.7 b
Guyana	35.4	4	0.8	174	0.0	X	X	0.0	X	0.1	X	34.1	43.0
Paraguay	X	X	10.3	233	0.0	X	X	X	X	0.0	X	11.0	2.8
Peru	5,986.7	88	31.5	130	0.5	0.8	X	3.3	0.2	4.8	X	488.5 b	23.6 b
Suriname	4.1	5	0.1	(15)	X	X	X	X	X	X	X	2.9	7.2
Uruguay	121.7	59	0.5	15	X	X	X	X	X	X	X	13.2 b	4.3 b
Venezuela	275.6	80	27.1	210	0.3	0.3	X	0.0	X	0.6	X	241.4	13.2

Fish Consumption

Table 23.4

	Average Annual Marine Catch		Average Annual Freshwater Catch		Average Annual Aquaculture Production 1987-89 (000 metric tons)							Average Annual Food Supply from Fish and Fishery Products 1986-88	
	(000 metric tons) 1987-89	Percent Change Since 1977-79	(000 metric tons) 1987-89	Percent Change Since 1977-79	Fresh-water Fish	Diad-romous Fish	Marine Fish	Crus-taceans	Molluscs	Total Fish and Shellfish	Other {a}	(000 metric tons)	Per Capita (kilo-grams)
ASIA	**34,752.1**	**35**	**9,091.9**	**115**	**4,944.8**	**405.0**	**259.4**	**428.6**	**2,019.1**	**8,057.0**	**3,125.1**	**33,529.1**	**11.4**
Afghanistan	X	X	1.5	0	X	X	X	X	X	X	X	1.5	0.1
Bahrain	7.9	88	0.0	X	X	X	X	X	X	X	X	9.4	20.4
Bangladesh	241.2	109	585.4	11	139.4	X	X	16.5	X	155.9	X	800.6 b	7.3 b
Bhutan	X	X	1.0	0	X	X	X	X	X	X	X	1.0	0.7
Cambodia	6.5	(34)	63.5	51	1.6	X	X	X	X	1.6	X	70.0	9.1
China	5,814.8	81	4,493.5	315	3,765.6	X	31.7	179.8	884.8	4,861.9	1,445.3	9,540.2 b	8.8 b
Cyprus	2.5	105	0.1	70	0.0	0.1	0.0	X	X	0.1	X	8.6	12.7
India	1,910.4	29	1,307.2	55	432.5	X	X	16.3	2.6	451.5	X	2,627.0	3.3
Indonesia	1,971.0	60	691.8	64	214.7	115.9	4.6	67.5	X	402.7	81.7	2,432.2	14.0
Iran, Islamic Rep	189.2	214	46.3	559	9.7	0.9	X	X	X	10.6	X	231.3 b	4.4 b
Iraq	5.0	(73)	13.9	(21)	4.8	X	X	X	X	4.8	X	19.7	1.1
Israel	16.3	56	15.8	5	13.8	0.4	0.7	0.0	X	14.9	X	94.7 b	21.3 b
Japan	11,455.5	16	207.9	(7)	24.9	87.9	215.3	3.1	434.9	766.1	575.1	8,839.0 b	72.1 b
Jordan	0.0	(94)	0.1	X	0.1	X	X	X	X	0.1	X	10.1	3.4
Korea, Dem People's Rep	1,600.1	34	100.0	61	X	X	X	11.0	162.7	173.7	315.2	873.2	42.4
Korea, Rep	2,768.6	33	43.3	30	7.1	2.3	1.9	0.2	409.9	421.4	457.5	2,066.2	49.6
Kuwait	8.7	83	0.0	X	X	X	0.0	X	X	0.0	X	20.0	10.8
Lao People's Dem Rep	X	X	20.0	0	2.5	X	X	X	X	2.5	X	20.0	5.3
Lebanon	1.7	3	0.1	0	X	0.1	X	X	X	0.1	X	1.7	0.7
Malaysia	598.6	(10)	14.7	431	6.1	2.1	0.3	1.5	39.6	49.6	X	497.2	30.1
Mongolia	X	X	0.3	(29)	X	X	X	X	X	X	X	2.5	1.3
Myanmar	552.5	40	145.2	0	6.0	0.0 d	X	X	X	6.0	X	599.4	15.3
Nepal	X	X	11.8	261	5.8	X	X	X	X	5.8	X	10.9	0.6
Oman	136.4	87	0.0	X	X	X	X	0.0	X	0.0	X	33.6	24.9
Pakistan	341.8	36	97.7	169	9.0	0.0 c	X	0.0	X	9.0	X	202.4	1.8
Philippines	1,478.1	25	554.5	81	84.7	192.8	X	44.0	26.4	347.9	248.6	1,961.5	33.8
Qatar	3.4	48	0.0	X	X	X	X	X	X	X	X	3.1	9.5
Saudi Arabia	48.9	93	0.5	X	0.6	X	0.0	0.0	X	0.6	X	101.2	8.0
Singapore	14.7	(5)	0.1	(77)	0.2	X	0.2	0.4	1.1	1.9	X	78.4 b	29.6 b
Sri Lanka	158.8	15	38.1	142	4.8	X	X	0.6	X	5.4	X	250.1 b	14.9 b
Syrian Arab Rep	0.9	(28)	4.5	88	1.6	0.1	X	X	X	1.7	X	5.9	0.5
Thailand	2,629.0	35	179.1	35	86.5	1.3	1.0	58.1	56.2	203.1	0.0	1,106.6	20.8
Turkey	538.8	132	48.3	132	2.1	1.1	0.1	X	X	3.3	X	378.0 b	7.0 b
United Arab Emirates	88.6	38	0.0	X	0.0	X	0.0	X	X	0.0	X	36.7	25.2
Viet Nam	620.8	51	250.3	39	115.0	X	X	29.5	X	144.5	1.7	815.5	13.0
Yemen (Arab Rep)	21.9	22	0.0	X	X	X	X	X	X	X	X	24.8	3.0
(People's Dem Rep)	50.9	(6)	0.0	X	X	X	X	X	X	X	X	37.4	16.4
EUROPE	**12,116.4**	**(2)**	**466.5**	**50**	**158.3**	**308.7**	**6.2**	**3.2**	**655.4**	**1,131.8**	**0.0**	**9,352.4 b**	**18.8 b**
Albania	7.6	(25)	5.6	57	0.4	0.2	0.0	X	2.3	2.8	X	10.1 b	3.2 b
Austria	X	X	4.9	43	1.3	3.1	X	X	X	4.3	X	61.0 b	8.0 b
Belgium	40.0	(16)	0.7	X	0.2	0.4	X	X	X	0.7	X	199.2 b	19.4 b
Bulgaria	97.5	(2)	12.4	30	10.5	1.5	X	0.1	X	12.1	X	57.6 b	6.4 b
Czechoslovakia	X	X	21.1	22	20.1	1.0	X	X	X	21.1	X	106.8 b	6.8 b
Denmark	1,843.9	6	24.7	55	X	29.2	X	X	X	29.2	X	107.4 b	20.9 b
Finland	103.8	3	8.8	(69)	X	15.9	X	X	X	15.9	X	153.6 b	31.0 b
France	827.1	10	41.4	X	7.8	32.9	0.2	0.2	187.1	228.3	X	1,681.9 b	30.1 b
Germany (Fed Rep)	189.0	(51)	26.0	69	6.0	16.5	0.0	X	22.6	45.1	X	680.3 b	11.0 b
(Dem Rep)	161.3	(18)	22.0	51	14.4	7.5	X	X	X	21.8	X	220.6 b	13.3 b
Greece	120.1	26	10.0	8	0.4	2.2	0.5	X	1.0	4.1	X	182.3 b	18.2 b
Hungary	X	X	36.9	10	18.6	0.3	X	X	X	18.9	X	52.6 b	5.0 b
Iceland	1,631.8	7	0.6	12	X	1.2	X	X	X	1.2	X	23.0 b	92.4 h
Ireland	249.9	159	0.6	X	X	6.1	X	X	13.8	18.9	X	58.3 b	16.5 b
Italy	504.5	18	58.3	131	2.8	36.8	4.2	X	85.3	129.1	X	1,164.6 b	20.3 b
Luxembourg	X	X	0.0	X	X	X	X	X	X	X	X	X b	X b
Malta	0.9	(28)	0.0	X	X	X	X	X	X	X	X	5.3	15.3 b
Netherlands	416.9	31	5.3	114	0.4	0.4	X	X	95.8	96.6	0.0 c	118.2 b	8.0 b
Norway	1,896.0	(34)	0.4	12	X	88.3	0.0	X	0.1	88.4	X	185.0 b	44.0 b
Poland	597.2	2	33.0	46	21.1	3.0	X	X	X	24.1	X	522.0 b	13.8 b
Portugal	354.1	32	1.9	X	1.9	X	0.4	0.0 d	X	2.3	X	592.9 b	57.7 b
Romania	181.9	72	70.3	40	38.7	X	X	0.0	7.9	46.6	X	203.0 b	8.8 b
Spain	1,368.1	5	29.7	39	0.4	14.4	0.6	2.9	233.2	251.5	X	1,446.5 b	37.1 b
Sweden	236.2	27	4.9	(51)	X	6.7	X	0.0	1.2	7.9	X	230.4 b	27.3 b
Switzerland	X	X	4.4	12	0.1 d	0.5	X	X	X	0.6	X	85.9 b	13.0 b
United Kingdom	892.8	(9)	17.1	787	0.1	35.4	X	0.0	3.8	39.4	X	1,120.6 b	19.6 b
Yugoslavia	49.3	39	25.6	4	13.2	0.3	0.3	X	1.3	15.0	X	79.4 b	3.4 b
U.S.S.R.	**10,266.1**	**24**	**1,001.2**	**26**	**343.6**	**8.2**	**0.1**	**X**	**0.2**	**352.1**	**3.8**	**8,236.8 b**	**28.9 b**
OCEANIA	**825.5**	**151**	**22.9**	**897**	**0.1**	**3.7**	**0.0**	**0.6**	**33.4**	**37.9**	**0.6**	**597.4**	**23.9**
Australia	194.5	55	3.3	154	0.0	2.6	X	0.3	10.2	13.1	0.1	301.4 b	18.2 b
Fiji	29.1	155	4.4	411	0.0	X	0.0	0.0	X	0.0	0.1	31.1 b	42.4 b
New Zealand	482.2	356	0.5	205	X	1.1	X	X	23.1	24.2	X	120.6 b	36.5 b
Papua New Guinea	10.5	(71)	14.6	X	X	X	X	X	X	0.0	X	89.6	24.8
Solomon Islands	52.2	83	0.0	X	X	X	X	0.0	X	0.0	X	16.8 b	55.9 b

Source: Food and Agriculture Organization of the United Nations.
Notes: a. Includes production of aquatic plants and seaweeds, which are excluded from marine catch; their harvest is to be subtracted as appropriate. b. Data are for 1987-89. c. Two years of data. d. One year of data.
Total of aquaculture production is included in the country totals for marine and freshwater catches.
World and regional totals include countries not listed and unallocated quantities.
0 = zero or less than half of the unit of measure; X = not available; negative numbers are shown in parentheses.
For additional information, see Sources and Technical Notes.

Sources and Technical Notes

Table 23.1 Coastal Areas and Resources

Sources: Length of marine coastline: United Nations Office of Ocean Affairs and the Law of the Sea, unpublished data (United Nations, New York, June 1989); U.S. Central Intelligence Agency, *The World Factbook 1988* (U.S. Government Printing Office, Washington, D.C., 1988). Shelf area to 200-meter depth: John P. Albers, M. Devereux Carter, Allen L. Clark, *et al. Summary Petroleum and Selected Mineral Statistics for 120 Countries, Including Offshore Areas*, Geological Survey Professional Paper 817, (U.S. Government Printing Office, Washington, D.C., 1973). Exclusive economic zone: United Nations Office of Ocean Affairs and the Law of the Sea, unpublished data (United Nations, New York, June 1989); French Polynesia and New Caledonia: Anthony Bergin, "Fisheries Surveillance in the South Pacific," *Ocean & Shoreline Management*, Vol. 11 (1988), p. 468.

Population in coastal urban agglomerations: United Nations Centre for Human Settlements (Habitat), unpublished data (United Nations, Nairobi, Februrary 1990).

Average volume of goods loaded and unloaded: United Nations Statistical Office, *Monthly Bulletin of Statistics*, Vol. XLIV, No. 12 (December 1990).

Offshore oil and gas resources: Offshore Magazine (PennWell Publishing Company, Tulsa, Oklahoma, July 20, 1984 and June 1991).

The United Nations Office for Ocean Affairs and the Law of the Sea compiles information concerning coastal claims from the following sources: the United Nations Legislative Series, official gazettes, communications to the Secretary General, legal journals, and other publications. National claims to maritime zones fall into five categories: territorial sea, contiguous zone, exclusive economic zone (EEZ), exclusive fishing zone, and continental shelf. The extent of the continental *shelf to 200-meter depth* and the *exclusive economic zone* for those countries with marine coastline are presented in the table. Only the potential and not the actual established area of the EEZ are shown. At present, only about half of the world's countries have established a full EEZ.

Under currently recognized international principles, an EEZ may be established by a nation out to 200 nautical miles to claim all the resources within the zone, including fish and all other living resources; minerals; and energy from wind, waves, and tides. Nations may also claim rights to regulate scientific exploration, protect the marine environment, and establish marine terminals and artificial islands. The EEZ data shown do not reflect the decisions of some countries, such as those in the European Community, to collectively manage fishing zones on EEZs in some areas. When countries' EEZs overlap—such as those of the United States and Cuba, which both have 200-mile EEZs, yet are only 90 miles apart—they must agree on a maritime boundary between them, often a halfway point.

The shelf area to the 200-meter isobath represents one indicator of potential offshore oil and gas resources because of sedimentation from continental areas. Other indicators are geologic and geographic. Accessibility and water depth place economic constraints on exploration and production operations in water deeper than 200 meters. Significant deep-water operations currently take place in the North Sea and off the Brazilian coast.

Population in coastal urban agglomerations was calculated using maps in scales from 1:500,000 to 1:2,000,000. Coastal area is defined as a zone no more than 60 kilometers inland. Projected population for the year 2000 is based on the medium variant of the 1988 United Nations Population Division assessment. Definitions of urban agglomeration vary greatly among countries. (See Technical Note for Table 17.2.) The most recent country-level estimates are for years from 1970 to 1986. Hence, a direct comparison of urban agglomerations among countries should be done with caution.

The United Nations Statistical Office based its estimates of *average annual volume of goods loaded and unloaded* in maritime transport mostly on information available in external trade statistics. *Petroleum products* exclude bunkers and those products not generally carried by tanker, namely, paraffin wax, petroleum coke, asphalt, and lubricating oil, which are included with the data for *dry cargo.*

Offshore Magazine annually queries national governments for statistics on *offshore oil and gas resources.* These data are supplemented with figures from oil- and gas-producing companies, expert sources, and published literature. National governments often have difficulty providing offshore gas production figures; the data are more frequently obtained from alternative sources. Figures for offshore *oil* and *gas* production in Middle Eastern countries are particularly difficult to obtain and, as a result, are less reliable.

Proven reserves of offshore crude oil and gas represent the fraction of total resources that can be recovered in the future, given present and expected economic conditions and existing technological limits.

Table 23.2 Nutrient Discharges and Predicted Concentrations in U.S. Estuaries

Sources: NOAA/EPA Team on Near Coastal Water, *Strategic Assessment of Near Coastal Waters, Susceptibility of East Coast Estuaries to Nutrient Discharges: Passamaquoddy Bay to Chesapeake Bay, Summary Report* (Department of Commerce, Washington, D.C., June 1989); *Strategic Assessment of Near Coastal Waters, Susceptibility of East Coast Estuaries to Nutrient Discharges: Albemarle/Pamlico Sound to Biscayne Bay, Summary Report* (Department of Commerce, Washington, D.C., June 1989); *Strategic Assessment of Near Coastal Waters, Susceptibility and Status of Gulf of Mexico Estuaries to Nutrient Discharges, Summary Report* (Department of Commerce, Washington, D.C., June 1989); *Strategic Assessment of Near Coastal Waters, Susceptibility and Status of West Coast Estuaries to Nutrient Discharges: San Diego Bay to Puget Sound, Summary Report* (Department of Commerce, Washington, D.C., October 1991).

Physical and hydrological characteristics of an estuary determine its susceptibility to concentrate dissolved and particulate pollutants. Susceptibility can be quantified by two parameters: dissolved concentration potential (DCP), which is the relative ability of an estuary to concentrate dissolved pollutants (in this case, phosphorus and nitrogen); and particle retention efficiency (PRE), which is the relative ability of an estuary to trap suspended particles and attached pollutants (primarily toxic materials). The DCP, a function of the total volume of an estuary, the volume of freshwater in the estuary, and the rate of freshwater inflow, assesses the effect of flushing and estuarine dilution on a load of dissolved pollutants. The PRE, also a function of estuary volume and annual freshwater inflow, equates an estuary's relative ability to retain sediment to its ability to concentrate particulate pollutants.

Total drainage area, the sum of estuarine and fluvial drainage areas, includes all river basins discharging into an estuary. *Fluvial drainage area* extends over the entire watershed upstream of the estuarine drainage area. *Estuarine drainage area* is measured from the head of tide and the seaward estuarine boundary as cataloged by the U.S. Geological Survey (USGS). Estuarine drainage area may include a coastal portion, which is the extent of all the counties bordering the estuary directly, and a noncoastal portion, which is the area of estuarine drainage beyond the coastal counties. Upstream is defined as the total of noncoastal estuarine area plus the fluvial drainage area.

Excessive nutrient loads, mainly nitrogen and phosphorus, are responsible for the eutrophication of estuaries, which may lead to algal blooms, emissions of noxious odors, and massive kills of marine organisms. The annual loadings of nitrogen and phosphorus entering each estuary were estimated separately for coastal and upstream areas.

Coastal point sources include wastewater treatment plants and land-based industrial facilities discharging directly to surface water within a coastal county portion of the estuarine drainage area. The transport of nutrients from surface waters is calculated separately for four land-use classes (agriculture, forest, urban, and other nonurban). The total nutrient discharge resulting from these four land-use categories within the coastal county portion of estuarine drainge area is defined as *coastal nonpoint* discharge.

Upstream sources contain point and non-point sources and include discharge from all riverine sources with an average annual flow greater than 1,700 liters per minute.

Estimates for annual nitrogen and phosphorous loadings do not account for other possible sources such as ocean influx, groundwater inflow, bottom sediments, wetlands, barren lands, and direct atmospheric deposition. The estimates for point and nonpoint sources are "end of pipe" and "edge of field" loadings, which represent a high estimate because they ignore transport phenomena (e.g., phosphorus tied with sediments or nitrification).

The *predicted concentration* of nitrogen and phosphorus is based on the DCP and annual nutrient loadings. This estimate does not account for nutrient recycling in the estuary, which in some systems may be responsible for a greater percentage of nutrient concentration in the estuary than new loadings entering the system each year. Low predicted concentrations (less than 0.1 milligram of nitrogen per liter and less than 0.01 milligram of phosphorus per liter) suggest maximum potential in the diversity of aquatic life. High predicted concentrations (more than 1 milligram of nitrogen per liter and more than 0.1 milligram of phosphorus per liter) are associated with high chlorophyll levels, low species diversity, and occasional red tides. The predicted concentration is a general indicator of the potential for eutrophication in an estuary. The degree to which real eutrophication occurs is dependent on other factors: nutrient recycling in the estuary and temporal changes in loading resulting from stratification phenomena, and/or changes in the agricultural runoff and freshwater inflow. Actual and long-term measurements of nutrient concentrations in U.S. estuaries do not currently exist.

Table 23.3 Marine Fisheries, Yield and Estimated Potential

Sources: Marine fishery production: Food and Agriculture Organization of the United Nations (FAO), *Yearbook of Fishery Statistics 1983, 1984,* and *1989* (FAO, Rome, 1984, 1986, and 1991). Estimated fishery potential: M.A. Robinson, *Trends and Prospects in World Fisheries,* Fisheries Circular No. 772 (FAO, Fisheries Department, Rome, 1984).

FAO divides the world's oceans into 19 marine statistical areas and organizes *annual catch* data by 840 "species items," species groups separated at the family, genus, or species level. *Marine fish* include the following FAO species groupings: flounders, halibuts, soles, etc.; cods, hakes, haddocks, etc.; redfishes, basses, congers, etc.; jacks, mullets, sauries, etc.; tunas, bonitos, bill-fishes, etc.; herrings, sardines, anchovies, etc.; mackerels, snoeks, cutlassfishes, etc.; sharks, rays, chimeras, etc.; and miscella-

neous marine fishes. *Cephalopods* include squids, cuttlefishes, octopuses, etc. *Crustaceans* are the total of the following categories: seaspiders, crabs, etc.; lobsters, spiny-rock lobsters, etc.; squat lobsters; shrimps, prawns, etc.; krill, planktonic crustaceans, etc.; and miscellaneous marine crustaceans. Years shown are three-year averages. *Total marine catch* differs from marine catch in Table 23.4 because the following mollusc categories are not included: abalones, winkles, conchs, etc.; oysters; mussels; scallops; clams, cockles, arkshells, etc.; miscellaneous marine molluscs. Please refer to the Technical Note for Table 23.4 for the definition of nominal fish catch and additional information on FAO's fishery data base.

Estimates of *potential* are FAO estimates of marine fisheries' biologically realizable potential. These estimates refer to the maximum harvest that can be sustained by a fishery year after year, given average environmental conditions. An assumed level of incidental take (catching one species while fishing for another) is subtracted from estimates of potential. The figures exclude the potential harvest from marine aquaculture.

Table 23.4 Marine and Freshwater Catches, Aquaculture, and Fish Consumption

Sources: Marine and freshwater catch: Food and Agriculture Organization of the United Nations (FAO), *Yearbook of Fishery Statistics 1983, 1984, 1986,* and *1989* (FAO, Rome, 1984, 1986, 1988, and 1991). Aquaculture production: Food and Agriculture Organization of the United Nations (FAO), Fisheries Department, *Aquaculture Production (1986–1989),* Fisheries Circular No. 815, Revision 3, (FAO, Rome, July 1991). Food supply from fish and fishery products: Edmondo Laureti, Food and Agriculture Organization of the United Nations (FAO), Fisheries Department, *Fish and Fishery Products—World Apparent Consumption Statistics Based on Food Balance Sheets (1961–1989),* Fisheries Circular No. 821, Revision 1, (FAO, Rome, July 1991).

Marine and *freshwater catch* data refer to marine and freshwater fish killed, caught, trapped, collected, bred, or cultivated for commercial, industrial, and subsistence use. Crustaceans, molluscs, and miscellaneous aquatic animals are included. Statistics for mariculture, aquaculture, and other kinds of fish farming are included in the country totals. Quantities taken in recreational activities are excluded. Figures are the national totals averaged over a three-year period; they include fish caught by a country's fleet anywhere in the world. Catches of freshwater species caught in low-salinity seas are included in the statistics of the appropriate marine area. Catches of diadromous (migratory between saltwater

and freshwater) species are shown either in the marine or inland area where they were caught.

Data are represented as nominal catch, which is the landings converted to a live-weight basis, that is, weight when caught. Landings for some countries are identical to catches.

International fishery data are continually revised. The *Yearbook of Fishery Statistics 1989,* the latest edition, contains FAO's most up-to-date published figures.

Data are provided annually to the FAO Fisheries Department by national fishery offices and regional fishery commissions. Some countries' data are provisional for the latest year. If no data are submitted, FAO uses the previous year's figures or makes estimates based on other information.

Years are calendar years except for Antarctic fisheries data, which are for split years (July 1–June 30). Data for Antarctic fisheries are given for the calendar year in which the split year ends.

Aquaculture is defined by FAO as "the farming of aquatic organisms, including fish, molluscs, crustaceans, and aquatic plants. Farming implies some form of intervention in the rearing process to enhance production, such as regular stocking, feeding, and protection from predators, etc. [It] also implies ownership of the stock being cultivated . . .." Aquatic organisms that are exploitable by the public as a common property resource are included in the harvest of fisheries.

FAO's global collection of aquaculture statistics by questionnaire was begun in 1984; today, these data are a regular feature of the annual FAO survey of world fishery statistics.

FAO's 840 "species items" are summarized in six categories. *Freshwater fish* include carps, barbels, tilapias, and other freshwater fishes. *Diadromous fish* include, among others, sturgeons, river eels, salmons, trouts, and smelts. *Marine fish* include a variety of species groups such as flounders, halibuts, and redfishes. *Crustaceans* include, among others, freshwater crustaceans, crabs, lobsters, shrimps, and prawns. *Molluscs* include freshwater molluscs, oysters, mussels, scallops, clams, and squids. *Other* includes frogs, turtles, and aquatic plants. Data on whales and other mammals are excluded from this table. For a detailed listing of species, please refer to the most recent *FAO Yearbook of Fishery Statistics.*

Average annual food supply from fish and fishery products is the quantity of fish and fish products available for human consumption. It is calculated as apparent consumption—production minus nonfood uses, minus exports, plus imports—of eight groups of primary fishery commodities and nine groups of processed products and estimated in the food balance sheets of FAO.

24. Atmosphere and Climate

The Earth's atmosphere is changing, and we do not fully understand what the effect of those changes will be on our own lives, much less the lives of our children. It is easy to imagine effects that could be catastrophic for life on this planet. Yet, in the face of these possibilities and our inadequate understanding of Earth processes, anthropogenic emissions of trace gases—pollutants that affect climate, the ozone layer, and human health—continue.

Industrial emissions of carbon dioxide (CO_2), from the burning of fossil fuels and the production of cement, continue and grow. Table 24.1 shows that these emissions differ considerably from country to country on both a total and a per capita basis. Measured on a per capita basis, a disproportionate share of these gases are emitted by industrialized and oil-producing countries. For example, per capita emissions in the United States reached 19.7 metric tons in 1989. In contrast, per capita emissions in China were only 2.2 metric tons and in India only 0.8 metric tons. CO_2 is the most important of the greenhouse gases. (See Chapter 13, "Atmosphere and Climate.")

Table 24.2 shows estimates by country of the CO_2 emitted in the course of deforestation, as well as emissions of methane (CH_4) and chlorofluorocarbons (CFCs), other important greenhouse gases. This table describes the global anthropogenic emissions and their distribution by source and by country.

Deforestation remains an important source of CO_2 in the atmosphere, making up about one quarter of total anthropogenic emissions. Although deforestation in Brazil has declined considerably in recent years (see Chapter 8, "Forests and Rangelands"), it accounts for almost 15 percent of CO_2 from deforestation and is the largest single country source. The countries of South and Southeast Asia together, however, account for fully 41 percent of CO_2 emissions from deforestation.

Overall China emits the most CH_4 at 40 million metric tons, followed by the United States (37 million), India (36 million), and the U.S.S.R. (34 million). Animal husbandry provides the largest component of anthropogenic emissions of CH_4, and India—the country with the largest number of cattle—emits almost 14 percent of the global livestock total. Another anthropogenic source of CH_4 is wet rice agriculture. India and China each emit 26 percent of CH_4 attributable to this source; only small amounts are emitted outside Asia. The U.S.S.R. is the largest emitter of CH_4 from gas produc-tion and transmission (35 percent) and is second (19 percent) only to China (33 percent) in CH_4 emissions from coal production. Large and populous countries are also the sources of the largest emissions from solid waste disposal. The United States leads at 37 percent, with the U.S.S.R. a distant second.

CFC emissions, as well as being potent greenhouse gases, cause depletion of the ozone layer. Policy mechanisms for their control are already in place. Nevertheless, an estimated 580,000 metric tons were emitted in 1989. The United States (22 percent) and Japan (16 percent), the two leading industrial powers, were also the leaders in the use and emission of these gases.

Table 24.3 shows the increasing atmospheric concentrations of trace gases with greenhouse and ozone-depleting effects. Since preindustrial times, CO_2 concentrations have increased 26.5 percent; CH_4 has increased 143.5 percent—although CH_4 concentrations are a tiny fraction of CO_2 concentrations—and the chlorinated trace gases appeared for the first time (they are the consequence of modern industrial processes).

Most of the increase in CO_2 concentrations is due to the burning of fossil fuels. Table 24.4 shows that total annual emissions have reached almost 22 billion metric tons. Indeed, they have increased by 260 percent since 1950 (on a per capita basis they have increased more than 75 percent). Emissions from solid fuel consumption have more than doubled, those from liquid fuel consumption have increased almost 500 percent, and those from gas consumption have increased almost 900 percent.

Not all anthropogenic emissions of pollutants are increasing inexorably. Data from the industrialized countries (Table 24.5) show that sulfur and nitrogen emissions have declined in countries that have attempted to control them. In general, the countries in Europe (including the European part of the U.S.S.R.) have made headway in controlling sulfur dioxide emissions over the past 20 years. However, efforts to control nitrogen emissions have had mixed results. Sulfur and nitrogen emissions are precursors of acid rain as well as air pollutants that affect human health.

Table 24.6 shows that the United States has decreased emissions of carbon monoxide (CO), particulate matter (PM), and hydrocarbons (HC) since 1980. In contrast, the United Kingdom's CO and HC emissions increased over the same time period; PM emissions decreased only slightly.

Table 24.1 CO₂ Emissions from Industrial Processes, 1989

	Carbon Dioxide Emissions (000 metric tons)						Per Capita Carbon Dioxide Emissions (metric tons)
	Solid	Liquid	Gas	Gas Flaring	Cement Manufacture	Total	
WORLD	8,764,288	8,863,216	3,466,144	205,184	556,928	21,863,088	4.21
AFRICA	270,029	256,462	51,985	45,162	23,867	647,352	1.03
Algeria	3,019	20,731	17,034	2,466	3,243	46,492	1.91
Angola	0	1,707	319	2,440	498	4,965	0.51
Benin	0	418	0	0	249	667	0.15
Botswana	1,700	0	0	0	0	1,700	1.36
Burkina Faso	0	520	0	0	0	520	0.07
Burundi	18	158	0	0	0	176	0.04
Cameroon	4	5,771	0	0	0	5,774	0.51
Cape Verde	0	77	0	0	0	77	0.22
Central African Rep	0	264	0	0	0	264	0.07
Chad	0	202	0	0	0	202	0.04
Comoros	0	51	0	0	0	51	0.11
Congo	0	1,576	4	169	29	1,773	0.81
Cote d'Ivoire	0	7,247	0	0	348	7,595	0.66
Djibouti	0	326	0	0	0	326	0.81
Egypt	2,939	59,349	12,355	0	4,836	79,483	1.54
Equatorial Guinea	0	106	0	0	0	106	0.29
Ethiopia	0	2,440	0	0	125	2,565	0.04
Gabon	0	4,983	531	2,242	70	7,826	6.89
Gambia, The	0	183	0	0	0	183	0.22
Ghana	7	3,232	0	0	282	3,521	0.26
Guinea	0	1,000	0	0	0	1,000	0.18
Guinea-Bissau	0	147	0	0	0	147	0.15
Kenya	355	4,232	0	0	605	5,192	0.22
Lesotho	0	0	0	0	0	0	0.00
Liberia	0	729	0	0	44	773	0.29
Libya	4	23,629	11,168	1,682	1,356	37,842	8.65
Madagascar	37	850	0	0	18	901	0.07
Malawi	176	425	0	0	37	634	0.07
Mali	0	414	0	0	15	425	0.04
Mauritania	15	2,964	0	0	44	3,023	1.54
Mauritius	202	802	0	0	0	1,000	0.95
Morocco	4,994	15,107	121	0	1,898	22,120	0.92
Mozambique	172	835	0	0	198	1,205	0.07
Namibia	0	0	0	0	0	0	0.00
Niger	421	575	0	0	15	1,008	0.15
Nigeria	264	32,826	8,295	36,131	1,744	79,263	0.77
Rwanda	0	381	4	0	0	381	0.04
Senegal	0	2,964	0	0	191	3,151	0.44
Sierra Leone	0	671	0	0	0	671	0.18
Somalia	0	960	0	0	0	960	0.15
South Africa	239,362	34,768	0	0	4,338	278,468	8.06
Sudan	0	3,265	0	0	73	3,338	0.15
Swaziland	443	0	0	0	0	443	0.59
Tanzania	11	1,938	0	0	150	2,099	0.07
Togo	0	432	0	0	194	627	0.18
Tunisia	344	8,904	2,154	33	2,488	13,923	1.76
Uganda	0	876	0	0	4	879	0.04
Zaire	887	2,708	0	0	227	3,822	0.11
Zambia	887	1,535	0	0	191	2,612	0.33
Zimbabwe	13,769	1,931	0	0	359	16,059	1.72
NORTH & CENTRAL AMERICA	1,955,110	2,616,103	1,109,584	21,629	58,422	5,760,830	13.60
Barbados	0	810	55	0	106	971	3.81
Belize	0	180	0	0	0	180	0.95
Canada	107,352	209,383	128,130	4,789	5,877	455,530	17.33
Costa Rica	0	2,286	0	0	271	2,557	0.88
Cuba	601	33,778	62	0	1,854	36,292	3.44
Dominican Rep	0	5,976	0	0	769	6,745	0.95
El Salvador	0	2,037	0	0	315	2,352	0.44
Guatemala	0	3,268	0	0	806	4,071	0.44
Haiti	0	616	0	0	110	725	0.11
Honduras	0	1,682	0	0	297	1,979	0.40
Jamaica	0	4,719	0	0	180	4,899	2.02
Mexico	20,445	234,624	49,255	3,671	11,710	319,702	3.70
Nicaragua	0	2,129	0	0	51	2,180	0.59
Panama	26	2,437	95	0	176	2,730	1.14
Trinidad and Tobago	0	5,518	7,251	5,621	191	18,580	14.73
United States	1,826,149	2,075,685	924,735	7,548	34,892	4,869,005	19.68
SOUTH AMERICA	67,044	345,193	102,610	18,881	23,563	557,298	1.91
Argentina	4,316	62,834	42,850	5,932	2,228	118,157	3.70
Bolivia	0	3,111	1,385	315	253	5,064	0.70
Brazil	39,124	146,816	6,533	2,023	12,458	206,957	1.39
Chile	9,200	18,294	3,177	300	857	31,833	2.45
Colombia	13,212	28,290	8,533	678	3,118	53,831	1.65
Ecuador	0	12,769	191	1,363	993	15,316	1.47
Guyana	0	660	0	0	0	660	0.84
Paraguay	0	1,557	0	0	161	1,722	0.40
Peru	484	18,423	997	282	993	21,174	0.99
Suriname	26	1,385	0	0	26	1,440	3.48
Uruguay	0	4,514	0	0	231	4,749	1.54
Venezuela	667	46,042	38,945	7,988	2,246	95,887	4.98

Table 24.1

	Carbon Dioxide Emissions (000 metric tons)						Per Capita Carbon Dioxide Emissions (metric tons)
	Solid	Liquid	Gas	Gas Flaring	Cement Manufacture	Total	
ASIA	**3,147,431**	**1,948,556**	**392,605**	**66,670**	**256,795**	**5,812,064**	**1.93**
Afghanistan	388	1,810	3,660	363	51	6,273	0.40
Bahrain	0	2,554	9,607	0	0	12,161	24.37
Bangladesh	480	6,031	7,416	0	187	14,114	0.11
Bhutan	4	29	0	0	0	33	0.04
Cambodia	0	451	0	0	0	451	0.07
China	1,964,032	292,699	28,817	0	103,068	2,388,613	2.16
Cyprus	202	3,561	0	0	429	4,192	6.05
India	461,803	143,929	15,535	9,688	20,980	651,936	0.77
Indonesia	8,999	81,722	15,334	24,648	7,024	137,726	0.77
Iran, Islamic Rep	4,170	110,191	42,590	2,884	6,240	166,074	3.11
Iraq	4	50,794	2,481	9,384	6,240	68,898	3.77
Israel	9,318	22,376	77	0	1,129	32,903	7.25
Japan	303,995	603,157	92,816	81	40,506	1,040,554	8.46
Jordan	0	8,530	0	0	887	9,416	2.42
Korea, Dem People's Rep	136,946	9,570	0	0	4,972	151,488	7.07
Korea, Rep	97,037	103,468	5,415	0	15,187	221,104	5.20
Kuwait	0	11,263	17,353	2,114	447	31,181	15.76
Lao People's Dem Rep	0	227	0	0	0	227	0.07
Lebanon	0	8,266	0	0	451	8,720	3.26
Malaysia	2,972	30,419	9,732	3,550	2,389	49,061	2.82
Mongolia	7,694	2,308	0	0	297	10,303	4.84
Myanmar	271	2,378	2,074	99	187	5,009	0.11
Nepal	216	586	0	0	132	934	0.04
Oman	0	3,986	4,455	1,341	473	10,259	7.07
Pakistan	7,181	29,037	19,218	2,059	3,481	60,973	0.51
Philippines	5,097	33,874	0	0	1,990	40,960	0.66
Qatar	0	2,631	10,527	0	150	13,308	37.59
Saudi Arabia	0	110,261	51,270	7,497	4,749	173,776	12.79
Singapore	44	34,962	0	0	850	35,860	13.34
Sri Lanka	0	3,836	0	0	198	4,034	0.22
Syrian Arab Rep	0	25,230	443	740	1,744	28,154	2.34
Thailand	9,673	50,604	9,915	0	7,486	77,680	1.43
Turkey	50,036	58,118	6,064	0	11,860	126,078	2.31
United Arab Emirates	0	15,766	31,210	2,173	1,795	50,944	32.94
Viet Nam	13,187	4,188	0	0	795	18,170	0.29
Yemen (Arab Rep){a}	0	3,147	0	0	348	3,495	0.40
(People's Dem Rep){a}	X	X	X	X	X	X	X
EUROPE	**1,970,071**	**1,616,223**	**623,972**	**15,129**	**122,440**	**4,347,794**	**8.74**
Albania	3,895	4,679	762	0	399	9,732	3.04
Austria	13,549	25,919	9,842	0	2,393	51,699	6.82
Belgium	40,253	37,856	16,558	0	3,437	98,104	9.97
Bulgaria	60,544	31,998	11,692	0	2,759	106,989	11.87
Czechoslovakia	156,138	44,979	19,808	0	5,426	226,347	14.47
Denmark	20,691	22,222	3,081	18	993	47,009	9.16
Finland	20,313	25,981	4,261	0	747	51,300	10.33
France	74,409	214,813	55,964	0	11,981	357,163	6.38
Germany (Fed Rep){a}	283,623	247,478	96,568	531	13,201	641,398	10.48
(Dem Rep){a}	X	X	X	X	X	X	X
Greece	29,195	34,936	282	4	6,511	70,920	7.07
Hungary	28,015	13,139	20,976	0	1,946	64,076	6.05
Iceland	238	1,649	0	0	59	1,942	7.69
Ireland	14,073	10,263	4,199	0	813	29,352	7.95
Italy	52,710	241,938	76,926	0	18,173	389,747	6.82
Luxembourg	7,072	1,000	927	0	275	9,266	24.92
Malta	692	982	0	0	0	1,674	4.76
Netherlands	31,228	27,667	64,105	227	1,762	124,990	8.43
Norway	3,811	24,717	6,540	10,259	685	46,009	10.96
Poland	370,005	43,939	19,529	0	7,460	440,929	11.54
Portugal	9,655	28,271	0	0	2,982	40,912	3.99
Romania	86,628	52,439	66,165	0	6,962	212,193	9.16
Spain	73,635	107,231	10,010	147	12,205	203,227	5.20
Sweden	13,659	43,184	949	0	1,096	58,888	7.00
Switzerland	1,488	31,631	3,488	0	2,722	39,326	5.94
United Kingdom	251,277	201,560	104,710	3,942	6,962	568,451	9.89
Yugoslavia	74,203	42,704	11,747	0	4,250	132,901	5.61
U.S.S.R.	**1,328,885**	**1,237,842**	**1,129,996**	**37,530**	**69,752**	**3,804,001**	**13.26**
OCEANIA	**146,985**	**100,764**	**39,758**	**0**	**3,745**	**291,248**	**11.16**
Australia	141,932	81,748	30,558	0	3,239	257,480	15.46
Fiji	37	645	0	0	0	678	0.92
New Zealand	4,609	11,893	9,200	0	476	26,176	7.77
Papua New Guinea	4	2,246	0	0	0	2,250	0.59
Solomon Islands	0	161	0	0	0	161	0.51

Source: Carbon Dioxide Information Analysis Center.
Notes: a. Data for Yemen and Germany combine data from their previous divisions.
Estimates are of the carbon dioxide emitted, 3.664 times the carbon it contains.
World and regional totals include countries not listed.
0 = zero or less than half the unit of measure; X = not available.
For additional information, see Sources and Technical Notes.

Table 24.2 Other Greenhouse Gas Emissions, 1989

	Carbon Dioxide Emissions from Land-Use Change (000 metric tons)	Methane from Anthropogenic Sources (000 metric tons)						Chlorofluoro-carbons (000 metric tons)
		Solid Waste	Coal Mining	Oil and Gas Production	Wet rice Agriculture	Livestock	Total	
WORLD	6,400,000	46,000	39,000	37,000	72,000	76,000	270,000	580
AFRICA	1,500,000	2,000	2,000	4,200	2,300	9,500	19,000	16
Algeria	X	56	X	770	X	140	970	1
Angola	33,000	22	X	180	8	130	340	X
Benin	9,500	10	X	X	2	43	54	X
Botswana	2,600	3	3	X	X	91	97	X
Burkina Faso	17,000	17	X	X	14	140	170	X
Burundi	530	12	X	X	6	18	34	X
Cameroon	60,000	25	X	X	8	190	230	X
Cape Verde	X	1	X	X	X	1	2	X
Central African Rep	13,000	6	X	X	4	90	100	X
Chad	15,000	13	X	X	9	200	220	X
Comoros	X	1	X	X	6	4	11	X
Congo	12,000	4	X	12	2	4	21	X
Cote d'Ivoire	350,000	26	X	X	140	50	200	1
Djibouti	X	1	X	X	X	10	11	X
Egypt	X	120	11	99	260	220	670	3
Equatorial Guinea	1,800	1	X	X	X	0	1	X
Ethiopia	30,000	93	X	X	X	1,300	1,400	X
Gabon	9,300	3	X	170	0	1	170	0
Gambia, The	1,900	2	X	X	4	13	18	X
Ghana	31,000	34	X	X	25	69	120	1
Guinea	37,000	14	X	X	250	68	300	X
Guinea-Bissau	18,000	2	X	X	63	14	72	X
Kenya	13,000	52	X	X	8	590	640	0
Lesotho	X	X	X	X	X	X	X	X
Liberia	39,000	5	X	X	61	4	63	0
Libya	X	10	X	230	X	53	290	X
Madagascar	120,000	25	X	X	740	370	860	0
Malawi	58,000	18	X	X	14	45	73	X
Mali	7,700	20	X	X	51	240	310	X
Mauritania	X	5	X	X	2	130	140	X
Mauritius	X	2	X	X	0	2	4	X
Morocco	X	57	12	1	2	230	310	1
Mozambique	30,000	35	X	X	47	51	130	X
Namibia	X	X	X	X	X	X	X	X
Niger	7,400	16	X	X	6	210	230	X
Nigeria	270,000	240	X	2,700	140	630	3,700	0
Rwanda	2,100	15	X	0	1	29	46	0
Senegal	11,000	17	X	X	15	120	160	0
Sierra Leone	4,600	9	X	X	100	14	97	X
Somalia	5,200	14	X	X	1	740	760	X
South Africa	X	680	1,900	X	1	820	3,400	7
Sudan	98,000	54	X	X	1	1,100	1,200	X
Swaziland	X	2	X	X	X	25	27	X
Tanzania	21,000	55	X	X	190	550	740	X
Togo	2,900	8	X	X	9	20	34	0
Tunisia	X	18	X	8	X	64	90	0
Uganda	10,000	40	X	X	10	160	210	X
Zaire	130,000	87	X	X	120	71	290	X
Zambia	27,000	15	0	X	6	100	120	X
Zimbabwe	16,000	21	42	X	0	240	310	1
NORTH & CENTRAL AMERICA	420,000	19,000	8,800	7,400	1,000	8,900	45,000	150
Barbados	X	1	X	0	X	1	2	0
Belize	X	0	X	X	0	2	2	X
Canada	X	1,700	560	1,100	X	740	4,100	11
Costa Rica	26,000	6	X	X	8	64	78	0
Cuba	890	24	X	0	120	190	310	0
Dominican Rep	1,300	15	X	X	49	88	160	0
El Salvador	1,600	14	X	X	3	43	59	0
Guatemala	41,000	21	X	X	6	81	110	1
Haiti	860	13	X	X	8	70	90	X
Honduras	42,000	10	X	X	3	95	110	0
Jamaica	810	6	X	X	0	13	18	1
Mexico	200,000	190	130	660	30	1,300	2,300	5
Nicaragua	59,000	8	X	X	18	63	87	0
Panama	19,000	5	X	X	13	56	75	0
Trinidad and Tobago	330	3	X	470	0	4	470	0
United States	22,000	17,000	8,100	5,200	740	6,000	37,000	130
SOUTH AMERICA	1,800,000	660	180	2,200	940	14,000	18,000	15
Argentina	X	73	0	740	16	2,900	3,800	3
Bolivia	37,000	16	X	68	13	260	360	0
Brazil	950,000	340	4	200	430	7,700	8,800	6
Chile	X	30	15	48	8	170	270	0
Colombia	420,000	71	160	120	270	920	1,500	2
Ecuador	160,000	23	X	100	40	160	330	0
Guyana	1,100	2	X	X	19	9	27	X
Paraguay	67,000	9	X	X	5	290	310	0
Peru	140,000	48	2	29	53	220	330	0
Suriname	1,100	1	X	X	45	3	43	0
Uruguay	X	9	X	X	22	500	530	0
Venezuela	59,000	43	2	900	18	480	1,400	2

	Carbon Dioxide Emissions from Land-Use Change (000 metric tons)	Methane from Anthropogenic Sources (000 metric tons)						Chlorofluoro-carbons (000 metric tons)
		Solid Waste	Coal Mining	Oil and Gas Production	Wet rice Agriculture	Livestock	Total	
ASIA	**2,600,000**	**9,100**	**16,000**	**6,000**	**67,000**	**25,000**	**130,000**	**140**
Afghanistan	X	45	2	72	110	250	480	X
Bahrain	X	1	X	77	X	0	79	0
Bangladesh	8,700	250	X	60	5,100	970	6,900	X
Bhutan	860	4	X	X	30	16	40	X
Cambodia	11,000	18	X	X	740	110	1,100	X
China	X	2,600	13,000	230	19,000	5,300	40,000	12
Cyprus	X	2	X	X	X	5	6	0
India	120,000	1,900	1,600	830	19,000	11,000	36,000	4
Indonesia	870,000	400	12	580	5,100	600	6,500	1
Iran, Islamic Rep	X	110	6	550	240	550	1,500	3
Iraq	X	40	X	760	34	120	950	1
Israel	X	120	X	1	X	15	140	3
Japan	X	2,400	150	37	1,400	280	4,100	95
Jordan	X	7	X	X	X	10	17	1
Korea, Dem People's Rep	X	49	600	X	410	52	1,200	X
Korea, Rep	X	99	360	X	640	82	1,200	5
Kuwait	X	5	X	240	X	3	250	1
Lao People's Dem Rep	240,000	11	X	X	180	83	370	X
Lebanon	X	5	X	X	X	5	10	X
Malaysia	280,000	39	X	480	270	38	890	2
Mongolia	X	5	5	24	X	250	260	X
Myanmar	380,000	95	X	X	3,100	470	3,200	X
Nepal	32,000	41	X	X	430	400	1,000	X
Oman	X	3	X	130	X	15	150	X
Pakistan	4,000	250	1	300	1,100	1,700	3,400	6
Philippines	190,000	140	1	X	1,500	230	2,400	1
Qatar	X	1	X	85	X	3	88	X
Saudi Arabia	X	29	X	960	X	90	1,100	3
Singapore	X	6	X	X	X	0	7	1
Sri Lanka	22,000	39	X	X	410	120	540	0
Syrian Arab Rep	X	25	X	58	X	100	190	1
Thailand	290,000	130	X	80	5,700	480	6,300	3
Turkey	X	120	29	3	33	700	880	1
United Arab Emirates	X	3	X	460	X	15	480	1
Viet Nam	150,000	150	84	X	3,200	270	3,600	X
Yemen (Arab Rep)	X	17	X	X	X	63	80	X
(People's Dem Rep)	X	6	X	X	X	20	26	X
EUROPE	**X**	**9,400**	**3,900**	**3,600**	**250**	**8,400**	**26,000**	**180**
Albania	X	50	X	6	2	37	95	X
Austria	X	150	X	12	X	150	310	3
Belgium	X	220	54	0	X	170	450	4
Bulgaria	X	150	2	0	8	170	330	1
Czechoslovakia	X	250	270	11	X	290	820	4
Denmark	X	100	X	30	X	140	270	2
Finland	X	98	X	X	X	79	180	1
France	X	1,100	120	33	14	1,300	2,600	24
Germany (Fed Rep)	X	1,200	790	170	X	890	3,000	27
(Dem Rep)	X	300	X	26	X	360	680	7
Greece	X	200	X	2	12	150	360	4
Hungary	X	170	20	92	9	120	410	3
Iceland	X	5	X	X	X	11	16	0
Ireland	X	70	X	23	X	340	430	2
Italy	X	1,100	X	100	110	600	2,000	25
Luxembourg	X	7	X	X	X	X	7	0
Malta	X	8	X	X	X	1	8	0
Netherlands	X	290	X	630	X	260	1,200	6
Norway	X	83	0	1,100	X	71	1,300	1
Poland	X	600	1,200	57	X	650	2,500	5
Portugal	X	200	3	X	22	130	350	4
Romania	X	380	41	440	33	600	1,500	2
Spain	X	770	230	27	32	520	1,600	17
Sweden	X	170	X	X	X	99	270	3
Switzerland	X	130	X	0	X	110	240	2
United Kingdom	X	1,100	1,200	750	X	900	3,900	25
Yugoslavia	X	460	3	34	6	240	750	4
U.S.S.R.	**X**	**4,600**	**7,600**	**13,000**	**370**	**7,900**	**34,000**	**67**
OCEANIA	**12,000**	**1,200**	**1,600**	**320**	**75**	**3,000**	**6,200**	**9**
Australia	X	1,100	1,600	250	68	2,000	5,000	8
Fiji	X	2	X	X	6	7	18	0
New Zealand	X	64	18	74	X	980	1,100	1
Papua New Guinea	12,000	9	X	X	X	5	15	X
Solomon Islands	X	1	X	X	0	1	X	X

Source: World Resources Institute.
Notes: Carbon dioxide mass is 3.664 times its carbon content.
0 = zero or less than half the unit of measure; X = not available.
For additional information, see Sources and Technical Notes.

Table 24.3 Atmospheric Concentrations of Greenhouse and Ozone-Depleting Gases, 1959–90

Year	Carbon Dioxide (CO2) ppm	Carbon tetrachloride (CCl4) ppt	Methyl chloroform (CH3CCl3) ppt	CFC-11 (CCl3F) ppt	CFC-12 (CCl2F2) ppt	CFC-22 (CHClF2) ppt	CFC-113 (C2Cl3F3) ppt	Total Gaseous Chlorine ppt	Nitrous Oxide (N2O) ppb	Methane (CH4) ppb	Carbon Monoxide (CO) ppb
Preindustrial	280.0 a	0	0	0	0	0	0	0	285.0 a	700 a	X
1959	315.8	X	X	X	X	X	X	X	X	X	X
1960	316.8	X	X	X	X	X	X	X	X	X	X
1961	317.5	X	X	X	X	X	X	X	X	X	X
1962	318.3	X	X	X	X	X	X	X	X	1,354	X
1963	318.8	X	X	X	X	X	X	X	X	X	X
1964	X	X	X	X	X	X	X	X	X	X	X
1965	319.9	X	X	X	X	X	X	X	X	1,386	X
1966	321.2	X	X	X	X	X	X	X	X	1,338	X
1967	322.0	X	X	X	X	X	X	X	X	1,480	X
1968	322.8	X	X	X	X	X	X	X	X	1,373	X
1969	323.9	X	X	X	X	X	X	X	X	1,385	X
1970	325.3	X	X	X	X	X	X	X	X	1,431	X
1971	326.2	X	X	X	X	X	X	X	X	1,436	X
1972	327.3	X	X	X	X	X	X	X	X	1,500	X
1973	329.5	X	X	X	X	X	X	X	X	1,624	X
1974	330.1	X	X	X	X	X	X	X	X	1,596	X
1975	331.0	104	70	120	200	X	X	1,386	291.4	1,541	X
1976	332.0	106	78	133	217	X	X	1,491	293.3	1,490	X
1977	333.7	115	86	148	239	X	X	1,640	294.6	1,471	X
1978	335.3	123	94	159	266	X	X	1,783	296.4	1,531	X
1979	336.7	116	112	167	283	46	X	1,913	296.3	1,545	X
1980	338.5	121	126	179	307	52	X	2,065	297.6	1,554	X
1981	339.8	122	127	185	315	59	X	2,113	298.5	1,569	72
1982	341.0	121	133	193	330	64	X	2,186	301.0	1,591	72
1983	342.6	126	144	205	350	71	24	2,393	300.9	1,615	70
1984	344.3	130	150	213	366	76	27	2,498	300.4	1,629	73
1985	345.7	130	158	223	384	85	31	2,609	301.5	1,643	75
1986	347.0	127	169	232	404	98	35	2,722	302.5	1,656	75
1987	348.8	X	X	X	X	X	X	X	304.5	1,667 b	X
1988	351.4	126 b	166 b	256 b	416 b	109 b	44 b	2,843	306.3	1,681 b	X
1989	352.8	126 b	172 b	265 b	433 b	X	51 b	2,834	X	1,694 b	X
1990	354.0	127 b	182 b	275 b	466 b	X	53 b	2,970	X	1,704 b	X

Sources: Charles D. Keeling of Scripps Institution of Oceanography for Carbon dioxide and Oregon Graduate Center for other gases.
Notes: a. Approximately. b. Preliminary data, previous years are not calibrated to the same standard. All estimates are by volume; ppm = parts per million; ppb = parts per billion; ppt = parts per trillion. X = not available. For further information, see Sources and Technical Notes.

Table 24.4 World CO$_2$ Emissions from Fossil Fuel Consumption and Cement Manufacture, 1950–89

Year	Carbon Dioxide Emissions (millions of metric tons)						Per Capita Emissions (metric tons)
	Total	Solid Fuels	Liquid Fuels	Gas Fuels	Gas Flaring	Cement Manufacture	
1950	6,002	3,946	1,550	355	84	66	2.38
1951	6,504	4,166	1,755	421	88	73	2.53
1952	6,606	4,129	1,847	454	95	81	2.53
1953	6,771	4,148	1,953	480	99	88	2.56
1954	6,855	4,115	2,041	506	99	99	2.53
1955	7,511	4,452	2,290	550	114	110	2.71
1956	8,006	4,694	2,488	590	117	117	2.86
1957	8,347	4,825	2,616	652	128	125	2.93
1958	8,566	4,924	2,682	703	128	132	2.93
1959	9,054	5,093	2,895	784	132	147	3.04
1960	9,475	5,199	3,114	861	143	158	3.15
1961	9,534	4,968	3,316	931	154	165	3.11
1962	9,922	4,976	3,594	1,015	161	180	3.15
1963	10,461	5,144	3,858	1,099	172	187	3.26
1964	11,051	5,283	4,170	1,202	187	209	3.37
1965	11,556	5,379	4,474	1,286	202	216	3.48
1966	12,142	5,441	4,855	1,392	220	231	3.55
1967	12,531	5,331	5,218	1,502	242	238	3.59
1968	13,176	5,335	5,687	1,630	267	256	3.70
1969	13,956	5,474	6,134	1,784	293	271	3.85
1970	14,989	5,756	6,734	1,891	319	286	4.07
1971	15,543	5,756	7,130	2,030	322	308	4.10
1972	16,155	5,815	7,533	2,136	344	326	4.21
1973	17,030	5,840	8,207	2,228	403	348	4.32
1974	17,060	5,829	8,222	2,264	392	352	4.25
1975	16,961	6,178	7,808	2,283	341	348	4.14
1976	17,935	6,313	8,475	2,371	399	377	4.32
1977	18,445	6,544	8,757	2,367	381	396	4.36
1978	18,620	6,603	8,731	2,470	392	425	4.32
1979	19,661	6,958	9,288	2,616	366	436	4.51
1980	19,287	7,039	8,827	2,656	326	440	4.32
1981	18,793	7,072	8,325	2,693	264	443	4.14
1982	18,664	7,302	7,980	2,689	253	443	4.07
1983	18,631	7,321	7,925	2,697	231	458	3.99
1984	19,210	7,650	8,010	2,876	209	469	4.03
1985	19,672	8,046	7,947	3,001	202	480	4.07
1986	20,339	8,255	8,332	3,063	191	498	4.10
1987	20,742	8,464	8,372	3,210	176	520	4.14
1988	21,607	8,750	8,750	3,356	202	550	4.21
1989	21,863	8,764	8,863	3,466	205	557	4.21

Source: Carbon Dioxide Information Analysis Center.
Notes: Mass of carbon dioxide. Totals differ from the sum of other columns because of rounding. For additional information, see Sources and Technical Notes.

World Resources 1992–93

Table 24.5 Sulfur and Nitrogen Emissions, 1970–89

	Sulfur Emissions (000 metric tons of SO2)					Nitrogen Emissions (000 metric tons of NO2)				
	1970	1975	1980	1985	1989	1970	1975	1980	1985	1989
NORTH & CENTRAL AMERICA										
Canada	6,677	5,319	4,643	3,704	X	1,364	1,756	1,959	1,959	1,943 a
United States	28,400	25,900	23,400	21,100	20,700 b	18,300	19,200	20,400	19,800	19,800 b
ASIA										
Japan	4,973	2,586	1,263	X	X	1,651	1,781	1,400	X	X
Turkey	X	X	276	322	354	X	X	X	(175)	(175)
EUROPE										
Albania	X	X	(50)	(50)	(50)	X	X	X	(9)	(9)
Austria	X	X	346	158	124	X	X	232	219	211
Belgium	X	X	828	452	414	X	X	317	281	297
Bulgaria	X	X	1,034	1,140	1,030	X	X	X	150	150
Czechoslovakia	X	X	3,100	3,150	2,800	X	X	X	1,127	950
Denmark	574	418	450	340	242	X	178	241	263	267
Finland	515	535	584	372	318	X	160	264	240	255
France	2,966	3,328	3,510	1,846	1,520	1,322	1,608	1,834	2,400	1,688
Germany (Fed Rep)	3,743	3,334	3,200	2,400	1,500	2,381	2,571	2,980	2,950	3,000
(Dem Rep)	X	X	5,000	5,000	5,210	X	X	X	955	708
Greece	X	X	400	360	360	X	X	X	150	150
Hungary	X	X	1,634	1,420	1,218	X	X	X	300	259
Iceland	X	X	6	6	6	X	X	X	12	12
Ireland	X	X	220	138	148	X	60	71	68	77
Italy	2,830	3,331	3,800	2,504	2,410	1,410	1,507	1,585	1,595	1,700
Luxembourg	X	X	24	16	12	X	X	23	19	19
Netherlands	807	429	464	276	290	456	464	558	544	565
Norway	171	137	142	98	74	159	176	192	203	220
Poland	X	X	4,100	4,300	3,910	X	X	X	1,500	1,480
Portugal	116	178	266	204	204	72	104	166	96	96
Romania	X	X	200	200	200	X	X	X	(390)	(390)
Spain	X	3,003	3,250	3,250	3,250	X	625	951	950	950
Sweden	930	690	502	270	220	302	308	394	301	301
Switzerland	125	109	126	96	74	149	162	196	214	194
United Kingdom	6,424	5,370	4,848	3,676	3,552	2,510	2,427	2,442	2,278	2,513
Yugoslavia	X	X	1,176	1,500	1,650	X	X	350	(190)	(190)
U.S.S.R. {c}	X	X	12,800	11,100	9,318	X	X	X	2,930	4,190

Sources: Co-operative Programme for Monitoring and Evaluation of the Long Range Transmission of Air Pollutants in Europe (EMEP); and the Organisation for Economic Co-operation and Development (OECD).
Notes: a. 1990 estimate. b. 1988 data. c. European part of the U.S.S.R. under the purview of EMEP.
X = not available. Emissions in parentheses were estimated by EMEP.
For additional information, see Sources and Technical Notes.

Table 24.6 Common Anthropogenic Pollutants, 1980–89

	Carbon Monoxide (000 metric tons)			Particulate Matter (000 metric tons)			Hydrocarbons (000 metric tons)		
	1980	1985	1989	1980	1985	1989	1980	1985	1989
NORTH & CENTRAL AMERICA									
Canada	10,273	10,781	X	1,907	1,709	X	2,099	2,315	2,256 a
United States	79,600	69,600	60,900	8,500	7,100	6,900 b	22,300	20,000	18,500 b
ASIA									
Japan	X	X	X	X	X	X	X	X	X
Turkey	X	X	X	X	X	X	(700)	(700)	X
EUROPE									
Albania	X	X	X	X	X	X	(30)	(30)	X
Austria	1,268	1,205	1,161 b	75	55	39 b	382	2,315	466 b
Belgium	X	X	X	X	X	X	374	374	X
Bulgaria	X	X	X	X	X	X	2,594	2,594	X
Czechoslovakia	X	X	X	X	X	X	400	400	X
Denmark	X	X	X	X	X	X	197	146	X
Finland	X	X	X	X	X	X	163	181	X
France	6,616	6,295	X	427	304	298	1,975	1,877	X
Germany (Fed Rep)	12,006	8,894	8,872	517	397	268	2,754	2,624	2,536
(Dem Rep)	X	X	X	X	X	X	550	550	X
Greece	X	X	X	X	X	X	(260)	(260)	X
Hungary	X	X	X	X	X	X	(270)	(270)	X
Iceland	X	X	X	X	X	X	(13)	(13)	X
Ireland	497	456	X	94	117	X	62	64	X
Italy	5,487	5,426	5,923	386	390	452 b	696	737	827 b
Luxembourg	X	240	X	X	3	X	13	20	X c
Netherlands	1,413	1,162	1,152	163	101	76	502	416	399
Norway	606	588	592	27	23	20	158	224	245
Poland	X	X	X	X	X	X	700	700	X
Portugal	533	X	X	119	X	X	55	134	156 b
Romania	X	X	X	X	X	X	(440)	(440)	X
Spain	3,780	X	X	X	X	X	843	X	X
Sweden	1,250	X	X	170	X	X	410	446	440 b,c
Switzerland	711	X	462	28	X	21	311	339	304
United Kingdom	4,829	5,318	6,522	570	555	512	1,887	1,926	2,066
Yugoslavia	X	X	X	X	X	X	(600)	(600)	X
U.S.S.R. {d}	X	X	X	X	X	X	8,056	8,056	X

Sources: Co-operative Programme for Monitoring and Evaluation of the Long Range Transmission of Air Pollutants in Europe (EMEP); and the Organisation of Economic Co-operation and Development (OECD).
Notes: a. 1990 estimate. b. 1988 data. c. All hydrocarbons. d. European part of the U.S.S.R. under the purview of EMEP.
X = not available. Emissions in parentheses were estimated by EMEP.
For additional information, see Sources and Technical Notes.

Sources and Technical Notes

Table 24.1 CO_2 Emissions from Industrial Processes, 1989

Source: Carbon Dioxide Information Analysis Center (CDIAC), Environmental Sciences Division, Oak Ridge National Laboratory, "1989 Estimates of CO_2 Emissions from Fossil Fuel Burning and Cement Manufacturing Based on the United Nations Energy Statistics and the U.S. Bureau of Mines Cement Manufacturing Data," ORNL/CDIAC-25, NDP-030 (an accessible numerical data base), (Oak Ridge, Tennessee, July 1991).

This table includes data on industrial additions to the carbon dioxide flux from *solid* fuels, *liquid* fuels, *gas* fuels, *gas flaring*, and *cement manufacture*. CDIAC annually calculates emissions of CO_2 from the burning of fossil fuels and the manufacture of cement for most of the countries of the world. Estimates of country emissions do not include "bunker fuels" used in international transport.

CDIAC calculates emissions from data on the net apparent consumption of fossil fuels (based on the World Energy Data Set maintained by the United Nations Statistical Office), and from data on world cement manufacture (based on the Cement Manufacturing Data Set maintained by the U.S. Bureau of Mines). Emissions are calculated using global average fuel chemistry and usage.

Although estimates of world emissions are probably within 10 percent of actual emissions, individual country estimates may depart more severely from reality. CDIAC points out that the time trends from a consistent and uniform time series "should be more accurate than the individual values." Each year, CDIAC recalculates the entire time series from 1950 to the present, incorporating their most recent understanding and the latest corrections to the data base. As a result, the carbon emissions estimate data set has become more consistent, and probably more accurate, each year.

Emissions of CO_2 are often calculated and reported in terms of their content of elemental carbon. CDIAC reports them that way. For this table, their figures were converted to the actual mass of CO_2 by multiplying the carbon mass by 3.664 (the ratio of the mass of carbon to that of CO_2).

Solid, liquid, and *gas* fuels are primarily, but not exclusively, coals, petroleum products, and natural gas. *Gas flaring* is the practice of burning off gas released in the process of petroleum extraction, a practice that is declining. During *cement manufacture,* cement is calcined to produce calcium oxide. In the process, 0.498 metric ton of CO_2 is released for each ton of cement production. *Total* emissions consist of the sum of the carbon in CO_2 produced during the consumption of solid, liquid, and gas fuels, and from gas flaring and the manufacture of cement.

Combustion of different fossil fuels releases CO_2 at different rates for the same energy production. Burning oil releases about

1.5 times the amount of CO_2 released from burning natural gas; coal combustion releases about twice the CO_2 of natural gas.

It was assumed that approximately 1 percent of the coal used by industry and power plants was not burned, and an additional few percent were converted to non-oxidizing uses. Other oxidative reactions of coal are assumed to be of negligible importance in carbon budget modeling. CO_2 emissions from gas flaring and cement production make up about 3 percent of the CO_2 emitted by fossil fuel combustion.

These data from CDIAC represent the only complete global data set of CO_2 emissions. Individual country estimates, based on more detailed information and a country-specific methodology could differ. An experts meeting, convened by the Organisation for Economic Co-operation and Development (OECD) in February 1991, has recommended (*Estimation of Greenhouse Gas Emissions and Sinks,* OECD, Paris, August 1991) that when countries calculate their own emissions of CO_2, they use a more detailed method when the data are available. Such data are available for only a few countries, and resulting inventories, if any, are not readily available. CDIAC's method has the advantage of calculating CO_2 emissions from a single common data set available for all countries.

Table 24.2 Other Greenhouse Gas Emissions, 1989

Sources: Land-use change: R.A. Houghton, R.D. Boone, J.R. Fruci, *et al.,* "The Flux of Carbon from Terrestrial Ecosystems to the Atmosphere in 1980 Due to Changes in Land Use: Geographic Distribution of the Global Flux," *Tellus,* Vol. 39B, No. 1–2 (1987), pp. 122–139; World Resources Institute (WRI) recent assessments of rates of deforestation (See Table 19.1, Sources and Technical Notes); and R.A. Houghton, "Tropical Deforestation and Atmospheric Carbon Dioxide," *Climate Change,* in press.

Methane (CH_4) from municipal solid waste: Jean Lerner, personal communication (National Aeronautics and Space Administration [NASA] Goddard Space Flight Center, Institute for Space Studies, May 1989); H.G. Bingemer and P.J. Crutzen, "The Production of CH_4 from Solid Wastes," *Journal of Geophysical Research,* Vol. 92, No. D2 (1987), pp. 2181–2187.

CH_4 from coal mining: David W. Barns and J.A. Edmonds, *An Evaluation of the Relationship Between the Production and Use of Energy and Atmospheric Methane Emissions* (U.S. Department of Energy, Office of Energy Research, Carbon Dioxide Research Program, No. TR047, April 1990); World Energy Conference (WEC), *1989 Survey of Energy Resources* (WEC, London, 1989).

CH_4 from oil and gas production and distribution: David W. Barns, J.A. Edmonds, *An Evaluation of the Relationship Between the Production and Use of Energy and Atmospheric Methane Emissions* (U.S. Department of En-

ergy, Office of Energy Research, Carbon Dioxide Research Program, No. TR047, April 1990); CDIAC, Environmental Sciences Division, Oak Ridge National Laboratory, "1989 Estimates of CO_2 Emissions from Fossil Fuel Burning and Cement Manufacturing Based on the United Nations Energy Statistics and the U.S. Bureau of Mines Cement Manufacturing Data," ORNL/CDIAC-25, NDP-030 (an accessible numerical data base), (Oak Ridge, Tennessee, July 1991); American Gas Association (AGA), "Natural Gas and Climate Change: The Greenhouse Effect," Issue Brief 1989-7 (AGA, Washington, D.C., June 14, 1989); A.A. Makarov and I.A. Basmakov, *The Soviet Union: A Strategy of Energy Development with Minimum Emission of Greenhouse Gases* (Pacific Northwest Laboratory, Richland, Washington, U.S.A., 1990); and S. Hobart, David Spottiswoode, James Ball *et al., Methane Leakage from Natural Gas Operations* (The Alphatania Group, London, 1989).

CH_4 from wet rice agriculture: Food and Agriculture Organization of the United Nations (FAO), *Agrostat PC* (FAO, Rome, 1991); Elaine Mathews, Inez Fung, and Jean Lerner, "Methane Emission from Rice Cultivation: Geographic and Seasonal Distribution of Cultivated Areas and Emissions," *Global Biogeochemical Cycles,* Vol. 5, No. 1 (March 1991), pp. 3–24.

CH^4 from livestock: Jean Lerner, Elaine Mathews, and Inez Fung, "Methane Emissions from Animals: A Global High-Resolution Data Base," *Global Biogeochemical Cycles,* Vol. 2, No. 2 (June 1988), pp. 139–156; Food and Agriculture Organization of the United Nations (FAO), *Agrostat PC (FAO, Rome, 1991).*

Chlorofluorocarbon (CFC) emissions: WRI estimate based on information in the U.S. Environmental Protection Agency, Stratospheric Protection Program, Office of Program Development, Office of Air and Radiation, *Appendices to Regulatory Impact Analysis: Protection of Stratospheric Ozone* (Washington, D.C., August 1988), Vol. 2, Part 2, Appendix K, pp. K-2-4–K-2-6; Alliance for Responsible CFC Use, unpublished data (Alliance for Responsible CFC Use, Arlington, Virginia, 1989); United Nations Environment Programme (UNEP), *Environmental Data Report* (Basil Blackwell Ltd., Oxford, 1991), pp. 26-27; and UNEP, *Report of the Secretariat on the Reporting of Data by the Parties in Accordance with Article 7 of the Montreal Protocol,* 1991.

Carbon dioxide, CH_4, CFC-11, and CFC-12 are the four most important greenhouse gases. This table provides estimates of annual emissions of CO_2 from land use change (i.e., deforestation), methane emissions by source, and current annual emissions of CFC-11 and CFC-12 combined. Nitrous oxide, tropospheric ozone, and other chlorofluorocarbons are also important to the greenhouse effect but less well studied and more difficult to estimate, especially at the national level. Tropospheric ozone has an average lifetime measured in hours and is a product of particular chemical processes involving the precursors CH_4, carbon monoxide, nitrogen oxides, and non-methane hydrocarbons in the presence of sunlight. Nitrous oxide emissions by country have proven difficult to estimate, in part because significant emissions are poorly understood. Production estimates and emission parameters from chlorofluorocarbons other than CFC-11 and CFC-12 are not available.

The Organisation for Economic Co-operation and Development (OECD) hosted an experts meeting in February 1991 on greenhouse emissions (a final report was published in August 1991, *Estimation of Greenhouse Gas Emissions and Sinks* [OECD, Paris]) to discuss methodologies that countries could use to estimate their own inventories of greenhouse gases (other than CFCs) and to point to areas requiring further research. Although these discussions served to illuminate and define the methods used here, the final published recommendations were directed toward informing governments on what data they could collect and what kind of basic country-specific (and even ecosystem-specific) research is required if they are to "assess their contribution to greenhouse gas emissions in an international context." The final report of the OECD experts meeting included additional suggested data sets and methods not fully discussed or validated during the meeting (such as a suggested source of deforestation data).

The estimates of emissions in this table can be controversial but are believed to be accurate estimates of the relative magnitudes of emissions and are believed to be the best possible, given the available data sets. WRI would welcome independent estimates of anthropogenic emissions of greenhouse gases from the countries of the world. The methods used here were chosen to maximize the use of the available international data so as to be comparable among countries. The international data set on any subject is limited, and so these estimates are also limited. Until most of the countries of the world publish their own independent estimates—based on common methods and scientifically valid parameters—global comparisons will require the use of these methods of the least common data set. Common methods and parameters were used between countries unless differing, but explicit and published, parameters were available that covered all countries. For example, estimates of CH_4 from coal mining were based on published data on the differing CH_4 content of differing coals and their production in each country of the world. More complex calculations—that might have been possible for one or two data-rich countries—are inappropriate for the world as a whole and were not attempted even for those few countries that might have sufficient (and uncontroversial) data.

Carbon releases from *land-use change* are based originally on the work of R.A. Houghton, R.D. Boone, J.R. Fruci, *et al.* They estimated the world flux of carbon in 1980 from deforestation, reforestation, logging, and changes in agricultural area for most of the world's tropical countries. The burning of biomass, however, does not necessarily contribute to the CO_2 flux. Fire is a natural process, and as long as burning and growth are in balance, there is no net movement of carbon from biomass to the atmosphere.

The carbon densities used here are based on more recent work by Houghton (1991) and used different estimates of carbon densities (including carbon sequestered in soils). These CO_2 emissions estimates explicitly include shifting cultivation and the diversion of forest fallow to permanent clearing. They are also consistent, based on a sound methodology, and global in scope. New estimates of carbon densities by forest type are expected from Brazil in 1992. (See Chapter 19, "Forests and Rangelands.") They are the most complete estimates available but are subject to modification should better data become available. More recent estimates of deforested areas were used to update Houghton's 1987 study where appropriate. Please consult the sources for more detail.

Although, in principle, emissions from land-use change should include the emissions of other gases from the burning of forest land, as well as emissions from the burning of grassland, the conversion of grassland to cropland, the creation of wetlands, and the burning of crop and animal residues, the international data sets needed to estimate these emissions do not exist (OECD experts meeting). Except for CO_2 emissions from deforestation, then, emissions from biomass burning in general are not available. Grass or trees that grow back after fire merely recycle the carbon and do not contribute CO_2 to long term greenhouse heating.

WRI also subtracted the weight of carbon contained in sawlogs and veneer logs (Food and Agriculture Organization of the United Nations [FAO], *Agrostat PC*, [FAO, Rome, 1991]) produced in each tropical country from CO_2 releases calculated from land-use change. Carbon was estimated as making up 45 percent of the weight of these wood products. This step was taken to approximate the carbon sequestered from the global carbon cycle by the production of durable wooden goods in each country. This is only an estimate because portions of other forest products are also sequestered (e.g., books in libraries, pit props, utility poles); and portions of saw and veneer logs are consumed (e.g., wastewood, disposal of plywood sheets used in concrete form building). This should lead to a small underestimate of total CO_2 emissions because it includes logs from areas not counted as deforested. The OECD, in its report on the experts meeting, suggested using a data set on global deforestation (Norman Myers, *Deforestation Rates in Tropical Forests and Their Climatic Implications* [Friends of the Earth, London, 1989]) that is inadequate and so was not used in this table. The methods for estimating emissions from land-use change, suggested by the OECD experts meeting, requires data and research into processes that do not yet exist. The method used here parallels that of R.A. Houghton, which has received peer review.

Choices must be made regarding the exact parameters to use in these calculations, but the deforestation and carbon density measures used here are the best general set available. The parameters used for this calculation were based on consistent definitions and common data sources. Even if slightly lower values were used for deforestation and biomass per area, the magnitude of carbon emissions would remain about the same. These estimates then are a good first approximation to current (i.e., circa 1989) emissions that result from land-use changes. There is some suggestion that northern temperate and boreal forest areas are net sinks for atmospheric carbon, although this, too, is controversial.

CH_4 emissions from municipal *solid waste* were calculated by multiplying the 1989 population by per capita emission coefficients developed for each country by H.G. Bingemer and P.J. Crutzen, in "The Production of CH_4 from Solid Wastes," *Journal of Geophysical Research,* Vol. 92, No. D2 (1987), pp. 2181–2187. R.J. Cicerone and R.S. Oremland, "Biogeochemical Aspects of Atmospheric Methane," *Global Biogeochemical Cycles,* Vol. 2, No. 4, (December 1988), pp. 299–327, suggest a likely range for annual world emissions from landfills at 30 million to 70 million metric tons. The method used here parallels that recommended by the OECD experts meeting.

Methane from *coal mining* was estimated using information on the average methane content of anthracite and bituminous coals, subbituminous coals, and lignite mined (WEC) in each country of the world. This latter data set is updated only every three years, and so the most recent year for which the necessary data are available is 1987. Less detailed data sets are available but inadequate to the task. This estimate assumed that 100 percent of the CH_4 in extracted coal was emitted, although this is a slight exaggeration. CH_4 is emitted from mines in larger quantities than that contained only in the coal removed—although in the long run, the CH_4 in an extractable deposit of coal will be emitted, on average, at the rate that it is mined. CH_4 trapped within the rock is released by mining, and it is one of the hazards of underground coal mining. Cicerone and Oremland (*Aspects of Atmospheric Methane*) show a likely range of 25–45 million metric tons of CH_4 emitted annually in the course of mining coal. No international data set exists that would allow internationally comparable estimates using a methodology suggested by the OECD in its report on the experts meeting.

Substantial quantities of CH_4 are released to the atmosphere in the course of oil and gas production and distribution. CH_4 vented in the course of oil production is estimated at 25 percent of the amount that is flared (Gregg Marland, Carbon Dioxide Information and Analysis Center [CDIAC], Oakridge, Tennessee [personal communication], 1990). Estimates of CO_2 from gas flaring in Table 24.1 also include gas that is vented (see also Barns and Edmonds, p. 3.9). CH_4 emissions from natural gas production were estimated at 0.5 percent of production (Barns and Edmonds, pp. 3.2–3.3). Recent estimates are that CH₄ leakage from distribution systems is no more than 1 percent in the United States (American Gas Association, "Natural Gas and Climate Change: The Greenhouse Effect") and no more than 1.7 percent in the Soviet Union (Makarov and Basmakov, *The Soviet Union: A Strategy of Energy Development with Minimum Emission of Greenhouse Gases*), although careful surveys have not been done. There is reason to believe that pipeline leaks in the U.S.S.R. are grossly understated—although U.S.S.R. natural gas volume is sometimes mistakenly overstated—but other estimates are non-existent. For these estimates, the U.S. experience was extended to Western Europe, Canada was counted at half the United States rate, and the Soviet estimate was used for Central Europe and the developing world because their situations were thought to be similar (S. Hobart *et al., Methane Leakage from Natural Gas Operations*). Cicerone and Oremland (*Aspects of Atmospheric Methane*) suggest a likely range of 25 million to 50 million metric tons of CH₄ emitted because of leaks associated with natural gas drilling, venting, and transmission. The OECD experts meeting developed a general conceptual model on how to go about estimating emissions from these production and distribution systems, but it was unable to identify data on the factors leading to emissions or any individual data source for this purpose.

CH₄ from the practice of *wet rice agriculture* was calculated from the area of rice production (as reported by the FAO, *Agrostat PC*, FAO, Rome, 1991) subtracting those areas devoted to dry (upland) and deepwater (floating) rice production in each country or, in the case of China and India, in each province (Dana G. Dalrymple, *Development and Spread of High-Yielding Rice Varieties in Developing Countries*, Bureau of Science and Technology, U.S. Agency for International Development, Washington, D.C., 1986; and Robert E. Huke, *Rice Area by Type of Culture: South, Southeast, and East Asia*, International Rice Research Institute, Los Baños, Laguna, Philippines, 1982). This estimate follows the method suggested in the OECD report of its experts meeting and calculates the number of days of rice cultivation and the percentage of total rice area in each crop cycle by country or, in the case of China and India, by province (Elaine Mathews, Inez Fung, and Jean Lerner, "Methane Emissions from Rice Cultivation: Geographic and Seasonal Distribution of Cultivated Areas and Emissions," *Global Biogeochemical Cycles*, Vol. 5, pp. 3–24).

There are many different studies of CH₄ emissions from wet rice agriculture. In the past, many of these studies had been criticized because they had been undertaken on temperate rices grown in North America or Europe. Recently published studies, based on similar rigorous methods, from subtropical China have dispelled some of that criticism. Studies using similar methodologies are expected soon from Indonesia and India. The OECD report of its experts meet-

ing recommended using a range of emissions found in a study in China (0.19–0.69 grams of CH₄ per square meter per day, H. Schütz, W. Seiler, and H. Rennenberg, presentation by Rennenberg at the International Conference on Soils and the Greenhouse Effect, August 14–18, 1989, Wageningen, the Netherlands, reported by the OECD experts meeting). The estimate here used the midpoint of that range (0.44 grams of CH₄ per square meter per day), assuming that this range is an unbiased estimate of the normally distributed range of emissions of methane. Alternate estimates are possible.

A two-year study in the subtropical rice bowl of China (Szechuan province) produced an estimated median flux (from some 3,000 flux estimates) of about 1.2 grams of CH₄ per square meter per day and a mean flux of 1.39 grams of CH₄ per square meter per day (M.A.K. Khalil, R.A. Rasmussen, Ming-Xing Wang, and Lixin Ren, "Methane Emissions from Rice Fields in China," *Environmental Science and Technology*, Vol. 25, No. 5, pp. 979–981). Studies in Europe and North America seem to support the range suggested by the OECD experts meeting. See the sources for more information. In general, estimates of CH₄ flux are based on a technique that captures CH₄ produced anaerobically before the growth of the rice plant as well as capturing the bulk of CH₄ production that is transported through the rice plant throughout the growing period. Growing periods, rice cultivar, fertilizers, temperature, and possibly pesticides, could influence methanogenesis. In the tropics, with modern varieties, sufficient fertilizer, and adequate water, two or even three rice crops per year are possible.

The cultivation of rice uses common techniques in both temperate and tropical climes—even if the cultivars are not so well adapted. The preparation of the impoundments wherein wet rice is grown—the creation of a hardpan overlain by soft anaerobic muck—creates similar environmental and chemical regimes wherever it occurs. Nonetheless, variations in water quality, soils, ambient temperature, precision of water control, and presence of cultivated algae or fish could also affect the total flux of methane.

Wet rice agriculture is practiced under four main water regimes: irrigated (52.8 percent of the world's total rice area), rainfed (similar to irrigated, 22.6 percent of the total), deep water (often dry in the early part of the season, may be planted to floating rice, 8.2 percent of the world's rice area), and tidal (3.4 percent of the area). Cicerone and Oremland (*Aspects of Atmospheric Methane*) suggest a likely range of 60 million to 170 million metric tons for CH₄ emissions associated with wet rice agriculture.

CH₄ emissions from domestic *livestock* were calculated using FAO statistics on animal populations and published estimates of methane emissions from each animal. The animals studied included cattle and dairy cows, water buffalo, sheep, goats, camels, pigs, horses, and caribou. P.J. Crutzen, I. Aselmann, and W. Seiler ("Methane Produc-

tion by Domestic Animals, Wild Ruminants, Other Herbivorous Fauna, and Humans," *Tellus*, Vol. 38B [1986], pp. 271–284) estimated animal methane production on the basis of energy intake under several different management methods for several different feeding regimes. These differing emission coefficients were then assigned to each country, based on the specifics of that country's animal husbandry practices and the nature and quality of feed available. Cicerone and Oremland's *Aspects of Atmospheric Methane* shows a likely range of 65 million to 100 million metric tons of emissions from enteric fermentation in domestic animals. Alternate methods of estimation, such as a complex modeling method suggested in the OECD report, are not yet possible because of the lack of basic data.

The only other major anthropogenic sources of CH₄, unaccounted for here, are the emissions consequent to the burning of biomass. Extensive biomass burning, especially in the tropics, is believed to release large amounts of CH₄. Cicerone and Oremland (*Aspects of Atmospheric Methane*) put the likely range of those emissions at 50 million to 100 million metric tons. The OECD experts meeting elaborated on the data that would be necessary if countries were to estimate CH₄ emissions from biomass burning.

Other natural sources of CH₄ include wetlands, methane hydrate destabilization in permafrost, termites, freshwater lakes, oceans, and enteric emissions from other animals. Natural sources account for an estimated 25 percent of all CH₄ emissions. Cicerone and Oremland (*Aspects of Atmospheric Methane*) estimate likely ranges of CH₄ emissions at 100 million to 200 million metric tons from natural wetlands, 10 million to 100 million metric tons from termites, 5 million to 25 million metric tons from the oceans, 1 million to 25 million metric tons from freshwater, and possible current releases of 5 million metric tons (potentially rising to 100 million metric tons if temperatures increase in the high arctic) from methane hydrate destabilization.

WRI has estimated total *chlorofluorocarbon* use (CFC-11 and CFC-12) for many countries. It used data on 1986 per capita production/use from 47 countries and the European Community (EC) to peg consumption in other similar countries, and updated these estimates using consumption data for 15 countries plus the EC in 1989. This estimate was based in part on the general level of total CFC (including CFC-113 and CFC-22) consumption (i.e., less than 0.3 kg, 0.3–0.5 kg, and over 0.5 kg, from the Alliance for Responsible CFC Use) and other relevant information. These data are, therefore, a mix of reported and estimated numbers. Consumption data for the EC, as reported by the EC and UNEP, were allocated to each member country in proportion to its share of the total EC population. Thus, all EC members are tied and among the highest per capita consumers of CFCs. (The EC could have reported consumption by country but chose not to.)

Table 24.3 Atmospheric Concentrations of Greenhouse and Ozone-Depleting Gases, 1959–90

Sources: Carbon dioxide: Charles D. Keeling, R.B. Bacastow, A.F. Carter, *et al.*, "A Three-Dimensional Model of Atmospheric CO_2 Transport Based on Observed Winds: 1. Observational Data and Preliminary Analysis," *Aspects of Climate Variability in the Pacific and the Western Americas,* American Geophysical Union (AGU) Monograph No. 55 (AGU, Washington, D.C., 1989), pp. 165–236; and Charles D. Keeling, personal communication (Scripps Institution of Oceanography, La Jolla, California, 1991). Other gases: R.A. Rasmussen and M.A.K. Khalil, "Atmospheric Trace Gases: Trends and Distributions Over the Last Decade," *Science,* Vol. 232, pp. 1623–1624. Concentrations after 1985 of CCl_4, CH_3CCl_3, CCl_3F (CFC-11), CCl_2F_2 (CFC-12), and N_2O: M.A.K. Khalil and R.A. Rasmussen, unpublished data (Oregon Graduate Center, Beaverton, September 1989). $C_2Cl_3F_3$ (CFC-113):M.A.K. Khalil and R.A. Rasmussen, unpublished data (Oregon Graduate Center, Beaverton, September 1989). CH_4 data, 1979–88: M.A.K. Khalil, R.A. Rasmussen, "Atmospheric Methane: Recent Global Trends," in preparation (1989). CH_4 data, 1962–78: M.A.K. Khalil, R.A. Rasmussen, and M.J. Shearer, "Trends of Atmospheric Methane During the 1960's and 70's," *Journal of Geophysical Research,* Vol. 94, No. D15 (December 1989), pp. 18,279–18,288. Recent data 1986–90: M.A.K. Khalil, personal communication, 1991.

The trace gases listed here affect atmospheric ozone or contribute to the greenhouse effect or both.

Carbon dioxide (CO_2) accounts for about half the increase in the greenhouse effect and is emitted to the atmosphere by natural and anthropogenic processes. See the Technical Notes for Tables 24.1 and 24.2 for further details.

Atmospheric CO_2 concentrations are monitored at many sites worldwide; the data presented here are from Mauna Loa, Hawaii (19.53° North latitude, 155.58° West longitude). Trends at Mauna Loa reflect global trends, although CO_2 concentrations differ significantly among monitoring sites at any given time. For example, the average annual concentration at the South Pole in 1988, for example, was 2.4 parts per million (ppm) lower than at Mauna Loa.

Annual means disguise large daily and seasonal variations in CO_2 concentrations. The seasonal variation is caused by photosynthetic plants storing larger amounts of carbon from CO_2 during the summer than in the winter. Some annual mean figures were derived from interpolated data.

Data are revised to correct for drift in instrument calibration, hardware changes, and perturbations to "background" conditions. Details concerning data collection, revisions, and analysis are contained in C.D. Keeling, *et al.*, "Measurement of the Concentration of Carbon Dioxide at Mauna Loa Observatory, Hawaii," *Carbon Dioxide Re-*

view: 1982, W.C. Clark, ed. (Oxford University Press, New York, 1982).

Calibration is necessary for all instruments used to measure trace gases. Although collected at the same site by the same investigators, trace gas concentrations before 1986 have not been recalibrated as have measurements from 1986 to 1990, which themselves should be considered preliminary. *Carbon tetrachloride (CCl_4)* is an intermediate product in the production of CFC-11 and CFC-12. It is also used in other chemical and pharmaceutical applications and for grain fumigation. Compared with other gases, CCl_4 makes a small contribution to the greenhouse effect and to stratospheric ozone depletion.

Methyl chloroform (CH_3CCl_3) is used primarily as an industrial degreasing agent and as a solvent for paints and adhesives. Its contribution to the greenhouse effect and to stratospheric ozone depletion is also small.

CFC-11 (CCl_3F), *CFC-12 (CCl_2F_2)*, *CFC-22 ($CHClF_2$)* and *CFC-113 ($C_2Cl_3F_3$)* are potent depletors of stratospheric ozone. Together, their cumulative effect may equal one fourth of the greenhouse contribution of CO_2.

Total gaseous chlorine is calculated by multiplying the number of chlorine atoms in each of the chlorine-containing gases (carbon tetrachloride, methyl chloroform, and the CFCs) by the concentration of that gas.

Nitrous oxide (N_2O) is emitted by aerobic decomposition of organic matter in oceans and soils, by bacteria, by combustion of fossil fuels and biomass (fuelwood and cleared forests), by the use of nitrogen fertilizers, and through other processes. N_2O is an important depletor of stratospheric ozone; present levels may contribute one twelfth the amount contributed by CO_2 toward the greenhouse effect.

Methane (CH_4) is emitted through the release of natural gas and as one of the products of anaerobic respiration. Sources of anaerobic respiration include the soils of moist forests, wetlands, bogs, tundra, and lakes. Emission sources associated with human activities include livestock management (enteric fermentation in ruminants), anaerobic respiration in the soils associated with wet rice agriculture, and combustion of fossil fuels and biomass (fuelwood and cleared forests). CH_4 acts to increase ozone in the troposphere and lower stratosphere; its cumulative greenhouse effect is currently thought to be one third that of CO_2, but on a molecule-for-molecule basis, its effect, ignoring any feedback or involvement in any atmospheric processes, is 20–30 times that of CO_2.

Carbon monoxide (CO) is emitted by motor traffic, other fossil fuel combustion, slash-and-burn agriculture, and chemical processes in the atmosphere such as the oxidation of CH_4. Increasing levels of CO can lead to an increase in tropospheric ozone and a buildup of other trace gases, particularly CH_4, in the atmosphere.

Data for all gases except CO_2 and CO are from values monitored at Cape Meares, Oregon (45° North latitude, 124° West longitude). Although gas concentrations at any

given time vary among monitoring sites, the data reported here reflect global trends. Data for CO were taken from several sites and averaged to reflect global concentrations and trends.

Table 24.4 World CO_2 Emissions from Fossil Fuel Consumption and Cement Manufacture, 1950–89

Source: Carbon Dioxide Information Analysis Center (CDIAC), Environmental Sciences Division, Oak Ridge National Laboratory, Oak Ridge, Tennessee, unpublished data, July 1991.

CDIAC calculates world emissions from data on the global production of fossil fuels (based on the World Energy Data Set maintained by the United Nations Statistical Office), and from data on world cement manufacturing (based on the Cement Manufacturing Data Set maintained by the U.S. Bureau of Mines). Emissions are calculated using global average fuel chemistry and usage. These data account for all fuels including "bunker fuels" not accounted for in Table 24.1. For further information, see the Technical Notes for Table 24.1.

Table 24.5 Sulfur and Nitrogen Emissions, 1970–89

Source: J.M Pacyna and K.E. Joerss, *Co-operative Programme for Monitoring and Evaluation of the Long Range Transmission of Air Pollutants in Europe (EMEP), Proceedings of the Workshop on International Emission Inventories, Regensburg, Federal Republic of Germany, July 3–6, 1990,* EMEP/CCC-Report 7/90 (Norsk Institutt for Lurtforskning, Lillestrom, Norway, 1991), pp. 67–68; and Organisation for Economic Co-operation and Development (OECD), *OECD Environmental Data Compendium 1991* (OECD, Paris, 1991), pp. 17–18.

Emissions of *sulfur* in the form of sulfur oxides and *nitrogen* in the form of its various oxides together contribute to acid rain and adversely affect agriculture, forests, aquatic habitat, and the weathering of building materials. Sulfate and nitrate aerosols impair visibility. These data on anthropogenic sources should be used carefully. Because different methods and procedures may have been used in each country, the best comparative data may be time trends within a country.

Sulfur dioxide (SO_2) is created by natural as well as anthropogenic activities. High concentrations of SO_2 have important health effects, and there is particular concern for the health of young children, the elderly, and people with existing respiratory illness (e.g., asthma). SO_2 in the presence of moisture contributes to acid precipitation as sulfuric acid.

Anthropogenic sources of nitrogen oxides come mainly from industrial sources and contribute to photochemical smog and the production of tropospheric ozone—an important greenhouse gas. All oxides of nitrogen also contribute to acid precipitation, in the form of nitric acid.

This table combines data from both EMEP and the OECD. EMEP is an activity of the 1979 Convention on Long-Range Transboundary Air Pollution. Data on sulfur and nitrogen emissions are submitted to EMEP by parties to the 1985 Protocol on SO_2 emissions and the 1988 Protocol on emissions of nitrogen oxides. Parties to these protocols should submit preliminary estimates of sulfur and nitrogen emissions by May of the year following and final estimates within a year after that. In the event of missing official data, EMEP interpolates between years of official data. In the event that this is not possible, EMEP will use its own—or others'—estimates of emissions.

OECD polls its members on emissions with questionnaires that are completed by the relevant national statistical service or designee. OECD does not have any independent estimation capability.

EMEP reports emissions in terms of the elemental content of sulfur, whereas OECD reports its emissions in terms of tons of oxides of sulfur. EMEP emission estimates were converted to their weight in SO_2. EMEP and OECD report nitrogen emissions in terms of nitrogen dioxide.

Please consult the sources for further information.

Table 24.6 Common Anthropogenic Pollutants, 1980—89

Source: J.M Pacyna and K.E. Joerss, *Co-operative Programme for Monitoring and Evaluation of the Long Range Transmission of Air Pollutants in Europe (EMEP)*, *Proceedings of the Workshop on International Emission Inventories, Regensburg, Federal Republic of Germany, July 3–6, 1990*, EMEP/CCC-Report 7/90 (Norsk Institutt for Lurtforskning, Lillestrom, Norway, 1991), p. 69; and Organisation for Economic Co-operation and Development (OECD), *OECD Environmental Data Compendium 1991* (OECD, Paris, 1991), pp. 21–26.

This table reports OECD data for carbon monoxide and particulate matter emissions and combines both EMEP and OECD data to describe the emissions of hydrocarbons. See the sources and the notes to Table 24.5 for additional information. Differences in definition can limit the comparability of these estimates.

Carbon monoxide (CO), is formed both naturally and from industrial processes, including the incomplete combustion of fossil and other carbon-bearing fuels. Emissions from automobiles are the most important source, especially in urban environments. CO interferes with oxygen uptake in the blood, pro-ducing chronic anoxia leading to illness or, in the case of massive and acute poisoning, even death. CO scavenges hydroxyl radicals that would otherwise contribute to the removal of methane—a potent greenhouse gas—from the atmosphere.

The health effects of *particulate matter* (PM) are in part dependent on the biological and chemical makeup and activity of the particles. Heavy metal particles or hydrocarbons condensed onto dust particles can be especially toxic. PM arises from numerous anthropogenic and natural sources. Among the anthropogenic sources are combustion, industrial and agricultural practices, and the formation of sulfates from sulfur dioxide emissions.

In the presence of sunlight, *hydrocarbons* are, along with oxides of nitrogen, responsible for photochemical smog. Anthropogenic emissions of hydrocarbons arise in part from the incomplete combustion of fuels or the evaporation of fuels, lubricants, and solvents as well as the incomplete burning of biomass. These data combine hydrocarbon emission data from OECD with volatile organic compound data from EMEP. EMEP uses OECD hydrocarbon data as volatile organic compound data for selected countries.

25. Policies and Institutions

Two indicators of a country's commitment to environmental protection are its effective participation in relevant international agreements and its collection and dissemination of environmental information. International cooperation on the environment continues to grow and will be a focus of discussion at the United Nations Conference on Environment and Development (UNCED) in June 1992. International conventions on global climate change, biological diversity, and forestry, if signed and ratified, would add to the inventory of agreements to safeguard the global environment.

Tables 25.1 and 25.2 present information on current country participation in critical international conventions and regional agreements protecting the environment. In Africa, for example, realization of the dangers of uncontrolled toxic wastes has led to a convention on hazardous waste movement and management that was signed in 1991 in Bamako, Mali by 17 countries and is in the ratification process. In Europe and North America, the Convention on Environmental Impact Assessment in a Transboundary Context, which would help prevent, mitigate, and monitor significant transboundary environmental impacts, was signed in 1991 in Helsinki by 26 countries and two republics of the U.S.S.R. In response to increasing levels of air pollutants from industrial sources, 27 industrialized nations (26 listed here, plus Liechtenstein) and two republics of the U.S.S.R. have ratified the 1979 Geneva Convention on Long-Range Transboundary Air Pollution. In response to the Chernobyl nuclear accident in April 1986, two conventions were created on nuclear accident notification and assistance.

The most recent global environmental convention, the Basel Convention on the Control of Transboundary Movements of Hazardous Wastes and Their Disposal, March 1989, was not yet in force in late 1991. At that time, 13 countries had ratified the convention and another 41 countries had signed it (including Liechtenstein, which is not listed in Table 25.2).

An amendment has been made in 1990 to the Protocol on Substances That Deplete the Ozone Layer to gradually reduce and finally phase out fully halogenated chlorofluorocarbons, carbon tetrachloride, and methyl chloroform between 1990 and 2005. As of late 1991, this amendment had not yet been ratified by enough countries to enter into force.

Countries continue to sign and ratify older conventions such as the Antarctic Treaty of 1959. The Protocol on Environmental Protection to the Antarctic Treaty was signed by the contracting parties to the Antarctic Treaty on October 4, 1991, in Madrid. This protocol designates Antarctica as a natural reserve and prohibits mineral mining for the next 50 years.

Table 25.3 lists sources of national environmental and natural resource information. These sources provide comprehensive assessments of natural resource and environmental conditions and often document trends and suggest policies for resource management. These assessments are becoming more comprehensive and analytical as complex environmental issues become better understood.

An increasing number of countries are preparing country and regional natural resource and environmental assessments, strategies, action plans, and compendia of environmental statistics. In addition, in preparation for UNCED, country reports are being produced by UN member states to reflect national experiences and perspectives on environment and development. Much environmental information is requested or instigated by foreign aid donors, development planners, resource policymakers, and finance ministers. This information is often an adjunct to action plans (e.g., the Tropical Forestry Action Plan, the National Conservation Strategy) or describes a sector or special issue (Biological Diversity Profile).

The World Bank has increased its support of national environmental assessments and action plans for developing nations (particularly in Africa) that are produced by, or in cooperation with, governments. However, more resources are needed to help countries develop their own capacity for monitoring and assessing environmental problems.

Table 25.4 lists sources of global and regional environmental information. The OECD state of the environment report and the Asian and Pacific state of the environment report are examples of the increasing number of regional environmental assessments. Large gaps remain in environmental information on the Soviet Union, the newly independent Baltic republics, and Central Europe.

Table 25.1 Participation in Major Global Conventions—

| | Antarctic Treaty and Convention 1959 & 1980 | Wildlife and Habitat | | | | Oceans | | |
		Wetlands (Ramsar) 1971	World Heritage 1972	Endangered Species (CITES) 1973	Migratory Species 1979	Ocean Dumping 1972	Ship Pollution (MARPOL) 1978	Law of the Sea {a} 1982
WORLD								
AFRICA								
Algeria		CP	CP	CP			CP	S
Angola								CP
Benin			CP	CP	CP			S
Botswana				CP				CP
Burkina Faso		CP	CP	CP	CP			S
Burundi			CP	CP				S
Cameroon			CP	CP	CP			CP
Cape Verde			CP			CP		CP
Central African Rep			CP	CP	S			S
Chad		CP		CP	S	S		S
Comoros								S
Congo			CP	CP				S
Cote d'Ivoire			CP		S	CP	CP	CP
Djibouti							CP	S
Egypt		CP	CP	CP	CP		CP	CP
Equatorial Guinea								S
Ethiopia			CP	CP				S
Gabon		CP	CP	CP		CP	CP	S
Gambia, The			CP	CP				CP
Ghana		CP	CP	CP	CP			CP
Guinea			CP	CP				CP
Guinea-Bissau				CP				CP
Kenya		CP		CP		CP		CP
Lesotho		CP		S		S		S
Liberia				CP		S	CP	S
Libya			CP			CP		S
Madagascar			CP	CP	S			S
Malawi			CP	CP				S
Mali		CP	CP		CP			CP
Mauritania		CP	CP					S
Mauritius				CP				S
Morocco		CP	CP	CP	S	CP		S
Mozambique			CP	CP				S
Namibia				CP				CP
Niger		CP	CP	CP	CP			S
Nigeria			CP	CP	CP	CP		CP
Rwanda			CP	CP				S
Senegal		CP	CP	CP	CP	S		CP
Sierra Leone								S
Somalia				CP	CP	S		CP
South Africa	CP, MLR	CP		CP		CP	CP	S
Sudan			CP	CP				CP
Swaziland								S
Tanzania			CP	CP				CP
Togo				CP	S	S	CP	CP
Tunisia		CP	CP	CP	CP	CP	CP	CP
Uganda		CP	CP	CP	S			CP
Zaire			CP	CP	CP	CP		CP
Zambia			CP	CP				CP
Zimbabwe			CP	CP				S
NORTH & CENTRAL AMERICA								
Barbados								S
Belize			CP	CP				CP
Canada	NCP, MLR	CP	CP	CP		CP		S
Costa Rica			CP	CP		CP		S
Cuba	NCP		CP	CP		CP		CP
Dominican Rep			CP	CP		CP		S
El Salvador				CP				S
Guatemala		CP	CP	CP		CP		S
Haiti			CP			CP		S
Honduras			CP	CP		CP		S
Jamaica			CP		S			CP
Mexico		CP	CP	CP		CP	S	CP
Nicaragua			CP	CP				S
Panama		CP	CP	CP	CP	CP	CP	S
Trinidad and Tobago				CP				CP
United States	CP, MLR	CP	CP	CP		CP	CP	
SOUTH AMERICA								
Argentina	CP, MLR		CP	CP		CP		S
Bolivia		CP	CP	CP	S			S
Brazil	CP, MLR		CP	CP		CP	CP	CP
Chile	CP, MLR	CP	CP	CP	CP	CP		S
Colombia	NCP		CP	CP		S	CP	S
Ecuador	CP	CP	CP	CP			CP	
Guyana			CP	CP				
Paraguay			CP	CP				S
Peru	CP, MLR		CP	CP			CP	CP
Suriname	CP {b}	CP		CP	CP	CP	CP	S
Uruguay	CP, MLR	CP	CP	CP	CP	S	CP	S
Venezuela		CP	CP	CP		S		

Wildlife and Habitat, Oceans, 1991

Table 25.1

	Wildlife & Habitat					Oceans		
	Antarctic Treaty and Convention 1959 & 1980	Wetlands (Ramsar) 1971	World Heritage 1972	Endangered Species (CITES) 1973	Migratory Species 1979	Ocean Dumping 1972	Ship Pollution (MARPOL) 1978	Law of the Sea {a} 1982
ASIA								
Afghanistan			CP	CP		CP		S
Bahrain								CP
Bangladesh			CP	CP				S
Bhutan								S
Cambodia				S		S		S
China	CP		CP	CP		CP	CP	S
Cyprus			CP	CP		CP	CP	CP
India	CP, MLR	CP	CP	CP	CP		CP	S
Indonesia			CP	CP			CP	CP
Iran, Islamic Rep		CP	CP	CP				S
Iraq			CP					CP
Israel				CP	CP		CP	
Japan	CP, MLR	CP		CP		CP	CP	S
Jordan		CP	CP	CP		CP		
Korea, Dem People's Rep	NCP						CP	S
Korea, Rep	CP, MLR		CP				CP	S
Kuwait				S		S		CP
Lao People's Dem Rep			CP					S
Lebanon			CP			S	CP	S
Malaysia			CP	CP				S
Mongolia			CP					S
Myanmar							CP	S
Nepal		CP	CP	CP		S		S
Oman			CP			CP	CP	CP
Pakistan		CP	CP	CP	CP			S
Philippines			CP	CP	S	CP		CP
Qatar			CP					S
Saudi Arabia			CP		CP			S
Singapore				CP			CP	S
Sri Lanka		CP	CP	CP	CP			S
Syrian Arab Rep			CP				CP	
Thailand			CP	CP				S
Turkey			CP				CP	
United Arab Emirates				CP		CP		S
Viet Nam		CP	CP	S				S
Yemen (Arab Rep)			CP					S
(People's Dem Rep)			CP					CP
EUROPE								
Albania			CP					
Austria	NCP	CP		CP			CP	S
Belgium	CP, MLR	CP		CP	CP	CP	CP	S
Bulgaria	NCP	CP	CP	CP			CP	S
Czechoslovakia	NCP	CP	CP				CP	S
Denmark	NCP	CP	CP	CP	CP	CP	CP	S
Finland	CP, MLR	CP	CP	CP	CP	CP	CP	S
France	CP, MLR	CP	CP	CP	CP	CP	CP	S
Germany	CP, MLR	CP	CP	CP	CP	CP	CP	
Greece	NCP, MLR	CP	CP		S	CP	CP	S
Hungary	NCP	CP	CP	CP	CP	CP	CP	S
Iceland		CP				CP	CP	CP
Ireland		CP		S	CP	CP		S
Italy	CP, MLR	CP	CP	CP	CP	CP	CP	S
Luxembourg			CP	CP	CP	S		S
Malta		CP	CP	CP		CP		S
Netherlands	CP, MLR	CP	CP	CP	CP	CP	CP	S
Norway	CP, MLR	CP	CP	CP	CP	CP	CP	S
Poland	CP, MLR	CP	CP	CP		CP	CP	S
Portugal		CP	CP	CP	CP	CP	CP	S
Romania	NCP		CP					S
Spain	CP, MLR	CP	CP	CP	CP	CP	CP	S
Sweden	CP, MLR	CP	CP	CP	CP	CP	CP	S
Switzerland	NCP	CP	CP	CP		CP	CP	S
United Kingdom	CP, MLR	CP	CP	CP	CP	CP	CP	
Yugoslavia		CP	CP			CP	CP	CP
U.S.S.R.	CP, MLR	CP	CP	CP		CP	CP	S
OCEANIA								
Australia	CP, MLR	CP	CP	CP		CP	CP	S
Fiji			CP					CP
New Zealand	CP, MLR	CP	CP	CP		CP		S
Papua New Guinea	NCP			CP		CP		S
Solomon Islands						CP		S

Sources: Environmental Law Information System of the IUCN Environmental Law Centre and United Nations Environment Programme.
Notes: a. Convention not yet in force.
b. Extended through the Netherlands.
CP = contracting party (has ratified or taken equivalent action); S = signatory (has signed but not ratified); MLR = contracting party to the Convention on the Conservation of Antarctic Marine Living Resources; NCP = nonconsultative contracting party to the Antarctic Treaty.
Some small countries--signatories or contracting parties to the conventions and protocols listed--are not included in this table.
For formal titles of the conventions and protocols listed, and for additional information, see Sources and Technical Notes.

Table 25.2 Participation in Major Global Conventions—

	Global Conventions							Regional Agreements {b}	
	Atmosphere			Hazardous Substances					
	Nuclear Test Ban	Ozone Layer	CFC Control	Biological and Toxin Weapons	Nuclear Accident Notification	Nuclear Accident Assistance	Hazardous Waste Movement {a}	UNEP Regional Seas	Other Regional Agreements
	1963	1985	1987	1972	1986	1986	1989		
WORLD									
AFRICA									
Algeria	S			S	S			M+	AFC
Angola									
Benin	CP			CP				WCA*	AFC*, HW*
Botswana	CP			S					AFC*
Burkina Faso	S	CP	CP						AFC, EC, HW*
Burundi	S			S					AFC*, HW*
Cameroon	S	CP	CP		S	S		WCA	AFC, HW*
Cape Verde	CP			CP					
Central African Rep	CP			S					AFC, HW*
Chad	CP	CP							AFC*
Comoros									AFC*
Congo			S	CP				WCA	AFC
Cote d'Ivoire	CP			S	S	S		WCA	AFC, HW*
Djibouti									AFC
Egypt	CP	CP	CP	S	CP	CP		M+, RS	AFC, HW*
Equatorial Guinea	CP	CP							
Ethiopia	S			CP					AFC*
Gabon	CP			S				WCA	AFC*
Gambia, The	CP	CP	CP	S				WCA	AFC*
Ghana	CP	CP	CP	CP				WCA	AFC
Guinea								WCA	AFC*, HW*
Guinea-Bissau	CP			CP					HW*
Kenya	CP	CP	CP	CP				EA+	AFC
Lesotho				CP					AFC*, HW*
Liberia	CP							WCA*	AFC
Libya	CP	CP	CP	CP		CP		M+	AFC*, HW*
Madagascar	CP			S				EA*	AFC
Malawi	CP			S					AFC
Mali	S			S	S	S			AFC, HW*
Mauritania	CP							WCA*	AFC*
Mauritius	CP			CP					AFC*
Morocco	CP		S	S	S	S		M+	AFC
Mozambique									AFC
Namibia									
Niger	CP			CP	S	S			AFC, HW*
Nigeria	CP	CP	CP	CP	CP	CP	CP	WCA	AFC
Rwanda	CP			CP					AFC
Senegal	CP		S	CP	S	S		WCA	AFC, EC, HW*
Sierra Leone	CP			CP	S	S			AFC*
Somalia	S			S				EA*, RS	AFC*, HW*
South Africa	CP	CP	CP	CP	CP	CP			
Sudan	CP			S	S			RS	AFC
Swaziland	CP								AFC
Tanzania	CP			S					AFC
Togo	CP		S	CP				WCA	AFC, HW*
Tunisia	CP	CP	CP	CP	CP	CP		M+	AFC
Uganda	CP	CP	CP						AFC, HW*
Zaire	CP			CP	S	S			AFC
Zambia	CP	CP	CP						AFC
Zimbabwe				CP	S	S			AFC
NORTH & CENTRAL AMERICA									
Barbados				CP				C	
Belize				CP					
Canada	CP	CP	CP	CP	CP	S	S		LR+, EIA*
Costa Rica	CP			CP	S	S			
Cuba				CP	S	S		C	
Dominican Rep	CP			CP					
El Salvador	CP			S			S		
Guatemala	CP	CP	CP	CP	CP	CP	S	C	
Haiti	S			S			S		
Honduras	CP			CP				C*	
Jamaica	S			CP				C	
Mexico	CP	CP	CP	CP	CP	CP	CP	C	
Nicaragua	CP			CP				C*	
Panama	CP	CP	CP	CP	S	S	CP	SEP+, C	
Trinidad and Tobago	CP	CP	CP					C	
United States	CP	CP	CP	CP	CP	CP	S	C, SP*	LR+, EIA*
SOUTH AMERICA									
Argentina	CP	CP	CP	CP	CP	CP	CP		
Bolivia	CP			CP			S		AMC
Brazil	CP	CP	CP	CP	S	S		SEP+	AMC
Chile	CP	CP	CP	CP	S	S	S	SEP+, C	
Colombia	CP	CP					S		AMC
Ecuador	CP	CP	CP	CP			S	SEP+	AMC
Guyana				S					AMC
Paraguay	S			CP	S	S			
Peru	CP	CP		CP				SEP+	AMC
Suriname									AMC
Uruguay	CP	CP		CP	CP	CP	S		
Venezuela	CP	CP	CP	CP			S	C	AMC

Atmosphere, Hazardous Substances, 1991 — Table 25.2

	Global Conventions							Regional Agreements {b}	
	Atmosphere			Hazardous Substances					
	Nuclear Test Ban	Ozone Layer	CFC Control	Biological and Toxin Weapons	Nuclear Accident Notification	Nuclear Accident Assistance	Hazardous Waste Movement {a}	UNEP Regional Seas	Other Regional Agreements
	1963	1985	1987	1972	1986	1986	1989		
ASIA									
Afghanistan	CP			CP	S	S	S		
Bahrain		CP	CP	CP			S	K+	
Bangladesh	CP	CP	CP	CP	CP	CP			
Bhutan	CP			CP					
Cambodia				CP					
China	CP	CP		CP	CP	CP	S	M+	EC
Cyprus	CP			CP	CP	CP	S		
India	CP		S	CP	CP	CP	S		ASC
Indonesia	CP		CP	S	S	S			
Iran, Islamic Rep	CP	CP		CP	S	S		K+	
Iraq	CP			S	CP	CP		K+	
Israel	CP		S	CP	CP	CP	S	M+	
Japan	CP	CP	CP	CP	CP	CP			
Jordan	CP	CP	CP	CP	CP	CP	CP	RS	
Korea, Dem People's Rep				CP	S	S			
Korea, Rep	CP			CP	CP	CP			
Kuwait	CP			CP			S	K+	
Lao People's Dem Rep	CP			CP					
Lebanon	CP			CP	S	S	S	M+	
Malaysia	CP	CP	CP	S	CP	CP			ASC
Mongolia	CP			CP	CP	CP			
Myanmar	CP			S					
Nepal	CP			S					
Oman								K+	
Pakistan	CP			CP		CP			
Philippines	CP		S	CP			S		ASC
Qatar				CP				K+	
Saudi Arabia				CP	CP	CP	CP	K+,RS	
Singapore	CP	CP	CP	CP					ASC
Sri Lanka	CP	CP	CP	CP					
Syrian Arab Rep	CP	CP	CP	S	S	S	S	M+	
Thailand	CP	CP	CP	CP	CP	CP	S		ASC
Turkey	CP			CP	S	S	S	M+	EC, LR
United Arab Emirates		CP	CP	S	CP	CP	S	K+	
Viet Nam	S			CP	CP	CP			
Yemen (Arab Rep)	S							RS	
Yemen (People's Dem Rep)	CP			CP					
EUROPE									
Albania								M+	EIA*
Austria	CP	CP	CP	CP	CP	CP	S		EC, LR+, EIA*
Belgium	CP	CP	CP	CP	S	S	S		EC, LR+, EIA*
Bulgaria	CP	CP	CP	CP	CP	CP			EC, LR+, EIA*
Czechoslovakia	CP	CP	CP	CP	CP	CP	CP		LR+
Denmark	CP	CP	CP	CP	CP	S	S		EC, LR+, EIA*
Finland	CP	CP	CP	CP	CP	S	S		EC, LR+, EIA*
France		CP	CP	CP	CP	S	CP	M+,C,EA+,SP+	EC, SPC, LR+, EIA*
Germany	CP	CP	CP	CP	S	CP	S		EC, LR+, EIA*
Greece	CP	CP	CP	CP	S	S	S	M+	EC, LR, EIA*
Hungary	CP	CP	CP	CP	CP	CP	CP		EC, LR+, EIA*
Iceland	CP	CP	CP	CP	CP	S	S		LR, EIA*
Ireland	CP	CP	CP	CP	S	S	S		EC, LR, EIA*
Italy	CP	CP	CP	CP	CP	S	S	M+	EC, LR+, EIA*
Luxembourg	CP	CP	CP	CP	S		S		EC, LR+, EIA*
Malta	CP	CP	CP	CP				M+	
Netherlands	CP	CP	CP	CP	S	S	S	C {c}	EC, LR, EIA*
Norway	CP	CP	CP	CP	CP	CP	CP		EC, LR, EIA*
Poland	CP	CP	CP	CP	CP	CP	S		LR+, EIA*
Portugal	S	CP	CP	CP	S	S	S		EC, LR, EIA*
Romania	CP			CP	CP	CP	CP		EIA*
Spain	CP	CP	CP	CP	CP	CP	S	M+	EC, LR+, EIA*
Sweden	CP	CP	CP	CP	CP	S	CP		EC, LR+, EIA*
Switzerland	CP	CP	CP	CP	CP	CP	CP		EC, LR+
United Kingdom	CP	CP	CP	CP	CP	CP	S	C {d},SP*	EC, LR+, EIA*
Yugoslavia	CP	CP	CP	CP	CP			M+	LR
U.S.S.R.	CP	CP	CP	CP	CP	CP	S		LR+
OCEANIA									
Australia	CP	CP	CP	CP	CP	CP		SP+	SPC
Fiji	CP	CP	CP	CP				SP+	SPC
New Zealand	CP	CP	CP	CP	CP	CP	S	SP+	
Papua New Guinea	CP			CP				SP+	SPC*
Solomon Islands				CP				SP+	

Sources: Environmental Law Information System of the IUCN Environmental Law Centre and United Nations Environment Programme.

Notes: a. Convention not yet in force. b. Regional agreement letter codes (M, ML, etc.) indicate ratification of specific regional agreement. c. Ratified on behalf of Aruba and the Netherlands Antilles Federation. d. Ratified on behalf of British Virgin Islands, Cayman Islands, and the Turks and Caicos Islands.
CP = contracting party (has ratified or taken equivalent action); S = signatory; + = has signed or ratified at least two protocols to this convention.
* = signatory to regional agreement.
UNEP Regional Seas agreements: M = Mediterranean convention against pollution; WCA = West and Central African convention on environmental cooperation; EA = East African convention on environmental protection; RS = Red Sea and Gulf of Aden convention on conservation; C = Caribbean convention on environmental protection; SEP = South-East Pacific convention on environmental protection; SP = South Pacific convention on environmental protection; K = Kuwait convention on environmental cooperation.
Other Regional Agreements: AFC = African conservation convention; HW = African hazardous waste convention; EC = European conservation convention; LR = transboundary air pollution convention; EIA = environmental impact assessment convention; AMC = Amazonian cooperation treaty; ASC = ASEAN conservation agreement; SPC = South Pacific conservation convention.
Some small countries--signatories or contracting parties to the conventions and protocols listed--are not included in this table.
For formal titles of the conventions and protocols listed, and for additional information, see Sources and Technical Notes.

Table 25.3 Sources of Environmental and Natural Resource

	INFOTERRA Member	National State of the Environment Report	Environmental Statistical Compendium	Country Environmental Profile	Tropical Forest/ Biodiversity Assessment	Biological Diversity Profile	National Conservation Strategy	Environmental Action Plan	Tropical Forestry Action Plan
AFRICA									
Algeria	Yes								
Angola	Yes								
Benin	Yes								
Botswana	Yes	1990			1988, 1989	1991 {b}	1990		
Burkina Faso	Yes			1980, 1982				IP	FSR IP
Burundi	Yes			1981	1989				
Cameroon	Yes			1981		1989			TFAP 1989
Cape Verde	Yes			1980					FSR IP
Central African Rep	Yes								FSR IP
Chad	Yes								
Comoros	Yes								
Congo	Yes					1990			
Cote d'Ivoire	Yes					1991 {b}	IP	IP	FSR IP
Djibouti	No								
Egypt	Yes			1980	1988				
Equatorial Guinea	No								FSR IP
Ethiopia	Yes	IP				1991 {b}	IP		FSR IP
Gabon	Yes					1990			FSR IP
Gambia, The	Yes			1981	1989 {d}				FSR IP
Ghana	Yes			1980		1988 {c}		IP	FSR 1988
Guinea	Yes			1983	IP	1988 {c}		IP	TFAP1988
Guinea-Bissau	Yes					1991 {b}	IP		FSR IP
Kenya	Yes	1987			1988 {d}	1988 {c}	IP		FSR 1987/TFAP IP
Lesotho	Yes			1982				1991	FSR IP
Liberia	Yes			1980	1987				
Libya	Yes								
Madagascar	Yes	1987				1988, 1991 {b}	1984	1988	FSR IP
Malawi	Yes			1982	IP		IP		
Mali	Yes			1980	1989				
Mauritania	Yes			1979, 1981			1988	IP	FSR 1990
Mauritius	Yes		1985					1991	
Morocco	Yes	IP		1980					
Mozambique	Yes		1985						
Namibia	No								
Niger	Yes			1980					FSR IP
Nigeria	Yes					1988	1990	1991	FSR IP
Rwanda	Yes			1981, 1987				IP	FSR IP
Sao Tome and Principe	Yes								
Senegal	Yes			1980		1991 {b}	IP		FSR IP
Seychelles	Yes	1990					IP		
Sierra Leone	No						IP		TFAP 1990
Somalia	Yes			1979			1990		FSR 1990
South Africa	No						1980		
Sudan	Yes			1989					FSR 1986
Swaziland	No			1980					
Tanzania	Yes					1988	IP		TFAP 1989
Togo	Yes						IP		FSR IP
Tunisia	Yes			1980	1988				
Uganda	Yes			1982	IP	1988 {c}			
Zaire	Yes			1981	1988	1990			TFAP 1990
Zambia	Yes	1988		1982			1985		FSR IP
Zimbabwe	Yes	1988, 1990		1982			1987		FSR IP
NORTH & CENTRAL AMERICA									
Barbados	Yes			1982			IP	IP	
Bahamas	Yes								
Belize	Yes			1984	1988		IP	IP	TFAP 1989
Canada	Yes	1986, IP	1986				1986		
Costa Rica	Yes	1988		1982			1990		TFAP 1990
Cuba	Yes								TFAP 1991
Dominican Rep	No			1981	1988				TFAP 1990
El Salvador	Yes			1985	1988				
Guatemala	Yes			1984	1988		IP		TFAP 1991
Haiti	Yes	IP		1985					FSR IP
Honduras	Yes			1982					TFAP 1988
Jamaica	Yes	IP		1987					TFAP 1990
Mexico	Yes	1991				1988			TFAP 1991
Nicaragua	No			1981			IP		FSR IP
Panama	Yes		1985	1980			IP		TFAP 1991
St. Lucia	Yes			1991			1987	IP	
Trinidad and Tobago	No						IP	IP	FSR IP
United States	Yes	1989, 1990, 1991	1983, 1990				IP		
SOUTH AMERICA									
Argentina	Yes	IP							TFAP 1988
Bolivia	Yes			1986	1988				TFAP 1989
Brazil	Yes	1984	1985			1988			
Chile	Yes	1985	1984	1990					FSR IP
Colombia	Yes			1990		1988	IP		TFAP 1989
Ecuador	Yes	IP		1987	1989	1988		IP	TFAP 1991
Guyana	Yes			1982					TFAP 1990
Paraguay	Yes	1985		1985					
Peru	Yes			1986	1988	1988	IP		TFAP 1988
Uruguay	Yes								
Venezuela	Yes	IP							FSR IP

Information, 1991

Table 25.3

		Sources of National Environmental Information {a}							
	INFOTERRA Member	National State of the Environment Report	Environmental Statistical Compendium	Country Environmental Profile	Tropical Forest/ Biodiversity Assessment	Biological Diversity Profile	National Conservation Strategy	Environmental Action Plan	Tropical Forestry Action Plan
ASIA									
Afghanistan	No								
Bahrain	Yes	1988							
Bangladesh	Yes			1980	1990		1987		MPFD IP
Bhutan	Yes								MPFD IP
Cambodia	No			1989					
China	Yes	IP	1988						
Cyprus	Yes	1987, 1989							
Hong Kong	Yes	1988							
India	Yes	1985		1980		1989	IP	IP	TFAP IP
Indonesia	Yes	1990	1983	1987	IP		IP		TFAP 1990
Iran, Islamic Rep	Yes								
Iraq	Yes								
Israel	Yes	1988							
Japan	Yes	1991	1980						
Jordan	Yes	IP		1979			IP		
Korea, Dem People's Rep	Yes								
Korea, Rep	Yes	1988							
Kuwait	Yes	1987							
Lao People's Dem Rep	No								TFAP 1990
Lebanon	Yes								
Malaysia	Yes	1990				1988	IP		TFAP 1991
Mongolia	Yes								
Myanmar	No			1982	1987	1989			
Nepal	Yes	IP		1979			1987		MPFD 1988
Oman	Yes	IP		1981			IP		
Pakistan	Yes	1986	1984	1986, 1988		1991 {c}	1986		MPFD IP
Philippines	Yes	1986	1979	1980	1989	1988	IP	1991	MPFD 1990
Qatar	Yes	1987							
Saudi Arabia	Yes	1989							
Singapore	Yes	1990		1988					
Sri Lanka	Yes	1991		1988	1988		1988	IP	MPFD 1989
Syrian Arab Rep	Yes	IP		1981					
Thailand	Yes	IP		1987			IP		MPFD IP
Turkey	Yes	1989							
United Arab Emirates	Yes								
Viet Nam	Yes						1985		FSR IP
Yemen (Arab Rep)	Yes			1982					
Yemen (People's Dem Rep)	Yes								
EUROPE									
Austria	Yes	1988, 1989	1985						
Belgium	Yes	1979	1989						
Bulgaria	Yes								
Czechoslovakia	Yes								
Denmark	Yes	1982	1990						
Finland	Yes	1988, IP	1987				IP		
France	Yes	1990	1989						
Germany (Fed Rep)	Yes	1989, 1990	1989						
Germany (Dem Rep)	Yes	1990							
Greece	Yes	1983							
Hungary	Yes	1990	1981						
Iceland	Yes	1986							
Ireland	Yes	1985	1987						
Italy	Yes	1989	1987, 1989				ND		
Luxembourg	Yes	1988							
Malta	Yes								
Netherlands	Yes	1989, 1990	1987						
Norway	Yes		1988				IP		
Poland	Yes	1989, 1990	1987						
Portugal	Yes	1989							
Romania	Yes								
Spain	Yes	1977					IP		
Sweden	Yes	1984	1990						
Switzerland	Yes	1989					IP		
United Kingdom	Yes	1990	1989				1983, 1990		
Yugoslavia	Yes	1987	1985				IP		
USSR	Yes	1988							
OCEANIA									
Australia	Yes	1987, 1988	1985				1988		
Fiji	Yes						IP		FSR 1990/TFAP IP
New Zealand	Yes	1988					1985		
Papua New Guinea	Yes								TFAP 1990
Samoa	Yes								
Solomon Islands	No								
Vanuatu	Yes	1986			1988		IP		FSR IP

Sources: World Resources Institute, International Institute for Environment and Development, IUCN-The World Conservation Union, U.S. Agency for International Development, World Conservation Monitoring Centre, and the United Nations Environment Programme.

Notes: a. Publication date of most recent edition; multiple dates indicate different reports.
b. Accompanied with poster maps.
c. draft.
d. Natural Resource Management Study.
INFOTERRA: member of INFOTERRA, the global environmental information system; FSR = Forestry Sector Review; TFAP = Tropical Forestry Action Plan; MPFD = Master Plan for Forestry Development; IP = in preparation; ND = published, no date.
For additional information, see Sources and Technical Notes.

Table 25.4 Sources of Published Global and Regional Environmental Information, 1991

World:

Lester R. Brown, et al., State of the World 1992 (W.W. Norton, New York, 1992). {a}*

Global Environment Monitoring System (GEMS), Global Freshwater Quality: A First Assessment (World Health Organization and United Nations Environment Programme, Oxford, 1989).

IUCN-the World Conservation Union, United Nations Environment Programme (UNEP), and World Wide Fund for Nature (WWF), Caring for the Earth: A Strategy for Sustainability (IUCN, UNEP, and WWF, Gland, Switzerland, 1991).

United Nations, World Population Prospects 1990 (Population Division, United Nations, New York, 1991).

United Nations, Department of International Economic and Social Affairs (DIESA), Prospects of World Urbanization 1988 (United Nations, New York, 1989).

United Nations Environment Programme (UNEP) and United Nations Children's Fund (UNICEF), The State of the Environment 1990: Children and the Environment (UNEP and UNICEF, Nairobi and New York, 1990).

United Nations Children's Fund (UNICEF), The State of the World's Children 1991 (Oxford University Press, New York, 1991). {a}

United Nations Development Programme (UNDP), Human Development Report 1991 (Oxford University Press, New York, 1991). {a}

United Nations Environment Programme (UNEP), Environmental Data Report (Basil Blackwell, Oxford, 1991). {b}

United Nations Environment Program (UNEP), State of the Environment: 1972-1992 (UNEP, Nairobi, 1992).*

United Nations Environment Programme (UNEP), The State of the Environment 1990 (UNEP, Nairobi, 1990). {a}

United Nations Environment Program (UNEP), The World Environment 1972-82: A Report (UNEP, Nairobi, 1982).

The World Bank, World Development Report (Oxford University, New York, 1991). {a}

World Commission on Environment and Development, Our Common Future (Oxford University Press, New York, 1987).

World Conservation Monitoring Centre (WCMC), Global Biodiversity 1992: The Status of the Earth's Living Resources (WCMC, Cambridge, 1992).

World Health Organization, World Health Statistics Annual (WHO, Geneva, 1990). {a}

World Resources Institute, in collaboration with the United Nations Environment Programme and the United Nations Development Programme, World Resources 1992-93 (Oxford University Press, New York, 1992) {b}

All Regions:

United Nations Environment Programme (UNEP), Regional Seas Programme Studies and Reports (UNEP, Nairobi). Regional series include West and Central Africa, Eastern Africa, Wider Caribbean, Mediterranean, Kuwait Action Plan, Red Sea and Gulf of Aden, East Asian Seas, South Asian Seas, South East Pacific, South Pacific, and South West Atlantic Regions.

Africa:

Food and Agriculture Organization of United Nations (FAO), Natural Resources and the Human Environment for Food and Agriculture in Africa (FAO, Rome, 1986).

IUCN-the World Conservation Union, Biodiversity in Sub-Saharan Africa and Its Islands: Conservation, Management and Sustainable Use (IUCN, Gland, Switzerland, 1990).

IUCN-the World Conservation Union, IUCN Sahel Studies, 1989 (IUCN, Gland, Switzerland. 1989).

L.O. Lewis and L. Berry, African Environments and Resources (Unwin Hyman, Boston, 1988).

The World Bank, Sub-Saharan Africa: From Crisis to Sustainable Growth (World Bank, Washington, D.C., 1989).

Latin America:

Eric Cardich, ed., Conservando el Patrimonio Natural de la Region Neotropical (IUCN, Gland, Switzerland, 1986).

Inter-American Development Bank (IDB), Natural Resources in Latin America (IDB, Washington, D.C., 1983).

Latin American and Caribbean Commission on Development and Environment, Our Own Agenda (IDB and UNEP, Washington, D.C., 1990).

Jeffrey Leonard, Natural Resources and Economic Development in Central America: A Regional Environmental Profile (Transaction Books, Oxford, 1987).

Jorge Morello, Perfil Ecologico de Sudamerica (Instituto de Cooperacion Iberoamericana, Barcelona, 1984).

United Nations Economic Commission for Latin America and the Caribbean (UNECLAC), Sustainable Development: Changing Production Patterns, Social Equity and the Environment (UNECLAC, Chile, 1991).

Asia and Oceania:

Asian Development Bank (ADB), Economic Policies for Sustainable Development (ADB, Manila, 1990).

Mark N. Collins, Jeffrey A. Sayer, Timothy C. Whitmore, The Conservation Atlas of Tropical Forests: Asia and the Pacific (IUCN, Gland, Switzerland, 1991).

A.L. Dahl and L.L. Baumgart, The State of the Environment in the South Pacific (UNEP, Geneva, 1983).

United Nations Economic and Social Commission for Asia and the Pacific (UNESCAP), State of the Environment in Asia and the Pacific 1990, (UNESCAP, Bangkok, 1990).

Europe, North America, and Other Developed Countries:

Commission of the European Communities (CEC), The State of the Environment in the European Community 1989 (CEC, Luxembourg, 1990).

DocTer Institute for Environmental Studies, Milan, European Environmental Yearbook 1991 (DocTer International U.K., London, 1991). {a}

European Community, The European Community and the Environment (European Community, Luxembourg, 1987).

Eurostat, Environment Statistics 1989 (Eurostat, Luxembourg, 1990).

Stanley P. Johnson and Guy Corcelle, The Environmental Policy of the European Communities (Graham and Trotman/Kluwer, London, 1989).

Organisation for Economic Co-operation and Development (OECD), Environmental Indicators (OECD, Paris, 1991).

Organisation for Economic Co-operation and Development (OECD), OECD Environmental Data Compendium 1991 (OECD, Paris, 1991).

Organisation for Economic Co-operation and Development (OECD), The State of the Environment 1991 (OECD, Paris, 1991).

United Nations Statistical Commission and United Nations Economic Commission for Europe, Environment Statistics in Europe and North America: An Experimental Compendium (United Nations, New York, 1988).

Source: Compiled by World Resources Institute.

Notes: * = forthcoming; {a} = annual series; {b} = biennial series.

For additional information, see Sources and Technical Notes.

Sources and Technical Notes

Table 25.1 Participation in Major Global Conventions—Wildlife, Habitat, and Oceans, 1991

Sources: United Nations Environment Programme (UNEP), UNEP Governing Council, *Register of International Treaties and Other Agreements in the Field of the Environment* (UNEP, Nairobi, May 1991); Environmental Law Information System of the World Conservation Union (IUCN-the World Conservation Union) Environmental Law Centre, unpublished data (IUCN-the World Conservation Union, Bonn, August 1991).

A country becomes a signatory of a treaty when a person given authority by the national government signs it. Unless otherwise provided in the treaty, a signatory is under no duty to perform the obligations stipulated before the treaty comes into force for the country. The authorized signature indicates a commitment to undertake domestic action to ratify, accept, approve, or accede to the treaty. A country is a contracting party when the treaty comes into force with respect to the country. Typically, this occurs when the country has ratified the treaty or otherwise adopted the provisions of the treaty as national law and when a prescribed number of countries indicates consent to be bound by the treaty and register instruments of ratification, acceptance, approval, or accession with the treaty's depository (which may be a national government, a United Nations organization, or another international organization; some treaties have multiple depositaries).

The complete titles of the conventions and treaties summarized in Table 25.1, and their places and dates of adoption, are as follows:

■ *Antarctic treaty and convention*: The Antarctic Treaty (Washington, D.C., 1959) is to ensure that Antarctica is used for peaceful purposes, for international cooperation in scientific research, and that Antarctica does not become the scene or object of international discord. The Convention on the Conservation of Antarctic Marine Living Resources (Canberra, 1980) is to safeguard the environment and protect the integrity of the ecosystem of the seas surrounding Antarctica, and to conserve Antarctic marine living resources.

■ *Wetlands (Ramsar)*: The Convention on Wetlands of International Importance Especially as Waterfowl Habitat (Ramsar, Iran, 1971) is to stem the progressive encroachment on and loss of wetlands now and in the future, recognizing the fundamental ecological functions of wetlands and their economic, cultural, scientific, and recreational value, by establishing a List of Wetlands of International Importance, and providing that parties will establish wetland nature reserves and consider their international responsibilities for migratory waterfowl.

■ *World heritage*: The Convention Concerning the Protection of the World Cultural and Natural Heritage (Paris, 1972) establishes a system of collective protection of the cultural and natural heritage sites of outstanding universal value, organized on a permanent basis and in accordance with modern scientific methods.

■ *Endangered species (CITES)*: The Convention on International Trade in Endangered Species of Wild Fauna and Flora (CITES) (Washington, D.C., 1973) protects endangered species from overexploitation by controlling trade in live or dead animals and in animal parts through a system of permits.

■ *Migratory species*: The Convention on the Conservation of Migratory Species of Wild Animals (Bonn, 1979) protects wild animal species that migrate across international borders, by promoting international agreements.

■ *Ocean dumping*: The Convention on the Prevention of Marine Pollution by Dumping of Wastes and Other Matter (London, Mexico City, Moscow, Washington, D.C., 1972) controls pollution of the seas by prohibiting the dumping of certain materials and regulating ocean disposal of others, encouraging regional agreements, and establishing a mechanism for assessing liability and settling disputes.

■ *Ship pollution (MARPOL)*: The Protocol of 1978 Relating to the International Convention for the Prevention of Pollution from Ships, 1973 (London, 1978) is a modification of the 1973 convention to eliminate international pollution by oil and other harmful substances and to minimize accidental discharge of such substances.

■ *Law of the sea*: The United Nations Convention on the Law of the Sea (Montego Bay, Jamaica, 1982) establishes a comprehensive legal regime for the seas and oceans, establishes rules for environmental standards and enforcement provisions, and develops international rules and national legislation to prevent and control marine pollution.

The United Nations Convention on the Law of the Sea has not yet entered into force. Sixty ratifications are required and until now only 43 countries have ratified it.

The European Community has signed the Convention on the Conservation of Migratory Species of Wild Animals and the United Nations Convention on the Law of the Sea.

Information on the number of Natural World Heritage Sites and Wetlands of International Importance is contained in Chapter 20, "Wildlife and Habitat," Table 20.1. For information on treaty terms, refer to the sources.

Table 25.2 Participation in Major Global Conventions—Atmosphere, Hazardous Substances, and Regional Agreements, 1991

Sources: United Nations Environment Programme (UNEP), UNEP Governing Council, *Register of International Treaties and Other Agreements in the Field of the Environment* (UNEP, Nairobi, May 1991); UNEP, *Status of Regional Agreements Negotiated in the Framework of the Regional Seas Programme*, Rev. 3 (UNEP, Nairobi, August 1991); Environmental Law Information System of the World Conservation Union (IUCN) Environmental Law Centre, unpublished data (IUCN, Bonn, August 1991).

See Technical Note for Table 25.1 for general information on the meaning of conventions, signing, and ratification.

The complete titles of the conventions and treaties summarized in Table 25.2, and places and dates of adoption, follow:

■ *Nuclear test ban*: The Treaty Banning Nuclear Weapon Tests in the Atmosphere, in Outer Space, and Under Water (Moscow, 1963) prohibits atmospheric and underwater nuclear weapons tests and other nuclear explosions and prohibits tests in any other environment if radioactive debris would be present outside the territory of the country conducting the test.

■ *Ozone layer*: The Vienna Convention for the Protection of the Ozone Layer (Vienna, 1985) is to protect human health and the environment by conducting research on ozone layer modification and its effects and on alternative substances and technologies, monitoring the ozone layer, and taking measures to control activities that produce adverse effects.

■ *CFC control*: The Protocol on Substances That Deplete the Ozone Layer (Montreal, 1987) requires nations to cut consumption of five chlorofluorocarbons (CFCs) and three halons by 20 percent of their 1986 level by 1994 and by 50 percent of their 1986 level by 1999, with allowances for increases in consumption by developing countries.

■ *Biological and toxin weapons*: The Convention on the Prohibition of the Development, Production, and Stockpiling of Bacteriological (Biological) and Toxin Weapons, and on Their Destruction (London, Moscow, Washington, D.C., 1972) prohibits acquisition and retention of biological agents and toxins that are not justified for peaceful purposes and of the means of delivering them for hostile purposes or armed conflict.

■ *Nuclear accident notification*: The Convention on Early Notification of a Nuclear Accident (Vienna, 1986) provides relevant information about nuclear accidents as early as possible in order that transboundary radiological consequences can be minimized.

■ *Nuclear accident assistance*: The Convention on Assistance in the Case of a Nuclear Accident or Radiological Emergency (Vienna, 1986) facilitates the prompt provision of assistance in the event of a nuclear accident or radiological emergency.

■ *Hazardous waste movement*: The Basel Convention on the Control of Transboundary Movements of Hazardous Wastes and their Disposal (Basel, 1989) sets up obligations to reduce transboundary movement of wastes; to minimize the amount and toxicity of hazardous wastes generated and to ensure their environmentally sound management; and to assist developing countries in environmentally sound management of hazardous wastes.

■ The *UNEP Regional Seas* Programme, initiated by UNEP in 1974, has developed regional action plans for controlling marine pollution and managing marine and coastal resources. The action plans usually include regional environmental assessments, environmental management, environmental legislation, institutional arrangements, and financial arrangements. The regional conventions and associated protocols that are a part of these action plans are included in the table and they address region-specific marine-related environmental issues.

Some of the symbols used to indicate participation in a Regional Sea convention denote several related conventions and protocols. An asterisk (*) follows the convention abbreviation if a country has signed, but not ratified the regional convention. A plus (+) sign follows the convention abbreviation if a country has signed or ratified at least two of the associated protocols to the regional convention. The abbreviations and full titles of Regional Seas conventions, dates of adoption, and associated protocols mentioned in the table are listed below.

■ *M:* Convention for the Protection of the Mediterranean Sea against Pollution (1976). Protocol for the Prevention of Pollution of the Mediterranean Sea by Dumping from Ships and Aircraft (1976). Protocol Concerning Co-operation in Combating Pollution of the Mediterranean Sea by Oil and Other Harmful Substances in Cases of Emergency (1976). Protocol for the Protection of the Mediterranean Sea against Pollution from Land-based Sources (1980). Protocol Concerning Mediterranean Specially Protected Areas (1982).

■ *WCA:* Convention for Co-operation in the Protection and Development of the Marine and Coastal Environment of the West and Central African Region (1981). Protocol Concerning Co-operation in Combating Pollution in Cases of Emergency (1981).

■ *EA:* Convention for the Protection, Management and Development of the Marine and Coastal Environment of the Eastern African Region (1985). Protocol Concerning Protected Areas and Wild Fauna and Flora in the Eastern African Region (1985). Protocol Concerning Co-operation in Combating Marine Pollution in Cases of Emergency in the Eastern African Region (1985).

■ *RS:* Regional Convention for the Conservation of the Red Sea and Gulf of Aden Environment (1982). Protocol Concerning Regional Co-operation in Combating Pollution by Oil and Other Harmful Substances in Cases of Emergency (1982).

■ *C:* Convention for the Protection and Development of the Marine Environment of the Wider Caribbean Region (1983). Protocol Concerning Co-operation in Combating Oil Spills in the Wider Caribbean Region (1983). Protocol Concerning Specially Protected Areas and Wildlife to the Convention for the Protection and Development of the Marine Environment of the Wider Caribbean Region (1990).

■ *SEP:* Convention for the Protection of the Marine Environment and Coastal Area of the South-East Pacific (1981). Agreement on Regional Co-operation in Combating Pollution of the South-East Pacific by Hydrocarbons or Other Harmful Substances in Cases of Emergency (1981). Supplementary Protocol to the Agreement on Regional Co-operation in Combating Pollution of the South-East Pacific by Hydrocarbons or Other Harmful Substances in Cases of Emergency (1983). Protocol for the Protection of the South-East Pacific Against Pollution from Land-Based Sources (1983). Protocol for the Conservation and Management of Protected Marine and Coastal Areas of the South-East Pacific Against Radioactive Contamination (1989).

■ *SP:* Convention for the Protection of the Natural Resources and Environment of the South Pacific Region (1986). Protocol Concerning Co-operation in Combating Pollution Emergencies in the South Pacific Region (1986). Protocol for the Prevention of Pollution of the South Pacific Region by Dumping (1986).

■ *K:* Kuwait Regional Convention for Co-operation on the Protection of the Marine Environment from Pollution (1978). Protocol Concerning Regional Co-operation in Combating Pollution by Oil and Other Harmful Substances in Cases of Emergency (1978). Protocol concerning Marine Pollution resulting from Exploration and Exploitation of the Continental Shelf (1989). Protocol for the Protection of the Marine Environment against Pollution from Land-Based Sources (1990).

Other regional agreements include a variety of agreements addressing region-specific environmental issues. The abbreviations and full titles of the agreements, and their date and place of adoption, are listed below.

■ *AFC:* African Convention on the Conservation of Nature and Natural Resources (Algiers, 1968).

■ *HW:* Bamako Convention on the Ban of the Import into Africa and the Control of Transboundary Movements of Hazardous Wastes Within Africa (1991).

■ *EC:* Convention on the Conservation of European Wildlife and Natural Habitats (Bern, 1979)

■ *LR:* Convention on Long-Range Transboundary Air Pollution (Geneva, 1979); Protocol to the 1979 Convention on Long-Range Transboundary Air Pollution on Long-Term Financing of the Co-operative Programme for Monitoring and Evaluation of the Long-Range Transmission of Air Pollutants in Europe (EMEP) (Geneva, 1984); Protocol to the 1979 Convention on Long-Range Transboundary Air Pollution on the Reduction of Sulphur Emissions or Their Transboundary Fluxes by at Least 30 Percent (Helsinki, 1985); Protocol to the 1979 Convention on Long-Range Transboundary Air Pollution Concerning the Control of Emissions of Nitrogen or their Transboundary Fluxes (Sofia, 1988).

■ *EIA:* Convention on Environmental Impact Assessment in a Transboundary Context (Espoo, Finland, 1991).

■ *AMC:* Treaty for Amazonian Cooperation (Brasilia, 1978).

■ *ASC:* ASEAN Agreement on the Conservation of Nature and Natural Resources (Kuala Lumpur, 1985).

■ *SPC:* Convention on Conservation of Nature in the South Pacific (Apia, Western Samoa, 1976).

The Convention on the Control of Transboundary Movements of Hazardous Wastes and Their Disposal has not yet entered into force. This will happen when 20 countries have ratified it. The Vienna Convention for the Protection of the Ozone Layer entered into force on September 22, 1988, after the required 20 countries ratified it. The Protocol on Substances That Deplete the Ozone Layer entered into force January 1, 1989, when the requirement of ratification by at least 11 countries, accounting for at least two thirds of 1986 estimated world chlorofluorocarbon consumption, had been met.

The European Community has signed the Vienna Convention for the Protection of the Ozone Layer and the Protocol on Substances That Deplete the Ozone Layer. It has also signed conventions on three regional seas with associated protocols, on the conservation of wildlife, on environmental impact assessments, and on long-range transboundary air pollution.

The Eastern African and South Pacific Regional Seas conventions and their protocols have not yet entered into force. For information on treaty terms, refer to the sources.

Table 25.3 Sources of Environmental and Natural Resource Information, 1991

Source: Compiled by the World Resources Institute.

INFOTERRA, the global environmental information system, is a network of national information centers established by the United Nations Environment Programme (UNEP) for the exchange of environmental information. Each member country compiles a register of institutions willing to share expertise in environmentally related areas, such as atmosphere and climate, energy, food and agriculture, plant and animal wildlife, and pollution. An international directory is developed from the national registers; the national offices use the directory to select experts who can answer the queries. In 1990, the network answered more than 18,000 queries, over half of which came from developing countries.

National State of the Environment Reports are published by government agencies, multilateral organizations, universities, and nongovernmental organizations. They analyze the condition and management of a country's natural resources and document its progress or failure in sustaining its natural resource base. UNEP supports the development of state-of-the-environment reports in several countries. Their goal is to help developing countries improve their knowledge of their environment and thus formulate more environmentally sound national strategies. UNEP provides consultants on a short-term basis and helps prepare and publish the final report.

Environmental Statistical Compendium, usually prepared by a government agency, reports national environmental statistical data primarily through graphs and tables, and contains little analysis.

Country Environmental Profiles are sponsored by the United States Agency for International Development (U.S. AID). These profiles assess a country's natural resource potential in relation to economic growth and development. The environmental profile program helps to establish an information base that can be used in planning and policy development.

Tropical Forest/Biodiversity Assessments are also sponsored by U.S. AID. These assessments provide a background on tropical forest and biodiversity conservation needs in each developing country and include information on laws and institutions affecting biological resources, the status and management of protected areas, the status and protection of endangered species, conservation efforts outside protected areas, major issues in tropical forest and biological diversity conservation, and recommendations and proposed activities.

Biological Diversity Profiles are published by the Habitats Data Unit of the World Conservation Monitoring Centre (WCMC) and the Tropical Forest Programme of the World Conservation Union (IUCN) in support of the conservation of biological diversity. The profiles provide basic background on species diversity, major ecosystems and habitat types, protected area systems, and legislative and administrative support; they identify the status of sites of critical importance for biological diversity and ecosystem conservation; and they provide a concise report on the values, threats, and conserva-

tion needs of these sites for decisionmakers and development agencies.

National Conservation Strategy (NCS) reports involve the consideration of current and future needs and aspirations of the people, the institutional capacities of the country, the prevailing technical conditions, and the status of its natural resources. On the basis of review, analysis, and assignment of priorities, an NCS seeks to define the best possible allocation of human and financial resources to achieve the goals of sustainable development. Host governments bear the main responsibility for implementing NCSs and must take the lead in their preparation. For more information on the status of National Conservation Strategies, see past issues of the *IUCN Bulletin Supplement.*

Environmental Action Plans (EAP) are sponsored by the World Bank and prepared by Bank staff and consultants in close collaboration with governments, various international organizations, NGOs, and other donors. These plans are detailed studies that culminate in the implementation of environmental projects and policies. Some EAPs provide a framework for integrating environmental considerations into a nation's overall economic and social development programs. The EAPs also make recommendations for specific actions, outlining the environmental policies, investment strategies, legislation, and institutional arrangements required.

Tropical Forestry Action Plan (TFAP) is a global strategy developed by the Food and Agriculture Organization of the United Nations (FAO), the United Nations Development Program, the World Bank, and the World Resources Institute, with the cooperation of some 40 bilateral donors, international organizations and NGOs. It provides a framework for concerted national and international action to manage, protect, and

restore forest resources in the tropics. TFAP exercises are developed by individual countries with the assistance of the international community and must produce informed decisions and action programs with explicit national targets on policies and practices to halt deforestation, the contribution of forest resources to sustainable economic development through afforestation and forest management, the conservation of forest resources, and the integration of forest-related issues in the priorities of other sectors. The planning phase usually involves a comprehensive forestry sector review (FSR) leading to the formulation of a national TFAP, which includes a long-term strategy, mid-term programs, and immediate projects. The Master Plans for Forestry Development (MPFD) are linked to the TFAP effort but are carried out by the Asian Development Bank (ADB) for its member countries (Bhutan, China, Laos, Nepal, Pakistan, the Philippines, and Thailand). MPFDs aim at long-term development of the forestry sector, including a five-year plan and annual programs and projects for implementation. The goal is to increase institutional capacity in these countries, coordinate donor assistance, and increase funding for forestry.

Table 25.4 Sources of Published Global and Regional Environmental Information, 1991

Source: Compiled by the World Resources Institute.

The bibliography of Sources of Published Global and Regional Environmental Information includes general statistical and analytical publications. It includes neither specialized reports nor journal articles.

Index

Page numbers in italics refer to tables or figures.

This index does not include page numbers for specific country data shown in Part IV tables. See Table of Contents for list of table titles. Most tables include data for 146 countries.

Index

tillage practices, 36, 100, 101, 102, 170
  water management, 163
  weed control, 100
  yields, 100, 101, 107
Aluminum, *320*
Amazon Basin
  agroforestry project, 124
  area, 166
  biological diversity, 46
  conservation, 46
  deforestation, 46, 51, 119, 121
  hydroelectric projects, 123
  precipitation, 160
  tribal people, 123-25, 135, 230-31
American Fisheries Society, 132
Ammonia, 61, 65, 104, 153
Amphibians, threatened species, *304-05*
Amu Darya, 166, 168-69
Angola, 11, 96
Antarctic Treaty and Convention, *358-39*
Anticancer drugs, 133
Aquaculture
  and mangrove forest losses, 49, 135-36, 180
  production, 96, 181, *340-41*
  sewage used in, 169
Aquino, Corazon, 220
Arabian orynx, 128
Aral Sea, 166, 168-69
Arfak Mountains, 138
Argentina, 82, 123, 130, 148
Arsenic, 61, 177
Ascension, 131
Asia
  see also specific countries
  child mortality, *78*
  deforestation, 118
  energy production and consumption, *144*
  energy reserves, *148*, 149
  fertility rates, 77
  food production, 96
  freshwater, 160
  infant mortality, *78*
  malnutrition in, 84
  mangrove losses, *178*
  nongovernmental organizations, 218, 220
  population growth, *76*, 77
  protected areas, 136
  rapidly industrializing countries, 41
  soil degradation, *112*, 114, 116
Asian Development Bank, 98
Asian NGO Coalition for Agrarian Reform and Rural Development, 224, 230
Association of African Women for Research and Development, 230
Association of Southeast Asian Nations, 53
Asthma, 42
Atlantic Ocean, 131, *338-39*
Atmosphere
  see also Air pollution
  conventions, 8, 152-53, 199, *360-61*
  levels of greenhouse and ozone-depleting gases, *205, 350*
Australia
  agriculture, 105
  biodiversity, 131
  energy production, 145
  Great Barrier Reef Marine Park, 137, 139
  land conservation, 106
  precipitation, 160
  soil degradation, 102, 112, 115
  water conservation, 106
Austria, *64, 65, 66*, 105, 106, 107, 145
Aylwin, Patricio, 50
Azerbaijan, 150

Azov Sea, 185, 186

B

Baltic Marine Environment Protection Commission, 68
Baltic Sea, 65, 68, 175, 176, 181, 184, 186
Bangladesh
  aquaculture, 169
  children's health, 34, 83-84
  education, 31
  energy sources, 37, 144, 148
  floods, 160
  health services, 32
  nongovernment organizations, 33, 218, 224
  poverty alleviation, 33
Bank for European Reconstruction and Development, 68
Bauxite, *322-23*
Bavaria, 102, 103-04
Belgium, *64, 65*, 161
Belize, 140
Benin, 223
Bhutan, 140
Bicycle industry, 54
Bioaccumulation of toxic substances, 165, 168, 177
Biodiversity losses, 4
  assessment, *362-63*
  causes, 96, 129-30, 134-36, 138
  conservation and, 10, 54, 136-38, 140
  convention, 10, 134
  crops, 104, 132-33
  deforestation and, 118, 120, 125, 127
  demand reduction and, 141
  ecosystem, 128
  estimation, 128, 139
  genetic, 10, 47, 54, 128, 132-33
  global strategy, 130, 133-34, 138-39
  habitat fragmentation, 118
  high-level areas, 46, 130, 132-33
  human cultural, 128
  ignorance about species and ecosystems, 134-35
  local aspects, 130
  national policies and, 130, 138-41
  natural resource consumption and, 134
  policies contributing to, 135, 139
  population growth and, 96, 134
  profile, *362-63*
  resource consumption and, 134
  resource distribution inequities and, 135
  species, 127-28
  trade and, 135
  valuation of, 135, 139
Biogas, 195, 223
Biohydrometallurgy, 26
Biomass energy, 36-37, 144, 148, 155, 195
Bioparks, 137
Bioregional management, 137
Biosphere reserves, 137, 138, *298-99*
Biotechnology, 10, 26
Birds
  species losses, 132
  losses to oil spills, 150
  threatened species, 129, 132, *304-05*
  trade in, 27, *300-01*
  waterfowl populations, 163
Births
  attended by trained personnel, *254-55*
  rates, 32, 45, 81, *248-49*
Black Forest, 160, 197
Black Sea, pollution, 65, 176, 182-83, 185, 186
Blacks, poverty and illness among children, 83, 88
Bolivia, 123, 231

Botanical gardens, 136-37, *306-08*
Botswana, 30, 80, 81, 96, 129, 133, 135
Brazil, 41
  air pollution, 88
  child mortality, 86
  cholera epidemic, 81
  contraceptive use, 77
  debt-for-nature swaps, 51, 53
  deforestation, 46, 47, 51, 119, 121
  energy consumption and production, 46, *51*, 53, 148, 151
  energy efficiency, 157
  exports, 47, 155
  family planning programs, 45
  income distribution, 79, 81
  lead poisoning, 88
  literacy rates, 43
  nongovernment organizations, 219, 220, 227, 231
  pollution control, 53
  population growth, 45
  poverty in, 45, 46, 86
  profile, 46
  transportation, 157
  Xingu River dam, 123
Breastfeeding, 83, 85
Brown tree snake, 132
Buffaloes and camels, *276-77*
Buffer zones, 137
Bulgaria, *61, 63, 64, 65, 66*, 146
Burkina Faso, 36, 220, 223, 224, 225
Burundi, 129
Byelorussia, *66*

C

Cadmium, 64, 66, 107, 177, 186, *320*
California, wind power, 22
Cambodia, 11
Canada, 19, 101-02
  child mortality, *78*
  Cree community property system, 135
  energy sources, 145
  forestry initiative, 123
  infant mortality, 82
  lead pollution, 161
  marine pollution, 176, 177
  population distribution, 177
  resource/material consumption, *18*, 145
  species diversity, 130
  temperate rainforests, 131
Canalization, 185
Canary Islands, 131
Cancer, 62, 79, 168, 195
Captive breeding, 128, 132, 136-37
Carbon dioxide emissions
  atmospheric levels, 2, 5, 21, *350*
  from cement manufacture, *350*
  by country, *211*
  deforestation and, 205-06
  industrial, *211, 346-47*
  from fossil fuel consumption, 151, 163, 205-06, *350*
  and global warming, 205
  from land-use change, *348-49*
  natural sinks, 209
  projections, *5*, 149
  reduction strategies, 8, 21, 22, 27, 71, 147, 196, 204
  sources, 5, 7, 21-22, 23, 25, 149, 200, *348-50*
  target limits, 210
  taxes on, 10, 23
  worldwide, 5
Carbon monoxide emissions, 196-97
  atmospheric levels, 196, *350*
  by country, *351*
  health effects, 88, 197
  indoor, 195
  reduction, 70, 196, 203

and smog formation, 197
  sources, 61, 62-63, 65, 70, 104, 149, 196, *351*
Carbon tetrachloride, *350*
Cardiovascular diseases, 62, *79*
CARE, 217
Caribbean Sea, 131
Caspian Sea, 185
Catholic church, grassroots organizations, 220, 225
Catholic Relief Services, 217
Cattle, 96, *276-77*
Cement manufacture, *350*
Central America
  see also Latin America; *specific countries*
  deforestation, 118
  mangrove losses, *178*
  nongovernmental organizations, 220
  soil degradation, *112*, 114, 116
  species diversity, 130
Central Europe
  agriculture, 65
  auto emissions, 62-64
  atmospheric pollution, 11, 57, 61-64
  banking institution initiatives, 68
  cause of environmental problems, 57-58, 60
  coal belt, 57
  coal dependence, 61, 67, 70-71, 143
  countries of, 58
  democratization, 57-58, 59, 66-67, 143, 146
  employment, 57
  energy policies, 60-61, 66-69, 71-72, 143, *144*, 145-46, 151
  energy reserves, *148*
  environmental damage, 57, 60, 61-66
  environmental protection options, 66-67, 70-72
  forest damage, 66
  government-to-government aid programs, 68
  health prospects, 57, 62-63
  industrial development, 58, 60-61
  infrastructure projects, 68
  laws and regulations, environmental, 72
  life expectancy, 62, 63
  market forces management, 67-70
  motor vehicles, 69-70
  nature conservation opportunities, 59
  nuclear energy, 71
  pollution control, 60
  smokestacks, 61-62
  soil damage, 66
  transboundary pollution, 66, 68
  water pollution, 11, 64-66, 72
  Western partnerships with, 68
Central government expenditures, *240-41*
Cephalopods, *339*
Cereals
  consumption, 94
  feed, 105
  food aid, 94, *278-80*
  prices, 97
  production and yields, 94, *272-73*
  surpluses, 107
  trade, 105, *278-79*
Cerebral palsy, 88
Chad, 11, 34, 129
Charcoal, *288-89*
Chemical companies, environmental strategies, 25
Chernobyl nuclear accident, 13, 71, 78, 145
Chesapeake Bay, watershed management, 184-89
Chickens, 96, *276-77*

Index

Vaccine-preventable disease, 83-84
Vaginal barrier contraceptives, *256-57*
Vanadium, *322-23*
Venezuela, 148
Victoria, Lake, 132
Viet Nam, 37, 169
Volatile organic compounds, 61, 62, 194, 195, 196, 198, 199

Wadden Sea, 176
Ward, Barbara, 219
Wars and conflicts, 11, 94, 150
Waste
  composition, *319*
  disposal methods, *319*
  disposal sites, 25
  energy conversion, 155
  methane emissions, *348-49*
  incentives for reducing, 10-11
  industrial, 17, 53
  municipal, *319*
  reduction, 159, 170
  solid, *348-49*
Wastewater
  from agriculture, 161
  costs of treatment, 72
  in OECD countries, *167*
  reuse of, 159
  treatment, 164, *167*, 168, 175
  untreated, 64, 65
Water
  see also Drinking water; Freshwater
  conservation, 6, 135, 163
  desalination, 159, 163, 164
  disputes, international, 171
  erosion of soils, *290*
  quality, 64-65, 67, 86, 163
  prices, 163
  supply, 6, 93
  treaties, 171
Water pollution
  see also Oceans; River basins
  acids, 162

from agriculture, 6, 10, 24, 42, 65, 97, 103-04, 168-69
areas of concern, 162-63
biochemical oxygen demand, 65, 67, 161
in Central Europe, 64-65, 72
chlorides, 162
effect on aquatic organisms, 162
health problems, 162, 165, 177
heavy metals, 162
from human settlements, 167-68
industrial, 88-89, 162, 168
from livestock farming, 169
from logging, 169
marine, 139, 141, 175
measure of, 67
from mining, 168
monitoring, 171
in newly industrializing countries, 42
nitrates, 65, 100-01, 103-04, 107, 172
from nutrients, 25, 97, 103, 104, 162, 163, 176-77
pathogens, 162
in poor countries, 30
reduction strategies, 68, 72, 169-71, 180-81, 183-85
regional approach to, 141, 171-72, 180—81
salinization, 64, 72, 163, 168
sediments, 162
sources, 162, 165, 166
target reductions, 67
temperature elevation, 162
from toxic chemicals, 162, 177
Watersheds
  management, 117-18, 187-91
  pollution, 182-83
  protection areas, 140
  temperate forests and, 131
Waterways, transport, *266-67, 332-33*
West Africa, 35, 36
Wetlands, 6
  convention, 140, *358-59*
  conversion to cropland, 23, 106
  ecological role of, 166, 167

internationally important, 140, *298-99*
losses, 129, 163, 177
sewage treatment in, 159, 169-70
Wheat, 101, 103, 118, 132
Wilderness areas
  land area by country, *262-63*
Wildlands, 6
Wildlife
  overexploitation, 5, 30, *302-03*
  pesticide effects on, 103
  poaching, 136
  at world heritage sites, *302-03*
Wind power, 22-23, 144, 145, *314-15*
Women
  and children's health care, 35, 37, 85, 86-87
  conferences, 218
  contraception, 6, 77
  earnings, 35
  economic opportunities in poor countries, 34-35
  education, 6, 34, 35, 87
  employment, 34
  forest management by, 130
  health, 6, 34, 77
  labor force population, *264-65*
  literacy rates, 35, 49, 77, 85, *254-55*
  loans for, 33
  maternal mortality, 34-35, *250-51*
  nongovernmental organizations for, 33, 225-26, 230
  poverty, 31
  role in developing countries, 6
  role in nongovernmental organizations, 225
  rural, 87
World Bank
  agricultural lending, 98
  Central European investments, 68
  criticisms of development projects, 187, 217-18, 221-22
  dam construction projects, 187, 217, 221-22
  nongovernmental organizations and, 217-18, 221-22

review of biodiversity conservation projects, 138
stabilization and structural adjustment policies, 32, 33
World Commission on Environment and Development, 2
World Conservation Union, 3-4, 69, 133, 140, 219
World Council of Churches, 217
World Environment Center, 69
World Health Organization
  child survival strategy, 89
  malaria meeting, 84
  particulate limits, 82
  sulfur dioxide limits and ratings, 42, 62
World Heritage Sites, 136, 140, *298-99, 302-03, 358-59*
World Meteorological Organization, 2, 204, 205
World Parks Endowment, 140
World Resources Data Base Index, 381-82
World Summit for Children, 81, 86, 89, 90
World Wide Fund for Nature, 51, 218
World Wildlife Fund, 218

Yarkon/Taninim aquifer, 163
Yarmuk River basin, 163
Yosemite National Park, 136 ·
Yugoslavia, *61, 63, 64, 65*
  energy consumption, 146
  forest defoliation, *66*
  modernization projects, 68
  political stability, 58

Zambia, 25, 133, 222
Zebra mussel, 130
Zimbabwe, 81, 88, 133, 220, 221, 222, 226, 231
Zinc, 67, 88, 183, 186, *321-23*
Zoos, 128, 132, 136-137

World Resources Data Base Index

The data base contains data in electronic form on diskette. Except where unavailable, the data range for each variable includes annual data for the years listed and data for up to 153 countries, except where noted with an asterisk (*). The data can be searched by variable, by country, or by year; it can also be exported to other electronic formats or graphed or put in chart form. For technical notes and sources, refer to the corresponding chapter of *World Resources 1992-93*.

Basic Economic Indicators
Gross national product in constant 1987 U.S. dollars, 1970–89
Gross national product in current U.S. dollars, 1970–89
Official development assistance data, 1982–89
Gross national product per capita in current dollars, 1970–89
Gross domestic product (GDP) in local currency, 1970–89
Agricultural share of GDP in local currency, 1970–89
Industrial share of GDP in local currency, 1970–89
Services share of GDP in local currency, 1970–89
Conversion factors between local to U.S. currency, 1970–89
Central government spending in local currency, 1970–89
Disbursed long-term public debt in U.S. dollars, 1970–89
Total external debt in U.S. dollars, 1970–89
Current borrowing in U.S. dollars, 1970–89
Total debt service in U.S. dollars, 1970–89
Total exports of goods and services in U.S. dollars, 1970–89
Selected world commodity indexes and prices in constant 1987 U.S. dollars, 1975–89 *
Selected central government expenditures for the most recent year available

Population and Human Development
Total population, 1950–2025
Population growth rate, 1950–2025
Total economically active population, 1950–2005
Crude birth rate, 1950–2025
Life expectancy—both sexes, 1950–2025
Life expectancy—females, 1950–2025
Life expectancy—males, 1950–2025
Total fertility rate, 1950–2025
Total population over age 65, 1950–2025
Crude death rates, 1950–2025
Infant mortality, 1950–2025
Maternal deaths
Child malnutrition—wasting
Child malnutrition—stunting
Safe drinking water availability—urban (1980 and 1988)
Safe drinking water availability—rural (1980 and 1988)
Sanitation services availability—urban (1980 and 1988)
Sanitation services availability—rural (1980 and 1988)
Health services availability—all
Health services availability—urban
Health services availability—rural
Number of doctors
Number of midwives and nurses
Number of other medical personnel
Adult female literacy (1970 and 1990)
Adult male literacy (1970 and 1990)
Percentage of population over age 25—completed primary school
Percentage of population over age 25—some postsecondary education
Percent of 1-year-olds immunized against TB
Percent of 1-year-olds immunized against DPT
Percent of 1-year-olds immunized against polio
Percent of 1-year-olds immunized against measles
Percent of married couples using any birth control method
Percent of married couples using female sterilization
Percent of married couples using male sterilization
Percent of married couples using oral contraception
Percent of married couples using injectable contraception

Percent of married couples using IUDs
Percent of married couples using condoms
Percent of married couples using vaginal barrier contraception
Percent of married couples using other birth control methods
Percent of married couples with affordable access to female sterilization
Percent of married couples with affordable access to the pill
Percent of married couples with affordable access to condoms
Percent of married couples with affordable access to abortion
Percent of married couples with affordable access to other methods of birth control

Land Cover and Settlements
Total area, 1970–89
Land area, 1970–89
Cropland area, 1970–89
Permanent pasture area, 1970–89
Forest and woodland area, 1970–89
Other land area, 1970–89
Wilderness area
Total urban population, 1970–90
Total rural population, 1970–90
Number of cities with one or more million inhabitants
Percentage of population residing in cities with at least 1 million inhabitants, 1950–2000
Number of people residing in cities with at least 1 million inhabitants, 1950–2000
Occupants per household
Rooms per household
Percentage of households without electricity
Total labor force, 1950–2005
Percentage of labor force in agriculture
Percentage of labor force in industry
Percentage of labor force in services
Total extent of paved and unpaved road
Total extent of paved road
Total extent of rail track
Total extent of inland navigable waterway
Total extent of paved road per 1,000 square km land area
Total extent of rail track per 1,000 square km land area
Total extent of inland navigable waterway per 1,000 square km land area
Total number of cars
Passenger-km transported by public car/bus
Passenger-km transported by private car/bus
Passenger-km transported by train
Passenger-km transported by commercial aircraft
Ton-km of freight transported by road
Ton-km of freight transported by rail
Ton-km of freight transported by inland waterway
Ton-km of freight transported by air

Food and Agriculture
Index of agricultural production, total, 1970–90
Index of agricultural production, per capita, 1970–90
Index of food production, total, 1970–90
Index of food production, per capita, 1970–90
Production of cereals, 1971–90
Area harvested for cereals, 1971–90
Production of roots and tubers, 1971–90
Area harvested for roots and tubers, 1971–90
Total cropland area, 1970–89
Total irrigated land, 1970–89
Total fertilizers consumed, 1970–89
Total tractors in use, 1970–89
Total harvesters in use, 1970–89
Total number of cattle, 1971–90
Total number of sheep, 1971–90
Total number of goats, 1971–90
Total number of pigs, 1971–90
Total number of horses, 1971–90
Total number of mules, 1971–90
Total number of asses, 1971–90
Total number of buffaloes, 1971–90
Total number of camels, 1971–90
Total number of chickens, 1971–90
Grain fed to livestock
Total cereal imports, 1970–89
Total cereal exports, 1970–89
Total pulse imports, 1970–89
Total pulse exports, 1970–89
Total edible oil imports, 1970–89
Total edible oil exports, 1970–89

Total cereal donations
Total cereal receipts
Total edible oil donations
Total edible oil receipts
Total milk donations
Total milk receipts
Total cereal aid
Total cereal aid from Canada
Total cereal aid from USA
Total cereal aid from Japan
Total cereal aid from EC
Total cereal aid from others
Total arid land area
Total semiarid land area
Total humid land area
Total land area with no inherent soil constraints
Arid land area with no inherent soil constraints
Semiarid land area with no inherent soil constraints
Humid land area with no inherent soil constraints
Cold land area with no inherent soil constraints
Total tropical land area
Total subtropical land area
Total temperate land area

Forests and Rangelands
Extent of closed forest
Extent of open forest
Extent of plantation
Extent of other wooded area
Average annual deforestation, closed forest
Average annual deforestation, total forest
Average annual reforestation
Extent of managed closed forest
Extent of protected closed forest
Roundwood production, total, 1970–89
Fuel and charcoal, production, 1970–89
Industrial roundwood, production, 1970–89
Sawnwood, production, 1970–89
Panels, production, 1970–89
Paper, production, 1970–89
Net trade, roundwood, 1970–89
Exports, roundwood, 1970–89
Imports, roundwood, 1970–89
Soil degradation—total area, by region *
Soil degradation—degraded area as percent of vegetated land, by region *
Soil degradation—total area affected by water erosion, by region *
Soil degradation—total area affected by water induced topsoil loss, by region *
Soil degradation—total area affected by water induced terrain deformation, by region *
Soil degradation—total area affected by wind erosion, by region *
Soil degradation—total area affected by wind induced topsoil loss, by region *
Soil degradation—total area affected by wind induced terrain deformation, by region *
Soil degradation—total area affected by overblowing, by region *
Soil degradation—total area affected by chemical degradation, by region *
Soil degradation—total area affected by nutrient loss, by region *
Soil degradation—total area affected by salinization, by region *
Soil degradation—total area affected by pollution, by region *
Soil degradation—total area affected by acidification, by region *
Soil degradation—total area affected by physical degradation, by region *
Soil degradation—total area affected by compaction, by region *
Soil degradation—total area affected by waterlogging, by region *
Soil degradation—total area affected by subsidence of organic soils, by region *
Undegraded area classified as permanent agriculture and stabilized terrain, by region *
Undegraded area classified as natural area, by region *
Undegraded area classified as nonvegetated land, by region *
Soil degradation—total area degraded by vegetation removal *
Soil degradation—total area degraded by overexploitation *
Soil degradation—total area degraded by overgrazing *
Soil degradation—total area degraded by agricultural activities *

Soil degradation—total area degraded by industrial and bioindustrial activities *

Wildlife and Habitat
Number of IUCN category I-V protected areas
Total area under IUCN category I-V protection
Number of IUCN category I-III protected areas
Total area under IUCN category I-III protection
Number of IUCN category IV and V protected areas
Total area under IUCN category IV and V protection
Number of protected marine and coastal areas
Total marine and coastal area protected
Number of biosphere reserves
Total area protected as biosphere reserves
Number of natural and mixed natural/cultural heritage sites
Number of wetlands of international importance
Total area protected as wetlands of international importance
Percent of CITES reporting requirement met
Number of live primates imported
Number of live primates exported
Number of cat skins imported
Number of cat skins exported
Number of live parrots imported
Number of live parrots exported
Number of reptile skins imported
Number of reptile skins exported
Number of live cacti imported
Number of live cacti exported
Number of live orchids imported
Number of live orchids exported
Number of known mammal species
Number of threatened mammal species
Threatened mammal species per 10,000 square km
Number of known bird species
Number of threatened bird species
Threatened bird species per 10,000 square km
Number of amphibian species
Number of threatened amphibian species
Threatened amphibian species per 10,000 square km
Number of freshwater fish species
Number of threatened freshwater fish species
Number of plant taxa
Endemic flora as a percentage of total
Rare and threatened plant taxa per 1,000 existing taxa
Rare and threatened plant taxa per 10,000 square km
Number of botanical gardens
Number of botanical gardens that are BCGI members

Energy and Materials
Commercial energy production, total, 1970–89
Commercial energy production, solid fuel, 1970–89
Commercial energy production, liquid fuel, 1970–89
Commercial energy production, gaseous fuel, 1970–89
Commercial energy production, geothermal and wind, 1970–89
Commercial energy production, hydro, 1970–89
Commercial energy production, nuclear, 1970–89
Commercial energy consumption, total, 1970–89
Commercial energy consumption per capita
Commercial energy consumption per constant 1987 U.S. dollars of GNP
Imports as percentage of consumption, 1970–89
Energy requirements in conventional fuel equivalent, total
Energy requirements in conventional fuel equivalent per capita
Energy requirements in conventional fuel equivalent per constant 1987 U.S. dollars of GNP
Traditional fuels consumption, 1970–89
Traditional fuels as percentage of total requirements
Percentage of commercial energy used, industry, 1971–89
Percentage of commercial energy used, transport, 1971–89

Percentage of commercial energy used, agriculture, 1971–89
Percentage of commercial energy used, commercial, 1971–89
Percentage of commercial energy used, residential, 1971–89
Percentage of commercial energy used, other, 1971–89
Energy intensity, industry
Energy intensity, agriculture
Annual municipal waste generation, total
Annual municipal waste generation, per capita
Composition of municipal waste, paper, and cardboard
Composition of municipal waste, plastic
Composition of municipal waste, glass
Composition of municipal waste, metals
Composition of municipal waste, organic as percentage of inorganic
Disposal of municipal waste, landfill
Disposal of municipal waste, total incineration
Disposal of municipal waste, incineration with energy recovery
Disposal of municipal waste, other
Production, bauxite
Consumption, aluminum
Production, cadmium
Consumption, cadmium
Production, copper
Consumption, copper
Production, lead
Consumption, lead
Production, mercury
Consumption, mercury
Production, nickel
Consumption, nickel
Production, tin
Consumption, tin
Production, zinc
Consumption, zinc
Production, iron ore
Consumption, iron ore
Production, steel crude
Consumption, steel crude
Reserves, copper
Reserves, lead
Reserves, tin
Reserves, zinc
Reserves, iron ore
Reserves, manganese
Reserves, nickel
Reserves, chromium
Reserves, cobalt
Reserves, molybdenum
Reserves, tungsten
Reserves, vanadium
Reserves, bauxite
Reserves, titanium
Reserves, lithium
Metal reserves index

Freshwater
Annual internal renewable water resources—total
Annual internal renewable water resources—per capita
Annual river flows from other countries
Annual river flows to other countries
Year of data: annual withdrawal
Annual withdrawal—total
Annual withdrawal—percentage of water resources
Annual withdrawal per capita
Sectoral withdrawal—domestic
Sectoral withdrawal—industry
Sectoral withdrawal—agriculture
Number of large dams over 15 meters in height (1977 and 1986)
Number of large dams over 30 meters in height
Number of large dams under construction
Gross theoretical hydropower potential
Exploitable hydropower potential
Total installed hydropower capacity
Installed microhydro hydropower capacity
Total hydropower generation
Hydropower generation as a percentage of capacity

Oceans and Coasts
Length of coastline
Maritime area—shelf to 200 meter depth
Maritime area—exclusive economic zone
Percentage of urban population in large coastal cities
Goods loaded—crude petroleum
Goods unloaded—crude petroleum
Goods loaded—petroleum products
Goods unloaded—petroleum products
Goods loaded—dry cargo
Goods unloaded—dry cargo
Offshore annual production—oil (1980 and 1990)
Offshore annual production—gas (1980 and 1990)
Offshore proven reserves—oil
Offshore proven reserves—gas
Average annual marine catch, by region, 1970–89
Average annual freshwater catch, 1970–89
Average annual aquaculture production—freshwater fish
Average annual aquaculture production—diadromous fish
Average annual aquaculture production—marine fish
Average annual aquaculture production—crustaceans
Average annual aquaculture production—molluscs
Average annual aquaculture production—total fish and shellfish
Average annual aquaculture production—other
Total average annual food supply from fish and fishery products
Per capita average annual food supply from fish and fishery products

Atmosphere and Climate
Carbon dioxide emissions from industrial sources—solid fuels, 1970–89
Carbon dioxide emissions from industrial sources—liquid fuels, 1970–89
Carbon dioxide emissions from industrial sources—gas fuels, 1970–89
Carbon dioxide emissions from industrial sources—cement manufacture, 1970–89
Total carbon dioxide emissions from industrial sources, 1970–89
Carbon dioxide emissions from deforestation
Methane emissions from solid waste
Methane emissions from coal mining
Methane emissions from oil and gas production
Methane emissions from wet rice agriculture
Methane emissions from livestock
Total methane emissions
Total emissions of chlorofluorocarbons
Atmospheric concentrations of greenhouse and ozone depleting gases—carbon dioxide, 1959–90
Atmospheric concentrations of greenhouse and ozone depleting gases—carbon tetrachloride, 1975–90
Atmospheric concentrations of greenhouse and ozone depleting gases—methyl chloroform, 1975–90
Atmospheric concentrations of greenhouse and ozone depleting gases—CFC11, 1975–90
Atmospheric concentrations of greenhouse and ozone depleting gases—CFC12, 1975–90
Atmospheric concentrations of greenhouse and ozone depleting gases—CFC22, 1979–88
Atmospheric concentrations of greenhouse and ozone depleting gases—CFC113, 1983–90
Atmospheric concentrations of greenhouse and ozone depleting gases—total gaseous chlorine, 1975–90
Atmospheric concentrations of greenhouse and ozone depleting gases—nitrous oxide, 1975–88
Atmospheric concentrations of greenhouse and ozone depleting gases—methane, 1965–90
Atmospheric concentrations of greenhouse and ozone depleting gases—carbon monoxide, 1981–86

The World Resources Institute (WRI) is a research and policy institute helping governments, the private sector, environmental and development organizations, and others address a fundamental question: How can societies meet human needs and nurture economic growth without destroying the natural resources and environmental integrity that make prosperity possible?

Through its policy studies, WRI aims to generate accurate information about global resources and environmental conditions, analyze emerging issues, and develop creative yet workable policy responses. In seeking to deepen public understanding, it publishes a variety of reports and papers; undertakes briefings, seminars, and conferences; and offers material for use in the press and on the air.

In developing countries, WRI provides technical support, policy analysis, and other services for governments and nongovernmental organizations that are trying to manage natural resources sustainably.

A central task of WRI is to build bridges between scholarship and action, bringing the insights of scientific research, economic analysis, and practical experience to the attention of policymakers and other leaders around the world.

WRI's projects are now directed at two principal concerns:

■ The effects of natural resources deterioration on economic development and on the alleviation of poverty and hunger in developing countries; and

■ The new generation of globally important environmental and resource problems that threaten the economic and environmental interests of all the nations of the world.

WRI is an independent, not-for-profit corporation that receives its financial support from private foundations and corporations, governmental and intergovernmental institutions, and interested individuals.

WRI is currently carrying out policy research in six major areas: Climate, Energy, and Pollution; Forests and Biodiversity; Economics; Technology; Resource and Environmental Information; and Institutions.

In developing countries, WRI's Center for International Development and Environment provides policy advice, technical assistance and other supporting services to governments, nongovernmental organizations and local groups charged with managing natural resources and economic development.

World Resources Institute

1709 New York Avenue, N.W.
Washington, D.C. 20006 U.S.A.

WRI's Board of Directors:

Officers:

United Nations Environment Programme

P.O. Box 30552
Nairobi, Kenya

Executive Director
Mostafa K. Tolba

Deputy Executive Director
William H. Mansfield III

Regional and Liaison Offices

Latin America and the Caribbean:
UNEP Regional Office for Latin America and Caribbean
Edificio de Naciones Unidas
Presidente Mazaryk 29
Apartado Postal 6-718
Mexico 5, D.F., Mexico

West Asia:
UNEP Regional Office for West Asia
1083 Road No. 425
Jufair 342
P.O. Box 26814
Manama, Bahrain

Asia and the Pacific:
(UNEP Regional Office for Asia and the Pacific)
United Nations Building
Rajadamnern Avenue
Bangkok 10200 Thailand

Europe:
UNEP Regional Office for Europe
Palais des Nations
CH-1211 Geneva 10, Switzerland

Africa:
UNEP Regional Office for Africa
UNEP Headquarters
P.O. Box 30552
Nairobi, Kenya

New York:
UNEP Liaison Office
UNDC Two Building
Room 0803
Two, United Nations Plaza
New York, New York 10017 U.S.A.

Washington:
UNEP Liaison Office
Ground Floor
1889 F Street, N.W.
Washington, D.C. 20006 U.S.A

The United Nations Environment Programme (UNEP) was established in 1972 and given by the United Nations General Assembly a broad and challenging mandate to stimulate, coordinate, and provide policy guidance for sound environmental action throughout the world. Initial impetus for UNEP's formation came out of the largely nongovernmental and antipollution lobby in industrialized countries. This interest in pollutants remains, but right from the early years, as perceptions of environmental problems broadened to encompass those arising from the misuse and abuse of renewable natural resources, the promotion of environmentally sound or sustainable development became a main purpose of UNEP.

From the global headquarters in Nairobi, Kenya, and seven regional and liaison offices worldwide, UNEP's staff of some 200 scientists, lawyers, administrators, and information specialists carry out UNEP's program, which is laid down and revised every two years by a Governing Council of representatives from its 58 member states. These members are elected on a staggered basis for three years by the United Nations General Assembly.

Broadly, this program aims to stimulate research into major environmental problems, promote environmentally sound management at both national and international levels by encouraging the application of research results, and make such actions and findings known to the public—from scientists and policymakers to industrialists and school children.

By the terms of its mandate, UNEP runs its program in cooperation with numerous other United Nations agencies, governments, intergovernmental organizations, and nongovernmental organizations. Its main concerns are climate change, pollution, water resources, desertification control, forests, oceans, and regional seas' biological diversity, human settlements, renewable sources of energy, environmentally sound management of industry, toxic chemicals, and international environmental lawmaking.

The essential base for environmentally sound management is provided by UNEP's work on the monitoring and assessment of the state and trends of the global environment. This is carried out in conjunction with agency partners, through the Global Environment Monitoring System (GEMS). The Global Resource Information Database (GRID) stores and analyzes geographically referenced environmental and resource data, and provides the essential link between monitoring and assessment and sound environmental management by putting information in forms useful to planners and managers. GEMS, the Geneva based International Register of Potentially Toxic Chemicals, and INFOTERRA provide both the international community and individual countries and organizations with the vital environmental information they need to take action.

The United Nations Development Programme (UNDP) is the world's largest multilateral source of grant funding for development cooperation. It was created in 1965 through a merger of two predecessor programs for United Nations technical cooperation. Its funds, which total $1.5 billion for 1991, come from the yearly voluntary contributions of member states of the United Nations or its affiliated agencies. A 48-nation Governing Council composed of both developed and developing countries approves major programs and policy decisions.

Through a network of offices in 114 developing countries, and in cooperation with over 30 international and regional agencies, UNDP works with 152 governments to promote higher standards of living, faster economic growth, and environmentally sound development. Currently, it is providing financial and technical support for over 6,000 projects designed to build governments' management capacities, train human resources, and transfer technology. These projects cover such fields as agriculture, forestry, land reclamation, water supply, environmental sanitation, energy, meteorology, industry, education, transport, communications, public administration, health, housing, trade, and development finance. Currently, projects valued at approximately $500 million are targeted on activities concerned with environmental aspects of development.

All UNDP-supported activities emphasize the permanent enhancement of self-reliant, sustainable development. Projects are therefore designed to:
■ Survey, assess, and promote the effective management of natural resources; industrial, commercial, and export potentials; and other development assets.
■ Stimulate capital investments to help realize these possibilities.
■ Train people in a wide range of vocational and professional skills.
■ Transfer appropriate technologies that respect and enhance the environment and stimulate the growth of local technological capabilities.
■ Foster economic and social development, with particular emphasis on meeting the needs of the poorest segments of the population.

In each developing country, UNDP also plays the chief coordinating role for operational development activities undertaken by the whole United Nations system. Globally, UNDP has been assigned numerous coordinating roles—from administering special-purpose funds such as those entrusted to the United Nations Sudano-Sahelian Office, to chairing the interagency steering committee of the International Drinking Water and Supply and Sanitation Decade. It also focuses on bringing women more fully into the process, fostering participatory grassroots development, and encouraging entrepreneurship.

United Nations Development Programme
1 U.N. Plaza
New York, New York 10017 U.S.A.

Administrator
William H. Draper III

Associate Administrator
Luis María Gómez

Bureau for Programmes and Policies
Assistant Administrator and Director
Gus Edgren

Regional Bureau for Asia and the Pacific
Assistant Administrator and Director
Krishan G. Singh

Regional Bureau for Arab States and Europe
Assistant Administrator and Director
Ali A. Attiga

Regional Bureau for Latin America and the Caribbean
Assistant Administrator and Director
Fernando Zumbado

Regional Bureau for Africa
Officer-in-Charge
Garth ap Rees

Bureau for External Relations
Assistant Administrator and Director
Aldo Ajello

Office for Project Service
Assistant Administrator and Director
Daan Everts